BEN
JONSON

Garrick as Kitely
From the portrait by Sir Joshua Reynolds at Windsor Castle
Reproduced by gracious permission of Her Majesty the Queen

BEN

JONSON

Edited by C. H. HERFORD

PERCY *and* EVELYN SIMPSON

VOLUME IX

An Historical Survey of the Text
The Stage History of the Plays
Commentary on the Plays

OXFORD
At the Clarendon Press

Oxford University Press, Ely House, London W.1

GLASGOW NEW YORK TORONTO MELBOURNE WELLINGTON
CAPE TOWN SALISBURY IBADAN NAIROBI LUSAKA ADDIS ABABA
BOMBAY CALCUTTA MADRAS KARACHI LAHORE DACCA
KUALA LUMPUR HONG KONG TOKYO

FIRST PUBLISHED 1950

REPRINTED LITHOGRAPHICALLY IN GREAT BRITAIN
AT THE UNIVERSITY PRESS, OXFORD
FROM SHEETS OF THE FIRST EDITION
1960, 1967

PREFACE

THE text having been completed in Volume VIII, the remaining volumes are devoted to interpretation. This covers textual history, stage history, and commentary. The present volume takes the commentary as far as *Volpone*; Volume X will include the commentary on the remaining plays and the masques; Volume XI will add the commentary on the poems and the prose works, supplementary matter, and an index. So will end the work begun in the year 1888.

In the present volume the frontispiece of Sir Joshua Reynolds's portrait of David Garrick as Kitely is reproduced by gracious permission of His Majesty the King. We have to thank Mr. Benedict Nicolson, Deputy Surveyor of the King's Pictures, for obtaining the permission, and Mr. W. C. Ellis, Superintendent of Windsor Castle, for allowing us to see the picture. Thomas Walkeley's petition on pages 100, 101, from the House of Lords' MSS. of December 1648, is printed by permission of Sir Henry J. F. Badeley, K.C.B., Clerk of the Parliaments. The discussion of the divided authorship of *Eastward Ho* is reprinted by permission of the Modern Language Association of America; it first appeared in *P.M.L.A.*, volume lix, in 1944.

Help in procuring information about the stage history of the plays has been given by Mr. Donald Beves, Vice-Provost of King's College, Cambridge, and Mr. A. P. Rossiter of Jesus College, for performances of *Epicoene*, *Volpone*, and *Bartholomew Fair* by the Marlowe Society; by Mr. John Parker, editor of *Who's Who in the Theatre*, for the performance of *Every Man in his Humour* at

Manchester in 1903; by Mr. Van Lennep for the performance of *Eastward Ho* at Harvard University in
1903; and by Miss Constance M. Winchell, the Reference Librarian, for the performance of *Eastward Ho* at
Columbia University, New York, in 1947.

William Trumbull's description of the *Masque of
Oberon* on pages 522–3 of Vol. X would in ordinary
circumstances have been printed from the original manuscript belonging to the Marquess of Downshire, but the
Trumbull papers have been removed from their original
home at Easthampstead Park and were not accessible
when we went to press. We have therefore printed from
the Historical Manuscripts' Commission's *Report on the
Manuscripts of the Marquess of Downshire* in the third
volume published in 1938. For permission to print this
report we are indebted to Sir Norman Scorgie, C.V.O.,
C.B.E., the Controller of His Majesty's Stationery
Office.

Various personal friends have helped not only by the
important work which they have published, but also by
private correspondence while the edition was taking
shape; Sir Edmund K. Chambers, Sir W. W. Greg, the
late Sir Charles Firth, the late George Thorn-Drury,
the late G. C. Moore Smith, Professor F. P. Wilson, and
Professor John Dover Wilson have always liberally
given their advice and help. Mr. C. F. Bell has been
consulted about the illustrations and has enriched the
edition by his Essay on the lighting of the masque. In
addition to special references made from time to time
in the commentary we gratefully acknowledge our
obligations to Mr. H. S. Bennett, Sir William A. Craigie,
the late Bertram Dobell, Mr. Percy J. Dobell, Professor

A. Ewert, Mr. H. L. Ford, Professor G. B. Harrison, the late W. J. Lawrence, Mr. John Munro, the late B. H. Newdigate, Dr. C. T. Onions, Mr. H. Sellers, Professor C. J. Sisson, Professor D. Nichol Smith, Mr. Francis Thompson, Mr. M. R. Trappes-Lomax, and Miss Marie-Thérèse d'Alverney of the Bibliothèque Nationale.

Our best thanks are due to the staff of the Public Record Office and to the Superintendent of the Literary Research Room, Mr. R. E. Latham, for the help we have received on manuscripts relating to the masques in Vol. X.

We have once again to express our gratitude to the printer and staff of the Clarendon Press for the skill and care with which they have threaded their way through the intricacies and difficulties of the text.

P. S.

Oriel College, Oxford.

May 1950.

CONTENTS

x   *Contents*

COMMENTARY

ILLUSTRATION

THE FRONTISPIECE

DAVID GARRICK AS KITELY, from the portrait by Sir Joshua Reynolds at Windsor Castle.

Garrick revived *Every Man in his Humour* in 1751 and chose the part of Kitely; he acted it again at Bath in 1766 in aid of a fund to help retired actors. After this he sat for his portrait to Reynolds in 1767. Reynolds, says Sir Lionel Cust, 'has rendered the actor's features with great truth and subtlety, and in none of the numerous portraits which he painted of Garrick has he touched a more sympathetic note' (*The Royal Collection of Paintings*, ii, p. 276).

The portrait is half-length with the body turned to the right. The head is full face with dark deep-set eyes looking right, a straight nose, and thin sensitive lips. The right hand is hidden in the folds of the cloak; the left hand with the fingers doubled lies on the right wrist. The wig is dark brown, fuzzed at the sides; a curl falls over the right ear.

The dress has an historic interest. As we noted on page 172, Garrick's revival was remarkable for an innovation in stage costume. The actors wore Stuart dresses. Garrick has a doublet of glossy brown, embroidered and slashed with white lace, a pointed white lace ruff, white lace cuffs, and a brown cloak thrown over his shoulders and covering his left arm. The inscription painted on the back of the picture is 'David Garrick aet 52, 1768. J. R. pinx'.

Reynolds gave the picture to Edmund Burke. At Burke's sale on 5 June 1812 it was bought for the Prince Regent and so passed into the royal collection.

LIST OF FACSIMILES

Robert Vaughan's portrait of Jonson, which was not later than 1627,
was re-used in John Benson's quarto edition of the *Execration against
Vulcan, with divers Epigrams . . . to severall Noble Personages in this
Kingdome*, 1640. We reproduced it as the frontispiece to our third
volume, and we printed Sir Henry M. Hake's analysis of it in our fifth
volume on pages xii, xiii.

To the Duodecimo edition Benson prefixed another portrait. The
engraver, whose initials are in the bottom left-hand corner, was William
Marshall. He engraved from 1591 to 1646, chiefly portraits. For
instance he prefixed to Milton's *Poems* of 1645 a shocking likeness with
four satiric lines in Greek underneath it, saying how worthless it was;
he evidently engraved these without understanding their meaning. His
Jonson portrait fares only a little better. It is a bust set in a niche
with a festoon stretched above it. The head is turned to the right. The
features and the thin beard are copied from Vaughan. A narrow cloak
is fastened to the poet's right shoulder and drapes the bust below. The
laurel wreath is exaggerated from Vaughan. The hair shows at the top
and below the right ear. Abraham Holland's couplet on the Vaughan
portrait—

> O could there be an art found out that might
> Produce his shape soe lively as to Write—

was wisely omitted here.

ABBREVIATIONS
USED IN THE COMMENTARY

A.P. = translation of the *Ars Poetica*.
Alch. = The Alchemist.
B.F. = Bartholomew Fair.
B.M. = the British Museum.
Beauty = The Masque of Beauty.
Blackness = The Masque of Blackness.
C. is A. = The Case is Altered.
C.R. = Cynthia's Revels.
Cat. = Catiline.
Ch. Tilt = A Challenge at Tilt.
Christmas = The Masque of Christmas.
Chlor. = Chloridia.
Conv. Drum = The Conversations with William Drummond.
D. is A. = The Devil is an Ass.
Disc. = Timber, or Discoveries.
E.E.T.S. = Early English Text Society.
E.H. = Eastward Ho.
E.M.I. = Every Man in his Humour.
E.M.O. = Every Man out of his Humour.
E. Althorp = The Entertainment at Althorp.
E. Blackfriars = The Entertainment at Blackfriars.
E. Bols. = Love's Welcome at Bolsover.
E. Highgate = The Entertainment at Highgate.
E. Welb. = The Entertainment at Welbeck.
Engl. Gr. = The English Grammar.
Ep. = The Epigrams.
F.I. = The Fortunate Isles.
For. = The Forest.
G.A.R. = The Golden Age Restored.
G.M. = The Gypsies Metamorphosed.
H.W. = For the Honour of Wales.
Hadd. M. = The Haddington Masque.
Hym. = Hymenaei.
I.M. = The Irish Masque.
K. Ent. = The King's Coronation Entertainment.
L.F. = Love Freed from Ignorance and Folly.
L.M.M. = Lovers made Men.
L.R. = Love Restored.
L.T. = Love's Triumph through Callipolis.
M.A. = The Masque of Augurs.
M.L. = The Magnetic Lady.
M.L.N. = Modern Language Notes.
M.L.R. = Modern Language Review.

M. Owls = The Masque of Owls.
M. of Q. = The Masque of Queens.
M.V. = Mercury Vindicated from the Alchemists.
Mod. Phil. = Modern Philology.
Mortimer = Mortimer his Fall.
N.I. = The New Inn.
N.T. = Neptune's Triumph.
N.W. = News from the New World in the Moon.
O.E.D. = The Oxford English Dictionary.
Oberon = The Masque of Oberon.
P.A. = Pan's Anniversary.
P. Hen. Barriers = Prince Henry's Barriers.
P.M.L.A. = Proceedings of the Modern Language Association of America.
P.R. = Pleasure Reconciled to Virtue.
R.E.S. = Review of English Studies.
S.N. = The Staple of News.
S.S. = The Sad Shepherd.
S.W. = Epicoene, or The Silent Woman.
Sej. = Sejanus.
T.L.S. = Times Literary Supplement.
T.V. = Time Vindicated.
1 Theob. = The Entertainment of the Two Kings at Theobalds.
2 Theob. = An Entertainment of the King and Queen at Theobalds.
U.V. = Ungathered Verse.
Und. = The Underwood.
V.D. = The Vision of Delight.
Volp. = Volpone, or The Fox.

AN HISTORICAL SURVEY OF THE TEXT

I

THE MANUSCRIPTS

OF these the autograph manuscripts are the most important:

(i) Ode to the Earl of Desmond, who died in 1601. Christ Church MS. 184, f. 40a. See *The Underwood*, xxv, with a facsimile of two verses.

(ii) Letter to Lord Salisbury on the imprisonment for *Eastward Ho*. Cecil MS. at Hatfield, cxiv. 58. Printed in vol. i, pp. 194–6.

(iii) Letter to Lord Salisbury on Gunpowder Plot, 8 November 1605. *Domestic State Papers, James I*, xvi. 30. Printed in vol. i, p. 202; facsimiled in part in Greg's *Literary Autographs*, plate xxiii.

(iv) Opening lines of the *Entertainment of the Two Kings at Theobalds*, July 1606. Cecil MS. cxliv. 272. Printed in vol. vii, p. 147.

(v) Letter to Queen Anne on sending her a gift-copy of *The Masque of Queens*, 1609. Printed in vol. vii, p. 279; facsimiled in Greg's *Literary Autographs*, plate xxiv.

(vi) Holograph of *The Masque of Queens*, 1609, a gift-copy to Prince Henry. British Museum Royal MS. 18 A xlv. Printed in vol. vii, pp. 277–317.

(vii) Letter to George Gerrard, enclosing an epitaph on Cecilia Bulstrode, August 1609. Harvard College Library. Printed in vol. viii, pp. 371–2.

(viii) Poem to the Earl of Somerset on his marriage, December 1613. British Museum, in a copy of the 1640 Folio with press-mark C. 28. m. 11. Printed in vol. viii, p. 384.

(ix, x) Poems to Lord Salisbury, *Epigrams* xliii, lxiii. Cecil MS. cxliv, f. 266. Facsimiled in *The Connoisseur*, vol. viii, p. 36.

(xi) Poem to Sir Horace Vere, *Epigram* xci. British Museum Additional MS. 23229, f. 87.

(xii) Poem to Alexander Glover, in a gift-copy of the Folio. Printed in *Inscriptions*, xi, vol. viii, p. 666.

(xiii) Letter to Richard Briggs, 10 August 1623, in a copy of Farnaby's *Juvenal*, 1615. Folger Shakespeare Library, Washington. Printed in vol. i, pp. 215–16: the correction 'vigiliis' in line 14 is sound, but in line 13 Jonson wrote 'Martialiticis'.

(xiv–xvi) *An Expostulation with Inigo Jones, To Inigo Marquess Would-be, To a Friend, an Epigram of him*. Lord Ellesmere's Library. Printed in *Ungathered Verse*, vol. viii, pp. 402–8.

(xvii, xviii) Translation of Martial, *Epigrams*, x. xlvii, and

Wotton's poem of *A Happy Life*. Dulwich College MS. I, articles 135, 136. Printed in *The Underwood*, xc, and in vol. i, p. 157.

(xix) 'Ad defensorem suum J. Seldenum protrepticon Ric. Jamesij' written in Jonson's copy of Selden's *Marmora Arundelliana*, 1628. Facsimiled in Sotheby's Catalogue of the Christie-Miller Library, sold 7 April 1927.

(xx) Letter to Sir Thomas Cotton, *circa* 1635. Printed in vol. i, p. 215; facsimiled in Greg's *Literary Autographs*, plate xxiii.

Next in importance to the autograph manuscripts are the manuscripts of the Masques. There are no manuscripts of the Plays.

(i) *An Entertainment of the King and Queen at Theobalds*. An earlier draft is in British Museum Additional MS. 34218, ff. 23*b*–4*b*, and in MS. clv of All Souls College, Oxford, ff. 319–21*a*. See vol. vii, p. 153.

(ii) *The Masque of Blackness*. An earlier draft is in British Museum Royal MS. 17 B xxxi, entitled 'The twelvth nights Reuells'. Jonson has signed the transcript at the end 'Hos ego versiculos feci. Ben: Jonson'. Printed in vol. vii, pp. 195–201.

(iii) *Christmas his Masque*. A seventeenth-century manuscript in the Folger Shakespeare Library, Washington, MS. 2203. 1, ff. 168–74, entitled 'Christmas his Showe'. See vol. vii, pp. 433–4.

(iv) *Pleasure Reconciled to Virtue*. A manuscript at Chatsworth in the Duke of Devonshire's Library, written by Ralph Crane for the performance on 6 January 1618. Printed in vol. vii, pp. 473–91.

(v) *The Gypsies Metamorphosed*. Richard Heber's manuscript, now in the Henry E. Huntington Library at Pasadena. Printed in vol. vii, pp. 565–615.

A second manuscript of this masque is in Harley MS. 4955 of the British Museum, on ff. 2–30, made for the Earl of Newcastle. See vol. vii, pp. 541, 560–1.

(vi) *An Entertainment at the Blackfriars*. British Museum Harley MS. 4955, ff. 48–52. Printed in vol. vii, pp. 767–78.

(vii) *The Entertainment at Welbeck*. An early draft in Harley MS. 4955, ff. 194–8. See vol. vii, pp. 789–90.

(viii) *Love's Welcome at Bolsover*. In Harley MS. 4955, ff. 199–202[r]. See vol. vii, p. 806.

Of the miscellaneous manuscripts Harley MS. 4955[1] in the British Museum has a special value. It contains more work of Jonson's than of any other writer. The following is a list of his poems and letters in this manuscript; they are collected in three groups on ff. 2–55, 173–82, 192–204.

[1] Described and collated by W. D. Briggs in *Anglia*, 1913, xxxvi, pp. 463–93.

POEMS

Ff. 2–30. *The Gypsies Metamorphosed*, mainly the text of 1640, without title.

Ff. 31–4ʳ. 'To a Freind', the epistle to Colby. *Und.* xv.

Ff. 34ᵛ, 35ʳ. 'The Man', *Und.* ii. 9 in the 'Celebration of Charis'.

F. 35ᵛ. 'The Bodie', the third poem of 'Eupheme'. *Und.* lxxxiv. 3.

F. 36, 37ʳ. 'The Minde', the fourth poem of 'Eupheme'. *Und.* lxxxiv. 4.

Ff. 37, 38. 'The Praises of a Country Life.' *Und.* lxxxv.

F. 39ʳ. 'To the Right Honorable William Earle of Newcastle', the epigram on his skill in fencing. *Und.* lix.

F. 40ʳ. 'To the Right Honorable William viscount Mansfield: On his Horsemanship, and Stable.' *Und.* liii.

F. 40ᵛ, 41ᵛ. Extract without heading from *The Vision of Delight*, ll. 57–125, 'Bright Night, I obey thee . . . And makes another face of things appeare'.

F. 41ᵛ. 'The Paynter to yᵉ Poet', Sir W. Burlase's poem. *Und.* lii.

F. 42ʳ. 'The Poet to yᵉ Paynter', Jonson's reply. *Und.* lii.

F. 42ᵛ. The epistle to Lady Covell, without title. *Und.* lvi.

Ff. 43–6ʳ. 'An Execration on vulcan.' *Und.* xliii.

Ff. 46ᵛ, 47ʳ. Christmas's song in *Christmas his Masque*, ll. 71–8, 93–101, 172–9, 182–245.

Ff. 47ᵛ. Verses on his 'Picture' left in Scotland. *Und.* ix.

Ibid. Verses by Craven on Jonson's journey to Scotland and Jonson's reply. *U.V.* xlvi.

Ff. 48–52. *An Entertainment at the Blackfriars*, without title. See vol. vii, pp. 767–78.

F. 52ᵛ. A song of welcome to the King, 'Fresh as the Day'. *U.V.* xliv.

F. 53. 'A Song of the Moon', without title. *U.V.* xlv.

F. 54ʳ. Epitaph on Jane, Countess of Shrewsbury. *U.V.* xxviii.

F. 54ᵛ. Epitaph on Charles Cavendish. *U.V.* xxii.

F. 55ʳ. Epitaph on Katherine, Lady Ogle. *U.V.* xxxi.

F. 173ʳ. 'To the Right Honoᵇˡᵉ⠆ my Lo: Weston L: Thresʳᵉʳ⠆ An Epigramme.' *Und.* lxxvii.

F. 173ᵛ. John Eliot's verses on Jonson, and Jonson's reply 'To my Detractoʳ'. *U.V.* xxxvii.

F. 174ʳ. 'To my Lord Weston, Lo: Tresurer. A Letter.' *Und.* lxxi.

Ff. 174ᵛ, 175ʳ. An Expostulation with Inigo Jones. *U.V.* xxxiv.

F. 176ʳ. To Inigo Marquess Would-be. *U.V.* xxxv.

Ibid. To a Friend, an Epigram of him. *U.V.* xxxvi.

F. 176ᵛ–9ᵛ. 'Epithalamion, or A Song, celebrating The Nuptialls of
. . . Mʳ Hierome Weston.' *Und.* lxxv.

F. 180–1. 'To Sʳ Lucius Carey, on the death of his Brother Morison.'
Und. lxx.

F. 192ʳ. 'A Song at Court to inuite the Ladies to Daunce.' *Neptune's
Triumph*, ll. 472–503.

F. 192ᵛ. 'To the great and Gratious King Charles. On the Vniuer-
sary day of his Raigne, 1629.' *Und.* lxiv.

F. 193ʳ. Epigram on the Prince's birth. *Und.* lxv.

Ibid. 'An Epigramme, To the Queenes Health.' *Und.* lxvi.

Ff. 194–8. 'The Kings Entertainement at Welbeck. 1633.' Vol. vii,
pp. 790–803.

Ff. 199–202. 'The King and Queene's Entertainement at Boulsouer,
in July. 1634.' Vol. vii, pp. 805–14.

LETTERS

F. 182. 'To the Right Honᵇˡᵉ˙ the Earle of Newcastle.' Printed in
vol. i, p. 210.

F. 202ᵛ. 'A Letter to the Earle of New Castle.' Printed in vol. i,
p. 211.

F. 203ʳ. 'An other Letter' to the Earl of Newcastle. Printed in
vol. i, pp. 211–12.

Ibid. 'An other Letter' to the Earl of Newcastle. Printed in vol. i,
p. 212.

F. 203ᵛ, 204ʳ. 'An other Letter' to the Earl of Newcastle. Printed
in vol. i, pp. 213–14.

Further, there are a number of poems addressed to Jonson.
(i) John Eliot's 'Epigramme. To my kind freind Mʳ Ben: Johnson
upon his Epigram to the Lo: Treasurer' (fol. 173ᵛ), with Jonson's
retort. (ii) Sir Lucius Cary's Anniversary, on Sir Henry Morison,
'wᵗʰ an Apostrophe, to my Father: Jonson'—'Our Metropolitane
in Poetry', as Cary calls him—followed by an 'Epistle To his
Noble Father, Mʳ Jonson' (f. 184). (iii) 'A Letter to Ben Jonson',
by Nicholas Oldisworth (f. 185). (iv) 'Vindiciæ Ionsonianæ' by
R. Goodwin (ff. 186–7). (v) Thomas Carew 'To Ben Jonson
upon occasion of his Ode' on the failure of *The New Inn* (f. 214). (vi)
Feltham's similar ode (f. 216).

The poems by other writers include a group by Donne on ff. 88–
144, and three groups of verse by Doctor Francis Andrews on ff. 57–
87, 145–72, 189–90, whose friend 'W. M.' in a dedication of Andrews's poems to William, Earl of Devonshire, describes him as
'an humble servant of your Lordships'. The first group of these

poems ends with lines to 'Sweet Lady Jane' Cavendish, dated 14 August 1629, and signed 'Franc: Andrilla'. He lived in London and was (apparently) a doctor of medicine, perhaps with a foreign degree, for his name does not appear in the Roll of the College of Physicians. He may be the Dr. Andrews to whom Donne addressed a Latin poem when his children tore up a book which Donne had lent him.[1]

It is clear that the collection was made for the Earl of Newcastle. Hence we have called it the Newcastle MS., marked 'N' in the critical apparatus. There are two hands in the manuscript: the first copies as far as f. 172, the second begins on f. 173 and also writes f. 39, the poem on Newcastle's fencing (*Und.* lix), and f. 55, the epitaph on Lady Ogle (*U.V.* xxxi). The first of these is inserted at f. 39 in order to accompany the poem on Newcastle's horsemanship, the second in order to place the lines on Lady Ogle with the Cavendish epitaphs.

The first scribe was painstaking and honest, but uneducated: he has many bad readings which are also found in the 1640 Folio text of *The Gypsies Metamorphosed*.[2] Lines frequently begin with lower-case letters and end without punctuation. The scribe had much trouble with classical allusions and out of the way words. He made a shocking muddle of the song in *Christmas his Masque*.

The poems were probably copied at different dates, but the outer limits are 1621, with which the collection opens, King James's verses at Burley-on-the-hill, and 1634, *Love's Welcome at Bolsover*. Nothing is copied from the 1616 Folio. The earliest poem in point of time is the Song of Christmas in the show of 1616, which was not included in the Folio of that year. Evidently Jonson was in the habit of sending the Earl of Newcastle copies of his poems. Writing to the Earl in 1631 he says, 'I haue here obeyed your commaunds, and sent you a packet of mine owne praises' by Lord Falkland and others, and that he would not have sent these tributes but that the Earl 'commanded it' (f. 182). Hence a number of the copies give the poems in an earlier form than that of the printed text: such are in *The Underwood*, Charis's description of her ideal lover (ii. 9); 'My Picture left in Scotland' (ix); the Epistle to Colby (xv); the 'Execration upon Vulcan' (xliii); the Epistle to Lady Covell (lvi); the birthday poem to King Charles (lxiv); the Epigram to the Queen (lxvi); the Epithalamion on the marriage of Jerome Weston (lxxv); and the Epigram to Lord Weston (lxxvii). The *Entertainment at Welbeck* also appears in an early form. More important still is the work not printed in Jonson's lifetime which this manuscript has preserved—the

---

[1] *Poems of John Donne*, ed. Grierson, i, p. 397.
[2] See vol. vii, p. 541.

epitaphs on members of the Cavendish family (*U.V.* xxii, xxviii, xxxi), the song of welcome to the King (xliv), the 'Song of the Moon' (xlv), the *Entertainment at the Blackfriars*, and the five letters to Lord Newcastle.

MS. Rawlinson poetry 31 in the Bodleian is also noteworthy. It is a collection of poems by Sir John Harington, Lord Herbert of Cherbury, Lord Pembroke, and Sir Benjamin Rudyard, as well as poems by Jonson, all of these last unsigned. It has a number of these in common with Harley MS. 4064 in the British Museum. Five of these are poems in *The Forest*—the epistle to Sir Robert Wroth (iii), the two poems to Celia (v, vi), 'Why, Disease, dost thou molest' (viii), and the epistle to the Countess of Rutland (xii), this last with the original ending. From *The Underwood* there are the Ode to himself, 'Where dost thou careless lie?' (xxiii), followed by the similar 'If men and times were now . . .' (*U.V.* xlviii), Horace's epode in praise of a country life (*Und.* lxxxv), and an alternative form of the epistle to a friend (*U.V.* xlix), beginning 'Censure not sharply then, but me advise'. It also has the epitaph on Cecilia Bulstrode (*U.V.* ix), 'A Speech out of Lucan' (*U.V.* l), and the poem, possibly Jonson's, 'Scorn or some humbler fate' (App. XVI, ix). It has a version of the poem in *Love's Martyr*, 'Splendor, oh more than mortal' (*U.V.* v), headed 'To L: C: off: B', i.e. To Lucy, Countess of Bedford. Finally, it includes two poems of Sir John. Roe to Jonson in 1603, 'The State and mens affairs are the best plays' and 'If great men wrong me, I will spare my self'.[1]

Copies of poems in seventeenth-century commonplace books are often very poor, but the chief value to be derived from a wide examination of them is the discovery of first drafts, sometimes very suggestive when a poem has been recast. In our introduction to the text of the *Poems* we have given ample illustration of the way in which Jonson retouched his early work.

---

[1] Printed in Grierson's *Poems of Donne*, i, pp. 414–16.

II

THE QUARTOS

The following are known to have been published in Quarto.

1600. *Every Man out of his Humour.* Three editions: (1) printed for William Holme, probably by Richard Bradock, who is identified by the ornaments; (2) printed for William Holme, probably by Peter Short; (3) printed 'for Nicholas Linge. 1600'. The printer is unknown, and the date is doubtful. Ling transferred the copyright to John Smethwick in 1607.

1601. *Every Man in his Humour.* Printed for Walter Burre; the printer is unknown.

1601. *Cynthia's Revels, or The Fountain of Self-Love.* Printed for Walter Burre; the printer is unknown.

1602. *Poetaster.* Printed for Matthew Lownes, probably by Richard Bradock.

1604. Jonson's part of the King's *Entertainment through the City of London,* together with the *Entertainment of the Queen and Prince at Althorp.* Printed for Edward Blount by Valentine Simmes.

1605. *Sejanus his Fall.* Printed for Thomas Thorpe by George Eld.

1605. *Eastward Ho.* Three editions, printed for William Apsley by George Eld.

1606. *Hymenaei.* Printed for Thomas Thorpe by Valentine Simmes.

1607. *Volpone, or The Fox.* Printed for Thomas Thorpe; the printer is unknown.

1608. *The Masques of Blackness and Beauty* together with *The Masque at Lord Haddington's Marriage.* Printed for Thomas Thorpe; the printer is unknown.

1609. *The Masque of Queens.* Printed for Richard Bonion and Henry Walley by Nicholas Okes.

1609. *The Case is Altered.* Printed for Bartholomew Sutton and William Barrenger by Nicholas Okes.

1611. *Catiline his Conspiracy.* Printed for Walter Burre; the printer is unknown. A second quarto printed for John Spencer by Nicholas Okes appeared in 1635, and was reprinted in that year (W. W. Greg). Andrew Crooke also issued a quarto in 1669, and William Crook a quarto in 1674.

1612. *The Alchemist.* Printed for Walter Burre by Thomas Snodham.

1617. *Lovers made Men.* No imprint.

1620. *Epicoene, or The Silent Woman.* Printed by William Stansby.

1621. *The Masque of Augurs.* No imprint.
1623. *Time Vindicated to Himself and to his Honours.* No imprint.
1623. *Neptune's Triumph for the Return of Albion.* No imprint.
1624. *The Fortunate Isles and their Union.* No imprint.
1630. *Love's Triumph through Callipolis.* Printed for Thomas Walkley by John Norton.
1631. *Chloridia.* Printed for Thomas Walkley; the printer is unknown.

These editions are described, and their collations given, in the textual introductions to each play or masque. The identification of Richard Bradock as the printer of the first Quarto of *Every Man out of his Humour* and *Poetaster* is taken from Dr. W. W. Greg's *Bibliography of the English Printed Drama to the Restoration*. Dr. Greg has also elucidated the problem of the corrections in the outer forme of sheet C and in sheet F of the Quarto of *Cynthia's Revels*.[1] These are not, as we supposed, Jonson's proof corrections of the printer's original errors, but for some reason—such as an accident at the printer's or a miscalculation causing a shortage—this portion of the text had to be reset, and the printer reset it very carelessly. We therefore cancel our attempt to adjust the irregular readings made in volume v on pages 552–4. The correct readings are the original, the incorrect and irregular are the later errors of the printer. Thus in the outer forme of C we should read:

C: 1. iii. 25 garbe; *A, C, D, E*   Reset: garbe *B*.
       27 illiterate; *A, C, D, E*   Reset: illiterate, *B*.
       31 Trauaile; *A, C, E*   Reset: Trauaile: *B, D*.
          gesture; *A, C, E*   Reset: gesture, *B, D*.
C3ᵛ: 1. iv. 147 all times, *A, C, E*   Reset: alltimes *B, D*.

The reprint of the 1635 quarto of *Catiline* is recorded by Dr. Greg.[1] It is a copy in the Harvard College Library with the first sheet of the preliminaries printed from the first issue, but the text reset. It is a curious testimony to the popularity of 'tedious but well-labour'd *Catiline*' that a publisher thought that these reprints would find a market as late as 1635, 1669, 1674.

A final point is the printing of five masque quartos—*Lovers made Men, The Masque of Augurs, Time Vindicated to Himself and to his Honours, Neptune's Triumph for the Return of Albion*, and *The Fortunate Isles and their Union*—without any imprint. Were they, as Professor W. A. Jackson has suggested, privately printed, primarily with a view to the performance, so that copies could be distributed to performers and to courtiers? or had Jonson a vague intention,

[1] See *R.E.S.* xiv, p. 218.

abandoned later, of publishing a collection of masques to which he would have prefixed a general title-page?

It may be added here as a footnote that one play, *The New Inn*, was printed in octavo by Thomas Harper for Thomas Alchorne in 1631.

An important bibliographical note by Dr. A. K. McIlwraith on the printing of Jonson's *Part of the King's Entertainment*, 1604, appeared in the fourth series of *The Library*, xxiv, pp. 181–6, revising the collations, working them out as they appear in two outer and two inner formes, and deducing from this the states of correction in the printing. He summarizes the result thus:

Forme	1st state	2nd state	3rd state	4th state
Part I, outer A	C1, C2, D	A1, A2, F	E, G	B, H
outer B	A2, C2	A1, C1, D, F	E, G	B, H
inner D	F	A1, A2, C1, C2, D, E, G	B, H	
Part II, inner A	A3, C2, D	A1, B, C1	A2, G, H	

The four states of Part I, outer A, are (1) C1, C2, D have eighteen uncorrected readings; (2) these are corrected in A1, A2, F; (3) but in making these corrections three marginal notes on A3^r were misplaced; these were corrected in E, G; (4) finally there was in B, H a rearrangement in the layout of the marginal note at line 69.

The four states of Part I, outer B, are (1) A2, C2 are without the final marginal note to line 364 (B4^v); (2) the note is inserted in A1, C1, D, F; (3) in E, G further changes were made in the marginal notes to ll. 349, 354 (B4^v); (4) finally in B, H a correction was made in the marginal note to l. 286.

The three states of Part I, inner D, are (1) F has ten incorrect readings in D1^v and D2^r; (2) these are corrected in A1, A2, C1, C2, D, E, G; (3) finally B, G, H make a further change in l. 570.

The three states of Part II, inner A, are (1) A3, C2, D have no page-numbers on sigs. A2^r, A3^v, A4^r, and the marginal note on l. 80 (A3^v) has 'folowing' with a comma; (2) in A1, B, C1 the missing page-numbers are inserted, and the comma after 'folowing' is replaced by a full stop; (3) A2, G, H have the correct spelling 'following' and many further corrections.

The main fact that emerges from this investigation is the general correctness of the Bodleian copies (B) and the invariable correctness of the Wise copy in the British Museum (H).

We take this opportunity to make two corrections in our textual introduction in volume vii, p. 74, notes 1 and 2. At sig. D1^v, l. 590, the original setting must have been that of F (the Rylands copy), in which the last line of the page was 'who brings with him a greater

ANNE then shee', with the catchword 'Whose' for l. 591. Jonson's notes forced the compositor to carry over the line to D2ʳ. Similarly on D2ʳ it would seem that originally the last line (615) read 'To sacrifice, saue my deuotion comes' and that the line 'That brings in stead of those thy masculine gummes' (616) was brought over from D2ᵛ. We owe this correction to Mr. F. C. Francis.

On page 71 of volume viii, sig. A3ʳ, l. 60 note and l. 69 note, delete 'G' from the critical apparatus in the first column.

In *The Gypsies Metamorphosed* we have to make two corrections. (1) We stated (vol. vii, p. 542) that the fortune of the Countess of Rutland (ll. 457–78) was not in D1, the early state of the Duodecimo text; it is found there on page 64. (2) We should have noted in the critical apparatus that lines 707–32 are not in D1.

III
THE FOLIO OF 1616

JONSON was the first Elizabethan dramatist to publish a collected edition of his works. The Folio of 1616, extending to more than a thousand pages, set a precedent which was followed by the First Folio of Shakespeare in 1623 and the First Folio of Beaumont and Fletcher in 1647. It excited some contemporary criticism. The epigrams (nos. 269, 270) preserved in *Wits Recreations*, though not printed till 1640, are obviously earlier.

> *To Mr. Ben. Johnson demanding the reason*
> *why he call'd his playes works.*
>
> Pray tell me *Ben*, where doth the mystery lurke,
> What others call a play you call a worke.
>
> *Thus answer'd by a friend in Mr.*
> *Johnsons defence.*
>
> The authors friend thus for the author sayes,
> *Bens* plays are works, when others works are plaies.

Thomas Heywood twice alluded to Jonson's venture into the book-market. In the address to the reader before *The Fair Maid of the West*, 1631, A4, he said, '*Curteous Reader, my Plaies have not beene exposed to the publike view of the world in numerous sheets, and a large volume; but singly (as thou seest) with great modesty, and small noise.*' And in *The English Traveller*, 1633, A3, he also told the reader, '*True it is, that my Playes are not exposed vnto the world in Volumes, to beare the title of* Workes, *(as others).*' Similarly, in Suckling's *Session of the Poets*, printed in his *Fragmenta Aurea*, 1646,

> The first that broke silence was good old *Ben*,
> Prepar'd before with Canary wine,
> And he told them plainly he deserv'd the Bayes,
> For his were calld Works, where others were but Plaies.

The printer and publisher was William Stansby, a man of high position in the London book trade. Writing from the Court of the Great Mogul in 1616, *Thomas Coriate Traueller for the English Wits*, included him with Jonson and Donne among the 'louers of vertue, and literature' to whom he sent his 'dutifull respect'. The Jonson Folio was one of the finest books he produced. He himself held the copyright only of *Certayne Masques at the Court never yet printed* which he registered at Stationers' Hall on 20 January 1615—*The Entertainment at Highgate*, the two *Entertainments at Theobalds*, the *Speeches at Prince Henry's Barriers*, the masque of *Oberon, Love*

Freed from Ignorance and Folly, Love Restored, A Challenge at Tilt of a Marriage, The Irish Masque, Mercury Vindicated from the Alchemists at Court, and *The Golden Age Restored.* These he printed for the first time. For the right to print the rest of the volume he had to negotiate with various booksellers. Two of these copyrights are acknowledged: some copies of the title-page of *Every Man out of his Humour* have the name of John Smethwicke on the imprint, and *Poetaster* is 'Printed by William Stansby, for Matthew Lownes'. Walter Burre owned a share in *Every Man in his Humour,* and the full copyright of *Cynthia's Revels, Sejanus,* and *Volpone* (transferred to him by Thomas Thorpe in 1610), *Epicoene* (transferred to him by John Browne and John Busby junior in 1612), *The Alchemist,* and *Catiline.* William Welby had acquired Cuthbert Burby's share in *Every Man in his Humour,* which had been transferred to him by Burby's widow in 1609. Thorpe, who had parted with other copyrights, retained those of *The Masques of Blackness and Beauty, Hymenaei,* and *The Haddington Masque.* Edward Blount had the copyright of Jonson's part of the King's *Coronation Entertainment,* if Man had not deprived him of it.[1] He retained at any rate his rights over *The Entertainment at Althorp.* Richard Bonion and Henry Walley had the copyright of *The Masque of Queens.* Two early plays not included in the collection were *The Case is Altered,* which Jonson probably discarded as a crude experiment in romantic comedy after he had evolved the Humour plays, and *Eastward Ho,* of which he was only part author. The plays end with *Catiline,* so that *Bartholomew Fair,* acted in 1614, was also excluded.

After the publication of the Folio in 1616 Stansby went on acquiring copyrights as opportunity offered. In 1618 Thomas Snodham acquired Welby's share in *Every Man in his Humour*; after his death his widow on 23 February 1626 transferred it to Stansby. On 4 July 1635 Stansby acquired from Burre and Lownes their rights over *Every Man in his Humour, Cynthia's Revels, Sejanus, Volpone, Epicoene, The Alchemist,* and *Catiline.* After his death his widow on 4 March 1639 transferred these copyrights to Richard Bishop, who thus acquired them for publication in the Folio of 1640.

At what date did the copy for the Folio go to the printer? Various clues point to 1612 or at latest 1613 as a likely year for its preparation. The last play included in it was *Catiline,* acted in 1611; *Bartholomew Fair,* acted in 1614, was not included. Two entries in the Stationers' Register are suggestive: on 15 May 1612 John Stepneth entered the *Epigrams*; on 28 September the copyright of *Epicoene* was trans-

[1] See vol. vii, pp. 77-8.

ferred to Walter Burre, who published *The Alchemist* in that year and may have published *Epicoene*.[1] Both these plays had been originally registered in 1610. No separate edition of the *Epigrams* is known, but William Drummond enters them among the books which he read in 1612 and 1613.[2]

Contemporary allusions in the *Epigrams* are innumerable, but none can be dated later than 1612, and two poems of 1614 which might have found a place in this collection were not printed till 1640—the Epistle before Selden's *Titles of Honor* and the lines before Raleigh's *History of the World*, printed in *The Underwood* (xiv and xxiv).

Between September 1612 and June 1613 Jonson was in France, but his literary output for these years was only three Court masques —*Love Restored* in January 1612, *The Irish Masque* in December 1613, and *A Challenge at Tilt* on New Year's Day 1614. He would be amply occupied in collecting and revising his works for a publisher.

If the copy went to press in 1612 or 1613 and the work was not published till 1616, why was Stansby so slow in producing it? In these years Charles Sayle records an output of thirty-nine books,[3] and they included another great folio, Raleigh's *History of the World*, licensed on 15 April 1611, but not issued till late in 1614. This formidable volume had prior claims. The only clue to the date of Stansby's printing of the Jonson Folio is his entry on the Stationers' Register on 20 January 1615 of the unprinted entertainments and masques of which he had the copyright. The most significant change in the text of these was to suppress the occasion of *Hymenaei*; the reference to the marriage of the Earl of Essex and the infamous Lady Frances Howard was omitted. This was caused by the exposure of the Overbury murder in 1615. Definite evidence of the murder was forthcoming in July of that year, so that by that date a proof correction could be made on page 907 if the printing had got so far.

The frontispiece, engraved by William Hole, is an emblematic title-page with figures personifying the different types of drama. It is reproduced as the frontispiece to our fourth volume.

At the top is a small tower with a low curved pediment. Before it stands Tragicomedy; she has a tragic crown and sceptre, but she wears the comic sock. In two niches on either side are diminutive figures of Bacchus with an ivy-clad thyrsus and Apollo, ray-crowned, with a lyre. Below on either side of a fantastic pediment are a Satyr

---

[1] See vol. v, pp. 142–3. [2] See vol. viii, p. 16.
[3] *Early Printed Books in the Library of the University of Cambridge*, vol. ii, pp. 636–60.

playing reeds and a Shepherd playing a pipe. In an oval frame
between them is an ancient theatre the form of which is modelled
on the Colosseum, a segment of a circle, greater than a semicircle.
In the classical theatre the background was a decorated wall with
two wings which served as dressing-rooms and store-rooms for the
properties. In Jonson's 'theatrum' there is only one wing, making
the building behind the stage L-shaped. 'The object of a jut forward
would be to facilitate the descents and ascents from and to the
heavens, which formed popular features in many plays, and which
must have been contrived by some kind of machinery from above.'[1]
Running along the frieze beneath these figures is the Horatian quotation 'Singula quaeque locum teneant sortita decenter'.[2] Interpreted
in terms of the drama this means, 'Let each type of play be fitly
apportioned and keep its proper place'. Below the frieze standing
in two pillared side-arches are two larger figures. On the left is
Tragedy, crowned and sceptred and wearing buskins, with a hel-
meted tragic mask fixed on the outer pillar; behind her is an embroidered curtain. On the right is Comedy in plainer dress, wearing
the sock; a hatted comic mask is fixed on her pillar, and the curtain
behind her is not embroidered. In the opening between the arches
is the title, 'The Workes of Beniamin Jonson', with another Horatian motto,

> neque, me vt miretur turba, laboro:
> Contentus paucis lectoribus.[3]

The base of the archway consists of a central recess with the imprint
and two sculptured plinths on either side of it. Below Tragedy is
Thespis driving his cart through an Attic landscape: a jar of wine
is fastened at the back of the cart, and a sacrificial goat is tethered
to it. For Jonson τραγῳδία was 'goat-song' from τράγος, 'goat'.
Below Comedy is a circular space cut out of a hill-side with rising
tiers of seats, a lighted altar in the centre, and a chorus of eight
men and women dancing round it. It has the unclassical label of
'Visorium', and it does not correspond to any historical plan: the
ancient ὀρχήστρα, or 'dancing ground', was a semicircular space
with the stage running along one side of it.

The imprint is found in three forms. (1) The commonest, which
we have reproduced, is 'LONDON, *printed by W. Stansby, and are to
be sould by Rich. Meighen. An⁰ D. 1616*'. (2) 'LONDON *Printed by*

---

[1] Chambers, *Elizabethan Stage*, ii, p. 546. For an example of its use in
Jonson see *Sejanus*, iv. 93 ff.
[2] *Ars Poetica*, 92. The motto applies to tragedy, comedy, pastoral, and the
ancient satyric drama, but the romantic blend of Elizabethan tragicomedy
rather falls outside it.
[3] Adapted from *Satires*, I. x. 73–4.

William Stansby An° D. 1616'. (3) A certain number of copies were printed on large paper, mostly perhaps for presentation, and these have the imprint, '*Imprinted at London by Will Stansby An° D. 1616.*' This is found in some small-paper copies also.

There is a table of contents which follows the title-page.

The Catalogue

Euery Man in his Humor,	To Mr. CAMBDEN.
Euery Man out of his Humor,	To the INNES of COVRT.
Cynthias Reuells,	To the COVRT.
Poëtaster,	To Mr. RICH. MARTIN.
Seianus,	To ESME Lo. Aubigny.
The Foxe,	To the VNIVERSITIES.
The silent Woman,	To Sir FRAN. STVART.
The Alchemist,	To the Lady WROTH.
Catiline,	To the Earle of PEMBROK.
Epigrammes,	To the same.

The Forrest,
Entertaynments,
Panegyre,
Masques,
Barriers.

The collation is as follows: ¶⁶, A–Z⁶, Aa–Zz⁶, Aaa–Zzz⁶, Aaaa–Pppp⁶, Qqqq⁴: pages x, 1–1016. Eee3 is misprinted 'Ee3', and Lll3 is mis-signatured Kkk3. Pages 5–8 were originally misnumbered 3–6; as page 5 ('3') begins the text of *Every Man in his Humour*, this led to pages 6, 7 being miscorrected 4, 5, a blunder which was not put right, but '3' was corrected to 5, and '6' to 8. Page 34 was misprinted '43', and page 713 '317'. In three large-paper copies page 75 is '81', page 999 '9999'. There are variations in the catch-words: 'as' for 'As' on page 193; 'Or,' correctly for 'Or' on page 350; 'O're' for 'O're-' on page 402; 'Dissolue' for 'Dissolue,' on page 489; 'I will' for 'I wil' on page 511. Or the type varies, as with 'THE' for 'The' on page 851; '*As*' for '*As*' on page 907; '*other*' correctly for 'other' on page 916; 'The' for 'THE' on page 944. Marked blunders are 'CAVP.' for 'DAVP.' on page 546, and the sub-stitution of 'DAVP.' for 'DAW.' on page 555. The catchword is omitted on pages 348 and 909, and sometimes at the end of a section. Occasionally it abbreviates the following word: an extreme example is 'E-' for 'EPITHALAMION' on page 922.

The collation in detail is:

¶ 1 blank, not found; ¶ 2 recto, the engraved title-page with the verso blank; ¶ 3 recto, 'The Catalogue'; ¶ 3 verso, ¶ 4 recto, 'Carmen protrepticon' of John Selden; ¶ 4 verso, 'TO BEN. IONSON, *on his workes*' by Edward Heyward; ¶ 4 verso–¶ 5 verso, 'Vpon SEIANVS' by George Chapman; ¶ 6 recto, '*To his worthy friend, the Author*' by Hugh Holland, 'Amicissimo, & meritissimo BEN: IONSON by 'I. D.' (i.e. John Donne), 'AD VTRAMQVE ACADEMIAM, DE BENIAMIN IONSONIO' by E. Bolton; ¶ 6 verso, 'To my deare friend, M. BEN: IONSON' by Francis Beaumont '*Vpon his Foxe*', 'VPON THE SILENT WOMAN' by Francis Beaumont, 'To my friend M. BEN: IONSON' by Francis Beaumont '*Vpon his Catiline*'.

EVERY MAN IN HIS HUMOUR, A1–F6 verso, pp. 1–72. A1 recto, the Title, with the verso blank; A2 recto, the Dedication to William Camden; A2 verso, 'The Persons of the Play', and the Scene; A3 recto–F6 recto, the text of the play; F6 verso, historical note on the performance and a list of the chief actors.

EVERY MAN OUT OF HIS HUMOUR, G1–P4 verso, pp. 73–176. G1 recto, the Title, with the verso blank; G2 recto, the Dedication to the Inns of Court; G2 verso, 'The Names of the Actors'; G3–G4 verso, the 'Characters'; G5 recto–H3 recto, the Induction; H3 recto–P3 verso, the text of the play; P4 recto, the alternative ending at Court, a speech by Macilente; P4 verso, historical note on the performance and a list of the chief actors.

CYNTHIA'S REVELS, OR THE FOUNTAIN OF SELF-LOVE, P5–Z3 verso, pp. 177–270. P5 recto, the Title, with the verso blank; P6 recto, the Dedication to the Court; P6 verso, 'The Persons of the Play' and the Scene; Q1–Q3 verso, the Induction; Q3 verso–Z3 recto, the text of the play; Z3 verso, historical note on the performance and a list of the chief actors.

POETASTER, Z4–Gg3 verso, pp. 271–354. Z4 recto, the Title, with the verso blank; Z5 recto, the Dedication to Richard Martin; Z5 verso, 'The Persons of the Play' and the Scene; Z6–Aa recto, the Induction; Aa1 recto–Ff6 verso, the text of the play; Ff6 verso–Gg3 recto, 'Apologetical Dialogue' for the play; Gg3 verso, historical note on the performance and a list of the chief actors. Z6 verso carries over from the previous play the running title '*Cynthias Reuells*'.

SEJANUS HIS FALL, Gg4–Oo3 verso, pp. 355–438. Gg4 recto, the Title, with the verso blank; Gg5 recto, the Dedication to Lord Aubigny; Gg5 verso, 'The Argument'; Gg6 recto, 'The Persons of the Play' and the Scene; Gg6 verso–Oo3 recto, the text of the play; Oo3 verso, historical note on the performance and a list of the chief actors.

VOLPONE, OR THE FOX, Oo4–Xx4 verso, pp. 439–524. Oo4 recto, the Title, with the verso blank; Oo5 recto–Pp2 recto, the Dedication to the two Universities; Pp2 verso, 'The Persons of the Play' and the Scene; Pp3 recto–Xx4 recto, the text of the play; Xx4 verso, historical note on the performance and a list of the chief actors.

EPICOENE, OR THE SILENT WOMAN, Xx5–Ddd6 verso, pp. 525–600. Xx5 recto, the Title, with the verso blank; Xx6 recto, the Dedication to Sir Francis Stuart; Xx6 verso, 'The Persons of the Play' and the Scene; Yy–Ddd6 recto, the text of the play; Ddd6 verso, historical note on the performance and a list of the chief actors. The running title is 'The silent Woman'.

THE ALCHEMIST, Eee1–Lll3 verso, pp. 601–78. Eee1 recto, the Title, with the verso blank; Eee2 recto, the Dedication to Mary, Lady Wroth; Eee2 verso, 'The Persons of the Play' and the Scene; Eee3–Lll3 recto, the text of the play; Lll3 verso, historical note on the play and a list of the chief actors.

CATILINE HIS CONSPIRACY, Lll4–Sss4, pp. 679–764. Lll4 recto, the Title, with the verso blank; Lll5 recto, the Dedication to Lord Pembroke; Lll5 verso, 'The Persons of the Play' and the Scene; Lll6–Sss4 recto, the text of the play; Sss4 verso, historical note on the play and a list of the chief actors.

THE EPIGRAMS, Sss5–Zzz1 verso, pp. 765–818. Sss5 recto, the Title, with the verso blank; Sss6, the Dedication to Lord Pembroke; Ttt1–Zzz1 verso, the text.

THE FOREST, Zzz2–Aaaa6, pp. 819–40.

PART OF THE KING'S ENTERTAINMENT IN PASSING TO HIS CORONATION, Bbbb1–Cccc5 verso, pp. 841–62. Bbbb1 recto, the Title, with the verso blank; Bbbb2–6 recto, At Fenchurch; Bbbb6 verso–Cccc4 recto, At Temple Bar; Cccc4 verso–5 verso, In the Strand.

A PANEGYRE on the King's Entrance to Parliament, Cccc6–Dddd2 verso, pp. 863–8. Cccc6 recto, the Title, with the verso blank; Dddd–Dddd2 verso, the text.

THE ENTERTAINMENT AT ALTHORP, Dddd3–Eeee1 verso, pp. 869–78. Dddd3 recto, the Title, with the verso blank; Dddd4 recto–Eeee1 verso, the text.

THE ENTERTAINMENT AT HIGHGATE, Eeee2–5 recto, pp. 879–85.

THE ENTERTAINMENT OF THE TWO KINGS AT THEOBALDS, Eeee5–6 recto, pp. 885–7.

THE ENTERTAINMENT OF THE KING AND QUEEN AT THEOBALDS, Eeee6 recto–Ffff1 verso, pp. 887–90.

MASQUES AT COURT, Ffff2 recto, the Title, with the verso blank. The Masques which follow have head-titles only.

THE MASQUE OF BLACKNESS, Ffff3–Gggg1 recto, pp. 893–901.

THE MASQUE OF BEAUTY, Gggg1–5 verso, pp. 901–10.

HYMENAEI, Gggg6–Iiii5 recto, pp. 911–33.

THE MASQUE AT LORD HADDINGTON'S MARRIAGE, Iiii5 verso–Kkkk4 verso, pp. 934–44.

THE MASQUE OF QUEENS, Kkkk5–Mmmm2 verso, pp. 945–64.

THE SPEECHES AT PRINCE HENRY'S BARRIERS, Mmmm3–Nnnn1 verso, pp. 965–74.

OBERON THE FAERY PRINCE, Nnnn2–6 recto, pp. 975–83.

LOVE FREED FROM IGNORANCE AND FOLLY, Nnnn6 verso–Oooo3 recto, pp. 984–9.

LOVE RESTORED, Oooo3–6 recto, pp. 989–95.

A CHALLENGE AT TILT AT A MARRIAGE, Oooo6–Pppp2 verso, pp. 995–1000.

THE IRISH MASQUE, Pppp2 verso–4 verso, pp. 1000–4.

MERCURY VINDICATED FROM THE ALCHEMISTS AT COURT, Pppp4 verso–Qqqq1 recto, pp. 1004–9.

THE GOLDEN AGE RESTORED, Qqqq1 verso–4 recto, pp. 1010–15.

There are variations in the title-pages of three of the plays, *Every Man out of his Humour, Cynthia's Revels,* and *Poetaster.* They have two different settings reproduced in facsimile in our edition of these plays: (1) a compartment with a vase of flowers at the top, pillars wreathed with grapes at the sides, and a lion and a unicorn above them;[1] (2) a setting in plain type. The imprints vary. Thus the bordered title of *Every Man out of his Humour* has 'Printed by *W. Stansby* for *I. Smithwicke*'; the plain title has 'Printed by WILLIAM STANSBY for *Iohn Smithwicke*', and in the large-paper copies we have simply 'Printed by WILLIAM STANSBY'.[2] In *Cynthia's Revels* the bordered title has 'Printed by *W. Stansby*'; the plain title 'Printed by WILLIAM STANSBY'. In *Poetaster* the bordered title has 'Printed by *W. Stansby* for *M. Lownes*'; the plain title has 'Printed by WILLIAM STANSBY for *Matthew Lownes*', shortened in the large-paper copies to 'Printed by WILLIAM STANSBY'.

At three points in the text quires have been reset. The first of these is sheet Yy, pages 529–40, the text of *Epicoene* up to Act II, scene

[1] No. 224 in McKerrow and Ferguson's *Title-page Borders.*

[2] A minor variant is the omission of 'HOR.' in both forms of the title-page, its insertion in the right margin in some copies, and the centring of it above the quotation in the large-paper copies.

ii, line 64. This has been discussed in the textual introduction to the play.[1] We append the list of variant readings.

Yy recto, page 529

	First state	Resetting
Title	EPICOENE,	EPICOENE
	PROLOGVE	PROLOGVE
Prol. 8	feasts)	(feasts,
	(make publique	make publique
9	guests	guestes
19	thought	thought.

Yy verso, page 530

	First state	Resetting
27	ord'naries	ordinaries
2nd Prol. margin	*Occasion'd . . . exception.*	*Note omitted*
1	ends	endes
8	Lest . . . iudge you.	Least . . . iudge you,
10	truths) . . . fain'd	truthes) . . . fayn'd
I. i. 1 margin	*making himselfe* | *ready*	*making him-* | *selfe ready*
8	ladie . . . it: where	lady . . . it, where
9	vnder a man | that	vnder a | man that
15	shee . . . oil'd	she . . . oyld
16	an' | I will	an' I | will

Yy2 recto, page 531

	First state	Resetting
I. i. 27	gallant	Gallant
35 margin	*Horses . . . time.*	*Note omitted*
35	*Puppy*	Puppy
36	*Pepper-corne, White-foote,*	Pepper-corne, White-foot,
	Franklin	Franklin
	White-maynes partie	White-maynes party
38	bee able	be able
40	companie	company
44	moist	moyst
50	Yes:	Yes;
54	indeede	indeed
60	nor heare	not heare

Yy2 verso, page 532

	First state	Resetting
I. i. 75	Collegiates, an or-|der	Collegiates, | an order
76	country-	countrey-
	from their hus-|bands	from | their husbands
77–8	*Wits,* and *Braueries* o' the time, | as	Wits, and Braueries | o' the time, as
78	crie	cry
79	· dislike in a braine, | or	dislike | in a braine, or
80	*hermaphroditicall* authoritie: | and	*hermaphrodical* | authoritie: and
82	President	president

[1] Vol. v, pp. 148–9.

fir, here i' the towne, of ladies, that call themfelues the Collegiates, an order betweene courtiers, and country-madames, that liue from their huf-
bands; and giue entertainement to all the *Wits*, and *Braueries* o' the time,
as they call 'hem : crie downe, or vp, what they like, or diflike in a braine,
or a fafhion, with moft mafculine, or rather *hermaphroditicall* authoritie:
and, euery day, gaine to their colledge fome new probationer.

    CLE. Who is the Prefident?

    TRV. The graue, and youthfull matron, the lady HAVGHTY.

    CLE. A poxe of her autumnall face, her peec'd beautie : there's no
man can bee admitted till fhee be ready, now adaies, till fhee has painted,
and perfum'd, and wafh'd, and fcour'd, but the boy here; and him fhee
wipes her oil'd lips vpon, like a fponge. I haue made a fong, I pray thee
heare it, o' the fubiect.

                    SONG.

S *Till to be neat, ftill to be dreft,*
    As, you were going to a feaft;
Still to be pou'dred, ftill perfum'd :
Lady, it is to be prefum'd,
Though arts hid caufes are not found,
All is not fweet, all is not found.

Giue me a looke, giue me a face,
That makes fimplicitie a grace;
Robes loofely flowing, haire as free :
Such fweet neglect more taketh me,
Then all th'adulteries of art.
Thy ftrike mine eyes, but not my heart.

    TRV. And I am, clearely, o' the other fide : I loue a good dreffing, be-
fore any beautie o' the world. O, a woman is, then, like a delicate garden;
nor, is there one kind of it : fhe may varie, euery houre; take often coun-
fell of her glaffe, and choofe the beft. If fhee haue good eares, fhew 'hem;
good haire, lay it out; good legs, weare fhort cloathes; a good hand, difcouer it often; practife any art, to mend breath, clenfe teeth, repaire eye-
browes, paint, and profeffe it.

    CLE. How? publiquely?

    TRV. The doing of it, not the manner : that muft bee priuate. Ma-
ny things, that feeme foule, i' the doing, doe pleafe, done. A lady
fhould, indeed, ftudie her face, when wee thinke fhee fleepes : nor, when
the dores are fhut, fhould men bee inquiring, all is facred within, then.
Is it for vs to fee their perrukes put on, their falfe teeth, their complexion,
their eye-browes, their nailes? you fee guilders will not worke, but
inclos'd. They muft not difcouer, how little ferues, with the helpe
of art, to adorne a great deale. How long did the canuas hang afore
                                                                      Ald-

The first state of Yy2 verso in the 1616 Folio.

sir, here i'the towne, of ladies, that call themselues the Collegiates, an order betweene courtiers, and countrey-madames, that liue from their husbands ; and giue entertainement to all the Wits, and Braueries o'the time, as they call 'hem : cry downe, or vp, what they like, or dislike in a braine, or a fashion, with most masculine, or rather *hermaphroditicall* authoritie: and, euery day, gaine to their colledge some new probationer.

CLE. Who is the president?

TRV. The graue, and youthfull matron, the lady HAVGHTIE.

CLE. A poxe of her autumnall face, her peec'd beauty : there's no man can bee admitted till she be ready, now adaies, till shee has painted, and perfum'd, and wash'd, and sour'd, but the boy heere ; and him shee wipes her oyld lippes vpon, like a sponge. I haue made a song, I pray thee heare it, o'the subiect.

SONG.

Still to be neat, still to be drest,
As, you were going to a feast ;
Still to bee pou'dred, still perfum'd:
Lady, it is to be presum'd,
Though arts hid causes are not found,
All is not sweet, all is not sound.

Giue me a looke, giue me a face,
That makes simplicity a grace ;
Robes loosely flowing, haire as free:
Such sweet neglect more taketh me,
Then all th'adulteries of art.
They strike mine eyes, but not, my heart.

TRV. And I am, clearely, o'the other side : I loue a good dressing, before any beauty o'the world. O, a woman is, then, like a delicate garden; nor, is there one kind of it : shee may varie, euery houre ; take often counsell of her glasse, and chuse the best. If shee haue good eares, show 'hem ; good haire, lay it out ; good legges, weare short cloathes ; a good hand, discouer it often ; practise any art, to mend breath, clense teeth, repaire eye-browes, paint, and professe it.

CLE. How? publiquely?

TRV. The doing of it, not the manner : that must bee priuate. Many things, that seeme foule, i'the doing, doe please, done. A lady should, indeede, study her face, when we thinke she sleepes : nor, when the dores are shut, should men bee inquiring ; all is sacred within, then. Is it for vs to see their perrukes put on, their false teeth, their complexion, their eye-browes, their nayles ? you see guilders will not worke, but inclos'd. They must not discouer, how little serues, with the helpe of art, to adorne a great deale. How long did the canuas hang afore *Ald-gate* ? were the people suffer'd, to see the Cities *Loue* and *Charitie*, while they were rude stone, before they were painted,
                                                                    and

Yy2 verso reset.

	First state	Resetting
I. i. 84	HAVGHTY	HAVGHTIE
85	beautie	beauty
86	shee be	she be
88	scour'd . . . here	sour'd . . . heere
88–9	oil'd lips	oyld lippes
89	pray thee | heare	pray | thee heare
93	*be pou'dred*	*bee pou'dred*
98	*simplicitie*	*simplicity*
102	*Thy . . . not*	*They . . . not,*
104	beautie	beauty
106	She . . . often coun-|sell	shee . . . often | counsell
107	choose	chuse
108	shew 'hem; | good . . . legs	show | 'hem; good . . . legges
109	a good hand, dis-|couer	a good | hand, discouer
110	teeth, repaire eye-|browes	teeth, | repaire eye-browes
115	indeed, studie	indeede, study
116	wee thinke shee	we thinke she
117	inquiring,	inquiring;
119	complexion, | their . . . nailes	com-|plexion, their . . . nayles
120	not worke, but | inclos'd	not | worke, but inclos'd
121	with the helpe | of	with | the helpe of
122	canuas hang afore |	canuas | hang afore
	Ald-	

On this page there are two additional lines ending with the words
'before they were painted' in the resetting: room was found for
these by printing the two stanzas of the Song closer, and leaving no
space between the Song and Truewit's speech that follows it.

Yy3 recto, page 533

	First state	Resetting
I. i. 123	suffer'd . . . cities	suffer'd, . . . Cities
	Loue, and *Charitie*, while | they	*Loue* | and *Charitie*, while they
124	painted, and	painted, | and
125	and burnish'd? No. No | more	and burnish'd? no: No more
	seruants approch	Seruants approach
126	mistresses, but when they are com-|pleat	Mistrisses, | but when they are compleat
128	ladie	lady
129	shee	she
131	her per-|ruke	her | perruke
134	held	helde
135	houre,	houre
136	t'other	'tother
137	Why, . . . should'st . . . re-leeu'd	Why? . . . shouldst . . . re-leiu'd
138	wee'l	wee'll

		First state	Resetting
I. i.	143	vncle . . . hee	vnckle . . . he
	144	formalitie	formality
	149	him, as it is | made . . . hee	him as it | is made . . . he
	151	mary,	mary
	153	He	Hee
	156	Hãmer-man	Hammer-man
	157	dwel in the pa-|rish	dwell in the | parish
	158	once vp | on a	once | on a
		-tuesdaies	-tuesdayes
	159	were quit. |	were | quit.
	161	Hau'-boyes	Hau'boyes
	163	him, . . . neere	him . . . nere
	165	hee	he
	166	aire	ayre
	167	sir! hee	sir? he
	169	noises	noyses
	170	bring him in	bring him
	171	grow	growe
	172	ease. His	ease: his
	173	Beare-ward	Beareward
	174	dogs . . . pa-|rishes	dogges . . . pari-|shes
		him,	him
	175	& cryed	and cried
		games vnder master |	games vnder master | Mo-
		Morose's	rose's windore . . . made
			a (*adding an extra line to the page*)

Yy3 verso, page 534

		First state	Resetting
I. i.	178	marching	going
	179	for ta-|king that	for taking | that
	182	clock . . . holy-day-eues	clocke . . . holyday eues
	183	of the | sicknesse	of | the sickenesse
	184	roome, with | double walls	roome, | with double walles
	185	and calk'd: | and	and | calk'd: and
	186	he . . . candle-light. He	hee . . . candlelight. Hee
	186–7	man, last weeke, for | hauing	man, | last weeke, for hauing
	188	fellow waits on him, | now	fel-|low waites on him, now
	188–9	Socks . . . with wooll: and	Sockes . . . with | wooll: and
		they talke | each	they talke each
	190	comes here. |	comes | heere.
I. ii. heading		Trve-wit	Trv-wit
	1	aile	ayle
	2	Strooke	Stroke
	3	of.	of,
	4	Davp.	Dav. (*so throughout the scene*)
	8	Hee thinks	He thinkes
	9	companie	company
	10	acts, . . . moniments	acts . . . mon'ments
	14	almanack	almanacke

	First state	*Resetting*
I. ii. 15	*tower*-wharfe	tower wharfe
16	hee	he
17	bloud	blood
22	Yes: why,	Yes, why
23	trick . . . yeere	tricke . . . yeare
24	harken	hearken
25	qualitie . . . shee bee	quallitie . . . she be
26	saies	sayes
29, 30	soft-spoken . . . sixe	soft spoken . . . six

Yy4 recto, page 535

	First state	*Resetting*
I. ii. 33	Mary, a Barber, one Cvt-berd:	Mary a Barber; *omitted*
33–4	one that | tells Davphine all here	one that tells Davphine all | heere
36	noise	noyse
37	trims	trimes
40	counsell	councell
47	wee can	we can
48	treatie	treaty
49	to tor-|ment him	to torment | him
51	He	Hee
52	lie	lye
53	guiltie .	guilty
54	doe	do
56	hee . . . Innocent!	he . . . Innocent.
57	lyes shee . . . innocent	lies she . . . Innocent
58	Why,	Why
59	lyes	lies
62	Do's	Dos
66	i'th' towne!	i'th towne*!*
67	he . . . speake—	hee . . . speake,
75	hee	he
79	sorry . . . belie	sory . . . belye
83	denie that:	deny that.

Yy4 verso, page 536

	First state	*Resetting*
I. ii. 83	gentlemen	gentleman
I. iii. 4	Davp.	Dav. (*throughout the scene*)
5	not for | secrets	not for se-|crets
6, 7	Nay, . . . he	Nay . . . hee
14	out! . . . do's	out, . . . dos
15–16	Hee . . . praises	He . . . prayses
19	stamps	stampes
20	he . . . a counsel-|lor	hee . . . a coun-|sellor
21	let's	lets
24	La-Foole	La Foole
25	mannikin!	mannikin.
26	Doe	Do
29	praiers. Hee	prayers. He

	First state	Resetting
I. iii. 30	Iudge	iudge
31	Bishop . . . Lawyer . . . hee	bishop . . . lawyer . . . he
32	Lady . . . shee	lady . . . she
34	guests	guestes
35	*Strand*	strand
36	purpose. Or	purpose: or
37	houses, or | the	houses, | or the
	Exchange	Exchange
	hee . . . meet	he . . . meete
38	'hem presents, | some	'hem | persents, some
	pounds-worth	pounds worth
39	laught at. He | is	laught | at. He is
40	chamber, for their | women	chamber, | their women
41	bait	bayt
42–3	but . . . he	bnt . . . hee
43	christen-name	christen name
45	Sir . . . LA-FOOLE	Sis . . . LA FOOLE

Yy5 recto, page 537

I. iii. 46	below,	*omitted.*
	ownes	owes
50, 51	let's . . . Boy	let's . . . BOY
54	he	hee
55	guests	guestes
	the whole | course	the | whole course
I. iv. 4	my lodg-|ing	my | lodging
6	a lodging, | as mine	a lodging, as | mine
8	*Strand*	Strand
14	companie	company
15	sir. The	sir: the
17	but	*omitted*
19	extremely	extreamely
23	DAVP.	DAV. (*throughout the scene*)
24	gamster:	gamster,
25	he	hee
28	visi-|ted so often,	vìsited | so often;
	entertainment	entertainement
30	Captaine	captaine
31	she . . . kins-woman	shee . . . kinswoman

Yy5 verso, page 538

I. iv. 40	*Europe* . . . selfe	Europe . . . self
41	*french* . . . wee	*French* . . . we
42	for	*Omitted.*
	coate | *Yellow*, or	coat yellow, | or
43	colours | more, which	coulors more, | which
44	coate . . . some-times	coat . . . sometimes
	solemnely | worne by	solemnly worne | by
45	nobilitie . . . antiquitie	nobility . . . antiquity

	First state	*Resetting*
I. iv. 46	is | not respected	is not respe-|cted
	Does . . . me	does . . . mee
47	& halfe | a dosen	and halfe a do-|sen
48	fowle, which	foule, which
49	company— | there will bee	company—there | will be
51	Cen-|tavre, mistris	Centavre, | mistris
52	si-|lent gentlewoman	silent gentle-|woman
53	has | promis'd to bring	has promis'd to | bring
54	wo-|man, will be there	woman, will bee | there
55	Knight	knight
56	with | your selfe, master	with your selfe, | master
	bee	be
57	haue | fidlers, and daunce	haue fidlers, and | daunce
	beene	bene
58	and haue spent | some crownes	& haue spent some crownes|
	since	since
59–60	after, | my ladies gentleman-	after, my ladies gen-|tle-
	vsher	man vsher
60	mee	me
61	it | pleas'd my elder brother	it pleas'd my elder | brother
62	ierkin	Ierkin
	that | day, as any was worne	that day, as any was worne|
	in	in
	Iland-	Iland-
63	and | I came ouer in it hither	and I came ouer in it hi-|
		ther
64–5	after | went downe to my	after went downe to | my
66	let | new leases, tooke their	let new leases, tooke | their
67	vpon la-|dies—and now I	vpon ladies—and now I |
	can	can
71	commoditie—	commodity.
72	La-F.	Cle.
74	gentlemen	Gentlemen
76	Wee . . . La-Foole	We . . . Lafoole
81	'tis	tis
II. i. 1	Cannot . . . find	Can not . . . finde
3	Let mee	Let me
4	mee . . . harsh . . . irksome	me . . . harshe . . . irkesome

Yy6, pages 539–40

II. i. 6	answere	answer
11	flock-bed	flockbed
12	bricke-bats	brickbats
13	leg . . . answere	legge . . . answer
14	otherwise (—)	otherwise, (—)
16	beene	been
18	not | but with . . . leg	not but | with . . . legge
19	be . . . be	bee . . . bee
20	shrug (—) so	shrug. (—) So
21	and | it is . . . grauitie	and it | is, . . . grauity
23	your	you

	First state	Resetting
II. i. 26	is | the lock oild	is the | lock oyld
27	of the | staires no	of the staires | no
28–9	much | doctrine, and impul-sion	much doctrine, and | impul-sion
30	this | diuine discipline	this diuine disci-|pline
31	earth; | still waited on	earth; still waited | on
	euen | in the warre (as	euen in the warre, (as
33–4	charges, and | directions	chardges, and directi-|ons
35	am | heartily	am hear-|tely
	angrie often-times	angry oftentimes
36	*Barbarian*	Barbarian
37	felicitie	felicity
39–40	man kind . . . throat, cut	mankinde . . . throate, cut
	throat: what | murderer	throat: | what murderer
	deuill	diuell
44	Alas	Alasse
45	hee	he
	with	*Omitted.*
46	Paine	Payne
II. ii. 1	sir (I . . . here)	sir, I . . . here:
3	all! . . . strange!	all? . . . strange.
4	here	heere
5	to bee | the	to | be the
7	at court | commend	at | court commend
9–10	*By saving a line at the opening of the scene, this speech (MOR. O . . . impudence?) is added to page 539; originally it began page 540. The catchwords are '(MOR.' and 'TRV.' respectively.*	
14	taste	taste,
16	mee	me
20	Mary	Marry
21	drowne	drowne,
22	low fall, | with	low | fall, with
23	delicate | steeple	deli-|cate steeple
25	as *Pauls,* | or	as | *Pauls*; or
	neerer	nearer
26	an excellent | garret	an | excellent garret
	windore	window
27	garret, with this | halter;	garret, | with this halter
28–9	sooner commit | your	soon-|er commit your
	wed-lock nooze; or, take a | little	wedlocke | nooze; or, take a little
31	rat; or a flie (as one | said	rat; | or, a flye (as one said
32	rather, then to follow this goblin | *matrimony*	rather, | then to follow this goblin *matrimony*
	Alas	Alasse
33	thinke to find a chaste wife, in these |	thinke | to finde a chaste wife, in these
34–5	many masques, plaies, puritane preachings, | mad-folkes	many | masques, playes, puritane parlee's, mad-folkes

	First state	Resetting
II. ii. 35–6	sights to be seene daily, pri-uate and pub-|lique	sights | to bee seene, dayly, priuate and publique
36–7	liu'd in king Etheldred's time, sir, or Edward the | Confessors	liu'd, in king E-|thelred's time, or Edward the Confessor's
38	haue found in some cold countrey-ham-|let	haue | found in some cold countrey hamlet
39	dull,	dull
40	man: | now, . . . pleas'd with	man: now, . . . pleas'd | with
41–2	you, | sir, . . . you shall runne	you, sir, . . . you | shall runne
43	sir! . . . cosen'd	sir, . . . cosen'd,
44	yours	yours,
45	begg'd	beg'd
54	centuple, | for	centu-|ple, for
56	Alas	Alasse
60	If	if
61	*Frenchman*	*Frenchman,*
62	iig . . . fencer	jig . . . fencer,

Only two of the readings in the second column are really cor-rections, and those are obvious—'*They strike*' for '*Thy strike*' in I. i. 102 and 'Ethelred's' for 'Etheldred's' in II. ii. 37. The most curious variant is 'puritane parlee's' for 'puritane preachings' in II. ii. 34, which seems to have no more point than 'going' instead of 'marching' in I. i. 178. Otherwise the errors are mostly errors of omission, such as the important marginal note to the Second Pro-logue, explaining the occasion of it, and the dropping of 'one Cvt-berd' in I. ii. 33. A sign of careless printing is the substitution of roman for italic type in proper names. But actual changes of reading derive a fictitious importance from the fact that the Folio reprint of 1640 was set up for the opening pages of this play from a copy containing sheet Yy reset.

Different settings are found later in the whole of quire 4M except 2 recto, in the inner forme of 4N1 and 6 and the outer forme of 4O3 and 4. Resettings of these are found in the British Museum copy with press-mark C.39.k.9, in the Douce copy in Bodley, in the copy belonging to Jesus College, Oxford, given to the college by Owen Wynne in 1656, and in a copy belonging to the editor, formerly Lord Birkenhead's. The printer's variations are given in detail below: there are a few variations of reading, but the differences are mainly of type, spacing, spelling, and punctuation; in a number of passages the line-arrangement varies. It is clear that the readings given in the second column are the later of the two.

How are they to be explained? In each of these quires some portions of the older setting are found intact: for example, the whole of 4M2 recto, the last fourteen lines of 4M3 verso, and the upper half of 4N3 recto. This rules out any question of accidents either to the type during the printing or to the stock of sheets after they had been printed off. What seems to have happened is that, in these three quires, the printer miscalculated the number of pulls required and did not discover the fact until he had printed off 4O. He had to make up the shortage by printing extra copies. But in 4M the type of all but one page had been distributed, and he had to reset most of the quire. In 4N and 4O only two formes had been distributed, and even these not completely: so he reset the missing portions and reused the original setting where it had been preserved.

Mmmm (4M) recto, page 961

	First state	Resetting
Masque of Queens		
566	à	d
567	queene	Queene
	note 'a' *Beronic.*	*Beronis.*
571	habit	habite
572	beautie	beauty
576	Shee	She
	solemnely	solemnly
577	*authour*	*Authour*
	president	*President*
578	rayse . . . equalitie	raise . . . equality
579	*queene . . . queene*	*Queene . . . Queene*
580	*deitie.*	*deitie*
586	note 'd' *Hist. lib.* | 6. *cap.*	*hist. lib.* 6. | *cap.*
587	doth	doeth
589	*Maximi*	*Maximi*
591	*appellatæ.* She | gouern'd	*appellatæ.* | She gouern'd
592	*Meroe*	*Meroe*
595	*East-anglia*	*East-Anglia*
596	compre-|hended,	com-|prehended
	Norfolke	*Norfolke*
597	shee	she
598	te-|stimony	testi-|mony
600	*Britonesse*	*Britonesse*
603	*weaknesse*	*weakenesse*
605	storie . . . &	story . . . and
	Note 'f' ranged even.	*Note 'f' between 605 and 6.*
		Note 'g' dropped with it.
607	libertie . . . Countrie	liberty . . . Countrey
	later	latter
609	description	desciption
	orta | *stirpe Regia*	*orta stirpe* | *Regia*
611	*bellum* | *omne administrauit*	*bellum omne ad-*|*ministrauit*
	animas	*animus* (a correction)

	First state	*Resetting*
612	after-|wards, *Fœmina*	afterwards, | *Fœmina*
613	waigh | the more	waigh the | more
614	*Romanes,* | and enemies	*Romanes,* and | enemies
617	chast . . . *Palmyrenes*	chaste . . . *Palmerynes*

4M verso, page 962

	she	shee
626	she	shee
627	she . . . always	shee . . . alwaies
634	She	Shee
637	languages,	languages
645	*tyranny*	*tyrannie*
650	yeeres	yeares
651	*Amazons*	*Amazons*
note 'k'	*In*	*In*
653	*Polytopiensis ci-|uis) inter*	*Polytopiensis | ciuis) inter*
656	dignitie	dignity
657	*scope* | of the *inuention*	*scope* of the | *inuention*
658	you a-|gaine here, might but	you againe here, might | but
659	heares | any testimony of others	heares any testimonie of | others
660-1	praise. | Shee being plac'd aboue	praise. Shee being plac'd | aboue
661	ceremony, &	ceremonie, and
662	prince-|ly vertue, against the witnesse.	princely vertue, against | the witnes
663	Bel-|anna I deuis'd, to honour hers	Bel-anna I deuis'd, to honor | hers
664	attribute | of *faire*: And is kept by me, in	attribute of faire: And is kept by mee, | in
666	*Ma-|iestie* with any shaddow, or figure.	*Maiestie* with any shaddow, or fi-|gure.
667	with | a longer *destinie*, then this *age*	with a longer *destinie*, then this | *age*
668	but | help'd to light by her gracious	but help'd to light by her graci-|ous
670	here	heere

4M2 recto, page 963, is identical in all copies collated; for example, in line 680, 'the description (we promis'd of the *scene*', the closing bracket after 'promis'd' is omitted.

4M2 verso, page 964

	First state	*Resetting*
732	immediately	immediatcly (?)[1]
739	*Musique*	*Musique*
740	voyce	voice
741	Maiesties | seruant, M^r.	Maiesties ser-|uant M.

[1] Possibly a broken *e*.

	First state	Reset
742	SONG *centred in the page.*	SONG *moved slightly to the right.*
748	*Queene*	*Queene*
750	*numerous* | composition	*numerous* com-|position
751	and ho-|nouring the	& honouring | the
752	*Prince,* CHARLES, | *Duke* of *Yorke.*	*Prince* CHARLES *Duke of Yorke.* |
753-4	the | motions were so euen	the motions were so | euen
754-5	*Mathe-|maticians* had lost *Proportion*	*Mathematicians* had lost *Pro-|portion*
756	The *Author* | was Mʳ. THO. GILES.	The *Author* was M. THO. GILES. |
757	Corrantoes. | And then their last *dance,*	Corrantoes. And then their last *dance,* |
758-9 760	with | which they tooke their stage, | had their returne to the	with which they tooke their | stage, had their returne to the |
761	*Song;* | whose notes (as the former)	*Song;* whose notes (as the former) |
762	worke excellent | friend, ALFONSO FERRABOSCO.	work excellent friend, ALFONSO FERRABOSCO. |

The last fourteen lines of this page are from the same setting, but the position of the list of the masquers' names has been moved more to the left. In each form it is badly centred.

4M3 recto, page 965

	First state	Reset
Barriers		
2	raysd	rays'd

In this line of the speech 'feet' is misprinted 'fee', a letter having dropped out in the printing. It is reset as 'feet'.

7	stild	stil'd
13	bene	bin
19, 21	æquall	equall
22	or'e-thirsty . . . vnæquall	or'e-thirstie . . . vnequall
23	liu'd	liu'd,
24	reuiu'd!	reuiu'd!
26	loue! . . . feare!	loue! . . . feare!
29	maiesty	maiestie

4M3 verso, page 966

38	strooke	stroke
40	Cob-webd[1]	Cob webd
46	maiesty	maiestie
52	so,	so
55	seats . . . knights	seates . . . knights.
56	watchd . . . nights	watch'd . . . nights,

[1] The hyphen faintly printed.

	First state	*Reset*
57	filld	fill'd
58	old	olde
62	cloudes	clouds
63	ARTHVR *centred in the page.*	*Moved more to the right.*
64	st. dir. Discouerd as a starre ab oue	Discouercd as a starre aboue.
68	calld of mee	call'd for mee
73	my flame	thy flame

4M4 recto, page 967

80	take	take,
87	List	list
92	duely . . . state, . . . throne	duly . . . state . . . throne
96	not be	not to be
97	deuisd	deuis'd
98	maiden	mayden
100	Indowe . . . LADY . . . lake	Indow . . . *Lady* . . . Lake
104	honor	honour
109	error	errour
115	Æternally	Eternally
118	Neither	Neyther
	st. dir. tombe	Tombe
120	She	Shee
122	MELIADVS, . . . knight	MELIADVS . . . knight,

4M4 verso, page 968

128, 141, 148	LADY *centred in the page.*	*Moved distinctly to the right.*
131	*sixe*	*six*
132, 148	MERLIN *centred in the page.*	*Moved to the right.*
135	vndemolishd . . . built!	vndemolish'd . . . built/
136	St. GEORGE'S	Saint GEORGES
138	honord	honor'd
143	armor	armour
145	Græcian HEROES . . . died	*Græcian Heroes* . . . dyed
146	raisd	rays'd
149	all . . . LADY	al . . . *Ladie*
154	GLory	GLorie
156	hower	houre

4M5 recto, page 969

167	copy . . . incitement . . . deedes	copie . . . inticement . . . deeds
168	knights . . . steedes	Knights . . . steeds
169	ladies	Ladies
170	vn-horse	vnhorse
172	*stage*	*Stage*
173	*scene*	*Scene*
175	lawes	Lawes
177	empire	Empire
179	shee	she
182	*Britayne* . . . flie.	*Britaine* . . . flye,

	First state	Reset
185	*iustice*	*Iustice*
186	*planet*	*Planet*
192	land	Land
194	arte	art
197	fleece . . . forrayne	Fleece . . . forraine
202	thunder,	thunder;
204	trayn'd	train'd

4M5 verso, page 970

210	ayde . . . nigh	aide . . . high
211	worthyest	worthiest
213	honors . . . gayne	honours . . . gaine
214	maintayne	maintaine
217	shee	she
218	*Britayne*	*Britaine*
220	king	King
221	*lyons hart*	*Lyons heart*
225	*lion*	*Lyon*
227	Deedes	Deeds
228	armies	Armies
230	begin	beginne
232	cullors	cullours
235	Fortunes	*Fortunes*
241	S. GEORGES	Saint GEORGES
243	*red sea*	*Red Sea*
249	remaynes	remaines
250	traynes	traines

4M6 recto, page 971

256	black	blacke
258	Here	Heere
260	farre	farre.
263	*french*	*French*
267	here	heere
279	*french*	*French*
283	here	heere
300	here . . . *eightie eight,*	heere . . . *eightie eight.*

4M6 verso, page 972

301	*Spaine*	*Spaine,*
308	windes	winds
311	shee	she
316	ordinance	ord'nance
322	bloud	blood
324	thunderer	Thunderer
325	*Countries . . . Spayne*	*Countreys . . . Spaine*
327	conquests	conquest
337	glorie	glory
342	Of SATVRNES	OfSATVRNES
343	*roses*	*Roses*

In the next quire, 4N, there are different settings of the inner forme of 4N1 verso and 6 and the outer forme of 4N3 and 4.

4N1 verso, page 974

First state		Reset
393	mee	me
404	*After*	*After*
407	blood	blood,
414	*heauen*	heauen
417	prophesy	prophesie
421	shal . . . euery	shall . . . euerie
434	*nations*	*Nations*
436	fly	flie
438	sky	skie

Minor changes on this page include omitting line spaces after the speech of Chivalry and before the speech of Merlin and by reducing the size of the type in which 'THE BARRIORS' is printed from great primer to pica.

4N3 recto, page 977 (*Oberon*, 66–114)

In this page only the lower half is reset. The sole change in the upper half is to tamper with the misprinted Greek in note 'e', '$\chi\rho\upsilon\sigma\pi\acute{\eta}\lambda\epsilon\xi\ \H{a}\rho\eta s$', which should have been corrected to '$\chi\rho\upsilon\sigma\sigma\pi\acute{\eta}\lambda\eta\xi\ \H{A}\rho\eta s$'. Apparently the corrector meant to have a capital '*X*': the compositor, not understanding this, reversed the small 'χ', so that we get a new atrocity '$X\rho\upsilon\sigma\pi\acute{\eta}\lambda\epsilon\xi$'. The resetting begins after the note '$\pi\alpha\rho\grave{a}\ \tau\grave{o}\ \lambda\acute{\upsilon}\omega$, soluo'. The lyric dialogue which follows is printed in double columns, separated by small vilely printed broken rules, which are different in the two states.

Oberon

90	Column 1, 11	ayme	aime
107	Column 2, 11	shells	shels

It may be noted in passing that the type of the marginal note on 4N3 verso was deranged and was blunderingly reset: thus, in the opening lines,

* *Erat solenne*	* *Erat solenne*
Baccho in pomp.	*Baccho in pomo.*
tenerorum mo-	*tenerorum more*
re puerorum	*purorum gestaui*
gestaui à Sileno,	*à Sileno, & Sa-*
& Satyris, Bac-	*tyris, Bacchis*
chis præcedenti-	*præcedentibus,*
bus, quarum v-	*quarum vna*

> *na semper erat* | *semper erat Tym-*
> *Tympanistria,* | *panistria, altera*
> *altera Tibicina,* | *Tibicina, &c.*
> *&c. vide Athe-* | *vide Atheanæ.*
> *næ.*

The one blunder of the original setting, '*gestaui*' for '*gestari*', is not corrected, and three new blunders are foisted in by the compositor, '*pomo.*', '*purorum*', and '*Atheanæ*'. But the text is identical; the wrong-fount italic notes of exclamation at lines 133, 143 are carefully preserved.

4N4 verso, page 980

	First state	*Reset*
274	Column 1, 1 cōfesse	confesse
278	Column 2, 2 rough,	rough
280	3 Euery	Euerie
288	Tells	Tels
290	Euery	Euerie
299	SONG *correctly centred.*	*Moved to the right.*
300–1	ayre	aire
302	Whilst . . . chayre	Whil'st . . . chaire
305	*IAMES* . . . flyes	IAMES . . . flies
306	eyes	eies
307	seene,	beene;
310	very	verie
311	buryed	buried
313	eyes	eies
317	*began*	*beganne*
318	SYLVANE	SYLVANI

4N6 recto, page 983

	First state	*Reset*
409	SONG. *correctly centred.*	SONG. *moved to the right.*
410, 414	1.	1
412, 417	2.	2
418	*Faery*	*Faerie*
419	dairy	dairie

In the first state this line is correctly ranged with the preceding; in the reset it is pushed out to range with the numbers '1' in lines 2 and 6.

422	*inuited home*	*inuited home*
423	*song*	*Song*
424	SONG. *centred*	*Moved away to the right.*
425	knights	Knights
429	aery	ayrie
430	vary	varie
431	*Faery*	*Faerie*
432	tarry	tarrie
436	*Moone*	*Moone*
444	*After . . . And*	*After . . . And*
445	song, the | starre	Song, | starre

	First state	*Reset*
450	Though . . . *ranged with ll. 448–9*	*Ranged with ll. 451–2*
	bed!	bed*!*
452	fiery	fierie
453	head!	head*!*

403 recto, page 989

Love Freed

350	out ward	outward
353	wee	we
356	*Masque-daunce*	*Masque-dance*
361, 364	euery	euerie
363	hee	he
372	With . . . *set back so as to be under* 'now' *in l. 371.*	*Correctly ranged*
373, 377	*Muses*	*Muses*
375	angry	angrie
378	West	west

In the last lines of the page, the initial letter of *Love Restored*, and the spacing of the head-title are changed.

403 verso, page 990

	First state	*Reset*
Love Restored		
8	wil	will
11	attired	attyred
12	be	bee
14	Morrice-dance	Morricc-dance
16	musique	musicke
17	Cvpid . . .	*Cupid* . . .
	maiestie	Maiesty
18	chayre	chaire
21	been	beene
22	Plvtvs.	Plvt.
24, 27, 40	Mas.	Masq.
27	rayle	raile
28, 44, 48	Plv.	Plvt.
29	masquer	Masquer
31	sur-|quedry.	surque-|drie
32	finde,	finde
32–3	but | you may	but you | may
34	I | will haue	I will | haue
35	delight | so deare	delight so | deare
	merry	merrie
36	hower . . . mee	houre . . . me
37	How! no masque, no, masque	How*!* no Masque, no Masque
38	you | say, are	you say, | are
	masque indeede	Masque indeed
39	Can | you tell	Can you | tell
41	bee no maske	be no Masque
43	A masque	A Masque
47	maske	Masque

	First state	Reset
50	*ioy*	*Ioy*
52	countrey	countrie
53	mare . . . . red-brest	Mare . . . Red-brest
54	masque:	Masque:
56	countrey . . . harmelesse:	countrie . . . harmelesse:
56–7	ROBBIN good-fellow	ROBBIN-good-fellow
58	countrey	Countrey
60	court	Court
61	*catchword* run	runne

4O4, page 991

61	run	runne
62	was | so put	was so | put
63	difficulties | as I haue	difficulties as I | haue
64	masque	Masque
64–5	*Reuells.* | I would you	*Reuels.* I would | you
66	o' that | ifaith, you let	o' that ifaith, you | let
68	good fellow-ship	good-fellow-ship
70	porter . . . me	Porter . . . mee
73	nonentry	nonentrie
76	me	mee
77	me . . . acorne	mee . . . Acorne
78	sow	Sow
79	carpenters	Carpenters
82	mazarded	amazed
86	cockscombe	Cockescombe
89	belie	belye
90	ingineer	Ingineer
91	ask'd . . . beare	asked . . . Beare
94	*masquers*	*Masquers*
96	be a musician,	bee a Musician
	mary . . . instrument	marie . . . Instrument
98	feather-maker	Feather-maker
99	*black-fryers* . . . told 'hem,	*Blacke-fryers* . . . tolde 'hem.
100, 102	be	bee
103	We . . . *masquers*	Wee . . . *Masquers*
105	countrey lady	Countrie Ladie
106	he	hee
107	clock . . . me	clocke . . . mee
109	me	mee
110	Mary	Marie
111	o' the whimlen's	of the Whimlen's
116	citizens	Citizens.

4O4 verso, page 992

120	be . . . me	bee . . . mee
122	be	bee
125–6	money . . . be . . . be	monie . . . bee . . . bee
128	whome	whom
130	interpreter . . . be	Interpreter . . . bee
131	a Co-|lossus	as a | *Colossus*
132	carrie me	carrie mee

	First state	Reset
137	fayl'd me	fail'd mee
140	deuice:	deuice:
141	be	bee
145	thou,	thou
148	riots . . . ruine	ryots . . . ruines
150	me . . . entertaining	mee . . . entertayning
152–3	*Poſt* and *payre*	*Poſt* and *Payre*
154	Tables ?	*Tables?*
156	gentlewomen	Gentlewomen
157	twentie . . . charges,	twẽty . . . charges
158	old	olde
159	*Dreames*	*Dieames*
160	then	then,
161	embroydred	embroydered
163	me	mee
164	countrey	countrie
165	be	bee

Finally there are some mysterious resettings made after the Folio had been published, apparently in order to make up incomplete sets. They are signatures T2 and 5, pages 219–20, 225–6; Xx1 and 6, pages 517–18, 527–8; Aaa1 and 6, pages 553–4, 563–4; Ttt1 and 6, pages 769–70, 779–80. The paper, the watermarks, the type, and the actual text are not those of the Folio. We have collated fully only one copy, lent us by Mr. H. L. Ford, the 'A' copy described in his *Collation of the Ben Jonson Folios*; the owner of another copy sent us photostats of Xx1. Both of these copies are on large paper, and if, as we think, large-paper copies were printed after the ordinary issue, there may have been a shortage of these sets, making it worth a publisher's while to complete the stock he had in hand. We give a collation and indicate by the symbol 'F2' the readings where the resetting agrees with the text of the 1640 Folio, a point which has some bearing on the possible date of this curious transaction.

T2, pages 219–20
Cynthia's Revels, IV. i. 112–215

		Original reading	Reset
IV. i.	132	march-pane	march-bane (*F2*)
	144	what by coach	what coach
	146	owne	own
	149	*Nymph* . . . be	*Nympth* . . . bee
	180–1	as a deyrie wench, I would dance at *may*-poles, and make silla-bubbes;	omitted as in *F2*.

T5, pages 225–6
Cynthia's Revels, IV. iii. 151–249

IV. iii.	164	*thing*	*thinge*
	166	ARGVRION	ARCVRION

		Original reading	Reset
IV. iii.	167–8	PHILAVTIA, | *What*	PHILAV-|TIA, *What*
	169	*would haue done* | *it*	*would* | *haue done it*
	172	*Who*	*Who*
	193	*thing*	*thinge*
	210	page:	page:
	223	't is	t' is
	231	the*lyra*	the *lyra*

XX1, pages 517–18

Volpone, v. viii. 13–x. 39

v. viii.	18	you, hither	you hither (*F2*)
	19–20	You shall perceiue, sir, I dare beate you. Approch. | VOLP. No haste, sir, I doe know your valure, well:	You shall perceiue, sir I doe know your valure, well: (*F2*)
	25	saue me,	Saue mee
	25 margin	*Mosca walkes by 'hem.*	omitted.
	26	ayre's	ayr's
v. ix.	4	madame	madam
	6	sir. VOLP.	sir VOLP.
	9	you. I	you, I
v. x, heading		AVOCATORI, 4.	AVOCATORI, 4.
	8	he . . . himselfe?)	be . . . himselfe) (*F2*)
	9–10	I haue abus'd, out of most couetous endes— | (CORV. The man is mad! CORB. What's that? CORV. He is possesst.)	*omitted as in F2.*
	17	onely	only
		(fathers	
	20	CORV. Graue	Graue fathers
	21	it, now	it now (*F2*)

XX6, pages 527–8

Epicoene, Dedication and Persons of the Play

Dedication	10	*Vndertaker*	*Vndertaker*
	13	*And*	*And*
	18	*honorable*	*honourable*
	19	*wip'd*	*wiped*
Persons	1	*loues no noise*	*loues noise*
	12	*Collegiates*	*Collegiate* (*F2*)
	14	Mrs. TRUSTY	Mrs. MAVIS (*F2*)

Aaa1, pages 553–4

Epicoene, III. i. 21–ii. 68

III. i.	31	polluted	poluted
	40	mans-meat	mans meat (*F2*)
	42	cleane linnen	cleanelinnen
	47	lady . . . married	ladie . . . maried

		Original reading	*Reset*
III. i.	48	Whitson-	whitson-
	49	WHITING,	WHITING.
	53	thence,	thence.
	54	elbowes	eldowes (*F2*)
	56	worry	worrie
III. ii.	12	we	wee
	14	he	hee
	17, 21	Mrs· OT.	M. OT.
	21	Mr· TRVE-WIT	M. TRVE-WIT (*F2*)
	23	some body	somebody
	25, 30	Mrs· OT.	M. OT. (*F2*)
	32	gouernes	go vernes
	34, 36	Mrs· OT.	M. OT. (*F2*)
	38	sir:	sir, (Sir, *F2*)
	40	he hopes	hee hopes
	41	he, for	hee, for
	48	DAV. . . . be	DAV. . . . bee
	54, 57	Mrs· OT.	M. OT. (*F2*)
	55	vnfortnnate	unfortunate
	62	ARTEMIDORVS	ARTEMIDORTS (*F2*)
	66	Mrs· OT.	M. OT. (*F2*)
	67	staynd	staind

Aaa6, pages 563–4

Epicoene, III. vi. 63–vii. 45

III. vi.	67	Mr.	M.
	69	miraculously	miracalously
	72	vs.	vs,
	81	we	wee
	88	you.	you, (*F2*)
	91	already	alreadie
	99	mee	me
	107	mistake	mtstake
III. vii, heading		Mrs.	Mrs.
	1	anymusique	any musique
	16 st. dir.	*La-Foole . . . meate.*	*Stage-direction at l. 15.*
	19	Mrs. . . . rump	M. (*F2*) . . . rumpe
	34, 36	Mrs.	M. (*F2*)
	37	in ordinary	inordinarie
	38	Mrs.	M. (*F2*)
	41	sent . . . Captayne	Sent . . . Captaine
	42	OTTER,	OTTER
	44	trumpetters	trumpeters

Ttt1, pages 769–70

Epigrams i–vii

ii.	1	for, booke	for Booke (for Book *F2*)
	7	Deceiue	Deceive
	9	couetous . . . selfe fame	covetous . . . selfe-fame
	10	shame:	shame. (*F2*)

		Original reading	Reset
ii.	11	lesse	lesse, (*F2*)
iii.	3	giue . . . leaue . . . craue	give . . . leave . . . crave
	4	haue	have
	5	lye vpon	lie upon
	7	haue	have
	8	-sticks, aduanced	-stickes, advanced
	9	clarke-like seruing-man	clerk-like serving-man
iv.	1	do'st . . . scepter	dost . . . Scepter (*F2*)
	2	do'st	do st
	3	things,	things (*F2*)
	4	gaue	gave
	6	t'haue	t'have
	7	wee	we
v.	1	driuen	driven
	3	king	King (*F2*)
vi.	2	pouertie liues	poverty lives
vii, heading		NEW	NEVV
	1	harbour'd	harbourd (*F2*)
	2	vpon	upon
	3	So	so
	4	*Synonima*	*Synonyma*

Ttt6, pages 779–80

Epigrams xl–xlv. 8

xl.	1	couer	cover
	2	vnder-neath	under-neath
	3	R ich,	R ich (*F2*)
	4	remoue	remove
	6	heauens	heavens
	9	Rare, as wonder,	Rare as wonder (*F2*)
	10	euer	ever
	13	L ife,	L ife (*F2*)
	14	times. Few	times few (*F2*)
		haue ru'de	have ru'd (*F2*)
	15	F ate,	Fate (*F2*)
xli.	2	gold, . . . colledge	gold . . . Colledge (*F2*)
	3	quaint	qnaint
	4	shee gaue,	she gave (*F2*)
xlii.	2	obseruing	observing
	3	euer	ever
	4	neuer	never
	8	home,	home (*F2*)
	9	Oft-times,	Oft-times (*F2*)
	11	long yearn'd	long-yearn'd (*F2*)
	12	out-spun.	out-spun
	15	shee	she
	17	be	bee (*F2*)
xliii, heading		OF	Of (*F2*)
	2	themselues	themselves
	3	loue	love
	6	couetous	covetous

		Original reading	Reset
xliii.	7	not, . . . thought, lest	not . . . thought least
	9	booke	Booke (Book *F2*)
		CECILL's	CECIL's (*F2*)
	11	seruile	servile
xliv, heading		BANCKS	BANKS (*F2*)
	3	blacks	blackes
xlv.	1	ioy	joy
	2	lou'd	lov'd
	3	Seuen yeeres	Seven yeares
	4	fate,	fate (*F2*)
		iust	just
	5	loose	lose
	6	enuie	envie
	7	haue	have

Of these four resettings signatures Aaa 1 and 6 have no watermark; the watermark of the others is a stopper surmounted with a crescent, instead of a cluster of grapes in T2 and 5 and Xx1 and 6, and a small jug in Ttt1 and 6. The type is coarser and by comparison blurred. Mr. C. E. Batey, who has analysed it, dates it about 1640; this is avowedly conjecture, but there is something more than confirmation in the fact that the resetting reproduces some of the worst blunders of the 1640 Folio, for instance, 'MRS. MAVIS' instead of 'MRS. TRVSTY' in the list of characters prefixed to *Epicoene*, 'eldowes' for 'elbowes' in Act III, scene i, line 54 and in scene ii, line 62 'ARTEMIDORTS' for 'ARTEMIDORVS'; in *Volpone*, v. viii. 19–20, it copies the blundering text of 1640 in reading

> You shall perceiue, sir, I doe know your valure, well:

for the two lines

> You shall perceiue, sir, I dare beate you. Approch.
> VOLP. No haste, sir, I doe know your valure, well:

and similarly in Act v, scene x, it omits lines 9 and 10 which are omitted in the 1640 Folio. Another point in which the printing points to 1640 rather than 1616 is the use of lower-case 'j' and 'v' for 'i' and 'u'. Signatures Ttt1 and 6 are full of examples of this, 'Deceive', 'covetous' in the second *Epigram*. There does not appear to be the slightest doubt that the owner of the stock, wishing to make up his sets, reprinted from the Folio of 1640, and not, as he should have done, from the Folio of 1616.

What new work was published in the Folio? First both in place and in importance was the revised version of *Every Man in his Humour*, which we believe to have been written for it,[1] with the

---

[1] See the introduction to the play, *infra*.

scene laid in England instead of Italy and a prologue which is a
literary manifesto setting forth Jonson's ideals in comedy. It was
probably to this play specially that Selden alluded when in the
'Carmen protrepticon' prefixed to the Folio he looked forward to
the new edition:

> *Efflictìm petimus nouúmque librum,*
> *Qui nullo sacer haùt petatur œuo,*
> *Qui nullo sacer exolescat œuo,*
> *Qui curis niteat tuis secundis.*

The texts of the early plays were carefully revised, and passages
which had to be cancelled at the time of publication in quarto were
restored. Examples of the minute textual revision have been quoted
in the textual introduction to the plays.[1] The inserted passages in
Cynthia's Revels are satire on the Court, which it was impolitic to
print in 1601. The chief additions of the Folio are Act III, scene iv,
lines 22–42; Act IV, scene i, lines 136–214, scene iii, lines 159–203,
and the first four scenes of the fifth act. In *Poetaster* the chief insertions are Act I, scene ii, lines 98–136; Act III, scene iv, lines 306–14;
Act III, scene v, which we believe to have been written for the Folio;
and the important 'Apologetical Dialogue', suppressed by authority
after it had been spoken once on the stage, and invaluable for its
personal history. *Epicoene* may have been printed in 1612, but, if
so, the Quarto of that year has disappeared since Gifford wrote in
1816 that he had seen it. The Folio is therefore, so far as we know,
our earliest extant text, and Jonson claimed in the dedication to
Sir Francis Stuart that '*There is not a line, or syllable in it changed
from the simplicity of the first Copy*'. The book of *Epigrams* and *The
Forest* were new. The new entertainments and masques were those
which Stansby registered on 20 January 1615. He printed these
continuously with a title-page *Masques at Court*, but without title-
pages for the separate masques, so that the collection could be
registered for sixpence.

Jonson watched carefully over the details of the printing. In his
copy of Lipsius's *Opera Omnia*, 1623, now in the library of Emmanuel
College, Cambridge, he has marked an instruction to the printer in
volume vii before the *Politica*, 'Minuta quædam hîc seruauimus, in
Punctis, Interuallis, Notulis, Verborum discriminibus, haud facilè
per te seruanda: Sed quæ negligi tamen aut inuerti sine noxa Operis
non possunt.' His noting such a passage is characteristic.

---

[1] *Every Man out of his Humour*, vol. iii, pp. 412–17; *Cynthia's Revels*, vol. iv,
pp. 17–22; *Poetaster*, ibid., pp. 193–5; *Sejanus*, ibid., pp. 335–43; *Volpone* has
very little change; *The Alchemist*, vol. v, pp. 278–80; *Catiline*, ibid., pp. 413–15.

In contrast to the form in which other people's plays and his own earlier quartos were printed, he copied the setting of the old Greek and Latin comedians originally adopted in the first editions of Plautus (Venice, Merula, 1472), Terence (Strassburg, Rusch, 1470), Aristophanes (Aldus, 1498). The speeches in dialogue are printed continuously, running on in even lines. With these classical authors the system continues to this day. The scene headings in these early texts gave only a list of the speakers. Thus in the *editio princeps* of the *Andria* of Terence we have for headings in the first act 'Simo. Sosia' for the first scene; 'Simo. Senex Dauus' for the second; 'Misis. Serua' for the third; 'Pamphilus. Misis' for the fourth scene. The scenes, and originally even the acts, were not numbered. Entrances and exits were not marked. Jonson, while putting in the act and scene numbers, followed this system of grouping at the beginning of the scene the names of all speakers who took part in it. When a new character or characters entered in the following scene, if the earlier characters remained on the stage, he put only the new-comers' names with a marginal note '*To them*' or '*To the rest*'. Occasionally, when a character entered later in the scene, he put the name by itself at the end of the other names, as in *Every Man out of his Humour*, Act IV, scene viii, where we have 'FVNGOSO' with a marginal '*To them*'. One consequence of this system is that the Folio increases the number of the scenes: there are three in the Quarto, nine in the Folio, in the third act of *Every Man out of his Humour*. He began the system in the Quartos of *Cynthia's Revels* and *Poetaster*, though here he recorded a number of entrances and exits; but the full classical form was adopted in the Quartos of *Sejanus*, *Volpone*, and *The Alchemist*, and these were taken as a model for the Folio. In *Sejanus* and *Catiline* Jonson numbered only the acts, feeling that in these Roman plays he could adhere strictly to the classical precedent. Lyly had anticipated Jonson in heading his scenes with a list of the characters, whether they were present at the opening or not.

Printing the names at the head of the scenes in capital letters, he adopted these for names of persons in the body of the text, where the Quartos, following the printer's convention of the day, had used lower-case italic. Thus in *Sejanus*, ii. 289, 'Sacrouir', at first printed as in the Quarto, was corrected to 'SACROVIR'.[1] There is also a suggestive correction in *Volpone*, II. iii. 8: the printer set up 'And cald the PANTALONE DI BESOGNIOSI'; Jonson corrected it to

---

[1] Occasionally the printer copies the Quarto and Jonson did not correct him: '*Signior Insulso*' and '*Signior Puntaruolo*' in *E.M.O.* II. i. 142, 144, for instance.

'PANTALONE *di besogniosi*'. Place-names are in lower-case italic, e.g. '*Cripple-gate*' (*E.M.O.* Ind. 72):[1] so are technical terms ('*stoccata*', *E.M.I.* I. v. 151), quotations, songs, foreign words and phrases, Greek derivatives, and words which, in their context, have a special point. For Greek derivatives we have examples in *Every Man out of his Humour*, Induction, 103, and *Cynthia's Revels*, v. vi. 84, where '*Metaphore*' and '*Hyperbole*', at first printed in roman, were corrected to italic. As an example of a word which derives its emphasis from the context we may take '*Countenance*' and '*Resolution*' in *Every Man out of his Humour*, IV. v and following scenes.

The classical manuscripts did not mark entrances and exits, and here Jonson follows them, though there are at times passages where a note would have been helpful. '*Exit.*' is found only once in the induction to *Every Man out of his Humour*, l. 353, and there it is accidentally taken over from the Quarto. He has a few marginal stage-directions such as '*The Consul goes out*'. '*Returnes*': '*Goes out againe.*' in *Sejanus* (v. 116, 121, 127, 149), '*One knocks without.*' in *Volpone* (I. ii. 82), or '*Discouers Catiline in his study.*' in the opening lines of *Catiline*. Other marginalia are references to the classics or slight explanatory notes such as '*Pedarij*' of senators who had no vote (*Sej.* I. 48), '*Fortuna equestris*' of the statue dedicated by the Senate at Antium (ibid. 510), '*Cestus*' of the 'strange poeticall girdle' of Venus (*Volp.* v. ii. 103).

Another feature of Jonson's classicism was his attempt to get back to the Greek and Latin forms of classical derivatives, such as— adhære, ædify, æmulous, æquall, æquiuocate, æternall, apprênded (*Sej.* v. 648), cœlestiall, commune, cortine, fornace, fruict, moniments, œconomic, phant'sie, pœnance, pœne (*C.R.* v. ii. 43), præcede, præcept, præcipitate, præcise, prægnant, præiudice, prælude, præscribe, prætext, præuaricate, præuent, pretious, solœcisme, sphære, syllabe, tædious (*Poet.* I. i. 47, Quarto), tragœdie, trophæe, tyran, voluptary. The climax of this pedantry was '*porcpisce*' for porpoise (*Sej.* v. 622; *Volp.* II. i. 40; *S.W.* IV. iv. 144), for here the classical name was *porcus marinus*; but Jonson was following Spenser (*Colin Clout*, 251), and he was followed in his turn by Dryden. These forms were sometimes too much for the printer, who normalized them: the Quartos have more of them than the Folio. The same thing happened to Milton, whose similar spellings, preserved in the Trinity College MS. of *Comus*, are not reproduced in the printed text.

---

[1] Frequently the Folio prints these with a lower-case initial capital, especially in *Cynthia's Revels* ('*spanish*, or *italian*', I. iv. 81); '*Venetian*' is corrected to '*venetian*' in this play, IV. i. 48. Such unusual spellings as '*liburnean*', '*cretan*' (*Sej.* v. 458; *Volp.* III. vii. 216) are not likely to have been a printer's.

The free use of capital letters in the Quartos was much restricted in the Folio. Thus in the opening lines of *Volpone* the Quarto has

> Good morning to the Day; and next, my Gold:
> Open the shrine, that I may see my *Saint*.

The Folio has

> Good morning to the day; and, next, my gold:
> Open the shrine, that I may see my *saint*.

Similarly in Act I, scene ii, ll. 124–5,

> Now, my fain'd *Cough*, my *Phthisick*, and my *Goute*,
> My *Apoplexie, Palsie*, and *Catarrhe*, . . .

in the Quarto become in the Folio

> Now, my fain'd cough, my phthisick, and my gout,
> My apoplexie, palsie, and catarrhes, . . .

The usage is too common to illustrate further.

The Folio, in contrast with the Quartos, shows a fully developed system of punctuation. In the earlier Quartos the punctuation is lighter, more akin to contemporary practice where the stops marked pauses in speech rather than the logical arrangement of clauses. When we edited the first play which Jonson issued, *Every Man out of his Humour*, we noted points of difference in the printing and quoted side by side two specimen passages.[1] We note here the main points of difference. First, with vocatives. 'Alas sir no' and 'Cling to my necke and wrists my louing Wormes' of the Quarto text of *Poetaster* (I. ii. 190, and induction 6) become 'Alas, sir, no' and 'Cling to my necke, and wrists, my louing wormes' in the Folio. The first of a pair of adjectives is marked off by a comma in the Folio: 'Sweet, and deare father' (*E.M.O.* III. vii. 28)—a significant example, for Jonson put the comma in while correcting the proofs of the Folio. Similarly with alternative words: 'two, or three', 'three, or foure' (ibid. II. vi. 23, 90). Adverbs and adverbial phrases are marked off with commas. For example, 'You deale, now, with a noble fellow' (*Alch.* I. ii. 34); and the instructions to Dapper,

> onely, take
> Three drops of vinegar, in, at your nose;
> Two at your mouth; and one, at either eare;
> Then, bath your fingers endes; and wash your eyes;
> To sharpen your fiue senses; and, cry *hum*,
> Thrise; and then *buz*, as often; and then, come.

> (Ibid. 165–70.)

[1] See vol. iii, pp. 414–15: these included changes of type. Similarly with *Poetaster*, vol. iv., pp. 190–1.

Or Drugger's petition to Subtle,

> And I would know, by art, sir, of your worship,
> Which way I should make my dore, by *necromancie*.
> And, where my shelues. And, which should be for boxes.
> And, which for pots.   (Ibid. iii. 10–13.)

In *The Alchemist* the Quarto has, for the most part, the elaborate punctuation: in the above passages it agrees with the Folio.

In the Folio the use of the exclamation mark is much freer. Fallace's rhapsody about Fastidius Briske is appropriately pointed with it: 'Oh, sweete FASTIDIVS BRISKE! ô fine courtier! thou art hee mak'st me sigh, and say, how blessed is that woman that hath a courtier to her husband! and how miserable a dame shee is, that hath neyther husband, nor friend i' the court! O, sweet FASTIDIVS! ô, fine courtier! How comely he bows him in his court'sie! how full he hits a woman betweene the lips when he kisses! how vpright hee sits at the table! how daintily he carues! how sweetly he talkes, and tels newes of this lord, and of that lady!' (*E.M.O.* iv. i. 29–38). Here the Quarto and the Folio at first read 'kisses?' 'table?' 'carues?' 'Lady?' Jonson changed the marks of interrogation in the proof.

Brackets play a distinct part in Jonson's system. They are used with an adverb or an adverbial phrase: 'Shee (late) hath found much fault' (ibid. ii. iv. 83); 'I feare, I haue (forgettingly) transgrest' (*Volp.* iv. vi. 5); 'onely your nose enclines (That side, that's next the sunne) to the queene-apple' (ibid. ii. 73–4); 'part of the grot (About the entrie) fell' (*Sej.* iv. 51). In a more subtle use brackets mark off anything which interrupts the grammatical movement of the sentence or the current of the thought: 'What (great, I will not say, but) sodayne cheare' (*The Forest*, ii. 82); 'I', says Cupid, 'haue beene contented (not to put off, but) to conceale my deitie' (*Ch. at Tilt*, 24–6); and Cynthia's pronouncement,

> Such is our chastitie: which safely scornes
> (Not *Loue*, for who more feruently doth loue
> Immortall honour, and diuine renowne?
> But) giddie CVPID, VENVS franticke sonne.
> (*C.R.* v. vi. 51–4.)

Here the Quarto brackets only '(for who more feruently . . . Renowne?)'. An innuendo in *The Forest* (xii. 68–9)—the reference to Lady Bedford—shows how Jonson could barb this point:

> Who, though she haue a better verser got,
> (Or *Poet*, in the court account) then I . . . .

Any other poet would have punctuated 'Or *Poet* (in the court account)', but Jonson puts the entire alternative as a contemptuous afterthought. Brackets are also used for quotations: 'wee can force no answere from him, but (ô reuenge, how sweet art thou! I will strangle him in this towell)' (*S.W.* IV. v. 181–3). And for stage-asides, as for those of Arrúntius or the Senators during the reading of Tiberius' letter in the fifth act of *Sejanus*, lines 564 following.

One other device of Jonson, his use of an apostrophe between two unelided but lightly sounded syllables to indicate that they are metrically equivalent to one syllable, has been already illustrated in the introductions to the *Grammar* and to the texts of *Every Man in his Humour*, *Sejanus*, and *Catiline*.[1] For instance, 'Before our hands be'at worke. I can accuse . . .' (*Catiline*, III. 588). The printers, especially the printers of the 1640 Folio, frequently blundered over this punctuation, omitting the mark or eliding one of the vowels, so that they printed 'T' a princes state' in *Sejanus*, I. 448, where the Quarto has 'To' a princes state', and 's'exceede' for 'so' exceede' in *Underwood*, xiv. 54, as contrasted with 'so' out-shone' (*Pr. Hen. Barriers*, 79). In the introduction to *Sejanus* we gave as illustration the similar practice of Donne. We may add here that this metrical apostrophe appears in the autograph manuscript of Milton, though it is not reproduced in his printed text. In *Comus*, 538 the manuscript has 'to' inveigle & invite th' unwarie sense', and in 723 'th' all giver would be' unthank't would be unprais'd'.

'Sentences', or moral maxims on life and conduct—the *sententiae* of the ancients—are printed with inverted commas at the beginning only of the verse or the sentence. They are exemplified in the introduction to *Sejanus*, and they are a common feature in the printing of the time.[2]

The authority for Jonson's punctuation, and for the changes which he made in it in reading the proofs of the Folio, is the autograph manuscript of *The Masque of Queens*, from which we printed our text.[3] Here are a few sentences (ll. 670–7): 'But, here, I discerne a possible Obiection, arising agaynst mee, to wch I must turne: As, *How I can bring* Persons, *of so different* Ages, *to appeare, properly, together*? Or, *Why* (wch is more vnnaturall) wth Virgil's Mezentius, *I ioyne the liuing*, w^th *the dead*? I answere to both these, at once, Nothing is more proper; Nothing more naturall: For these all liue; and together, in they^r *Fame*; And so I present them.' Here again (ll. 663–6) 'The *Name* of BEL-ANNA I deuis'd to honor hers

---

[1] See vol. ii, pp. 430–1; vol. iii, pp. 295–6; iv, pp. 338–42; v, p. 414.
[2] See P. Simpson, *Shakespearian Punctuation*, § 42.
[3] See vol. vii, pp. 277–317.

proper, by; as adding, to it, the attribute of *Fayre*: And is kept by
mee, in all my *Poëmes*, wherin I mention her *Maiesty* wᵗh any
shadow, or *figure*'. And the description of Zenobia (ll. 628–30), 'In
Trebellius Pollio, reade the most noble description of a *Queene*, and
her; that can be utter'd, wᵗh the dignity of an *Historian*'. A few
smaller points are 'Call vs one, by one,' (l. 115); 'Mixe Hell, wᵗh
Heauen,' (l. 147); 'Cast them, vp;' (l. 265); 'You, that (to arme
vs) haue yoʳ selues disarmd' (l. 221). And for emphasis in the
unusual punctuation we may quote (ll. 70, 71):

> Quickly, come away:
> For we, all, stay.

and the final reference to greatness (ll. 771–2), which

> soone decayes;
> But so *good Fame* shall, neuer.

    The Folio was much corrected in the course of its passing through
the press. As with so many books of the time, corrected and uncorrected sheets are bound up together, so that it is necessary to collate
a number of copies in order to present the text in the form in which
Jonson wished it to appear. The following copies have been collated:
The Grenville copy in the British Museum, a beautiful copy on large
paper ('M1' in the following list); a second Museum copy with press-
mark C.39.k.9 ('M2'); two copies in the Bodleian, with shelf-marks
A.A. 83. Art, Douce I. 302 ('B1, B2'); the Oriel College copy; and
three copies belonging to the editor, a copy bought from Bernard
Quaritch in 1888 for eighteen shillings ('S1'), the late Lord Birkenhead's copy ('S2'), and a large-paper copy (defective at beginning
and end) which was formerly Sir Charles Firth's ('S3'). By the
permission of that generous scholar, the late Professor W. Bang, we
printed our text of the early plays from his edition of the Folio in
the *Materialen zur Kunde des älteren englischen Dramas*. Even so,
we have had to push the search further for the press-variants of
Cynthia's Revels, recording from Dr. Judson's edition exceptional
variants from the Yale University copy and from a copy belonging
to Professor W. L. Phelps.

    It was the exception, not the rule, for a seventeenth-century
printer to send out proofs to an author. The author dropped in at
the press once or twice a day, looked over the newly taken pulls,
and corrected such errors as caught his eye in a cursory reading.
The uncorrected sheets were not kept separate, still less were they
destroyed; they were bound up at haphazard with those which the
author had corrected, as we see from the lists on the following pages.

Dr. R. B. McKerrow was the first to cope with this problem editorially in his edition of the *The Devil's Charter* by Barnabe Barnes, which he edited for Professor Bang's series in 1904. The only editor of Jonson who has followed him is Dr. A. C. Judson in his edition of *Cynthia's Revels* in the Yale Studies in English, 1912. A sheet of the Folio consists (usually) of three leaves of four pages each, bound together so that the first leaf has pages 1, 2, 11, and 12; the second has 3, 4, 9, and 10; and the third 5, 6, 7, and 8. Pages 1 and 12, 3 and 10, 5 and 8 constitute the outer forme; pages 2 and 11, 4 and 9, 6 and 7 the inner forme. The two formes were printed at different times, the inner forme probably being printed first; the outer being printed on the back of this when it had had time to dry. Hence we may find a corrected inner forme with an uncorrected outer, and vice versa. In checking the following lists we have therefore to remember that the pages corrected together were

> A1 recto, page 1, with A6 verso, page 12;
> A1 verso, page 2, with A6 recto, page 11;
> A2 recto, page 3, with A5 verso, page 10;
> A2 verso, page 4, with A5 recto, page 9;
> A3 recto, page 5, with A4 verso, page 8;
> A3 verso, page 6, with A4 recto, page 7.

An asterisk is added to readings which have not been recorded in the critical apparatus of the text; a few of these were overlooked, and others were obtained by collating fresh copies. Some new variants were sent us by Mr. H. L. Ford. It is, of course, possible that more may come to light in copies which we have been unable to collate. Twice in our text of the plays we have been mistaken about a correction: in *Cynthia's Revels*, III. v. 54, 'adore,' and 'adore' is a case of a comma dropping out in the printing; and in *Poetaster*, III. iv. 237, where the Folio assigns the line to the first Pyrgus, there is no authority for '2. Pyr.', which the sense requires. In the preliminary quire

> ¶ 6^r the side-notes '*Vpon Seianus.*' against H. Holland's verses, '*In Vulponem*' against the Latin verses of Donne and Bolton, inserted in *S1*, are not found in the other copies. Without them it would not be clear that Donne's verses referred to *Volpone*.

Every Man in his Humour

A2^r, p. 3.	Dedication, 5	CLARENTIAVX *not in M2,*	*Inserted in the rest*
		O	
A3^r, p. 5.	Prologue 3	stage *M2, S2*	stage, *the rest*
	14	day . . . be; *M2, S2*	day, . . . be. *the rest**

A4ᵛ, p. 8.	i. ii. heading	Knowell *M2, S2*	Kno'well the rest*
	4	you . . . vncle, here, *M2, S2*	you, . . . * vncle here *the rest*
	10	a very *M2, S2*	very *the rest*
	13	you *M2, S2**	you, *the rest**
	31	cannot *M2, S2*	can not, *the rest*
	43 c.w.	Knowell *M2. S2*	Kno'well *the rest**
A5ᵛ, p. 10.	i. ii. 107	t'haue *M2, O*	then t'haue *the rest*
	125	in-kind *M2, O*	in kind *the rest*
	i. iii 12	Blayne-*all but B2*	Brayne- *B2**
A6ʳ, p. 11.	i. iii. 16	lettler *B1, S1*	letter *the rest*
D6ᵛ, p. 48.	iv. ii. 115	you companions *M2, B1, 2, O, S1, 2*	your companions *M1, 2, S3*
F4ʳ, p. 68.	v. iii. 83	metamorphosis *B1, O, S1, 2*	*metamorphosis* M1, 2, B2, S3

Every Man out of his Humour

For this play we have also collated Mr. H. L. Ford's 'A' copy on large paper. Quire G, pp. 73–84, was reset with a plain title-page. This quire embodies Jonson's corrections and Stansby's re-spacings. The removal of the stage-direction between ll. 50, 51 on p. 82 lost the space of three lines, and 'whites' were left before and after Mitis' speech in 37, 'Forbeare, good Asper' and before Asper's speech, 51, 'I not obserued', giving the page an irregular look. Stansby improved the printing of this sheet and must have told Jonson about it. For corrections of the text see pp. 82, 84, ll. 139, 145, and for respacing see the resetting in the Ford copy.

G2ʳ, p. 75.	Dedication,* 2–4	HVMA- | NITY, AND LIBERTY, | IN THE KINGDOME *M2, B1, 2, O, S1, 2*	HVMA- | NITY, AND LIBERTY, IN THE |KINGDOME *M1, Ford, S3**
	13	*Now M2, B1, 2, O, S1, 2*	*Now,* S3, M1, Ford*
	15	*promise*; *M2, B1, 2, O, S1, 2*	*promise,* M1, Ford, S3*
	19	*publike. For so M2, B1, 2, O, S1, 2*	*publike: For so,* M1, Ford, S3*
	24	true Honorer *M2, B1, 2, O, S1, 2*	honorer *M1, Ford, S3*
G2ᵛ, p. 76.	The Actors,* 5	Pvntervolo *M2, B1, 2, O, S1, 2*	Pvntarvolo *M1, Ford, S3**
		Seruingmen 2. *M2, B1, 2, O, S1, 2*	Seruingmen, two *M1, Ford, S3*
	10	*Cinedo* his Page *M2, B1, 2, O, S1, 2*	Cinedo, *his* Page *M1, Ford, S3*
	13	*Fido* their Seruant *M2, B1, 2, O, S1, 2*	Fido, their Seruant *M1, Ford, S3*
	15	Hinde, *M2, B1, 2, O, S1, 2*	Hine *M1, Ford, S3*
	23	*Rustici* (ranged with 'Shift') *M2, B1, 2, O, S1, 2*	Rvstici (*above* 'Fungoso') *M1, Ford, S3*
	29	Orenge *M2, B1, 2, O, S1, 2*	Orange *M1, Ford, S3**

G3ʳ, p. 77. Characters, 5 *of | danger* M1, 2, B1, 2, *of dan-|ger* Ford*
O, S1, 2, 3

G3ᵛ, p. 78. 42 *and | backs* M1, 2, B1, 2, O, *and backs |* Ford*
S1, 2, 3

43 *into | credit* M1, 2, B1, 2, O, *into credit* Ford*
S1, 2, 3

44–5 *the | jerke of his* M1, 2, B1, 2, *the jerke of |* his Ford*
O, S1, 2, 3

G4ʳ, p. 79. 68 *pray'd, | but* M1, 2, B1, 2, O, *pray'd, but |* Ford*
S1, 2, 3

85 *liues | vpon* M1, 2, B1, 2, O, *liues vp-|on* Ford*
S1, 2, 3

88 *shil-|lings* M1, 2, B1, 2, O, *shillings* Ford*
S1, 2, 3

89 *of | seruices* M1, 2, B1, 2, O, *of serui-|ces* Ford*
S1, 2, 3

90 *came | new* M1, 2, B1, 2, O, *came new |* Ford*
S1, 2, 3

G4ᵛ, p. 80. 101 *Twins* M1, 2, B1, 2, O, S1, *twins* Ford*
2, 3

104 *Plaiers* M1, 2, B1, 2, O, S1, *Players* Ford*
2, 3,

G5ʳ, p. 81. Heading. *Sounding* M2, B1, 2, O, S1, 2 *sounding* M1, Ford, S3*
5 he *M2, B1, 2, O, S1, 2* hee *M1, Ford, S3*
7 cañot wake | *M2, B1, 2, O,* cannot | wake *M1,*
S1, 2   Ford, S3*
11 vs. *M2, B1, 2, O, S1, 2* vs! *M1, Ford, S3*
13 I: my soule *M2, B1, 2, O,* I. My language *M1,*
S1, 2   Ford, S3
14 oyly *M2, B1, 2, O, S1, 2* oily *M1, Ford, S3*

In M1, Ford, S3 the page ends at l. 14 'such oily colours', with catchword 'To'. In the other copies the page ends at l. 17 'follies of the
time', with catchword 'Naked'.

G4ᵛ, p. 82. 15 daube *M2, B1, 2, O, S1, 2* dawbe *M1, Ford, S3*
17 time, *M2, B1, 2, O, S1, 2* time *M1, Ford, S3*
22 publicke, *M2, B1, 2, O, S1, 2* publike *M1, Ford, S3*
24 luxuries; *M2, B1, 2, O, S1, 2* luxuries: *M1, Ford, S3*
34 howerly *M2, B1, 2, O, S1, 2* hourely *M1, Ford, S3*
41 Sanctitie *M2, B1, 2, O, S1, 2* sanctitie *M1, Ford, S3*
44 than the Ocean *M2, B1, 2,* then the ocean *M1,*
O, S1, 2   Ford, S3
45 Counters *M2, B1, 2, O, S1, 2* Counters M1, Ford, S3

Between 50 and 51 a stage-direction *Here hee makes adresse to the People.*
In M2, S1 on the left, extending into the outer margin; in B2 and the Bang
copy on the right, extending to the inner margin; not found in B1, O,
S2, leaving a white line-space; not in M1, Ford, S3, with the line
closed up.

In M1, Ford, S3 the page ends at l. 58 'your applause', with catchword 'Like'; in the other copies at l. 60 'austerest brow', with catchword 'Where'.

G6ʳ, p. 83.	59	merit: *M2, B1, 2, O, S1, 2*	merit. *M1, Ford, S3**
	62	Censors . . . eyes *M2, B1, 2, O, S1, 2*	censors, . . . eyes, *M1, Ford, S3*
	63	me; . . . fauour. *M2, B1, 2, O, S1, 2*	me, . . . fauour, *M1, Ford, S3*
	69	fury *M2, B1, 2, O, S1, 2*	furie *M1, Ford, S3**
	72	Cripple-gate *M2, B1, 2, O, S1, 2*	*Cripple-gate* M1, Ford, S3
	74	peremptory *M2, B1, 2, O, S1, 2*	peremptorie *M1, Ford, S3*
	76	Nay *M2, B1, 2, O, S1, 2*	Nay, *M1, Ford, S3*
		Mɪᴛ. Answere? what? *as a new line in M2, B1, 2, O, S1, 2*	*Ranged with* 'Nay . . . answere.' *in* M1, *Ford, S3*
	81	O *M2, B1, 2, O, S1, 2*	O, *M1, Ford, S3*
	85	I; I *M2, B1, 2, O, S1, 2*	I, I *M1, Ford, S3*
	86	Cᴏʀ. For the abuse of Humour. *as a new line in M2, B1, 2, O, S1, 2*	*Ranged with* 'Asᴘ. Ha? . . . is't.' *in* M1, *Ford, S3**
	88	Why . . . it *M2, B1, 2, O, S1, 2*	Why, . . . it, *M1, Ford, S3*
	89	aire *M2, B1, 2, O, S1, 2*	aire, *M1, Ford, S3**
	91	Moisture *M2, B1, 2, O, S1, 2*	Moisture, *M1, Ford, S3*
	93	horne *M2, B1, 2, O, S1, 2*	horne, *M1, Ford, S3*
	96	what so'ere *M2, B1, 2, O, S1, 2*	vvhatso'ere *M1, Ford, S3**
	98	Humour: so *M2, B1, 2, O, S1, 2*	Humour. So *M1, Ford, S3*
G6ᵛ, p. 84.	103	Metaphore *B2, S1*	*Metaphore* M1, 2, B1 O, S2, 3, Ford
	105	quality *M2, B1, 2, O, S1, 2*	qualitie *M1, S3, Ford**
	110	Rooke *M2, B1, 2, O, S1, 2*	rooke *M1, Ford, S3*
	112	shoe-tie *M2, B1, 2, O, S1, 2*	shooetye *M1, Ford, S3*
	114	'tis *M2, B1, 2, O, S1, 2*	it is *M1, Ford, S3**
	115	truth: now *M2, B1, 2, S1, 2*	truth now, *M1, Ford, S3*
	117	Apes *M2, B1, 2, O, S1, 2*	apes *M1, Ford, S3*
	120	deformity *M2, B1, 2, O, S1, 2*	deformitie *M1, Ford, S3*
	121	euery *M2, B1, 2, O, S1, 2*	euerie *M1, Ford, S3**
	123	Asᴘᴇʀ *M2, B1, 2, O, S1, 2*	Asᴘᴇʀ. *M1, Ford, S3*
	127	men; *M2, B1, 2, O, S1, 2*	men, *M1, Ford, S3**
	129	Yes . . . be *M2, B1, 2, O, S1, 2*	Yes, . . . be, *M1, Ford, S3*
	130	either *M2, B1, 2, O, S1, 2*	eyther *M1, Ford, S3*
	132	phisicke *M2, B1, 2, O, S1, 2*	physicke *M1, Ford, S3**
	133	And . . . camels *M2, B1, 2, O, S1, 2*	And, . . . camels, *M1, Ford, S3*
	139	this, . . . *M2, B2, S1*	this? *M1, B1, O, S2, 3*
		no *M2, B1, 2, O, S1, 2*	No *M1, Ford, S3*
	140	any here *M2, B1, 2, O, S1, 2*	any, here, *M1, Ford, S3*

G6ᵛ, p.84. 142 For *M2, B2, O, S1*   For, *B1, M1, Ford, S2, 3*
           145 Crush *B2, S1*   Squeeze *M1, 2, B1, O, S2, 3*

                    soules *M2, B1, 2, O, S1, 2*   natures *M1, Ford, S3*

This quire shows a corrected state in lines 103, 139, 140, 142, and 145. (The readings found in M1, Ford, and S3 alone are a resetting.)

H3ᵛ, p. 90. I. i. 20 lou'd *M2, B2, S2*   lou'd, *M1, B1, O, S1, 2*
             27 wild-fire *M2, B2, S2*   wild-fire, *M1, B1, O, S1, 3*

             34 *incutitᵷ,* Bang copy   *incutitᵷ* all other copies collated

         ii. 3 Gentleman *M2, B2, S2*   Gentleman, *M1, B1, O, S1, 3*

             4 CAR. A . . . resolution. *om. M2, B2, S2 (with catchword* 'CAR.')   *Inserted in the rest, with catchword* 'SOG.'

The last line of page 90, brought over from page 91, but at first accidentally dropped.

H4ʳ, p. 91. I. ii. 24 signior *M2, B2, S2*   Signior *M1, B1, O, S1, 3*
             45 all: *M2, B2, S2*   all; *M1, B1, O, S1, 3*
I3ᵛ, p. 102. II. i. 166 Saies *M2, B2, S1*   saies *M1, B1, O, S2**
I4ʳ, p. 103. II. ii. 7 aboue. *M2, B2, S1*   aboue! *M1, B1, O, S2*
             40 edifice; *M2, B2, S1*   edifice! *M1, B1, O, S2*
L1ᵛ, p. 122. III. iii. 23 and *acute,* M2, B2, S2   & acute *M1, B1, O, S1, 3*
             28 her; *M2, B2, S2*   her— *M1, B1, O, S1, 3*
             29 me. *M2, B2, S2*   me! *M1, B1, O, S1, 3*
             30 admiration, *M2, B2, S2*   admiration *M1, B1, O, S1, 3*

             33 (margin) The first bill. *not in M2, B2, S2*   *Inserted in the rest*

           44–5 *giuen.* This is *M2, B2, S2*   *giuen.* | PVNT. This is *M1, B1, O, S1, 3*

             47 (margin) The second bill. *not in M2, B2, S2*   *Inserted in the rest*
             47 PVNT. *If* M2, B2, S2   *If* M1, B1, O, S1, 3
             48 *any* | *yong* M2, B2, S2   *any young* | *M1, B1, O, S1, 3*

             57 EVRIPVS . . . *whiffe* M2, B2, S2   Euripus . . . *Whiffe the rest*

L2ᵛ, p. 124. III. iv. 48 Harrots *M2*   *Harrots* the rest
             48 st.-dir. *in M2 at l. 46*   *At l. 48 in the rest*
             52 god *M2*   them *the rest*
             60 *Bore* M2   Bore *the rest*
             62 Bore *M2*   Boore *the rest*
             64 Heralds . . . Swine *M2*   *Heralds* . . . swine *the rest*
             79 PROPER *M2*   *Proper* the rest
             81 head, PROPER *M2*   head *Proper* the rest
             82 st.-dir. *Puntaruolo* M2   *Puntaruolo* the rest
             83 Hogs-cheeke *M2*   hogs-cheeke *the rest*
             88 pan . . . crest *M2*   pan, . . . crest, *the rest*

L5ʳ, p. 129. III. vi.	136	time, sir, *M2*	time, sir; *the rest*
	137	head, . . . those *M2*	head: . . . these *the rest*
	145	sir, *M2*	sir: *the rest*
	162	whiffes *M2*	*whiffes* the rest
	171	Dogge *M2*	dogge *the rest*
	178	*Affrick, M2*	*Affrick:* the rest
	179	face, you *M2*	face. You *the rest*
	183	argue . . . day *M2*	argue, . . . day, *the rest*
L6ʳ, p. 131. III. vii.	22	*seruice!* by *M2, B2, S2*	*seruice* ? by *M1, B1, O, S1, 3*
	28	(margin) The letter. *not in M2, B2, S2*	*Inserted in the rest*
	28	*Sweet* M2, B2, S2	*Sweet, M1, B1, O, S1, 3*
	30	*gold* M2, B2, S2	*gold, M1, B1, O, S1, 3*
	32	*dancing,* M2, B2, S2	*dancing:* M1, B1, O, S1, 3
	33	*shew in truth*; M2, B2, S2	*shew, in truth,* M1, B1, O, S1, 3
	37	*law: therefore* M2, B2, S2	*law. Therefore* M1, B1, O, S1, 3
	38	*sake* M2, B2, S2	*sake,* M1, B1, O, S1, 3
	41	*gentilitie,* M2, B2, S2	*gentilitie:* M1, B1, O, S1, 3
	45	*Yours, if his owne.* M2, B2, S2 *in a line by itself.*	Yours, if his owne. *B1, O, S1, ranged with the end of the letter.* Yours, if his owne. *M1, S3, in a line by itself.*
	46	this ? *M2, B2, S2*	this! *M1, B1, O, S1, 3*
	47–8	Belike . . . kinde . . . Wel, *M2, B2, S2*	Belike, . . . kind . . . Wel! *M1, B1, O, S1, 3*
	49	indeede; *M2, B2, S2*	indeede! *M1, B1, O, S1, 3*
	57	there *M2, B2, S2*	there, *M1, B1, O, S1, 3*
	61	now, *M2, B2, S2*	now! *M1, B1, O, S1, 3*
	63	No, aliue *M2, B2, S2*	No. Aliue *M1, B1, O, S1, 3*
	64	preserue it, *M2, B2, S2*	preserue it; *M1, B1, O, S1, 3*
	65	touch it, *M2, B2, S2*	touch it: *M1, B1, O, S1, 3*
	66	hell *M2, B2, S2*	hel, *M1, B1, O, S1, 3*
L6ᵛ, p. 132. III. viii.	1	(margin) *To him.* Not in S2	*Inserted in the rest*
M2ʳ, p. 135. III. ix.	40	would *B2, S1, 2*	that you would *M1, 2, B1, O, S3*
M2ᵛ, p. 136. III. ix.	101	fingers *B2, S1, 2*	fingers, *M1, 2, B1, O, S3*
	113	ladie *B2, S1, 2*	ladie. *M1, 2, B1, O, S3*
	115	Good, *B2, S1, 2*	Good! *M1, 2, B1, O, S3*
	116	fire: *B2, S1, 2*	fire. *M1, 2, B1, O, S3*
	118	And *B2, S1, 2*	And, *M1, 2, B1, O, S3*
	132	*Simile* B2, S1, 2	*simile* M1, 2, B1, O, S3
	136–7	*March . . . agoe. B2, S1, 2*	(*March . . . ago.) M1, 2, B1, O, S3*
	137	comet *B2, S1, 2*	Comet *M1, 2, B1, O, S3*

M3ʳ, p. 137.	IV. i. 5	ano-|god *S1*	ano-|ther, god *the rest*
M3ᵛ, p. 138.	IV. i. 34	courtesie *S1*	court'sie *the rest*
	35	betwixt . . . kisses? *S1*	betweene . . . kisses ! *the rest*
	36	table? . . . carues? *S1*	table! . . . carues! *the rest*
	38	lady? . . . spoone *S1*	lady! . . . spoone, *the rest*
	40	Oh, sweet *S1*	O, sweet *the rest*
	ii. 1	you'le *S1*	you'll *the rest*
	3	tell you, *S1*	tell you: *the rest*
	8	yfaith, . . . her, *S1*	yfaith! . . . her. *the rest*
	18	supper time *S1, O*	supper time, *the rest*
	26	from the court *S1*	from court *the rest*
	27	mistris *S1*	Mistris *the rest*
	34	gallants't *S1*	gallant'st the *rest*
	37	Fearefull *S1*	fearefull *the rest*
M4ʳ, p. 139.	IV. ii. 40	counterfeits, *S1*	counterfeits. *the rest*
	44	*Zani* S1	*Zani*, the rest
	49	him. *S1*	him! *the rest*
	50	'hem *S1*	'hem, *the rest*
	52	*Chesse*, S1	*Chesse*: the rest
	54	O, *S1*	O *the rest*
	56	me *S1*	me, *the rest*
	59	hand *S1*	hand, *the rest*
	61	still *S1*	still, *the rest*
	63	see him *S1*	see him, *the rest*
	65	*Notaries* S1	*Notaries*, the rest
	66	*Exchange* presently, *S1*	*Exchange*, presently: *the rest*
	75	here . . . gold *S1*	here, . . . gold, *the rest*
	81	st.-dir. Deliro . . . *wife.* not in S1	*Inserted in the rest*
	88	sute; *S1*	sute: *the rest*
	91	malitious *not in S1* and tell *S1*	*Found in the rest* & tel *the rest*
	92	heauens *S1*	heuens *the rest*
M5ʳ, p. 141.	IV. iii. 22	cat, *B2, S1, 2*	cat *M1, 2, B1, O, S3*
	24	physicians *B2, S1, 2*	physicians, *M1, 2, B1, O, S3*
	29	meanes; as magique *B2, S1, 2*	meanes, as magicke *M1, 2, B1, O, S3*
	32	enchantments; *B2, S1, 2*	enchantments, *M1, 2, B1, O, S3*
	36	vnderstand you? . . . bee *B2, S1, 2*	(vnderstand you?) . . . be *M1, 2, B1, O, S3*
	37	fraud *B2, S1, 2*	fraud, *M1, 2, B1, O, S3*
	41	traine *B2, S1, 2*	traine, *M1, 2, B1, O, S3*
	44	said, sir: *B2, S1, 2*	said, sir, *M1, 2, B1, O, S3*
	49	That...departure *B2, S1, 2*	that . . . departure, *M1, 2, B1, O, S3*

M5ʳ, p. 141. IV. iii.	52	hindered *B2, S1, 2*	hindered, *M1, 2, B1, O, S3*
	55	sir; *B2, S1, 2*	sir, *M1, 2, B1, O, S3*
	58	CARLO, *B2, S1, 2*	CARLO! *M1, 2, B1, O, S3*
	66	him; *B2, S1, 2*	him: *M1, 2, B1, O, S3*
	67	houre; *B2, S1, 2*	houre, *M1, 2, B1, O, S3*
	69	smooth? *B2, S1, 2*	smooth! *M1, 2, B1, O, S3*
M5ᵛ, p. 142. IV. iii.	88	chamber *B2, S1, 2*	chamber, *M1, 2, B1, O, S3*
	98	awaie *B2, S1, 2*	away *M1, 2, B1, O, S3*
	99	How? *Bang copy*	How! *all other copies*
N1ʳ, p. 145. IV. iv.	112	table *M2, B1, O, S1*	table, *M1, B2, S2, 3*
	113	citie *M2, B1, O, S1*	citie, *M1, B2, S2, 3**
	115	'hem *M2, B1, O, S1*	'hem, *M1, B2, S2, 3**
	116	then: *M2, B1, O, S1*	then, *M1, B2, S2, 3**
	118	man; *M2, B1, O, S1*	man! *M1, B2, S2, 3**
	V. 1	GALLANTO'S *M2, B1, O, S1*	*Gallanto's* M1, B2, S2, 3
		come *M2, B1, O, S1*	come, *M1, B2, S2, 3**
N1ʳ, p. 145. IV. v.	11	any's *M2, B1, O, S1*	any is *M1, B2, S2, 3*
	13	with you; *M2, B1, O, S1*	with you. *M1, B2, S2, 3*
	16	him; *M2, B1, O, S1*	him, *M1, B2, S2, 3*
	22	place *M2, B1, O, S1*	place, *M1, B2, S2, 3*
	28	manhood; *M2, B1, O, S1*	manhood: *M1, B2, S2, 3*
N2ʳ, p. 147. IV. vi.	1	(margin) *To them.* not in M2	*Inserted in the rest*
	9	me: I know *M2*	me. I know *the rest**
	10	one *M2*	one, *the rest**
	19	disgrace, indeed, *M2*	disgrace (indeed) *the rest*
	25	there's *M2*	there were *the rest*
	26	I; *M2*	I: *the rest*
	28	an ingenious tall *M2*	as ingenious a tal *the rest*
	32	robbery *M2*	robbery, *the rest*
	35	was't *M2*	was it *the rest*
	37	that *M2*	occasions *the rest*
	41	respects, *M2*	respects: *the rest**
	43	for *M2*	for, *the rest*
N5ᵛ, p. 154. IV. viii.	100	SOGLIARDO *M2*	SOGLIARDO, *the rest**
	102	for court *M2*	for the court *the rest*
	103	court *M2*	court, *the rest*
	105	selfe; *M2*	selfe, *the rest**
	106	miter *M2*	Mitre *the rest*
	110	*manfrede* it *M2*	vndertake *the rest*
	115	monsieur . . . Courtier *M2*	Monsieur . . . courtier *the rest*
	122	himselfe: *M2*	himselfe, *the rest*
	129	safe; *M2*	safe: *the rest*
	132	gentlemen *M2*	gentlemen, *the rest**
	137	protest; *M2*	protest, *the rest*

N6ᵛ, p. 156.　v. i. 10　you're *M2, B1, O, S1*　you were *M1, B2, S2, 3*

21　Pray thee *M2, B1, O, S1*　Pray thee, *M1, B2, S2, 3*

24　command *M2, B1, O, S1*　a command, *M1, B2, S2, 3**

26　no; *M2, B1, O, S1*　no, *M1, B2, S2, 3*

31　harke you *M2, B1, O, S1*　harke you, *M1, B2, S2, 3*

42　sweet; *M2, B1, O, S1*　sweet: *M1, B2, S2, 3*

43　short *M2, B1, O, S1*　short, *M1, B2, S2, 3*

51　no: you *M2, B1, O, S1*　no. You *M1, B2, S2, 3*

54　inough; *M2, B1, O, S1*　inough, *M1, B2, S2, 3**

55　how, . . . at' *M2, B1, O, S1*　how . . . o't *M1, B2, S2, 3**

O1ᵛ, p. 158.　v. ii. 23　he's *M2, B2, O*　h'is *M1, B1, S1, 2, 3*

O6ʳ, p. 167.　v. vi. 57　houres: *M2, B2, O*　houres— *M1, B1, S1, 2, 3*

57 st.-dir. *The knight . . . him.*　*Inserted in the rest*
not in *M2, B2, O*

76　enter: On, *M2, B2, O*　enter. One *M1, B1, S1, 2, 3*

81　eyes *M2, B2, O*　eyes, *M1, B1, S1, 2, 3*

P3ʳ, p. 173.　v. x. 31　hether *Bang copy*　hither *all other copies*

35　*when | one is* Bang copy　*when one | is* the rest
by silence Bang copy　*either by silence* the rest

xi. 27　perceiue . . . ladies, *Bang copy*　perceiue, . . . ladies *all other copies*

Cynthia's Revels

P5ʳ, p. 177. Plain t-p.　selfe-loue *Bang copy*　self-Loue *all other copies*

R1ᵛ, p. 194.　I. iv. 97　BENEFACTOR? | or *Phelps copy*　Benefactor? or | *the rest*

98　church *Phelps*　church, *the rest*

108　curious . . . band *Phelps*　curious, . . . band, *the rest*

122　clothes *Phelps*　clothes, *the rest*

124　vntrauel'd *Phelps*　vn-trauel'd *the rest*

131　sir, I protest *Phelps*　sir. I protest. *the rest*

The original readings of I. iv are all found in the Quarto.

R2ᵛ, p. 196.　I. v. 38　Floate *Bang*　Floates *all other copies*

R3ʳ, p. 197.　I. v. 41　il-affected *M2, B1, O*　ill-affected *M1, B2, S1, 2, 3*

42　follies: *M2, B1, O*　follies. *M1, B2, S1, 2, 3*

50　woe *Bang and Phelps copies*　woo *the rest*

53　betray *M2, B1, O*　betray, *M1, B2, S1, 2, 3*

II. i. 1　by diuine *M2, B1, O*　my diuine *M1, B2, S1, 2, 3*

12　easinesse *M2, B1, O*　easinesse, *M1, B2, S1, 2, 3*

14　mine; *M2, B1, O*　mine: *M1, B2, S1, 2, 3*

Here there are two states of correction: 'woe' in l. 50 was probably corrected by the compositor before the other corrections were made.

R4ᵛ, p. 200. II. ii. 59 and 60   Cioppini *M2, B1, O*   cioppini *M1, B2, S1, 2, 3*

    65   Rogue *M2, B1, O*   rogue *M1, B2, S1, 2, 3*

    68–9   on them time enough; *M2, B1, O*   on 'hem time enough: *M1, B2, S1, 2, 3*

    74   stratagems *M2, B1, O*   strangenes *M1, B2, S1, 2, 3*

    79   *ordinarie* M2, B1, O   ordinarie *M1, B2, S1, 2, 3*

    82   *laughter* M2, B1, O   *laughter,* M1, B2, S1, 2, 3

    94   healths; *M2, B1, O*   healths, *M1, B2, S1, 2, 3*

    101   *cockatrice* M2, B1, O   *cockatrice,* M1 B2, S1, 2, 3

R5ʳ, p. 201. II. iii. 34   gratuitie *Bang copy*   grauitie *all other copies*

R6ʳ, p. 203. II. iii. 100   clockes; *Phelps copy*   clockes: *the rest*

    101   *whetstone* Phelps   *whetstone,* the rest

    105   anchouies Phelps, O   *ænchouies* the rest

    108   clothes *Phelps*   clothes, *the rest*

    127   cholericke; *Phelps*   cholericke, *the rest*

    128   and order'd . . . *nature* Phelps   & order'd . . . *Nature* the rest

    137   injurie *Phelps*   iniurie *the rest*

    148   prayses; *Phelps*   prayses: *the rest*

Here '*anchouies*' and '*ænchouies*' show two states of correction: the Quarto has '*Anchoues*', and '*anchouies*' is a first correction of this. No other example is recorded of the fantastic spelling '*ænchouies*'; it is probably an error due to foul case, the ligature *æ* having found its way into the *a* division. It may have been recorrected in *O*.

S1ᵛ, p. 206. II. iv. 86   metaphysically; *Phelps copy*   metaphysically: *the rest*

    99   too *Phelps*   too, *the rest*

    110   knowledge; *Phelps*   knowledge: *the rest*

S6ʳ, p. 215. III. v. 55–6   *in this court . . . kingdome* Phelps   in this court . . . kingdome *the rest*

    57   all *Phelps*   all, *the rest*

    75   Nymph *Phelps*   *Nymph* the rest

    89   LINDABRIDES *Phelps*   LINDABRIDES.— *the rest*

    94   exotickes *Phelps*   exoticke *the rest*

T1ʳ, p. 217. IV. i. 9   he *M2, B1, O*   hee *M1, B2, S1, 2, 3*

    10   MERCVRY . . . me *M2, B1, O*   mercurie . . . mee *M1, B2, S1, 2, 3*

    26   be; *M2, B1, O*   be: *M1, B2, S1, 2, 3*

    29   trunesse . . . hee's *M2, B1, O*   trewnesse . . . he's *M1, B2, S1, 2, 3*

    37   propitious *M2, B1, O*   propitious, *M1, B2, S1, 2, 3*

    43   them *M2, B1, O*   'hem *M1, B2, S1, 2, 3*

    48   *venetian* M2, B1, O   *Venetian* M1, B2, S1, 2, 3

T1^v, p. 218.	IV. i. 90	ARGVRION, *M2, B1, O*	ARGVRION *M1, B2, S1, 2, 3*
	97	fashion; *M2, B1, O*	fashion: *M1, B2, S1, 2, 3*
T6^r, p. 227.	IV. iii. 253	*dye* M2, B1, O	dye, *M1, B2, S1, 2, 3*
	257	die-note *M2, B1, O*	die-note *M1, B2, S1, 2, 3*
	268	kings . . . dukes *M2, B1, O*	Kings . . . Dukes *M1, B2, S1, 2, 3*
	269–70	*Brunswicke*, the *Lantgraue M2, B1, O*	Brunswick, the Lant-graue *M1, B2, S1, 2, 3*
		Count M2, B1, O	Connt *M1, B2, S1, 2, 3 (type deranged)*
	294	him; *M2, B1, O*	him, *M1, B2, S1, 2, 3*
	302	that brought *M2, B1, O*	who brought *M1, B2, S1, 2, 3*
T6^v, p. 228.	IV. iii. 314	*loues* M2, B1, O	loues *M1, B2, S1, 2, 3*
	327	judgement *M2, B1, O*	judgement, *M1, B2 S1, 2, 3*
	338	you *M2, B1, O*	you, *M1, B2, S1, 2, 3*
	343	hope *M2, B1, O*	hope, *M1, B2, S1, 2, 3*
	347	vpon *M2, B1, O*	vpo' *M1, B2, S1, 2, 3*
V1^r, p. 229.	IV. iii. 355	*tuff-taffata* All but M1, S3	tuft-taffata *M1, S3*
	358	chinne; *All but M1, S3*	chinne, *M1, S3*
	367	MOR. *All but M1, S3*	MORV. *M1, S3*
		So also 370, 375, 377, 383	
	377	Yes, master *All but M1, S3*	Yes. Master *M1, S3*

The object of the correction 'MORV.' is to distinguish the speeches of Moria and Morus, both originally headed 'MOR.'. In line 383 'MORV.' is probably a miscorrection: the Quarto has '*Moria*'. She might have sent her page to summon Asotus, but his statement, 'I am call'd to the ladies', suggests that Moria herself called him.

V3^r, p. 233.	IV. v. 43	twice *S2*	twice, *the rest*
	61	alter *S2*	alter all *the rest*
V4^v, p. 236.	V. ii. 7	your *S2*	your own *the rest*
	18	greene, and yellow *S2*	*greene*, and *yellow* the rest
	29	greene *S2*	*greene* the rest
	34	truenesse; *S2*	truenesse, *the rest*
V6^v, p. 240.	V. iii. 118	retrogade *Bang and Yale copies*	retrograde *the rest*
	121	Encounter *all but M1, S3*	Encount'rer *M1, S3*
	iv. 14	*prizer*, all but M1, S3	*prizer:* M1, S3
	15	too choose *Bang and Yale*	to choose *the rest*
	23	ANOR. *Bang and Yale copies*	AMOR. *the rest*

Two states of correction, (1) the obvious misprints of the Bang and Yale copies, (2) the improved reading of v. iii. 121 and the stronger punctuation of v. iv. 14. The former may be compositor's corrections, the latter are clearly Jonson's.

X1ʳ, p. 241. v. iv. 33	*Courtling* B1, O, S1	*courtling* M1, 2, B2, S2, 3
37	elixi'r *B1, O, S1*	*elixi'r* M1, 2, B2, S2, 3
40	*court* B1, O, S1	court *M1, 2, B2, S2, 3*
48	*pothecarie* B1, O, S1	pothecary *M1, 2, B2, S2, 3*
49	reciprick commerce; *B1, O, S1*	reciprock commerce, *M1, 2, B2, S2, 3*
X6ʳ, p. 251. v. iv. 587	(appeare *B1, O*	appeare *M1, 2, B2, S1, 2, 3*
X6ᵛ, p. 252. v. iv. 613	taxe, *B1, O, S1*	taxe *M1, 2, B2, S2, 3*
625	see't *B1, O, S1*	see it *M1, 2, B2, S2, 3*
Y2ᵛ, p. 256. v. vi. 52	*Loue;* M2, B2	*Loue,* M1, B1, O, S1, 2, 3
57	Any *M2, B2*	Any, *M1, B1, O, S1, 2, 3*
77	argument *M2, B2*	argument, *M1, B1, O, S1, 2, 3*
84	hyperbole *M2, B2*	*hyperbole* M1, B1, O, S1, 2, 3
Y3ᵛ, p. 258. v. vii. 24	thus *S1*	thus, *the rest*
26	natural affection *S1*	*naturall Affection the rest*
27	Storge, and *S1*	STORGE, & *the rest*
29	allowable selfe-loue *S1*	*allowable selfe-loue* the rest
30	perfection *S1*	*Perfection* the rest
31–2	perpendicular leuell *S1*	*perpendicular Leuell* the rest
32	Cube, or Square *S1*	*Cube,* or *Square* the rest
36	delectable and pleasant Conuersation *S1*	*delectable and pleasant Conuersation* the rest
41	Word *S1*	word— *the rest*
42	Allegorie *S1*	*allegorie* the rest
45	*wittinesse* S1	*Wittinesse* the rest
48	Word *S1*	word *the rest*
53	*simplicitie* S1	*Simplicitie* the rest
56	*Siluer* S1	*siluer* the rest
62	*Quaternion* S1	*quaternion* the rest
Y4ʳ, p. 259. v. viii. 12	wane. *S1*	wane! *the rest*
15	pall . . . thankes *S1*	paule . . . thanks *the rest*
37	praise; *S1*	praise *the rest*
46	my'ndeuours *S1*	m'indeuours *the rest*
Y5ʳ, p. 261. v. x. 1 st. dir.	*The Maskes* | *ioyne, and* | *dance.* M2, B2	*The Masques* | *ioyne, and they* | *dance.* M1, B1, O, S1, 2, 3
7, 9	*comedie* M2, B2	*comœdie* M1, B1, O, S1, 2, 3
14	little *M2, B2*	little, *M1, B1, O, S1, 2, 3*
41 st. dir.	*They hauc dan-|ced the first straine.* M2, B2	*The first* | *straine done* M1, B1, O, S1, 2, 3

Y6ᵛ, p. 264.   v. xi. 50   comtemn'd *Bang and Yale*   contemn'd *all other copies*

Zıᵛ, p. 266.   v. xi. 120   ARETE; *Bı, O, S2*   ARETE, *Mı, 2, B2, Sı, 3*

            131   vnpunished *Bı, O, S2*   vnpunished: *Mı, 2, B2, Sı, 3*

            134   doome; *Bı, O, S2*   doome, *Mı, 2, B2, Sı, 3 (a miscorrection for 'doome.')*

            147   *Weeping* Bı, O, S2   *weeping* Mı, 2, B2, Sı, 3

Z3ʳ, p. 269.   THE END. *enclosed between two rules in B2, Sı. The top rule was taken out and placed below the quotation from Martial in Mı, 2, Bı, O, S2, 3.*

Poetaster

Z5ʳ, p. 273. Dedication 4   FRIEND. *B2, Sı*   FRIEND, *the rest*

Z6ʳ, p. 275. Induction 11   Stay: *Bı, O, S2*   Stay! *Mı, 2, B2, Sı, 3*

            14   not . . . These *Bı, O, S2*   not, . . . these *Mı, 2, B2, Sı, 3*

            16   lights *Bı, O, S2*   lights, *Mı, 2, B2, Sı, 3*

Aa2ᵛ, p. 280. I. ii. 25   Master, *Mı, 2, B2, S2**   Master, *Bı, O, Sı, 3*

            30   OVID. SE. *B2, S2 (so 56, 68, 72)*   OVID. *se.* Mı, 2, Bı, O, Sı, 3

            35   *camrades* B2, S2   *cam'rades* Mı, 2, Bı, O, Sı, 3

            48   'hem, *B2, S2*   'hem: *Mı, 2, Bı, O, Sı, 3*

            49   *punke* B2, S2   punke, *Mı, 2, Bı, Sı, 3*

            56   alone; *B2, S2*   alone, *Mı, 2, Bı, O, Sı, 3*

            61   OVID. Iv. *B2, S2 (so 70)*   OVID. *iu.* Mı, 2, Bı, O, Sı, 3

            75   reuennew *B2, S2*   reuenew *Mı, 2, Bı, O, Sı, 3*

Aa3ᵛ, p. 282. I. ii. 133   himselfe *O, Sı*   himselfe, *Mı, 2, Bı, Sı, 3**

            136   Boy *O, Sı (so 150)*   boy *Mı, 2, Bı, 2, S2, 3*

            141   *law*; Intend that: I *O, Sı*   *law:* Intend that. I *Mı, 2, Bı, 2, S2, 3*

            146   farewel, *Bang copy*   farewel. *the rest*

            151   I. *O, Sı*   I— *Mı, 2, Bı, 2, S2, 3*

            155   Now, captaine *O, Sı*   Now Captaine *Mı, 2, Bı, 2, S2, 3*

            183   -cracker: *O, Sı*   -cracker, *Mı, 2, Bı, 2, S2, 3*

            185   him and *O, Sı*   him, an' *Mı, 2, Bı, 2, S2, 3*

Aa4ʳ, p. 283. I. ii. 188   now: *O, Sı*   now. *Mı, 2, Bı, 2, S2, 3*

            192   *Sixe* O, Sı   *sixe* Mı, 2, Bı, 2, S2, 3

            194   *Time* O, Sı   Time *Mı, 2, Bı, 2, S2, 3*

            205   CALLIMACHVS. Thy *O, Sı*   CALLIMACHVS, thy *Mı, 2, Bı, 2, S2, 3*

            206   so: *O, Sı*   so, *Mı, 2, Bı, 2, S2, 3*

Aa4ʳ, p. 283. I. ii. 207   must: They *O, S1*   must, they *M1, 2, B1, 2, S2, 3*

                starued *O, S1*   staru'd *M1, 2, B1, 2, S2, 3*

            208   linnen: *O, S1*   linnen; *M1, 2, B1, 2, S2, 3*

            210   No: *O, S1*   No, *M1, 2, B1, 2, S2, 3*

            211   Lawyer *O, S1*   lawyer *M1, 2, B1, 2, S2, 3*

            212   Ist *O, S1*   ist *M1, 2, B1, 2, S2, 3*

            217   me *O, S1*   me, *M1, 2, B1, 2, S2, 3*

            220   horse *O, S1*   horse, *M1, 2, B1, 2, S2, 3*

            231   *Romane artes* O, S1   artes *M1, 2, B1, 2, S2, 3*

Aa4ᵛ, p. 284. I. ii. 249   knowledge *O, S1*   knowledge, *M1, 2, B1, 2, S2, 3*

Aa5ʳ, p. 285. I. iii. 29, 30   house, The iewellers, | where *B2, S2*   house, | The iewellers, where *M1, 2, B1, O, S1, 3*

            41   *elyzium* B2, S2   *elyzian* M1, 2, B1, O, S1, 3

            51   new *B2, S2*   now *M1, 2, B1, O, S1, 3*

In Bb3ʳ, p. 293 (II. ii. 201) all copies print 'hat', but the spacing before it shows that the initial *t* had been set up originally.

Dd1ᵛ, p. 314. IV. ii. 49   A God; but *B1, O, S1, 2*   A God, but *M1, 2, B2, S3*

            56   Court; *B1, O, S1, 2*   Court: *M1, 2, B2, S3*

Dd5ᵛ, p. 322. IV. v. 179   *drouzinesse*, Bang and Yale copies   *drouzinesse* all other copies

Dd6ʳ, p. 323. IV. v. 216   Ovid; *B1, O, S1, 2*   Ovid: *M1, 2, B2, S3*

Ee1ʳ, p. 325. IV. vii. 8   humours *M2*   *humours* the rest

            14   truncheon; *M2*   truncheon. *the rest*

          31–2   Stay, Asinivs; you, . . . *Lictors* one line in M2   Stay, Asinivs; | You, . . . *Lictors* two lines in the rest

Ee3ʳ, p. 329. IV. ix. 80 st. dir.   *Shee . . . backe.* not in B2, S1, 2   *Inserted in the rest*

            81   vndescern'd *B2, S1, 2*   vndiscern'd *M1, 2, B1, O, S3*

            85   descerne *B2, S1, 2*   discerne *M1, 2, B1, O, S3*

         88–9 st. dir.   *He . . . backe.* not in B2, S1, 2   *Inserted in the rest*

Ee4ᵛ, p. 332. V. i. 102   reason *B2, S1, 2*   reasons *M1, 2, B1, O, S3*

           105   bodie; *B2, S1, 2*   bodie: *M1, 2, B1, O, S3*

           106   himselfe: *B2, S1, 2*   himselfe, *M1, 2, B1, O, S3*

Ff3ʳ, p. 341. V. iii. 285   —(Tvcca. *B1, O, S1, 2*   (Tvcca. *M1, 2, B2, S3*

           288   *brawles.* B1, O, S1, 2   *brawles,* M1, 2, B2, S3

           302   poet: *B1, O, S1, 2*   poet, *M1, 2, B2, S3*

Ff.3ʳ, p. 341. v. iii. 306		—(Tvcc. *B1*, *O*, *S1*, 2 (*so* 309, 314)	(Tvcc. *M1*, 2, *B2*, *S3*
	308	*arrogance:* B1, O, S1, 2	*arrogance.* M1, 2, B2, S3
	325	snake; *B1*, *O*, *S1*, 2	snake, *M1*, 2, *B2*, *S3*
Ff4ᵛ, p. 344. v. iii. 430		Captaine; *B1*, *O*, *S1*, 2	Captaine, *M1*, 2, *B2*, *S3*
	433	him: *B1*, *O*, *S1*, 2	him: doe. *M1*, 2, *B2*, S3
	436	fiends. *B1*, *O*, *S1*, 2	fiends! *M1*, 2, *B2*, *S3*
	438	now; *B1*, *O*, *S1*, 2	now, *M1*, 2, *B2*, *S3*
	442	Commander; *B1*, *O*, *S1*, 2	Commander, *M1*, 2, *B2*, *S3*
	456	still; *B1*, *O*, *S1*, 2	still, *M1*, 2, *B2*, *S3*
	470	and *reciprocall*, B1, O, S1, 2	*reciprocall* and *M1*, 2, and *reciprocall B2*, *S3*
Ff5ᵛ, p. 346. v. iii. 566		Cae *M2*, *B1*, *O*, *S2*	Caesar *M1*, *B2*, *S1*, 3

Sejanus

G5ᵛ, p. 358. Argument 3		*court*: M2, S1	*court*; M1, B1, 2, O, S2, 3
	7, 8	*dislikes, it . . . out*, M2, S1	*dislikes (it . . . out)* M1, B1, 2, O, S2, 3
	14–15	*and more* S1	*& more* M1, 2, B1, 2, O, S2, 3
	15–16	*Em-|pire: where* S1	*Empire: | where* M1, 2, B1, 2, O, S2, 3
	16–17	*and hard, | in respect* S1	*& hard, in re-|spect* M1, 2, B1, 2, O, S2, 3
	17–18	*in hope) he |* S1	*in hope for the suc- | cession) he* M1, 2, B1, 2, O, S2, 3
	19	*and instill's into his | eares* S1	*& instill's in-|to his eares* M1, 2, B1, 2, O, S2, 3
	20	*and their | mother* S1	*and | their mother* M1, 2, B1, 2, O, S2, 3
	21	*coue-|tously* S1	*co-|uetously* M1, 2, B1, 2, O, S2, 3
	23	*he labours to marry* Li-|uia M2, S1	Seianus *labors to marry |* Liuia *M1*, *B1*, 2, O, S2, 3
	26	*separated* S1	*retyred* M1, 2, B1, 2, O, S2, 3
	29	*eares . . . there* S1	*feares . . . there,* M1, 2, B1, 2, O, S2, 3
	36–7	*with one letter, and in one | day* M2, S1	*and with a long doubt-full | letter, in one day* M1, B1, 2, O, S2, 3
	37–8	*and torne in pieces, by | the* M2, S1	*and torne | in pieces by the* M1, B1, 2, O, S2, 3

S1 on this page shows throughout the first state of the text; the readings of *M2* in the second column show the first attempt to correct it,

notably the bracketing of '(*it one day breaking out*)' in lines 7, 8, and
the substitution of Sejanus' name for the pronoun '*he*' in line 23. The
other copies in the second column show the final state, notably in
the readings '*in hope for the succession*', which is clearer than '*in hope*'
in lines 17, 18, and the epithets '*long doubtfull*' added to describe
Tiberius' letter in lines 36, 37. The changes caused some respacing
of the lines.

Ii4ᵛ, p. 380.   II. 289   *Sacrouir* M*1*, O, S*1*, 2, 3   Sacrovir M*2*, B*1*, 2

The only correction in this quire: it looks like a belated attempt to
bring it into line with III. 157, 185, 267, where 'Sacrovir' is printed:
this is also the form adopted in the Folio of 1640.

Kk2ʳ, p. 387.	III. 82	go'ds M*2*, S*2*	gods, M*1*, B*1*, 2, O, S*1*, 3

Probably a printer's correction.

Ll1ᵛ, p. 398.	III. 532	we faintly, such, M*2*, S*1*, 2	we, faintly, such M*1*, B*1*, 2, O, S*3*
	539	marrie M*2*, S*1*, 2	marrie, M*1*, B*1*, 2, O, S*3*
	547	forth; M*2*, S*1*, 2	forth: M*1*, B*1*, 2, O, S*3*
	551	Livia who was wife M*2*, S*1*, 2	Livia, first the wife M*1*, B*1*, 2, O, S*3*
	552	to Drvsvs M*2*, S*1*, 2	my Drvsvs M*1*, B*1*, 2, O, S*3*
	570	vs, M*2*, S*1*, 2	vs; M*1*, B*1*, 2, O, S*3*
	571	Only M*2*, S*1*, 2	Only, M*1*, B*1*, 2, O, S*3*
	572	Beleeue M*2*, S*1*, 2	Beleeue, M*1*, B*1*, 2, O, S*3*
	574	merit; M*2*, S*1*, 2	merit. M*1*, B*1*, 2, O, S*3*
Ll2ʳ, p. 399.	III. 586	shall. Dull M*2*, B*2*, S*1*, 2	shall: dull M*1*, B*1*, O, S*3*
Ll3ʳ, p. 401.	III. 662	awhile!) when M*1*, B*2*, O, S*1*, 3	awhile.) When M*2*, B*1*, S*2*
	663	your sending M*1*, B*2*, O, S*1*, 3	our sending M*2*, B*1*, S*2*, 3
	666	choise or M*1*, B*2*, O, S*1*, 3	choise, or M*2*, B*1*, S*2*
	667	ambition, M*1*, B*2*, O, S*1*, 3	ambition: M*2*, B*1*, S*2*
	673	*Capua*; Th'other M*1*, B*2*, O, S*1*, 3	*Capua*, th'other M*2*, B*1*, S*2*
	681	eare; M*1*, B*2*, O, S*1*, 3	eare, M*2*, B*1*, S*2*
	682	Drvsvs; M*1*, B*2*, O, S*1*, 3	Drvsvs, M*2*, B*1*, S*2*
	685	him; M*1*, B*2*, O, S*1*, 3	him. M*2*, B*1*, S*2*
	690	too much humour M*1*, B*2*, O, S*1*, 3	too fit matter M*2*, B*1*, S*2*
	693	apprehends: M*1*, B*2*, O, S*1*, 3	apprehends. M*2*, B*1*, S*2*
	695	nature: M*1*, B*2*, O, S*1*, 3	nature. M*2*, B*1*, S*2*
	696	Affections M*1*, B*2*, O, S*1*, 3	Affections, M*2*, B*1*, S*2*
	702	Thinke M*1*, B*2*, O, S*1*, 3	thinke M*2*, B*1*, S*2*
Ll4ᵛ, p. 404.	IV. 34	they M*1*, B*2*, O, S*1*, 3	they, M*2*, B*1*, S*2*
	39	For M*1*, B*2*, O, S*1*, 3	for M*2*, B*1*, S*2*
	52	Others M*1*, B*2*, O, S*1*, 3	others M*2*, B*1*, S*2*

Ll5ᵛ, p. 406.	IV.	124	hate, M2, B2, S1, 2	hate; M1, B1, O, S3
		140	*Vultures* M2, B2, S1, 2	vultures M1, B1, O, S3
		141	first M2, B2, S1, 2	first, M1, B1, O, S3
		146	fooles M2, B2, S1, 2	fooles, M1, B1, O, S3
		154	facile, M2, B2, S1, 2	readie M1, B1, O, S3
Ll6ʳ, p. 407.	IV.	164	soueraigne; M2, S1, 2	soueraigne, M1, B1, 2, O, S3
		172	SEIANVS? M2, S1, 2	SEIANVS! M1, B1, 2, O, S3
		177	Empire M2, S1, 2	empire M1, B1, 2, O, S3
		194	That M2, S1, 2	that M1, B1, 2, O, S3
		198	the easie M2, S1, 2	The easie M1, B1, 2, O, S3
		200	comment: M2, S1, 2	comment; M1, B1, 2, O, S3
		201	there, M2, S1, 2	there; M1, B1, 2, O, S3
Mm1ᵛ, p. 410.	IV.	288	men. B1, 2, O, S2	men! M1, 2, S1, 3
		290	*patriot* B1, 2, O, S2	patriot M1, 2, S1, 3
Mm3ʳ, p. 413.	IV.	414	MAR. B1, 2, O, S1	MIN. M1, 2, S2, 3
		434	choke him.) B1, 2, O, S1	choke him, M1, 2, S2, 3
		435	That . . . ARRVNTIVS.) *not in* B1, 2, O, S1	*Inserted in* M1, 2, S2, 3
		438	By CASTOR . . . By POLLVX B1, 2, O, S1	By POLLVX . . . By HERCVLES M1, 2, S2, 3
		444	owne; B1, 2, O, S1	owne, M1, 2, S2, 3
		446	st. dir. *They . . . Terentius.* not in B1, 2, O, S1	*Inserted in* M1, 2, S2, 3
		449	Mixing B1, 2, O, S1	Mingling M1, 2, S2, 3
		455	strong, B1, 2, O, S1	strong; M1, 2, S2, 3
		456	deuotion, B1, 2, O, S1	deuotion; M1, 2, S2, 3
Mm4ᵛ, p. 416.	V.	19	So B1, 2, O, S1	so M1, 2, S2, 3
		23	fortune B1, 2, O, S1	fortune, M1, 2, S2, 3
		24	strife, B1, 2, O, S1	strife: M1, 2, S2, 3
		26	No B1, 2, O, S1	no M1, 2, S2, 3
		30	furnace B1, 2, O, S1	fornace M1, 2, S2, 3
		31	you, goe see B1, 2, O, S1	(you, goe see) M1, 2, S2, 3
		33	'tis. B1, 2, O, S1	'tis— M1, 2, S2, 3
			imposture B1, 2, O, S1	imposture, M1, 2, S2, 3
	Before	35	*To them.* not in B1, 2, O, S1	*Inserted in* M1, 2, S2, 3
		37	serpent. B1, 2, O, S1	serpent! M1, 2, S2, 3
		48	lord? B1, 2, O, S1	lord! M1, 2, S2, 3
		54	vs, B1, 2, O, S1	vs; M1, 2, S2, 3
		57	ominous: B1, 2, O, S1	ominous! M1, 2, S2, 3
Mm6ʳ, p. 419.	V.	149	st. dir. *Returnes.* not in B1, 2, O, S2	*Inserted in* M1, 2, S1, 3
		153	palace; B1, 2, O, S2	palace. M1, 2, S1, 3
		156	By B1, 2, O, S2	by M1, 2, S1, 3
		157	Let B1, 2, O, S2	let M1, 2, S1, 3
		163	me, B1, 2, O, S2	me: M1, 2, S1, 3

Mm6ʳ, p. 419.	v. 165	colleague; *B1, 2, O, S2*		colleague, *M1, 2, S1, 3*
	172	*farre; Farre* B1, 2, O, S2		*farre. Farre* M1, 2, S1, 3
	173	now; *B1, 2, O, S2*		now, *M1, 2, S1, 3*
	173 st. dir.	These sound, | while the *Fla-|men* washeth. *B1, 2, O, S2*		Sound, while | the *Fla-men* | washeth. *M1, 2, S1, 3*
	174	*minds:* B1, 2, O, S2		*minds.* M1, 2, S1, 3
Mm6ᵛ, p. 420.	v. 185	away *B1, 2, O, S2*		away! *M1, 2, S1, 3*
Nn2ᵛ, p. 424.	v. 339	Which *O, S2*		With *M1, 2, B1, 2, S1, 3*
	347	Macro, *O, S2*		Macro! *M1, 2, B1, 2, S1, 3*
Nn5ʳ, p. 429.	v. 543 st. dir.	The Epistle | is read *M1, O, S2*		*The Epistle is | read* M2, B1, 2, S1, 3
	557	*libels* O, S2		*libels,* M2, B1, 2, S1, 3
	571	*hohe* Bang copy		*hope* all other copies
Oo1ᵛ, p. 434.	v. 765	theatre; *M2, S1, 2*		theatre, *M1, B1, 2, O, S3*
	766	circke, *M2, S1, 2*		circke; *M1, B1, 2, O, S3*
	768	sensitiue *M2, S1, 2*		sensiue growne *M1, B1, 2, O, S3*
	769	furie; *M2, S1, 2*		furie, *M1, B1, 2, O, S3*
	772	garlands *M2, S1, 2*		gyrlands *M1, B1, 2, O, S3*
	773	reuerenced. *M2, S1, 2*		reuerenced! *M1, B1, 2, O, S3*
	782	knaues, *M2, S1, 2*		knaues; *M1, B1, 2, O, S3*
	791	Aske *M2, S1, 2*		aske *M1, B1, 2, O, S3*
	795	roofe *M2, S1, 2*		proofe *M1, B1, 2, O, S3*

Volpone

Oo6ʳ, p. 443.	Dedication 47	scene: *And* M2, S1, 2		Scene. *And* M1, B1, 2, O, S3.
Pp3ᵛ, p. 450.	Prologue 20	Playes . . . No *B2*		playes . . . no *the rest*
	27	Play *B2*		play *the rest*
	I. i. 4	Sunne *B2*		sunne *the rest*
	5	*Ram* B2		*ram* the rest
	7	That *B2*		That, *the rest*
Pp4ʳ, p. 451.	I. i. 34	-shares, I fat *B2*		shares; fat *the rest*
	40	priuate *B2*		priuate— *the rest*
	48	But *B2*		But, *the rest*
	51	roofes: . . . vengeance. *B2*		roofes; . . . vengeance. — *the rest*
	53	a thresher *B2*		the thresher *the rest*
	57	marchant *B2*		merchant *the rest*
	58	*Romagnia* B2		*Romagnia* the rest
Qq2ʳ, p. 459.	I. iv. 63	As . . . good— *S1*		(As . . . good—) *the rest*
	70	sir. *S1*		sir! *the rest*
	75	cordiall. *S1*		cordiall! *the rest*
	87	recouer; *S1*		recouer— *the rest*
	94	will; *S1*		will: *the rest*

Qq5ᵛ, p. 466. II. i. 78   meat; *S1*   meat: *the rest*
                        88   *Babiouns* S1   *Bab'ouns* the rest
                        94   aduices *S1*   aduises *the rest*
                        98   POLL: *S1*   POLL. *the rest*
                       115   blouds, *S1*   blouds; *the rest*
                       116   pedants, *S1*   pedants: *the rest*
Rr2ᵛ, p. 472. II. iii. 1 st. dir. *He beates ... &c.* not   *Inserted in the rest*
                           in S1
                         5   *Piazza* S1   *piazza* the rest
                         8   DI BESOGNIOSI *S1*   *di besogniosi* the rest
                        12   'Tis *S1*   It is *the rest*
                   iv. 6   some ambitious *S1*   an ambitious *the rest*
                        11   sir, *S1*   sir! *the rest*
Rr3ʳ, p. 473. II. iv. 30   of o' *Yale copy*   o' *all other copies*

The 'of' of the Quarto was altered to 'o'' and not picked out originally;
there is a space before and after the 'o'.

Rr5ʳ, p. 477. II. vi. 78   him, *S1*   him: *the rest*
                        93   it; *S1*   it: *the rest*
                   vii. 6   not I *S1*   not, I *the rest*
Tt5ʳ, p. 501. IV. v. 48   Af thankes *Bang copy*   Of thankes *all other
                                                              copies*

Epicoene

Yy, pp. 529–40.   *Reset in M1 and S3*
Zz2ʳ, p. 543. II. iii. 20   Daw. *M2, S2*   DAW. *M1, B1, 2, O, S1, 3*
                        24   recite his own | workes *M2,*   recite his | owne workes
                           S2   *M1, B1, 2, O, S1, 3*
                           madrigall *M2, S2*   *madrigall* M1, B1, 2, O,
                                                                 S1, 3
                        47   gentlemen. *M2, S2*   gentlemen! *M1, B1, 2,*
                                                                 *O, S1, 3**
                        57   There is *M2, S2*   There's *M1, B1, 2, O,*
                                                                 S1, 3
Zz5ᵛ, p. 550. II. v. 87   print *M2, S2*   print, *M1, B1, 2, O, S1, 3*
                        94   soft-low *M2, S2*   soft, low *M1, B1, 2, O,*
                                                                 S1, 3
                        97   now—mistris *M2, S2*   now-mistris *M1, B1, 2,*
                                                                 O, S1, 3
Aaa3ᵛ, p. 558. III. iv. 36   Speake, out *M1, B1, 2, O,*   Speake out *M2, S2*
                           S1, 3
Ddd2ʳ, p. 591. v. iii. 58   pertinencies *S1*   impertinencies *the rest*
                        59   bee *S1*   be *the rest*
Ddd3ᵛ, p. 594. v. iii. 213   can not *M1, 2, B1, 2, S1,*   cannot *O*
                           2, 3
Ddd5ᵛ, p. 598. v. iv. 177   DAVPHINE, *S1*   DAVPHINE *the rest*
                       195   nephew, *S1*   nephew *the rest*

The Alchemist

Ggg3ʳ, p. 629. II. iii. 271   treacherou'st *S1*   trecherou'st *M1, 2, B1,*
                                                                 2, O, S2, 3
Ggg4ᵛ, p. 632. II. v. 29   *Malleation,* S1   *Malleation.* M1, 2, B1,
                                                                 2, O, S2, 3

Hhh4^v, p. 644. III. iv. 84   long) *B2*   long(*M1, 2, B1, O, S1, 2, 3*

92   without, *B2*   without *M1, 2, B1, O, S1, 2, 3*

The inverted bracket in line 84 must have been due to some disturbance of the type.

Iii2^v, p. 652.   IV. ii. 1   cleare *B2, S1*   cleare. *M1, 2, B1, O, S2, 3*

Kkk2^r, p. 663. IV. vii. 57   fiend. *B2, S2*   fiend) *M1, 2, B1, O, S1, 3*

Catiline

Rrr4^v, p. 752.   V. 212   Neyther *M1, 2, B1, 2, S1,*   Neither *O*
2, 3

A printer's correction. The spelling 'neither' is found everywhere else in the play, but 'neyther' and 'eyther' were spellings of Jonson. In *EMO.* Induction 130 he corrected 'either' to 'eyther', and he writes 'neyther' in the holograph of the *Masque of Queens*, line 334, where the printed texts have 'neither'.

The Epigrams and the Forest

One trivial error corrected by the compositor as soon as he made it— 'with' for 'wits' (Ttt4^r *Epigram* xxiii. 5) in a fragment of the Folio used as a press-copy, and not found in any copy which has been collated, is all that we have discovered in the text of these poems.

Masques and Entertainments

Dddd5^v, p. 874. *Entertainment at Althorp*, 143
succeed, *press-copy*   succeed. *all other copies*
Mmmm, *except 2 recto, reset*
Nnnn4 and 6, *the inner forme, reset.*
Ooo3 and 4, *the outer forme, reset*
Pppp1^v, p. 998. *A Challenge at Tilt*, 166
I ? *S1*   O, *the rest*
Pppp5^v, p. 1006. *Mercury Vindicated*, 85–6
nothing of nothing *M2, B1,*   a thing of nothing *M1,*
2, O, S1, 2   S3
87   a | any lease *M2, B1, 2, O,*   a | toy, a lease *M1, S3*
S1, 2
Qqqq4^v–5^r, pp. 1014–15. *The Golden Age Restored*, 199–240
199–220 PALLAS . . . heauen. precede 221–40 ASTRÆA . . . *Corantós.* in M2, B1, 2, O, S1, 2. Transposed in M1.[1]

On pages 988–1008 the running-title varies between '*Masques*' and '*Masques*': *S1* has the plain capital on pages 988, 993, 997, 999, 1001, 1002, 1005, 1006, 1008, and the swash italic capital on page 1004; the other *S* copies vary. The corrector tried to make the letter uniform.

[1] The page is missing in S3.

In this imposing array of over six hundred corrections a small number are obviously those of the compositor or the corrector. For example, in *Every Man out of his Humour*, IV. i. 5, he corrected 'ano-|god', where a syllable had dropped out at the beginning of a new line, to 'ano-|ther, god'; similarly 'retrogade' and 'ANOR.' (for 'AMOR.') in *Cynthia's Revels*, V. iii. 118, IV. 23; and in *Mercury Vindicated*, 87, finding that he had printed 'a | any lease', he looked up his copy and got the correction 'a | toy, a lease'. But most of the corrections are the author's, made at the printing-office where he would present himself for this purpose every morning. With work corrected hastily, sometimes in gloomy weather or in an ill-lighted room, we must not expect the accuracy of a modern press-reader, and in fact Jonson did overlook a number of errors. The worst perhaps is 'GVEVENER' for 'GVENEVER' or Guinevere in *Every Man out of his Humour*, II. iii. 68; the misspelling is in all the texts, and in view of Jonson's passing the text twice, in the First Quarto and in the Folio, we have not ventured to correct it. On the other hand, we have not printed '*metaposcopie*' in *The Alchemist*, I. iii. 44, because here we feel confident that Jonson knew the Greek word μέτωπον and the *a* is a printer's blunder.

Two points are obvious to anyone who studies the corrections. First, there is a heavy proportion of them in the older works, plays which had appeared in quarto, *Every Man out of his Humour*, *Cynthia's Revels*, *Poetaster*, and *Sejanus*. They are fewer in *Volpone*, *Epicoene*, and *The Alchemist*, and they all but disappear in *Catiline* and in the *Epigrams*, which Jonson called 'the ripest of my studies'. The newer work needed no revision in 1612. The *Masques*, of which Stansby registered a number in 1615, show no sign of the author's correction except on the last two pages, where he transposed effectively the final speeches, making Astraea decide that she would return to earth in order to bask in the sunshine of King James's court. The text of the entertainments and the masques is often carelessly printed, and the Latin and Greek quotations in the notes are especially bad.[1] Jonson cannot have read the proofs. It is probable that the printer, registering this section of the work in 1615 and producing it in 1616, hurried the printing.

Of changes in the text the chief are the insertion of Camden's title of 'Clarentiaux' in the dedication of *Every Man in his Humour*; of 'Your honorer' for 'Your true Honorer' in the dedication of *Every Man out of his Humour*, 'language' for 'soule', 'Squeeze' for 'Crush' in the Induction (ll. 13, 145), 'malitious intent' for 'intent' (IV. ii. 91), 'make occasions publike' for 'make that publike' (IV. vi. 37),

[1] See vol. vii, pp. 79, 206, 273–4, 375–6.

and 'vndertake' for the unintelligible '*manfrede* it' (IV. viii. 110) in
the body of the text. In *Sejanus* (III. 551–2) we may note

> LIVIA, first the wife
> To CAIVS CAESAR, then my DRVSVS,

for

> LIVIA, who was wife
> To CAIVS CAESAR, then to DRVSVS,—

'too fit matter' for 'too much humour' (ibid. 690), 'readie sword'
for 'facile sword' (IV. 154), and the changes in the Roman oaths
(ibid. 438)

> POM. By POLLVX, that's the worst. (ARR. By HERCVLES, best.)

for 'By CASTOR, that's the worst', and 'By POLLVX, best', because
in ancient Rome women, not men, swore by Castor.[1]

A second point is that most of the changes are made in the type
and the punctuation, altering roman type to italic or vice versa,
initial capitals to lower-case, and regulating the stops: for instance,
a semicolon is changed to a colon in *Cynthia's Revels*, Act II, scene i.
14, scene iii. 148, scene IV. 86, 110. There is an interesting change
in the song of the kiss (IV. iii. 252–3):

> *It should be my wishing*
> *That I might dye, kissing.*

The comma after '*dye*' was inserted in the proof, and Amorphus
adds an explanation of it in the comment 'your long *die*-note did
arride me most, but it was somwhat too long'. On the use of the
colon to make an emphatic pause, substituted for a comma in
Sejanus, V. 23–4, we have already commented.[2] We may illustrate
it here from *Volpone*, II. ii. 118–19:

> But *Alchimy*,
> I neuer heard the like: or BROVGHTONS bookes.

The colon in such sentences might be represented in a modernized
text by a dash. For an effective introduction of the parenthesis we
may instance *Volpone*, I. iv. 61–4:

> Mos. He smelt a carcasse, sir, when he but heard
> My master was about his testament;
> (As I did vrge him to it, for your good—)
> CORB. He came vnto him, did he? I thought so.

The Quarto and the Folio originally had no parenthesis. We have
already discussed very fully Jonson's principles of punctuation, and
these few instances of his application of them may suffice here.

---

[1] See vol. iv, pp. 336–7.   [2] See vol. iv, pp. 342–3.

APPENDIX XVII

AN ATTACK UPON THE FOLIO

A SUSTAINED attack on the authority of the Folio was made at Louvain by Professor H. de Vocht in four volumes of the *Materials for the Study of the Old English Drama*, viz. in his editions of *Poetaster*, 1934, *Sejanus*, 1935, *Volpone*, 1937, printed from the Quartos, and in his *Comments on the Text of Ben Jonson's Every Man out of his Humour*, 1937. He denies that the Folio text is Jonson's revision of the Quartos, and that Jonson had anything to do with it except to supply dedications; the six hundred-odd proof corrections which we have recorded were not Jonson's. All deviations from the Quarto texts, all proof-readers' corrections were made in the office of the publisher, William Stansby. This excellent printer provided the Folio with a 'coat of dulling varnish', 'disfiguring touches', and a 'procrustean frame'—by which we suppose he means the verse arrangement.[1] Previously Dr. B. A. P. van Dam had contributed to the *Herinneringsbundel Professor S. S. Rosenstein* at Leyden an article on the closing scene of *Every Man out of his Humour* entitled 'Een Merkwaardig Geval' (1902), which, in collaboration with Dr. C. Stoffel, he recast in *Anglia*, xiv, 1903, pp. 377–92, 'The Authority of the Ben Jonson Folio of 1616'. They attributed all changes in this scene to the corrector. In *Anglia*, xlix, 1937, pp. 398–415, 'The Folio Text of Ben Jonson's "Sejanus"', Evelyn Simpson entered a *caveat* against Dr. de Vocht's theory with reference to *Sejanus* and *Poetaster*; we have made occasional use of it here.

Obviously the investigation must begin in Stansby's printing-office. We search Dr. de Vocht's pages for some well-defined account of it and find nothing but a confused haze. All he tells us finally[1] is that 'if documents were brought to light indicating the details of the transaction between Jonson and Holme on the subject of *Every Man out of his Humour*', we should find out 'what right Jonson had to interfere with a work of his, which he had let go out of his hand'. Matters are not helped by calling William Holme the 'editor' of the first and second Quartos: he was the publisher, not the editor. We are put off with casual remarks here and there: 'William Stansby—or whoever is responsible for the *Folio*-edition';[2] the Folio 'shows at every page that it was edited by an average printer's corrector';[3] 'whoever is answerable for the bringing out and the shaping of the *Folio*,—be he printer, press-corrector, or compositor, one man or more'.[4] Light is thrown on this last comment by the statement[5] that Stansby used more than one press to print the Folio, 'more than one reader will have been required' for this, and 'the multiplicity of readers seems a fit explanation for the diversity of the corrections'. How many readers were there in Stansby's office? Stansby himself, a well-educated man and an expert printer,

[1] *Comments*, p. 151.   [2] Ibid., p. 8.   [3] Ibid., p. 46.
[4] Ibid., p. 116.   [5] Ibid., p. 139.

no doubt read proofs of the books he printed, and he may also have employed one corrector. But a 'multiplicity' of them? A final touch of incoherence is given by the suggestion[1] that the copy was dictated to the compositor, and it seems with lamentable results. The compositor could not keep in his head the exact words dictated; when he was told 'filthy' or 'Spirit' (*E.M.O.* I. iii. 26, v. xi. 60) he set up 'dirty' or 'spleene'. The chaos in Stansby's office must have been appalling, and yet Dr. de Vocht pays a high tribute to his technical skill as a printer.

Meanwhile, with his texts rewritten both in the copy and the proofs, with cancels and additions which blurred his meaning and tricked his metre, how was Jonson likely to behave? Remembering his remark on the 'lewd printer' of some later plays, John Beale,[2] we can only echo de Vocht's hypothesis that, if documents could be brought to light, they would tell us something—and something very pungent! Jonson was the last man in the world to tolerate any tampering with his work.

Dr. de Vocht says of the plays: 'Each of them starts—apparently quite unnecessarily—with a separate title-page, splendid in its large capitals, providing full information about the first performance and about the players, together with the solemn device[3] and due indication of printer and date. . . . On each third page begins a stately dedicatory letter—probably Jonson's *only* contribution to the *Folio*—; it is followed by the *Persons of the Play* and the play proper.'[4] Jonson's 'only contribution'! We have already pointed out the new work published in the Folio.[5] Dr. de Vocht does not discuss the additions in *Cynthia's Revels*, but he has to admit the genuineness of the 'lengthy passages' added to the Quarto text of *Poetaster*, and this is how he accounts for them:

> The criticisms on lawyers, players, and officers were certainly part of the original redaction; they were spoken when the *Poetaster* was first acted, in the Summer of 1601, in so much that they caused their author to be all but condemned for calumny. They were repressed by authority when the play was printed in 1602; but the publisher Matthew Lownes, who must have been duly informed of what was going on, most probably had the incriminated passages, and kept them in store for further use. As to the subsequent additions, the dialogue Horatius–Trebatius and the final *apologeticall Dialogue*, they were, no doubt, composed soon after the performance of the *Satiromastix*, two or three months later, about September or October 1601. They certainly were in existence when the *Poetaster* came out in 1602, and probably were in Lownes's possession ever since they had been composed.[6] Even the dedicatory letter to Martin, no doubt, was

---

[1] Ibid., p. 57. [2] See vol. i, p. 211.
[3] There is no printer's device on any of the title-pages.
[4] *Comments*, pp. 116–17. [5] See pp. 42–3.
[6] Not true of the dialogue between Horace and Trebatius (III. v). Jonson says he wrote '*an* apologeticall Dialogue: *which was . . . all the answere I euer gaue, to sundry impotent libells . . .*' (see vol. iii, p. 317). Dr. de Vocht alters

written in the heat of the Stage-Quarrel, when Jonson hoped to follow up the first edition of the *Poetaster* by a second, which was to revenge victoriously his honour. . . . A man as jealous of his literary fame as Jonson, can hardly have awaited the possible chance of a collected edition of his—mostly still unborn—works to vindicate himself from enemies who had appealed to justice against him: in all probability the text of a second, and complete, edition of the *Poetaster* must have been ready, and in Lownes's hands, ever since 1602, so that it could be brought out at the first opportunity.

Notice in this paragraph the phrases which are the stock-in-trade of the conjecturalist. Facts failing him, he falls back on 'must have been', 'most probably', 'no doubt', 'probably', 'can hardly', and, finest of all, 'in all probability must have been'. There is not a scrap of evidence that a second Quarto was ready for the printer in 1602; if it was, why did a second edition wait till 1616?

On the most crucial point of all the oracle is silent. What of the rewritten version of *Every Man in his Humour*? Was that a fabrication of Stansby's? The failure to mention it may be an oversight, but the explicit statement that only the dedications to the plays were new seems to rule it out. If Dr. de Vocht would tell us, with the ready assurance which marks all his utterances, that this great version was not written by Jonson, we could give up the task of refuting him and leave him to enjoy his mare's-nest undisturbed.

There is a serious misrepresentation of the Folio in his treatment of the end of *Every Man out of his Humour* in the Folio text. Here he is following Drs. van Dam and Stoffel.[1] At the end of the play, where the original conclusion of the Quarto had been changed because of its impersonation of Queen Elizabeth on the stage, which had given offence,[2] an extract from the original eulogy of the Queen is appended in the Folio with this heading

Which, in the presentation before

Queene E. was thus varyed,

By MACILENTE.

Macilente abandons his envious humour at the sight of the Queen.

> Neuer till now did obiect greet mine eyes
> With any light content: but in her graces,
> All my malicious powers haue lost their stings.

The trio, van Dam, Stoffel, and de Vocht, actually suggest that the play was not performed at Court at all; in other words, though they do not

---

this to '*apologeticall Dialogue* . . . as well as "all the answere ⟨he⟩ euer gaue"', and says 'by which he probably meant the evidently apologetic scene between Horace and Trebatius . . .'. (*Poetaster*, p. 103.) 'As well as' is an interpolation.

[1] *Comments*, pp. 104–16.

[2] See vol. iii, pp. 602–4.

put it so bluntly, that the heading was a lie of Stansby's or of one of
his compositors or of one of his multitude of readers. Dr. de Vocht
thinks it probable that 'the very first performance is referred to' in this
Court presentation. But in the revised epilogue of the first Quarto there
is a clear reference to the Globe Theatre—the address to

> The happier spirits in this faire-fild Globe.

And, as Sir Edmund Chambers says, it is 'a little difficult to believe
that the play was given at Court before it had been "practised" in
public performances'; he concludes 'that, having suppressed the address
to a mimic Elizabeth at the Globe, Jonson revived it in a slightly altered
form when he took the play to Court at Christmas'.[1] The address would
then be spoken, not to a boy actor dressed up as the Queen, but to
Elizabeth herself, and there is a change in the wording which fits in
with this: instead of

> that Shee (whose *Figure* hath effected
> This change in me) may neuer suffer Change
> In her Admir'd and happie Gouernment:

the Folio has

> that shee (whose presence hath effected
> This change in me) may suffer most late change
> In her admir'd and happie gouernment.

Dr. de Vocht, denying that there was a Court performance, makes great
play with the alteration of '*Figure*' to 'presence'. The Folio editor
altered it to bolster up his clumsy fabrication!

A further point in which Dr. de Vocht hopelessly misunderstands the
Folio concerns the scene arrangement and Jonson's habit of grouping
at the head of each scene the names of all the characters taking part
in it. We have explained that he was following the model supplied him
in the texts of the ancient classical comedies.[2] Thus, the opening scene
of *Sejanus* is headed 'SABINVS, SILIVS, NATTA, LATIARIS, CORDVS,
SATRIVS, ARRVNTIVS, EVDEMVS, HATERIVS, &c'. At line 1 Gifford has
a note 'Enter Sabinus and Silius, followed by Latiaris'; at line 20 'Enter
Satrius and Natta at a distance'; after line 72 'Enter Cordus and
Arruntius'; at line 85 'Exeunt Natta and Satrius', Latiaris being accidentally overlooked; at line 105 'Drusus passes over the stage, attended
by Haterius, &c.'. At line 175 the text has 'Here comes SEIANVS';
Gifford closes the scene at this point, the Folio continuing it for two
lines to enable the next scene to begin with the words of Sejanus to
Terentius, 'I note 'hem well'. Criticizing this system in *Every Man out
of his Humour* and not understanding how it originated, Dr. de Vocht
assumes that these scene headings mark the entrance of the characters.[3]
'The audience are made dupes of, by the arrangement into nicely defined

[1] *Elizabethan Stage*, iii, p. 362.   [2] See p. 44.
[3] *Comments*, pp. 16–23.

scenes and acts, since they are told that they see persons who do not appear.' At line 290 of the Induction to *Every Man out of his Humour*:

> CORD. O, here comes the *Prologue*: Now sir! if you had staid a little longer, I meant to have spoke your prologue for you, I faith.

The third sounding.

PROLOGVE.

> PROL. Mary, with all my heart, Sir, you shall doe it yet, and I thanke you.

'Taking the *Folio* at the letter', says Dr. de Vocht, 'it is certain that, when Cordatus speaks those words, the *Prologue* has not yet appeared'; and only at line 293 'the *PROLOGVE*, at last, enters'. The Folio says 'Here comes the *Prologue*'; but, if you 'take it at the letter', literally, that is, it says nothing of the kind. How do you take it? Spiritually? Notice too the Quartos of *Sejanus* (1605) and *Volpone* (1607), which Dr. de Vocht has edited and in which he has implicit faith, also have this alleged misarrangement; so has the Quarto of *The Alchemist* (1612) —a clear proof that Jonson adopted this setting for his plays before 1616. Dr. de Vocht is discreetly silent about these Quartos in this connexion. The system reappears in the Folio of 1640, and in the octavo edition of *The New Inn* in 1631.

Dr. de Vocht's remarks on metre are the worst feature of his books. He belongs to a school of metrists who scan lines by cutting out syllables, leaving a residuum of unpronounceable jargon. To save space, we confine ourselves to some examples from *Volpone*, where he supposes that he has disproved new readings of the Folio. In I. iv. 28 the Quarto has

> Before they kill him. CORB. Right, I conceiue you.

The Folio improves the line by reading 'Right, I doe conceiue you'. But, according to Dr. de Vocht, 'conceiue you' is a 'coalition', the Quarto is right, and the line scans

> Befóre they kíll him.—Ríght, I cón-ci'yé.[1]

The songs are mauled. Three lines of the song on fools (I. ii. 69, 74, 79) are in the Quarto:

> *Themselues, and others merry making . . .*
> *His very face begetteth laughter . . .*
> *When Wit shall waite vpon the Foole.*

It is the metre of *L'Allegro* and *Il Penseroso*, octosyllabic but frequently varied by trochaic openings without the initial unaccented syllable. Jonson in the Folio chose the trochaic opening for these lines:

> *Selues, and others merry-making . . .*
> *Eene his face begetteth laughter . . .*
> *When wit waites vpon the foole.*

[1] *Volpone*, p. 187.

But these, it seems, were substitutions of the printer, who failed to scan the Quarto lines thus:

> 'msélues and óthers mérry máking . . .
> 's véry fáce begétteth laúghter . . .
> Whén wit'll waít vpón the fool.[1]

'*Them-* of *Themselues* pronounced as *'em*, *'um*, or even *'m*, forms one syllable with *selues*.' Of course we can only get this *'m* after a vowel, as in 'I'm'. Similarly the mountebank's song (II. ii. 120 f.) is 'reduced into a regular rhythm'.

> *Had old* HIPPOCRATES, *or* GALEN,
> (*That to their bookes put med'cines all in*)
> *But knowne this secret, they had neuer*
> (*Of which they will be guilty euer*)
> *Beene murderers of so much paper,* . . .

This reads easily and naturally, but 'pronunciation cannot have been modelled on orthography, which merely represents, as well as possible, the spoken word'. So here we are when once we make up our minds to soar above orthography: scan thus:

> Hád old Híp-po-crátes or Gálen—

('Hippocrates' is apparently three syllables)—

> Thát to'er boóks put méd'cines áll in—

('to' and 'their' make one syllable)

> Bút known thís secrét they'd néver,
> Óf which théy'll be guílty éver,
> Múrd'rers béen of só much páper.

'Been murderers' is 'corrupt: it does not seem possible to adapt it to the rhythm'.[2] In Dr. de Vocht's hands a smooth line like

> But knówn this sécret théy had néver

becomes a hideous cacophony; he has not even an elementary understanding of metre.

To the point of classical scholarship involved in Jonson's alteration of the Roman oaths in *Sejanus*, IV. 438, Dr. de Vocht devotes seven pages.[3] Jonson wrote in the Quarto:

> POM. By *Castor*, that's the worst. (ARR. By *Pollux*, best.)

[1] Ibid., pp. 189 f.
[2] The verse of two lines in the Folio is attacked for misprints which Jonson corrected, 'I fat' corrected to 'fat' in I. i, and the accent on '*Romagnia*' (ibid. 58) inserted in proof. Dr. de Vocht could have learnt this from our critical apparatus. In IV. iv. 14 the 'indispensable' comma, which the Folio is attacked for omitting, is found in some copies; it dropped out in the printing.
[3] *Sejanus*, pp. 198–205.

The Folio set this up at first, but corrected it to

POM. By POLLVX, that's the worst. (ARR. By HERCVLES, best.)

We discussed the passage in our introduction to the play,[1] quoting the *locus classicus* in Aulus Gellius, which states that Roman women did not swear by Hercules nor men by Castor, but that both sexes might swear by Pollux. 'That knowledge', says Dr. de Vocht airily, 'was quite trivial, being duly pointed out by dictionaries', such as Thomas Cooper's. The 'average *tiro*' knew it; for a blunder in it 'schoolboys were whipped'. With profound but misguided erudition the professor has discovered two erroneous lines in fifteenth- and sixteenth-century texts of Plautus which put the oath 'by Castor' on the lips of a man (*Asinaria*, v. ii. 46 and 80). Modern texts correct these blunders and give the speeches to women. Working up a hint from an old commentator, Dr. de Vocht suggests that Jonson accepted these false readings, rejected the statement of such a competent authority as Aulus Gellius, and put the Castor oath in the mouth of Pomponius to show his effeminacy. To such hard shifts is the critic driven in order to make good his attack on the Folio.

He is less subtle over *Every Man out of his Humour*, III. ix. 123, where he credits Jonson with the spelling 'abhominable' because the Quarto has it and the Folio corrects it to 'abominable'. Jonson was so ignorant of Latin that he accepted the vulgar derivation for this word, *ab homine*, 'away from man', that is, 'beastly', and did not know the word *abominari*. Jonson, in fact, is on a level with Holofernes in *Love's Labour's Lost* (v. i. 21), who stoutly defended 'abhominable'.

Ignorance of Elizabethan English is another melancholy feature of Dr. de Vocht's criticism. In *Every Man out of his Humour*, II. iv. 27, Deliro says to Fido, 'Cast in more franckincense, yet more, well said'. The Folio reproduces this 'enigmatic' reading, 'which does not refer to anything that has been mentioned'. '*Said* seems an incomprehensible stopgap, . . . it would be more consistent to have *well done*.'[2] It is a pity that Dr. de Vocht did not notice three other passages of this play where 'well said' is similarly used (Induction 330, IV. ii. 7, V. v. 55). 'Said' here is 'sayed', 'assayed', and virtually means 'well done'. It is a common use in Jonson and other writers. See Dyce's note in his *Beaumont and Fletcher*, vol. i, p. 328.

At the climax of the play (v. xi. 58–60) Macilente, finding nothing more to envy, says in the Quarto:

> their vertue,
> Being now rak't vp in embers of their Follie,
> Affords no ampler Subject to my Spirit.

The Folio has

> their folly,
> Being now rak't vp in their repentant ashes,
> Affords no ampler subiect to my spleene.

---

[1] Vol. iii, pp. 336–7. Professor W. D. Briggs in his edition of the play was the first to explain the alteration.   [2] *Comments*, pp. 46, 60 n. 3.

Dr. de Vocht, imagining that 'rak't vp' means 'revived' (instead of 'gone over with a rake', 'smoothed out'), easily reduces the Folio reading to nonsense.[1]

There is an extraordinary outburst[2] over the correction of IV. viii. 110: 'My selfe shall *manfrede* it for them' in the Quarto; 'My selfe shall vndertake for them' in the Folio. 'The change is an actual loss to the language: . . . no author would ever dream of taking away from the picturesque dress in which he wraps his conceptions, a fine, though quaint, jewel like: "I'll manfrede it", to replace it by a worthless piece of glass, or a practical button: "I'll undertake it", just because a few people are unable to appreciate it! For this ill-favoured substitution can hardly be explained otherwise than by the ignorance of a press-reader, who coming across a word which was above his understanding, concluded at a mistake, and set it right according to his own scanty lights.' The word was also above the understanding of the late Dr. Henry Bradley, the late Professor W. W. Skeat, and Dr. C. T. Onions, all of whom we have consulted, and above the understanding of the *Oxford Dictionary*, which omits it. We turn to Dr. de Vocht for a sorely needed elucidation, and he gives us four wild guesses at verb-forms which do not exist: 'Possibly *mainferre*, used as a verb, for: to manage with an iron gauntlet;—or *manred*, also made into a verb, meaning: to conduct as a lord does his vassals; or *maufrey*, for *gallimaufry* (cf. *O.E.D*), viz., to treat with sharp, violent means;—maybe a playful adaptation of the Norman *manuvre*, Low-Latin *manoperare*, which entered the language at a later period.' So *manfrede* is wrong even if any of these ridiculous hypotheses could be entertained. In fact the word is a misprint, as its absence from the *Oxford Dictionary* shows.

In *Volpone*, III. ix. 53

Defame my patron; defeate you—VOLT. Where's her husband?

'the word *defeate* stands for *'feate*, as the verse requires'. This is suggested on the analogy of the aphetic forms ' 'gan ' and ' 'cause ' for ' began ' and ' because '; does Dr. de Vocht know that the *de-* here is a negative prefix and that the verb ' feat ' in the sense which he assigns to it does not exist? The pauses in the line make it perfectly metrical.[3]

It is unfortunate that one who has such an imperfect command of the language should attempt conjectural emendation, especially in a text so sound as Jonson's. We begin with further metrical freaks.

Tis true; but, Stoique, where (in the vast world)—*E.M.O.* I. i. 2.

The Folio editor 'unfortunately . . . passed over' this line.[4] For 'the' he should have read 'this' or 'our', and 'the stress in the last foot would come out better'. Here the slight pause after 'Stoique' and the metrical stress on 'where' are followed quite naturally by two light

[1] Ibid., p. 98.
[2] Ibid., pp. 134–5.
[3] *Volpone*, p. 176.
[4] *Comments*, pp. 71–2.

syllables before the voice lingers over the final 'vast world'. Exactly similar is *Volpone*, III. iv. 68:

> I'am all for musique: saue, i' the fore-noones . . .

which Dr. de Vocht would scan 'I ám all fór musíque: saue ín the fórenoones'. And compare Shakespeare's

> Look where he goes, even now, out at the portal.[1]

In *Every Man out of his Humour*, II. iv. 86, the Quarto has the unmetrical line

> And so through all: All which I haue alter'd—

corrected in the Folio to

> And so through all: all which, now, I haue alter'd.

The Folio 'fails to reproduce the original text, in which there is only an apparent mistake'. Read

> And so through all: all which I'ue alterèd.

Then the verse is 'quite regular' and does not 'prop up the line with a stiff *I haue*, and a trivial *now*'.[2]

In I. iii. 70–1 the Quarto has

> Where heauen cannot see him? Sbloud (one thinkes)
> 'Tis rare and admirable, that he should breath, and walke. . . .

The Folio correction ''Tis rare, and strange' is 'entirely wrong'. In the first line 'heauen cannot' is two syllables, and the line is short. Read

> Where heav'n can't see him? Sblood, me thinks 'tis rare
> And admirab', that he should breathe, and walk.

'Admirable' is pronounced, 'as very often, *admirab*'.[3]

Two lines in *Volpone*, 'metrically defective' in the Quarto, are not cured in the Folio:

> Crocodile, that hast thy teares prepar'd (III. vii. 119)
> Streight, giue out, about the streetes, you two (v. ii. 60).

'Although instances are found in the verses of Chaucer, Marlowe, Shakespeare, and especially of Milton, those monosyllabic initial feet may not have been in Jonson's intention at all.' So 'You, crocodile' and 'Go! straight give out' were 'possibly' written by Jonson.[4]

In *Poetaster*, III. i. 244–5, Crispinus offers to oust 'VIRGIL, VARIVS, and the best of them' in Maecenas' household. Dr. de Vocht conjectures

---

[1] *Hamlet*, III. iv. 136.
[3] Ibid., pp. 74–5.
[2] *Comments*, pp. 73–4.
[4] *Volpone*, pp. 172–3.

'the rest of them'—a good reading if it had authority, but 'best' is merely Crispinus' exaggeration.

In *Sejanus*, I. 563–5,

> SEI. Why, then giue way.
> DRV. Giue way, *Colossus*? Doe you lift? Aduance you?
> Take that.

'Do you lift?' 'seems incomprehensible'. The *Oxford Dictionary* in section 3 *sub voce* gives examples of this intransitive force in the sense 'lift yourself', and, of course, it fits in with '*Colossus*'. Dr. de Vocht ruins the dramatic movement of the line by making Drusus turn from Sejanus to his friends with the feeble apostrophe 'Do you list?'—'you' addressing the friends at one moment and Sejanus at another.

In I. 304–5, Sejanus' words to the doctor,

> Why, sir, I doe not aske you of their vrines,
> Whose smel's most violet?

Dr. de Vocht conjectures 'violent' in the form 'violēt'. He sagaciously remarks that Jonson probably did not allude to the effect of 'a drop of terebic essence taken with a piece of sugar', complains that 'violet' is neither adjective nor adverb, and says we should expect 'as violet' or 'like violet'. The delicate irony of the phrase has escaped him.[1] Indeed we have a suspicion that Dr. de Vocht is rather impervious to any form of irony other than his own, which is apt to be elementary. In *Volpone*, v. vii. 18–21, the disguised Volpone baits Voltore, who has lost the legacy:

> VOLT. What doe I know?
> VOLP. Mary no end of your wealth, sir, god decrease it.
> VOLT. Mistaking knaue! what, mock'st thou my misfortune?
> VOLP. His blessing on your heart, sir, would 'twere more.

It seems incredible that an editor should propose to change 'god decrease it' to 'god increase it', and justify it by the sarcasm on Voltore's misfortune, 'would 'twere more'. The Folio editor 'either did not notice the mistake or felt unable to rectify it'.[2]

In I. i. 66–7 Volpone, giving gold, says

> Hold thee, MOSCA,
> Take, of my hand.

'Here is an evident mistake: the compositor mixed up two words; no doubt, Jonson wrote: "Take thee, *Mosca*, Hold of my hand."'[3] 'Hold thee' is a Jonsonian phrase: compare *A Tale of a Tub*, II. iv. 36,

> Nay, say not so *Hilts*: hold thee; there are Crownes—

and in *Catiline*, v. 578, Cato, handing a letter to Caesar, says 'Hold thee, drunkard'.

---

[1] *Sejanus*, p. 186.   [2] *Volpone*, p. 201.   [3] Ibid., p. 199.

In *Volpone*, IV. iv. 20, Mosca, after telling Corbaccio that he shall
'enioy the crop of all', mocks Corvino and Voltore. In the Quarto,

> But you shall eat it. Much. Worshipfull Sir
> *Mercury* sit vpon your thundring tongue . . .

'You shall eat it' is addressed to Corvino; 'Much.' is a stage aside;
'Worshipfull Sir' is Voltore the lawyer. The Folio by printing 'Much!'
makes the irony a little clearer. Dr. de Vocht reads 'Much excellent
Sir', which he thinks a natural English greeting. He adds, quite
unjustly, that the exclamation 'Much!' has been a puzzle to all commentators, including Whalley and Gifford, both of whom understood
it and annotated it as ironic, meaning 'not at all'. Nor has it puzzled
the *Oxford Dictionary*, which duly records it *s.v.* 'Much', C.d. with
examples from Marlowe, Shakespeare, and Jonson.

'*Ineptissime Voctius*'—to borrow a formula from the critical apparatus
in old classical texts—is all we can say of these conjectures.

We have now shown in detail how ill equipped Dr. de Vocht is for
the task which he has set himself. Nothing that the Folio prints can
win from him even a grudging approval. 'It would almost be useless
to state', he observes, 'that some of the many mistakes and misprints
in the first *Quarto*' of *Every Man out of his Humour* 'were set right' in
the Folio.[1] He pounces on any scrap of evidence on which he can lay
his hands; his citations and references run into thousands. He has never
seriously considered the two obvious objections to his theory—that
Jonson would not have tolerated this systematic sabotage of his text,
and that Stansby would not have wasted time, money, and ink in
rewriting copy and inserting new readings in the proof. A casual reader
might find Dr. de Vocht's vast accumulation of evidence plausible; a
critical sifting soon shows its weakness. This it has been our unpleasant
task to supply, and we gladly take leave of one of the most futile efforts
ever made to discredit the authority of a great classic text.

[1] *Comments*, p. 43.

IV

THE PLAYS OF 1631

AFTER his paralytic stroke in 1628 Jonson evidently thought of publishing his unprinted work in a second Folio to accompany the collection of 1616. The design began to take shape in 1631 when *Bartholomew Fair*, *The Devil is an Ass*, and *The Staple of News* were printed. The printer was John Beale, the publisher Robert Allot, who entered only one of these plays, *The Staple of News*, on the Stationers' Register. John Waterson had entered it on 14 April 1626 but assigned it to Allot on 7 September 1631. The other two plays, though not entered, were transferred by his widow Mary Allot to John Legatt the younger and to Andrew Crooke on 1 July 1637. Jonson in his letter to the Earl of Newcastle complained bitterly of the 'lewd printer' Beale, from whom he could not get a copy of *The Staple of News* to send with *The Devil is an Ass*; he had already sent a copy of *Bartholomew Fair*.[1]

Probably this sending out of private gift-copies to friends and patrons was the only use made of this issue in 1631.[2] Copies survive of a single one of these plays in a contemporary binding: we ourselves have a copy of *The Devil is an Ass* bound in vellum, with wide margins and with end-leaves having one of the watermarks found in the body of the text. Copies of the three plays are occasionally found as a separate volume: Messrs. Dobell sold a copy in contemporary binding in 1929, and there is one in the library of Jesus College, Oxford. Dr. Greg possesses a copy in what appears to be an eighteenth-century binding. Further, only these three plays were printed in folio. But Jonson published in octavo *The New Inn* in the course of the year; it was printed by Thomas Harper for Thomas Alchorne, who registered it on 17 April. Stung by the failure of this play two years earlier, Jonson determined to vindicate himself in the eyes of the reading public by the only remedy that remained to him—publication. A wider audience was given an opportunity of reversing the judgement of the playhouse.

Why did the 'Second Volume' go no farther than the three plays? Jonson's state of health is a possible, though it is not a likely, explanation. He looked after the proofs of *The New Inn* effectively.[3] Probably John Beale was the cause of the stoppage; Jonson's stormy

---

[1] See vol. i, p. 211.
[2] In vol. ii, p. 131, we wrote '*Bartholomew Fair* was first published in 1631': for 'published' read 'printed'.
[3] See vol. vi, pp. 386–93, for the list of his proof-corrections.

relations with him made further co-operation impossible. Allot too may have been glad to be rid of an enterprise which, if he was any judge of printing, he could not have regarded as satisfactory. As it was, the sheets of the edition were on his hands at the time of his death in 1635.

THE
VVORKES
OF
BENJAMIN JONSON.

The second Volume.

CONTAINING
THESE PLAYES,
Viz.

1 Bartholomew Fayre.
2 The Staple of Newes.
3 The Divell is an Asse.

LONDON,
Printed for RICHARD MEIGHEN.
1640.

V

THE FOLIO OF 1640

In certain features of the printing the Second Folio shows a departure from the methods of its predecessor. It economizes space by printing fifty lines to a page where the earlier folio had forty-seven.[1] In the 1616 Folio the date of performance, the company, and a list of the chief actors followed the plays in a final page; the 1640 Folio prints this historical note on the back of the title-page after the mention of the scene, omitting the reference to the company because that was already on the title-page. The result was that the 1,016 pages of text in the First Folio were reduced to 896 in the Second.

In this volume proper names of characters are printed in lower-case italic instead of the roman capitals of the First Folio.

As might be expected, the Second Folio modernized to some extent. In lower-case 'j' and 'u' are the rule; this was becoming the practice towards the middle of the seventeenth century. But by a curious inconsistency 'I' and 'V' are often retained as capitals, especially in titles. Thus 'AS IT WAS PRESENTED AT COVRT BEFORE KING IAMES' in the heading to *News from the New World Discovered in the Moon*. 'IONSON', 'IOHNSON', 'JONSON', and 'JOHNSON' are all found. In Hugh Holland's preliminary verses the heading is 'To His worthy friend, BEN. IONSON. *Vpon his* SEJANUS'.

The spelling is modernized, though inconsistent survivals of the older forms are found occasionally. Thus, 'than' for 'then', 'marry' for the oath 'mary', 'lose' for 'loose', 'hither' and 'whither' for 'hether' and 'whether', 'gifts' for 'guifts', 'guests' for 'ghests', 'valour' for 'valure', 'velvets' for 'vellets', 'Paules' for 'Poules', 'sheriffs' for 'shrieffs', 'struck' for 'strooke', 'authenticall' for 'autenticall'; a significant example, because it affects the metre, is '*atomes*, to undoe' for '*atomi*, to 'vndoe' in *Sejanus*, I. 257. A minor point is that 'god' in oaths, the common form in the First Folio, which modified the profanity at least to the eye, usually attains to the dignity of a capital letter in the Second Folio.

THE FIRST VOLUME

This is a reprint of the Folio of 1616 in two sections. The collation is A to Kkkk[6], Lll[4], the plays; A–T[6], the *Epigrams, Entertainments*,

[1] In the second volume the part printed by Beale had forty-seven lines; afterwards the number is inconsistent, but the printer aimed at a page of fifty lines.

and *Masques*. In detail: A1 recto blank; A1 verso, Robert Vaughan's portrait inlaid; A2 recto, William Hole's engraved title-page, re-touched by altering the *i* of 'Beniamin' to *j* and re-engraving the shield with the imprint and date to 'LONDON. *Printed by* Richard Bishop, *and are to be sold by* Andrew Crooke *in St Paules Church-yard. An^o D. 1640*'; A2 verso blank; A3 recto, 'The Catalogue'; A3 verso–A6 verso, poems by John Selden, Edward Heyward, William Hodgson, George Chapman, Hugh Holland, John Donne, George Lucy, Edmund Bolton, Francis Beaumont. Richard Bishop in 1635 bought William Stansby's business from Stansby's widow for £700, and he acquired the copyright of *Every Man out of his Humour* from John Smethwick on 28 April 1638.

Every Man in his Humour. B1, title-page, with the imprint of Richard Bishop facsimiled in vol. iii, p. 299; B1 verso blank; B2 recto, the dedication to Camden; B2 verso, the persons of the play, the scene, and the list of the principal comedians; B3 recto–G1 verso, the text. Pages 1–62.

Every Man out of his Humour. G2 recto, title-page, with the imprint of Richard Bishop, facsimiled in vol. iii, p. 420; G2 verso blank; G3 recto, the dedication to the Inns of Court; G3 verso, 'the Names of the Actors' (i.e. characters) and the list of the principal comedians; G4, character-sketches of the persons; G5 recto–O4 recto, the text; O4 verso, the epilogue at the Court performance. Pages 63–152, with page 135 misnumbered 125.

Cynthia's Revels. O5 recto, the title-page, with the imprint of Richard Bishop, facsimiled in vol. iv, p. 29; O5 verso blank; O6 recto, the dedication to the Court; O6 verso, the persons of the play, the scene, and the list of the principal comedians; P1 recto–X4 recto, the text; X4 verso blank. Pages 153–235.

Poetaster. X5 recto, the title-page, with the imprint of George Young and Richard Bishop's device, facsimiled in vol. iv, p. 199; X5 verso blank; X6 recto, the dedication to Richard Martin; X6 verso, the persons of the play, the scene, and the list of the principal comedians; Y1 recto–Dd5 verso, the text, concluding with the Apologetical Dialogue. Pages 237–310.

Sejanus his Fall. Dd6 recto, the title-page, with Richard Bishop's imprint, facsimiled in vol. iv, p. 347; Dd6 verso blank; Ee1 recto, the dedication to Lord Aubigny; Ee1 verso, the argument; Ee2 recto, the persons of the play, the scene, and the list of the principal tragedians; Ee2 verso–Kk6 verso, the text. Pages 311–84.

Volpone, or The Fox. Ll1 recto, the title-page, with the imprint of Richard Bishop, facsimiled in vol. v, p. 15; Ll1 verso blank; Ll2 recto–3 recto, the dedication to the Universities of Oxford and

Cambridge; Ll3 verso, the persons of the play, the scene, and the principal comedians; Ll4 recto–Qq6 verso, the text. Pages 385–456.

Epicoene, or The Silent Woman. Rr1 recto, the title-page, with the imprint of Richard Bishop, facsimiled in vol. v, p. 159; Rr1 verso blank; Rr2 recto, the dedication to Sir Francis Stuart; Rr2 verso, the persons of the play, the scene, and the list of the principal comedians; Rr3 recto–Yy3 verso, the text. Pages 457–522.

The Alchemist. Yy4 recto, the title-page, with the imprint of Richard Bishop, facsimiled in vol. v, p. 287; Yy4 verso blank; Yy5 recto, the dedication to Mary, Lady Wroth; Yy5 verso, the persons of the play, the scene, and the list of the principal comedians; Yy6 recto–Eee2 recto, the text; Eee2 verso blank. Pages 523–91.

Catiline. Eee3 recto, the title-page, with the imprint of Richard Bishop, facsimiled in vol. v, p. 425; Eee3 verso blank; Eee4 recto, the dedication to the Earl of Pembroke; Eee4 verso, the persons of the play, the scene, and the list of the principal tragedians; Eee5 recto–Lll4 verso, the text. Pages 593–668.

Epigrams. A1 recto, the title-page, with the imprint and device of Richard Bishop; A1 verso blank; A2, the dedication to the Earl of Pembroke; A3 recto–D5 verso, the text. Pages 1–46. A new epigram was added after cxxviii, 'To Edward Filmer, on his Musicall Work dedicated to the Queen. Anno, 1629'.

The Forest. D6 recto–F3 recto, the text, with title heading on the first page; F3 verso blank. Pages 47–65.

Part of the King's Entertainment in Passing to his Coronation. F4 recto, title-page with Richard Bishop's imprint and device; F4 verso blank; F5 recto–H1 verso, the text. Pages 67–86.

A Panegyre on the King's Entrance to Parliament. H2–H3, the text, with title heading on the first page. Pages 87–90.

The Entertainment at Althorp. H4 recto, the title-page with Richard Bishop's imprint and device; H4 verso blank; H5 recto–I2 recto, the text, headed 'A SATYRE'. Pages 91–9.

The Entertainment at Highgate. I2 verso–I5 recto, the text, with title heading on the first page. Pages 100–5.

The Entertainment of the Two Kings at Theobalds. I5 verso, I6 recto, the text, with title heading on the first page. Pages 106–7.

The Entertainment of the King and Queen at Theobalds. I6 verso–K1 verso, with title heading on the first page. Pages 108–10.

Masques at Court. K2 recto, general title-page with Richard Bishop's imprint and device; K2 verso blank. Pages 111–12. The masques which follow have title-headings on the first page.

The Masque of Blackness. K3 recto–K6 verso, pages 113–20.

The Masque of Beauty. K6 verso–L5 recto, pages 120–9.

Hymenaei. L5 verso–N3 verso, pages 130–50.

The Haddington Masque. N4 recto–O2 verso, pages 151–60.

The Masque of Queens. O3 recto–P6 recto, pages 161–79.

The Speeches at Prince Henry's Barriers. P6 verso–Q4 verso, pages 180–8.

Oberon the Fairy Prince. Q5 recto–R3 recto, pages 189–97.

Love Freed from Ignorance and Folly. R3 verso–R6 recto, pages 198–203.

Love Restored. R6 recto–S2 verso, pages 203–8.

A Challenge at Tilt. S2 verso–S4 verso, pages 208–12.

The Irish Masque at Court. S5 recto–S6 verso, pages 213–16.

Mercury Vindicated from the Alchemists at Court. T1 recto–T3 verso, pages 217–22.

The Golden Age Restored. T3 verso–T6 verso, pages 222–8.

The first scholarly examination of Jonson's text was made by Dr. Brinsley Nicholson in an article contributed in 1870 to *Notes and Queries*, 4th Series, vol. v, pp. 573–5, 'Ben Jonson's Folios and the Bibliographers'. He collated and criticized the text of both folios. He stated that, except for dropped words and trifling errors, 'as a rule, both words and punctuation' of the earlier folio 'have been very carefully followed' in the reprint of 1640. 'Words, stops, and the apostrophes that indicate the scansion are occasionally corrected in a manner not to be accounted for by the care and pains of any ordinary or mechanical press reader, especially if the uncorrected errors . . . be also taken into account.' Then he instanced the notes to some of the masques, 'in which a press error hardly ever occurs, and where the errors of the original in references and in Latin and Greek are invariably corrected'. Unfortunately this high praise of Bishop's printing is unjustified. Certainly he corrected a number of errors, and he tried, not very successfully, to correct the Greek and Latin of the masques; he also tried to improve the punctuation, chiefly by means of a larger use of the semicolon. But Nicholson's conclusion that some of the corrections 'must have been made' and others 'probably were made by the author' can hardly be accepted. It would have been characteristic of Jonson to have left a copy of the 1616 Folio marked with his corrections, but there is not a scrap of evidence that he ever did so.

We have from time to time criticized the text of the Second Folio in the introductions to the several plays.[1] The misprints are mostly

[1] See vol. iii, pp. 294–6, 417–18, for *Every Man in* and *Every Man out of his Humour*; vol. iv, pp. 23, 195–6, 343–4, for *Cynthia's Revels, Poetaster*, and *Sejanus*; vol. v, pp. 9, 10, 150–1, 416–17, for *Volpone, Epicoene*, and *Catiline*.

commonplace printers' blunders, such as 'snowie' for 'sinowie'
(*E.M.O.* ii. vi. 157), 'wrapt' for 'warpt' (*C.R.* iv. i. 28), 'searching'
for 'searcing' (ib. v. iv. 325), 'difference' for 'diffidence' (*S.W.* iv.
i. 68), '*dispositions*' for '*depositions*' (*Volp.* ii. ii. 139), 'porter' for
'potter' (*Cat.* iii. 542), 'intimate' for 'inanimate' (*K. Ent.* 119),
'Ladder' for 'Larder' (*Merc. Vin.* 72). More important are the
occasional corrections or attempts at a correction: for instance,
'*some*', though this is obvious because of the rhyme, for '*fame*'
(*E.M.I.* v. v. 81), '*Yea, fright all aches*' for '*Yet fright all aches*'
(*Volp.* ii. ii. 202), 'I could desire, grave *Fathers*' for 'I could desire,
Fathers' (*Cat.* iv. 209), because the corrector thought that 'desire'
must be a dissyllable; '*anima*' correcting '*animas*', a misprint for
'*animus*' in *The Masque of Queens*, 611; '*straight*' similarly correcting '*starre*', a misprint for '*the starre*' in *Oberon*, 445; 'no' affection', which is a Jonsonian punctuation, for 'no affection' in
Epigram xxiii. 6; 'lock'd' for 'look'd' (ibid. xcii. 17). The worst of
the Latin and Greek blunders corrected are—ἀντίθεον Πολυφῆμον for
ἀντι.θεὸν Πολύφημον (*K. Ent.* 341, note 'e'); 'PULCHERRIMÆ' and
'FVNESTISSIMAM' for 'PVLCHERIMÆ' and 'FVNESSIMAM' (ibid. 656,
662); ταυρόκρανος and ἀγκάλαις for ταυρόκρανος and ἀγκάλαις (*M.
Blackness*, 46, note 'h'); σύμβολον and γενέσθαι for σὺμβολον and
γενὲσθαι (*Hym.* 288 note 'a'); θάλλειν for θαλέιν (ibid. 436, note *);
'*silices*' for '*silicet*' (*M. Queens*, 265, note 'g'); '*hircinis*' and λευκὸς
for '*hircints*' and λουκός (*Oberon*, 66, note 'a'); '*gestari*' for '*gestaui*'
(ibid. 130, note *). Blunders almost as bad are left uncorrected,
and there is some slight excuse in the fact that they occur in
marginal notes printed in small type. We ourselves have sometimes
missed them in a first proof and have only been saved by the revise.

A few large-paper copies of the first volume of the 1640 Folio have
survived, but they are rare. Swinburne had one, which was sold at
Messrs. Sotheby's in June 1916. They have a few corrections. Two
copies have been collated—Selden's copy in the Bodleian (G.2.5.
Art. Seld.) and a copy belonging to the editors. The following
corrections of the text and accidental deviations from it such as
dropped letters have been noted.

Every Man in his Humour

P. 9.	i. ii. 91	wind-mill]	wind-m[111] (the letters broken)
P. 17.		Act II. Scene II.]	Act II. Scene I.
P. 20.	ii. ii. 21, 25, 30	and]	an
	25	lucke]	luck
	34	he brewes]	hee brews

P. 44.   IV. iii. 14   de-|vill!]   de-!|vill!
                15   trash!]   trash¹
P. 52.   IV. viii. 145   counsell.]   counsell
P. 57.   IV. xi. 50   I'le-keep it]   I'le keep it

Every Man out of his Humour

P. 66. The Names of the Actors, 5 PUNTER-   PUNTARVOLO
                            VOLO]
P. 67. Characters, 5   *iether*]   *either*
                14   PUNTERVOLO]   PUNTARVOLO
P. 75. Induction, 334   *Elixi'r*]   Elixer
P. 84.   I. iii. 181   *envie*]²   *envie*
P. 149.   V. x. 2   sower]   sowre

Cynthia's Revels

P. 177.   II. iii. 153   against;]   against,

Poetaster

P. 237. Title-page, 5   1601 By. the]   1601. By the
P. 240. The Persons, 5   . GALLUS]   *Readjusted*
                    COR
P. 251.   II. i. 35   mightely]   mightily
P. 289.   IV. ix. 95–6   stay | In]   st | In
             V. i. 1–2   conquer'd, | And]   conqu | And
                2–3   felt; | Griev'd]   felt | Griev'd

Sejanus

P. 349.   III. 515   AUGUSTUS | In   AUGU | In

Volpone

P. 387. Dedication, 12   *of it | heare*]   *of | heare*
                13   *It is | certaine*]   *It | certayne*
                14   *licence of | Poëtasters*]   *licence | Poëtasters*
P. 391. Heading   VOLPONE,]   VOLPONF³
P. 392.   I. i. 15   the best;]   the best
P. 402.   I. v. 17   Beshrew't]   Best shew't
Pp. 402–3.   I. v. 26   Vo TORE]   VOLTORE
                84   Vo LP.]   VOLP.
                89   Vo PONE]   VOLPONE
P. 403.   68   aith]   Faith
                69   Fs well]   As well
                70   A CORV.]   CORV.⁴
                71   is]   It is
                92   moneth]   month

¹ The type disturbed, and the note of exclamation has moved up a line.
² The 'I' is faintly printed.
³ The final 'E' is broken.
⁴ In ll. 68–70 the initial letter dropped a line.

The Alchemist

P. 566.	IV. i. 35	suffer that,]	suffer that;	
	49	guilt]	gilt	
P. 574.	IV. iv. 46	Foot-men]	Fo ot-men	
	48	*Bet'lem*]	*B et'lem*	
P. 575.	IV. v. 17	Sh's]	Sh'is	
	25–32	And so . . . interprete Rome.]	*And so . . . interprete* Rome.[1]	
	27	*Philosophers*]	*Philosophers stone*	
	29	Brimstoni]	*Brimstony*	
P. 576.	IV. v. 36	O]	O,	

Catiline

P. 613.	II. 219	sulennesse]	sullennesse
P. 647.	IV. 550	fortunes,][2]	fortunes
P. 658.	V. 180, 188	there? . . . books, *misplaced above the line*	*Adjusted*

Epigrams

P. 4.	Dedication	BEN. JONSON]	. . N. JONSON

Part of the King's Coronation Entertainment

P. 69.	17	CEOLO]	COELO

Hymenaei

P. 131	52 note 'a'	For, which]	For which,
	note 'e'	quasi. Minister]	quasi Minister

THE SECOND VOLUME

The second volume opens with the three plays printed by John Beale for Robert Allot in 1631—*Bartholomew Fair, The Devil is an Ass,* and *The Staple of News.* Though this is the order of composition, performance, and printing, *The Devil is an Ass* is placed third in the group and is so numbered on the title-page which Richard Meighen prefixed to copies of these plays when they were published in the Folio of 1640. Only one of these plays was entered on the Stationers' Register, *The Staple of News,* on 14 April 1626, shortly after its performance. Such evidence as there is suggests that these plays were not published by Allot in 1631. Jonson's complaint to the Earl of Newcastle that he could not extract from the printer a copy of *The Staple of News* to send as he had sent the two other plays[3] shows that they were not on sale at Allot's shop, the sign of

---

[1] In Q and F1 Dol's speech was printed in small roman parallel with the agitated comments of Face and Mammon: the size of the type compelled this. F2 printed the speech and the comments separately in large type, with Dol's speech first. Originally F2 set this last in roman; the large-paper copy corrected it to italic so as to be uniform with her other quotations.

[2] The comma faint.

[3] See vol. i, p. 211.

the bear, in Paul's churchyard. John Hansley's licensing note on 6 June 1640, 'Let this be entered . . . but not printed . . .',[1] shows that he knew nothing of the printing nine years earlier.

After Allot's death his widow Mary on 1 July 1637, 'by order of a full Court holden the Seauenth day of Nouember last', i.e. in 1636, transferred her husband's rights in sixty-one books, including *Bartholomew Fair* and *The Staple of News*, to John Legatt and Andrew Crooke.[2] Crooke had been Allot's servant and had received from him a legacy of twenty pounds on condition that he remained three years in Mary Allot's service. The omission of *The Devil is an Ass* in this large transfer of stock can only be explained as an oversight. Crooke attempted to remedy it in 1640 when the Folio, which would contain these plays, was under way. This is the licenser's note found in manuscript in a copy of the Folio with the 1631 text of *The Devil is an Ass*: 'June 6 1640. Let this be entered for Andrew Crooke but not printed till I give further directions. John Hansley.'[3] All the evidence suggests that Crooke was fully entitled to the copyright, but the licenser's caution was justified by the legal difficulties which beset the publication of the 1640 Folio.

Over the first three plays, however, there was finally no trouble. Richard Meighen issued them with a title-page dated 1640, which described them as 'The Second Volume' of Jonson's 'Workes'. Once again there was no legal transfer, but Meighen probably came to terms with Crooke and bought up the sheets.

The greater portion of this 1640 volume—that is to say, the masques, the latest plays, *The Underwood*, the translation of the *Ars Poetica*, and the prose-works—was issued by Thomas Walkley, probably in the early months of 1641.[4] He neglected to enter it in time on the Stationers' Register, and he had reason to regret that he had not secured his rights. His own account was that Jonson before his death presented Sir Kenelm Digby with 'seuerall' of his 'writings and workes' in 'true & perfect' manuscript copies, giving him full authority to dispose of them. Walkley bought the manuscripts from Sir Kenelm for forty pounds and spent two hundred pounds on printing them. 'Before they were fully perfected', John Benson and Andrew Crooke secured 'false & imperfect Copies of the said workes' and entered them at Stationers' Hall. Walkley complained to one

---

[1] See vol. vi, p. 146.
[2] Arber, *Transcript*, iv. 387.
[3] Published by Professor S. G. Dunn in *The Times Literary Supplement*, 28 July 1921.
[4] He had published in 1631 the masque of *Chloridia*, the last work issued in Jonson's lifetime.

of the Secretaries of State, who issued an injunction against Benson and Crooke. Matters took a new turn. Benson and Crooke evaded the injunction. John Parker, a stationer of London, with Benson and Crooke's connivance, successfully entered an action at the Guild-hall and attached all Walkley's edition that had so far been printed on the pretext that the stock belonged to Benson and Benson owed him money. On 20 January 1640 Walkley filed a bill in Chancery, stating his case and adding that Benson and Crooke, relying of course on their entries in the Register, announced that they would go forward with their own edition. They carried out their threat, at least in part, but Walkley presumably won his case, for there is no counter-plea by any of the defendants, and Walkley succeeded in getting the book out in 1641. It was probably late in 1640 before the case was heard in the Court of Chancery and later still before Walkley's stock was restored to him. His statement that it was attached before the work was 'fully perfected' is borne out by the fact that two imprints in the volume, those of *The Sad Shepherd* and of *Timber, or Discoveries*, are dated 1641. In both these works there are clear signs of hasty printing, especially in the *Discoveries* where there are serious omissions, for instance, in the passage bor-rowed from Hoskyns (ll. 2128–289). All the other imprints have the date 1640, when he had originally planned to publish the whole work. He had not completed it when his stock was seized. In 1648 he was still appealing to the House of Lords for a licence, but he stated that he had printed the book 'by authority'. This could only have been the authority of the Court of Chancery. For an entry on the Stationers' Register he had to wait till 1658 when he entered the contents of 'the third volume' and added at the end of the list the hitherto-unregistered *The Devil is an Ass*. His rights at last secured, he transferred them to Humphrey Moseley.

Such in brief is the story of the painful steps by which the second volume of the 1640 Folio found its way into the market. It remains to authenticate it. First, as to Benson and Crooke and what they succeeded in publishing. They paved their way adroitly by a series of entries on the Register.

4°. Nouembris 1639 . . .

John Benson. Entred for his Copie vnder the hands of Doctor Bray and Master ffetherston warden An Addicion of some excellent Poems to Shakespeares Poems by other gentlemen. viz[t]. His mistris drawne. and her mind by Beniamin: Johnson. An Epistle to Beniamin Johnson by ffrancis Beaumont. | His Mistris shade. by R. Herrick. &c. vj[d].

(Arber, *Transcript*, iv. 487.)

The Jonson poems are the third and fourth of the 'Eupheme' series in honour of Lady Digby, printed at the end of *The Underwood*.

16º. die Decembris 1639 . . .

John Benson. Entred for his Copie vnder the hands of Master Clay and Master Bourne warden a booke called Ben Johnsons Execration against Vulcan with other his smaller Epigrams   vj[d].

Ibid. 493.

8º. ffebruarij 1639. [i.e. 1640.]

John Benson. Entred for his Copie vnder the hands of Master Clay and Master Bourne warden a booke called Quintus Horatius fflaccus his booke of the Art of Poetry to the Piso's. translated into English by Beniamin: Johnson   vj[d].

Ibid. 498.

20º. ffebruarij. 1639. [i.e. 1640.]

John Benson. Entred for his Copie vnder the hands of doctor wykes and Master Bourne warden a booke called The Masque of the Gypsies by Beniamin: Johnson   vj[d].

Ibid. 500.

So far the nefarious Benson, and he followed up the entries with publication. He published in quarto *Ben Ionson's Execration against Vulcan. With divers Epigrams . . . Never published before* in 1640; Matthew Clay's imprimatur is dated 14 December 1639. He followed this up with a duodecimo in 1640—*Q. Horatius Flaccus: His Art of Poetry . . . With other Workes of the Author, never Printed before*—viz. *The Masque of Gypsies*; Clay's imprimatur is dated 21 February 1640. Walkley in his bill of 20 January mentions that Benson and Crooke were threatening publication, and it followed in due course with Benson.

What of Crooke? He too made an entry of Jonson manuscripts on the Register, with Richard Serger for his accomplice:

20º. Martij 1639 [i.e. 1640.] . . .

Master Crooke and Richard: Seirger   Entred for their Copie vnder the hands of doctor wykes and master ffetherston warden four Masques viz[t]   vj[d].

> The Masque of Augures
> Tyme vindicated
> Neptunes triumphes. and
> Panns Anniuersary or the sheapards holy day.
> with sundry Elegies and other Poems by Beniamin: Johnson

Ibid. 503.

The four masques specified in this entry are the next in order in the Folio to *The Masque of Gypsies*, which Benson had just printed. It looks as if Crooke and his partner made that masque a starting-point for further raids on Jonson's work, and here not improbably on Walkley's text, though Benson's copies of the *Ars Poetica* and *The Masque of Gypsies* were from a different manuscript than that which Walkley printed. That is why Walkley calls their copies 'false and imperfect'. Crooke and Serger did not print these four masques; evidently this was the 'further printing' after the two issues of the *Poems* in 1640 which Walkley stopped.

Here is the full text of Walkley's bill in the Public Record Office, Chancery Proceedings before 1714, Mitford, 90–38:[1]

| xx. Januarij. 1640. | To the right hono^ble Sr Edward Littleton |
| Pindar[2] | K^t Lord keeper of the greate seale of England |

Humbly complayning sheweth vnto y^r good lopp. yor Daylie Orato^r Thomas Walkeley Cittizen & stationer of London.

That whereas seuerall of the writings and workes of Beniamin Johnson late deceased and not before printed were some shorte tyme before his decease presented vnto & giuen by the said Beniamin to Sr Kenelme Digby to dispose thereof at his will and pleasure.

To whose care & trust the said Beniamin left the publishing and printing of them and delivered him true & perfect Copies for his better & more effectual dooing thereof,

And the said Beniamin shortly after dyeing, the said Sr Kenelme Digbye in pursuance of the said truste reposed in him deliuered the same Copies to yor Orato^r to haue them published and printed according to the intencon of the said Beniamin Johnson freely bestowing the benefitt of the printing thereof on yor Orato^r,

Wherevpon yor Orator having procured licence for the printing thereof and having to his great charge caused them to be printed before such tyme as yor Orato^r had the same from the printing house or that they were fully perfected, one John Benson & Andrew Crooke having notice that yor Orato^r was in hand wth the printing of the same bookes and that there was like to bee some profitt made thereby

They the said Benson & Crooke having obtayned by some casuall or other indirect meanes false & imperfect Copies of the same works did make an Entry in the Hall of the Company of Stationers of London in their owne name for the printing & publishing of the same workes, the Company not knowing of yor Orato^res interest therein or of yor Orato^res printing thereof,

wch vndue and irregular proceeding of them the said Benson & Crooke com̃ing accidentally to the knowledge of your Orato^r yor Orato^r did

---

[1] Printed by Frank Marcham in an article in *The Library*, 4th Series, 1930–1, vol. xi, pp. 225–9, 'Thomas Walkley and the Ben Jonson "Workes" of 1640'.

[2] Matthew Pindar, one of the six clerks from 21 Mar. 1640 till 26 Oct. 1683.

thervpon make complaynt thereof to one of his Ma^tes Secretaries of State who having heard & vnderstood the trueth of the proceeding did graunt a warrant, thereby prohibiting the sayd Benson & Crooke from further printing or publishing the same workes or any of them.

But nowe soe it is may it please yor good lopp. that one John Parker a stationer also of London p^rtending the said Benson to be greatly indebted to him and finding the name of the said Benson to be entred in the hall of the stationers for the printing & publishing of the said workes and knowing that diverse of the said bookes wch yor Orato^r had at his owne proper charge caused to be printed were accordingly printed and ready for to be published, And knowing also where they were, the said Parker did by some private practice or agreem^t wth them the said Benson & Crooke cause the said bookes wch yor Orato^r had soe caused to be printed to be attached in London as the wares of him the said Benson at the suite of him the said Parker for a p^rtended debt supposed to be owing to him the said Parker by the said Benson and proceeding therevpon in the Guildhall London obteyned a Judgem^t thervpon, yor Orato^r being noe way privy thereto or knowing thereof

Which said wares soe attached and for wch the said Parker had obtayned Judgem^t in maner as aforesaid are the proper goodes and wares of yor Orato^r onely and are of the value of three hundred poundes at the least,

Soe as now yor Orato^r having been at aboue two hundred poundes charge in & concerning the printing the same bookes, they are detayned from yor Orato^r by him, by whom the same were printed for yor Orato^res vse in respect of the said Attachment & Judgem^t, yor Orato^r being noe way indebted to the said Confederates or any of them, And the said Benson & C⟨r⟩ooke doe giue out that they will in the meane tyme proceed wth the printing and publishing their Copies whereby yor Orato^r is like to be greatly dampnifyed contrary to all equity & good Conscience.

In tender Consideracon whereof, and for that yor Orato^r hath noe way to helpe himselfe against the said Judgem^t soe surreptuously obtayned without yor hono^res privity as aforesaid nor to be releiued in the p^rmisses but by yor lopps. ayd in this hono^ble Courte, yor Orato^res witnesses who should proue the p^rmisses living remotely in places vnknowne to yor Orato^r

May it therefore please yor lopp, the p^rmisses considered to graunt to yor Orato^r his Maties most gracious processe of Subpena to be directed to the said John Benson Andrew Crooke & John Parker Comanding them & every of them at a certayne day and vnder certayne paine therein to be limited personally to be & appeare before yor lopp. in his Ma^tes high Court of Chancery then & there to answere the p^rmisses

And further to stand to and abide such order sentence & Judgem^t therein as shalbe agreeable to equity and good conscience

And yor Orato^r shall daylie pray &c.
John Vernon[1]

pk.

---

[1] Walkley's counsel.

If Walkley won the case, as seems probable, his troubles were not over. We find him complaining in 1648 that the book was still unlicensed. This would explain why he did not print a title to his portion of the work, corresponding to Richard Meighen's title-page for the three plays of 1631. Two House of Lords MSS., dated 20 December 1648, are a petition of nineteen London stationers—Crooke, Benson, and Walkley among them—and a special petition of Walkley to the House of Lords to appoint additional licensers of books. The stationers complain that though three licensers had been appointed 'to lycence for the presse all bookes of history poetry humanity and philosophie . . . diuers bookes lye vnprinted that would be beneficiall to ye Common Wealth, and trade is much hindred'. Of the three appointed, Thomas Farnaby was dead—he had died the year before—Sir Nathaniel Brent 'since imployed in greater business—and 'Mr Langly the Scholemaster of Paules' was too busy with his school to do the work. Walkley's petition was as follows:

To the Right hono^ble the House of Peeres in Parliam^t Assembled

The humble peticon of Thomas Walkley Station^r

Humbly sheweth

That about 6 yeares ago yor Pet^r bought a peece of Poetry of Mr Ben: Johnsons which cost him 40^li, and printed it by Authority wch caused him to disburse 300^li more, to the greate weakeninge of yor pet^r in his estate.

That since Sr Nathaniell Brent and Mr Langley the Schoolemaster of Pauls haue bin appoynted and still are authorized by the Authority of Parliam^t to lycence all bookes of Poetry and humanity, soe that yor Pet^rs former Authority is excluded, and become invalid.|

Now in reguard Sr Nathaniell Brent is gon out of ye Towne about Publique affaires which may detaine him long, and Mr Langley p^rtends busines soe as hee cannot pvse it

Yo^r Pet^rs humble suite to yor hono^r is, that yor Hono^rs would be pleased to desyre Mr Langley or some other whome he shall appoynt to pvse ye said Coppie, and relycence it Soe that it may be entred in ye Common Hall according to Custome That yor Pet^r may not loose his right.|

And yor Pet^r shall pray &c

Tho. Walkley.

Walkley's description of the Jonson manuscripts which he wished to get 'relicenced' as 'a peece of Poetry' is odd, but his statement that he bought them for forty pounds is very interesting. The 'peece' must have been at least the collection of *The Underwood* and probably also the translation of the *Ars Poetica*. In the Chancery suit he estimated that the printing had cost 'above two hundred pounds' and he put the value of the stock at three hundred pounds. In the petition to the Lords he put his total expenses at three hundred pounds for the printing and forty pounds for the purchase of the manuscript. Presumably he would be awarded damages by the Court of Chancery, so that he was not throwing in his legal expenses. At any rate, he was a hundred pounds out in his reckoning.

The registration which Walkley should have made in 1640 was effected in 1658.

17 September 1658

Thomas Walkley. Entred for his copie under the hand of Master Pulleyn warden a booke called Ben Johnsons Workes ye 3^d volume containing these peeces, vizt, ffifteene masques at court and elsewhere. Horace his art of Poetry Englished. English Grammar. Timber or Discoveries. Underwoods consisting of divers poems. The Magnetick Lady. A Tale of a Tub. The sad shephard or a tale of Robin Hood. The Devill is an asse. Salvo jure cuiuscunque   vj^d

(Eyre and Rivington, Transcript, vol. ii, p. 196.)

On 20 November Walkley transferred his rights to Humphrey Moseley.[1] The inclusion of *The Devil is an Ass* in 'the third volume', to which it did not belong, is all the more curious because its two companion plays of 1631, *Bartholomew Fair* and *The Staple of News*, are ignored. This is the first registration of the play; it had not been transferred to Crooke in 1637, nor by Crooke to Meighen in 1640. Meighen's title-page to the three plays is the only evidence of his claim, but at any rate it was not disputed.

So ends the record of muddle, evasion, and dishonesty which characterizes the history of this volume and is suitably reflected in the amorphous arrangement of its contents. Printing and paper are poor, the type on one page of a leaf showing through on the next, and not only in workmanship but in accuracy the 1640 Folio as a whole compares unfavourably with Stansby's Folio of 1616.

But the most interesting revelation afforded us by these legal documents is not a point of law or copyright, but Walkley's statement that he acquired the manuscripts from Sir Kenelm Digby, whom Jonson had made his literary executor. It is supremely important to know on trustworthy evidence that this new text was set up from the poet's autograph. Realizing that he was not likely to bring out his later works himself, he trusted Digby with his

---

[1] *Transcript*, vol. ii., p. 206.

papers. In a poem addressed to Lady Digby, whom he called his Muse, he had drawn an intimate picture of his relations with Sir Kenelm:

> Goe, *Muse*, in, and salute him. Say he be
>> Busie, or frowne at first; when he sees thee,
> He will cleare up his forehead. . . .
> For he doth love my Verses, and will looke
>> Upon them, (next to *Spenser*'s noble booke.)
> And praise them too. O! what a fame 't will be?
>> What reputation to my lines, and me,
> When hee shall read them at the Treasurer's bord,
>> The knowing *Weston*, and that learned Lord
> Allowes them? Then, what copies shall be had,
>> What transcripts begg'd? how cry'd up, and how glad,
> Wilt thou be, *Muse*, when this shall them befall?
>> Being sent to one, they will be read of all.[1]

Jonson died in 1637, and within six months Bryan Duppa, then Dean of Christ Church, published the collection of contemporary tributes to him entitled *Jonsonus Virbius*. Digby, hearing that this work was in hand, wrote to Duppa a letter of warm appreciation, urging him to publish, saying that he too intended a similar act of devotion: 'I will,' he said, 'as soone as I can do the like to the world, by making it share with me in those excellent pieces (alas that many of thē are but pieces!) wᶜʰ he hath left behind him and that I keepe religiously by me to yᵗ end.'[2] When Humphrey Moseley published in 1659 *The Last Remains of Sʳ John Suckling. Being a Full Collection Of all his Poems and Letters which have been so long expected and never till now Published*, he said in a prefatory address to the reader in apology for printing the unfinished tragedy of *The Sad One*:

Nor are we without a sufficient President in Works of this nature, and relating to an Author who confessedly is reputed the Glory of the English Stage (whereby you'll know I mean *Ben: Johnson*) and in a Play also of somewhat a resembling name, *The SAD SHEPHERD*, extant in his Third Volume; which though it wants two entire *Acts*, was nevertheless judg'd a Piece of too much worth to be laid aside, by the Learned and Honorable Sir *Kenelme Digby*, who published that Volume. We have also in Print (written by the same hand) the very Beginning only (for it amounts not to one full *Scene*) of a Tragedy call'd *MORTIMER*. So that we find the same fate to haue hapned in the Works of two of the most celebrated and happy Wits of this Nation.

---

[1] *The Underwood*, lxxviii, 19–32.
[2] Autograph letter in B.M. Harley MS. 4153, ff. 19ᵛ, 20ʳ.

And he aptly quoted Donne,

> A hand or eye
> By Hilliard drawn, is worth a History
> By a worse Painter made.

Moseley composed this preface a year after he had bought the Jonson copyrights from Walkley; Walkley was his authority for the reference to Digby.

An interesting association of Digby with the 1640 Folio came to light in 1925 when Mr. P. J. Dobell offered for sale a copy of the second volume with the Meighen title-page and the 1641 text of *The Devil is an Ass*, inscribed by Digby 'for the Queene of Bohemia'. The copy came from the Craven collection at Combe Abbey, Coventry; Elizabeth of Bohemia was believed, after the death of the Elector Palatine, to have been secretly married to William, first Earl of Craven, and she bequeathed her books to him. The copy was bound in contemporary blue morocco with gold tooling.

The light thrown on the history of the volume and the circumstances of its publication is helpful when we come to consider the text. The plays of 1631—'the second Volume', as Meighen calls it on his title-page—make the first section. Next comes a section containing the Masques, *The Underwood*, the Welbeck and Bolsover Entertainments, and *Mortimer his Fall*. A third section includes the translation of *The Ars Poetica*, *The English Grammar*, and *Timber, or Discoveries*. The last section includes *The Magnetic Lady*, *A Tale of a Tub*, and *The Sad Shepherd*. The date on the title-pages of the last three sections is 1640, with the exception of *Timber* and *The Sad Shepherd*, which have the imprint 'LONDON, Printed M.DC.XLI'. Probably the second section was printed off, but the third and fourth, which were being set up simultaneously, were unfinished when John Parker swooped down on the printing-office and impounded the stock.

What printer did Walkley employ? Mr. Charles Sayle tentatively suggested John Haviland,[1] because the factotum initial of *Christmas his Masque*, with Salome receiving the head of John the Baptist,[2] was used by him in printing the fifth edition of Andrew Willet's *Synopsis Papismi* in 1637. No other initial border or decorated letter is found in Walkley's portion of the Folio, and this slender link has not been strengthened by any other evidence.

A likelier printer has been suggested by Professor W. A. Jackson.

---

[1] *Early English Printed Books in the University Library, Cambridge*, vol. ii, p. 905.
[2] See the facsimile in vol. vii, p. 435.

Bernard Alsop printed in 1640 the general title-page to the 1631 plays; it has his device, no. 339 in McKerrow. Alsop was in partnership with Thomas Fawcett (or Forsett) in 1625 and later. These partners were probably the printers employed by Walkley. The second part opens on signature B without a general title-page. We should expect 'Printed by Bernard Alsop and Thomas Fawcett for Thomas Walkley'. Walkley's troubles probably account for the omission. After his dealings with Sir Kenelm Digby, he might in happier circumstances have procured some commendatory verses from him and his friends.

The collation of the four sections is as follows:

(i) *The Beale and Allot plays of 1631*

Bartholomew Fair. Six leaves of A, the first originally blank; A2, the title-page; A3–6, unpaged, the prologue, the persons of the play, the induction. B to M in fours, pages 1 to 88, the text of the play; pages 12, 13, and 31 are misnumbered '6', '3', and '13' respectively.

In 1640 Richard Meighen printed a general title to the three first plays on the blank leaf A1, which is conjugate with A6; Dr. Greg possesses a copy with the original A1 in its blank state. As he notes, 'for a sheet to be passed through the printing-press again, after it had once been perfected, must have been an unusual occurrence'.[1]

The Devil is an Ass. The collation is continuous with that of *Bartholomew Fair*: N1, page 91, the title-page; N2, pages 93, 94, the persons of the play and the prologue; N3 and 4, O to Y in fours, pages 95 to 170, the text of the play. Two numbers, 89 and 90, have been dropped in the pagination at the beginning; page 99 is misnumbered '97', and page 137 misnumbered '129'.

[At this point it is necessary to make an interpolation. When the sheets of the 1631 edition ran out in 1641, Thomas Harper reprinted it. The collation is A1, the title-page, and A2 the persons of the play and the prologue, both unpaged; B to I in fours and one leaf of K, pages 1 to 66, the text of the play; K2 blank, preserved in a copy belonging to the editor. Page 35 is mispaged '39'.]

The Staple of News. Both signatures and paging are erratic. The double lettering Aa is kept as far as Cc2; then it changes over to the single letter C3, and this is kept to the end of the play, except that F2 was misprinted F3 with the genuine F3 following it, but the printer corrected it. Thus we get Aa recto, page 1, the title-page; Aa verso,

---

[1] See his article on 'The Printing of Jasper Mayne's Plays' in the *Proceedings of the Oxford Bibliographical Society*, vol. i, p. 259.

page 2, the persons of the play; Aa2, pages 3–4, the induction; Aa3 recto, page 5, the prologue for the stage and Aa3 verso, page 6, the prologue for the Court; Aa4 to H4, and six leaves of I, pages 7 to 76, the text of the play, ending with the epilogue on I6 verso. There are three mispagings, '9' for 19, '16' for 22, and '36' for 63.

(ii) *The Masques*, The Underwood, *the later Entertainments, and the fragment of* Mortimer

This section opens abruptly with *Christmas his Masque*; Walkley did not prefix a title-page, though this is supplied to two of the masques, the Masque at Lord Hay's in honour of the Baron De Tour on page 9, with '1617' at the foot as if that were the date of printing, and *The Masque of Gypsies* on page 47, with the date of performance at the end of the title 'Avgvst, 1621'.

The collation of the Masques is B–Q⁴, R², S–X⁴, Y², pages 1 to 160, with pages 8 and 160 blank and page 93 misnumbered '87', but corrected in the Bodleian copy and in one copy belonging to the editor. The Masques are *Christmas, his Masque* (page 1), *A Masque presented in the house of the Right Honorable the Lord Haye* (page 9), *The Vision of Delight* (page 16), *Pleasure Reconciled to Vertue* (page 22), *For the Honour of Wales* (page 30), *Newes from the New World discover'd in the Moone* (page 39), *A Masque of the Metamorphos'd Gypsies* (page 47), *The Masque of Augures with the severall Antimasques* (page 81), *Time Vindicated to Himselfe, and to his Honors* (page 92), *Neptunes Triumph for the Returne of Albion* (page 105), *Pans Anniversarie; or, The Shepherds Holy-day* (page 118), *The Masque of Owles at Kenilworth* (page 125), *The Fortunate Isles, and their Vnion* (page 129), *Loves Triumph through Callipolis* (page 144), *Chloridia. Rites to Chloris and her Nymphs* (page 151).

Under-Woods, Z–Mm⁴, Nn1–4 recto, pages 161–271, with the title-page on Z1 recto, an editorial note 'To the Reader' on Z1 verso, and the text of the poems beginning on Z2 recto; signature Bb2 is misprinted 'B2'. The running title is *Vnderwoods* or *Vnder-woods* on pages 163 to 200, *The Vnder-wood* on page 201, *Vnder-woods* on pages 202 to 207, *The Vnder-wood* on pages 208–71; in some copies a correction on pp. 164–5. This title by a blunder of the printer is carried on to the two entertainments which follow.

The Kings Entertainment at Welbeck in Nottinghamshire, Nn4 verso, Oo⁴, pages 272–80.

Loves Welcome. The King and Queenes Entertainment at Bolsover, Pp², Qq1, pages 281 to 286, the last page blank and page 285 misnumbered '283'.

Mortimer his Fall, three unsignatured leaves Qq2–4, pages 287 to 292, the title on Qq2 recto with the verso blank, 'The Persons Names' on Qq3 recto, 'Arguments' on Qq3 verso, and the fragment of the opening scene of Act 1 on Qq4.

(iii) *The translation of the* Ars Poetica, The English Grammar, *and* Timber

Horace his Art of Poetrie. Made English by Ben. Iohnson; Printed M.DC.XL, A–C⁴, D1–3, pages 1–30, the last page blank. The title is on page 1, and the translation faces the Latin text.

The English Grammar. Made by Ben. Iohnson. The title on D4 recto; four Latin aphorisms on grammar at the foot of D4 verso; the preface on E1 recto; the text illustrated with Latin notes, E1 verso, F–K⁴, L², pages 34–84.

Timber: or, Discoveries; Made vpon Men and Matter: as they have flow'd out of his daily Readings; or had their refluxe to his peculiar Notion of the Times. 'Printed M.DC.XLI.' The title on M1 recto; a Latin note 'Sylva' on M1 verso; the text headed *Explorata: or, Discoveries*, M2–4, N–R⁴; pages 85–132. The running title is '*Discoveries*'.

(iv) *The Magnetic Lady, A Tale of a Tub. The Sad Shepherd*

The Magnetick Lady: or, Humors Reconcil'd. The title on A1 recto; A1 verso blank; A2 recto, the Scene; A2 verso, blank; A3–4, the Induction; B–H⁴, the text of the play: pages 1–64.

A Tale of a Tub. The title on I1 recto; I1 verso, blank; I2 recto, 'The Persons that act'; I2 verso, the prologue; I3–4, K–P⁴, Q², the text of the play: pages 65–114, the last page blank. Pages 70 to 79 are duplicated, so that the pagination should have been 65–124.

The Sad Shepherd: or, A Tale of Robin-Hood. 'Printed M.DC.XLI.' The title is on R1 recto; R1 verso, blank; R2 recto, 'The Persons of the Play'; R2 verso, 'The Argument of the first Act'; R3, the prologue. R4, S–V⁴, the text of the play: pages 115–56, the last page blank. Pages 123–32 are omitted in the pagination, pages 151 and 154 are misnumbered '143' and '146'.

To sum up: Jonson's handwriting, even to the last, was legible, as is proved by the autograph letter which 'Youʳ infirme Ben. now' sent from his sick-bed to Thomas Cotton asking for the loan of a scholarly book.[1] The printer had no excuse for misreadings of the text. His press-work was abominable; he made no attempt to arrange his copy and present it in a logical sequence of plays, masques,

---

[1] See vol. i, p. 215: facsimiled in Greg's *English Literary Autographs*, part i, no. xxiii (c).

poems, and prose-works. He may have got the manuscripts in odd parcels; if so, he set them up just as they came in. Jonson was mercifully spared the sight of the disorganized proofs; that might have provoked an epigram 'To his lewd Printer' or another 'Execration'. The utmost that could be said for Walkley's printer is that, after all, he was a better workman than John Beale.

An occasional defect of the Folio is the dropping out of words. Three such passages have been accounted for by Professor P. Maas; he attributes the omission to physical damage in the copy used by the printer.[1]

(1) In *The Masque of Augurs*, 314 and 377, the words '*King*' and '*Addes*' at the beginning of the lines are dropped in the Folio without any sign of omission; we have retrieved them from the Quarto. 'Such omissions are rare', says Professor Maas; 'their recurrence so close together at the same place in the verse-line raises the suspicion that one and the same physical cause had damaged both passages in the copy for the Folio. In the Quarto the two words stand exactly at the same place on the recto of signatures B2 and B3, the corresponding places on the versos being blank. This proves that in this masque the copy for the Folio was a copy of the Quarto in which these two words had been destroyed, perhaps by a spark.'

(2) In *Pleasure Reconciled to Virtue*, '*tune*' in the first half of line 292 and '*ever*' in the first half of line 316 are similarly omitted, but here the Folio marks lacunae in the text. The missing words are recovered from the contemporary Chatsworth MS. 'In the copy for the Folio, which for this Masque must have been a MS., they probably stood on corresponding places of recto- and verso-page; ll. 313–16 must then have been deeply indented.'

(3) A lacuna is also marked in the text of *The Magnetic Lady*, iv. ii. 55, 't'ingage him—the busines'; we have inserted 'i'. Earlier in the scene (l. 20) is the defective line 'And had up for honour to her blood'. 'A page of 35 lines', says Professor Maas, 'is not improbable for the MS. from which this play was printed.'

Thirteen copies of this volume have been collated for the text in volumes vi, vii, and viii. Some additional variants have been found and are asterisked in the following lists. We prefix the symbols used to indicate the copies.

M1 = British Museum copy with press-mark C. 39. k. 9.
M2 = British Museum copy with press-mark C. 28. m. 12., containing the autograph copy of Jonson's verses to Somerset on his wedding.

[1] *Review of English Studies*, xviii (1942), pp. 464–5.

M3 = British Museum copy with press-mark 79. l. 3.

M4 = the Museum copy of the three plays of 1631 with press-mark 642. l. 29.

M5 = 'The Third Volume', 1640–1, to which is prefixed the 1641 reprint of *The Devil is an Ass*, with press-mark fol. 1482. d. 15, given by Dr. Greg.

B1 = the Douce copy in the Bodleian (Douce I. 303).

B2 = the Bodleian copy with shelf-mark Don. d. 66.

Seld = Selden's copy of *The Devil is an Ass* in the Bodleian.

O = the Oriel College copy.

A1 = the copy presented by Dudley Digges to All Souls College, Oxford, lacking *Bartholomew Fair* and *The Staple of News*.

A2 = the All Souls College copy with shelf-mark pp. 4. 18.

S1 = a copy belonging to the Editor with the title-page to the 1631 plays.

S2 = another copy with the 1641 text of *The Devil is an Ass*.

S3 = another copy, formerly Lord Birkenhead's.

S4 = another copy, without the induction to *Bartholomew Fair*, and without *The Sad Shepherd*, formerly Sir Charles Firth's.

S5 = a copy of *The Devil is an Ass*.

The corrections made in these copies while the volume was printing are as follows:

(i) *The Plays of 1631*

Meighen's Title-page

Found in M1, M2, M3, B2, O, A2, and S1

Bartholomew Fair

C2ʳ, p. 11.	I. v. 93	you head *M1, 2, 4, B2, O, S3*	your head *M3, B1, A2, S1, 2, 4*
D1ᵛ, p. 18.	II. ii. 40	*Wou'ld* S3	*Who'ld* the rest
	46	Heere. *M1, B1, O, S3*	Heere, *M2, 3, 4, B2, A2, S1, 2, 4*
	56	*Egdeworth* S3	*Edgeworth* the rest
	59	morning. *M1, B1, O, S3*	morning, *M2, 3, 4, B2, A2, S1, 2, 4*
D4ʳ, p. 23.	II. iv. 37	st. dir. *This . . . not.* not in S3	*Inserted in the rest*
	39	sing *M1, B1, O, S3*	sing, *M2, 3, 4, B2, A2, S1, 2, 4*
	58	on on *M1, B1, O, S3*	one on *M2, 3, 4, B2, A2, S1, 2, 4*
	65	here *M1, B1, O, S3*	here, *M2, 3, 4, B2, A2, S1, 2, 4*
E3ᵛ, p. 30.	II. vi. 115	bold *B1, S2*	bold, *the rest*

E4ʳ, p. 31. II. vi. 146 st. dir. Instice *M3, O,*   Iustice *the rest*
             Manchester College copy
          150 Parent of the of the *M1,*   Parent of the *B1, 2*
             2, 3, 4, O, A2, S1, 2, 3, 4
H4ʳ, p. 55. IV. ii. 108 am if *S3, 4*   am, if *the rest*
L2ʳ, p. 75, and L3ᵛ, p. 78, are reset (V. iii. 92–137, 'green gamesters . . . fitted';
     v. iv. 90–138, 'Come, come . . . *you need.*'). The original setting is in
     M2, 3, 4, O, A2, S1, 3, 4.

			Originally	*Reset*
L2ʳ, p. 75.	v. iii.	102	Sir.	Sir,
		103–4	—And heere	——And here
		113	hight	height
		114	do	doe
		118	Mʳ. *Littlewit* ?	Mʳ *Littlewit.*
		124	go-|ing	go|ing
		125	*Trigsstayers*	*Trigsstayres*
		127	hee	he
		130	iudgement	Iudgement
		132	I'll be	Ile be
		136	*drum*	*Drum*
Signature after		137	L 2	L2
Catchword			ACT.	Aᴄᴛ.
L3ᵛ, p. 78.	v. iv.	90	ready	readie
		93	bare headed	bare-headed
		96	Stocks	stocks
		100	in himselfe	himselfe
		101	*Numps*	*Numpes*
		108	pray you . . . me	pray . . . mee
		109	Well then,	Well, then
		111	neither, now . . . mee	neirher, now, . . . me
		112	Wɪɴ-w. . . . care, he	Wɪɴ-ᴠᴠ. . . . care hee
		113	to expresse	expresse
		117	*chief*	*chiefe*
		118	*cloth,*	*cloth*
		120	*Which . . . call it*	*VVhich . . . call*
		122	*he*	*hee*
		123	*to come*	*to'come*
		128	Pᴠᴘ.L. *Cole*	Pᴠᴘ. L.*Cole*
			(So 130, 132, 135, 137)	
		129	*That is . . . controle.*	*That's . . . controle:*
		131	We	Wee
		133	*cole . . . do*	*Cole . . . doe*
		135	*your . . . here,*	*you . . . here*
		136	*maners . . . here,*	*manners . . . here*
		137	*say,*	*say*
	After	138	c.w. Pᴠᴘ.	*omitted*

The Devil is an Ass (1631)

N3ʳ, p. 95.   I. i. 20 for't. *M2, 3, O, A2, S1, 3*   for't, *M1, B2, Seld, S4, 5*
P2ʳ, p. 109.   I. vi. 185 Kings *M1, 2, B2, Seld,*   *Kings* M3, O, S4, 5
             A2, S1, 3

P2ʳ, p. 109. I. vi. 186   Stage-garment *M1, 2, B2,*   *Stage*-garment *M3, O,*
                        Seld, A2, S1, 3   *S4, 5*

187   norhings else, *M1, 2, B2,*   norhing else: *M3, O, S4,*
       Seld, A2, S1, 3   *5*[1]

193 st. dir. *Hee . . . againe* not *Inserted in M3, O, S4, 5*
       in M1, 2, B2, Seld, A2,
       S1, 3

213   you *M1, 2, B2, Seld, A2,*   you, *M3, O, S4, 5*
       S1, 3

215   ayre in: yes *M1, 2, B2,*   ayre in. Yes *M3, O,*
       Seld, A2, S1, 3   *S4, 5*

224   mine owne *M1, 2, B2,*   mine *M3, O, S4, 5*
       Seld, A2, S1, 3

P3ᵛ, p. 112. II. i. 20 st. dir. *To a third.* not in M1, *Inserted in M3, O, S4,*
       2, B2, Seld, A2, S1, 3   *5*

22   dispatch it: *M1, 2, B2,*   dispatch it. *M3, O, S4, 5*
      Seld, A2, S1, 3

22 st. dir. *He . . . Fitz-dottrel.* *Inserted in M3, O, S4, 5*
      not in M1, 2, B2, Seld,
      A2, S1, 3

26   Proiect . . . Duke *M1, 2,*   proiect . . . *Duke* M3, O,
      B2, Seld, A2, S1, 3   *S4, 5*

33 st. dir. *He . . . Ingine.* not *Inserted in M3, O, S4, 5*
      in M1, 2, B2, Seld, A2,
      S1, 3

42   Commoners, and Alder- *Commoners,* and *Alder-*
      men *M1, 2, B2, Seld,*   *men* M3, O, S4, 5
      A2, S1, 3

45   Land *M1, 2, B2, Seld, A2,*   land *M3, O, S4, 5*
      S1, 3

46   Crown's . . . a moiety *M1,* *Crowne's . . .* his moiety
      2, B2, Seld, A2, S1, 3   *M3, O, S4, 5*

47   Crowne *M1, 2, B2, Seld,* *Crowne* M3, O, S4, 5
      A2, S1, 3

50   Throughout *M1, 2, B2,*   Thorowout *M3, O, S4, 5*
      Seld, A2, S1, 3

51   millions *M1, 2, B2, Seld,* *millions* M3, O, S4, 5
      A2, S1, 3

53   acre, *M1, 2, B2, Seld, A2,*   acre. *M3, O, S4, 5*
      S1, 3

58   Gallant *M1, 2, B2, Seld,*   gallant *M3, O, S4, 5*
      A2, S1, 3

65   Proiect; foure dogs skins Proiect. 4. *Dog-skinnes*
      M1, 2, B2, Seld, A2,   M3, O, S4, 5
      S1, 3

S2ᵛ, p. 134. III. iii. 129 In corrigible *M2, 3, O,* Incorrigible *M1, B2, Seld,*
      A2, S1   *S3, 4, 5*

V1ᵛ, p. 148. IV. iv. 31 *Abezzo.* M1, 2, 3, O, A2, *Abezzo,* B2, Seld, S1, 4, 5
      S3

45   *Carrnuacins* M1, 2, 3, O, *Carrauicins* B2, Seld, S1,
      A2, S3   4, 5

---

[1] 'norhing' should be 'nothing'.

V1ᵛ, p. 148.	iv. iv. 47	well, *M1, 2, 3, O, A2, S3*
X2ᵛ, p. 158.	v. i. 4	With, *M2, A2*
	9	Wtih *M2, A2*
X3ᵛ, p. 160.	v. ii. 21	st. dir. *sterts* B2
	41	tame *B2*
Y1ʳ, p. 163.	v. v. 8	fo rme *B2*
Y2ʳ, p. 165.	v. vi. 64	*heaters* M2, 3, A2, S3
Y2ᵛ, p. 166.	v. vii. 2	esteem e of *M2, 3, B2, Seld, O, A2, S1, 3, 5*
Y3ᵛ, p. 168.	v. viii. 58	to be the merrier *M2, 3, A2, S3*
	59	Sir. *M2, 3, A2, S3*
	60	insolence *M2, 3, A2, S3*
	67	st. dir. *They whis-|per*, M1, 2, 3, Seld, A2, S3, 4
	69	st. dir. *And giue* M2, 3, A2, S3
	74	Yellow, yellow, yellow, yellow *M2, 3, A2, S3*
	76	clapping *M2, 3, A2, S3*
	81	st. dir. *a Iuglers game* M2, 3, A2, S3
	86–7	to such a fellow, | I'd rather fall. *M2, 3, A2, S3*
	87	ò they whisper, they whisper, whisper, &c. *M2, 3, A2, S3*
	95	meanes, *M2, 3, A2, S3*
	102	Sir: *M2, 3, A2, S3*

Right column readings:

well *B2, Seld, S1, 4, 5*

VVith *the rest*

VVith *the rest*

starts M1, 2, 3, Seld, O, S1, 3, 4, 5*

name *M1, 2, 3, Seld, O, S1, 3, 4, 5**

for me *M1, 2, 3, O, Seld, S1, 2, 3, 4, 5**

Cheaters M1, B2, Seld, O, S1, 4, 5

a steeme of *M1, S4*[1] (M1 like a broken *e*, not *a*)

the merrier man *M1, B2, Seld, O, S1, 4, 5*

Sir! *M1, B2, Seld, O, S1, 4, 5*

impudence *M1, B2, Seld, O, S1, 4, 5*

They whi \| *per* O *They w hi\|per* B2, S1, 5

and giue him M1, B2, Seld, O, S1, 4, 5

Yellow, yellow, yellow, yellow M1, B2, Seld, O, S1, 4, 5

with clapping *M1, B2, Seld, O, S1, 4, 5*

to be a Iuglers game M1, B2, Seld, O, S1, 4, 5

to such a foole, \| He makes himselfe. *M1, B2, Seld, O, S1, 4, 5*

O they whisper, whisper, whisper. M1, B2, Seld, O, S1, 4, 5

meanes? *M1, B2, Seld, O, S1, 4, 5*

Sir. *M1, B2, Seld, O, S1, 4, 5*

Two of the catchwords differ from the text. On O1 verso, page 100, the catchword is 'An'', the text on page 101 has the incorrect 'And''. On O3 recto, page 103, the catchword is 'ACT.', but two lines of the unfinished scene begin the next page before 'ACT. I SCENE. V.' is reached.

[1] The correction is made by erasure: it is found also in the Christ Church, Jesus College, Oxford, and Manchester College copies. In M1 the first *e* of 'steeme' is half taken out. In all copies the letters of 'steeme' are brought together; there is a bad blur for the *a*. The *p* of 'piece' in line 1 is nearly obliterated, the *b* of 'but' in line 3 is disturbed. See vol. vi, p. 153.

The chief errors of the Harper reprint of 1641 have been tabulated by Mr. H. L. Ford in his *Collation of the Ben Jonson Folios*, pages 26–8 ; a rather fuller list of the variants from the 1631 text has been included in our critical apparatus. They are not worth repeating here, but we may note that there is a misprint in the Latin motto on the title-page—*Ficta voluptatis causa*—where ‘*Ficta*’ becomes ‘*Fucta*’, which the printer of the 1669 title-page corrected, as he hoped, to ‘*Facta*’. But Harper’s text was corrected while it was passing through the press, and we record such variants as we have found in a copy of Mr. Ford’s and a copy of our own : they occur chiefly in quire G.

		Uncorrected copy	*Ordinary copy*
A2ᵛ, [p. ii.] Prologue,	2	Play	Play,
	21	fac	face
G1ʳ, p. 41. III. vi.	27	her	her,
	49	treachery.	treachery!
IV. i. scene heading		Act. IV	Act. VI.
G1ᵛ, p. 42. IV. i.	8	*madame*	*Madame*
	16	to day	to day,
	20	Unquited	Vnquieted
	30	do wonder	doe wonder
	35	you Ladiship	your Ladiship
	38	soulder’d	solder’d
	42	Cosins	Cousins
	44	Unto	Vnto
G4ʳ, p. 47. IV. iv.	59	But yet	But, yet,
	63	you Sir	you, Sir
	84	onl’ allow’d	onel’ allow’d
	90	That’s	This’s
	96	honest *Tayl-bush*	honest, *Tayle-bush*
G4ᵛ, p. 48. IV. iv.	108 marg.	*satisfied*	*satisfied*,
	110	into the schoole	in the schoole
	120	eies	eyes
	121	she’ hath	sha’ hath[1]
	122	helpe	helpes
	127	will ; be great	will ; be great[2]
	129	*Madame. Tay.*	*Madam. Tai.*[3]
	132	Usher	Vsher
	135	Ground	ground
	137	presupose	presuppose
	140	*Ladyship*	*Ladiship*
	142	*Postillos*	*Pastillos*
	150	*privety*	*pivety*
	151	sweten	sweeten
H3ᵛ, p. 54. IV. vii.	81	pray you	pray you,
I3ʳ, p. 61. V. vi.	47	endangerdd’st	endangered’st

[1] Probably a misprint for ‘sh’ hath’, the printer meaning to treat the metrical apostrophe as a mark of elision : see p. 50.

[2] The spacing between the words is adjusted.

[3] The spelling is altered to adjust an overlong line.

The Staple of News

In copies of the 1640 Folio this play is usually printed after *Bartholomew Fair* and before *The Devil is an Ass*, which was both acted and printed earlier. No satisfactory reason can be given for this anomalous arrangement. Richard Meighen's general title-page put the plays in this order—*The Devil is an Ass* last of the three. The binder may have followed this arrangement.

The variants in this play are fewer than in the two preceding. Jonson's corrections in *The Devil is an Ass* may have made Beale chary of sending him proofs; even when the play was printed off Jonson found it difficult to extract a copy from him to send to the Earl of Newcastle.

This play has many examples of careless printing, such as deranged type, dropped letters, and lost stops. For example, the last word on Cc1 recto (I. vi. 17) 'wardship' appears as 'ward ship', 'wardsh ip', 'ward sh ip', and 'ward shi p'; 'miracles' in the first line of F1 verso (III. ii. 153) appears as 'mirac l'. The apostrophe disappears in some copies in 'pickl d' (D2 recto, II. iv. 11) 'sow d' (I2 recto, v. ii. 22), and 'gi ' (I5 recto, v. v. 24). But the worst blunder is in the change of signatures: after Cc2 there is a reversion to single letters, D to I. F2 is misprinted F3 in most copies.

The variants in the text follow.

Bb2ᵛ, p. 12.	I. iii. 52 st. dir.	*tr* B2	*to* the rest
F1ʳ, p. 41.	III. ii. 124	1. *Cu_{st.}* |	
		A she | baptist *M1, 2, 3, B1, O, A2, S1, 3, 4*[1]	
		1. *Cust.* | *A she* An-| baptist *S2*	1. *Cust.* | *A she* Ana-| baptist *B2, W. W. Greg's copy*
F2ʳ, p. 43, signature.		F3 *in all copies examined*	F2 *W. W. Greg's copy*
F4ʳ, p. 47.	III. iv. 27	moyetie *S1*	*moyety* the rest
	32	paths *S1*	paths, *the rest*
F4ᵛ, p. 48.	III. iv. 49	tyssues *S2, 3*	tissues *the rest*
I4ʳ, p. 71.	v. iv. 25	*sixtee* M2	*sixteen* the rest
I4ᵛ, p. 72.	v. iv. 68	Aagainst *S3*	Against *the rest*
	v. 5	baile, or mainprise *S3*	*baile*, or *mainprise* the rest

(ii) *The Masques*, The Underwood, *the later Entertainments, and* Mortimer

The Masques

B2ʳ, p. 3.	*Christmas*, 66	BABIE-COCKE *M1, 2, 3, 5, B1, A1, S1, 3, 4*	BABIE-CAKE *B2, O, A2, S2*

[1] We conjecture that this was the first state because of the derangement of the type in '*Cust*'. Deranged in M1, not in 2, 3.

C3ʳ, p. 13. *Lovers Made Men*, 163 glory in *M1* | glory in! *the rest*

D4ᵛ, p. 24. *Pleasure Reconciled*, 80 ȷf *press-copy* | if *the rest*

E1ʳ, p. 25. | 131 *their, feet* press-copy | *their feet* the rest
| 133 *Pigmees* press-copy | *Pigmies* the rest
| 139 three, . . . foure, . . . ten, *press-copy* | three ? . . . foure ? . . . ten ? *the rest*

E2ʳ, p. 27. | 254 *enterweave* M5, B1, S4 | *interweave* the rest

E3ᵛ, p. 30 heading, *For the Honour of Wales* before M5, B1, S4 | before, B2, O, S1, 2, 3, M1, 2, 3

F1ʳ, p. 33. | 155 cannow *M1, 2, O, A1* | can now *the rest*

F2ᵛ, p. 36. | 305 st. dir. *ot* press-copy | *of* the rest

F4ʳ, p. 39. *News from the New World*, 3 Newes S1, 2 | Newe *the rest*

G1ᵛ, p. 42. | 161 flow *S3* | flow, *the rest*
| 195 *catchword not in M1, 2, 3, 5, B1, O, A1, 2, S1, 2, 4* | ces *B2, S3*

H2ᵛ, p. 52. *Gypsies Metamorphosed*, 143 *heare* M3, 5, B1, A1, 2, S1, 4 | here M1, 2, B2, O, S2, 3

I4ʳ, p. 63. | 620 owne, *M1, 3, 5, B1, 2, O, A1, S1, 3, 4* | ow *M2, A2, S2,* ¹
| 642 adoe, *M1, 3, 5, B1, O, A1, S3, 4* | ado *M2, B2, A2, S1, 2,* ¹

I4ᵛ, p. 64. | 735 Olive-colour'd *M2, A2, S2, 4* | Olive-colou r'd *M1, 3, 5, B1, 2, O, A1, S3*²

K1ᵛ, p. 66. | 854 honayles *M3, 5, B1, 2, O, S4* | hobnayles *M1, 2, A1, 2, S1, 2, 3*

K3ᵛ, p. 70. | 1079 *Tyrcwomen* M1, 2, 3, 5, O, A1, S1, 2 | *Tyrewomen* B1, 2, A2, S3, 4
| 1080 *perfumes* M1, 2, 3, O, A1, S1, 2 | *perfumers* B1, 2, A2, S3, 4

L1ᵛ, p. 74. | 1244 *defedendo* M3, A1, S1, 2 | *defendendo* M1, 2, 5, B1, 2, O, A2, S3, 4

M1ᵛ, p. 82. *The Masque of Augurs*, 67 chimney ? M3, 5, B1, 2, S4 | chimney! *M1, 2, O, A1, 2, S1, 2, 3*

M4ʳ, p. 87. | 286, note 'h' Janees *M3, 5, B1, 2, S4* | Jances *M1, 2, O, A1, 2, S1, 2, 3*
| 286, note 'i' valer. *M3, 5, B1, 2, S4* | Valer. *M1, 2, O, A1, 2, S1, 2, 3*
| *cemarum* M3, 5, B1, 2, S4 | *comarum* M1, 2, O, A1, 2, S1, 2, 3

V3ʳ, p. 145. *Love's Triumph*, 58 margin. *No note in M3, B2, O, S3, 4* | Porus, *and* Penia *M1, 2, 5, B1, A1, 2, S1, 2*

The Underwood

In addition to the thirteen copies here collated some special readings are quoted from the copy in the Columbia University Library recorded by Hoyt H. Hudson in the facsimile edition of

---

¹ The final letters, coming at the end of a line, have failed to print.
² The type begins to shift in *S1*.

Epigram, The Forest, Underwoods published for the Facsimile Text Society, 1936 (= Col.).

Aa2ʳ, p. 171.	ii. 9. 6	Gop *M1, S1*	God *the rest*
Aa3ᵛ, p. 174.	iv. 9	*Tares* M1, S1	*Teares* the rest
Cc4ʳ, p. 191.	xxii. 21	An . . . them, *M2, 3, 5, O, A1, 2, S3*	And . . . them *M1, B1, 2, S1, 2, 4*
Dd1ʳ, p. 193.	xxv. 16	fight *M1, 5, A2, S1, 3*	sight *M2, 3, B1, 2, O, A1, S2, 4*
Ee1ʳ, p. 201.	Headline before xxxvi. 5 *Vnder-woods.* A1, S2, Col.		The *Vnder-wood* the rest
	xxxvi. 13	*still'd* A1, S2, Col.	*stil'd* the rest
Ee2ʳ, p. 203.			
	xxxviii. 75	weather *S2, Col.*	weather, *the rest*
Ee2ᵛ, p. 204.			
	xxxviii. 88	Steight *Col.*	Streight *the rest*
	94	apply *Col.*	apply; *the rest*
	111	Fivers . . . doth *S2, Col.*	Fibres . . . doe *the rest*
	115	away *Col.*	away; *the rest*
Ee3ʳ, p. 205.	xxxix. 15	othes *Col.*	oathes *the rest*
	29	back *Col.*	back, *the rest*
	30	streames *Col.*	streames: *the rest*
	44	infamie *Col.*	infamie; *the rest*
Ee3ᵛ, p. 206.	xl. 14	made, *S2, Col.*	made; *the rest*
Ee4ᵛ, p. 208.	Headline before xlii. 5 *Vnder-woods.* A1, S2, Col.		The *Vnder-wood.* the rest
	xlii. 53	And Officer *A1, S2, Col.*	An O fficer *the rest*
Ff1ʳ, p. 209.	xlii. 80	roiots *M3, S2*	riots *the rest*
	xliii. 1	this *M3, S2*	this, *the rest*
Ff4ᵛ, p. 216.	xlv. 7	friendship, *M3, S2*	friendship *the rest*
	11	ends *M3, S2*	ends, *the rest*
	xlvi. 1	Hнe *M3, S2*	Hᴇ *the rest*
Gg1ʳ, p. 217.	xlvi. 7	man *M1, 2, 3, B1, A1, S2, 4*	mans *M5, B2, O, A2, S1, 3*
	xlvii. 4	them, not *M1, 2, 3, B1, A1, S2, 4*	them not, *M5, B2, O, A2, S1, 3*
Gg2ʳ, p. 219.	xlviii. 16	beginst *B1, S4*	begin'st *the rest*
Hh1ʳ, p. 225.	lvi. 21	stoole *M3, 5, O, A1, S2, 4*	stoole, *M1, 2, A2, S1, 3*
	22	afternoones *M3, 5, B1, 2, O, A1, S2, 4*	afternoones, *M1, 2, A2, S1, 3*
Hh2ʳ, p. 227.	lxi. 5	heare *M2, 3, B1, A1, S3*	heare, *M1, B2, O, A2, S1, 2, 4*
Hh2ᵛ, p. 228.	lxii, heading	*No date in M1, 3, S1, 2*	1629. *the rest*
	lxii. 13	wish, *M1, 3, S1, 2*	wish *the rest*
	lxiii, heading	*No date in M1, 3, S1, 2*	1629. *the rest*
Hh3ʳ, p. 229.	lxiv, heading	*No date in M1, 3, S1, 2*	1629. *the rest*
	lxiv. 6	majestie *M1, 3, S1, 2*	Majestie *the rest*
	17	ease *M1, 3, S1, 2*	ease, *the rest*
	lxv, heading	*birth* M1, 3, S1, 2	*birth.* the rest
		No date in M1, 3, S1, 2	1630. *the rest*
Hh4ᵛ, p. 232.	lxvi. 14	*Teirce* M3, 5, B1, 2, O, A1, S2, 4	*teirce* M1, 2, A2, S1, 3

Hh4ᵛ, p. 232.	lxix. 14	flatt'rer *M3*, *5*, *B1*, *2*, *O*, *A1*, *S2*, *4*	flattrer, *M1*, *2*, *A2*, *S1*, *3*
Iiᵛ, p. 234.	lxx. 85	*Johnson*: B1, S4	*Johnson*, the rest
Ii4ʳ, p. 239.	lxxv. 9	day! *B1*, *S4*	day *the rest*
Ii4ᵛ, p. 240.	lxxv. 64	stay *S4*	stay! *the rest*
Mm1ᵛ, p. 258.	lxxxiv. 8. 2	illustirous *M2*, *S1*	illustrious *the rest*
Mm2ʳ, p. 259.	lxxxiv. 9. 1	ty'd *M1*, *O*, *S3*	dy'd *the rest*
	2	dy'd *M1*, *O*, *S3*	sey'd *the rest*
	11	faite *M1*, *O*, *S3*	faire *the rest*
	27	one, *M1*, *O*, *S3*	one: *the rest*
	46	*sheepe* M1, O, S3	*Sheepe* the rest
Mm3ʳ, p. 261.	102	heaven *Empyre*, and *M1*, *O*, *S3*	heav'n *Empire*, and *the rest*[1]
Mm3ᵛ, p. 262.	lxxxiv. 9. 159	nobilitie *M1*, *O*, *S3*	Nobilitie *the rest*
	195	Infirmer *M1*, *O*, *S3*	Infirmery *the rest*
Nn2ʳ, p. 267.	lxxxvi. 10	Swans *M1*, *2*, *3*, *B2*, *O*, *A2*, *S1*, *2*, *3*	Swans, *B1*, *A1*, *S4*

Mortimer his Fall

Qq3ᵛ, p. 292.	After 69	Left unfinished. *A2*, *S1*, *3*	Hee dy'd, and left it unfinished, *the rest*

(iii) *Horace his Art of Poetry, The English Grammar, The Discoveries*

Art of Poetry

B1ʳ, p. 9.	174	so 'above *M3*, *B2*	so 'bove *the rest*
B3ᵛ, p. 14.	233	*Ne*; M2, *5*, B1, S2	*Ne*, the rest
B4ᵛ, p. 16.	243	*Davus ne* M3, B2	Davus*ne* the rest
	264	*similis: sibi* M3	*similis sibi:* the rest
C1ʳ, p. 17.	355	beware. *M2*, *3*, *B1*, *S1*, *2*	beware, *M1*, *5*, *B2*, *O*, *A1*, *2*, *S3*, *4*[2]
C3ʳ, p. 21.	471	ownce *M2*, *3*, *B1*, *A1*, *2*, *O*, *S2*, *3*, *4*	ounce *M1*, *5*, *B2*, *S1*
	479	and priest, a speaker *M2*, *3*, *B1*, *O*, *A1*, *2*, *S2*, *3*, *4*	a priest, and speaker *M1*, *B2*, *S1*
C4ʳ, p. 23.	487	profaane to seperate *B1*, *S2*	profane to separate *the rest*
	490	crave *B1*, *S2*	carve *the rest*

The English Grammar

E2ᵛ, p. 36.	I. iii. 17	in: *M2*, *B1*, *2*	in *the rest*
	19	Syllabes *M2*, *B1*, *2*	Syllables *the rest*[3]
	27	shé, | in all . . . Article th*è* two lines in *M2*, *B1*, *2*	One line in the rest
	41	Syllabe *M2*, *B1*, *2*	Syllable, *the rest*[3]

[1] A miscorrection: read 'Heav'n *Empyrean*'.
[2] The comma has failed to print clearly in most copies.
[3] A miscorrection: the printer did not know that Jonson spelt 'syllabe' to correspond with συλλαβή.

E2ᵛ, p. 36. I. iii. 55 *her, hir* M2, B1, 2   *her,* for *hir* M1, 3, O, A1, 2, S1, 2, 3, 4

E3ʳ, p. 37. note (r), line 8 *dro* M2, B1, 2   *pro* the rest

F1ᵛ, p. 42. note (g), line 1 Latines B1, S2   Latinis *the rest*

    note (h), line 9 *quam* B1, S2   *quám* the rest

    line 11 vi. B1, S2   vi: *the rest*

F2ʳ, p. 43. 22 force *Chi.* or the | S1, M1   force of *Chi.* or | the *the rest*

F3ʳ, p. 45. G note (p), line 7 *Qoudᶍ* M1, S1, B2, A2   *Quodᶍ* M2, 3, B1, O, A1, S2, 3, 4

F4ʳ, p. 47. 108 these B1, S2   these, *the rest*

    124 *O* B1, S2   *P* the rest

    130 reputation, B1, S2   reputation *the rest*

G3ᵛ, p. 54. vii. 16 *Adjectivè* S2   *Adjectivè* the rest

G4ʳ, p. 55. viii. 3, 9 *No side notes in* M2, 3, 5, O, A1, 2, S3, 4   *Genus. Figura.* the rest

Discoveries

M1ᵛ, p. 86. 2 *va-rietate* M2   *varietate* the rest

    6 *Antiqui.* M2   *Antiqui:* the rest

    c.w. THE M2   EX- the rest[1]

M4ʳ, p. 91. 233 litterature M2   literature *the rest*

    240 (margin) *Icuncolor | motio* M2   *Icuncula-|rum motio* the rest

    289–90 misinterpreted M2   mis-interpreted *the rest*

N1ʳ, p. 93. 354 judgement, M1, S1   judgement, or measure. *the rest*

    357 ἀνθρώποιον M1, S1   ἀνθρώποισιν *the rest*

    358 πγείστη . . . ἰ οὔσης M1, S1   πλείστη . . . ἰούσης *the rest*

    362 (margin) *Pindar:* M1, S1   *Pindari* the rest

    370 *Zeno,* M1, S1   *Zeno* the rest

    381 one, M1, S1   one *the rest*

    384 Ward- M1, S1   Ward *the rest*

    E'χεμυθία, . . . γλωσσῆς M1, S1   E'χεμυθία. . . . γλωσσῆς *the rest*

    387 com | pesce M1, S1   com-|pesce the rest

    391 to, M1, S1   to *the rest*

    400 blasted, M1, S1   blasted; *the rest*

    402 stood M1, S1   stood, *the rest*

    bald, M1, S1   bald *the rest*

    405 (margin) *Vulgi expectatio.* at line 404 M1, S1   *At line 406 in the rest*

    408 now M1, S1   new *the rest*

N1ᵛ, p. 94. 445 seeke . . . good, . . . *Mis-chefe* M1, S1   seek . . . good . . . *Mis-chiefe* the rest

N2ᵛ, p. 96. 545 it. As A2, S4   it: as *the rest*

---

[1] In the press-copy, M5, O, A1, S2 and 4, there are clear signs of the 'EX-' having been stamped in over an erasure; the letters were stamped in separately as they are not quite in line, but in A2, S1, and S3 they appear to be normally printed.

N2ᵛ, p. 96	570	(margin) *verè* S4, A2	*verè* the rest
	585	in, *S4, A2*	in; *M1, 2, 3, 5, B1, 2, O, S1, 2, 3*
N4ᵛ, p. 100.	777	*Tamer-Chams,* M1, S1	*Tamer-Chams* the rest
	779	them | them *M1, S1*	them *the rest*
	789	Readers: . . . sweetnesse, *M1, S1*	Readers; . . . sweetnesse *the rest*
	790	inveighing: *M1, S1*	inveighing, *the rest*
	797	avoyded, *M1, S1*	avoyded *the rest*
	808	things, *M1, S1*	things *the rest*
	809	is: *M1, S1*	is; *the rest*
	813	selfe: *M1, S1*	selfe; *the rest*
	834	(margin) *No side note in M1, S1*	*Studiorum* the rest
O4ʳ, p. 107.	1250	(margin) *Character.* M5, O, S3, 4	*Character. Principis.* the rest
Q1ᵛ, p. 118.	1881	benefit, *M1, S1*	benefit *the rest*
	1881	(margin) *De oratio-|nis. | dignitate.* M1, S1	*De oratio-|nis dignita|te.* the rest
	1886	sense is, *M1, S1*	sense is *the rest*
Q3ʳ, p. 121.	2063	short, *M2*	short *the rest*
	2102	truth, *M2*	truth *the rest*
Q4ʳ, p. 123.	2226	timts *M1, S1*	times *the rest*
	2232	is, but *M1, S1*	is but, *the rest*
	c.w.	time *M1, S1*	times *the rest*
R1ᵛ, p. 126.	2397	*Poesie* O, S3	*Poesie:* the rest
	2407	(margin) *Ethicr* O, S3	*Ethica* the rest
	2409–10	Titleour *O, S3*	Title our *the rest*
R2ᵛ, p. 128.	2500	*Stobus* S3	*Stobæus* the rest
	2502	κεκτημένη. *S3*	κεκτημένη· *the rest*

(iv) *The Magnetic Lady, A Tale of a Tub, The Sad Shepherd*

The Magnetic Lady

A2ʳ, p. 3.	Persons, 15	*Bias* A1	*Bias,* the rest
A3ᵛ, p. 6.	Induction, 67	securities, *A1*	securities: *the rest*
	78	*Magnum!* A1	*Magnum.* the rest
B1ᵛ, p. 10.	I. i. 66	terme *S4*	termes *the rest*
	75	ym *S4*	my *the rest*
B2ʳ, p. 11.	I. ii. 10	health, *M1, 5, B1, O, S1, 4*	health *M2, 3, B2, A1, 2, S2, 3*
	13	What? *M1, 5, B1, O, S1, 4*	What *M2, 3, B2, A1, 2, S2, 3*
B3ᵛ, p. 14.	I. v. 12	*Rut.* The *Armenians* M1, 5, B1, O, S1, 4	*Rut.* The *Arminians* M2, 3, 4, B2, A1, 2, S2, 3
C2ʳ, p. 19.	I Chorus, 6	no Act *B2, A2*	noAct *the rest*[1]
	9	*Comedy,* had reserv'd, *B2, A2*	*Comedy* had reserv'd *the rest*
	20	land, . . . Pannims, *B2, A2*	land . . . Paynims *the rest*
	21	Monsters: *B2, A2*	Monsters; *the rest*

[1] The type has been deranged.

C2r, p. 19.	I Chorus, 22	Daughter: M1, B2, O, A2, S1	Daughter M2, 3, 5, B1, A1, S2, 3, 4
	24	lame, . . . miracles: M5, B2, A2	lame . . . miracles. the rest
	27	ꝗhen M1, B2, O, A2, S1	then M2, 3, 5, B1, A1, S2, 3, 4
	29	then, your People; B2, A2	then; your People, the rest[1]
	30	Tudeske B2, A2	Tudesko the rest
	38	well. B2, A2	well: the rest
	44	degrees! B2, A2	degrees: the rest
C3v, p. 22.	II. iii. 7	Especially 'in B2, A2	Especially in the rest[2]
	10	darker: what B2, A2	darker? What the rest
	11	English— M1, B2, O, A2, S1	English—. the rest
	12	it. B2, A2 it.— M1, O, S1	it—. M2, 3, B1, A1, S2, 3, 4
		Give heaven B2, A2	Give her vent the rest
	14	with B2, A2	with; the rest
	16	hers, B2, A2	hers the rest
	30	weekes! B2, A2	weekes: the rest
	42	(To B2, A2	To the rest
	44	too B2, A2	to the rest
	45	Practise!. . . man? B2, A2	Practise: . . . man, the rest
C4r, p. 23.	II. iii. 73	large M2	large! the rest
C4v, p. 24.	II. iv. 33	family? M3, S3, 4	family! the rest
	II. v. 16	veines M3, S3, 4	veines, the rest
D1v, p. 26.	II. vi, scene heading	Rnt. M5, B2, S3	Rut. the rest
	21	more, M5, B2, S3	more the rest
	23	in open sale M5, B2, S3	sale in open the rest
D2v, p. 28.	II. vi. 100	Legacie? M1, 5, O, S1	Legacie, the rest
D3v, p. 30.	2 Chorus 64	ten, M1, 5	ten the rest
D4r, p. 31.	2 Chorus 77	Dam. By whom, Boy? added to the preceding speech in B2, S3	Printed as a separate speech in the rest
	III. i. 1	Iem. B2, S3	Item. the rest
	17	name: B2, S3	name:) the rest
E4v, p. 40.	III. vi. 123	other sword free M2, B2, O, A2, S1	other, sword free. M1, 3, B1, A1, S2, 3, 4
F1v, p. 42.	III. vii. 23	Captaine! M1	Captaine: the rest
	25	hence,! M1	hence; the rest
F4r, p. 47.	IV. v. 14	travell? M1	travell the rest
	15	sake. M1	sake? the rest
	24	you, Mr. Practise. M1	you. Mr. Practise, the rest
	vi. 8	trke M1	take the rest
G1r, p. 49.	IV. vii. 10	another. M3, O, A2, S1, 2, 4	another? M1, 2, 5, B1, 2, A1, S3
G2r, p. 51.	IV. viii. 64	Daugh M1, O, S1, 4[3]	Daughter; M2, 3, 5, B1, 2, A1, 2, S2, 3

[1] A miscorrection.

[2] Read 'Especially, in' . . .

[3] A long line; the end letters have failed to print.

G4ᵛ, p. 56.	v. vi. 2	Counsels. *M3, B1, O, A2, S1, 2, 4*	Counsels? *M1, 2, 5, B2, A1, S3*
H1ʳ, p. 57.	v. vii. 21 st. dir.	*Not in M3, 5, A1, S3*	Inserted in *M1, 2, B1, 2, O, A2, S1, 2, 4*
	32	is, *M3, 5, A1, S3*	is *M1, 2, B1, 2, O, A2, S1, 2, 4*
H2ʳ, p. 59.	v. viii. 37	Boulting-tub. *M2, B2, A2*	Boulting-tub, *M1, 3, 5, B1, O, A1, S1, 2, 3, 4*
H3ᵛ, p. 62.	v. x. 61	charity *M2, B2, A2*	charity— *M1, 3, 5, B1, O, A1, S1, 2, 3, 4*
	98	unnarurall *M2, B2, A2*	unnaturall *M1, 3, 5, B1, O, A1, S1, 2, 3, 4*
	100	havǝ *M2, B2, A2*	have *M1, 3, 5, B1, O, A1, S1, 2, 3, 4*

A Tale of a Tub

I2ʳ, p. 67.	*The Persons* 19, 20, 21	IONE . . . MADGE ... KATE, *S2*	IONE, ... MADGE, ... KATE. *the rest*
I3ʳ, p. 69.	I. i. 6	keepe, *S2*	keepe *the rest*
	11	errand, *S2*	errand *the rest*
	12	What! Squire, *S2*	What, Squire! *the rest*
	17	danger *S2*	dagger *the rest*
	20	spirit her sonne *S2*	spirither, sonne[1] *the rest*
	28	would *S2*	would, *the rest*
	29	*Tripoly. S2*	*Tripoly;* the rest
	31	morning; *S2*	morning, *the rest*
	33	y-styl'd *S2*	y-styl'd, *the rest*
I4ᵛ, p. 72.	I. ii. 32	zay, . . . *Turfe; M2*	zay. *Turfe,* the rest
	iii. 20	uppi-nions *M2*	uppinions *the rest*
	29	married: *M2*	married? *the rest*
K3ᵛ, p. 78.	I. vii. 27	Poets; *S3*	Poets, *the rest**
	29	me! *M2, 3, 5, B1, A2, S2, 3**	me: *M1, B2, O, A1, S1, 4*
	31	Conntre-Madam's *S3*	Countri-Madams *the rest**
	33	sake, *M2, 3, B1, S3.* Stop lost in *A2, S2*	sake: *M1, 3. 5, B2, O, A1, S1, 4*
		dispose *S3*	dispense *the rest*
L1ʳ, p. 81 (71).	II. ii. 75	Hine! . . . you. *S4*	Hine. . . . you? *the rest*
	97	valew *S4*	value *the rest**
	100	death,... *Tiburne; S4*	dead; . . . *Tiburne,* the rest*
L4ᵛ, p. 88 (78).	II. v. 38	was.—. Well *M1, 2, 3, 5, B1, 2, O, A1, 2, S1, 2, 3*	was. Well *B1, S4*
	41	me? *M1, 2, 3, 5, B2, O, A1, 2, S1, 2, 3*	me. *B1, S4*
	vi. 6	Sir? speake? *M1, 2, 3, 5, B2, O, A1, 2, S1, 2, 3*	Sir, speake. *B1, S4*[2]
	14	obey. *M1, 2, 3, 5, B2, O, A1, 2, S1, 2, 3*	obey! *B1, S4*
M3ʳ, p. 93 (83).	III. iv. 15	see, *M3, S3*	see *the rest**
	16	pa rdee: *M3, S3*	pardee! *the rest**
	17	zaith, *M3, S3*	zaith *the rest**

¹ A miscorrection for 'spirit, her sonne'.   ² A miscorrection for 'Sir? speake'.

M3^v, p. 94 (84).   III. iv. 29   me; *S3*   me, *the rest**

    v. 21   *Wispe!* S3   *Wispe.* the rest*

M4^r, p. 95 (85). III. v. 58   sonne! *M5, B1, O, S1, 4*   sonne. *M1, 2, 3, B2, A1, 2, S2, 3*

    62   soune *M5, B1, O, S1, 4*   sonne *M1, 2, 3, B2, A1, 2, S2, 3*

O1^v, p. 106 (96). IV. ii. 49   weekes, *B2, A2*   weekes *the rest*

    51   this . . . blade, *B2, A2*   this, . . . blade ? *the rest*

    52   thee, *B2, A2*   thee *the rest*

    59   heare, *B2, A2*   heare; *the rest*

    65   not I, *B2, A2*   not I; *the rest*

O4^r, p. 111 (101). IV. vi. 16   yet, *B2, A2*   yet *the rest*

P1^v, p. 114 (104). v. ii. 26   I man *B1, A1, S2*   my man *the rest*

    52   Ladies *B1, A1, S2*   Ladie *the rest*

P3^r, p. 117 (107). v. iv. 16   it. *A1*   it! *the rest**

P4^r, p. 119 (109). v. vii. 31   old *B1, A1, S2*   oild *the rest*

Q2^r, p. 123 (113). v. x. 81   enter! *M1, 3, 5, B1, 2, O, A1, 2, S1, 2, 3, 4*   enter. *Yale copy, M2*[1]

Epilogue,   after l. 16   *FINIS.* not in M1, 3, 5, B1, O, A1, S1, 2, 3, 4   Added in B2, A2, M2

The Sad Shepherd

R4^r, p. 131 (121). I. ii. 2   *Robin-hood?* O, S1   *Robin-hood* the rest

    3   Wood. *O, S1*   Wood ? *the rest*

S3^v, p. 148 (138). I. vi. 24   su1e *M1, 2, 5, A1, 2*   sure *the rest*

Peculiarities of printing in this play are ''em' for 'them' in II. i. 1, vii. 16; elsewhere it is Jonson's usual ''hem'. 'O' stands for 'oh' in II. v. 1, 23, 41, vi. 75, 76, III. ii. 33, iii. 1; ô is used for 'o'' in I. vi. 51, 57, and also for 'oh' in II. vi. 75. In II. ii. 7 'na'se' is found for 'nase'.

One fact is clear from the texts themselves, and proved by the miscorrections, that the printers modified and conventionalized Jonson's elaborate punctuation. In such passages as the following the comma, at first printed in the text, was removed: 'i' the holy land, or else where' (*Magnetic Lady*, 1 chorus, 20); 'lame, and all to be laden with miracles' (ibid. 24); 'short, and succinct *Periods*' (*Discoveries*, 2063); 'Discoveries of truth, and fitnesse' (ibid. 2102). The comma taken out in the following clauses was in Jonson's manuscript:

He expects no more, then that summe to be tendred. (*M.L.* II. vi. 21)
On such an errand, as a Mistris is (*T. of T.* I. i. 11).

Jonson's habit of enclosing adverbs like 'still' and 'yet', and adverbial clauses, led to miscorrections. Such lines as

And Na-ture ioyes still, in equality (*D. is A*. I. vi. 126)
He is groune too much, the story of mens mouthes (ibid. 160)

[1] A miscorrection; there should be no stop.

have kept the second comma only. These, on the other hand, have kept only the first, which was removed in the proof:

> So doth the flatt'rer, with faire cunning strike (*Und.* lxix. 14)
> Nor is that worthy speech of *Zeno*, the philosopher to be past over
> (*Discov.* 370).

In the *Art of Poetry*, 174, the text had originally 'so 'above'; this was miscorrected to 'so 'bove'. Jonson's spelling also suffered. His attempt to copy classical spellings such as 'æquall', 'œconomy' received a short shrift: the *English Grammar* gives a good illustration, in which 'Præposition' is found once only, though Jonson must have used it throughout. In the *Grammar*, too, 'syllabe', which reproduces συλλαβή, is 'corrected' to 'syllable' (I. iii. 19).

VI

THE POEMS OF 1640

In 1640, while the Folio was still at the press, its publication was anticipated by two small collections of Jonson's verse for which the bookseller John Benson was responsible. He had secured the manuscripts of a number of Jonson's poems, and he printed them early in the year in two volumes, quarto and duodecimo.

T.-p. of Quarto. The title of the Quarto is 'Ben: Ionson's Execration against VVLCAN. With divers epigrams by the same Author to severall Noble Personages in *this Kingdome. Never Published before. LONDON.* Printed by *J. O*', i.e. John Okes, 'for *John Benson,* and are to be sold at his shop at St. *Dunstans* Church-yard in Fleet-streete. 1640.' The collation was originally A to G in fours, but finding an unprinted poem to Henrietta Maria, '*An Epigram to the Queens Health*' (*Und.* lxvi), Okes clumsily inserted a subsidiary signature 'f' of two leaves after F4 where it comes between Sir William Burlase's poem to Jonson, '*The Painter, to the Poet*' and Jonson's reply '*The Poet, to the Painter*' (*Und.* lii). The collation is, in detail: A1 recto blank; A1 verso, Robert Vaughan's portrait of Jonson with the underline 'Are to be Sould by William Peake' erased;[1] A2 recto the title-page set in a border of printer's ornaments, with the verso blank; A3–A4 recto, the 'Epistle Dedicatory' to Lord Windsor; A4 verso, 'Imprimatur Matth. Clay. Decemb. 14. 1639'; B1 recto–C1 recto, the Execration against Vulcan; C1 verso–G3 recto (with the two leaves of 'f' noted above) the so-called *Epigrams,* some of which are lyrics; G3 verso, a commendatory poem by Zouch Townley; G4 recto, with the verso blank, a short list of errata, with this appeal: 'Courteous Reader, some litterall faults are escaped, by oversight of the Corrector to the Presse, which I entreat thee to mend with thy Pen as thou espyest them, which are these.' By a further oversight of the corrector one reference is wrong: 'P. 19. l. ult. r. Aromaticke for stromaticke'; 'P. 19' should be 'page 27'. With a few exceptions the poems are printed alternately in italic and roman type. Another freak of the printer was in the Elegy on Lady Paulet (*Und.* lxxxiii) to print the word 'And' at the beginning of lines 52, 56, 61, 69, 75, 81, 84, 86, in italic on D1 verso, D2 recto. Another pointless proceeding is to print Jonson's name or initials at the end of every poem.

T.-p. of Duodecimo. The Duodecimo has for frontispiece a title-page engraved by William Marshall. At the top, laurel-crowned and

---

[1] See vol. iii, pp. ix–x.

set in a niche is a bust of Jonson; the head is a copy in reverse of
Robert Vaughan's portrait, but it is copied so badly as to be almost
a caricature, and it has even been described as a portrait of Horace!
Below the bust is the title set in two half-circles of scroll-work:
'Q. HORATIVS FLACCUS, his Art of POETRY. *Englisht by* Ben:
Jonson. London, *Printed for John Benson*, 1640.' There is a second
state of the imprint, 'London, *Printed for J. Benson and are sold by
W. Ley at Paules-Chayne*, 1640.' A printed title-page follows:
'Q: Horatius Flaccus: *His Art of Poetry*. ENGLISHED By Ben:
Jonson. With other Workes of the Author, never Printed before.
LONDON: Printed by *J. Okes*, for *John Benson*. 1640.' The other
works were *The Gypsies Metamorphosed* and a reprint of the *Epi-
grams* already published in the Quarto. Both have half-titles: 'The
Masque of the GYPSIES. Written by BEN: JONSON. LONDON:
Printed by *J. Okes*, for *J. Benson*, and are to bee sold at his shop
in St. *Dunstans* Church-yard in Fleet-street. 1640.' 'EPIGRAMS
to Severall Noble Personages in this Kingdome. The Author *Ben:
Ionson*.' with the previous imprint re-used. All these titles are
framed in a border of printer's ornaments.

Of the original issue only one imperfect copy survives, Syn. 8.64.13
in the Cambridge University Library.

The full collation would be A–G in twelves. In detail this is as
follows: A1 blank; A2 recto, with the signature in a factotum block;
A2 verso, 'Imprimatur: Mat. Clay. And by other Authority. Febr.
21. 1639.'; A3 recto blank; A3 verso, the engraved title-page; A4
recto, the printed title-page, with the verso blank; A5–A6 verso, the
dedication to Lord Windsor; A7–12, complimentary verses, by Sir
Edward Herbert (A7 recto), Barton Holyday (A7 verso–A9 verso),
Zouch Townley (A10 recto), I. C. (A10 verso–A12 verso)[1]; B12–C2
recto, pages 1–27, Horace's *Art of Poetry*;[2] C2 verso blank; C3 recto,
page 29, title-page of the Execration against Vulcan, with the verso
blank; C4–C8 verso, pages 31–40, the text of the Execration; C9,
pages 41–2, blank; C10, page 43, the title of *The Masque of the
Gypsies*, with the verso blank; C11–E11 verso, pages 45–94, the text
of the masque; E12 (not included in the pagination) blank; F1 recto
(not included in the pagination), the title-page of the Epigrams,

---

[1] It may be noted that the Locker-Lampson copy (no. 400 in A. F. Griffiths's
Bibliotheca Anglo-Poetica, 1815, pp. 179–80) has inserted leaves in quire A:
leaf *a* from Sir John Beaumont's *Bosworth Field*, 1629, with verses by George
Fortescue and Jonson, which has been identified; and two leaves, not identified, after the imprimatur, verses by R. H., 'To the Reader vpon the Author,
his Kinsman', and verses in English 'Ad Lectores'. These last are from Henry
Hutton's *Follies Anatomie, Or Satyres and Satyricall Epigrams*, 1619.

[2] In C1 recto, p. 25, there is an error in the catchword: '930 In' should be
'630 In'.

with the verso blank; F2–G11, pages 95–138, the text of the Epigrams; G12, pages 139–40, blank. The Cambridge copy has the blank leaves A1 and G12, but C3–C8, pages 29–44, and E5–E8, pages 81–8, are missing. It has the original eight leaves D6–10, E9–11, slashed for cancel; the binder should have destroyed them, of course, after the sewing.

After he had set up the volume, Benson acquired a copy of the fuller version of *The Gypsies Metamorphosed* acted at Windsor in the third performance: he decided to make room for it. To do this he had to cancel D6–10, pages 59–68, and E5–8, pages 81–8. D5 is followed by an additional quire ' d ' of fourteen leaves; E4 is followed by another quire ' e ' of twelve leaves. These additions run the pagination up nominally to 104, but as pages 69 to 82 are duplicated, this is really page 118; the text of the *Epigrams*, which begins two leaves later, keeps its old numbering, pages 95–138: either this section had been printed off, or Okes did not trouble to adjust the pagination.

In the textual introduction to *The Gypsies Metamorphosed* we have used the early state of the Cambridge copy to determine the Burley and Belvoir version before it was changed and amplified for the performance at Windsor.[1]

Benson dedicated both collections to Thomas, sixth Baron Windsor, but he varied the wording. 'Affectionate servant' in the subscription is not a usual form of address from a publisher to a patron.

Quarto	*Duodecimo*
To the Right Honourable THOMAS Lord WINDSOR, &c.	¶ To the Right Honourable THOMAS Lord .*WINDSORE.*

Quarto

My LORD:

THE assurance the Author of these Poems received of his Worth from your Honour, in his life time, was not rather a marke of his desert, than a perfect demonstration of your Noble love to him: Which consideration, has rais'd my bold desire to assume presumption, to present these to your Honour, in the person of one deceased; the forme whereof somewhat disperst, yet carry with them the Prerogative of truth to be Mr. *Ben: Jonsons*; and will so appeare to all, whose Eyes, and Spirits are rightly plac'd. You are (my Lord) a Person

Duodecimo

My Lord:

THE Extension of your *Noble Favours* Commands, and my *Gratitude* no lesse binds me to present this *Elaborate Peece*, of our learned and judicious Poet *Ben Ionson* his Translation of *Horace de Arte Poetica*, to your *Lordships* perusall: which *Book* amongst the rest of his *Strenuous* and *Sinewy* Labours, for its rare profundity, may challenge a just admiration of the Learned in this and future Ages, and crowne his *name*

[1] See vol. vii, pp. 542–5, 551–5.

who is able to give value and true esteeme to things of themselves no lesse deserving: such were his, strong, and as farre transcendent ordinary imagination, as they are conformable to the sence of such who are of sound judgement: his Strenuous Lines, and sinewey Labours have rais'd such Piramydes to his lasting name, as shall out-last Time. And that these may, without any diminution to the glory of his greater Workes, enjoy the possession of publicke favour, (by your Honours permission) I shall be glad by this small Testimony ⟨to⟩ account it a fit opportunity to assure your Honour, my Lord, that

I am

Your most humble and affectionate Servant,

JOHN BENSON.

with a lasting memory of never dying glory! You rightly knew (my *Lord*) the worth and true esteeme both of the *Author* and his Learning, being more perspicuous in the candid judgement of *Your Lordship*, and other sublime *Spirits* that rightly knew him, then my capacity can describe. But there is from me a iust duty and service, due to *your Honour*, which makes me assume this boldnesse, yet in some good assurance that *your Goodnesse* will be pleas'd to accept of this as a true acknowledgment, and profession of my most humble *thankfulnesse*, by which my *Lord you* shall dignifie the purpose of him who shall always study to be accounted

Your Honours most observant and affectionate servant.

I. B.

The tortuous history of the publication of these two volumes has been given in the previous chapter.[1] The true owner of the copyright was Thomas Walkley, who had bought the manuscripts from Sir Kenelm Digby. But late in 1639 Benson acquired all the poems printed in the Quarto; Clay's imprimatur is dated 14 December, and Benson registered the volume two days later. That these were the only poems he had at that date is proved by the fact that the text ended on G3 recto, and he filled in the verso with Zouch Townley's lines '*To Mr. Jonson*', beginning '*Ben*; the *world* is much in debt'. He registered *Horace's Art of Poetry* on 8 February 1640, and *The Masque of Gypsies*, as he called it, on 20 February; these he printed in the Duodecimo, in which the imprimatur is dated February 1640. In March he planned a further instalment—*The Masque of Augurs, Time Vindicated, Neptune's Triumph, Pan's Anniversary* 'with sundry Elegies and other Poems'; but he was stopped from printing these, probably by the appeal Walkley made 'to one of his Maties Secretaries of State'.[2]

All but three of these minor poems afterwards appeared in *The Underwood*. These exceptions were '*Another* ⟨Epigram⟩ *on the Birth of the Prince*', beginning '*Another Phœnix, though the first is dead*'; '*A Parallell of the Prince to the King*', beginning '*So Peleus when he faire* Thetis *got*'; John Eliot's gibe at Jonson's poem to Lord

[1] See pp. 93–101.
[2] See p. 99.

Engraved title-page of the Duodecimo, 1640

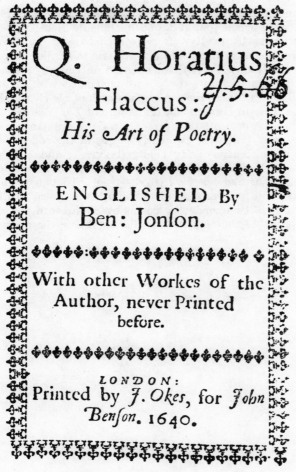

Q. Horatius Flaccus:

His *Art of Poetry.*

ENGLISHED By Ben: Jonson.

With other Workes of the Author, never Printed before.

LONDON: Printed by *J. Okes*, for *John Benson*. 1640.

Title-page of the Duodecimo. Q. Horatius Flaccus: His Art of Poetry, 1640

Weston (*Und.* lxxvii), and Jonson's ferocious answer to it.[1] The two first are not genuine; the third was below the literary level of *The Underwood*, in which Jonson did not include it. Benson's collection has four poems to royalty, afterwards *Underwood* lxv, lxvi, lxvii, lxxii; two poems to the Earl of Newcastle (*Und.* liii, lix); two to Lord Weston (lxxiv, lxxvii); the epigram on Digby, here called an epigram to him (lxxviii); the poems exchanged with Sir William Borlase (lii); the 'Ode Pindaric on the death of Sir Henry Morison' (lxx); the 'Ode to Himself' on the failure of *The New Inn*; 'Upon my Picture left in Scotland' (ix); 'On a Gentlewoman working by an Hour glass' (viii); the two early poems of the collection called 'Eupheme' celebrating Lady Digby (lxxxiv. 3 and 4); the song 'Come, noble Nymphs, and do not hide' in *Neptune's Triumph*; and the song in *The Sad Shepherd* (I. v. 65–80), 'Though I am young and cannot tell'. A certain outward finish was given to the book by the group of commendatory poems by Sir Edward Herbert and others; probably the contributors did not know the questionable antecedents of the volume.

[1] See *U.V.* xxxvii.

VII

THE FOLIO OF 1692

THIS edition was produced by a syndicate of leading booksellers, Henry Herringman, Edward Brewster, Thomas Bassett, Richard Chiswell, Matthew Wotton, and George Conyers. The chief partner, Herringman, had long contemplated such an edition. When he and John Martyn and Richard Mariot published in 1652 *The Wild-Goose Chase* as a supplement to the First Folio of Beaumont and Fletcher, they told the reader in a prefatory address:

If our care and endeavours to do our Authors right (in an incorrupt and genuine Edition of their Works) and thereby to gratifie and oblige the Reader, be but requited with a suitable entertainment, we shall be encouraged to bring Ben Johnson's two volumes into one and publish them in this form; and also to reprint Old Shakespeare: both which are designed by

Yours,
Ready to serve you.

They repeated this offer in the preface to the Second Folio of Beaumont and Fletcher which they published in 1679. Herringman had the copyright of Walkley's portion of the 1640 Folio; he had acquired it on 19 August 1667 from Humphrey Moseley's widow.

The edition waited till 1692, after Herringman, Brewster, Chiswell, and R. Bentley had carried out the second half of their programme by publishing the Fourth Folio Shakespeare in 1685. It was advertised in *The Gentleman's Journal: or. The Monthly Miscellany* in May 1692 and it appeared in *The Term Catalogues* in the Trinity term, as 'Printed by Tho. Hodgkin; and sold by most Booksellers in London'.[1]

The edition had for frontispiece William Elder's idealized portrait of Jonson reproduced as the frontispiece to our sixth volume. The original measures 11½ by 7¼ inches. The title runs: 'THE WORKS OF BEN JONSON, Which were formerly Printed in Two Volumes, are now Reprinted in One. To which is added A COMEDY CALLED THE NEW INN. With Additions never before Published. — *neque, me ut miretur turba laboro:* | *Contentus paucis lectoribus.* [Four ornaments, the crowned rose, thistle, fleur-de-lis, and harp.] LONDON, Printed by *Thomas Hodgkin,* for *H. Herringman, E. Brewster, T. Bassett, R. Chiswell, M. Wotton, G. Conyers,* M DC XCII.' The frontispiece and the *Leges Convivales* belonged to Thomas Bassett,

---

[1] Ed. Arber, ii. 414.

'at the George in Fleet-street, near St. Dunstan's Church'. The title-page of the *Leges Convivales* has his imprint, and Elder's portrait was on sale separately at his shop.

The novel features of the edition were that it included *The New Inn*, the *Leges Convivales*, and the lines over the entrance to the Apollo room at *The Devil*, and it recast *The English Grammar*. The revision of the *Grammar* is a remarkable achievement; it was largely rewritten by a competent scholar who eliminated archaisms and brought the work thoroughly up to date. Otherwise the Folio of 1640 was reprinted, and no attempt was made to rearrange its contents; the plays, the masques, and the poems are still in two separate sections. *The Devil is an Ass* was printed from a copy of the 1631 Folio in which P2 recto and P3 verso were uncorrected, and *The New Inn* from a copy of the 1631 octavo in which C1 was uncorrected.[1] The printer was Thomas Hodgkin, and of course he simplified the punctuation of the original, which he did not always understand. When Cob after his beating by Bobadill produces Justice Clement's warrant, 'I have it here in black and white; for his black, and blew: shall pay him' (*E.M.I.* IV. iv. 20–2, as the Second Folio punctuates, following the First), the grammatical construction is 'I have that here which shall pay him'. Hodgkin reproduced it, 'I have it here in black and white; for his black and blue shall pay him'. He modernized the spelling, especially in substituting ''em' for ''hem'. So we find in the second Act of *The Alchemist* 'Solomon' for 'Salomon', 'Cornwall' for 'Cornwaile', 'furnace' for 'fornace', 'Seraglio' for '*seraglia*'. He is lavish of capital letters, as was the fashion in the later seventeenth century. Take this sentence from *The Silent Woman* (III. iii. 126–9): 'I, she must hear Argument. Did not *Pasiphae*, who was a Queen, love a Bull? and was not *Calisto*, the Mother of *Arcas*, turn'd into a Bear, and made a Star, Mistris *Ursula*, i' the Heavens?' The only capitals in the First Folio are in the personal names; the Second Folio has one additional one, 'Bull'. Some bad blunders are copied from the Second Folio: 'bets' for 'lets' in *Sejanus*, II. 400; 'Mrs. MAVIS, *the Lady* HAUGHTIES *Woman*' in the character-list before *Epicoene*, the name being repeated from the line before, whereas it should be 'Mrs. TRUSTY'; 'With the *Philosophers*' for 'With the *Philosophers stone*' in *The Alchemist*, IV. v. 27; 'Sallance' and 'pish ass' for 'balance' and 'parish ass' in *The Gypsies Metamorphosed*, 323, 746; '*Clementia tutelat opima*' for '*Clementia tutela optima*' in the *Discoveries*, 1175 n. There is also a bad crop of new blunders. Cob, with his herring cob, refuses to 'eate my own fish, and bloud' (*E.M.I.* III.

---

[1] See vol. vi, pp. 154, 393.

iv. 54–5); the 1692 text stupidly alters to 'my own Flesh and Blood'. For misprints we may quote 'acceptably' for 'acceptedly', 'this bulk of ignorance' for 'this hulke', and 'eats not those that feed him' for 'eats on those' (*E.M.O.* I. ii. 117, 195, 232); 'I have seen less Roses grow upon sweeter Faces' for 'less noses', because the *n* was imperfectly printed in the Second Folio (ibid. IV. iv. 49, 50); 'Sums' for 'Suns', and '*Centurions*' for '*centuries*', caught up from the following line, and leaving three centurions for Sejanus's full bodyguard at the crisis of his fate (*Sej.* III. 62, v. 133); 'timely' for 'timeless' in *Volpone*, IV. v. 41, probably because the printer did not reflect that 'timeless' means 'untimely'; 'quiet' for 'quit' in *Epicoene*, I. i. 159, because he did not see that 'quit' meant 'acquitted' and thought it the proper antithesis to 'riot'; 'puss' for 'pase' in *The Magnetic Lady*, v. ii. 23, a misprint for 'pass'; 'wisely' for 'wildly' in *The Entertainment at Highgate*, 198, where the satyrs 'wildly stand at gaze'. There are occasional corrections, but they are few. The song in *Poetaster*, II. ii. 163, has the opening line as in the First Folio, '*If I freely may discover*', where the Second Folio has '*freely can discover*'; the printer may have known a musical setting which read '*may*'. In *Volpone*, v. x. 8–10, he tried his hand at emendation: here the First Folio read

(CORV. Will he betray himselfe?) VOLT. Whom, equally,
I haue abus'd, out of most couetous endes—
(CORV. The man is mad! CORB. What's that? CORV. He is possesst.)

The Second Folio omitted the second and third lines, so the 1692 text supplies as a stopgap

whom equally
I have abus'd, by my false Accusation:

In *A Tale of a Tub*, IV. iii. 21, 'empty-handed' for 'empty-headed', in *Underwood*, xxix. 15, 'Art' for 'are'; xl. 20, 'rarified' for 'ratified', and in *The Gypsies Metamorphosed*, 247, 'Viands' for 'urands' are correct.

To save space the text was printed in double columns on each page, a full column usually having seventy-four lines of text. There are two gaps in the pagination and signatures, between *Catiline*, the last of the First Folio plays, and the *Epigrams* (omitting pages 265–80, quires Mm, Nn), and between *The Golden Age Restored*, the last of the First Folio masques, and *Bartholomew Fair*, which begins the Second Folio (omitting pages 383–92, Ccc3, 4 and Ddd). In the sixteenth century it was the rule to print large books on two, or more often on three, presses; the dividing-points can generally be found. There are occasional examples in the seventeenth century:

for instance, in the First Folio of Beaumont and Fletcher's plays in 1647 a postscript of the publisher at the end of the preliminary leaves states, 'After the *Comedies* and *Tragedies* were wrought off, we were forced (for expedition) to send the *Gentlemens* Verses'— twenty-two leaves—'to severall Printers, which was the occasion of their different Character; but the *Worke* it selfe is one continued Letter, which (though very legible) is none of the biggest, because (as much as possible) we would lessen the Bulke of the Volume'. 'Foure printers dwelling farre asunder' printed the Folio of *All the Workes of Iohn Taylor the Water Poet Being 63 in number collected in one volume*, Taylor tells us in some prefatory lines on the errata. William Masters compiling a list of errata in his *Λόγοι "Ευκαιροι, Essayes and Observations Theologicall and Morall*, 1653, notes 'The mistakes of the Presses (for more than one was made use of for expedition sake) which seem most likely to endanger the sense are here corrected'. Evidently the Jonson Folio of 1692 was printed in this manner on three presses simultaneously; the printer cast up the copy and miscalculated, leaving gaps. This was at any rate better than the treatment of Fuller's *History of the Worthies of England* in 1662: his son tells us in a preface to the reader, 'The discounting of Sheets (to expedite the Work at severall Presses) hath occasioned the often mistake of the Folio's'; in consequence signatures and paging are duplicated, the repeated numbers being bracketed to distinguish them.

The collation is A⁶, B–Z⁴, Aa–Ll⁴, Oo–Zz⁴, Aaa–Bbb⁴, Ccc², Eee– Zzz⁴, Aaaa–Yyyy⁴, Aaaaa1 (= Zzzz1), Zzzz2–4, Aaaaa–Bbbbb⁴. [Ccccc² unsignatured.] R2 is signed R. Pages 1–264 (228–9 mispaged 218–19), 281–374 (369, 370 mispaged 371–2), 377–82, 393–744 (412–13 mispaged 406–3, 540–1 mispaged 538–9). [745–8 unpaged.] Sheet Ccc is discoloured, as Dr. Greg has pointed out; the only explanation that can be suggested is that the paper was of inferior quality.

In detail the collation is as follows:

Preliminary pages: A1 recto blank; A1 verso, Elder's portrait; A2 recto, the title-page, with the verso blank; A3 recto, the catalogue; A3 verso–A5 recto, complimentary verses; A5 verso blank. Pages i–x, not numbered.

Every Man in his Humour: A6 recto, title and the dedication to Camden; A6 verso, the persons of the play, the scene, and the actor-list; B–D⁴, the text. Pages xi, xii, 1–24.

Every Man out of his Humour: E1 recto, title and the dedication to the Inns of Court; E1 verso, the persons of the play, the actor-list, and the character sketches; E2 recto–I2 verso, the text. G1 is not signatured. Pages 25–60.

Cynthia's Revels: I3 recto, the title and the dedication to the Court; I3 verso, the persons of the play, the scene, and the actor-list; I4 recto–N3 verso, the text. Pages 61–94.

Poetaster: N4 recto, the title and the dedication to Richard Martin; N4 verso, the persons of the play, the scene, and the actor-list; O1 recto–R2 recto, the text. R2 is misprinted R; R2 verso is blank. Pages 95–124.

Sejanus: R3 recto, the title and the dedication to Lord Aubigny; R3 verso, the argument, the persons of the play, the scene, and the actor-list; R4 recto–V4 recto, the text. V4 verso blank. Pages 125–52.

Volpone: X1, the title, the dedication to the Universities, the persons of the play, the scene, and the actor-list; X2 recto–Aa2 recto, the text. Aa2 verso blank. Pages 153–80.

Epicoene: Aa3 recto, the title and the dedication to Sir Francis Stuart; Aa3 verso, the persons of the play, the scene, and the actor-list; Aa4 recto–Dd4 verso, the text. Pages 181–208.

The Alchemist: Ee1 recto, the title and the dedication to Mary Lady Wroth; Ee1 verso, the persons of the play, the scene, and the actor-list; Ee2 recto–Hh2 verso, the text. Pages 209–36.

Catiline: Hh3 recto, the title and the dedication to the Earl of Pembroke; Hh3 verso, the persons of the play, the scene, and the actor-list; Hh4 recto–Ll4 verso, the text. Pages 237–64.

Here at the end of these plays is a break in the text; quires Mm and Nn, pages 265–80, are missing.

Epigrams: Oo1 recto, the title and the dedication to the Earl of Pembroke; Oo1 verso–Pp4 verso, the text. Pages 281–96.

The Forest: Qq1 recto–Qq4 recto, the text. Pages 297–303.

The King's Entertainment at his Coronation: Qq4 verso–Rr4 recto, the text. Pages 304–11.

A Panegyre: Rr4 verso, Ss1 recto, the text. Pages 312–13.

The Entertainment at Althorp: Ss1 verso–2 verso, the text. Pages 314–16.

The Entertainment at Highgate: Ss3 recto–4 recto, the text. Pages 317–19.

The Entertainment of the Two Kings at Theobalds: Ss4 verso, the text. Page 320.

The Entertainment of the King and Queen at Theobalds: Tt1, the text. Pages 321–2.

The Masque of Blackness: Tt2 recto–3 verso, the text. Pages 323–6.

The Masque of Beauty: Tt4 recto–Uu1 verso, the text. Pages 327–30.

Hymenaei: Uu2 recto–Xx2 recto, the text. Pages 331–9.

The Haddington Masque: Xx2 verso–4 verso, the text. Pages 340–4.

The Masque of Queens: Yy1 recto–Zz1 verso, the text. Pages 345–54.

Prince Henry's Barriers: Zz2 recto–3 verso, the text of the speeches. Pages 355–8.

Oberon: Zz4 recto–Aaa2 recto, the text. Pages 359–63.

Love Freed from Ignorance and Folly: Aaa2 verso–4 recto, the text. Pages 364–7.

Love Restored: Aaa4 verso–Bbb1 verso, the text. Pages 368–70.

A Challenge at Tilt: Bbb1 verso–2 verso, the text. Pages 370–2.

The Irish Masque: Bbb3, the text. Pages 373–4.

Mercury Vindicated from the Alchemists: Bbb4 recto–Ccc1 recto, the text. Pages 377–9 (dropping out pp. 375–6).

The Golden Age Restored: Ccc1 verso–2 verso, the text. Pages 380–2.

Here at the end of the masques is a second break in the text; Ccc3, 4, and quire Ddd, pages 383–92, are missing.

Bartholomew Fair: Eee1 recto, title and prologue at Court; Eee1 verso, the persons of the play; Eee2, the induction; Eee3 recto–Iii2 recto, the text. Iii2 verso blank. Pages 393–428.

The Staple of News: Iii3 recto, title, the persons, the scene; Iii3 verso, the induction; Iii4 recto, the prologues for the stage and for the Court; Iii4 verso–Mmm4 recto, the text. Mmm4 verso blank. Pages 429–56.

The Devil is an Ass: Nnn1 recto, the title, the persons, the scene; Nnn1 verso, the prologue; Nnn2 recto–Qqq2 verso, the text. Pages 457–84.

The Magnetic Lady: Qqq3 recto, the title, the scene, the persons; Qqq3 verso–4 recto, the induction; Qqq4 verso–Ttt2 recto, the text. Ttt2 verso blank. Pages 485–508.

A Tale of a Tub: Ttt3 recto, the title and the prologue; Ttt3 verso, the persons and the scene; Ttt4 recto–Yyy2 recto, the text. Yyy2 verso blank. Pages 509–32.

The Sad Shepherd: Yyy3 recto, the title, the persons, the scene; Yyy3 verso, the argument of Act I, the prologue; Yyy4 recto–Zzz4 verso, the text. Pages 533–44.

Underwoods: Aaaa1 recto, title and address to the reader, with the verso blank; Aaaa2 recto–Eeee4 verso, the text. Pages 545–84.

The Entertainment at Welbeck: Ffff1 recto–2 verso, the text. Pages 585–8.

Love's Welcome at Bolsover: Ffff3, the text. Pages 589–90.

Mortimer: Ffff4 recto, the title and the persons; Ffff4 verso, the arguments; Gggg1 recto, the text. Pages 591–3.

Christmas his Masque: Gggg1 verso–2 verso, the text. Pages 594–6.

Lovers made Men: Gggg3 recto–4 recto, the text. Pages 597–9.

The Vision of Delight: Gggg4 verso–Hhhh1 verso, the text. Pages 600–2.

Pleasure Reconciled to Virtue: Hhhh2 recto–3 recto, the text. Pages 603–5.

For the Honour of Wales: Hhhh3 verso–Iiii1 recto, the text. Pages 606–9.

News from the New World in the Moon: Iiii1 verso–3 recto, the text. Pages 610–13.

The Gypsies Metamorphosed: Iiii3 verso, the title, the prologue at Windsor, the address to the King at Burley; Iiii4 recto–Llll1 verso, the text. Pages 614–26.

The Masque of Augurs: Llll2 recto–4 recto, the text. Pages 627–31.

Time Vindicated: Llll4 verso–Mmmm2 verso, the text. Pages 632–6.

Neptune's Triumph for the Return of Albion: Mmmm3 recto–Nnnn1 recto, the text. Pages 637–41.

Pan's Anniversary: Nnnn1 verso–2 verso, the text. Pages 642–4.

The Masque of Owls: Nnnn3, the text. Pages 645–6.

The Fortunate Isles: Nnnn4 recto–Oooo2 verso, the text. Pages 647–52.

Love's Triumph through Callipolis: Oooo3 recto–4 recto, the text. Pages 653–5.

Chloridia: Oooo4 verso–Pppp2 recto, the text. Pages 656–9.

Horace's Art of Poetry: Pppp2 verso–Qqqq3 recto, the text. Pages 660–9.

The English Grammar: Qqqq3 verso, the title and the preface; Qqqq4 recto–Tttt2 recto, the text. Pages 670–91.

The Discoveries: Tttt2 verso, the title and note on 'Sylva'; Tttt3 recto–Yyyy4 recto, the text. Yyyy4 verso blank. Pages 692–720.

The New Inn: Zzzz1 recto, here called 'Aaaaa', the title and the dedication to the reader; Zzzz1 verso, the argument; Zzzz2 recto, the scene, the persons, and the prologue; Zzzz2 verso–Bbbbb4 verso, the text, followed by Jonson's 'Ode to Himself'. Pages 721–44.

Leges Convivales: [Ccccc1 recto], the title; [Ccccc1 verso], the Latin text; [Ccccc2], a translation in English verse, followed by the verses 'Over the Door at the Entrance into the Apollo'. Pages 745–8, not numbered.

VIII

THE BOOKSELLERS' EDITION
OF 1716–17

IN *The Evening Post*, 9–11 May 1717, was the advertisement, 'This Day is publish'd, The Works of Ben Jonson In 6 Volumes'. This edition was produced by a syndicate, John Walthoe, Matthew Wotton, John Nicholson, John Sprint, George Conyers, Benjamin Tooke, Daniel Midwinter, Thomas Ballard, Benjamin Cowse, Jacob Tonson, and William Innys. Volumes i, v, and vi have the imprint of 'J. Wotton' instead of 'Matthew Wotton'. Volume ii is dated 1717, the rest 1716. The first volume has a title-page, '*The Works of Ben. Johnson in six volumes. Adorn'd with Cuts. —neque me ut miretur turba laboro: Contentus paucis lectoribus*' with London imprint and date 1716. Vertue's engraving of Jonson is reproduced as a frontispiece, and Louis Du Guernier's illustrations are in the text for all plays up to *The Devil is an Ass*; they failed at this point because Du Guernier died on 19 September 1716.

Volume i contains the preliminary verses (pp. 1–16), *Every Man in his Humour* (17–119), *Every Man out of his Humour* (121–268), *Cynthia's Revels* (269–400), *Poetaster* (401–512).

Volume ii has *Sejanus* (1–110), *Volpone* (111–228), *Epicoene* (229–346), *The Alchemist* (347–448).

Volume iii has *Catiline* (1–112), *The Epigrams* (113–76), *The Forest* (177–202), *The Entertainments* (203–71), *The Masques* (272–488).

Volume iv has *Bartholomew Fair* (1–136), *The Staple of News* (137–248), *The Devil is an Ass* (249–361), *The Magnetic Lady* (363–415).

Volume v has *A Tale of a Tub* (1–89), *The Sad Shepherd* (90–134), *Underwoods*, including the Welbeck and Bolsover Entertainments (135–301), *Mortimer* (302–7), *The Masques* up to *The Masque of Augurs* (308–432).

Volume vi has *The Masques* concluded (1–96), *Horace* (97–137), *The English Grammar* (138–221), *The Discoveries* (222–323), *The New Inn* and the *Ode* (324–418), *Leges Convivales* (419–22), the verses at the entrance to the Apollo (423).

The book is reprinted from the Folio of 1692, except where it makes blunders of its own, such as 'glad camels' for 'gald' (*E.M.O.* Ind. 133), 'dangerous bastard' for 'degenerous' (*Sej.* III. 387), 'mouth' for 'moth' (*Alch.* v. i. 20), 'look day In the full face' for 'dull face' (*Cat.* I. 297–8), 'Senator' for 'Stentor' (*S. of N.* v. vi. 49), 'ingenious strong words' for 'inginous' (*N.I.* II. vi. 66), 'every stop he made' for 'every stoop' (ibid. IV. iii. 15), 'laughing herds' for 'loughing', i.e. lowing (*For*. iii. 16), 'He knows the flattering colours' for 'Ne knowes he flatt'ring Colours' (*Und*. lii. 21), 'season' for 'seisin' (ibid. lxxxii. 8). But the printer's best effort was to change Jonson's reference to his own death in *Ep*. xxxiii. 4, 'Breathe to expect my when, and make my how' to 'make my bow'. He also states that *Epicoene* was first acted 'By the King's Majesty's Servants'—a blunder which Whalley copied.

IX

WHALLEY'S EDITION OF 1756

The Works of Ben. Jonson. In seven volumes. Collated with All the former Editions, and Corrected; with Notes Critical and Explanatory. By Peter Whalley, Late Fellow of St. John's College in Oxford.—Neque me ut miretur turba laboro, Contentus paucis lectoribus. HOR. *Rudem esse omnino in nostris poetis, aut inertissimæ segnitiæ est, aut fastidii delicatissimi.* CIC. *de Fin. L. 1.* A group of publishers is given in the imprint: D. Midwinter, W. Innys and J. Richardson, J. Knapton, T. Wotton, C. Hitch and L. Hawes, J. Walthoe, D. Browne, J. and R. Tonson, C. Bathurst, J. Hodges, J. Ward, M. and T. Longman, W. Johnston, P. Davey and B. Law. The edition was in octavo, and was advertised in the book catalogue of *The Monthly Review* for August 1756. Already in January 1752 *The Gentleman's Magazine* had published some notes on *Every Man in his Humour*, supplied by Whalley, 'by whom a complete edition' of Jonson's works, 'with critical and explanatory notes, is preparing for the press'.[1] In 1787, when recording payments of booksellers to editors, the same paper stated that Whalley received £210 for the edition.[2]

It had for frontispiece Vertue's engraving of the supposed Honthorst portrait. Whalley prefixed a life of Jonson with illustrative documents, including the warrant of 1630 for the poet's pension. He took over Du Guernier's illustrations from the 1717 edition. He collected the plays, masques, and poems printed in the two Folios and put them together, and he included *The Case is Altered* in an edition of Jonson for the first time.

The collation is: Volume i. A1 recto, general title-page; A2 recto, title-page of vol. i; A3–6, list of subscribers; a–b⁸, preface; c–d⁸, life of Jonson. A–Dd⁸, pages 1–432, commendatory verses, *Every Man in* and *Every Man out of his Humour, Cynthia's Revels.*

Volume ii. Three preliminary leaves of title-page, errata, and illustration. A–Kk⁸, Ll⁴, Mm¹, *Poetaster, Sejanus, Volpone, Epicoene.*

Volume iii. Three preliminary leaves as in vol. ii. A–Cc8, the last leaf blank, pages 1–414, *The Alchemist, Catiline, Bartholomew Fair.*

Volume iv. Two preliminary leaves of title-page and errata. A–Ff⁸, Gg⁴, pages 1–472, *The Devil is an Ass, The Staple of News, The New Inn, The Magnetic Lady.*

Volume v. Two preliminary leaves of title-page and errata. A–Ee⁸, the last leaf blank, pages 1–448, *A Tale of a Tub, The Sad Shepherd, Mortimer, Entertainments, Masques at Court.*

[1] Vol. xxii, p. 3. [2] Ibid. lvii, part i, p. 76.

Volume vi. Two preliminary leaves of title-page and errata. A–Ee^8, pages 1–448, *Masques at Court, Epigrams, The Forest, Underwoods*. Volume vii. Two preliminary pages of title-page and errata. A–Z^8, Aa^6, the last page blank, pages 1–380, *Underwoods, The Discoveries, Horace's Art of Poetry, The English Grammar, Leges Convivales, The Case is Altered.*

In his preface Whalley laid down the lines on which the edition would proceed. Commenting on the two Folios of 1616 and 1640, he noted that the former was printed in Jonson's lifetime, 'and under his own inspection, so that we have an authentic copy for our pattern, and which we found of great use in correcting the mistakes of subsequent editions'; the latter, published after Jonson's death, 'was undoubtedly printed from his original manuscripts; but as they had not the benefit of the author's revisal, there are many more [misprints] as well as more material blunders in that volume, than in the volume I have just now mentioned'. Discussing some critical principles, he anticipated a great maxim of Dr. Johnson in the preface to his Shakespeare, 'The mere improvement of a writer's sense, can never authorize the alteration of his words.' It will be noticed that Whalley is silent about the Quartos, though he thanks Garrick, Rawlinson, and Theobald for lending him a few. On the other hand, he used the Duodecimo edition of the *Poems* of 1640 to correct the bad Folio text of *The Gypsies Metamorphosed*.

Whalley printed from the Booksellers' edition of 1717. He had Theobald's copy, and quotes from time to time the conjectures written in the margin. He was helped by Seward and Sympson, the editors. of an edition of Beaumont and Fletcher commenced by Theobald, in which, says Dyce, 'the most unwarrantable liberties were taken with the text'. Whalley adopted for Jonson the system which they had used in Beaumont and Fletcher, and which excited the derision of Gifford. 'None of them', he says, 'printed from the earliest editions; they took up the latest which they could find, and went smoothly on till they were stopt by some palpable error of the press. This, as the clown says, was *meat and drink to them*; they immediately set themselves to conjecture what the word should be, and after a little burst of vanity, at which it is impossible to forbear a smile, they turned, for the first time, to the old copy, and invited the public to witness their sagacity, and partake in their triumph.' Whalley often quotes these ridiculous readings of the 1717 edition. In *Sejanus*, III. 387, for instance—'*Which never yet* DANGEROUS *bastard did* | *Upon his parent.*] The sense and measure are both defective; the first editions read *degenerous*, which, being right, I have admitted into the text.' In *The Alchemist*, v. i. 19, 20, Lovewit, who has left Face only his hangings and his bedding, says

> If he haue eate 'hem,
> A plague o' the moath, say I.

By a sheer misprint the 1717 text had 'mouth'. Of this Whalley says, 'Though the expression . . . may be admitted with some explanation, it is better, I think, to adopt the reading of the first folio, which gives us *moath*; as clothes laid up, and not used or aired, are apt to be eaten by those insects.' In *Prince Henry's Barriers*, 155, the Lady of the Lake summons the Prince, 'Come forth; your fostresse bids.' The 1717 text has 'Fortress': '*Fortress* is an error, and the true word *fostress* is given us by the folio editions. Mr. Sympson likewise saw the mistake, and ingeniously sent me *fautress* as his conjecture, which I should have made use of, had not the old books prevented me.' In *Oberon*, 445, the 1616 Folio reads '*the starre vanished*'; the 1640 Folio, printing from a reset page, copied its blunder by omitting '*the*'; the 1692 Folio, trying to correct this, printed '*straight vanished*'. Whalley, printing in his text '*strait vanished*', has a footnote, 'The folio of 1616 reads, and I think more correctly, the *star* vanished.' In *Epigram* xxxiii. 3, 4, Jonson, moved by Sir John Roe's death to think of his own, says

> And I, now,
> Breathe to expect my when, and make my how.

The reading of 1717, 'rather too ludicrous', says Whalley, is 'make my bow'. He conjectured 'how'—'And this, upon examination, I find is likewise the lection of the folio.'

Whalley corrected a number of obvious errors. He rearranged faulty verse, for instance in *Every Man in his Humour*, iv. viii. 141–3, and in *The Case is Altered*, ii. vi. 1–11, where he substituted '*Christophero*' for '*Christopher*'. As examples of his corrections we may quote *A Tale of a Tub*, ii. ii. 87, 'Some mile o' this Towne, [we] were set upon', where the pronoun had disappeared before the repeated 'we' of 'were'; 'gust' for 'guest', 'With' for 'Which', '*mutat*' for '*mutuat*', '*In minimo, mundus*' for '*En minimo*, mundus' in *The Case is Altered*, iii. iv. 31, v. 7, iv. ii. 24, v. xii. 39; 'a sauer i' the main' for 'i' the man' in *Epicoene*, iii. iii. 34; 'He that did liue in Oxford' for 'loue in Oxford' in *The New Inn*, i. v. 59; 'reparation' for 'reputation' and 'Vogue' for 'Rogue' in *The Magnetic Lady*, iii. iv. 21, v. iv. 1; 'lines' for 'liues' in *Love Freed from Ignorance and Folly*, 350; 'a *Colossus* of the companie' for 'a *Colossus*, the companie' in *Love Restored*, 131; 'fæces' for 'faces' in *Mercury*

Vindicated, 168; 'breath' for 'breadth' in *Pan's Anniversary*, 44; 'canore' for 'cauore', 'Corvus' for 'Cornus', 'Contemplatio dicta' for 'Contemplatio dicti' in *The Masque of Augurs*, 326 note '1', 350 note 'p', 336 note 'o'; 'offering' for 'offspring', 'bald' for 'bold' in *The Underwood*, xxii. 29, lxx. 68; the insertion of Benn's name, ibid. xxxiii. 6; and 'Eliot' for 'Cliot' in *Discoveries*, 903.

Whalley hoped to bring out a second edition and, with a view to this, left a revised copy behind him. After his death it passed to F. G. Waldron, the editor of *The Sad Shepherd*. Waldron intended to edit Jonson, but his edition entitled *The Works of Ben Jonson. Volume the first. Containing Every Man in his Humour. Every Man out of his Humour. . . . Printed for the Editor, and sold at no. 54, Drury-Lane. M, DCC, XCII.* got no farther than Act II, scene i, line 117 of the first play and, in this fragmentary form, was included in *The Literary Museum; or Ancient and Modern Repository*, a small collection of reprints in which it is incongruously placed. He incorporated and amplified Whalley's notes; Whalley's edition was reprinted by John Stockdale in 1811 in *The Dramatic Works of Ben Jonson, and Beaumont and Fletcher*, the latter from George Colman's text.

X

GIFFORD'S EDITION OF 1816

WILLIAM GIFFORD's edition marked an epoch in the history of Jonson's text. It is easy in an age when bibliography has reinforced textual criticism and scholarship has transformed our notions of the text of Shakespeare to indicate Gifford's weaknesses, but in his day he rendered a great service to Jonson's memory and revived an interest in his writing. Above all, he had profound sympathy with his author, and as the translator of Juvenal and editor of Massinger he had some obvious qualifications for his task. The edition appeared in 1816, with the title *The Works of Ben Jonson, in nine Volumes. With Notes critical and explanatory, and a biographical Memoir, By W. Gifford, Esq.* For motto he quoted the lines in *Jonsonus Virbius*, at that time attributed to Cleveland, 'The Muses' fairest light in no dark time'. The imprint was *London: Printed for G. and W. Nicol; F. C. and J. Rivington; Cadell and Davies; Longman and Co.; Lackington and Co.; R. H. Evans; J. Murray; J. Mawman; J. Cuthell; J. Black; Baldwin and Co.; Rodnell and Martin; and R. Saunders; By W. Bulmer and Co. Cleveland-row, St. James's. 1816.* The collation is—

Volume i. Portrait of Jonson, drawn by W. Behnes, engraved by J. Fittler, published July 9 1816 by R. H. Evans, Pall Mall, London. π1 recto, the title-page; π2 recto, the dedication to George Canning, dated July 3d, 1816; a–p⁸, q⁴, Memoirs of Ben Jonson; q5–8, r–s⁸, t², Proofs of Ben Jonson's Malignity, from the Commentators on Shakspeare; t3–8, u², Characters of Jonson; u3–8, x–y⁸, z², Ancient Commendatory Verses on Jonson; z3, 4, Portraits of Jonson, by Octavius Gilchrist; z5, autograph inscription in Jonson's gift-copy of *Sejanus* to Francis Crane; z6 recto, note on the preceding; z6 verso, errata. A³, B–K⁸, L⁶, *Every Man in his Humour.* Pages, 6 preliminary+ccclxii+162.

Volume ii. A1 recto, title-page; B2, C–P⁸, Q1 recto, *Every Man out of his Humour*; Q2 recto–8 verso, R–Bb⁸, Cc⁶, *Cynthia's Revels*; Cc7–8, Dd–Nn⁸, Oo², *The Poetaster.* Pages ii+551.

Volume iii. A1 recto, title-page; B–L⁸, M1 recto, *Sejanus*; M2–8, N–Y⁸, Z1 recto, *Volpone*; Z2 recto–8 verso, Aa–Ii⁸, Kk⁴, *Epicoene.* Pages ii+500.

Volume iv. A1 recto, title-page; B⁴, C–N⁸, O⁴, *The Alchemist*; O5–8, P–Z⁸, Aa⁶, *Catiline*; Aa7, 8, Bb–Mm⁸, Nn³ (misprinted N), *Bartholomew Fair.* Pages ii+542.

Volume v. A1 recto, title-page; B–I⁸, L⁷, *The Devil is an Ass*;

L8, M–U⁸, X⁴, *The Staple of News*; X5–8, Y–Ff⁸, Gg⁴, *The New Inn*. Pages ii+455.

Volume vi. A1 recto, title-page; B–I⁸, *The Magnetic Lady*; K–Q⁸, R1 recto, *A Tale of a Tub*; R2–8, S–U⁸, X², *The Sad Shepherd*; X3–7, *The Fall of Mortimer*; X8, Y–Dd⁸, Ee3, *The Case is Altered*; Ee4–Ll1, *Entertainments*. Pages ii+514.

Volume vii. A1 recto, title-page; B–Ff⁸, *Masques at Court*. Pages ii+447.

Volume viii. A1 recto, title-page; B–I⁸, L², *Masques, Love's Welcome at Welbeck, Love's Welcome at Bolsover*; L3–8, M–Q⁸, R⁴, *Epigrams*; R5–8, S–T⁸, U1 recto, *The Forest*; U2–8, X–Gg⁸, *Underwoods*. Pages ii+464.

Volume ix. A1 recto, title-page. B–F⁸, *Underwoods* (continued); G⁴, *Leges Convivales*; G5–8, H–K⁸, L1, 2 recto, *Translations from the Latin Poets*; L2 verso–8, M–Q⁸, R⁶, *Discoveries*; R7, 8, S–Y⁸, Z⁵, *The English Grammar*; Z6–8, Aa–Dd⁸, Ee², *Jonsonus Virbius*; Ee3–8, Ff⁴, Gg², *Glossarial Index*. Pages ii+444.

Cancels are found in the edition. In vol. ii, D3, pages 25 and 26 are pasted on to a stub, and page 25 is numbered '2' at the foot. In vol. iii, R3–5, pages 241–6 are similarly pasted on to the second of two stubs showing after R2; here both R3 recto and R4 recto are numbered '3' at the foot of the page. It looks as if R4 and R5 were cancelled first, and R4 numbered '3', and then it was found that R3 also had to be cancelled. In vol. iv the first two leaves of *Bartholomew Fair*, Aa7 and 8, pages 357–60, are pasted on to a stub; the half-title is numbered '4'. In the Bodleian copy of vol. v, S7, pages 269–70, which are not numbered, are clumsily pasted in between pages 256 and 257. In vol. vi, T3, pages 277–8 are pasted on to a stub and numbered '6'. There must have been some bad blunders in the printing which Gifford insisted on correcting. The numbers at the foot of the page seem to mark the cancels, though we have not found number '1'.

The text was set up from a copy of Whalley's edition. The Quartos and the Folios were collated, but not thoroughly: a number of errors derived from the editions of 1692 and 1716 remain uncorrected; but Gifford made a distinct advance on his predecessors. He modernized in order to increase the circle of Jonson's readers by making the text easier to follow. He marked the scene divisions on the modern system, put in scene locations and stage-directions. He preferred the modern forms, 'window', 'tyrant', 'venture', 'coach', to Jonson's 'windore', 'tyran', 'venter', 'carroch'; and when he found a phrase like 'is he made of' (that is, is he valued) 'at court?' (*E.M.O.* iv. iv. 73), he made it easier for the reader by writing, 'is he made much of?' Sometimes he misunderstood the original. 'A wench of a stoter' (*D. is A.* III. iii. 32) means 'a twopenny whore'; Gifford's note is, 'Either by accident or design Whalley reads *storer* for *stoter*, and I have retained his variation.' In *E.M.O.* III. ix. 38–40 Brisk says of his mistress, 'her braine's a very quiuer of iests! and she do's dart them abroad with that sweet loose, and iudiciall aime, that you would——'. 'Loose' is the noun, meaning 'discharge', but Gifford by printing 'with that sweet, loose, and judicial aim' reduced the text to nonsense. Sometimes he missed the old pronunciation: as in *Hymenaei*, 781, '(Like to beg'd *monopólies*) all their pride. . .'. Pronouncing 'monópolies', he wrote 'Most like to begg'd monopolies . . .'. In such passages he never stopped to think whether a printer, having in his copy 'Most' at the beginning of a line, would be likely to leave it out. He ruined the last line of the song in *Cynthia's Revels*, IV. iii. 242–53, '*O, that ioy so soone should waste*'—'*That I might dye, kissing*'—by printing 'That I might die with kissing'. Jonson commented in the context on the 'long *die*-note', and when reading the proof he inserted a comma after '*dye*' to emphasize this. In *A Tale of a Tub*, I. i. 77, 'A testie Clowne: but a tender Clowne, as wooll', we have an example of the fluid line of Jonson's later work; Gifford makes it 'A testy, but a tender clown as wool'. On the other hand, he continually fills out elisions and expands contracted words, so that he is quite inconsistent in the handling of metre. Thus, 'My heart is not so light, as 'twas i'the morning' (*T. of T.* II. v. 44) becomes 'My heart is not so light as it was in the morning', and 'Thou serv'st him rightly, *Hilts. Hil.* Ile seale az much' (ibid. IV. iii. 25) is even more unwarrantably 'Thou wilt serve him rightly, Hilts. *Hilts.* I'll seal to as much.'

In one point Gifford adopted the critical methods of his day— namely, to pick and choose between Quarto and Folio readings. He does this although he believes the Folio of 1616 to have been printed under Jonson's personal supervision. In the first scene of *Every Man in his Humour* the Quarto has 'Very good, sir.' (l. 5) and 'buzzard' (l. 59), where the Folio has 'well sir' and 'kite': Gifford takes the Quarto readings, remarking of the first, 'It signifies little which is taken, though it may be just necessary to note the variation', and of the second, 'I prefer this to *kite*, which is the reading of the folio'. In *Every Man out of his Humour*, v. xi. 32, Fastidius Briske affectedly calls Fallace 'this poore spinster'; Gifford follows the Quarto, 'this poor dame'. In *Sejanus*, IV. 93, he prefers the 'Lord Sejanus' of the Quarto to 'great Sejanus' of the Folio. In *Catiline*, I. 425, 'Differring hurts, where powers are so prepar'd', the Folio reading, he takes the Quarto 'where powers are most prepared', and in III. 729 the easier rhythm of the Quarto appeals to him, 'To strangle headstrong husbands' instead of 'To betray headie husbands', which the Folio substitutes.

Sometimes it is not clear whether an unauthorized reading is an emendation or simply careless writing or even a printer's blunder. The printer may be responsible for '' He is now the court-god' for ' He is the now court-god' in *Sejanus*, I. 203 ; and in *The New Inn*, III. ii. 101–2,

> Or, like to glasses, so their minds take in
> The formes of their beloved, and *then* reflect—

for '*them* reflect'. But in *E.M.I.* II. i. 37 'both' for 'but' is an emendation to avoid a second 'but' in the sentence. In *The Case is Altered*, v. i. 7, there is no authority for 'coying tricks' instead of 'wooing tricks', and in the *Discoveries*, 370–1, 'Nor is that speech of Zeno . . . to be passed over, *with* the note of ignorance' instead of '*without* the note of ignorance'.

Gifford's readings are rarely an improvement. In *The Devil is an Ass*, IV. vii. 54, he is probably right in reading 'Sous'd' for the 'Sou't' of the first edition; in the fragment of *Mortimer*, I. i. 31, he rightly read 'scale' for 'seale'. He corrected a number of blunders in the Latin notes to the masques: for instance, '*de plectendo*' in *The Coronation Entertainment*, 83 note 'a', where the early texts have '*deplectendo*', and '*horrore comarum*' for '*honore comarum*' in *The Masque of Augurs*, 286 note 'i'. Gifford's most attractive correction of the text was his conjecture in *Love Restored*, 85–6, 'I would not imitate so catholic a coxcomb as Coryat, and make a case of asses', where the 1616 Folio has 'and make a case: vses'. Unfortunately the original is past cure. Palaeographically there is no support for Gifford's brilliant guess.

The notes he supplied for the edition are a great improvement on Whalley's. He himself defined their scope: 'They are chiefly illustrative of obsolete phrases and customs, of personal and historical notices connected with the subject, together with such incidental touches on the characters and conduct of the respective pieces, as the occasion seemed to demand. There will also be found some explanatory remarks on the language of Shakspeare. . . .' The notes also elucidate many of Jonson's borrowings from the Greek and Roman classics. One other purpose of the edition was to vindicate Jonson's memory from the charge of being an enemy and a calumniator of Shakespeare ; Gifford pursues it till it becomes an obsession with him. In a note on *Epicoene*, IV. iv. 17–18, he expressly says that he entered upon the task of reprinting Jonson with this aim in view. 'If I cannot silence malice, I will at least shame it: if I cannot disencumber the pages of Shakspeare from the scurrility, and false-hood, with which they are disgraced, I will, at all events, show that nothing but the grossest stupidity can, in future, attend to them with decency and credit.' Hence a series of onslaughts on Shiels, Steevens, Chalmers, Malone, and—what is worse—on Dryden and Drummond. Dryden's offence was that he considered Jonson's verse-tribute to Shakespeare in the First Folio parsimonious; Drum-mond's, that he lured Jonson to his house on a pretence of hospitality merely in order to vilify him. Gifford pushed his vindication so far as to deny that the references to the 'Servant-monster' and the 'nest of Antiques' in the induction to *Bartholomew Fair* (ll. 127–8) referred to Shakespeare at all, but he cleared up a number of pas-sages in which Jonson was absurdly supposed to have penned a sneer at Shakespeare. One of the worst is in *The Case is Altered*, II. vii. 140–2, where Martino has broken Onion's head in a fencing-match and Juniper advises him 'go, get a white of an egge, and a little flax, and close the breach of the head, it is the most conducible thing that can be'. When a servant says in *King Lear*, III. vii. 105–6, 'I'll fetch some flax and whites of eggs To apply to his bleeding face', Steevens said this passage was ridiculed 'in the *Case is Altered*, 1609'. This was the date of publication, not of performance; *The Case is Altered* preceded *King Lear* by eight years or more, and, even if it had not preceded, this homely remedy was used by any housewife. 'The *ridicule*, therefore,' says Gifford, 'if any there be, (which assuredly there is not) is Shakspeare's.—But now comes Mr. Malone,—(who is much too just to fabricate dates, or to conceal them for a bad purpose, but whose hatred of Jonson is so excessive that he will consent to avail himself of the insinuation which he could not make,)—exposes Steevens's dishonesty with respect to the priority of *The Case is Altered*; but unwilling to lose a charge against Jonson, seeks to bolster up his crazy accusation by a supposition as full of malice, as the other is of falsehood. "The *sneer* at Shak-speare," he says, "though not originally there, might be introduced by Jonson between the appearance of *King Lear* and the publication of his own play."'

Epigram lvi 'On Poet-ape'—

> Poore POET-APE, that would be thought our chiefe,
>   Whose workes are eene the fripperie of wit, . . .
> At first he made low shifts, would picke and gleane,
>   Buy the reuersion of old playes; now growne
> To'a little wealth, and credit in the *scene*,
>   He takes vp all, makes each mans wit his owne,
>   And told of this, he slights it.—

is the occasion for a caustic note. 'Mr. Chalmers will *take it on his death* that the person here meant is Shakspeare! Who can doubt it? For my part, I am persuaded, that GROOM IDIOT in the next epigram is also Shakspeare; and, indeed, generally, that he is typified by the words "fool and knave", so exquisitely descriptive of him, wherever they occur in Jonson.'

Stephen Jones, 'a name utterly unworthy of notice, but as the booksellers have connected it with the drama'—he continued Baker's *Biographia Dramatica*—stated that all Jonson's masques were first printed in 1640. His ignorance of the Folio of 1616 provokes the comment: 'He could grovel in falsehood for the gratification of his senseless enmity to Jonson; but to open one of his volumes for the purpose of ascertaining the truth, appears to have been thought a mere loss of time' (vol. vii, p. 198).

The misstatements of Shakespeare's commentators are fair game, and an edition of Jonson is an appropriate place in which to expose them; but Gifford from time to time obtrudes his politics. Two objects of his savage attacks are Horace Walpole and the City of London. Walpole in his *Catalogue of the Royal and Noble Authors of England* had spoken with contempt of Jonson's patrons, the first Duke and Duchess of Newcastle, as a 'picture of foolish nobility', 'retired to their own little domain and intoxicating one another with circumstantial flattery. . .'. Says Gifford, 'Dead to every generous feeling, selfish, greedy, and sneakingly ostentatious, Walpole, in the midst of a baby-house, surrounded with a collection of childish trumpery, had the audacity to speak in this manner of a man, who, after strenuously fulfilling every duty of life, as a patriot, a soldier, and a statist, retired to his paternal seat, where he lived in the practice of a magnificent hospitality, the friend of genius, the liberal patron of worth, employing the close of an active and honourable life in innocent and elegant pursuits, which might benefit many, and could injure none' (vol. viii, p. 444). Walpole also attacked Lord Falkland, trying to refute Clarendon's noble character of him. Quoting Clarendon's tribute to his generosity, Gifford says, 'Walpole, who never bestowed a sixpence on any worthy object or person, and who continued, to extreme old age, to fumble with his gold, till his fingers, like those of Midas, grew encrusted with it, must have been greatly scandalized at this, and probably drew from it his shrewd conclusion that lord Falkland "had much debility of mind". To have done with this calumniator of true patriotism, loyalty and virtue—though gorged to the throat with sinecures, he was always railing at corruption, and indulging, with the low scribblers whose flattery he purchased with praise (for he gave nothing else, except the hope of a legacy, which he never intended to realize) in splenetic sneers at kings and courtiers: he called himself a republican, and uttered many grievous complaints of the loss of liberty, &c., and yet went crying out of the world because the French were putting his hopeful maxims of reform in practice' (vol. ix, pp. 6, 7).

The satire on Penyboy Senior's meanness in *The Staple of News*, II. iv. 99–101—

> Hee minds
> A curtesie no more, then *London*-bridge,
> What Arch was mended last—

provokes the comment: 'Two hundred years have nearly elapsed since this was written, and the observation still holds. This pernicious structure has wasted more money in perpetual repairs than would have sufficed to build a dozen safe and commodious bridges, and cost the lives, perhaps, of as many thousand people. This may seem little to those whom it concerns—but there is blood on the city; and a heavy account is before them. Had an alderman or a turtle been lost there, the nuisance would have been long since removed.' This note at least is relevant and illustrates a point in the text, but a tirade appended to a note on *The Entertainment at Althorp*, 262–3, digresses altogether from Hatton's house at Holmby to the Giants of Guildhall, because Corbett happened to have mentioned them together in his *Iter Boreale*: 'The Giants of Guildhall, thank heaven, yet defend their charge: it only remains to wish that the citizens may take example by the fate of Holmeby', which was destroyed in the Civil War, 'and not expose them to an attack to which they will assuredly be found unequal. It is not altogether owing to their wisdom that this has not already taken place. For twenty years they were chained to the car of a profligate buffoon', viz. John Wilkes, 'who dragged them through every species of ignominy to the verge of rebellion; and their Hall is even yet disgraced with the statue of a worthless negro-monger', viz. Beckford, 'in the act of insulting their sovereign with a speech, of which (factious and brutal as he was) he never uttered one syllable.' These are good examples of what Gifford calls in his preface 'the occasional warmth of my language'.

Gifford's notes stopped short at the end of his ninth volume. He left the *Discoveries* and *The English Grammar* alone. To the latter he was not a good enough philologist to contribute anything of value, especially as he reprinted from Whalley the version of 1692. But in the *Discoveries* we might have had a note of several pages on 'Would he had blotted a thousand', with a last torrent of invective against the calumniators. The edition of *Jonsonus Virbius*, with which the volume concluded, was edited by Octavius Gilchrist, who had already done pioneer work in exposing the untruth of Jonson's supposed enmity to Shakespeare in two pamphlets, *An Examination of the Charges maintained by Messrs. Malone, Chalmers, and others, of Ben Jonson's Enmity, &c. towards Shakespeare*, 1808, and *A Letter to William Gifford, Esq., on the late Edition of Ford's Plays; chiefly as relating to Ben Jonson*, 1811. Gifford explained his own failure to edit the two last pieces as a consequence of his being 'overwhelmed with affliction for an irreparable loss, and incapable of the slightest exertion'. The loss was the death on 6 February 1815 of his old servant Ann Davies, who had worked for him more than twenty years and who, according to Sir Walter Scott, used to sit with him in his study when he wrote (Lockhart, *Life of Scott*, 1838, vii, p. 23).

In 1838 Gifford's text, with such errors as 'vicious' for 'viscous' (*Alch.* II. iii. 145), was reprinted in a single volume with an introductory essay by 'Barry Cornwall' (B. W. Procter). But what was really a second edition of Gifford appeared in 1871, partially revised by Lieutenant-Colonel Francis Cunningham, in three volumes. It was published by John Camden Hotten, and taken over by Messrs. Chatto and Windus in 1872. In 1875 this editor also reprinted Gifford, 'with introduction and appendices', in nine handsome volumes printed at the Chiswick Press and published by Bickers and Sotheran. In the 1871 text Cunningham introduced a number of corrections and very occasionally supplied an additional note. But in the 1875 edition he reprinted Gifford's text exactly, and then pointed out its errors and added a fair number of supplementary notes in an appendix to each volume. Swinburne has commented severely upon this method, or want of method.[1] Cunningham in his editions of Elizabethan dramatists was never more than an amateur.

He added to the text a number of poems, in particular the fine *Ode ἀλληγορική* before Holland's *Pancharis* (*U.V.* vi) and the translation of Martial's *Vitam quae faciunt beatiorem* (*Und.* xc), and he set out clearly the Jonson pieces in the Newcastle MS., which Gifford had shuffled into a footnote. He printed the full version of the Drummond *Conversations*; Gifford had had them only from the summary in the Drummond Folio of 1711. He supplied new facts and documents about Jonson—the notices in the Edinburgh Archives of Jonson's visit in 1618, and the examination by the Attorney-General in 1629, and Jonson's appointment as City Chronologer. He discussed J. P. Collier's suggestion of an early date for *A Tale of a Tub*, and he added to the list of commendatory poems Francis Beaumont's letter to Jonson on the meetings at the Mermaid,

[1] *A Study of Ben Jonson*, p. 118.

inexcusably omitted by Gifford. Many of Cunningham's notes are
useful and suggestive. If all this new matter had been worked in
at the proper points in Gifford's text, and the errors of Gifford
excised, Cunningham would have ranked as an independent editor
rather than as a camp-follower of Gifford.

Cunningham's weakness betrays itself in the textual notes. He
frequently corrects Gifford's misreadings from a copy, first of the
1616, and secondly of the 1640, Folio, which he had collated. But
he did not know that each of these editions had been corrected while
passing through the press, and that sometimes the reading which he
condemns is to be found in a quarto. Thus in the argument of
Sejanus (ll. 17, 18) Jonson wrote originally '*the issue of* Germanicus
(*who were next in hope*)' and in the proof expanded this to '*next in
hope for the succession*'. Cunningham's note is 'Whalley was wrong
about these words. They are *not* in the folio 1616, but appear for
the first time in the folio 1640, which Whalley had before him'.
Similarly, in Act IV, ll. 434–5, Cunningham, not knowing of Jonson's
corrections in proof, imagined the added words, which he calls
'essential to the dialogue', to be an addition of the 1640 Folio. In
the *Speeches at Prince Henry's Barriers*, l. 210, Elizabeth with her
navy is described as 'The ayde, or feare of all the nations nigh'.
Cunningham comments, '"Nations *nigh*" is a sorry substitute for
"the nations *high*". When the editors made this sagacious change,
did they reflect on the poor compliment conveyed by the word they
substituted, as compared to the other?' The Folio reads 'nigh', but
the page in which the line is found, page 970, was reset, and it
was the printer who substituted 'high'. Similarly in *Love Restored*,
l. 82, 'I had beene mazarded' (page 991 in the First Folio), there
was also a resetting, and the blundering printer changed this to
'amazed'. Cunningham's note is, 'Here Gifford has quietly thrown
aside the folio of 1616, and followed that of 1640. In the former
the reading is, "I had been *amazed*", which is certainly feeble and
almost unmeaning, compared to the other. I suppose the correction
must have been derived from Jonson himself.' In the elegy on Lady
Pawlet (*Und.* lxxxiii. 71–2)—

> Speakes Heavens Language! and discourseth free
>   To every *Order*, ev'ry *Hierarchie*!—

the note is, '"I am not aware of Gifford's authority for the word
discourseth. . . . The folio has *discovereth*, and I have no doubt it is
right.' Gifford took the reading from the Quarto and Duodecimo
editions of the *Poems*, 1640, which print 'discourses', and the context shows clearly that he was right. How blurred Cunningham's

notions of textual criticism were is revealed in his note on *Volpone*,
III. iv. 5, 6, where Lady Would-be, complaining of her tire-women,
says 'I am drest Most fauourably, to day.': 'Upton may be right
in supposing that Lady W. is speaking ironically, but I think it
more likely that the printer is in error, a rare case in this 1616 folio
—*carelessly* would do or *shamefully*.' He excused himself for not
correcting the text of *The English Grammar* because of the 'want
of general interest in the subject'. He did not know that Whalley
and Gifford had reprinted the rewritten text of 1692. He supposed
that Gifford had done the rewriting, and, as our critical apparatus
shows, he would have had to fill pages with the corrections.

XI

EIGHTEENTH-CENTURY SELECTIONS

THE famous plays were frequently reprinted in the eighteenth century. Jacob Tonson led the way in 1709 with *Volpone, Epicoene,* and *The Alchemist* in quarto editions as they were 'acted at the Theatre Royal by Her Majesty's Servants'.

Four plays of Jonson, together with Shadwell's *Timon of Athens,* were printed in duodecimo and published by Henry Hills, junior, in 1710. They are *Epicoene, Volpone, Catiline, The Alchemist.* Each play has a separate title-page, undated, with the imprint ' *LONDON* : Printed and Sold by *H. Hills,* in *Black-Fryars,* near the *Water-side* '. Each play is separately paged, so that it could be sold by itself. The date is fixed by advertisements of *Epicoene* and *Volpone* in *The Post-boy,* 16 March $170\frac{9}{10}$, 'Just publish'd, Epicoene' . . . , 'This day is publish'd, Volpone . . .'. Further light is thrown on the publication by an advertisement in *The Evening Post,* 'From Saturday July 14 to Tuesday July 17, 1711'—'Five Plays by Mr. Congreve, pr. 3s. Four of Ben Jonson, and Timon of Athens, pr. bound 3s. Hudibras compleat with the Original Cuts, Annotations to the whole, and an Index, pr. in 1 Vol. 3s. Dr. Wellwood's Memoirs, pr. 2s. 6d. Sold by J. Baker at the Black Boy in Pater-Noster-Row.' Mr. P. J. Dobell had a copy with a title-page, in which unfortunately the imprint is defective: ' *Four Select Plays, viz., The Silent Woman;* *Volpone. or the Fox. Catiline's Conspiracy. The Alchemist. By Ben Johnson. To which is Added, Timon of Athens, or, The Man-Hater. By M^r. Shadwell. London:* Printed for J. Baker, at the ⟨Black Boy in⟩ Pater-Noster-Row. M⟨ .⟩' Henry Hills died in 1713, and Baker may have acquired his stock: in any case the plays were not originally printed for him. The collation is *Epicoene,* A–D¹², E,³ E4 blank, pages 1–102 ; *Volpone,* A⁷, B–D¹², E⁴, with E4 verso blank, pages 1–95 ; *Catiline,* A⁸, B–D¹², E⁴, pages 1–96 ; *The Alchemist,* A–B¹², C⁸, D¹², pages 1–96 ; *Timon,* A–C¹², D⁸, with D8 verso blank, pages 1–87.

Volpone, 'Printed for T. Johnson. In the Year 1714', was published at The Hague and included in *A Collection of the best English Plays,* vol. xii, small octavo, A–H⁶, 124 pages.

A duodecimo edition of selected plays was published at Dublin in 1729. *Ben. Johnson's Plays, Vol. I. Containing, Volpone; or, the Fox Catiline his Conspiracy Bartholomew Fair. Sejanus his Fall. Dublin: Printed by S. Powell, For George Risk, George Ewing, and William Smith, Booksellers in Dame's-street. MDCCXXIX.* The same imprint is in *Vol. 11. Containing Epicœne: or, the Silent Woman. Every Man in his Humour. Every Man out of his Humour. The Alchemist.* The names of forty-six subscribers are printed on a leaf following the general title-page. There are separate titles to each play, but, in order to save space, the scenes are not marked; thus 'ACT I. SCENE I' covers the whole act. The collation is: Volume I. *Volpone*, A–C¹², D⁹; *Catiline*, D10–12, E–G¹², H⁸; *Bartholomew Fair*, I⁴, K–N¹², O⁶; *Sejanus*, P–S¹². Pages iv+180. Volume II. *Epicoene*, A–D¹²; *Every Man in his Humour*, E–G¹², H⁸; *Every Man out of his Humour*, I–N¹², O⁸; *The Alchemist*, O12, P–R¹², S¹⁰. Pages vi+398.

In 1732 there appeared in duodecimo *The Three Celebrated Plays Of that Excellent Poet Ben Johnson. Viz. The Fox, a Comedy. The Alchymist, a Comedy. The Silent Woman, a Comedy. To which is added, A compleat Catalogue of all the Plays that were ever printed in the English Language, to the Year 1732. London, Printed for W. Feales at Rowe's Head, over-against Clement's-Inn Gate. Where may be had Variety of Plays.* The catalogue of plays is 'Continu'd down to *April* 1732'. The frontispiece is an engraving by J. Van der Gucht of the mountebank scene in *Volpone* with Celia dropping the handkerchief. The Catalogue was sold separately, 'Price 6d.'.

Each play has a title-page, separate signatures and pagination. The collation is—π recto blank, verso the engraved title-page; π2, the general title-page, with the verso blank. *Volpone*, A–D¹², pages 1–96; *The Alchemist*, A–D¹², pages 1–96; *Epicoene*, A–D¹², E², pages 1–100. Catalogue, A–C⁶, pages 1–36. On the last page is advertised *The English Theatre. In Three Parts.* running to twenty volumes. Part III, vol. iv, has *Volpone*, vol. v *Epicoene*, and vol. vi *The Alchemist*. All the plays 'may be had single'. These appear with the date '1732' and the imprint 'Printed for J. Walthoe, G. Conyers, J. Knapton, R. Knapton, D. Winter and A. Ward, A. Bettesworth and C. Hitch, B. Lintot, J. Tonson, W. Innys, J. Osborn and T. Longman, R. Robinson, T. Wotton and B. Motte: And sold by W. Feales, at Rowe's Head, over-against Clement's-Inn-Gate.' These plays were reissued in 1739 with the addition of *Bartholomew Fair*.

Another duodecimo appeared in 1738—*O Rare Ben Johnson! or, The Favourite and Celebrated Comedies Of that Excellent Poet Ben Johnson. viz. The Fox, The Alchymist, The Silent Woman; and Bartholomew Fair. The Whole Newly Corrected from the Errors of former Impressions. The Last never before Printed in a Pocket Edition. London: Printed and Sold by the Booksellers in Town and Country.* Undated, but the edition is advertised in *Common Sense: or, The*

Englishman's Journal, no. 92, 4 November 1738, as 'just publish'd, And sold by J. Torbuck, in Clare-Court, Drury-Lane'. 'Price 2s. 6d.' The frontispiece is a badly engraved bust of Jonson on a mural tablet. Each play is separately paged and signatured. The collation is: two preliminary leaves with frontispiece and general title-page; *Volpone* and *The Alchemist* each on A–D¹², 96 pages; *Bartholomew Fair*, A–D¹², E⁶, 108 pages.

Robert Urie, of Glasgow, published *Volpone*, *The Alchemist*, and *Epicoene* in octavo in 1752.

This century produced a number of acting versions and adaptations. Garrick's version of *Every Man in his Humour*, 'With Alterations and Additions. As it is Perform'd at the Theatre-Royal in Drury Lane', printed by J. and R. Tonson and S. Draper in 1752, may be said to have had a longer run with the booksellers than it had with the playgoers. Editions are recorded in 1755, 1759, 1761, 1765, 1774 (in Garrick's *Dramatic Works*), 1776, 1780, 1789, 1791, and 1797. *Bell's British Theatre, Consisting of the most esteemed English Plays*, and running finally to twenty-four volumes, 'Printed for John Bell, near Exeter Exchange, in the Strand, and C. Etherington, at York', contained *Every Man in his Humour*, Garrick's version, in vol. i, 1776, *The Alchemist* in vol. xvii, 1777, and *Volpone* in vol. xix, 1778; passages omitted in the theatre were marked with inverted commas, and insertions were printed in italic. The text is 'Regulated from the Prompt-Book, By Permission of the Manager', 'By Mr. Hopkins, Prompter' for the first two plays, 'By Mr. Wild, Prompter' for the third. As late as 1808 this version was reproduced 'With remarks by Mrs. Inchbald'. A curious pendant to these— presumably pirated—is an American edition, giving the text 'as performed at the Theatres Covent-Garden, New-York, Philadelphia and Boston', published at New York by D. Longworth 'at the Dramatic Repository, Shakespeare-Gallery, Feb.—1811'.

After Garrick the most important stage-editor was George Colman, who adapted *Epicoene* and published it in 1776 'As it is Acted at the Theatre Royal in Drury-Lane'; it was 'Printed for T. Becket, Corner of the Adelphi, Strand'.

Freer adaptations were made by Francis Gentleman of *Sejanus* in 1752 and of *The Alchemist* in 1771. Garrick refused to act this hotch-potch of *Sejanus*, in which Tiberius stopped at Rome to preside at the conviction of Sejanus and made a pious speech at the end of it, promising to redress his cruelties, thus preserving poetic justice, to which 'History should give way'. But *The Alchemist* was altered to a farce in two acts and renamed *The Tobacconist*, of which there was an edition in 1771, reprinted in 1815, 1821, and 1824.

The opera also went briskly to work at Jonson. In 1771 there was *The Fairy Prince: A Masque as it is performed at The Theatre-Royal in Covent-Garden. London: Printed for T. Becket, in the Strand: Bookseller to Their Royal Highnesses the Prince of Wales and Bishop of Osnaburgh.* This was an adaptation by George Colman, who in 1772 altered *Comus* for Covent Garden. The Jonson portion is from *Oberon,* with scraps from other masques. The second part has the scene at Windsor Castle, with a procession of the King and the Knights of the Garter, and ends with a chorus from Dryden and a dance of fairies. In 1774, and running into three editions, appeared *Airs, Duets, Chorusses, &c. In the new masque called the Druids. As performed at the Theatre-Royal, Covent-Garden. The words chiefly taken from Ben Jonson; the music composed by Mr. Fisher. London: printed for T. Evans, near York-Buildings, Strand.*

XII
LATER TEXTS

BEFORE Gifford's edition of 1816 Sir Walter Scott brought out in *Modern British Drama The Alchemist*, 1804, and *Volpone*, 1811. Similar collections since have rung the changes on the famous plays. Thus *The Alchemist, Epicoene*, and *Every Man in his Humour* appeared in J. S. Keltie's *The Works of the British Dramatists*, 1870; *The Alchemist, Volpone*, and *Epicoene* in Henry Morley's *Plays and Poems of Ben Jonson*, 1885. In the Mermaid Series of *The Best Plays of the Old Dramatists*, 1893–5, with an introduction by C. H. Herford, Brinsley Nicholson prepared the first volume containing *Every Man in* and *Every Man out of his Humour*, and *Poetaster*, but died before it appeared; the second and third volumes reproduced without acknowledgement Gifford's text and introductions to *Bartholomew Fair, Cynthia's Revels, Sejanus, Volpone, Epicoene*, and *The Alchemist*. *The Chief Elizabethan Dramatists*, 1911, edited by W. A. Neilson, had *Every Man in his Humour, Sejanus, Volpone*, and *The Alchemist*; the second volume of C. M. Gayley's *Representative English Comedies*, 1913, had *Every Man in his Humour*, edited by C. H. Herford, *Epicoene*, edited by C. M. Gayley, and *The Alchemist*, edited by G. A. Smithson; *Masterpieces of the English Drama*, 1915, edited by Ernest Rhys, had *Every Man in his Humour, Volpone, Epicoene*, and *The Alchemist*; *Typical Elizabethan Plays*, 1926, edited by F. E. Schelling, had *Volpone, The Hue and Cry after Cupid* [i.e. *The Haddington Masque*], and *The Sad Shepherd*; *Great English Plays*, 1928, edited by H. F. Rubinstein, had *Epicoene*. *Shakespeare and his Fellow Dramatists*, 1929, edited by E. H. C. Oliphant, had *Volpone, The Alchemist*, and *Bartholomew Fair*; *Eight Famous Elizabethan Plays*, 1932, edited by E. C. Dunn, had *Volpone*; *English Drama 1580–1642*, 1933, edited by C. F. Tucker Brooke and N. B. Paradise, had *Every Man in his Humour, Volpone, Epicoene*, and *The Gypsies Metamorphosed*; *Elizabethan Plays*, 1933, edited by Haselton Spenser, had *Every Man in his Humour, Volpone, The Alchemist, Bartholomew Fair*, and *Eastward Ho*; *Ben Jonson, Selected Works*, 1939, edited by H. Levin, viz. *Sejanus, Volpone, Epicoene, The Alchemist, Every Man in his Humour, Bartholomew Fair*, the masques of *Oberon, The Vision of Delight, The Fortunate Isles*, followed by an anthology of verse and criticism.

There are many editions of separate plays. The chief are—*Every Man in his Humour*, edited by H. B. Wheatley, 1877, by W. M. Dixon, 1896, by P. Simpson, 1919; *Poetaster*, edited by J. H. Penni-

man, together with Dekker's *Satiro-mastix*, 1913; *Sejanus*, edited
by W. D. Briggs, 1911; *Volpone*, the Quarto text edited by V.
O'Sullivan, 1898, with the drawings of Aubrey Beardsley; the Folio
text edited by H. B. Wilkins, a Paris dissertation, 1906; *The
Alchemist*, edited by H. C. Hart, 1903, by F. E. Schelling together
with *Eastward Ho*, 1909. *The Sad Shepherd* was edited in the Cambridge Plain Texts by L. J. Potts in 1929. Carl Grabau issued in
the *Shakespeare-Jahrbuch*, 1902, vol. xxxviii, a reprint of the Quarto
of *Every Man in his Humour*, and the Noel Douglas Replicas issued
a facsimile of the Quarto of *The Alchemist* in 1927.

The only complete text of the plays which has been issued of late
years is that in the 'Everyman Library', 1910, with an introduction
by F. E. Schelling; it includes the Quarto version of *Every Man in
his Humour*, but the text is a lax reprint of Gifford. H. C. Hart
began an edition in Methuen's 'Standard Library' in 1906, but owing
to his death it got no farther than *Poetaster*. What is virtually an
edition of the plays is contained in the *Yale Studies in English* issued
play by play from 1903 to 1917; these are noticed in our textual
introductions. The plays not included in the series are *Every Man
out of his Humour*, *Sejanus*, and *A Tale of a Tub*, but this last,
edited by Dr. F. M. Snell, was published by Longmans, Green & Co.
in 1915. These editions are doctorate theses and vary in quality.
Dr. A. C. Judson's edition of *Cynthia's Revels*, 1912, has a scholarly
discussion of the variants in the text of the 1616 Folio and is excep-
tionally good. Dr. H. H. Carter's edition of *Every Man in his
Humour*, 1921, reproduces on opposite pages very accurate texts
of the Quarto and the Folio. Dr. H. S. Mallory's edition of *Poetaster*,
1905, and Dr. W. E. Selin's edition of *The Case is Altered*, 1917, are
also trustworthy texts.

What would have been an outstanding edition came to an untimely
end—Professor W. von Bang's careful type-facsimile of the 1616
Folio at Louvain in his series *Materialen zur Kunde des älteren
englischen Drama*, Band vii: two parts appeared in 1905 and 1908,
taking the reprint up to page 552 of the Folio at the opening of the
third Act of *Epicoene*. The Germans burnt what was left of the stock
when they destroyed Louvain in 1914. In the same series Bang also
issued scholarly reprints of four Jonson Quartos: *Every Man in his
Humour*, x, 1905; *Every Man out of his Humour* 'from Holme's
Quarto of 1600'—the second Quarto—xvi, 1907, and the third
Quarto, 'from Linge's Quarto of 1600', xvii, 1907, edited by W. Bang
and W. W. Greg; *Cynthia's Revels*, xxii, 1908, edited by W. Bang
and L. Krebs. Two plays were reprinted from the Folio of 1640:
The Sad Shepherd, with Waldron's continuation, xi, 1905, edited

by W. W. Greg; and *A Tale of a Tub*, xxix, 1913, edited by H. Scherer.

The series was revived by Professor H. de Vocht. He edited *Poetaster*, ix, 1934; *Sejanus*, xi, 1935; *Volpone*, xiii, 1937; and published *Comments on the Text of Ben Jonson's Every Man out of his Humour*, xiv, 1937. These volumes have already been discussed.[1] His texts are accurate—as accurate as his theories about them are fantastic.

When Bang's original series appeared, Holme's First Quarto of *Every Man out of his Humour* had not been identified. A copy had lurked unrecognized in the British Museum. This was reprinted for the Malone Society, 1921, in a type-facsimile edited by F. P. Wilson and W. W. Greg.

Jonson's masques and entertainments were reproduced in their historic setting and carefully annotated by the antiquary John Nichols in *The Progresses, Processions and Magnificent Festivities of King James the First* (4 vols., 1828). Henry Morley's *Masques and Entertainments of Ben Jonson*, 1890, reprinted all but the entertainments at Welbeck and Bolsover and the Cavendish entertainment at the Blackfriars. H. A. Evans's *English Masques* in 'The Warwick Library', 1897, was mainly a Jonson reprint; it included *The Haddington Masque, The Masque of Queens, Oberon, The Golden Age Restored, Lovers made Men, News of the New World discovered in the Moon, The Masque of Augurs, Pan's Anniversary, Neptune's Triumph for the Return of Albion*, and *The Fortunate Isles*. Peter Cunningham's *Life of Inigo Jones*, printed for the Shakespeare Society, 1848, printed what he fondly believed to be a type-facsimile of the holograph of *The Masque of Queens* and the British Museum manuscript of *The Masque of Blackness. The Masque of Queens* was beautifully reproduced by the King's Printers in 1930, with an introductory note by Guy Chapman and with reproductions of Inigo Jones's drawings for this masque. *The Gypsies Metamorphosed* was reproduced in facsimile from the Heber-Huntington manuscript by G. Watson Cole, who fully discussed its relation to the Duodecimo and Folio texts of 1640; it was published by the Century Company for the Modern Language Association of America in 1931.

The poems which were printed in the Folios, *Epigrams, The Forest*, and *The Underwood*, were, of course, included in the two great collections of Robert Anderson, *Works of the British Poets*, Edinburgh, 1793, vol. iv, and Alexander Chalmers's *The Works of the English Poets*, 1810, vol. v. They were edited with a memoir and notes by Robert Bell in 1856.

<hr>

[1] See pp. 74–84.

In 1936 they were edited by B. H. Newdigate, who added the loose pieces not found in the collected texts of 1616 and 1640 and an anthology of the songs in the plays. A facsimile of the Folio texts of the *Epigrams*, *The Forest*, and *The Underwood*, with a bibliographical note by H. H. Hudson, was published by the Columbia University Press for the Facsimile Text Society in 1936. *The Underwood* was printed, not very correctly, in type-facsimile by the Cambridge University Press in 1905. Jonson's earlier version of Horace's *Art of Poetry* was included in E. H. Blakeney's edition and translation of the *Ars Poetica* published by the Scholartis Press in 1928.

Miss A. V. Waite edited *The English Grammar* in 1909. A more scholarly edition is Strickland Gibson's, beautifully printed by Stanley Morison at the Lanston Monotype Press in 1928; a collation of the 1692 revision was included.

The Discoveries, which, after Swinburne's praise of them, were regarded at the time as a literary revelation, went through a number of editions. Henry Morley issued them at once in Cassell's National Library, volume 169. F. E. Schelling was the first to produce a well-annotated edition in 1892; he was followed by Sir Israel Gollancz in the Temple Classics edition of 1898. A further advance was made in 1906, when Maurice Castelain published 'a critical edition with an introduction and notes on the true purport and genesis of the book', tracing the source of most of the sections. G. B. Harrison in 1923 issued a type-facsimile, no. 5 in the Bodley Head Quartos, to which he appended the *Drummond Conversations*.

In 1932 H. L. Ford published a bibliographical pamphlet, *Collation of the Ben Jonson Folios 1616–31–1640*.

In 1938 Dr. S. A. Tannenbaum issued *Ben Jonson* (*A Concise Bibliography*), the second volume of a series of Elizabethan Bibliographies, which is a careful and well-arranged record of Jonson's work.

Altogether, the work of the last fifty years has made a sounder approach to the study of Jonson and yielded a clearer interpretation of it. We hope in the commentary which follows to profit by the labours of our predecessors and to round off their research.

THE STAGE HISTORY
OF THE PLAYS

A TALE OF A TUB

THIS play was licensed to Queen Henrietta's men on 7 May 1633 and produced at the Cockpit. There was a performance at Court, where it was 'not likt', on 14 January 1634.[1] There is no record of any further performance. The failure of such a piece at Court at that date is intelligible. It was a theme of rustic homespun told in an archaic manner; the love-making was crude and the heroine without a vestige of romance. The other plays acted at Court in the same month were *Cymbeline* and *The Winter's Tale*, both of which were 'likt'; Fletcher's *The Faithful Sheperdess* and *The Night Walker*, the former brilliantly mounted, the latter 'Likt as a merry play'; Massinger's *The Guardian*, 'well likte'; and Davenant's *The Wits*, of which 'the kinge commended the language, but dislikt the plott and characters'.[2] Whatever the critical standard at Court may have been, Jonson was both out of favour and out of fashion.

Herbert had licensed the play on condition that 'Vitru Hoop's parte'[3] should be 'wholly struck out, and the motion of the tubb'; so the Lord Chamberlain had directed because of a complaint of Inigo Jones that the part and the motion were 'a personal injury unto him'.

In the version which has come down to us Vitruvius Hoop has disappeared, except for an incidental reference,[4] but he is replaced by the Islington cooper, In-and-In Medlay, who certainly gives us a Motion of a Tub; however, it is a harmless epitome of the five acts of the play in a puppet-show of five scenes. The satire on Inigo Jones is limited to depicting him as the puppet-master, a counterpart of Lanthorn Leatherhead in *Bartholomew Fair*, and far more insipid.

Was this the text that finally satisfied (or evaded) the requirements of the censor? and was it acted at the Cockpit and at Court? We think it was, though we have to face the possibility that, after the play was done with, Jonson recast it in a form suitable for publication. But there is one slight piece of external evidence which supports our view that in the Folio text we have the acting version.

---

[1] See vol. iii, p. 3, for the quotations from Herbert's Office Book. His fee of £2 was perhaps of a penal character; he levied this charge on *The Duchess of Suffolk* in 1624, 'which being full of dangerous matter was much reformed by me; I had two pounds for my pains' (quoted in Chalmers's *Supplementary Apology*, p. 217). Herbert's usual fee at this date for a revived play was £1.
[2] See Malone, *Variorum Shakespeare*, vol. iii, pp. 234–6.
[3] 'Vitru.' is the short form of 'Vitruvius' used in the speech headings.
[4] See v. ii. 71–3.

Chapman, writing on his death-bed in 1634 an 'Invective' against Jonson, gibed at the losses of his fire and advised him—

> Some pore thinge wright new; a Riche Caskett Ben
> All of riche Jems t'adorne most learnèd men
> or a Reclaime of most facete Supposes
> To teach full-habited men to blowe their noses
> make the king merrie.[1]

What was this 'reclaim of most facete Supposes'—a 'poor thing' originally—which Jonson was advised to rewrite? 'Reclaim' implies recovery or re-use of something which had been laid aside; 'most facete' suggests that it was a comedy; 'Supposes' is a side-glance at the actual title of *A Tale of a Tub*. 'To teach full-habited men to blow their noses'—a variation of 'to teach your grandmother to suck eggs'—means 'to teach a fully equipped artist the ABC of his art'. In this obscure way, thoroughly characteristic of Chapman, the figure of Inigo Jones emerges dimly from the involved irony.[2] It suggests that the Motion of the Tub in the form in which it was printed in 1640 was known to Chapman in 1634. This could only be the stage version, and Chapman's final gibe—'Make the king merry'—further suggests that it was played at Court as well as at the Cockpit.

It is unlikely that this was the version of which Inigo complained. Unlikely, because for Jonson to have persisted in it would have been an open defiance of the Master of the Revels which Herbert would not have tolerated. We are driven to infer that Inigo Jones complained of something that went much deeper than the superficial satire of the extant version. The catchwords 'feasible' and 'conduce', the bad Latin 'to *infinito*', the puppets mounted on an old saltpetre tub as the nearest approach he could make to the antique, even the egotism that refused to work with a collaborator—

> But I must be alone then, joyn'd with no man—[3]

were at most the petty failings of a famous man hardly calling for the august intervention of the Lord Chamberlain when anyone made jokes about them. But, according to Drummond, Jonson told King Charles the First 'that when he wanted words to express the greatest Villaine jn ye world he would call him ane Inigo'.[4] With such a conception of his opponent, it was dangerous for Jonson to attempt a satirical portrait, and he may easily have produced something which goaded Inigo to action.

---

[1] Ashmole MS. 38, p. 17.
[2] See the full treatment of the question in Appendix XXIV, 'Jonson, Chapman, and Inigo Jones', added to the commentary on the Masques.
[3] Act v, scene vii, l. 14.   [4] *Conv.* xvii. 468–9.

Changes made by Jonson to meet the requirements of the censor stand out clearly in the extant text. Squire Tub's reference to Vitruvius Hoop in Act v, scene ii, lines 71–3—

> Spare for no cost, either in bonds, or hoops,
> To architect your Tub: Ha' you nere a Cooper
> At *London* call'd *Vitruvius*? send for him.—

is evidently a blind: it means, 'Observe, no Vitruvius Hoop come to Finsbury; he is a minor architect in London.' Whether he appeared early in the original text, hobnobbing with his classically named associates, Diogenes Scriben, To-Pan, and Rasis Clench, or made a triumphal entry at the end to architect the tub, cannot be determined now; the allusion in the text suggests the latter alternative. But, when the part had to be cancelled, Jonson turned for a substitute to the joiner, In-and-In Medlay, who is depicted as a particularly shallow and stupid character. It is he who suggests that Saint Valentine was 'a deadly *Zin*, and dwelt at *High-gate*' (I. ii. 7); he tells the blustering Hilts that he 'must' obey the Queen's officers, and when Hilts snorts 'Why must I?' he replies 'You must, an' you wull' (II. ii. 34); when Clay is advised to tell the truth if he has really done the robbery, Medlay says 'Speake man, but doe not convesse, nor be avraid' (ibid. 141); and it is he who transforms 'dictator' to 'Dick: Tator' (III. vi. 22). It showed a petty spite to single out this dolt as a medium through which to satirize the brilliant architect.

Before he was forced to take on new duties, Medlay was a joiner (v. ii. 14, 32, 36, 61). He is to put a carved panel over Turfe's chimney-piece (III. vi. 8–10). When they are choosing topical tunes for Rosin the fiddler to play at the wedding—'Tom Tiler' for the tileman Clay, 'The Jovial Tinker' for To-Pan—Medlay calls for 'The Jolly Joyner, for mine owne sake' (I. iv. 41). And he remains a joiner even in the interpolated or 'interloping' scene of the fourth Act, suitably named In-and-In by his father, the weaver In-and-In Shittle

>   bycause that wee doe lay
> Things in and in, in our worke.

Further, this fits in with the satire on Inigo's desire to monopolize any task on which he was engaged:

> Hee'll do't alone Sir, He will joyne with no man,
> Though he be a Joyner: in designe he cals it,
> He must be sole Inventer: *In-and-In*
> Drawes with no other in's project, hee'll tell you.
> (v. ii. 35–8.)

But elsewhere he becomes 'In-and-In Medlay, Of Islington, Cooper' as he is described in the list of characters before the play (I. i. 36, ii. 10). And the change to coopering was necessitated by his having to make a tub.

Jonson in his haste to patch up the play did not clear up this confusion; he even added to it, as we see, in the 'interloping' scene where he comes to close quarters with Inigo, elevating In-and-In Medlay to the status of '*Architectonicus professor*'. This scene, together with the performance of the Motion, is Jonson's final addition to the text.

Another clue to the rewriting is furnished by 'Diogenes' Scriben: why 'Diogenes'? His ramshackle explanation that he was a descendant of the Greek cynic (IV, the scene interloping, 26–35) takes us nowhere. But the question propounded in V. ii. 34, 'who shall write' the masque? answered by Hilts, '*Scriben*, the great Writer', suggests that he wrote the original motion of the Tub. This gives him a real kinship with Diogenes. Though here and in the dramatis personae he is called 'the Great Writer', he does nothing in the extant play to justify this description. His one effort of the kind is fathered on Inigo in the revision.

THE CASE IS ALTERED

THE title-page of the 1609 Quarto professes to print the play 'As it hath been sundry times acted by the Children of the Blackfriars'. The company did not take this title till about 1606.[1] When formed in 1600, it was 'the Children of Queen Elizabeth's Chapel', and after 1603 it was for a time 'the Children of her Majesty's Revels'. When did this company produce *The Case is Altered*?

We have given 1598 as a probable date for the composition of the play,[2] and it must have been early in the year. Nashe's reference in *Lenten Stuffe*, 1599 (*Works*, ed. McKerrow, iii, p. 220), to Juniper as the 'merry cobler . . . in that witty Play of *the Case is altered*' suggests not only that the play had made a hit but also that it was still fresh in the memory of the playgoer; *Lenten Stuffe* was entered in the Stationers' Register on 11 January in that year. But the play which has come down to us shows clear signs of interpolation, which can only have been made for a revival. In the second scene of the play the portrait of Antonio Balladino, who appears here only in order to satirize himself, is an afterthought. Its sole purpose was

---

[1] E. K. Chambers, *The Elizabethan Stage*, ii, pp. 52–3.
[2] Vol. i, pp. 305, 325.

to enable Jonson to relieve his feelings about Antony Munday, especially after Meres in *Palladis Tamia*, registered on 7 September 1598, had ludicrously overestimated his skill in plot-making: 'you are in print already for the best plotter', says Onion. The sting lies in the word 'already': 'A good start, but you will go far.' The only suggestion of a link with the plot is Juniper's request that Balladino will help Onion in his love-making by writing for him 'some pretty paradox or some allegory' to send his wench; but Jonson omitted to alter a later reference (IV. v. 32–9) in which it is clear that originally Valentine was to have performed this office for Onion.

In a private letter to us Mr. W. J. Lawrence suggested that the criticism of the contemporary English theatre in Act II, scene vii, lines 26–82, was a further interpolation. Valentine talks of 'the publicke *Theater*' and 'the common *Theaters*' (ll. 26, 40). Now, the actual terminology of public and private theatres does not emerge before the revival of the boy companies in 1599 and 1600. Thus we find *Cynthia's Revels* and *Poetaster* described on the Quarto title-pages as 'Sundry times privately acted in the Blackfriars by the Children of her Majesty's Chapel'. Further, Balladino (scene ii, 75–6) prefers writing 'for the peny, I care not for the Gentlemen I, let me have a good ground'—as distinct from the roofed theatre with its higher prices. And his satire that you 'haue some now (as, for example, in plaies) that will . . . write you nothing but humours' (ibid. 60–2) could not have been written before 1600 at the earliest when the vogue of the Humour Play had begun.

These interpolations obtrude an alien note into the play. They are satire, and they are in keeping with the hardening of Jonson's style after he had quitted his early romantic writing. And of course they have not the remotest bearing on the plot.

The play was acted at Chicago University at the Auditorium Playhouse on 17 May 1902. An acting-copy with a revised text was published, and a souvenir volume with illustrations of some of the characters. The principal actors were W. A. Averill, Count Ferneze; E. T. Robertson, Paulo Ferneze; E. Goettsch, Camillo; A. P. Solberg, Maximilian; C. G. Larsen, Angelo; D. A. R. Robertson, Jacques de Prie; W. J. Sherman, Christophero; H. Woodhead, Onion; H. J. Lurie, Juniper. The female parts were taken by men, Aurelia by Herbert Mellinger, Phoenixella by Frederick Bramhall, and Rachel de Prie by John Weddell.

The only modern performance in England was at Birkbeck College on 12 and 13 December 1924.

EVERY MAN IN HIS HUMOUR

Every Man in his Humour was first acted in the autumn of 1598
by the Chamberlain's men who were then playing at the Curtain
theatre in Shoreditch. The Quarto title-page speaks of performances
being given 'Sundry times'. A letter of Tobie Mathew to Dudley
Carleton on 20 September, preserved among the Domestic State
Papers,[1] gives one date, evidently an early one, precisely. Mathew
describes a French visitor at Nonesuch, well received in Court
circles: 'There were with him divers Almans, where of, one, lost out
of his purse, at a play 3 hundred crownes. A new play called, Euery
mans humour.' The reference to repeated performances implies a
theatrical success. This was the tradition with regard to this comedy.
Aubrey records that, after previous failures at the Curtain, Jonson
'vndertooke againe to write a Playe and hitt it admirably well, viz.
Every man . . . wch was his first good one'.[2] Dryden says the same
in the *Essay of Dramatic Poesy*.[3]

At the end of all plays in the 1616 Folio Jonson appended a list
of the principal actors. In *Every Man in his Humour* Shakespeare
heads the list. The prominence thus given to him has suggested
that he played the part of the elder Kno'well.[4] There is also a tradition that, when the manuscript was on the point of being rejected
at the playhouse, Shakespeare intervened in its favour and got it
accepted. Rowe, in the account of Shakespeare prefixed to his edition of 1709, has preserved the tradition for us in a report which is
clearly open to criticism. There is exaggeration in the statement
that Jonson 'was at that time altogether unknown to the world',
and in the picturesque account of the people at the playhouse
turning the manuscript over 'carelessly and superciliously', and
Shakespeare 'luckily casting his eye upon it'. But the main fact
may be true.

Dr. T. W. Baldwin in *The Organization and Personnel of the Shake-
sperean Company*, appendix viii, has attempted to apportion the
parts in the Jonson plays which they acted. Combining these with
their possible parts in Shakespeare plays, he infers what was likely
to suit each individual actor. He distributes the ten actors named
by Jonson as follows: Shakespeare, the elder Kno'well; Burbage,

---

[1] Elizabeth cclxviii. 61.
[2] Aubrey MS. 8, f. 108. Aubrey left a blank because he was not sure which
of the humour plays was referred to.
[3] *Essays*, ed. Ker, vol. i, p. 81.
[4] First suggested by Thomas Davies, *Dramatic Miscellanies*, 1785, vol. ii,
p. 56.

Brainworm; Cob, Kemp (three very probable assignments); Phillips, Kitely; Pope, Bobadill; Heminges, Clement; Sly, Downright; Condell, Wellbred; Beeston, the younger Kno'well; Duke, Matthew. For Stephen he suggests Cowley, whom Jonson does not name. There is no clue to the actors of the women's parts, who would be boys.

The play was revived at Court by the King's men on 2 February 1605. In 'The Accompte of the Office of the Revelles of the whole years Charges in An°. 1604' (A.O. 3/908/13), dated 1605 'By his Maties Plaiers': of 'On Candlemas night. A playe Euery on In his Vmor'. It is for this revival that Sir E. K. Chambers believes the revised version to have been made.[1] Though we place the revision later, Sir Edmund's date has much to recommend it. Seven years had passed since the first performance, and Jonson had produced four comedies in that interval; the revision, whenever it was made, brought *Every Man in his Humour* into line with his later work. The one thing certain is that it was revised in the period of Jonson's dramatic mastery. Sir Edmund places it before *Volpone*; we ourselves favour a date near to *The Alchemist*.

In 1631 the King's men gave the play as a benefit performance for Sir Henry Herbert, the Master of the Revels; occupying the Globe in the summer and the Blackfriars in the winter, they gave him the benefit of two performances every year. The entry in his office book is: 'Received of Mr. Taylor and Lowins, in the name of their company, for the benefit of my winter day, upon the second day of Ben Jonson's play of Every Man in his Humour, this 18 day of February, 1630—12*l*. 4*s*. 0*d*.'[2] Under the date of 17 February the play is entered in a list of the year's plays in MS. 2068. 8 of the Folger Shakespeare Library.[3]

The play was revived at the Restoration. Killigrew's company acted it occasionally at the Theatre Royal in Drury Lane after they received their patent on 7 May 1663.[4] Along with *Catiline, Bartholomew Fair, The Devil is an Ass, Every Man out of his Humour*, and *Sejanus*, it was an 'Old Stock Play'. It was allotted to the company in January 1669. It was produced before 1673 when the epilogue written for it by Charles Sackville, Earl of Dorset, was printed in *A Collection of Poems Written upon several Occasions By several Persons*, 1673, pages 29–32. This was again printed in the Earl of Dorset's *Poems upon several occasions*, 1675, page 29.

---

[1] *Elizabethan Stage*, iii, p. 360.
[2] Malone, *Variorum Shakespeare*, iii, p. 177.
[3] First printed by G. E. Bentley, *The Jacobean and Caroline Stage*, i, p. 28.
[4] Downes, *Roscius Anglicanus*, 1708, pp. 8, 9.

EPILOGUE[1]

To every Man in his humour.

INtreaty shall not serve nor violence,
To make me speak in such a Playes defence.
A play where Wit and Humour do agree
To break all practis'd Laws of *Comedy*:
The Scene (what more absurd) in *England* lies,
No Gods descend, nor dancing Devils rise;
No captive Prince from nameless Country brought,
No battel, nay, there's not a duel fought.
And something yet more sharply might be said,
But I consider the poor Author's dead;
Let that be his excuse— Now for our own,
Why— Faith, in my opinion, we need none.
The parts were fitted well; but some will say,
Pox on 'em Rogues, what made 'em chuse this Play?
I do not doubt but you will credit me,
It was not choice, but meer necessity;
To all our writing friends, in Town, we sent,
But not a Wit durst venture out in *Lent*;
Have patience but till *Easter*-Term, and then
You shall have Jigg and Hobby-horse agen.
Here's Mr. *Matthew*, our domestique Wit,
Does promise one of the ten Plays h'as writ;
But since great bribes weigh nothing with the just,
Know, we have merits, and in them we trust
When any Fasts, or Holy-days, defer
The publick labours of the *Theatre*,
We ride not forth, although the day be fair,
On ambling Tit to take the Suburb-air,
But with our Authors meet, and spend that time
To make up quarrels between sence and rhyme.
Wednesdays and *Fridays* constantly we sate
Till after many a long and free debate,
For divers weighty reasons 'twas thought fit
Unruly sence shu'd still to rhyme submit.
This the most wholesom Law we ever made.
So strictly in this *Epilogue* obey'd,
Sure no man here will ever dare to breake.

Enter Johnson's *Ghost.*

Hold, and give way, for I my self will speak,
Can you encourage so much insolence,
And add new faults still to the great offence

[1] The punctuation has been slightly retouched.

Your Ancestors so rashly did commit
Against the mighty Powers of Art and Wit?
When they condem'd those noble works of mine
Sejanus, and my best lov'd *Catiline*:
Repent, or on your guilty heads shall fall
The curse of many a rhyming Pastoral:
The three bold *Beauchamps* shall revive again,
And with the *London* Prentice conquer *Spain*.
All the dull follies of the former age
Shall rise and find applause upon this *Stage*.
But if you pay the great arrears of praise,
So long since due to my much injur'd Plays,
From all past crimes I first will set you free,
And then inspire some one to write like me.

'Mr. *Matthew*, our domestique Wit', was Matthew Medbourne, who
translated Molière's *Tartuffe*; for this Dorset also wrote an Epilogue.
The 'three bold Beauchamps' is a lost play attributed to Thomas
Heywood; it evidently resembled his play of *The Four Prentices of
London, with the Conquest of Jerusalem*. Both were satirized in *The
Knight of the Burning Pestle*. That Ben should threaten to revive
them as a punishment for the audience is a quaint touch of
archaism.

John Rich revived the play at Lincoln's Inn Fields in 1725. The
bill in *The Daily Post* of 12 January described the play inconse-
quently as 'Never acted Before' and 'Revis'd with Alterations'.
The alterations meant the omission of seven characters—Matthew,
Cash, Cob, Formal, Wellbred's servant, Bridget, and Tib—and the
addition of three new characters—Marwit, Clara, and Lucinda.
Hippisley was Kitely; Hall, Bobadill; Quin, old Kno'well; Ryan,
young Kno'well; Spiller, Brainworm; William Bullock, Stephen;
Hulet, Downright; Walker, Wellbred; Christopher Bullock, Clement;
Egleton, Marwit; Mrs. Moffett, Clara; and Mrs. Butcher, Lucinda.
Hippisley was a low comedian, unsuitably cast for Kitely; Bullock
was a mature Stephen of sixty-eight years; Spiller was famous for
his portrayal of old men.[1] There were only three performances; the
receipts on the first night were £51. 18s., on the second night £28,
and on the third, a benefit night, £100. 15s. 6d.[2]

On 29 November 1751 the memorable revival of Garrick took
place at Drury Lane. He had been three years preparing for it,
because 'The Language & Characters of Ben Jonson (and particularly of the Comedy in question) are much more difficult than

---

[1] R. G. Noyes, *Ben Jonson on the English Stage*, pp. 250, 251.
[2] British Museum Additional MSS. 32249–52, quoted ibidem.

those of any other Writer'.[1] There was no acting tradition to draw upon, but ten of the actors whom Garrick engaged had played in the revivals of *Volpone*, *The Alchemist*, and *Epicoene*. Garrick himself took the part of Kitely, and he assigned Bobadill to Henry Woodward. The other parts were—old Kno'well, Edward Berry; young Kno'well, David Ross; Brainworm, Richard Yates; Downright, Richard Winstone; Wellbred, William Palmer; Cash, Charles Blakes; Stephen, Edward Shuter; Matthew, Henry Vaughan; Cob, Thomas Mozeen; Clement, Taswell; Formal, Costello; Dame Kitely, Mrs. Ward; Bridget, Miss Minors; Cob's wife, Mrs. Cross.

The General Advertiser, for 29 November 1751, which printed the cast, also made the interesting announcement that 'the Characters will be dressed in the old English Manner', an early example, perhaps even the earliest, of the use of historic costume at the theatre. Sir Joshua Reynolds painted Garrick in his dress as Kitely—a Spanish cloak, a satin doublet embroidered and slashed with white lace, a pointed lace collar, with a dark wig parted down the middle and fuzzed out at the sides. Garrick left out in his version Kitely's complaint (II. i. 110) that Wellbred and his smart companions mocked him all over

> From my flat cap, vnto my shining shoes.

And, though he does not mention them, he might have included his worsted stockings.

Garrick published his stage-version at once—*Every Man in his Humour. A Comedy. Written by Ben Jonson. With Alterations and Additions. As it is Perform'd at the Theatre-Royal in Drury-Lane*—with an advertisement: 'It is hoped the Liberty that is taken with this celebrated Play of *Ben Jonson*, in leaving out some Scenes, with several Speeches and Parts of Speeches in other Places, and in adding what was necessary for Connexion, and a whole Scene in the Fourth Act, will be excused; as the Distance of 150 Years from the Time of Writing it, had occasioned some of the Humour to be too obsolete, and dangerous to be ventur'd in the Representation at present.'

Garrick spoke the following Prologue, written for the performance by William Whitehead, the future Poet Laureate:

> CRITICKS! *your Favour is our Author's Right—*
> *The well-known Scenes, we shall present to-night,*
> *Are no weak Efforts of a modern Pen,*
> *But the strong Touches of immortal* Ben;

[1] *Some Unpublished Correspondence of David Garrick*, ed. G. P. Baker, pp. 79, 80.

A rough old Bard, whose honest pride disdain'd
Applause itself unless by Merit gain'd—
And wou'd to-night your loudest Praise disclaim,
Shou'd his great Shade perceive the doubtful Fame,
Not to his Labours granted, but his Name.
Boldly he wrote, and boldly told the Age,
'He dar'd not prostitute the useful Stage,
'Or purchase their Delight at such a Rate,
'As, for it, he himself must justly hate:
'But rather begg'd they wou'd be pleas'd to see
'From him, such Plays, as other Plays shou'd be:
'Wou'd learn from him to scorn a motley Scene,
'And leave their Monsters, to be pleas'd with Men.'
Thus spoke the Bard—And tho' the Times are chang'd,
Since his free Muse, for Fools the City rang'd;
And Satire had not then appear'd in State,
To lash the finer Follies of the Great;
Yet let not Prejudice infect your Mind
Nor slight the Gold, because not quite refin'd;
With no false Niceness this Performance view,
Nor damn for Low, *whate'er is just and true:*
Sure to those Scenes some Honour shou'd be paid,
Which Cambden *patroniz'd, and* Shakespear *play'd:*
Nature was Nature then, and still survives;
The Garb may alter, but the Substance lives.
Lives in this Play—where each may find complete,
His pictur'd Self—Then favour the Deceit—
Kindly forget the hundred Years between;
Become old Britons, *and admire* old Ben.

Naturally Garrick had to excise anything that had grown obsolete. Most of the literary allusions had lost their point: the mention of John Trundle, the ballad-monger (I. iii. 63); Nashe's Herring the king of fish; Roger Bacon and his brazen head (I. iv. 10–33, 63–4); the eulogy on *The Spanish Tragedy* (I. v. 47–64); the references to pilfering from Marlowe's *Hero and Leander* (IV. ii. 46–9, 53–60) and Daniel's *Delia* (v. v. 23–7). Of local references those to Picthatch (I. ii. 93), to Drake's old ship at Deptford (I. iii. 121), to beggars on the outskirts of the city (III. v. 12–23), and to the quarrelsome carmen in Thames Street or at Custom-house Quay (III. ii. 61–71) were omitted. Symmachus and the Seven Wise Masters (III. i. 35, v. 9) also drop out.

The structural alterations were important. Cob's part was drastically cut. Dryden had already commented on it as 'mechanic humour' depending on the tankard.[1] Cob was a typical figure of

---

[1] Epilogue to the second part of *The Conquest of Granada*.

Elizabethan low comedy. Garrick omitted the opening lines of Act II, scene iii, in which Cob appears; the fourth scene of the third Act, Cob's protest against fasting days; the seventh scene, his visit to Clement; the fourth scene of the fourth Act, his interview with Tib. His tirade against tobacco (III. v. 105–16) was also shortened.

The scenes were reduced in number. The second Act had two scenes, the first taking in the first three scenes of the original, the second taking in the rest of the Act, Kno'well delivering his soliloquy in Moorfields. The third Act again had two scenes: Jonson's scenes i and ii were run together and located at the Stocks-Market; the second scene took in scenes iii and v, the fourth scene being omitted. There were two scenes in the fourth Act, the first three scenes of Jonson making scene i, the fifth, sixth, and seventh scenes making scene ii, scene iv of the original being omitted. Garrick began his fifth Act with Jonson's Act IV, scene ix, the Stocks-Market again. Scene ii was Act IV, scene x, scene iii was Act IV, scene xi, and scene iv concluded the piece, with i, ii, and iii of the original, scene iv being omitted, and scene v much shortened.

This simplified the task of the scene-shifter and saved space for additions. Garrick resorted to the well-known device of the actor-manager to improve his own part. Apart from minor touches he inserted an entire scene of 270 lines at the end of his fourth Act to give a long-drawn display of Kitely's vacillating jealousy. The scene was a chamber in his house.

Enter Kitely and Cash.

Kite. Art thou sure, *Thomas*, we have pry'd into all and every part throughout the house? Is there no By-place, or dark Corner has escap'd our Searches?

Cash. Indeed, Sir, none; there's not a Hole or Nook unsearch'd by us, from the upper Loft to the Cellar.

Kite. . . . While we were searching of the dark Closet by my Sister's Chamber, did'st thou not think thou heard'st a rustling on the other side, and a soft tread of Feet?

Cash. Upon my Truth, I did not, Sir; or if you did, it might be only the Vermin in the Wainscot; the House is old, and overrun with 'em.

Kite. It is indeed, *Thomas*—we should bane those Rats—dost thou understand me—we will—they shall not harbour here; I'll cleanse my House from 'em, if Fire or Poison can effect it—I will not be tormented thus—They knaw my Brain, and burrow in my Heart—I cannot bear it.

Cash. I do not understand you, Sir!

Cash expostulates with him and argues that 'some whispering Knave' has deceived him. For a few moments Cash makes him give up his suspicions. But they return with twofold force, though he tries to stifle them.

> I'll silence
> The Sneers of Envy, stop the Tongue of Slander;
> Nor will I more be pointed at, as one
> Disturb'd with Jealousy—
>
> *Dame.* Why, were you ever so?
>
> *Kite.* What!—ha! never, never—ha, ha, ha!
> She stabs me home. ⟨*Aside.*⟩ Jealous of thee!
> No, do not believe it—speak low, my Love,
> Thy Brother will o'erhear us—No, no, my Dear,
> It cou'd not be, it cou'd not be—for—for—
> What is the time now?—I shall be too late—
> No, no, thou may'st be satisfy'd
> There's not the smallest Spark remaining—
> Remaining! What do I say? there never was,
> Nor can, nor ever shall be—so be satisfy'd—
> Is *Cob* within there?—Give me a Kiss,
> My Dear, there, there, now we are reconcil'd—
> I'll be back immediately—Good bye, good-bye—
> Ha! ha! jealous! I shall burst my Sides with laughing;
> Ha! ha! *Cob*, where are you, *Cob*! Ha! ha!—

Playgoers in the eighteenth century, we are told, found Jonson's style too antiquated: this is how Garrick brought it up to date. But it gave good opportunity for the play of feature and the inflexion of voice in which he excelled. He made the part. Theophilus Cibber, a hostile critic of Garrick, who criticized his 'studied Tricks, his Over-fondness for extravagant Attitudes, frequent affected Starts, convulsive Twitchings, Jerkings of the Body, sprawling of the Fingers', said his performance of Kitely was 'so excellent a Piece of Nature,—so truely comic,—it makes Amends for all the Farce with which that indelicate Piece of low Humour abounds'.[1]

Two other actors markedly contributed to the success of the revival—Woodward as Bobadill and Shuter as Master Stephen. Contemporary opinion regarded Woodward's Bobadill as his masterpiece of acting. Thomas Davies in his *Dramatic Miscellanies*[2] has left on record a description of a rehearsal which speaks well both for Garrick and Woodward:

During the greatest part of the rehearsals of *Every Man in his Humour*, Woodward seemed very attentive to Garrick's ideas of Bobadil. But, in his absence one morning, he indulged himself in the exhibition of his own intended manner of representation. While the actors were laughing

---

[1] *Two Dissertations on the Theatres*, pp. 46, 47, 56, quoted by Noyes, op. cit., p. 267.   [2] Vol. ii, p. 69.

and applauding Woodward, Garrick entered the playhouse, and, unperceived, attended to the transaction of the scene. After waiting sometime, he stept on the stage, and cried, 'Bravo, Harry! bravo! upon my soul, bravo!—Why, now this is—no, no, I can't say this is quite my idea of the thing—Yours is, after all—to be sure, rather—ha!' Woodward perceiving the manager a little embarrassed, with much seeming modesty, said, 'Sir, I will act the part, if you desire it, exactly according to your notion of it.'—'No, no! by no means, Harry. D—n it, you have actually clenched the matter.—But why, my dear Harry, would you not communicate before?'

Churchill in the *Rosciad*, 1761,[1] criticized Woodward severely as an actor, but was forced to make an exception for his Bobadill:

> . . . endow'd with various powers of face,
> Great master in the science of Grimace, . . .
> His wit and humour in Distortion lye,
> And all his merit enters at the eye.
> We laugh, we clap,—but, on Reflexion's birth,
> We wonder at ourselves, and curse our mirth.
>
> .　　.　　.　　.　　.
>
> Merit he had, some merit in his way,
> But seldom found out in what part it lay.
> In BOBADIL, indeed, such praise he bore,
> Such worthy praise, that KITELY scarce had more.

He 'acted in more performances of *Every Man in his Humour* than any other actor in the period, with a total of one hundred thirty-one nights in comparison with Garrick's ninety; he chose the comedy seven times for his benefit, and it is not strange that Bobadill and Woodward became almost synonymous in the poetical squibs and reviews.'[2]

The third famous player in the revival was Ned Shuter—

> Shuter, who never car'd a single pin
> Whether he left out nonsense, or put in,

to quote a malicious couplet of *The Rosciad*.[3] Thomas Wilkes in his *General View of the Stage*, 1759, pp. 300–1, gave him high praise. And *The Rational Rosciad*, by 'F— B— L—', 1767, p. 30, said of him

> SHUTER, the muse a perfect master deems,
> Who is in every part the thing he seems;
> His tones so various and so just surprize,
> His vast command of features charms our eyes;

---

[1] Page 11. The passage was revised in Churchill's *Poems* of 1763.
[2] Noyes, op. cit., p. 270.　　　　　　　　　[3] Page 31, ed. 1763.

> His strict propriety in all he plays,
> Critics themselves, into applause, betrays;
> What beauties he exhibits to the sight,
> When master STEPHEN is in fearful plight.

A travelling company from Drury Lane performed in the provinces in 1752 and 1754.[1] The play was given at Richmond on 15 July 1752: Cross was Kitely; Burton, old Kno'well; Blakes, Bobadill; Phillips, Clement; Cross, Stephen; Davis, Downright; Vaughan, Matthew; Shuter, Brainworm; Macgeorge, Cash; Miss Helm, Bridget; Miss Ibott, Dame Kitely. Only Vaughan kept his old part, Blakes took another part. On 21 July they acted the play again at the Twickenham Theatre, with *The King and Miller of Mansfield* as an afterpiece.

On 2 August 1754 the play was given at the Jacob's Well Theatre at Bristol for the benefit of Blakes. The cast was—Kitely, Palmer; Bobadill, Blakes; old Kno'well, Berry; young Kno'well, Mozeen; Brainworm, Barrington; Stephen, Green; Downright, Winstone; Wellbred, White; Clement, Arthur; Matthew, Smith; Cash, Olivier; Cob, Cox; Dame Kitely, Mrs. Bland; Bridget, Mrs. Simpson; Tib, Mrs. Pit.

Garrick continued to revive the play at intervals up to his final appearance on 25 April 1776. There were various changes in the cast, but the most serious was the desertion of Woodward, who went over to Covent Garden in 1759. Yates, the Brainworm of the first performance, changed over to the part. 'His Brainworm', said Wilkes, 'was no less a masterpiece than Woodward's Bobadil; nay, if we consider the various powers it required to support differently the serving-man, the disbanded soldier, the justice's clerk, and the varlet of the city or bailiff, and how he excelled in each, in all, we shall perhaps rank him next to Kitely.'[2]

At Covent Garden William Smith played Kitely from October 1762 and at Drury Lane from 1778 to 1798. The feeling that the play was obsolete finds expression from time to time. Thus *The General Evening Post* for 13–16 February 1773:

When the heap of theatrical rubbish is thus reviewed, which passes under the title of Every Man in his Humour, it may not be unnecessary to ask, how a play can be frequently exhibited with applause, which is so egregious a compound of absurdity? To this we answer, that nobody goes to see the *play*, but the *performers*. Garrick's Kitely is so exquisite a piece of acting, that it would croud fifty theatres: Woodward at the other house, is to the last degree masterly in Bobadil, and Shuter

---

[1] See *Notes and Queries*, vol. clxxiii, p. 238.   [2] Noyes, op. cit., p. 274.

inimitable in Stephen. Let us not, therefore, compliment the *poet* at the expense of the *player*, nor suppose, when we run to the representation of Ben Johnson's pieces, that it is the *composition* with which we are captivated; his works are as heavy on the stage, as they are tiresome in the closet, and will fall into oblivion the instant they cease to be capitally executed.

'Smith the genteel, the airy, and the smart', as Churchill described him,[1] was successful as Kitely, but the author of *The Rational Rosciad*, p. 28, while paying a tribute to his fine elocution, accused him of lifeless acting:

> Frantic and mad with jealousy and rage,
> In desp'rate mood when Kitely quits the stage,
> Why can with SMITH's good sense that *noke* prevail,
> His arm t'envelope in his garments tail.

The garments, by the by, were historical: Garrick's innovation was followed in the Covent Garden performance.

On 15 March 1763 Woodward, playing Bobadill for his own benefit, prefaced the performance with a prologue of his own composition:

> *'Tis strange* (excuse my gravity) *'tis passing strange*
> How much the giddy world is given to change!
> The days, the seasons change, and men and women,
> All change their minds—and all that can their linen.
> Ler the grave moralist, with curious eye
> Observe the busy throng that vend and buy—
> *Change*, Sir, I must have *change*—is all the cry.
> The World, a mere *Change-alley* we may call;
> Stars, stocks, and tides, and actors, rise and fall—
> Thus I, who late with worse than tragic face,
> With shrug repentant, and with sad grimace,
> Most humbly sued you'd take the wand'rer in,
> Am tempted now to more than comic grin;
> Am forc'd to give these deep reflections birth,
> And show my wisdom to disguise my mirth.—
> Truth is, the strange delight your smiles impart, ⎫
> Has often rais'd too high my conscious heart; ⎬
> Inspir'd my airs, and sometimes—spoil'd my part. ⎭
>   Hence has a *Giant-Bard*—you all know who,[2]
> In lines most sage, and as 'tis said, most true,
> Remark'd on *Woodward's tricks, his starts, and whims,*
> *His twisted features, and his tortur'd limbs,*
> *His wink impertinent, his saucy stare,*
> *His grin ridiculous, his careless air,*

---

[1] *The Rosciad*, 1761, p. 16.   [2] Churchill.

His more than Idiot *vacancy of face,*
His monkey arts, and mountebank grimace,
That furrow'd cheeks with *untaught laughter fill,*
And make sad Critics *smile against their will.*
Alas, poor wisdom! doom'd to vile disgrace,
While antic laughter sits upon her face!
While grins detested, and usurping mirth,
That makes her *hate herself,* and curse her birth—
I'm sorry—but these pangs she must endure,
Unless *you* force me to apply the cure;
If *you* indeed should threat to *lay the switch on,*
I straight shall own myself a *grave physician;*
To cure all lamentable mirth profess,
All grief phantastical, and droll distress.—
　　This when we need—to-night I cannot fear
Th'extorted simper, or the ready sneer,
When all around such partial smiles I see,
And each kind aspect seems to beam on me.—
Oh! should your favour haply be misplac'd, ⎫
Let it, like my imputed errors, last; ⎬
And *inclination kindly take for taste;* ⎭
So shall I still indulge a grateful heart,
And feel unchecked the pleasure you impart.
　　Yet under *Bobadil's* grave masque tonight,
I'll hide the antic bauble from your sight,
In calm composure smoak my *Trinidado,*
And taste, for all my faults, the *bastinado.*[1]

Woodward was better at declaiming verse than at writing it. The prologue met with a savage criticism in *The Theatrical Review* of 1 April 1763.

On 17 December 1800 William Cooke revived the play at Covent Garden. Fawcett was Bobadill, and Munden Brainworm. 'Cooke has the praise', wrote Mrs. Inchbold,[2] of having given the part of Kitely 'all its former power over the town, and to have fully supplied the vacant part of Garrick'. It was considered Cooke's best part after Iago.

On 5 June 1816 Kean revived the play for his benefit at Drury Lane. He played Kitely, with Munden for Brainworm and Harley for Bobadill. Hazlitt reviewed it in *The Examiner* on 8 June.

This play acts much better than it reads. . . . Brainworm is a particularly dry and abstruse character. We neither know his business nor his motives; his plots are as intricate as they are useless, and as the

[1] *The Public Advertiser,* 16 March 1763, and elsewhere.
[2] *The British Theatre,* vol. iv, edition of *Every Man in his Humour.*

ignorance of those he imposes on is wonderful. This is the impression in reading it. Yet from the bustle and activity of this character on the stage, the changes of dress, the variety of affected tones and gipsey jargon, and the limping distorted gestures, it is a very amusing exhibition, as Mr MUNDEN plays it. Bobadil is the only actually striking character in the play, . . . The rest, Master Matthew, Master Stephen, Cob and Cob's Wife, were living in the sixteenth century. But from the very oddity of their appearance and behaviour, they have a very droll and even picturesque effect when acted. It seems a revival of the dead. . . .

The pathos in the principal character Kitely, is 'as dry as the remainder biscuit after a voyage'. There is, however, a certain good sense, discrimination, or *logic of passion* in the part, which Mr. KEAN pointed in such a way as to give considerable force to it. In the scene where he is about to confide the secret of his jealousy to his servant, Thomas, he was exceedingly happy in the working himself up to the execution of his design, and in the repeated failure of his resolution. The reconciliation-scene with his wife had great spirit, where he tells her, to shew his confidence, that 'she may sing, may go to balls, may dance', and the interruption of this sudden tide of concession with the restriction—'though I had rather you did not do all this'—was a master-stroke.[1] It was perhaps the first time a parenthesis was ever spoken on the stage as it ought to be.

The Bobadill of Harley is cautiously praised.

He delivered the Captain's well-known proposal for the pacification of Europe, by killing twenty of them each his man a day, with good emphasis and discretion. Bobadil is undoubtedly the hero of the piece; his extravagant affection carries the sympathy of the audience along with it, and his final defeat and exposure, though exceedingly humorous, is the only affecting circumstance in the play. Mr. HARLEY's fault in this and other characters is, that he too frequently assumes mechanical expression of countenance and bye-tones of humour, which have not anything to do with the individual part.

Mr. HUGHES personified Matthew to the life: he appeared 'like a man made after supper of a cheese-paring'. MUNDEN did Brainworm with laudable alacrity. OXBERRY's Master Stephen was very happily hit off; nobody plays the traditional fool of the English stage so well; he seems not only foolish, but fond of folly.[2]

The next revival was at Covent Garden in May 1825 with Young as Kitely, W. Farren as Brainworm, Keeley as Matthew, Blanchard as Clement, and Mrs. Chatterley as Dame Kitely.

On 29 July 1838 Macready revived the play at the Haymarket.[3]

---

[1] In Garrick's version, amplifying Act IV, scene viii.
[2] *A View of the English Stage*, 1818, pp. 300–3.
[3] Macready had brought out the play at Bath on 10 Feb. 1816 (Genest, *English Stage*, viii, p. 563).

The performance generally was described as disappointing in *The Theatrical Examiner* of 29 July, but high praise was given to Macready.

A singular proof of the masterly skill of the actor ... consists in his excluding from Kitely every particle of sympathy or pity. We laugh at him, and are glad that his business suffers such serious interruptions from his jealousy. That is all. Such an effect is more surprising in Mr. Macready's hands, since it is the characteristic of his acting to idealize his characters, and venture everything, even to a fault now and then, for the sympathies of his audience.—And we are really, after all, not sure that a remote touch of pity did not cross us, when, in the closing scene of the third act with Cobb, after that worthy person had asked—'By my troth, sir, will you have the truth of it?'—Kitely was made to drop his voice with fear, and falter out with an agonized effort to seem calm and ready to hear—'Ay, good Cobb, I pray thee, heartily.'[1] Yet this was a subtle touch of nature, which we could not wish away.

Robert Browning was among the audience, and wrote in a private letter, 'Macready is looking well; I just saw him the other day for a minute after the play; his Kitely was Kitely—superb from his flat cap down to his shining shoes.'[2]

In this performance Webster was Bobadill, Buckstone and Hill were the two town gulls, Strickland was Brainworm, and Worrell Cash.

The memorable revivals of Charles Dickens and his company of literary amateurs began on 20 September 1845 at Miss Kelly's Theatre, 73 Dean Street, Soho, the bill being headed 'Strictly Private'.[3] It was repeated publicly as a charity performance at St. James's Theatre on 15 November.

John Forster gives an account of the production in the *Life and Letters of Charles Dickens*.[4]

We had chosen EVERY MAN IN HIS HUMOUR, with special regard to the singleness and individuality of the 'humours' portrayed in it; and our company included the leaders of a journal[5] then in its earliest years, but already not more renowned as the most successful joker of jokes yet known in England, than famous for that exclusive use of its laughter and satire for objects the highest and most harmless which makes it still so enjoyable a companion to mirth-loving right-minded men, Maclise took earnest part with us, and was to have acted, but fell away on the eve of the rehearsals; and Stanfield, who went so far as to

---

[1] Act III, scene vi, ll. 35–6.
[2] Mrs. Sutherland Orr's *Life and Letters of Robert Browning*, pp. 99, 100.
[3] A copy is in the Forster Library at South Kensington.
[4] Edition 1872, vol. ii, pp. 182–6.   [5] *Punch.*

rehearse Downright, then took fright and also ran away: but Jerrold, who played Master Stephen, brought with him Lemon, who took Brainworm; Leech, to whom Master Matthew was given; A'Beckett, who had condescended to the small part of William;[1] and Mr. Leigh, who had Oliver Cob. I played Kitely, and Bobadil fell to Dickens, who took upon him the redoutable Captain long before he stood in his dress at the footlights; humouring the completeness of his assumption by talking and writing Bobadil till the dullest of our party were touched and stirred to something of his own heartiness of enjoyment. . . .[2]

The play was played on the 21st of September[3] with a success that out-ran the wildest expectation; and turned our little enterprise into one of the small sensations of the day. The applause of the theatre found so loud an echo in the press, that for the time nothing else was talked of in private circles; and after a week or two we had to yield (we did not find it difficult) to a pressure of demand for more public performance in a larger theatre, by which a useful charity[4] received important help, . . .

Of the thing itself, however, it is necessary to be said that a modicum of merit goes a long way in all such matters, and it would not be safe now to assume that ours was much above the average of amateur attempts in general. Lemon certainly had most of the stuff, conventional as well as otherwise, of a regular actor in him, but this was not of a high kind; and though Dickens had the title to be called a born comedian, the turn for it being in his very nature, his strength was rather in the vividness and variety of his assumptions, than in the completeness, finish, or ideality he could give to any part of them. . . . At the same time this was in itself so thoroughly genuine and enjoyable, and had in it such quickness and keenness of insight, that of its kind it was unrivalled; and it enabled him to present in Bobadil, after a richly coloured picture of bombastical extravagance and comic exaltation in the earlier scenes, a contrast in the later of tragical humility and abasement, that had a wonderful effect. But greatly as his acting contributed to the success of the night, this was nothing to the service he had rendered as manager. It would be difficult to describe it. He was the life and soul of the entire affair. . . . He was stage-director, very often stage-carpenter, scene-arranger, property-man, prompter, and bandmaster. . . . He adjusted scenes, assisted carpenters, invented costumes, devised playbills, wrote out calls, and enforced as well as exhibited in his proper person everything of which he urged the necessity on others. Such a chaos of dirt, confusion and noise, as the little theatre was the

[1] Clement's servant.
[2] The bill has the actors' names added in manuscript: in addition to the above old Kno'well, H. Mayhew; young Kno'well, Frederick Dickens; Downright, G. Costello; Wellbred, Thompson; Cash, Augustus Dickens; Clement, F. Stone; James, Wellbred's servant, young Jerrold; Dame Kitely, Miss Fortescue. To these the *Athenaeum* of 22 Nov. adds Bridget, Miss Hinton, and Tib, Miss Bew.   [3] The bill says 20 Sept. for the first performance.
[4] The Sanatorium.

day we entered it, and such a cosmos as he made it of cleanliness, order, and silence, before the rehearsals were over!

Not all the audience were as enthusiastic as Forster and the London press. 'Everybody seemed pleased', said *The Times*, but there is a hostile notice in *The Greville Memoirs*:[1]

All the world went last night to the St. James's Theatre to see the second representation of *Every Man in his Humour*, by Dickens and the *Punch* people. House crammed full. I was in a bad place, heard very ill, and was so bored that at the end of the third act I went away. Dickens acted Bobadil very well indeed, and Douglas Jerrold (the author of the Caudles) Master Stephen very well also; the rest were very moderate and the play intolerably heavy. . . . The audience were cold as ice'. The aged Lord Melbourne, who said it was a dull play 'with no μῦθος in it', exclaimed between the acts in a stentorian voice, heard across the pit, 'I knew this play would be dull, but that it would be so damnably dull as this I did not suppose.'

In 1847 Dickens revived the play at Manchester on 26 July and at Liverpool on 28 July for the benefit of Leigh Hunt. At Manchester he realized £440. 12s., at Liverpool £463. 8s. 6d. There were a few changes in the cast: George Cruikshank, the caricaturist, was Formal, and G. H. Lewes was Kno'well; Miss Emmelin Montague was Dame Kitely, and two professional actresses, Mrs. A. Wigan and Mrs. Caulfield, were Bridget and Tib.

Sergeant Talfourd wrote a prologue for the first performance,[2] Sir Edward Bulwer (afterwards Lord) Lytton for the second, which Forster has preserved:[3]

> Mild amid foes, within a prison free,
> He comes . . . our grey-hair'd bard of Rimini!
> Comes with the pomp of memories in his train,
> Pathos and wit, sweet pleasures and sweet pain!
> Comes with familiar smile and cordial tone,
> Our hearths' wise cheerer!—Let us cheer his own!
> Song links her children with a golden thread,
> To aid the living bard strides forth the dead.
> Hark the frank music of the elder age—
> Ben Jonson's giant tread sounds ringing up the stage!
> Hail! the large shapes our fathers loved! again
> Wellbred's light ease, and Kitely's jealous pain.
> Cob shall have sense, and Stephen be polite,
> Brainworm shall preach, and Bobadil shall fight—
> Each, here, a merit not his own shall find,
> And *Every Man* the *Humour* to be kind.

---

[1] Vol. v, ed. L. Strachey and R. Fulford, 1938, p. 236, with Reeve's note.
[2] Printed in *Dickens and Talfourd*, by Cumberland Clark, pp. 41–3; it was devoted entirely to a plea for Hunt. [3] *Life of Dickens*, ii, p. 343 note.

On 17 May 1848 Dickens repeated the play at the Haymarket, giving the proceeds to the indigent playwright Sheridan Knowles. In this cast Dudley Castello was old Kno'well; Frank Stone, Downright; Augustus Egg, Stephen; Willmott, Clement; Cole, Formal; Miss Kenworthy, Bridget; and Mrs. Cowden Clarke, Tib. Mrs. Clarke has recorded some touches of Dickens's by-play. In the second scene of Act II he went to the back of the stage before bawling out his parting taunt 'Scavenger!' and then darted off at full speed; at 'This a *Toledo*? pish' (III. i. 163) he bent the sword into a curve; he leaned on his companion's shoulder when puffing out his tobacco smoke as 'your right *Trinidado*'; and he rattled off his arithmetic in Act IV, scene vii, making an invisible sum of addition in the air and scoring it underneath with an invisible line. When he reappeared in the fifth Act after his drubbing, he had wetted his plume of feathers and taken some of them out, in order to add to his crestfallen appearance. He and Leech (Master Matthew) had their wigs made of a different cut; Bobadil's fuzzed out at the side and extremely bushy, Matthew's flat at the ears and highly peaked above his forehead.[1]

On 25 April 1903 Mr. (afterwards Sir) F. R. Benson produced the play at the Memorial Theatre of Stratford-on-Avon as one of the dramatic performances of the Shakespeare Festival. Shakespeare's original connexion with the play warranted its revival on such an occasion. Benson himself played Bobadill; Charles Bibby, old Kno'well; Walter Hampden, young Kno'well; H. O. Nicholson, Brainworm; B. A. Pittar, Downright; J. S. Hamilton, Wellbred; Arthur Whitby, Kitely; Cyril Keightley, Stephen; P. D. Owen, Matthew; G. W. Johnson, Cash; G. F. Hannam-Clark, Cob; Henry Herbert, Clement; Eustace Le Grand, Formal; Miss Alice Arden, Dame Kitely; Miss Dorothy Green, Bridget; Miss Leah Hanman, Tib. The performance brought out the important fact that *Every Man in his Humour* is 'essentially an acting play', said *The Times*, 'one which needs the bustle and movement of the stage for its effect'. It praised specially the acting of Brainworm and Stephen.

Two amateur performances took place in March 1905 and December 1934, the former by the English Club of the Leland Stanford University, on an Elizabethan stage modelled on the old sketch of the Swan Theatre; they published as a record of it *Elizabethan Humour and the Comedy of Ben Jonson*, San Francisco, 1905, illustrated with pictures of Bobadill and Cob: the second by the Literary Society of Birkbeck College, London, with Elizabethan music.

The next revival was at the Gaiety Theatre, Manchester, where

[1] C. and M. Cowden Clarke, *Recollections of Writers*, 1878, pp. 310–11.

Miss Horniman's company played it on 29 November 1909. The producer was Mr. B. Iden Payne. Ian Maclaren was Bobadill; Charles Bibby, Cob; Esmé Percy, Justice Clement; Clifton Alderson, Kitely; Edyth Goodall, Dame Kitely; Hilda Bruce-Potter, Bridget; and Ada King, Tib.

The second revival of the play at the Shakespeare Memorial Theatre at Stratford-upon-Avon took place on 6 August 1937, and later, under the direction of Mr. B. Iden Payne. Dudley Jones spoke the prologue, and the cast was as follows: old Kno'well, Stanley Howlett; young Kno'well, Michael Goodliffe; Brainworm, Kenneth Wicksteed; Stephen, Patrick Crean; Downright, Clement McCallin; Wellbred, Norman Wooland; Kitely, Godfrey Kenton; Cash, Donald Layne-Smith; Bobadill, Donald Wolfit; Matthew, George Hagan; Cob, Dennis Roberts; Clement, Andrew Leigh; Formal, Richard Blatchley; Dame Kitely, Valerie Tudor; Bridget, Rosalind Iden; Tib, Clare Harris. The elder Kno'well was made up to represent Shakespeare in view of the ascription of the part to him, though that is not older than J. P. Collier. *The Times* justly said of the production that without unduly prolonging any situation or labouring any joke it made every incident lucid and 'brought out many diversions half hidden in the text'. There was 'no burlesque' and nothing that did not spring easily from the words of the play. Cob and Brainworm were excellent—the former a difficult part because of his fantastic and obsolete jokes—and Clement's eccentricity was brought out to perfection. As the intrigue developed, the performance rose to a climax. The uproar in Kitely's house and the comedy of errors outside Cob's were admirably done. The performance brought out the dramatic life and meaning of the play in a manner that would not be realized on merely reading it. It was a revelation of accomplished stage-craft.

EVERY MAN OUT OF HIS HUMOUR

THIS comedy was acted by the Chamberlain's men at the newly built Globe Theatre, 'in the yeere 1599', says the First Folio. The revised epilogue[1] entreats

> The happier spirits in this faire-fild Globe, . . .
> That with their bounteous *Hands* they would confirme
> This, as their pleasures *Pattent*: which so sign'd,
> Our leane and spent Endeauours, shall renue
> Their Beauties with the *Spring* to smile on you.

[1] Printed in vol. iii, pp. 603-4.

And the induction refers to the time 'when the house was a building' (l. 329). Sir Edmund Chambers estimates that the theatre was ready for the occupation of the Chamberlain's men by the beginning of the autumn season of 1599.[1]

The date of the performance can be fixed approximately by a letter of Rowland Whyte to Sir Robert Sidney, dated 13 November 1599, 'My Lord Darby hath put up the playes of the children in Pawles to his great paines and charge.'[2] One of their plays at this date was *Histriomastix*—a play alluded to in Act III, scene iv, line 29. *Every Man out of his Humour* followed before the end of the year. Jonson at this stage adopted the Calendar date which began the year on 1 January.

The Court performance, for which Jonson wrote a special epilogue addressing the Queen in person instead of addressing an actor made up to resemble the Queen,[3] took place about Christmas. The *Declared Accounts*, 543, *m.* 57, record payment to John Heminges for the Chamberlain's men on 26 December 1599 and on Twelfth Night 1600.

On 8 January 1605 the play was revived at Court by the King's men, who had succeeded the Chamberlain's company in 1603; it is entered in 'The Accompte of the Office of the Revelles of the whole yeres Charge in An°: 1604: Vntill the last of October 1605' (A.O. 3/908/13).[4] It is dated 1605, 'By his Ma^tis plaiers: The 8: of Ianuary: A play Cauled *Euery on out of his Vmor*'. *Every Man in his Humour* followed on Candlemas night.

At the Restoration Downes speaks of *Every Man out of his Humour* as one of the old plays acted 'but now and then',[5] but the only recorded performance was at the Theatre Royal in 1675, 'at which time', says Langbaine,[6] 'a new Prologue, and Epilogue were spoken by *Jo. Heyns*, which were writ by Mr. *Duffet*. See his *Poems*[7] 8° pag. 72, &c. This is an excellent Old Comedy.' Here is Thomas Duffett's 'doleful nonsense', to use his own phrase about the Puritans. The 'nun' alluded to in the opening lines is Anne Reeve.

Prologue to Ev'ry Man out of his Humor
Spoken by Mr. Hayns, July, 1675.

So fast from Plays approv'd and Actors known,
To drolling, stroling Royal Troop you run,
That *Hayns* despairing is Religious grown.

[1] *Elizabethan Stage*, ii, p. 415.
[2] In the De L'Isle and Dudley Papers, which supplement Collins's *Sidney Papers*: Collins omitted this passage. It has been communicated to us by Dr. G. B. Harrison.　　　　　[3] See vol. iii, pp. 599, 600, 602–3.
[4] So too in Bodleian MS. Malone 29, f. 69*b*.
[5] *Roscius Anglicanus*, pp. 8, 9.
[6] *English Dramatic Poets*, 1691, pp. 290–1.　　　　　[7] Published in 1676.

So Crack enjoy'd, the queazy Gallants slight,
And she, though still her beauty's in its height,
In rage turns Nun and goes to Heav'n in spight:
O Novelty, who can thy pow'r oppose!
Polony Bear or strange Grimace out-goes
Our finest language and our greatest shows.
　　As thick-scul'd Zealots, who from Churches fly,
Think doleful nonsense good that makes them cry;
Y'are pleas'd and laugh because—you know not why.
There ign'rant crouds round travel'd Gallants sit,
As am'rous youths round Vizards in our Pit,
And by their motions judg the Farces Wit.
　　If they but grin, a jest is understood,
All laugh outright and cry—I'gad that's good;
When will our damn'd dull silly rogues do so?
Y'are very complaisant, I fain would know
Where lies the wit and pow'r of (*il ohe.*)
　　The modish Nymphs now ev'ry heart will win,
With the surprising ways of *Harlequin.*
O the fine motion and the jaunty mene,
While you Gallants—
Who for dear Missie ne'r can do to much,
Make Courtships *alamode* de *Scarramouch.*
Ha——ha——
I could have taught you this, but let that pass,
Y'have heard I've wit, now you shall know I've grace,
I will reform——
But what Religions best in this, lewd Town,
My friends I'm yet like most of you, of none.
If I commence, I fear it will not do.
Religion has its *Scarramouchys* too,
Whose hum's and ha's get all the praise and pence,
For noise has still the upper hand of sense.
Well since 'tis so——
I'll keep my Station till your humours come,
Though like the longing woman, now you rome,
And leave all dainties for the Butchers thumb.
　　You and vile husbands equally proceed
Like rambling Bees, you quit your balm to feed
On ev'ry gaudy flow'r and painted weed.
When Winter comes you will again grow wise,
And visit home the wife that you despise,
With empty purses and with laden thighs.
　　　Epilogue to Ev'ry Man out of his Humor.
How crosly and how kindly things do go!
Though foreign troop does very pow'rful grow,
Kind Justice beats down our domestick foe.

The' inchanted Castle's once more overthrown,
That Nursery where all the youth in Town,
Such deeds of Valour and of Love have shown.
Britains Low Countreys, where at mighty rates
The younger Brothers urg'd their needy Fates,
And th' Elder got diseases for Estates.
    See how the scatter'd Cracks in parties fly,
How like a nest of Wasps disturb'd they ply,
And fiercely fix on any Fop that's nigh.
I warn you, though your presence theirs will bring,
Be not too eager for the pretty thing.
The bag of Honey's sweet, but 'ware the sting.
Play round the light, but from the heat retire;
For if y'are joyn'd between hot Love and Ire,
Like *Samsons* Foxes you'l set all on fire.
Reform your selves, Reformers of the Stage,
Blame not my Zeal, who can suppress their rage?
When Love and Wrath spare neither Sex nor Age.
For our Play we say nothing—
The merit of it will your plaudits gain,
Or else new Wit would strive to prop in vain,
What *Johnsons* sacred mem'ry can't sustain.

No later performance than this of 1675 is recorded, though Thomas Davies thought it might be revived 'with some judicious alterations'.[1]

CYNTHIA'S REVELS

Cynthia's Revels was 'first acted, in the yeere 1600. By the then Children of Queene Elizabeths Chappell', who played at the Black-friars. We learn from a contract which he made on 2 September 1600 with Richard Burbage for the use of this theatre, that Henry Evans 'intended then presentlye', i.e. at once, 'to erect or sett vp a company of boyes',[2] so that the play was performed late in the year.

It was presented at Court on 6 January 1601, when Nathaniel Gyles, master of the Children of the Chapel, was paid £5 for what is described as 'a showe wth musycke and speciall songes p'pared for the purpose'.[3] The description fits *Cynthia's Revels* with the four lyrics in Act I, scene ii, Act IV, scene iii, and Act V, scene vi, and the Court masques in Act V, scenes vii and ix.[4]

[1] *Dramatic Miscellanies*, ii, p. 74.
[2] E. K. Chambers, *Elizabethan Stage*, ii, p. 42.
[3] Ibid. iii, p. 364; iv, p. 166.
[4] This corrects the statement in vol. i, p. 393, that there is no evidence that the play was performed at Court.

Two of the boy-actors were addressed in the Quarto text by their christian names in the Induction, 'resolute *Iacke*' (l. 21: cf. 33, 218) and '*Sall.*' at line 222. Jack is probably John Underwood, but John Frost is possible. 'Sall.' is Salomon (or Solomon) Pavy, who played Anaides (l. 59).

That the Court performance was not a success may be inferred from the motto in the Quarto, 'Quod non dant Proceres, dabit Histrio.' And Dekker's reference in *Satiromastix*, 1602, sig. M verso —'when your Playes are misse-likt at Court, you shall not crye Mew like a Pusse-cat, and say you are glad you write out of the Courtiers Element', can, as a matter of date, refer only to this play[1] and possibly to the impersonation of Elizabeth in *Every Man out of his Humour*, which had been criticized.[2] The motto 'Quod non dant Proceres' had also been on the title-page of the Quarto of *Every Man in his Humour*.

POETASTER

Poetaster was acted 'sundry times priuately in the Blacke Friers, by the Children of her Maiesties Chappell', the Quarto title-page tells us; the Folio gives the year as 1601. This must have been early in the year, for the performance is proved to have taken place in the spring by the admission of the player Histrio in Act III, scene iv, lines 328–9, 'this winter ha's made vs all poorer, then so many staru'd snakes'. Dekker's reply to Jonson's attack, *Satiromastix, or the Untrussing of the Humorous Poet*, was entered on the Stationers' Register on 11 November 1601 and published early in 1602; Jonson retorted by entering *Poetaster* on 21 December, and this also was published in Quarto in 1602. He wrote the play in fifteen weeks, with a speed unusual for him, to anticipate an attack which he knew Dekker was planning (III. iv. 323–35, IV. vii. 26–7). Jonson got in the first blow, and Dekker, to lose no time, tacked his untrussing on to an unfinished romance of William Rufus and his Court. The ephemeral character of the satire in both plays made later performances impossible.

Mr. William Poel's has been the only revival in modern times. Performed on Shakespeare's birthday, 26 April, in the Shakespeare tercentenary year, 1916, in the Apothecaries' Hall built on the site of the old Blackfriars Theatre, with the actor who played Virgil dressed as a living replica of the Stratford bust, the revival gave the play a new orientation. On 27 April it was repeated in the Small

---

[1] So Penniman, *The War of the Theatres*, p. 127. [2] See vol. iii, pp. 602–3.

Theatre of the Albert Hall. All the actors were young, to suggest a link with the Children of the Chapel. In October 1916 Mr. Poel gave the performance at the Carnegie Institute, Pittsburgh, U.S.A., with college students for the actors.

The cast was as follows: Augustus Caesar, I. Greenleaf, who also played Envy in the prologue; Mecoenas, S. Geoffries; Ovid, G. Rees; Marcus Ovid, Y. Pienne; Tibullus, C. H. Morgan; Cornelius Gallus, M. James; Virgil, E. D. Rees; Horace, F. Allardy; Lupus, G. Brunswick; Tucca, B. Dyne; Luscus, C. Telford; Crispinus, M. Carey; Hermogenes, I. Hearne; Albius, A. Lubimoff; Minos, W. Fairbairn; Histrio, K. Harrison; Lictors, C. Renaud, L. Simpson; Pages, E. Renaud, M. Rowland; Julia, V. Foucheux; Cytheris, O. A. Jettley; Plautia, P. Bryan; Chloe, I. Hayter; Maid, A. Scamell. Mr. J. Fisher White appeared as Ben Jonson and spoke the Apologetical Dialogue during the interval. A few characters were omitted. Choristers of Westminster Cathedral sang before the performance to the lute and virginal accompaniment of Mr. Arnold Dolmetsch.

SEJANUS

THE play was acted by the King's men in 1603, as Jonson himself tells us. There was no public playing from 19 March 1603 to March 1604, the theatres being closed for Elizabeth's death and then because of the plague. Sir E. K. Chambers suggests that the 1603 performance may have been at Court in the autumn or the winter (*Elizabethan Stage*, iii, p. 367). When the theatres reopened, *Sejanus* was acted at the Globe and hissed off the stage. Jonson in his dedication to Aubigny refers to the 'violence' which the play received. In the lines which he prefixed to the Quarto, 'Ev. B' described how 'in the GLOBES faire Ring, our Worlds best Stage' he

> veiw'd the Peoples beastly rage,
> Bent to confound thy graue, and learned toil.

In William Fennor's *Descriptions*, 1616, B2, is 'The Description of a Poet':

> But sweet Poesye
> Is oft conuict, condemn'd, and iudg'd to die
> Without iust triall, by a multitude
> Whose iudgements are illiterate, and rude.
> Witnesse *Sceianus*, whose approued worth,
> Sounds from the calme South, to the freezing North,
> And on the perfum'd wings of *Zephyrus*,
> In triumph mounts as farre as *Æolus*,

With more then humane art it was bedewed,
Yet to the multitude it nothing shewed;
They screwed their scuruy iawes and look't awry,
Like hissing snakes adiudging it to die:
When wits of gentry did applaud the same,
With Siluer shouts of high and sounding fame:
Whil'st vnderstanding grounded men contemn'd it,
And wanting wit (like fooles to iudge) condemn'd it.

British Museum Additional MS. 25348 is an anonymous attempt at a play on the Essex divorce of 1613, *The True tragi-Comedie formerly acted at Court & now reui⟨u⟩ed by ane Eie witness*; the date is *c*. 1654. The writer says on f. 1*b*, 'I a monst others hissed Seianus of the stage, yet after sate it out, not only patiantly, but with content, & admiration'.[1]

In the actor-list printed in two columns at the end of the play Burbage heads the first column and Shakespeare heads the second. Burbage heads these lists in *Every Man out of his Humour*, *Sejanus*, *Volpone*, *The Alchemist*, and *Catiline*. The Burbages owned the Globe Theatre, at which all these plays were acted. It seems natural to suggest that Richard Burbage played the leading part in them. If so, did Shakespeare play Tiberius? In the epigram which John Davies of Hereford wrote 'To our English Terence, Mr. Will. Shakespeare', printed in *The Scourge of Folly*, 1610, Epig. 159, there is an obscure reference to Shakespeare's playing royal parts.

Some say (good *Will*) which I, in sport, do sing,
Had'st thou not plaid some Kingly parts in sport,
Thou hadst bin a companion for a *King*;
And, beene a King among the meaner sort.
Some others raile; but, raile as they thinke fit,
Thou hast no rayling, but, a raigning Wit:
And honesty *thou sow'st, which they do reape;*
So, to increase their Stocke *which they do keepe.*

Rowe first told us that Shakespeare played the Ghost in *Hamlet*, but there is nothing in the part to give offence. But, if it is possible to suggest that he played Tiberius in *Sejanus*, this might have involved some trouble in view of the fact that the author was summoned before the Privy Council for this play.

Sejanus is one of the plays of Killigrew's company vaguely indicated in Downes's *Roscius Anglicanus*, 1708, p. 8, as acted at the Restoration. Probably it was acted after the revival of *Catiline*, but we have no record of it.

The only revival in modern times was that of Mr. William Poel

[1] Quoted by B. M. Wagner in *Philological Quarterly*, 1928, vii, pp. 306–8.

at the Holborn Empire Theatre on 12 February 1928. To secure
the effect of continuity Mr. Poel built out a platform stage over the
auditorium level, beginning at the proscenium edge and ending at
the fifth or sixth row of the stalls; there was a background of dark
curtains and there were arched entrances at the sides. The cast was
as follows: Tiberius, Roy Byford; Drusus senior, George E. Ban-
croft; Drusus junior, Pat Beveridge; Nero, Lewis Shaw; Caligula,
Iris Roberts; Arruntius, Robert Speaight; Silius, Gordon Douglas;
Sabinus, Frank Macey; Lepidus, Arthur Brough; Cordus, Wilfred
Walter; Gallus, Alan Edmiston; Regulus, Laurier Lister; Terentius,
Wilfred Walter; Laco, Lionel Ridpath; Eudemus, Esmé Percy;
Sejanus, D. A. Clarke-Smith; Varro, Keith Pyott; Clerk, John K.
Maclean; Macro, George Skillan; Afer, Norman Claridge; Pom-
ponius, Noel Dixon; Satrius, Charles Maunsell; Natta, Richard Coke;
Agrippina, Margaret Scudamore; Livia, Viola Lyel; Sosia, Violet
Gould. The make-up of Arruntius suggested Ben Jonson; that of
Cremutius Cordus Shakespeare. Cordus had affirmed in his history
that 'Cassius was the last of all the Romans'; this suggested Julius
Caesar. Further, Shakespeare was an admirer of Essex, and his *King
Richard II* had been played on the eve of the Essex rising; in the
original edition of the play the deposition scene was left out. The
play, as Mr. Poel saw it, was not written to give prominence to any
individual character in it, but to show the sudden rise and fall of
a people's favourite; it was a political satire.

It is unnecessary to do more than mention Francis Gentleman's
worthless adaptation, *Sejanus, a Tragedy. As it was intended for the
Stage*, published in 1752. Garrick rejected it. Gentleman cut out
nineteen minor parts, developed the parts of Livia and Agrippina,
and made Tiberius preside at the overthrow of Sejanus in the Senate.
Poetic justice, 'to which I think History should give way', was
satisfied by making Tiberius in a final speech promise 'To heal those
wounds by base SEJANUS made', to free his nephews and end the
reign of terror.

EASTWARD HO

THIS comedy, as the title-pages of the Quartos state, was acted at
the Blackfriars by the Children of the Queen's Revels. The prologue
refers to Dekker and Webster's *Westward Ho*, staged late in 1604.
The play was acted at some date in 1605 before the imprisonment
of the authors for its unlicensed publication; the imprisonment was
over by November 1605, because Jonson was then at large, working
in the service of the government about the Gunpowder Plot.

In August 1613 Daborne, writing to Henslowe about a play on which he is engaged and which is not ready, suggests that the stage-keeper should 'set vp bills agst munday', 9 August, 'for Eastward hoe'.[1] The play had passed to the Lady Elizabeth's men, and they also gave it at Court on 25 January 1614. The accounts of the Treasurer of the Chamber have the following notice: 'To Joseph Taylor for himselfe and the reste of his fellowes servauntes to the Lady Eliz her grace upon the Councells Warraunt dated at Whitehall 21 June 1614 for presenting before his Ma^{ty} a Comedy called Eastward Howe on the xxvth of January last past—vj^{li}. xiij^s. iiij^d. and by way of his Ma^{ts} reward lxvj^s. viij^d.'[2]

It is probably to this play that Daborne again alludes in his letter to Henslowe of 13 November 1613, asking for a further loan of ten shillings, and 'if y^u please not to stay till Johnsons play be playd the kings men hav bin very earnest wth me to pay y^u in y^r money'. . . .[3]

In 1685 Nahum Tate's alteration of the play entitled *Cuckold's Haven, or an Alderman no Conjuror* was brought out at Dorset Garden as a farce in three acts. Touchstone's character was degraded to suit the buffoon Nokes, and Security pretended to be bewitched— an episode copied from Fitzdottrel's exploit in *The Devil is an Ass*.

In 1751 Garrick revived the play at Drury Lane on Lord Mayor's day, 29 October, substituting it for the customary performance of Edward Ravenscroft's *The London Cuckolds*. Garrick renamed it *The Prentices*. Garrick's attempt to substitute a decent play for an indecent one was resented, and the play failed.

That Henry Woodward played in this, and apparently some further, performance of *Eastward Ho* is clear from the epitaph on him printed in *The Thespian Magazine* for September 1794:

> thy blithe *Mercutio*
> Our spirits cheer'd, and banished all our woe.
> At *Bobadill's* fierce strut, or fiercer stare,
> At *Tuchstone's* quipps, at *Fopplington's* grand air
> Say who the well-earn'd plaudit could forbear?

In 1751 the play was successfully revived in an adaptation by Mrs. Charlotte Lennox, *Old City-manners*, and performed at Drury Lane. Garrick had recommended the alteration and helped with it. The chief actors were Touchstone, Baddeley; Flash, Palmer; Quicksilver, Dood; Golding, Brereton; Security, Parsons; Bramble,

---

[1] *Henslowe Papers*, ed. Greg, p. 71.
[2] Chambers, *Elizabethan Stage*, iv, p. 129.
[3] Greg, *Henslowe Papers*, p. 78: along with Malone and Fleay he refers this to *Bartholomew Fair* acted on 31 Oct. 1614. E. K. Chambers suggests *Eastward Ho* (op. cit. iii, p. 372).

Hurst; Mrs. Touchstone, Mrs. Johnston; Gertrude, Mrs. Wrighten; Mildred, Miss P. Hopkins; Winifred, Mrs. Whitfield; Sindefy, Miss Platt. Colman wrote the Prologue, which was spoken by King.

> In Charles the Second's gay and wanton days,
> When Lords had wit, and Gentlemen wrote plays,
> A rural 'Squire was term'd a country-put,
> And the grave City was the standing butt!
> To town, like oxen, honest Knights were led,
> To shew in droves huge antlers on their head;
> Gallants, in quest of game, cry'd *Eastward hoe*!
> And oft sprung puss within the sound of Bow;
> While every 'prentice in the galleries chuckl'd,
> At London Alderman, dubb'd London Cuckold.
>
> But now the times are chang'd, and chang'd the jest;
> For horns, some say, sprout nobly in the West.
> The murrain 'mongst horn'd cattle spreads so far,
> It rages on each side of Temple-bar.
> The modish Alderman o'erleaps his ward,
> And the gay Cit plants horns upon my Lord;
> While beaux, whose wives of flattery chew the cud,
> Are Dupes full blown, or Cuckolds in the bud.
>
> Artists, who furnish'd pictures for the stage,
> In good Queen Bess's memorable age,
> With a just pencil city portraits drew,
> Mark'd every vice, and mark'd each virtue too.
> The city Madam's vanities display'd,
> Prais'd *honest gains*, but damn'd the *tricks* of trade;
> Artists, like these (old Ben the chief!) to-night,
> Bring idleness, and industry to light;
> Their sketch by time, perhaps, impair'd too much,
> A female hand has ventur'd to retouch;
> Hence too our Hogarth drew, nor scorn'd to glean,
> The comic stubble of the morall scene,
> Shew'd to what ends both good and evil stretch,
> To honour one, and t'other to Jack Ketch;
> Turn'd ridicule 'gainst folly, fraud, and pride,
> And fought with humour's lance on virtue's side.
>
> Such be henceforth each comick artist's aim,
> Poets or painters, be their drift the same.
> Such are the lessons which to-night we read,
> And may next sessions prove that we succeed![1]

Mrs. Lennox kept in the main to the original. Her chief innovations were the introduction of 'poor Mr. Fig the grocer', a jilted

---

[1] Printed in *The Gentleman's Magazine* for Nov. 1775.

lover of Gertrude. Then Sir Petronel turns out to be no knight; he
had married an innkeeper's daughter at Mile-end and robbed his
father-in-law. So Gertrude is freed from him. Archaic phrases and
allusions disappear: the *Hamlet* references are suppressed, but the
drunken Quicksilver quotes in Act II—

> *Touch.* Why, how now, Sirrah? what vein's this?
> *Quick.* *Save me, and hover o'er me with your wings,*
> *You heavenly guards?* What would your gracious figure?

And Petronel, when he first enters, addresses Gertrude, 'My charm-
ing bride, may I presume to taste the hanging cherry of your lip?—
Nectar! ambrosia! orgeat and capilaire!'

The only performance of this century was at Harvard University
in 1903. It was given by the Harvard Chapter of Delta Upsilon
fraternity at Brattle Hall, Cambridge, on 14 and 16 April and at
the Bijou Theatre, Boston, on 17 April. Touchstone was played by
J. D. Williams, Mistress Touchstone by Elijah Swift, Gertrude and
Mildred by Edward F. Breed and Daniel C. Manning, Quicksilver and
Golding by J. T. Hoguet and H. C. De Long, Flash by S. B. Hall,
Security by F. E. Ames, and Bramble by F. R. Fitzpatrick. The
performance was directed by John T. Malone of the Players, New
York, who made an acting version cutting out the minor characters,
Winifred, Sir Petronel Flash, Sindefy, Beatrice, and Poldavy. The
tavern scene, in which R. S. Wallace as the sea-captain terrified
the tapster by smoking the newly introduced Virginia tobacco, was
especially amusing, and the performance was a great success.

On 22–5 October 1947 the play was performed at Columbia University, New York, at the Brander Matthews Hall. Michael Wyler
was Touchstone, William Markham Altman and Kenneth Buckridge
were Quicksilver and Golding, G. Rose Raph was Mistress Touchstone, Caroline Couche and Mary Lou Neilson were Gertrude and
Mildred, Adolph Anderson was Security and Ruth Witwer his wife,
William Bijur was Sir Petronel Flash, and Gloria Kunnel Sindefy.
A contemporary criticism singles out Golding and Flash for special
praise, comments on the slow movement of the play in the first two
acts, but notes the quickening of the action and the dialogue in the
rest of the play. The actors made the most of the delightful fun
poked at a number of the characters.

VOLPONE

Volpone was acted by the King's men at the Globe, and 1605 is given in the Folio as the year of the first performance. This might, on Jonson's reckoning, be early in 1606, and this is probably the date, as Sir Politic Would-be's whale at Woolwich (II. i. 47) appears to be the whale mentioned by Stow as seen at West Ham late in the January of that year. Jasper Mayne in *Jonsonus Virbius*, 1638, ll. 67–8, pays a tribute to the popularity of the play and notes the higher prices of the earliest performances:

> So when thy Foxe had ten times acted beene,
> Each day was *first*, but that 'twas cheaper seene.

The performances at Oxford and Cambridge followed in 1606 or 1607, probably in 1607 if the date of the dedication in the Quarto, 11 February 1607, means, as it is likely to mean, 1608. The tribute in the stately dedication to the 'love and acceptance' which the play won from the Universities points to an unqualified success.

The King's men revived the play at various dates; there was a Court performance on 27 December 1624,[1] and another on 19 November 1630.[2] Sir Humphrey Mildmay saw it at the Blackfriars on 27 October 1638,[3] and this was followed by a Court performance on 8 November.[4]

Wright in his *Historia Histrionica*, 1699, p. 4, says Lowin acted Volpone, among other Jonson parts, 'with mighty applause' 'in my time, before the Wars'. Presumably this was after the death of Burbage in 1619; Lowin was in the original cast, but Burbage must have acted the title part. Joseph Taylor, who joined the King's men in 1619, acted Mosca: Flecknoe commemorated him in *Enigmaticall Characters* (1658, p. 10), describing a parasite, 'He is on, who now the stage is down, Acts the *Parasites* part at Table; and since *Tailors* death, none can play Musco's part so well as he.'

After the Restoration the King's Company revived the play; it was one of the stock plays which was the special property of the Theatre Royal. Their earliest performance was in 1662, when Edward Browne, son of Sir Thomas, saw *Volpone* 'at the New Theatre in Lincolnes Inne fields';[5] he paid 2*s*. 6*d*. Mr. Noyes

---

[1] *Variorum Shakespeare*, iii, p. 228.
[2] G. E. Bentley, *The Jacobean and Caroline Stage*, i, p. 28, quoting from a bill in the Folger Library.
[3] Ibid. ii, p. 678.
[4] Adams, *The Dramatic Records of Sir Henry Herbert*, p. 77.
[5] British Museum Sloane MS. 1900, f. 37.

identifies this as the theatre of the King's Company in Vere Street.[1]
Killigrew's company also acted *Volpone* at Court that year on
16 October, as Evelyn records.[2]

An amateur performance was given at Oxford in 1663. Antony
à Wood records that he paid 6*d*. 'to see Volponey acted at the town
hall by prentises and tradesmen' on 1 January and again on 6
January.

Downes gives the cast of the King's Company at this period.[3]
Michael Mohun was Volpone; Charles Hart, Mosca; William Cartwright, Corbaccio; Robert Shatterel, Voltore; Nicholas Burt, Corvino; John Lacy, Sir Politic Would-be; Edward Kynaston, Peregrine;
Mrs. Corey, Lady Would-be; Mrs. Marshall (presumably Ann), Celia.
This would be the company Pepys saw on 14 January 1665: 'To
the King's house, there to see "Vulpone", a most excellent play; the
best I think I ever saw, and well acted.'

The company played *Volpone* at Court on 28 August 1667 and
received £20 for the performance.[4] They also played it on 17 January
1676, when the King was present and they received £10.[5] The
Theatre Royal closed in April 1682, but the King's Company and
the Duke of York's at Drury Lane and Dorset Garden united and
continued to play Jonson. Langbaine stated in 1691 that *Volpone*
'is still in vogue at the Theatre in *Dorset Garden*'.[6]

Mr. R. G. Noyes has recovered a manuscript prologue of this
period, printed by him for the first time in *Modern Language Notes*,
lii, pp. 198–200:

> Did Ben now live, how would he fret, and rage,
> To see the Musick-room outvye the stage?
> To see French Haut-boyes charm the listning Pitt
> More than the Raptures of his God-like wit!
> Yet 'tis too true that most who now are here,
> Come not to feast their Iudgment, but their Ear.
> Musick, which was by Intervals design'd
> To ease the weary'd Actors voice and mind,
> You to the Play judiciously prefer,
> 'Tis now the bus'ness of the Theatre:
> They Act, and if o're spent, for breath they stay,
> We Serve but as the Chorus to their Play;
> In vain we chuse the best Poetick strain,)
> The teeming head's choice labours cull in vain, }
> Whilst plyant fingers quite putt down the brain.)

[1] *Jonson on the English Stage*, p. 41.
[2] *Diary*, ed. Bray and Wheatley, 1879, ii. 153, 211.
[3] *Roscius Anglicanus*, 1708, p. 4.
[4] Nicoll, *Restoration Stage*, p. 306.   [5] Ibid., p. 308.
[6] *An Account of the English Dramatic Poets*, p. 298.

> The Fox above our boasting Play-bills shew,
> Variety of musick stands below.
> This fills the Pitt so full, and solid sense
> Is clear outweigh'd by empty circumstance.
> So to charm beasts Orpheus in vain did use
> The lofty Transports of his heav'nly Muse,
> Till waving those, all Fidler he appear'd,
> And drew with Musick the unthinking herd.

Mr. Noyes dates the prologue approximately during the second decade of the Restoration owing to the complaint about the triumphs of opera. Davenant's operatic version of *Macbeth* was brought out in 1673, and Shadwell's operatic version of *The Tempest*, the Davenant and Dryden version, in 1674.

There was a regular series of revivals in the eighteenth century. *Volpone* was acted at the Theatre Royal on 2 May and 27 December 1700, and 18 March 1701. We learn this from Mr. Hotson's discovery of the accounts rendered to Penelope, Lady Morley, for plays at Drury Lane, where she was a box-holder.[1] In the Easter term of 1701 the actors were presented before the grand jury for Middlesex for producing indecent plays, of which *Volpone* was one.[2] The indecency of *Volpone* was confined, apparently, to Lady Would-be's speech to Peregrine (IV. iii. 18–19), misquoted in this form: 'Pray, Sir, make use of me, pray while you stay make use of me and the oft'ner you use me I shall take it for granted you have forgotten the Injury I have done you. ⟨*Peregrine.*⟩ Be damn'd.' The action failed, and there was one more performance this year on 19 June. This was announced in *The English Post* of June 11/13, with the statement, 'The Part of the Fox attempted by Mr. Cibber. For his own Benefit.'

In 1703 there were five performances, on 21 May, 25 May, 12 June, 3 November, and 24 November. In the first of these *The Daily Courant* (20 May) stated that the part of Corbaccio was 'to be acted by Ben Johnson for his own benefit'. It was played again for this actor's benefit in 1708, 1712, and 1716. From 1703 to his death in 1742, Mr. Noyes notes,[3] there were only seven years in which he failed to play Corbaccio. Steele in *The Spectator* of 29 April 1712 paid a tribute to his acting: '*Johnson* by acting *Corbaccio* the other night, must have given all who saw him a thorough detestation of aged Avarice.' And Chetwood stated that he 'arrived at as great

---

[1] *The Commonwealth and Restoration Stage*, pp. 306–8. Lady Morley brought an action against Davenant and the patentees of the theatre to recover the arrears on her husband's shares. The accounts are summarized on pp. 378–9.
[2] See the notice in Noyes, *Ben Jonson on the English Stage*, p. 54.
[3] Op. cit., p. 63.

a Perfection in Acting, as his great Namesake did in Poetry. He seemed to be proud to wear that eminent Poet's double Name, being more particularly great in all that Author's Plays that were usually performed, *viz.*, *Wasp* in the Play of *Bartholomew-Fair*, *Corbaccio* in the *Fox*, *Morose* in the *Silent Woman*, and *Ananias* in the *Alchymist*.'[1]

In the performance of 12 June 1702 Robert Wilks played Mosca, 'for his own Benefit', says *The Daily Courant* of 11 June. Downes describes him as 'Proper and Comely in Person, of Graceful Port, Mein and Air; void of Affectation. . . . He is indeed the finisht Copy of his Famous Predecessor, Mr. *Charles Hart*.'[2] Hamlet was one of his famous parts. He acted Mosca for the last time on 5 October 1731.

In 1704 there were performances on 23 February, 17 June, and 29 November, and in 1705 performances on 5 June and 7 November. George Powell played Volpone to Wilks's Mosca. Musical entertainments and displays by such un-Jonsonian characters as Scaramouch, Harlequin, and Puncinello varied the performance.

The staff of Drury Lane joined that of the Haymarket in 1706, and *Volpone* was performed on 3 December. John Mills was Volpone; Wilks, Mosca; Theophilus Keen, Voltore; Benjamin Johnson, Corbaccio; Colley Cibber, Corvino; Henry Norris, Politic Would-be; Barton Booth, Bonario; Mrs. Leigh, Lady Would-be; Mrs. Oldfield, Celia.[3] Mills shared the title-part with George Powell until 1712, and shared Corvino with Cibber. On 15 January 1708 the united companies returned to Drury Lane, and on 27 April *Volpone* was played for Johnson's benefit. Mrs. Rogers was Celia, Mrs. Kent Lady Would-be. The acting version of the play printed for J. Tonson in 1709 gives a cast. There were performances on 26 February and 27 May. This last is memorable as inspiring a criticism by Steele in *The Tatler*[4] on the effect the play would have on the playgoer. The cast gives Powell for Volpone, Cibber for Corvino, Mrs. Kent for Lady Would-be, Fairbank for Peregrine, and Corey, Carnaby, Smith, and Cross for the four Avocatori: otherwise the performers were as in 1706.

From 1712 to 1726 there were one or two performances a year, except for a break in 1719 when *Volpone* was not played. During this period Wilks was famous in the part of Mosca.

In 1727 the Drury Lane company had to compete with a new theatre in Lincoln's Inn Fields and in 1732 with the new Covent

[1] *A General History of the Stage*, 1749, p. 174.
[2] *Roscius Anglicanus*, p. 51.   [3] Genest, ii. 360.
[4] No. 21, ed. Aitken, i. 177–8.

Garden theatre. Of the performances at Drury Lane in 1731 and 1733–5 Thomas Davies has given an account in his *Dramatic Miscellanies* (ii. 99, 100):

> In the year 1731, the elder Mills acted Volpone; Wilks, Mosca; Colley Cibber, Corvino; Ben Jonson, Corbaccio; Mrs. Horton, Lady Would-be; and Celia by Mrs. Butler. About three years after, it was acted to still more advantage, for Quin excelled Mills in Volpone. In the Mountebank he assumed all the art, trick, and voluble impudence, of a charlatan; though W. Mills, who succeeded Wilks[1] in Mosca, fell below his predecessor, yet his father, who submitted to play Corvino, was superior to C. Cibber in that part. Cibber seemed, I thought, to jest with the character. Mills was in earnest, and had a stronger voice to express passionate and jealous rage than the other. Jonson kept his old part, but Milward's Voltore was a fine copy of law oratory. Mrs. Clive, I need not say, gave infinite entertainment in Lady Wou'd-be. Though Celia is but a short part, to Mrs. Butler's great commendation, she rendered it extremely interesting.

'The venerable Mr. Boman', then close on eighty, is praised as the first avocatore. 'This actor was the last of the Bettertonian school.'

At Covent Garden *Volpone* was played on 15 November 1727 with James Quin as Volpone, Lacy Ryan as Mosca, Boherne as Voltore, John Hippisley as Corbaccio, William Milward as Bonario, Thomas Chapman as Peregrine, James Spiller as Sir Politic, Mrs. Younger as Lady Would-be, and Mrs. Bullock as Celia.[2] Quin was famous for such Shakespearian parts as Benedick, King Lear, and Richard III, and Davies's tribute to him in *Volpone* has been quoted above. He acted the part until 1750, not only at Covent Garden, but at Lincoln's Inn Fields and Drury Lane. One record of his acting which has come down to us exhibits him as practising a method of declamation which appeals to actors from time to time, in tragedy as well as comedy. Sir John Hill in *The Actor*, 1750, gives advice on the manner of recitation in comedy:

> Nothing can be more evident, than that rhyme and measure always tend to take off greatly from the air of truth, nature and reality, which the dialogue would otherwise have. In consequence of this, the actor's principal care and study ought to be, wherever he is encumber'd with these fetters, to break the one, and, as much as possible, sink and lose the other in the reciting. Several of our *Shakespear's* and *Ben Johnson's* plays have passages in rhyme and measure, in some parts; and that excellent composition *Comus* abounds too much in them, in the character of the God of Revels; yet, to the honour of *Volpone* and *Comus*, we mean when Mr. *Quin* represents those characters, perhaps it has not

---

[1] Wilks died in 1732.   [2] Genest, iii. 218.

been found out by any body, that has not read as well as seen those pieces, that there is a line in measure, or a single rhyme in either of them.[1]

The verse-rhythm could be destroyed by keeping to the modern logical punctuation and dropping or varying the emphasis;[2] but it is difficult to see how rhyme was sacrificed, unless by substituting a synonym for the rhyming word, saying 'brave' instead of 'bold', for example. In *Volpone*, of course, the title-character speaks no rhyming verse; rhymes are confined to the prologues, the epilogue, the songs, and a few couplets at the end of scenes.

Of Hippisley's performance Thomas Davies says that 'no comedian ever excelled him in describing the excesses of avarice and amorous dotage. . . . Corbaccio . . . is a strong portrait of covetousness, a vice which predominates in the man when almost all his faculties of body and mind are extinguished. Corbaccio can neither see nor hear perfectly: Hippisley's look told the audience that he was a deaf man, for his dim eyes seemed to enquire out the words which were spoken to him. In this character it is acknowledged that he excelled his great competitor Johnson.'[3]

There were seven performances of *Volpone* in 1733 and five in 1734 at Covent Garden and Drury Lane, and also at the Haymarket, to which there had been a secession from Drury Lane headed by Cibber; the seceders returned in March 1734. *The Universal Spectator* for 8 December 1733 reviewed the Covent Garden performances of 1733 and described the visit of an old-fashioned knight, Sir Jasper Truby, who made amusing comments on the characters.[4] At the Haymarket Adam Hallam played Mosca; William Milward, Voltore; Edmund Berry, Corvino; Oates, Bonario; Winstone, Peregrine; Benjamin Griffin, Sir Politic Would-be; Charlotte Clarke (Cibber's daughter), Lady Would-be; and Mrs. Butler, Celia.[5]

In 1736 came a change in the cast at Covent Garden: Dennis Delane acted Volpone, and the beautiful Mrs. Horton Celia: she had been Lady Would-be at Drury Lane from 1725 to 1731; she played

---

[1] Quoted by R. G. Noyes, op. cit., pp. 80–1.

[2] See a correspondence in *The Times* from 30 Jan. to 4 Feb. 1920, about a performance of *Julius Caesar* in which the actors overrode the rhythm and turned poetry into prose.

[3] *Memoirs of the Life of David Garrick*, 1784, i. 36–7.

[4] Mr. Noyes quotes from *The Gentleman's Magazine*, iv, p. 624, the prologue and epilogue of a performance at Bury School on 5 Nov. 1734. Mr. Stebbing spoke the prologue—a diatribe against popery, as exhibited in Gunpowder Plot; and Master Rustal, who acted Volpone ('To night as mountebank I have been drubb'd'), made this the starting-point in the epilogue for an attack on the mountebanks Sir William Read and Dr. Joshua Ward.

[5] Quoted from Griffin's diary, Egerton MS. 2320, by Noyes, op. cit., p. 70.

Celia from 1736 to 1746, and Lady Would-be finally in 1750. The famous actress Mrs. Clive played Lady Would-be at Covent Garden in 1743, and Anne Bellamy was Celia there from 1745 to 1753. Luke Sparks, after playing Corvino, succeeded Quin as Volpone in 1753, and Edward Shuter was Corbaccio. Then for seventeen years the play was dropped at Covent Garden.

Garrick planned a revival of the play at Drury Lane in 1757 and again in 1769, but abandoned the project. It was actually revived at Covent Garden on 26 November 1771. William Smith was Volpone, Robert Bensley was Mosca; Thomas Hull, Voltore; Edward Shuter, Corbaccio; Matthew Clarke, Corvino; Richard Wroughton, Bonario; Kniveton, Sir Politic; Mrs. Gardner was Lady Would-be and Miss Miller Celia. In 1773 John and Mrs. Bulkley took over Sir Politic and Celia. The text was shortened. A touch of Shuter's by-play is quoted in *The Theatrical Review* which gave a full notice of the performance:[1] 'His strokes of Bye-play, of endeavouring to hasten the death of *Volpone*, (whom he supposes to be sick, and near his end, on the Couch) by pressing his stomach with his cane, while *Mosca* is engaged with *Voltore*, are well imagined, when we consider, that in this Character, Nature is rather caricatured, which is the general, tho' only fault of this Author, in his Comic Writings.'

Bell's edition of the play in *The British Theatre*, 1778, with a frontispiece of Hull as Voltore, gives the text 'As altered from Ben Jonson and performed at the Theatre-Royal in Covent Garden. Regulated from the Prompt-Book, By Permission of the Managers, By Mr. Wild, Prompter'. There was no rewriting, and only one structural change: after I. iii. 80 Corvino entered, not Corbaccio; of the two Corvino gives less scope to the actor, and the Corbaccio scene, being put later, leads up to a climax in the proposal to disinherit his son. The changes were omissions only, of scenes, passages in long speeches, lines, or phrases; thus Volpone's opening speech was shortened by over thirteen lines.

> Good morning to the day; and next my gold;
> Hail the world's soul and mine!
> That lying here, amongst my other hoards,
> Shew'st like a flame by night, or like the day
> Struck out of chaos, when all darkness fled
> Unto the centre.
> Well did wise poets by thy glorious name,
> Title that age which they would have the best;
> Thy looks, when they to Venus did ascribe,

[1] Vol. i (1772), pp. 226–32.

They should have giuen her twenty thousand Cupids;
Such are thy beauties and our loves!
        Thou art virtue, fame,
Honour, and all things else. Who can get thee,
He shall be noble, valiant, honest, wise—

The general effect of the cuts was to speed up the action, and the omission of archaisms, contemporary and scholarly allusions, and details on which the poet was apt to insist made the play easier to follow. The larger omissions are the show in I. ii. 1–82 and the sports of III. iii. 1–20; the reduction of Sir Politic Would-be almost to a nonentity by omitting the portents in II. i. 33–97, and the projects in IV. i. 11–147, and the whole of v. iv; Lady Would-be loses the reference to her red nose (III. iv. 14–16), some of her literary criticism (ibid. 90–7), and her moralizing (102–12). The mountebank speech in Act II has three cuts (ii. 47–68, 134–73, 185–203 (one song being considered sufficient)). In II. v the detailed picture of the mountebank (ll. 3–24) was considered superfluous after the audience had seen him. Details were also omitted in Volpone's proffers to Celia (III. vii. 213–20, 224–32) and only the first two lines were retained of the song 'Come, my Celia' (ll. 166–7). In the fifth Act scenes v to ix were shortened, and scene x was omitted. Elizabethan allusions naturally disappear—the reference to the lawyer's mule (I. ii. 106–7), to the bells in plague-time and the cockpit (III. v. 5–11), to the entertainment of Henry III of France at Venice (III. vii. 157–64), to the French Hercules (IV. iv. 22), and the scholarly reference to Lollia Paulina (III. vii. 195–7). Coarse details were omitted, and phrases which savoured of indecency—the reference to Volpone's incontinence (I. v. 54–5), the slimy eyes (ibid. 57–8), and the running nose (65), and Corvino's abuse of Celia (II. v. 26) and his coarse threat (57–66).

The final performances of the century were at the Haymarket on 12 September 1783 and at Drury Lane in February and on 13 April 1785. Colman managed the former and gave eight performances: John Palmer was Volpone; Bensley, Mosca;[1] John Bannister, Voltore; William Parsons, Corbaccio; James Aickin, Corvino; R. Palmer, Bonario; and Mrs. Inchbold, Celia.

The play was not performed again until the twentieth century; as Gifford put it in 1816, 'the age of dramatic imbecility was rapidly advancing upon us, and the stage already looked to jointed-dolls, water-spaniels, and peacocks'-tails for its main credit and support'.

---

[1] For a criticism of Bensley see J. Boaden, *Memoirs of Kemble*, 1825, i, p. 57, and of Parsons, with his hands like the claws of a harpy clutching the will (ibid., p. 62).

The twentieth century has seen a number of revivals which did justice to the acting merits of the play. The Phoenix Society twice played it, on 30 January 1921 at the Lyric Theatre, Hammersmith, and on 29 June 1923 at the Regent Theatre, King's Cross. The cast at the Lyric Theatre was—Volpone, Balliol Holloway; Mosca, Ion Swinley; Voltore, D. Lewin Mannering; Corbaccio, Stanley Lathbury; Corvino, George Zucco; Bonario, Murray Kinnell; Peregrine, William Armstrong; Sir Politic, Eugene Leahy; Lady Would-be, Margaret Yarde; Celia, Isabel Jeans. At the second performance Rupert Harvey played Mosca. The producer was Allan Wade. The setting was specially designed for an Elizabethan play—a set scene, either drab or green, unchanged throughout the play, with three openings below and above, against this dull background; the actors in bright dresses stood out clearly. It was a brilliant performance, especially by the two chief characters. Mr. Holloway caught the Renaissance touch in Volpone, interpreting him as a grim moralist with a deep sense of humour and doing full justice to the aesthetic beauty of the play at such moments as the grandiose wooing of Celia.

The Marlowe Dramatic Society gave seven performances of the play at Cambridge on 3 March 1923 to 10 March. Dennis Arundell was Volpone; F. L. Birch, Mosca; A Goodden, Corbaccio; D. L. Herbage, Peregrine; V. Clinton Baddeley, Sir Politic Would-be; Cecil Barton, Lady Politic. Criticism of the acting centred on one main point—the difference between the serious part dominated by Volpone and the farcical element of the minor characters. High praise was given to the performance of the latter, while more than one critic spoke doubtfully of the former. The play, mainly no doubt because of its length, was taken at a good pace, and no distinction was made between the serious and the farcical elements in this respect; the great poetry of Volpone's wooing of Celia gives a higher tone to the style. The quick-moving action was helped by the setting. The stage was arranged in three parts with an inner arch and an apse-shaped innermost stage. The full stage had a curtain with Aesop's fable of the fox and crow in pink, red, and black. Volpone's bedroom and the Senate House were within this, the latter draped in black, hung with blue patterned in silver; the crimson robes of Senators and advocates stood out against this. The music was almost entirely Ferrabosco's; an 'almaine' and 'curranta' before Act I, the Fool's song in Act I. ii. 66–81 adapted from 'Alfonsoes Toy', Volpone's song in Act III. vii. 166–83 adapted from one of his lute lessons, and a 'coranto' before Act IV. 'Greensleeves' as set by William Ballet was also given in Act III, scene ii; and the mountebank songs in Act II, scene i, were adapted from Laudi Spirituali, 'Amor fals' ingrato, ovvero Ballo di Mantova', 'Gioia et amore'.

The play was next given at the Malvern Festival of 1935 on 30 July. Wilfrid Lawson was Volpone; Stephen Murray, Mosca; Arthur Ridley, Voltore; Charles Victor, Corbaccio; Cecil Trouncer, Corvino; Donald Eccles, Bonario; Harold Chapin, Peregrine; Clifford Marle, Sir Politic Would-be; Eileen Beldon, Lady Would-be; Curigwen Lewis, Celia. Mr. Herbert Prentice was the producer. 'A fox in his flaming make-up', *The Times* said of the performer of the title-part, 'he was in essence a man whose cruelty and cunning and intellect had grown with age and were ripe for mischief on the grand scale. Mr. Lawson's performance had breadth and drive, and all the other performances were nicely adjusted to its movement.'

On 19 December 1936 the students of Eliot House, Harvard University, revived the play. The director was Dr. Harry Levin. Norton Goodwin played Volpone.

The performances of Mr. Donald Wolfit were given at the Westminster Theatre in January and February 1938, at Cambridge on 19, 20 February 1940, and at the St. James's Theatre in March 1942. There were also revivals in 1944 and 1947. At the Westminster Theatre Donald Wolfit was Volpone; Alan Wheatley, Mosca; Mark Dignam, Voltore; Stanley Lathbury, Corbaccio; Raymond Lovell, Corvino; Niall McGinnis, Bonario; Rachel Kempson, Celia. The sub-plot of Sir Politic and Lady Would-be was omitted. The suggestion of animal symbolism which runs through the play in the names of the characters was developed by making the Avocatori look like owls. It was a good performance. Volpone in the scene where Mosca introduced the would-be heirs leered through the curtains and twiddled his toes under the bedclothes for sheer enjoyment as the gifts kept coming in. He was very effective in the mountebank scene, and when he wooed Celia began by flinging pearls into her lap. Mosca, a visible hypocrite from the start, rather emphasized this aspect of the character, perhaps as a clue to the sequel, and Miss Kempson gave a powerful rendering of the impotent part of Celia—the utmost that could be done with it. At the St. James's Theatre Frank Thornton was Mosca, and Nigel Clarke, Eric Maxon, and Reginald Jarman were the legacy-hunters.

On 30 April 1940 the play was given in the Clarendon Press Institute at Oxford by the Hertford College Dramatic Society under the direction of Mr. Nevill Coghill. William Goodger played Volpone; Ronald Ellen, Mosca; Maurice Chandler, Corbaccio; Gerald Lester, Corvino; Patrick Carmody, Sir Politic; John Reynolds, Peregrine; Frances Fraser, Lady Would-be; Daphne Levens, Celia;

and John Wilson, Bonario. The setting was eighteenth-century baroque to get the effect of richness; in the scrutineo scene Volpone was brought in in a sedan chair. The acting of the principal characters reached a high level. Mr. John Masefield wrote a prologue for this performance.

> Eleven generations have gone sere
> Since Oxford 'bounty' brought Ben Jonson here
> To show this poem in a College Hall.
>
> Our learned watched Volpone's rise and fall
> With 'love' and with 'acceptance' in such measure
> As gave the poet never-dying pleasure;
> Pleasure so deep, that when the play was printed,
> He offered it, with gratitude unstinted,
> (Together with himself), to these two Cities
> Where so much love of Learning and of Wit is.
>
> Now, for two hours, or a little more,
> We need not think, nor talk about, the war;
> But, (thanks to Hertford College), watch the while
> Volpone and his Mosca practise guile.
>
> Quite possibly, unheard, unseen, but near,
> Ben's truculent and burly ghost is here
> Trembling with joy that living scholars share
> His estimate of what his Muses bare,
> And promising to pledge us in a cup, . . .
>
> But I must stop;—the Curtain's going up.

In June 1944 there were five performances at the Shakespeare Memorial Theatre, Stratford-on-Avon. The principal actors were Robert Atkins (who produced the play), Volpone; John Byron, Mosca; David Read, Voltore; Clement Hamelin, Corbaccio; Raymond Rollett, Corvino; Helen Cherry, Celia; Peter Upcher, Sir Politic; Viola Lyel, Lady Would-be. The parts of Volpone and Mosca were admirably played; the pair fitted in to one another at first in a good-humoured conspiracy to defraud the legacy-hunters whom they moved about like chessmen before they changed over to the grim contest of checkmating each other. The play was given fully except for Sir Politic's tortoise. Lady Would-be stood out amusingly in the sombre group with which she was associated. The comic side of the play was well maintained by the owl-like magistrates, W. E. Holloway, Jack Lynn, and David March, but the antics of the dwarf, hermaphrodite, and eunuch were rather elementary; they largely consisted of tumbling tricks. The elocution of all the actors was so good that not a syllable was missed. Altogether it was a memorable revival.

Three translations of *Volpone* have appeared in France, by Amédee Pichot and J. Defauchompret in 1835 ('Collection du théâtre étranger', fascicules 6 & 7), by Ernest Lafond in 1863 ('Librairie Hetzel'), and in 1934 by Maurice Castelain ('Collection du théâtre anglais de la Renaissance'), the last with a text of the play printed opposite the translation.

It is a tribute to the dramatic power of *Volpone* that there have been three foreign adaptations of it. The earliest by Ludwig Tieck, a keen student of Jonson, *Herr von Fuchs. Ein Lustspiel in drei Aufzügen, nach dem Volpone des Ben-Jonson*, was in 1793. Tieck omitted the mountebank scene and the interludes in Volpone's house, and he renamed the characters. Volpone was Herr von Fuchs, Mosca Fliege, Bonario Karl von Krähfeld, and Celia Louise. Louise was von Krähfeld's (Corvino's) ward and at the end of the play was betrothed to Karl. This change recalls a comment of W. B. Yeats when he saw the Phoenix performance: in the trial scene Bonario and Celia sat below the tribune of the judges in the centre of the stage facing the audience, and Yeats said, 'They looked so pathetic, they were not even lovers.'

Émile Zola's adaptation, which he rightly called a farce, *Les Héritiers Rabourdin*, was a burlesque on *Volpone*; if he had not in his preface pointed to Jonson as his source, few would have detected it. Rabourdin, an absolute pauper credited with having saved vast wealth, dupes rich relatives and friends, who give him presents and money; his niece, for instance, loses favour because for many days she has sent him nothing more than a leg of mutton. The visitors also dose him heavily with medicines. He is threatened with exposure because he cannot raise a few pounds to pay his bills. He has a sham death-scene, and when the victims unlock his safe they find it empty. Played at the Théâtre Cluny in Paris on 5 November 1874, the piece was a disastrous failure.

An English version by A. Teixeira de Mattos was played at the Independent Theatre on 23 February 1894 under the management of Mr. J. T. Grein. The translation also failed completely on the stage.

Thirdly there was the adaptation of Stefan Zweig and Jules Romains, played very successfully at the Théâtre d'Atelier, Paris, in December 1928. An English translation has been made by Ruth Langner. The difference in tone between the adaptation and the original is marked by the authors' note, 'To be played as a *commedia dell' arte*, lightly, quickly, caricatured rather than realistic; *allegro conbrio*'. Volpone is a rich Levantine, not a Venetian; Corbaccio's son is a sea-captain, Leone; Corvino's wife is Colomba; the underplot disappears, but Lady Would-be is amply replaced by Canina, a prostitute, who wants Volpone to marry her in order to father her unborn child. The character of Mosca is changed; he looks indifferently on while Volpone rhapsodizes over his gold, thinks that treasure locked up in money chests is wasted, and would give it wings. He agrees reluctantly to the final duping of the victims over Volpone's supposed death. Leone is outwitted and put in the pillory for a time. Finally Mosca secures the treasure, and prepares to spend it. Volpone flies to Genoa where he has a ship with a rich cargo; the Judge, after the exposure of all the trickery, had decided to nail Volpone's supposedly dead body to the gallows.

Charles Dullin played Volpone; Daniel Lecourtois, Mosca; M. Vibert, Corvino; M. Decroux, Corvino; G. Seroff, Corbaccio: the last used the same by-play as Shuter in prodding Volpone with a cane to make him cough.[1]

EPICOENE, OR THE SILENT WOMAN

'THIS Comoedie', says the note appended to the play in the 1616 Folio, 'was first acted, in the yeare 1609. By the Children of her Maiesties Reuells.' The theatre was the Whitefriars, to which there is a local reference in line 24 of the prologue. The date may be the end of 1609, 'or, if Jonson's chronology permits,' says Sir E. K. Chambers, 'early in 1610'.[2] We accept the latter date for the reasons we gave in the similar problem of *Volpone*. F. G. Fleay declared for the early months of 1610 because the Children of the Chapel who acted the play were not entitled to call themselves the Children of the Queen's Revels before their patent of 4 January 1610, which authorized them 'to practice and exercise in the quality of playing, by the name of Children of the Revells of the Queene, within the white ffreyers in the Suburbs of our Citty of London'.[3] This company was called successively Children of the Chapel, Children of the Queen's Revels, Children of the Blackfriars, and Children of the Whitefriars. We cannot therefore call Jonson's historic note a certain proof of the date, 1610: looking back on the performance when

---

[1] See p. 202.
[2] *Elizabethan Stage*, iii, p. 370. In our general introduction to the play (vol. ii, p. 69) we declared for 1609, through misdating the entry in the Stationers' Register, the date of which was 20 Sept. 1610.
[3] Chambers, op. cit. ii, p. 56.

he edited the Folio, he may by a slip of memory have antedated the official title of that year by a few months. But it fits his system of chronology, and it is at any rate a confirmation. Note that the second prologue (l. 5) speaks of the play being presented at night.

Sir Henry Herbert's Office Book records 'The Silent Woman playd at Court of St. James on thursday y\e 18 Febr. 1635', i.e. 1636.[1] This would be by the King's men. They acted the play again at Court on 21 April 1636. This is entered in the Audit Office accounts for that year; the King's men were claiming their fee. Wright says (*Historia Histrionica*, 1699, p. 4) that 'in my time, before the Wars' John Lowin used to act Morose; this would be after the play was taken over by the King's men. Wright also says that Joseph Taylor played Truewit; this would be after he joined the King's men in 1619.

A performance of *Epicoene* June 1660 is the first which is recorded at the Restoration. Pepys noted on 6 June that the 'two Dukes' of York and Gloucester 'haunt the Park much' and 'were at a play, Madam Epicene, the other day'.[2] It was played by 'the Red Bull actors' in St. John's Street, Clerkenwell, a company of old players who had survived the Commonwealth, and Malone quotes from a paper of Sir Henry Herbert's *The Silent Woman* as one of their stock plays.[3] They merged into a new company of Killigrew's, which received its patent on 21 August and acted in Gibbon's tennis-court in Vere Street near Clare-market; they played *Epicoene* on 10 November and 4 December. Between the two performances, on 19 November, they acted the play at the Cockpit at Whitehall in an entertainment provided by General Monk. The prologue, preserved in a broadside, is ascribed to Denham in the Bodleian copy (Wood 398. 16).

THE PROLOGUE TO HIS MAJESTY
At the first PLAY presented at the Cock-pit in
WHITEHALL
Being part of the Noble Entertainment which Their MAIESTIES
received *Novemb.* 19. from his *Grace* the Duke of
ALBEMARLE

Greatest of Monarchs, welcome to this place
Which Majesty *so oft was wont to grace*
Before our Exile, to divert the Court,
And ballance weighty Cares with harmless sport.
This truth we can to our advantage say,
They that would have no KING, *would have no* Play:

[1] Malone, *Variorum Shakespeare*, iii, p. 273.
[2] *Diary*, ed. Wheatley, i, pp. 172–3.
[3] *Variorum Shakespeare*, iii, pp. 272–3.

> *The* Laurel *and the* Crown *together went,*
> *Had the same* Foes, *and the same* Banishment:
> *The Ghosts of their great Ancestors they fear'd,*
> *Who by the art of conjuring Poets rear'd,*
> *Our* HARRIES &- *our* EDWARDS *long since dead*
> *Still on the Stage a march of Glory tread:*
> *Those Monuments of Fame (they thought) would stain*
> *And teach the People to despise their Reign:*
> *Nor durst they look into the Muses Well,*
> *Least the clear Spring their ugliness should tell;*
> *Affrighted with the shadow of their Rage,*
> *They broke the Mirror of the times, the Stage;*
> *The Stage against them still maintain'd the War,*
> *When they debauch'd the* Pulpit *and the* Bar.
> *Though to be Hypocrites, be our Praise alone,*
> *'Tis our peculiar boast that we were none.*
> *What e're they taught, we practis'd what was true,*
> *And something we had learn'd of honor too,*
> *When by Your Danger, and our Duty prest,*
> *We acted in the Field, and not in Jest;*
> *Then for the* Cause *our Tyring-house they sack't,*
> *And silenc't us that they alone might act;*
> *And (to our shame) most dext'rously they do it,*
> *Out-act the Players, and out-ly the Poet;*
> *But all the other Acts appear'd so scarce,*
> *Ours were the* Moral Lectures, *theirs the* Farse:
> *This spacious Land their Theater became,*
> *And they* Grave Counsellors, *and* Lords *in Name;*
> *Which these Mechanicks Personate so ill*
> *That ev'n the Oppressed with contempt they fill,*
> *But when the Lyons dreadful skin they took,*
> *They roar'd so loud that the whole Forrest shook;*
> *The noise kept all the Neighbourhood in awe,*
> *Who thought 'twas the true Lyon by his Pawe.*
> *If feigned Vertue could such Wonders do,*
> *What may not we expect from this that's true!*
> *But this Great Theme must serve another Age,*
> *To fill our Story, and adorne our Stage.*

Edward Kynaston, the boy actor, famous for his success in women's parts, played Epicoene. Pepys records on 7 January 1661:

Tom and I and my wife to the Theatre, and there saw 'The Silent Woman', the first time that euer I did see it, and it is an excellent play. Among other things here, Kinaston, the boy, had the good turn to appear in three shapes: first as a poor woman in ordinary clothes, to please Morose; then in fine clothes, as a gallant, and in them was clearly the prettiest woman in the whole house, and lastly, as a man; and then likewise did appear the handsomest man in the house.[1]

The play was performed at Cambridge in 1662, probably in the month of March. There is a tantalizing reference to it in the epilogue to S. Brooke's *Adelphe*, a play of 1612 and 1613, revived in 1662, probably at Trinity College: the text is in Trinity MS. R. 10. 4. The audience are asked which play they prefer—the *Adelphe* or *The Silent Woman*, which had just been acted.

> Peregimus, et vosmet jam sciscitamur serio
> Quænam e duabus maxime arridet fabula,
> Quam nunc apertis oculis spectastis hodie,
> An audijstis auribus quam occlusis nuperrime
> Miri, reor, subsidio Otocoustici?
> Titulo scilicet lepidam, silentem fœminam,
> Qualis nec extat modo, nec extabit uspiam;
> Versutus edidit quam Alastor improbus,
> Qui primus omnium simulavit se Hypocritam,
> Proteus Academicus, Centaurus Scenicus, . . .

There is no clue to the 'Alastor improbus' who produced the play.[2]

Killigrew's company moved to Drury Lane in April 1663, and Downes gives the cast for a performance of *Epicoene* on 7 May. Cartwright was Morose; Mohun, Truewit; Burt, Cleremont; Kynaston, Dauphine; Wintershall, La Foole; Shatterel, Daw; Lacy, Otter; Mrs. Knepp, Epicene; Mrs. Rutter, Lady Haughty; Mrs. Corey, Mistress Otter. Mrs. Knepp was the first of a number of actresses who made the part of Epicene ridiculous by posing as a woman in disguise. Pepys, however, admired her: on 18 September 1668 he writes, 'At the end of the play, thinking to have gone abroad with Knepp, but it was too late, and she to get her part against to-morrow, in "The Silent Woman"';[3] and again on 19 September, 'To the King's playhouse, and there saw "The Silent Woman", the best comedy, I think, that ever was wrote; and sitting by Shadwell the poet, he was big with admiration of it. . . . Knepp did her part mighty well.'[3] On 16 April 1667 he had said of the play, 'I was never more taken with a play than I am with this "Silent Woman", as old as it is, and as often as I have seen it. There is more wit in it than goes to ten new plays.'[4]

In 1664 the King's Company played *Epicoene* at the Inner Temple, and on 1 June at Drury Lane where Pepys saw it, 'not so well done

---

[1] *Diary*, ed. Wheatley, i, p. 320.
[2] See the letter of G. C. Moore Smith to *The Cambridge Review* of 4 Feb. 1919.
[3] *Diary*, viii, pp. 107–8.   [4] Ibid. vi, p. 274.

or not so good a play as I formerly thought it to be'.[1] About 12 January 1669 it was 'allowed of to his Maties Servants at ye New Theatre'.[2] In 1673 the Company went to Oxford, probably early in July; they were in money difficulties. They acted *Epicoene*; 'there was no permanent theatre there, other than the Sheldonian, and this was never let to professional actors'; they acted in one of the Oxford tennis-courts.[3] Dryden contributed a prologue and epilogue, which have been preserved in *Miscellany Poems*, 1684, pp. 263–7.

PROLOGUE,

To the University of *Oxon*.

Spoken by Mr. Hart, *at the Acting of the*

Silent Woman,

Written by Mr. Dryden.

What *Greece*, when Learning flourish'd, onely Knew,
(*Athenian* Judges) you this day Renew.
Here too are Annual Rites to *Pallas* done,
And here Poetique prizes lost or won.
Methinks I see you, Crown'd with Olives sit,
And strike a sacred Horrour from the Pit.
A Day of Doom is this of your Decree,
Where even the Best are but by Mercy free:
A Day which none but *Johnson* durst have wish'd to see.
Here they who long have known the usefull Stage,
Come to be taught themselves to teach the Age.
As your Commissioners our Poets goe,
To Cultivate the Virtue which you sow:
In your *Lycæum*, first themselves refind,
And Delegated thence to Humane kind.
But as Embassadours, when long from home,
For new Instructions to their Princes come;
So Poets who your Precepts have forgot,
Return, and beg they may be better taught:
Follies and Faults elsewhere by them are shown,
But by your Manners they Correct their Own.
Th' illiterate Writer, Emperique like, applies
To minds diseas'd, unsafe, chance Remedies:
The Learn'd in Schools, where Knowledge first began,
Studies with Care th'Anatomy of Man;
Sees Vertue, Vice, and Passions in their Cause,
And Fame from Science, not from Fortune, draws.

---

[1] *Diary*, ed. Wheatley, iv, p. 148. Edward Browne saw it at Drury Lane, and paid 2s. (Sloane MS. 1900, f. 37).   [2] Nicoll, *Restoration Drama*, p. 315.
[3] H. Macdonald, *John Dryden, a Bibliography*, p. 138.

So Poetry, which is in *Oxford* made
An Art, in *London* onely is a Trade.
There Haughty Dunces whose unlearned Pen
Could ne'er Spell Grammar, would be reading Men.
Such build their Poems the *Lucretian* way,
So many Huddled Atoms make a Play,
And if they hit in Order in some Chance,
They call that Nature, which is Ignorance.
To such a Fame let mere Town-Wits aspire,
And their Gay Nonsense their own Cits admire.
Our Poet, could he find Forgiveness here
Would wish it rather than a *Plaudit* there.
He owns no Crown from those *Prætorian* bands,
But knows *that* Right is in this Senates hands.
Not Impudent enough to hope your Praise,⎫
Low at the Muses feet, his Wreath he lays,⎬
And where he took it up Resigns his Bays.⎭
Kings make their Poets whom themselves think fit,
But 'tis your Suffrage makes Authentique Wit.

EPILOGUE, *Spoken by the Same.*

Written by Mr. Dryden.

No poor *Dutch* Peasant, wing'd with all his Fear,
Flies with more haste, when the *French* arms draw near,
Than We with our Poetique train come down
For refuge hither, from th'infected Town;
Heaven for our Sins this Summer has thought fit
To visit us with all the Plagues of Wit.
    A *French* Troop first swept all things in its way,
But those Hot *Monsieurs* were too quick to stay;
Yet, to our Cost in that short time, we find
They left their Itch of Novelty behind.
    Th' *Italian* Merry-Andrews took their place,
And quite Debauch'd the Stage with lewd Grimace;
Instead of Wit, and Humours, your Delight
Was there to see two Hobby-horses Fight,
Stout *Scaramoucha* with Rush Lance rode in,
And ran a Tilt at Centaure *Arlequin.*
For Love you heard how Amorous Asses bray'd,
And Cats in Gutters gave their Serenade.
Nature was out of Countenance, and each Day
Some new born Monster shewn you for a Play.
    But when all fail'd, to strike the Stage quite Dumb,
Those wicked Engines call'd Machines are come.
Thunder and Lightning now for Wit are Play'd,
And shortly Scenes in *Lapland* will be Lay'd:

Art Magique is for Poetry profest,
And Cats and Dogs, and each obscener Beast
To which *Ægyptian* Dotards once did Bow,
Upon our *English* stage are worship'd now.
Witchcraft reigns there, and raises to Renown
Macbeth, the *Simon Magus* of the Town.
Fletcher's despised, your *Johnson* out of Fashion,
And Wit the onely Drug in all the Nation.
In this low Ebb our Wares to you are shown, ⎱
By you those Staple Authours worth is known, ⎰
For Wit's a Manufacture of your Own. ⎰
When you, who onely can, their Scenes have prais'd,
We'll boldly back, and say their Price is rais'd.

With Dryden's criticism, here of the contemporary stage, and especially his reference to Davenant's operatic version of *Macbeth* at Dorset Garden, compare the anonymous prologue to *Volpone* quoted on pages 197–8.

From 4 May 1682 to 22 December 1694 the King's Company united with Killigrew's; they played *The Silent Woman* before the King and Queen on 15 January 1685. Langbaine said of it in 1691 that, in spite of its borrowings from the classics, it was 'Accounted by all, One of the best Comedies we have extant; and those who would know more, may be amply satisfied by the perusal of the judicious Examen of this Play made by Mr. Dryden'.[1]

Lady Morley[2] saw the play on 21 December 1700 and on 5 June 1701. Twice in 1703, 'with several entertainments of Singing and Dancing' as *The Daily Courant* advertised on 7 October, twice in 1704, and once in 1706 *The Silent Woman* was played at Drury Lane: Betterton, now the important actor of the company, played Morose three times—the only part he ever took in a piece of Jonson's. There were six performances in 1707 and two in 1708 by the Drury Lane Company and Betterton's, which had united at the Haymarket. The cast was Benjamin Johnson, Morose; Booth, Dauphine; the elder Mills, Clerimont; Wilks, Truewit; Norris, Cutbeard; Colley Cibber, Sir John Daw; Epicoene, Mrs. Oldfield. Johnson played Morose up to 1742, and Wilks played Truewit till his death in 1732. Of Johnson Davies says, 'Such an exhibition of comic distress . . . I have hardly ever seen in any other actor. He and Weston are the only comedians I can remember, that, in all the parts they represented, absolutely forgot themselves. . . . Jonson stayed on the stage to the last, within about two years of eighty.'[3] Booth played

---

[1] *The English Dramatick Poets*, p. 296.   [2] See p. 198.
[3] *Dramatic Miscellanies*, ii, p. 106.

Dauphine till 1729; Mills played Clerimont till 1736; Cibber played Daw till 1735; and Norris was Cutbeard till 1729. W. R. Chetwood noted the 'inimitable Perfection of the cast from 1712 to 1730'.[1]

The union of the Drury Lane and Haymarket companies came to an end in 1709 with the temporary closing of Drury Lane. The actors went from this theatre to the Haymarket and performed *Epicoene* on 11 January 1710. A performance on 9 February for the benefit of Richard Estcourt, actor and mimic, was recommended by Steele in *The Tatler*; he spoke of *Epicoene* as 'that admirable play'.[2] The Haymarket Company returned to Drury Lane in November 1710 and revived the play on the 28th of that month. Up to 1733, when there was another revolt to the Haymarket, it was given at least once a year with minor changes in the cast.[3] Benjamin Johnson was Morose, William Mills was Truewit, Mrs. Butler was Epicoene. There were four performances that year. From December 1733 to October 1736 there were thirteen performances; then the play was acted once a year till 1742 and not resumed at Drury Lane till 1752. On 22 May 1735 there was a benefit performance for Hewitt, Winstone, and Miss Cole; and the epilogue, spoken by Miss Cole and Master Green, repeats in a lighter form Dryden's criticism of the current attractions of the stage—French comedians, Italian singers, and harlequins. Even Jonson's plays suffered from inroads of buffoonery. On 31 May 1709 William Pinkethman had ridden in on a donkey to speak the epilogue of *Epicoene*. He was parodying Joseph Haines, who used to ride in on an ass, apparently after more than one play in which he acted, and recite an epilogue written for him by Tom Brown;[4] he wore the uniform of a cavalry officer.

> *He.* What shall we say—come Miss, do you begin.
> *She.* I can't, this odious Play has given me the *Spleen*,
> Must we be teaz'd with *Ben's* old Writings still!
> *He.* How should we please, or ever hope Advance,
> I'm no *Italian*——
> *She.*   Nor am I from *France*.
> O Faugh! I hate my self—an *English* Wench!—
> O dear, dear Ribaldry, and ⟨all in⟩ *French*.
> *He.* Must *Shakespeare's* Nature, *Johnson's* Humour cease;
> And to Buffoons and empty Sounds give place?
> *She.* Lord! can your Humour like a Caper charm,
> Or *Hamlet* like a soft *Piano* warm;
> What's *Caesar's* Death to a *French* Comic-Scene?
> Or what is *Cato* to a Harlequin?

---

[1] *Ben Jonson*, p. 72.   [2] No. 130, ed. Aitken, iii, p. 92.
[3] All these are chronicled by Mr. Noyes, op. cit.
[4] Printed in Tom Brown's *Works*, 1720, v, p. 233.

But let us still your kind Applauses share,
And to deserve the Boon shall be our Care;
To rise in *Merit* justly by *Degrees*,
And tho' we're *English*, yet we hope to please.[1]

There were seven performances of *Epicoene* at Covent Garden under the management of Christopher Rich between April 1745 and March 1748. Bridgewater was Morose; Oliver Cashel, Dauphine; Ridout, Clerimont; Hale, Truewit; Woodward, the brilliant actor of Bobadill, La Foole; Theophilus Cibber, Daw; Marten, Otter; and Mrs. Pritchard, Epicoene.

Garrick was interested in the play and planned a careful revival of it in 1752. It was acted at Drury Lane on 26 November, with 'the Characters New Dress'd after the manner of the Time'. The actors whom he chose had been well trained in Jonson parts. Richard Yates was Morose; Scrase was Clerimont; William Havard, Dauphine; William Palmer, Truewit; Shuter, La Foole; Woodward, Daw; Thomas Davies, Cutbeard; Edward Berry, Otter. In the women's parts Mrs. Pritchard was Epicoene; Mrs. Clive, Lady Haughty; Mrs. Bennett, Centaure; Mrs. Price, Mavis; Mrs. Cross, Mistress Otter. Davies writing in 1784 gave his recollections of the performance.

When it was revived, about thirty years since, under the management of Mr. Garrick, with perseverance it was dragged on for a few nights. The managers acquired neither profit nor reputation by the exhibition of it. Some expressions met with severe marks of the spectators' displeasure. The character of Morose, upon whose peevish and perverse humour the plot of the comedy depends, is that of a whimsical recluse, whose disposition can bear no sound but that which he utters himself. If this were the whole of his character, he would still be a good object for comic satire, but the melancholy of Morose degenerates into malice and cruelty.

Davies instances his schemes to disinherit his nephew.

But, beside the licentiousness of the manners, and quaintness of expression, in the Silent Woman, the frequent allusions to forgotten customs and characters render it impossible to be ever revived with any probability of success. To understand Jonson's comedies perfectly, we should have before us a satirical history of the age in which he lived.[2]

Undeterred by his earlier failure, Garrick made a second attempt to produce the play at Drury Lane on 13 January 1776. George Colman made an acting-version for him, which was printed later in

---

[1] Printed in *The Delights of the Muses: Being a Collection of Poems Never before Published*, 1738, pp. 175–6.   [2] *Dramatic Miscellanies*, ii. 101–3.

the year. Robert Bensley played Morose, Palmer his old part of Truewit; Davies, Clerimont; Brereton, Dauphine; Parsons, Daw; King, La Foole; Yates, Otter; Baddeley, Cutbeard; Mrs. Siddons, Epicoene; Miss Sherry, Lady Haughty; Mrs. Davies, Centaure; Miss Platt, Mavis; Mrs. Millidge, Trusty; and Mrs. Hopkins, Mistress Otter. After three nights' performance Mrs. Siddons gave up Epicoene, and a male actor Philip Lamash took the part; there had been criticism of an actress attempting what Jonson had explicitly written as a male part. Colman wrote a prologue which was spoken by Palmer.

> Happy the soaring bard who boldly wooes,
> And wins the favour of, the tragic muse!
> He from the grave may call the mighty dead,
> In buskins and blank verse the stage to tread;
> On Pompeys and old Cæsars rise to fame,
> And join the poet's to th' historian's name.
> The comick wit, alas! whose eagle eyes
> Pierce Nature thro', and mock the time's disguise,
> Whose pencil living follies brings to view,
> Survives those follies, and his portraits too;
> Like star-gazers, deplores his luckless fate,
> For last year's Almanacks are out of date.
>
> "The Fox, the Alchemist, the Silent Woman,
> "Done by Ben Jonson, are out-done by no man.'
>
> Thus sung in rough, but panegyrick, rhimes,
> The wits and criticks of our author's times.
> But now we bring him forth with dread and doubt,
> And fear his *learned socks* are quite worn out.
> The subtle Alchemist grows obsolete,
> And Drugger's humour scarcely keeps him sweet.
> Tonight, if you would feast your eyes and ears,
> Go back in fancy near two hundred years;
> A play of Ruffs and Farthingales review,
> Old English fashions, such as then were new!
> Drive not Tom Otter's *Bulls and Bears* away;
> Worse *Bulls and Bears* disgrace the present day.
> On fair Collegiates let no critick frown!
> A Ladies' Club still holds its rank in town.
> If modern Cooks, who nightly treat the pit,
> Do not quite cloy and surfeit you with wit,
> From the old kitchen please to pick a bit!
> If once, with hearty stomachs to regale,
> On old Ben Jonson's fare, tho' somewhat stale,
> A meal on Bobadil you deign'd to make,
> Take *Epicœne* for his and Kitely's sake!

Colman wrote very little into the play; he chiefly concerned himself with lightening the dialogue and so speeding up the action. There are constant small parings of the speeches; a phrase or a sentence disappears. He expurgated carefully, even taking out, for instance, 'bastarded their issue' (II. ii. 46). This entailed a toning down of the Collegiate ladies, and he lessened their importance. In the opening scene lines 87 ('and wash'd')–127 are omitted; when the ladies enter after the marriage, the only speeches retained between lines 11 and 52 ('Where's your husband? . . . CENTAURE?') are 'Is this the silent woman?' (34) and 'A gentlewoman . . . of a good race' (39, 40). The third scene of the fourth Act stops at line 29 ('the miracle of a kingdom'), losing just over thirty lines. The sixth scene of the fourth Act is shortened by forty-three lines, suppressing the desire of the Collegiates to get Dauphine to the College; hence the attempts to make an assignation in Act v, scene ii (1–67) also go. Truewit's tirade against marriage (II. ii) is well pruned, and the cursing of the barber by Truewit and Morose (III. v. 59–120) is omitted altogether. The scene of the preparation for divorce at the climax of the play (v. iii) abbreviates Otter and Cutbeard's Latin, omits Morose's confession of impotence, and stops short at line 170, after which the women rush in.

Only at one point of the play did Colman make a structural change. In the original Epicoene gives up her pretence of silence immediately after the marriage (III. iv. 27–8). Colman thought it more effective to postpone it. Morose enters with Epicoene and Cutbeard: 'How much happier am I', he says, 'than in old time Pigmalion, possessing a statue, on whom Heaven hath already bestowed animation! Approach, thou living marble! thou rich vein of beauty, approach! Grieve not that thou art poor, and thy friends deceased, love! Thou hast brought a wealthy dowry in thy silence; and in respect of thy poverty, I shall have thee more loving and obedient.' The guests arrive and fill the house with noise. Morose is left alone with his bride. 'I have wedded a lamb; no tempests shall henceforth disturb us, no sound annoy us, louder than thy still, small voice, my love, soft as the whispering of summer breezes, or sweet murmur of turtles. Wives are wild cats; but thou shalt be a tame domestic animal, with velvet feet entering my chamber, and with the soft purring of delight and affection, inviting the hand of thy husband to stroke thee.'

Epicoene throws off the mask at the point where Morose enters with his long sword and drives off the shrieking Mistress Otter (IV. ii. 123 in the original). Epicoene intervenes: 'Fie, master Morose, that you will use this violence to a gentlewoman!'

From his own point of view Colman certainly succeeded: he modernized the play. Of course, he cut out obsolete allusions such as the prentices' Shrove-tuesday riot (I. i. 158) and Dr. Forman (IV. i. 149), and archaic words and phrases such as 'porcpisce' (IV. iv. 144) and 'giue the dor' (III. iii. 28) for which he substituted 'pig' and 'give the slip'. The erudition in which Jonson delighted was reduced to a minimum; Daw's 'sackful' of classical authors in II. iii. 57 foll., for instance, and his Greek and Latin in the discussion on Morose's madness (IV. iv. 68–73) is cut down to 'The disease in Greek is called Mavía, in Latin, Insania'.

Mr. Noyes gives the receipts for the first three performances, £265. 17s. on 13 January, £200. 13s. 6d. on 15 January, and £146. 8s. on 18 January. There was also a performance on 23 January, when the receipts were £134. 6s.

The final performance of the century was at Covent Garden on 26 April 1784 for the benefit of John Edwin; Colman's version was used. The Public Advertiser of 26 April printed the cast. James Aickin was Morose, Whitfield was Dauphine; Davies, Clerimont; Wroughton, Truewit; Quick, Daw; Edwin, La Foole; Booth, Otter; Wewitzer, Cutbeard; Mrs. Bates played Epicoene; the Collegiate ladies were played by Mrs. Wilson, Miss Platt, Miss Stuart; Mrs. Webb was Mistress Otter.

The first performance of the nineteenth century was at Harvard University, where the play was performed in the Sanders Theatre by students of the American Academy of Dramatic Arts on 30 March 1895. The version used was a shortened text arranged by Mrs. Abbey Sage Richardson, who cut down the fifth act much as Colman did, omitting the dialogue of Dauphine with the Collegiate Ladies (v. ii) and La Foole's and Daw's confessions about the bride, and shortening the discussion on divorce at v. iii. 153. All the characters were played by men. An Elizabethan stage was built for the revival.

On 8 May 1905 the Mermaid Repertory Company under the direction of Philip Carr gave the play at the Great Queen Street (now Kingsway) Theatre. Cyril Cattley played Epicoene; Arthur Goodsall, Clerimont; Michael Sherbrooke, Truewit; Milton Rosmer, Dauphine; George Ingleton, Morose; Ashton Pearse, La Foole; Henry Twyford, Daw; E. C. Buffum, Cutbeard; W. H. Kemble, Otter; Miss Ada Potter, Miss Stuart, Miss Violet Bazalgette, the Collegiate Ladies; Miss Sime Seruya, Mistress Otter; and Miss Inglis, Trusty. The text was pruned, not only of coarse passages, but of such characteristic turns of phrases as Daw's 'As I hope to finish Tacitus' (IV. v. 50). The Collegiates, said The Times, should have been made 'less suggestive of a "ladies college" in the modern sense'; they were not grotesque enough. Cyril Cattley gave an excellent performance of Epicoene, and Morose, Truewit, Amorous, and Daw were all good.

The spring term of 1909 saw *Epicoene* performed at Cambridge for the second time. It was played by the Marlowe Dramatic Society on 19 and 20 February, with simple scenery of green hangings and old music, by Orlando Gibbons, for instance, and 'Still to be neat' was sung to John Wilson's air accompanied by a lute. Rupert Brooke spoke the prologue. W. Frost was Morose; H. M. Butler, Sir Dauphine Eugenie; C. C. Brown, Clerimont; W. Foss, Truewit; W. Phillips, Epicoene; R. W. Poley, Daw; W. H. Malleson, La Foole; F. Arundel, Otter; H. L. Birrell, Mistress Otter; Cosmo Gordon, Lady Haughty; W. H. Haslam, Centaure. In *The Times* of 22 February there was a masterly review, which, we understand, was written by William Poel. All the parts were played by men, and Poel commented,

the essential thing is that the principal female character must be played by a boy or youth. It is true that English audiences in the days of Pepys, and for nearly a century later, were accustomed to see, and apparently to enjoy, the play with a woman in the part of Epicoene; but by the last year of Garrick's professional life this incomprehensible error of taste and sense had been dissipated. He took Mrs. Siddons out of the part (it is really impossible to imagine Mrs. Siddons, even at the age of twenty, appearing as a squeaking hobbledehoy!) and gave it to a man. But if one of the female parts is played by a male, while the others are in the hands of females, it must be very difficult for the audience not to see the difference, and not to know all through that Epicœne is really a boy. Once that feeling is allowed to enter, the point of the joke is lost.

The boyishness of the Cambridge actors 'was one of the pleasantest features of the performance', but there was 'no great loss of femininity. Certainly the Cambridge Lady Haughty was so convincingly feminine as to be a complete puzzle.'

There is a criticism of the actor who took Morose.

Was it by accident or design that he behaved throughout as if he were deaf? If by design, his interpretation offers a valuable piece of criticism on the character. Mere dislike of noise is hardly what Jonson meant by a 'humour', and if Morose were really hard of hearing and invented a dislike of noise to cloak his churlish hatred of his kind, he becomes at once a more Jonsonian character and a more interesting study.

And he would be literally morose. But the actor may merely have stuffed his ears to deaden sounds.

Incidentally Poel gave a literary criticism of the play.

There is no play at once so Jonsonian and so 'Elizabethan' as this. It has all the characteristics of the literary giant—his huge, rumbling laugh, as huge as Rabelais', yet sometimes as bitter as Swift's; his invincible desire to be 'classical', which leads him not only to give strength and shape to his intrigue by cramming the complicated bundle of plots and persons into a mould as near that of 'the unities' as he can get, but to make his very innkeepers and barbers talk Latin, so that he may introduce an elaborate burlesque of the contest between canon and civil law; his scorn of fops and fools, liars and rogues, male and female, his keen eye for all the 'humours' which went to make up the variegated, frank world of his time; and his downright, brutal love of a farcical joke at the expense of affectation and folly. *Epicoene* is the most farcical play he ever wrote; and at the same time the least savage, and the most faithful to the facts and characters of the contemporary life which he knew at least as well as he knew his classics. It contains a whole gallery of vivid, clearly differentiated portraits, some of them drawn with an incisive skill which can only be compared with Molière.

A very important revival of the century was the twenty-first production of the Phoenix at the Regent's Theatre, King's Cross, on 16 November 1924, under the direction of Mr. Allan Wade. Cedric Hardwicke was Morose; Raymond Massey, Dauphine; H. C. Hewitt, Clerimont; George Zucco, Truewit; Godfrey Winn, Epicoene; Melville Cooper, Daw; Harold Scott, La Foole; Alfred Clark, Otter; Wallace Evennett, Cutbeard; the Collegiates were played by Miss E. Lodge, Miss Hilda Sims, Miss Winifred Evans; Miss Marion Lind was Mistress Otter.

The Oxford Summer Diversions of August 1938 included a performance of *Epicoene* produced by Nevill Coghill. C. Thomas was Morose; R. Benn, Dauphine; V. Peskett, Clerimont; D. Bishop, Truewit; H. Moore, La Foole; K. Sanders, Daw; H. Cardwell, Epicoene; J. Good, Cutbeard; A. Dunn, Otter; the Collegiates were Miss Joan Yeaxlee, Miss P. Riley, Miss V. Maynard; Mrs. Fraser, Mistress Otter. There was an epilogue by John Masefield, who suggested that the play suited a man of Jonson's temperament, loud and hearty. Mr. Thomas's Morose and Mr. Bishop's Truewit were particularly good, and the play was lucidly presented, with its element of caricature preserved, but not unduly marked.

Two other amateur performances were (1) on 11 May 1912 at the Theatre of Birkbeck College, by a cast entirely of women, under the direction of Miss C. M. Edmondston; Cordelia Minnion was Morose, Irene Palmer was Epicoene; (2) an abbreviated version of the play made by Miss A. G. Caton, given in the Palmer Hall,

Fairford; Commander F. Cadogan was Morose, S. Beck was Epicoene, and the adapter was Truewit.

On 16 June 1948 the O.U.D.S. at Oxford performed the play in the open air in Mansfield College garden. The cast was: Sir Dauphine Eugenie, Alan Cooke; Clerimont, Michael Godley; Truewit, Charles Lepper; Morose, Brian Badcoe; Daw, Norman Painting; La Foole, Robert Hardy; Cutbeard, David Raeburn; Tom Otter, John Schlesinger. The part of Epicoene was once again given to a woman, G. Rowe-Dutton; Jennifer Ramage was Mrs. Otter; Daphne Levens, Haughty; Ann Clamp, Centaure; Pat Hackwood, Mavis. The producer was Frank Hauser. The vigour and gusto of the performance were delightful; the elocution was excellent. The actors behaved as if they thoroughly enjoyed the play, and they gave it a freshness and quickness of movement by utilizing three entrances, so that the action was continuous. Morose was skilfully made up as a picture of comic senility; Truewit played upon his nerves with unfailing dexterity. Epicoene, whether demure or strident, played her part with skill. A good point was made at the climax of the play when Dauphine dismisses his crushed and baffled uncle: 'Now you may go in and rest as private as you will, sir. I'll not trouble you, till you trouble me with your funeral, which I care not how soon it come.' Morose left the stage just at the words 'I'll not trouble you', and the actor turned to the audience to finish the sentence. It toned down an ugly touch.

The adaptations and translations of *Epicoene* began with Jean-Baptiste Rousseau's *L'Hypocondre, ou la femme qui ne parle point*, printed in the *Portfeuille de J.-B. Rousseau, 1751*, Amsterdam, 1751.[1] Morose's nephew is Léandre and Truewit Eutrapel, Epicoene Androgyne; Clerimont is suppressed. The opening scene is a monologue by the barber. Details of London life are carefully eliminated. Thus in Act ii, scene ii. 17–25 there are French equivalents.

> EUTRAPEL: Vous prétendez, dit-on, vous marier en forme!
> Vous marier! vous, vous!
> MOROSE: Ah, quelle voix énorme!
> EUTRAPEL: Comme si dans Paris vous manquiez de secours
> Pour abréger le fil de vos malheureux jours!
> Que la Seine, épuisée et tarie en sa source,
> Ne vous pût de ses flots présenter la ressource;
> Ou que vous n'eussiez pas, si c'est votre plaisir,
> Pour vous précipiter cent clochers à choisir!
> Vous marier, morbleu!

---

[1] Recorded by H. A. Grubb in *Modern Language Notes*, 1940, lv, pp. 170–6.

Morose finally leaves the stage with a violent tirade.

Richard Twiss, in his *Travels through Portugal and Spain, In 1772 and 1773* (1775, p. 457, quoted by Gifford), says: 'In 1769 a Portuguese translation in three acts, in prose, was published of Ben Johnson's *Epicoene*: it was acted at Lisbon, though miserably disfigured.'

In 1771 Francis Gentleman treated *Epicoene* as he had treated *The Alchemist* in 1770, degrading it to farce; he called his production *The Coxcombs*. The prologue and one scene survive.[1]

Ludwig Tieck, a devoted student of Jonson, translated the play in 1800, *Epicoene oder Das stille Frauenzimmer. Ein Lustspiel in fünf Akten von Ben Jonson*. He gave a close translation.[2]

A Russian translation by E. and R. Blokh was published at Petrograd in 1921.[3]

An adaptation, *La Femme Silencieuse de Ben Jonson*, by Marcel Achard, was acted at the Théâtre Atelier at Paris in 1926. Mélot du Dy, reviewing it in *La Nouvelle Revue Française* for February, pp. 246–7, wrote 'M. Ben Jonson, jeune dramaturge anglais, assisté d'un confrère français plein d'expérience, vient de faire une invention', and asked 'mais qui est Ben Jonson?'

An adaptation, *Lord Spleen*, by Hugo F. Köningsgarten was published at Berlin in 1930.

In 1935 Stephan Zweig, the adapter of *Volpone*, wrote the libretto for Richard Strauss's opera *Die schweigsame Frau: Komische Oper in 3 Aufzügen*. The text was published at Berlin.

THE ALCHEMIST

The Alchemist was performed by the King's men at the Globe in 1610. It soon won its way to a secure place with London playgoers; but apparently some personal satire was detected in it at first, and Herrick denounced

> Such ignorance as theirs was, who once hist
> At thy unequal'd Play, the *Alchymist*:
> Oh fie upon 'em![4]

Lowin, who is in Jonson's actor-list, played Mammon according to Wright, *Historia Histrionica*, 1699, p. 4. Joseph Taylor, who, according to Wright, acted Face, joined the company in 1619.

---

[1] Printed in *The Oxford Magazine*, for September 1771, and reprinted by Mr. Noyes, op. cit. pp. 201–3.
[2] Printed in *Tieck's Schriften*, 1829, ii, pp. 155–354.
[3] Tannenbaum, *A Concise Bibliography of Ben Jonson*, p. 7.
[4] *Works*, ed. Moorman, p. 150, '*Upon M*. Ben. Johnson. *Epig.*'.

The precise date of performance in 1610 is not easy to fix. Ana-nias's confused chronology, giving 17 November in III. ii. 131–2, and 24 October in V. v. 102–3, as the supposed day of the action, cannot be taken as the date, real or anticipated, of the performance. The plague was in London from 12 July to 29 November; it was not serious till August, and it decreased by the end of the year.[1] Playing would be possible up to July. Further, the fact that the play was entered for publication on 3 October indicates that the performance had taken place. We therefore withdraw our earlier conjecture that the play was written a few weeks before the registration,[2] and we incline to the view of Sir E. K. Chambers[3] that it was produced in the earlier half of the year before the deaths from plague amounted to thirty or forty a week and the theatres were closed lest they should spread infection. The action is set in plague-time, but the disease had been virulent in 1609, and this would account for Love-wit's running away from London to his hopfields.

It is some confirmation of this view that the King's men took the play to Oxford, along with *Othello*, in September. August and September would be their time for autumn tours, which would pre-suppose an earlier performance in London; in any case the plague would have stopped them from playing there in October.

The evidence for this Oxford performance, discovered by Mr. Geoffrey Tillotson,[4] is in the Fulman papers of Corpus Christi College, Oxford.[5] It is a copy of the Latin correspondence of Henry Jackson made by William Fulman, both of whom were fellows of the college. There are three excerpts of a letter dated September 1610, which relate to *The Alchemist*.

— Postremis his diebus adfuerunt Regis Actores Scenici. Egerunt cum applausu maximo, pleno theatro. Sed viris piis et doctis impii merito visi sunt, quod non contenti Alcumistas perstringere, ipsas Sanctas Scripturas foedissimè violarint. Anabaptistas scilicet vellica-bant; ut sub hac persona lateret improbitas.—

— Theologos nostros, qui (pudet dicere) avidissimè confluebant.—

— nusquam majori plausu theatra nostra sonuisse, quam cum in-traret personatus ille nebulo, qui, ut fictam Anabaptistarum sancti-tatem spectatoribus deridendam proponeret, Scripturas impiè, et prodigiosè contaminavit. (He goes on to say that the tragedy of Desdemona moved the audience to tears.)

Jackson's horror at the profanity put in the mouths of Wholesome and Ananias is in keeping with his character; he was a friend of

---

[1] F. P. Wilson, *The Plague in Shakespeare's London*, pp. 120–2.
[2] In vol. ii, p. 87.   [3] *Elizabethan Stage*, iii, p. 371.
[4] See *The Times Literary Supplement*, 20 July 1933.
[5] Vol. x, ff. 83*b* and 84*a*.

John Rainolds, President of Corpus, the author of *Th' ouerthrow of stage-playes*; and he is bitter about the 'theologi'—query, the doctors of divinity—who flocked to the performance. Where was *The Alchemist* played at Oxford? Dr. F. S. Boas quotes[1] from the Oxford City audited accounts a payment in 1609-10—the accounts running from Michaelmas to Michaelmas—of 10s. to the King's men by the mayor. It is, as he says, a natural inference that this payment was for *The Alchemist*, which would just come within the period covered by the accounts. 'Theatra nostra' probably means an inn-yard, such as the yard of the King's Arms which was used for this purpose at a later date; the Town Hall is also a possibility.[2]

The Alchemist was revived at Court in 1612 or 1613, probably in 1613, early in the year. The accounts of the Lord Treasurer, Lord Stanhope of Harington, running from Michaelmas 1612 to Michaelmas 1613, are preserved in a Bodleian manuscript, MS. Rawlinson A 239, formerly Pepys MS. 78. On f. 47*b* is a payment of £20 made to John Heminges, dated 20 May 1613, 'for presentinge sixe severall playes', including *The Alchemist*. It was also acted at Court on 1 January 1623.[3]

Sir Henry Herbert had an agreement with the King's men that they should give him the benefit of two days in the year, one in summer and one in winter, 'to bee taken out of the second daye of a revived playe, att my owne choyse'. In 1631 he records that he 'Received of Mr. Blagrave, in the name of the kings company, for the benefit of my winter day, taken upon The Alchemist, this 1 of Decemb. 1631—13*l*. 0*s*. 0*d*.'.[4]

A last revival before the Puritans closed the theatres is recorded incidentally in the *Domestic State Papers* of 1639. On 21 January Madam Ann Merricke wishes she were with her friend Mrs. Lydall 'to see the Alchymist, which I heare this tearme is revived'; (S.P. 16/409/167) she has to console herself with the study of Shakespeare and the History of Women—query, Thomas Heywood's Γυναικεῖον —which were 'all her country library'. On 18 May Sir Humphrey Mildmay saw it; his seat cost him five shillings.[5]

Of the actors in the original performance we know that Lowin played Mammon.[6] Burbadge must have played Face, because John Taylor succeeded him. Dr. Baldwin assigns the other parts as

---

[1] *The Times Literary Supplement*, 31 Aug. 1933.   [2] See p. 197.
[3] Malone, *Variorum Shakespeare*, iii, p. 147.   [4] Ibid., pp. 176-7.
[5] Bentley, *The Jacobean and Caroline Stage*, 'The Records of Sir Humphrey Mildmay', p. 678.
[6] Wright, *Historia Histrionica*, p. 424.

follows:[1] Heminges was Subtle; Condell, Surly; Ostler, Lovewit;
Eccleston, Kastril; Armin, Drugger; Tooley, Tribulation Wholesome. This leaves Cooke for Ananias, and Underwood for Dapper.

James Shirley, the dramatist, was responsible for a performance
of *The Alchemist* in Dublin at the Werburgh Street Theatre, which
had been opened in 1635 by John Ogilby, Strafford's master of the
revels. Shirley went to Ireland probably in 1636 to manage this
theatre, for which he edited plays, wrote new plays of his own, and
contributed prologues and epilogues to plays that he revived. A
prologue which he wrote for a performance of *The Alchemist* is
printed among his poems of 1640, pp. 36–7.

A Prologue to the

ALCHIMIST

Acted ⟨in *Ireland*⟩.

The *Alchemist*, a Play for strength of wit,
And true Art, made to shame, what hath been writ
In former Ages (I except no worth
Of what or Greeks or Latines have brought forth),
Is now to be presented to your eare,
For which I wish each man were a Muse here,
To know, and in his soule be fit to be
Judge of this Master-piece of Comedie;
That when we hear but once of *Johnsons* name,
Whose mention shall make proud the breath of Fame
We may agree, and Crownes of Laurel bring,
A justice unto him the Poets King.
But he is dead, Time envious of that blisse,
Which we possest in that great Braine of his,
By putting out this light, hath darkned all
The sphere of Poesie, and we let fall
At best, unworthy Elegies on his Herse,
A Tribute that we owe his living Verse;
Which, though some men that never reacht him, may
Decry, that love all folly in a Play,
The Wiser few shall this distinction have,
To kneele, not tread upon his honour'd grave.

Shirley stayed at Dublin till 1640, and *The Alchemist* was probably
one of his early revivals.

W. R. Chetwood quotes Benjamin Johnson junior as often 'giving
most extravagant praises to one *Baker*, a Master-Paver in *Dublin*,

---

[1] *The Organization of the Shakespearean Company*, p. 427.

for excelling in Sir John Falstaff, the Spanish Fryar, Sir *Epicure Mammon* in the *Alchymist*, and many other Parts. He would be studying in the Streets, while he would be overlooking his Men at their Work.'[1] Chetwood is not a very trustworthy authority, but he knew something of the Dublin stage.

The play was at once revived at the Restoration. There is in the library of Worcester College, Oxford, a broadside *Prologue to the Reviv'd Alchemist* reprinted by Mr. C. H. Wilkinson in the *Proceedings and Papers* of the Oxford Bibliographical Society, vol. i, pp. 281–2. 'It is certain', Mr. Wilkinson notes, 'from the pieces among which it was bound that it was published in 1660, and this early revival throws an interesting light on the popularity of the play. It is printed on one side of the leaf in two columns, and was probably sold at the theatre door.'

> *The Alchemist*; Fire, breeding Gold, our *Theme*:
> Here must no Melancholie be, nor Flegm.
> Young *Ben*, not Old, writ this, when in his Prime,
> Solid in Judgement, and in Wit sublime.
> The *Sisters*, who at *Thespian* Springs their Blood
> Cool with fresh Streams, All, in a Merry Mood,
> Their wat'ry Cups, and Pittances declin'd,
> At *Bread-Street's Mer-maid* with our *Poët* din'd:
> Where, what they Drank, or who plaid most the Rig,
> Fame modestly conceals: but He grew big
> Of this pris'd Issue; when a *Jovial* Maid,
> His Brows besprinkling with *Canarie*, said,
> Pregnant by Us, produce no Mortal Birth;
> Thy active Soul, quitting the sordid Earth,
> Shall 'mongst Heav'ns glitt'ring *Hieroglyphicks* trade,
> And *Pegasus*, our winged Sumpter, jade,
> Who from Parnassus never brought to *Greece*,
> Nor *Romane* Stage, so rare a Master-piece.
> This Story, true or false, may well be spar'd;
> The Actors are in question, not the *Bard*:
> How they shall humour their oft-varied Parts,
> To get your Money, Company, and Hearts,
> Since all Tradition, and like Helps are lost.
> Reading our Bill, new pasted on the Post,
> Grave Stagers both, one to the other said,
> *The* ALCHEMIST? What! are the Fellows mad?
> Who shall *Doll Common* Act? Their tender Tibs
> Have neither Lungs, nor Confidence, nor Ribs.
> Who *Face*, and *Subtle*? Parts, all Air and Fire:
> They, whom the *Authour* did Himself inspire,

---

[1] *A General History of the Stage,* 1749, p. 174.

Taught, Line by Line, each Tittle, Accent, Word,
Ne're reach'd His Height; all after, more absurd,
Shadows of fainter Shadows, wheresoe're
A *Fox* be pencil'd, copied out a *Bear*.
    Encouragement for young Beginners small:
Yet howsoe're we'll venture; have at All.
Bold Ignorance (they say) falls seldome short
In *Camp*, the *Country*, *City*, or the *Court*.
    Arm'd with the Influence of your fair Aspects,
Our Selves we'll conquer, and our own Defects.
A thousand Eyes dart raies into our Hearts,
Would make Stones speak, and Stocks play well their Parts:
Some few Malignant Beams we need not fear,
Where shines such Glory in so bright a Sphere.

There is no clue to the authorship of these vigorous lines. It is unlikely that Killigrew, the manager of the company which was acting the piece, could have written them; and Davenant, as the manager of the rival company, is ruled out.

Three performances in 1661 are definitely dated; there may have been more in that year. Pepys saw the play at the King's Theatre in Vere Street on 22 June—'The Alchymist, which is a most incomparable play', and again on 14 August. The list of plays acted by the King's Company from 1660 to 1662 records a performance of *The Alchemist* on 16 December.[1]

In 1662 Dr. Edward Browne paid 2s. 6d. to see the play performed by the King's Players, at the same theatre; he calls it in 'the new Theatre in Lincoln's Inn Fields'.[2] The Rev. John Ward in his *Diary* (1648–79, ed. Severn, p. 174) similarly records that he saw *The Alchemist* there: 'two parts were acted wel, the Dr. and the Puritan, the latter incomparably well.'

Downes gives the cast after the Theatre Royal in Bridges Street was opened in May 1663. Wintersel was Subtle; Mohun, Face; Cartwright, Mammon; Burt, Surly; Lacy, Ananias; Bateman, Wholesome; Mrs. Rutter, Dame Pliant; and Mrs. Corey, Dol Common. Mrs. Corey's acting of this last part was so famous that she acquired the nickname of 'Doll Common'; Pepys so calls her.[3] Up to 3 August 1664 the part of Subtle had been taken by Walter Clun, who had made his mark in the parts of Iago and Falstaff. Returning home from the play, he was robbed and murdered near Tottenham Court as he was riding to his country house in Kentish Town. 'One of the rogues taken', says Pepys, 'an Irish fellow. It seems most

[1] Malone, *Variorum Shakespeare*, iii, p. 275.
[2] B.M. Sloane MS. 1900, f. 36.
[3] *Diary*, ed. Wheatley, vi, p. 115; viii, p. 200.

cruelly butchered and bound. The house will have a great miss of him.'[1] So much so that the play was not acted again till 17 April 1669. 'Learning that "The Alchymist" was acted', says Pepys, 'we did go . . . to the King's house; and it is still a good play, . . . but I do miss Clun, for the Doctor.'[2] The King was present, and the actors received the usual £10; similarly on 12 November 1674 and 26 October 1675—the last performances recorded in this century.[3]

The Alchemist was played throughout the eighteenth century, usually at Drury Lane. Lady Morley[4] saw it there on 27 March and 1 April 1701; it was advertised in *The Daily Courant* of 8 October as to be revived on 9 October 'at the New Theatre in Lincoln's Inn Fields'; this was by Betterton's company. Mr. Noyes has reconstructed a possible cast at this date, partly from the cast of 1709, for the Drury Lane players: Subtle, Colley Cibber; Face, George Powell; Dapper, Henry Norris; Drugger, Pinkethman; Surly, John Mills; Kastril, William Bullock; Ananias, Johnson; Dol Common, possibly Mrs. Rogers.[5] The other parts cannot be assigned.

There is a gap in the performances till 1709, when the first acting quarto of the play was published with the following cast: Subtle, Colley Cibber; Face, George Powell; Mammon, Richard Estcourt; Surly, John Mills; Lovewit, John Bickerstaff; Tribulation, George Pack; Ananias, Benjamin Johnson; Drugger, William Pinkethman; Dapper, Henry Norris; Kastril, William Bullock; Dame Pliant, Mrs. Cox; Dol Common, Mrs. Saunders. There were six performances that year. Steele noted the performance of 11 May briefly but appreciatively in *The Tatler*.[6]

In September 1709 most of the Drury Lane company revolted from the manager Rich and went to the Haymarket, where they acted *The Alchemist* on 14 and 23 January 1710. Robert Wilks played Face, and Dogget, whom Downes describes as 'very Aspectabund, wearing a Farce in his Face',[7] had a congenial part in Dapper; John Mills, already at the Haymarket, probably kept his old part of Surly, and Mrs. Saunders was probably Dol Common. These players returned to Drury Lane in November 1710, and the old cast of 1709 was revived in 1712 and 1713.

The play took on a new lease of life in 1721, the period of the South Sea bubble and the national craze for speculation; the ruthless exposure of projectors in the comedy had something of a topical appeal. The point was driven home in the epilogue to the revival

[1] *Diary*, iv, p. 195.
[2] Ibid. viii, p. 279.
[3] Nicoll, *Restoration Drama*, pp. 306–7.
[4] See p. 198.
[5] Op. cit., p. 110.
[6] Ed. Aitken, i, pp. 125–6.
[7] *Roscius Anglicanus*, p. 52.

'By His Royal Highness's Command' from 25 to 27 October, and again on 22 November; the allusions are to the French Mississippi Company and to the South Sea failure.

> *An Epilogue spoke to a Play* Call'd the Alchymist.
> *Old Surly* Ben, *to Night, hath let us know,* ⎫
> *That in this Isle a Plenteous Crop did Grow* ⎬
> *Of* Knaves *and* Fools, *a Hundred* Years ago: ⎭
> Chymists, Bauds, Gamesters & *a Numerous Train*
> *Of humble Rogues, Content with moderate Gain.*
> *The* Poet *had he liv'd to see this* Age
> *Had brought Sublimer* Villains *on yᵉ Stage;*
> *Our* Knaves *Sin higher Now then those of* Old,
> Kingdoms, *not Private Men, are* Bought & Sold,¹
> *Witness the* South-sea *Project, which hath shown* ⎫
> *How far Philosophers may be out done* ⎬
> *By Modern S—m—n that have found yᵉ* Stone. ⎭
> *Well might it take its Title from the* Main,
> *That* Rose *so swift and* Sunk *so soon again;*
> Fools *have been always* Bit *by artfull* Lyes,
> *But here the* Cautious *were deceiv'd &* wise,
> *And Yet, in these Flagitious Monstrous Times,*
> *The* Knaves *detected* Triumph *in their* Crimes
> Wallow *in* Wealth, *have all things at Command,*
> *And Brave the Vengeance of an* Injur'd Land;
> *Well! since wee've Learn'd Experience at our Cost,* ⎫
> *Let us preserve the* Remnant *not yet* Lost, ⎬
> *Though* L—w, *from* France, *be landed on the* Coast, ⎭
> *By Sober Arts Aspire to* Guiltless *Fame,*
> *And Prove that* Virtue's *not an Empty Name.*²

'L-w from France' is an allusion to the celebrated projector, John Law of Lauriston, the founder of the Mississippi scheme; idolized by the French at first, he narrowly escaped with his life after the financial collapse. He returned to England on 13 October 1721, and was present at the performance on 25 October. 'Last night', says *The Whitehall Evening Post* for 26 October, 'their Royal Highnesses the Prince and Princess of Wales were at the Theatre in Drury Lane, and saw the *Alchymist* acted. There was a splendid appearance of the Nobility and Gentry; the famous Mr. Law and his son were there also.'

The cast in 1721 included Colley Cibber as Subtle, John Mills as

¹ Joseph Gage, who profited from the Mississippi scheme, offered three millions sterling to Augustus, King of Poland, to resign the crown in his favour. When Augustus refused, Gage tried to get the sovereignty of Sardinia.

² Printed as an engraved broadside and in *The Gentleman's Magazine*, 1825, xcv, part i, pp. 100–2, with historical notes by 'Eu. Ho', i.e. Hood, which we have used. The punctuation has been slightly corrected.

Face, Henry Norris as Dapper, Pinkethman as Drugger, Johnson as Ananias, and six new players—John Harper as Mammon, William Wilks as Surly, Benjamin Griffin as Tribulation Wholesome, Josias Miller as Kastril, Mrs. Markham as Dame Pliant, and Mrs. Wethereld as Dol Common. Mr. Noyes[1] notes Johnson and Griffin continued in their parts till 1740, Harper in his part till 1739, Mills till 1737, Cibber till 1733, Wilks till 1726, Miller till 1726, resuming the part from 1733 to 1738, Mrs. Markham till 1726, and Mrs. Wethereld till 1732. Thomas Davies criticizes the actors of the period:

> Colley Cibber I have seen act Subtle with great art; the elder Mills at the same time played Face with much shrewd spirit and ready impudence. The two Palmers have successively acted Face with much archness and solid characteristic bronze.[2] Ben Griffin and Ben Jonson were much admired for their just representation of the canting puritanical preacher and his solemn deacon the botcher; there was an affected softness in the former which was finely contrasted by the fanatical fury of the other.—Griffin's features seemed ready to be relaxed into a smile, while the stiff muscles and fierce eye of the other admitted of no suppleness or compliance. There is still to be seen a fine print of them in these characters, from a painting of Vanbleek: they are very striking resemblances of both comedians. . . .
>
> I have never seen an adequate representer of Sir Epicure, from Harper down to Love.[3] The first seemed to have been taught by one who had juster conceptions of what was to be done in the part than the player could execute.[4]

There were four performances in 1723 and two in 1726, after which the play was acted with few breaks till 1776, when Garrick played in it for the last time. The most important change in the cast was the appearance of Theophilus Cibber in the part of Abel Drugger in 1731, a part which he played till 1746. Davies commented on the contrast of his performance with Garrick's: 'Mr. Garrick freed the stage from the false spirit, ridiculous squinting, and vile grimace, which, in Theophilus Cibber, had captivated the public for several years, by introducing a more natural manner of displaying the absurdities of a foolish tobacconist.'[5] Cibber's farcical treatment of the part was also criticized by Samuel Foote in his attempt to differentiate the comic from the comical:

> Cast your Eye on the *Abel Drugger* of G. and the *Abel Drugger* of C. I call the simple, composed, grave Deportment of the former Comic, and the squint-ey'd grinning Grimace of the latter Comical. The first obtains your Applause, by persuading you that he is the real Man. The

---

[1] Op. cit., p. 119.   [2] In Garrick's company.
[3] 'The bloody murderer of blank verse', according to *The Dramatic Censor*, ii, p. 492.   [4] *Dramatic Miscellanies*, ii, pp. 108–9.   [5] Ibid., p. 107.

latter indeed opens your Eyes, and gives you to understand, that he is but personating the Tobacco-Boy: But then to atone for the Loss of the Deception, you are ready to split with Laughter, at the ridiculous Variations of his Muscles. It may indeed be objected, that this Conduct destroys all Distinction of Characters, and may as well become *Sir John Daw* or *Sir Amorous La Fool*[1] as honest *Nab*. Well, and what then? Don't Folks come to a Play to laugh? And if that End be obtained, what matters it how?[2]

There were four performances of the play at Drury Lane in 1733, five in 1734, and six in 1736, as well as one performance at the Haymarket in 1734 by actors who had seceded from Drury Lane. Mrs. Charlotte Clarke was Dol Common, except for one evening when Mrs. Clive took the part; Mrs. Pritchard played it from 1736 to 1768. Davies wrote: 'Dol Common fell into Mrs. Clive's hands about fifty years ago . . . by lessening the vulgarity of the prostitute, ⟨she⟩ did not give so just an idea of her. . . . Mrs. Pritchard, by giving a full scope to her fancy as well as judgement, produced a complete resemblance of the practised and coarse harlot in Madam Doll.'[3] In 1737 Charles Macklin was Face, a part which he played till 1748, William Havard was Surly, and Woodward, the great actor of Boba-dill, was Kastril.

In 1740 Cibber was playing at Covent Garden as Abel Drugger, but returned to Drury Lane in 1742. Richard Neal played Kastril till 1745 and then Ananias till 1749; Mrs. Cross played Dol Common. In 1742 Edward Berry, the performer of old Kno'well, was Abel Drugger, and on 21 March 1743 Garrick first took the part, his playing of which marked an epoch in the history of the play, at a performance for the benefit of Macklin.

The one important change he made was to encroach on the part of Kastril when Surly, with the odds hopelessly against him, is driven off the stage (IV. vii). Garrick eked out the part of Drugger by making him the protagonist of the mêlée. As *The Theatrical Review* of 1 February 1763 pointed out, 'The character, as drawn by Johnson, is that of a most credulous, timid, pusillanimous wretch; the Broughtonian attitudes, into which Mr. Garrick throws himself, are utterly inconsistent with the part.' How well Garrick interpreted the psychology of the character apart from this scene is shown by a contemporary criticism quoted in the Biographical Memoir[1] prefixed to *The Private Correspondence of David Garrick*, 1831, pp. x–xi:

Abel Drugger's first appearance would disconcert the muscular eco-

[1] Misprinted '*Tool*'.
[2] *The Roman and English Comedy Consider'd and Compar'd*, 1747, pp. 38–9.
[3] Davies, op. cit. ii, p. 110.

nomy of the wisest. His attitude, his dread of offending the doctor, his saying nothing, his gradual stealing in farther and farther, his impatience to be introduced, his joy to his friend Face, are imitable by none. Mr. Garrick has taken that walk to himself, and is the *ridiculous* above all conception. When he first opens his mouth, the features of his face seem, as it were, to drop upon the tongue; it is all caution; it is timorous, stammering, and inexpressible. When he stands under the conjurer to have his features examined, his teeth, his beard, his little finger, his awkward simplicity, and his concern, mixed with hope and fear, and joy and avarice, and good-nature, are above painting.'[1]

The critic next notices the eager *running up* to inform Subtle that he himself *sells* the tobacco which the philosopher commended; the struggle to make his intended present *two* pounds.[2] His *breaking the bottle* in the Doctor's absence, while curiously examining the implements around him. His *beating off* Surly, disarming him, and throwing away the sword in contempt. He does not know friend from foe in his triumphant perambulation, and is going even to strike his favourite Captain Face. Garrick seemed to say, to the very sides scenes, 'Will *you* fight me?'

The breaking the urinal in Subtle's absence originated in an accident which happened to the elder Cibber:

He, while the other personages were employed, rather than stand idle, was fiddling about the table of the Alchymist; and by way of filling up time, took up the urinal, and held it to the light, when it by chance slipping through his fingers, broke to pieces; and he had the presence of mind to put on an air of distress happy to the time and place; it told to admirable purpose. He played the part afterwards as usual; but the audience obliged him to restore the accidental addition; and it has been ever since retained by every other performer.[3]

Garrick's elaborate handling of this episode is set forth, not without a touch of the grotesque, in detail in a pamphlet which he wrote against himself to forestall criticism:

Drugger [he said] is *mentally absorb'd* with the different Ideas of the *invaluable* Price of the *Urinal*, and the Punishment that may be inflicted in Consequence of a Curiosity, no way appertaining or belonging to the Business he came about. [If that is his mental condition,] How are the different Members of the Body to be agitated? Why Thus,—His *Eyes* must be revers'd from the Object he is most intimidated with, and by dropping his *Lip* at the same[4] Time *to* the Object, it throws a

---

[1] Attributed to James Boaden in *The Dictionary of National Biography*.
[2] In Garrick's version of II. vi. 80.
[3] Wilkes, *A General View of the Stage*, 1759, pp. 257–8.
[4] Misprinted 'some'.

trembling *Languor* upon every *Muscle*, and by declining the right Part of the Head *towards* the *Urinal*, it casts the most *Comic Terror* and *Shame* over all the *upper* Part of the Body, that can be imagin'd; and to make the *lower* Part equally ridiculous, his *Toes* must be *inverted* from the *Heel*, and by *holding* his *Breath*, he will unavoidably give himself a *Tremor* in the *Knees*, and if his *Fingers*, at the same Time, seem *convuls'd*, it finishes the compleatest low Picture of *Grotesque Terror* that can be imagin'd by a *Dutch* Painter.[1]

A test of the popularity which the play obtained through Garrick's revival is the way it passed into political and other allusions in current speech and writing. The most remarkable was the scene in the House of Commons on 12 February 1783, when Pitt, the twenty-four-year-old Chancellor of the Exchequer, furiously attacking Sheridan, had the questionable taste to allude to his connexion with the drama; Sheridan retorted that, if he should ever again engage in the occupation alluded to by Pitt, he might attempt to improve on the Angry Boy.[2] The House took up the allusion with zest.

Garrick's text was a modification of the original. His insertions were trivial, but he cut out much. He expurgated freely; even the 'vnctuous paps of a fat pregnant sow' (II. ii. 83–4) had to go. He made a clean sweep of obsolete allusions, the Hollands (I. ii. 109), Lully and Ripley (II. v. 8), and he changed Picthatch to Drury Lane (II. i. 62). He shortened drastically the alchemical jargon; thus in Act II, scene iii, he deleted lines 35–40, 53–66, 83–5, 96–8, 141–210. The satire on the Puritans had lost its freshness; in the third act lines 7–47 of scene i, 21–101 of scene ii disappear. The serious excisions were in the part of Sir Epicure Mammon. In order to make Drugger more conspicuous, the wings of Mammon's soaring ambition were ruthlessly clipped. The mythology of his concluding speech in the first scene of the third act shared the fate of the alchemical allusions later, and though he was allowed to contemplate a harem as large as Solomon's, his other immoral aspirations were pruned away; among luxuries of which he was deprived were

> The tongues of carpes, dormise, and camels heeles,
> Boil'd i' the spirit of SOL, and dissolu'd pearle,
> (APICIVS diet, 'gainst the *epilepsie*)

and he was not allowed to

> eate these broaths, with spoones of amber,
> Headed with diamant, and carbuncle.   (II. ii. 75–9.)

---

[1] *An Essay on Acting: In which will be consider'd The Mimical Behaviour of a Certain fashionable faulty Actor*, pp. 6–8.
[2] Sir Nathaniel Wraxall's *Historical Memoirs of my own time*, ed. H. B. Wheatley, 1884, ii, p. 431.

So too with the prospect he held out later to Dol of eating mullets 'Sous'd in high-countrey wines', pheasant eggs, cockles boiled in silver shells, shrimps swimming in a batter of dolphins' milk;

> and with these
> Delicate meats, set our selues high for pleasure,
> And take vs downe againe, and then renew
> Our youth, and strength, with drinking the *elixir,*
> And so enioy a perpetuitie
> Of life and lust.   (IV. i. 156–66.)

The cures of disease that Mammon would have effected (I. iv. 17–29) and the silver ditch running with cream from Hogsden to the rebuilt London (V. v. 76–80) also vanish from the text. The 'arrogant pretension personified', which Charles Lamb singled out as Mammon's characteristic, was deliberately toned down by Garrick.

Garrick's insertions in the text chiefly concern Drugger, and are such slight speeches that it is clear the success of the acting depended upon the by-play. Drugger's portague, which he has kept this half-year (I. iii. 87)—

> And I would fain keep it half a year longer—

would help the point of Face's ''Shalt keep it no longer'. In the sixth scene of the second act there are a number of trivial additions to show Drugger's simplicity. 'He's busy with his spirits, but wee'll upon him', says Face: 'Where are they?' Drugger asks. He is told of the mystic character of the sign to be given him—'As thus'— 'I don't understand it', he says: 'that's Abel' evoked the comment 'So it is'. When Subtle praises the tobacco and asks 'What is't a pound?' he answers

> I'll sell your worship a hogshead of it.
> *Face.* He'll send you a hogshead, Doctor. [*Abel runs out, and Face
> brings him back.*

When Face dispatches him, 'Away, be gone', he says

> I'll give him a pound.—I'll give him two pound. [*Exit.*

In one passage Garrick showed obtuseness, but he may have felt that his version better suited the matter-of-fact playgoer. After the explosion Face suggests as a 'good penance' to the disconsolate Mammon that he should send a hundred pounds to the box at the Bethlehem Hospital 'For the restoring such as ha' their wits' (IV. v. 87). Garrick substituted 'such as ha' lost their wits'.

The chief actors with Garrick in 1743 were Bridges as Subtle, Macklin as Face, Berry as Mammon, Havard as Dapper, Brownsmith as Tribulation, Phillips as Ananias, Mrs. Pritchard as Dol Common, and Mrs. Bennett as Dame Pliant. There were many changes in the succeeding years. The most memorable was Thomas Weston's performance of Abel Drugger in 1763 when Garrick went to Italy; Weston played the part with a fine simplicity, wisely discarding Garrick's method. Hugh Kelly, attacking the Drury Lane actors, made an exception in favour of Weston,

> Tho' bold, yet simple; forcible, tho' cool;
> Fine without trick; and finish'd without rule—

and commemorated his

> sublime stupidity of face,
> As dead to sense as destitute of grace.[1]

The part of Subtle was played by John Burton in 1753, by Woodward from 1755 to 1758, and again by Burton from 1758 to 1772. Cross was Face from 1748 to 1753, when Woodward took the part for two years; William Palmer then took it for fourteen years, and John Palmer played it till 1768. Henry Vaughan was Dapper from 1748 to 1766; John Packer was Lovewit from 1759 to 1776; Charles Blaker was Surly from 1746 to 1763; Robert Baddeley succeeded him and, except for two years, kept the part till 1776. Clough was Tribulation in 1759; Hartry succeeded him from 1766 to 1774. The part of Mammon was played by Robert Bransby in 1759 and James Love in 1762 and again by Bransby in 1774. Davies criticized in Love 'a deficiency of glowing and warm tints which such a rich dupe in folly required, and the character amply afforded'.[2] The glowing and warm tints, as we have already noted, had been to some extent subdued in Garrick's version. Till his farewell performance on 11 April 1776 Garrick produced the play once or twice every year.

In the nineteenth century[3] the Elizabethan Stage Society under the direction of William Poel acted the play at Apothecaries' Hall, Blackfriars, partly on the site of the old Blackfriars Theatre, on 24 and 25 February 1899. The cast was: Lewis Mannering, Subtle; Michael Sherbrooke, Face; Ernest Meads, Mammon; Harold Graham, Dapper; Samuel Allen, Drugger; Charles Gellet, Lovewit; Edgar Playford, Surly; Frank Vernon, Tribulation; Leonard Howard, Ananias; Percy Bryett, Kastril; Edith Ashby, Dol Common;

---

[1] *Thespis; or, A Critical Examination into the Merits of all the Principal Performers belonging to Drury-Lane Theatre*, 1766, p. 24.

[2] *Dramatic Miscellanies*, ii, p. 109.

[3] Dickens thought of producing the play in 1848, with himself as Mammon, but only got as far as two or three rehearsals. See Forster's *Life*, ii. 19.

Dorothy Cacey, Dame Pliant. The performance was a highly finished piece of work, and the leading parts were well sustained. Poel revived the play at the New Theatre, Cambridge, in August 1902.

The Marlowe Dramatic Society performed the play at Cambridge on 5 March 1914. Dennis Robertson was Subtle; F. L. Birch, Face; W. T. R. Rawson, Dol Common; W. Hedley, Mammon; A. G. Harman, Dapper; A. S. C. Goullet, Drugger; R. W. Mallison, Surly; W. G. D. Butcher, Kastril; W. F. A. Chambers, Dame Pliant; H. Barnsly, Tribulation Wholesome; and J. Burnaby, Ananias. *The Times* described the acting as excellent throughout; 'Subtle and Face could hardly be bettered'. Subtle took his lines at great speed with a parsonic accent; Face brought off a personal triumph and kept the others on the move. Mammon was not quite enough of the voluptuary, not quite convincing in his raptures. But his part suffered badly, as Dol's, from motives of prudery, was badly cut. It was all-important that Mammon, who was far above a Dapper or a Drugger, should be trapped, and Dol, as Jonson conceived her, was just the person to do it. F. M. Cornford in *The Cambridge Review*, parodied the censor by proposing to read in IV. i. 15–17,

> Physic or mathematics,
> Poetry, State, the white slave traffic . . .
> She will endure and never startle.

The scenery consisted largely of hangings and curtains made of a patchwork of bright-coloured stuffs sewed upon canvas. For Subtle's laboratory there was a futurist backcloth with cubist squares and weird creatures emblematic of alchemy.

On 8 April 1916 the play was revived by the Birmingham Repertory Company. The cast was as follows: Subtle, Felix Aylmer; Face, Joseph A. Dodd; Dol Common, Margaret Chatwin; Dapper, Frank D. Clewlow; Drugger, E. Stuart Vinden; Lovewit, James Smith; Mammon, William J. Rea; Surly, Frank Moore; Wholesome, Scott Sunderland; Ananias, Walter Turner; Kastril, A. C. Rose; Dame Pliant, Maud Gill.

The Phoenix Company gave a very successful performance of the play at the Regent Theatre, King's Cross, on 18 and 19 March 1923. Subtle was played by Baliol Holloway, Face by George Desmond, Mammon by Frank Collier, Dapper by J. L. Firth, Drugger by Andrew Leigh, Lovewit by Orlando Barnett, Surly by Rupert Harvey, Tribulation Wholesome by H. R. Hignett, Ananias by Stanley Lathbury, Dol Common by Margaret Yarde, and Dame Pliant by Nell Carter. Allan Wade was the producer. Subtle was played with a dry humour which brought out his cynicism; the

Puritans, one expansive and the other portentously solemn, stood out among the performers; Mammon too was admirably acted, especially in the rendering of the great lines on his imaginary future when he achieved the stone. Face and Dol Common were also good.

On 9 and 10 December 1927 Birkbeck College gave a performance with a prologue by J. H. Lobban.

In August 1932 there was a very good performance of the play at the Malvern Festival. The chief actors were William Rea as Subtle, Ralph Richardson as Face, Kelso as Sir Epicure Mammon, Cedric Hardwicke as Drugger, and Eileen Beldon as Dol Common.

On 12 November 1934 the students of Kirkland House, Harvard University, performed the play under the direction of Dr. Huntingdon Brown, who acted Ananias.

On 1 April 1935 the play was produced at Princes Theatre, Shaftesbury Avenue, by Olga Katzin, with Hugh Miller as Subtle, Austin Trevor as Face, Bruce Winston as Mammon, Iris Hoey as Dol Common, Alan Trotter as Tribulation, and Brember Wills as Ananias. The play was treated mainly as boisterous modern comedy; the *Daily Herald* called it ' a rollicking farce', but Mr. Bruce Winston rose to the poetry of Mammon's part at the appropriate moments.

The Durham Colleges Dramatic Society presented *The Alchemist* at Neville's Cross College, Durham, on 2 December 1938. Face was played by A. S. Haydon, Subtle by D. P. Jenkins, Doll by Elizabeth Manners, Sir Epicure by J. Fernsby. Dr. Clifford Leech was the producer.

A performance was given by the Wadham College Dramatic Society in Wadham Gardens, Oxford, on 19 and 25 May 1946. Timothy Bateson was Subtle; Stuart Jolly, Face; Russell Smith, Mammon; and Margaret Pugh, Dol Common.

In January 1947 the Old Vic Theatre company revived the play at the New Theatre, St. Martin's Lane. George Relph was Subtle; Ralph Richardson, Face; Nicholas Hannen, Mammon; Michael Warre, Surly; Frank Duncan, Dapper; Alec Guinness, Drugger; Peter Copley, Ananias; Michael Raghan, Wholesome; Joyce Redman, Dol Common. The play was acted as a kind of harlequinade, swift and vigorous, but with a boisterousness hardly suited to Jonson. The actors, except the Puritans, were dressed in eighteenth-century costume, which also seemed incongruous. The excuse given in the programme that charlatanism flourished a century after Jonson's death overlooked the fact that this was not true of alchemy.

In the 1672 edition of *The Wits: or, Sport upon Sport* (pp. 159–66) Francis Kirkman published an abridgement of *The Alchemist*, two scenes in which Abel Drugger appears, I. iii, II. vi, and one scene of Ananias, II. v.

Side by side with Garrick's performance of the play a low farce by Francis Gentleman called *The Tobacconist* ran from 1770 to 1815. The hero was a great-grandson of Abel Drugger and named after him; Weston played the part, and later Edmund Kean. Mr. Noyes has summarized the plot.[1] The only passage worth quoting from it is in the prologue.

> BEN JOHNSON's *name, in ev'ry ear of taste,*
> *Must with respect, and countenance be grac'd;*
> *No pen the lines of nature better drew,*
> *No wit or satire ever higher flew;*
> *An early pillar of the English stage,*
> *His pieces were true pictures of the age;*
> *Time-worn they feel impair—yet still must please;*
> *Nervous and just, though void of modern ease.*
>
> .   .   .   .   .
>
> *Search all the world, examine ev'ry part;*
> *You'll find each man an alchymist at heart.*
> *In ev'ry clime we find, if truth be told,*
> *The universal deity is gold.*
> *Whate'er of merit you perceive this night,*
> *Grant your old bard as his undoubted right.*
> *My brain has laboured—feebly I confess,*
> *Only to furnish a more modern dress.*
> *My weak endeavours let your candor raise,*
> *They hope indulgence, though they reach not praise.*

The London Evening Post, reviewing the first performance, said, 'To analize this piece particularly, would be soiling the pen of criticism, as it was nothing more than an incoherent mixture of obsolete humour and low buffoonery'.

Dryden made a curious mistake about the origin of *The Alchemist* when he wrote in 1668 a prologue for a revival of Thomas Tomkis's *Albumazar*, first acted before King James at Trinity College, Cambridge, on 10 March 1614–15; the bursar's account-book of Trinity College records a fee of £20 to Tomkis for 'penning and ordering' the play. Dryden, who was also a Trinity man, thought *The Alchemist* a copy of *Albumazar*. The prologue is attributed to Dryden in *Miscellany Poems*, 1684, p. 279: it was first printed in *Covent Garden Drollery*, 1672.[2]

> To say this Commedy pleas'd long ago,
> Is not enough to make it pass you now:

[1] Op. cit., p. 155.   [2] Ed. G. Thorn-Drury, p. 87.

Yet gentlemen, your Ancestors had witt,
When few men censurd, and when fewer writ.
And Johnson of those few the best, chose this,
As the best modell of his master piece;
Subtle was got, by our *Albumazar*,
That *Alchimist* by this Astrologer.
Here he was fashion'd, and I should suppose,
He likes my fashion well, that wears my Cloaths.
But *Ben* made nobly his, what he did mould,
What was anothere's Lead, became his Gold:
Like an unrighteous Conqueror he Raigns.
Yet Rules that well, which he unjustly gains. . . .

CATILINE

Catiline was acted and published in 1611. It must have been played
before 29 August when Eccleston joined the Lady Elizabeth's men.
The company was the King's men, and Jonson printed a list of the
'principall Tragoedians', headed by Burbadge, who may be inferred
to have played the part of Cicero. Richard Robinson's name
appears in Jonson's actor-lists for the first time, and, as he became
famous in women's parts (*D. is A.* II. viii. 69–77), he may have
played Sempronia. Dr. Baldwin assigns Catiline to Lowin, Cethegus
to Condell, Caesar to Ostler, Cato to Heminges, Lentulus to Underwood, Petreius to Eccleston, Curius to Cooke, and the Ghost of Sylla
to Tooley (op. cit., p. 427).

The play was damned. The first two acts went well, Jonson tells
the reader in the preliminary address, but the audience 'disliked the
Oration of Cicero' in the fourth act. The commendatory verses prefixed to the Quarto hint delicately at the failure. Beaumont implies
that Jonson had not 'itch'd after the wild applause of common people':

But thou hast squar'd thy rules, by what is good;
And art, three Ages, yet, from vnderstood.

And Field echoes Jonson's reference in the dedication to 'these Iig-
giuen times':

But, in this Age, where Iigs and dances moue,
How few there are, that this pure worke approue!

Leonard Digges, in the verses he prefixed to Shakespeare's *Poems*,
1640, contrasted the failure of *Catiline* with the brilliant success of
Julius Caesar which delighted the audience

When some new day they would not brooke a line,
Of tedious (though well laboured) *Catiline*.

And it is possibly to *Catiline*, in spite of the play being described as a comedy, that Gayton alluded in his *Pleasant Notes upon Don Quixot*, 1654, p. 271; he described how 'the only *Laureat* of our stage (having compos'd a Play of excellent worth, but not of equall applause) fell downe upon his knees, and gave thanks, that he had transcended the capacity of the vulgar; yet his protestation of their ignorance, was not sufficient to vindicate the misapplication of the argument; for the judicious part of the Auditory condemn'd it equally with those that did not understand it, and though the Comœdy wanted not its *prodesse, & delectare*, had it been exhibited to a scholastick confluence; yet men come not to study at a Play-house, but love such expressions and passages, which with ease insinuate themselves into their capacities.' The statement that the judicious as well as the vulgar condemned the play fits in with the Latin motto prefixed to it, an adaptation of Horace, *Epistles*, II. i. 186–8, 'Such writing as this gives no pleasure to the rabble; even with the upper class enjoyment has flitted from the ear to the restless eyes and the hollow delights of spectacle.'

The title-page of the second Quarto, 1635, describes the play as 'now Acted by his MAIESTIES Servants with great Applause', and Downes included it in his list of old plays acted before 1663 at the Theatre Royal 'but now and then; yet being well Perform'd, . . . very Satisfactory to the Town' (*Roscius Anglicanus*, 1708, p. 8). But the earliest revival of which we have any record is that of 1668. This was at the Theatre Royal in Bridges Street on 18 December before King Charles II, and on 19 December. Pepys saw it on the second day, 'a play of much good sense and words to read, but that do appear the worst upon the stage, I mean, the least diverting, that ever I saw any, though most fine in clothes; and a fine scene of the Senate, and of a fight, that ever I saw in my life'.[1] 'Of a fight' is interesting; the actors evidently worked up a spectacular effect in the fifth act for which there is no warrant in the text.

The King's men had planned to act the piece a year earlier. Pepys heard on 7 December 1667 that it was 'likely to be soon acted', but a quarrel between the actors Hart and Moone was an obstacle[2] to a performance at the Theatre Royal. On 11 December he heard, however, that it was 'to be suddenly acted at the King's house; and there all agree that it cannot be well done, . . . there not being good actors enow: and Burt acts Cicero, which they all conclude he will not be able to do well. The King gives them £500 for robes, there being, as they say, to be sixteen scarlett robes'.[3] But on

---

[1] *Diary*, ed. H. B. Wheatley, viii. 182.   [2] Ibid., vii. 230.
[3] Ibid. 235.

11 January 1668 he learned from Mrs. Knepp that 'for want of the clothes which the King promised them' the piece 'will not be acted for a good while'.[1]

Catiline was played again on 2 January 1669, and on 13 January when the King saw it. These performances involved a piquant court scandal. Pepys on 15 January writes:

> Up, and by coach to Sir W. Coventry, where with him a good while in his chamber, talking of one thing or another; among others, he told me of the great factions at Court at this day, even to the sober engaging of great persons, and differences, and making the King cheap and ridiculous. It is about my Lady Harvy's being offended at Doll Common's[2] acting of Sempronia, to imitate her; for which she got my Lord Chamberlain, her kinsman, to imprison Doll: when my Lady Castlemayne made the King to release her, and to order her to act it again, worse than ever, the other day, where the King himself was: and since it was acted again, and my Lady Harvy provided people to hiss her and fling oranges at her: but it seems the heat is come to a great height, and real troubles at Court about it.[3]

The revival was commemorated by a new edition of the play published in quarto in February 1669. Following Jonson's own precedent in the Folio, it gave a list of 'The Principal Tragœdians', namely, Hart, who played Catiline; Burt, who played Cicero; Mohun, who played Cethegus; Beeston, Kynaston, Reeves, Winterson, Cartwright, Gradwell, Bell. Mrs. Corey, in spite of her notoriety as Sempronia, is not mentioned. The Prologue and Epilogue spoken by Nell Gwynn are quoted:

A

PROLOGUE

To *Catiline*,

To be Merrily spoke by Mrs. *Nell*.[4]

A Woman's Prologue! This is vent'rous News;
But we, a Poet wanting, Crav'd a Muse.
Why should our Brains lye fallow, as if they
Without His fire, were mere Prometehan (sic) *Clay?*
In Natur's Plain-Song we may bear our parts;
Although We want choise Descant from the Arts,
Amongst Musicians; so the Philomel
May in Wild-Notes, though not in Rules excell.
And when i'th weaker Vessel Wit doth lye;
Though into Froth it will work out, and flye.

---

[1] *Diary*, ed. H. B. Wheatley, vii. 277.   [2] Mrs. Corey.   [3] Ibid. viii. 199, 200.
[4] The Quarto of 1674 adds 'in an *Amazonian* Habit'.

But Gentlemen, You know our formal way,
Although we're sure 'tis false, yet we must say,
Nay Pish, Nay Fye, in troth it is not good,
When we the while, think it not understood:
Hither repair all you that are for Ben;
Let th' House hold full, We're sure to carry't then.
Slight not this Femal Summons; Phoebus-rayes,
To Crown his Poets, *turn'd our sex to* Bayes.
And Ladies sure you'l vote for us entire,
(This Plot doth prompt the Prologue to conspire)
Such inoffensive Combination can
But show, who best deserve true worth in Man.
And You, with Your great Author taking Part;
May chance be thought, like him to know the Art,
Vouchsafe then, as you look, to speak us fair,
Let the Gallants dislike it, if they dare:
They will so forfeit the repute of Judges,
You may turn Am'zons, and make them Drudges,
Man's claim to Rule is, in his Reason bred;
This Masculine Sex of Brain may make you Head.
'Tis real Skill, in the Right place to praise;
But more, to have the Wit, not to Write Playes.

THE
EPILOGUE.

By the same.

No Dance, no Song, no Farce? His lofty Pen,
How e're we like it, doubtless Wrote to Men.
Height may be his, as it was Babel's *fall;*
There Bricklayers *turn'd to Linguists, ruin'd all.*
I'de ne're spoke this, had I not heard by many,
He lik't one silent Woman, above any:
And against us had such strange prejudice;
For our applause, he scorn'd to write amiss,
For all this, he did us, like Wonders, prize;
Not for our Sex, but when he found us Wise.
A Poet *runs the Gantlet, and his slips,*
Are bare expos'd to regiments of Whips;
Among those, he to Poetick Champions Writ;
As We to gain the Infancy of Wit.
Which if they prove the greatest Number, then
The House hath cause to thank Nell, *more than* Ben.
Our Author *might prefer your praise, perhaps,*
Wee'd rather have your Money, than your Claps.

On 8 March 1675 *Catiline* was acted before the King at the Theatre Royal in Drury Lane. Langbaine wrote in 1691 (*Account of the*

English Dramatick Poets, p. 288), 'This Play is still in Vogue on the Stage, and always presented with success.' Verbruggen played Cethegus about 1690, a part for which his rough, wild manner fitted him.[1]

In *The Life Of the Late Famous Comedian, Jo. Haynes. Containing, His Comical Exploits and Adventures* . . . 1701, pp. 23–4, written by Tom Brown, one comical exploit is recorded during a performance of *Catiline*.

There happen'd to be one Night, a Play Acted, Call'd, *Catilines Conspiracy*, wherein there was wanting a Great Number of Senators.

Now Mr. *Hart* being chief of the House, wou'd oblige *Jo.* to dress for one of these Senators. Altho *Jo*'s Sallary being then 50s. *per* Week, freed him from any such obligation.

But Mr. Hart, . . . being sole Governour of the Play-House, and at a small variance with *Jo.* commands it, and the other must obey. *Jo.* being vex'd at the slight Mr. *Hart* had put on him, found out this method of being reveng'd on him: He gets a Scaramouch dress, a large full Ruff, makes himself Whiskers, from Ear to Ear, puts on his head, a long Merry Andrews Cap, a short Pipe in his mouth, a little three Leg'd stool in his hand, and in this manner, follows Mr. *Hart* on the Stage, sets himself down behind him, and begins to smoke his Pipe, to Laugh, and Point at him.

Which Comical Figure, put all the House in an uproar, some Laughing, some Clapping, and some Hollowing. Now Mr. *Hart*, as those that knew him can aver, was a Man of that Exactness and Grandeur on the Stage, that let what wou'd happen, he'd never discompose himself, or mind any thing but what he then Represented, and had a Scene fall'n behind him, he wou'd not at that time look back, to have seen what was the matter, which *Jo.* knowing, remain'd still Smoaking, the Audience continued Laughing, Mr. *Hart* Acting, and Wondering at this unusual occasion of their Mirth, sometimes thinking it some disturbance in the House; again, that it might be something amiss in his dress; at last, turning himself towards the Scenes, he discover'd *Jo.* in the aforesaid Posture, whereupon he immediately goes off the Stage, Swearing, Swearing he would never set foot on it again, unless *Jo.* was immediately turn'd out of Doors; which was no sooner spoke, but put in Practice. So our grave Senator, was presently dismis'd the Senate, and turn'd out of the House in *Querpo*.

Unfortunately this story does not square with the facts of stage history. In the 1668 and 1669 performances Hart played Catiline, and the only scene in which he appears in the Senate is in the fourth act; his speeches in that scene are few and curt. Haines could have played this trick only in the long speech of Cicero, and there is no

---

[1] Noyes, *Ben Jonson on the English Stage*, p. 311.

evidence that Hart took that part. But in the Bodleian copy of Haines's life (Godwin Pamphlet 384) there is a contemporary note in manuscript, 'In 1672', and Malone, quoting the Catiline story in his *Variorum Shakespeare*, iii, p. 289, dates it about 1673. If Hart changed his part of Catiline for Cicero in the later performance, Haines's buffoonery was credible, but we have no evidence to authenticate it. The 1674 Quarto has no actor-list.

BARTHOLOMEW FAIR

THIS comedy was acted at the Hope Theatre on the Bankside by the Lady Elizabeth's men on 31 October 1614 according to the mock-indenture quoted in the Induction, ll. 64–72.[1] Two actors of this company are noticed in the text—Nathan Field, 'your best *Actor*', and Joseph Taylor (v. iii. 88, 81). Mr. W. J. Lawrence suggested that Field played Littlewit.[2]

The play was promptly acted at Court on 1 November. Nathan Field received £10 for it 'in the behalfe of himselfe and the rest of his fellowes' by a Lord Chamberlain's warrant dated 11 June 1615;[3] and the Pipe Office Declared Accounts (Revels, 2805) include 'Canvas for the Boothes and other necessaries for a play called Bartholomewe Faire'.[4] Strange to say, there is no further record of any performance of the play during the reigns of James I and Charles I. In the latter reign the rising power of Puritanism may have been a deterrent.

Naturally, it was popular at the Restoration. It was the second of Jonson's plays to be acted by the King's players at Vere Street on 8 June 1661. Pepys wrote of this performance: 'Then to the Cook's with Mr. Shepley and Mr. Creed, and dined together, and then I went to the Theatre and there saw Bartholomew Faire, the first time it was acted now-a-days. It is a most admirable play and well acted, but too much prophane and abusive.'[5] A second performance followed on 27 June. In both these revivals the puppet-show was omitted, but it was given on 7 September, when Pepys again saw it:

So I having appointed the young ladies at the Wardrobe to go with them to a play to-day, . . . my wife and I took them to the Theatre,

---

[1] The reference to 'Johnsons play' in Daborne's letter of 13 Nov. 1613 (Greg, *Henslowe Papers*, p. 78) was probably to *Eastward Ho*, but Malone, Fleay, and Greg explain it of *Bartholomew Fair*. See p. 193.
[2] *Speeding up Shakespeare*, p. 92.   [3] A.O. 1/390/52.
[4] Chambers, *Elizabethan Stage*, iv. 183.
[5] *Diary*, ed. Wheatley, ii. 50–1.

where we seated ourselves close by the King, and Duke of York, and Madame Palmer, which was great content; and, indeed, I can never enough admire her beauty. And here was 'Bartholomew Fayre', with the puppet-show, acted to-day, which had not been these forty years (it being so satyricall against Puritanism, they durst not till now, which is strange they should already dare to do it, and the King do countenance it), but I do never a whit like it the better for the puppets, but rather the worse. Thence home with the ladies, it being by reason of our staying a great while for the King's coming, and the length of the play, near nine o'clock before it was done.[1]

On 12 November Pepys went again and repeated his criticism of the puppets: 'though I love the play as much as ever I did, yet I do not like the puppets at all, but think it to be a lessening to it.'[2] The last performance of the year was on 18 December.

Meanwhile, an outrageous farce, in part worked up from *Bartholomew Fair* presumably by some courtier, had been given at Whitehall before the King. It is described in a letter of a Puritan, the Rev. William Hooke, to a friend in New England on 12 October 1661. The letter is in the Mather Papers published by the Massachusetts Historical Society:[3]

You will heare by the bearer of the play of the Puritan before the Highest, where were p^rsent (as they say) the E: Manchester & 3 Bpp^s, and London one of them. In it were rep^rsented 2 Presbiterians vnder the forme of M^r. Baxter & M^r. Callamy, whose Habitt & actions were sett forth: prayers were made in imitation of the Puritan, with such scripture expressions as I am loath to mention, the matter such as might have been vsed by any godly man in a right maner: The case of Syon lying in the dust was spreade before, &c: & God's former deliverances of his peo: vrged in such phraises as would amaze yo^w if yo^w heard them, with eyes lifted vp to heaven, one representing the Puritan put in the stockes for stealing a pigg, & the stockes found by him vnlockt, which he admires at as a wonderfull pvidence & fruite of prayer, vpon which he consults about his call, whether he should come forth or not, & at last pceived it was his way, & forth he comes, lifting vp his eyes to heaven, & falls to prayse & thankesgiving; I canot tell yo^w all of it, being large, but such as that some p^rsent, who were farr from liking the Puritan, were gr^tly astonished, wondring the house did not fall vpon there heades. The play I heere, was taken out of one or two of Ben: Johnson's, &c: for which Ben. would say, that, if he were damn'd, it would be for these 2 playes. I heere it hath beene acted againe.[4]

---

[1] *Diary*, ed. Wheatley, ii. 98–9.   [2] Ibid., p. 135.
[3] Fourth Series, viii. 177–8.
[4] In the same papers, p. 174, is a slightly different version that the Puritans 'preached as they doe agst Babilon, & at last came some Souldiers, & puled one out of the Pulpit, & put him in a payre of stockes, and then a company of Ho: bⁿ: & sisters bemoaning him & prayed, & after some space of time

It is strange, after what Pepys says of the risk incurred in satirizing Puritanism, that such a performance should have been permitted at Court. It was revived at Dublin with the play before the Lord Lieutenant of Ireland in 1670. Here our authority is Richard Baxter; in the *Reliquiæ Baxterianæ*, 1696, part III, p. 84, he says:

> There happened a great rebuke to the Nobility and Gentry of *Dublin* in *Ireland*, which is related in their *Gazette* in these words. [*Dubl. Dec. 27.* 'Yesterday happened here a very unfortunate Accident: Most of the Nobility and Gentry being at a Play, at a publick Playhouse, the upper Galleries on a sudden fell all down, beating down the second, which together with all the People that were in them, fell into the Pit and lower Boxes: His Excellency, the Lord Lieutenant, with his Lady, happened to be there, but thanks be to God escaped the Danger without any harm, part of the Box where they were remaining firm, and so resisting the Fall from above; only his two Sons were found quite buried under the Timber. The younger had received but little hurt, but the eldest was taken up dead to all appearance, but having presently been let Blood, &c. recovered. There were many dangerously hurt, and seven or eight killed outright.][1]

So far the *Gazette*. About seventeen or eighteen died then, and of their Wounds. The first Letters that came to *London* of it, filled the City with the report, that it was a Play in scorn of Godliness, and that I was the Person acted by the Scorner, as a Puritan, and that he that represented me was set in the Stocks, when the fall was, and his Leg broke. But the Play was *Ben Johnson's Bartholomew-Fair*, with a scene added for the times, in the which the Puritan is called a *Banbury* Man, and I cannot learn that I was named, nor medled with more than others of my Condition, unless by the Actor's dress they made any such reflecting Intimations.

The play proper continued intermittently. There is a record of its performance in 1662 when Dr. Edward Browne paid 1s. 6d. to see it at Killigrew's theatre.[2] It was assigned to the King's men on 8 April 1663, and was one of the plays which Downes noted as acted occasionally.[3] We learn from him that William Wintershall, 'good in Tragedy, as well as in Comedy', acted Cokes so well 'that the Famous Comedian *Nokes* came in that part far short of him'.[4]

Pepys saw the play on 2 August 1664: 'To the King's play-house, and there saw "Bartholomew Fayre", which do still please me; and

the lock of the stockes flew open, & then the same before mentioned gave God thankes'.
[1] The accident was noted by Robert Bowyer in a letter from Dublin to Robert Southwell, quoted in the Historical Manuscripts Commission's *Report on the Manuscripts of the Earl of Egmont*, Dublin, ii. 24; Bowyer states it was the complete play which was acted.
[2] British Museum Sloane MS. 1900, f. 63ᵛ.
[3] *Roscius Anglicanus*, p. 9.   [4] Ibid., p. 17.

is, as it is acted, the best comedy in the world, I believe.'[1] His next
visit was during the fair on 4 September 1668:

> Up . . . and at noon my wife, and Deb. and Mercer, and W. Hewer
> and I to the Fair, and there, at the old house, did eat a pig, and was
> pretty merry, but saw no sights, my wife having a mind to see the play
> 'Bartholomew-Fayre', with puppets. Which we did, and it is an excel-
> lent play; the more I see it, the more I love the wit of it; only the
> business of abusing the Puritans begins to grow stale, and of no use,
> they being the people that, at last, will be found the wisest. And here
> Knepp came to us, and sat with us.[2]

In 1669 *Bartholomew Fair* was 'allowed of to his Maties Servants
at ye New Theatre', and on 22 February there was a command
performance at the Cockpit at Whitehall, the company receiving
£20.[3] Pepys took his wife and two girls to Whitehall, 'and there
did without much trouble get into the playhouse, there in a good
place among the Ladies of Honour, and myself also sat in the pit;
and there by and by come the King and Queen, and they begun
"Bartholomew Fayre". But I like no play here so well as at the
common playhouse; besides that, my eyes being very ill since last
Sunday and this day se'nnight, with the light of the candles, I was
in mighty pain to defend myself now from the light of the candles.'
The play was again acted at Court on 30 November 1674, the actors
receiving £10.[4]

For the rest of the century there are only vague references. The
play was in the repertory of the King's Company, formed out of
the union of the two patent companies in 1682,[5] and Langbaine
noted in 1691 that it had 'frequently appear'd on the Stage, since
the Restoration, with great applause'.[6]

In the eighteenth century the play was performed up to 1731 and
then disappeared from the stage. It was played at Drury Lane on
18 August 1702 and 25 March, 8 April, and 28 September 1704. The
first complete cast is for the performance at the Haymarket on
12 August 1707 by the actors who revolted from Drury Lane. Littlewit was played by Henry Norris, Cokes by William Bullock, Quarlous
by John Mills, Waspe by Benjamin Johnson, Overdo by Theophilus
Keen, Nightingale by Henry Fairbank, Ursula by a male actor Cross,
Mistress Welborn by Mrs. Porter, and Dame Purecraft by Mrs.
Powell. Josias Miller succeeded Bullock as Cokes in 1715. Bullock,
Mills, and Miller owned theatrical booths in the Fair; there was also

---

[1] *Diary*, ed. Wheatley, iv. 206.
[2] Ibid. viii. 98.
[3] Nicoll, *Restoration Drama*, pp. 306, 315.
[4] *Diary*, ibid. p. 235.
[5] Downes, *Roscius Anglicanus*, pp. 39, 40.
[6] *The English Dramatick Poets*, pp. 287–8.

a 'Ben Jonson's booth' there,[1] for which Elkanah Settle wrote. George Pack, Colley Cibber, and John Bickerstaff successively played the Rabbi; Booth, Ryan, and Tom Walker played Edgworth. Charles Shephard succeeded to the part of Overdo from 1715 to 1722.

From 1708, when the Drury Lane and Haymarket comedians reunited, *Bartholomew Fair* was played in most seasons up to 1722, when it was acted at Court on 21 December. There was only one revival, on 30 October 1731. Johnson was Waspe; Theophilus Cibber, Cokes; Shephard, Overdo; John Harper, Ursula; and Kitty Clive, Win Littlewit.

On 25 August 1735 an altered version of the play was performed at Lincoln's Inn Fields. Meanwhile the Fair had steadily deteriorated. Tom Brown noted in 1699 that '*Smithfield* is another sort of a Place now to what it was in the Times of *Honest Ben*; who, were he to rise out of his Graue, wou'd hardly believe it to be the same numerical spot of Ground where Justice *Overdo* made so busie a Figure, where the *Crop-ear'd Parson* demolish'd a *Gingerbread Stall*, where *Nightingale*, of harmonious memory, sung *Ballads*, and fat *Ursula* sold *Pig* and *bottled Ale*'.[2] The City authorities intervened; acting at the Fair was forbidden in 1735 and the veto was enforced in 1762; the Fair was held for the last time in 1855.

There was a performance of the play by the Phoenix Society at the New Oxford Theatre on 26 June 1921. The cast was as follows: Littlewit, Eric Cowley; Win Littlewit, Angela Baddeley; Dame Purecraft, Margaret Yarde; Busy, Ben Field; Winwife, Tristan Rawson; Quarlous, Howard Rose; Cokes, Ernest Thesiger; Waspe, Stanley Lathbury; Overdo, Frank Cellier; Dame Overdo, Helena Millais; Grace Welborn, Clare Harris; Leatherhead, H. K. Ayliff; Joan Trash, Elsie French; Edgworth, Edward Combermere; Nightingale, John Clifford; Ursula, Roy Byford; Mooncalf, Edwin Greenwood; Knockhum, Eugene Leahy; Whit, Richard Grenville; Alice, Silvia Young; Trouble-all, Edwin Greenwood. In the Induction P. H. Vernon was the Stage-keeper, F. Harker the Bookholder, and Allan Wade, who produced the play, the Scrivener. The parts of Busy and Cokes were admirably played, and the general level of the acting was high. But there was a certain heaviness of movement, due perhaps to the episodic treatment of the characters; they do not move to a defined goal as the characters in *The Alchemist* clearly do.

On 30 April 1940 the ladies of Bryn Mawr College, Pennsylvania,

---

[1] Errol Sherson, *London's Lost Theatres of the Nineteenth Century*, 1925, p. 329, quoted by Noyes.   [2] *Works*, i. 212.

performed the play. Ursula was played by Miss Follanbee, the Ginger-bread woman by Miss Joan Trash, and Mooncalf by Miss Copeland. An eyewitness records that the performance went unexpectedly well.

In March 1947 the Marlowe Society acted the play at Cambridge. The actors were: Littlewit, P. Collins; Busy, J. Money; Winwife, D. Eves; Quarlous, A. Edinborough; Cokes, J. Sleap; Waspe, R. Lewis; Overdo, N. Forward; Leatherhead, J. Myers; Edgworth, M. Manton; Nightingale, C. Parker; Mooncalf, D. Pocock; Knockhum, S. Joseph; Whit, A. Knowles; Trouble-all, E. Junge; Win-the-fight Littlewit, Elizabeth Cunningham; Dame Purecraft, Gillian Webb; Dame Overdo, Stella Forwood; Grace Wellborn, Margaret Dewhirst; Joan Trash, June Hooper; Ursula, Elvira Evans; Alice, Sylvia Clark. The producer was Donald Beves; the sets were designed by Pat Robertson.

THE DEVIL IS AN ASS

THE stage history of this play, *The Staple of News*, and *The Magnetic Lady* is confined to a record of the original performances. *The Devil is an Ass* was performed at the Blackfriars[1] playhouse in 1616 by the King's men. The Blackfriars was their second house, a roofed theatre which they could use in winter. The performance took place towards the end of the year. Professor G. L. Kittredge has brought evidence to bear on this point.[2] He cites the case of a pretended demoniac, John Smith, a nephew of 'silver-tongued Smith', who suffered from hystero-epilepsy, 'of which lying and imposture are well-recognized symptoms'. He was twelve or thirteen years of age at the time, and Professor Kittredge shows the significance of Merecraft's comment to Fitzdottrel,

> 'Tis no hard thing to'out doe the *Deuill* in:
> A Boy o' thirteene yeere old made him an *Asse*
> But t'other day. (v. v. 49–51.)

This must have been something more recent than the boy of Burton in 1596. Smith lived at Husbands Bosworth, Leicestershire, and he accused nine women, who were hanged at Leicester on 18 July 1616. Smith continued his fits and accused six more women in August. Fortunately King James visited Leicester on 15 August, and interested himself in the case. He examined Smith, detected the fraud, and sent him to Archbishop Abbott at Lambeth, to whom he made

---

[1] See I. vi. 31.
[2] *Modern Philology*, ix. 195–209, 'King James I and *The Devil is an Ass*'.

a full confession. He afterwards exhibited his tricks to the King. Five of the accused women were released on 15 October; the sixth had died in prison. Smith described the familiars of the six women—a horse, a cat, a polecat, a fish, a toad, a dog. When the horse tormented him, he whinnied; when the cat did, he would miaow, and so on. There is no record of any punishment of Smith: the only people inconvenienced by his brutality were Justice Winch and Serjeant Crow, who had hanged the nine women earlier; they were 'discountenanced' by the King's action.

The play must therefore have been acted late in the year, probably in November or December.

Minor points which help to confirm a late date are the references to the widgeon being in season (v. ii. 39)—this bird appears late in September or early in October—and to the fieldfare—Chaucer's 'frosty feldefare'—which comes early in October (III. vi. 3, 4).

Downes includes *The Devil is an Ass* among the 'old plays' acted 'now and then' by the King's men at the New Theatre in Drury Lane at the Restoration.[1] It is very doubtful if this means more than that they acquired the right to act it; the theme was far too antiquated for a Restoration audience. That persistent playgoer Pepys never mentions the play.

THE STAPLE OF NEWS

THIS comedy was acted by the King's men at the Blackfriars in 1626 during Lent. The second Intermean refers 'to the time of yeer, in Lent', and the Dutch eel-boats (III. ii. 84) came over at that season. There is also the reference 'now, at the Coronation' (ibid. 301), which took place on 2 February 1626. There is a reference to the death of the actor William Rowley early in February (ibid. 205–6 n.). F. G. Fleay suggested with much probability a public performance at Candlemas and a Court performance at Shrovetide, 19 February.

THE NEW INN

The New Inn was licensed by Sir Henry Herbert on 19 January 1629,[2] and was a complete failure, as the title-page of the first edition, 1631, plainly indicates. It was 'most negligently play'd' by the King's Company; in the description of 'The Persons of the Play' only two of the actors are commended, those who played the Host

---

[1] *Roscius Anglicanus*, p. 8.   [2] Malone, *Variorum Shakespeare*, i. 421.

and Lovel. It was 'more squeamishly beheld, and censured' by the audience, who hissed at the references to Cis or Cecily, the chambermaid. This we learn from the second epilogue, less militant than an apologia of Jonson's usually is, because of his illness; it was written in anticipation of a Court performance which never took place. Robert Wild in his *Poem In Nova Fert Animus* (Broadside 1679) alludes to the failure of the play:

> Poets, who others can Immortal make,
> When they grow *Gray*, their Lawrels them forsake;
> And seek young Temples where they may grow Green;
> No Palsie-hands may wash in *Hippocrene*;
> 'Twas not Terse Clarret, Eggs and Muskadine,
> Nor Goblets Crown'd with *Greek* or *Spanish* Wine,
> Could make new Flames in Old *Ben Johnsons* Veins,
> For his Attempts prov'd lank and languid strains:
> His *New Inn* (so he nam'd his youngest Play)
> Prov'd a blind Ale-house, cry'd down the first Day:
> His own dull Epitaph—*Here lies Ben Johnson*,
> (Half drunken too) He Hickcupt—*Who was once one*.[1]

We do not know what reception the audience gave to the concluding scene, but we should imagine that the grotesque incidents of the disguised Lady Frampul removing the patch which she had kept over one eye for seven years (with what effect upon her eyesight we are not told) and the disguised Lord Frampul pulling off his beard and cap, so that he at once became visible, must have excited derision. Jonson seems to have thought that he could have remedied matters by bringing in the drunkards in the last act,[2] but Owen Feltham's criticism had much point:

> *Jug, Pierce, Peck, Fly*, and all
> Your Jests so nominall,
> Are things so far beneath an able Braine,
> As they do throw a stain
> Through all the unlikely plot.[3]

There was one modern revival of the play at the Chelsea Arts Club in 1903 by members of the Old Vic Company under the direction of C. R. Ashbee. We have failed to obtain any account of it.

---

[1] See vol. i, p. 184.   [2] 1 Epilogue, 13–16.
[3] *Lusoria*, p. 17 in *Resolves*, 8th ed., 1661.

THE MAGNETIC LADY

THE earliest reference to the play is a letter of the news-writer John Pory to Sir Thomas Pickering on 20 September 1632, 'Ben Jonson (who, I thought, had been dead) hath written a play against next terme called the Magnetick Lady'.[1] Accordingly we find Herbert licensing the play on 12 October. Knight, the book-keeper of the Blackfriars playhouse, paid Herbert's fee.[2] A Court performance is recorded in the epilogue.

There was trouble with the Court of High Commission over the oaths in the play. A 'second petition' of the actors to the Court is our authority. The first petition, of which we are not informed, had evidently given the impression that the oaths were in the play and that Herbert had passed them. Summoned to Lambeth, Herbert cleared himself before Archbishop Laud, the actors 'doing him right', that is, acquitting him of any responsibility for a text which they had themselves interpolated.[3]

We get an entertaining glimpse of the first performance from some scurrilous lines of Alexander Gill the younger, preserved in Ashmole MS. 38, page 15. The failure of the play was witnessed by two victims of Jonson's satire—Nathaniel Butter and Inigo Jones.

> O, how thy frind, *Natt Butter* gan to Melte
> When as the poornes of the plott he smelte,
> And Inigo with laughter ther grewe fatt
> That thear was Nothing worth the Laughing att.

Gill speaks of the play having 'three shamfull foyles', that is, only three performances which failed. Jonson's epilogue to the King suggests a Court performance, but he may have written this for a performance which never came off. Gill mentions the two leading actors at this date of the King's men, John Lowin and Joseph Taylor, who evidently performed in the play: were they the two actors whom Jonson praised as the Host and Lovel in *The New Inn*? There is also in the lines a puzzling reference to Ironside's dress—the 'Rosie Foole' with 'his strang habitt, and Indiffinett Nott'. 'Nott' means with his hair close-cropped; Chaucer's Yeoman had 'a not-head' 'with a broun visage' (*Prol.* 109). All that we are told about this point in the play is that Ironside

> got his head into a Beaver,
> With a huge feather. (III. iv. 61–2.)

---

[1] B.M. Harley MS. 7000, f. 336.
[2] *Variorum Shakespeare*, 1821, iii. 231.
[3] Ibid., p. 233. See our textual introduction in vol. vi, p. 501.

THE SAD SHEPHERD

In a British Museum manuscript, Sloane MS. 1009, on ff. 373–4, a prologue and epilogue are found for what was evidently a private performance, probably at a nobleman's house in the time of Charles II. There is a reference to the two chief Restoration companies in line 10: Davenant died in 1668, and Killigrew's company existed from 1660 to 1682. A definite date might be possible if we could identify Mr. Portlock, who spoke the prologue.

Evidently they had some by-play, or perhaps a dumb show, at the end, in which Earine was taken out of the tree and restored to Aeglamour. The form of the epilogue, with Aeglamour intervening, is like Lord Dorset's prologue and epilogue to *Every Man in his Humour*, with Jonson similarly breaking in.[1]

We print the manuscript as it stands, except for the insertion of a few stops. Lines 56 to 63 are torn.

> Prologue spoken by Mr Portlock who comeing in at first
> wonders and speaks to himselfe.
>
> Hey Hey! what means all this; what is 't I see?
> How, a theater, lights and Company
> Mongst which I fantcy y^t I heare some say
> They hither come, In hopes to see a Play
> I'le undeceive 'um for I'le let 'um know
> Theres noe such thing and therefore they may goe
> If tis for that they came; I was within
> Where I was told they for theyr comeing in
> Did nothing pay, and sure I am the Crew
> Neither of Davenant nor Tom Killegrew
> E're play'd for nothing, 'lesse somtymes at Court
> Wether they goe to make the King some sport.
>
> To ye Company.
>
> Gentle Spectators; who are hither come
> With resolution to pronounce a doome
> On the Sad Sheepheard, and as some doe say
> Swel'd bigg with the expectation of a Play
> ffaith you're deceived; It must not by noe means
> Be called a Play; where there's nor Acts, nor Scenes.
> Tis true; the Iolly Robbin at his feast
> Does for the entertainement of his Guest
> Intend a Pastorall which some commend
> Though brave Ben Iohnson did not make the end.

[1] See p. 170.

If therefore some with witt 'mongst you spy a fault
Let him remember that 'thas cost him naught
And hold his tongue; for soe to heare and see
And be exceptious would ill manners bee,
But harke! that's the Sad Sheepheard sure I heare
Who malancholy perhaps is comeing here.
 Tis he; he loves noe company, I'le be gone
 His whole delight's always to be alone.

   The Epilogue begun by Mr Portlock
Well what thinke you now? was I i'th right?
Was what you long expected worth the sight?
I am sure of this whether well or ill content
You'le all agree and each will give's consent
I told you true and that it was no Play
You've seen, nor worth halfe this delay,
Yett take a care rash Iudge least that you be
Both of your censure and your witt too free.
Remembring still what I before did say
That 't cost you nothing nor it was noe Play.
Had old Ben lived what witt amongst you durst
Have censured what he wrote though n'ere soe curst?
Tis not for what he wrote then that we feare
But how you liked us that I am come here.
But here's the Sheepheard's 'selfe and I would fayne
Heare how he'll begg your suffrages now he's well againe.

   Eglamour or the Sad Sheepheard
    answeres him first, then speak⟨s⟩ to yᵉ company.
ffortune has been soe kind to me too day
As I can't feare but they will like our Play.
At least they will not with an angry looke
Damne us downe right, they 'le give us sure our ⟨booke.⟩
I'le try and aske them.
You that to Robbins bower are hither come
ffrom you they say wee must expect our Doome
Whether we'hve done or well or Ill too day
And which you'le call it Pastorall or Play.
I pray be Gracious doe it
If you mislike it we wi
Tis the first fault th
See how they trembleing
Take my advice, and free
To Iolly Robbin and hi
And feare not that her
I will engage you ne're
ffor the Sad Sheephard who soe long has mourn'd
Is now recoverd Earine is return'd

His Joys are full and banisht is his Greife
And all his sorrows now have found releife
He wants but this that each of you will give
His full consent and leave that he may live
And be a sharer since he is a Guest
Invited to the Jolly Robbins feast.

Two attempts have been made to complete the play—F. G. Waldron's in 1783 and Alan Porter's in 1935. Jonson marked out the action to the end of the third act in his completed 'Argument'. The devout hermit, Reuben the Reconciler, evidently brought about a peaceful and happy ending; and there is some clue to Maudlin's fate in Puck-hairy's comment upon her (III. i. 6–8),

This Dame of mine here, *Maud*, growes high in evill,
And thinkes she doe's all, when 'tis I, her Divell,
That both delude her, and must yet protect her.

In the closing lines of the fragment he cautions her to 'pull in her sailes'. She must have gone too far at last and succumbed to Alken and the huntsmen.

F. G. Waldron edited the play with some useful notes and appended his continuation: 'sequiturque patrem non passibus aequis' is his modest motto. It was reprinted in Dr. Greg's edition of the play, 1905.

Waldron developed the love-making of Karolin and Amie and began that of Lionel and Mellifleur. Earine was recovered from the tree after a tough fight in which Lorel overthrew three of the rescuers but was himself knocked out by Little John. Aeglamour, despairing of finding her, drowned himself in Trent,

Thinking her spirit hover'd in the air,
Waiting till his from mortal bands was clear.[1]

Puck-hairy changed his nature,

No more a witch's goblin and Puck-hairy,
But mankind's friend, a pure and gentle fairy,

and in this capacity he revived Aeglamour. Maudlin and Lorel repented, and Clarion married Douce. Reuben's reconciliation was very thorough.

Alan Porter's reconstruction, appended to our text of the original play, was published by the John Day Company, New York, with a foreword by H. N. MacCracken and R. A. E. Brooks, in 1944. The fourth act opens with love-scenes between Lionel and Mellifleur,

[1] Cf. III. ii. 24–32.

Karol and Amie. Puck-hairy tortures the Cook again and destroys the venison and the dinner, but Clarion makes good the loss. Douce shows him the tree which is Earine's prison; he releases her and takes her to Robin's bower. Puck recovers Maudlin's girdle, but wearies of her service. He will perform one more trick for her and then return to his old employments; for instance,

> Turn the milk sour when sluttish maids have left it
> Uncover'd in the dairy.

In other words, he will become Robin Goodfellow again; as he is the source of Maudlin's evil power, she is doomed. In the form of Earine she woos Clarion to cause more confusion. But all is cleared at the Hermit's Cell. Reuben teaches Aeglamour to reconcile himself to sorrow before he knows that his love is recovered. He gives Robin a message that King Richard has annulled his sentence of outlawry and created him Earl of Huntingdon and keeper of Sherwood Forest—a curious intrusion into history, and false history at that. He pleads for the now harmless Maudlin:

> Temper reproof with pity. . . . She is a woman
> Crost with misfortune, age, and penury,
> . . .   baited,
> Dup'd and deceiv'd and mock'd-at by Puck-hairy.

Coming in again as Earine, she is detected and seized. She 'storms out' when invited to the feast, now actively preparing. Clarion and Douce round off the marriages, and the play ends merrily with Robin Hood's banquet.

On 23 July 1898 the Elizabethan Stage Society, under the direction of William Poel, gave a beautiful performance of the pastoral in the courtyard of Fulham Palace. The archers in Lincoln green moved naturally in that Tudor setting. The players were: Robin, Paget Bowman; Marian, Miss Marian Morris; Friar, Edgar Playford; John, Lovell Fry; Scarlet, Percy Varley; Scathlock, Frederic Bohun; George, Arthur Broughton; Much, J. H. Brewer; Clarion, Charles Bright; Lionel, Miss Alice Arden; Alken, Mr. Mackersy; Aeglamour, Mrs. John Gott; Karolin, Mr. Crampton; Mellifleur, Miss Deane; Amie, Miss Virginia Carlisle; Earine, Miss Edith Clegg; Maudlin, Michael Sherbrooke; Douce, Miss Armine Grace; Lorel, Mr. Howard; Puck, Master Gauntlett. At the close of the performance the archers returned, Robin Hood holding out in his hand the captured hare, the form which Maudlin had assumed. A short masque followed at the end of the play, to round it off with a suggestion of Robin Hood's entertainment. Mr. Arnold Dolmetsch directed the old music used in the piece, Nicholas Lanier's setting of 'Though I am young', 'The King's Hunt' by John Bull, and 'The Hunt's up' by William Byrd, introduced into the hunting scene.

The latest performances of the play were at Vassar College, Poughkeepsie, on 18 May 1935 and 24 May 1947, when Jonson's fragment and Alan Porter's completion of it were performed by the Philalethean Society in a semi-natural amphitheatre fringed with dark evergreens. 'It was hard to tell', says an eyewitness, 'which part of the staging was artificial, so well did the little lake and tree prison harmonize with the natural surroundings.' Elizabethan music was used, including Lanier's setting of the song, 'Though I am young and cannot tell . . .'. The performers were: Esther Stapley, Robin Hood; Cynthia Hathaway, Marian; Edith Thacker, Tuck; Pamela Reilly, Little John; Frances Holt, Scarlet; Sarah Floyd, Scathlock; Susan Johnstone, George-a-Greene; Elizabeth Smith, Much; Sally Jenkins, Aeglamour; Helga Freeman, Clarion; Sara Woolrey, Lionel; Anne Oliver, Alken; Jane Raoul, Karolin; Esther Vanamee, Mellifleur; Mary Stewart, Amie; Priscilla Brownell, Earine; Frances Campbell, Maudlin; SaLees Smith, Douce; Mary Large, Lorell; Hyacinthe Kaufman, Puck-Hairy; Ruth Coffin, Reuben.

APPENDIX XVIII

CONTEMPORARY ACTORS IN JONSON'S PLAYS

RICHARD ALLEN (Allin or Alleyn) played in *Epicoene* as one of the Children of the Queen's Revels in 1609 and joined the Lady Elizabeth's men in 1613.

ROBERT ARMIN, probably a member of the Chamberlain's company in 1599, was one of the King's men in 1603, and as a member of that company he acted in *The Alchemist* in 1610. He was author of *Foole upon Foole* (1599 and 1605), enlarged as *A Nest of Ninnies* (1608); of *Quips upon Questions* (1600), of a play *Two Maids of Moreclacke* (1609), acted by the King's men; and of *Phantasma, the Italian Tailor and his Boy* (1609). He acted in Shakespeare's plays. He died in 1615.

HUGH ATTWELL (Attawel) played in *Epicoene* as one of the Children of the Queen's Revels in 1609; he joined the Lady Elizabeth's men in March 1613. His signature is in the *Henslowe Papers* at Dulwich, as witness of a debt of Daborne to Henslowe on 25 April 1613 (MS. I. 72) and as one of the signatories of a letter to Edward Alleyn in 1616 or 1617 (ib. 110). He died on 25 September 1621.

WILLIAM BARKSTED (or Backsted), author as well as actor, published *Myrrha* in 1607 and *Hiren* in 1611, and was reviser or part author of Marston's *Insatiate Countess*, published in 1613. He played in *Epicoene* as one of the Children of the Queen's Revels in 1609, joined the Lady Elizabeth's company in 1611 and the Prince's men in 1616. He is one of the signatories in the *Henslowe Papers* to a bond of £500 on 29 August 1611 (Greg, p. 18).

ROBERT BAXTER acted in *Cynthia's Revels* in 1601 as one of the Children of the Chapel.

CHRISTOPHER BEESTON acted in *Every Man in his Humour* in 1598 as one of the Chamberlain's men. He joined Worcester's men in 1602 and in 1603 passed with them to the Queen's men. He became a leading actor and owned the Cockpit Theatre. He probably died in 1639.

JOHN BLANEY acted in *Epicoene* in 1609 as one of the Children of the Queen's Revels, and was one of the Queen's men from 1616 to 1619.

RICHARD BURBADGE, son of James Burbadge, builder of the Black-friars Theatre, joined the Chamberlain's men in 1594, became a prominent member, and continued till his death on 13 March 1619 as one of the King's men. He acted in *Every Man in his Humour*, *Every Man out of his Humour*, *Sejanus*, *Volpone*, *The Alchemist*, and *Catiline*. Dr. Baldwin assigns to him the parts of Brainworm, Brisk, Sejanus, Mosca, Face, and Cicero. His name heads the actor-lists in the Jonson Folio of all these plays except the first, where Shakespeare's name is at the head of the first column and Burbadge's at the head of the second column. In *Bartholomew Fair*, v. iii. 86–8, Jonson paid a tribute to him: '*Cokes*. Which is your *Burbage* now? *Lanterne*. What meane you by that, Sir? *Cokes*. Your best *Actor*.—Your *Field*?' It was a fitting tribute to the actor who had played the title-parts in *Hamlet, King Lear*, and *Othello*.

GILES CARIE (or Gary), acted in *Epicoene* as one of the Children of the Queen's Revels, and later joined the Lady Elizabeth's men. His signature in the form 'Gilles Gary' is appended to the bond given to Henslowe on 29 August 1611 (Greg, *The Henslowe Papers*, p. 18).

HENRY CONDELL, as a Chamberlain's man and later as a King's man, played in *Every Man in his Humour, Every Man out of his Humour, Sejanus, Volpone, The Alchemist*, and *Catiline*. He acted also in the plays of Beaumont and Fletcher and Shakespeare. Along with Heminges he edited the First Folio of Shakespeare. He was one of the original sharers of the Blackfriars Theatre and he acquired a share in the Globe. He died at Fulham in December 1627.

ALEXANDER COOKE as a member of the King's men played in *Sejanus, Volpone, The Alchemist*, and *Catiline*. 'The fact that in the first two of these his name occurs at the end of the lists has been somewhat hazardously accepted as an indication that he played women's parts' (E. K. Chambers, *The Elizabethan Stage*, ii, p. 312). He acted in Shakespeare's plays. He died in February 1614.

THOMAS DAY played in *Cynthia's Revels* and *Poetaster* as one of the Children of the Chapel.

JOHN DUKE as one of the Chamberlain's men played in *Every Man in his Humour* in 1598. He afterwards joined Worcester's company, which became Queen Anne's, 1602–9.

WILLIAM EGLESTONE (or, as he signs himself in a bond to Henslowe, 'Ecclestone') played in *The Alchemist* in 1610 and *Catiline* in 1611 as one of the King's men. After an interval in which he joined the Lady Elizabeth's company (1611–13), he rejoined the King's men. He acted in the Beaumont and Fletcher plays and in Shakespeare's.

NATHAN FIELD, born in 1587, was a pupil of Jonson, with whom he read the *Satires* of Horace and *Epigrams* of Martial (*Conv. Dr.* xi. 164–5). He prefixed a copy of verse to the Quarto of *Volpone* in 1607; Jonson had invited him to contribute it along with the eulogies of Donne, Beaumont, Fletcher, Chapman.[1] He also contributed a copy to Fletcher's *Faithful Shepherdess* and to Jonson's *Catiline* in 1611. He had acted in *Cynthia's Revels, Poetaster*, and *Epicoene* as one of the Chapel Children; he joined the company of the Queen's Revels in 1610 and the Lady Elizabeth's company in 1613; with these last he played in *Bartholomew Fair*, 1614, and earned from Jonson the tribute which coupled him with Burbadge; it has been quoted in the notice of Burbadge.[2] He also acted in a number of the Beaumont and Fletcher plays. He wrote two plays, *A Woman is a Weathercock* (1612), *Amends for Ladies* (1618), and was joint-author with Massinger of *The Fatal Dowry* (1632). Three autograph letters of his are preserved in the *Henslowe Papers*, ed. Greg, pp. 66, 67, 84.

[1] See vol. v, pp. 5, 6.   [2] See above.

JOHN FROST acted in *Cynthia's Revels* as one of the Chapel Children in 1601.

JOHN HEMINGES (or Heming), as one of the Chamberlain's and afterwards of the King's men, acted in *Every Man in his Humour, Every Man out of his Humour, Sejanus, Volpone, The Alchemist*, and *Catiline*. Thereafter, according to the evidence accumulated by Sir E. K. Chambers,[1] he appears as a business manager, and he is named as overseer and trustee in the wills of several actors. Jonson's allusion to him in *Christmas his Masque*, 135–7, where he and Burbadge are represented as trying to hire a boy for the King's players, would tally with this. He acquired considerable financial interest in the Globe and Blackfriars Theatres. Along with Henry Condell he arranged the publication of the First Folio of Shakespeare. He died in October 1630.

WILLIAM KEMP, the famous comedian, acted in only one play of Jonson's, *Every Man in his Humour*, as one of the Chamberlain's men in 1598. The allusion in *Every Man out of his Humour*, iv. viii. 145–6, 'would I had one of *Kemps* shoes to throw after you' suggests that he had left that company in 1599. His famous morris-dance from London to Norwich took place in the following year.

JOHN LOWIN joined the King's men in 1603, when he acted in *Sejanus*, and became one of the most prominent members of the company. He acted in *Volpone, The Alchemist*, and *Catiline*; after the death of Burbadge he took such parts as Volpone and Mammon, and also Morose in *Epicoene* (Wright, *Historia Histrionica*, 1699), and possibly Catiline. He acted in Shakespeare's plays, playing Falstaff, and in Beaumont and Fletcher's.

THOMAS MARTON acted in *Poetaster* as one of the Children of the Chapel.

WILLIAM OSTLER acted in *Poetaster* as one of the Children of the Chapel. Passing on to the King's men, he acted in *The Alchemist* and *Catiline*. He also acted in Webster's and Fletcher's plays. He died on 16 December 1614.

SOLOMON PAVY, as one of the Chapel Children, played Anaides in *Cynthia's Revels* (Induction, 59, and the Quarto reading of 222), and a part in *Poetaster*. When he died in July 1602, aged thirteen, Jonson wrote his epitaph in *Epigram* cxx, which tells us he had acted for three years and made his mark in old men's parts.

WILLIAM PEN (or Penn), as one of the Children of the Revels, acted in *Epicoene*. He later joined the Prince's men.

AUGUSTINE PHILLIPS, a member of the Chamberlain's company, acted in *Every Man in his Humour, Every Man out of his Humour*, and *Sejanus*. He was one of the original shareholders of the Globe Theatre in 1599. He acted in Shakespeare's plays. He died in May 1605, probably at his house in Mortlake.

THOMAS POPE, as one of the Chamberlain's men, acted in *Every Man in his Humour* and *Every Man out of his Humour*. Samuel Rowlands

---

[1] *Elizabethan Stage*, ii, p. 321.

commemorated him in 1600 along with John Singer of the Admiral's men in *The Letting of Humour's Blood in the Head-Vein*, sat. iv:

> What meanes Singer then,
> And Pope, the clowne, to speak so boorish, when
> They counterfaite the clownes upon the Stage?

He died early in 1604.

RICHARD ROBINSON 'first appears in the *Catiline* actor-list of the King's men in 1611, and as playing the Lady in a stage-direction (l. 1929) to *The Second Maiden's Tragedy* of the same year'.[1] In *The Devil is an Ass* (1616), II. viii. 64 f., he is called 'a very pretty fellow' and praised for his skill in masquerading as a lawyer's wife at a supper. He acted in Shakespeare's plays and is a signatory to the dedication of the Beaumont and Fletcher Folio of 1647. He died in March 1648.

Wright in *Historia Histrionica*, 1699, describes him as killed at the taking of Basing House on 14 October 1645, but this is a confusion with the actor William Robins.[2]

WILLIAM SHAKESPEARE acted twice in Jonson's plays, in *Every Man in his Humour* and in *Sejanus*. Rowe in the *Life* of Shakespeare prefixed to his edition of 1709 says with regard to the first: 'His Acquaintance with *Ben Johnson* began with a remarkable piece of Humanity and good Nature; Mr. *Johnson*, who was at that Time altogether unknown to the World, had offer'd one of his Plays to the Players, in order to have it Acted; and the Persons into whose Hands it was put, after having turn'd it carelessly and superciliously over, were just upon returning it to him with an ill-natur'd Answer, that it would be of no service to their Company, when *Shakespear* luckily cast his Eye upon it, and found something so well in it as to engage him first to read it through, and afterwards to recommend Mr. *Johnson* and his Writings to the Publick.' This may not be altogether legendary, but Rowe has embroidered the details.[3] Shakespeare's name heads the list of actors appended to the play in the Folio of 1616. In the similar list appended to *Sejanus* Burbadge heads the names in the first column and Shakespeare the names in the second column. Did Burbadge play the title-part in *Sejanus*, and Shakespeare play Tiberius? In John Davies's *The Scourge of Folly*, 1610, Epigram 159 '*To our English Terence Mr.* Will. Shake-speare' there is a cryptic remark about his acting in royal parts:

> Some say (good *Will*) which I, in sport, do sing,
> Had'st thou not plaid some Kingly parts in sport,
> Thou had'st bin a companion for a *King*;
> And, beene a King among the meaner sort.

The natural interpretation of the second line, as Howard Staunton said, is that Shakespeare once played a royal part in a way that gave offence at Court. Two plays to which this might apply are Shakespeare's *King*

---

[1] E. K. Chambers, *Elizabethan Stage*, ii, p. 336. Dr. Baldwin suggests that he played Sempronia in *Catiline*.
[2] E. Nungezer, *A Dictionary of Actors*, pp. 299, 302.   [3] See p. 168.

Richard II and Jonson's *Sejanus*. Augustine Phillips put the former on the stage in 1601 the day before the Essex rising; the company which played it was the Chamberlain's, but we have no evidence that Shakespeare acted in it, still less that he played Richard. *Sejanus* got Jonson into trouble with the Privy Council for treasonable matter which it was supposed to contain.[1] It is just possible that some confused echo of this trouble explains Davies's allusion.

WILLIAM SLY, as one of the Chamberlain's men, acted in *Every Man in his Humour*, *Every Man out of his Humour*, *Sejanus*, and *Volpone*. He acted also in Shakespeare's plays. He died in August 1608.

JOSEPH TAYLOR joined the Lady Elizabeth's men in 1611 and is mentioned in *Bartholomew Fair*, v. iii. 81, which they played. In 1619 he joined the King's men after the death of Burbadge, and played some important parts. Wright praises him as Truewit in *Epicoene* and Face in *The Alchemist* (*Historia Histrionica*, 1699, p. 405). He died in November 1652.

NICHOLAS TOOLEY (or Tooly), one of the King's men, acted in *The Alchemist* and *Catiline*. He acted in Shakespeare's plays. He died in June 1623.

JOHN UNDERWOOD, one of the Chapel Children in 1601, acted in *Cynthia's Revels* and is probably the ' Jack' addressed by name in the text of the Induction, 21, 33, 218, though this might possibly be John Frost. He joined the King's men later and acted in *The Alchemist* and *Catiline* and in Shakespeare's plays. He died in October 1624.

[1] See *Conv. Drum.* xiii. 326–7; vol. ii, pp. 4, 5.

COMMENTARY

A TALE OF A TUB

THE title, while primarily referring to the adventures of Squire Tub, has a quibbling allusion to the proverbial expression for a stupid or nonsensical story; cf. Clarke, *Parœmiologia*, 1639, 'You tell us a Tale of a Tub *sine capite fabula*', and the motto from Catullus xxii. 14 quoted on Jonson's title-page. In literature the phrase was first used by Sir Thomas More, who seems to have been fond of it; see his *Works*, 1532, pp. 371–2 (*Confutation of Tindale*), 'consyder the placys and his wordes to gyther and ye shal fynde al his processe therin a fayre tale of a tubbe'; and *The second parte of the cõfutacion of Tyndals answere*, 1533, p. 106, 'thys is a fayre tale of a tubbe tolde vs of hys electes'. Sir J. Macintosh in his *Life of More* (Lardner, p. 107) also has this anecdote: 'An attorney in his Court, named Tubb, gave an account in court of a cause in which he was concerned, which the chancellor (who with all his gentleness, loved a joke) thought so rambling and incoherent, that he said at the end of Tubb's speech, "This is a tale of a tub".' For Jonson's use of the phrase see I. iv. 25, IV the scene interloping 27–37, and *Hon. Wales*, 321. On 16 January 1638 there was entered on the Stationers' Register for Francis Grove *A Tale of a Tubb or a Gallimaufrey of Merriment* by N: D:' of which nothing is now known; at that date the title may well have been suggested by Jonson's play.

The origin of the phrase is from a story in Apuleius, *Metamorphoses*, ix, chs. v–vii, which Boccaccio copied in the *Decameron* (7th day, 2nd *novella*, 'Peronella mette un suo amante in un doglio').[1] An adulterer surprised by the unexpected return of the husband was hidden by the guilty wife in an old tub 'multifariam rimis hiantibus quassum'. The husband announces that he has sold the tub for five denarii and is going to take it away. The wife replies that she has already sold it for seven denarii, and that the purchaser is inside at the moment, examining it. He asks the husband for a light and begins scraping and cleaning the tub. When it is cleared, the seven denarii are paid for it, and the husband has to carry the tub to the adulterer's house.

Thomas Nabbes may be glancing at Jonson's play in his *Tottenham Court*, v. iii, acted in 1634, 'There was a Tub at Tottenham: you know the success of it', but the primary reference is to a trick played on a lover hidden in a tub in Act III, scenes iv and v, who has water thrown over him: the scene reads like a feeble suggestion caught up from Boccaccio.

[1] G. Métivier in *N. & Q.* I. iv. 242–3.

The *Unity of Time* is strictly observed in this play. The action takes place within one day. In the first scene the household at Totten are in bed, and it is still dark (l. 56). The wedding-party assembles in scenes ii and iii; the intended bridegroom arrives in scene iv. In scene vi an hour has passed since Squire Tub left in scene i (l. 41). The second act opens with the wedding-party on their way to church. At the opening of the third act (i. 13) Turfe says they have spent the morning 'in privie search' for the supposed robber. In iii. v. 54–6 the sun has risen two hours earlier. In the first scene of Act iv, where Turfe goes to Justice Preamble's, the time is twelve o'clock (see v. ii. 6). The time in Act iv, scene iv, when Metaphor is on his way back with Turfe's money is two o'clock (see v. iii. 24). In iv. vi. 13 ''tis late'. In v. ii. 7 it is close on four o'clock. The company are invited by the Squire to supper in v. iv. 30; the ordinary time for this at this date was six o'clock, and it is ready in scene vii, line 53.

The Early Element in the Play

A Tale of a Tub confronts an editor with peculiar difficulties. Though performed for the first time, as far as we know, in 1633, it is a composite play in which work of a much earlier date can be clearly traced. This has to be considered in any attempt to determine the date of composition. Our own view, set forth by C. H. Herford in his essay on the play in volume i, is that Jonson wrote the piece in its original form about 1596 or 1597, but reshaped it in 1633, rewriting old work and adding new scenes. It is an example of Jonson in his old age, when his powers of invention flagged, re-using old work. On the other hand, Dr. W. W. Greg, while agreeing that there 'are two distinct layers, or at least styles, in the composition', believes the play to have been composed in 1633: we must regard it, 'so far as actual composition is concerned, as a late work in which are embedded here and there fragments of strongly contrasted and possibly early writing'.[1]

The loss of Jonson's early work is a serious difficulty in any attempt to discuss this question. He told Drummond in 1618 or 1619 that the half of his comedies were not in print.[2] We have only *The Case is Altered*, which we believe to be his, especially in view of the fact that his name was inserted in the second title-page after

---

[1] In 'Some Notes on Ben Jonson's Works', *R.E.S.* ii, pp. 129–45, a review of our first two volumes. It is perhaps unnecessary to do more than refer to F. G. Fleay's theory that the play was written in 1601; Sir E. K. Chambers rejects it (*Eliz. Stage*, iii, p. 373).

[2] *Conv.* xvi. 393.

it had been omitted by an oversight.[1] But his authorship of this play has been questioned, and any evidence based upon it has to be used with caution—for instance, the points of resemblance between the primitive clown Puppy in *A Tale of a Tub* and Onion in *The Case is Altered*.[2] In Jonson's dramatic gallery these two figures stand apart.

To read *A Tale of a Tub* after the plays which preceded it on the stage—*The Staple of News*, *The New Inn*, and *The Magnetic Lady*—gives something of a shock. The only point of resemblance is that it is written in verse. The effect on Dr. Greg is noteworthy. Criticizing our view of an early play afterwards revised, he writes 'we have to suppose that in his nonage Jonson wrote a comedy of easy and ingenious construction, more amusing than his Humours and vastly more legitimate than his impossible Satires. And what is even more surprising, we have to imagine him, at the very end of his life, practically rewriting the piece, and imparting to the language a raciness and gusto which it certainly did not originally possess, but miraculously avoiding intoxication from the heady fumes of his unmanageable—or at least often ill-managed—erudition'.[3] Why was Jonson as a young man incapable of writing a 'comedy of easy and ingenious construction'? He was a keen student of Plautus and Terence; throughout his life he worked at plot construction with a care and closeness which mark him out among his contemporaries. As for 'raciness and gusto', pray are these senile qualities? And if there is no misplaced erudition[4] in the play, why does that suggest late rather than early work? The point is not established by saying that this characteristic of Jonson's mature style and art was 'miraculously avoided'. In making his own suggestions Dr. Greg finally asserts, that 'assuming the *Tale* as we have it to be a revision of an earlier piece', this was not Elizabethan, it was 'practically' a new play, and 'there is no reason to suppose that the original version was by Jonson at all'. What evidence has Dr. Greg that Jonson ever took over and reworked a play by another writer?

In two important features *A Tale of a Tub* stands apart from the normal Jonsonian play. The Humours are completely absent from it, and the characters are superficially drawn. 'Quelques esquisses de caractères assez amusantes, mais restées à l'état embryonnaire', to quote M. Castelain's happy description.[5] Chanon Hugh, the contriver of the comic harms, is a good illustration. He is merely a

---

[1] See vol. iii, pp. 95–6.   [2] Vol. i, pp. 298–9.   [3] Loc. cit., p. 136.
[4] Dr. Greg is probably thinking of such references as the enumeration of the 'Lovers' Scriptures' in *The Sad Shepherd*, I. v. 96–7.
[5] *Ben Jonson*, p. 457.

shrewd trickster and a quick-change artist—the nearest analogue in Jonson to the cunning slave of Plautus, without a vestige of the subtlety or the intellectual wit which Jonson infused into the character as his art developed. Mosca is the consummation of the type, but it begins with Brainworm in 1598, and the finer handling of this early example of the servant-intriguer shows a marked advance on Hugh. Brainworm, for instance, is a shrewd judge of character and hits off Old Kno'well and Master Matthew with nice judgement. The glorification of Brainworm at the end of *Every Man in his Humour* sets the stamp of Jonson's self-approval on the superior pattern produced after a stage of experiment. Consider too Miles Metaphor: in his childish effort to live up to his name he is insipidity itself:

> Let not the mouse of my good meaning, Lady,
> Be snap'd up in the trap of your suspition,
> To loose the tail there, either of her truth,
> Or swallow'd by the Cat of misconstruction. (IV. iv. 25–8.)

He seems to have been named for no other purpose than to let him talk like this.[1] Contrast Carlo Buffone with his 'stabbing similes' in *Every Man out of his Humour*.[2]

The archaic setting also distinguishes *A Tale of a Tub* from other plays. The time is in Queen Mary's reign,[3] as Sir E. K. Chambers has pointed out. She is the queen referred to more than once.[4] And Edward VI is 'our late Leige, and soveraigne Lord' (I. v. 33). So with the ecclesiastical references to 'Chanon' Hugh, who reads the marriage service in Latin (III. vii. 9–11), Turfe's oath, 'by our Lady o' *Walsingham*' (III. i. 3), or Hugh's '*Sancti Evangelistæ!*' (III. vii. 25). In keeping with this is Hugh's quotation from the Latin grammar—

> If I fit you not . . .
> Call me, with Lilly, *Bos, Fur, Sus, atq; Sacerdos.*
> (III. vii. 69–72.)

Now in 1633 there would be at least an historical memory of the great Queen who shattered the Armada; but who at that date kept alive any recollection of her predecessor? The struggle between Catholic and Protestant was over; Englishmen would not even talk of 'Bloody Mary'. And Lily's Latin grammar had ceased to supply

---

[1] Compare II. vi. 49–52.
[2] Characters 26, II. i. 10, ii. 86–91, iii. 101–2; IV. iii. 100–3, iv. 10, 11, 109–13, v. 59–61; v. iv. 1, vi. 33–5.
[3] Not in Queen Elizabeth's, as we stated in vol. i, p. 280.
[4] In I. iv. 53, vii. 22; II. i. 31, 53, ii. 2, 30–1, 33, 78, v. 5, vi. 14; IV. i. 3; v. ii. 1.

material for stage jokes as it did in John Lyly's plays when the Paul's boys acted them and when 'because I don't want you' could be phrased '*quia non egeo tui vel te*' because *egeo* in Latin could govern either the genitive or the ablative.[1] If Jonson wrote this in 1633, he was archaizing with a vengeance.

In v. ii. 74 Squire Tub proposes to call in as a helper 'old John Heywood', the dramatist of Henry the Eighth's reign, who broke with the tradition of the moralities by his 'new and very mery enterludes'. They were printed in 1533 and 1534. Memories of him as a pioneer in English comedy might survive in the reign of Elizabeth, but who remembered him in 1633? By that date the drama had travelled a long way from the play of *The Weather* and *The Foure P.P.*

The English setting of the play is noteworthy. If it is early, it is the only instance of Jonson's doing this openly before 1610, and this fact has been cited as a proof of the late date of the play.[2] The Florentine setting of the first draft of *Every Man in his Humour* and the Londoners masquerading as Italians in *Every Man out of his Humour*, where, contrary to Jonson's practice, no scene location is given to the play, have also been adduced as evidence. But in this latter play Sordido and the farm-labourers talk the same educated English as the rest of the actors, while *A Tale of a Tub* is a picture of life in a village where the characters talk in dialect. How could Jonson have pretended that they were Boeotians, for instance? Because Jonson from 1610 onwards regularly staged his plays in England, why was it impossible for him to do this earlier in a setting which imperatively required it?

Then there are the two styles of the play fully discussed in our general introduction.[3] Dr. Greg handsomely admits that this point has been proved conclusively.[4] We will add only a single passage here, Squire Tub's description of Awdrey.

> Now th'adventurous Squire hath time, and leisure,
> To aske his *Awdrey* how she do's, and heare
> A gratefull answer from her. Shee not speakes:
> Hath the proud Tiran, Frost, usurp'd the seate
> Of former beauty in my Loves faire cheek;
> Staining the roseat tincture of her blood,
> With the dull die of blew-congealing cold?
> No, sure the weather dares not so presume
> To hurt an object of her brightnesse. (ii. iv. 49–57.)

---

[1] *Campaspe*, ed. Bond, ii. i. 42.
[2] By Wolfgang Keller in the *Shakespeare Jahrbuch*, lxiii, pp. 212–13.
[3] Vol. i, pp. 284–9.
[4] Op. cit., p. 134.

The verse has the movement of Jonson's early work; the style is early too. For a passage tinged with the same faint colouring of the romantic manner we may compare *Every Man in his Humour*, I. i. 186–8 in the Quarto text, describing Prospero's ribald letter, lines which were cancelled in the Folio later:

> The modest paper eene lookes pale for griefe
> To feele her virgin-cheeke defilde and staind
> With such a blacke and criminall *inscription*.

Here again, in verse fully representative of Jonson's early manner, is the prelude to his satire on the Court in *Cynthia's Revels*, III. iv. 3–11: we quote the Quarto of 1601—

> Where I haue seene (most honor'd *Arete*,)
> The strangest Pageant, fashion'd like a Court,
> (At least I dreamp't I saw it) so diffus'd,
> So painted, pied, and full of *Raine-bow* straines;
> As neuer yet (eyther by Time, or Place)
> Was made the foode to my distasted Sence:
> Nor can my weake imperfect Memorie
> Now render halfe the formes vnto my tongue,
> That were conuolu'd within this thriftie Roome.

We do not accept Dr. Greg's estimate that 'the abrupt change of style' marks a turn-over as late as the third scene of the third act: 'Up to that point', he writes, 'the verse has mainly been typical of Jonson's latest manner.' We find frequent traces of the old manner earlier. Besides the romantic passage we have quoted from the second act, we may cite the crude soliloquy of Hilts, as unlike as possible to the mature work of Jonson, in II. iii. 36–49; his description of the chief robber, II. ii. 120–7; and the opening lines of II. iv. 1–28. Sometimes a scene in the older manner, the opening scene of Act IV for instance, has a sprinkling of freer lines such as 65, 75. The whole of the first act has been worked over, though layers of the older style remain. Jonson always watched over the openings of his plays with scrupulous care.

Closely connected with this evidence of style is the intermittent use of rhyme. The first scene of the second act opens with eight lines of it; there is a rhyming couplet at lines 25–6 and a rhyming passage in lines 36–43. Jonson's early work has this laxity, but here there has possibly been a rewriting of lines 14–24, where Turfe insists on a small wedding party, and of lines 48–55, where he cuts down the wedding music; these lines are inconsistent with Puppy's rhapsody on the lavish food preparations in III. ix. 54–72 and Turfe's order in I. iv. 50–1 to 'Press all noises', i.e. all musicians, 'Of *Fins*-

bury in our name'.[1] Compare the occasional rhyme in *The Case is Altered*, II. iv. 15–20, 53–64. In Jonson's mature work rhyme is used only at a critical moment or to express strong emotion.[2] When he revised *Every Man in his Humour*, he changed over from rhyme to blank verse in a significant speech. In the Quarto (II. ii. 1–36) Lorenzo senior indulged in an abstract discussion on reason as a law of life—'a tame, and rather uninteresting homily, in rhyme', Gifford calls it. In the Folio version (II. v. 1–66) this disappears, and in place of it old Kno'well reads a blank-verse lecture on parents ruining the morals of the young. The new version had more point dramatically, and it showed a clearer perception of the metre appropriate to the occasion.

Hitherto the only test which has been made of the metre of the play is Miss Snell's analysis of the percentage of extra syllables within the blank-verse lines.[3] She gives the statistics of eight plays which she has fully collated. The percentage rises from 2·5 in *The Case is Altered*, 5 in the first draft of *Every Man in his Humour*, 4·5 in *Every Man out of his Humour*, 4 in *Cynthia's Revels*, 5 in *Poetaster*, to 24 in *The Staple of News*, 16·6 in *The New Inn*, 24·8 in *The Magnetic Lady*, and 24·6 in *A Tale of a Tub*. This proves, according to Miss Snell, that '*A Tale of a Tub* is a late play, and it was all written at about the same time', namely, in 1633.

We passed over Miss Snell's statistics rather summarily in our introductory essay,[4] and Dr. Greg has twitted us with 'disregarding inconvenient evidence'. We therefore examine it in detail here. Miss Snell claims that the percentage of extra syllables in the 'so-called "early" portions' is 24·7, and in the 'so-called "revised" portions' 24·3. She obtains this amazing result by describing as 'so-called "early" portions' the whole of the play except 'The Scene Interloping' in the fourth act, Act v, scene ii, lines 28–75, and apparently[5] Act v, scene vi, lines 22–7, and scene vii. Miss Snell unfortunately fails to state the authority who has adopted this lop-sided arrangement, by which only 183 lines are included in the 'revised' portion, and all the rest of the play is held to be early work. We ourselves made it clear that in our opinion a large part of the play in its present form was written about 1633, and that the opening scenes in particular contained a style of verse closely resembling that of the Inigo scenes.

[1] For other rhyming fragments see III. vi. 30–1, 34–5, 43–4, 46–7; vii. 1, 2, 23–4, 51–2.
[2] The rhyming passages in *Sejanus*, II. 174–209, III. 625–60, are a good example.
[3] *A Tale of a Tub*, 1915, pp. xxiv–xxviii.   [4] Vol. i, p. 285, note.
[5] Miss Snell gives a wrong reference for the last scenes '5. 6. 22–103'.

Miss Snell has based her elaborate statistics on the Cunningham–Gifford text of Jonson's plays as 'presenting the most uniform text'.[1] Any editor of a play of Jonson who has had access to the Folio texts should have been aware that Gifford constantly expanded the metrical contractions of the original without recording such changes. A few examples from *A Tale of a Tub* will show his method. 'If't be' becomes 'If it be', making I. i. 272 an alexandrine; 'for't' is expanded in scene v. 17; Jonson's contractions are disregarded in 'Gent'man' (II. ii. 79), 'Gen'woman' (II. iii. 49); ''conciles' (v. x. 96) becomes 'reconciles'. Metrical apostrophes are ignored in 'you'all' (I. iii. 1), 'I'am' (II. ii. 35), 'To th'mangy Knight' (II. iv. 15), 'the sole o'the head', 'the crowne o'the foot' (IV. ii. 81–2). The line 'I' the Church bookes, *D'oge*; not the'high Constables' (I. ii. 17) is expanded to 'In the church-books, D'oge; not in the high constable's'. So 'Have Ore in every thing' (II. ii. 112) becomes 'Have an oar', and 'Ile seale az much' (IV. iii. 25) 'I'll seal to as much'. Further, the lines (II. vi. 8–9)—

> How then, Sir? what if I doe? peradventure yea:
> Peradventure nay, what's that to you Sir? Say.

found in a scene where the verse is mostly early, are quite normal with the contemporary pronunciation 'paraunter' for 'peradventure'. Miss Snell's analysis based on a text with these spurious extra syllables is hopelessly untrustworthy.

Using the Folio text, we have ourselves applied Miss Snell's method of analysis to three scenes which we believe to contain early work, Act II, scene iv; Act III, scenes iii and ix. These scenes contain a total of 228 lines. The percentage of the extra syllables amounts to 5·7, a near approach to the 5 per cent. which she gives for the first draft of *Every Man in his Humour*. Miss Snell, although she has edited the play, has failed to notice the two distinct styles in its composition. The problem of deciding the date of the play turns mainly on this distinction, and we have little faith in an editor who has ignored it.

Finally, no metrical problem can be conclusively solved by a single test. The use of extra syllables within the line is only one of the variations which a poet can play on his instrument. The study of Shakespeare's verse includes such questions as feminine, weak, and light endings to the line, lines with a final pause, lines with an extra syllable after the caesura, lines starting with a single stressed syllable equivalent to a foot, and the alexandrine. Miss Snell has merely counted syllables. Jonson's early verse, formal as it was apt to be,

---

[1] Yale edition, p. xxv, note.

had its touches of variety. He occasionally used the alexandrine
and the stressed opening syllable.

> And had more store of breath: you call me Pursyvant!
>
> (III. vii. 29.)
>
> Body o'me, how came this geare about? (Ibid. 3.)

And he used the extra syllable in such lines as

> This sword shall shred thee as small unto the grave,
>
> (IV. ii. 52.)
>
> Which were opprest with a darke melancholly. (IV. iii. 3.)

It is obvious that Jonson in his later work wrote a looser and more
fluid line. But any study of his verse must be based on the best
available text, and it must be handled by someone who does not
imagine that all extra syllables are of equal importance. Such a
study would reveal striking differences between the different scenes
of *A Tale of a Tub*, and set in clear perspective the early portions
embedded in it.

The points then on which we rest our case for *A Tale of a Tub*
being early work revised and slightly enlarged in 1633 are:

1. The delineation of character, which it is the chief glory of Jonson
   to have achieved in drama, is entirely lacking here. With the
   possible exception of Basket Hilts—and he is an underling—
   the personages are colourless.
2. The appearance in the same play of two entirely different styles,
   a corresponding difference in the verse, and the fitful intrusion
   of rhyme.
3. Archaism carried to a point where the allusions would hardly
   be intelligible in 1633.

Each of these points is significant: collectively they constitute a
powerful case.

The Persons that act

1. *Chanon*, influenced by the French *chanoine* and common in the
fourteenth and fifteenth centuries; this is a late survival.

Vicar of Pancrace. Besides the local reference, there is an allusion to
'Pancridge Parson', a term of contempt for a priest easily secured for
irregular marriages: cf. Middleton and Rowley, *A Fair Quarrel*, v. i.
372–4 (ed. Bullen), 'For we were wedded by the hand of heaven | Ere
this work was begun. | *Chough*: At Pancridge, I'll lay my life on't'; and
in Field's *A Woman is a Weathercock*, II. i. Scudamore reproaches
Neville who is disguised as a parson, 'Thou Pancridge parson'.

2. *Squire Tripoly*. There was a tavern named Tripoly at Hoxton: cf. *Pimlico. Or Runne Redcap. Tis a mad world at Hogsdon*, 1609, D3ᵛ, praising Pimlico ale: '*Tripoly* from the *Turke* was taken, | But *Tripoly* is againe forsaken; | What news from *Tripoly*? Would you know? | *Christians flye thence to Pimlico.*' 'A ballad of *Tripoli*' was entered in the Stationers' Register on 19 June 1587 (Arber, *Transcript*, ii. 472).

3. *Basket Hilts*. Cf. Waspe in *Bartholomew Fair*, who is 'governour' to Cokes (*B.F.* III. v. 247); the name is explained by the description there given of him (II. vi. 59, 60) as 'a fellow that knowes nothing but a basket-hilt, and an old Fox in't': see also Lady Tub's description I. vi. 27–9. Basket Hilts is also the name of a servant in Cooke's *Greenes Tu Quoque*, 1614, sig. L3.

4. *Preamble . . . alias Bramble*. See I. v. 12–17, and Lawyer Bramble in *Eastward Hoe*. Cf. also I. v. 9 n.

9. *Tobie Turfe*. 'Peter Turph' is one of the boon companions of Christopher Sly in the induction to *The Taming of the Shrew*, sc. ii, l. 92.

13. *In-and-In*. Explained IV, scene interloping, 3–9. This character was reworked as a satire on Inigo Jones. Vertue has preserved a tradition on the authority of 'Dr. Harwood from Sʳ Crist. Wren' that Inigo 'was put apprentice to a Joyner in Paul's churchyard' (B.M. Add. MS. 23069,f. 19ᵛ).

Headborough. Here = a parish peace-officer or constable: originally, the chief of a frank-pledge, responsible for the ten members who constituted it. Cf. IV, scene interloping, 49:

> Head-borough, or Tithing-man;
> Or meanest Minister o' the peace

14. *Rasi'*. Explained IV, scene interloping, 19–22.

15. *To-Pan*. This must be τὸ πᾶν, as the 'merry *Greeke, To-Pan*, of *Twyford*', in the interloping scene of Act IV, l. 23, clearly shows. 'Pan' suggests tinker, and Lyly has the quibble on the Greek word in *Midas*, IV. i. 60–1 (ed. Bond), '*Pan* is all, and all is *Pan*; thou art *Pan* and all, all *Pan* and tinkerly.' Cf. *P.A.* 70–2. The combination of tinker and thirdborough (or under-constable) is hardly extensive enough to warrant us in interpreting 'jack of all trades'. The prefix seems purely whimsical. The earliest example of τὸ πᾶν quoted in the *Stanford Dictionary* is in the sense of 'the universe', or 'the whole Frame of things', by J. Worthington, *Life*, in Joseph Mede's *Works*, p. iii, published in 1664.

Third-borough, petty constable.

16. *Chalcot*, now Chalk Farm. In 1556 the name appears as 'Chawcoot's Farm' (*Hist. MSS. Commission Rep.* xv, App. ii, p. 259, quoted in *N. & Q.* 25 July 1905). The name Chalcot Gardens survives in Hampstead.

Scriben. The name is puzzling. 'Could Jonson have known the form *scrivein* (obsolete in the fifteenth century), of which *scrivener* is an extended form?' (C. T. Onions). *Do'ge* = Diogenes (I. i. 39, iii. 9), and the abbreviation suggests 'dog', or 'cynic', but nothing he says or does in the play justifies this aspersion. This 'great writer' is a clerk (I. iii. 14, 15), not a satirist.

17. *Ball*, i.e. Hannibal. 'Ball' was a common name for a dog: see Spenser, *Shepheardes Calender*, Sept., 164, S. Rowlands, *Knave of Clubbes*, 1611, C 2b, 'Swaggring Ball, the butchers dog', Drayton, *Moone-Calfe*, l. 1128, 'Ball, Eateall, Cuttaile, Blackfoot'. Cf. *'Ball-Hanny'* in v. v. 7.

22. *Black Iack*. Another quibble: the 'black jack' was a leather jug for holding beer.

Prologue, 8, 9. *Whitson-Lads . . . at Wakes and Ales*. Cf. Stubbes, *The Anatomie of Abuses*, 1583 (ed. Furnivall, p. 150): 'In certaine Townes where drunken *Bacchus* beares all the sway, against a *Christmas*, an *Easter*, *Whitsonday*, or some other time, the Church-wardens (for so they call them) of euery parish, with the consent of the whole Parish, prouide half a score or twenty quarters of mault, wherof some they buy of the Church-stock, and some is giuen them of the Parishioners them selues, euery one conferring somewhat, according to his abilitie; which mault, beeing made into very strong ale or beere, it is set to sale, either in the Church, or some other place assigned to that purpose.'

I. i. *Sir Hugh*. Clergy were entitled 'Sir', a translation of 'dominus' applied to bachelors of arts in some universities.

1–7. The opening lines recall the first verse of Donne's 'Epithalamion, Or mariage Song on the Lady Elizabeth, and Count Palatine being married on St. Valentines day' (*Poems*, i. 127, ed. Grierson):

> Haile Bishop Valentine, whose day this is,
> > All the Aire is thy Diocis,
> > And all the chirping Choristers
> And other birds are thy Parishioners,
> > Thou marryest every yeare
> The Lirique Larke, and the grave whispering Dove,
> The Sparrow that neglects his life for love,
> The household Bird, with the red stomacher,
> > Thou mak'st the black bird speed as soone,
> As doth the Goldfinch, or the Halcyon;
> The husband cocke lookes out, and straight is sped,
> And meets his wife, which brings her feather-bed.
> This day more cheerfully then ever shine,
> This day, which might enflame thy self, Old Valentine.

The popular belief that the birds coupled on St. Valentine's day was very old: see Chaucer, *The Parlement of Foules*, 309–15.

2, 3. *Februere . . . sheare*. Quoted in Ray's *Proverbs*, 1678.

8. *Makes*, mates.

13. *Salt-peeter-man*. 'Before the discovery and importation of Indian nitre, saltpetre was manufactured from earth impregnated with animal matter, and being the chief ingredient of gunpowder, was claimed by the Government and in most cases became a State Monopoly. Patents for making saltpetre were expressly exempted in 1624 from the Statute against Monopolies (21 Jac. I. c. 3, 5. 10) and the saltpetre-man was

empowered to break open all premises and to dig up the floors of stables, and even dwelling-houses.'—*Remembrancia*, p. 114, n. 2.

20–1. *conjur'd up the spirit* . . . *In Priests-lack-Latine*. The service of exorcism prescribed by the Church was in Latin; hence frequent references to the language for invoking or allaying spirits. Cf. Fletcher, *The Night-walker*, ii. i, 'Lets call the butler up, for he speaks Latine, | And that will daunt the devil.' For the bad Latin, cf. 'Sir John Lack-latin' as a popular name for an ignorant priest.

23–4. *wa'hoh!* . . . *the call*. Cf. *Hamlet*, i. v. 115–16, 'Hillo, ho, ho, boy; come bird, come'—the falconer's cry to recall the hawk. The 'lure' (25) was a sham bird, usually made of pigeons' wings, with hawk's food attached.

24. s.d. *night Gowne*, dressing-gown.

30. *Who hath my heart, as I have his*. From Sir Philip Sidney's poem, 'My true loue hath my heart and I haue his', first printed in Puttenham's *Arte of English Poesie*, 1589 (p. 233, ed. Arber), and reprinted in the 1593 text of the *Arcadia*, iii, f. 177.

46. It was the custom to draw lovers' names by lot on the eve of St. Valentine. See Brand, *Popular Antiquities*, ed. Ellis, i, p. 53.

56. *Cham*, earlier *icham*, = I am. In 76 *Che* = I, is an expanded syllabic form.

59. *At's little a hole*. . . . *through a Milstone*. Cf. *Iohn Heywoodes woorkes*, 1562, Ciij, Proverbs, i. x, 'I see daie at this little hole'; and 'She thought Ales, she had seene far in a milstone | Whan she gat a husbande.'

60–1. *Bilke* . . . *a word signifying Nothing*. A word of uncertain origin; this is the earliest use recorded in the *O.E.D.* Blount tried to explain it in his *Glossographia*, 1681, p. 83, as 'an Arabic word, and signifies *nothing*: cribbography-players understand it best'. To 'bilk' in cribbage = to balk anyone's score in his crib, and may have been a mincing pronunciation of the latter. Gifford illustrated from *Certain verses to be reprinted with* [D'Avenant's] *Gondibert* (1653), p. 24:

> Some say by Avenant no place is meant,
> And that this Lombard is without descent,
> And as by Bilke men mean there's nothing there,
> So come from Avenant, means from No-where.

For the trick of verbal criticism, here characteristically displayed by Jonson, cf. i. ii. 13–20, iv. 43–5.

66–7. Cf. Plutarch, *De Garrulitate*, ix, Μέτελλος δὲ ὁ γέρων ἕτερόν τι τοιοῦτο ἐρωτώμενος ἐπὶ στρατείας [i.e. some such thing as the watchword] εἰ, φησὶν, ᾤμην τὸν χιτῶνά μοι συνειδέναι τοῦτο τὸ ἀπόρρητον, ἀποδυσάμενος ἂν αὐτὸν ἐπὶ πῦρ ἔθηκα. Thence transferred to various historical personages, e.g. to Louis XI of France (Pierre de Matthieu, *Histoire de Louys XI*, 1610, pp. 550–1), and Henry VIII (Cavendish, *Life of Wolsey*, Temple Classics ed., p. 252), and Bethlem Gabor, whose 'usuall motto' it was (*The Negotiations of Sir Thomas Roe*, 1740, p. 662).

70 s.d. *making himself ready*, dressing. Cf. the stage-direction *E.M.I.* I. v. 71.

73. *knots.* Cf. *B.F.* II. ii. 52, *S. of N.* II. iii. 15–16

74. *'casions*, needs. *Merchant of Venice*, I. i. 138–9:

> My purse, my person, my extremest means
> Lie all unlock'd to your occasions.

75. *'Cham no mans wife*, i.e. no dependant. Cf. II. ii. 64.

86. *Angell.* The usual pun: cf. *C. is A.* IV. viii. 73–4.

89. *for the next.* A proverb in Ray, *Collection*, 1678, p. 273, 'I'll thank you for the next, for this I am sure of.'

95. *the Bason.* Cf. *M.L.* v. x. 64, and Vaughan, *The Golden Grove*, 1608, O4, 'Afterwards, the marriage day being come, the inuited ghests do assemble together, and at the very instant of the marriage, doe cast their presents, (which they bestow vpon the new-married folkes) into a bason, dish, or cup, which standeth vpon the Table in the Church, ready prepared for that purpose. But this custome is onely put in vse amongst them, which stand in need.'

Bride-ale, the drinking at a wedding: originally the bride sold the ale to the guests who paid what price they chose for it.

99. *Tile-Kill*, tile-kiln. 'In ME. the final -*n* became silent (in most districts), hence the frequent spelling *kill* in place of the etymological *kiln*; cf. *miln, mill.*' *O.E.D.*

100. *come off*, pay up.

I. ii. 2. *Zin Valentines.* Swinburne, *Study*, pp. 83–4, compares with this personification 'one of George Eliot's exquisite minor touches— Mr. Dempster's derivation of the word Presbyterian from one Jack Presbyter of historic infamy'.

cursin'd, christened.

10. *woundy*, great, very great. Cf. IV, scene interloping, 14.

brag, brisk. Cf. the epilogue, 9.

21. *rememory.* The word actually occurs in Harding's *Chronicle*, XIV. ii, dated *c.* 1470 (*O.E.D.*), but here it is no doubt a confused blending of 'memory' and 'remembrance'.

27. *bear a brain*, have a shrewd memory, like the Nurse in *Rom. and Jul.* I. iii. 30, 'nay I doe beare a braine'.

34–5. *'scourse.* Puppy interprets the word to mean 'exchange', and 'Charty' suggests 'cart-horse' to his mind. Cf. 'Jordan Knock-hum', the 'Horse-courser', who is a character in *Bartholomew Fair*.

36. *Smithveld*, the chief horse fair. Cf. *Disc.* 471, and *2 Henry IV*, I. ii. 55–60.

37. *Fabians.* Robert Fabyan, a Londoner, whose *newe Cronycles of Englande and of Fraunce*, recording events to the battle of Bosworth, were published in 1516; editions, continued by other hands, appeared in 1533, 1542, and 1559.

38. *In any new.* Hall (1542), Fox (1563), Holinshed (1577), and Stow (1598).

43. *Vlat cheating: all your Law.* A theme which Jonson developed in *Poet.* i. ii. 117–32.

i. iii. 11. *That verse gees upon veete* recalls Bacon's saying to Jonson just before the Scottish journey that 'he loved not to sie poesy goe on other feet yn poetical dactilus and spondæus' (*Conv-Dr.* 333–5).

14. *The greatest Clarkes* . . . See Chaucer, *The Reeves Tale, C.T.* A. 4054, and Skeat's note.

23. *strewings.* Cf. the wedding preparations with which Dekker's *Satiromastix* opens, '*Enter two Gentlewomen strewing of flowers. 1.* Come bedfellow come, strew apace, strew, strew: in good troth tis pitty that these flowers must be trodden vnder feete as they are like to bee anon.'

25. *twelve smocks.* Elsewhere we read only of the wife, daughter, and six maids (ii. i. 30, iii. ii. 30).

34. *A Midlesex Clowne.* Fuller (*Worthies*, 1662, 'Middlesex', p. 177) quotes this name as proverbial and an instance like 'churl' of the degradation of words. He derives it 'Clown from *Colonus, one that plougheth the ground*', and comments that 'some endeavour to fix the *Ignominious sense* upon them' [i.e. in Middlesex] 'as if more arrant *Rusticks* than those of their condition elsewhere'. So Richard Stanihurst in his Description of Ireland in Holinshed's *Chronicles*, 1577, p. 2, etymologizes the word 'clown'; he is describing the region near Dublin: 'But Fingall especially from tyme to tyme hath bene so addicted to all the poyntes of Husbandry, as that they are nicknamed by their neighbors, for their continuall drudgery, Collonnes [? Coloumes] of the Latin worde *Coloni*, wherunto the clipt English worde Clowne, seemeth to be aunswerable.'

49. *Out-cept.* Used also in ii. iv. 31, *G.M.* 913, *Ent. Welbeck,* 61.

50. *Kindome,* 'of parallel formation to *king-dom*, and much more frequent in Old English', *O.E.D.*, citing examples from A.D. 700 to 1406.

55. *monumental copper.* Evidently like the old cauldron of beaten copper, 'Mother Ludlam's Kettle' in Frensham church near Farnham. Aubrey believed that the churchwardens used it for love-feasts. Mother Ludlam was a local witch.

i. iv. 1. *wusse,* certainly. Originally the Old English adjective *Gewis,* 'certain'; in Middle English the neuter form was used adverbially. Finally it came to be regarded as a verb: 'I wusse', *Poet.* v. iii. 251, 'y'wisse', *Chr.* 106, and 'wis', *D. is A.* v. viii. 31.

3. *wispes.* For this rustic substitute for boots, cf. *E.M.I.* i. iii. 31, and Carlyle, *French Revolution,* vol. iii, book v, ch. vi, of the Sansculotte army, 'These Soldiers have shoes of wood and pasteboard, or go booted in hay-ropes, in dead of winter.' For Clay's excuse, that he could not 'dance in boots' (7), cf. the bridegroom Stub in the *Entertainment at Welbeck,* 156–7, who wore 'yellow Stockings, and Shooes, for being to dance, he would not trouble himself with Bootes'.

4. *Originous.* The only example of the word: doubtless a blunder of Turfe.

11. *long sawsedge-hose.* Cf. II. ii. 125 'a paire of pin'd-up breech's, like pudding bags'. Cf. the fashion of 'tall stockings, Short blister'd breeches', *Hen. VIII*, I. iii. 30, 31.

14. *leere side,* left side, as in II. ii. 127. For the form cf. 'leerebord', a sixteenth-century form of 'larboard'.

18. *Rosemary.* Cf. *E.H.* III. ii. 83 s.d., and Fletcher, *The Womans Prize*, I. i, '*Enter* Moroso, Sophocles, *and* Tranio, *with Rosemary, as from a wedding.*'

19–20. Imitated in *The Marrow of Complements*, 1655, p. 49, where a rustic lover tells his mistress, 'Wee'l have Rosemary and bayes to vill a bow pot, and with the zame Ile trim that vorehead of my best vore-horse.'

19. *Bow-pot,* bough-pot.

20. *Bride-laces,* fringed strings of various material given to the wedding-party to tie up their sprigs of rosemary. Cf. *G.M.* 939, *Ent. Welbeck,* 247.

21. *points,* the tagged laces which fastened the breeches to the doublet. 'To show the impatience of the bridegroom, it was the custom . . . to tear them off, instead of untying them, and throw them, to be scrambled for, amongst the guests.'—Gifford on *N.I.* v. iv. 35.

22. *Mary Ambry,* an unhistorical character in a ballad of the Percy Folio *The valorous acts performed at Gaunt by the brave bonnie lass Marye Aumbree* (Hales and Furnivall ed. i. 513). This refers to the effort made, with the aid of English volunteers, to recapture Ghent in 1584 after Parma's successes in the Netherlands. Hence 'Mary Ambry' comes to mean 'Amazon', 'virago': cf. *S.W.* IV. ii. 123, and Fletcher, *The Scornful Lady*, v. iv. 99–100, 'my large Gentlewoman, | My *Mary Ambree*'.

23. *sur'd,* affianced.

30. *Cloath-breech.* An allusion probably to Greene's tract *A Quip for an Upstart Courtier or a Quaint Dispute between Veluet Breeches and Cloth Breeches,* 1592 (based on F. T.'s *The Debate between Pride and Lowliness, c.* 1570–80). F. G. Fleay, who dated the play 1601, preferred to trace the allusion to the play *A morall of Cloth Breches and veluet hose* acted by the Chamberlain's men, and entered on the Stationers' Register 27 May 1600.

32. *wives,* wife's. A common form as in Peele's *Old Wives Tale,* which is usually misprinted *Wives'* in modernized references.

39. *Tom Tiler.* An old dance tune, alluded to by Heywood, *A Woman Kilde with Kindnesse,* 1607, I. ii, in a discussion of dance tunes, 'For my part, I like nothing so wel as Tom Tyler', and *The Fair Maid Of The West,* 1631, II. i, 'I have so tickled them with our Countrey dances, Sellengers round, and Tom Tiler.' Clench's desire to have the tune specially for the bridegroom's sake refers to the use of 'Tom Tiler' for 'a henpecked husband', as in Fletcher's *The Womans Prize*, II. vi.

41. *the jolly Joyner.* Untraced.

42. *the joviall Tinker.* Identified by Chappell, *Old English Popular Music,* i. 187, with the song *Joan's Ale is new,* which was licensed on

the Stationers' Register 26 October 1594. There was also a ballad entitled *The Jolly Tinker* licensed to John Trundle, 22 March 1616 (Arber, *Transcript*, iii. 585).

43. *jovy*. Cf. *Alch.* v. v. 144.

50. *noises*, bands of musicians. Cf. *S.W.* iii. iii. 86, and Psalm xlvii. 5, 'God is gone up with a merry noise, and the Lord with the sound of the trump.'

i. v. 8. *pitch'd his rest*. The common form is 'set up his rest' as in ii. v. 37, *E.M.O.* v. xi. 52. Originally a gambling term, taken from the game of primero: 'rest' = 'remainder', and 'to set up one's rest' = to stand upon the cards in one's hand, on the chance that they are superior to those of one's adversary—to stake all: hence, various figurative uses tabulated in the *O.E.D.*, but specially, 'to make up one's mind', 'to take a resolution'.

9. *winding wit*. So. v. x. 56. Of course a quibble on 'bramble', but it can hardly be a coincidence that it is found also in *Eastward Ho*, v. iii. 87 in reference to the lawyer Bramble.

22. *Knot-headed*, close-cropped, short-haired. 'Not-headed' would be a better spelling: cf. *N.W.* 278, 'not heads and broad hats', and Drayton, *The Muses Elizium*, 1630, p. 12 (of a lamb), 'Of the right kind, it is notted', with the marginal note 'Without hornes'.

23. *eat Sallads*. A thin diet compared with (say) roast beef. Cf. *Hymen*. 26–8.

28. *ad unguem*, perfectly, to a hair. An expression borrowed from sculptors who in modelling give the finishing touch with the nail, or from joiners who test the accuracy of joints in wood by the nail. See Horace, *A.P.* 417 (B. J.'s transl.), and *C. is A.* iv. v. 28, *M.L.* iii, chorus, 32, 'to the nail'.

36–8. There are mistakes in Jonson's heraldry. See the discussion on this passage in Mr. A. H. Nason's *Heralds and Heraldry in Ben Jonson's Plays*, pp. 124–5, who points out (1) that if the messengers wore the royal arms as pursuivants of the king, their tabards would not be 'minor' coats; (2) that, though Henry VII had the rouge dragon for the dexter supporter of his arms and the greyhound of the House of York on the left, Edward VI had other supporters, viz. a lion *or*, and a dragon *gules* or a greyhound *argent*.

54. *diviner*, divine—in reference to his cloth.

59. *spraying*. This word is unintelligible: the context in 58 'for feare of falling' suggests that 'sprayning' is a likely correction.

68–9. For the alchemical terms, *faeces* and *terra damnata*, cf. *Alch.* ii. iii. 63, v. 5.

i. vi. 7, 8. *the Lambe . . . the Larke*. Cf. Lyly, *Euphues and his England* (*Works*, ed. Bond, ii. 16), 'Goe to bed with the Lambe, & rise with the Larke.'

21. *Full-mart*, polecat.

24–5. *not to be pronounc'd Without a reverence.* 'Save-reverence' (*salva reverentia*), especially in the corrupted form 'sir-reverence', was used apologetically in quoting indecency. Cf. Harington, *The Metamorphosis of Aiax*, 1596, sig. Aiiij, 'And as old Tarlton was wont to saie, this same excellent word saue-reuerence makes it all mannerlie'; John Taylor, *Waterworke*, 1614, E4ᵛ, 'If to a foule discourse thou hast pretence, | Before thy foule words name Sir *reuerence.*' Cf. *B.F.* IV. i. 61, *Ent. Welbeck*, 97, and the adverb 'surreverently', *M.L.* I. ii. 12. For ironic extensions of the phrase, cf. *B.F.* Ind. 28, *E.H.* II. i. 163, IV. ii. 145.

26. *earn'd*, yearned, grieved poignantly.

33. *Fore-man.* An affectation, or quibble. The gentleman-usher walked in front of his mistress when she went out of doors.

45–7. Curiously like Kitely in *E.M.I.* IV. viii. 139–41 when he learns that his wife has gone away under the escort of his trusted servant Cash.

58. *Out-fitting*, beyond what fits. This use is not recorded in the *O.E.D.*

I. vii. 4. *proper*, handsome. So l. 26.

32–3. *you—For . . . sake: dispense.* The punctuation marks an aside.

36. *jealous.* Here, as in the first Quarto of *Hamlet*, xiv. 13, 'For murderous mindes are alwayes jealous', the metre can be cured by reading the trisyllable form 'jealious'. Cf. *Rich. III*, I. i. 92, 'Well strooke in yeares, faire, and not iealious'; *Arden of Fevershame*, i. 48, 'In any case be not too Jelyouse'; ib. 134, 'Because my husband is so Jelious'; ib. 213, 'Yet pardon me, for loue is Jelious'; ib. 381, 'Your louing husband is not Jelious'.

37. *Pusse.* Cf. *Alch.* v. iii. 38.

II. i. 1. *the better leg avore.* Dr. Scherer illustrates from *King John*, IV. ii. 170; *Titus Andronicus*, II. iii. 192.

4. *a dog his day.* Cf. *Iohn Heywoodes woorkes*, 1562, Pt. I, ch. xi, Diijᵛ, 'But as euery man saith, a dog hath a daie'; *A new Enterlude . . . entituled new Custome*, II. iii, ed. 1573, D1ᵛ, 'Well if it chaunce that a dogge hath a daye, | Woe then to Newcustome.'

8. *Wedding, and hanging.* Cf. *Schole-house of women*, 1560, B1ᵛ, 'It gooeth, by destenye To hange or wed', and *Iohn Heywoodes Proverbs*, 1546 (*Works*, 1562, I. iii. Aiv), 'Be it far or nie, weddyng is desteny, | And hangyng likewise, saith that prouerbe, sayd I.'

17. *geare*, business.

18. *lick zalt*, leave a salt taste in the mouth: *zalt* is an adverb. Turfe's apologetic 'by her leave' denotes that the phrase contains something equivocal: probably then *zalt* is used in the sense of 'lascivious' ,in reference to the proposed meeting of 'All the young Batchelers and Maids . . . O' the zixe Parishes'. For this use cf. *E.M.O.* IV. iii. 80, n.

20. *Upstantiall* is one of Stilt's vulgarisms in Chettle's *Tragedy of Hoffman*, 1631, F3.

22. *Deare meate's a theife*. Cf. Udall, *Apophthegmes* of Erasmus, 1542, f. 40*b*, 'And (as our englishe prouerbe saith) hous keepyng is a priuie theef'.

23. Cf. *Iohn Heywoodes woorkes*, 1562, Proverbs, pt. i, ch. xi:

> Men know (quoth I) I haue herd now and then,
> How the market goth by the market men.

Mercat- Jonson's usual spelling, like the Latin *mercator*, *D. is A*. I. i. 10; *S. of N*. I. ii. 86, II. iv. 86; *M.L*. IV. vii. 33.

24. *Hum drum I cry*, the commonplace for me! Stephen in *E.M.I*. I. i. 45 took the opposite line, scorning to be 'a consort for euery *hum-drum*'.

27. *as true as a Gun*. Fletcher, *The Prophetess*, I. iii, 'You are right, Master, Right as a Gun.' Cf. 'As right as a Club', II. ii. 71.

37. *traines o' Kent*. An allusion to the 'Kentish long-tails' of the legend. For *traines* cf. *E.M.O*. IV. iii. 41, 'the traine, or taile of a *Thracian* rat'.

Kent, or Christendome. Fuller, *The Worthies of England*, 1662, ii, p. 63, '*Neither in Kent nor Christendome*. This seems a very *insolent expression*, and as *unequal a division*. Surely the first Authour thereof had small skill in *even distribution* to measure an *Inch* against an *Ell*; yea to weigh a *grain* against a *pound*. But know Reader, that this *home-Proverb is calculated* onely for the *elevation* of our *own Country*, and ought to be restrained to *English-Christendome*, whereof *Kent* was first converted to the Faith. So then *Kent* and *Christendome*, (parallel to *Rome* and *Italy*) is as much as the *First cut*, and all the *Loafe* besides.' F. Grose, *A Provincial Glossary*, 1811, p. 72, explains the phrase as irony, 'the Kentishmen formerly claiming the right of marching in the van of the English army'.

26. *need not veare his stake*, will not lose by it, will get the equivalent to what he has put in the bride-bason.

44. *Such another*. Cf. *B.F*. II. iii. 54; *Respublica*, 1553, III. vi. 864 (E.E.T.S.), '*Avarice*. This same ⟨bag⟩ I got by sectourship of my Mother. | A vengeaunce on hir, old witche, for suche an other'; Shakespeare, *Troilus and Cressida*, I. ii. 263.

49. *the great Feates, and the lesse*. Perhaps connected with the adjective 'feat' in the sense of 'smart', 'adroit' (see *O.E.D*.), and so 'the superior and inferior artists'. But the italicizing of the name in the Folio suggests a personal allusion; e.g. to the juggler Feates who was well known about 1580. See Reginald Scot, *The discouerie of witchcraft*, 1584, p. 144: 'This fellowe by the name of *Feats* was a iugler, by the name of *Hilles* a witch or coniurer, euerie waie a cousener'; and '*Bomelio Feates* his dog' is classed with Mahomet's pigeon, ib., p. 252. Other references are given in the note to *Volp*. II. ii. 22.

53. *rondels*, roundels, dancing in a ring. Cf. *M.N.D*. II. ii. 1.

59. *sussified*, satisfied. Cf. III. viii. 38, and *Every Woman in her*

Humour, 1609, F3ʳ, '*Scil.* S'lid I cannot be sussified, I pray you Signior what meanes he by *occuput*?'

II. ii. 9. *snorle*, snarl, apparently; the *O.E.D.* suggests that it is a misprint for 'snarle'.

11. *costard*, head.

12. *growse*, as a term of contempt is rare. No other example is quoted in *O.E.D.*

13. *who's*, whoso.

14. *not bate . . . an ace*, not make the slightest abatement.

15. Cf. *Poet.* 1. ii. 24–5, 'How now, good man slaue? what, *rowle powle*? all riuals, rascall?' *O.E.D.* explains 'rowle powle' as 'A worthless fellow; a rascal'. But both the Jonson passages and their context suggest a levelling of social distinction: similarly S. Rowlands, *Hell's broke loose*, 1605, B3, 'Wee'le ayme our thoughts on high, at Honors marke: | All rowly, powly; Tayler, Smyth, and Clarke', where *O.E.D.* queries the word as an adverb, meaning 'Pell-mell, without distinction'.

Maple-face, with a face mottled like the grain of maple. Cf. Middleton, *Your Five Gallants*, IV. vii. 113 (ed. Bullen), 'you unlucky, maple-faced rascal'.

17. *brended*, literally tawny, brindled, but with a quibble on 'brand'. With *bitch* cf. 'fox' as a cant name for a sword, and *The Faithful Friends*, 1660, I. ii, where Bellario, a broken-down soldier, says 'Pay? Tis against my profession: | I have a bitch shall bite him to the bone | Dares ask but such a question.'

24. *rung noone o' your pate*. The cook knocked on the dresser as a signal to the servants to serve up dinner: 'The dresser, the cookes drum', says Massinger in *The Unnatural Combat*, 1639, III. i. For Puppy's metaphor cf. T. Heywood, *England's Elizabeth*, 1631, p. 156, 'As for the Ringers, he made their pates ring noone, before they were releast out of the stocks.'

25–6. *That would I faine zee, quoth the blind George Of Holloway.* In the earliest forms of the proverb other names appear: Heywood in *The Pardoner and the Friar*, 1533, Biij, has a context very like the text—

> And yf thou playe me suche another touche,
> Ish knocke the on the costarde, I wolde thou it knewe.
> *Pard.* Marry that I would see, quod blind Hew.

Latimer (1555) is quoted in Foxe's *Acts and Monuments*, 1563, p. 1349, 'Now that would I see, quod long Roben, *vt dicitur vulgariter*.' But in Jonson's day the saying was fastened on a character actually living at Holloway to the north of London. Taylor in *The Pennyles Pilgrimage*, 1618, B1ʳ, after leaving Islington, writes:

> At *Hollywell* [i.e. Holloway] I was inforc'd carrowse
> Ale high, and mightie, at the Blind-mans house.
> But there's a helpe to make amends for all,
> That though the Ale be great, the Pots be small.

And Dr. F. Andrews, describing a ride out of London (Harley MS. 4955, f. 61), has:

> Py-pudding Islington we past, . . .
> At holy-well we druncke a can
> At the blewe-bell with the blynd man,
> Who can at tables play as right,
> As if he wanted not his sight,
> But yet he hath this oddes I thinke
> That he can cog for a blynde sinque.

Iacke Dawe, *Vox Graculi*, 1623, A2, 'As on a time I sate musing on the very verticke point of *Hie-gate-hil*, . . . To make experiment of my skill, if it could reach so high, as to take the iust *Altitude* of the *Blindmans* Bottle-ale at *Holloway*.' Ray (*Proverbs*, 2nd ed., 1678, p. 268) quotes: 'That would I fain *see* said blind *George* of *Hollowee*' as a 'Proverbial Phrase'.

34. *wull. Ep.* xc. 17.

35. *Gentleman.* The apostrophe in *I'am* points to the pronunciation 'Gent'man', as printed in l. 79.

39. *continente.* A misprint for *continenter*, 'continuously', 'for a long spell'? By *Verbatim*, Turfe apparently means 'Upon my word'.

43. *Bun.* As a term of endearment in Drayton's *Nimphidia*, 1627, p. 175.

> Where she was wont to call him her deare sonne,
> Her little Play-feere, and her pretty Bun.

46. *Bride-cake* carried in the bridal procession: cf. *Ent. Welbeck*, 251, 'The two Bride Squires, the *Cake-bearer*, and the *Boll-bearer*'.

50. *Hine*, hind.

52. *This's.* A frequent metrical contraction in Jonson; it goes back to Middle English (see Skeat's *Chaucer*, i, p. 522). Cf. in the First Folio of Shakespeare, *Meas. for Meas.* v. i. 132, 'this' a good Fryer belike'.

62. *a dog of waxe.* An unexplained term used to cap an expression which the speaker treats with incredulity or contempt: cf. *Sir John Old-castle*, ii. ii, ed. 1600, D1ᵛ, where Murley, a brewer, hesitates to accept a colonelcy—'will lusty Caualiering captaines gentlemen come at my calling, goe at my bidding? Daintie my deere, theile doe a dogge of waxe, a horse of cheese, a pricke and a pudding, no, no, ye must appoint some lord or knight at least to that place'; Wilkins, *The Miseries of Inforst Mariage*, 1607, i. ii, where Scarborough objects to the wife designed for him—'*Scar.* O but my Lord— *Lord.* But me a Dog of wax, come kisse and agree'; Beaumont and Fletcher, *Philaster*, 1620, p. 7 (i. i), 'Oh, tis a Prince of wax. *Gal.* A dog it is'; Field, *Amends for Ladies*, 1618, E3 (iii. iii), '*Bould.* How like you Master *Pert*? *Wid.* Fie vpon him, when he is in his skarlet clothes, he lookes like a man of waxe, and I had as leue a dogge a waxe.'

old Blurt. Based on the phrase 'blurt, master constable (= 'a fig for the constable'), which was the title of a play of Middleton published in 1602. *O.E.D.* quotes from the *North Riding Records* of 1606 the case of one William Forde who was fined for using the expression to a constable.

63. *I am no mans wife.* Cf. I. i. 75.

69, 70. *'twill be his owne . . . another day*, he will gain by it in the long run. Cf. J. Cooke, *Greenes Tu quoque*, 1614, K3, '*Gart.* Wee'le be instructed by you. *Rash.* Well, if you bee, it will be your owne another day'; *The Life and Death of the Lord Cromwell*, 1602, III. i. 29–32 (ed. Brook), 'haue not I manie a time and often said, *Tom,* or *Maister Thomas, learne to make a Horse-shooe, it will be your owne another day*: this was not regarded'; Middleton, *The Witch*, II. iii. 21–3 (ed. Bullen), 'The boy will do well certain: give him grace | To have a quick hand and convey things cleanly! | 'Twill be his own another day.'

Che vore 'hun, I warrant him. Cf. *King Lear*, IV. vi. 242, 'che vor'ye', and Gill, *Logonomia Anglica*, 1621, ed. Jiriczek, p. 90: '*Pro* s. *substituunt z vt* zing *pro* sing *cano*: *&* Ich *pro* J *ego*: cham, *pro* J am *sum*: chol, *pro* I wil *vel volo*: chi vor ye, *pro* I warrant you, *certum do.*'

71. *As right as a Club.* Cf. Day, *Peregrinatio Scholastica* (p. 55, ed. Bullen), 'He is his owne as sure as a clubb.'

76. *Mass:* = Master. The colon is a mark of abbreviation: in *Volp.* II. i. 55 Jonson prints 'Mass' Stone'.

79. *Gent'man.* Cf. *Poet.* III. iv. 2, *Alch.* II. iii. 122, and 'Gen'woman' *infra*, II. iii. 49.

88. *sort*, set. Cf. *E.M.I.* I. v. 20.

93. *apperill.* Cf. *D. is A.* v. iv. 34, *M.L.* v. x. 50.

94. *raise Hue and Cry i'the hundred. The Order of keeping a Court Leet and Court Baron, with the charges appertaining of the same*, 1625, specifies the '*Huy and crie*' among other matters 'to be presented in Leet, and to be punished there': see p. 65,

    '59 Also you shall enquire if the inhabitants after robberies and felonies committed, doe make fresh suite from towne to towne, or from county to county, or from hundred to hundred according to the Statute of *Winchest. 13. E. 1. cap. 2.* For if a man be robbed in the day time, and the thiefe escape, and is not taken within forty daies after the robberie, for lacke of huy and crie, the borough or hundred shall answer to the party all his goods and dammages: also if any person be killed in a towne in the day time, and the murderer or manslayer escape, not taken or arrested by those of the towne, then the towneship shall be amerced. 18. Ed. 2.'

107. *and your Cap be of wooll,* 'as much as to say most certainly, As sure as the clothes on his back'—Ray, *Proverbs*, 4th ed., 1768, p. 181. An Act of Parliament passed in 1571 for the benefit of cappers ordered all citizens to wear woollen caps on Sundays and holidays upon penalty of a fine of ten groats: these caps are the 'plain statute caps' of *Love's Labour's Lost*, v. ii. 281. Cf. Marston, *The Dutch Curtezan*, 1605, E3ᵛ, 'nay, though my husband be a Citizen and's caps made of wooll, yet

I ha wit'. Nares refers to a popular song with the burden 'An if thy cap be wool'.

112. *Have Ore in every thing.* So *B.F.* III. v. 56, *M.L.* II. ii. 27: cf. *Iohn Heywoodes woorkes*, 1562, pt. i, ch. x, Cij: 'She must haue an ore in euery mans barge'; and Cotgrave, 1611, s.v. *Fretillon*, 'A little nimble dwarfe or hop-on-my-thombe; a Jacke of the Clock-house; a little busie-bodie, medler, Jacke-stickler; one that hath an oare in euerie mans Boat, or his hand in euerie mans dish.'

118. *nere the nere,* no nearer. Cf. the epilogue, 16.

123. *swad,* bumpkin.

127. *leere.* See I. iv. 14.

129. *be nought,* efface yourself, keep quiet. Cf. the interlude of *new Custome*, 1573, Biij, 'With all my harte and auengeance come vp and be nought'; and *As You Like It*, I. i. 31–2, 'Marry sir be better employed, and be naught a while.'

phrensick. A rare form for which the *O.E.D.* cites uses in 1547 and 1570: 'frenzical', however, survived much later.

136. *where were your eyes then? out at washing?* A variation on the phrase in *Volp.* III. iv. 12, 'you ha' not wash'd your eies, yet?'

139. *tell troth, and shame the Divell.* This proverb is found in *1 King Henry IV*, III. i. 58: Jonson applies it in *D. is A.* v. viii. 142, *M.L.* IV. iv. 24. Rabelais, *Pantagruel*, III. xxxvi, 'Nostre feal, faisons honte au diable d'enfer, confessons verité.'

144. *Hare,* harry, scare.

five wits, And seven senses. Dame Turfe was hardly capable of differentiating the 'wits' or intellectual powers (see Malone's note on *Tw. Night*, IV. ii. 83) from the 'senses', but for her second phrase cf. Motteux's *Rabelais*, 1694, IV. xiii, 'The Filly was scar'd out of her seven Senses' (*O.E.D.*).

148. *Kyrsin.* Cf. I. ii. 2.

168. *prejudiciall.* Hilts has a few illiterate phrases: cf. II. iii. 25.

II. iii. 3. *A word, or two, cold with you.* Cf. Porter, *The two angry women of Abington*, 1599, F4ᵛ, 'Giue me leaue to talke two or three cold words with my yong Master.'

18. *a slippery Merchant.* Cf. Carleton, *Jurisdiction Royall, Episcopall, papall,* 1610, vii. 172, 'The King to hold this slippery Merchant . . . required all the Bishops to set to their approbation, and seales to these Lawes.'

29–30. *the red-Lyon In Paddington.* W. Robins, *Paddington Past and Present*, [1853], pp. 181–2, discusses the ancient Lion inns of the district. In the Red Lion in the Edgeware road, near the commencement of the Harrow road, there was a tradition that Shakespeare had played; another Red Lion in the Harrow road was formerly situated near the bridge which carried the Harrow road over the burn. Robins also records a tradition that Jonson frequently visited the Wheat Sheaf in the Edgeware road.

38. *monger.* The *O.E.D.* has one instance dated 1706 of this word in the sense of 'whoremonger'.

40. *I' my tother hose,* not a bit of it! Cf. Withal, *Dictionary,* 1616, p. 584, 'Zonam perdidit: hee hath left his purse in his other hose'; and Middleton, *Blurt, Master-Constable,* II. ii. 270 (ed. Bullen), 'I'll play, sir. *Hip.* Come. *Cur.* But in my t'other hose.'

41. *fooles finger.* Cf. Cotgrave, 1611, '*Le doigt sale,* the middle finger which we (after the Latines) call the fooles finger'. This is the 'digitus impudicus' of Martial, VI. lxx. 5, pointed derisively at a pathic. The phrase in the text seems merely to point a quibble at the name of Captain Thum(b)s. Compare the metaphor in the interloping scene of Act IV, 59, 60.

II. iv. 3. *You'ld ha' the Calfe with the white face.* (1) A proverbial phrase deriding extravagance: 'You want too much.' Cf. Chettle and Day, *The Blind-Beggar of Bednal-Green,* 1659, D3ᵛ (ed. Bang, l. 833), 'You'd have the Calf with the white face I think.' (2) A term of endearment for a pretty girl. Cf. J. C., *The Two Merry Milke-Maids,* 1620, C2ᵛ, 'yet beshrew me they are a couple of handsome Calues with white Faces'; Fletcher, *The Scornful Lady,* 1616, IV. i, '*Elder Lo.* Lord, how I lou'd this woman, how I worshipt this pretty calfe with the white face heere.'

9. *Like Bungy's dog,* the familiar in the old legend of Friar Bacon.

13. *Lard.* For this form at this date see Field and Massinger, *The Fatal Dowry,* 1632, IV. i, 'O Lard, hee has made me smell (for all the world) like a flaxe.'

14–16. *Like . . . vish.* Quoted by Ray, 1678: a variant on 'Like will to like, quoth the Devil to the collier.' Cf. too *Iohn Heywoodes woorkes,* Proverbs, I. xi (1562), 'But hakney men saie, at mangy hackneis hyer, | A scalde horse is good inough for a scabde squyre.'

17. *not a barrell better Hering among you,* nothing to choose between you. Cf. *Nashes Lenten Stuffe,* 1599, K4 (*Works,* iii. 222, ed. McKerrow), 'Other disgraceful prouerbes of the herring there be, as *Nere a barrell better herring, Neither flesh nor fish, nor good red herring,* which those that haue bitten with ill bargaines of either sort haue dribd forth in reuenge and yet not haue them from Yarmouth.'

18. *fram-pull,* peevish, cross. Cf. *N.I.* v. ii. 29, and *The Merry Wives,* II. ii. 81–2, 'hee's a very iealousie-man; she leads a very frampold life with him, (good hart.)'

19. *Turne not the bad Cow, after thy good soape.* Explained in H. Porter's *The two angry women of Abington,* 1599, I4, 'be not you like the Cowe that giues a good sope of milke and casts it downe with hir heeles': cf. *Iohn Heywoodes woorkes,* 1562, pt. ii, ch. vii, Iiijᵛ,

> Margery good cowe (quoth he) gaue a good meele,
> But than she cast it downe again with her heele.

soape, draught, sup: cf. Lodge and Greene, *A Looking Glasse, for*

London and Englande, 1598, B4, of a cow, 'you haue had her milke, and I tell you sir, she giues a pretie soape'.

29. *geances*. *O.E.D.*, citing no other instance, doubtfully explains, 'An imagined rustic pronunciation of *chance*'. But Skeat's explanation seems preferable, that *geances* is 'jaunts-es', an illiterate double plural of 'jaunt'. He compares *Rom. and Jul.* II. v. 26, Quarto 2, 1599, 'Fie how my bones ake, what a iaunce haue I': so Q3, but F1, Q1, Q4, and Q5 read 'jaunt'. The verb follows in ll. 49–50:

> Beshrewe your heart for sending me about
> To catch my death with iaunsing vp and downe.   (Q2.)

Here again F1, Q4, and Q5 read 'jaunting'. The *O.E.D.* suspects that the noun 'iaunce' in the above passage is a scribal error or a misprint for 'iaunte'. One parallel is quoted from Sussex dialect, 'I doant justly know how far it is to Hellingly, but you'll have a middlin' jaunce before you get there' (*Sussex Glossary*, 1875).

30. *send me to Iericho*, i.e. to any distant or out-of-the-way spot. The earliest instance of the phrase appears to be in R. B.'s *Apius and Virginia*, 1575, Malone Reprint, l. 787, 'Well sith here is no company haue with ye to Ierico.'

34–5. *get a flap With a fox-taile*, be mocked for his pains. The phrase may have originated from the fact that the fox-tail was one of the badges of the fool. Cf. T. Wilson, *Rhetorique*, 1553, f. 21*b*, 'So that he [i.e. the lawyer] gaineth alwaies . . . wheras the other get a warme sonne often tymes, and a flappe with a foxe taile, for al that euer thei haue spent'; *King Darius*, 1565 (ed. Brandl, 192), 'I gaue him a blow with a foxtail.'

41. *neither-nother*. So 'eder-oder' *B.F.* v. iv. 53, and both forms in the *Irish Masque*, 34–5.

45. *were there no worse*, would there were no worse!

46. *All is not Gold* . . . Cf. Chaucer, *House of Fame*, i. 272, 'Hit is not al gold that glareth.'

52. *Tiran*. A frequent form in Jonson, closer than 'tyrant' to the Latin *tyrannus*.

76. *there goe two word's to a bargaine*. Cf. Bacon, *Coulours of Good and Evill* (in *Essayes*, 1597, p. 68), 'The second blow makes the fray, The seconde worde makes the bargaine'; Fletcher, *The Wild-Goose Chase*, II. iii. 10–11:

> Yet two words to a bargain; he slights us
> As skittish things, and we shun him as curious.

84. *Margery Turne-up*. In *G.M.* 940 '*Ione Turnup*' is a rustic girl at Windsor.

II. v. 37. *set my rest up*. Cf. I. v. 8.

38–9. *fortune* . . . *Thou art a blind Bawd*. Cf. *Cat.* v. 600, *N.I.* II. v. 132–3.

40–1. *let . . . To get.* For the use of *to* see *O.E.D.* s.v. 'Let', v.¹ 12b.
43. *Court . . . Councell.* Alluding to the proverb, 'I was neither of court nor of counsayle made', *Iohn Heywoodes woorkes*, 1562, Eijʳ, Proverbs, pt. i, ch. xi.

II. vi. 1. *Hoiden*, dolt. Cf. Cotgrave, 1611, '*Badault*, a foole, dolt, sot . . . gaping hoydon'.
a Hare. *O.E.D.* quotes 'to make a hare of' = 'to make ridiculous': there is a quibbling reference to the hare's doubling and Hilts's long journeys.
5. *nere halt afore a Criple*, don't assume a defect before one who really has it and will find you out. Cf. Chaucer, *Troilus and Criseyde*, iv. 1457–8:

> It is ful hard to halten unespyed
> Bifore a crepil, for he can the craft;

Iohn Heywoodes woorkes, 1562, pt. ii, ch. v, Hij, 'It is harde haltyng before a creeple ye wot.'
8, 9. *peradventure.* Scan 'peraunter': for this form see Gower, *Confessio Amantis*, ii. 563. Puttenham, *Arte of English Poesie*, III. xi, gives as a 'figure of *rabbate*' '*paraunter* for *parauenture*'.
30. *Blade; . . . looke.* The semicolon emphasizes: see *Shakespearian Punctuation*, § 29.
dead-doing. The epithet is Spenserian: cf. *The Faerie Queene*, II. iii. 8, 'Hold, O deare Lord, hold your dead-doing hand.'
40. *beseek.* Cf. *2 Henry IV*, II. iv. 152, 'I beseeke you now, aggrauate your Choler'.
51. *vallies*, valise. Metaphor tries to live up to his name: cf. IV. iv. 25–8.

III. i. 2. *Arsie-Varsie; upside downe.* Cf. Drayton, *Elegies* (added to *The Battaile of Agincourt*), 1627, p. 191, 'All arsey varsey, nothing is it's owne, | But to our prouerbe, all turnd vpside downe.' The phrase is still used in the Oxfordshire dialect.
3. *our Lady o' Walsingham.* The shrine of the Virgin at Walsingham in Norfolk was famous for pilgrimages: see Erasmus's account in the Colloquy, *Peregrinatio Religionis ergo*. The chapel dated back to the twelfth century and was reputed to be an exact copy of the holy cottage at Nazareth.
28. *moulded in clay.* Modelled on the phrase 'moulded in wax' = well-modelled, handsome, shapely; cf. *G.M.* 430–1: 'He's as handsome a man, as euer was *Adam*, | A Man out of waxe.'
32. *Justices of Coram nobis*, i.e. of the Court of the King's Bench.
38. *thick*, thilk, that.
53. *Muckinder*, handkerchief.
60. *On his owne head.* On, of. See *O.E.D.* s.v. 'Head', 35b.
61–2. A trite joke of the stage-clown: Eckhart (*Die lustige Person in älteren englischen Drama*, p. 325) cites *The Tragicall raigne of Selimus*,

1594, H2ᵛ (Malone Reprint, 1976–9): '*Bulli*. A good well nutrimented lad: well if you will keepe my sheepe truly and honestly, keeping your hands from lying and slandering, and your tongues from picking and stealing, you shall be maister *Bullithrumbles* seruitures'; and *A most pleasant Comedie of Mucedorus*, 1598, I. iv. 128–31, ed. Brook, 'I can keepe my tongue from picking and stealing, and my handes from lying and slaundering, I warrant you, as wel as euer you had man in all your life.'

here hence. Cf. *Poet.* v. iii. 355.

65. *burrough*, pledge.

76. *Receive me*. A blundering version of 'God refuse me!'

80. *ra'tempt* is meaningless, though such forms as 'revise' (II. ii. 44) and 'Returney' (IV. i. 58) may faintly justify it. But *n'atempt* is possible as a survival in dialect of the older *n'* (= ne) in combination with a verb, as in Gower's *Confessio Amantis*, iv. 1134–5:

That time schal noght overpasse
That I naproche hir ladihede.

Compare Jonson's own use of 'not' (= 'ne wot') in IV. i. 821.

III. ii. 31–2. *Pride Would be paid one day, her old vi'pence*. Cf. *Misogonus*, II. i. 12 (ed. Bond, *Early Plays from Italian*), 'Ile giue him his olde fippens'; Barnes, *The Divils Charter*, 1607, v. i, K2, 'A pox on him, micher, faith ile pay him his olde fippence for't now.'

III. iii. 34. *vetch*, fetch, dodge. Tub's lapse into dialect here and in line 33 is either an oversight or a trace of the earlier text.

46–7. *though I doe not turne the spit; I hope yet the Pigs-head*. Puppy's mind runs much on food (see III. ix. 56–74). He asks for a solid taste of it, though he has not done the menial work.

Jack-sauce. Cf. R. Edwards, *Damon and Pithias*, 1571, F1, 'I sayde well enough, what Iacke sauce, thinkst cham a foole?'; *New Custome*, 1573, Biij, 'Marie auaunt Iackesauce, and pratling knaue.'

III. iv. 28. *Colstaves*, cowlstaves, poles on which men carry a burden between them. The cowlstaff was sometimes used as a weapon: cf. *Christmas*, 46.

III. v. 4. *Mad-dame*. Cf. *D. is A.* iv. iii. 39; H. Hutton, *Follies Anatomie*, 1619, A6ᵛ, 'Salute a Mad-dame with a french cringe grace.'

16. *a man of marke*. The noble was worth 6s. 8d., the mark 13s. 4d. The quibble is found in *M.L.* iv. vi. 26–7, and *The Puritaine*, i. iii, ed. 1607, B3, where Corporal Oth is denouncing the Puritan Servants, 'proud Cocks-combes? not once to doe dutie to a man of Marke. *Frail*. A man of Marke quotha, I doe not thinke he can shew a Beggers Noble.'

30. *has kept levell coyle*. For *lever le cul*, 'to lift the buttock', an old Christmas game of changing chairs, the loser being displaced by another player. *To keep level coil* = to change about, and so to create a dis-

turbance. Cf. Armin, *Nest of Ninnies*, 1608, D2ᵛ, 'and so they did, and entred the Parlour, found all this leuell coyle and his pate broken'.

43. *Surreverence*. Cf. I. vi. 25 n.

52. *may be . . . Lady*. This assonance was not uncommon: cf. *Iohn Heywoodes woorkes*, 1562, Hiij, pt. ii, ch. vi,

> Wherfore my wyfe will be no lorde, but lady,
> To make me, that should be her Lorde, a baby.

and *Much Ado*, v. ii. 33–4, 'I can finde out no rime to Ladie but babie, an innocent rime'; the rhyme 'may be' occurs in *Love's Labour's Lost*, II. i. 206, and Peele, *The Araygnement of Paris*, l. 312 (Malone Reprint). For the phrase cf. Chaucer, *The Miller's Tale* (*C.T.*, A. 3783–4),

> Therof, quod Absolon, be as be may,
> I shal wel telle it thee to-morwe day.

III. vi. 1. *triùmph*. For the accent cf. *Alch.* v. iv. 12, *U.V.* xxvi. 41.

3–6. The mock-titles here quoted were borne by the Finsbury Archers whom Henry VIII constituted into a fraternity of St. George in 1539 (Entick, *History and Survey of London*, 1766, i. 497). The title of 'Prince Arthur' commemanted the King's elder brother who had taken a keen interest in archery. Mulcaster in the *Positions*, 1581, pp. 101–2, ch. 26, 'Of Shooting', refers to 'the friendly and franke fellowship of prince *Arthurs* knightes in and about the citie of *London*, which of late yeares haue so reuiued the exercise' of archery, and expressly mentions 'my good friend in the citie maister *Hewgh Offley*, and the same my noble fellow in that order Syr *Launcelot*' and 'prince *Arthur* himself maister *Thomas Smith*'. The 'Duke of Shoreditch' dates from an archery contest at Windsor in Henry VIII's reign when Barlo, one of the King's guard, won the prize. 'This *Barlo* drew his Bow, and shooting won the best. Whereat the King greatly rejoiced, commending him for his good Archery; and for that this *Barlo* did dwell in *Shoreditch*, the King named him *Duke* of *Shoreditch*.'—William Wood, *A Remembrance Of the worthy Show and Shooting by the Duke of Shoreditch, and his Associates the Worshipfull Citizens of London, upon Tuesday the 17th of September*, 1583, p. 41, printed as Part II of *The Bow-mans Glory*, 1682. This work mentions the following: 'the Marquess *Barlo*, alias *Covell*', 'the Marquess of *Clarkenwell*', 'the Earl of *Pancridge*' (p. 43), 'the Marquess of *Islington*' (p. 45), 'the Marquess of *Hogsden*' (p. 49), 'the Marquess of *Shackelwell*' (p. 50). Once a year the Archers had a State procession—the 'Arthur's show' of *2 Henry IV*, III. ii. 212, in which Shallow was 'Sir Dagonet'. Jonson has several sneers at these sham aristocrats: see *D. is A.* II. i. 64, IV. vii. 65; *U.V.* xxxv. 20.

6. *Bevis, or Sir Guy*. For the popular knowledge of the romances compare Cob in *E.M.I.* III. iv. 36, 56.

22. *Dick: Tator*. Whalley noted the reappearance of this joke in *The Last Speech and Dying-Words of Thomas (Lord, alias Colonel) Pride . . . Taken in Short-hand by T. S.*, 1680, p. 10, 'They talk indeed of a

Roman General who came from the plough (*Dick Tator* I think they call him).'

26. *Vadian.* Untraced. 'Vadianus' is the Latin form of 'Watt' or 'Watts', like 'Vadius' for 'Wade', and there may have been a Richard Watt, a 'toter', or piper, of the City.

43. *grow thick; but thin are sowne* reverses the farmers' saying 'Thick sown, but thin come up', perhaps with a quibble on 'thick' in the sense of 'stupid': line 44 suggests this.

III. vii. 2. *Hodge hold thine eare, faire, while I strike.* Apparently proverbial, as in the proverb quoted in Ray's *Proverbs*, 1670, p. 1, 'When you are an *Anvil* hold you still; | When you are a hammer strike your fill.' There may be an answer to it in *N.I.* IV. ii. 74, 'Then *Hodge* sings *Sampson*, and no ties shall hold.'

5. An Alexandrine: Jonson admitted this in his early verse; see *E.M.I.* II. i. 89.

13. A proverb of incompatibles, found in various forms: e.g. Clarke, *Parœmologia*, 1638, p. 97 (ed. 1639), 'That which was good never loved the frier. *Quae semel ancilla nunquam hera (Dissimilitudo)*'; Ray, *Proverbs*, 1670, 94, 'What was good, the Frier never lov'd'; and Davies, *The Scourge of Folly*, c. 1611, p. 210, 'But that that was, the Fryer neuer lou'd.'

15. *inter*—sc. calicem supremaque labra, a rendering of 'Graecus ille παροιμιώδης versus: Πολλὰ μεταξὺ πέλει κύλικος καὶ χείλεος ἄκρου' (Aulus Gellius, XIII. xvii, § 3).

19. *Give a man a fortune, throw him i' the Sea.* The Stationers' Register for 24 July 1600 records the entry of 'Two plaies or thinges thone called the *maides metamorphosis* thother *gyve a man luck and throw him into the sea.*' Clarke, *Parœmologia*, 1639, p. 125, has 'Give a man fortune and cast him into the sea. *si lubeat servare, procul quoque numina possunt.*'

20. *The properer man, the worse luck.* Cf. Day, *Ile of Guls*, 1606, sig. C3, 'The properer women, the worse luck', and Clarke, *Parœmologia*, 1639, p. 165.

21. *Tempus edax rerum*, Ovid, *Met.* xv. 234.
In time the stately Oxe. Cf. Kyd, *The Spanish Tragedie*, II. i. 3 (C2ᵛ in Allde's Quarto), 'In time the sauuage Bull sustaines the yoake.' Quoted in *Much Ado*, I. i. 226, in the form 'In time the sauage Bull doth beare the yoke.'

22. *lightly*, usually.

36. *rule . . . Squire.* A quibble: 'squire' is a form of 'square', as in IV, scene interloping, 38–45, 51. Cf. IV. ii. 74–5, 'The Chanon has his rules Ready.'

40. *Allegory.* So Puttenham sums up allegory as 'a long and perpetuall Metaphore' (*The Arte of English Poesie*, III. xviii, p. 197, ed. Arber).

42–3. *like tops In Lent.* Cf. Taylor the Water Poet, *The Praise of*

Clean Linen, 1630 (*Works*, ed. Spenser Society, ii. 169), 'Round like a whirligigge or lenten Top', explained by the *O.E.D.* as 'some kind of toy, ? used at Shrovetide'. No doubt it was like the 'town' or 'parish top' (*N.I.* II. v. 43). The 'Jack of Lent' (IV. ii. 49) was a similar amusement.

43. *Hoblers-hole.* A quibble on 'hobbler' in the sense of 'A child's top that wobbles or spins unsteadily' (*O.E.D.*). 'Hobler's hole', 'hobler-hole', or 'hoblies hole' appears to have been 'a hole into which such a top was thrown, as a mark to be aimed at'. Cf. W. de Britaine, *Humane Prudence*, 1686, xix. 85, 'Like a Top, which hath been for a long time scourged, and run well, yet at last to be lodged up for a Hobler'.

46. *Hercules, the Porter.* The life-size picture of Elizabeth's giant porter, eight and a half feet high, dated 1580, still hangs in the King's Guard Chamber at Hampton Court. At the revival of the play in 1633 the reference would be to William Evans, similarly alluded to in *M.L.* III. iv. 83 (see note).

72. *with Lily.* The reference is to W. Lily's *Brevissima Institutio seu Ratio Grammatices*, 1567, Bj^v. For a parson, 'Sacerdos' is an amusing climax.

74. *regulars.* A quibble on (1) regular nouns suggested by line 72, and (2) Hugh's position as one of the regular clergy.

76. *point in his devise.* Originally in the phrase 'at point device' = to the point of perfection, precisely, as in Chaucer, *The Squire's Tale*, *C.T.*, F. 560–1:

> So peynted he, and kembde at point-devys,
> As wel his wordes as his countenaunce.

Then as an adjective: 'Properly drest, All poynte deuyse', Skelton, *Magnyficence*, 1526, l. 852. Hence the irregular use here: other irregular extensions occur in *E.H.* III. ii. 250.

III. viii. 20. *Canbury*, now Canonbury in north London. Originally a grange belonging to the priory of St. Bartholomew in Smithfield.

27. *haunts unto.* For the construction cf. *Cursor Mundi*, c. 1300, l. 13691, 'Mont oliuet it es an hill þat iesus hanted mikel till.'

32. *hang'd, or married.* Cf. II. i. 8.

34. *mount'nance*, amount. 'Apparently a corruption of *Mountance*, assimilated to *maintenance*', O.E.D.

38. *sussifie.* Cf. II. i. 59.

III. ix. 4. *Soldado.* Cf. *E.M.I.* IV. ii. 117.

15. *at Saint Quintins.* In this battle fought on 10 August 1557 the French were defeated by the troops of Philip II of Spain. As to Hugh's service there, the English did not take part in the battle, but came up in time to share in the pillage of the town. Jonson may have meant the allusion for irony. Cf. *The Merry Devill of Edmonton*, I. ii. 31–2 (ed. Tucker Brooke), 'my souldier of S. Quintins'.

42. *whom the Divell drives.* Cf. *Iohn Heywoodes woorkes*, 1562, pt. ii, ch. vii, Hiv^v, 'And that he must needes go, whom the diuel dooth driue.'

47. *wee have brought our egges to a faire Market.* Cf. Beaumont and Fletcher, *Cupid's Revenge*, I. i (ed. Waller, ix. 224), 'we have Brought our Eggs and Muskadine to a fair Market'. The proverb also appears in the form, 'Tis one that brought his Pigs to the wrong market' (Cartwright, *The Ordinary*, 1638, IV. iii).

50. *the still Sow eates up all the draffe.* Cf. *Iohn Heywoodes woorkes*, 1562, *Proverbs*, pt. i, ch. x, Ciij^v, 'Well the still sowe eats vp all the draffe Ales'; and ib., Tiij^v, 'Epigrammes vpon Prouerbs', 142. Applied as in the text in T. Heywood's *The Seconde Part of If you know not me*, 1606, C2^v, 'Timothie you know the Prouerbe good *Timothy, That the still Sow eates all the draffe*: and no question the most smooth-tongu'd fellow, the more arrant knaue.' *Draffe*, swill.

51–2. *the patterne Of all the painefull a'ventures, now in print.* On 17 July 1576 William Howe obtained a licence to print *the most excellent pleasant and variable historie of the strange adventures of prince* APOLLONIUS LUCINA *his wife and* THARSA *his Daughter*: the Stationers' Register adds, 'This booke is sett foorth in print with this title *The patterne of peynfull aduentures*' (Arber, *Transcript*, ii. 301). Hazlitt quotes a title-page of that year ascribing the work to 'Laurence Twine Gentleman', who was admitted a fellow of All Souls in 1559. See also Collier, *Bibliographical Catalogue*, ii. 455. In the edition of 1607 the translator is described as 'T. Twine *Gent*.' In 1608 there was also published *The Painfull Adventures of Pericles Prince of Tyre. Being the true History of the Play of Pericles, as it was lately presented by the worthy and ancient Poet John Gower*, by George Wilkins, based on Twine's novel and itself the source of the play of Pericles.

56. *an Oxe did speake.* Perhaps an allusion to the portents of speaking oxen recorded in Roman history by Livy; cf. *Ep.* cxxxiii. 74, and Nashe, *Haue with you to Saffron-walden*, 1596 (*Works*, ed. McKerrow, iii. 62), 'Should I reckon vp but one halfe of the miracles of his conception, . . . one or other like *Bodine* wold start vp and taxe mee for a miracle-monger, as hee taxt *Liuy*, saying that he talkt of nothing else, saue how oxen spake. . . .'

58. *flead*, flayed.

67. *verven*, fervent.

70. *Cry'd out his eyes.* Cf. *B.F.* II. iv. 57–9, *Und.* xliii. 53, and Lamb's *Dissertation upon Roast Pig*.

76. *drive a Buck.* Puppy's ornate equivalent for 'do the washing'.

IV. i. 11. *demeanes*, demesnes.

20. Bramble makes a deprecatory gesture.

30. *defie*, repudiate, cast off, as in *1 Henry IV*, I. iii. 228.

50. *ought be punish'd.* At this date an archaism: cf. *Julius Caesar*, I. i. 3, 'you ought not walk'.

59. *make Legges*, bend the knee as a courteous salute to a superior: cf. *Alch.* II. vi. 26.

62. *district*, harsh, exacting (Lat. *districtus*).

ransackle. Cf. *G.M.* 912.

74. *hab, nab*, get or lose, hit or miss, however it may turn out. 'Conjectured to represent some part of the verb HAVE, presumably the present subjunctive, OE. *hæbbe*, early southern ME. *habbe*, in conjunction with the corresponding negative form OE. *næbbe*, ME. *nabbe*.'— O.E.D., quoting as the earliest instance Udall, *Apophthegmes* of Erasmus, 1542 (f. 186), 'putte to the plounge of . . . habbe or nhabbe, to wynne all, or to lose all'.

82. *not* = ne wot, 'knows not'. Cf. Gower, *Confessio Amantis*, i. 56–7 (ed. Macaulay), 'He not, til that the chance falle, Wher he schal lese or he schal winne.' Jonson uses the form in *Poet.* III. v. 57, '*Lucanian, or Apulian*, I not whether.' It is noticeable that Gascoigne thought it needed a gloss: see his *Works*, 1587, 'Flowers', p. 56—'Saue that I not his name, and though I could it tell, | My fraendly pen shall let it passe, because I loue hym well'—where a marginal note explains 'not' as 'know not'.

96. *Tom Long*. The Stationers' Register has an entry between 22 July 1561 and 24 July 1562 'Recevyd of william shepparde for his lycense for printinge of a ballad intituled TOM LONGE ye Caryer. iiijᵈ' (Arber, *Transcript*, i. 177). Thomas Hackett was fined 2s. 6d. for printing it later (ib. 184). Collier, *Bibliographical Catalogue*, ii. 532, notes *The merry Conceits of Tom Long*, 'the Carrier of Gotham', 1608, and Taylor the Water Poet's *Tom Long the Carrier*, 1630. But the name was used as a proverbial expression for dilatoriness: cf. *Iohn Heywoodes woorkes*, 1562, pt. i, ch. xi, Diij, 'But for my rewarde, let him be no longer tarier. | I will send it hem, by John Longe the carier'; and Davies, *Scourge of Folly*, p. 175, *Proverbs*, no. 348, 'That which is sent by Iohn long the Carrier, | Makes him that lookes for't a passing longe tarrier.' '*Tom Long*, carrier, of a person that loiters, and is long in coming or returning'—S. Pegge's *Derbicisms*, late eighteenth century (*E.D.S.*, no. 76, 1896, p. 129).

97. *call me his curtall*. A curtal horse or dog was one whose tail had been docked: hence the abbreviations 'cur' and 'cut', used as terms of contempt. Cf. *Sir Thomas More*, sc. viii (Addition IV. 230–1, Malone Society Reprint), 'haue the fates playd the fooles am I theire Cutt?' said by Falkner after his shag hair has been cropped. *O.E.D.* illustrates from H. Medwall, *A goodly interlude of Nature* [*c.* 1490], biᵛ, 'yf thou se hym not take hys owne way | Call me cut when thou metest me a | nother day'; *Tw. Night*, II. iii. 176; and *The London Prodigal*, 1605, Cijᵛ, 'And I doe not meete him, chill giue you leaue to call me cut.' Falstaff's 'if I tell thee a Lye, spit in my face, call me Horse' (*1 Henry IV*, II. iv. 186–7) is similar.

99. *to crambe*, to play crambo, a game in which one player gives a word or line of verse and another has to cap the rhyme. For specimens

in Jonson see *D. is A.* v. viii. 109–10, *N.I.* I. iii. 114–15. It was evidently a tavern amusement: Dekker in *The Seuen deadlie Sinns of London*, 1606, p. 3, associates 'Crambo' with 'Vpsy-Freeze', 'Parmizant', &c., as one of 'the learned rules of *Drunkennes*'.

106. *not a word but mum*. Cf. the interlude of *Welth and Helth*, C1 (l. 461 Malone Soc.), 'Peace no mo wordes but mum'; *Iohn Heywoodes woorkes*, 1562, pt. ii, ch. v, Giij, 'I will say nought but mum, and mum is counsell.'

108. *in coney* or 'incony', a cant word, apparently meaning 'rare', 'fine', 'delicate': here associated with 'super-dainty', as with 'sweet' in *Love's Labour's Lost*, III. i. 128, 'My sweete ounce of mans flesh, my in-conie Iew'; IV. i. 135, 'most sweete iests, most inconie vulgar wit'. The rhyme with 'money' indicates the probable pronunciation.

126. *Apt*. Cf. *Poet.* I. ii. 101.

The Scene interloping.

It is strange that Jonson, with his scrupulous regard for the canons of dramatic art, should emphasize the foisting in of this additional scene with such a tell-tale title. The object is to satirize Inigo Jones. Compare the introduction of Clove and Orange into *Every Man out of his Humour* (III. i) to parody Marston's fustian vocabulary, and the candid admission of the 'Grex' (ib. 17–19) that they are 'meere strangers to the whole scope of our play; only come to walke a turne or two, i' this *Scene of Paules*, by chance'. The sudden appearance of characters 'by chance' was alien to the whole spirit of Jonson's art. Here the 'interloping' scene does not advance the action, but Gifford pointed out that it allows an interval for Metaphor to get to Kentish Town.

10. *Architectonicus professor*. For Inigo's latinity cf. v. vii. 12, 13.

12. *Visicarie*, physician and apothecary—a 'portmanteau-word'.

19. *God-phere*, godfather.

21. *Rasis*. Mohammed-ben-Zakaria, born about 850 at Ray in Irak on the frontiers of Khorassan. He was celebrated in medieval Europe under the name of Rhazes, and his writings formed the basis of higher medical teaching up to the seventeenth century. Cf. *M.L.* III. iii. 19.

22. *King Harry's Doctor*. Henry VIII founded the Royal College of Physicians. Two of his doctors were Thomas Linacre and Sir William Butts.

23. *merry Greeke*, or 'merry grig', one full of frolic. It is uncertain which of these synonyms is the earlier; it is easier to account for 'grig' —'*Anguillette*, a Grig, or little eele' (Cotgrave)—than for 'Greek', which is more likely to be a perversion (*O.E.D.*). *N.I.* II. v. 42; *U.V.* xi. 38.

29. *pest'lence poore*, plaguy poor. Cf. *B.F.* II. ii. 1.

33. *rowting*, roaring.

41. *streake*, strike.

46, 51. *Squire*. For the quibble cf. III. vii. 36.

55. *Cyning and Staple*. Once the accepted etymology. Gifford refers to R. Verstegan, *A Restitution of Decayed Intelligence*, 1605, p. 326:

'I do fynd this name of office anciently to haue bin *Cuningstable*, and I haue shewed before that *Cuning* and *Cyning* beeing both one, our now name of *King* is thereof deruyed, and *Cunstable* might accordingly be more rightly bee *Kingstable*. The etymologie thereof is *Columen Regis*.'

57. *Iohn's for the King*. 'John' was a typical servant's name, and there is a reference to the song *John for the King* entered as a 'new Ballet' to Edward White in the Stationers' Register, 24 October 1603 (Arber, *Transcript*, iii. 245). But Nashe in *Haue with you to Saffron Walden*, 1596, speaks of it as a 'jig' of Thomas Deloney (*Works*, ed. McKerrow, iii. 84), and in Heywood's *Rape of Lucrece*, 1609 (E2ᵛ, 1638 ed.), there is a clown's song:

> Iohn for the King has beene in many ballads,
> Iohn for the King downe dino,
> Iohn for the King has eaten many sallads,
> Iohn for the King sings hey ho.

IV. ii. 12. *wee rose on the wrong side*. Contrast *Iohn Heywoodes woorkes*, 1562, pt. ii, ch. iv, Gij, 'And that you rose on your right syde here right'; Marston, *What You Will*, 1607, F1ᵛ, 'Byd you rise on your right side to-day.'

14–15. *zet my sword . . . wee'll take*. Cf. Palsgrave, *Acolastus*, 1540, IV. vi, X1ʳ, 'Which way so euer my staffe falleth, that waye will I take'; and Holinshed's *Chronicles*, 1578, ii. 1704 (the account of the murder of Arden of Feversham in 1551), 'The seruing man knew black Wil, and saluting him, demaunded of him whither he went, he answered by his bloud (for his vse was to sweare almost at every word) I know not, nor care not, but set vp my staffe, and euen as it falleth I goe.'

18. *The unlucky Hare hath crost us*. A common superstition at this date: cf. Bishop Joseph Hall, *Characters of Vertues and Vices*, 1608, p. 87, of the superstitious man, 'if but an Hare crosse him ⟨in⟩ the way, he returnes'; and Sir T. Browne, *Pseudodoxia Epidemica*, 1646, Bk. V, ch. xxi, 'If an Hare crosse the high way there are few above three score that are not perplexed thereat: which notwithstanding is but an Auguriall terror, according to that received expression, *Inauspicatum dat iter oblatus Lepus*.'

27. *pannell*. Originally the cloth placed under the saddle to protect the horse's back from being galled; then, as here, a rough treeless pad.

32. *is the Surbater*, makes footsore, wearies out by walking. This is the only example in the *O.E.D.*, but 'surbated' is found in *The Master of Game* (c. 1410), and 'Surbate' in *The Faerie Queene*, III. iv. 34.

33. *treslesse*, trestles. *treslesse dormant* is an absurd variant of 'table dormant' (*Alch.* v. v. 103)—a quibbling antithesis to 'currant' in l. 32.

34. *who*, whom. Cf. *Poet.* v. i. 57, and the examples in Franz, *Shakespeare-Grammatik*, § 201.

35. *neither nick*, i.e. the devil. *nor in the nick*, in a tight place, cornered. Cf. the quibble in *S.W.* IV. iv. 165, 'A very sharke, he set me i' the nicke t'other night at *primero*.'

40–1. *Lubber . . . Lover.* Dr. Scherer cites the same quibble in *The Two Gentlemen of Verona*, II. v. 38–42.

43. *Scrape-hill.* An inexact but intelligible word: 'hill' is probably an abbreviation of 'dunghill'; cf. Face's abuse of Subtle, *Alch.* I. i. 33–4.

44. *orange-tawny-coated.* The dress of an apparitor.

49. *sixe weekes the Iack of Lent.* The Jack-a-Lent was a stuffed puppet used as a cockshy from Ash Wednesday to Good Friday; it was then burnt. Cf. *S. of N.* v. v. 35, and Heywood, *The Foure Prentices of London*, 1615, Dj^v, 'Clown. Nay you old Iack a lent, sixe weekes and vpwards'; Quarles, *Argalus and Parthenia*, 1621, Introduction:

> That he may stand like a Jack a lent,
> Or a shroving Cock, for Everyone to spend a Cudgel at.

59. *put thy smiter up.* Cf. Lyly, *Endimion*, I. iii. 88–9 (ed. Bond), No, it is my Simiter; which I by construction often studying to be compendious, call my Smyter'; and Nashe, *Foure Letters Confuted*, 1592, Di^v, 'Put vp thy smiter, O gentle Peter, | Author and halter make but ill meeter.'

IV. iii. 27. *get the Lasse from Dargison.* 'Dargison' or 'Donkin Dargeson' is an old tune, the music of which is given in Chappell, i, p. 230. Two other allusions to the song are preserved in Day's *The Ile of Guls*, 1606, Oi^r, 'No, no, we are guls, Innocent sots, but lante tanta, the girles are ours we haue won em away to dargison', and a few lines later, 'An ambling nag, and a down, a down, | We haue borne her away to dargison.'

IV. iv. 6. *sleevelesse*, useless. For the quibble cf. *The Fair Maid of the Inn*, IV. ii (Beaumont and Fletcher, *Works*, ed. Waller, ix, p. 200), 'Foro. Then will I convey thee stark naked to *Develing* to beg a pair of *brogs*, . . . Clow. And no doublet to 'em? Foro. No sir, I intend to send you of a sleeveless errand.'

20–2, 25–8. Professor Koeppel suggests that the extravagance of metaphor in this passage is a satire on euphuism or arcadianism, but the language does not naturally suggest either. The talk of Hirtius and Spungius in *The Virgin Martyr*, II. iii, which he compares (e.g. 'The petticoat of her estate is unlaced', 'the smock of her charity is now all to pieces') is certainly similar, but hardly a 'reminiscence' of it. Metaphor is trying desperately to live up to his name, and it is an interesting sign of early work that Jonson has not overdone this mannerism; it is only occasional.

IV. v. 5. *I am not for your mowing.* Cf. Udall's translation of Erasmus's *Apophthegmes*, 1542, f. 342, 'Lais, an harlot of Corinthe of excellent beautie, but so dere and costely that she was no morsell for mowyers'.

31. *And*, if.

32. *your own.* Cf. *E.M.I.* IV. viii. 9, *Alch.* IV. v. 70; Chaucer, *Troilus*, ii. 750, 'I am my owne womman wel at ese.'

34. *you tooke me . . . tardie,* 'surprised me', with a suggestion of 'caught me tripping'. Cf. Lyly, *Mother Bombie,* II. iv. 1, '*Dro.* We were all taken tardie' (said of the pages caught by their masters in a tavern).

38. *leave your linnen.* A contemptuous phrase on the lips of a 'velvet' madam: contrast Dame Turfe's 'reverence' for Lady Tub's 'velvet Gowne' (III. v. 10–11).

63. *see for.* See *O.E.D.,* s.v. 'see', 19.

69. *jumpe.* Cf. *D. is A.* IV. i. 6.

81. *dispos'd.* Awdrey quibbles on the sense, 'inclined to merriment'. Cf. Beaumont and Fletcher, *The Maid's Tragedy,* IV. i. 14–15, '*Evadne.* You are strangely disposed, sir. *Melantius.* Good madam, not to make you merry.'

95. *a french Hood.* Regarded by city dames as a genteel fashion long after it was out of date elsewhere: cf. Dekker, *The Shomakers Holiday,* 1600, E^v, where Eyre's wife, expecting her husband to be nominated sheriff, asks, 'Art thou acquainted with neuer a fardingale-maker, nor a French-hoode maker, . . . how shall I looke in a hoode I wonder'; Eyre, when elected, brings her one as a present (sig. F)—'I shal make thee a Lady, ther's a French hood for thee, on with it, on with it, dresse thy browes with the flap of a shoulder of mutton, to make thee looke louely.' Jonson also refers to this hood in *Alch.* II. vi. 33, *B.F.* I. v. 15, 16, and *Und.* xlii. 69.

IV. vi. 2. *Ruffin.* The name of a fiend: cf. the epithet 'ruffinous' in Chapman's *Iliad,* vi. 456.

7. *on my . . . holy-dom.* Cf. *Two Gentlemen of Verona,* IV. ii. 131, 'By my hallidome'.

11. *wish her trust.* Cf. Franz, *Shakespeare-Grammatik,* § 493*a.*

16. *The black Oxe.* A type of adversity: cf. *E.H.* v. v. 80, and *Iohn Heywoodes woorkes,* 1562, pt. i, ch. vii, Biij^v, 'The blacke oxe had not trode on his nor hir foote', and ib. Sij, *Epigrammes vpon Prouerbs,* no. 79. Still an Albanian proverb (von Hahn, *Albanische Studien,* i. 196, note G).

26. *legion.* An echo of the cry of the Gadarene demoniac, 'My name is Legion: for we are many' (Mark v. 9). Hence it is better to read 'Spirit Legion' as the name of the supposed devil.

31–2. Marlowe's *Doctor Faustus* probably dates 1592, and Greene's *Friar Bacon* 1589.

54. *neare.* The old comparative of 'nigh'; cf. epilogue, 16.

69. *Loggets,* lit. small logs. The form in the First Folio text of *Hamlet,* v. i. 90: 'loggits' in Q2. The Clarendon Press edition describes the game as resembling bowls, but with notable differences. It is played on a floor strewed with ashes. 'The Jack is a wheel of lignum vitae or other hard wood, nine inches in diameter and three or four inches

thick. The loggat, made of apple-wood, is a truncated cone 26 or 27 inches in length, tapering from a girth of 8½ or 9 inches at the one end to 3½ or 4 inches at the other. Each player has three loggats which he throws, holding lightly the thin end. The object is to lie as near the Jack as possible. The only place we have heard of where this once popular game is now played is the Hampshire Hog Inn, Norwich.'

72. *pluck it off.* Cf. *C. is A.* I. vii. 48.

v. i. 8. *by and by,* immediately.

v. ii. 21. *longs* (*az one would zay*). The phrase refers to the longing humours of a pregnant woman, but is also applied to men. Cf. *D. is A.* I. ii. 31–2, '*Fitz-dottrell.* I long for thee. An' I were with child by him, | And my wife, too; I could not more'; *F.I.* 195, '*Mere-Foole.* I long, saue this great belly, I long.'

30–1. *A disguise . . . Is the true word.* Cf. *M. Augurs,* 49, 50, 'Disguise was the old English word for a Masque sir, before you were an implement belonging to the *Revels*'; and Jonson uses the term in *F.I.* 276, 285. Sir E. K. Chambers notes 'disguising' as a vernacular name in the fourteenth century for the *ludus regis,* a court entertainment by masked dancers at Christmas (*Mediaeval Stage,* i, p. 393). Bacon in his *History of King Henry VII,* 1622, p. 245, writes of 'Masques (which they then called Disguises)'.

35. *He will joyne with no man.* For this trait of Inigo's character see the 'Expostulation with Inigo Jones' (*U.V.* xxxiv. 64–5), 'He is, or would be ye mayne Dominus doe | All in ye Worke!'

36. *in designe he cals it.* Cf. *U.V.* xxxiv. 55–6, 'which by a specious fyne | Terme of ye Architects is called Designe!' and *Disc.* 1134–5, 'The other remoue themselues upon craft, and designe (as the *Architects* say). . . .'

39. *feazable.* Jonson himself uses the word in *S.W.* III. iii. 102 and IV. iv. 111, where it is spelt 'fæsible', *D. is A.* II. i. 37, *S. of N.* I. vi. 54 ('feizible'). Like 'conduce' it is a satisfactory word; it is Inigo's parrot use of it that is satirized. But exception appears to have been taken to it in academic Oxford as late as 1698. Humphrey Wanley writes to Arthur Charlett on 13 May, 'I most humbly thank you for your last kind letter, by which I understand that I used the word *Feasible* to the Vice-Chancellor. I have no Copy of what I wrote: but so far as I remember, I meant no more, than that such a thing is *Feasible,* or *Possible to be done, or brought to pass*' (Bodleian Ballard MS. 13, f. 64).

60. *Ingine.* Here virtually = 'mechanics'.

72–3. *a Cooper . . . call'd Vitruvius.* Revived later in 1633 in the 'Coronel Vitruvius' of *Love's Welcome at Bolsover.* See pages 163–5.

74. *Iohn Heywood.* There is one other reference to him in the *Drummond Conversations,* 573–7. He was attached to the retinue of the Princess (afterwards Queen) Mary and received a payment of forty

shillings in March 1538 for 'pleying an interlude with his children' before her.

v. III. 51. *set Cock a hoope*. Cf. *Grammar*, II. vii. 82, 'Take the cock of(f) the hoope'. Originally a drinking phrase, meaning 'turn on the tap'; then, as here, 'give oneself up to sheer enjoyment'. Cf. Bale's *A Comedy concernynge thre Lawes*, 1548? f.ij^v,

> Cheare now maye I make, & set cocke on the houpe.
> Fyll in all the pottes, and byd me welcome hostesse.

Blount in his *Glossographia*, 1670, and Phillips in the 1678 edition of his dictionary explain it of taking out the spigot and laying it on the hoop of the barrel so that the ale can run out and the company drink without intermission. The *Oxford Dictionary* points out that this is an impossible explanation, but no other has been offered.

55. *as vull as a Pipers bag*. Cf. *B.F.* IV. iv. 12.
60. *Burroughs*, pledges.

v. iv. 24. *she did not know her selfe*. Cf. *C. is A*. v. vi. 47.

v. vi. 20. *Ghests*. The aspirate, Italian in origin, denotes the hard *g*; so Jonson has 'ghirland'.

v. vii. 3. *stand-still*. A clumsy expression for 'permanent foundation', the form perhaps due to a confusion with 'stand-point'.

11–13. Inigo's latinity appears to have been weak: Jonson further satirizes it in the induction to *The Magnetic Lady*, 76–8, and the *Welcome at Bolsover*, 42.

24. *Skelton . . . Elinour Rumming*. Skelton's poem *The Tunnyng of Elynour Rumming*, the ale-wife of Letherhead, is also alluded to in the masque of *The Fortunate Isles*, 1624, 369, in which Skelton himself appears as a character. On all his title-pages he is described as 'Laureate' or 'Poet Laureate'.

31. *oild Lanterne-paper*. Cf. the 'Expostulation', *U.V.* xxxiv. 72 foll.
32. *every Barber*. Cf. *S.W.* III. v. 85–6.
39–40. *her Huisher . . . bareheaded before her*. A very important point of etiquette, noted again in scene x, line 26. Similarly with a coachman in *N.I.* IV. i. 12–17.
48. *his whistle*. Also sneered at in the 'Expostulation', *U.V.* xxxiv. 66. Cf. scene x, line 7.
50. *virge*, wand.
52. *briefe*, abstract.

v. viii. 13. *halfe Lord Chamberlin, i' my Masters absence*. 'A severe hit at Herbert; Astley being the nominal, but he the acting, Master of the Revels.'—Fleay, *Biogr. Chron.* i, p. 387.

16. *sage sentences*. The phrase suggests (1) Peter Lombard's compilation *The Book of the Sentences*, an authoritative pronouncement on points of doctrine; (2) a judicial tribunal: cf. I. i. 32 foll.

v. ix. 11. *a Hall!* Originally the cry to a crowd when an open space was required for dancers; then, as here, a summons to an entertainment. Cf. *Hon. Wales*, 332; *P.A*. 234–5.

12. *'Tis merry* . . . The proverbial phrase, slightly adapted. Cf. *King Alisander* [*c.* 1300], 1164, 'Swithe mery hit is in halle | When the burdes waven alle'; and *Iohn Heywoodes woorkes*, 1562, 'Epigrammes vpon Prouerbs', sig. Rij, 'It is mery in hall when beardes wagge all.' Jonson also quotes the phrase, *Christmas*, 10; *G.M*. 1280, 1288; and *U.V*. xlv. 13.

v. x. How was the Motion staged? There was a large tub 'like a Salt-Peeter Tub' (v. vii. 5), 'capt with . . . A fine oild paper which we'— the producers of masques—'use'. It contained 'the light to the busines', apparently a huge lantern with a solitary candle, the 'vapour' of which 'drove all the motions of our matter about' (ibid. 30–6). Thus the figures of the motion were shadow-shapes which revolved on the top of the tub. Before the performance the tub and lantern were hidden by a curtain (stage-direction at v. x. 9). Medlay draws the curtain and 'discovers the top of the Tub', turning round the apparatus to exhibit the figures—an elementary parody of the *machina versatilis*.[1] In the 'Expostulation' (*U.V*. xxxiv. 72–4) Jonson expressed his contempt for Inigo's feat

> Of Lanterne-lerry, with fuliginous heat
> Whirling his Whymsyes, by a subtilty
> Suck't from the Veynes of shop-philosophy.

The sneer at 'shop-philosophy' is elucidated by To-Pan's comment on Medlay's 'fine oild Lantern-paper'—'Yes every Barber, every Cutler has it', and by the reference in *Epicoene*, iii. v. 85–6, to the barber's 'inuention of caruing lanterns in paper'.

v. x. s.d. *on the by*. Cf. *Cat.* iii. 377, 'i' the *rere*, or o' the *by*'.

9. *To run the meaning over in short speeches*, i.e. act as 'interpreter' to the motions. Cf. *Hamlet*, iii. ii. 240–1, 'I could interpret betweene you and your loue: if I could see the Puppets dallying.' Lanthorn Leatherhead, another satirical sketch of Inigo Jones, in *Bartholomew Fair* 'interprets Master *Littlewit's* Motion' (iii. iv. 142).

17 s.d. *Ha' peace*. Similarly in *Christmas*, 79, 141.

The first Motion. Sir E. K. Chambers (*Mediaeval Stage*, ii. 158 n.) calls attention to the use of 'motion' for a shadow-play.

24. *sad*, dark-coloured.

29. *page*. As if Tub had his sets of verse written out in five separate sheets.

40. *&c*. Usually an indication that the actor could improvise, as in Marlowe's *Doctor Faustus*, l. 967 (ed. Tucker Brooke), 'I scorne you: and you are but a &c.'. The object of the '&c.' was to mark appropriate moments in which the clown could 'speak more than was set down for him'. But that would be pointless here where the scene is

[1] *M. of Q.* 446–7.

all clownery and the interpreter makes only 'short speeches' (l. 9). It would also be very unlike Jonson to leave the actor free play. '&c.' probably marks the unfinished speech, when Tub interrupts it; cf. the parallel in III. vii. 21.

59. *Hart root*, sweetheart. For the origin of the phrase see *Iohn Heywoodes woorkes*, 1562, pt. ii, ch. v, H1ᵛ, 'He loueth hir better at the sole of the foote, | Than euer he loued me at the hert roote'.

92. εὐφονία *gratiâ*. Whose error is this? Tub's, or the printer's? Even if we correct to εὐφωνίας the phrase is a jumble of Greek and Latin. Marston has it correctly in *The Dutch Curtezan*, 1605, H4, 'whatsoere he has don, has bin only *Euphoniæ gratia*, for Wits sake'. 'Euphony' had not been naturalized: Joseph Webbe in *An Appeale to Truth*, 1622, p. 30, talks of 'the sweet sound of words and voices called *Euphonia* by the Grecians'. The earliest anglicized example in the *Oxford Dictionary* is from H. Cockeram's *The English Dictionarie, or an interpreter of hard English words*, 1623, '*Euphonie*, accent in words'.

94. *stan' on*, rhyming with 'Chanon', is an instance of the slurred or lightly sounded final -*d*. Cf. *Forest*, xi. 49, 50, 'combines . . . mindes'; and *A.P.* 612–13, 'groun'. . . swoune', where Jonson uses the apostrophe.

95. *Giles* is possible in the text only if it was the original name afterwards changed to Miles.

97. *to pay . . . his Club*. The earliest instance in *O.E.D.* is from Pepys, and strictly used of expenses involving a joint payment. Jonson seems to mean vaguely 'contribution' or 'payment'.

Epilogue

4. *rubs*. A metaphor from the game of bowls in which, when a bowl was diverted from its course by some impediment, it was said to 'rub'. Cf. *King Richard II*, III. iv. 3–5.

9. *brag*. Cf. I. ii. 11.

11. *poore Iohn*. Dried and salted hake, often noticed as an inferior kind of food, was popularly called 'poor John'.

16. Cf. *Iohn Heywoodes woorkes*, 1546, pt. i, ch. ii, ed. 1562, Aiij, 'earely vp, and neuer the nere'; Munday and Chettle, *The Death of Robert Earle of Huntingdon*, 1601, F4 (to Bruce who has come too late to save his castle), 'In you yfaith the Prouerb's verified: | Y'are earely vp, and yet are nere the neare.' *Neare* is the old comparative as in IV. vi. 54.

THE CASE IS ALTERED

THE title of the play was a proverb of legal origin. Its common form was 'The case is altered, quoth Plowden.' This is a reference to the distinguished jurist, Edmund Plowden (1518–85). Fuller was the first to explain the proverb in *The History of the Worthies of England*, 1662, *Shrop-shire*, p. 2:

This Proverb referreth its originall to *Edmund Plowden*, an eminent

Native and great Lawyer of this County, though very various the relations of the occasion thereof. Some relate it to *Plowden* his faint pleading at the first for his Client, till spurred on with a better *Fee:* which some will say, beareth no proportion with the ensuing Character of his Integrity.[1] Others refer it to his altering of his Judgement upon the Emergencie of new matter formerly undiscovered: It being not Constancie but Obstinacie to persist in an old error, when convinced to the contrary by cleer and new Information. Some tell it thus, That, *Plowden* being of the Romish perswasion, some Setters *trapanned* him (pardon the *prolepsis*) to hear Masse: But afterwards *Plowden* understanding, that the *pretender* to Officiate was no Priest, but a meer Lay-man (on designe to make a discovering) Oh! *The case is altered quoth Plowden: No Priest, no Masse.* As for other meaner Origination of this Proverb, I have neither List nor Leasure to attend unto them.'

Ray in the second edition of his *Proverbs*, 1768, p. 175, accepts Fuller's explanation, and says the proverb was 'usually applied to such Lawyers or others as being corrupted with larger fees shift sides, and pretend the case is altered; such as have *bovem in lingua*'. Compare B. Rich, *The Irish Hubbub*, 1619, p. 35, 'We haue so many *Ploydens* in these daies, that can alter the case, and for their owne lucre, will take money to set men at strife and variance.' Ray also quotes this anecdote—no doubt the 'other meaner Origination' ignored by Fuller—'*Plowden* being asked by a neighbour of his, what remedy there was in Law against his neighbour for some hogs that had trespassed his ground, answered, he might have very good remedy; but the other replying, that they were his hogs, Nay then neighbour (quoth he) the case is altered.' Plowden was a Catholic and did have trouble with the authorities: in a list of London papists in 1578 he appears as 'Mr. Ployden who hears mass at Baron Brown's, Fish Street Hill' (*D.N.B.*).

Whetstone quotes the phrase in his *Historye of Promos and Cassandra*, v. iv. 1, '*Ros.* A Sir, in fayth, the case is altred quight' (1578, Fijᵛ). This appears to be the earliest example in literature. It was also used as a title by F. T. in his slight dialogue *The Case is Altered. How? Aske Dalio and Millo*, published by Crede in 1604. This was entered to John Smethwicke in the Stationers' Register on 16 February, 'provided that this copie be not taken from my [? any] other to the hurt of another mans book'; the licensing authorities seem to have had an uneasy feeling that the title was familiar to them, or they may have been definitely thinking of Jonson's play. Shakespeare has the phrase in *3 Henry VI*, iv. iii. 31.

[1] Referring to the biography which follows (p. 7) where Fuller quotes Camden's tribute to Plowden: 'Vitae integritate inter homines suae professionis nulli secundus.'

The play touches slightly upon history. In 1510 Chaumont d'Amboise, Lord Chaumont, father of the Chamont of this play, recaptured Vicenza for the French from Maximilian of Germany. The inhabitants had decamped with most of their goods to Padua—not Verona, as Jonson implies in I. ix. 79, 80, for that town was already in the hands of the French. The action of the play is dated 1529 (ibid. 67).

In 1512 the Pope appointed Maximilian Sforza Duke of Milan. He is the Maximilian of the play.

PLACE AND TIME IN THE PLAY

In this comedy we have more freedom in the setting than in Jonson's mature work. The scene is Milan, shifting from the palace of Count Ferneze to the humble dwelling of the beggar Jaques de Prie. In the palace we have at one moment the state-rooms and at another the servants' hall. The play opens in the latter (scenes i–v) and returns to it in Act II, scenes ii and vii: a special feature of this is the cobbler's shop specified in I. i, '*Iuniper a Cobler is discouered, sitting at worke in his shoppe and singing*' and IV. v, '*Enter Iuniper in his shop singing*'; probably a bench with boots and tools was pushed out to indicate the shop and withdrawn when he takes off his cobbler's apron and puts on the servingman's blue dress (I. i. 23). The action is in the state-rooms in Act I, scenes vi–ix, Act IV, scenes i and ii, x and xi, and Act V, scene ix to the end. In Act II, scenes iii–vi are set in what Angelo describes as 'a solitary walk' (IV. 5), probably in the garden where the Count sends to look for his son when he is not in the house. The sixth and seventh scenes of Act V are apparently in the street before the palace.

The scenes at Jacques de Prie's house are partly in front of it— Act I, scene x (which is an abrupt transition from the palace), and the first four scenes of Act III, with another abrupt change in the fifth scene to the back of the house where Jaques hides his gold under a heap of manure. This 'back-side', as he calls it, is the scene of his soliloquies in Act II, scene i, Act III, scene v; so in Act IV, scenes vi–ix; it has a tree up which Onion climbs; the first five scenes of Act V are also enacted here.

Act V, scene viii, is in the open country near Milan.

The time indications are rather indefinite. There are four clearly marked intervals: the first when Maximilian and Lord Paulo Ferneze go off to the wars after Act I, scenes ix and x; the second when Maximilian returns with prisoners at the opening of the fourth act: news had come to Count Ferneze of Lord Paulo's capture in Act III, scene iv. The third after arrangements had been made for an exchange of prisoners and Camillo (the supposed Chamont) leaves to effect it in Act IV, scene iv. Finally in Act V, scene viii, Chamont and Paulo return; they reach Count Ferneze in scene xii.

1. i. s.d. *Iuniper . . . is discouered,* i.e. by drawing a curtain covering the central space at the back of the stage. Cf. the opening stage-direction of *Eastward Ho*: '*At the middle dore, Enter Golding discouering a Gold-smiths shoppe*'; and *E.M.I.* 1. v stage-direction. In Lyly's *The Woman in the Moone,* 1. i. 56, the direction is 'They draw the Curtins from before Natures shop.'

sitting at worke . . . and singing. Similar stage-directions are found in *The Coblers Prophesie* by R. Wilson, 1594, A3ᵛ–A4, where Ralph enters 'with his stoole, his implements and shooes, and, sitting on his stoole, falls to sing'; *Locrine,* 1595, C4ᵛ (II. iii), 'Enter *Strumbo, Dorothie, Trompart* cobling shooes and singing'; and *George a Greene,* 1599, E3ᵛ (IV. iii), '*Enter a* Shoomaker *sitting vpon the stage at worke*' (C. R. Baskervill).

in his shoppe. On the ground floor of Ferneze's palace (cf. 15, 'go vp'), in accordance with the Italian custom of leasing this part of the house to artisans and shopkeepers.

19. *a mourning creature.* He must put on a black coat instead of a blue one (1. vii. 27), as the family are in mourning for Lady Ferneze.

21. *a word to the wise.* Cf. Plautus, *Persa,* 729, 'Dictum sapienti sat est.'

23. *Lye there . . .* From Marlowe's *Tamburlaine,* Part I, 1. ii (237, ed. Brooke), 'Lie here ye weedes that I disdaine to weare.'

1. ii. *Antonio Balladino* is Antony Munday, who was much scoffed at by his contemporaries. In *Histriomastix, Or, The Player whipt,* 1610, he is satirized in the character of 'Post-haste', with several parallels to the present play, as F. G. Fleay noted. Middleton also gibed at him in his pageant, *The Triumphs of Truth,* 1613.

The name *Balladino* alludes to his ballads, which are not extant. One in particular would be sufficient to wake the animosity of playwrights—

> *A Ringinge Retraite Couragiouslie sounded*
> *wherein Plaies and Players are fytlie Confounded—*

entered on the Stationers' Register on 10 November 1580. In *Histriomastix,* when his company is cashiered, he says, 'Ile boldly fall to ballading againe' (H1ᵛ), and in Chettle's *Kind-Harts Dreame,* 1593 ?, he appears as 'Antony Now-now', protesting against the abuses of ballad-makers.

He is to 'make some prety *Paradox* or some *Aligory*' (15). Munday had published *The Defence of Contraries, Paradoxes,* &c., from the French, in 1593.

He is '*Pageant* Poet to the City of *Millaine*' (29). No city pageant by Munday earlier than 1605 is now known, but the set from 1592 to 1604 is missing. In the first draft of *Every Man in his Humour,* Prospero writing to Lorenzo brackets 'the *Hall-Beadle*' and the '*Poet*

Nuntius' for 'penurie of wit and Inuention' (*Quarto*, I. i. 174–5); this is probably a fling at Munday. It has been conjectured that 'antony the poyete' to whom Henslowe advanced money on a lost play, 'a widowes Charme' in July, August, and September 1602 (*Henslowe's Diary*, ed. Greg, pp. 169–70) was the 'pageant poet' of Jonson; but the fact that Munday is mentioned elsewhere by name in all other plays for which Henslowe paid him tells against this suggestion.

For the 'stale stuffe' of his pageants (48–9) see the onslaught in *The Triumphs of Truth*, summed up in the title-page as 'All the Showes, Pageants, Chariots; Morning, Noone, and Night Triumphes. *Directed, Written*, and *redeem'd into Forme, from the Ignorance of some former times, and their Common Writer*, By Thomas Middleton', who complains that 'the miserable want' of art and knowledge 'in the *impudent common Writer*, hath often forc'd from me much pitty and sorrow; and it would heartily grieue any vnderstanding spirit to behold many times so glorious a fire in bounty and goodnesse offering to match it selfe with freezing Art, sitting in darknesse, with the candle out, looking like the picture of *Blacke Monday*' (ed. 1613, A3).

He 'writes so plaine, and keepes that old *Decorum*' (58–9). In *Histrio-mastix* (sig. C) Post-haste gives a sample of his play of the 'Prodigal Child', and Gulch exclaims,

> Heer's no new luxurie of blandishment,
> But plenty of old Englands mothers words.

He refuses to 'raise his vaine' even if they will give him 'twenty pound a play' (72–3). The 'vaine' is also alluded to in Antony Brewer's *The Love-sick King*, II. i (1655, B4): 'Let mee see, what day's this; O Monday! I shall love Mondays vein to poetize as long as I live, for this trick.' In *Histriomastix* (sig. D4 and verso, sig. E) ten pounds is the price claimed for a play; Henslowe at this date usually paid six.

Finally, Antonio is 'in print already for the best plotter' (79) in Meres's *Palladis Tamia*, 1598, and his use of the undramatic device of the dumb show (80) may be illustrated from *The Downfall of Robert, Earle of Huntington*, 1601, A2ᵛ (licensed for the stage 15 February 1598):

> Sk⟨elton⟩. And gentlemen, since you are thus prepar'd,
>   Goe in, and bring your dumbe scene on the stage,
>   And I, as Prologue, purpose to expresse
>   The ground whereon an Historie is laied.

The dumb show follows to illustrate events which precede the play, and then (A3)—

> Sk. Sir Iohn once more, bid your dumbe shewes come in;
>   That as they passe I may explane them all.

The show is actually given a second time. Similarly in *The Death of Robert*, 1601, D3, the action is broken by presenting three visions of King John in dumb show.

3. *Ingle*, intimate, originally in a bad sense. The *O.E.D.* accuses Scott

of misusing the word in *Kenilworth*, iii, 'Ha! my dear friend and ingle, Tony Foster', but this is the use throughout the present play: see II. vii. 86, IV. v. 33.

14, 15. But contrast IV. v. 36.

19. *with a powder*, with a rush, impetuously. Cf. Fuller, *Pisgah*, v. v. 151, 'Jordan . . . comes down with a powder, and at set times overflowes all his bankes'; *Northward Ho*, 1607, H2ᵛ, 'send him hither with a powder presently. *Phil.* Hees blowne vp already.'

42. *my mind* . . . Sir Edward Dyer's song in Byrd's *Psalmes, Sonets, & songs of sadnes and pietie, made into Musicke of fiue parts*, 1588, no. xiv, Dijᵛ. Similarly quoted as a hymn of the contented in *E.M.O.* I. i. 14.

52. *Mæcen-asses*. Cf. *E.M.O.*, Induction, 179, 'an ARISTARCHVS, or starke-asse', and Dekker's dedication of *The Guls Horne-booke* to 'all Guls in generall' as his 'most worthie *Mecæn-asses*'.

61-2. *write you nothing but humours*. A reference to *the comodey of vmers* of Henslowe's *Diary*, Chapman's *Humorous Day's Mirth*, played 11 May 1597, and thence till 13 July, and again in October and November. No doubt the reference also covers *Every Man in his Humour*. It would be thoroughly in Jonson's manner to allude thus to his own play, and even if *The Case is Altered* originally preceded *Every Man*, this opening scene was rewritten later in order to satirize Munday.

69, 70. *the foole came not out a iot*. Cf. *S. of N.*, 1st Intermean, 23–36, n.

76. *ground*. What we now call the pit: cf. 'groundling'. Cf. II. vii. 69, *B.F.* Ind. 49, 'the vnderstanding Gentlemen o' the ground'.

I. iii. Stage direction. *an armd Sewer . . . with seruice*. The 'sewer' (Fr. *essayeur*) was (1) the taster of each dish to prove that it contained no poison, (2) afterwards the chief servant who directed the placing of the dishes on the table. Cf. *Macbeth*, I. vii. s.d., 'Enter a Sewer, and diuers Seruants with Dishes and Seruice over the Stage', where the Clarendon Press editors illustrate 'service' from Heywood's *A Woman Kilde with Kindnesse*, 1607, F, '*Enter Butler, and Ienkin with a table cloath, bread, trenchers, and salt.*'

10. *setting vp of a rest*. Here and in *E.M.O.* v. xi. 52, *N.I.* I. ii. 11 = 'to take up permanent quarters', and the *O.E.D.* illustrates this use from Lamb and Dickens. Originally a gambling term, 'to stake one's all', as in Gascoigne's *Supposes*, 1566, III. ii, where a full illustration is given from primero.

I. iv. Juniper's misuse of words begins with this scene. In a series of articles contributed to *Notes and Queries* from March to November 1903, H. C. Hart pointed to Gabriel Harvey as Juniper's special model. But the parallels are not complete, though it is not unlikely that Jonson used Harvey among other sources. If so, the satire is general and not unlike Clove's vacuous use of Marston's words in *Every Man out of his Humour*, III. iv.

From the first Jonson showed a marked interest in the study of words and style. Bobadill's fencing jargon and Daniel's conceits were satirized in *Every Man in*, and Puntarvolo's arcadianism in *Every Man out of his Humour*. 'Pure and neat Language I love, yet plaine and customary'—words written long after the date of this play (*Disc.* 1870)—sum up Jonson's consistent attitude. The tendency to make other characters comment on a speaker's oddities of phrase becomes almost a mannerism with him. Compare in this play Valentine's aside, 'O how pittifully are these words forc't. As though they were pumpt out on's belly' (18 *infra*); Maximilian's need of a comment before he can understand Juniper (I. viii. 14); and Jaques's bewildered repetition of 'Ortographie, Anatomy' (IV. viii. 27) even at the moment when he suspects his gold to have been stolen.

4. *frolicke*, simply 'cheerful', its original sense.

5. *I am no changling*. A favourite phrase with Harvey. Cf. 'His behaviour is no turne coat, though his stile be a changeling' (*Works*, ed. Grosart, ii. 288); 'Indeed, I saw you to be no changeling' (iii. 16); 'Would not you should think me a changeling' (iii. 86). (Hart.)

6. *keepe the pristinate*. No parallel in *O.E.D.* Whalley compares Terence, *Andria*, 817, 'pol, Crito, antiquom obtines'.

mad Hierogliphick. Cf. Dekker, *Old Fortunatus*, 1600, K2, '*Amp.* Brother, what misteries lie in all this? *Andel.* Trickes, Ampedo, trickes, deuises, and mad Herogliphickes, mirth, mirth, and melody.'

10. *Absconde*. Italicized in Q: query, not the English word, but the Latin. Juniper 'has the phrases' in Latin occasionally (e.g. II. vii. 23).

17. *What fortuna de la Guerra?* Cf. *Love's Labour's lost*, v. ii. 527–8: 'But we will put it (as they say) to *Fortuna de la Guarra*.'

27–8. *no marle . . . another*. Cf. *E.M.O.*, Induction, 281–6.

32. *O sea sicke Iest*. Cf. *The Wisedom of Doctor Dodypoll*, 1600, D3, '*Doct.* A plage a de Marshans, blowe win⟨d⟩e. *Han.* You need not curse him sir, he has the stormes at Sea by this time. *Doct. O forte bien*, a good Sea-sick ieast, by this faire hand.'

1. v. 6. *Alla Coragio*. Popular slang: Parolles in *All's Well*, II. v. 90, 'Bravely, coragio'; Stephano in *The Tempest*, v. i. 258, 'Coragio, Bully-Monster, Coragio'. The prefix *Alla* is merely Balthasar's blundering.

42. *for* in asseverations = 'before'. Cf. *E.M.O.* II. iii. 154, where F2 reads ''fore'.

43. *Capriccio*. Introduced by Harvey to denote 'a fantastic person': cf. his 'Signor Capricio' for Nashe (ii. 109)—(Hart). 'Caprichious' occurs as a new word in II. vii. 74–5.

hold hooke and line. Cf. B. Rich, *The Irish Hubbub*, 1617, p. 56, 'give the Deuill his due, for hee hath done his deuoure, hee hath brought the world to a good passe, he may now sit him downe and rest him, and hee may cry with the Angler: *Hould hooke and line, and all is mine*'; Sharpham, *The Fleire*, 1607, E3, '*Fleir*: Caught I hope: hold hooke and line, hee's fast by heauen.'

i. vi. 7 foll. The dialogue between Kitely and Cash in *E.M.I.* iii. iii. 40–112 is an interesting parallel, worked out rather more elaborately.

16. *iniury.* 'Supplanted *c.* 1600 by the current *injure*', *O.E.D.* Thus in *E.M.O.* iii. vi. 50 Holme's and Linge's Quartos print 'iniurie', the Folios 'iniure'.

30–2. Cf. *Hamlet*, iii. ii. 61–9.

47. *a happy mixture of our soules.* Cf. *D. is A.* i. vi. 196–8:

> . . . I had taught
> Our lips ere this, to seale the happy mixture
> Made of our soules.

85. Gifford calls attention to Jonson's favourite practice of indicating his characters to the audience by anticipatory touches before they actually appear. Dryden commended it in his *Examen of the Silent Woman* (*Essays*, ed. Ker, i. 87). In Shakespeare's *Julius Caesar* the keen characterization of Cassius put on Caesar's lips (i. ii. 191–210) follows the dialogue in which Cassius first whets Brutus against Caesar; Jonson would have made it precede.

i. vii. 9. *fennell*, the flatterer's herb. Gifford compares Lyly, *Sapho and Phao*, ii. iv. 60–1 (ed. Bond), 'Flatter, I mean lie; litle things catch light mindes, and fancy is a worme, that feedeth first vpon fenell.'

18. *sort*, set. Cf. *E.M.I.* iv. iii. 13.

motly braines. Cf. *As You Like It*, v. iv. 40, of Touchstone: 'This is the Motley-minded Gentleman.'

27. *the blew order.* Blue coats were worn by servingmen: cf. *E.M.I.* ii. iv. 12, *E.H.* iii. ii. 9, *M. Chr.* 52, 'In a blew Coat, serving-man like'.

32. *do.* Cf. *E.M.I.* i. i. 28, 'How doe my coussin EDWARD, vncle?'

48. *pull his cloth ouer his eares.* The sign of dismissal from service: cf. *T.T.* iv. vi. 71–2.

69. *manage my affections*, control my feelings, with a suggestion of the primary use, the art of training horses. Cf. *E.M.O.* ii. iii. 211, 'O, manage your affections.'

71. *the property* . . . Had Maximilian been dipping into the spurious poems of Ausonius? See the *Septem Sapientum Sententiae* once attributed to him, I Bias, 6–7:

> Quid prudentis opus? cum possis, nolle nocere.
> Quid stulti proprium? non posse et velle nocere.

i. viii. 4. *conden't.* A blunder, or a misprint? Query, 'condeuc't' in the sense of 'conducted'.

5. *procliue*, headlong, hasty. The *O.E.D.* has a parallel only from Mrs. Browning, *Aurora Leigh*, iii. 756, for the absolute use.

6. *preiudicate.* 'A favourite and constant word with Harvey.'—Hart, who quotes 'prejudicate judgements' (ii. 14) and 'prejudicate assertions' (ii. 134).

9. *compunction.* Cf. 'pitiful compunction', Harvey, i. 196 (Hart).

19. *allacrity of spirit*. This phrase occurs in *Rich. III*, v. iii. 73: cf. also Harvey, i. 222, 'alacrity of courage' (Hart).

25–6. *his tongue . . . sleepes*. Repeated in *Poet*. III. i. 36–7, 'Doubtlesse, this Gallants tongue has a good turne, when hee sleepes.'

I. ix. 24. *Fortunatus hat*. The first part of a play of *Fortunatus* is recorded by Henslowe as acted by the Admiral's men in 1596; the 'whole history', for which three payments were made to Dekker, in November and December 1599. Dekker's recast was entered on the Stationers' Register 20 February 1600 and published in that year. For literary allusions cf. *F.I.* 186, Marston's *Antonio and Mellida*, Part II, II. ii, 'Ould Fortunatus wishing cappe', and *The Honest Man's Fortune*, IV. ii.

36. *speake i' the nose, and turne puritan*. An early expression of Jonson's contempt for the sect he was afterwards to satirize so mercilessly. Cf. II. iii. 26.

41. *disclaime in*, renounce all part in, disown. The preposition is found in v. xii. 68, *E.M.I.* (Quarto), III. i. 76 (where the Folio has 'disclaim'), v. iii. 126 (to which the Folio has no corresponding words); *Poet*. I. ii. 102 (where F2 omits the 'in'); *Volp.* III. ix. 32, IV. v. 107; *S.S.* I. iv. 19.

affects, affections (Lat. *affectus*). Cf. I. x. 10, *Poet*. IV. ix. 19.

57. *repercussiue*. Cf. *C.R.* I. i. 122.

94. s.d. *tucket*, flourish on the trumpet.

I. x. 25. *genius*. In *Cat*. iv. 565 Catiline addresses Cethegus, 'thou my better Genius', and in *For*. xiv. 21, of Sir William Sidney, 'For he with his best *Genius* left alone'. In medieval theology the rational spirit temporarily lodged within the body and directing the bodily faculties for good or for evil. Cf. Spenser, *The Faerie Queene*, II. xii. 47; *Julius Caesar*, II. i. 66.

38. *in virtue then in bloud*. Cf. *D. is A*. I. vi. 167–8, 'you seeme a Gentleman of vertue, No lesse then blood'.

44. *Lar*, the *Lar familiaris* of old Roman belief, or tutelary spirit of the family: cf. v. ii. 8, 10, 16. He appears as a character in the *Aulularia* of Plautus.

45–6. *ghost . . . In an vnsauory sheet*. Cf. *A Warning for Faire Women*, 1599, Induction, A2ᵛ,

> a filthie whining ghost,
> Lapt in some fowle sheete, or a leather pelch,
> Comes skreaming like a pigge halfe stickt.

For the incorrect form *Satrapas* cf. Marston, *Pigmalions Image*, 1598, p. 27, *Sat*. i, 'For shame leaue running to some *Satrapas*.'

48. *Well lets go*. For closing a scene with words which overlap the metre cf. II. v, and *King Lear*, III. vi (Quarto text). Sometimes they even overlap the rhyme; cf. *A Warning for Faire Women*, 1599, B2,

> *Dru*. Hope you the best, she shal haue much adoe,
> To hold her own when I begin to wooe: come Hodge. *Exit*.

II. i. 1, 2. *So now* . . . Like the miser in the *Aulularia*, 79, 80:

> Nunc defaecato demum animo egredior domo,
> postquam perspexi salva esse intus omnia.

13, 14. Ibid. 113–15,

> Nam nunc quom celo sedulo omnes ne sciant,
> omnes videntur scire et me benignius
> omnes salutant quam salutabant prius.

31. „*That* . . . Gnomic lines are frequently punctuated with inverted commas at the beginning of the line. For the form of those employed here cf. III. v. 17, 18, and Drayton, *The Moone-Calfe*, 1627, p. 182, '„(Nothing as hunger sharpeneth so the sent)', and p. 183, '„T'was done by sleight, that was not done by strength.'

37. *And this his daughter.* Hegio in the *Captivi*, 101–3:

> Perdidi unum filium,
> puerum quadrimum quem mihi servos surpuit,
> neque eum servom unquam repperi neque filium.

38. This redeeming trait in Jaques's character recalls in a distant manner Shylock's pang at the loss of the turquoise ring which he had of Leah when he was a bachelor. It stands out as a happy touch in this crude soliloquy of fifty lines.

64 foll. Based on Plautus' *Aulularia*, 90–100: see the closer reproduction in *D. is A.* II. i. 168–76.

II. ii. 7. *checke* . . . *at.* The hawking phrase used in *Tw. Night*, III. i. 61–2:

> And like the Haggard, checke at euery Feather
> That comes before his eye.

Cf. *Mortimer*, I. i. 11–12:

> There is a Fate, that flies with towring spirits
> Home to the marke, and never checks at conscience.

16. *vaile*, give gratuities.

17. *chaw.* Cf. *D. is A.* IV. ii. 53.

27. *talkes in quiddits.* Cf. *1 Henry IV*, I. ii. 50–1, 'What, in thy quips and thy quiddities?'

35. *That were not so good, me thinkes.* A polite formula of disapproval also found *E.M.O.* I. ii. 139, *S.N.* II. v. 68 (n.).

37. *thy pappes.* Cf. *C.R.* III. iv. 67 (A courtier) 'Playes with his mistresse pappes'; *D. is A.* II. vi. 71, where the stage-direction runs, '*He growes more familiar in his Court-ship, playes with her paps, kisseth her hands, &c.*' S. Purchas, *Microcosmus*, 1619, pp. 257–8, '. . . whom neither scorching Heat in Summer, nor pinching Cold in Winter, nor nipping vnseasonable Winds, nor that Haile-shot (Hell-shot) of lustfull Eyes, *fierie Darts*, can make so much as to interpose a Shield, or any Couering of Attire, before their delicater parts, the tender Pappes:

except we call that a Couering, the false Brests, lately bought, not of the Dawber, Plaisterer, Painter, but the German Artificer (O Mysterie of Iniquitie!) as the *nakednesse* of the Brest was before borrowed of the Italian Curtizan; which with better right might keepe *open her shopwindowes*, as professing common sale.'

Mumps. Blunderingly used as a term of endearment: the elder Loveless applies it insultingly to Abigail in Beaumont and Fletcher's *Scornful Lady*, v. i. 99. *O.E.D.* hesitates whether to explain as a contraction of 'mumpsimus' or to connect with the verb 'mump' (= to mumble with the gums).

Pastorella. The name of Sir Calidore's love in *The Faerie Queene*, IV. ix and x.

II. iii. 1. *case*, pair.

13. *You take too much Tobacco.* A libel on the gentle Phoenixella, but for the fact of women smoking cf. Dekker, *Satiromastix*, 1602, C2ᵛ, '*Asin.* I burnt my pype yesternight, and twas neuer vsde since, if you will tis at your seruice gallants, and Tobacco too, tis right pudding I can tell you; a Lady or two, tooke a pype full or two at my hands, and praizde it for the Heauens, shall I fill, Flannius?' H. P., *Thalia's Banquet*, 1620, Epigram 18 'Vpon Gellia':

> When *Gellia* went to schoole and was a girle,
> Her teeth for whitenesse might cōpare with pearl,
> But after she the taste of sweete meates knew,
> They turn'd all *Opals* to a perfect blew,
> Now *Gellia* takes Tobacco, what should let
> But last they should conuerted be to Iet?

John Swan, *Speculum Mundi*, 1635, p. 266, 'The women of America ... do not use to take *Tobacco*, because they perswade themselves it is too strong for the constitution of their bodies: and yet some women of England use it often, as well as men.'

15. *true-stich.* Cf. *P.A.* 138, 'Goe through-stitch with all.'

22. *at eleuen and sixe.* Cf. Harrison, *A Description of England*, 1577, II. vi (ed. Furnivall, i. 166), 'With vs the nobilitie, gentrie, and students doo ordinarilie go to dinner at eleuen before noone, and to supper at fiue, or betweene fiue and sixe at afternoone. The merchants dine and sup seldome before twelue at noone, and six at night especiallie in London.'

26. *Præcisianisme*, Puritan preciseness. *O.E.D.* quotes J. Jones, *Bathes of Bath*, 1572, iii. 24, 'The Puritanes, but better we may terme them piuish precisians.'

II. iv. 16. *hearted* For the absence of a stop to mark the unfinished speech see Simpson, *Shakespearian Punctuation*, § 41.

40. *a Decade in the art of memory. Ars memoriae* in Cicero, *Acad.* ii. 2, *de Orat.* ii. 74, and Quintilian, XI. ii = a memoria technica. *Decade*, the

points to be memorized arranged in sets of ten. Cf. the elaborate scheme of Hugh Platte in *The Jewell House of Art and Nature*, 1594, § 98, pp. 81–5, '*The Art of memorie which master Dickson the Scot did teach of late years in England, and wherof he hath written a figuratiue and obscure treatise, set down briefly and in plaine termes according to his owne demonstration, with the speciall vses thereof.*'—'You must make choice of some large edifice or building, whose Chambers or Galleries bee of some reasonable receipt, and so familiar vnto you, as that euerie part of each of them may present it selfe readily vnto the eyes of your minde when you call for them. In euerie of these roomes you must place ten seuerall subiects at a reasonable distaunce one from the other, least the neerenesse of their placing shoulde happen to confound your Memorie. Your subiectes must consist of Decades, whereof the first is a man, and the fifth a woman, or rather the wife of that man which beginneth the Decade. And by this meanes your first, your fift, your tenth, your fifteenth, and your twentieth subiect, &c. both forwarde and backe-warde is easily brought to minde. The rest of the subiects in euerie Decade may be such as are meerly differing the one from the other, vnlesse you shall like to haue some few of them resembling the pro-fession of him that beginneth the Decade.' *Alexandri Dicsoni Arelii de vmbra rationis & iudicij, siue de memoriæ virtute Prosopopoeia*, 1583, to which Platte alludes, suggests on pp. 68 and 69 a method of dividing each sign of the zodiac into ten and working through the hundred and twenty. For the metaphor cf. Fletcher and Massinger, *The Lovers Pro-gress*, II. ii, 'I would learn the art of memory in your table book', and Marston, *Antonio and Mellida*, Part I, II. i (1602, D3): '*Fel.* Faith, I haue nineteene mistresses alreadie, and I not much disdeigne that thou shold'st make vp the ful score. *Fla.* Oh, I heare you make common places of your mistresses, to performe the office of memory by.'

48. *my refuge.* This trick of inventing 'new tearmes' in the relations of love and friendship was carried to absurd lengths by the gallants of the day; cf. the parody of it in *E.M.O.* IV. v. 56–79.

51. *Plouer*, i.e. simpleton, dupe. Cf. *B.F.* IV. ii. 60, 'Was there euer greene Plouer so pull'd?' *S. of N.* II. iii. 82–3:

and what Plouer's that
They haue brought to pull? BRO. I know not, some green Plouer,
I'le find him out.

Chapman, *Cæsar and Pompey*, 1633, C4 (II. i):

Why thou art a most greene Plouer in policy, I
Perceiue.

52. *take away the P.* For this childish play with the letter cf. Sonnet 14 appended to Barnfield's *Cynthia*, 1595:

Here, hold this gloue . . .
. . . place this gloue neere thy hart,
So shalt thou rid my payne, and ease my smart.

> How can that be (perhaps) thou wilt reply,
> A gloue is for the hand, not for the hart. . . .
> To this, thus answere I.
> If thou from gloue do'st take away the g,
> Then gloue is loue: and so I send it thee.

53–4. *borrow Cupids wings . . . do strange things.* Seemingly a quotation: compare *M. of Owls*, 3, 4, of Captain Cox's hobby-horse, the 'Pegasus' of the '*Warwick* Muses':

> And though he have not on his wings,
> He will doe strange things.

II. vi. 48. *Loue hates delays.* Cf. Ovid, *Ars Amat.* ii. 229, 'Amor odit inertes'; Seneca, *H.F.* 588, 'Odit verus amor nec patitur moras.'

II. vii. 2. *hilts*, foils.

3. *I cannot resolue you.* Cf. *S.W.* III. ii. 25–7, 'Mᴿˢ. Oᴛ. But he departed straight, I can resolue you. ` Dᴀᴠ. What an excellent choice phrase, this lady expresses in!' Used also in *E.M.I.* I. v. 44, *Alch.* I. ii. 151, *T.T.* III. viii. 5.

4. *ingenuity.* Harvey has the word (i. 179), 'Young blood is hot: youth hasty: ingenuity open' in the sense of ingenuousness, apparently the earliest instance. Nashe pilloried this with other instances of 'ouerrackt absonisme' in *Strange Newes, Of the intercepting of certaine Letters*, 1592 (*Works*, ed. McKerrow, i, p. 316). The earliest recorded use of 'ingenuity' in the sense of quickness of wit is *E.M.O.* III. ix. 78–82, where Macilente comments on the misuse of it by Fastidius Briske (Hart).

8. *Epitaphs.* This malapropism recurs in *C.R.* IV. iv. 16.

9. *misbegotten of some fencer.* Cf. *S.W.* IV. ii. 125–7.

15. *performe* (or more frequently, play) *their prizes.* A technical term for engaging in a fencing-match: cf. *C.R.* v. iii. 9, 95.

29–82. Jonson's habit of criticism was irrepressible, and his combative instincts made him take a delight in lecturing and criticizing his audiences. It is also characteristic that one part of the present passage (53–7) reappears in the truculent Induction to *Every Man out of his Humour*, 177–84:

> How monstrous, and detested is't, to see
> A fellow, that has neither arte, nor braine,
> Sit like an Aʀɪsᴛᴀʀᴄʜᴠs, or starke-asse,
> Taking mens lines, with a tabacco face,
> In snuffe, still spitting, vsing his wryed lookes
> (In nature of a vice) to wrest, and turne
> The good aspect of those that shall sit neere him,
> From what they doe behold! O, 'tis most vile.

Jonson was apt to repeat his phrases and, above all, to re-use old material which for any reason he had discarded.

32. *a man is nobody, till he has trauelled.* Cf. Nashe, *The Vnfortunate Traueller*, 1594 (*Works*, ed. McKerrow, ii, p. 297), 'hee is no bodie that hath not trauelled'.

54. *rookes*, gulls, simpletons.

59. *censure*, judgement.

62. *acceptiue*. Cf. *Poet.* iii. iv. 87.

69. *grounded iudgements*. Cf. *B.F.*, Induction, 76, *K. Ent.* 266.

74. *Caprichious*. Cf. 107–8 below, and the satirical reference in Dekker and Chettle's *Patient Griesill*, 1603, ii, sig. Cᵛ–C.

'*Far.* Sirha *Vrcence*, this is one of those changeable Silke gallants, who in a verie scuruie prid, scorne al schollers, and reade no bookes but a looking glasse, and speake no language but sweet Lady, and sweet *Signior* and chew between their teeth terrible words, as though they would coniure, as complement and Proiects, and Fastidious, & Caprichious, and Misprizian, and the Sintheresis, of the soule, and such like raise-veluet tearmes.

Vrc. What be the accoutrements now of these gallants?

Far. Indeed thats one of their fustian outlandish phrases to, marie sir their accoutrements, are al yᵉ fantasticke fashions, yᵗ can be taken vp, either vpon trust or at second hand.'

So also C2ʳ:

'*Ric.* He that shall deny it Sir ile make him eate his words.

Emu. Good friend I am not in the Negatiue, bee not so Caprichious, you misprize me, my collocution tendeth to S. Owens dignifiing.'

It is important to note, from the evidence of Henslowe's *Diary*, that this play was composed in 1599.

Harvey apparently introduced the word 'capricious' into English—a fact overlooked by the *O.E.D.* H. C. Hart quotes 'capricious Dialogues of rankest bawdry' (i. 290), 'the capricious flocke' (ii. 52), in which the word means 'lecherous'; and, for the modern usage, 'a queint and capricious nature' (ii. 278), 'capricious and transcendent witte' (i. 201), 'capricious veine' (ii. 53), 'capricious humour' (54), 'capricious panges' (ib.).

The word quickly took root in English, and even Jonson became reconciled to the use of it: cf. *C.R.* ii. i. 7, 'act freely, carelessly, and capriciously', and *Hadd. M.* 171, 'a subtle capriccious Daunce'.

75. *stay, that word's for me*. Dr. Selim illustrates from *S. of N.* i. ii. 48–9:

P. Iv. *Emissaries*? stay, there's a fine new word, *Thom!*
'Pray God it signifie any thing, what are *Emissaries*?

83. *well sayd*, well done. A common phrase in this sense: cf. Davies of Hereford, *The Scourge of Folly*, 1620, p. 102:

Now wipe thine Nose (sweete Babe) vpon thy sleeue:
What, wilt, Ifaith? Why, well sedd, I perceiue
Th'wilt do as thou art bidde.

94. *in statu quo prius*. Cf. Harvey, i. 68, 'Remayning still, as we say, *in statu quo*'.—Hart, who points out that this quotation is the earliest use in print.

112. *a Plantan.* Cf. Tomkis, *Albumazar*, 1615, IV. ii:

> *Tri.* Help *Amellina*, help, I am falne i'th Cellar:
> Bring a fresh Plantane leafe I haue broke my shinne.

The Two Noble Kinsmen, 1634, CIᵛ (I. ii. 61):

> these poore sleight sores,
> Neede not a plantin.

124. *double locke.* Cf. *Arden of Feversham*, 1592, G2ᵛ:

> When he should haue lockt with both his hilts,
> He in a brauery florisht ouer his head.

125–6. *single.* A quibble on the sense 'weak' or 'silly'. Cf. *E.M.O.* II. iii. 292–5, '. . . hee might haue . . . explicated 'hem better in single *Scenes.* COR. That had beene single indeed'; and *U.V.* xxiv. 3, 'To say but one, were single.'

127. *a cob-web.* Cf. *S. of N.* II. iv. 175–6; *Mids. N. D.* III. i. 190–1.

130. *breake my head, and then give me a plaister.* A proverb: cf. *Iohn Heywoodes woorkes*, 1562, II. ix, Kiijᵛ:

> Your tales haue lyke tast, where temprance is taster,
> To breake my heade, and then geue me a plaster.

And *Florios Second Frutes*, 1591, p. 137, 'You breake my head, and then giue me a plaster, I can not tell how it will falle out quoth the good wife that gaue her husband a glister with a good cudgell.'

135. *Mephistophiles.* Cf. Dekker, *The Shomakers Holiday*, 1600, K (V. iv), 'auaunt, auaunt, auoide Mephostophilus'.

136. *the signe . . . in Aries.* Cf. Chaucer, *The Squieres Tale* (*C.T.*, F. 51), 'In Aries, the colerik hote signe'.

141. *white of an egge, and a little flax.* Cf. *B.F.* II. v. 186, and *King Lear*, III. vii. 105–6 (First Quarto, 1608, H2), '2 Ser. Goe thou, ile fetch some flaxe and whites of egges to apply to his bleeding face.'

144. *beare away the bucklers*, conquer, come off winner. Cf. Nashe, Preface to *Menaphon*, 1589 (*Works*, ed. McKerrow, iii. 323), '. . . would carry the bucklers full easily from all forraine brauers'; Cotgrave, s.v. 'Gaigné', '*Ie te le donne gaigné.* I grant it, I yield to thee; I confesse thy action; I giue thee the bucklers.'

III. i. 5. *much.* For this ironic use cf. *E.M.O.* I. iii. 99.

6. *True to my friend.* Cf. Proteus's saying in *The Two Gentlemen of Verona*, V. iv. 53–4, 'In Loue, Who respects friend?' (C. R. Baskervill).

11–15. Cf. *E.M.O.* II. iv. 9–14.

18. *louers periuries are ridiculous?* Cf. Tibullus, III. vi. 49, 'periuria ridet amantum | Iuppiter', and Ovid, *A.A.* i. 633, 'Iuppiter ex alto periuria ridet amantum.'

III. ii. 14. From Plautus' *Aul.* 184–5:

> Evc. Non temerarium est ubi dives blande appellat pauperem.
> iam illic homo aurum scit me habere, eo me salutat blandius.

From the same source come Jaques's abrupt exits to see that his gold is safe, and his ceaseless suspicions concerning the wooers: e.g. 194, 'Nunc petit quom pollicetur; inhiat aurum ut deuoret.'

21. *he has smelt it.* Ibid. 216, 'Aurum huic olet.'

38. *passionate*, deeply stirred. Cf. 'passions', line 46, and *E.M.I.* v. iii. 18.

42–3. Cf. Plautus, *Aul.* 238–9: 'Evc. At nihil est dotis quod dem. Me. Ne duas. | dum modo morata recte veniat, dotata est satis.'

III. iii. 38. *stockings* For the punctuation cf. II. iv. 16.

44. Cf. *Aulularia*, 220–4:

> Evc. Heia, Megadore, hau decorum facinus tuis factis facis,
> ut inopem atque innoxium aps te atque aps tuis me inrideas.
> Nam de te neque re neque verbis merui uti faceres quod facis.
> Me. Neque edepol ego te derisum venio neque derideo,
> neque dignum arbitror.

III. iv. 31. *flawe*, squall.

52. *seeme-les*, unseemly.

III. v. Charles Lamb printed in his *Specimens* three extracts from this play—II. iii, I. vi. 9–21, and this soliloquy—beginning at line 4, ''tis not to be told'. He commented upon the last:

> 'The passion for wealth has worn out much of its grossness in tract of time. Our ancestors certainly conceived of money as able to confer a distinct gratification in itself, not considered simply as a symbol of wealth. The old poets, when they introduce a miser, make him address his gold as his mistress; as something to be seen, felt, and hugged; as capable of satisfying two of the senses at least. The substitution of a thin, unsatisfying medium in the place of the good old tangible metal, has made avarice quite a Platonic affection in comparison with the seeing, touching, and handling pleasures of the old Chrysophilites. A bank note can no more satisfy the touch of a true sensualist in this passion, than Creusa could return her husband's embrace in the shades. See the Cave of Mammon in Spenser; Barabas' contemplation of his wealth in the *Rich Jew of Malta*; Luke's raptures in the *City Madam*; the idolatry and absolute gold-worship of the miser Jaques in this early comic production of Ben Jonson's. Above all hear Guzman, in that excellent old translation of the *Spanish Rogue*, expatiate on the "ruddy cheeks of your golden ruddocks, your Spanish pistolets, your plump and full-faced Portuguese, and your clear-skinned pieces of eight of Castile", which he and his fellows the beggars kept secret to themselves, and did privately enjoy in a plenti-

ful manner. "For to have them, to pay them away, is not to enjoy them; to enjoy them, is to have them lying by us; having no other need of them than to use them for the clearing of the eye-sight, and the comforting of our senses. These we did carry about with us, sewing them in some patches of our doublets near unto the heart, and as close to the skin as we could handsomely quilt them in, holding them to be restorative."'

5. *for gold.* Cf. Virgil, *Aeneid*, iii. 56–7, 'Quid non mortalia pectora cogis, Auri sacra fames?'

9. *enuies*, vies with, seeks to rival. Cf. *The Forest*, xii. 70, 'And, who doth me (though I not him) enuỳ'.

16. *In* is, of course, a verb.

17, 18. ,,*Scarce* . . . ,, *And*. Cf. II. i. 31. An echo of Horace's 'Rem facias, rem, | recte si possis, si non, quocumque modo rem' (*Ep.* I. i. 65–6), which Jonson reset in *E.M.I.* II. v. 49–51.

IV. i. The opening dialogue of this scene has been misunderstood. Maximilian turns to Camillo in the first instance, believing him to be Chamont. Pacue starts on hearing this, but Chamont quells him with a word and a warning gesture. He does not 'take' Pacue 'aside', as Gifford suggested in a stage-direction: he follows the conversation closely as he was bound to do. But the speech 'Marry with my Lord's leaue' (22 foll.)—assigned by the Quarto and all editors to '*Cam.*'—must be his. He steps forward, nominally as the inferior, but really in order to assert his right.

15. *semblably.* Cf. *1 Henry IV*, v. iii. 21.

20. *your ransomes.* The offer of two prisoners for one is from the *Captivi*, 332, but the ingenious adaptation of this in ll. 22 foll. is quite original.

38. *misprize*, misunderstand: the earliest example of this use in the *O.E.D.*, but Shakespeare has 'a mispris'd mood' (*Mids. N. D.* III. ii. 74) in the sense of a mistaken humour or caprice. 'Misprision' is one of the 'raise-veluet tearmes' satirized in *Patient Grissill* (quoted II. vii. 74, above).

43. *regression.* An affected use of the word here: Maximilian's style is apt to be precious.

46–9. Pacue here and later speaks the conventional stage-dialect of the foreigner—a broken English, in which the suffix 'a' and a frequent use of 'de' were the most prominent sounds. Thus in *The Wisedome of Doctor Dodypoll*, 1600, the Doctor, who is a German, talks like the French Pacue: cf. C3ᵛ, 'No? by garr me giu'a de high cōmendation'; C4, 'Me no stay, me go seek'a my faire *Cornelia*'; D2ᵛ, '. . . I will giue a de proue a dee good reason, reguard Monsieur, you no point eate a de meate to daie, you be de empty, begar you be emptie, you be no point vel, you no point vell, be gare you be vere sicke, you no point leaue a de prouision, be gare you stay, spit your nose.' It should be remembered that Jonson did not know French at this date (see *Ep.* cxxxii. 4).

58. *iealousie*, suspicion.

62–4. Perhaps it is merely a coincidence, but Plautus uses the simile in *Captivi*, 116–18.

71. *foole* is addressed to Maximilian 'within'. Pacue turns with a gesture of derision to the door by which Maximilian made his exit.

IV. ii. 4, 5. Compare the similar touch of pathetic suggestion in Euripides' *Ion*, 353–4. Could it have suggested this? The denouement also recalls the Greek play, with the corresponding situation of a parent unconsciously seeking the life of a son and the clue to discovery being a token worn in childhood.

24. *Fortuna*. Horace, *Epod*. iv. 6.

25–31. Cf. *Captivi*, 342–8.

33. *Passe*. Maximilian's order to the soldiers. Cf. *Julius Caesar*, I. ii. 24.

43. *motley*. Quibbles on the 'browne' and 'blacke' of 45.

44. *somewhat in the wind*. Cf. *Com. of Errors*, III. i. 69.

45. *browne study*. The *O.E.D.* quotes as the earliest instance *A manifest detection of the moste vyle and detestable vse of Diceplay* (Percy Society's reprint, no. lxxxviii, p. 6), of which an edition appeared in 1532—'lack of company will soon lead a man into a brown study'.

51. *Cupid . . . in both your eyes*. Dr. Selin quotes John Heywood's 'A praise of his Ladye' in *Tottel's Miscellany*, 1557, Vii,

> In eche of her two cristall eyes,
> Smileth a naked boye'—

and Dekker, *Old Fortunatus*, 1600, B2ᵛ,

> Wish but for beautie, and within thine eyes,
> Two naked Cupids amorously shall swim.

54. *Bridget*. Probably the Irish patron saint, *c*. 452–523, known in England as St. Bride. But St. Bridget of Sweden (*c*. 1302–73), founder of the order of Bridgittines, was known in England from the convent of Syon at Isleworth founded by Henry V in 1415.

57. *turne tippet*. A phrase to denote a complete change of habit or condition. Cf. *Iohn Heywoodes woorkes*, 1562, pt. ii, ch. i, Fijᵛ,

> So turned they their typpets by way of exchaunge,
> From laughyng to lowryng, . . .

Ibid., sig. S, in the *Epigrammes vpon Prouerbs* he writes 14 epigrams on the phrase. Nares quotes *Monsieur Thomas*, II. ii. 4–7:

> ye stand now
> As if ye had worried sheep: you must turn tippet,
> And suddenly, and truely, and discreetly
> Put on the shape of order and humanity.

58. *A packing penny*, literally a penny given at dismissal. Cf. 'packing-penny day', the last day of a fair when cheap bargains could be made.

59. *Cypries Ile.* Venus—'diva potens Cypri'—was specially worshipped at Paphos. There is a quibble on the 'cypress black as any crow', the crêpe which the ladies are wearing.

60. *at the length.* 'At the last' and 'at last' are in common use, but 'at the length' is a rarer form: cf. Proverbs xxix. 21 (1611), 'He that delicately bringeth vp his seruant from a child, shall haue him become his sonne at the length.'

IV. iii. This scene is interesting as giving in a rough and simple form what Jonson afterwards elaborated so tediously in *Cynthia's Revells*, II. iii and III. v. Compare B. Rich, *Faultes Faults, And nothing else but Faultes*, 1606, f. 6:

> 'But see here a companie now presenting themselues, that I cannot say are affected, but I think are rather infected with too much courtesie; you shall know them by their salutations. For first with the kisse on the hand, the bodie shall be bowed downe to the ground: then the armes shall bee cast out, like one were dauncing the old Antike, not a word but, at your seruice, at your commaund, at your pleasure: this olde protestation, *Yours, in the way of honestie*, is little cared for: euerie Gull was woont to haue it at his tongues end, but now it is forgotten. And these *Flowers of courtesie*, as they are full of affectation, so they are no lesse formall in their speeches, full of fustian phrases, many times deliuering such sentences as doe bewray and lay open their maisters ignorance: and they are so frequent with the kisse on the hand, that a word shall not passe their mouthes, till they haue clapt their fingers ouer their lippes.'

10–12. For Onion's object in looking for Valentine see IV. v. 32 foll.

16. *your Cousan.* So Cob in *E.M.I.* III. iv. 54 addresses a 'cob-herring' as 'My princely couz'.

S.dd. 17, 22. *Vnder the arme. The shoulder.* Probably to be explained by Puttenham's remark (*The Arte of English Poesie*, 1589, ed. Arber, p. 292) that it is the custom 'In Fraunce, Italie, and Spaine to embrace ouer the shoulder, vnder the armes, at the very knees, according to the superiors degree'. Perhaps the embrace at the knees is the trick that 'cannot be cleanly done abroad' (42). But the first might, as Gifford suggested, refer to 'making a profound bow, and conveying the hat with the right hand under the left arm while perpendicular to the floor'; the second might refer to throwing the cloak over the shoulder. Cf. Massinger and Field, *The Fatall Dowry*, II. ii (1632, D4ᵛ), 'A husband in these dayes is but a cloake, . . . Sometimes you may weare him on your shoulder, now & then vnder your arme.' The challenger in *C.R.* V. iii. 87 is told, 'your cloke on your halfe-shoulder falling'.

80. *time was . . . be.* The speech of the Brazen Head in the story of Friar Bacon. Cf. *E.M.I.* I. iv. 63–4.

IV. iv. 1. *Iasper.* A spelling found only here; it leads up to the play on the name in line 17. Cf. I. viii. 22–5, '*Iuniper*. . . . a sweete youth';

E.M.O. Induction, 37, where Mitis, the gentle, says to Asper, 'be not like your name'; *Cat.* II. 348, 'my FVLVIA lookes, like her bright name'; and *S.S.* I. iv. I, 'Welcome bright *Clarion*, and sweet Mellifleur.'

14. *the Lady*, i.e. Aurelia.

19, 20. *mine eyes Haue euer tasted.* Cf. *E.M.I.* IV. vii. I, 'Did your eyes euer tast the like clowne of him?'

IV. v. I. *songs and sonets.* The phrase originated in 1557 with *Tottel's Miscellany*, which was entitled *Songes and Sonettes, written by the right honorable Lorde Henry Howard late Earle of Surrey, and other.* Here and in *Poet.* I. i. 5 used for 'verse', but perhaps with a shade of depreciation: cf. the contemptuous use in *E.M.I.* IV. iii. 17.

4. *Academy*, deep study.

7. *downe the wind*, literally of a worthless hawk dispatched along the course of the wind to get rid of her, hence a phrase for decline or ruin.

13. *super nagulum*, like the German *die Nagelprobe trinken*, to leave no heel-taps, explained by Nashe in a marginal note to *Pierce Pennilesse*, 1592, E4ʳ, '*Drinking super nagulum, a deuise of drinking new come out of Fraunce; which is, after a man hath turnd vp the bottom of the cup, to drop it on his naile, & make a pearle with that is left; which, if it shed, & he cannot make stand on, by reason thers too much, he must drinke againe for his pennaunce.*'

19. *surquedry.* Cf. *L.R.* 31, 'all licence of surquedry'. Chaucer explained the word in *The Persones Tale*—'Presumpcion, is whan a man undertaketh an empryse that him oghte nat do, or elles that he may nat do; and that is called Surquidrie' (*C.T.* i. 403, ed. Skeat). Hart notes from Harvey 'Surfeited with pleasure's surquedrie' (i. 297), 'toad-swoln in surquidry' (ib. 291), and the adjective 'surquidrous' (ii. 101).

28. *ad vnguem* = *super nagulum* (13), *vpsie freeze* = *op zijn Friesch*, in Frisian, or Dutch, fashion, as in line 13. Cf. *Alch.* IV. vi. 23, '*vpsee Dutch*'.

32. *Valentine.* A clear proof that Valentine originally performed the part that is assigned to Antonio Balladino in the text of I. ii. 14, 15.

37. *handkerchier.* 'Hand-kercher', *C.R.* IV. iii. 26, *D. is A.* IV. iv. 89; 'handkercher', *B.F.* III. v. 180.

40. *O in diebus illis.* A catch-phrase for the past, 'once upon a time'. Hart notes that Harvey used it in 1589: 'But old Aristotle was a deepe politician *in diebus illis*' (ii. 191). Cf. Nashe, *The Terrors of the Night*, 1594, '*In diebus illis*, when *Corineus* and *Gogmagog* were little boyes' (*Works*, ed. McKerrow, i. 367), and *Nashes Lenten Stuffe*, 1599 (ib. iii. 188); and J. M., *A Health to the Gentlemanly profession of Seruingmen*, 1598, F1ᵛ and G2ᵛ. McKerrow suggests for its origin Genesis vi. 4, 'Gigantes autem erant super terram in diebus illis.' It is found as late as 1642 in *A Discovery of divers sorts of Asses*, A2, where Smithfield is the speaker, 'It is well known that *in Diebus illis*, in former times, I was a very dirty myry *Smithfield*.'

44. *curuet.* Hart compares Harvey, iii. 35, 'corvettest and showest

thy crankes among a company of valorous Captaines, whose stirrop thou art not worthy to hold', and he quotes Nashe's gibe at Harvey—'some of his nimblest Pommados and Sommersets'—in *Haue with you to Saffron-walden*, address to the Reader, *ad fin.*, as explaining the gibe in Marston's *Scourge of Villany*, xi. 99–103:

> Room for Torquatus, that ne'er oped his lip
> But in prate of *pommado reversa*,
> Of the nimble tumbling Angelica.
> Now on my soul his very intellect
> Is nought but a curvetting sommerset.
> *(Notes and Queries, 11 April 1903.)*

prognosticat. 'A favorite term with Gabriel Harvey, as well as with his brother Richard, the almanack-maker'—Hart.

48. *Meridian slaue.* A comic adaptation of 'meridian devil', the 'daemonium meridianum' of Psalm xci. 6.

50. *tolerable.* Cf. Dogberry in *Much Ado*, III. iii. 33, and Heywood, *The Fayre Mayde of the Exchange*, 1607, G4. *Much Ado* dates *c.* 1599.

IV. vi. 9. *turne turtle.* The type of constancy. Selin quotes Lyly's *Euphues* (*Works*, ed. Bond, ii, p. 54), 'the Turtle hauing lost her mate, wandreth alone, ioying in nothing, but in solitarinesse'. Cf. *S.S.* I. iv. 65–6.

11. *And* = 'an', 'if', as the colon after 'die' in line 10 shows.

13, 14. Cf. *E.M.O.* II. iv. 133–4, 'blind *Fortune* still Bestowes her gifts on such as cannot vse them'.

IV. vii. 2. *Hay my loue, O my loue . . . 4. trip and goe.* 'Trip and go' was the title of a morris dance; for the tune see Chappell's *Old English Popular Music*, 1893, i. 309. Nashe alludes to it in the preface to the pirated edition of *Astrophel and Stella*, 1591: 'Indeede, to say the truth, my stile is somewhat heauie gated, and cannot daunce trip and goe so liuely, with oh my loue, ah my loue, all my loues gone, as other Sheepheards that haue beene fooles in the Morris time out of minde.' 'Ales trype and go' is a character in *Jacke Jugeler*; and the phrase became proverbial. In Munday's *The Death of Robert, Earle of Huntingdon*, 1601, K, Brand calls girls who refuse their lover's advances

> these no forsooths,
> These pray awayes, these trip and goes, these tits.

12. *hity tity.* The muddled Juniper seems to mean 'bo-peep'.

19. *Horizons*, a confusion with 'orisons' in the sense of 'entreaties'.

21. *crotchets*, mental twists. Cf. *Volp.* v. xi. 16.

28. *Radamant.* 'Probably Juniper means Rodomont', says Hart, who quotes from Harvey, 'To bate Sir Rodomont an ace' (ii. 296), 'Such another Rodomont' (ib. 225). Query, a distortion of 'Bradamante' (*Alch.* II. iii. 225). But there is no need to alter the text: in

the company of Machiavelli Rhadamanthus will serve. 'Machiavel is frequent in Harvey's pages' (Hart).

40. *march paine wench.* Cf. *C.R.* iv. i. 132, 'the very march-pane of the court'. *Marchpaine*, marzipan, as the type of something delicious.

42. *apple-squire*, a harlot's attendant. Cf. *E.M.I.* iv. x. 57.

43–4. *Sweetheart . . . bag pudding.* Cf. Day, *Humour out of Breath*, 1608, ii. i, C4, '*Pa.* Farewell sweet heart. *Exit.* | *Boy.* Gad a mercy, bagpudding.' Halliwell quotes Howell, *English Proverbs*, p. 6, 'Sweetheart and bag-pudding'.

52. *conni-catching*, cheating. Cf. *E.M.I.* iii. i. 181.

iv. viii. From the fourth act of the *Aulularia*. Euclio, hiding his gold in the temple of Fides, discovers that Lyconides' slave has overheard him; he searches the slave—an episode which Jonson has improved. He then removes his gold in order to hide it in the Grove of Silvanus; the slave, again overhearing, runs on ahead, hides in a tree, and secures the treasure.

12–22. *Aulularia*, 634–5, 640–2, 646–7:

> *Euc.* Redde huc sis. *Lyconidis Servus.* Quid tibi vis reddam ? *Euc.*
>   Rogas ?
> *L. S.* Nil equidem tibi apstuli. . . .
>   *Euc.* Ostende huc manus.
> *L. S.* Em tibi, ostendi, eccas. *Euc.* Video. Age ostende etiam ter-
>   tiam.
>   . . . *Euc.* Agedum, excutedum pallium.
> *L. S.* Tuo arbitratu. *Euc.* Ne inter tunicas habeas.

25. *not true Ortographie*? Originally a legal phrase: cf. *S.W.* v. iv. 201–3, and Chapman, *May-Day*, 1611, ii. v, '*Quin.* I haue examin'd the particulars of your bill Master *Taylor*, and I finde them true *Orthographie*.' Hart notes this as a Harvey word, along with 'inviolable', 'predicament', and 'intimate'—'all as yet pedantic terms'.

35. *bombard slops*, the 'huge tumbrell-slop' of *E.M.I.* ii. ii. 24, the wide puffed breeches in fashion under Elizabeth. The 'bombard' was (1) an early cannon, (2) a large vessel of liquor, perhaps resembling it in shape. Falstaff is jeered at as a 'huge Bombard of Sacke' (*1 Henry IV*, ii. iv. 436).

73–4. The usual quibble on the gold coins called angels in use from Edward IV to Charles I, having the figure of the archangel Michael.

79. *fortune my foe.* Also alluded to *G.M.* 883. The words are printed in the *Bagford Ballads*, ed. Ebsworth, iv, pp. 962–3. For the tune see Chappell, ed. 1893, i, p. 77; the metrical laments of great criminals were sung to it.

78. *my soule. Aulularia*, 181, 'Nunc domum properare propero, nam egomet sum hic, animus domi est.'

iv. ix. 3. *panurgo.* Cf. Bobadill's 'GARGANTVA breech', *E.M.I.* ii. ii. 25. The allusion is not to Rabelais's own work but to the early English chapbooks about Gargantua, e.g. *Gargantua his prophesie*, entered on the Stationers' Register 6 April 1592, and the *History of Gargantua*, 4 December 1594, as well as the earlier references in Edward Deering's letter prefixed to *A Briefe and necessary Instruction*, 1572, and Captain Cox's Library in *Robert Laneham's Letter*, 1575 (Halliwell, note on *As You Like It*, III. ii. 210).

7. *contagious*, a malapropism for 'outragious', perhaps as in Middleton, *Blurt, Master-Constable*, II. ii. 298–300 (ed. Bullen), '*Imp.* Fie, fie, fie, fie, fie; though I hate his company, I would not have my house to abuse his countenance; no, no, no, be not so contagious.'

23. *inexorable.* Cf. *E.M.O.* v. iii. 70.

36. *stigmaticall.* Cf. Harvey, III. 41: 'Thou will be cosmoligized, if thou beest catcht here, for calling our Masters of Arte stigmatical, that is, burnt with a hot Iron' (Hart). For the misuse of the word cf. *Dick of Devonshire*, IV. i (ed. Bullen, p. 61), 'as you & your brother *Manuell* lay in the high Bed, & I trondling underneath, I heard one of you talke most stigmatically in his sleepe—most horriferously'.

37. *go in my foot-cloth*, literally to ride on a horse caparisoned with a large and richly ornamented cloth—a sign of rank. Cf. *Volp.* I. ii. 105, *Und.* xv. 107.

39. *cullison*, cognizance, often of silver, worn on the sleeve of the servant's coat. Cf. *E.M.O.* I. ii. 145, and the Stationers' preface to the First Quarto of *Othello*, 1622, '*To set forth a booke without an Epistle, were like to the old English prouerbe*, A blew coat without a badge.' So too one of the stock jokes of the vulgar clown quoted in the First Quarto of *Hamlet* in the player scene (ix. 35, *Cambridge Shakespeare*, ix, p. 727) is 'my coate wants a cullison'.

41. *harrot*, herald. Cf. *E.M.I.* I. iv. 16, *E.M.O.* III. iv. 48.

47. *God boy ye*, one of the various colloquial shortenings of 'goodbye'—'God be wy you', 'God b'uy ye', 'God b'y you', 'God b'wy'.

IV. x. 4. *subiect of your mirthe.* *Capt.* 656, 'Ita mihi stolido susum vorsum os subleuere offuciis.'

30. *Amurath.* Cf. the contemporary allusion in *2 Henry IV*, v. ii. 48. Amurath IV, on his accession in 1574, invited his brothers to a feast and had them all strangled.

IV. xi. 43. *sets.* A euphonic form of the second person singular, also found in *E.M.I.* II. v. 112 'insist's'; *M.L.* IV. viii. 21, 'eates'; *Ep.* lviii. 5, 'disioints'. The Shakespearian instances are collected in Abbott, § 340. There is an interesting recognition of the idiom in P. G.'s (P. Greenwood's?) *Grammatica Anglicana*, 1594, p. 15, '*De Verbo.* Contractionibus fere utimur in Carmine. Præsens. 1. *Hate.* 2. *Hatest.* 3. *Hateth.* . . . Contract 2 *Hates*, 3 *Hates*.'

45–7. *Captivi*, 681–2:

> HE. At cum cruciatu maxumo id factumst tuo.
> TY. Dum ne ob male facta peream, parvi existumo.

70. *engraue it on his burgonet.* Maximilian borrows a tragic phrase in order to be impressive. Cf. *The First Part of the Contention betwixt the two famous Houses of Yorke and Lancaster*, 1594, v. i. 113–15:

> *Clif.* I am resolu'd to beare a greater storme,
> Then any thou canst coniure vp to day,
> And that ile write vpon thy Burgonet;

and *The First part of the Tragicall raigne of Selimus*, 1594, H4ᵛ (ll. 2420–1, Malone reprint)—

> But we shall soone with our fine tempered swords,
> Engraue our prowesse on their bu⟨r⟩ganets.

78. *speare*, an irregular form of spire, perhaps influenced by the spelling of 'spear', a lance (*O.E.D.*).

v. i. 14. *Rooke*, simpleton, as in II. vii. 54, *E.M.I.* I. v. 88. There is a quibble with 'wethercocke', l. 15. The 'kooke' of Q. is impossible: either a 'k' was accidentally duplicated by the printer or a form of 'R' in seventeenth-century script, bearing some resemblance to 'k', was misread.

24. *bald french crownes*. The same quibble as in *E.M.O.* II. i. 113–18.

36. *behind S. Foyes.* Evidently suggested by Euclio's hiding his gold in the temple of Fides: 'Nunc hoc mihi factust optumum ut ted auferam, aula, in Fidei fanum' (*Aul.* 582–3).

39. *geere*, matter in hand.

v. ii. The belief in fairies made such a trick as is here played on Jaques possible: cf. S. S., *The Honest Lawyer*, 1616, C, where Valentine, plotting to rob Gripe the usurer, says, 'I haue often heard the gripulous Dotard talke of Fairies: and how rich the house proues that they haunt. . . . Two or three nights we'le scatter some small peeces of silver, till opportunitie plumpe our proiect'; ib. F2ᵛ, '*Gripe.* These three or foure nights I ha' bene haunted with Fairies: they dance about my bed-side, poppe in a peece of gold betweene the sheetes, scatter here and there fragments of siluer, in euery corner. I keepe my chamber swept, cleane linnen, fire to warme them euery night. I was at first afraide, they had beene spirits; now I see, they are good harmlesse Fairies.'

v. iii. 17. *when can you tell?* The ironic use of 'when' found in *1 Henry IV*, II. i. 37–9: Gadshill tries to borrow the lanterns of the carriers: 'I pray thee, lend me thine. *Second Carrier.* Ay, when? canst tell. Lend me thy lantern, quoth he? marry, I'll see thee hanged first.'

v. iv. 7. *faire fethered . . . birds.* The word 'angel' has twice done duty for a quibble on the name of the coins (IV. viii. 73–4, v. ii. 5), and 'angel' is used for bird in the fanciful mythologizing of poets of the time. Cf. *N.I.* v. i. 23, and Fletcher, *The Spanish Curate*, III. iv. 13–15 (ed. Waller, II. 105):

O my sweet soul, I have brought thee golden birds home,
Birds in abundance: I have done strange wonders:
There's more a hatching too.

The Coxcomb, II. i, where the Tinker and his trull rob Viola: 'look in the Pockets *Doll*, there may be birds. *Dor.* They are flown, a pox go with them' (ibid. VIII. 330).

Red-brested is due to the old phrase 'red gold'.

12. *comes.* Cf. IV. xi. 43.

19. *Hienna*, hyena, described in a marginal note of the Geneva Bible on Ecclesiasticus xiii. 18 as 'a wilde beaste that counterfaiteth the voyce of men, and so entiseth them out of their houses and deuoureth them'.

v. vi. 1. *catso.* A pointless exclamation: for a different use see *E.M.O.* II. i. 20.

11. *addicted.* Hart notes that 'addicted to Theory' is one of Harvey's phrases pilloried by Nashe in *Foure Letters Confuted* (*Works*, ed. McKerrow, i. 316).

16. *princocks*, coxcomb.

31. *A french boy.* Cf. *E.H.* I. i. 6, and *Sir Gyles Goosecappe*, 1606, ed. Bang and Brotanek, ll. 2626–7:

> Three things there be, that shood thine anger swage,
> An English mastife, and a fine french page.

34. *crusado*, a Portuguese silver coin, worth about 2s. 4d.

35. *imbecell*, the same word as 'embezzle'. Here = 'entice away from service'. The erroneous attempt to connect the word with Lat. *imbecillare* seems to have been made in the sixteenth century: see *O.E.D.*

39. *portmantu.* Onion means 'portague', another Portuguese coin, 'the great crusado' which was of gold. Harrison, *Description of England*, II. xxv (ed. Furnivall, i. 364), notes that it was 'a peece verie solemnelie kept of diuerse'.

47. *aparel . . . forget himself.* Perhaps proverbial: cf. the anecdote of John Heywood, *Conv. Dru.* 573–7.

52. *Speake legibly.* Repeated *E.M.I.* I. iv. 83.

v. vii. 9. *We*, i.e. 'Oui'. Cf. *Englishmen for my Money*, I. i, 'Pigs and Frenchmen speak one language, *awee, awee.*'

19. *exhibition*, allowance. Cf. *E.M.O.* II. v. 27.

27. *semitary*, scimitar.

30. *ile stand to nothing.* Cf. Freeman, *Rubbe, and A great Cast*, 1614, C3ᵛ, Epigram 39:

> Starke drunke, *Demetrius* word is: *Hee'l stand too't,*
> When he hath neither vse of hand nor foot,
> But iostles this, and shoulders vp that wall,
> And stands to nothing, yet hee'l stand to all.

35–40. Repeated in *E.M.I.* I. iii. 75–90.

v. viii. Compare the similar scene in *The Two Gentlemen of Verona.*

7. *stale,* decoy. Cf. *Volp.* IV. v, 85, *Cat.* III. 723.

9. *like a puppet,* showing no independence, colourless.

35. *euented,* found vent. Cf. *K. Ent.* 324, 'the apt euenting of her heat'.

48. *To take into,* to strike into. An extension of such a use as

> then no Planets strike,
> No Faiery takes   (*Hamlet,* I. i. 162–3.)

and

> strike her yong bones
> You taking Ayres, with Lamenesse.
>   (*King Lear,* II. iv. 161–2.)

61. *Like the rude clapper.* Cf. *Much Ado,* III. ii. 12–14, 'he hath a heart, as sound as a bell, and his tongue is the clapper, for what his heart thinkes, his tongue speakes'.

v. xi. 15. *hares eyes.* Cf. the Greek proverb λαγὼς καθεύδων of a person feigning sleep, and Chapman, *An Epicede,* 1612, D, '*Frantick Distemper*; & *Hare-eyd vnrest*', with a marginal note, 'Out of the property of the Hare that neuer shuts her eyes sleeping'.

v. xii. 28. So literally in Plautus, *Capt.* 980. The form 'twentith' is found occasionally in Jonson's text.

30. *three and foure.* The age is given as two years in I. ix. 64–5.

35. *tablet.* For the syllabic *l,* cf. 'doublets' *Alch.* III. ii. 81.

52. *Drownds. O.E.D.* illustrates from Palsgrave, 1530, 'I drownde, *je noye*.'

54–6. No hint is given of this in the play. Jonson in his later work would not have allowed an isolated touch of this kind.

88. *starting hols,* ways of escape. Cf. *Disc.* 1338.

90. *Ill gotten goods* . . . Plautus, *Poenulus,* 844, 'Male partum male disperit.'

102. *Your cake is dow.* A proverb of spoilt hope: cf. *The Taming of the Shrew,* v. i. 125.

v. xiii. 31. *helogabolus.* It is worth noting that on 19 June 1594 'the lyfe and Death of Heliogabilus' was licensed on the Stationers' Register as an interlude to John Danter.

62. *splendidious,* Hart's correction. This form occurs *E.M.O.* II. ii. 79, *C.R.* v. x. 43; and 'splendidous' in *Volp.* II. ii. 80.

65. *passe not of,* care not for, regard not.

57. *March faire.* Cf. Dekker, *Satiromastix,* 1602, D2ᵛ: '*Tuc.* Come Iacke. *Dem.* Nay Captaine stay, we are of your band. *Tuc.* March faire then.'

a faire March . . . Cf. John Heywood, *The play of the weather,* 1565? D1:

> And now to mind there is one olde prouerbe come
> One bushell of marche dust is worth a kyngs raunsome.

Still current in the form 'a peck of March dust'.

EVERY MAN IN HIS HUMOUR

PREFATORY NOTE

THERE are several contemporary references to *Every Man in his Humour*. They are interesting as showing that the play had made its mark. A Puritan expressed his disapproval of it at once. Richard Schilders, a Protestant refugee, who had settled in England and become a member of the Stationers' Company, returned to the Low Countries in 1580 and issued from his press at Middelburg a number of Puritan books. Among them was *Th'overthrow of Stage-Playes*, 1599 and 1600; it included the controversial letters of the Oxford scholar, John Rainoldes. People who 'can hardly be drawen to spare a penie in the Church', he complains, 'can yet willingly and chearefullie afoord both pence and testers' to see a play. He attacks the *Comedy of Humours*, appealing even to those 'that haue not bene afraied of late dayes to bring vpon the Stage the very sober countenances, graue attire, modest and matronelike gestures & speaches of men & women to be laughed at as a scorne and reproch to the world. . . . Well to heale, if it may be, or at least, to correct the bad humour of such humorists as these (who in their discouery of humours doe withall fouly discouer their own shame and wretchedness to the world) here is now laied before thee (good Reader) a most excellent remedie and receipt, if thou canst be so happie to make thy profite of it.'

In 1601 'W. I.', a writer not certainly identified,[1] published *The Whipping of the Satyre*, a poem on three censorious critics of the age whom he dubs 'the Satyrist, Epigrammatist, and Humorist'. The Satirist is Marston, the Humorist is equally clear, but the Epigrammatist is doubtful; perhaps he is Edward Guilpin. In the prose introduction W. I. pungently attacks them as 'Asses of Coram', who supposed they 'had sate of a commission, *ad Jnquirendum de moribus*', and took upon them 'to taxe all the world, like Augustus Cesar':

> . . . it is not long since, that a friend of mine being merily disposed, told me for great newes, that there were three persons in the Realme, had vndertaken a notable peece of trauell, at their owne costs and charges. Whither, said I? Marry, quoth he, to discouer a whole Iland, and the maners of the people, bidding me gesse, who these three were. I, after a

[1] He seems to have been a Cambridge man, judging from allusions in his book and in the replies to it; Dr. Brinsley Nicholson suggested William Ingram, see vol. i, p. 29 n. A. Davenport (*Poems of J. Hall*, p. xxxiii) has suggested John Weever with the initials reversed.

long demurre, thought (God forgiue me) that the one should be Sir Frauncis Drake, the other Sir Martin Frobysher, and the third Captaine Candish: but then the remembrance of their deaths, was the death of my opinion: at last I told him, I could not tell, demaunding to what Countrie they were bound, and who might be their Pilote? Faith (quoth hee) their Pilote is better for iudgement, then euer Pontius Pilate was, and for experience the best in the world. The diuell as soone (quoth I.) At that he smiled (vnmasking the Iest) and told mee, it was the diuell indeed, that had playd the Pilote, in guiding these three vessels of iniquitie, the *Satyrist, Epigrammatist,* and the *Humorist,* to discouer and lay open the infirmities of their Countrie men. (Sigg. A2 ᵛ—A3.)

W. I. then addresses the writers individually: this is the advice he gives to Jonson:

Now by your leaue, *Monsieur Humorist,* you that talke of mens humours and dispositions, as though you had bene a Constellation-setter seuen yeres in the firmament, or had cast account of euery mans natiuitie with the starres: but if I were as the Astronomers, I would call you into question for it, seeing you haue so abused their Art. But, had you bene but so meane a Philosopher, as ⟨to⟩ haue knowne, that *mores sequuntur humores,* you would questionles haue made better humours, if it had bene but to better our maners, and not in stead of a morall medicine, to haue giuen them a mortall poyson: but I consider of you, as of a yonger brother: you wanted this same *multis nimium,* and *nulli satis* coyne (a goodyere of it) and therefore *opus & vsus* put you to such a pinch, that you made sale of your Humours to the Theater, and there plaid Pee boh with the people in your humour, then out of your humour. I doe not blame you for this: for though you were guilty of many other things, yet I dare say, you were altogether without guilt at that time, notwithstanding I suppose you would haue written for loue, and not for money: but I see you are one of those that if a man can finde in his purse to giue them presently, they can finde in their hearts to loue him euerlastingly: for now adaies *Æs in præsenti perfectum format amorem.*

England is depicted as an earthly paradise under Elizabeth, but two majestic sisters, Church and Commonwealth, complain of the unfilial conduct of three of their sons, who have been false to their baptismal vows and their upbringing and have changed their names:

> Each to his name his disposition fram'd,
> *Sat.* rough, severe: *Ep.* skip-Iacke iester like:
> *Hu.* with newfangled neuterisme enflam'd,
> Al naught.

'Neuterism' is no doubt intended for 'neoterism' in the sense of 'novelty'; it may be a misprint. The charge is interesting: it is the earliest recognition of the fact that Jonson had created a new type in comedy.

Sharp correction is recommended as the only cure for Marston: then the corrector may

> take the other two apart,
> And shewe how lewdly they their time mispent,
> Who being of a milder-moulded heart,
> May happily in Christian sort relent.

W. I. offers himself for the task, deals first with Marston, alluding to his *Satires* of 1599, and writes a lengthy admonition *In Epigram-matistam & Humoristam*, which concludes:

> It seemes your brother *Satyre* and ye twayne,
> Plotted three wayes to put the Diuell downe;
> One should outrayle him by inuectiue vaine,
> One all to flout him like a countrey clowne;
> And one in action, on a stage out-face,
> And play vpon him to his great disgrace.
>
> You *Humorist*, if it be true I heare,
> (*d*) An action thus against the Diuell brought,
> Sending your humours to each Theater,
> To serue the writ that ye had gotten out.
> (*e*) That Mad-cap yet superiour praise doth win.
> Who out of hope euen casts his cap at sin.
>   (*d*) *Against the booke of Humours.*
>   (*e*) *Pasquils Mad-cap.*   (Sig. F3ᵛ.)

Two anonymous replies to W. I. were issued in the same year—*No Whippinge nor trippinge: but a kinde friendly Snippinge*, entered on the Stationers' Register on 11 August, and *The Whipper of the Satyre his pennance in a white Sheete: Or, The Beadles confutation*, registered on 6 November. The latter is a colourless retort, with which Marston's vigorous pen has been unwisely credited. The first has been plausibly assigned to Breton; in style and method it closely resembles Breton's acknowledged work. The author deprecates all this satirical writing, and especially personal attacks. He incidentally puts in a plea for 'poore Mad-cap', who, as he says, was never personal.

One other critic has left us a vivid glimpse of the arch-humorist, as he appeared to his enemies or his victims. Dekker's *Satiromastix* was hurriedly brought out in 1601 as a counterblast to Jonson's *Poetaster*. This is how a captain in the play lectures Horace, the character in which Jonson impersonates himself:

A Gentleman or an honest Cittizen, shall not Sit in your pennie-bench Theaters, with his Squirrell by his side cracking nuttes; nor sneake into a Tauerne with his Mermaid; but he shall be Satyr'd, and Epigram'd vpon, and his humour must run vp o' th Stage; you'll ha *Euery Gentleman in's humour* and *Euery Gentleman out on's humour*: wee that are heades of Legions and Bandes, and feare none but these same shoulder-clappers,[1] shall feare you, you Serpentine rascall. (H2ʳ.)

At the end of the play Horace, who has been tossed in a blanket and whipped, meekly receives instructions on his future conduct:

Besides, you must forsweare to venter on the stage, when your Play is ended, and to exchange curtzies, and complements with Gallants in the Lordes roomes, to make all the house rise vp in Armes, and to cry that's Horace, that's he, that's he, that pennes and purges Humours and diseases. (M1ʳ.)

Barnaby Riche, in his *Faultes Faults, And nothing else but Faultes*, 1606, f. 4ʳ included a number of pen portraits which show clearly the influence of Jonson, and he made an indirect acknowledgement of his debt: 'As for the humorous', he said, 'they haue beene alredie brought to the Stage, where they haue plaide their parts, *Euerie man in his humour.*'

THE DATE OF THE REVISION

The question has been discussed in our introduction (vol. i, pp. 332–5). A few points are added here.

Could the original version printed in the Quarto of 1601 have been placed, unchanged, at the head of the plays in the 1616 Folio? The English setting, the countless improvements in the text, the Prologue with its air of mature conviction and ripe experience transform the play; in tone and texture it harmonizes completely with the later work.

We believe Jonson to have been at work on it in or about the year 1612. In 1609 in *Epicoene* he had laid the scene in London and discarded the convention of a foreign setting; in 1610 in the prologue to *The Alchemist* he advertises this literary innovation.

Our *Scene* is *London*, 'cause we would make knowne,
No countries mirth is better then our owne,
No clime breeds better matter, for your whore,
Bawd, squire, impostor, many persons more,
Whose manners, now call'd humours, feed the stage.

The choice of an English setting made the characters more lifelike— an important point when they were types of humour—and this closer reality is reflected in the new version of *Every Man in his Humour*.

The last play included in the 1616 Folio was *Catiline*, acted in

[1] Bailiffs.

1611. *Bartholomew Fair*, first acted on 31 October 1614, was not included. Entries in the Stationers' Register of other work near these dates are:

20 September 1610. *The Silent Woman*, entered to John Browne and John Busby, junior.

3 October 1610. *The Alchemist*, to Walter Burre.

15 May 1612. The *Epigrams*, to John Stepneth.

28 September 1612. *The Silent Woman*, transferred to Walter Burre.

20 June 1615. *Certayne Masques at the Court never yet printed*, assigned to William Stansby (i.e. all the Masques after *The Masque of Queens* published in 1609).

The Alchemist was published in 1612 by Burre. Gifford speaks of a 1612 Quarto of *The Silent Woman*, though no copy of this has been traced. Burre had previously published *Every Man in his Humour* and *Cynthia's Revels* in 1601, *Sejanus* in 1605, *Volpone* in 1607, and *Catiline* in 1611. Why did he keep back *The Alchemist* and *The Silent Woman*? Did he hold them over for the collected edition, and then resolve to publish them when Stansby failed to make headway with it? No separate edition of the *Epigrams* is known, but the poet William Drummond enters 'Ben Jhonsons epigrams' among the 'bokes red be me anno 1612'. Contemporary allusions in the *Epigrams* are innumerable, but none can be dated later than 1612, and Jonson's description of this collection as 'the ripest of my studies' means that it contained new work and that any old work in it had been scrupulously revised.

If Jonson was actively preparing the Folio for the printer in 1612, when did it go to press? Stansby is not likely to have begun the printing of it so early. He was not the man to turn out raw and hasty work, and he had his hands full at the time with another folio, which occupied his presses for three years—Raleigh's *Historie of the World*, licensed for publication on 15 April 1611, but not issued till late in 1614. The registration of the *Masques* in 1615 shows that he was free to go forward with the Jonson Folio, and possibly shows the point which he had then reached in the printing.

On 6 January 1612 the masque of *Love Restored* was performed at Court; the next masques were *The Irish Masque* on 29 December 1613, *The Golden Age Restored* on 6 January 1615, and *Mercury Vindicated from the Alchemists at Court* on 1 January 1616. His only play was *Bartholomew Fair* in 1614. This is all the output for the period of his life when his art had fully ripened. Was the zenith of his career marked by a lapse into sterility? The editing of the Folio (with a number of corrections in the earlier plays, *Every Man out of his Humour, Cynthia's Revels, Poetaster,* and *Sejanus,* over which he worked carefully), the polishing and the completion of the book of *Epigrams,* and the recast of *Every Man in his Humour* would explain his inactivity just when to all appearance he was idlest.

THE QUARTO OF 1601

The mottoes on the title-page, *Quod non dant proceres* and *Haud tamen inuideas vati,* are from Juvenal, *Satire* vii, ll. 90 and 93.

I. i. 13. *Académies.* The regular pronunciation at this date: cf. *Alch.* III. iv. 43; *D. is A.* II. viii. 20; *N.I.* I. iii. 57, v. 37; *S.S.* III. i. 3.

51. *Buzzard* ('Kite' Folio). Nares quotes *Comenii Janua Linguarum,* 1662, § 146, '*Between hawk and buzzard,* means between a good thing and a bad of the same kind: the hawk being the true sporting bird, the buzzard a heavy lazy fowl of the same species.' So Dryden, *The Hind and the Panther,* iii. 1121–3 (of the Buzzard):

> Of small Renown, 'tis tru; for, not to lye,
> We call him but a *Hawk* by courtesie.

174–5. *Poet Nuntius.* The letter is rewritten in the Folio, but contains, in a different context, the phrase 'Poet-maior, *o' the towne*' (I. ii. 84). Probably a fling at Antony Munday, satirized in *The Case is Altered* (I. ii. 29, 30) as '*Pageant* Poet to the City of *Millaine*'.

I. ii. 22. *halfe an houre ago.* At II. iii. 43, the interval is 'some houre'; this need not be inconsistent with the text, but Jonson suppressed the reference to the hour, perhaps because he anticipated misconstruction.

24. *with heaue and ho.* An old refrain found in Skelton, *The Barge of Courte,* 250–2:

> Holde vp the helme, loke vp, and lete God stere:
> I wolde be mery, what wynde that euer blowe,
> Heue and how rumbelow, row the bote, Norman, rowe.

The reference is to a 'roundell or songe' made by the watermen in praise of John Norman, Lord Mayor of London, in the thirty-second year of Henry VI, who went to Westminster by water. The phrase *with heaue and ho* is a survival of this sailor chorus.

Cf. Marlowe, *King Edward II,* 1598, D3 (II. ii. 188), quoting Fabyan's *Chronycle*:

> Maids of England, so⟨r⟩e may you mourne
> For your lemmons you haue lost, at Bannocks borne,
> With a heaue and a ho.

55–7. The pun on 'stile' is an old one: see Chaucer, *The Squire's Tale* (*C.T.,* F. 105–6),

> Al be it that I kan nat sowne his stile,
> Ne kan nat clymben over so heigh a style.

Cf. Dekker, *Satiromastix*, 1602, C4. *Asinius* of a book he is reading, 'The whoorson made me meete with a hard stile in two or three places as I went ouer him. *Dem.* I beleeue thee, for they had need to be very lowe & easie stiles of wit that thy braines goe ouer.' Shakespeare has the quibble in *Much Ado*, v. ii. 6–7, and Heywood in *Love's Mistris*, II. ii. It is noticeable that in a few passages stock jokes of this kind, found in the Quarto, are eliminated in the Folio text: e.g. III. iv. 85–7, v. iii. 255–8.

117. *Catso.* Cf. *C. is A.* v. vi. 1.

I. iii. 67. *abhominable.* This spelling was due to an absurd etymology, *ab homine*, which Jonson was too good a scholar to accept. In *E.M.O.* III. ix. 123 *C.R.* Induction, 124, and *Poet.* v. iii. 83, the Quartos spell 'abhominable', but the Folio, as in the present passage, corrects to 'abominable'.

75. *By the life of Pharaoh.* Modified in the Folio to 'the foot of PHARAOH', in order to avoid a direct Biblical quotation. The oath was popular judging from plays, e.g. *The History of the Trial of Chivalry*, 1605, I3ᵛ 'Bow. Not we, by this beard: not we, by the life of Pharo'; Dekker, *The Shoomakers' Holiday*, 1600, B3ᵛ, 'by the life of Pharo, a braue resolute swordsman' (so D2ᵛ and H4); Dekker and Webster, *West-ward Hoe*, 1607, H1ᵛ, 'Play, life of Pharao play.'

84 s.d. *Bobadilla discouers himselfe: on a bench.* The Folio corrects 'Bobad. is discouered lying on his bench.' A curtain is drawn at the back of the stage below: cf. *Eastward Hoe*, I. i (opening stage-direction) '*At the middle dore, Enter Golding discouering a Gold-smiths shoppe.*'

II. i. 17. *Rex Regum.* Perhaps deleted in the Folio because of its scriptural ring (cf. I. iii. 59, and *infra* 228), but the context suggests that Musco is quoting, from Plautus, *Captivi*, 825, 'Non ego nunc parasitus sum sed regum rex regalior'.

II. iii. 102. *Ghibelletto* was the ancient Byblus, the modern Jebail in Syria; the *Tortosa* of line 107 is therefore the Syrian town anciently known as Orthosias (Ferrarius, *Lexicon Geographicum*, Paris, 1670). According to Heyd, *Histoire du Commerce du Levant* (1885, ed. Reynaud, i. 139), Count Raymond took Tortosa in 1101 or 1102 and Gibelet in 1104; Saladin captured them in 1188; they were finally evacuated by the Christians in 1291 after the fall of Acre (ib., p. 358). Does the text refer to these long-forgotten struggles?

184. *a Barbers virginals.* Cf. *S.W.* III. v. 64.

228. *in secula seculorum.* Brainworm parodies the concluding formula of a homily: 'Qui cum patre et spiritu sancto vivit et regnat per omnia saecula saeculorum. Amen.' Cf. Chaucer, *The Summoner's Tale* (*C.T.*, D. 1733–4):

> And when this frere had seyd al his entente
> With *qui cum patre* forth his wey he wente.

The phrase is used in several plays, e.g. Peele, *King Edward the first*, 1593, B4ᵛ (Malone Society Reprint, ll. 489–90), 'heere I entertaine thee,

thy boye, and thy trull, to follow my fortune, in *Secula seculorum*';
Beaumont and Fletcher, *Philaster*, 1620, p. 58: 'I'le see you Chronicled,
. . . And sung in sonets, and bath'd in braue new ballads, | That all
tongues shall troule you in *Secula seculorum*'; and Shirley, *The Gamester*,
III. ii, 'I am your humble servant in secula seculorum.'

III. 22–9. These lines make a belated reappearance in John Cotgrave's anthology, *The English Treasury of Wit and Language*, 1655,
p. 28 ('Of Beauty').

57. *Rimarum plenus* from Terence, *Eunuchus*, 105, also quoted by
Beaumont and Fletcher, *The Scornful Lady*, 1616, C4, II. i, 'Our Comick
Poet giues the reason sweetly; *Plenus rimarum est*, he is full of loope-
holes.'

72. *I not think*. This idiom, which restores the metre, is a favourite
one with Jonson: to take only one play, he has it in *Sejanus*, I. 375, III.
39, 242, 418, 572. Puttenham comments upon it in *The Arte of English
Poesie*, 1589, III. xxii (ed. Arber, p. 262), as an instance of ὕστερον
πρότερον or 'preposterous placing', which is 'a pardonable fault, and
many times gives a pretie grace vnto the speech'.

157–8. *by selfe loue, and affectation*. The Folio text (III. iv. 20–2)
answers Cob's question, 'Mary, Ile tell theé, COB: It is a gentleman-like
monster, bred, in the special gallantrie of our time, by affectation; and
fed by folly.' 'As tis generally receiued in these daies' suggests the
popular misconception of it denounced in the Induction to *Every Man
out of his Humour* (110–17), eccentricity in dress and 'an apish, or phan-
tasticke straine', or Nym's vacuous use of it in *The Merry Wives of
Windsor*. But the omission of self-love as one of the main ingredients of
'humour' is less easy to explain, in view of the fact that *The Fountaine
of Selfe-Loue. Or Cynthias Reuels*—to quote the Quarto title—was to
follow shortly. Here again the Folio inverted the titles, putting *The
Fountayne of selfe-Loue* in the second place. Jonson may have altered
the emphasis because of the relatively small part that the fountain
plays after the opening.

III. ii. 10. *Disparuiew's*, poor beggars. Cf. Chettle and Day, *The Blind-
Beggar of Bednal-Green*, 1659 (acted 1600), Dɪᵛ, II. i (ed. Bang, 657–8),
'Come you desper-view. | Deliuer me the Iewel or I'll hang thee.'

16. *Pirgo's*. The Folio substitutes '*Reformado's*'. Perhaps connected
with '*Pirgo, a companie of horsemen in battell containing fortie soldiers*' in
Florio's *New World of Words*, 1611. *The Tincker of Turvey*, 1630, p. 11,
also has, in reference to a noisy cobbler, 'note what a spruce Lether-
Pergo it is'.

21. *Tamberlaine*. Marlowe's play was acted probably in 1587: Jonson
in later life sharply criticized its '*scenicall* strutting and furious vocifera-
tion' (*Disc.* 777).

Agamemnon. A play with this title, by Dekker and Chettle, was
licensed for publication on 3 June, 1599.

47. *Gonfalionere.* Query, a misprint for 'Gonfallonere' or 'Gonfaloniere'.

82. *exposing* ('expulsion' Folio). The sense of 'expelling' is rare: the earliest instance in the *O.E.D.* is from Lithgow, 1632.

III. iii. 52. *an ingratitude wretch.* For this colloquial misuse cf. Onion, *C. is A.*, IV. v. 53, 'I will not be ingratitude.'

96. *set*, set down.

III. iv. 47. *so long as he doth not forsweare himself.* Like Touchstone's comment on the knight that swore 'by his honour' that the pancakes were good and the mustard naught; he was not forsworn, 'swearing by his honour, for he never had any' (*As You Like It*, I. ii. 57–72). The point is altered in the Folio revision (IV. ii. 27–30) by substituting 'by the foot of PHAROAH'.

85–7. The joke on bearing appears in *The Taming of the Shrew*, II. i. 198–200.

90. *Oh God . . . so sir* anticipates Clove in *E.M.O.* III. i. 25.

101. *By this fayre heauen* is proved to be the right reading by III. ii. 121, 154.

174. *signior Pythagoras.* Cf. *C.R.* IV. iii. 146–7, 'Breeches *Pythagoricall*, by reason of their transmigration, into severall shapes'.

IV. i. 56–7. *so happy as to light upon an ounce now of this doctors clarke.* The Folio revises this to 'so happy, as to light on a nupson, now, of this Iustices nouice'. 'Nupson' = simpleton, but no such meaning can be extracted from 'ounce', which seems an impossible word in this context. Was the original 'dunce', with the 'd' faintly written, and 'a ounce' then corrected by the printer?

IV. ii. 19. *for a more instance.* It shows the minute care which Jonson spent on the revision that he interchanged the opening of this speech with that of 39 'upon my first comming to the citie' in the Folio text.

34. *hath* ('haue' Folio). The singular after 'trickes of preuention' is a well-known idiom of Elizabethan English (see Folio version, IV. x. 46, and Abbott, *Shakespearian Grammar*, § 412), but it is noteworthy that, in this passage, Jonson corrected it.

IV. iii. 109. *though not in thee.* An attempt to correct the aposiopesis 'not in the' —, which is found in the first state of the Quarto text and reproduced in the Folio: see the discussion in the Quarto note on IV. viii. 114.

131. *1. 2. 3. 4. and 5.* The clock strikes. Cf. the opening sentence of Dekker's *Match mee in London*, 1631, B1ᵛ (a midnight scene), '*Malevento. Tormiella* Daughter—nor in this roome—Peace: 1. 2. 3. 4. 5. 6. 7. 8. 9. 10. 11. 12.'

v. ii. 31. *flincher* is pointless; the 'filtcher' of the Folio text (IV. xi. 34) is probably the right word here.

v. iii. 312. *for God sake.* 'For God's sake' elsewhere, in this play, but cf. *E.H.* v. i. 94, 'for God-sake', and *King John*, IV. i. 78, 'For heauen sake'.

210–12. *Pro . . . opus.* Ovid, *Ars Amat.* III. 413–14, 'Quis nosset Homerum . . .' 'Pro superi! ingenium magnum' is Jonson's own addition to the quotation.

236. *Qui . . . nihil.* Seneca, *Medea*, 163.

239. *and will noe sunshine on these lookes appeare?* Probably from a ballad: we have not succeeded in tracing it.

241. *ile be the porpuis, ile daunce.* Cf. *Sej.* v. 622–4.

242. *thou hast a cloake for the rayne.* Originally from Varro, *Menippeae*, fragm. 571 (ed. Bücheler), 'non quaerenda est homini qui habet virtutem paenula in imbri'; still an Italian proverb, but the sense is 'a means of protection or support'. Cf. *A new Enterlude . . . entituled new Custome*, 1573, Cij, 'Shee can finde out a cloke for euery rayne', and *A Warning for Faire Women*, 1579, B4:

> The cause he doth frequent my house, thou seest,
> Is for the loue he beares vnto my daughter.
> *Rog.* A verie good cloake mistres for the raine,
> And therein I must needes commend your wit.

255–8. Shakespeare has this quibble twice, *As you Like It*, II. iv. 11–14, and *2 King Henry IV*, I. ii. 212–13.

263. *Dic . . . virum.* The opening words of the *Aeneid*.

274. *From Catadupa. . . .* Now Chellal, the cataract of the Nile near Syene, referred to in Macrobius, *Somnium Scipionis*, II. 4, § 14. The allusion, deleted in the Folio, appears to have had point at this date. Lodge in 1596 published *Wits Miserie, and the Worlds Madnes: Discouering the Deuils Incarnate of this Age*, in which the affected speech of the devil of Contempt is satirized (p. 23): 'Get him write letters to his friend, and marke mee his Method: Sien of my Science in the Catadoupe of my knowledge, I nourish the Crocodile of thy conceit.'

294. *Maddona* and 'Madona' are seventeenth-century spellings, showing the pronunciation. So *E.M.O.* II. iii. 195.

297. *In Sommer time.* This ballad was long popular: a transfer of copyright is noted in the Stationers' Register on 14 December 1624. A version in the Pepys Collection (iv. 42) has the title 'A pleasant Song made by a Souldier whose bringing up had been dainty'.

309. *brize*, gadfly. The phrase recurs in *Poet.* III. i. 248, *Und.* xv. 71.

312. foll. The first and perhaps the finest passage in which Jonson gave expression to his high ideal of poetry; for other utterances see *Poetaster*, v. i, the dedication of *Volpone*, and *Discoveries*, 2381–408.

313. *Barathrum*, the abyss, hell. Derived from the Greek βάραθρον, a deep pit at Athens into which the bodies of criminals condemned to death were thrown.

340–4. Cf. *Poet.* I. ii. 240–8:

> When, would men learne but to distinguish spirits,
> And set true difference twixt those jaded wits
> That runne a broken pase for common hire,
> And the high raptures of a happy *Muse*,
> Borne on the wings of her immortall thought,
> That kickes at earth with a disdainefull heele,
> And beats at heauen gates with her bright hooues;
> They would not then with such distorted faces,
> And desp'rate censures stab at *poesie*.

364–5. *Who list to leade and a souldiers life.* The tune is given in Chappell, *Old English Popular Music*, 1893, i, p. 303. Peele refers to the song in *King Edward the first*, 1599, C, '*Enter the Harper and sing to the tune of Who list to lead a Souldiers life.*' For the redundant 'and' of the ballads cf. *M. of Christmas*, 215, 238, *Tw. Night*, v. i. 375, 'When that I was and a little tiny boy', and *King Lear*, III. ii. 74, 'He that has and a little tiny wit'. It adds an emphasizing touch, virtually meaning 'and that too'.

389. *a spice of the yealous.* Yellow was the colour of jealousy: there is a similar quibble in *E.H.* v. v. 185–6.

422. *plentuous.* Cf. Jasper Heywood's translation of Seneca's *Hercules Furens*, 1561, D4, 'The plentuous places of the towne'.

448. *Claudite. . . .* Virgil, *Eclogue*, iii. 111.

THE REVISED VERSION

Dedication to Camden. In 1601, when Jonson's position as a dramatist was assured by the two Humour plays, he seized an occasion to show his gratitude to Camden. In a gift-copy of the first quarto of *Cynthia's Revels* he inserted a special dedication to his old schoolmaster, speaking of himself as 'Alumnus olim, æternum Amicus'. When he issued his collected works in 1616 he significantly transferred his tribute to the opening play, and he included among the *Epigrams* a further tribute to that 'most reuerend head' (*Ep.* xiv). Camden is also quoted as an authority in the text of the Masque at Lord Haddington's wedding, 28, 29, and in Jonson's part of *The King's Entertainment in passing to his Coronation*, 28–31, 'the glorie and light of our kingdome, M. CAMDEN.'

On the subject of dedications to plays see D. Nichol Smith on 'Authors and Patrons' in *Shakespeare's England*, vol. ii, p. 211. He suggests that Jonson established the practice. All the more significant is the experimental dedication of the gift-copy to Camden. There is an earlier example in *Fidele and Fortunio*, 1585, which A.M. or M.A. dedicated to 'Maister M.R.' and 'Maister John Heardson Esquier'.

4. *so solemne a vice.* Cf. *M.L.* II. Chorus, 34, 'the solemne vice of interpretation'.

The Persons

Downe-right, A plaine Squier. Cf. the old tune 'Downright Squire', mentioned in Clement Robinson's *A Handful of Pleasant Delights*, 1584 (ed. Arber, pp. 7, 30).

Cob, A Water-bearer. Before water was laid on to the houses, it had to be fetched from the conduits. Hired men carried it in 'tankards', or hooped wooden vessels, broad at the bottom and narrow at the top, holding about three gallons; these 'tankards' are depicted in R. Treswell's plan of Westcheap, 1585, grouped round 'yᵉ litle cundit' east of St. Michael's Church at the end of Paternoster Row (reproduced in Furnivall's *Harrison's England*, Part III, Supplement, § 1). In the epilogue to the second part of *The Conquest of Granada*, Dryden instanced 'Cobb's tankard', along with 'Otter's horse' in *The Silent Woman*, as typical of the 'coarse' and 'mechanic humour' of the drama before the Restoration.

Bobadill. The last king of the Moors in Spain, who fell when Granada was taken in 1492, was named Bobadil. The name should be Boabdil, a corruption of Abu 'Abd Allah (R. Brown in his edition of Leo Africanus's *The History and Description of Africa*, Hakluyt Society, vol. i, p. xi).

The name soon came to connote braggart: see Chapman, *The Gentleman Vsher*, v. 1 (1606, H2ᵛ):

> The noble *Medice*, that man, that Bobbadilla,
> That foolish knaue, that hose and dublet stinckard.

Quips vpon Questions, or, A Clownes conceite on occasion offered, 1600, by 'Clunnyco de Curtanio Snuffe', has a reference to the character in the mock-dedication 'To the right worthy Sir Timothie Truncheon: alias Bastinado, euer my part-taking friende, Clunnico de Curtanio sendeth greeting; wishing his welfare but not his meeting.' The passage is, 'I shal . . . like a Burgomaister walke from Stationers shop to Stationers shop, to see what entertainement my Booke hath; and who so disgraces it enuiously, and not iesting at it gently, at the least bastinado them, that bobbadillo like as they censure, so with him they may receiue reward.'

A Paules-man meant a lounger in the middle aisle of Paul's, then a fashionable resort and a centre of business: see *E.M.O.* III, scenes i–vi.

The Scene London

This location appears here in the revised text of *Every Man in his Humour*, in *Epicoene*, 1609, and in *The Alchemist*, 1610, where the Prologue calls attention to the fact:

> Our *Scene* is *London*, 'cause we would make knowne,
> No countries mirth is better then our owne.
> No clime breeds better matter, for your whore,
> Bawd, squire, impostor, many persons more,
> Whose manners, now call'd humours, feed the stage.

This rejection of the Italian convention, accepted in the Quarto version, is a further step in the direction of realism, which reaches a climax in the play of *Bartholomew Fair*. The pointed announcement in *The Alchemist* further suggests that this adoption of a London scene was something of an innovation in 1610; when Jonson had once decided to 'shew an Image' of contemporary London, it was characteristic of him to justify the fact in a prologue. For *A Tale of a Tub* see page 271.

The notices of time in the play

The action takes place in one day, as Jonson points out with comic pertinacity. The clock ticks audibly in every act. The first scene is early morning, 'A goodly day toward!' (I. i. 1), and Edward Kno'well 'scarse stirring yet' (ib. 29, 30). In the thi d scene he is just up, and has received Well-bred's letter, but an hour has passed: 'my father had the full view o' your flourishing stile, some houre before I saw it', he tells Well-bred later (III. i. 47–9). At I. iv. 58 'It's sixe a clocke'; at v. 29 'some halfe houre to seuen'. At II. ii. 45 the bell rings for breakfast at Kitely's house. In III. iii. 44 it is 'Exchange time, sir'. The Quarto version of the corresponding scene (III. i) defines minutely: at the beginning of the scene it is 'New striken ten', and at line 37 'Past ten'. Kitely calculates that his business will take him two hours: he will then be either at the Exchange or at Justice Clement's (Folio, III, iii. 118–19). The sixth scene finds him at Clement's, i.e. about noon. In IV. ii. 64 Matthew refers to the verses which he made 'this morning'; in scene vi Kno'well left Brainworm with Formall 'betweene one and two'(v. i. 11). The false message of IV. viii. 134 was delivered 'After two' (v. i. 14). In v. iii. 94 the newly married pair are on the point of ordering their wedding supper; at the end of the act the entire party sup at Clement's house. Six o'clock was the usual hour with Londoners of that class.

In no other play is the day so elaborately mapped out; Jonson must have worked from a time-table.

Prologue

Found only in the Folio: see the Introduction, vol. i, pp. 333–5.

The view that the Prologue was a literary manifesto with an historical retrospect has been attacked by Mr. R. G. Howarth in a lecture on *Shakespeare's Tempest* (Sydney, 1936): 'Though there is no external evidence for its delivery, it must have been spoken, if it was to make the impression obviously designed by Jonson, and at a rival theatre to the "Globe", perhaps with Shakespeare there to listen and profit. What point would there have been in perfecting an early comedy and furnishing it with a proud explanatory preface, if that comedy were not to be acted, but just issued for reading? What point would there have been in so thoroughly revising the play?' To take the last point first: if the Folio had opened with the Quarto text of *Every Man in his Humour*, would this have harmonized with the humour plays which follow? Even the second play, *Every Man out of his Humour*, is far maturer in tone, and Jonson published it before its predecessor. There was ample point in revising it to present his plays in sequence as one balanced and harmonious whole.

As Mr. Howarth says, there is no record of the prologue being spoken. Where will he get his 'rival theatre'? The King's men played *Every Man in his Humour* in 1605, when Sir E. K. Chambers believes they played the revised version, but this will not suit Mr. Howarth, who dates it 1612. The only other company who acted Jonson's plays up to *Catiline* was the Chapel children, and the 1605 performance shows that they had no right to it.

That Jonson was capable of writing a prologue purely as a literary apologia is proved by the parallel instance of *Epicoene*, for which he wrote a second prologue 'Occasion'd', says the Folio ,'by some persons impertinent exception'. He had been accused of personal satire; he rebuts the charge with a statement of the aims of drama.

> The ends of all, who for the *Scene* doe write,
> Are, or should be, to profit, and delight.
> And still 't hath beene the praise of all best times,
> So persons were not touch'd, to taxe the crimes.

Art must approximate to truth, not

> By writing truths, but things (like truths) well fain'd.

Finally he tells his detractors,

> They make a libell, which he made a play.

Even this short disclaimer of fourteen lines is cast in the form of critical exposition, and there is nothing to indicate that it was ever spoken on the stage at all.

7–9. Jonson recurs to this in the first chorus of *The Magnetic Lady*. It is an echo of an old complaint. Whetstone in the dedication to *Promos and Cassandra*, 1578 (A ii^v), had objected to the licence of the English dramatist: 'in three howres ronnes he throwe the worlde: marryes, gets children, makes children men, men to conquer kingdomes . . .' Cf. Sidney, *Apology* (*Elizabethan Critical Essays*, i, p. 197), 'Now, of time, they are much more liberall'—i.e. than of place—'for ordinary it is that two young Princes fall in loue. After many trauerces, she is got with childe, deliuered of a faire boy; he is lost, groweth a man, falls in loue, and is ready to get another child; and all this in two hours space.'

Steevens instanced Lyly's *Endimion*, 1588, and Fleay (*Life of Shakespeare*, p. 290) suggested *Vortiger* (acted 4 December 1596) and *Uter Pendragon* (29 April 1597).

9. *with three rustie swords*. Cf. Sidney (op. cit., p. 197), 'while in the meantime two Armies flye in, represented with foure swords and bucklers . . .' and the 'foure or fiue most vile and ragged foyles' of *Henry V*, iv, Chorus, 50.

10. *foot-and-halfe-foote words*. So Jonson renders Horace's *ampullas et sesquipedalia verba* by 'Their bombard-phrase, and foote-and-halfe-foot words' (*A.P.* 139). Gayton, *Pleasant Notes upon Don Quixot*, 1654,

p. 24. 'I have heard that the Poets of the Fortune and red Bull had alwayes a mouth-measure for their Actors (who were terrible teare-throats) and made their lines proportionable to their compasse, which were *sesquipedales*, a foote and a halfe.'

11. Probably a fling at the whole group of plays on the Wars of the Roses—*The First Part of King Henry VI*, 'new' in March 1592; *The first part of the Contention betwixt the two famous Houses of Yorke and Lancaster*, licensed in March 1594; *The True Tragedy of Richard, Duke of Yorke*, published in 1595; *The Tragedy of King Richard the second*, licensed in August 1597; *The Tragedy of King Richard the third*, licensed in October 1597; *The First Part of King Henry IV*, licensed in February 1598; *The Second Part*, printed in 1600.[1]

It is difficult to see the point of Jonson's accusation that these plays were characterized by an element of ponderous bombast. Are the 'foot-and-halfe-foote words' to be found in the comic extravagance of 'I am ioyned with no Foot-land-Rakers, no Long-staffe six-penny strikers, none of these mad Mustachio-purple-hu'd-Maltwormes, but with Nobility, and Tranquilitie; Bourgomasters, and great Oneyers' (*1 Henry IV*, II. i. 70–4) or—to quote a later example—the 'beesome Conspectuities' of *Coriolanus*, II. i. 59?

Malone's suggestion that Jonson referred to the compound epithets in *King Richard III*, e.g. 'childish-foolish' (I. iii. 142), 'gallant-springing, brave Plantagenet' (I. iv. 218), 'senseless-obstinate' (III. i. 44), 'beauty-waning widow' (III. vii. 185), 'mortal-staring war' (v. iii. 90), is unconvincing. Jonson himself used such compounds: e.g. 'sordid-base' in II. v. 96. But Sidney affected the compound adjective in the *Arcadia*, and Hall noticed it as a trick of his style, abused by other writers:

> In Epithets to ioyne two words in one,
> Forsooth for Adiectiues cannot stand alone,
> As a great Poet could of *Bacchus* say,
> That he was *Semele-femori-gena*.
>
> (*Virgidemiarum*, 1598, Book VI, Sat. 1, p. 93.)

15. So in the induction to *Every Man out of his Humour*, 281–3, Jonson refers to the 'admirable dexteritie' with which the playwrights travel over sea and land. Many contemporary illustrations could be given, in addition to *King Henry V*, of this function of the Chorus; e.g. in Heywood's *The Four Prentises of London*, possibly acted in 1594, the Chorus at the end of Act I wafts the audience to Boulogne, France, Italy, and Ireland by successive stages of description and dumb show.

16. *creaking throne*. Cf. Lodge and Greene, *A Looking Glasse, for*

---

[1] Mr. W. J. Lawrence (*Pre-Restoration Stage Studies*, pp. 209, 248, 316) worked out a theory that Shakespeare's *Henry VI* plays were not glanced at in this passage of the Prologue. He thought the plays attacked were what he called the Contention Plays, and he conjectured that *The True Tragedie of Richard, Duke of Yorke* was acted in 1610, not knowing, when he wrote in 1927, that this play was a mutilated copy of the third part of *King Henry VI* and never was acted in that form.

London and England, 1598, B, 'Enters brought in by an Angell *Oseas* the Prophet, and set downe ouer the Stage in a Throne'; and at the end of Greene's *Alphonsus*, 1599, 'Exit Venus; Or if you can conueniently, let a chaire come downe from the top of the Stage and draw her vp.'

17. *nimble squibbe.* Sometimes dropped from the garret over the stage: see R.M., *Micrologia*, 1629, B3, describing a player: 'If his Action presages passion, he raues rages, and protests much by his painted Heauens; and seemes in the heighth of his fit ready to pull *Ioue* out of the Garret, where perchance he lies leaning on his elbowes, or is employed to make Squips [*sic*] and Crackers to grace the May.' In Shirley's *The Doubtful Heir*, 1653, the audience are warned in the prologue that the play has 'No clown, no squibs, no devil in't'.

18. *roul'd bullet.* 'It was the stage practice to make theatrical thunder by rolling a cannon ball along the floor, until the critic Dennis obtained a more satisfactory sound by the shaking of thin sheets of copper. The old plan is still, however, occasionally resorted to.' (H. B. Wheatley.)

19. *tempestuous drumme.* Possibly an allusion to *The Tempest*; the epithet is unusual. If so, the 'monsters' graced by the public in line 30 would include Caliban, the '*Seruant-Monster*' of *B.F.* (ind. 127).

21–3. Imitated by Glapthorne in the prologue to *The Ladies Privilege*, 1640:

> It starts our Authors confidence, who by me
> Tels you this much t'excuse the Comedy.
> You shall not here be feasted with the sight
> Of anticke showes; but Actions, such as might
> And have been reall, and in such a phrase,
> As men should speake in.

22. *Comœdie.* Similar spellings affected by Jonson are 'Tragœdie', 'æquall', 'idæa', 'præiudice', 'Chimæra', 'æmulation', 'pœnance'.

23. *an Image of the times.* Cf. 'Ciceros definition'—'*Imitatio vitae, Speculum consuetudinis, Imago veritatis*', quoted admiringly in *E.M.O.* III. vi. 205–7. So Sidney, *Apology* (ed. Gregory Smith, pp. 176–7), . . . 'Comedy is an imitation of the common errors of our life, which he representeth in the most ridiculous and scornefull sort that may be; so as it is impossible that any beholder can be content to be such a one . . . with hearing it we get as it were an experience, what is to be looked for of a nigardly *Demea*, of a crafty *Dauus*, of a flattering *Gnato*, of a vaine glorious *Thraso*, and not onely to know what effects are to be expected, but to know who be such, by the signifying badge giuen them by the Comedian.'

24. *sport with humane follies, not with crimes.* In accordance with the Aristotelian distinction that Comedy is μίμησις φαυλοτέρων μέν, οὐ μέντοι κατὰ πᾶσαν κακίαν (*Poetics*, v, § 1). *Volpone* is, of course, a marked violation of this law.

I. i. 1. *toward.* Cf. *C.R.* v. x. 7, 'I have a *comœdie* toward'; *Poet.* IV, v. 170, 'here's a song toward'.

5. *be'at.* The first example in the 1616 Folio of a metrical punctuation used by some poets of the time to indicate a syllable lightly pronounced in scansion. The 1640 Folio omits the apostrophe. See the discussion on the use in the introduction to *Sejanus*, vol. iv, pp. 338–42.

11. *in both our vniuersities.* Jonson was honorary M.A. of both Oxford and Cambridge.

12. *graces*, degrees.

17–20. Adapted from *The Spanish Tragedie*, VI. i. 70–3 (Allde's Quarto, I4):

> When I was yong I gaue my minde,
> And plide my selfe to fruitles poetrie:
> Which though it profite the professor naught,
> Yet is it passing pleasing to the world.

19. *professors*, those who follow it as a serious pursuit.

25–8. Dr. Brinsley Nicholson here calls attention to Jonson's habit of interposing lines of rhythmic prose in his verse; in this passage they bridge over the transition to prose pure and simple. Cf. I. ii. 27–9; II. ii. 45–8, iii. 54–5; IV. iii. 24–6. Sometimes these loose rhythms are used with dramatic effect, as in the voluble excitement of Lupus in *Poet.* v. iii. 9–11:

> I pronounce you all traytors, horrible traytors:
> What? Doe you know my affaires?
> I have matter of danger, and state, to impart to CAESAR.

or in the hurried aside of *Alch.* III. iv. 109–10.

28. *doe.* Here and in *E.M.O.* ind., 342, 'he do'not heare me I hope', 1640 corrects this vulgarism, but it suits Stephen; cf. *C. is A.* I. vii. 32, '*Oni.* What, do not this like him neither?' and *E.M.O.* II. iii. 257, 'CARL. He do'not goe bare foot, does he?'

31, 32. Not only is Stephen remarkably like Slender in the *Merry Wives of Windsor*, but each relies much upon his books: compare Slender's 'Book of Songs and Sonnets' and his 'Book of Riddles' (I. i. 179–82) (J. Dover Wilson).

32. *a booke of the sciences of hawking, and hunting.* Gifford notes Gervase Markham's reissue in 1595 of *The Gentlemans Academie, or the Booke of S. Albans: Containing three most exact and excellent Bookes: the first of Hawking* . . . originally put forth by Dame Juliana Berners in 1486. George Turbervile's two adaptations from the French, *The Booke of Faulconrie or Hauking for the onely delight and pleasure of all Noblemen and Gentlemen* and the *Noble Art of Venerie or Hunting* both appeared in 1575, and William Gryndall's *Hawking, Hunting, Fouling, and Fishing, With the true measures of blowing* . . . *Whereunto is annexed, the maner and order in keeping of Hawkes, their diseases, and cures: and all such speciall poynts, as any wise, appertaine to so Gentlemanlike qualitie* in 1596.

36. *wusse*, certainly. See *T. of T.* I. iv. 1.

41–2. *the hawking, and hunting-languages.* One of the affectations of the time: cf. *Und.* xliv. 70–2:

> What need we know?
> More then to praise a Dog? or Horse? or speake
> The Hawking language?

And J. Stephens, *Satyrical Essayes*, &c., 1615, pp. 257–8 (*A Falkoner*), 'Hee hath in his minority conuersed with Kestrils, and yong Hobbies; but growing vp he begins to handle the lure, and look a Faulcon in the face. All his learning makes him but a new linguist: for to haue studied and practised the termes of Hawkes Dictionary, is enough to excuse his wit, manners, and humanity.' Jonson's appreciation of the 'science' itself is recorded in *Epigram* lxxxv.

46. *scroyles,* scroundrels. Cf. *Poet.* iv. iii. 33, 'I crie thee mercy (my good scroile)'; *King John*, ii. i. 373, 'these scroyles of Angiers'.

47. *Hogsden,* Hoxton, which Stow notes as 'a large street with houses on both sides' (*Survey*, ed. Kingsford, ii, p. 74). It was in Hoxton fields that Jonson killed the actor Gabriel Spencer in a duel fought on 20 September 1598, not long after the first performance of *Every Man in his Humour*.

47. *What doe you talke on it?* Why! do you mean to tell me that . . .

48. *the archers of Finsburie.* Stow in his *Survay*, 1603, p. 430, notes that 'In the yeare 1498 all the Gardens which had continued time out of mind without Moregate, to witte, aboute and beyonde the Lordship of Finsbery, were destroyed. And of them was made a playne field for Archers to shoote in.' In Jonson's day, when archery was valueless in war, the practice continued as a sport, especially by the Society of Archers, with Arthur's Show and the Duke of Shoreditch.

49, 50. *a ducking to Islington ponds.* A favourite sport of citizens: cf. Middleton and Dekker, *The Roaring Girle*, ii. i (1611, D4), where gallants enter 'with water Spaniels and a ducke': 'we're going all to Hogsden . . . Push, let your boy lead his water Spaniel along, and weele show you the brauest sport at parlous pond'; and Brome, *The Damoiselle*, ii. i (1653, C3): '*Amp.* And know of him what Gamesters came to the Ponds now adayes, and what good dogs . . . And ask him—Dost thou heare? If he ha'not done away his own dog yet, *Blackswan* with the white foot? If I can but purchase him, and my own whelp prove right, I will be Duke of the Ducking-pond.' Perilous Pond was enclosed in 1743, converted into a bathing-place, and renamed 'Peerless Pool'. The site is in Baldwin Street, City Road.

50. *mun.* Cf. *Alch.* v. v. 129, 'Death, mun' you marry?'

63. *on it.* Gifford printed 'on't', but the line is probably an Alexandrine: see the note on ii. i. 87.

68. *bable.* The old form, found also in *Volp.* i. ii. 73.

74. *respectlesse in his courses,* inconsiderate in his actions.

80. *like an vnsauorie snuffe.* Jonson is fond of this metaphor: cf. *Ep.* lix, and *Und.* xliii. 187–8.

88. *and none of yours.* Cf. in a similar context Seneca, *Ep.* xliv. 5, 'Nemo in nostram gloriam vixit, nec quod ante nos fuit nostrum est.'

I. ii. 2. *do' not*. The apostrophe indicates a monosyllabic pronunciation.

5–8. Not unlike Slender's 'I keep but three men and a boy yet, till my mother be dead: but what though? Yet I live like a poor gentleman born' (*The Merry Wives*, I. i. 249–51).

6. *as simple as I stand here*. Cf. *The Merry Wives*, I. i. 199 (spoken by Slender); Sidney, *Arcadia*, 1590, p. 163, 'I, simple though I sit here, thought once my pennie as good siluer, as some of you do'; *The Returne from Pernassus*, II. iv, 'I am . . . his father Sir, simple as I stand here.'

9. *In good time*. In Jonson a formula of polite acquiescence, like *à la bonne heure*. But it could be ironical or incredulous, as in *The Taming of the Shrew*, II. i. 194.

14. *here bee them*. Cf. v. ii. 4.

26. *will this nere be left?* isn't it about time you stopped this?

28. *for shame*. Compare Bobadill's aristocratic reluctance, III. v. 128–9. It apes the etiquette of the knights of romance:

> For loth he was his noble hands t'embrew
> In the base blood of such a rascall crew.
> (*The Faerie Queene*, v. ii, st. 52.)

30. *peremptorie*, absolute. Cf. I. v. 82, 91.

49–52. *pray you remember your court'sie . . . pray you be couer'd*. Cf. the etiquette in *Love's Labour's Lost*, v. i. 83–4 (Armado to the Pedant), 'I doe beseech thee remember thy curtesie. I beseech thee apparell thy head.'

57. *the old Iewrie*. The name at this date was an historical survival; the Jews who returned to England under Cromwell settled in Aldgate (Wheatley).

73. *change an olde shirt, for a whole smocke*, exchange an old man (i.e. Kno'well) for a wench free from disease. Cf. 'A shirt and a smock' = a man and a woman in *Romeo and Juliet*, II. iv. 99.

73. *fripperie*, old-clothes shop. Cf. *Ep*. lvi. 2, 'the fripperie of wit'.

79. *coddling*, stewing (with an equivoque).

82. *our Turkie companie* received its charter in 1581 for trade in the Levant. Records of presents to the Sultan are in Hakluyt's *Voyages*, 1599, ii, p. 171—a present from Elizabeth in March 1583, and again (ib. ii. 306) in October 1593: the latter was '12 goodly pieces of gilt plate, 36 garments of fine English cloth of al colors, 20 garments of cloth of gold, 10 garments of sattin, 6 pieces of fine Holland, and certaine other things of good value; al which were carried round about the court, each man taking a piece, being in number very neere 100 parcels, and so 2 and 2 going round that all might see it, to the greater glory of the present, and of him to whom it was giuen'; as a present to the Sultana, 'a iewel of her maiesties picture, set with some rubies and diamants, 3 great pieces of gilt plate, 10 garments of cloth of gold, a very fine case of glasse bottles silver & gilt, with 2 pieces of fine Holland'; there were also presents to viziers and court officials. In 1605 the Levant Company was

reconstituted; to help them out of their difficulties the King made them a grant of £5,322 'for a present to the Grand Seignior'. (*State Papers, Domestic*, 1605, 13 Dec, xvii. 35, and 1606 (April?), xx. 27.) Dekker in *The Wonderfull yeare*, 1603, B1^r, speaks of new-year's gifts 'more in number, and more worth then those that are giuen to the great Turke, or the Emperour of *Persia*'.

83. *batch*, strictly the quantity of bread baked at once; *leuin*, leaven. For the combination cf. *Cat.* iv. 222, 'Except he were of the same meale, and batch'.

85. *willing . . . seene*. This sounds like a part of a caption advertising some prodigy or monster at a fair; compare i. iii. 125–7. (J. Dover Wilson.)

88–9. *as vnconscionable, as any Guild-hall verdict*. Repeated in *D. is A*. i. i. 20–3 ('a *Middlesex* Jury') and *M.L.* iii. iv. 55–7 ('*London*-Iury'). 'A London jury would find Abel guilty of the murder of Cain' was, according to Gifford on the last passage, the saying of a Tudor bishop of London; the source of this is Hall's Chronicle of *The triumphant reigne of Kyng Henry the .viii.* (ed. 1550, L iii^v). Richard Hun, a merchant tailor, committed to 'Lollers tower' in St. Paul's, had been found dead in his cell; at the inquest on 5 and 6 December 1514 the jury found the Chancellor of the diocese and his servants guilty of murdering Hun. The bishop, Richard Fitz-James, wrote to Wolsey in their favour, saying, 'If my Chaunceller be tryed by any .xii. men in London, they be so maliciously set *In fauorem heretice prauitatis*, that they wyl cast and condempne any clerke though he were as innocent as Abell.'

Later complaints are frequent. Cf. Middleton, *A Trick to Catch the Old One*, 1608, iv. v. 176–80 (Bullen), 'Why, thou great Lucifer's little vicar! I am not so weak but I know a knave at first sight: thou inconscionable rascal! thou that goest upon Middlesex juries, and wilt make haste to give up thy verdict because thou wilt not lose thy dinner'; and Nabbes, *Tottenham Court*, 1638, i. iv, 'Why let but an honest Iury (which is a kind of wonder in *Middlesex*) finde you not guilty of any thing that may make compassion deafe'—.

91. *the wind-mill*. Originally a Jewish synagogue 'at the north Corner of the old Iury'; then assigned to the Friars of the Sack as their chapel; then a private house. '*Robert Large* Mercer, Mayor in the yeare 1439. kept his Mayoralty in this house, and dwelled there vntill his dying day. This house standeth and is of two parrishes, as opening into Lothberie, of S. *Margarets* parrish, and opening into the Old Iury of S. Olaues parrish. . . . *Hugh Clopton* Mercer, Mayor 1492. dwelled in this house, and kept his Mayoralty there: it is now a Tauerne, and hath to signe a Windmill.' —Stow, *Survay*, 1603, p. 280. There is a woodcut of the tavern in the *Notorious Life and Ignominious Death of John Lambe, otherwise called Doctor Lambe* 1628. Lambe is being mobbed, and the inn in the background has the sign of the windmill.

92. *Burdello*, brothel.

93. *Spittle*, hospital, especially for foul diseases. Cf. *Alch.* i. iv. 22,

'Searching the spittle, to make old bawdes yong'; *Henry V*, v. i. 75–6, 'my *Doll* is dead i'th Spittle of a malady of France'.

Pict-hatch. A notorious haunt of prostitutes at the back of a turning called Rotten Row, opposite the Charterhouse wall in Goswell Road.

95. *the times hath.* In Elizabethan writers this old plural in *th* survived chiefly in the forms 'hath' and 'doth'. Cf. *Henry V*, prol. 9, 'The flat vnraysed Spirits, that hath dar'd . . .' and Fletcher, *The Faithfull Shepheardesse*, II. iii. 70–3, 'By it doth growe . . . all hearbs which witches vse, All simples . . . All sweetes . . .'

99. *guifts*, a frequent spelling in Jonson, to mark the hard *g*.

104. *th' Hesperian Dragon*, *N.I.* III. ii. 11.

105. *I'had thought* (1640 ignores the apostrophe). Whalley, whom Gifford followed, tried to eke out the line by printing 'I had thought you', but they overlooked the slow deliberate rhythm which lengthens it sufficiently in delivery.

106. *Y'had.* So Jonson prints 'Th'art': cf. Gill, *Logonomia*, 1619, p. 128, 'in Ðou' (i.e. Thou) 'ante *art* dipththongus sæpe deficit'.

108. *geering.* So spelt *B.F.* v. iii. 97, *D. is A.* I. vi. 99.

gamsters, people who make game of everything. Cf. *Henry VIII*, I. iv. 45, 'You are a merry Gamster, My Lord Sands.'

129–34. Whalley quoted Terence, *Adelphoe*, 57–8, 69–75:

> Pudore et liberalitate liberos
> retinere satius esse credo quam metu. . . .
> Malo coactus qui suom officium facit,
> dum id rescitum iri credit, tantisper pavet;
> si sperat fore clam, rursum ad ingenium redit.
> Ille quem beneficio adiungas ex animo facit,
> studet par referre, praesens absensque idem erit.
> Hoc patriumst, potius consuefacere filium
> sua sponte recte facere quam alieno metu.

I. iii. 15. *a what-sha'-call-him doublet.* Cf. *Poet.* III. iv. 245, 'the t'other fellow there, hee in the—what sha' call him—'.

26. *horson scander-bag rogue.* Cf. Tucca's greeting in Dekker's *Satiromastix*, 1602, H1ᵛ, 'away, flie Scanderbag flie'; and *The Shomakers Holiday*, 1600, D3ʳ, 'no, we haue beene bargaining with Skellum Skanderbag,' where 'Skellum' = 'scoundrel'. 'Scanderbag' (properly Iskanderbeg, 'Prince Alexander') was the Turkish name of George Castriot (1414–67), the patriot chief who won the freedom of Albania in twenty-two battles. In 1562 there appeared *Two very notable Commentaries the one of the Originall of the Turcks and Empire of the house of Ottomanno, written by Andrewe Cambine, and thother of the warres of the Turcke against George Scanderbeg, prince of Epiro, and of the great victories obteyned by the sayd George, aswell against the Emperour of Turkie, as other princes, and of his other rare force and vertues, worthye of memorye, translated oute of Italian into Englishe by John Shute*; and in 1596, *The*

Historie of George Castriot Surnamed Scanderbeg, King of Albanie. Containing his famous actes, his noble deedes of Armes, and memorable victories against the Turkes, for the Faith of Christ. . . . By Iaques de Lavardin. . . . Newly translated out of French into English by Z. I., Gentleman, published by W. Ponsonby: Spenser, in a prefatory sonnet, described Castriot as 'matchable to the greatest' of the ancient heroes. A play was entered for Allde on the Stationers' Register on 3 July 1601, 'the true historye of George Scanderbarge as yt was lately playd by the right honorable the Earle of Oxenford his servantes' (Arber, *Transcript,* iii. 187).

31. *wispe of hay.* Cf. *T. of T.* i. iv. 1–5.

34. *trusse,* tie the 'points' or tagged laces which fastened the breeches to the doublet. This clumsy substitute for buttons often necessitated assistance: Tucca, in *Poet.* iii. iv, calls his pages 'my little point-trussers'. Brainworm in his reply quibbles on 'truss'd' in the sense of beaten.

38. *foundre you.* Compare the intransitive use, 'come to grief' in *Henry VIII,* iii. ii. 39, 40, 'But in this point | All his trickes founder.'

43. *the woollen stocking.* Whalley quotes R. Tailor, *The Hogge hath lost his Pearle,* i. i. (1614, B2), 'Good parts without any abilements of gallantry, are no more set by in these times, than a good legge in a woollen stocken.' Cf. ii. i. 105 below.

47. *in a silke-hose.* Similarly Sir Andrew Aguecheek fancied the look of his own leg in a 'colour'd stocke' (*Tw. Night,* i. iii. 127). Cf. *C.R.* ii. iii. 115–16, 'He treades nicely, . . . especially the first *sunday* of his silke-stockings.' Stow records in his *Annales* (ed. Howes, p. 867) that in 1561 Queen Elizabeth was presented with a pair of black silk stockings by her silk-woman, Mrs. Montague, and gave up cloth hose from that time. This appears to have set the fashion.

61. *Costar'-monger.* So spelt *Alch.* iv. i. 57, *S.W.* i. i. 154, and *B.F.* passim.

familiar Epistles. The use of italics in the Folios suggests a title, as in the letters of Cicero or Pliny, or the *Familiar Epistles of Sir Anthonie of Gueuara,* 1574.

63. *Mʳ. Iohn Trundle, yonder,* bookseller from 1603 to 1626, and in 1613 at the sign of Nobody in Barbican. In co-operation with Nicholas Ling he published the First Quarto of *Hamlet* in 1603, but he was specially a publisher of ballads and light literature. Alexander Gill, in his splenetic verses on *The Magnetic Lady,* tells Jonson,

As for the press, if thy play must come to't,
Let Thomas Purfoot or John Trundell do't.

71. *messe,* a set of four (originally one of the groups into which the company at a banquet were divided). Cf. *Love's Labour's Lost,* iv. iii. 201–3, 'confesse . . . That you three fooles, lackt me foole, to make vp the messe'.

78. *melancholy'.* So spelt here and at iii. i. 100 in F1 ; and at *B.F.* iii. iv. 74, 'How melancholi' Mistresse *Grace* is yonder!' in F2. Jonson sup-

posed that the adjective 'melancholy' was abbreviated from 'melancholic'. So '*Iouy*' Boy', *Alch.* v. v. 144.

94. *More-gate*. Then a postern gate in the City wall near Colman Street.

99–101. *protest*. An affectation, as Whalley notes: cf. *Rom. and Jul.* II. iv. 167–73, where the Nurse considers that Romeo's I protest' is 'a gentleman-like offer', and the incessant use of it by Lampatho in Marston's *What You Will*, II. i. 37 foll. (Bullen), and in *Sir Giles Goosecappe*, v. v (1606, I4, but acted *c.* 1601): '*Wil.* . . . I protest she does most abhominablie miscarrie her selfe. *Ia*: Protest you sawsie Iack you, I shood doe my countrie and courte shippe good seruice to beate thy coalts teeth out of thy head, for suffering such a reuerend worde to passe their guarde; why, the oldest courtier in the world man, can doe noe more then protest. *Bul*. Indeede page if you were in Fraunce, you wood bee broken vpon a wheele for it, there is not the best *Dukes* Sonne in Fraunce dares saie I protest, till hee bee one and thirtie yeere old at least, for the inheritance of that worde is not to bee possest before.'

102. *By my fackins*. Cf. *Alch.* I. ii. 131, 'Sweare by your fac?'

108. *sort*, rank.

109. *i' this companie*. A jocular allusion to the audience. (J. Dover Wilson.)

118. *a Millaners wife*. A milliner was originally an importer, then a vendor, of Milan goods. Cf. *A Warning for Faire Women*, 1599, C2:

> *Man.* She told me sir the Draper would be here,
> And George the Milliner with other things.

And *The Winter's Tale*, IV. iv. 191, 'No Milliner can so fit his customers with Gloues.'

120. *cypresse*, 'a light transparent material resembling cobweb lawn or crape' (*O.E.D.*). For the contrast with lawn cf. *Ep.* lxxiii. 14, and *The Winter's Tale*, IV. iii. 215–16, 'Lawne as white as driven Snow, | Cypresse blacke as ere was Crow'.

answer'd, excused, justified.

121. *Drakes old ship, at Detford*. The *Golden Hind*, laid up at Deptford by order of Queen Elizabeth; she visited it on 4 April 1581 and knighted Drake on board. It became a holiday resort: cf. *E.H.* III. iii. 150, and Peacham's verses prefixed to Coryat's *Crudities*, 1611, k4ᵛ.

124. *Idea* (italicized in Ff), in the Platonic sense of 'archetype' or 'perfect pattern'.

131. *melancholy, and gentleman-like*. It was a fashionable trait of the contemporary gallant to be 'as sad as night Onely for wantonnisse' (*King John*, IV. i. 15, 16). In *The Life and Death of the Lord Cromwell*, III. ii (ed. 1602, C4ᵛ), Hodge, disguised as the Earl of Bedford, says: 'How do I feele my selfe, why, as a Noble man should do, O how I feele honor come creeping on, My Nobilitie is wonderfull melancholie: Is it not most Gentleman like to be melancholie.'

131. *ensure*, guarantee.

138. *goe before*, 'Serving-man-like' (*T. of T.* IV. iv. 9).

1. iv. 8. *linage.* 'The spelling *lineage*, which appears late in the seventeenth century, is probably due to association with *line.'—O.E.D.* 'Lineage' is found at III. iv. 50.

13. *Herring the King of fish.* See *Nashes Lenten Stuffe* . . . *With a new Play neuer played before, of the praise of the Red Herring,* 1599, which tells 'howe the Herring scrambled vp to be King of all fishes' (Nashe's *Works,* iii. pp. 201–4, ed. McKerrow). Taylor, *Jacke-a-Lent (Works,* 1630, p. 116), also speaks of ' The maiesticall king of Fishes, the heroicall most magnificent *Herring*'.

16. *Harrot,* herald. Cf. *C. is A.* IV. ix. 41, 'some harrot of armes'.

17. *Cob,* the head of a herring. Cf. Dekker, *The Second Part of Honest Whore,* 1630, G2ᵛ, 'he can come bragging hither with foure white Herrings . . . but I may starue ere he giue me so much as a cob'.

29–31. *Roger Bacon . . . broyl'd o' the coles?* Cob knew his history (cf. l. 63) probably from a chapbook, which may have had him burnt as a necromancer.

32. *vpsolue,* clear up. A vulgarism?

52. *cast,* a quibble on the sense 'to vomit'. Cf. Porter, *The Two Angry Women of Abington,* 1599, E2, (of a drunkard) 'he were good Now to play at dice, for he castes excellent well'.

55. *swallow'd a tauerne-token.* T. Heywood in *Philocothonista, Or, The drunkard, Opened, Dissected, and Anatomised,* 1635, p. 60, gives as one of the euphemisms for drunkenness, 'He hath swallowed an *Haire* or a *Tauerne-Token.*' Halfpenny and farthing tokens were issued by victuallers and tradesmen generally, for use as small change: with the exception of the 'Haringtons' (*D. is A.* II. i. 83) no royal issue of farthings was made till 1672. Jonson's most frequent mention of them is, as might be expected, in *Bartholomew Fair* (I. ii. 35; II. iv. 5; III. iv. 16).

57. *God b'w'you, sir.* Cf. *Love's Labour's Lost,* III. i. 141, 'God be wy you', and *Henry V,* IV. iii. 6, 'God buy' you Princes all.'

58. *carried two turnes.* Cf. R. W., *The three Lordes and three Ladies of London,* 1590, C2ᵛ:

> Enter painfull *Penurie,* attired like a waterbearing woman with her Tankard.
> . . . you may see poore painful *penury*
> Is faine to carry three Tankards for a penie, . . .
> I shall loose my draught at *Conduit,* and therefore Ile away.

61. *hauings.* Cf. *C.R.* v. iv. 34 (a man) 'of goodly hauings'; *D. is A.* III. iii. 133, 'A man of meanes and havings'.

63. *the Brasen-head.* An allusion to the legend of Roger Bacon. See the old romance *The famous Historie of Fryer Bacon,* 1627, ch. v, 'How Fryer Bacon made a Brasen head to speake, by the which he would haue walled England about with Brasse'. Jonson has a further allusion in *C.R.* IV. ii. 32, 'Who answeres the brazen head? it spoke to some bodie.'

64. *Mo fooles yet.* The traditional words of the Brazen Head are 'Time is', 'Time was', 'Time will be' (quoted *C. is A.* IV. iii. 80). But cf. *Vlysses vpon Aiax,* 1596, C1ᵛ, 'I could tell you more as hee hath done

(out of that most learned author the booke of merrie tales from whence his best iestes are deriued) but that as the olde *Manciple* of *Brasennoze* Colledge in *Oxforde* was wont to say; There are more fooles to meete with'.

66–7. *worshipfull fish-monger*, i.e. a member of the city company.

77. *poyetrie*. Cob's broad pronunciation is a survival of an older form: cf. 'Plato þe Poyete' in Langland, *Piers Plowman*, A text, xi. 129 (1362), and 'poyet' in Tindale's version of Titus i. 12 (1526).

81. *There's an oath*. The gallant of the period made a study of oaths. Cf. *Euerie Woman in her Humor*, 1609, B1^v, where Servulus, learning to become a gentleman, swears 'By this bright horizon'—'no common oath', as his follower remarks: he replies, 'Were it common, it past not these doores: Sir, I shift my oathes as I wash my hands, twice in the artificial day.' The variant then is 'By this illuminate welkin'.

83. *sweare the legiblest*. Cf. *C. is A*. v. vi. 52, 'Speak legibly.'

84–5. *as I am a gentleman, and a souldier*. A sharking captain also uses this oath in Nashe's *Vnfortunate Traveller*, 1594 (ed. McKerrow, ii. 223).

88. *at's tonnels*, through his nostrils (lit. tunnels). For the practice see *E.M.O.* iv. iii. 93–6, 'there wee might see SOGLIARDO sit in a chaire, holding his snowt vp like a sow vnder an apple-tree, while th' other open'd his nostrils with a poking-sticke, to giue the smoke a more free deliuerie'.

91. *the next Action*. Bobadill, like Shift in *E.M.O.* ('Characters') and Captain Hungry in *Ep.* cvii, 'way-layes the reports of seruices', and gets meals and money by them.

91–2. *Helter . . . hang-man*. So in Dekker, Chettle, and Haughton's *Patent Grissill* (acted 1599), ed. 1603, H4, a beggar says 'Make him a cuckolde Madame, and vpon that I drinke to you: helter skelter here roagues, top and top gallant, pell mell, huftie tuftie, hem, God saue the Duke and a fig for the hangman.'

care'll kill a cat. Ray in his *Proverbs*, 1670, p. 67, comments 'And yet a cat is said to have nine lives. *Cura facit canos.*'

92. *vp-tailes all*, the refrain of an old song, the tune of which is in Queen Elizabeth's *Virginal Book* and in *The Dancing Master*, 1650: see Chappell's *Popular Music in the Olden Time*, 1893, i, p. 149. Gifford quotes Sharpham, *The Fleire*, 1607, F1^v, 'she euerie day sings *Iohn for the King*, and at *Vp tailes all*, shees perfect'.

I. v. s.d. *Bobad. is discouered* by drawing the curtain covering the central space at the back of the stage. Compare the opening stage-directions of *The Case is Altered*, 1609, and *Eastward Hoe*, 1609.

5. *small beere*. Cf. Middleton, *The Roaring Girl*, ii. i. 128–9, ed. Bullen, 'This shows like small beer i'th' morning after a great surfeit of wine o'ernight.'

20. *sort*, company. Cf. *T. of T*. ii. ii. 87–8, 'were set upon By a sort of country fellowes'.

33. *possesse*. Cf. IV. v. 9, *D. is A.* v. v. 44.

37. *Cabbin*. Bobadill speaks modestly, but he may be thinking of the military use for 'tent', as in III. vii. 69.

44. *I resolue so*, I am convinced. For this affectation compare *C. is A.* II. vii. 3.

47. *Goe by, Hieronymo!* i.e. Kyd's *The Spanish Tragedie*, which Bobadill identifies by a stock quotation at sig. G4 in Allde's undated quarto (III. xii. 27–31, ed. Boas):

> *Hiero.* Iustice, o iustice to *Hieronimo*.
> *Lor.* Back, seest thou not the King is busie?
> *Hiero.* O, is he so.
> *King.* Who is he that interrupts our busines?
> *Hiero.* Not I, *Hieronimo* beware, goe by, goe by.

'Perhaps no single passage in Elizabethan drama became so notorious as this. It is quoted over and over again, as the stock phrase to imply impatience of anything disagreeable, inconvenient, or old-fashioned.'— Boas: who gives passages in *The Taming of the Shrew*, Dekker, Middleton, Deloney, and Taylor. Jonson has the words again in *The New Inn*, II. v. 82.

50–1. For similar ignorance on the part of a gallant, Mr. Baskerville (*English Elements*, p. 126) compares Davies, *Epigram* 22, on 'the fine youth *Ciprius*' and his fashions:

> Yet this new fangled youth, made for these times,
> Doth aboue all praise old George *Gascoines* rimes.

55. *againe* rounds off a clause or sentence with a cry of assurance: cf. II. ii. 34, *Poet.* III. i. 32, iv. 163; IV. v. 54.

57. *O eyes*. From *The Spanish Tragedie*, III. ii. 1–4 (E1ᵛ in Allde's quarto). Cf. *The Wandering-Jew, Telling Fortunes to Englishmen*, 1640, G2, where a lover enters to the fortune-teller: 'Young-man, you are welcome, What ayle your eyes? have you bin crying? Crying (said he) O eyes! no eyes but fountains full of Teares. A line in *Ieronimo* (cryed the Boy) . . . I Confesse it, said the Lover, 'tis in *Ieronimo*, and I am *Ieronimo*; for I have a son murdred; the sonne of my mother is made away by the cruelty of a Maid; I am *Iphis*, She *Anaxarete*.'

65–70. Matthew 'vtters nothing, but stolne remnants' (IV. ii. 57), but this blend of his pilfering has not been traced. It opens with a suggestion of the style of Daniel.

70. *Hast made the wast*. Cf. *Iohn Heywoodes woorkes*, 1562, Pt. I, ch. ii, A iij,

> Som things that prouoke young men to wed in haste,
> Show after weddyng, that hast maketh waste.

And Harrison, *A Description of England*, 1587, II. v (i, p. 136), of scamped work, 'whereby the buier is often sore defrauded, and findeth to his cost, that hast maketh wast, according to the prouerbe'.

71. s.d. *making him ready*, dressing. Cf. *T. of T.* i. i. 69, s.d. 'Hilts *enters, and walkes by, making himselfe ready.*'

81. *hanger*, the loop or strap in a sword-belt from which the weapon was hung. A fashionable gallant had embroidered hangers, the 'liberal-conceited carriages' of Osric's eulogy (*Hamlet*, v. ii. 148 ff.). Gifford, on *Poet.* iii. iv. 84, quoted John Cooke's *Greene's Tu Quoque* (Flesher's ed., G4), where Joyce tells her brother, 'since you came to th' Inn's a Court', she had wrought him 'a faire payre of Hangers'; and the song *Jockie is grown a gentleman*:

> The belt that was made of a white leather thonge,
> Which thou and thy father wore so longe,
> Is turned to hangers of velvet stronge,
> With gold and pearle embroydered amonge.

82. *peremptory-beautifull.* Cf. i. ii. 30.

88. *rooke*, gull, simpleton. Cf. *C. is A.* ii. vii. 54, 'such rookes as these should be asham'd to iudge'.

no more iudgement than a malt-horse. Cf. *B.F.* ii. vi. 109, 'no, no, I am a dull malt-horse, I know nothing'; *Comedy of Errors*, iii. i. 32, 'Mome, malt-horse, capon, coxcomb, idiot, patch!'

97. *prouerbes.* Nicholas Proverbs in Henry Porter's *The two angry women of Abington*, acted in 1598, is a kindred spirit to Downright.

111. *chartel.* 'Challenge' in *Q.*

112. *dependance*, a duellist's ground of quarrel. Cf. *D. is A.* iii. iii. 62 ff., *Vision of Delight*, 113.

113. *Caranza.* Jeronimo de Carranza, author of *De la Filosofia de las Armas*, first published in 1569, the pioneer of a long series of Spanish treatises on fencing: in *The New Inn*, ii. v. 87, iv. iv. 83, he is spoken of as superseded. In Fletcher's *Love's Pilgrimage*, v. iv (Folio text, 1647), Sanchio tells the Governor, who demands his sword from him in a street riot:

> Stay heare me. Hast thou ever read *Curanza*?
> Understandest thou honour, Noble Governour?

When the Governor afterwards orders all weapons to be restored, he stands out stiffly:

> It seems thou hast not read *Curanza*, fellow.
> I must have reparation of honour,
> As well as this: I finde that wounded.
>   *Gov.* Sir,
> I did not know your quality, if I had
> Tis like I should have done you more respects.
>   *Sanch.* It is sufficient, by *Caranza's* rule.

115. *stoccata*, thrust. Cf. *Vincentio Saviolo his Practise*, 1595, H1ᵛ, 'if your enemie bee cunning and skilfull, neuer stand about giuing any foine or imbroccata, but this thrust or stoccata alone'; Mercutio agreed—

'*Alla stocatta* carries it away' (*Rom. and Jul.* III. i. 72). A rival school of theorists favoured the cut.

121. *vn-in-one-breath-vtter-able.* Cf. *D. is A.* III. iii. 51, 'an ore vn-to-be-melted'; *N.I.* v. iv. 24–5, 'a neglect Vn-to-be-pardon'd'; and Chapman, *May-day,* III. v (1611, p. 53), 'of an vn-cole-carrying spirit'.

126. With *accommodate* as a 'worde of Action', cf. of course *2 Henry IV,* III. ii. 75–6, 'a Souldier-like Word, and a Word of exceeding good Command'. Jonson brands it as an affectation in *Disc.* 2275, 'You are not to cast a Ring for the perfumed termes of the time, as *Accommodation, Complement, Spirit,* &c.'

bed-staffe. Bed-staves were of various sizes and had various uses; but here the bedroom has only one ('*another* bed-staffe', says Bobadill), and it is the right length for fencing. This was the kind used for beating up the bed in making it. See a picture in the series of nineteen plates depicting home life designed by the French artist Abraham Bosse and engraved by J. le Blond and M. Tavernier, Paris, 1633: the bedroom scene 'La Nourrice', engraved by Tavernier, shows a bed in the corner, which a servant is just making; she reaches over it and smoothes the coverlet with a stick.

129. *state,* position. An affectation?

let your poynard maintain your defence. 'The dagger was held in the left hand and used to ward off the opponent's thrust with his rapier, the while one thrust with one's own.'—J. Dover Wilson on *Hamlet,* v. ii. 222: see the whole note.

139. *passe vpon you.* Matthew is confused by the unfavourable senses of the term—(1) to pass sentence upon (*Meas. for Meas.* II. i. 19, 23), (2) to impose upon (*Tw. Night,* v. i. 355).

142. *carreere,* lunge.

144. *passada,* a forward thrust while the fencer advances one foot, the 'immortal passado' of Mercutio. Cf. Saviolo, op. cit., H3, 'If your enemy be first to strike at you, and if at that instant you would make him a passata or remoue, it behoueth you to be very ready with your feet and hand.'

149. *venue.* The French term was out of fashion: cf. *Hamlet,* v. ii. 161, 'in a dozen passes', where the corresponding reference in the First Quarto (sc. xv. 18) reads 'in twelue venies'.

165. '*Tis somewhat with the least.* Cf. *N.I.* II. i. 2, 'It was a great deale with the biggest for me'; and Chaucer, *Troilus and Criseyde,* I. 281, 'She n'as nat with the leste of her stature.'

166. *redish . . . to tast our wine.* Cf. the admonition to two needy poets in Randolph, *The Jealous Lovers,* 1632, III. v:

> I will not have you henceforth sneak to Taverns,
> And peep like fidlers into Gentlemens rooms,
> To shark for wine and radishes.

167. *to close the orifice of the stomach.* Cf. Aeneas Silvius (Pope Pius II), *De Curialium miseriis,* c. 19, 'alii modico pane vel caseo prægustato

orificium stomachi clauserunt.' (Quoted by E. Bensly, *R.E.S.* vi, p. 207.)

169. *the Coridon.* Cf. Dekker and Webster, *West-ward Hoe*, 1607, H4, 'Will you then turne *Coridons* because you are among clowns? shal it be said you haue no braines being in *Brainford*?'

II. i. 6. *with th' pieces.* So III. iii. 42–3, 'with th' bonds', but in *Ep.* cxxxiii. 153, 'with' the'. This is only Jonson's meticulous way of writing 'wi' the'. Cf. W. Goddard, *A Mastif Whelp*, [Dort? 1615?], B4 (of a woman repeating like an echo the last words of her lover), 'Quoth shee [entwind] thus loue with' last words dus shee binde'; and 'This's' (*T. of T.* II. ii. 52), which is common in Jonson and found in other writers.

pieces of eight. The Spanish silver *peso* or piece of eight reales value (*pieza de á ocho*). Cf. *Alch.* III. iii. 15.

9. *grogran*, or grogram, 'a coarse fabric of silk, of mohair and wool, or of these mixed with silk; often stiffened with gum' (*O.E.D.*). This cloth deteriorated in England in the seventeenth century. When badly worn and with its cords threadbare it made a very shabby dress (Linthicum, *Costume in the Drama*, p. 78). Cf. *C.R.* III. ii. 6, 'poore grogran-rascall'; *M.L.* IV. i. 6, 'A new silke-Grogoran Gowne'.

18. *the Hospitall*, Christ's Hospital, which in addition to the 'children of the house', the sons of City freemen, educated foundlings and other children admitted from the City parishes. Cf. *N.I.* IV. ii. 7–9:

> He had no Father, I warrant him, that durst own him;
> Some foundling in a stall, or the Church porch;
> Brought vp i' the *Hospitall*; and so bound Prentise.

And Middleton, *The Widdow*, II. i (1652, D2ᵛ):

> I ha' no charge at all, no child of mine own,
> But two I got once of a scowring woman,
> And they'r both well provided for, they'r i' th' Hospitall.

60. Cf. *Julius Caesar*, I. ii. 72–4:

> Were I a common Laughter, or did vse
> To stale with ordinary Oathes my loue
> To euery new Protester.

69. *'Sdeynes*, a shortened form of 'God's deynes' or 'God's dines' (in Porter's *Two angry women of Abington*, 1599, ll. 1804 and 2342, Malone Society's reprint). The *O.E.D.* doubtfully suggests a corruption of 'dignesse', so that the phrase is 'by God's dignity'. Cf. 'God's dentie' in W. Bullein, *A Dialogue*, &c., 1573, p. 91.

70. *a crackt three-farthings.* Silver pieces coined by Elizabeth, thin and liable to crack: behind the Queen's head was a rose: cf. *King John*, I. i. 141–3.

71–2. *It will neuer . . . bone.* Cf. *Iohn Heywoodes woorkes*, 1562, Pt. II, ch. viii, I iv^v:

> This prouerbe prophecied many yeres agone.
> It will not out of the fleshe that is bred in the bone.

74. *a shoulder . . . horse.* Cf. E. Gosynhill, *The Schole house of women*, 1540 (misprinted 1560), A ii^v:

> As handsome for a man, is a womans corse
> As a shulder of mutton, for a syck horse.

And *Iohn Heywoodes woorkes*, 1562, Pt. I, ch. vii, I iij:

> Thou art, to be plaine, and not to flatter thee,
> As holsome a morsell for my comely cors,
> As a shoulder of mutton for a sicke hors.

75. *for, 'fore.* So in II. ii. 32. Cf. *E.M.O.* II. iii. 153–5, 'Some ten or eleuen pound would doe it all, and suit me *for the heauens*', where the Folio of 1640 reads '*fore the heauens*'.

78. *the Counters.* The two City prisons, each under the control of a sheriff. At this date one was in Wood Street, Cheapside; the prisoners from an older Counter in Bread Street were first lodged in it in 1555. It is described by William Fenner in *The Compters Commonwealth*, 1617, p. 9. The other was in the Poultry near St. Mildred's church. Cf. Middleton, *The Phoenix*, IV. iii. 18–22 (Bullen): 'in that notable city called London stand two most famous universities Poultry and Wood-street, where some are of twenty years' standing, and have took all their degrees, from the Master's side down to the Mistress' side, the Hole'; *E.H.* II. ii. 263–5, 'Let 'hem take their choice, eyther the *Kings Benche*, or the *Fleete*, or which of the two *Counters* they like best.' The plays of *Every Man out of his Humour* and *Eastward Ho* both end in one of the Counters.

has the wrong sow by the eare. The proverb is in *Iohn Heywoodes woorkes*, 1562, Pt. II, ch. ix, K ij. Contrast *E.H.* II. ii. 278, 'You haue the Sowe by the right eare, Sir.'

79. *claps his dish at the wrong mans dore.* In Ray's *Proverbs*, 2nd ed., 1678, p. 239, 'at a wrong man's door'. Beggars carried a wooden dish with a cover which they clapped to attract notice and collect alms. Cf. Heywood, *King Edward IV*, Part II, 1605, V₄, 'Enter M⟨istress⟩ Blage very poorely a begging, with her basket and clap-dish'; *The History of the tryall of Cheualry*, 1605, B2^v, 'I know him as well as the Begger knowes his dish.'

79–80. *I'le lay my hand o' my halfe-peny.* In Ray, 1678, p. 250. Cf. *Iohn Heywoodes woorkes*, 1562, Pt. I, ch. vi, B ij:

> I perfectly feele euen at my fyngers ende.
> So harde is your hande set on your halfpeny,
> That my reasonyng your reason setteth nought by.

83–4. *eate . . . anger.* Cf. III. i. 181–2.

87. Jonson's verse admits an occasional Alexandrine: that it was intentional is shown by the fact that the Quarto in this passage reads 'disswade me', and in *Poet*. I. ii. 231, 'O sacred *poesie*, thou spirit of *Romane* artes', where 'Romane' is an insertion of the Folio in the Quarto text, and in *Alch*. III. iv. 4, 'He neuer heard her *Highnesse* dote, till now (he sayes)' where 'he sayes' is a similar addition. Occasionally the line has a middle pause which makes it effective: 'Safe from the wolues black iaw, and the dull asses hoofe' (*Poet*. Apol. Dial. 239).

104. *blow the eares*. Cf. *Poet*. I. ii. 61–2, 'They wrong mee, Sir, . . . That blow your eares with these vntrue reports.'

106. *flat cap*. Stow in his *Survay*, 1603, p. 545, relates how in the reign of Henry VIII 'The youthfull Citizens also tuke them to the new fashion of flatte caps, knit of woollen yearne blacke, but so light that they were forced to tye them vnder their chins, for else the wind would be maister ouer them.' When the fashion changed at court, 'flat-cap' became a term of derision for a citizen: cf. *E.H.* I. i. 101, 'Mary fough, goodman flat-cap.'

shining shooes, i.e. blackened shoes. Cf. Mayne, *The City Match*, 1639, I. iv:

> *New*. But for thee, Franck, O Transmutation!
> Of Satin chang'd to Kerseyhose I sing.
> Slid his shooes shine too. *Br*. They have the Gresham dye.
> Dost thou not dresse thy selfe by 'em? I can see
> My face in them.

Gifford quoted Massinger, *The Guardian*, II. iii (*Three New Playes*, 1655, p. 32), where 'owners of dark shops' are identified,

> If they walk on foot, by their Rat-colour'd stockings,
> And shining shooes. If Horsmen, by short Boots,
> And riding furniture of several Counties.

And Shirley, *The Doubtful Heir*, 1652, II. ii (*Six New Playes*, 1653, p. 16):

> *Capt*. Will you to your Shops agen?
> *Ant*. I have no mind to Woosted Stockings agen,
> And Shoos that Shine, I would were colours still.

118–19. *quarrell'd My brother*. For the transitive use cf. *Gram*. I. iv. 8, 'we are not now to quarrel *Orthographie*'.

123–4. *Like . . . quack-saluers . . . set the bills vp*. Cf. *Alch*. v. i. 12, 13:

> You saw no Bills set vp, that promis'd cure
> Of agues, or the tooth-ach?

II. ii. 9. *to night*, last night, like 'hac nocte' in Plautus, *Captivi* 127, *Amphitryo* 731. So III. i. 2, *D. is A*. IV. i. 18.

19. (*god forgiue me I should sweare*). Cf. Fallace in *E.M.O*. IV. i. 19, 20, 'By the faith of a Gentlewoman, (beast that I am to say it)'. The qualifying clause is added to preserve middle-class respectability: cf.

Hotspur's contempt for the 'Sunday-citizens'' mild oaths in *1 Henry IV*, III. i. 248–51.

21–2. *draw my sword in . . . Fleet-street*. Lodge, *Wits Miserie*, 1596, p. 63, describes the fiend of Brawling-contention: 'In a fray in Fleet-street you shall daily see him foremost, for but in fighting, chiding, and scolding, hee hath no countenance.' Cf. Sir W. Cornwallis, *Essays*, 1600, N4, 'I can remember no sight more offensiue to me then a variable old man, that can speake of nothing but the fashions of his Time, the wench then in price, how many hacks he hath had in his Buckler in a Fleet-streete fray, or the friskes of the Italian Tumblers.'

23. *Madge-howlet*. 'Madge-Owle', *S.S.* II. iii. 8. 'Madge' was a popular name for the owl: 'Also there is Vlula; and this is that which we call the Howlet, or the Madge.'—Swan, *Speculum Mundi*, 1643, p. 397.

24. *tumbrell-slop*. Cf. *C. is A.* IV. viii. 35, 'Stay let me see these drums, these kilderkins, these bombard slops.'

25. *Garagantua*. Rabelais began to publish his *Gargantua and Pantagruel* in parts in 1535. But the reference here is to Gargantua, the hero of the folk-tale, rather than to Rabelais, whose great work was little known in England at this date. The earliest English reference is in *The book of Merchants*, 1547, C3. In the Stationers' Register 'Gargantua his prophesie' was entered on 6 April 1592, and 'A booke entituled the historie of Gargantua' on 4 December 1594 (Arber, *Transcript*, ii. 607, 667). Shakespeare's reference in *As You Like it*, III. ii. 210, to 'Gargantua's mouth' is closely contemporary with Jonson's here. A lost translation of the *Croniques admirables* of Francis Girault is probably the source of these allusions (see Huntington Brown's edition).

30. *right hangman cut*, dressed ready for the hangman. One of Jonson's elliptical phrases.

31. *ging*, company. Cf. *Alch.* V. i. 21, *N.I.* I. v. 46.

34. *as he brewes. . . .* Cf. *Iohn Heywoodes woorkes*, 1562, B iiij, pt. i, ch. viii:

> For had I lookt afore, with indifferent eye,
> Though haste had made me thurst neuer so drye:
> Yet to droune this drought, this must I needes thynke,
> As I woulde needes breue, so must I needes drynke.

II. iii. Margin [*To them*]. Jonson usually heads a new scene with the full list of characters who take part in it. But when new characters enter to those already on the stage and Jonson marks a new scene with their entrance, he usually gives a list of the newcomers only and adds a note in the margin '*To them*', as in IV. iii. Here and in IV. vii and ix this is wrongly done, and in the fifth act this stage-direction is given inconsistently in the 1616 Folio, which omits it for scenes ii and iii.

9, 10. Kitely's consummate fatuity is sustained in minor touches throughout the play: cf. ll. 22–4, III. iii. 80–2, IV. viii. 38–9, 45.

20. *in the pride of blood*, in the full flush of passion.

35. *rose-water*. Mr. Wheatley quotes Venner's *Via Recta ad Vitam longam*, 1620, p. 129, to show that fruit was frequently eaten with rose-water: 'Raspis or Framboise being ripe, . . . may bee eaten by themselues . . . or if there be neede of cooling with Rose, or Violet-water and Sugar.'

38. *Musse*, mouse. Cf. *Hamlet*, iii. iv. 183. 'Pinch Wanton on your cheeke, call you his Mouse'. Edward Alleyn begins a letter to his wife 'My good sweett harte and loving mouse' (*Henslowe Papers*, ed. Greg, p. 34). Jonson would know the terms of endearment in Martial, *Ep.* xi. xxix. 3, 'Cum me murem, cum me tua lumina dicis'.

46. *this new disease*. The title seems to have included forms of fever which were imperfectly diagnosed. Cf. G. Wapull, *The Tyde taryeth no Man*, 1576, G iij:

> Yes truely he dyed in a great madnesse,
> And went with the Tyde boate straight into hell . . .
> And some sayd he dyed of the new sicknesse.

And Sir C. Cornwallis, *The Life and Death of Henry, Prince of Wales*, 1641, p. 29, 'the Feauer, (called for the strange diversitie) *The new Disease*'. Prince Henry died of it (typhoid fever probably in his case).

47–8. *come in, out of the aire*. The medical science of Jonson's day thought fresh air bad for an invalid: cf. *B.F.* v. vi. 95, 'Get your wife out o' the ayre, it wil make her worse else'; and *Hamlet*, ii. ii. 205, where Polonius, thinking Hamlet to be ill, suggests that he should 'walk out of the air'. Night-air was even worse: see *Julius Caesar*, ii. i. 263–7.

54. *shee has me i' the wind*. Cf. *Sej.* ii. 406, 'They haue vs in the wind.' A hunting metaphor: cf. Turbervile, *The Noble Arte of Venerie*, 1575, p. 242, 'When he', i.e. the hart, 'smelleth or venteth anye thing, then we saye he *hath* (*this or that*) *in the winde*'. The game was intercepted on the windward side to force it into the toils laid in the opposite direction.

57–69. Quoted in R. Allot's anthology, *Englands Parnassus : Or the choysest Flowers of our Moderne Poets*, 1600, p. 143, under the heading '*Iealousie*'.

60. *the houses of the braine*. The old anatomists divided the brain into three houses or cells or ventricles: imagination was the foremost, reason the middle, and memory the hindmost cell. See Vicary, *The Anatomie of the Bodie of Man*, 1577, E.E.T.S., Extr. Ser. 53, pp. 30–1. 'The substaunce of the braine is diuided into three partes or ventrikles. . . . First, in the foremost Ventrikle God hath founded and set the . . . fyue Wittes. . . . And also there is one part of this Ventrikle, the vertue that is called Fantasie. . . . In the other parte of the same Ventrikle is ordeyned and founded the Imaginatiue vertue. . . . In the middest sel or ventrikle there is founded and ordeyned the Cogitatiue or estimatiue vertue. . . . In the thirde Ventrikle, and last, there is founded and ordeyned the vertue Memoratiue. . . .' And *The whole worke of that famous Chirurgion Maister Iohn Vigo*, 1586, f. 6 *b*, 'The braine is a substance full of marrowe diuided into three ventricles, of which there is one in the fore part which is greater then the other three. The second is in the middest. The third

hath his residence in the hinder part. And therefore, after *Galens* iudgement, it is the foundation of imagination, and of deuising, and of
remembrance.' The ventricles are elaborately described ff. 6–8. Gregory
Reisch's *Margarita Philosophica*, 1503, X, ch. xxi, gives a diagram of the
head, showing the formation of the ventricles.

60–1. *it begins . . . vpon the phantasie*. The medical theories of Jonson's
time always made this the starting-point of any form of brain trouble.
Cf. Burton, *Anatomy*, 1621, pp. 121–2, 'So that the first steppe and
fountaine of all our grieuances in this kinde', [viz. melancholy or choler]
'is *læsa Imaginatio*, which misinforming the Heart, causeth all these
distemperatures, alteration and confusion of spirits and humors'; he
explains apparitions and noises in the head (p. 267) : 'The Organs corrupt
by a corrupt phantasie, as *Lemnius lib. i. cap.* 16 well quotes. *cause a
great agitation of spirits, and humors, which wander too and fro in all the
creekes of the braine, and cause such apparitions before their eyes.*' Timothy
Bright's *A Treatise of Melancholy*, 1586, ch. xvii (pp. 99–107), discusses
the whole subject '*How melancholie procureth feare, sadnes, dispaire, and
such other passions*'.

67. *sensiue*. Cf. *Sej.* v. 768, where the line 'As if his statues now were
sensitiue' is corrected in the Folio to 'now were sensiue grown'.

II. iv. 4. *the lye*. Cf. IV. iv. 11–14; and *Othello*, III. iv. 1–5, '*Des*. Do you
know, Sirrah, where Lieutenant *Cassio* lyes? *Clo*. I dare not say he lies
anywhere. *Des*. Why man? *Clo*. He's a Soldier, and for me to say a
Souldier lyes, 'tis stabbing.'

5. *the Fico*. 'To give the fico' was to thrust the thumb between the
forefingers or swell out the cheek by putting it into the mouth: cf.
2 Henry IV, v. iii. 117–18:

> I speake the truth
> When Pistoll lyes, do this, and figg-me, like
> The bragging Spaniard.

At the words 'do this' he makes the gesture. So Lodge in *Wits Miserie*,
1596, p. 23, 'Behold next I see *Contempt* marching forth, giuing mee the
Fico with this [*sic*] thombe in his mouth.' It is to this form of insult that
Brainworm alludes, not to the poisoned fig of Italy and Spain.

9. *drie foot*, by the mere scent. Later Brainworm varies the metaphor:
'he has follow'd you ouer the field's, by the foot, as you would doe a hare
i' the snow' (III. ii. 46–8).

11. *conspiracie*, plot. 'The notion of combination being lost sight of'
O.E.D. s.v. 'conspire', Ib.

12. *blew-waiters*. Serving-men were dressed in blue. Cf. *C. is A.* I. vii.
26–7, 'euer since I belongd to the blew order'; and J. Cooke, *Greenes Tu
Quoque*, 1614, D2 (of a serving-man), 'and for his colours, they are
according to the season, in the Summer hee is apparrelled (for the most
part) like the heauens, in blew, in the winter, like the earth, in freeze'.

13. *motley*, the fool's coat. Cf. *Ep.* liii. 9. *Wee may weare motley at the*

yeeres end, we may be made fools of in the end: or does Brainworm refer to something that might happen at his old master's death to a servant who fell into disfavour with the heir? (J. Dover Wilson.)

20. *true garb.* Cf. an excised passage of the Quarto text, v. iii. 163, where Brainworm describes himself as 'begging . . . in the most accomplisht and true garbe (as they tearme it)'. Moorfields was a noted haunt of soldier-beggars: cf. *E.H.* I. i. 137–8, 'mee thinkes I see thee already walking in Moore fields without a Cloake, with halfe a Hatte, without a band, a Doublet with three Buttons, without a girdle, a hose with one point and no Garter, with a cudgell vnder thine arme' (cf. l. 88 below) 'borrowing and begging three pence'; and Field, *A Woman is a Weathercocke*, IV. ii (1612, G4), 'God a mercy, zoones methinkes I see my selfe in Moore-fields, vpon a woaden leg, begging three pence.' Robert Anton in *The Philosophers Satyrs*, 1616, p. 20, notes among the characters that haunt Moorfields:

> *lymping Souldiers*, and *wild trauellers*,
> That sit a Sunning vnder some *greene tree*,
> Wondring what *riches* are, or *rich men* be.

21. *Lance-knights*, mercenary footsoldiers, especially those armed with a lance or pike. The word is an adaptation of the German *Lanzknecht*.

35. *iet ring.* Cf. *Gipsies Metamorphosed*, 932–3, 'They haue robd me too of . . . a Iett ringe I had, to drawe *Iacke Strawe* hether a holidayes.' Jet was a favourite material for cheap rings owing to its electrical attraction: cf. III. iii. 25, *N.I.* I. iii. 142. Mr. Thorn-Drury comments, 'When jet rings had posies in them were they lined with silver? Cf. *Manningham's Diary*, p. 83, "Posies for a jet ring lined with sylver."'

36. *the poesie.* Cf. *C.R.* IV. v. 114–15, 'please you, sir, to accept this poore ruby, in a ring, sir. The *poesie* is of my owne deuice. *Let this blush for me*, sir.'

42. *the deeper, the sweeter.* A drinking proverb. Cf. Cooke, *Greenes Tu Quoque*, 1614, D2, 'And againe the Prouerbe sayes, The deeper the sweeter: There has the seruing-man the vantage againe, for he drinks still in the bottome of the pot'; S. S., *The Honest Lawyer*, 1616, H4, Gripe, giving drink, says, 'So, off with't bottome and all: the deeper the sweeter.'

49. *foll.* Compare Shirley's burlesque in *The Schoole of Complement*, IV. v (1631, p. 56):

> '*Gorg.* Good your worship bestow a small piece of siluer vpon a poore souldier, new-come out of the Low-Countries, that haue beene in many hot seruices, against the Spaniard, the French, and great Turke. I haue beene shot seuen times thorow the body, my eyes blowne vp with gun-powder, halfe my skull seard off with a Canon, and had my throat cut twice in the open field: good your worship, take compassion vpon the caterwaking [sic] fortunes of a forlorne Gentleman, that haue lost the vse of my veines: good your generous nature take compassion vpon me, I haue but foure fingers and a

thumbe vpon one hand: can worke, and woonnot: one small piece of gratefull siluer, to ⟨pay⟩ for my lodging, I beseech you venerable sir.'

54. *rather die with silence, then liue with shame.* The antithesis recalls *Euphues*, quoted in the text of *E.M.O.* v. x. 34–6, and the slightly elevated style indicates the gentleman. Shift affects it in *E.M.O.* III. vi. 64–7, and his 'Hard is the choice' is another euphuistic touch (ib. 79, 80).

59. *Bohemia, Hungaria, Dalmatia.* Ferdinand (afterwards the Emperor Ferdinand I) was crowned king of Hungary in 1527, but he only nominally ruled it. He had to fight a rival John Zapolya, who was a vassal of Selim II; Zapolya died in 1540, and next year the country passed under Turkish rule for nearly a hundred and fifty years, and became a battle-ground.

63. *Alepo,* taken by Selim I in 1516; the capture added Syria to his empire.

Vienna, relieved in 1529.

64. *the Adriatique gulfe.* Perhaps suggested by the battle of Lepanto, 1571.

76, 83. *veluet scabberd . . . siluer hilt.* Cf. Stubbes, *The Anatomie of Abuses,* 1583, ed. Furnivall, i, p. 62: 'To these haue they their Rapiers, Swoords and Daggers, gilt twise or thrise ouer the hilts, with good Angell golde, or els argented ouer with siluer both within and without, and if it be true as I heare say it is, there be some hiltes made all of pure siluer itself, and couered with golde. Othersome at the least are Damasked, Vernished, and ingrauen marueilous goodly: and least any thyng should be wantyng to set forthe their pride, their scaberds and sheathes of Veluet or the like; for leather, though it be more proffitable and as seemely, yet wil it not carie such a porte or countenance like the other.' Fynes Moryson in his *Itinerary,* 1617, Part III, IV. ii, comments on the use of the velvet scabbard as a 'peculiar fashion, which I neuer obserued in any other part', of the French and the English.

82. *a Spaniard!* Stephen does not know that Toledo is in Spain.

87. *there's another shilling.* Like Sir Andrew Aguecheek in *Tw. Night,* II. iii. 30–3.

88. *Higgin-Bottom.* Not certainly identified. Gifford referred to the correspondence in Lodge's *Illustrations,* ii, pp. 215–18, about the dispute which the Earl of Shrewsbury had with his tenants in May, 1579. One of these, Otwell Higgenbotham, was examined before the Privy Council. Elizabeth interested herself in the case, and the tenants seem to have won it.

II. v. 8, 9. From Ovid, *Fasti,* v. 57, 69–70:

> Magna fuit quondam capitis reverentia cani . . .
> verba quis auderet coram sene digna rubore
> dicere? censuram longa senecta dabat.

8. *buffon.* The usual form in Jonson (*C.R.* III. iv. 41; *Poet.* v. iii. 372,

Apol. Dial. 189; *Volp.* ded. 57, *Entertainment at Althorp*, 289, *M.L.* I. ii. 42), but 'buffoon' came in later: see Drayton, *The Moone-Calfe*, 1627, p. 163, 'Him to associate some Buffoon doth get.'

14–34. From Quintilian, i. 2. 6–8 'Utinam liberorum nostrorum mores non ipsi perderemus! Infantiam statim deliciis solvimus. Mollis illa educatio, quam indulgentiam vocamus, nervos omnes mentis et corporis frangit. Quid non adultus concupiscet, qui in purpuris repit? Nondum prima verba exprimit, iam coccum intellegit, iam conchylium poscit. Ante palatum eorum quam os instituimus... Gaudemus, si quid licentius dixerint: verba ne Alexandrinis quidem permittenda deliciis risu et osculo excipimus. Nec mirum: nos docuimus, ex nobis audiunt, nostras amicas, nostros concubinos vident, omne convivium obscaenis canticis strepit, pudenda dictu spectantur. Fit ex his consuetudo, inde natura.'

22. *dearling.* This spelling is found here and in *Volp.* I. ii. 71 in the 1616 Folio; in *Alch.* III. iv. 3 in the Quarto and both Folios; in *D. is A.* v. vi. 74 in the 1640 Folio.

24. *mother' her selfe.* See II. i. 6 n.

39. *to seale.* Cf. *Alch.* II. i. 12, *Und.* xlvii. 15.

45. *the Venetian cortezans.* Coryat in his *Crudities*, 1611, devotes a chapter to them; in Day's *Humour out of breath*, 1608, II. i, Venice is described as 'the best flesh-shambles in *Italie*'.

48, 49. From Horace, *Ep.* I. i. 53, 65, 66:

> O cives, cives, quaerenda pecunia primum est . . .
>   rem facias, rem,
> si possis recte, si non, quocumque modo rem.

50–5. From Juvenal, *Sat.* xiv. 7–10, 13–14:

> . . . iuvenis, qui radere tubera terrae,
> boletum condire et eodem iure natantis
> mergere ficedulas didicit nebulone parente
> et cana monstrante gula . . .
>   cupiet lauto cenare paratu
> semper et a magna non degenerare culina.

58, 59. Ibid. 31–3:

>   velocius et citius nos
> corrumpunt vitiorum exempla domestica, magnis
> cum subeunt animos auctoribus.

Similarly the language in ll. 61–4 is suggested by Juvenal, 59–69.

63. *leystalls,* dung-heaps: 'lay-stall', *Und.* xxi. 8.

80. *the price of two cannes of beere,* twopence. Cf. E. S., *The Discouerie of The Knights of the Poste,* 1597, A3ᵛ, 'I tolde you of as much money as filde a quart, which God wot was but one penny for the which I had a quart of ale at *Colbrooke*'; Lodge and Greene, *A Looking Glasse,* &c., 1598, D2ᵛ, '*Clowne.* I will not do a stroake of worke to day, for the ale is good ale, and you can aske but a peny for a pot, no more by the statute.'

89. *not . . . giuen in the course of time*, i.e. you will one day be repaid: 'Cast your bread upon the waters.'

96. *sordid-base.* Cf. *Sej.* III. 188, 'with sordide-base desire of gaine'.

108. *mettall* or mettle, spelling and sense being interchangeable. Cf. *Julius Caesar*, I. ii. 308–9:

> Thy Honorable Mettle may be wrought
> From that it is dispos'd.

112. *thou insist's.* A euphonic form of the second person singular, also found in *M.L.* IV. viii. 21, 'Envious Sir *Moath*, that eates on that which feeds thee'; *Epig.* lviii. 5, 'And so my sharpnesse thou no lesse dis-ioynts'. There is an interesting recognition of the idiom in P. G.'s (? P. Greenwood's) *Grammatica Anglicana*, 1594, p. 15, '*De Verbo.* Contractionibus fere utimur in Carmine. Præsens 1. *Hate.* 2. *Hatest.* 3. *Hateth.* . . . Contract 2. *Hates*, 3. *Hates.*'

116. *I.* For the extra syllable prefixed to the line cf. III. vi. 29, IV. vi. 2.

119. *purchast*, acquired.

143. *cassock*, a soldier's cloak or loose outer coat—the original sense of the word.

musket-rest. Cf. *E.M.O.* IV. iv. 25–6, 'he walkes vp and downe like a charg'd musket, no man dares encounter him: that's his rest there. PVNT. His rest? why has he a forked head?' A support was needed for the old unwieldy musket; it consisted of a pole of tough wood, with an iron spike at the end for fixing in the ground, and a semicircular piece of iron at the top to rest the musket on. The soldier carried it on his right shoulder by strings fastened below the head. The firelock, which did away with the necessity of a rest, was invented in France about 1635 and was generally used in the Civil War.

144. *Mile-end.* Then a common on the main eastern road out of London, used as a training-ground for the City bands. Thus Stow, *A Summarie of the Chronicles of England*, 1604, p. 420, records that on 27 August 1599, '3000 Citizens householders and subsidy men, shewed on the Miles end, where they trained all that day, and other vntill the fourth of September.' Cf. IV. vi. 73, and Barnaby Rich, *The Fruites of long Experience*, 1604, p. 33, in which Captain Skill argues with Captain Pill: 'God blesse me, my Countrey and friendes, from his direction that hath no better *Experience* then what he hath atteyned vnto at the fetching home of a Maye-pole, at a Midsomer fighte, or from a trayning at *Milende-Greene*.' Beaumont has a burlesque of the muster in *The Knight of the Burning Pestle*, v. ii.

145–6. *counterfeit . . . slip.* A 'slip' was a counterfeit coin: cf. Greene, *A Disputation, Betweene a Hee Conny-catcher, and a Shee Conny-catcher*, 1592, E4, 'and therefore he went & got him a certaine slips, which are counterfeyt peeces of mony being brasse, & couered ouer with siluer, which the common people call slips'. The play on words recurs *M.L.* III. vii. 26–8, *Und.* xlv. 17: cf. *Rom. and Jul.* II. iv. 44–8.

III. i. 8. *through*, throw.

13. *faces about*. Cf. *S. of N.* IV. iv. 51:

> *Faces about to the right hand*, the *left*,
> Now, *as you were*.

22. *quos . . . Iupiter*. From Virgil, *Aeneid*, vi. 129.

27. *Thespian girles*. In Ovid, *Metamorphoses*, v. 310, the Muses are 'Thespiades deae'.

35. *Symmachus*, a scholar, statesman, and orator, consul in A.D. 391, whose collected letters were published in ten books after his death; he modelled his style on that of Pliny.

38. *marle*, marvel: *E.M.O.* Ind. 322 'mar'le'. The noun is in *S.W.* III. i. 43 ''Tis mar'l' . . . .

camell. Cf. *Sej.* I. 568, 'Auoid mine eye, dull camell.'

94. *vtters*. A quibble on the commercial sense, 'to put into circulation': cf. IV. ii. 57.

95–6. *out of measure . . . in measure*. Cf. *The Triall of Treasure*, 1567, D iii (Lust to Lady Treasure), 'Ah lady, I loue thee in faith out of measure.' Inclination, in an aside, 'It is out of measure in deede as you saie.' Jonson repeated the quibble in *C.R.* II. iv, 52–4, 'PHI. And did I not dance mouingly the last night? MOR. Mouingly? out of measure (in troth) sweet *charge*. MER. A happy commendation, to dance out of measure.'

96. *I faith* = 'Ay, faith'—not, as Gifford and later editors print, 'I' faith'.

115. *Strigonium*, Graan in Hungary, which was retaken from the Turks in the year 1595, after having been in their possession nearly half a century. 'It should be observed, that the inroads which the Turks made into the Emperor's dominions, had made it fashionable to go a volunteering in his service; and we find that Thomas Lord Arundel of Wardour was created at this very time a Count of the Empire, as a reward of his signal valour; and because in forcing the water tower near Strigonium, he took a banner from the Turks with his own hand. (Whalley.)

141. *demi-culuerings*, cannon of about four and a half inches bore.

142. *giue on*, make the assault.

144. *linstock*, 'a staff about three feet long, having a pointed foot to stick in the deck or ground, and a forked head to hold a lighted match.'— *O.E.D.*

145. *petrionel*, a large pistol or carbine. The common form is 'petronel', but 'petrionel' is found in *E.M.O.* v. v. 32, and 'peitronell'—probably a misprint for this—in *S.W.* IV. v. 112. The Quarto spells 'Petrinell'.

150. *a good figure obseru'd*, i.e. in saying 'put them to the sword' he used a good old-fashioned expression.

155. *Morglay*, the sword of Bevis of Southampton. Selden refers to it in a note on Drayton's *Polyolbion*, 1613, Song II, p. 37: 'His sword is kept as a relique in *Arundell* Castle, not equalling in length (as it is now worne) that of *Edward the Third's* at *Westminster*.'

Excalibur was the sword of Arthur, and *Durindana* the sword of Orlando, with which he is fabled to have cleft the Pyrenees. Cf. Harington's *Orlando Furioso*, 1591, xiv, st. 57:

> Durindan, a blade of temper rare,
> That *Hector* erst, and now *Orlando* bare.

165. *guilder*, a Dutch silver coin worth about 1s. 8d.

170. *if you can take him, so*, if you can fathom him, well and good.

171. *prouant*, supplied by the government stores, and therefore inferior. Gifford quotes Massinger, *The Maid of Honour*, 1632, I. i, B2ᵛ:

> A knave with halfe a britch there,
> And no shirt, . . . if you beare not
> Your selves both in, and upright, with a provant sword
> Will slash your skarlets, and your plush a new way.

181. *connie-catching*, swindling. Cf. *C. is A.* IV. vii. 52.

183–4. *ostrich stomach*. The ostrich is attracted by bright metal, such as tin or a silver spoon, swallows it, and even digests it owing to the extreme acidity of its stomach. For the quibble cf. III. iv. 35–7.

III. ii. 12. *and you had not confest it*. Cf. Sir T. More, *Epigrammata*, 1563, 'Ridiculum, in Minacem':

> Thrasonis uxorem bubulcus rusticus
>   Absente eo uitiauerat.
> Domum reuersus miles ut rem comperit
>   Armatus & ferus insilit.
> Tandem assecutus solum in agris rusticum,
>   Heus clamat heus heus furcifer.
> Restat bubulcus, saxaq́; in sinum legit.
>   Ille ense stricto clamitat,
> Tu coniugem meam attigisti carnifex?
>   Respondit imperterritus,
> Feci. fateris, inquit? At ego omnes Deos
>   Deasq́; testor ô scelus,
> In pectus hunc ensem tibi capulo tenus,
>   Ni fassus esses, abderem.

18. *by his leaue . . . vnder his fauour*. Repeated *D. is A.* I. iii. 26–7:

> Nay, now, you ly:
> Vnder your fauour, friend, for, I'll not quarrell.

The virtue of a qualifying phrase is also shown in Randolph, *The Jealous Lovers*, 1632, I. vi:

> *Tyn.* Good impertinent.
> *Asot.* Impertinent? Impertinent in thy face.
> Danger accrues upon the word Impertinent!
> Tutour, draw forth thy fatall steel, and slash
> Till he devoure the word Impertinent.

> *Ball.* The word Impertinent will not beare a quarrell:
> The Epithite of Good hath nullified it.
> *Asot.* We are appeas'd - - - Be safe - - I say - - Be safe.

25. *farre the fitter*: a toy is a better comparison than a soldier's instrument; '*eueryone*' then includes children.

29. *conceipted*, pleasant, witty. Cf. *Sej.* 1. 286, 'your lordship is conceited'.

34. *of as bare a coat*, like a poor clergyman.

35. *extraordinarie*, i.e. I am not a regular soldier.

52. *Colman-street*, 'the Bond Street of the period' (Wheatley). It has won literary fame from the sharking colonel of Cowley's comedy, *Cutter of Coleman Street*, published in 1663.

69, 70. *Thames-street . . . the car-men*. In Fletcher and Shirley's *The Night-walker*, iv (*Beaumont and Fletcher*, vol. vii, p. 361, ed. Waller), a carman making a clumsy attempt to ring bells is told:

> You think you are in *Thames-street*
> Justling the Carts.

Diary of H. Machyn (Camden Society, ed. Nichols, p. 296), 'The xxvj day of November ⟨1562⟩ at night was slayne a carter by a Frenche-man, because that the carter cold ⟨not give⟩ hym roome for presse of cartes that was ther that tyme.'

Custome-house key. D. is A. 1. i. 63.

III. iii. 13. *oportunitie*. Cf. Shakespeare, *The Rape of Lucrece*, 876, 886:

> O opportunity thy guilt is great, . . .
> Thou fowle abettor, thou notorious bawd.

And Warner, *Albions England*, 1589, p. 154, of Aeneas and Dido, 'Being there all alone, vnknowne of and vnsought for of their Seruaunts, Oportunitie the chiefe Actresse in al attempts, gaue the Plaudiat in Loue his Comedie.'

19, 20. Milton has the same image in *Comus*, 393–7. For the artificial contrast of 'golden tree' and 'leaden sleepe' cf. *Poet.* III. v. 13–14, 'golden sleepe' and 'siluer *Tyber*'—a translation from Horace in which Jonson has inserted the epithets.

22. *caract*, carat. But Jonson confused the word with 'charact', a sign or mark. It is clear from the *Grammar*, I. iv. 219, that he preferred to spell it 'charact' from the Greek χαρακτήρ, as he does *Disc.*, 2295; but it is 'caract' in *Volp.* I. v. 14, *D. is A.* I. vi. 88, *M.L.* I. i. 44, *F.I.* 330, and 'carract' in *M.L.* I. vii. 38, *Und.* lxxv. 100, lxxxiii. 27, *U.V.* xlii. 30.

36. *little caps*. They were of velvet and fashionable in the City: cf. *B.F.* I. i. 19–23, 'Now you looke finely indeed, *Win!* this Cap do's conuince! you'ld not ha' worne it, *Win*, nor ha' had it veluet, but a rough country Beauer, with a copper-band. . . . Sweete *Win*, let me kisse it!' Gifford quotes *The Taming of the Shrew*, IV. iii. 64–70 (a passage expanded from the older play printed in 1594).

38. *three-pild akornes*. 'Three-pile' was velvet of the richest and

strongest quality. But there is a further quibble: Turbervile in *The Noble Art of Venerie*, 1575, p. 242, says of the hart's horns: 'His heade when it commeth first out, hath a russet pyll vpon it, the whiche is called *Veluet*, and his heade is called then, *a veluet head.*'

40, 50. *Carry' in . . . my' imaginations.* Cf. I. i. 5 n.

44. *Exchange time.* 'Past ten' in the Quarto, and the timetable in the contemporary play, *A Warning for Faire Women*, 1599, C1ᵛ, agrees with this:

> . . . in the morning, til twas nine a clocke,
> I watcht at *Sanders* doore til he came forth,
> Then folowed him to Cornhil, where he staied
> An hower talking in a marchants warehouse,
> From thence he went directly to the Burse,
> And there he walkt another hower at least,
> And I at 's heeles. By this it strooke eleuen,
> Home then he comes to dinner.

But eleven is given as the opening hour for business on the Exchange in Nashe, *The Returne of Pasquill*, 1589, D2ᵛ, and Haughton, *English Men for my Money*, 1616, B1ʳ, ''tis past aleauen, Exchange time full'.

59. *to*, to be compared with.

76. *my priuate.* Cf. *Cat.* III. 481, 'Nor must I be vnmindfull of my priuate.'

88. *precisian*, Puritan.

90. *Fayles*, 'a very old table-game, and one of the numerous varieties of backgammon that were formerly used in this country. It was played with three dice and the usual number of men or pieces. The peculiarity of the game depended on the mode of first placing the men on the points. If one of the players threw some particular throw of the dice he was disabled from bearing off any of his men, and therefore *fayled* in winning the game, and hence the appellation of it.'—F. Douce in Gifford.

Tick-tack, or tric-trac, was also a variety of backgammon. It was played on a board with holes along the edge, in which pegs were placed for scoring. The rules are given in *The Compleat Gamester*, 2nd ed., 1680, p. 112.

96. *But; if.* A good instance of the dramatic value of the old punctuation.

108. *not taken lawfully.* A point in casuistry, for which Gifford quotes *3 Henry VI*, I. ii. 22–4:

> An Oath is no moment, being not tooke
> Before a true and lawfull Magistrate,
> That hath authoritie ouer him that sweares.

138. Quoted in *Bel-vedére or The Garden of the Muses*, 1600, p. 145, under the heading '*Of Feare, Doubt, &c.*'

III. iv. 1. *Fasting dayes.* An Act of 1548, 2 & 3 Edward VI, c. 19, appointed Fridays, Saturdays, Ember days, vigils and Lent as fasting days for the benefit of the fishing trade, 'and that by eating of fish much flesh shall be saved and increased'. In 1562 *An Acte, towching certayne Politique Constitutions made for the maintenance of the Navye*, 5 Elizabeth, c. 5, section xii, added Wednesdays. The penalty for a breach of the Act was a fine of £3 or three months' close imprisonment. In 1585 an Act, 27 Elizabeth, c. 11, repealed the Wednesday fast, and in 1593, 35 Elizabeth, c. 7, the penalties were lessened. For the underlying principle see *A brief note of the benefits that grow to this Realme by the obseruation of Fish Days*, issued by the Privy Council in 1594 (reprinted in Arber's *Garner*, i. 299).

2. *on a light fire*, ablaze. A common expression from the sixteenth to the eighteenth centuries (*O.E.D.*).

7. foll. *choller . . . collar . . . slip your head out*. The same quibble as in *Rom. and Jul*. I. i. 4–6.

14. *rewme*. Cf. Lyly, *Midas*, 1592, III. ii. 56–8 (ed. Bond), '*Motto*. I did but rub his gummes, and presentlie the rewme euaporated. *Licio. Deus bone*, is that worde come into the Barbers bason?'; ibid. v. ii. 105–9, 'If thou encroach vpon our courtly tearmes, weele trounce thee: belike if thou shouldst spit often, thou wouldst call it the rewme. *Motto*, in men of reputation & credit it is the rewme; in such mechanicall mushrumpes, it is a catarre, a pose, the water euill'; and *E.H.* v. ii. 69, 'Pity is a Rheume, that I am subiect too.' But 'rewme' as an affectation had had its day; it was now superseded by 'humour'.

18. *mack*, a distortion of 'mass'. Cf. *Sir John Oldcastle*, 1600, C4, 'Now by the macke, a prettie wench indeed.'

25. *Feed my humour*. Found in Lyly, *Euphues and his England*, 1580, 'To the Ladies', *ad. fin. The Faerie Queene*, 1590, III. ii, st. 12, v. v, st. 55; Lodge and Greene, *A Looking Glasse*, 1598. B; *Richard III* (first published 1597), IV. i. 65.

36. Sr *Bevis his horse*, also celebrated in *Und*. liii. 9, 10:

> Or what we heare our home-borne Legend tell,
>   Of bold Sir *Bevis*, and his *Arundell*.

The 'Legend' was first printed by Wynkyn de Worde in 1500. Editions are entered on the Stationers' Register in 1558, 1560–1, and 1568–9. Cob's craving to eat the war-horse as a protest against fasting-days is his notion of hyperbole.

42. *Flemmish . . . rauen vp more butter*. Jonson alludes to this habit of the Dutch or the Flemings again in *Volp*. I. i. 42, and *B.F.* II. v. 100, 101. There is Alva's historic boast on entering the Netherlands, 'I have tamed men of iron in my day, I shall know how to deal with these men of butter.' Fynes Moryson in his *Itinerary*, 1617, Pt. III, II, ch. iv, p. 97, says of them: 'Touching this peoples diet, Butter is the first and last dish at the Table, whereof they make all sawces, especially for fish, and thereupon by strangers they are merrily called Butter-mouths . . . the Bawers . . ., passing in boates from City to City for trade, carry with them cheese, and boxes of butter for their foode, whereupon in like sort strangers call them

Butter boxes, and nothing is more ordinary then for Citizens of good accompt and wealth to sit at their dores, (euen dwelling in the market place) holding in their hands, and eating a great lumpe of bread and butter with a lunchen of cheese.'

53. *Hannibal.* Pistol reverses the blunder in *2 Henry IV*, ii. iv. 179–80, 'with *Caesar*, and with Caniballs, and Troian Greekes', and Elbow greets Pompey as 'thou wicked *Hanniball*' in *Measure for Measure*, ii. i. 167–70.

54. *fish.* F 3's humourless substitution of 'Flesh' looks like a compositor's attempt at a correction; it is accepted by Whalley and Gifford.

56. *rich as . . . Cophetua.* Two versions of a ballad *King Cophetua and the Beggar-maid* are extant—one in Richard Johnson's *Crown Garland of Goulden Roses*, 1612, 'A Song of a Beggar and a King', which Percy reprinted in the *Reliques*; the other in *A Collection of Old Ballads*, 1723, pp. 138–44, 'Cupid's Revenge, or, An Account of a King who slighted all Women, and at length was constrain'd to marry a Beggar, who prov'd a Fair and Virtuous Queen'. As for his wealth he was a king of Africa, and Pistol in *2 Henry IV*, v. iii. 99, in which there seems to be either a quotation from or a close allusion to the story of Cophetua, has 'I speake of Affrica, and Golden ioyes', which may be a hint on the subject.

64. *beaten like a stock-fish.* 'Stock-fish' was dried cod, which was beaten before it was boiled. Cf. Cotgrave, s.v. 'Carillon': '*Je te frotteray à double carillon*, I will beate thee like a stockfish, I will swinge thee while I may stand ouer thee.'

iii. v. (Heading) THOMAS. Cash is so designated in this scene only.

5. *artificer,* artist.

8, 9. *ioyn'd patten,* lit. of sharing by letters patent in a privilege or office. *O.E.D.* quotes Huloet, *Abcedarium Anglo-Latinum*, 1552, 'Ioynt patent with another, as where, ii. men haue one office ioyntly, *duumuir*.'

9. *the seuen wise masters.* Bias, Pittacus, Cleobulus, Periander, Solon, Chilon, and Thales.

12. *gentlemen of the round,* 'a watch under the command of an officer, which goes round a camp, the ramparts of a fortress, &c., to see that the sentinels are vigilant, or which parades the streets of a town to preserve good order; a military patrol'.—*O.E.D.*, quoting Blandy, *The Castle, or picture of pollicy*, 1581, 18*b*, 'Corporall, gentleman in a company or of the Rounde, Launce passado'.

12, 13. *sit on the skirts,* press hard upon, make themselves a nuisance. Cf. *Iohn Heywoodes woorkes*, 1562, Prouerbes, pt. I, ch. v, B^v:

> And also I shall to reueng former hurts,
> Hold their noses to grinstone, and syt on theyr skurts,
> That erst sate on mine.

And Puttenham, *The Arte of English Poesie*, 1589, pp. 252–3, 'to speake faire to a mans face, and foule behinde his backe, to set him at his trencher and yet sit on his skirts for so we vse to say by a fayned friend'.

16, 17. *a shoue-groat shilling.* A shilling used in the game of shovel-board (for which see Strutt, *Sports and Pastimes*). It was slid across the board by a stroke with the palm of the hand and aimed at one of the nine numbered spaces on the board; it needed to be smooth, in order to slip easily. Cf. *2 Henry IV*, II. iv. 182–3, 'Quoit him downe (*Bardolph*) like a shoue-groat shilling'; and John Taylor, *A Shilling, Or, The Trauailes of Twelue-pence*, 1622 ?, B2:

> For why with me the vnthrifts euery day,
> With my face downewards do at shoue-boord* play,

where Taylor has a marginal note '* Edw. shillings for the most part are vsed at shooue-bord'; one of these is figured in the frontispiece.

17. *Reformado's*, officers of a 're-formed' or disbanded company. Cf. *S.W.* v. ii. 67, 'Knights *reformados*'.

22. *Serieant-Maior.* In the seventeenth century a field officer, next in rank to the lieutenant-colonel, and corresponding partly to the 'major' and partly to the 'adjutant' of the modern army (*O.E.D.*).

23. *Coronell.* The original form from the French *coronel*, but 'colonel' appears *circa* 1580. See the interesting discussion in the *O.E.D.* The two forms were used indifferently; 'coronel' disappeared in writing *circa* 1650, but still survives in pronunciation.

27. *a weauer of language*, a spinner of yarns.

31. *a Hounds-ditch man.* Cf. S. Rowlands, *The Letting of Humours Blood in the Head-vaine*, 1600, D2ᵛ:

> . . . into *Hounds-ditch*, to the Brokers row:
> Or any place where that trade doth remaine,
> Whether of *Holborne Conduit*, or *Long-lane*;

and W. Parkes, *The Curtaine-Drawer of the World*, 1612, p. 4 (of the age of primeval innocence), '. . . not one Broker had all *Hounds-ditch*, which now is able to make ten Juries, and cloath all the naked Sauadges in *Virginia*, with the skins or cases that the vnwily serpents of our age haue cast, or rather haue beene puld from, and stript, by creeping into too narrow Angles and corners'; Dekker, *The Seuen deadlie Sinnes of London*, 1606, '. . . spying the Brokers of *Hownsditch* shuffling themselues so long together (like a false paire of Cards) till the Knaues be vppermost'.

One of the deuil's neere kinsmen. In *D. is A.* I. i. 143, Satan acknow-ledges the relationship—'Or let our tribe of Brokers furnish you'; cf. *Merry Conceited Jests of George Peele* (Peele's *Works*, ed. Bullen, ii, p. 376), 'at Beelzebub's brother the broker's'.

34. *a craftie knaue needs no broker.* Cf. *S. of N.* II. v. 83–4, and *2 Henry VI*, I. ii. 100–3:

> They say, A craftie Knaue do's need no Broker,
> Yet am I *Suffolke* and the Cardinalls Broker.
> *Hume*, if you take not heed, you shall goe neere
> To call them both a payre of craftie Knaues;

A Knacke to knowe a Knaue, 1594, C2ᵛ (Honesty, alluding to Conicatcher and Broker):

> . . . some wil say,
> A crafty knaue needs no broker,
> But here is a craftie knaue and a broker to:
> Then imagin there wants not a knaue.

36. *Well put off.* For this form of retort cf. *Richard III*, i. ii. 70–2.

62–3. *seruing of god.* Not unlike Dogberry's notion in *Much Ado*, iv. ii. 18–23.

69. *Fire on your match.* An artificial toning-down of the Quarto, 'A pox on your match.'

73. *Trinidado*, the best tobacco, according to Heylin, *Cosmographie*, 1652, iv, p. 173, 'TRINIDADO . . . abundantly well stored with such commodities as are of the natural growth of *America*, viz. *Maize*, . . . and the best kind of *Tobacco*, much celebrated formerly by the name of a *Pipe of Trinidado.*' Rowland White writes to Sir R. Sidney on 27 July 1600, 'I was desired by Mr. *Roger Manners*, that you will send him for a Token, a Ball of Tobacco, high Trinidado; you can send him nothing, that will more encrease his Loue towards you' (*Sidney Papers*, ii, p. 208).

77–81. For tobacco as a substitute for food see the account of Hawkins's second voyage in Hakluyt, *The Principall Nauigations*, &c., 1589, p. 541, 'The *Floridians* when they trauell haue a kinde of herbe dryed, which with a cane, and an earthen cup in the end, with fire, and the dried herbs put together, do sucke thorow the cane the smoke thereof, which smoke satisfieth their hunger, and therewith they liue foure or fiue dayes without meat or drinke, and this all the Frenchmen vsed for this purpose: yet do they holde opinion withall, that it causeth water and fleame to void from their stomacks'; and W. Lithgow, *The Totall Discourse, Of the Rare Aduentures, . . . of long nineteene Yeares Trauayles . . . in Europe, Asia, and Affrica*, 1632, p. 375, where he says that in seven days' wanderings in the Libyan desert 'our victuals and water done, we were forced to relye vpon Tobacco'.

82. *diuine.* A stock epithet at this period. Gifford quotes *The Faerie Queene*, iii. v, st. 32:

> Into the woods thenceforth in hast she went,
> To seeke for hearbes, that mote him remedy; . . .
> There, whether it diuine *Tobacco* were,
> Or *Panachœa*, or *Polygony*,
> She found, and brought it to her patient deare.

86. *Balsamum.* Gerard in his *Herball*, 1597, p. 560, says of balm, 'the iuice thereof glueth togither greene woundes'.

87. *Sᵗ. Iohn's woort.* Cf. G. Baker's translation of Gesner, *The Practise of the new and old phisicke*, 1599, f. 147ᵛ, 'The oyle of S. *Iohns* wort, is hot and drie, and stipticke, through which it closeth and healeth the wounds of sinewes cutte, and the burning of fire'; and N. Culpeper,

The English Physitian Enlarged, 1656, 'St. Johns-wort is as singular a Wound herb, as any other whatsoever, either for inward Wounds, hurts, or Bruises, to be boyled in Wine and drunk, or prepared into Oyl or Oyntment, Bath or Lotion outwardly.'

88. *Nicotian*, so named from Jaques Nicot, the French ambassador at Lisbon, by whom tobacco was introduced into France in 1560. But 'Nicotian' is a generic name for the plant: is Bobadill blundering?

89. 90. *expulsion . . . obstructions.* Cf. Sir John Davies's *Epigrammes* (added to the undated *Ovid* of Marlowe, 8vo, Mason copy in Bodley, G1ᵛ):

> It is *Tobacco*, whose sweet substantiall fume,
> The hellish torment of the teeth doth ease,
> By drawing downe, and drying vp the rewme,
> The Mother and the Nurse of each disease.
> It is *Tobacco* which doth colde expell,
> And cleares the obstructions of the Arteries,
> And surfets threatning Death digesteth well,
> Decocting all the stomackes crudities.

96. *tabacco-traders.* In the Quarto 'pothecaries'. In *The Alchemist* Abel Drugger, the apothecary, is 'A Tabacco-man' and sells 'good tabacco', unadulterated (I. iii. 21–7); and Henry Buttes in *Dyets Dry Dinner*, 1599, P6, observes '*Fumivendulus* is the best Epithite for an Apothecary.' When Jonson revised *Every Man in His Humour*, the 'drug' was widely sold in London; see B. Rich, *The Honestie of this Age*, 1614, p. 25, 'There is not so base a groome, that commes into an *Ale-house* to call for his pot, but he must haue his *pipe of Tobacco*, for it is a commoditie that is nowe as vendible in euery Tauerne, Inne, and *Ale-House*, as eyther Wine, Ale, or Beare, and for *Apothecaries Shops, Grosers Shops, Chaundlers Shops*, they are (almost) neuer without Company, that from morning till night are still taking of Tobacco.'

108. *foure dyed.* Carleton writes to Chamberlain, 29 Dec. 1601 (*Domestic State Papers, Elizabeth*, cclxxxiii. 48): 'one Jackson who frequented little Brittane street very of⟨ten⟩ died sodainely on monday last and being opened it was Judgd by the Surgens that he did efflare animā wᵗʰ the smoke of Tobacco wᶜʰ he tooke vnsatiably'; and John Deacon, *Tobacco Tortured, or, The Filthy Fume of Tobacco Refined*, 1616, A1, points to 'the vntimely deaths of sundry such excellent personages as (tampering too much therewith) haue (euen now of late) not onely bene sodainly sur-prised by an vnnaturall death, but (which more is) their dead bodies being opened, had all their entrails as blacke as a coale, and the very fat in their bodies resembling (in all outward appearance) the perfect colour of rustie, or reesed bacon', and he cites particularly (p. 43) the 'pitifull experience of *Parson Digbie* at Peterborough of late: who (hauing excessiuely taken *Tobacco* in a tippling house) did instantly fall downe starke dead in the open streets'. Whalley quoted King James, *A Counterblaste to Tobacco*, 1604, D, (Tobacco-smoking) 'makes a kitchin . . . oftentimes in the inward partes of men, soiling and infecting them,

with an vnctuous and oily kind of Soote, as hath bene found in some great *Tobacco* takers, that after their death were opened'.

115–16. *rats-bane, or rosaker*, different preparations of arsenic. Cf. *E.H.* IV. i. 221–2, 'Take *Arsnicke*, otherwise called *Realga* (which indeede is plaine *Ratsbane*).'

118. *cullion*, a coarse expression of abuse. Cf. *Henry V*, III. ii. 19.

121. *meddle with his match*. A proverbial phrase, on which Jonson also quibbles in *B.F.* I. iv. 102–3, where Waspe tells Littlewit, 'meddle you with your match, your *Win*, there, she has as little wit, as her husband'.

137. *drunke*. In common use for smoke, due to a quibble on the word 'pipe'. Cf. the interlude of *Wine, Beere, Ale, and Tobacco contending for superiority*, 1630, C4: '*Tobaco.* What do yee stand at gaze—Tobacco is a drinke too. *Beere.* A drinke? *Tobaco.* Wine, you and I come both out of a pipe'; and a 'tobacconist's', i.e. a smoker's, speech in *The Wandering-Jew*, 1640, D2, 'In one of these pipes is my mornings draught.'

141. (margin) *practises at a post*. These marks were in Finsbury Fields, upright stones or posts three or four feet high. All had names. See Raikes, *Hist. of Hon. Artillery Company*, ii, pp. 125–7. There is a plan, ibid. facing p. 30, and a picture of two, facing p. 126.

150. *the artillerie garden*. The Honourable Artillery Company was incorporated in 1507, revived in 1611, and continued without a break to the Civil War. Its headquarters from 1540 to 1685 were in the Tassell Close without Bishopsgate, where Artillery Lane and Artillery Street still preserve the name. The present ground in Finsbury was leased in 1641. Jonson pokes fun occasionally at the training of the Artillery-yard, e.g. in the epilogue to the *Masque of Christmas*, and in *Und.* xliv. 23–8:

> Well, I say thrive, thrive brave Artillerie yard,
> Thou Seed-plot of the warre, that hast not spar'd
> Powder, or paper, to bring up the youth
> Of *London*, in the Militarie truth,
> These ten yeares day; As all may sweare that looke
> But on thy practise, and the Posture booke.

170. *french dressing*. Cf. *E.H.* I. i. 6; *Sir Gyles Goosecappe*, I. ii (1606, B2ᵛ), '*Foul. O mon dew. Rud.* O doe not sware Captaine. *Foule.* Your Frenchman euer sweares Sir Cutt, vpon the lacke of his lacquay I assure you'; and Chapman, *Caesar and Pompey*, II. i (1631, D), 'Thou shalt . . . drinke with the Dutchman, sweare with the French man, cheat with the English man, brag with the Scot.'

larded, garnished. *Sej.* III. vi; *Hamlet*, IV. v. 29–36:

> White his shroud as the mountain snow,
> Larded with sweet flowers.

III. vi. 25. *Cornu-copiæ*. Etymologically the correct form: Jonson uses it in *S. of N.* III. ii. 119.

37. *Bride-well.* The old palace of Henry VIII was handed over by royal grant in 1553 'to be a Workehouse for the poore and idle persons of the Citie' (Stow, *Survay*, 1603, p. 398).

47. *I haue egges on the spit*, i.e. 'I am very busie. Egges if they be well roasted require much turning.'—Ray, *Proverbs*, 2nd ed., 1678, p. 241. Cf. *B.F.* I. iv. 15–16, 'I, quickly, good Mistresse, I pray you: for I haue both egges o' the Spit, and yron i' the fire.'

III. vii. 11. *the greene lattice.* A window of lattice-work (usually painted red), or a lattice-pattern—the chequers—was a common mark for an inn. Cf. Marston, *1 Antonio and Mellida*, 1602, v. i. 223, ed. Bullen, 'as well known by my wit as an ale-house by a red lattice'. Gifford notes that in his day there was a lane in the City called corruptly Green-Lettuce Lane from the alehouse which once stood in it.

scot, and lot, in its original sense of a parish assessment.

27–9. *life . . . death.* A quibble suited to the illiterate. Cf. Heywood, *Edward IV*, Part I, 1600, v. v, '*Sellinger.* I warrant thee, tanner, fear not thy son's life. *Hobs.* Nay, I fear not his life; I fear his death.'

31–1. *a twelue-moneth and a day*, the legal period for determining the cause of death due to injury or wounds. Skeat (Chaucer, *C.T.*, D 909) suggests as the origin of the phrase that 'it takes an extra day to make the date agree', e.g. from 21 November to 21 November. Gifford quotes Shirley, *The Wittie Faire One*, III. ii (1633, E1ᵛ), 'I, but I will not hurt her I warrant thee, and shee dy within a Tweluemonth and a day Ile be hangd for her.'

63. *Sweet Oliver.* A stock epithet for the rival of 'mad' Orlando in Ariosto's epic: cf. *Und.* xliii. 70, 'All the madde *Rolands*, and sweet *Oliveers*'. A 'ballad' beginning 'O swete Olyuer leaue me not behinde the' was entered on the Stationers' Register to Richard Jones on 6 August 1584, and 'The answeare of O sweete Olyuer' on 20 August (Arber, *Transcript*, ii. 434); and 'O sweete Olyuer altered to ye scrip- tures' on 1 August 1586 (ib. 451).

66. *mettle*, pewter. Cf. Marston, *The Scourge of Villainy*, Sat. ii. 125–7, ed. Bullen.

76. *feare*, frighten.

93. *your parcell of a soldier.* *C.R.* II. i. 28, 'what parcell of man hast thou lighted on for a master?'

IV. i. 7. *vp and downe, like . . . sprites.* Cf. *2 Henry IV*, I. ii. 154–5, 'You follow the yong Prince vp and downe, like his euill Angell', and Puck's song in *Mids. N. D.* III. ii. 396–7, 'Vp and downe, vp and downe, I will leade them vp and downe.'

15. *perboyl'd*, boiled thoroughly—the original sense. The modern sense is due to a confusion with 'part-boiled'.

IV. ii. 1. *Seruant*, lover, authorized admirer—a common use.

11. *To mock an ape withall*, a proverbial phrase for 'dupe a simpleton'.

Marston heads his 9th Satire in *The Scourge of Villainy*, 'Here's a Toy to mock an Ape indeed.'

21. *cheese*. Cf. Tomkis, *Albumazar*, 1615, III. ix:

> Is there no looking-glasse within't; for I hate glasses
> As naturally, as some do Cats, or Cheese.

22. *bag-pipe*. Cf. *Merch. of Venice*, IV. i. 49.

25. *censure of a* —— The aposiopesis is here a sign of vacuity; but in *Every Man out of his Humour* Jonson makes the courtier Fastidius Briske speak thus. He describes his grey hobby, 'a fine little fiery slaue, he runs like a (oh) excellent, excellent! with the very sound of the spurre' (II. i. 35–6); and 'There was a countesse gaue me her hand to kisse . . . did me more good by that light, then—and yesternight sent her coach twise to my lodging' (II. vi. 19–21). Was it an affectation in court circles? Jonson would regard it as a solecism. In III. v. 86–7, 'Your *Balsamum*, and your S^t. IOHN's woort are all mere gulleries', the Quarto text had 'your *Balsamum*, and your ——' as if Bobadill suffered from a lapse of memory.

37. *Incipere, in that sense*. Cf. Harington, *The Metamorphosis of Aiax*, 1596, p. 64, 'But I had almost forgot to English the argument, and then folkes might laugh indeede at me, and thinke I were *Magister incipiens* with an, *s*, and say I could not English these three words.'

39. *motte*, word.

40. *Benchers*, loungers on the benches in an ale-house.

pauca verba. A catch-phrase of the time, found in *S. W.* III. i. 1, *Love's Labour's Lost*, IV. ii. 155, *The Merry Wives*, I. i. 119. A printer's attempt at a Spanish form, 'Paucos Palabros', occurs in the *Masque of Augurs*, 268, and 'Paucas Pallabris' in *The Taming of the Shrew*, Ind. I. i. 5. The implication of the phrase in the ale house is 'Drink more, and talk less.'

42 foll. Quoted rather loosely from Marlowe's *Hero and Leander*, two editions of which appeared in 1598. Linley's Quarto reads at B3:

> Faire creature, let me speake without offence,
> I would my rude words had the influence,
> To leade thy thoughts, as thy faire lookes do mine,
> Then shoudst thou bee his prisoner who is thine.
> Be not vnkind and faire, mishapen stuffe
> Are of behauiour boisterous and ruffe.
>
> .   .   .   .
>
> And I in dutie will excell all other,
> As thou in beautie doest exceed loues mother.

The poem became a lover's handbook of quotations: cf. Sharpham, *The Fleire*, 1607, B3^v: '*Nan*. Faith I haue a dozen [i.e. suitors] at the least, and their deserts are all so good, I know not which I should loue most: and one last day did court me thus: *O had my tongue the influence to lead thy faire thoughts as thy faire lookes do mine : then shouldst thou be his prisoner who is thine.* I seeing my poore Gentleman likely to be drownd in the depth of *Hellespont*, deliuered him this verse to catch hold of: *O be not faire and so vnkinde : misshapen stuffe, is of behauiour boystrous and rough.'*

51. *shakes his head like a bottle.* Cf. *C.R.* ind. 215–17, 'A fift, only shakes his bottle-head, and out of his corkie braine, squeezeth out a pittiful-learned face, and is silent'; and Bacon, *Apophthegmes* 1625, '21. Many men, especially such as affect grauitie, haue a manner, after other mens speech, to shake their heads. Sir Lionell Cranfield would say; *That it was, as Men shake a Bottle, to see if there were any wit in their Head, or no.'*

56. *free of the wit-brokers.* A metaphor from admission to a City company: cf. 'Free of the *Grocers*?' (*Alch.* I. iii. 5).

60. *worse then sacrilege.* Cf. Synesius, *Opera*, 1612, p. 280, c, ἡγοῦμαι δὲ ἀσεβέστερον ἀποθανόντων λόγους κλέπτειν, ἢ θαιμάτια, ὁ καλεῖται τυμβωρυχεῖν.

68. *at the—the starre.* Matthew and Bobadill had adjourned to a tavern that morning (I. v. 166); Mathew affects to forget which tavern it was.

89. *tricks.* The word acquired an equivocal meaning from punning on the Latin *meretrix*: cf. Bullein, *A Dialogue bothe pleasaunt and pietifull*, 1573, p. 26, 'a kinde hearted woman, and full of meretrix, ha, ha, ha'; and *Iohn Heywoodes woorkes*, 1562, O ij, 'The fyrst hundred of Epigrammes':

> Madame, ye make my hert lyght as a kyx,
> To see you thus full of your *meretrix*.
> This tricke thus well tricked in the latine phrase, . . .

95. *a trick vyed, and reuyed.* 'To *vie* was to hazard, to put down a certain sum upon a hand of cards; to *revie*, was to cover it with a larger sum, by which the challenged became the challenger, and was to be *revied* in his turn, with a proportionate increase of stake.'—Gifford. Cf. *E. H.* IV. ii. 16, 17, 'Nay, and you'll show trickes, wee'l vie with you, a little.'

99. *you, lampe.* In modern punctuation 'you—lamp', as if the speaker paused a moment to choose his term of censure or ridicule: cf. *E.M.O.* II. iii. 103, 'Peace, you, ban-dogge, peace.'

lampe of virginitie. Thomas Bentley published in 1582, *The Monument of Matrones, conteining seuen seuerall Lamps of Virginitie, or distinct treatises* on prayer and on *the woorthie works, partlie of men, partlie of women:* the work was entered on the Stationers' Register on 7 November 1581, as *The lampe of virginitie and mirror for matrons.* Nashe in 1594 dedicated *The Terrors of the Night* to 'the new kindled cleare Lampe of Virginitie, . . . Mistress Elizabeth Carey'.

take it in snuffe, take offence at it. Originally of the unpleasant smell from the smoking snuff of a candle. 'The phrase was especially common between 1580 and 1660.'—*O.E.D.* Cf. *E.M.O.* ind. 180, 181:

> Taking mens lines, with a tabacco face,
> In snuffe;

and *S.W.* IV. v. 174, 'he went away in snuffe'.

101. *begg'd . . . for a concealment.* An allusion to the practice of begging old monastery lands and secularized property which had not passed into the hands of the Crown. Commissions of search for these were so grossly abused by courtiers that in 1572 and 1579 Elizabeth revoked them. Cf. *Sir Gyles Goosecappe*, 1606, D3, 'And Sir *Gyles* I can tell ye, tho he seeme something simple, is composed of as many good parts as any knight in England. *Hip.* He shood be put vp for concealement then, for he shewes none of them.'

104. *teston* = tester, or sixpence. This was, for instance, the price of an ordinary play in quarto. Wel-bred says 'a teston, at least': a vellum wrapper would raise the price to 8*d.* or 9*d.*, and a leather binding cost still more (R. B. McKerrow in *Shakespeare's England*, ii, p. 229).

110. *whose cow ha's calu'd?* Cf. Falstaff's exclamation on being arrested, 'How now? whose Mare's dead? what's the matter?' (*2 Henry IV*, II. i. 40).

114. *companions?* For the contemptuous use of the term cf. I. ii. 23, and *2 Henry IV*, II. iv. 132, 'I scorne you, scuruie Companion.'

116. *hang-byes*, hangers on, parasites.

117. *potlings.* Cf. the reference to a 'tauerne' and a 'drinking-schole', IV. ii. 108–9, and Kitely's account of revels, II. i. 61–5.

soldado's. Cf. *T. of T.* III. ix. 4, 'Disguis'd *Soldado* like'. The combination with the nonce-word *foolado's* is revived in a passage of *The Mohocks* quoted as the motto to Scott's *Fortunes of Nigel*, ch. xvii.

124. *cut a whetstone.* Cf. Chapman, *Bussy D'Ambois*, I. ii (1606, B2ᵛ), '*Gui.* Cease your Courtshippe, or by heauen Ile cut your throat. *D'Amb.* Cut my throat? cut a whetstone; good *Accius Næuius*, doe as much with your tongue as he did with a Rasor; cut my throat?' For the ancient Roman myth of Accius Naevius, who at the bidding of Tarquinius Priscus cut a whetstone through with a razor, see Livy, i. 36.

131. *Holofernes.* A play with this title was performed by the Paul's boys before Queen Mary when she visited Elizabeth at Hatfield in 1554. But with Bobadil it is a good mouth-filling name, for 'tyrant', 'dictator'. It is one of Tucca's playful methods of address in *Satiromastrix*, 1602, sig. M.

137. *coystrill.* Originally *custrel*, an attendant on a knight or man-at-arms. The secondary sense of knave 'seems to have originated from association with *custron*', a scullion (*O.E.D.*). In this sense *coistrel* is the commoner form. Cf. *Tw. Night*, I. iii. 37.

IV. iii. 9. *ancient*, old-fashioned, with a suggestion of 'out of date'.

17. *Songs, and sonnets.* Cf. *C. is A.* IV. v. 1, 'Fellow *Iuniper*, no more of thy songs and sonets.' The phrase originated in 1557 with *Tottel's Miscellany*, which was entitled *Songes and Sonettes, written by the right honorable Lorde Henry Howard, late Earle of Surrey, and other.* Slender in *The Merry Wives*, I. i. 179–80, says, 'I had rather then forty shillings I had my booke of Songs and Sonnets here.'

26. *'Sdeynes.* Cf. II. i. 69.

54. *find me a master.* 'Finde me bountiful' in the Quarto.

IV. iv. 12–14. *the lye . . . no souldier.* Cf. *Othello*, III. iv. 4, 5: '*Clo.* He's a Soldier, and for me to say a Souldier lyes, is stabbing.'

17. *foist*, rogue, lit. pickpocket: cf. iv. vii. 132; *Alch.* IV. vii. 16.

fencing Burgullian. In Marston's *The Scourge of Villanie*, 1598, H4ᵛ, Sat. ix, a fencer talks 'Of *Vincentio*, and the *Burgonians* ward'; and Dekker says of Jonson in the preface to *Satiromastix*, 1602, '*Horace* (questionles) made himselfe beleeue that his *Burgonian* wit might desperately challenge all commers.' Stow in *The Annales of England*, 1605, p. 1308, records among the executions in July 1598: 'Also *Iohn Barrose* a *Burgonian* by nation, and a Fensor by profession, that lately was come ouer and had chalenged all the Fencers of England, was hanged without Ludgate, for killing of an officer of the Citie which had arrested him for debt, such was his desperatnesse, and brought such reward as might be an example to other the like' (quoted by R. A. Small, *The Stage-Quarrel*, p. 6 n.).

26. *I was smok't*, I had a warm time. Cf. *Titus Andronicus*, IV. ii. 111, 'Some of you shall smoke for it in Rome.'

IV. v. 13. *Howsoeuer*, in any case, whatever happens.

17. *pretend'st*. Used in a good sense, as in *E.M.O.* II. iv. 49, 50:

> Is't possible shee should deserue so well,
> As you pretend?

IV. vi. 20. *scholler*. For scholarship and the black art cf. *Much Ado*, II. i. 227–8, 'I would to God some scholler would coniure her'; and *Hamlet*, I. i. 42, 'Thou art a Scholler; speake to it *Horatio*.'

31. *they seem'd men*. 'Seem' means 'to be seen'; so the Latin *videor* as the passive of *video*, as in Varro, *De Re Rustica*, I. ii. 4, 'ubi sol sex mensibus continuis non videtur'. So in *Alch.* I. iii. 70–1, 'The rest, They'll seeme to follow.' Cf. John Pikeryng, *Horestes*, 1567, Bjʳ, 'couldst thou wᵗ a good wil Contentyd be? that one should so, thy father seme to kyll'. and B iiijᵛ, 'If that the law doth her condemne, as worthy death to haue, Oh nature wouldst thou wil yᵗ I, her life should seme to saue?'

53. *Much wench, or much sonne!* Cf. *As You Like It*, IV. iii. 1, 2. 'Is it not past two o'clock? and here much Orlando!'

59. *nupson*, simpleton. Cf. *D. is A.* II. ii. 77.

73. *at Mile-end.* Cf. II. v. 144.

IV. vii. (margin) *To them.* This stage-direction, which is wrongly placed in F1, is rearranged in F2 in conformity with Jonson's practice elsewhere, e.g. in *E.M.O.* v. ii and iii.

1. *eyes . . . tast.* Cf. *C is A.* IV. iv. 18–20:

> Kind gentleman I would not sell thy loue,
> For all the earthly obiects that mine eyes
> Haue euer tasted.

14. *hay?* The Italian *hai*, 'you have it', on a thrust reaching the antagonist.

16. *punto*, an instant—with a quibble on the sense found in l. 77.

21. *trauaile*, (1) travel, (2) labour. Jonson often combines the meanings: see *E.M.O.* ind. 281–6: 'MIT. No? how comes it then, that in some one Play we see so many seas, countries, and kingdomes, past ouer with such admirable dexteritie? COR. O, that but shewes how well the Authors can trauaile in their vocation, and out-run the apprehension of their auditorie.'

44–5. *Turne-bull, White-chappell, Shore-ditch.* All disreputable quarters: the man of fashion, who was sensitive over being known to lodge at Cob's (I. v. 32–4), has forgotten himself. Turne-bull—or more correctly Turnmill—Street was a noted haunt of prostitutes near Clerkenwell Green: cf. Nashe, *Pierce Penilesse*, 1592 (*Works*, ed. McKerrow, i, p. 217), '*Lais, Cleopatra, Helen* . . . with the rest of our vncleane sisters in *Shorditch*, the *Spittle, Southwarke, Westminster, & Turnbull streete*'.

77. *Punto*, a thrust with the point.
Reuerso, a back-stroke.

78. *Stoccata.* Cf. I. v. 151.
Imbroccata, defined by Florio as 'a thrust at fence, or a venie giuen ouer the dagger'.
Passada. Cf. I. v. 143–4.

79. *Montanto*, an upright thrust.

87–8. *twentie score, that's two hundreth.* Bobadill's arithmetic exercised Gifford: 'This error in computation runs through all the editions, so that it was probably intended. Indeed Bobadill is too much of a borrower to be an accurate reckoner.'

121. *Gipsie*, canting rogue.

125. *Tall*, bold. Cf. the amusing passage IV. xi. 48.

126–7. Bobadill's scruples about fighting have a contemporary parallel in actual life. Dr. G. B. Harrison quotes in *The Second Elizabethan Journal* (*1595–1598*), p. 286, under the heading 'News from Paris', 23 June 1598, the year of the performance of this play, 'A certain Dutchman, Sir Melchior Leven, that was knighted by my Lord Essex at Cadiz, hath refused to fight Sir Charles Blount in Paris on the ground that the King hath forbidden duels, whereat all do mock him. Sir Charles who went with the Secretary on his embassage stayed behind on purpose to effect this challenge.' The full account is given in the Salisbury MSS. viii. 219, 224–31, see also Chamberlain's letters, pp. 10, 14.

132. *foist.* Cf. IV. iv. 17.

141. *strooke with a plannet.* A stroke or a sudden death was attributed to the malignant influence of a planet; and thus, as Gifford says, it was a convenient term for any fatal illness which doctors could not diagnose. Cf. *The Wisedome of Doctor Doddypoll*, 1600, C2ᵛ, where Alberdure, drinking wine into which a powder has been poured, goes out raving,

and Florio says, 'My Lord, 'tis sure some Planet striketh him'; and
E.M.O. v. xi. 5, 'Some *Planet* strike me dead.'

strooke F1: *struck* F2. F2 makes this change in sixteen passages,
but retains 'strook' or 'strooke' in seven. In two passages of later
work, for which F2 is the only authority—*S.N.* I. i. 28 and *Und.* xlix.
5—it also retains the old form. This suggests that Jonson always
used it, and that the changes in F2 may be a compositor's attempt to
modernize the spelling. Milton preferred the fuller sound of 'strook',
but varied it occasionally with 'struck': see Masson's note on the *Nativity Ode*, 95.

147–8. *that Nature should be at leisure to make 'hem!* Repeated in
D. is A. IV. iv. 191–2.

IV. viii. 5. *adiection.* Cf. *C.R.* III. v. 99, 100, 'See what your proper
GENIVS can perform alone, without adiection of any other MINERVA.'

9. *is neuer his owne man.* Cf. *E.M.O.* II. iv. 76, *Alch.* IV. v. 70, and
Greenes Neuer too late, 1590, Pt. II, G3ᵛ (Calena to her son who has
eaten little supper), 'I saw by thy stomacke to night thou art not
thine owne man.' Compare the Latin use of *suus* in Plautus, *Persa*, 472,
'Ita ancilla mea quae fuit hodie, sua nunc est', i.e. 'is now her own
mistress'.

10. *valure*, 1616: 'valour' 1640. So in *Alch.* II. i. 51 ('valor', 1640).

17. *poyson'd.* On this practice see Pedro Mexia, *The Treasurie of
Ancient and Modern Times*, 1613, Bk. II, ch. xvii, 'That a man may bee
impoysoned by Pomanders of sweet smell, Fumes of Torches, Tapers,
Candels; by Letters, Garments, and other such like things'. He gives
an instance of 'a great lady of *France* (some few yeares past)' poisoned
by a pair of envenomed gloves and a handkerchief; he quotes, without
believing, 'a common report, that the Saddles of Horses may be impoysoned, the Raines of their Bridles, the Stirrops, and Scabberds and
Sheathes of Swordes, thereby to impoyson such as sit, handle, or weare
them'. *The Domestic State Papers* of 1587 (*Elizabeth*, cxcvii. 10) contain
a confession of Michael Modye that he had discussed with the French
ambassador's secretary how to kill the Queen, 'either by gunpowder or
by poisoning her stirrup or her shoe, or some other Italian device', and
Stephen Powle (ib. ccxxii. 77) in 1589, acknowledging the receipt of £20
from Burleigh, describes his services in Italy where he discovered 'a plot
to take away the Queen's life by poisoned perfumes, for which purpose
Geraldi, a Bergamasco, was employed by the Pope'.

25. *mithridate*, an antidote against poison or infection. Mr. Wheatley
refers to *A Discourse of the medicine called Mithridatium, declaring the
firste beginninge, the temperament, the noble vertues, and the true vse of the
same*, 1585.

65. *the tower.* They could be married at once within the precincts of
the Tower, which was extra-parochial. Gifford quotes Rowley, *A Match
at Midnight*, 1633, G2ᵛ, 'She will . . . goe with you to your lodging, lie
there all night, and bee married i' th morning at the Tower, assoone as

you shall please.' Cf. *Witt's Recreations*, 1640, '148 *On a gentleman that married an heire privately at the Tower*': the angry father asks him

> how he did dare . . .
> Thus beare his onely daughter to be married,
> And by what Cannons he assum'd such power?
> He sayd the best in England sir, the Tower.

The Court of High Commission stopped the practice in 1632.

104. *I'ld returne him his owne*, I'd pay him back in kind.

113. *an' they doe not, a plague of all ceruse, say I*. Cf. *Alch.* v. i. 19–20, 'If he haue eate 'hem, A plague o' the moath, say I'. *Ceruse* was a cosmetic of white lead: cf. *Sej.* II. 63, and Jonson's note.

114. *though not in the* —— So in the Quarto, but with a full stop instead of the dash. Wellbred affects modesty and stops short of indecency. On the stage the dash might be represented by a cough. For 'touch' of sexual contact see *O.E.D.* 2 a.

117. *bone-fires*. Cf. *Forest*, xiv. 58–9, 'As with the light Of bone-fires'. The modern spelling, due to the natural shortening in pronunciation of the initial syllable, actually dates from the sixteenth century, though 'bone-fire' continued down to 1760 (*O.E.D.*).

122–3. *a minutes losse . . . is a great trespasse*. Cf. the refrain of the song 'O know to end' in *Hymenaei*, 398, 'A minutes losse, in *loue*, is sinne'.

131. *the squire*, i.e. the 'apple-squire' (IV. x. 57), or pandar.

139. *dors*, hoaxes. The verb is used in *B.F.* IV. ii. 21, 'Dorring the Dottrel'; the noun is more frequent, especially in the phrase 'to give the dor'; cf. *C.R.* v. ii–iv passim.

IV. ix. The wrong insertion of Downright's name at the head of this scene is curious. It suggests that Jonson, when revising the play, at one time planned his re-entrance here. Downright might be hunting for Matthew, with whom he still had an account to settle (IV. vii. 132–3). The incorrect marginal note 'To them' strongly confirms this possibility; the words are absurd where they stand, but would be appropriate one line lower, level with Downright's name. (Compare the error in the heading of scene vii.) It is true that the Quarto lends no support to such a suggestion, but the Folio is so carefully edited that this pointless intrusion needs to be explained. Downright need only have passed over the stage again. At the sight of the tall figure in the russet cloak Matthew would scud like a rabbit, and the damaged Bobadill acquire sufficient momentum to hobble after him. But if Jonson thought of any by-play of this kind, he reconsidered it. The masterly portraiture of the seventh scene would only be impaired by retouching: 'manum de tabula'.

10. *in Venice? as you say?* The Quarto has simply 'in *Venice*': the added words hardly transplant the passage naturally into Elizabethan England, but Jonson wished to keep the Italian ring of the *Gentelezza* and the *retricato*.

15. *retricato*. An unexplained word, of which there appears to be no other example. The passage is reprinted from the Quarto. Dr. C. T. Onions suggests the possibility of a confusion with *rintricato*, 'entangled', which is in Florio.

39. *a brace of angells*. Brainworm made the most of his brief opportunity: the lawful fee is quoted in the 'Character' of a Tailor added to the fifth edition of Overbury's *A Wife*, 1614, E1ᵛ, 'His actions are strong in Cownters, . . . A ten groates Fee setteth them a foote, and a brace of Officers bringeth them to execution.' Cf. Wapull, *The Tyde taryeth no Man*, 1576, Fij (where a debtor pleads for delay to get bail):

Sergeaunt ¶ At one word ten groates thou shalt pay,
Or else to the Counter we must out of hand.

But with Brainworm's charge cf. Greene, *A Quip for an Vpstart Courtier*, 1592, E2, where a serjeant arrests a man with money in his purse, and 'bids him send for some of his friends to bale him, but first he couenants to haue some brase of angels for his paines'.

43. *crosse*. The silver penny and halfpenny were so marked. 'By fortune' echoes the usual quibble.

48. *this iewell in my eare*. Cf. Harrison, *A Description of England*, 1587, II. vii (ed. Furnivall, i, p. 170), 'Some lustie courtiers also and gentlemen of courage, doe weare either rings of gold, stones, or pearle in their eares, whereby they imagine the workemanship of God not to be a little amended.' Stubbes in *The Anatomie of Abuses*, 1583 (ed. Furnivall, p. 70), says the practice of wearing ear-rings 'is not so muche frequented amongest Women as Men'; this was because of the style of head-dress worn by women at that date.

49, 50. *pull vp your bootes*. Cf. H. Parrot, *Laquei Ridiculosi*, 1613, B2ᵛ, 'Epig. 7. *Videantur quae non sunt*':

Saltus goes booted to the dauncing schoole,
As if from thence his meaning were to ride;
But *Saltus* says they keepe his legs more coole,
And which for ease he better may abide:
Tut, that's a cold excuse. It rather seem'd
Saltus silke stockings were not yet redeem'd.

70. *varlet*, originally servant to a knight: here technically of a city serjeant. Cf. *Poet*. III. iv. 19, *Volp*. v. vi. 12.

IV. X. 15. *copes-mate*, associate, and here paramour. The *O.E.D.* quotes *Tell-Trouthe's New Year Gift*, 1593, p. 17, 'Were taken by their husbands with other of their copesmates'.

37. *trecher*. Cf. *King Lear*, I. ii. 118.

46. *thy powers in chastitie is*. Syntax was not stereotyped in Jonson's day: thus, he writes *Cat*. IV. 593, 'The sight of such spirits hurt not, nor the store'; *Forest*, xiv. 17–19, 'When all the noyse Of these forc'd ioyes, Are fled and gone'; ib. 21–2, 'the number of glad yeeres Are justly

summ'd'. In the parallels here quoted the plural is logical; the composite noun phrase has a plural idea. But the text is different, and in *The Sad Shepherd*, I. iv. 17—a rhyming passage in which the preceding line ends with 'bough'—Jonson even writes 'Such were the Rites, the youthfull *Iune* allow'. This freedom is significant in so scrupulous a writer.

50 (margin). *By Thomas.* Against *B.F.* v. iv. 36 there is a similar note, '*By* Edgworth'. *By* = about, in reference to.

55. BA'D. A pun on 'bawd': Kitely spells the word. Not unlike Shakespeare's 'And for his meede, poor Lord, he is mewed vp' (*Rich. III*, I. iii. 139).

56. *hoddie-doddie,* or hoddidob. Literally a snail-shell (*Florio*, 1611); here cuckold and noddy, perhaps in reference to the 'horns'.

57. *apple-squire,* a harlot's attendant.

IV. xi. 4. *rests.* Cf. Wapull, *The Tyde taryeth no Man*, 1576, Fjᵛ (stage-direction), 'The Sergeaunt and the debtor rested entereth'.

6. *a mace.* The badge of the City serjeant: Gifford quotes Chapman, *All Fooles*, 1605, C3:

> If I write but my Name in Mercers Bookes,
> I am as sure to haue at sixe months end
> A Rascole at my elbow with a Mace.

And Shirley, *The Bird in a Cage*, II. i (ed. 1633, D3ᵛ), 'are you in debt and feare arresting, you shall saue your money in protections, come vp to the face of a Sergiant, nay walke by a Shole of these mankind horse-leaches, and be mace proofe'.

7. *carries pepper and salt.* There is a quibble on 'mace', the spice made of the dried rind of the nutmeg. Cf. Massinger and Dekker, *The Virgin Martir*, 1622, III. iii, '*Spun.* Does the diuell eate any *Mace* in 's broth? *Har.* Exceeding much, when his burning feauer takes him, and then hee has the knuckles of a Bailiffe boyld to his breakefast.'

46. *make,* prepare (as the Quarto reads). Cf. *Sej.* II. 123, 'Were LYGDVS made, that's done'; and *Volp.* II. vi. 57, IV. v. 110.

v. i. 46. *take downe my armor.* Collier in his *Bibliographical Catalogue*, i, pp. 156–7, pointed out a striking parallel in Antony Copley's *Wits, Fittes, and Fancies; Or, A generall & serious Collection, of the Sententious Speeches, Answers, Iests, and Behauiours, of all sortes of Estates, From the Throne to the Cottage*, 1595, p. 182, 'A Souldiour comming about a sute to a merrie Recorder of *London*,' (Collier suggests Fleetwood) 'the Recorder seeing him out at the window, ran hastilie into an inner roome, & there put on a Corslet and a head-peece, & then with a Launce in his hand came downe vnto him, and sayd: How now Sirra, are you the man that hath somwhat to say to mee? Begin now when you dare, for behold (I trow) I am sufficiently prouided for you.'

48. *gorget,* a piece of armour to protect the throat.

v. ii. 27. *this picture.* Cf. sc. v. 49, 'you signe o' the Souldier, and picture o' the *Poet*'. There is also an allusion to his dress.

28. *M*ʳ. *Fresh-waters suite.* A freshwater soldier was, literally, one without experience: '*White Shields* were accustomed to be bestowed vpon such as were *Nouices* in *Martiall affaires*, or (as wee commonly call them) *Freshwater Souldiers*' (Guillim, *A Display of Heraldrie*, 1610, p. 39). But the term is usually contemptuous: cf. *Greenes Neuer too Late*, 1590, H4, 'What seruant, are you such a fresh water souldier, that you faint at the first skirmish?'; and S. Rid, *Martin Mark-All*, 1610, B3 'you are most like to the whip-iacke, who . . . being an idle fellow, and a freshwater souldier, never sayling farther than Graues-end, will talke and prate of the low Countreys, of this battell, & that skirmish that he fought in, whereas indeed he neuer durst say so much as Boh to a Mouse'.

v. iii. 18. *passion*, used of strong emotion, here of sorrow. Cf. Fletcher and Rowley, *The Maid in the Mill*, ii. ii, '*Bust.* Oh, oh, oh, oh. *Jul.* So, here's a Passion towards.'
62. *with . . Edward, and I.* Cf. *C.R.* i. iv. 50, 'make this gentleman and I friends'; *Sej.* v. 670, 'betweene you, and I'.
78–9. *reform'd souldier.* Cf. iii. v. 17.
92. *sure.* Cf. 'to make sure' = to betrothe (*T. of T.* i. iv. 23).
95. *preuent*, anticipate.
115. *ingine*, wit. Cf. *Sej.*, argument 24, 'worketh (with all his ingine) to remoue *Tiberius* from the knowledge of publike businesse'.

v. iv. The episode of a walk through the streets of London in armour is found in the *Jests of George Peele*, entered on the Stationers' Register, 14 December 1605: see Peele's *Works*, ed. Bullen, ii, p. 400. The story is probably earlier, as Mr. Baskerville suggests (*English Elements*, p. 134).
12. *Gi' you ioy.* 'God give you joy' was the usual greeting to the newly married: see *E.H.* iii. ii. 85, *N.I.* v. iii. 8.

v. v. 11. *Mount vp thy Phlegon.* Quoted from the Quarto text ('Mount thee my Phlegon Muse') and with the variant 'on an ebon cloud' in Dabridgecourt Belchier's *Hans Beer-pot his Inuisible Comedie*, 1618, C2, in a passage full of literary satire. The tone suggests a parody; but no original has been traced. Dr. W. W. Greg points out that Greene parodies the idea in *Orlando Furioso*. In the Dulwich MS. version (ll. 260–3) Orlando, raving, enters as a poet, and in a passage which is unfortunately fragmentary, says he must 'talke in secrett to the starres'. The next words preserved are

          . . . doth lye
When Joue rent all the welkin wᵗʰ a crake
fye, fye tis a false verse.

Phlegon was one of the horses of the Sun. He is mentioned in the Quarto text of *Orlando*, 1594, D1ᵛ (Malone Society Reprint, l. 594).

12–13. *Saturne . . . podex.* 'Saturni podex' is a proverbial phrase in Erasmus's *Adagia*, ed. Stephanus, 1558, col. 808.

21. *realme . . . common-wealth.* 'Realm' was written and pronounced 'ream': Jonson rhymes 'realm' with 'stream' in the *Panegyre*, 5, 6, and *Hymenaei*, 427–8, but in *Und.* xxx, 9, 10, 'Realme' rhymes with 'Helme'. The same pun is found in Marlowe, *The Iew of Malta*, iv. iv (l. 1834, ed. Tucker Brooke), 'Giue me a Reame of paper, we'll haue a kingdome of gold for 't: and G. Harvey, *Pierces Supererogation*, 1598, (p. 138), 'For Stationers are already too-full of such Realmes, and Commonwealthes of Wast-paper'.

24–5. Burlesqued from the opening sonnet of Daniel's *Delia*, 1592. In the Quarto Jonson quoted the first four lines straightforwardly, and Matheo admitted that he 'translated that out of a booke, called *Delia*'. Echoes are found elsewhere: see the prologue to *The Maydes Metamorphosis*, 1600:

> Then to the boundlesse Ocean of your woorth,
> This little drop of water we present;

and in Taylor's *Workes*, 1630, p. 80, 'Laugh and be Fat', the 'Epilogue to Mr. Coriat' has:

> Thus to the Ocean of thy boundlesse fame,
> I consecrate these rude vnpolish'd lines.

35. *embleme*, in the literary sense of 'a picture and short posie expressing some particular conceit' (*Cotgrave*, 1611). For an instance see *Poet.* v. iii. 67–104.

38–9. *not borne euerie yeere, as an Alderman.* Pleasantly adapted from the lines of Florus:

> Consules fiunt quotannis et novi proconsules,
> solus aut rex aut poeta non quotannis nascitur.

This was a favourite maxim of Jonson's, who quotes it in the epilogue to *The New Inn*, 23–4, *Disc.* 2433, and *Panegyre*, 163, and refers to it in *Epig.* iv. 3.

45. *They haue it with the fact.* Cf. *Pan's Anniversary*, 239, 'They have their punishment with their fact'. The phrase is modelled on Seneca's epigrams on sin, *De Ira*, iii. 26, § 2 'Maxima est enim factae iniuriae poena fecisse', and *Ep.* 97, § 14 'Prima illa et maxima peccantium est poena peccasse'.

73–4. In the Quarto part of the alleged play-excerpt which follows has not been traced. But the lines are quoted by R. Tofte in *The Blazon of Iealousie*, 1615, p. 56, marginal note:

> *Most certaine t'is, where IEALOVSIE is bred,*
> *HORNES in the Mind, are worse then HORNES on the Head;*

and Dekker and Webster, *West-ward Hoe*, iv. ii (1607, F4), have 'Hornes feard, plague worse, than sticking on the head'. Apparently the aphorism appealed to contemporaries: it is quoted, under the head of 'Jealousy', in the two anthologies of 1600, *Englands Parnassus*, p. 145 (beginning 'Where iealousie', and assigned to Jonson), and *Bel-vedére*, p. 45 ('This still we find, where iealousie . . .' without the author's name).

81. Cf. Heywood, *The Iron Age*, Part I, 1 (1632, C4):

> Thus euery man is borne to his owne Fate.
> Now it raines Hornes. let each man shield his Pate.

APPENDIX XIX

THE THEORY OF THE FOUR HUMOURS

THE physiological theory that four humours entered into the composition of man's body, and that a right proportion of them constituted health, an irregular distribution of them brought about disease, was promulgated in the latter part of the fifth century B.C. by the great physician Hippocrates. The treatise '*Of the Nature of Man*' (Περὶ χυμῶν, ch. iv), written by his son-in-law Polybus, states the theory: 'The body of man has in itself blood, phlegm, yellow and black bile; these make up the nature of his body, and through these he feels pain or enjoys health. His health is most perfect when these elements are evenly proportioned to one another in combination, quality, and quantity, and are perfectly mingled. He has pain when one of these elements is defective or excessive or is isolated in the body, uncompounded with the others.'

It was Galen in the second century A.D. who developed Hippocrates' theory, combining with it the notion of spirit penetrating all parts and mingling with the humours in different proportions. Excess showed itself in various types: the element of fire predominated in the choleric man, air in the sanguine man, water in the phlegmatic man, and earth in the melancholy man. Fire was hot and dry, air hot and moist, water cold and moist, earth cold and dry. Galen's book *Of Temperaments* (Περὶ κράσεων) discussed the theory, and a Latin translation of it by Thomas Linacre, published by John Siberch at Cambridge in 1521, circulated the work in England. But it was Linacre's pupil, Sir Thomas Elyot, who did most to popularize the idea. His *Castel of Helth*, published by Berthelet in 1539, was 'corrected and in some places augmented' in 1541, and up to 1618 fifteen editions are recorded. On folio 8 of the second edition we have a discussion

¶ *Of humours.*

In the body of Man be foure principall humours, which contynuinge in the proportion, that nature hath lymytted, the body is free from all syckenesse. Contrary wise, by the increase or diminution of any of them in quantitie or qualytie, ouer or vnder their natural assignement, inequall temperature commeth in to the body, whiche syckenesse, foloweth more or lasse, accordynge to the lapse or decaye of the temperatures of the sayd humours, whiche be these folowinge.

| Bloudde, | Choler, |
| Fleume, | Melancoly. |

¶ Bloudde hath preeminence ouer all other humours in susteynynge of all lyuynge creatures, for it hath more conformitie with the originalle cause of lyuynge, by reason of temperatenes in heate and moysture, alsoo nourisheth more the body, and restoreth that whiche is decayed, beinge the very treasure of lyfe, by losse wherof, death immedyately foloweth. The dystemperature of bloud hapneth by one of the other thre humours by the inordinate or superfluous mixture of them.

Elyot goes on to discuss phlegm, choler, and melancholy. Then he connects them with the ages of man and the seasons of the year. The four ages are

Adolescency to .xxv. yeres, hotte and moyst, in the whiche tyme the body groweth.
Iuuentute vnto .xl. yeres, hotte and drye, wherin the body is in perfyte growthe.
Senectute, vnto .lx. yeres, colde and drie, wherin the bodye beginneth to decreace.
Age decrepite, vntil the last time of lyfe, accidently moist, but naturally cold and dry, wherin the powers and strength of the body be more and more minished. (Folio 13.)
Next 'The tymes appropried to euery naturall humour' (f. 69):
Fleume hath moste puissance in wynter, from the .viii. Idus of Nouember, vnto the .viii. Idus of Februarye, whereby are ingendred Catarres or reumes, the vuula, the cough, and the stytche . . .
Bloudde increaseth in Sprynge tyme, frome the .viii. Idus of February, vnto the .viii. Idus of May, wherof are ingendred, feuers, and swete humours, whyche do shortely putrifye, . . .
Redd choler hath power in sommer from the viii. Idus of May, vntyll the .viii. Idus of August, whereby are ingendred hotte and sharpe feuers, . . .
Yelowe choler, wherof is ingendred the fleme of the stomake, is nouryshed in Autumne, whyche begyneth the .viii. Idus of August, and dureth vnto the .viii. Idus of Nouember, and maketh shakynge feuers and sharpe, the blacke coler than increaseth.

Finally Elyot prescribes a diet for each humour, as Hippocrates had done centuries before him.

The diagnosis of the ages of man is also very old. A striking example of it is in Seneca's *De Ira* (II. xix. 1, 2), where he discusses the effect of humour on anger: he must have derived the data from Hippocrates.[1] Jonson would be familiar with this passage.

[1] Quoted by W. D. Briggs in the *Flügel Memorial Volume*, 1916, 'Cynthia's Revels and Seneca', p. 60.

Seneca, *De Ira*, II. xix. 1, 2.

'Opportunissima ad iracundiam fervidi animi natura est. Nam cum elementa sint quattuor, ignis aquae aëris terrae potestates pares his sunt, fervida frigida avida atque umida. Et locorum itaque et animalium et corporum et morum varietates mixtura elementorum facit et proinde in aliquos magis incumbunt ingenia prout alicuius elementi maior vis abundavit. Inde quasdam humidas vocamus aridasque regiones et calidas et frigidas. Eadem animalium hominumque discrimina sunt: refert quantum quisque humidi in se calidique contineat. Cuius in illo elementi portio praevalebit, inde mores erunt. Iracundos fervida animi natura faciet: est enim actuosus et pertinax ignis. Frigidi mixtura timidos facit: pigrum est enim contractumque frigus.'

Seneca is concerned with the effect of the humours on anger, and he discusses sex and age, boys and women, 'quibus umidi plus inest', the 'siccae aetates', maturity and old age, and the effect of wine in stimulating anger. His discussion owes something to Aristotle's analysis of the characteristics of three ages, youth, the prime of life, and old age in the *Rhetoric*, book II, chapters xii–xvii, a passage which would probably be known to Jonson. Of youth he says, 'And they are sanguine; like drunken men, they are saturated with their own natural warmth' (διάθερμοί εἰσιν ὑπὸ τῆς φύσεως); of old men, 'And they exceed the due measure in self-love (φίλαυτοι μᾶλλον ἢ δεῖ), which is a kind of little-mindedness'.

The only contemporary of Jonson who analysed the humours is Robert Burton in an introductory subsection to his great work.[1]

'A humour', he says, 'is a liquid or fluent part of the Body, comprehended in it, for the preservation of it . . . .' The 'foure first primary Humours' 'though they bee comprehended in the Masse of *Blood*, yet they have their severall affections, by which they are distinguished from one another . . .'

'*Blood*, is a hot, sweet, temperate, red humour, prepared in the *Meseraicke* veines, and made of the most temperate parts of the *Chylus* in the liver, whose office is to nourish the whole body, to giue it strength and colour, being dispersed by the veines, through euery part of it. And from it *Spirits* are first begotten in the heart, which afterwards by the *Arteries*, are communicated to the other parts.

'*Pituita*, or Fleagme, is a cold and moist humour, begotten of the colder part of the *Chylus*, (or white iuyce comming of the meat digested in the stomacke) in the Liver; his office is to nourish, and moisten the members of the body, which as the tongue, are moued, that they be not over dry.

'*Choler*, is hot and dry, bitter, begotten of the hotter parts of the

[1] *The Anatomy of Melancholy*, 4th ed., 1632, Partition 1, Section 1, Member 2, subsection 2.

Chylus, and gathered to the Gall: it helps the naturall heat and senses, and serues to the expelling of execrements.

'*Melancholy*, cold and drie, thicke, blacke, and sowre, begotten of the more fæculent part of nourishment, and purged from the spleene, is a bridle to the other two humours, *Blood* and *Choler*, preseruing them in the Blood, and nourishing the bones: These foure humors haue some analogie with the foure Elementes, and to the foure ages in man.'

To show the lengths to which the theory could be carried we print on p. 395 from John Jones's *The Bathes of Bathes Ayde*, 1571, a medical analysis given in a 'Table of the Seven Things Natural' facing folio 23.

Such was the theory which Jonson turned to literary account in the Comedy of Humours. In and after the sixteenth century the chemical doctrines, which were the result of the study of alchemy, began to displace the teaching of Galen, but the humour theory lasted up to the early part of the eighteenth century.

EVERY MAN OUT OF HIS HUMOUR

THIS was the first of Jonson's plays to be printed, and the text shows marked signs of editorial care. (1) The type of play is defined as a 'Comicall Satyre' on the title-page. (2) The printed text, as stated in the Quarto, 'contained more than hath been publikely Spoken or Acted'. Authors or editors sometimes reasserted themselves in this way when publication gave them the opportunity. Thus Webster puts on the title-page of *The Dutchesse of Malfy*, 1623: 'As it was Presented priuatly, at the Black-Friers; and publiquely at the Globe, By the Kings Maiesties Seruants. The perfect and exact Coppy with diuerse things Printed, that the length of the Play would not beare in the Presentment'; and Brome in *The Antipodes*, 1640, has a final note (L4ᵛ): 'Courteous Reader *You shal find in this Booke more then was presented upon the* Stage, *and left out of the* Presentation, *for superfluous length* (*as some of the* Players *pretended*) *I thought good al should be inserted according to the allowed* Original.' The actors' point of view is given in the prologue to *The Coxcomb* on its revival in 1636, as printed in the First Folio of Beaumont and Fletcher, 1647, p. 118:

> *This Comedy long forgot, by some thought dead,*
> *By us preserv'd, once more doth raise her head. . . .*
> *The worke it selfe too, when it first came forth, . . .*
> *Was well receiv'd, and favour'd, though some rude*
> *And harsh among th'ignorant multitude,*

Elementum is a simple and most pure bodie, and the best parte, of that wherein it is, can not be deuided into any other kind: and of it all things naturall haue their beginning without al generacion or corruptiō. Howbeit of Fire made thicke, commeth Ayre. Of Aire made thick commeth water. Of water made thick, cōmeth Earth. . . .

Elementes foure.

- **Fyre** — Absolutelie hot, and moderately dry.
- **Ayre** — Absolutely moist, and moderately hot.
- **Water** — Absolutely cold, & moderately moist.
- **Earth** — Absolutely dry, and moderately cold.

This is but a mutation of the parts onely. And the consent and agrement of them is, the fyre with the Ayre in heate, in drynes with the Earth, in moisture the Ayre with the water, & in heate with the fire, in coldnes the water with the earth and in moysture with the ayre, the earth in drines with the fyre, and in coldnes with the water & as the water to the fyre is extreme contrary, so is the aire to the earth.

Humors (which may be called the sonnes of Elements) is a part contained subsisting the bodie.

Humors foure.

Naturall

- **Blud.** Temperate, norishing the body contained in the vains swetish raigning in the spring.
- **Flewme.** Cold and moist, sowpling the drie and hard parts without proper măcion, tastles, raigning in winter.
- **Choler.** Hot and drie, clensing and quickning conteined in the gall bitter raigning in sommer.
- **Melācholie.** Cold and dry, staying and binding, contained in the Splene, sower, raigning in haruest.

Vnnatural (as)

- Blud distempered with other humors.
- Flewm, waterie, glassie, slimie, plastoie,[1] salt, sower, harsh, rugh.
- Choler, Citrine, yelkie like, cankrie.
- Melācholie cōmixed & adustid with other dangerous qualities, killing.

And eueri day they are thus moued as the blud betwen the ninth houre at night, and iij. in the morning. Choler between iiij. & ix afore none. Melācholie, betwen ix. and iij. Flewme between iij. & ix. at night.

Simple, as — Skin, fatte, flesh, muscles, fillets, guts, veins, artires, Synowes, chords, gristles, bones, tunicles, &c.

. . . you haue here in this Table noted vnto you, the things wherof the Natural bodies is made.

[1] Query, plastrie.

> *. . . wanting wit and strength,*
> *Truly to judge, condemn'd it for the length,*
> *That fault's reform'd.*

In Jonson's play the actors may well have omitted the running comments of the 'Grex'. (3) Jonson prefixed to the play 'the seuerall Character of euery Person', to indicate the bias of each 'humour'. He reverted to this practice in 1631 when he published *The New Inn* after its failure, and hit off 'The Persons of the Play. With some short Characterisme of the chiefe Actors'. In the characterization of *Every Man out of his Humour*, however, he expressly disclaimed any attempt to criticize the actors. (4) He used the Induction for the first time, and in a fuller and more elaborate form than he ever employed again, to formulate his theory of comedy. (5) The composite motto characteristically asserts that the play is a new type. It is a cento of Horace, *Epistles*, i. xix. 22, *Ars Poetica*, 361–2 and 367. Jonson had a trick of getting a great deal of personal point into his Latin mottoes.

With reference to the title of the play, it may be noted that Shakespeare used the phrase in *Much Ado about Nothing*, published in Quarto in 1600, and perhaps composed early in 1599. Benedick, 'the married man', exclaims at the end of the play (v. iv. 99–102): 'Ile tel thee what prince: a colledge of witte-crackers cannot flout me out of my humour, dost thou think I care for a Satire or an Epigramme? no, if a man will be beaten with braines, a' shall weare nothing hansome about him.'

'Comical Satire'

So Jonson described the three early plays of *Every Man out of his Humour*, *Cynthia's Revels*, and *Poetaster*. The term is on the title-pages in the Folio text, and it heads the actor-list and notice of date which Jonson appended to his plays in this edition; 'The Comical Satyre of *Every Man out of his Humour*' is also on the title-page of the Quartos. The term is not found elsewhere.

What is the point of it? Have these plays any special characteristics which call for a critical label? A monograph of great value has been written on them by Professor Oscar James Campbell—*Comicall Satyre and Shakespeare's Troilus and Cressida*, in which Shakespeare's one experiment in sustained dramatic satire is ranged with the models that preceded it. Marston's early plays also show some kinship with the type: he had had his literary training as a satirist, and in his first play, *Antonio and Mellida*, produced in 1599, probably in the summer, he has spasmodic outbursts of satirical portraiture and reflection, which are the outcome of habit rather than of theory: he had written satire, and he went on writing it.

Professor Campbell traces the origin of the comical satire to the restraining order of the Archbishop of Canterbury and the Bishop of London on 1 June 1599, when they prohibited all further printing of the works of Hall, Marston, Davies, and Nashe, ordered all copies on the market to be burnt, and decreed that 'noe *Satyres* or *Epigrams* be printed hereafter'. It is probable that Jonson, who was a slow writer, had been at work on *Every Man out of his Humour* before the order appeared; at any rate he produced the play later in the year. His calling it a 'Satyre'—with the emphasis on satire, not on comedy—was something of a challenge. And it outwitted the bishops because it castigated vice and folly:

> His sharpnesse, that is most excusable;
> As being forc't out of a suffering vertue,
> Oppressed with the licence of the time.

So he defended his point of view in *Poetaster*[1] where he makes the poet Virgil his mouthpiece.

Jonson had classical precedent for this. There was the Old Comedy of Greece, from 460 to 404 B.C., with which Horace and the Renaissance critics believed early Roman Satire to be closely connected. 'Prisca comoedia', says Horace of the Greeks, claimed the right to chastise vice.

> Si quis erat dignus describi quod malus ac fur,
> quod moechus foret aut sicarius, aut alioqui
> famosus, multa cum libertate notabant.[2]

And he goes on to describe Lucilius, the first Roman satirist, as 'entirely derived' from the Old Comedy: 'hinc omnis pendet Lucilius, hosce secutus.' This underrates the achievement of Lucilius, denying him originality; as Professor Sellar says, 'Greek comedy and Roman satire were the independent results of freedom of speech and criticism in different ages and countries'.[3] The function they discharged was identical, but not their literary form; they ran on parallel lines. And Jonson, a lifelong student of Horace, Juvenal, and Martial, followed their tradition.

He was not the first in England to hold this view. Sidney thought that the ideal comedy should be didactic, describing it as 'an imitation of the common errors of our life', represented 'in the most ridiculous and scornefull sort that may be; so as it is impossible that

---

[1] v. iii. 368–70.   [2] *Sat.* I. iv. 3–5.
[3] *Roman Poets of the Republic*, 3rd ed., 1889, p. 224.

any beholder can be content to be such a one'.[1] And Lodge even
showed some prevision of Jonson's method when, after explaining
that comic types reproved vice 'couertly in shadowes' while avoiding
all personal reference, he spoke of the moral purge that might be
effected 'if we had some Satericall Poetes nowe a dayes to penn our
commedies'.[2]

English satire before 1599 in its exposure of vice and folly also
helped to shape the new venture. Its main characteristics are
mapped out by Professor Campbell.[3] The satiric portrait of various
types of gull, for instance, often has in it a dramatic element; a scene
could be made out of it. Thus Marston's fencer in his gallery of
humours, the tenth satire in *The Scourge of Villanie*, 1598, is a
miniature Bobadill:

> Oh come not within distance, *Martius* speakes,
> Who nere discourseth but of fencing feates,
> Of *counter times*, *finctures*, slye *passataes*,
> *Stramazones*, resolute *Stoccataes*,
> Of the quick change, with wiping *mandritta*,
> The *carricado*, with th' *enbrocata*,
> *Oh, by Iesu Sir* (me thinks I heare him cry)
> *The honourable fencing misterie,*
> *Who doth not honour?* Then falls he in againe,
> Iading our eares, and some-what must he faine
> Of blades, and Rapier-hilts, of surest garde,
> Of *Vincentio*, and the *Burgonians* ward.
>   Thys bumbast foile-button I once did see
> By chaunce, in *Liuias* modest companie,
> When after the *God-sauing* ceremonie,
> For want of talke-stuffe, falls to foinerie,
> Out goes his Rapier, and to *Liuia*,
> He showes the ward by *puncta reuersa:*
> The *incarnata*. Nay, by the blessed light,
> Before he goes, he'le teach her how to fight
> And hold her weapon. Oh I laught amaine,
> To see the madnes of this *Martius* vaine.

In the Induction to *Every Man out of his Humour* Asper, the
presenter, is a satirist: he proposes to

> strip the ragged follies of the time,
> Naked, as at their birth, . . .
>   . . . and with a whip of steele,
> Print wounding lashes in their yron ribs.

[1] *An Apology for Poetry* (*Elizabethan Critical Essays*, ed. Gregory Smith,
i, pp. 176–7).
[2] *Defence of Poetry*, 1579 (ibid., p. 82).   [3] Op. cit., ch. ii.

Mitis warns him,

> take heed,
> The days are dangerous, full of exception,
> And men—

he might have added, especially bishops—

> growne impatient of reproofe.

But Asper's vein of mere denunciation is confined to the induction; it would have been futile in the body of the play. He leaves the stage to 'turne an actor and a Humorist', and reappears as Macilente, the embodiment of envy, who engineers the plot and dishumours the impostors.

He has a further mission to perform. It was necessary, Jonson felt, to make his conception of the comical satire clear to the audience. Hence he devised interpreters of the characters and of the action. Macilente and Carlo Buffone, in their different ways, discharge this duty in the present play; Professor Campbell well compares Ulysses and Thersites in *Troilus and Cressida*. In *Cynthia's Revels* Cupid and Mercury on the one hand, Crites on the other, describe or criticize the characters. But all are dramatic in that they take part in the action; still more does Horace, the archcommentator in *Poetaster*.

One other point to note in these plays is the severe punishment meted out to vice. Sordido's attempt at suicide is the penalty he pays for his cruel treatment of the poor. The immorality of Brisk and Fallace is nipped in the bud; but in *Poetaster*, where it is fullblown in Ovid and Julia, it meets with condign punishment.

THE CHARACTERS

The attempts of critics to trace portraits of Jonson's contemporaries in his dramatic characters have to be discussed in connexion with this play, which has been the starting-point for a number of identifications. These are set forth in *A Biographical Chronicle of the English Drama*, 1891, by F. G. Fleay in the articles on Jonson, Dekker, and Marston; *The War of the Theatres*, by Dr. Josiah H. Penniman, 1897, which is especially full and elaborate; *The Stage-Quarrel between Ben Jonson and the so-called Poetasters*, by Dr. R. A. Small, 1899, whose attitude to the identifications is keenly critical; and in Mr. H. C. Hart's edition of *The Works of Ben Jonson*, which stops short at *Poetaster* owing to his untimely death. Stray identifications are suggested by Dr. Brinsley Nicholson in the first volume of the *Mermaid* edition, and by writers in the *Dictionary of National*

Biography. Their chief results may be set forth instructively in tabular form:

	Fleay	Penniman	Small	Hart
Macilente .	Jonson	Jonson	..	..
Puntarvolo .	'May be' Sir J. Harington	Munday	..	[Gabriel Harvey,[1] afterwards] Sir W. Raleigh
Carlo Buffone	[Dekker, afterwards] Marston	Marston	Charles Chester	Charles Chester
Fastidius Briske	[Drayton,[2] afterwards] Daniel	Daniel	..	Daniel
Deliro .	'Possibly' Munday	..	..	..
Saviolina .	Elizabeth Carey	Daniel's 'Delia'	..	..
Sordido .	One of the Burbage family	Henslowe (?)	..	..
Fungoso .	..	Lodge	..	Lodge

Further suggestions by Mr. Fleay are that Cordatus and Mitis in the induction 'may be' Donne and Chapman; Dr. Nicholson identifies Clove and Orange as Marston and Dekker; Mr. A. H. Bullen, writing on Dekker in the *Dictionary of National Biography*, accepts Mr. Fleay's first view about Carlo; and Sir Sidney Lee in the article on Lyly suggests that he is caricatured in Puntarvolo.

'No one, I suppose,' writes Mr. Fleay, 'doubts that the "Comical Satires" of Jonson are personally satirical; but to give here all my grounds for identifying the persons satirized would require almost a history of contemporary poetry, non-dramatic as well as dramatic' (*Biographical Chronicle*, i, p. 359). The paradox that the great portrayer of the Humours, who is blamed for taking the life out of drama and making it unnatural by presenting abstractions in blind obedience to a theory, was, after all, a hard-and-fast caricaturist, could hardly be more sweepingly stated. But it does not inspire confidence in Mr. Fleay to find that at first he discerned Dekker in Buffone; the identification with Marston was an afterthought. Even then, the rival clues were so inextricable that he failed to disentangle them in his final proof-sheets: at page 97 of volume i he declares for Marston; at pages 360, 363, 364, 368-9 for Dekker, and again at page 71 of volume ii; but at page 75 he recurs to Marston. No one can mistake the portraiture of Marston and Dekker in *Poetaster*;

[1] In *Notes and Queries*, 9th Series, xii, p. 343.
[2] In *Shakespeariana*, iii, p. 30.

but if Buffone was an early sketch of Marston the features must be so blurred and uncharacteristic that, even after a close scrutiny, it is possible to confuse him with a totally different figure.

Dr. Penniman's results are set forth in his *War of the Theatres* with great clearness and precision, and with constant reference to the text. It is the fullest and most careful statement that has been presented for his side of the controversy. His treatment of Fungoso may be cited for the light which it throws upon these methods. He quotes Jonson's preliminary paragraph of characterization, and then gathers from the text the facts about Fungoso, noting what he does point by point. Dr. Penniman sums up:

> 'The reference to the tailor's bill which Fungoso was unable to pay[1] is, in itself, almost sufficient to identify him with Lodge, who was notorious for having been arrested in 1595 at the instigation of R. Topping, of the Strand, tailor. There are extant several documents which deal with the lawsuit concerning this bill. They date from 1595 to 1598. Lodge fled "beyond seas", and Henslowe, who had gone bail for him, refused to pay the bail or to disclose Lodge's hiding-place. Henslowe finally agreed to pay, and decision was rendered against him. When Lodge published *A Fig for Momus*, 1595, the title-page bore the name of the author as "T. L. of Lincolne's Inne, Gent". We find in Lodge's study of law the original of Fungoso's study of law, but Lodge, like Fungoso, did not persevere in the law. When Fungoso hides under the table (v. 6)[2] we have, perhaps, an allusion to Lodge's hiding during the trouble with the tailor. It is not improbable that the numerous references to a "suit" and to Fungoso's being "short a suit" may have a double meaning and include the lawsuit' (*War of the Theatres*, p. 56).

Now could a playwright with any faith in art make drama in this fashion? And was the lawsuit of Topping *versus* Lodge or the homely fact which led up to it—that Lodge could not pay for his clothes—a memorable event of the period? Topping was the marvellous person—not Lodge—for he waited seven years before he had Lodge arrested. But must the pother he then made fill

> The spacious times of great Elizabeth
> With sounds that echo still?

It misses the entire significance of the Comedy of Humours to subject its plastic material to this rigid pressure. Jonson, narrowing the scope of his art, was forced to repeat himself; types reappear with minor variations. Obviously in this kind of play the Pretender could play many parts; in *Every Man out of his Humour* alone we have the affectations of Puntarvolo, Briske, and Saviolina in high life, with middle-class supporters in Fungoso and Fallace, and with

---

[1] In IV. vii. 33–53.   [2] v. vii. 35 in this edition.

Shift, the 'thred-bare Sharke', and Sogliardo, 'the essentiall Clowne', still lower in the social scale. Or we have studies of Envy and Avarice in Macilente and Sordido, which show why Jonson postulated a serious element of satire in comedy. And types are taken over from play to play. Gifford notes that Fastidius Briske is 'a Bobadill at Whitehall', while 'Sogliardo and Fungoso are Master Matthew and Master Stephen thrown into new situations'. Still more marked is the affinity between the characters in the present play and those in *Cynthia's Revels*: Puntarvolo becomes Amorphus, Fungoso Asotus, and Fastidius Briske Hedon ; Saviolina is elaborated in Philautia. *Poetaster* ruthlessly develops Anaides in Demetrius, and Hedon in Crispinus ; surface personalities, which we should not have recognized in the earlier play if Dekker had not pointed them out to us,[1] were worked up minutely and set in clear relief.

One figure only in *Every Man out of his Humour*—the literary lecturer of the induction—stands out beyond mistake. It is the author to the life, and he recurs in the later plays, as Dekker pungently reminded him: 'you must haue three or foure suites of names . . . you must be call'd Asper, and Criticus,[2] and Horace, thy tytle's longer a reading then the Stile a the big Turkes: Asper, Criticus, Quintus, Horatius, Flaccus' (*Satiromastix*, 1602, D). But to see Jonson in Macilente is a perversity of which his worst enemies in his own day were not guilty. Did any man ever openly describe himself as falling 'into such an enuious apoplexie, with which his iudgement is so dazeled, and distasted, that he growes violently impatient of any opposite humor in another'? From the critical standpoint Macilente is one of the most significant figures in the play: he is at once the counterpart and antithesis to Brainworm in *Every Man in his Humour*. He plots and controls the intrigue which disillusions the whole motley group of humorists. But Brainworm, while unmistakably gifted with an intellectual element, is actuated by a sense of fun ; envy is the mainspring of Macilente's plotting.[3] It is suggestive that Jonson's handling of him appealed to a brother dramatist. Marston copied this phase of him in the Malevole of *The Malcontent*, inserting in the text a characterization which also owes something to the descriptive sketches in *Cynthia's Revels*. Malevole is thus hit off by Pietro before his first entrance:

'This *Maleuole* is one of the most prodigious affections that euer conuerst with nature; A man or rather a monster; more discontent

[1] See note to *C.R.* III. iii. 24–6.
[2] So the 'Crites' of *Cynthia's Revels* was originally named in the Quarto.
[3] Jonson emphasizes this: see the discussion of the 'Grex' at the end of the first act, and Macilente's renunciation of his envy in the epilogue.

then Lucifer when he was thrust out of the presence, his appetite is
vnsatiable as the Graue; as farre from any content as from heauen, his
highest delight is to procure others vexation, and therein hee thinkes
he truly serues heauen; for tis his position, whosoeuer in this earth can
be contented is a slaue and dam'd; therefore do's he afflict al in that
to which they are most affectted; the Elements struggle within him; his
owne soule is at variance: his speach is halter-worthy at all howers:
I like him fayth, he giues good intelligence to my spirit, makes me
vnderstand those weakenesses which others flattery palliates: harke
they sing.

SCENA TERTIA.

A Song.

Enter Maleuole *after the Song.*

See: he comes: now shall you heare the extremity of a Malecontent:
he is as free as ayre; he blowes ouer euery man. And sir, whence come
you now?
   Mal. From the publick place of much dissimulation. ( )¹

Quarto 1604, Biᵛ.

Mercifully no one has yet suggested that this is a portrait of Jonson.
   Some identifications are based on a single allusion, slight in
itself, limited in scope, and inconsistent with other traits when the
character is examined as a whole. Perspective is completely lost.
Browning's answer to a correspondent who questioned him about
the source of *The Lost Leader* has a far-reaching application. He
admitted, 'with something of shame and contrition, that I undoubtedly had Wordsworth in my mind—but simply as a "model";
you know, an artist takes one or two striking traits in the features
of his "model", and uses them to start his fancy on a flight which
may end far enough from the good man or woman who happens to
be "sitting" for nose and eye'.² Not even the tip of Daniel's nose
is visible in the features of Fastidius Briske. Nothing that he says
or does at any point of the play can be imputed, directly or indirectly,
remotely or superficially, to Daniel. This incongruous attribution
was reached by a devious route. Briske resembles Hedon in *Cynthia's Revels*; Hedon is the lover of Philautia; Philautia, just when
she is professing indifference to Hedon but deep interest in the
effects of her head-dress, exclaims 'I should be some LAVRA, or some
DELIA, me thinkes' (IV. i. 33–4); and 'Daniel in his *Delia* Sonnets
calls his lady "a Laura", *Sonnet* 40'.³ From this it follows that
Daniel 'swore tersely, and with variety', and borrowed other people's

---

¹ The second Quarto adds an explanation '(the Church)'.
² Mrs. Sutherland Orr's *Life and Letters of Robert Browning*, pp. 132–3.
³ Fleay, *Biographical Chronicle*, i, p. 364.

horses (*E.M.O.* Characters, 39 foll.). The plain fact is that Hedon
and his mistress are courtiers, and she refers to Daniel's poetry
because it was popular in Court circles. In exactly the same way
Gullio, a courtier in the first part of *The Returne from Parnassus*,
who quotes lines of Shakespeare as his own composition, is criticized
by a bystander—'I thinke he will runn throughe a whole buke of
Samuell Daniell's!'[1]

On one character of *Every Man out of his Humour*—or, at most,
on two—contemporaries did fasten with this accusation of stage-
caricature. Jasper Mayne in *Jonsonus Virbius*, writing of the moral
value of Jonson's satire in inspiring hatred of evil types, adds this
interesting information:

> So did thy sting not *bloud*, but *humours* draw,
> So much doth *Satyre* more correct then *Law*;
> Which was not *nature* in *thee*, as some call
> Thy *teeth*, who say thy *wit* lay in thy *Gall*.
> That *thou* didst quarrell first, and then, in spight,
> Didst 'gainst a *person* of such *vices* write:
> That 'twas *revenge*, not *truth*, that on the *Stage*
> *Carlo* was not presented, but *thy Rage*:
> And that when *thou* in *company* wert met,
> Thy *meate* tooke *notes*, and thy *discourse* was *net*.
> Wee know *thy* free-*veine* had this *innocence*,
> To spare the *partie*, and to brand th' *offence*.
> And the just *indignation thou* wert in
> Did not expose *Shift*, but his *tricks* and *ginne*.

Similarly Dekker asserted in the preface to *Satiromastix* that a Captain Hannam was the prototype or—in Browning's phrase—the
'model', of Captain Tucca in *Poetaster*; and it is noteworthy that
this insignificant trio—Buffone, Shift, and Tucca—were just common frequenters of taverns and ordinaries. Jonson is quite frank
on this question in the dedication to *Volpone* (ll. 47–58). He admits
that he 'cannot escape, from some, the imputation of sharpnesse,
but that they will say, I haue taken a pride, or lust, to be bitter,
and not my yongest infant but hath come into the world with all
his teeth'; but he pleads that he has never attacked any 'nation,
societie, or generall order, or state' or any 'publique person'. Then
comes the significant reservation: 'Where haue I beene particular?
Where personall? except to a mimick,[2] cheater, baud, or buffon,

[1] Gullio is almost a pale copy of Brisk, and H. C. Hart (i, pp. xlvi–xlvii)
claims him as another caricature of Daniel.
[2] Thus Puntarvolo has been alleged to be a representation of Sir Thomas
Conyngsby of Hampton Court, Herefordshire, M.P. for Leominster, knighted
by Essex in 1591, and ancestor of the Earls of Conyngsby. He died on 30 May

creatures (for their insolencies) worthy to be tax'd?' It was natural that the attempt to portray the vulgar parasite or sharker should come close to reality: this narrow type admitted of no idealizing touch. But here the character is lifted into the sphere of art—as in Bobadill with his 'high seriousness'; in Mosca with his transcendent cunning; or—to go farther afield—in Pistol, whom the genius of Shakespeare transmuted with a sublime infusion of the mock-heroic —contemporary gossip was discreetly silent, and the modern investigator fails to find a clue. Bobadill is a 'humorist' in the Jonsonian sense—the artistic incarnation of a type: characters like Buffone or Shift are in the main freaks or perversities—'humorists' only in the commonplace sense against which Jonson himself protested.

The gossip about Carlo, to which Mayne refers, is confirmed by Aubrey in his jottings on Sir Walter Raleigh (Aubrey MS. 6, f. 76); he quotes as his authority 'Dr. J. Pell', a noted mathematician and linguist, who studied both at Cambridge and at Oxford. Aubrey writes:

'In his youthfull time, was one *Charles Chester*, that often kept company with his acquaintance; he was a bold impertinent fellowe, & they could never be at quiet for him: a perpetuall talker & made a noyse like a druṁe in a roome: So, one time at a taverne, Sʳ W. R. beates him and seales up his mouth & his upper and neather beard with hard wax. From him Ben: Johnson takes his Carlo Buffone Jester in Every man ⟨out of ¹⟩ his Humour.'

Other references to Chester show that his scurrility was a byword. Harington refers three times to this characteristic of his: in *An Apologie* for his *Aiax*, 1596, Cc6, 'you know the booke well enough, I haue read you a sleepe in it, once or twice as we went from Greenwich to Westminster. Out vppon it haue you put it in print? did not I tell you then, Charles Chester & 2. or 3. such scoffing fellowes would laugh at you for it?'—in *Vlisses vpon Aiax*, 1596, D3, 'or (to vse *Charles Chesters* iest, because you are faced like *Platina*) would it not anger your harte strings, if a man shoulde saye that you looke like a sturdie Hostler that coulde guird a maie till shee fart againe?' —and in *A Treatise vpon Playe* (*Nugae Antiquae*, ii, p. 180) there is

1605. His journal at the siege of Rouen has been printed by the Camden Society. His portrait with his favourite dog 'Cricket' is preserved at Cassiobury. Mr. G. F. Townsend in *The Town and Borough of Leominster*, p. 89, quotes a dubious tale to the effect that the players went down to Hampton Court to be able to mimic Sir Thomas exactly, and secured a suit from his wardrobe by a trick, and that afterwards, when he saw the play acted in London, he stood up among the audience and asked in bewilderment, 'Am I Sir Thomas Conyngsby, or is that Sir Thomas Conyngsby?'
¹ These words are inserted in the MS. by Wood. Aubrey, uncertain which of the two Humour plays contained the character, left a blank space.

a sneer at 'some Chester-like elloquens'. Lastly there is a reference in Nashe's *Pierce Pennilesse*, 1592 (*Workes*, ed. McKerrow, i, pp. 190–1), to 'an odde foule mouthde Knaue, called *Charles* the Fryer', who lived 'not farre from Chester', whom 'a great personage' as a punishment for his scurrility, 'brickt vp in a narrow chimney', 'fed for fifteene dayes with bread and water through a hole', and then 'let out to see if he could learne to rule his tongue any better'. Nashe quotes some of his flowers of speech to noblemen whom 'he would liken to more vgly things than himself'; for instance, 'to guilded chines of beefe, or a shoomaker sweating, when he puls on a shoo', or 'to a Spanish Codpisse'; or he would tell a courtier 'that his face was not yet finisht, with such like innumerable absurd illusions: yea, what was he in the Court but he had a comparison in stead of a Capcase to put him in'. Jonson lays stress on Carlo's 'absurd' or 'adult'rate' similes, and his gift of 'transforming any person into deformity' 'more swift then *Circe*' (Characters, 25–7; induction, 356–69).[1] It is not improbable that Chester's grotesque talk[2] influenced Jonson in his choice of such a noted character to represent the parasite; the extravagance was at least distinctive, and the misuse of the English language Jonson never missed an opportunity of satirizing.

After a full weighing of the evidence, the general conclusion is that in this play Jonson did not use his carefully drawn representations of the humours to screen a series of personal attacks; that in *Cynthia's Revels* he did introduce lightly touched sketches of Dekker and Marston, indicated by a few satiric strokes only, which were clear at least to Dekker; and that it was not till *Poetaster* that he drew his full-length portraits of contemporaries. Even in the one figure of *Every Man out of his Humour*, in which we can definitely trace satirical impersonation, it is not difficult to see an underlying literary purpose.

THE INDUCTION

Jonson's use of the induction is characteristic.[3] The device of a presenter engaged in a preliminary dialogue was used by Kyd to

---

[1] Mr. Baskerville, *English Elements*, p. 176, compares Nashe with Jonson, and especially Carlo's comparison of Puntarvolo to 'a shielde of brawne, at *Shrouetide*' (IV. iv. 110), where, as he notes, the Quarto reads 'a Chine of Brawne'.

[2] Dekker specially comments on Tucca's copying the tricks of Hannam's speech: 'I wonder what language *Tucca* would haue spoke, if honest Capten *Hannam* had bin borne without a tongue?' In addition to his general scurrility, the special traits are his stammer and the number of nicknames he works off on the other characters.

[3] C. R. Baskerville has a useful discussion of the point (*English Elements*, pp. 146–9).

invest the action with an allegorical significance. Thus in *The Spanish Tragedy* (acted about 1587) Revenge and the Ghost of the murdered Andrea watch the progress of events while themselves remaining in the background; and in *Soliman and Perseda* (registered in 1592) Love, Fortune, and Death claim to control the action. The effect is to charge these plays with a peculiar atmosphere. But elsewhere the device involves comments—sometimes in the form of banter—either upon the piece or the players. In Peele's *The Old Wifes Tale* (acted about 1590) the old wife Madge is presenter and tells the story as a winter's tale to Fantastic and Frolic, two detached spectators; they question her about the action and the characters. In Greene's *The Scottish History of Iames the fourth*, and in the pre-Shakespearian *Taming of a Shrew* (both registered in 1594) the setting is similar in principle and more elaborately worked out. In *Wily Beguiled* (acted in 1596?) the play opens with 'Spectrum' posted up on the title-board, and this dialogue between the Prologue and a player:

'What hoe, where are these paltrie Plaiers? stil poaring in their papers and neuer perfect? for shame come forth, your Audience stay so long, their eies waxe dim with expectation.

[*Enter one of the Players.*]

How now my honest Rogue; what play shall wee haue here to night?

Play. Sir you may looke vpon the Title.

Prol. What, *Spectrum* once again? Why noble *Cerberus*, nothing but patch-pannell stuffe, olde gally-mawfreies and cotten-candle eloquence? out you bawling bandogge fox-furd slaue: you dried stockefish you, out of my sight. [*Exit the Player.*]

Well tis no matter: Ile set mee downe and see't, and for fault of a better Ile supply the place of a scuruy Prologue.'

He speaks four lines, and a Juggler enters, spirits away the title, and substitutes 'Wily Beguiled', which the company proceed to act. In Munday's *The Downfall of Robert, Earle of Huntington* (acted 1597–8) Skelton calls out some of the actors in the induction, and presents them with an actor for the part of Little John; he introduces the dumb-shows before the acts. The induction of four other plays bring us a step nearer to Jonson; they are touched with a faint suggestion of criticism. In *Mucedorus*, 1598, Comedy and Envy dispute which shall present the play; Envy is conquered in the epilogue. In *A Warning for fair women*, 1599, Tragedy prevails over Comedy and History at the outset; in Yarington's *Two Tragedies in One*, 1601, there is an allegorical contest of Truth with Homicide and Avarice; and in the first part of Marston's *Antonio and Mellida*, acted shortly before Jonson's play, eight actors discuss the parts they have to play.

Jonson availed himself of this crude device to read his audience a lecture on the true principles of comedy and to expound his conception of the Humours. He used the induction also in *Cynthia's Revels, Bartholomew Fair, The Staple of News,* and *The Magnetic Lady,* always with some implication of criticism, but never again as the elaborate manifesto of a literary theory. It is interesting that Marston copied this feature in the first part of *Antonio and Mellida,* printed in 1602, but perhaps acted in 1600; he discusses the acting. So does Webster in the induction added to the second edition of *The Malcontent,* 1604. The note of criticism recurs in Marston's last induction prefixed to the 1607 Quarto of *What You Will.* But by 1607 Beaumont could write in the prologue to *The Woman Hater,* '*Gentlemen, Inductions are out of date*'.

The acting date of *What You Will* is probably 1601. It was performed at a private theatre: the tireman entering to light the candles for the induction points to a roofed building. Not improbably the Paul's boys acted the piece; it contains none of the fustian terms ridiculed in *Poetaster,* but it also has no reference to *Poetaster* and the attack on Marston. Allusions to Jonson and his theorizing are unmistakable. Atticus, Doricus, and Philomuse speak the induction, and Doricus alludes to three formidable auditors 'Sir sineor Snuffe, Monsieur Mew, and Caualiero Blirt'. Philomuse expresses his contempt for ignorant critics. Doricus continues:

> Nay, nay, nay, Heauens my hope, I cannot smoth this straine,
> Witts death I cannot, what a leaprous humor
> Breaks from ranke swelling of these bubbling wits?
> Now out vp-pont: I wonder what tite braine:
> Wrung in this custome to mainetaine *Contempt*
> Gainst common *Censure*: to giue stiffe counter buffes
> To crack rude skorne euen to the very face
> Of better audience. Slight ist not odious,
> Why harke you honest, honest *Phylomuse*
> (You that indeauor to indeere our thoughts,
> To the composers Spirit) hold this firme:
> *Musike* and *Poetry* were first approu'd
> By common scence; and that which pleased most,
> Held most allowed passe: not[1] rules of Art
> Were shapt to pleasure, not pleasure to your rules,
> Thinke you if that his sceanes tooke stampe in mint
> Of three or foure deem'd most iudicious,

[1] Bullen reads 'know' for 'not'.

It must inforce the world to currant them
That you must spit defiance or dislike?
Now as I loue the light were I to passe
Through publick verdit, I should feare my forme
Least ought I offerd were vnsquard or warp'd,
,,The more we know, the more we know we want
,,What *Bayard* boulder then the ignorant?   (Sig. A2.)
,,Beleeue me Phylomuse: ifaith thou must
,,*The best best seale of wit, is wits distrust.*

Phy. Nay gentle *Doricus.*

Dor. Ile have no more of him, nay and your friend the Author, the composer: the *What you will*: seemes so faire in his owne glasse, so straight in his owne measure that hee talkes once of squinting *Critickes*, drunken *Censure*, splay-footed *Opinion*, iuicles huskes, I ha done with him, I ha done with him.

There is little doubt who 'rung in the custom' to express contempt for the common verdict on drama. The statement that

rules of Art
Were shapt to pleasure, not pleasure to your rules

openly rejects the Horatian ideal, which Sidney and Jonson followed, of combining instruction with delight in literary work; and it is too a bold anticipation of Dryden's attitude, for which Marston has not received credit. In the prologue to *The Dutch Courtezan*, 1605 (A2) he also emphasized this point:

Slight hastie labours in this easie Play,
Present not what you would, but what we may:
For this vouchsafe to know the onely end
Of our new studie is, not to offend.
Yet thinke not, but like others raile we could,
(Best art Presents, not what it can, but should)
And if our pen in this seeme ouer slight,
We striue not to instruct, but to delight,
As for some few, we know of purpose here
to taxe and scowt: know firme art cannot feare
Vaine rage: onely the highest grace we pray
Is, you'le not taxe, vntill you iudge our Play.

His final appeal is to ask the audience to

suruay
Nothing but passionate man in his slight play,
Who hath this onely ill: to some deem'd worst,
A modest diffidence, and selfe mistrust.

Again in Act III, scene ii, of *What You Will*, Lampatho, who is an acknowledged satirist,[1] mimics the vein of Asper:

> *Lam.* Dreadlesse of rackes, shappados, or the sword,
> Mauger Informer and slie intelligence,
> Ile stand as confident as *Hercules*,
> And with a frightlesse resolution,
> Rip vp and launce our times impieties.
> *Sim.* Vds so peace.
> *Lam.* Open a bounteous eare for Ile be free,
> Ample as *Heauen*, giue my speech more roome,
> Let me vnbrace my breasts, strip vp my sleeues,
> Stand like an executioner to vice,
> To strike his head off with the keener edge,
> Of my sharpe spirit.
> *Lau.* Roome and good licence, come on, when, when.
> *Lam.* Now is my fury mounted, fix your eyes,
> Intend your sences, bend your listning vp,
> For Ile make greatnesse quake, Ile tawe the hide
> Of thick-skind *Hugenes*.
> *Lau.* Tis most gratious weele obserue thee calmely.
> *Qua.* Hang on thy toungs end, come on pree-thee doe.
> *Lam.* Ile see you hang'd first, I thanke you Sir, Ile none,
> This is the straine that chokes the theaters:
> That makes them crack with full stufft audience,
> This is your humor onely in request
> Forsooth to raile, this brings your eares to bed,
> This people gape for, for this some doe stare,
> This some would heare, to crack the Authors neck,
> This admiration and applause persues,
> Who cannot raile, my humors chang'd 'tis cleare,
> Pardon Ile none, I prise my ioynts more deare. (E1ᵛ.)

A greater than Marston appears to have cast a passing glance on Asper. *As You Like it*, entered on the Stationers' Register on 4 August 1600, and probably acted in the previous year, contains in the character of Jaques the only attempt made by Shakespeare to portray a Jonsonian 'humour'. Jaques's speeches in Act II, scene vii, lines 1–87, repeat, in a changed setting, in a milder tone, and with a romantic touch alien to Jonson's art, the language of Asper:

> Give me leaue
> To speake my minde, and I will through and through
> Cleanse the foule bodie of th' infected world,
> If they will patiently receiue my medicine.

[1] Quadratus in II. i calls him 'Don Kynsader'—Marston's own pseudonym when he published *The Scourge of Villainy*.

Detached from their context, the words might pass for Asper's. But the context is Jaques's request to the Duke for leave to wear motley in order that he may rail with licence. The rebuke is delicately turned, keeping carefully within the limits of admissible allusion. And the Duke makes the severe reply that all Jaques, even in motley, could effect would be

> Most mischeeuous foule sin, in chiding sin.

Did 'narrow-eyed decipherers' among Jonson's contemporaries misread the character of Jaques for a caricature of Jonson? This may have been one of the literary attacks of which Jonson complained in the 'Apologetical Dialogue' added to *Poetaster* (ll. 96–8)—

> three yeeres,
> They did prouoke me with their petulant stiles
> On euery stage.

In all probability he gave the provocation himself—not by personal satire in his plays, but by the air of literary tutelage which he assumed towards the theatre in such writing as the induction to *Every Man out of his Humour*.

PLACE AND TIME IN THE PLAY

In the Induction Jonson dismisses as unnecessary the strict observance of the old laws of classical comedy—for instance, that the play should 'fall within the compasse of a dayes businesse' (ll. 235–45). There is no notice of the scene added to the list of the characters; it is vaguely described in the text as 'The Fortunate Island' (Ind. 273), which allows a certain amount of latitude and has a more classical ring than 'England' would have had.

The play opens in the country, in Sogliardo's lordship with its farms (I. ii. 18). Sordido has one of Sogliardo's farms (I. iii), for Macilente stays on at the close of the previous scene to observe him. 'The *Scene* is the country still, remember' (I. iii. 198).

Sogliardo is to visit Puntarvolo at his country house (I. ii. 223). The first three scenes of the second act take place there. Briske, Carlo, Sogliardo, and Fungoso call there and stay the night; 'neighbour Sordido' is included among the guests (II. iii. 251). Sogliardo is on his way to London (I. ii. 223–4) and intends to spend 'some weeke or so' there in order to get a coat of arms at the Heralds' office (II. iii. 287).

Scenes iv to vi are at Deliro's house in the City next morning. Except for a return to Sordido's farm in Act III, scenes vii and viii, London is the scene of the rest of the play—the middle aisle of

Paul's (III. i–vi), a room at Court (ix), Deliro's house again (IV. i, ii, vii; v. viii), Puntarvolo's lodgings (IV. iii–vi, viii), The Palace Stairs (v. i, iii), a room at Court (v. ii), the Mitre (v. iv–vii, ix), the Counter prison (v. x, xi).

Time is also liberally treated. A second night passes in the third act. Briske offers (II. vi. 81–2) to take Macilente to Court 'to morrow' if he can get good clothes. Deliro supplies them, and we find in Act IV, scene ii, lines 29–45, that Macilente has been to Court. In Act IV, scene iii, lines 84–5, Sogliardo has had his smoking lesson from Shift 'euer sin' yesterday noone', i.e. ever since he engaged Shift in Act III, scene vi.

In Act IV, scene viii, line 5, Puntarvolo is prepared to go to Court 'this afternoon': he goes in Act v, scene ii. Shift, who does not go there, will meet his patron about three or four o'clock (IV. viii. 81), which he does in the third scene of Act v.

The play ends at night. Deliro, who was going to bed in Act v, scene viii, line 25, goes to the tavern to redeem Fungoso. Fallace hurries off to the Counter to perform a similar service for Briske and is surprised by her husband there.

So far as the passage of a night in the action is concerned, Jonson could have pleaded classical precedents in the *Amphitryo* of Plautus and the *Heauton Timorumenos* of Terence, but no such precedent can be found for the scenes in which we learn that Sordido's almanacs have not kept faith with him (III. vii and viii). A week at least, if not a month, must have elapsed for Sordido to test their worthlessness.

Dedication

9. *friendship with diuers.* Possibly Benjamin Rudyerd, Richard Martin, John Hoskyns, John Donne; Selden did not enter at Clifford's Inn till 1602.

20. *But when the game . . .* The idea is from Martial, x. xx. 18–20 (lines addressed to Pliny, after a reference to his pleading in the courts).

the Lord of liberty raignes, i.e. the Lord of Misrule appointed at the Christmas revels. Gifford quotes Shirley, *The Sisters*, 1652, II. ii (in *Six New Playes*, 1653, p. 13):

> I have seen a Counterfeit
> With such a Majesty compose himself,
> He thought himself a Prince; could frown as scornfully,
> And give his hand out to great Lords to kiss,
> With as much grace, as all the Royall bloud
> Had musterd in his veins.
> *Lu.*   Some Monarch
> Of Innes a Court in *England* sure.

24. *your Honorer*. So Jonson, revising the proofs for the large-paper issue of the Folio, deliberately toned down 'your true Honorer'. Elsewhere he has epithets: 'Your Lo. most faithfull honorer' to Lord Aubigny in the dedication of *Sejanus*, and to Lord Pembroke in *Catiline* and the *Epigrams*; 'Your La: true honorer' to Mary, Lady Wroth, in *The Alchemist*. 'True' was retained when *Every Man in his Humour* was reprinted in 1640. Jonson carried his sturdy independence a step farther in dedicating *Cynthia's Revels* to the Court as 'Thy seruant, but not slaue'; and he had had a passage of arms with lawyers in *Poetaster*. He was accused of satirizing them personally in that play (see the 'apologeticall Dialogue' added to it in the Folio, l. 82, and his reply, ll. 116–27). Even in the present play lawyers are summarily grouped with brokers and usurers for their corruption and rapacity (Induction, l. 25).

The Characters

7. MACILENTE. Florio in his *Worlde of Wordes*, 1598, has 'Macilénte, *leane, meagre, gant, barren, thin*'.

8. *well parted*. Cf. III. ix. 14, 15, 'meanely clad, Though ne're so richly parted'; v. ii. 18, 'so courtly, and wel-parted a gentleman'; *C.R.* v. ii. 72, 'a man rarely parted'.

14. PVNTARVOLO. Cf. Florio, *Worlde of Wordes*, 1598, 'Puntaruolo, *a nice, coy, affected, scrupolus, selfconceited fellow. a bodkin. a man that stands vpon points, a carper, a findefault, a gouldsmiths pouncer*'.

16. *consecrated to singularity*. As Sir Walter Scott put in his 'Advertisement' to a reprint of *The Letting of Humours Blood*, 1815, 'The more ambitious coxcombs of our forefathers' day, affected to distinguish themselves, not only from the sober-minded public, and from the vulgar, but from each other, for which purpose each assumed a strain of peculiarity, however absurd and fantastic, and, in the phrase of heraldry, bore his folly with a difference.' 'Put thy selfe into the tricke of singularitie' is the advice of the letter to Malvolio (*Tw. Night*, II. v. 134).

Iacobs staffe, an obsolete instrument for taking altitudes. In Gregory Reisch's *Margarita Philosophica*, 1503, vi, ch. iv, is a description and a woodcut of one form of it, though he corrects it in the errata to the second edition, 1504. Cf. Fletcher and Massinger, *The Spanish Curate*, v. i (Folio, 1647, p. 45), where Jamy says to Violante:

> In stature you are a Giantesse: and your Tailour
> Takes measure of you with a Iacobs staffe,
> Or he can never reach you.

21. *returnes*. A common form of speculation: a traveller, starting on a long or dangerous voyage, deposited a sum of money on condition of receiving a high rate of interest on his return ('five for one' in *The Tempest*, III. iii. 48); the money was irrecoverable if he did not return. In *C.R.* I. iii. 34, the traveller Amorphus is 'one that hath now made the sixth returne vpon venter'.

26. *absurd similes.* Cf. Ind. 363, 'his adult'rate *simile's*', and II. i. 10, 'how he confounds with his *simile's*?' Examples are a timber column (Ind. 328); a musty bottle, new wickered (I. ii. 200); a motion in a great antique clock (II. i. 6); a fresh salmon kept in a tub (ib. 94); a shield of brawn at Shrovetide or dry pole of ling on Easter eve (IV. iv. 110–11); a Dutch purse with the mouth downward (V. vi. 34–5).

29, 30. *Oares . . . Sculler.* Cf. Dekker, *The Guls Horne-booke*, 1609, ch. vi, p. 31, of a gallant lodging on the waterside, 'it addes a kind of state vnto you, to be carried from thence to the staires of your Play-house: hate a Sculler (remember that) worse then to be acquainted with one ath Scullery. No, your Oares are your onely Sea-crabs, boord them, & take heed, you neuer go twice together with one paire'; and *Histrio-mastix*, 1610, C2, '*Lyar.* Let's Duck it with our Dogs to make vs sport, | And crosse the water to eate some Creame; | What hoe? Sculler. *Vel.* You do forget; *Plenty* affoords vs Oares.'

32. *posset.* 'Posset is hot Milk poured on Ale or Sack, having Sugar, grated Bisket, Eggs, with other ingredients, boiled in it, which goes all to a curd' (R. Holme, *Academy of Armory*, 1688, iii, p. 84).

35. FASTIDIVS BRISKE. See Burton's references in *The Anatomy of Melancholy*, 1621, p. 205: 'let him haue but a good outside, he carries it, most men are esteemed according to their clothes. In our gullish times, him, whom you peradventure in modesty would giue place to, as being deceived by his habit, and presuming him some great worshipfull man, beleeue it, if you shall examine his estate, he will likely be proved a serving-man of no great note, my Ladies taylor, or his Lordships barber, so some such gull, a *Fastidius Briske*, a Sᵣ *Petronell Flashe*, a meere outside'; and ibid., pp. 677–8 (of the causes of jealousy): 'If a young gallant come by chance into her presence, a *Fastidius Briske* that can weare his clothes well, in fashion with a locke, a gingling spurre, a feather, that can cringe and with all compliment, court a gentlewoman, she raues vpon him; *ô what a louely proper man he was*, how sweetly he carried himselfe, with how comely a grace, *sic vultus sic ora ferebat*, how neatly he did weare his clothes, sing and dance, &c, and then she beginnes to loath her husband, to hate him and his filthy beard, his gotish complection, how like a dizard, a foole, an asse he lookes, how like a clowne he behaues himselfe.'

36. *affecting.* Cf. *The Merry Wives*, II. i. 127, 'I neuer heard such a drawling-affecting rogue'.

37. *practiseth . . . how to salute.* C. R. Baskerville compares Nashe's account of a visitor's experience with Gabriel Harvey: 'Two howres good by the clocke he attended his pleasure, whiles he (as some of his fellow In-mates haue since related vnto mee) stood acting by the glasse all his gestures he was to vse all the day after, and currying & smudging and pranking himselfe vnmeasurably. . . . downe he came, and after the *bazelos manus*, with amplifications and complements hee belaboured him till his eares tingled and his feet ak'd againe. . . . The Gentleman swore to mee that vpon his first apparition (till he disclosed himselfe) he tooke

him for an Vsher of a dancing Schoole' (*Haue with you to Saffron-walden*, 1596, ed. McKerrow, *Works*, iii. pp. 91–2).

38. *Base-violl.* See III. ix. 30 n.

41. *the boot.* Cf. Dekker, *The Guls Horne-booke*, 1609, ch. i, p. 6, 'fine backes, and fat bellies are Coach-horses to two of the seuen deadly sins [namely, to Pride and Gluttony]: In the bootes of which Coach, *Lechery* and *Sloth* sit like the waiting-maide'; and Scott's description of the lord lieutenant's coach in *Old Mortality*, ch. i: 'The insides were their graces in person, two maids of honour, two children, a chaplain stuffed into a sort of lateral recess, formed by a projection at the door of the vehicle, and called, from its appearance, the boot, and an equerry to his Grace ensconced in the corresponding convenience on the opposite side.'

42. *praise*, appraise, value.

44. *the gingle of his spurre.* See II. i. 38–9, v. 23.

46. DELIRO. Cf. Burton's reference in *The Anatomy of Melancholy*, ed. 2, 1624, pp. 468–9, ''tis a great fault (as some men are *vxorij*) to bee too fond of their wiues, to dote on them as Senior *Deliro* on his, *Fallace*', with a marginal note 'Every man out of his humour'. Florio defines 'Deliro *doted, raued, fabled, become a foole. Also a foole, a sot, a gull, a dotrell, a swaruer from reason, bestraughted of his wit. Also peeuish and fond.*'

54. *iuniper.* Burton, *Anatomy*, 1624, p. 222, writes '*Bessardus Bisantius* preferres the smoake of Iuniper to melancholy persons, which is in great request with vs in *Oxford*, to sweeten our chambers'. Cf. *C.R.* II. iv. 75.

55. *villanous-out-of-tune musick.* Cf. *Poet.* III. iv. 283 and the opening of *The Malcontent* just before the Duke's return (1604, sig. B), '*The vilest out of tune Musicke being heard. Enter* Bilioso *and* Præpasso.' They stop it, and a perfumer enters. Deliro was aping the manners of court.

58. *Peat*, a spoilt, self-willed woman. Cf. *E.H.* v. i. 60, and *The Taming of the Shrew*, i. i. 78, 'A pretty peate, it is best put finger in the eye'.

60. *wants the face to be dishonest.* Cf. *Volp.* i. v. 106, 'Shee hath not yet the face, to be dishonest'.

62. SAVIOLINA. Cf. Florio, *A Worlde of Wordes*, 1598, 'Sauiolino, *prettie wise, warie, or wittie. Also nice, coy, puling, selfconceited, humorous.*'

65. SORDIDO. Florio (1598) among other meanings has '*a niggard, a paltrer, a dodger, a pennie-father, a mizer, a pinch-pennie, a couetous wretch*'.

66. *Chuffe*, churl, but also with a suggestion of 'miser', which attaches to the word: cf. *S. of N.* 4th intermean, 22, and Marlowe's translation of *Ouids Elegies*, III. vi. 50, 'Chuffe-like had I not gold and could not vse it?'

70. FVNGOSO used as the name of a type—'Some idle FVNGOSO, that hath got aboue the cup-board, since yesterday'—in *C.R.* IV. iii. 74–5. Florio (1598) has 'Fungoso, *spungie, airie, light, as a mushrome*'.

77. SOGLIARDO. Cf. Florio (1598), 'Sogliardo, *a mocker, a scoffer, a quipper, a flouter, a frumper, a iester. Also slouenly, sluttish, or hoggish. Also a lubbard, a loggerhead, a gull, a foole, a flattrer, a cogger'.

80. *Terme*, the London season, then fixed by the law-terms. The country gentlemen, who flocked to London with their families, were called 'termers' (*Ep*. iii. 9). For motions or puppet-plays in the season see *C.R.* IV. i. 182–3, 'As a countrey gentlewoman, keep a good house, and come vp to terme, to see motions'; and *Volp*. v. iv. 77–8, 'MER. 1. 'Twere a rare motion, to be seene in *Fleet-street!* MER. 2. I, i'the terme.' Tobacco 'was then a matter of serious study, and had its professors, like the rest of the liberal arts' (Gifford).

83. SHIFT. Cf. *Ep*. xii.

84–5. *neuer was Souldier . . . lendings.* Much like Bobadill (*E.M.I.* I. iv. 88–90), and Tucca (*Poet*. I. ii. 192–202).

85. *skeldring*, begging (but specially used of the disbanded or wounded soldier). Cf. *Poet*. I. i. 24, 'skeldring captaine'; ii. 49, 50, 'An honest decayed commander, cannot skelder' . . .; Dekker and Middleton, *The Roaring Girl*, v. i. (1611, K3), '*Trap.* Your Worship will not abuse a souldier? *Moll.* Souldier? . . . you skeldering varlet?' Hence, in the sense of 'cheating': *Poet*. III. iv. 155, 'A man may skelder yee, now and then, of halfe a dozen shillings, or so'.

odling. Found only here, and the context suggests the sense of 'cheating'. 'Perhaps an error of some kind' (*O.E.D.*).

86. *Poules.* So Bobadill is '*A Paules-man*' in the 'Persons' of *E.M.I. Pict-hatch.* See *E.M.I.* I. ii. 93.

87. *Takes vp.* Cf. I. ii. 119, 120, 'I will take vp, and bring my selfe in credit sure'.

testons, sixpences.

89. *way-layes . . . seruices.* Gifford quotes Gower on Pistol, *Henry V*, III. vi. 68–70, 'and such fellowes are perfit in the Great Commanders Names, and they will learne you by rote where Seruices were done'.

96. *Whiffe.* See III. iii. 57.

97. *Cockatrice*, prostitute. Cf. I. ii. 220 n.

Imparters. Cf. Tucca's inquiry *Poet*. III. iv. 369, 'Did not MINOS impart?' The delicacy of the word is brought out in III. vi. 64–7, 'Please you . . . to impart some ten groates, or halfe a crowne to our vse, till our abilitie be of grow'th to returne it'.

100. *case*, pair. Cf. *C. is A*. II. iii. 1.

109. *Cloue serues to sticke him.* Cf. *M. Christmas*, 154–5. The reference is to a housekeeper's practice elucidated in T. Lupton's *A Thousand Notable things* [1595], Book II, Fij^v, 'Wine will be pleasant in taste and in sauour, and cullour: it wyll much please thee if an Orenge, or a Lymon (stickt round about with Cloaues) be hanged within the vessel that it touche not the Wyne. And so the Wyne wyll be preserued from foystines and euyll sauor. *Mizaldus.*'

113. *Moderator*, lit. one who presides at a discussion; here, virtually, exponent.

The Induction

the second Sounding. This immediately precedes the Induction in *Cynthia's Revels* also and the speech of Envy in *Poetaster*: cf. H. Fitzgeoffery, *Notes from Black-Fryers*, 1620, E7ᵛ, of a playgoer arriving early:

> Come, let's bethink our selues what may be found:
> To deceive *Time* with, till the second sound.

A third sounding ushered in the prologue: see below 292–3, *C.R.*, prol., and Heywood, *The Foure Prentises of London*, 1615, A4, 'Doe you not know that I am the Prologue? . . . Haue you not sounded thrice?'

4. *who is so patient*. From Juvenal, i. 30–1:

> Nam quis iniquae
> tam patiens urbis, tam ferreus ut teneat se?

10. *saile-stretcht wings*. Cf. Massinger, *The Bond-man*, 1. iii (1624, B3):

> we are circled round
> With danger, o're our heads with sayle stretch'd wings,
> Destruction houers.

34. *howrly*, v.l. *howerly*. Cf. in v. x. 2 the correction of *sower* back to *sowre* in F2. Gill in *Logonomia*, 1619, B4, distinguishes the pronunciation of 'our' and '*ouer* hora': the latter '*e* interposito scribatur': Wither in *Abuses Stript, and Whipt*, 1617, p. 307, rhymes 'Fry'r' and 'Sy'r' as monosyllables, but in *Britain's Remembrancer*, 1628, f. 133ᵛ, prints

> how much the nigher
> They lay unto their *Altar*, or their *Choïre*.

Daniel's *Delia*, 1592, has among the errata on A1ᵛ, 'Sonneted desires, read desiers'.

39. *with the words of* HERCVLES, i.e. fearlessly. From Juvenal, ii. 19–21:

> peiores qui talia verbis
> Herculis invadunt et de virtute locuti
> clunem agitant.

In *Poet*. v. iii. 294–5, a parody of Marston is greeted with 'I mary, this was written like a HERCVLES in *poetrie*, now'.

43–4. *hair . . . eye-browes*. A reference to the cropped heads of the Puritans, but the phrase is from Juvenal, who applies it to the Stoics:

> Rarus sermo illis et magna libido tacendi
> atque supercilio brevior coma. (ii. 14–15.)

Cf. *B.F.* iii. vi. 24, *Ep*. xxi. 1.

45. *Counters*. See *E.M.I.* ii. i. 78.

51. *round*, the Globe Theatre.

60. *censur'd*, judged. So 'censors' in line 62 = 'critics', and in *Disc.* 889 Jonson describes Bacon's language as 'nobly *censorious*'.

70. *Thespian spring*, Aganippe on Mount Helicon near the town of Thespiae. *Ep.* ci. 33.

71. *leaps forth a Poet.* From Persius, more fully quoted in *Disc.* 2489.

72. *the founder of Cripple-gate*, St. Giles, the patron saint of cripples, because according to the myth he refused to be cured of lameness, so that he might mortify the flesh more effectively. The postern of Cripple-gate was at the north end of Little Wood Street, and the church of St. Giles was just outside it. But William Baldwin in his *Beware the Cat*, 1570 (ed. Halliwell, p. 16), describes the founder of Cripple-gate as 'a cripple, who begged so much in his life (as put to the silver weather cock which he stole from Powles steeple) after his death builded it'. As a matter of fact, Cripple-gate is glossed in old documents as *Porta contractorum*, and means sunk or covered gate: cf. OE. *crypel* (Kentish *crepel*), 'a narrow passage, burrow, drain'.

79. *well-spoken dayes.* Cf. *Rich. III*, i. i. 29, 'these faire well spoken dayes'.

88. *Why, Humour* ... In this passage Jonson launches the Comedy of Humours; in the induction to his last Humour play, *The Magnetic Lady or Humours Reconciled*, ll. 99–106, he surveys it in a brief glance of retrospect.

110. *But that a rooke* . . . To this vulgar misconception Jonson has several references: see *E.M.I.* iii. iv. 18–22, *Alch.* iv. vii. 39, *B.F.* i. iv. 60. This aspect is fully treated in Marston's 'Satire XI' appended to *The Scourge of Villanie*, 1598, and in S. Rowlands's *The Letting of Humours Blood in the Head-Vaine*, 1600, C, epigram 27.

111. *cable-hatband*, a twisted cord of gold, silver, or silk, worn round the hat. Apparently a novelty in fashion, for Briske explains at iv. vi. 84–6, 'I had on, a gold cable hatband, then new come vp', . . . 'it was massie, gold-smithes worke'. Cf. Marston, *Antonio and Mellida*, Part I, 1602, C3ᵛ (he cried for) 'more cable, till hee had as much as my cable hatband, to fence him'.

three-pild ruffe. Cf. Stubbes, *The Anatomie of Abuses*, 1583 (ed. Furnivall, pp. 70–1), discussing ruffs: 'beyond all this they haue a further fetch, nothing inferiour to the rest; as, namely, three or foure degrees of *minor* ruffes, placed *gradatim*, step by step, one beneath another, and all vnder the Maister deuil ruffe'; Dekker, *The Guls Horne-booke*, 1609, ch. i, p. 7, 'your trebble-quadruple *Dædalian* ruffes'.

112. *A yard of shoetye.* A French importation, according to *Ep.* lxxxviii. 4. 'A yard to a yard and a quarter of ribbon was allowed for each shoe-tie' (Linthicum, *Costume in the Drama*, p. 243, quoting the account of William Freke at Oxford, '2 yards Ribband to make shooe-strings'). Crashaw's *Wishes. To his (supposed) Mistresse*, 16–18, illustrate the accent on the first syllable of the word:

> I wish her Beauty,
> That owes not all his Duty
> To gaudy Tire, or glistring shoo-ty.

Switzers knot. Cf. T. Freeman, *Rubbe, and A great Cast*, 1614, Epig. 32, of a fop tricked out in the fashion of all countries, 'His Garter tyed with a Switzers knot'.

113. *French garters.* Cf. *Ep.* lxxxviii. 4.

114. *more then most ridiculous.* For this 'Arcadian phrase', as Cunningham calls it, see Spenser, *Amoretti*, 1595, Sonnet viii, 'More then most faire'. Plautus' 'Stultior stultissumo' for 'a consummate fool' may be compared with it. It was a courtier's expression: see v. i. 55, *C.R.* iii. v. 110–11—a rehearsal of courting—'Aso. No harme, more then most faire feature. Amo. That touch relished well'; and Marston, *What You Will*, i. i. (1607, B2):

> *Ran.* Then must my pretty peate be Fand and Coach'd.
> *Jaco.* Muffd Mask'd and Ladied, with my more then most sweete
> Madam.

115–21. *scourge . . . mirrour . . . Anatomiz'd.* Compare the titles of Marston's *The Scourge of Villanie*, 1598; Baldwin's *A Myrroure for Magistrates*, 1559; Stubbes's *The Anatomie of Abuses*, 1583; and Nash, *The Anatomie of Absurditie*, 1589.

121. *Anotamiz'd* (Qq). A common spelling; it is noteworthy that Jonson corrects it.

131. *sort*, set.

138. *intentiue.* Cf. 'intention', *C.R.* i. v. 42; 'intend', ib. v. ii. 3.

161. *armes thus wreath'd.* Repeated in *C.R.* iii. iv. 64–5:

> Then walkes of melancholike, and stands wreath'd,
> As he were pinn'd vp to the arras, thus.

Gifford quotes from *Love's Labour's Lost*, iii. i. 15–20, Moth's recipe of melancholy for success in love—'with your hat penthouse-like ore the shop of your eies, with your armes crost on your thinbellie doublet, like a Rabbet on a spit, . . . these are complements, these are humours'. Cf. the well-known couplet on Ford (*Choyce Drollery*, 1656, *On the Time-Poets*, B3ᵛ):

> Deep in a dumpe John Ford alone was got,
> With folded armes and melancholly hat.

162. *Cryes meaw.* Dekker taunted Jonson with doing this, in *Satiromastix*, 1602, M1ᵛ, '. . . when your Playes are misse-likt at Court, you shall not crye Mew like a Pusse-cat, and say you are glad you write out of the Courtiers element'.

shakes his empty head. Like Master Stephen in *E.M.I.* iv. ii. 51–2.

163–4. *motions*, puppet-shows. Jonson writes the libretto for one on *Hero and Leander* in the fifth act of *Bartholomew Fair*; it is spoken by the showman of 'master of the motions'. He gives a list of these shows: '*Ierusalem* was a stately thing; and so was *Niniue*, and the citty of *Norwich*, and *Sodom* and *Gomorrah*; with the rising o'the prentises; and pulling down the bawdy houses there, vpon *Shroue-Tuesday*; but the

Gunpowder-plot, there was a get-penny' (*B.F.* v. i. 8–12). Often these motions were burlesques of a play. Thus 'Niniveh' probably followed on Lodge and Greene's *A Looking Glasse, for London and Englande*: the stage-direction on F3ᵛ, ed. 1598, 'Ionas the Prophet cast out of the whales belly vpon the stage' would lend itself to marionette treatment. See below, II. iii. 146–8, 'They say, there's a new Motion of the city of *Nineueh*, with IONAS, and the whale, to be seene at Fleet-bridge?' This show is often noticed in old plays.

Rome may have been the puppet-play of 'Julius Caesar', which was a mixed performance. Cf. Dekker, *The Wonderfull Yeare*, 1603, F3ᵛ, 'like the fellow that described the villainous motion of *Iulius Cæsar* and the Duke of *Guize*, who (as he gaue it out) fought a combat together'; and Day and Chettle, *The Blind-Beggar of Bednal-Green*, acted 1600, IV. i (1659, G2), 'You shall likewise see the famous City of *Norwitch*, and the stabbing of *Julius Cæsar* in the *French* Capitol by a sort of Dutch *Mesapotamians*.' *London* is mentioned in *Lingua*, III. vi (1607, G3) in good company: 'the sight of *Nineuie, Babilon, London*, or some Sturbridge-faire-masters'.

165. *a drie bisquet iest*. Cf. *Euerie Woman in her Humor*, v. i (1609, H4), 'Will ye beleeue what such a bisket brain'd fellow as this saies?' And *As You Like It*, II. vii. 38–41:

> in his braine,
> Which is as drie as the remainder bisket
> After a voyage: He hath strange places cram'd
> With obseruation.

170. *Ieiunus . . .* Horace, *Satires*, II. ii. 38. Jonson's rendering is quoted in *Englands Parnassus*, 1600, p. 86, under the heading of 'Famine'.

179. ARISTARCHVS, *or stark-asse*. Cf. John Taylor, *Laugh and be Fat*, 1613?, p. 41:

> Great *Coriat*, mirrour of the 4-fold world, . . .
> The onely *Aristarck-asse* of this age.

In H. Parrot's *Laquei Ridiculi*, 1613, ii, Ep. 149, 'Stark AS' is substituted for 'Momus' of the earlier version in *Epigrams*, 1608, no. 152.

181. *In snuffe*. Cf. *E.M.I.* IV. ii. 99.

vsing . . . vice. Repeated from *The Case is Alter'd*, II. vii. 80–1.

202. *profit . . . pleasure*. A maxim of the *Ars Poetica*, 343–4:

> Omne tulit punctum qui miscuit utile dulci
> lectorem delectando pariterque monendo—

which became a fixed article in Jonson's literary creed: he is never tired of repeating it. In the prologue to *Volpone* he says that his

> true scope, if you would know it,
> In all his *poemes*, stil, hath been this measure,
> To mixe profit, with your pleasure.

The second prologue to *The Silent Woman* opens

> The ends of all, who for the *Scene* doe write,
> Are, or should be, to profit, and delight.

In *The Masque of Queens*, bearing in mind the dignity of the performers, he 'chose the argument, to be, *A Celebration of honorable, & true Fame, bred out of Vertue*: obseruing that rule of the best *Artist*, to suffer no obiect of delight to passe without his mixture of profit, & example'. Other references are *Alch.*, prol. 16, *S. of N.*, epil. 2, *Love's Triumph*, 6, 7, and *Disc.* 1516–17, where Jonson also applies the maxim to the art of painting.

Sidney had given currency to this view of poetry in England, but it was the common attitude of the Renaissance critics.[1] Marston's breaking away from it has been noted above (p. 409), but it was left for Dryden to state it effectively: 'delight is the chief, if not the only, end of poesy: instruction can be admitted but in the second place, for poesy only instructs as it delights' (*Defence of an Essay of Dramatic Poesy*, ed. Ker, p. 113).

207–8. *hang . . . eares.* Imitated by Randolph, *Poems*, 1638, p. 81, of Sir Rowland Cotton:

> And when great *Henry* did his Maxims heare,
> He wore him as a Iewell in his Eare.

Cf. Chapman, *Bussy D'Ambois*, ed. Boas, III. ii. 6, 'Truths words like jewels hang in th'eares of kings'.

219. *Arte* . . . From the old maxim incorrectly attributed in some old texts to Publilius Syrus, 'Nisi ignorantes ars osorem non habet'. Jonson's line is quoted in *Englands Parnassus*, 1600, p. 9, under the heading of 'Art'.

232. *Vetus Comœdia.* Jonson uses this term twice, once, as here, of the old classical comedy, and once, as in the *Drummond Conversations*, 410, of the medieval English interludes. So Nashe of an anti-Martinist play, apparently meaning interlude, in *The Returne of Pasquill* (*Works*, ed. McKerrow, i, p. 92). We have explained the present passage in our introductory essay in volume i, p. 376. The Old Comedy of Greece was Jonson's precedent for the satiric element in his own comedies. Then he passes to a new point—the technique: for this Terence is the model, chosen probably because of Horace's summary of the popular verdict on early Roman writers of comedy concluding with 'vincere Caecilius gravitate, Terentius arte' (*Ep.* II. i. 59).

Professor O. J. Campbell (*Comicall Satyre*, pp. 4–6) narrows down the interpretation of *Vetus Comœdia* to the Greek comedy which culminated in the work of Aristophanes and says, correctly enough, that Terence is not this type of comedy-writer. But Jonson here, and in the short survey of comedy which follows, is taking a wide sweep which ends with Menander and Roman comedy.

[1] See Spingarn, *Literary Criticism*, pp. 47 foll.

235. *obserue all the lawes of Comedie.* Jonson's attitude to the 'lawes' is interesting. Twice elsewhere he refers to these critical principles. In the prologue to *Volpone*, 30–2, drawn up

> As best Criticks haue designed,
> The lawes of time, place, persons he obserueth,
> From no needfull rule he swerueth.

But in the preface to the 1605 Quarto of *Sejanus*—where he was writing a Roman tragedy in classical form—he admits defects: 'First, if it be obiected, that what I publish is no true *Poeme*; in the strict Lawes of *Time*. I confesse it: as also in the want of a proper *Chorus*.'

The explanation is that Jonson was not an out-and-out classicist: he recognized development, and he claimed a corresponding freedom. The passage in the *Discoveries*, 129–42, which he translated from Vives on the theme 'Non nimium credendum antiquitati' is a valuable assertion of this principle.

239. *Grex*, company. Not an English word, but taken over from Plautus and Terence: cf. Plautus in the last line of the *Pseudolus*, 'sei voltis adplaudere atque adprobare hunc gregem et fabulam'.

250 foll. *'tis extant . . .* Jonson's precise statement, borrowed from some Renaissance critic, about the number of the actors in Greek comedy is quite untrustworthy; Aristotle expressly says in the *Poetics* (v, § 3) that nothing is known on the subject.

252. *Song*, probably κῶμος, 'the revel song', Comedy originating in the phallic choral songs; but Aristotle favours the derivation from κώμη, 'the village song' of actors wandering through the country-side.

Susario. Susarion of Megara first regulated primitive Greek comedy and introduced it into Attica between 580 and 564 B.C.

253–4. *Epicharmus* of Cos gave a literary form to the Doric comedy of Sicily. He wrote at Syracuse in the reigns of Gelo (485–478 B.C.) and Hiero (478–467 B.C.). His contemporary *Phormis* (called in later times Phormus) helped in the development.

254. *Chionides*, an Attic comedian 'eight years before the Persian War' (*Suidas*), 488–7 B.C. or 487–6 B.C.

255. *Cratinus*, 519–422 B.C.; first made the Old Comedy a weapon of personal attack. He is said to have limited the number of characters to three, whereas Susarion and his followers brought in their characters in a loose unmethodical manner.

256. *Eupolis*, 446–410 B.C., a rival of Aristophanes.

260. *Menander*, 342–291 B.C., the leading poet of the New Comedy, tamer than the Old, and mainly a comedy of manners.

Philemon (died in 262 B.C.), the first poet of the New Comedy; together with Menander he reduced it to a regular form.

262. *Cecilius.* Caecilius Statius, who died in 168 B.C., was by some considered the greatest of the Roman comic poets (Aulus Gellius, xv. 24).

268. *and not [to] be tyed*, Q3. Linge's Quarto has no authority, but the 'to' prefixed to the second of two infinitives is not uncommon in

Elizabethan syntax; see below, II. iii. 291, and *Julius Caesar*, I. ii. 172–3, 'Brutus had rather be a villager Than to repute himself a son of Rome'; IV. iii. 72–4, 'I had rather coin my heart And drop my blood . . . than to wring From the hard hands of peasants their vile trash'.

269–70. *a few (who are nothing but forme)*. Similarly in the preface to the *Sejanus* Quarto, 1605, Jonson speaks of the failure to reproduce the chorus, 'whose Habite, and Moodes are such, and so difficult, as not any, whome I haue seene since the *Auntients*, (no, not they who haue most presently affected Lawes) haue yet come in the way off'. The reference may be to Sackville and Norton's *Gorboduc*, acted in 1561, which won the praise of Sidney; perhaps even to such amateur plays as *Gismond of Salerne*, 1567–8, and *The Misfortunes of Arthur*, 1588, composed and acted by the members of the Inns of Court. But more probably Jonson is glancing at Kyd's *Cornelia*, 1594, translated from Garnier, and Daniel's *Cleopatra*, twice printed in 1594, and again in 1595, 1598, and 1599. Not only were these rigidly cast in the Senecan mould, but they were the composition of recognized men of letters.

273. *Insula Fortunata*. Revived as a compliment to James and his Queen in the *Entertainment at Highgate*, 1604, 51, and again at the Court of Charles I in the masque of *The Fortunate Isles*, 1625.

281. *in some one play*. Two plays of 1599, to which the poet may be pointing, are Shakespeare's *King Henry V* and *Old Fortunatus* as recast by Dekker: in each play the Chorus describes the changes of the scene. Cf. *E.M.I.*, prol. 15.

285. *trauaile*. This spelling, interchangeable with 'travel', helps the pun, which recurs in *C.R.* v. x. 1–3, *D. is A.* I. vi. 119.

299. *vnperfect*. Cf. *C.R.* III. iv. 58, 'Like an vnperfect *prologue*, at third musike'.

out. Cf. *Coriolanus*, v. iii. 40–2:

> Like a dull Actor now, I haue forgot my part,
> And I am out, euen to a full Disgrace.

312. *the two-penny roome*. C. B., *The Hospital of Incurable Fooles*, 1600, Ep. Ded., 'I beg it with as forced a looke as a Player that is speaking an Epilogue, makes loue to the two pennie roume for a plaudite'. It was not a very reputable part of the house. Cf. Dekker, *Newes from Hell*, 1606, B3ᵛ, 'you may take him . . . in the afternoones, in the twopeny roomes of a Play-house, like a *Puny*, seated Cheeke by Iowle with a Punke'; *Lanthorne and Candle-light*, 1608, ch. ii, C4ᵛ, 'pay thy two-pence to a *Plaier*, in his gallery maist thou sit by a harlot'; Beaumont, *The Woman-Hater*, 1607, prol., A2, '. . . I doe pronounce this, to the vtter discomfort of all two peny Gallerie men, you shall haue no bawdrie in it'.

319. *fustian protestations*. See *E.M.I.* I. iii. 99–103.

323. *sack-but*, 'a brass trumpet with a slide like that of a trombone for alternating the pitch' (*O.E.D.*). Cf. *Iacke Drums Entertainment*, I. ii (1601, D4ʳ), 'Along with me then, you droming *Sagbut*'.

324. *play vpon him*. Cf. *E.M.I.* III. ii. 24.

327. *well-timberd fellow. Volp.* IV. v. 124; Fletcher and Massinger, *The Spanish Curate*, 1622, II. i, 'A fine straite timber'd man'.

329. *when the house was a building.* The Globe Theatre, built by Richard Burbage with the materials from the demolished 'Theater', in 1598 or early in 1599.

330. *well said*, well done. See *C. is A.* II. vii. 83 n.

335. *Castalian. Poet.* III. i. 40. There is a half-pun on Castilian wine.

335–45. *Pace* Gifford, a half-humorous, half-satirical sketch of the poet himself. Compare the suggestion of a personal portraiture underlying the description of *Disc.* 821–45, with Swinburne's comment (*A Study*, pp. 147–8).

342. *he do'not.* Cf. II. iii. 257, and *C. is A.* I. vii. 32.

343. *ballac't.* A sixteenth- and seventeenth-century form of 'ballasted', the past participle of which would be 'ballass-ed'.

347. *Ile trust none* (F): *Ile n'ere trust none* (Qq). Jonson toned down this pleonasm also in III. vi. 173, 'were you neuer at any yet?' where the Quarto text was 'were you neuer at none yet?'; and v. ix. 46–7, 'be not made a shot-clog any more', which was originally 'bee not made a Shot-clog no more'.

348. *Gentiles* (F2). In F1 also at *C.R.*, ind. 116.

350. *No pledging your own health.* Cf. Middleton, *Women beware Women*, III. ii (1657, L3):

> *Duke.* Yes by the law of *Bacchus*; plead your benefit,
> You are not bound to pledge your own health Lady.

359–60. *sooner . . . iest.* Drummond applied this proverb to Jonson himself: see *Conv.* xix. 681. It goes back to Quintilian, VI. iii. 28, of joking, 'Laedere nunquam velimus, longeque absit illud propositum potius amicum quam dictum perdendi'.

368. *Atheistical policies.* This trait is suppressed in the text, perhaps from a fear of the censor.

I. i. 1. *Viri . . .* An untraced quotation. In Morelius's *Ex Veterum Comicorum Fabulis Sententiae*, Paris, 1553, p. 2, Ἀνδρὸς τὰ προσπίπτοντα γενναίως φέρειν is assigned to Menander, and rendered, 'Viri est, quae accidunt generoso animo ferre': and 'Fortunae caecitas' is a phrase of Apuleius, *Met.* xi. 15.

7. *cor'siue*, corrosive. Cf. *Und.* xxvi. 2, 'I send nor Balmes, nor Cor'sives to your wound'.

11. *pild*, beggarly. Cf. Becon, *Reliques of Rome*, 1563, p. 163, 'A pylde and beggarly ceremony' (*O.E.D.*).

14. *My mind . . .* Cf. *C. is A.* I. ii. 42 n.

15. *hungrie belly barkes.* Cf. Horace, *Sat.* II. ii. 18, 'Latrantem stomachum'.

25. *the organs of my sight.* In Qq, 'my *Optique* instruments', but elsewhere Jonson suggests that 'optic' in reference to eyesight is an affectation. It is Puntarvolo who says (II. iii. 28) '*Dazle, your organs to*

my optique sense', and Amorphus in *Cynthia's Reuels* (I. iii. 36), who talks of his 'optiques' drinking in the spirit of beauty. Puntarvolo's use is the earliest passage recorded in that sense in the *O.E.D.*, though 'optic sinews' or 'nerves', as a rendering of the medieval *nervi optici*, goes back to 1541. With the revised phrase cf. Othello's 'My speculative, and offic'd Instrument' for the eye in the First Folio of *Oth*. I. iii. 270, where the Quartos have a variant 'actiue Instruments'.

26–7. *cast Mine eye-balls . . . forth*. This explosive image recurs in *Volp*. v. viii. 2, and *D. is A*. II. vii. 17; cf. *Henry VI, Part I*, IV. vii. 79–80:

> Oh were mine eye-balles into Bullets turn'd,
> That I in rage might shoot them at your faces.

34–5. *Inuidus* . . . From an epigram 'De liuore' by Caelius Firmianus Symposius (in Lemaire's *Poetae Latini Minores*, 1824, ii, p. 442). 'Gemit' should be 'fremit'. In Mirandola's *Illustrium Poetarum Flores*, Strassburg, 1541, p. 187, and in Mignault's commentary on Alciati's *Emblemata*, Antwerp, 1574, no. lxxi, p. 211, attributed to Virgil; the latter reads 'gemit', probably by a false recollection of the line before the quotation 'Testatus gemitu graues dolores'.

41. *Rooke*. Cf. *E.M.I.* I. v. 88.

I. ii. 6. *like your taylors needle, I goe through*. Contrast *C. is A*. II. iii. 15–16:

> What true stich sister? both your sides alike?
> Be of a sleighter worke.

for my name. Gifford pointed out that Carlo's lessons in the art of becoming a gentleman are chiefly derived from the chapter in Erasmus's *Colloquies* entitled 'Ἱππεὺς ἄνιππος, *sive Ementita Nobilitas*; and that Dekker in *The Guls Horne-book* expanded several of Jonson's points. See Erasmus, *Omnia Opera*, 1540, i, p. 709: 'N. Restat cognomen. Hic illud in primis cauendum, ne plebeio more te patiaris uocari Harpalum Comensem: sed Harpalum à Como: hoc enim nobilium est.'

17. *a Constable for your wit*. Proverbial: cf. Dekker, *The Guls Hornbooke*, 1609, p. 2, 'all that are chosen Cunstables for their wit go not to heauen'; Middleton, *A Mad World*, v. ii (1608, H3), 'This is some new player now, they put all their fooles to the Constables part still'; and the title of Glapthorne's play, *Wit in A Constable*, 1640.

22. *complements*, accomplishments, as in *C.R.* IV. iii. 8. Branded by Jonson in *Disc.* 2275 as one of 'the perfumed termes of the time'.

32. *hine* = 'hind'. See *T. of T*. II. ii. 50.

38. *giue o're house-keeping in the countrey*. From Erasmus (*Opera*, 1540, i, p. 709): 'Primum fac procul te abducas à patria. HA. Memini. NE. Ingere te in conuictum iuuenum vere nobilium—' skilfully adapted to the economic facts of Jonson's time. The decay of country houses and the rush to town was the theme of the reformer and the satirist: see *Shakespeare's England*, i, pp. 33–5.

44. *least popular*, like Bobadill (*E.M.I.* i. v. 37).

46. *Primero*, a card-game of Spanish origin, so called because it was won by the holder of the 'prime', a sequence of the best cards (*Ep.* cxii. 22). Each player had four cards. The best hand for 'prime' was the ace, counting sixteen, and the seven, six, and five, which were trebled, making a total of 54; but this could be beaten by the 'flush', four cards of one colour. The combination was a record hand (*Alch.* i. ii. 47). The game is elaborately described in Harington's *Epigrams*, 1618, ii, ep. 99, '*The Story of* Marcus *Life at Primero*'.

Passage. Gifford quoted Cotton, *The Compleat Gamester*, 1680, p. 119: 'Passage is a Game at dice to be play'd at but by two, and it is performed with three Dice. The Caster throws continually till he hath thrown Dubblets under ten, and then he is out and loseth, or dubblets above ten, and then he *passeth* and wins.'

50. *with a safe conscience.* Cf. *E.M.I.* iv. ii. 30.

56. *picke your teeth.* Amorphus gives similar advice in *C.R.* iii. i. 24–5. Cf. Fletcher, *The Wild-Goose*, 1652, i. ii: '*Italie* for my money, . . . | The very pick-teeth speak more man than we do, | And season of more salt'; Earle, *Micro-cosmographie*, 1628, 19, 'A Gallant', 'His Pick-tooth beares a great part in his discourse'.

58. *ruffle . . . boot.* Cf. Earle, ib., 'Hee has learnt to ruffle his face from his boote'; Cartwright, *The Ordinary*, i. ii (1651, p. 8):

> *Sli.* Your playster'd face doth drop against moist weather.
> *Sha.* Fie, how you writh it; now it looks just like
> A ruffled boot.

For the fashion in boots compare T. M., *The Ant, and the Nightingale*, 1604, C4: 'I beheld a curious payre of Bootes of King *Philips* leather, in such artificiall wrinckles, sets and pleats, as if they had been starcht lately, and came new from the Laundresses.'

63. *sit o' the stage.* Cf. ii. vi. 52–3; *C.R.* Ind. 144–6; *D. is A.* i. vi. 31–8.

66. *kinred.* 'Kindred' first became common in the seventeenth century; the 1640 Folio so spells it.

73. *a great chain*, the steward's badge of office. Whalley quotes Middleton, *A Mad World*, ii. i (1608, B4), '*Sir Bonn.* Run sirrah, cal in my chief gentleman i'th' chaine of gold, expedite'. Cf. *Love's Cure*, i. ii (Beaumont and Fletcher Folio, 1647, p. 127), 'how dos't thou think I shall become the Stewards chaire ha? will not these slender hanches show well with a chaine, and a gold night-Cap after supper when I take the accompts?' and *Alch.* ii. iii. 329–30.

Jonson adapts Erasmus (*Opera*, i. 709), 'Iam quo firmior sit hominum opinio, fingito literas à magnatibus ad te missas, in quibus identidem appelleris eques clarissimus, magnarumque rerum fiat mentio. . . . Curabis ut huiusmodi literæ tibi uelut elapsæ, aut per obliuionem relictæ ueniant ad aliorum manus.'

80. *breakes it up*, opens, by breaking the seal. Cf. Lodge, *The Wounds of Ciuill War*, ii. iii (1594, D), '*Lectorius* read, and breake these letters vp'.

83–4. *breath'd vpon her picture.* Cf. Sir John Davies, *Epigram* 38, 3–4, 'the seller Of painting which with breathing will be thawd'.

88 foll. From Erasmus, op. cit., 'Interdum insue uesti, aut relinque in crumena, ut quibus sarciendi negocium dederis illic reperiant. Illi non silebunt, & tu simulac resciueris, compones uultum ad iracundiam ac mœsticiam, quasi doleat casus.'

110 foll. From Erasmus (l.c., p. 710): 'Iam ut ludas creditores, mille sunt artes. HA. Earum quidem rudis non sum. Sed tandem urgebunt, ubi perspexerint nihil esse nisi uerba. NE. Imò nulla est commodior ad regnum uia, quam debere quam plurimis. HA. Quî sic? NE. Primum creditor obseruat te non aliter quàm obligatus magno beneficio, uereturque ne quam præbeat ansam amittendæ pecuniæ. Seruos nemo magis habet obnoxios, quàm debitor suos creditores, quibus si quid aliquando reddas, gratius est quàm si dono dones. HA. Animaduerti. NE. Illud tamen caueto, ne cum tenuibus habeas commercium. Nam hi ob paruam summulam ingentes excitant tragœdias. Placabiliores sunt, quibus lautior est fortuna, cohibet illos pudor, lactat spes, deterret metus, norunt quid possint equites.' This passage was also copied by Rabelais, *Œuvres*, ed. Marty-Laveaux, 1868, III. iii, who, like Jonson, took the idea from Erasmus.

122. *Ludgathians*, bankrupts committed to the debtor's prison at Ludgate, and summarily calling in the money due to them. Dekker uses the term in *The Seuen deadly Sinnes of London*, 1606, p. 2, ch. i, 'Politick Bankruptisme'; and Sharpham in *Cupids Whirligig*, 1607, E3, 'I am none of these Ludgations that beg for fourescore and ten poore men: my suite is only for my selfe'.

132 foll. From Erasmus, op. cit., 'At famuli sunt alendi. NE. Sunt: at non ales famulos ἀχείρους, & ob id ἀχρείους. Mittantur huc & illuc: inuenient aliquid. Scis uarias esse talium rerum occasiones. . . . Ergo famulos ale non segnes, aut etiam sanguine propinquos, qui alioqui forent alendi. . . . Reperient aliquid in diuersorijs, aut in ædibus, aut in nauibus incustoditum. Tenes? Meminerint non frustra datos homini digitos.' A broken-down gallant in *Measure for Measure*, IV. iii. 13, is named 'Master Starve-lackey'.

137. *Mercuries.* Mercury, the messenger god, was also god of thieves.

145. *cullisen.* Cf. *C. is A.* IV. ix. 39.

159. *puck-fist.* Literally, the puff-ball fungus (cf. *Poet.* IV. vii. 21); hence an empty boaster (ib. V. iii. 37; *Alch.* I. ii. 63). Cf. also *N.I.* III. i. 151.

162. *mushrompe gentlemen.* Cunningham quotes Marlowe, *Edward II*, I. iv (1594, C1ᵛ):

> a night growne mushrump,
> Such a one as my Lord of Cornewall is.

Jonson spells 'mushrome' in *S.W.* II. iv. 153, *Cat.* II. 136, *M.L.* III. vi. 70. Cf. Plautus, *Trinummus*, 1851, 'Pol hicquidem fungino genere est'.

166. *wefts*, waifs. 'Weft' is a spelling of 'waift', which is apparently 'waif' with a parasitic *t*. Spenser has 'waift' once (*F.Q.* IV. xii. 31),

and 'weft' several times, and the latter is frequent in collocation with 'stray'. Cf. Fletcher and Massinger, *The Elder Brother*, IV. iv (1637, H3), 'you are Lord o' the soyle Sir, | *Lilly* is a Weft, a Stray, shee's yours, to use Sir'.

178. *those that fortune fauours*. Alluding to the proverb *Fortuna favet fatuis*, also quoted in the prologue to *The Alchemist*. Professor Skeat connected the proverb with the old 'Audentes fortuna iuvat' (Virgil, *Aen.* x. 284), 'fortis fortuna adiuvat' (Terence, *Phormio*, 203) by suggesting an extension of 'favours the hardy' to 'favours the fool-hardy'. Cf. Chaucer, *Troilus*, iv. 600–1:

> Thenk ek Fortune, as wel thy-selven wost,
> Helpeth an hardy man to his emprise.

184. *scorne to liue by my wits*. Cf. *S.W.* II. iii. 112–16.

192. *at euery tauerne*. Hence the point of Dekker's fling at Jonson in *Satiromastix*, 1602, MIᵛ: 'In brieflynes, when you Sup in Tauernes, amongst your betters, you shall sweare not to dip your Manners in too much sawce, nor at Table to fling Epigrams, Embleames, or Play-speeches about you (lyke Hayle-stones) to keepe you out of the terrible daunger of the Shot, vpon payne to sit at the vpper end of the Table, a'th left hand of Carlo Buffon.'

199. *a trout*. Cf. *Tw. Night*, II. v. 19, 20 (of Malvolio), 'heere comes the Trowte, that must be caught with tickling'.

210. *a blacke fellow*. From Horace, *Sat.* I. iv. 85, 'hic niger est, hunc tu, Romane, caveto'.

220. *Cockatrice*, or basilisk, a fabled reptile hatched by a serpent from a cock's egg, and reputed to kill by its mere glance. Cf. *Poet.*, prol. 36–7, *Volp.* v. viii. 27, *N.I.* I. v. 48, and Pliny's *Naturall Historie* (Holland's translation, 1601, p. 356), XXIX. iv: 'To come now unto the Basiliske, whom all other serpents doe flie from and are afraid of: . . . he killeth them with his very breath and smell that passeth from him; yea, and (by report) if he do but set his eye on a man, it is enough to take away his life.' Wyclif rendered Psalm xci. 13 (1382) 'Vpon the eddere and the kokatrice shalt thou go', where the Vulgate is *super basiliscum* and the LXX ἐπὶ βασιλίσκον. Hence, applied to persons in the sense of monster; and especially to a prostitute. Cf. *Poet.* IV. vii. 6, *Alch.* v. iii. 34, *Ep.* xii. 21.

227. *Búffon*. The old accent: cf. *E.M.I.* II. v. 8.

I. iii. It is interesting to note a case which came before the Star Chamber of Archer, a farmer of Southchurch in Essex, at 'Michaelmas 7º Caroli', printed in *Reports of Cases in the Courts of Star Chamber and High Commission*, edited by S. R. Gardiner for the Camden Society, 1886, pp. 43–9. Archer kept back his corn till June—8 quarters of wheat, 60 quarters of rye, 100 quarters of oats—and sold most of it at London and Chelmsford, none or very little of it in Rochford hundred where he lived, and where the Earl of Warwick had ordered him to sell it. He pleaded that his barn had not been visited by any justice or officer (cf. l. 131 in this scene) according to the King's proclamation. He had, as a blind, bought seed-corn in the market (cf. ll. 136–7). He was adjudged to pay a fine of 100 marks to the King and £10 to the poor, to stand on a pillory at Newgate market for an hour, with a paper put on his hat, 'For inhancing the price of corn', then to be led through Cheapside to Leadenhall market, and stand another hour on the pillory, and finally to be sent to Chelmsford market and be pilloried a third time.

6. *deadded.* First in Wyclif's version of 1 Samuel xxv. 37, 'And the herte of hym with yn forth is deed', where 'deadyd', 'deadid', and 'dedid' are variants (*O.E.D.*).

16. *a Prognostication.* The weather-forecast was a great feature of the early almanacs; see Mr. Eustace F. Bosanquet's illustrated monograph on *English Printed Almanacks and Prognostications* up to 1600. Thomas Askham, who printed them from 1548 to 1571, set the fashion for English prognosticators of omitting prophecies of peace and war, royal personages, towns and countries, and confined himself to the weather for the seasons and months and the diseases likely to prevail. The next important compiler was Thomas Buckminster, or Buckmaster, who issued them from 1565 to 1599. The British Museum possesses the following for 1599: *1599. An Almanacke and Prognostication for this yeere of our Lord Iesus Christ. M.D.XCIX. Which is from the worldes Creation 5561. Done according to Art by Gabriel Frend. Imprinted at London by Richard Watkins and Iames Roberts. Cum priuilegio Regiæ Maiestatis.* To his almanac for 1589 Frend appends *A briefe and playne Prognostication* including (Dvi) 'My opinion touching the condition of the weather for euery day in this present yeere of our Lord GOD', and concluding (Evi):

> Thou hast my gesse at dayly weather,
>   Here present in thy viewe,
> My credite shall not lie thereon,
>   That euery worde is true:
> Yet some to please I thought it best,
>   To shewe my mynde among the rest.

Samuel Rowlands in *Looke to it: For, Ile Stabbe ye, 1604*, D1ᵛ, addresses the 'Wretched Husband-man' in the style of Ben:

> You Husband-men that heape & hord vp Corne,
> And neuer laugh, but when it waxeth deere:
> You whom the poore do wish had nere bin borne,
> Because you famish and vndo them heere.
> You that an *Almanacke* still beare about,
> To search and finde the rainy weather out.
>
> You that at plentie euermore repine,
> And hang your selues for griefe, to see the same.
> You that will weepe when as the Sunne doth shine,
> And sigh to heare but of faire-weathers name.

You that for nothing but deare yeeres do pray,
To Gentlemen your Sonnes, another day.
            Ile Stabbe yee.

24. *S. Swithins*, 15 July. He had to 'turn back' as he is looking at
August (l. 15). In the Quarto he was looking at July already. This
minute revision is characteristic. Cf. T. Adams, *Workes* (1629), p. 836,
An engrosser of corn 'makes his Almanacke his Bible: if it prognosticate
raine on *Swithins* day, he loues and beleeues it beyond the Scripture'.

30. *reekes*. The old form, surviving in dialect.

38. *the next moneth* to August. 'He has kept his finger there, while
for the moment he turned to Saint Swithin's Day' (Nicholson). Very
ingenious; but Sordido runs on to the forty days after St. Swithin's,
and so arrives at September.

55. *penny*. See Bosanquet, op. cit., pp. 9–10. In Lodge and Greene's
A Looking Glasse, 1598, B4, the poor man pleading to the Usurer for
his cow says: 'she saued me euery yeare a peny in almanakes, for shee
was as good to me as a Prognostication, if she had but set vp her taile,
and haue galladt [*sic*] about the meade, my little boy was able to say,
oh father there will be a storme: her very taile was a Kalender to me.'
Gifford quotes Fletcher, *The Chances*, i. viii (1647 Folio, p. 3):

Why? all Physitians
And penny Almanacks allow the opening
Of veines this moneth.

And Massinger, *The City-Madam*, ii. ii (1658, p. 24):

Stargaze! sure
I have a penny Almanack about me . . .
In his name publish'd.

78. *fire (from heauen)*. As in 'a booke shewing *the miraculous Judgement of God showen in Herefordshire, where a mightie barne filled with
Corne was consumed with fire begynninge last Christmas Eeue, and Duringe
ffyftene Dayes after*' entered on the Stationers' Register on 22 February
1595; cf. 'A ballad intytuled *the iuste Judgement of God vpon a myserable
hard harted ffermour*', entered on 18 March 1587.

87. "*Wealth . . .* Quoted in *Englands Parnassus*, 1600, p. 258, under
the heading of 'Riches'.

90. *precept*, magistrate's order. Harrison in his *Description of England*, ii. xviii, 'Of faires and markets', shows how difficult it was for
the poor to buy corn. In the second edition of 1587 he added this
suggestion: 'Finallie, if mens barns might be indifferentlie viewed im-
mediatelie after haruest, and a note gathered by an estimat, and kept
by some appointed & trustie person for that purpose, we should haue
much more plentie of corne in our towne crosses than as yet is commonlie
seene: bicause each one hideth and hoordeth what he may, vpon purpose
either that it will be deerer, or that he shall haue some priuie veine by
bodgers, who doo accustomablie so deale, that the sea dooth load awaie

no small part thereof into other countries & our enimies, to the great hinderance of our common-wealth at home, and more likely yet to be, except some remedie be found.'

93. *in paper*. Pills were usually wrapped in gold or silver leaf: the three gilded pills in the arms of the Medici of Florence are a punning allusion to their name.

99. *I, much*. Cf. *C. is A.* III. i. 5.

107. *sort*, set.

110. *Like snakes*. Jonson's age believed in the theory of spontaneous generation: cf. *Sej.* III. 689–90, 'Wormes, and moaths | Breed out of too fit matter, in the things | which after they consume'; and *Merc. Vind.* 188–9, 'flies and insects, that are her'—i.e. Nature's—'trespasses and scapes'.

116. *exclaimes*. Cf. *Rich. II*, I. ii. 2. There is an irony in Sordido's contempt here and in his 'I'le hang first' (l. 141), in view of the sequel.

118 foll. Expanded from Horace, *Sat.* I. i. 64–7:

> ut quidam memoratur Athenis
> *Sordidus ac diues,* populi contemnere voces
> sic solitus: populus me sibilat, at mihi plaudo
> ipse domi simul ac nummos contemplor in arca.

121. *Knocking my head* . . . Cf. *Alch.* IV. v. 99, 'And hit our heads against the roofe for ioy'.

133 foll. The 'New and Choise Characters, of seuerall Authors' added to the sixth impression of Overbury's *Wife*, 1615, include '*An Ingrosser of Corne*' (L4ᵛ): 'when his Barnes and Garners are ful (if it be a time of dearth) he will buy halfe a bushell, i'th' Market to serue his Housholde: and winnowes his Corne in the night, lest, as the chaffe throwne vpon the water, shew'd plentie in *Ægypt*; so his (carryed by the winde) should proclayme his abundance.'

145. "*He that will thriue* . . . Quoted in *Englands Parnassus*, 1600, p. 106, under the quaint heading 'Frugalitie'. The principle is applied to politics in *Sej.* III. 736 foll.

157. *propriety*, or in technical language *decorum*. Cf. *Alch.* v. v. 159 n.

195. *Frenchefied courtier*. See *Ep.* lxxxviii, 'ON ENGLISH MOVNSIEVR'.

II. i. 6. *motions*, figures on the face of the clock moved by the vibration of the pendulum. Gifford compares Cartwright, *The Ordinary*, 1651, I. v:

> that old Emerit thing that like
> An Image in a German clock, doth move,
> Not walke, I meane that rotten Antiquary.

7. *a habberdashers stall*. In Jonson's day the haberdasher tended to become (1) a hatter, as in IV. vii, *S. of N.* I. ii, (2) a dealer in tape, thread, ribbons, and any articles connected with dress. But the 'haberdasher of small wares' dealt in a large variety of odds and ends: Stow in *The English Chronicle*, ed. Howe, 1615, p. 869*a*, tells us that in

Gresham's Exchange, under Elizabeth, 'the Milloners, or Haberdashers, . . . sould mousetrappes, bird Cages, shooing hornes, Lanthornes, and Iews trumpes'. Cf. A. Copley, *Wits Fittes and Fancies*, 1595, p. 182: 'An old Marchant had hanging at his girdle a pouch, a spectacle-case, a punniard, a pen and inck-horne, and a hand-kertcher, with many other trinkets besides: which a merie companion seing, said: it was like a Haberdashers shop of smal wares.'

16. *hot-house*, a bathing-house with hot baths. Cf. IV. iii. 70, viii. 35. For the association with a brothel see *Ep.* vii and the similar uses of 'bagnio'.

19. *Hee's gone now.* This trick of the unfinished sentence or idea seems to have been a courtly affectation. Fastidius uses it again in III. ix. 40, 78, and is criticized for it by Macilente in the former passage.

20. *Catso's*, scamps. Cf. *Wily Beguilde*, 1606, F4ᵛ, 'And so cunningly temporize with this cunning *Catso* | That he may thinke she loues him as her liffe.' The exclamatory use of the word is found in *C. is A.* v. vi. 1.

21–2. *ouer a bog like your wild Irish.* Thus Harington of Tyrone's followers: 'His guard for the most part were beardless boys without shirts, who, in the frost, wade as familiarly through rivers as water-spaniels' (*Journey to North of Ireland*, 1599, in *Nugæ Antiquæ*, 1804, i. 251). And Dekker, *Lanthorne and Candle-light*, 1608, D, 'the Diuells foote-man was very nimble of heeles, (for no wild-Irishman could out-runne him)'.

32. *when shall I see him?* No answer, because there is no horse to see: cf. the 'Character' of Fastidius, 41–3.

39. *gingle.* Also in the 'Character', 44. Gifford quotes Chapman, *Monsieur D'Olive*, 1606, F, 'you may heare 'am halfe a mile ere they come at you, . . . sixe or seauen make a perfect Morrice-daunce; they need no Bells, their Spurs serue their turne'. The noise was made by the large loose rowels: see T. M., *The Ant and the Nightingale*, 1604, C4, 'Lastly, he walkt the chamber with such a pestilent Gingle, that his Spurs ouersqueakt the Lawyer, and made him reach his voice three notes aboue his Fee: but after we had spied the Rowles of his Spurs, how we blest our selues, they did so much and so farre exceed the compass of our fashion, that they lookt more like the forerunners of wheele-barrowes.' As the rowels were blunt, they were useless for riding: see Sharpham, *The Fleire*, 1607, C3, 'Your swaggerer is but like your walking spur, a gingles much but heele neu'r pricke.'

40. *morris-dancer.* Cf. *G.M.* 738, 'They should be Morris dancers by theire gingle.'

46–7. *though I say it—That should not say it.* An old saying: in the fifteenth-century couplets on the Nine Worthies (Tanner MS. 407, f. 32ᵛ), Alexander the Great introduces himself:

> And in romaunce often am I leyt
> As conquerour gret thow I seyt.

62. *threeding of the needle.* Cf. the gipsy song in Middleton and Rowley, *The Spanish Gipsie*, III. i (1653, E):

> *Trip it Gipsies, trip it fine,*
> *Show tricks and lofty Capers;*
> *At threading Needles we repine,*
> *And leaping over Rapiers.*

65. *leigerity*, nimbleness in doing the tricks.

wigh-hie, neighing. Cf. Fletcher, *Women Pleas'd*, IV. i (1647 Folio, p. 38), where the player of the hobby-horse has a Puritanical fit:

> This Beast of *Babylon*, I will never back againe,
> His pace is sure prophane, and his lewd wihies
> The Son⟨g⟩s of *Hymyn*, and *Gymyn*, in the wilderness.

66. *daggers in the nose*. These appear in the Tollett window at Betley sticking out of the dancer's cheeks. Douce, *Illustrations of Shakespeare* (1807), ii. 468, suggests that they are survivals of a sword dance.

trauels of the egg. Another conjuring trick, of which this seems to be the only mention.

74–5. Benedick was of the same opinion: 'if a man doe not erect in this age his owne tombe ere he dies, hee shall liue no longer in monuments, then the Bels ring, & the Widdow weepes' (*Much Ado*, v. ii. 67–9).

80. *arrides me*. A latinism: *hoc mihi arridet*. This is the earliest recorded example: the courtier Amorphus uses it in *C.R.* III. v. 82, IV. iii. 257. Cunningham noted Charles Lamb's revival of it.

85. *garbe*, fashion. Another court-word: see IV. iv. 78, and *C.R.* I. iii. 25, IV. i. 27. Amorphus is described (ib. v. iv. 540) as 'your grand garbe-Master'. But Jonson has confused 'garb' in this sense, derived from Italian *garbo*, 'grace', with 'garb' = wheat-sheaf, a sense now obsolete except in heraldry. For *sheafe* cf. *M.L.* III. vi. 153–4, 'Noblemen, and Gentlemen, | Of the best sheafe'.

89. *Dum vitant . . .* From Horace, *Sat.* I. ii. 24.

93. *no salt in him*. Cf. the Greek proverb ἅλμη οὐκ ἔνεστ' αὐτῷ (Erasmus, *Adagia*, ed. Stephanus, 1558, col. 514).

98. *pomander chains*. 'Pomander' was a scented paste, made into balls, and worn round the neck or on the arm in a box, chain, or bracelet. See *C.R.* v. iv. 400–7, 'an excellent *diapasme* in a chaine'. It was not only a luxury, but a preservative: cf. *Alch.* I. iv. 21, where 'pomander-bracelets' are offered citizens' wives as a protection against the plague.

99. *complexion*, constitution.

101. *emptie puffe*. Cf. *C.R.* III. iii. 26, 'a strange arrogating puffe'; Shirley, *Love Tricks or Schoole of Complement*, II. ii (1631, D4ᵛ), 'A very puffe, a weak Canniball'.

110. *fore-runners*. For the quibble cf. Fletcher, *The Nice Valour*, III. i (1647 Folio, p. 157):

> *Pas.* . . . shut in my casements, that the breaths
> Of their Coach-mares reek not into my Nostrills;
> Those beasts are but a kinde of Bawdy fore-runners.

113. *french crown*. The 'two figures' on the coins of Henri IV of France were, on the obverse, the king's head, on the reverse a cross of four fleurs-de-lis with an 'H' in the centre.

117. *crowne*. There is a quibbling allusion to the baldness caused by the pox, or 'French disease', as it was often called: cf. *C. is A*. v. i. 24, 'Let these bald french crownes be vncouered.'

120. *damnation*. For this playful greeting cf. *The First Part of Iero-nimo*, 1605, B1ᵛ, where Lorenzo addresses the villain Lazarotto 'How might I crosse it, my sweet mischiefe: | Hunny damnation, now?' and Marston, *The Malcontent*, ii. v (1604, D4ᵛ), '*Mal*. I, I will come friendly Damnation.'

131. *taint*, break. The noun 'taint' and the verb 'attaint' originally mean 'hit' or 'touch' in tilting.

132. *like the signe of the George*. A phrase to denote marked stiffness and rigidity: cf. Lyly, *Euphues* (ed. Bond, i, p. 260), 'lyke *Saint George*, who is euer on horse backe yet neuer rideth'.

173. *tarras*, terrace. So 'the tarras' at Whitehall, *Love Restored*, 74.

11. ii. 14. *forsooth*, a servant's or a city-woman's attenuated oath.

17. *Humanum est errare*. Cf. Lucian, *Demonax*, 6 (of Socrates), ἡγεῖτο γὰρ ἀνθρώπου μὲν εἶναι τὸ ἁμαρτάνειν, θεοῦ δὲ ἦ ἀνδρὸς ἰσοθέου τὰ πταισθέντα ἐπανορθοῦν, and Augustine, *Sermones* (ed. Migne), 164. 14, 'Humanum fuit errare, diabolicum est per animositatem . . . in errore manere'.

18. *of his chaplaine*. A wise alteration from the Quarto 'of a Puritane': as 'hee goes to church', l. 68. And in *B.F*. iv. vi. 106, 'Zeal-of-the-land' Busy objects to quotations from Horace and Persius as 'the very rags of *Rome*, and patches of *Poperie*'.

22. *puntilio's*, fine or minute points. In *C.R*. ii. iii. 44 it is used for 'apex': 'hath not toucht the *puntilio*, or point of his hopes'.

37. *jigge after a play*. The 'jig' was a lyrical farce written in rhyme and sung or danced to ballad measure, or as Cotgrave, 1611, defines it s.v. 'Farce', 'the Iyg at the end of an Enterlude, wherein some pretie knauerie is acted'. Cf. *Iacke Drums Entertainment*, i (1601, C1ᵛ), 'As the Iigge is cald for when the Play is done'.

47. *the dogges*. Cf. Nashe, *The Vnfortunate Traueller*, 1594 (*Works*, ed. McKerrow, ii, p. 218), 'as melancholy as a dog'.

53. *As the skin betweene your browes*. This phrase is used to corroborate and emphasize an adjective: it is usually colloquial, as in Dogberry's testimonial to Verges, 'honest as the skin betweene his browes' (*Much Ado*, iii. v. 11–12), but Chapman makes poetry of it in *Hero and Leander*, 1598, 4th Sestiad, 14:

> *Venus* would seeme as farre from any spot
> Of light demeanour, as the very skin
> Twixt *Cynthias* browes; Sin is asham'd of Sin.

Staunton suggested that the reference was to the branding of notorious harlots, but this was merely his inference from some metaphorical expressions of Shakespeare, in *The Comedy of Errors*, II. ii. 135, 'And teare the stain'd skin of my Harlot brow'; *Hamlet*, IV. v. 115–17. 'brands the Harlot | Euen heere betweene the chaste vnsmirched browe | Of my true Mother', and III. iv. 42–4, 'takes off the Rose | From the faire forehead of an innocent loue, | And makes a blister there'. Similarly R. Wilson in *The Cobblers Prophecie*, 1594, G1^v, has

> But the foule horror of a harlots name,
> Euen of the Lecher counted as a scorne:
> Whose forehead beares the marke of hatefull shame,
> Of the lust-louer hated and forlorne.

79. *splendidious.* Cf. *C. is A.* v. xiii. 62 note.

89. *in a frame.* Cf. *S.W.* IV. vi. 27–8, 'not so superlatiuely neat as some, madame, that haue their faces set in a brake!'

90. *sute of wanescot.* Referred to by Brathwait, *A Strappado for the Diuell*, 1615, p. 124:

> Now heauen preserue mine eyesight what is here?
> A man made vp in Wainscot? . . . this's the Courtier,
> Braue *Pun-tevallo.*

94. *in east-cheape, among the butchers.* Cf. *E.H.* IV. i. 4, and Stowe, *Survay*, 1598, p. 170, 'This Eastcheape is now a flesh market of Butchers there dwelling, on both sides of the street, it had sometime also Cookes mixed amongst the Butchers, and such other as sold victuails readie dressed of all sorts.' So in the *London Lyckpeny*:

> Then I hyed me into Est-Chepe
> One cryes rybbs of befe & many a pye.

II. iii. 16. *ride vpon a moile*, as judges and serjeants at law did. Dugdale in *Origines Juridiciales*, 1666, p. 38 (quoted by Gifford), states that John Whiddon, justice of the Court of King's Bench, 1 March, 'was the first of the Judges who rode to Westminster Hall on a Horse or Gelding: for before that time they rode on Mules'. Cf. Warner, *Albions England*, xiv, ch. 91 (1612, p. 369):

> I knew when men-Iudiciall rode on sober Mules, whereby
> They might of Suters, these, and they aske, Answere, and Replie.

For the form 'moile' cf. *Poet.* I. ii. 173, *Sej.* III. 167, *Volp.* I. ii. 39, 41, 107.

55. *innated.* 'Frequent circa 1550–1650', *O.E.D.*

68. *Sir Lancelot, and queene Gueuenere.* It is tempting to emend to 'Guenevere': the form 'Gueuenere' is certainly wrong. But it appears, not only in the First Quarto, but in the First Folio, and Jonson passed it in the proof.

Hostile references to the 'Arthurs', 'Tristrams', and 'Lancelots' occur in the 'Execration upon Vulcan' (*Und.* xliii, 30, 69). But Arthur,

Merlin, and the Lady of the Lake play a part in *Prince Henry's Barriers*, and Jonson saw what might be made of the legend in a heroic poem (*Conv. Dr.* x. 148–50).

70. *copie*, supply, abundance. Jonson was fond of the word.

74. *porridge*. Apparently as bad as beef: see note on III. ix. 16.

83. *potato-pies* are mentioned as a luxury in *C.R.* II. ii. 55.

97. *grand scourge*; or, *second vntrusse of the time* refers to the title of Marston's *The Scourge of Villanie*, issued in 1598 and 1599, and to '⟨Mu⟩nday[s] ballet of vntrusse' (McKerrow's *Nashe*, v, p. 195). Note the innuendo that this 'impudent common iester' (Ind. 357) is carrying on the task of Marston and of Munday.

100. *yeoman pheuterer*, (1) a keeper of greyhounds, (2) the attendant who held the hound in the slips and loosed it. Massinger in *The Maid of Honour*, II. ii (1632, D2ᵛ), uses the term contemptuously:

> You yeoman phewterer, conduct mee to
> The Lady of the mansion, or my poniard
> Shall disembogue thy soule.

103. *you, ban-dogge*. In modern punctuation 'you—bandog': cf. *E.M.I.* IV. ii. 99, 'you, lampe of virginitie'.

104. *Nimfadoro*. An Italian term adopted by Jonson. Cf. Florio, 1598, '*Nimfadóro, Nimfodóro*, an effeminate wanton, milke-sop, perfumed ladies-courting courtier'; toned down in the 1611 edition to 'an effeminate fellow, a spruce ladies courting fellow'. 'Nimphadoro, a young courtier & a common louer', is a character in Marston's *Parasitaster, or The Fawne*, 1606.

109. *reall*. The Quartos have the emphatic spelling 'Reall'. Whether Jonson intended the sense of 'royal' or the scholastic use of 'real' as opposed to nominal is not clear; and a similar ambiguity clouds Marston's reference in the preface to *The Scourge of Villainy*, 1598, B4, to 'iudicial Torquatus' and his new-minted Epithets '(as Reall, Intrinsecate, Delphicke)'. But a cancelled line in *Every Man in his Humour* (Quarto version, I. i. 75)—'And entertaine a perfect reall substance'—favours the scholastic use. Other examples in Jonson are *E.M.I.* I. iii. 117, 'conceale such reall ornaments as these, and shaddow their glorie'; *M.L.* I. iii. 13, 'Pursue your project reall'—perhaps the legal sense; and *C.R.* I. i. 110, 'I shall really redeeme the minutes I haue lost'.

111. *Hesperide's*. So the plural is often marked: '*simile's*' (Ind. 364). '*Catso's*' (II. i. 20), '*room's*' (II. iv. 100), '*recipe's*' (*Alch.* II. iii. 233). The apostrophe should mark an elided *e*, but in a word like 'Hesperides' it was probably used as a mark of accent to suggest the right pronunciation.

137. *guilt spurre*. Cf. IV. iv. 86. Fennor notes in *The Compters Common-Wealth*, 1617, p. 32, that gallants 'scorned to weare any other then Beauer hats, and gold bands, rich swords and scarfes, silke stockings and gold fring'd garters, or russet bootes and gilt spurres'.

147. *Niniueh*. See Ind. 164.

at Fleet-bridge. Cf. *Volp.* v. iv. 77, 'MER. I. 'Twere a rare motion, to be seene in *Fleet-street!* MER. 2. I, i' the terme'.

165. *marke*, valued at 13*s*. 4*d*.

166. *Plowden* = Edmund Plowden, 1518–85, the eminent jurist. His chief work was entitled *Les Comentaries, ou les Reportes de Edmunde Plowden vn apprentice de le comen Ley, de dyuers cases esteantes matters en ley, & de les Argumentes sur yceux, en les temps des Raygnes le Roye Edwarde le size, le Roigne Mary, le Roy & Roigne Phillipp & Mary, & le Roigne Elizabeth*, first published in 1571; new editions or reprints appeared in 1578, 1579, 1599, 1613, and 1684. An *Abridgement* was published in 1607; a version by Fabian Hicks appeared in 1650, and again in 1659.

Diar = Sir James Dyer, 1512–82, Chief Justice of the Court of Common Pleas. A collection of cases reported by him was edited and selected by his nephews, R. Farewell and James Dyer, in 1585 under the title *Cy ensuont ascuns nouel cases, collectes per le iades tresreuerend Iudge, Mounsieur Iasques Dyer, chiefe Iustice del common banke.* The editors state that after earnest solicitation by their friends, they 'tooke in hand . . . to select and choose out of the whole bodie of the said worke, such cases and matters, as should be . . . most necessarie & profitable for the Students & professors of the Common Lawes'. Subsequent editions appeared in 1592, 1601, 1621, 1672, and 1688. An *Abridgement de touts les Cases, reportes per Mounsieur Iasques Dyer* was printed in 1602 and 1609, and was translated by Sir Thomas Ireland in 1651.

167. *Brooke* = Sir Robert Brooke, or Broke († 1568), Chief Justice of the Court of Common Pleas and Speaker of the House of Commons. His chief work is entitled *La Graunde Abridgement, collect & escrie per le Iudge tresreuerend Syr Robert Brooke Cheualier, nadgairs Chiefe Iustice del comon banke*, published in 1568; subsequent editions appearing in 1570, 1573, 1576, and 1586. It was founded on Fitzherbert's *Abridgement* (see below), but contained a number of recent cases and additional readings. Tottell published a selection of these in 1578 under the title *Ascuns Nouell cases de les ans et temps le Roy H. 8. Ed. 6, et la Roygne Mary, Escrie ex la grand Abridgement, compose per Sir Robert Brooke Chiualer &c*; further editions appeared in 1587, 1597, 1604, and 1625.

Fitzherbert = Sir Anthony Fitzherbert, 1470–1538, Justice of the Common Pleas. His *Graunde Abridgement* was first printed by Pynson in 1514 in three large folio volumes 'at the pryse of xls'; it is a digest of the year books arranged under appropriate titles in alphabetical order. Other important works published by Fitzherbert were *La Novel Natura Breuium* in 1534, and *Loffice et auctoryte des Justyces de peas côpyle et extrayte hors des aunciēt liures si bien del comen ley cōe dez estatutes oue moultes auts choses necessaries a scauoir* in 1538. These works were in great demand. Of the *Novel Natura Breuium* subsequent editions appeared in quick succession in 1537, 1553, 1567, 1576, 1581, 1588, 1609, 1616, and 1635; in 1652 it was translated into English, new editions appearing in 1666, 1687, 1730 with a commentary by Lord

Chief Justice Hale, 1755, and finally 1794. A translation of the *Office et auctoryte des Justyces de peas* appeared in 1538 under the title *The newe Boke of Justices of the peass by A. F. k. lately translated out of Frenche into Englyshe*: new editions or reprints followed in 1541, 1543, 1547, 1556, 1560, and 1566.

For these legal classics see Davies's 43rd *Epigram*, in which 'Publius student at the common law deserts his books for the bear-garden':

> Leauing old *Ployden*, *Dier* and *Brooke* alone,
> To see old *Harry Hunkes* and *Sacarson*.

176. *beholding*. So *Ep.* cxi. 4. 'Beholden' in *S.W.* v. i. 8, iv. 212.

182. *gloriously*, boastfully (Lat. *gloriose*).

187. *an vbiquitarie*. Cf. *C.R.* ii. iv. 100, 'an *vbiquitarie*, shee is euery where'; and Holinshed's *Chronicles*, 1587, iii, p. 579, 'Vnlesse we will grant the king and queene . . . to haue beene *Hic ibi simul* which priuilege is granted to none but Ubiquitaries.'

190. *the rack*. Cf. *Und.* xiii. 130.

192. *by the fire i' the presence*. Cf. the poem 'To Sᵣ Nicholas Smyth' by Sir John Roe in Donne's *Works* (ed. Grierson, i, p. 405):

> Hear how the Huishers Checques, Cupbord and Fire
> I pass'd; by which Degrees young men aspire
> In Court.

193. *ouer the stage, i' the lords roome*. Cf. Dekker, *The Guls Horne-booke*, 1609, p. 2, 'but when at a new play you take vp the twelue-penny roome, next the Stage, (because the Lords & you may seeme to be haile fellow wel met) . . .'; and p. 28, 'the Lords roome, (which is now but the Stages Suburbs'. Similarly in *Satiromastix*, 1602, M1ʳ, Jonson himself is directed not 'to venter on the stage, when your Play is ended, and to exchange curtezies, and complements with Gallants in the Lordes roomes'.

199. *slight fauours*. Allusions are frequent: cf. Marston, *What You Will*, i. i (1607, F2ᵛ), 'he that bought the half penny riband wearing it in his eare, swearing twas the duches of *Millans* fauor'; Rowlands, *Looke to it: For, Ile Stabbe ye*, 1604, C:

> You that protest the Feather in your Hat,
> Came from a Comtesse Fanne by way of fauour.

And Burton, *The Anatomy of Melancholy*, 1621, p. 614, 'If he get any remnant of hers, a buske-point, a feather of her fanne, a shoo-tie, a lace, he weares it for a fauour in his hat, or next his heart . . .; a garter or a bracelet of hers is more precious then any Saints relique, and he layes it vp in his casket, O blessed relique, and euery day will kisse it.' So *C.R.* iii. iv. 70.

205. *ingenious*. With the 'ingenous' of the Quartos cf. 'enginous', *C.R.* iii. iii. 40.

209. *cob-web lawne*, a transparent lawn. In *Satiromastix*, 1602, C2,

Horace [i.e. Jonson] describes Fannius [i.e. Dekker] as 'the slightest cob-web-lawne peece of a Poet, oh God!'

211. *manage your affections.* Also in *C. is A.* I. vii. 69.

214. *in the power of my purse.* From Plutarch, *Reg. et Imperat. Apophth.*, 'Philip', 6—Philip's comment when a poor man had abused, but afterwards praised him on receiving a present: ὁρᾶτε οὖν, εἶπεν, ὅτι παρ' ἡμᾶς αὐτούς ἐστι καὶ τὸ καλῶς καὶ τὸ κακῶς ἀκοῦσαι.

222. *exornation,* a term of the rhetoricians. Wilson, in *The Art of Rhetorique,* 1553, iii, p. 90, devotes a section to it and defines it, 'Exornation is a gorgiousse beautifiynge of the tongue with borowed wordes, and chaung of sentence or speache, with muche varietie.'

226. *the Arcadia.* Fungoso studied it (III. v. 28). Cf. J. Stephens, *Satyrical Essayes,* 1615, II. xi, p. 276, of '*A Lawyers Clarke*': 'hee woes with bawdery in text; and with Iests, or speeches stolne from Playes, or from the common-helping *Arcadia*'; and Antony Stafford, *The Guide of Honours,* 1634 (written 1624), A6ᵛ (of those who raile at the Ages past), 'Some of them lately have not spared even *Apollo's* first borne, incomparable and inimitable Sir *Phillip Sydney,* whose *Arcadia* they confine onely to the reading of Chambermaids; a censure that can proceede from none but the sonnes of Kitchinmaids.'

227. *in Greenes workes.* William Goddard in *A Mastif Whelp,* C2, Satire 33, points a gibe thus:

> Why could'st not beg or steale from *Green* on dramm of witt?
> And soe by blurd-endashed lynes haue sent him it.

Greene's works displaced the *Arcadia,* and kept up their popularity with the middle class: see the allusion to *The Groatsworth of Witte* (and note). The 'New and Choise Characters' added to the sixth edition of Overbury's *Wife,* 1615, describe '*A Chamber-Mayde*': 'Shee reades *Greenes* workes ouer and ouer, but is so carried away with the *Myrrour of Knighthood,* she is many times resolu'd to run out of her selfe, and become a Ladie errant' (¶4ᵛ). Cf. Wither, *Britain's Remembrancer,* 1628, f. 42ᵛ:

> That, which this age affects, as graue, and wise,
> The following generation may despise.
> *Greenes* phrase, and *Lillie's* language, were in fashion,
> And had among wits much commendation;
> But now, another garbe of speech, with vs
> Is pris'd, and theirs is thought ridiculous.

238. *associate you.* Cf. *Rom. and Jul.* v. ii. 6, 'to associate me'.

245. *put forth some fiue thousand pound.* This system of insurance on foreign travel was a common practice. The premium varied from one-third to one-fifth, so that the chance of a safe return was estimated from two to one to four to one against. Fynes Moryson (*Itinerary,* 1617, Part I, iii. 1) makes the interesting comment that 'this manner of giuing out mony vppon these aduentures, was first vsed in Court, and among the very Noble men', but he adds, perhaps with a glance at *Every Man*

out of his Humour, that 'in this age . . . bankerouts, stage-players, and men of base condition, haue drawne this custome into contempt'. He himself in 1595 'gaue out one hundred pound to receiue three hundred at my returne among my brethren, and some few kinsmen and dearest friends', as well as five sums of £100 for which he was to receive £150, which he notes as a 'disadvantageous aduenture to the giuer of the money'. Cf. *Ep.* cxxxiii. 28, 'three for one', and Barnaby Rich, *Favltes* (1606), 8, 'whipsters, that hauing spent the greatest part of their patrimony in prodigality, wil giue out the rest of their stocke, to be paid two or three for one, vpon their returne from *Rome*, from *Venice*, from *Constantinople*, or some other appoynted place'. For the higher rate cf. *The Tempest*, III. iii. 48, 'Each putter out of fiue for one', and *The Noble Gentleman*, I. i. (Beaumont and Fletcher's *Works*, 1647, p. 28):

> There is no remedy, this land must be,
> In *Paris* ere to morrow night.
> *Gent.* It shall, let me consider, some 300 acres
> Will serve the turne.
> *Wife.* 'Twill furnish at all points, . . .
> For the return will give ye five for one.

248. *Constantinople.* Cf. *S.W.* II. v. 125–7, 'It shall not haue hope to repaire it selfe by *Constantinople*, *Ireland*, or *Virginia*'; and Nashe, *The Terrors of the night*, 1594, A4 (*Works*, ed. McKerrow, i, p. 343), 'but such poore fellowes as I, that cannot put out money to be paid againe when wee come from *Constantinople*, either must haue our work dispatcht by the weeks end, or els we may go beg'.

283. *conduct.* Cf. *Rom. and Jul.* v. iii. 116, 'Come bitter conduct, come vnsauoury pride.'

290. *could haue . . . and t'haue.* Cf. note on Ind. 268.

295. *single*, simple, weak. Cf. *C. is A.* II. vii. 125–6.

302. *traded.* Cf. *Volp.* v. viii. 10. Cunningham quotes Udall's translation of Erasmus's *Paraphrase of the newe testament*, 1551, f. cccxcix (Udall's dedication to Queen Katharine of the Paraphrase of St. John's Gospel): 'what a noumbre is there of noble weomen (especially here in this realme of Englande) . . . not only aswel seen and as familiarly traded in the Latine and Greke tounges, as in theyr owne mother language.'

307. *happily.* This spelling is found frequently in Jonson; e.g. at III. vi. 23. In *C.R.* IV. ii. 45 the 1640 Folio alters to 'haply'; in *Alch.* II. vi. 71 the First Folio spells 'happ'ly'.

II. iv. 3. The 1640 Folio, reading 'at my house' for 'euen', converts the line into an alexandrine: cf. *E.M.I.* II. i. 87 note.

9–14. Similar in tone to *C. is A.* III. i. 11–15.

50. *pretend*, profess, claim. Cf. *E.M.I.* IV. v. 17.

73–4. Quoted in *Englands Parnassus*, 1600, p. 200, under the heading of 'Marriage'.

87. *back-side.* Cf. *C. is A.* IV. viii. 1. For this the rear stage would be used.

91. *flowers.* Cf. *Poet.* II. i. 20–2, and the description of Dr. Levinus Lemnius, travelling in England in 1560, in *The Touchstone of Complexions* (translated by T. Newton), 1576, f. 48, 'their Chambers, & Parlours strawed ouer with sweete herbes, refreshed mee; their Nosegayes finelye entermingled wyth sondry sortes of fragraunte floures in their bedchambers and priuie roomes, with comfortable smell cheered mee vp and entierlye delighted all my Sences.'

93. *perfumed gloues.* Autolycus in *The Winter's Tale*, IV. iv. 217, sells '*Gloues as sweete as Damaske Roses*'. Howes in his continuation of Stow's *Annales*, 1615, p. 868, notes that Edward de Vere, Earl of Oxford, brought perfumed gloves from Italy 'about the fourteenth or fifteenth yeare of the Queene', and that she 'had a payre of perfumed Gloues trimmed onely with foure Tuftes or Roses, of cullered Silke, the Queene tooke such pleasure in those Gloues, that shee was pictured with those Gloues vppon her hands, and for many yeeres after it was called the Earle of Oxfords perfume'. Cf. also Dekker's *Match me in London*, II. i (1631, D2): '*Bilbo.* What ist you lack sir! *King* [*of Spain*]. A gloue with an excellent perfume. *Bil.* For your selfe sir! *King.* I would fit my selfe sir, but I am now for a woman. . . . *Bil.* . . . the sent is aromaticall and most odorous; the muske vpon my word Sir is perfect Cathayne, a Tumbasine odor, . . . not a graine either of your Salmindy Caran or Cubit musk.' The price was 'foure double Pistolets', or about £2. 13s. 4d.

113. *sprightly riuer.* The image is varied in *Und.* xl. 25–8:

> No Mistris no, the open merrie Man
> Moves like a sprightly River, and yet can
> Keepe secret in his Channels what he breedes
> 'Bove all your standing waters, choak'd with weedes.

148. *naturalls.* Cf. *Alch.* 'To the Reader', 11, *Disc.* 746.

II. v. 19. *in print*, in a precise and perfect manner: cf. Burton, *Anatomy*, 1621, p. 619, of a lover, 'he must be in league with an excellent Tayler, Barber, haue neat shooe-ties, points, garters, speake in print, walke in print, eat and drinke all in print, and that which is all in all, hee must be mad in print', where the original Latin cited in the margin is 'cum cura'. Hence the adjective phrase as in the text: Whalley compares Massinger, *The Guardian*, II. i (1655, p. 20):

> Is he not madam
> A monsieur in print? what a garb was there! O rare!

20. *the last edition.* Echoed in II. vi. 11. Cf. Dekker, *The Honest Whore*, Part I, 1604, E2ᵛ, 'I would thou wouldst giue me fiue yards of Lawne, to make my *Punke* some falling bands a the fashion, three falling one vpon another: for that's the new edition now'; and Massinger, *The City-Madam*, I. ii (1658, p. 7):

> *Page.* Clown Sir! he is transform'd,
> And grown a gallant of the last Edition.

27. *exhibition*, payment of an allowance. Cf. *Poet.* I. ii. 76, *S.W.* III. i. 59.

46. *conferre*. Cf. IV. viii. 31, *Volp.* V. x. 33.

II. vi. 19–23. Cf. Marston, *Satire* iii, appended to *Pigmalions Image*, 1598: Duceus is asked whence he comes—

> And he straight answers vs,
> From Lady *Lilla*. And is going straight
> To the Countesse of (   ), for she doth waite
> His comming. And will surely send her Coach,
> Vnlesse he make the speedier approch.

The truth being that

> He neuer durst vnto these Ladies show
> His pippin face.

24. *her garter*. Cf. *C.R.* III. iv. 69, a lover at court 'will spend his patrimonie for a garter'; and Drayton, *The Battaile of Agincovrt*, 1627, lxi, p. 13 (of the young nobles starting for France):

> One ware his Mistris Garter, one her Gloue;
> And he a lock of his deare Ladies haire.

52. *two-shilling ordinarie*. For a varied list of prices see Dyce's note on Middleton, *The Phœnix*, IV. ii, 'the sixpenny ordinary'. Two shillings was rather dear. But cf. Dekker, *Lanthorne and Candle-light*, 1608, D2ᵛ (of a money-lender), 'Hee comes to an Ordinary, to saue charges of house-keeping, and will eate for his two shillings, more meat then will serue three of the guard at a dinner'; Marston, *What You Will*, 1607, F3ᵛ, 'Ile goe to the halfe crowne ordinary euery meale, Ile haue my Iuory boxe of Tobacco, Ile conuerse with none but Counts and Courtiers'; and Richard Turner, *Nosce te*, (*Humors*), 1607, E:

> What is thy Ordinary? now by *Pharoes* life,
> Ile leaue it, if 't be vnder halfe a crowne.
> Ti's but two shillings: O extreame disgrace,
> He scornes to suppe, when Suppers grow so base.

66. *seam-rent*. Cf. *Poet.* I. ii. 209.

94–9. A suggestion from Horace's ninth *Satire*, 'Ibam forte', afterwards elaborately worked up in *Poetaster*, III. i–iii.

108. *eate . . . gold, . . . drinke dissolu'd pearle*. Cf. *Volp.* III. vii. 190, 191, 217, 'See, here, a rope of pearle; . . . | Dissolue, and drinke 'hem. . . . Our drinke shall be prepared gold, and amber'; *Alch.* II. ii. 75, 76, 'The tongues of carpes, dormise, and camels heeles, | Boil'd i' the spirit of SOL'—i.e. in gold—'and dissolu'd pearle'. The 'cullises', or rich broths for invalids, made of game boiled to a jelly and seasoned with rich spices, sometimes had gold or pearl dissolved in them. 'If you put in certaine peeces of golde, it will be the better' is the suggestion in a recipe for cullises in T. Cogan's *The Haven of Health*, 1584, ch. 157, p. 133.

157. *sinowie*. Spelt 'sinnewye' in *Disc.* 2041. Cf. the noun-form 'sinnow' in *Hamlet*, I. v. 94 (Quarto 1604), and 'vnsinnow'd', ib. IV. vii. 10.

163–73. Jonson had more than once to resort to this kind of disclaimer. Thus in *Volpone*, ded. 56 foll., '*Where haue I beene particular? Where personall? except to a mimick, cheater, bawd, or buffon, creatures (for their insolencie) worthy to be tax'd?* . . . *Application, is now, growne a trade with many; and there are, that professe to haue a key for the decyphering of euery thing*'; in *Bartholomew Fair*, Ind. 137–41, Jonson stipulates that the audience is not to contain or conceal 'any *State-decipherer*, or politique *Picklocke* of the *Scene*, so solemnly ridiculous, as to search out, who was meant by the *Ginger-bread-woman*, who by the *Hobby-horse-man*, who by the *Costard-monger*, nay, who by their *Wares*'. In the second chorus of *The Magnetic Lady* he repeats the argument of the text: '*Dam*. But whom doth your *Poët* meane now by this—Mr. *Bias*? what Lords Secretary, doth hee purpose to personate, or perstringe? *Boy*. You might as well aske mee, what *Alderman*, or *Aldermans* Mate, hee meant by Sir *Moath Interest*? or what eminent Lawyer, by the ridiculous Mr. *Practise*? who hath rather his name invented for laughter, then any offence, or injury it can stick on the reverend Professors of the Law: And so the wise ones will thinke.' Such protests were common form: Nashe has a striking one in the preface to *Christs Teares ouer Ierusalem*, 1594 (*Works*, ed. McKerrow, ii. 182), where he complains that 'there be certaine busie wits abrode, that seeke in my *Iacke Wilton* to anagrammatize the name of Wittenberge to one of the Vniuersities of England, . . . Let one but name bread, they will interpret it to be the town of Bredan in the low countreyes; if of beere he talkes, then straight he mocks the Countie Beroune in France. . . . Infinite number of these phanatical strange hierogliphicks haue these new decipherers framed to them selues, & stretcht words on their tenter hooks so miserably, that a man were as good, considering euerie circumstance, write on cheuerell as on paper.' Nashe has a contemporary reference to the theatre (quoted here by Mr. Baskerville) in the prologue to his *Summers Last Will and Testament*, 1600, 'Moralizers, you that wrest a neuer meant meaning out of euery thing, applying all things to the present time, keepe your attention for the common Stage: for here are no quips in Characters for you to reade'.

175. *writing-tables*. Cf. the prologues to Beaumont, *The Woman Hater*, 1607, A2, '*if there bee any lurking amongst you in corners, with Table bookes, who haue some hope to find fit matter to feede his —— mallice on, let them claspe them vp, and slinke away, or stay and be conuerted*'; and Fletcher and Massinger, *The Custom of the Country* (Folio 1647, p. 25):

> . . . *wee dare looke*
> *On any man, that brings his Table-booke*
> *To write downe, what againe he may repeate*
> *At some greate Table, to deserue his meate*

> *Let such come sweld with malice, to apply*
> *What is mirth here, there for an injurie.*
> *Nor Lord, nor Lady we have tax'd; nor State,*
> *Nor any private person, their poore hate*
> *Will be starv'd heere, for envy shall not finde*
> *One touch that may be wrested to her minde.*

183. *The middle isle in Paules.* Francis Osborn, *Historical Memoires on the Reigns of Queen Elizabeth and King James*, 1658, pp. 64–5: 'It was then the fashion of those times, and did so continue till these . . . for the principall Gentry, Lords, Courtiers and men of all professions not merely Mechanick, to meet in *Pauls Church* by eleven, and walk in the middle Ile till twelve, and after dinner from three, to six, during which time some discoursed of Businesse, others of Newes.' In *Witt's Recreations Augmented*, 1641, P3, the motto for a Paul's walker is 'Defessus sum ambulando'. John Chamberlain, the news-monger, has an interesting reference in a letter of 19 November 1602, 'I am quite out of the trade, which may well be by reason of a new deuised order to shut the vpper doores in Powles in seruice time, whereby the old entercourse is clene chaunged, and the trafficke in newes much destroyed'. W. Rowley, *A Search for Money*, 1609, A4, dedication 'To all those that lack money': 'I knowe the walkes in *Paules* are stale to yee, yee could tell extemporally I am sure how many paces t'were betweene the quire and the West dore.'

184. *the west end of it.* Advertisements were posted up there: cf. B. R., *Greenes Newes both from Heauen and Hell*, 1593, C2ᵛ, '. . . Maister *White* walking into *Poules*, and seeing many bils sette vp on the West doore by such as wanted Maisters, perusing the bylles, and finding one that he thought might be fitte for his purpose . . . gaue notice vnder the bill, that he shoulde repaire into *Graties streete*, and at such a signe enquire for Maister *White*'; and Dekker, *The Guls Horne-booke*, 1609, p. 21, '*Si quis doore* (pasted & plaistred vp with *Seruingmens supplications*)'. Falstaff engaged Bardolph in Paul's (*2 Henry IV*, I. ii. 48).

190. *Apple Iohn.* The name seems to indicate his withered and shrivelled appearance: cf. *2 Henry IV*, II. iv. 1–9. But it carries with it also the suggestion of 'apple-squire' or pandar: cf. *B.F.* I. iii. 55.

194. *Siquis*, an advertisement or public notice. Cf. Hall, *Virgidemiarum*, 1597, ii, Sat. v. 1, 2:

> Saw'st thou euer *Siquis* patch'd on *Paul's* Church dore,
> To seek some vacant Vicarage before?

196. *hull vp and downe*, literally to drift to the wind with sails furled. Cf. John Smith's *A Sea Grammar*, 1627, ix. 40: 'Try the mizen, if that split, or the storme grow so great she cannot beare it; then hull, which is beare no saile. They call it hulling also in a calme swelling Sea, which is commonly before a storme, when they strike their sailes lest she should beat them in peeces against the mast by Rowling.'

the humorous world. Cf. *Ep.* cxxxi. 7, 'if the hum'rous world will talke at large'.

III. i. With the life-like picture of Paul's given in these scenes compare Dekker's *The Guls Horne-booke*, 1609, ch. iv, 'How a Gallant should behaue himselfe in Powles-walkes'. The chapter is a good commentary on Jonson. Cf. also *The burnynge of Paules church in London in the yeare of our Lord 1561*, Giiij, '*The South Alley* for Usurye and Poperye, *the North for Simony*, and *the Horse faire* in the middest for all kind of bargains, metinges, brawlinges, murthers, conspiracies, and *the Font* for ordinary paiments of money, are so well knowen to all menne as the begger knowes his dishe'; *The Meeting of Gallants at an Ordinarie*; *or, The Walkes in Powles*, 1604, B2ʳ, where Signior Ginglespurre tells Signior Shuttlecocke, 'But see yonder, *Signior Stramazoon* and *Signior Kickshawe*, now of a suddaine allighted in *Powles* with their durtie Bootes, lets encounter them at the fift Pillar, . . . What *Signior*, both well met vppon the old worne Brasse'; T. M., *The Blacke Booke*, 1604, B2, referring to country people:

> And how they grate with their hard nayly soales
> The stones in *Fleet-streete*, and strike fire in *Powles*:
> Nay, with their heauie Trot, and yron-stalke,
> They haue worne off the brasse in the mid-walke.

J. H. in the 'Characters' appended to *The House of Correction*, 1619, D2ᵛ, describes a courtesan: 'Faine would she haue beene a *Quirrister at Pauls*, but that she loues not to stand in a *Surplisse*: yet many times she repayres thither, especially vnto *the lower end of the Middle Ile*.'

1. *without discouery.* The variety would have exposed him. Cf. too *Alch.* I. i. 93, 'Write thee vp bawd, in *Paules*'. On a report of the Attorney-General Noye in 1631 the practice was stopped, and a notice posted up that it was the King's pleasure that 'no man, of what qualitie soeuer, shall presume to Walke in the Isles of the Quire, or in the Body, or Isles, of the Church, during the time of Diuine Seruice' (*Domestic State Papers, Charles I*, ccxiv, f. 94, ccxxix, f. 116).

10. *laugh, and be fat.* A proverbial phrase, also played on in *Ent. Highgate*, 236.

15. *store of gallants.* Cf. *Cat.* I. 171, 'store, and change of women'.

17. *strangers to the whole scope of our play.* An extraordinary confession for a dramatist to make: compare in *The Case is Altered* the insertion of a new character, Antonio Balladino, to satirize Anthony Munday, and the 'interloping scene' in Act IV of *A Tale of a Tub*, to satirize Inigo Jones.

18. *only . . . a turne or two.* Dekker is emphatic about the propriety of not being seen 'aboue foure turnes, but in the fift make your selfe away, either in some of the Sempsters shops, the new Tobacco-office, or amongst the Booke-sellers' (*The Guls Horne-booke*, 1609, pp. 18–19).

25. *O god, sir.* A fashionable stopgap when conversation flagged or

when an awkward question called for a reply. Cf. II. v. 50, and Shake-speare's satire on 'O Lord, sir' in *All's Well*, II. ii. 40–53, and Marston, *The Dutch Courtezan*, II. i. 197–9 (ed. Bullen), '*Hol*. O Lord, sir! *Cac*. Well spoken; good English'.

30. *in a booke-sellers shop*. Like Emulo in Dekker and Chettle's *Patient Grissill*, II. i (1603, C1), 'my briske spāgled babie wil come into a Stationers shop, call for a stoole and a cushion, and then asking for some greeke Poet, to him he falles, and there he grumbles God knowes what, but Ile be sworne he knowes not so much as one Character of the tongue'. This play, acted in 1599, has some striking parallels to Jonson's work: see especially Brisk's duel, IV. vi. 72 foll.

32. *the tongues, to his suits*. The international costume of the Eliza-bethan fop is a common topic of satire: see the commentators on *Much Ado*, III. ii. 27–35, *Merch. of Venice*, I. ii. 66–8. Jonson recurs to it in *N.I.* II. ii. 61–8. Cf. W. Goddard, *A Neaste of Waspes*, 1615, F1ᵛ, stanza 65:

> But speake I praie, who ist would gess or skann
> *Fantasmus* to be borne an Englisheman?
> Hees hatted spanyard-like, and bearded to,
> Ruft Itallyon-like; pac'd like them also,
> His hose and doublett's Frenche: his bootes and shoes
> Are fashond pole in heeles, but French in toes
> *Oh! hees compleate! what shall I descant an?*
> *A compleate Foole: noe compleate Englishe man.*

III. ii. 11. *out of her humour*. 'Jonson forgot to account for this', says Gifford, but her abrupt exit when she found spectators at her husband's comedy of euphuism gives a clear enough hint for so fugitive a character.

25. *yonder*, in Doctors' Commons.

29. *of as many colours, as . . . any fooles coat*. Cf. *S.W.* I. iv. 41–3.

III. iii. 1. *in Mediterraneo*. For the pun on 'aisle' and 'isle'—the words were confused from the fifteenth century onwards—cf. '*in Insula Paulina*', III. v. 32, and Dekker, op. cit., p. 18, 'Your *Mediterranean* Ile' . . . 'pick out such an howre, when the maine Shoale of Ilanders are swimming vp and downe'.

2. *but let that pass*. For this affectation, cf. III. vi. 53, and Holofernes in *Love's Labour's Lost*, v. i. 82–95. Variations are 'but let that vanish' (*C.R.* Ind. 43), and 'but let that scape' (ib. I. i. 37).

8. *predominant*, or 'fore-top', the front lock of hair which was allowed to grow and brushed upward. Portraits of the time show this fashion, e.g. the portrait of the third Earl of Southampton at Welbeck. Cf. *C.R.* III. iv. 13. No other example of 'predominant' in this sense is quoted.

10. *stroking vp*. Cf. *Sir Gyles Goosecappe*, IV. ii (1606, G1ᵛ), 'curling this My golden foretoppe, stept into the presence'; and Rowley, *A Match at Midnight*, I. i (1633, B1ᵛ), 'While I tye my Band, prethee stroke up my fore-toppe a little'.

23. *acute*. Italicized in the Quarto and originally in the Folio: the sense of 'keen-witted' was new and perhaps euphuistic. Cf. Armado in *Love's Labour's Lost*, III. i. 61, 'A most acute Iuuenall'; Fastidius here and in IV. viii. 49, and the affected Amorphus in *C.R.* IV. iii. 15, 'most ingenious, acute, and polite ladie'.

23. *sweet silent rhetorique* . . . A gird at Daniel who had written in *The Complaint of Rosamund*, 1592, stanza xviii [xix]:

> Ah beauty Syren, fayre enchaunting good,
> Sweet silent rethorique of perswading eyes;
> Dombe eloquence, whose powre doth moue the blood,
> More then the words, or wisedome of the wise;
> Still harmonie, whose diapason lyes
> Within a brow, ...

Daniel liked the fancy and repeated it in *The Queenes Arcadia*, 1606, V. ii, pp. 390–1:

> Ah what a silly messenger is Speech
> To be imploi'd in that great Embassie
> Of our affections, in respect of th' eye?
> Ah 'tis the silent rhetoricke of a looke,
> That works the league betwixt the states of hearts.

Davies played on the phrase in his 45th *Epigram* (*c.* 1599):

> *Dacus* with some good collour & pretence,
> Tearmes his loues beautie silent eloquence:
> For she doth lay more collours on her face,
> Then euer *Tullie* vsde his speech to grace.

And Jonson attacked it again in *S. of N.* III. ii. 270–2. As a matter of fact, Daniel only expressed a truism in epigrammatic form. Shakespeare writes in *Lucrece* (ll. 29, 30):

> Beautie it selfe doth of it selfe perswade
> The eies of men without an Orator.

Cf. Burton, *Anatomy*, 1621, p. 551: '*Plato* calls Beauty therefore a priuiledge of nature, *naturæ gaudentis opus*, a dumbe comment, *Theophrastus* a silent fraud, still Rhetoricke *Carneades*, that perswades without speech.'

26. *anatomie of wit* echoes the title of Lyly's famous treatise.

33. foll. In Greene's *The Scottish Historie of Iames the fourth*, 1598, C2, bills are set up; e.g. 'If any gentleman, spirituall or temporall, will entertaine out of his seruice, a young stripling of the age of 30. yeares, that can sleep with the soundest, eate with the hungriest, work with the sickest, lye with the lowdest, face with the proudest, &c. that can wait in a Gentlemans chamber, when his maister is a myle of, keepe his stable when tis emptie, and his purse when tis full, and hath many qualities woorse then all these, let him write his name and goe his way, and attendance shall be given.' Cf. B. R., *Greenes Newes*, 1593 (ed. McKerrow, p. 20): 'Theyr Lodgings being thus prouided, Maister *White*

walking into *Poules*, and seeing many bils sette vp on the West doore by such as wanted Maisters, perusing the bylles, and finding one that he thought might be fitte for his purpose . . . gaue notice vnder the bill, that he shoulde repaire into *Graties streete*, and at such a signe enquire for Maister *White*.'

37. *little legges*. Cf. Lenton, *Leasures*, 1631, Character 31, 'A Gentleman-Vsher'—'The smallnesse of his legs bewrayes his profession'; Randolph, *The Muses Looking-glasse*, 1638, IV. ii:

> let him be your Gentleman-usher;
> Madam you may in time bring down his legs
> To the just size, now over grown with playing
> Too much at foot-ball;

Glapthorne, *The Hollander*, II. i (1640, C4ᵛ), 'I might serve for a gentleman Usher, were my legges small enough.'

40. *lies in lauander*, a euphemism for 'in pawn'. Gifford quotes *E.H.* v. i. 56–7, 'Good faith, rather then thou shouldest pawne a ragge more, I'ld lay my Ladiship in lauender, if I knew where.' Cf. Massinger, *A New Way to Pay Old Debts*, v. i (1633, L1ᵛ), 'Put me in good security | Of some of your new possessions, . . . or I'le haue you | Dragg'd in your lauender robes to the Goale.'

47 foll. Compare R. Brathwaite's satire 'To Captaine Whiffe' in *The Smoaking Age, or The Life and Death of Tobacco*, 1617, pp. 182–3: 'You Captaine, that glory in your Art of vanity, making a high-Road-way 'twixt your mouth and your guttes, (and with a cunning retrait) bringing it backe same way it came; you, that set up bils for your Novice to reade; as thus: "Whosoever wil be Disciplined, or Matriculated in the Art, Science or Mystery of *Tobacco-whiffing*, let him subscribe his name, the place of his being; and Captaine *Whiffe* will be ready there to attend his yong master-ships pleasure, with the profoundst of his skil." O my impudent Sharke, Art thou fled from thy Captaine, & dar'st thou now usurpe the name of Valour? Thou that durst not smell Gunpowder art now turn'd Tobacco-whiffer?'

48. *of the first, second, or third head*, the first, second, or third gentleman of his family: Fungoso states (IV. i. 11), 'I must bee the first head of our house'. The term is derived from venery: cf. *The Returne from Pernassus*, 1606, II. v: 'I caused the Keeper to seuer the rascall Deere, from the Buckes of the first head: now sir, a Bucke the first yeare is a Fawne, the second yeare a Pricket, the third year a Sorell, the fourth yeare a Soare, the fift a Bucke of the first head, the sixt yeare a compleat Buck.' Hence the sense of 'upstart', as in Cotgrave, '*gentilhomme de ville*, a gentleman of the first head, an upstart gentleman', and the sneering use in *N.I.* IV. ii. 68, *M.L.* III. vi. 116.

56. *Cuban ebolition*. Cf. *The Returne from Pernassus*, IV. i, 'Good faith Maister *Prodigo* is an excellent fellow, he takes the *Gulan ebullitio* so excellently', where, however, the Halliwell-Phillipps MS. reads, 'Cuban ebullition'.

57. *Euripus*. Judging from its etymology, the strait of Euboea with the shifting tides, this should mean a rapid inhaling and emitting of the smoke. The Euripus had seven tides a day.

Whiffe. Cf. Dekker, *The Guls Horne-booke*, 1609, ch. v, p. 25, 'then let him shew his seuerall tricks in taking it. As the *Whiffe*, *the Ring*, *&c.* For these are complements that gaine Gentlemen no meane respect, and for which indeede they are more worthily noted, I ensure you, then for any skill that they haue in learning'; Rich, *My Ladies Looking Glasse*, 1616, p. 51 ('The Ninihammer'), 'his greatest *dexteritie* is in the managing his *Tobacco pipes*: and he hath the *gulpe*, the *whiffe*, and the *snuffe* very exactly and at his fingers ends'.

65. *Stet Quæso* . . . a request to the reader not to tear the bill down. Cf. J. Chamberlain's letter to Sir Dudley Carleton, 4 August 1620: 'The demolishment of the houses about Paul's is threatened every day, but the people either do not or will not seem to believe it, nor do, nor remove, nor avoid; but some make jests, as if it were not meant in earnest; and one in knavery wrote upon his door, *Stet quæso, candide lector*' (*Court and Times of James I*, 1848, ii. 209).

71. *good properties*. Cf. the 'Character' of Fastidius Briske, Ind. 41, 'a good property to perfume the boot of a coach', and *Julius Caesar*, iv. i. 39–40, 'Do not talke of him, | But as a property.'

73. *the Mitre*. Originally in Bread Street, Cheapside; afterwards moved to Fleet Street. Cf. iii. vi. 161, 'Your Miter is your best house'; Middleton in *Your fiue Gallants*, ii. i. 220 (ed. Bullen), says that for 'neat attendance, diligent boys' it 'far excels' the Mermaid, and praises its catering in *A Mad World*, 1608, v. i. 77–8, 'Sirrah, why this will be a true feast, a right Mitre supper.'

iii. iv. 7. *talke fustian*. Jonson, with a spice of malice, mainly uses Marston's uncouth vocabulary, which he was afterwards to satirize more systematically in *Poetaster*. *Patient Grissill*, 1603, ii. i, satirizes 'changeable Silke gallants' who 'reade no bookes but a looking-glasse, and speake no language but sweet Lady, and sweet Signior, and chew between their teeth terrible words, as though they would coniure, as complement, [cf. *Disc.* 2275] and proiects, and Fastidious, & Caprichious [cf. *C. is A.* ii. vii. 74], and Misprizian [cf. *C.R.* iv. iv. 31], and the Sintheresis of the soule, and such like raise-veluet tearmes'. For the figurative use of 'fustian' cf. *C.R.* Ind. 43.

22. *soules Synderesis*. Cf. *The Scourge of Villanie*, 1598, G6ᵛ, Sat. viii, 'Returne, returne, sacred *Synderisis*', and Iᵛ, Sat. x in ed. 1599, 'The poore soules better part so feeble is, | So cold and dead is his *Synderesis*.'

23. *panch of Esquiline*, the jakes. In *The Scourge*, 1598, F6ᵛ, G6ᵛ, and *Histrio-Mastix*, 1610, D4:

rotten stuffs,
More fit to fill the paunch of Esquiline,
Then feed the hearings of iudiciall eares.

450 *Plays*

Spenser originated the phrase in his allegorical description of the human body, *F.Q.* II. ix, stanza 32.

24. *Zodiack . . . Eclipticke line.* Cf. *Histrio-Mastix*, B2, 'In the Ecliptick line, which partes the Zodiack'.

opticke. See the note on I. i. 25.

26. *vegetable circumference.* Cf. *The Scourge*, 1599, H2ᵛ:

> *Ned* hath rauished my sense
> In a Poetick vaine circumference.

27. *ventositie.* Untraced in Marston, but he is made to disgorge it in the Quarto text of *Poet.* v. iii. 494; the Folio alters this to 'ventositous'.

intellectuall, or mincing capreall. Cf. *The Scourge*, 1599, H3ᵛ:

> His very soule, his intellectuall
> Is nothing but a mincing capreall.

29. *Plato's Histriomastix.* *Histrio-Mastix, Or, the Player whipt* was published anonymously by Thomas Thorp in 1610. Marston's part authorship is attested by the vocabulary, and confirmed by Jonson's treatment of it here. A possible reference to Jonson is found at sig. B4ᵛ, where Chrysoganus is thus addressed:

> How you translating-scholler? you can make
> A stabbing *Satir*, or an *Epigram*,
> And thinke you carry iust *Ramnusia*'s whippe
> To lash the patient; goe, get you clothes,
> Our free-borne blood such apprehension lothes.

33. *Reason . . . animalls.* Professor Koeppel first pointed out the parallel passage in *The Wisdome of Doctor Dodypoll*, ii (1600, E), where a madman commits an assault:

> *Alp.* Lay holde vpon him, helpe the Doctor there.
> *Alb.* Then reason's fled to animals I see,
> And Ile vanish like Tobaccho smoake. *Exit.*

The date of Jonson's play, 1599, and the 'Et tu Brute' in v. vi. 79, suggest a reference to Shakespeare's *Julius Caesar*, which was acted in London in September 1599. Antony in the funeral oration says (III. ii. 104-5):

> O Iudgement! thou art fled to brutish Beasts,
> And Men haue lost their Reason.

Antony's comment fits his context; Jonson is poking fun at a pseudo-Aristotelian idea. See J. Dover Wilson, 'Ben Jonson and *Julius Caesar*' in *Shakespeare Survey*, ii, 1949, pp. 36–43.

48. *Harrots.* Cf. *E.M.I.* I. iv. 16.

55 foll. Erasmus again: see *Omnia Opera*, 1540, i, p. 709: 'Sed adde clypeum cum insignibus. HA. Quænam mihi suades deligam? NE. Duo mulctra si uelis, & cantharum ceruisiarium. H. Ludis, age dic serio. NE. Nunquam fuisti in bello? HA. Ne uidi quidem. N. At interim opinor, decollasti anseres & capos rusticorum. HA. Persæpe, & quidem

fortiter. Pone machæram argenteam, tria anserum capita aurea. HA.
In quo solo? N. Quo? nisi sanguinolento, monumentum fortiter effusi
cruoris. . . . In uertice quid eminebit? HA. Expecto. NE. Caput canis
demissis auribus.' Cf. J. Stephens, *Satyrical Essayes*, 1615, p. 263, II,
Character viii, 'A Farmer': 'To purchase Armes (if he æmulate Gentry)
sets vpon him like an Ague: it breakes his sleepe, takes away his
stomacke, and he can neuer be quiet till the *Herald* hath giuen him the
Harrowes, the Cuckow, or some ridiculous Embleme for his Armory'.
Small, *The Stage-Quarrel*, p. 55, quotes Fuller, *Worthies of England*,
1661, pp. 47–8, ch. xvi, 'Of the Coats of Arms, affixed to such, as have
been Sheriffs of Counties': 'Two colours are necessary and most highly
honourable; . . . *three* are very honourable; *four* commendable; *five*
excusable; more, disgraceful. Yet have I seen a *Coat of Arms* (I mean
within the Escucheon) so piebald, that if both *Metalls*, and all the *Colours*
(*seven* in all) were lost elsewhere, they might have been found therein.
Such *Coats* were frequently given by the heralds (not out of want of
wit, but will to bestow better) to the new Gentry in the End of the
Reign of King *Henry* the Eighth. One said of a *Coat* that it was so
well victualled, that it might endure a Siege, such the plenty and variety
of Fowl, Flesh and Fish therein; though some done so small, one needed
a magnifying glass to discover them; but such *surfeited Coats* have since
met with a good *Physician, who hath cured many of them.' (A marginal note is '* Mr. *Camden*'.)

75–9. Jonson knew that to 'lay colour vpon colour' 'afforded but an
ill blazon' (*C.R.* II. iii. 159–60), so the fool's coat here is intentional.
In *S. of N.* IV. iv. 25–6 he even blazons metal upon metal to mark
an heraldic hyperbole. On the whole subject see A. H. Nason, *Heralds
and Heraldry in Ben Jonson's Plays*, 1907.

86. *word*, motto. Cf. *C.R.* v. vii. 32, 41, 48, 56.

Not without mustard. C. R. Baskerville suggests a reference to the
story in Nashe of the storm-tost sailor's vow: see *Pierce Penilesse*, ed.
McKerrow, i, p. 171, and the note on l. 6.

104. *stand vpon your gentilitie.* Cf. *E.M.I.* I. i. 86, ii. 2.

III. v. With the opening compare *The Guls Horne-booke*, 1609, ch. iv,
p. 20, on the fashions to be seen in Paul's: 'All the diseasd horses in
a tedious siege, cannot shew so many fashions, as are to be seene for
nothing euery day in Duke *Humfreyes walke*. If therefore you determine
to enter into a new suit, warne your Tailor to attend you in Powles
who, with his hat in his hand, shall like a spy discouer the stuffe, colour,
and fashion of any doublet or hose that dare be seene there, and stepping
behind a piller to fill his table-bookes with those notes, will presently
send you into the world an accomplisht man, by which meanes you shall
weare your clothes in print w^t the first edition.' So in *Ep.* lxxxviii
a copyist of French fashions is described as

> The new *french*-taylors motion, monthly made,
> Daily to turne in PAVLS, and helpe the trade.

2. *blush-colour'd sattin*, damask rose. Simplicius in Marston's *What You Will*, v. i. 100, has a 'blush-colour satin suit'.

5. *wing*, an upright shoulder lappet. 'This word was long retained for the particular kind of epaulet worn by light infantry and flank companies of regiments' (Cunningham). Ladies wore 'puff-wings' of lawn (*Poet.* IV. i. 16).

13. *beg him*, in fuller phrase 'beg him for a fool'. If a man was legally proved to be an idiot, an application could be made to the Court of Wards to obtain the custody of him and the profits of his estate. The King could grant this to any subject. Cf. Marston, *What You Will*, II. i (1607, B4ᵛ):

> *Qua.* I protest, beleeue him not, Ile beg thee *Lauerdure*
> For a conceal'd Ideot if thou credit him;

and *The Insatiate Countesse*, IV. iv (1613, H), 'If my husband had beene worth the begging some Courtier would haue had him: he might be begg'd well inough, for he knows not his owne wife from another.'

14. *the fustie world*. Marston, rounding off *The Scourge of Villanie*, 1598, with a note to the reader, ends, 'I take a solemne congee of this fusty world'.

28. *the Arcadia*. Cf. II. iii. 226.

34. *What is he, for a creature?* Like the German 'Was ist das für ein?' Cf. *S.W.* III. ii. 41. Spenser in *The Shepheardes Calender*, April 17, has 'What is he for a Ladde, you so lament?' and E. K. glosses, 'A straunge manner of speaking. s. what maner of Ladde is he?' The phrase lent itself to quibbles: cf. Sharpham, *The Fleire*, 1607, F3ᵛ, '*Sus.* But come, what was a for a man? *Nan.* What was a for a man? Why, a was a man for a woman, what should a be?'

III. vi. 16, 17. Untraced, but cf. J. C., *The Two Merry Milke-Maids*, III. i (1620, H4):

> *Smir.* Oh, Oh. *Fre.* What Oh? where lies the Crampe? *Smir.* Oh, Oh! *Strikes his breast.*
> *Smir.* With that the moody squire thumpt his breast,
>   And rear'd his eyes to heauen for reuenge.
> Speake sweet *Ieronimo.*

24–6. Wither, *Abuses Stript and Whipt*, 1613, D4:

> He weares such colours as for Louers be,
> Drinks vowed healths vpon his bared knee:
> Sue's mainly for a shoo-string, or doth craue her,
> To grant him but a busk-point, for a fauour.

29, 30. From Juvenal, *Sat.* iii. 152–3.

35. *seene a serjeant*, been arrested. Cf. IV. ii. 62.

48 foll. Copied by H. Parrot in *Laquei Ridiculosi*, Epig. 218, '*Cedant arma Nummis*':

> Oh spare you Syr, you offer great disgrace
> To wish me sell my Rapier? sir, t'were base:
> A Marshall Gentleman of my profession. . . .
> The blade Syr, Ile besworne is such a' one
> As farther came from hence then *Prester-Iohn*,
> Yet if it needs will please you looke vpon it,
> I would but borrow some small siluer on it.

50. *iniurie* (Qq). Cf. *C. is A.* I. vi. 16.

57. *my lord of Leyster's time.* Leicester's feeble campaign in the Netherlands took place in 1586 and 1587. He died in 1588. Brill, Flushing, and Ramequeens were the three towns handed over to Elizabeth as a guarantee to repay the expenses of her interference. Cunningham notes that Leicester in his correspondence spells 'Vlussingue' and 'Hage'.

59. *a gentleman of sort* ('good sort' in the Quartos). Cf. *Meas. for Meas.* IV. iv. 14–15, 'giue notice to such men of sort and suite as are to meete him'; and Barrey, *Ram-Alley*, IV. i (1611, F4), 'Her husband is a Gentleman of sort. | *Serjeant.* A Gentleman of sort, why what care I.'

74. *playing o' the Iewes trump.* For the suggestion of money-making attaching to the phrase cf. *E.H.* II. ii. 210, 211, 'what will not an vsurous knaue be, so he may bee riche? O 'tis a notable Iewes trump! I hope to liue to see dogs meate made of the old Vsurer's flesh.'

80. *clem*, lit. of the 'pinch' of hunger. The transitive form appears in *Poet.* I. ii. 186.

112. *Ianus.* Cf. the 'invocation' in *Merch. of Venice*, I. i. 50, 51:

> Now by two-headed *Ianus*,
> Nature hath fram'd strange fellowes in her time.

113. *Hercules.* From the *Apocolocyntosis* of Seneca, 5: Claudius, arriving in heaven, cannot speak intelligibly: 'Tum Iuppiter Herculem, qui totum orbem terrarum pererraverat et nosse videbatur omnes nationes, iubet ire et explorare quorum hominum esset.' (Whalley.)

152. *countenance*, patronage. Cf. *Alch.* I. i. 22, 43, and Selden's *Table Talk*, xliii ('Fines'): 'The old law was, that when a man was fined, he was to be fined *salvo contenemento*, so as his countenance might be safe; taking countenance in the same sense as your countryman does, when he says, if you will come unto my house, I will shew you the best countenance I can, that is, not the best face, but the best entertainment.'

more then countenance is a practical offer; it means maintenance or at least money. Cf. Shirley's picture of a country gentleman in *The Wittie Faire One*, I. ii (1633, B3):

> . . . humbly rides th'old fashion
> With halfe a douzen wholesome Liueries,
> To whom he giues Christian wages and not countenance
> Alone to liue on.

154–5. *high men, and low men*, loaded dice which were also called 'high' and 'low fullams'. Cf. Cotton, *The Compleat Gamester*, 1670

(1680), 9, 'This ⟨cheating⟩ they do by false Dice, as High-Fullams, 4, 5, 6, Low-Fullams, 1, 2, 3; and *The London Prodigall*, 1605, A4, 'Item, to my sonne *Mat Flowerdale* I bequeath two bayle of false dyce, *Videlliced*, high men, and loe men, fullomes, stop cater traies, and other bones of function'. *Fullan*, the oldest known form of the word (in *Dice-Play*, c. 1550), probably means 'full one'; but Fulham seems to have been a haunt of gamesters and may have originated the term. Cf. the quibble in Rowley's *A Woman Never Vext*, 1631, p. 19: '*Step*. Soft, this dye is false. *Hugh*. False? you doe him wrong Sir, hee's true to his Master. *Step*. Fullum: *Dick*. I'le be hang'd then: where's Putney then I pray you. *Step*. 'Tis false, and I'le have my money againe.'

169. *stiffeneckt gentleman*. Cf. II. ii. 88–90, IV. i. 36.

172. *ordinaries*. Cf. Chapman, *May-Day*, I. ii (1611, pp. 14, 15): '*Innoc*. But Captaine, did not you say that you would enter me at an Ordinary, that I might learne to conuerse? *Quint*. When thou wilt Lieftenant; No better time then now,' for now th'art in good clothes, which is the most materiall point for thy entrance there. *Innoc*. I but how should I behaue my selfe? *Quint*. Marry Sir, when you come first in, you shall see a crew of Gallants of all sorts: . . . Now will all these I say at your first entrance wonder at you, as at some strange Owle: Examine your person, and obserue your bearing for a time. Doe you then ath' tother side seeme to neglect their obseruance as fast, let your countenance be proofe against all eyes, not yeelding or confessing in it any inward defect. In a word be impudent enough, for thats your chiefe vertue of society. . . . , ther's no prescription for Gentility, but good clothes and impudence: for your place, take it as it fals, but so as you thinke no place to good for you; fall too with ceremony whatsoeuer the company be: and as neere as you can, when they are in their Mutton, be thou in thy Wood-cocke, it showes resolution. Talke any thing, thou car'st not what, so it be without offence, and as nere as thou canst without sence. . . . After dinner there will be play, and if you would be counted compleate, you must venture amongst them; for otherwise, theill take you for a Scholler or a Poet, and so fall into contempt of you.'

176–9. From Erasmus, *Omnia Opera*, 1540, i, p. 604, the account of German inns in the Colloquy on 'Diversoria': 'Quòd si quem conspexerint peregrinæ gentis, qui cultu dignitatis nonnihil præ se ferat, in hunc intenti sunt omnes defixis oculis, contemplantes quasi nouum aliquod animantis genus adductum sit ex Africa.' The last phrase refers to the Greek proverb, καὶ λέγεται δέ τις παροιμία ὅτι ἀεὶ Λιβύη φέρει τι καινόν (Aristotle, *Hist. An.* viii. 28), which Jonson uses again in *D. is A.* I. v. 8–10, *U.V.* xxx. 88.

190. *portcullice of coine*. 'A popular name for the silver halfpenny of Queen Elizabeth (the smallest silver coin issued by her), which bore on the obverse a portcullis and a mint-mark' (*O.E.D.*). These were the coins to which Bacon alluded in the dedication of the first edition of his *Essays*, 1597: 'The late new halfe-pence, which though the Siluer were good, yet the peeces were small.'

195–201. Not, as Steevens suggested, a gird at *Twelfth Night*, which was acted in 1602, but the whole passage defines Jonson's attitude towards romantic comedy, as Greene had already written it in *Frier Bacon and frier Bongay* (printed 1594) and as Shakespeare had already developed it. It is a terse restatement of the position taken up in the prologue to *Every Man in his Humour*.

204. *Ciceros definition.* 'Comoediam esse Cicero ait imitationem vitae, speculum consuetudinis, imaginem veritatis.'—*Donati fragmentum de Comoedia et Tragoedia* (in Gronovius's *Thesaurus Graecorum Antiquitatum*, 1697, viii, p. 1689). Cf. Quintilian's comment on Menander, 'Omnem vitae imaginem expressit' (x. i, § 69). So in *M.L.* ii, Chorus 38–41, Jonson speaks of 'the Glasse of custome (which is *Comedy*)' 'so held up to me, by the *Poet*, as I can therein view the daily examples of mens lives, and images of Truth, in their manners, so drawne for my delight, or profit, as I may (either way) use them'.

208. *the correction of manners.* Cf. the epilogue to Plautus' *Captivi*:

> Spectatores, ad pudicos mores facta haec fabula est . . .
> Huiusmodi paucas poetae reperiunt comoedias,
> ubi boni meliores fiant.

209. *the maker.* Cf. *Disc.* 2409.

III. vii. Sordido's attempt at suicide is not a literary exaggeration. Besides the reference in *Macbeth*, ii. iii. 4, Gifford quotes from *The Curse of Corne-horders: With The Blessing of seasonable Selling. In three Sermons, on Pro. 11. 26* [*Hee that with-holdeth Corne, the people shall curse him: But blessing shall be vpon the head of him who selleth it.*] *Begun at the general Sessions for the County of Cornwall, held at Bodmyn, and continued at Fowy. By Charles Fitz-Geffrie. . . . Printed at London by I. B. . . ., 1631.* The first page notes the royal proclamation authorizing the Justices to force corn into the market. The second sermon, on the people's curse, tells the story of Bishop Hatto, and then (p. 24)—'But these examples of ancient times doe lesse affect, and may be held fabulous. That God hath made the curses of the poore effectuall vpon such couetous Corne-horders, euen in recent remembrance, may appeare by this, that some of this cursed crue haue become their owne executioners, and in kindnesse haue saued the Hang-man a labour by haltering themselues, when contrary to their expectation, the price of corne hath sodainly fallen: and this both in other Countries, and among vs as a Diuiner of good reputation haue deliuered vpon their owne knowledge.' [Marginal note ᵃ mentions 'Lauater, Cartwright ad Text'.] Henry Peacham tells this story in *The Truth of our Times: Revealed out of one Mans Experience*, 1638, pp. 113–14: 'There was a miserable slave not long since, that had kept three or fourescore load of Hay two or three years, hoping it would bee still dearer, when it was at five pounds and ten shillings the load, but presently it falling to forty and thirty shillings, went into his barne, takes a stoole to stand on, and throwing a rope over a beame, kicks downe the stoole, and so hangs: his sonne being threshing on the other side of the wall, hearing the stoole fall, runs in, and seeing his father hanging, takes his knife, and cuts him downe, rubs him, and recovers him: his son a weeke after comming for his weekes wages for threshing, (for his father allowed him nothing but what hee dearely earned) he abated him twopence, which the sonne told him was wanting; his father answered, the rope which he cut cost him so much, and hee should pay for it.' Retelling this story in *The Worth of a Peny*, 1647, p. 19, Peacham locates it 'at Priors Thorne, neere to Swafham in Norfolke,' and deducts one penny for the spoilt rope. Finally John Taylor in *Part of this Summers Travels, Or News from Hell, Hull, and Hallifax*, 1640?, pp. 16–18, even gives the farmer's name: 'At a place called *Priors Thorns*, neere to two Towns, namely, *Northbery* and *Sapham*, [in Norfolk] there dwelt a man named *Frier*, who was rich in substance, but very poore and miserable in his conditions: belike hee had read or heard of a Play that was written 40 years since by Master *Benjamin Iohnson*, the Play is extant, and is called *Every Man out of his Humour*, in which Play was acted and personated a miserly Farmer, that had much corne in his Barnes, and did expect a scant or barren Harvest, that through want and scarcity hee might sell his corne at what deare rates hee pleased, but (contrary to his wicked hopes) the Harvest proved abundantly plentifull, wherefore hee being in an extraordinary merry or mad veine, put himselfe to the charge of the buying of a two peny halter, and went into his Barn as secretly as he could, and putting the halter about his neck with a riding knot, he fastned the other end to a beam, and most neatly hang'd himself: But (as ill luck would have it) his man presently came into the Barne, and espyde his Master so bravely mounted, the unlucky Knave drew his Knife and cut the halter, crying out for helpe as lowde as he could, rubbing and chafing his Master with all care and dilligence to recover him to life againe; at the last he awak'd out of his traunce, and fetch'd a deep groan, began to stare and look about him; and taking the end of the cut halter in his hand, his first words to his man was, Sirrah, who did cut this, O Master (said the fellow) it was I that did it, and I thank God that I came in good time to doe it, and I pray you to take God in your minde, and never more to hazard your soule and body in such a wicked manner: to which good counsell of the poor fellow, the Caitiffe replyde, Sirrah, If you would be medling (like a sawcy busie Rogue) you might have untyde it, that it might have serv'd another time, such an unthrifty Rascall as thou will never be worth such a halter, it cost me two pence, and I will abate the said two pence, for the which the fellow would dwell no longer with him, but went and got him another service: This was acted really and lately at the place aforesaid, in imitation of that part in the Play, of *Every Man out of his Humour*.'

And now for an object-lesson in the growth of a legend. The story goes back in England at least to 1561 when Hoby's translation of *The*

Courtyer of Count Baldessar Castilio appeared: at ii, sig. X, is the following: 'And *M. Augustin Beuazzano* toulde, that a couetous manne whiche woulde not sell hys corne while it was at a highe price, whan he sawe afterwarde it had a great falle, for desperacion he hanged himself vpon a beame in his chamber, and a seruaunt of his hearing the noise, made speede, and seeing his maister hang, furthwith cut in sunder the rope and so saued him from death: afterwarde whan the couetous man came to himselfe, he woulde haue had hys seruaunt to haue paide him for his halter that he had cut.' (See Professor W. Bang in *Englische Studien*, XXVI. ii, pp. 330–2; cf. note on v. ii *infra*.) The *Courtier* appeared originally in 1516.

10. *kept touch*, kept faith.

21. *rug-gownes*, made of hairy frieze and worn by astrologers and mathematicians, e.g. by Doctor Dee (*Alch.* II. vi. 21).

29. *your blessing*. Apparently a pious formula to be inserted in the model letter: cf. Thomas Sanders to his father in *Domestic State Papers (Elizabeth)*, 1580, Addenda xxvii. 12, 'I beg your daily blessing, more worth to me than any worldly treasure.'

31. *contrary to custome*. 'Fungoso imposes on his father; the revels were at Christmas' (Gifford).

42. *Ego sum ortus* . . . Cf. the spurious *Pro Nobilitate*, ascribed to Plutarch, 21: μεχρὶ δὲ τίνος ἀπειρόκαλος ἔσῃ τὸ Ἰφικράτους ἀπόφθεγμα εὐλογήσας; τοιούτῳ δὲ κέχρηταί ποτε καὶ ὁ Τύλλιος. ὁ μὲν οὖν Ἰφικράτης ἀστείως τινι ἑαυτὸν μέν ἀφ' Ἁρμοδίου γένος ἔχειν μεγαλαυχῶντι ἐκείνῳ δὲ ὀνειδίζοντι τὸ ἀγενές, ἀλλὰ μὴν τό μου γένος ἀπ' ἐμοῦ λαμβάνει τὴν ἀρχὴν, τὸ δὲ σὸν ἐν σοὶ λήγει. In Plutarch's *Reg. et Imper. Apophthegmata*, 'Iphicrates', 5, the story is told, but there is no mention of Cicero.

45. *Yours, if his owne*. Cf. *C.R.* v. iv. 605. Slightly varied as 'Youres or not his owne', George Turberville's letter in Gascoigne's *Adventures of Master F. J.* (*A Hundreth sundrie Flowers*, 1572, p. 205), 'More youres than his owne' (ibid., p. 206), or 'Yours as his owne Ihon Derricke' in Derrick's *The Image of Ireland*, 1581, address to the reader.

Simon Daines in his *Orthoepia Anglicana* (1640, p. 82) gives 'Certaine briefe Notes, or Directions, for writing of Letters'. He enjoins (p. 94) that in writing to a parent the 'subscription' should be: '*Your dutifull, your most dutifull*, or, *Most dutifull and respective, Dutifull and most obedient, till death*, &c. whether son or daughter.' While the 'new kind of subscription' used by Fungoso belongs to that class which Daines assigns (p. 93) 'to an adversary, *Yours as you use me. Yours to use, but not abuse. Yours if you please; if not mine owne. Yours as I see cause. Yours when not mine owne*, and the like, as your judgement, and the occasion offered suggest.'

63–5. Cf. Plautus, *Aulularia*, 9–12 (of a miser and his hoard):

Is quoniam moritur (ita avido ingenio fuit)
nunquam indicare id filio voluit suo,
inopemque optauit potius eum relinquere
quam eum thesaurum commonstraret filio.

III. viii. 7. *chance medley*. A popular abbreviation of the law term 'manslaughter by chance-medley', i.e. homicide by misadventure. Cf. *S.W.* III. v. 118.

22. *horse-bread-eating*. Cf. Harrison's *A Description of England*, II. vi (i, p. 153, ed. Furnivall). After saying that gentry eat wheaten bread, Harrison adds that 'their household and poore neighbours in some shires are inforced to content themselues with rie, or barlie, yea, and in time of dearth manie with bread made either of beans, peason, or otes, or of altogither and some acornes among, of which scourge the poorest doo soonest tast, sith they are least able to prouide themselues of better'. When 'the artificer and poore laboring man' cannot get corn, he 'is driuen to content himselfe with horssecorne, I meane, beanes, peason, otes, tares, and lintels: and therefore it is a true prouerbe, and neuer so well verified as now, that hunger setteth his first foote into the horsse manger. If the world last a while after this rate, wheate and rie will be no graine for poore men to feed on; and some caterpillars there are, that can saie so much alreadie.' Similarly J. M. writes in *A Health to the Gentlemanly Profession of Servingmen*, 1598, B1ᵛ, 'As the poore must mixe Beanes and Pease with their Breadcorne this deare yeere, for Wheat and Rie is too highly rated'.

49. *Like an vnsauourie muck-hill*. Cf. *C. is A*. IV. ix. 20. An old saying: cf. W. Bullein, *A Dialogue against the Feuer Pestilence* (1564), p. 4 (of a usurer), 'And like vnto great stinking mucle medin hilles, whiche neuer do pleasure vnto the lande or grounde, vntill their heapes are caste abrode to the profites of many'; and Bacon, *Apophthegmes*, 1625, p. 252, 'Mr. Bettenham vsed to say; *That Riches were like Mucke: When it lay, vpon an heape, it gaue but a stench, and ill odour; but when it was spread vpon the ground, then it was cause of much fruit.*'

57. Quoted in *Englands Parnassus*, 1600, p. 169, under the heading 'Life'.

62. *Acts, and Monuments*. So *S.W.* I. ii. 8–10, 'Hee thinks, I, and my companie are authors of all the ridiculous acts, and moniments are told of him.' A reference to Foxe's *Book of Martyrs*, the first English edition of which, published by John Day in 1563, had the title *Actes and Monuments of these latter and perillous dayes, touching matters of the Church, wherein are comprehended and described the great persecutions & horrible troubles, that haue bene wrought and practised by the Romishe Prelates, speciallye in this Realme of England and Scotlande, from the yeare of our Lorde a thousande, vnto the tyme nowe present*.

For the *Chronicle* of the Quarto cf. Cartwright, *The Ordinary*, 1651, IV. iii:

> *An.* I doubt not, but
> I shall be in the Chronicle for this,
> Or in a Ballad else.

65. *teares trill'd . . . like . . . bowles*. A quibble on the two verbs 'trill', (1) to twirl, (2) to flow in a slender stream.

73. *soggy*, lit. sodden, soaked, or swampy. Sir W. A. Craigie's con-

jecture 'foggie' blends the two senses (1) flabby, not solid, (2) thick, dull. With (1) compare Golding's *Ovid's Met.* xv (1567, p. 189), 'Then greene, and voyd of strength, and lush, and foggye, is the blade' (*insolida* in the original).

87. *Cistellaria.* In Act III. 639–50.

102. *Epitasis.* The old critics divided a comedy into protasis, epitasis, catastasis, and catastrophe. In the argument of *N.I.* 64–5, Jonson notes, '*Here begins, at the* third Act, *the* Epitasis, *or businesse of the* Play'. Cf. *M.L.*, chorus I. 7–13, II. 84.

III. ix. 9. *palme it beares.* A latinism: Varro, *De Re Rustica*, iii. 16. 14 has 'Siculum mel fert palmam'. Cf. *Poet.* v. iii. 321, *U.V.* iii. 6.

15. *richly parted.* Cf. *supra*, Characters, 8.

16. *beefe.* Cf. Sir Andrew Aguecheek's confession in *Tw. Night*, I. iii. 80–1, 'I am a great eater of beefe, and I beleeue that does harme to my wit'; and Burton, *Anatomy of Melancholy*, 1624, p. 87: '*Beefe*, a strong & hearty meat, (cold in the first degree, dry in the second *Galen lib. 3. cap. 1. de alim. sac.*) is condemned by him, and all succeeding Authors, to breed grosse melancholy blood.'

17. *rince his . . . guts.* A drinking phrase: cf. Marston, *What You Will*, III. ii (1607, D4), 'I was liquord soundly my guts were rinc'd for the heauens'.

22. *put off*, take off my hat. Dekker's advice to a gallant illustrates Maciente: 'Sucke this humour vp especially: Put off to none vnlesse his hatband be of a newer fashion then yours, & three degrees quainter: but for him that weares a trebled cipers about his hatte (though he were an Aldermans sonne) neuer moue to him' (*The Guls Horne-booke*, 1609, p. 20).

23. *Lord Chancelors tombe.* The tomb of Sir Christopher Hatton (ob. 1591) in Saint Paul's choir, a massive structure celebrated by Bishop Corbet:

> Nor need the Chancellor boast whose Pyramis
> Above the Host and Altar reared is.
> *(Iter Boreale, Poems, 1672, p. 30.)*

Near by were unpretending tablets to Sir Philip Sidney and his father-in-law Sir Francis Walsingham; hence the epigram in Stow (*Survay*, 1603, p. 340):

> Philip and Francis haue no Tombe,
> For great Christopher takes all the roome.

This monument was one of the sights of London: Dekker in *The Guls Horne-booke*, 1609, ch. iv, p. 21, advises the visitor to go up the steeple and cut his name on the leads, and then 'your next worthy worke is, to repaire to my Lord *Chancellors Tomb*'.

the Shriues posts. Set up before the doors of a sheriff's or a mayor's house for proclamations to be posted on them. Whalley says it was usual for people to uncover when reading them. Gifford compares *The*

Puritaine, III. v (1607, E), '*Pyb*. Wee will attend his worship—worship I thinke, for so muche the Posts at his doore should signifie.' Cf. *C.R.* I. iv. 101–2, 'The prouident painting of his posts against hee should haue beene *Prætor*'; *Lingua*, II. iii (1607, D3), 'knowes he how to become a Scarlet gowne, hath he a paire of fresh posts at his doore? . . . why then choose him Mayor vpon my credit, heele proue a wise officer'; *The Faire Maide of the Inne*, III. i, 'all as neate as a *Magnifi⟨c⟩o*'s post new painted, at his entrance to an office'.

30. *base violl* or *violl de Gambo* (2499), a viol held between the legs while being played, a violoncello (see *O.E.D.* s.v. 'Bass viol' and 'viol da Gamba'). For its use in courtship see Marston, *Pigmalions Image*, &c., 1598, p. 28, Sat. i:

> Come *Brisus*, by the soule of Complement,
> I'le not endure that with thine instrument
> (Thy Gambo violl plac'd betwixt thy thighes,
> Wherein the best part of thy courtship lyes)
> Thou entertaine the time, thy Mistres by:
> Come, now lets heare thy mounting *Mercurie*,
> What mum? giue him his fiddle once againe,
> Or he's more mute then a *Pythagoran*.

The wooer's name, methods, and ineffectiveness are closely parallel to Jonson.

39. *loose*. 'Th' Archers terme, who is not said to finish the feate of his shot before he giue the loose, and deliuer his arrow from his bow.'— Puttenham, *The Arte of English Poesie*, 1589, III. xvi, p. 145. Cf. *N.I.* II. vi. 229, *Disc.* 1717.

45. *shiuering*. Cf. Macilente's irony, III. iii. 12–16, and *C.R.* III. v. 9–12.

50. *vauting horse*, a wooden horse for gymnastic practice. For its use in courtship see *C.R.* II. i. 63–6, and Donne, *The Progresse of the Soule*, ll. 464–7, describing one who was the

> First that could make love faces, or could doe
> The valters sombersalts, or us'd to wooe
> With hoiting gambolls, his owne bones to breake
> To make his mistresse merry.

65. St. dir. *takes tobacco betweene*. Chapman, *Al Fooles*, II. i (1605, D3):

> And for discourse in my faire Mistresse presence,
> I did not as you barraine Gallants doe,
> Fill my discourses vp drinking Tobacco.

69. *as a parenthesis*. Cf. *C.R.*, Ind. 120–31, a speech punctuated with long dashes, and a marginal note '*At the breaches he takes his tobacco*'.

72. *rush*. *C.R.* II. v. 18, 19 n.

82. *wit, for ingenuitie*. So in Lord Falkland's *Epistle To his Noble ffather, Mʳ Jonson*:

> I thought you proud, for I did surely knowe,
> had I Ben: Jonson, bene, I had beene soe. . . .
> Now I recant; And doubt, whether your Store
> of Ingenuity, or Ingenie, be more!

'Ingenious' and 'ingenuous' were completely confused in the seventeenth century, and 'ingenuity' served as the abstract noun for either. In IV. iv. 73 the Folio has 'ingenuously', in *C.R.* IV. i. 33 'ingeniously', correctly in each instance, where the Quartos give the opposite reading.

104–5. *I haue wisht . . . that instrument.* The point of this 'good iest' is that it was a stale lover's conceit. Marston had already satirized it in *The Scourge of Villanie*, 1598, G4, Sat. viii:

> *Saturio* wish'd him selfe his Mistres buske,
> That he might sweetly lie, and softly luske
> Betweene her pappes, . . .
> . . .   But out on *Phrigio*,
> That wish'd he were his Mistres puppie cur, to goe
> And licke his Mistres fist, . . .
> But *Punicus*, of all I'le beare with thee,
> That faine would'st be thy Mistres smug Munkey,
> Here's one would be a flea, (iest comicall)
> Another his sweet Ladies verdingall
> To clip her tender breech; Another he
> Her siluer-handled fanne would gladly be,
> Here's one would be his Mistres neck-lace faine,
> To clip her faire, and kisse her azure vaine.
> Fond fooles, well wish'd, and pittie but should bee,
> For beastly shape to brutish soules agree.

Shakespeare played with the conceit in *Sonnet* cxxviii, and lifted it into poetry in *Rom. and Jul.* II. ii. 23–6:

> See how she leanes her cheeke vpon her hand.
> O that I were a Gloue vpon that hand,
> That I might touch that cheeke.

105. *a thousand times, and not so few.* Cf. IV. v. 47, *C.R.* I. iv. 187.

114. *dance after your pipe.* There was an old dance tune called 'The Shaking of the Sheets' or 'Dance after my Pipe', which is given in Chappell's *Popular Music of the Olden Time*, i. 228. Cf. *Iohn Heywoodes woorkes*, 1562, Part II, ch. vi, Hiij:

> she hath . . . suche toies in her hed.
> That to daunce after her pipe, I am ny led.

131. *a woodcockes head.* Gifford showed the point of the comparison by reproducing a drawing of an old pipe. Saviolina quibbles on 'woodcock' as a cant name for a fool, as Shift does at IV. vi. 46. Cf. the proverbial 'springes to catch woodcocke' (*Hamlet*, I. iii. 115) to denote obvious traps.

H h

135. *plaine-song . . . runne . . . diuision vpon it.* 'Divisions in the musical nomenclature of the seventeenth and eighteenth centuries were rapid passages, slow notes divided into quick ones, as naturally takes place in variations on a theme or ground. Hence the word can be applied to quick consecutive passages, like the long semi-quaver runs in Handel's *bravura* songs' (Grove, *Dictionary of Music*). C. B. Mount in *Notes & Queries*, 8th Series, viii, p. 281, comments: 'The division or breaking up of a series of notes may be done in either of two ways: by voice or instrument making florid variation on its own simpler theme; or by one instrument against another, the one giving the "ground", the other "dividing", the two producing harmony. This latter sort of division would be the same as "descant".' He quotes Christopher Simpson, *The Division-Violist*, 1659, p. 21, where it is stated that there are 'Three sorts of Division expressed on the Viol, *viz.* Breaking the Ground, Descanting upon it, and Mixture of these together'. Simpson defines them: 'Breaking the ground is the dividing its Notes into more diminute Notes' (ibid.) ; 'Diminutive, or Descant Division is That which maketh another distinct, and concording Part unto the Ground' (p. 28); 'Mixt-Division, I call that which mixeth Descant, & Breaking the Ground.' Jonson has the metaphor again in *C.R.* I. ii. 68, *Poet.* IV. v. 191, *S.S.* III. iv. 15.

IV. i. 12. *first head*: cf. III. iii. 48.
giue me the head: cf. v. xi. 22.
19. *beast that I am to say it.* Cf. *E.M.I.* II. ii. 19.
39. *case of pick-tooths.* A foreign importation, affected by courtiers. Overbury says of his 'affected traveller'—'his pick-tooth is a maine part of his behauiour' (*Characters*, 1614, E1v). Cf. *C.R.* I. i. 73, II. iii. 88; *D. is A.* V. i. 41.

IV. ii. 12. *peeke-boe* (F1). For this form cf. the verb 'peek' in Palsgrave, 1530, 655/2, 'I peke or prie, *je pipe* hors'. 'Peekbo' or 'peekabo' survives in the United States. F2 substitutes 'boe-peep', which Ff agree in reading in *C.R.* v. iv. 256.
16. *come vp to supper.* For this ironic invitation cf. *Iohn Heywoodes woorkes*, 1562, Pt. II, ch. i, Fij:

> Gup with a galde backe gill, come vp to supper.
> What mine old mare woulde haue a new crouper.

And Chapman, *The Blinde begger of Alexandria*, 1598, D2. Elinine says to her sister 'nymphs' boasting that they will have jewellery and fine clothes like her, 'Come vp to supper, it will become the house wonderfull well.'
34. *kissing ladies pumps.* Cf. *C.R.* III. iv. 67, *Poet.* I. ii. 47; Fletcher and Massinger, *The Little French Lawyer*, I. i (Fol. 1647, p. 52):

> Some times admitted, and vouchsaf'd to kisse
> Her glove, her skirt, nay, I have heard, her slippers.

35. *Holding the cloth for them.* Cf. *C.R.* v. iv. 40–1, of courtiers, 'This prouides coaches; This repeates iests; This presents gifts; This holds vp the arras.' Marston, *What You Will*, iv. i (1607, F2), 'He is a fine Courtier, . . . and holds vp the arras, supportes the tapistry, when I passe into the presence, very gracefully'.

44. *like the Zani*, attendant on a mountebank. Cf. *C.R.* ii. iii. 102, 'The other gallant is his *Zani*, and doth most of these trickes after him'; *Volp.* ii. i. 28, iii. i. 33; Dekker, *The Guls Horne-booke*, 1609, ch. vi, 'Your Inne-a-court man is Zany to the Knights, and (marry very scuruily) comes likewise limping after it.'

49. *vnrude*, rude, unmannerly, uncouth. A variant of *unride* (OE. *unȝerȳde*), rough, violent (*O.E.D.*). Jonson and his contemporaries probably associated the epithet with 'rude'. The earliest quotation in the *O.E.D.* is from William Fullwood's ballad, *A Supplication to Eldertonne for Leache's Vnlewdnes, Desiring him to pardone his manifest vnrudeness*, 1561–2 (printed in *Old Ballads*, Percy Society, p. 57), 'For you may see he is in deed An unrude simple man.' Jonson has the word again in *M. Christmas*, 106, and *Ent. Blackfriars*, 46.

79. *pease . . . peace.* Repeated *M.L.* iv. vii. 11. Beaumont and Fletcher also have the pun in *A King and No King*, ii. ii. 160 (ed. Bond).

81. Gifford wrongly marked a new scene here, ending at line 103. The comedy that follows is played with the help of the two doors on either side of the stage, often mentioned in the old stage-directions. Cf. Middleton, *The Changeling*, 1653, D3ᵛ, where the passage of Alonzo and de Flores through the fort to the vault in Act iii is indicated by the direction 'Ex. at one door & enter at the other'; *The Spanish Gipsie*, 1653, I3, where at the end of Act v, scene i, Alvarez says to Louis

> Walke off my Lord
> To the next Field, you shall know all,

and after Louis's reply, the stage-direction 'Ex. at one dore; Enter presently at the other' marks the prompt passage to the field.

99. *in Fetter-lane* near the Inns of Court.

100. *say on*, try on. Spelt ''ssayes', *Ep.* xii. 9.

iv. iii. 15. *turne Turke.* A phrase for a complete change, here ludicrously misapplied.

24. *autenticall*, licensed: cf. *All's Well*, ii. iii. 12–14, where Galen and Paracelsus are 'learned and authentic fellows'.

33. *vnctions, to make our skinnes impenetrable.* The 'vaine-glorious Knight' revives the faded memories of ordeal by battle when the combatants swore to make no use of magic to aid them.

33–4. *trauaile inuisible . . . a ring.* The powder is fern-seed, supposed to make those who carried it invisible. The ring is the fabled ring of Gyges, king of Lydia, which made him invisible when he turned the bezel inwards towards the palm of the hand (Cicero, *de Officiis*, iii. 19. 78) ; or the ring of Angelica in Boiardo's *Orlando Inamorato* and Ariosto's

Orlando Furioso, which had the same effect when put in the bearer's mouth. Cf. *N.I.* I. vi. 16–22; *1 Henry IV*, II. i. 83–4, 'we haue the receit of Fern-seede, we walke inuisible'; and Massinger, *The Fair Maid of the Inne*, I. i (Beaumont and Fletcher Folio 1647, p. 29):

> Why did you think that you had *Giges* ring,
> Or the herbe that gives invisibility?

35–6. *three-forked charme . . . into his collar.* Whalley refers to Cornelius Agrippa's dog as described by Paulus Iovius, *Elogia Doctorum Virorum*, 1596, p. 187: 'Excessit e vita nondum senex apud Lugdunum ignobili & tenebroso in diuersorio, multis eum tanquam Necromantiæ suspicione infamem execrantibus, quod Cacodæmonem nigri canis specie circumduceret, ita vt cum propinqua morte ad pænitentiam vergeretur, cani collare loreum magicis per clavorum emblemata inscriptum notis exsolverit, in hæc suprema verba irate prorumpens, Abi, perdita bestia, quæ me totum perdidisti.'

39–42. Fynes Moryson in his *Itinerary*, 1617, Part I, p. 235, mentions a certificate that was given him at the Latin Monastery at Jerusalem: 'Moreouer they gaue to each of vs freely and vnasked (as it seemes of custome) as well to vs Laymen as to the Friars, a testimony vnder the seale of their Monastery, that we had been at *Ierusalem*, and for better credit, they expressed therein some markable signes of our faces and bodies.'

75. *froted*, massaged. Cf. Marston, *What You Will*, III. iii (1607, E4^v): 'I curle his perriwig, painte his cheekes, perfume his breath, I am his froterer or rubber in a Hot-house, the prop of his lies, the bearer of his false dice.'

78. *our poxe.* Cf. Gayton, *Pleasant Notes upon Don Quixote*, 1654, p. 21: 'Father *Ben* (when one unhappily mulcted for peeping into holes, he had no right to, swore he had got a clap, which he called the *French* Pox) was worthily wroth at the expression, and in a fume, said, why not (Sr) the English Pox? we have as good and as large as they have any.'

81. *salt.* A quibble (1) pungent, stinging; (2) salacious. Cf. *Volp.* IV. iii. 23.

82. *porpuse.* Elsewhere Jonson spells 'porcpisce' (*Sej.* v. 622, *Volp.* II. i. 40, *S.W.* IV. iv. 144).

lieger, lit. a resident ambassador. Cf. *D. is A.* v. vi. 64, *S. of N.* I. v. 20, *For.* xiii. 72.

83. *Hornes ordinarie yonder.* Probably the Fleet-street tavern noticed in *Maroccus Extaticus*, 1595, B2^v, 'had you . . . taken some of the excellent Muscadine at the Horne'; and *Father Hubbards Tales*, 'his eating must be in some famous tavern, as the Horn, the Mitre, or the Mermaid' (Bullen's *Middleton*, viii, p. 77).

84. *droning a tabacco pipe.* Cf. *S.W.* IV. i. 65, 'as he lyes on his backe droning a tobacco pipe'. The phrase is a quibble on the 'drone' or brass pipe of a bag-pipe.

88 foll. For the point of this training see *The Guls Horne-booke*, 1609,

ch. v, pp. 24–5: 'Before the meate come smoaking to the board, our Gallant must draw out his Tobacco-box, the ladell for the cold snuffe into the nostrill, the tongs and prining [read priming] Iron: All which artillery may be of gold or siluer (if he can reach to the price of it) it will bee a reasonable vsefull pawne at all times, when the current of his money falles out to run low.'

89. *Patoun*, Gifford suggests, 'may be moulding tobacco, which was then always cut small, into some fantastic or fashionable form for the pipe': he refers the word to the French *pâton*, a pellet of paste to feed chickens. Brathwaite writes in *The Smoaking Age*, 1617, p. 94, 'So as, no meat can be well digested . . . till a pipe of *Tobacco* be exhaled, yea sometimes a whole *Petoun* of *Indian* fume be exhausted': this seems to mean a lump or a larger quantity. The form of the word is perhaps a variant of 'Petun', once a fairly common name for tobacco: see *O.E.D.*

90. *Receit reciprocall*, 'not improbably what Decker, in the *Gull's Hornbook*, calls the *ring*, that is, as I suppose, passing the pipe from one to another' (Gifford).

92. *piece of Perspectiue*, peep-show. Cf. *Alch.* III. iv. 87.

95. *poking-sticke*, a small steel rod for setting the plaits of a ruff.

100. *as a barber . . . bloud*. Barbers at this date performed minor operations in surgery: see *Poet.* III. iv. 103, *S.W.* III. v. 97–8.

109. *slicke*, sleek. The noun 'slicking' occurs in *C.R.*, palinode, 22; the verb 'sleek' in *Cat.* I. 562, II. 64.

110. *Lynceus*, the Argonaut, proverbially famous for his keen sight, also alluded to in *Sej.* IV. 473, *B.F.* II. i. 4.

IV. iv. 5. *figment*. Cf. *C.R.* I. iv. 22, of Lucian, 'He doth feed you with fittons, figments, and leasings.'

6. *pulse of my watch*. Cf. *S. of N.* I. i. 11, 12:

> Three, foure, fiue, six. Inough, inough, deare watch,
> Thy pulse hath beate inough.

8. *Patricians of Sparta*. Apparently chosen to suggest haughty exclusiveness, but Gifford suggests the term is as laxly used as 'Greek' or 'Trojan' in the literature of the time.

9. *tenne i'the hundred*, the legal rate of interest as fixed by a statute of the thirteenth of Elizabeth ('An Acte agaynst Vsurie'). Cf. *Poet.* III. iv. 175 (Quarto reading), *S. of N.* II. i. 4 n.

14, 15. *Sattin . . . Sathan*. A common pun. Cf. Heywood, *A Mayden-Head well lost*, 1634, III. ii: '*Lau.* Then take your Sattin farther. *Clow.* Your Ladiship hath coniur'd me, and I will auoide Satan'; and Taylor, *Superbiæ Flagellum*, 1621, C2v:

> That which kept twenty, in the dayes of old,
> By Sathan is turn'd sattin, silke, and gold.

For the satin doublet of a respectable tradesman see *E.H.* I. i. 114 n.

16. *darknesse . . . shop*. Dishonest tradesmen were accused of having

ill-lighted shops to enable them to palm off inferior goods undetected on their customers. See Middleton's *Michaelmas Terme*, 1607, where the woollen-draper Quomodo has Shortyard and Falselight for his attendants, and remarks (II. iii. 109–11), ''tis always misty weather in our shops here; we are a nation the sun ne'er shines upon'.

17. *blankes*, bonds ready drawn for mortgaging estates.

18. *the verge*. The Verge extended for twelve miles round the King's place of residence, wherever he happened to be. Cf. *C.R.* IV. i. 150, *Love Restored*, 78, and the metaphor in *M.L.* IV. vii. 41.

27. *rest*. A quibble (1) on the musket-rest (*E.M.I.* II. v. 143); (2) on its semicircular top in Puntarvolo's reply; (3) on its hanging from the shoulder, when not in use, in the further remark on 'Suspended' (l. 29).

49. *properer*, handsomer, as in 61.

73. *made of*. Cf. A. Dent, *The Plain Mans Path-way to Heauen*, 1617, p. 77, of a hawk 'which a man holdeth vpon his fist, stroketh her, maketh of her, taketh great delight and pleasure in her'.

75. *casting-glasse*, a bottle for sprinkling scent. Cf. Marston, *Antonio and Mellida*, Part I, 1603, E3, '*Enter Castilio and his Page. Castilio with a casting bottle of sweete water in his hand, sprinkling himselfe.* | *Cast.* Am not I a most sweete youth now.'

78. *garbe*. Cf. II. i. 85.

87. *Precisianisme*, Puritanism. Cf. *C. is A.* II. iii. 26.

93–4. Quoted in *Englands Parnassus*, 1600, p. 189, under the heading 'Loue'.

101. *starcht beard*. Gifford quotes John Taylor, *Superbiæ Flagellum* (1621, C7ᵛ), a *locus classicus* on beards:

> Some seeme as they were starched stiffe and fine,
> Like to the bristles of some angry swine.

110. *like a shield of brawne*. Cf. the introductory note on 'The Characters', 26.

119. *Sir Dagonet*, also alluded to in *C.R.* v. iv. 549, is the fool in the *Morte d'Arthur*, but the reference is to the archery club of Finsbury: see *T.T.* III. vi. 5 n. and Shallow's reminiscences in *2 Henry IV*, III. ii. 271–2, 'I remember at Mile-end-Greene, . . . I was then Sir *Dagonet* in Arthurs Show.'

IV. v. 18. *Europe*. Sogliardo is affected by his company: cf. II. i. 30, v. ii. 25; but the reference to the 'walls' is a heightening touch.

35. *Pickt-hatch*. Cf. *E.M.I.* I. ii. 93.

36. *Bid-stand*. Perhaps coined by Jonson. Gifford quotes Killigrew, *The Parson's Wedding*, I. i (*Comedies*, &c., 1664, p. 74): 'If you dare do this, I shall sing a song of one that bad stand, and made a Carrier pay a dear Rent for a little ground upon his Majesties high-way.'

37. *New-market . . . Gads-Hill*. Cf. J. M., *A Health to the Gentlemanly profession of Seruingmen*, 1598, 13ᵛ: (When a servingman is dismissed) 'What shall he then do? Shall he make his appearance at Gaddes hill,

Shooters hill, Salisburie playne, or Newmarket heath, to sit in Commission, and examine passengers?' And T. M., *The Blacke Booke*, 1604, C3, 'Sometimes they are Clarkes of *Newe-market Heathe*, sometimes the Sheriffes of *Salisburie Plaine*; and another time they commit Brothelrye, when they make many a man stand at *Hockley* in the Hole.'

Hockley i'the hole. 'Ray Street and Coppice Row, and the Clerkenwell Workhouse occupy the site, which still continues below the level of the neighbourhood' (Cunningham).

Gadshill between Gravesend and Rochester was notorious. Shakespeare's commentators refer to a ballad called *The Robery at Gaddes Hill* in 1558 (Arber, *Stationers' Register*, i. 96) and to Sir Roger Manwood's memorandum against Curtall, Manweringe, and other malefactors in Kent in Lansdowne MS. 63, no. 16. Cf. also S. Rowlands's reference to '*Burstow-causie, Gads-hill*, and *Coome-parke*' in *The Knave of Clubbs*, 1611, B4ᵛ, and John Clavell's *A Recantation of an ill led Life*, 1628, p. i: '*Gadd's-hill*, and those Red tops of Mountaines, where good people lose, Their ill kept purses.' *Shirburn Ballads*, xxxii, stanza 10, p. 132:

> Then, following his fancy and wicked lewde will,
>   watching for purses and robbing for gould,
> He traveled to *Kent*; and vpon *Gad's-hill*
>   at last he was taken, and layd vp in hould.   [J. M.]

55. *bell-ropes.* A joke on their 'hanging' from the bell-levers: cf. *Thierry and Theodoret*, II. i (ed. Waller, vol. x, p. 21), 'No more for feare o'th' bell ropes.'

61. *Elder tree.* A medieval tradition: Mandeville saw the tree in Jerusalem near the pool of Siloam (*Travels*, ed. Hamelius, i, p. 61). Cf. *Piers Plowman*, Passus I, 65–6 (A text, Trinity MS.):

> Judas he iapide . with Jewene siluer
> And siþen on an Eldir . hangide him affir.

And Gerrarde's *Herball* (1597, p. 1240), 'It [the Arbor Iudae] may be called in English Judas tree, whereon Iudas did hang himselfe, and not vpon the Elder tree, as it is said.'

62. *Captain Pod.* Cf. *B.F.* v. i. 8, with the marginal reference to Pod as 'a Master of motions', and the contemptuous references in *Ep.* xcvii. 2, cxxix. 16. He is 'Captain *Pod* of *Py-corner*' in Smithfield in Day and Chettle's play, *The Blind-Beggar of Bednal-Green*, 1659, G2, where puppet-shows are cried. Cf. Dekker and Wilkins's *Iests to make you Merie*, 1607, p. 32, 'he thought like *Bankes* his horse, or the *Baboones*, or captaine *Pold* with his motion, shee would haue showne him some strange & monstrous sight'.

64. *Holden.* His camel, says Gifford, was 'a beast of parts'. He is mentioned by Taylor, and in very good company:

> That for ingenuous study downe can put
> Old *Holden's* Camell, or fine *Bankes* his Cut.
>   *A Cast over the Water* (*Works*, 1630, p. 159).

68. *Countenance . . . Resolution.* Cunningham compares *Wit At seuerall Weapons*, IV. i (Beaumont and Fletcher Folio, 1647, p. 84):

> *Mir.* 'Tis very sociably done, Sir, farewell performance,
> I shall be bold to call you so.
> *Cun.* Do, sweet confidence.

IV. vi. 10. *bracelet of her haire.* Cf. *C.R.* palinode 19, and Brathwaite, *A Strappado for the Diuell*, 1615, p. 126 ('The Courtier'):

> He smells of Complement, in presence faire,
> And vses oft to weare bracelets of haire,
> Swearing they came from such, but tis not so,
> For 'twas some *tyre-woman* he tooke them fro.

44. *corroborated*, firmly (or, perhaps, securely) put to him.

46. *woodcocks.* A quibble, as in III. ix. 131.

60. *Bankes . . . with his horse.* Bankes exhibited his performing bay, Marocco, at the 'Crosse Keyes in Gracious-streete' before Tarlton's death in 1588, according to *Tarlton's Jests*, 1600; and at 'Bel-sauage without Ludgate' in 1595, according to the tract *Maroccus Extaticus*. A ballad 'shewing the strange qualities of a yonge nagge called Morocco' was entered on the Stationers' Register on 14 November 1595; and there are references, before the present play, in Nashe's *Haue with You to Saffron Walden*, 1596, Sir John Davies's *Epigrams*, and Bastard's *Chrestoleros*, 1598.

the fellow with the elephant. Another London performer about 1594: Gifford quotes Donne, *Satyre* i. 79–82 (dated 1593 in Harley MS. 5110):

> But to a grave man, he doth move no more
> Then the wise politique horse would heretofore,
> Or thou O Elephant or Ape wilt doe,
> When any names the King of Spaine to you.

Cf. Davies, *Epigrammes*, 30 (dated 1594 in Bodley MS. Rawl. Poet. 212), on 'Dacus', who writes prose speeches for showmen, among them 'the man y^t keepes ye Eliphant', Bankes, and 'him y^t with ye Ape doth playe'.

62. *his picture . . . in a cloth*: the showman's advertisement, as in *B.F.* v. i. 1.

70. *in-auspicious.* The first syllable is to be accentuated—an extension of the principle stated in *Gram.* i. ch. vii. 34–40.

72 foll. Fleay (i, p. 361) noted the similar duel in Dekker and Cheetle's *Patient Grissill*, which was probably acted early in 1600. See the Quarto of 1603, E3^v–E4^v:

> *Emu.* Sir *Owen* and my selfe encountring, I vailde my vpper garment, and enriching my head againe with a fine veluet cap, which I then wore, with a band to it of Orient Pearle and Golde, and a foolish sprig of some nine or ten pound price, or so, wee grewe to an emparlance. . . .

Emu. I was then encountred with a pure Toledo siluered: and eleuating mine arme, in the drawing (by Jesu sweete Madame, my rich cloake loaded with Pearle, which I wore at your sister *Grissils* bridall, I made it then (by God) of meere purpose, to grace the Court, and so foorth) that foolish garment dropped downe: the buttons were illustrious and resplendant diamonds, but tis all one. . . .

. . . the welsh Knight making a very desperate thrust at my bosome, before God fairely mist my imbroydered Ierkin that I then wore, and with my ponyard vapulating and checking his engine downe, it cut mee a payre of very imperiall cloth of golde hose, at least thus long thwart the cannon, at least.

Iul. And mist your leg?

Fa. I, and his hose too.

Emu. And mist my leg (most bright starre) which aduantagious signe I (   ) this legge (hauing a fayre carnation silke stocking on) stumbled, my spangled garters in that imprision fell about my feete, and he fetching a most valarous and ingenious careere, inuaded my Rapier hand, entred this gilded fort, and in that passado vulnerated my hand thus deepe I protest, and contest heauen.

Iul. No more, its too tragicall.

Emu. I conclude, I thought (by the *Synthorisis* of my soule) I had not been imperished, till the bloud shewing his red tincture, at the top of a faire enueloped gloue, sunke along my arme, & spoil'd a rich wastecoate wrought in silke, and golde, a toy *&c.*

Far. Hee'll strip himselfe out of his shirt anone, for Gods sake step in. (They do so, & expose a sound arm in the scarfe.)

Dekker and Chettle may have copied Jonson, but it is possible that there had been a courtiers' duel in which no damage was done to anything but their clothes (E. K. Chambers, *Elizabethan Stage*, iii, p. 292).

82. *rasht*, slashed. Cf. *The Faerie Queene*, iv. ii. 17, 'And shields did share, and mailes did rash, and helmes did hew'.

84. *cable hatband.* Cf. Ind. 111.

85. *murrey.* Cotgrave has '*morée*, a kind of murrey, or darke-red colour'.

90. *purles*, pleats, frills. Cf. *Ent. Bolsover*, 167; *Und.* ii (8), 23, xv. 65, xlii. 16.

Italian cut-worke band . . . cost me three pound. Cf. H. Peacham, *The Truth of our Times*, 1638, p. 61, 'hee is not a gentleman, nor in the fashion, whose band of Italian cut-work now standeth him not at the least in three or four pounds. Yea a Semster in Holborne told mee that these are of threescore pound price a piece.'

99. *stramazoun.* 'A vertical downward cut in rapier fence, which is delivered at the head with the part of the weapon close to the point' (Hutton, quoted in *O.E.D.*).

102. *hangers.* Cf. *E.M.I.* i. v. 81.

107. *wrought shirt.* Cf. Stubbes, *The Anatomie of Abuses*, 1583, ed. Furnivall, p. 53: 'And these shurts (sometimes it happeneth) are wrought

through out with nedle work of silke, and suche like, and curiouslie stitched with open seame, and many other knackes besydes, mo than I can describe.' Later editions add: 'In so much as I haue heard of Shirtes that haue cost some ten shillynges, some twentie, some fortie, some fiue pound, some twentie Nobles and (which is horrible to heare) some ten pounde a peece.'

111. *ruffle of my boot*, the top of the boot which turned over with a fringed and scalloped edge, and hung loosely over the leg. Cf. T. M., *The Ant and the Nightingale*, 1604, C4: 'I beheld a curious payre of Bootes of King Philips leather, in such artificiall wrinckles, sets and pleats, as if they had bene starcht lately, and came new from the Laundresses. . . . But that which struck vs most into admiration, vpon those fantasticall Bootes, stood such huge and wide tops, which so swallowed vp his thyes that had he sworne, as other Gallants did, this common Oath, Would I might sinke as I stand, all his body might very well haue sunke downe and bene damnd in his bootes.'

112. *Spanish leather*, the *cordovan*, highly valued. *D. is A.* IV. iv. 71-2; Massinger, *The City Madam*, 1658, I. i.

> *Ladye.*   Where are my Shoos.
> *Milliscent.* Those that your Ladyship gave order
> Should be made of the Spanish Perfum'd Skins.

143. *long of.* Cf. *Love's Labour's Lost*, II. i. 118, *Mids. N. Dream*, III. ii. 339.

euill angels. Cf. *C. is A.* IV. viii. 73.

IV. vii. 27. *master Snip*. Snipsnap, the tailor, is addressed in *The Faithful Friends*, II. iii, 'Spoke like a man, bold snip'; and Stuffe, the lady's tailor, in *N.I.* v. ii. 9, is dismissed with 'Hang him poore snip, a secular shop-wit!' For the origin of the name see Holme, *Academy of Armory*, 1688, iii, p. 290: 'That Proverb, or by Word . . . used to the Taylors. Snip-snap quoth the Taylors Shears. Alas poor Louse beware thy Ears.'

46. *white monie*, silver. Cf. *B.F.* II. vi. 137, and Middleton, *The Phœnix*, 1607, I. vi, 'Yet I hope he had so much grace before he died to turn his white money into gold, a great ease to his executor.'

52. *the philosopher*. Perhaps referring to Democritus' ὁ κόσμος σκηνή, ὁ βίος πάροδος· ἦλθες, εἶδες, ἀπῆλθες (T. Gale's *Opuscula Mythologica, Ethica*, &c., Camb., 1691). Cf. Sharpham, *Cupids Whirligig*, 1607, EIᵛ, 'Gentlemen, doe you not knowe the Philosopher saith this world is but a stage: *hodie mihi, cras tibi*: tis my part to day, it may be some of yours to morrowe.'

67. *depart with*, part with.

IV. viii. 19. *ninth heauen* . . . 26. *christall crowne of the skie*. Cf. *Ep.* cxxx. 11-14, and W. Alley, *The poore mans Librarie*, 1571, ii, p. 59: 'The philosophers do saye, that there be x. heauens: whereof seuen haue the names of the planets, as of: Saturnus. Iupiter. Mars. Sol. Venus. Mer-

curius. Luna. The eight heauen is called *cœlum sydereum, siue stellatum,*
the ninth they called *cœlum aqueum, vel crystallynum*: not of coldnesse,
but of clearnesse: because by that the starres did clearly appeare and
shine. The tenth they called *primum mobile.*'

29. *Adonis gardens.* Cf. *C.R.* v. x. 112. The Ἀδώνιδος κῆποι of the
Greeks (Plato, *Phaedrus* 276 B; Theocritus, xv. 113) were quick-growing
plants grown in pots for the festival of Adonis; hence a symbol of short-
lived pleasure. But the Elizabethans, headed by Spenser, misinterpreted
the phrase as a synonym for an earthly paradise: see *Colin Clout's come
home again,* 804–8, *The Faerie Queene,* iii. vi, st. 42–50. Fletcher in *The
Loyal Subject,* iii. vi (Folio 1647, p. 39), speaking of the Court, copies
Jonson:

> this place is pleasure,
> Preserv'd to that use, so inhabited;
> And those that live here, live delightfull, joyfull:
> These are the Gardens of Adonis, Ladies,
> Where all sweets, to their free and noble uses,
> Grow ever young and courted.

34. *too perfectly off.* No aposiopesis or 'bogg'd invention' (iii. ix. 41).
Jonson has these set speeches occasionally, and likes to comment on
them critically: cf. Bobadill's praise of tobacco in *E.M.I.* iii. v. 76–94,
with Kno'well's remark 'This speech would ha' done decently in a
tabacco-traders mouth'.

37. *stoues in Sweden.* Dekker in *The Dead Tearme,* 1608, C2, says of
the law: 'no *Stoues* in *Muscouy* can put a man into more violent
sweates'. For the 'Flaunders' of the Quarto cf. Coryat's reference in
the *Crudities,* 1611, p. 153, to the one 'stew, stoue, or hot house' that
he saw in Italy at Padua: 'but afterward when I came into Rhetia,
Heluetia, high Germany, and some parts of the Netherlands, there is
such frequent use of them in all those countries, especially in the winter,
that I lay not in any house whatsoeuer but it had a stoue.'

110. *manfrede it* (Q), revised, while the Folio was at the press, to
'vndertake', is an apparently impossible form. If sound, it depends for
its point on some allusion now completely lost. Possibly the word is
a misprint. Henry Bradley 'felt inclined to suggest that Ben may have
invented a verb *manprende* (French *mainprendre*), and when he found
that the printers had misread his copy, was led to the sensible decision
to stick to plain English'.

123. *Rosa-solis.* Originally a cordial made or flavoured from the plant
sundew (*ros solis*); then brandy or spirits entered into its composition.
Cf. *M.L.* iii. iii. 21, and J. Cooke, *Greenes Tu quoque,* 1614, B4ᵛ, '*Bub.*
How, stark dead? & could not *aqua vitæ* fetch him again? *Blank.* No
sir, nor *Rosa Solis* neither.'

145. *one of Kemps shooes.* Not a reference to the famous morris-dance
to Norwich in February and March 1600; *Kemps nine daies wonder*
describing it was entered on the Stationers' Register on 22 April.
'Creizenach . . . points out that in 1599 Thomas Platter saw a comedy

in which a servant took off his shoe and threw it at his master, and suggests that this was a bit of common-form stage clownery, in which case the Norwich dance would not be concerned. The performance described by Platter was in September or October, and apparently at the Curtain. Kempe may quite well have been playing at the Curtain with a fresh company after the Chamberlain's moved to the Globe.' (E. K. Chambers, *Elizabethan Stage*, iii, p. 362.)

For the throwing an old shoe as a sign of luck cf. *G.M.* 410, *Iohn Heywoodes woorkes*, 1562, Pt. I, ch. ix, C, 'Nowe for good lucke, caste an olde shoe after mee'; and H. Porter, *The two angrie women of Abington*, 1599, E1ᵛ, '*Phil.* Shall I fling an olde shooe after ye? *Nich.* No, you should say God send faire weather after me. *Phil.* I meane for good lucke.'

163. *discourse*, reasoning. Cf. *Poet.* v. i. 101, *Cat.* iii. 282, *B.F.* iv. iii. 36.

v. i. 9. *cormorants*. Gifford comments on the old treatment of servants: 'they were stripped and beaten at their master's pleasure; and *cormorants*, *eaters*, and *feeders*, were among the civilest terms bestowed upon them.' Cf. *S.W.* iii. v. 33–5, 'where are all my eaters? my mouthes now? barre vp my dores, you varlets'.

17. *carrie coales*. The Groom is carrying charcoal: Cunningham notes, 'From the earliest drawings of Whitehall, it would appear to have been charred in the immediate neighbourhood of the Palace.' The poorest drudges in greathouses were employed in carrying it. Hence the phrase 'to carry coals' = (1) to do any dirty work, as in this passage; (2) to submit to any insult, as in v. iii. 37. Gifford quotes Marston, *The Malcontent*, iv. v. (1604, G2), 'Great slaues fear better than loue, borne naturally for a coale-basket.'

hold my dogge. This was also a degrading office: see 77–80 below and iii. 24, and Rowlands quoted on *Poet.* iv. i. 13.

31. *chiefely . . . Briske*, who had a habit of abruptly changing the subject: see ii. i. 19.

55. *more then most faire*. Cf. Ind. 114.

58–60. *you must talke*. Chapman, *May-day*, 1611, i. ii, quoted on iii. vi. 172.

88. *leese*, lose. Cf. *Ep.* xxxvii. 1, *For.* iii. 61, *King's Ent.* 624, *Ent. Althorp*, 299, *Und.* xv. 56.

v. ii. The trick here played on Saviolina was worked up, as Professor Bang pointed out (*Englische Studien*, xxvi, Heft 2, pp. 330–2), from *The Courtyer of Count Baldessar Castilio*, Hoby's translation, 1561, Y3ᵛ, Y4, a '*Merrie Prancke*', that 'was wrought vnto a coople of greate Ladyes': 'Not manie dayes since in the Court that I meane, there arriued a manne of the Countrie about *Bergamo*, to be in seruice wyth a Gentilman of the Court: whyche was so well sett oute with garmentes and so finelye clad, that for all hys brynginge vp was alwayes in keapinge

Oxen and could doe nothinge elles, yet a manne that had not heard
him speake woulde haue iudged him a woorthie Gentilman. And so whan
those two Ladies were enfourmed that there was arrived a *Spaniarde*,
seruaunt to Cardinall *Borgia* whose name was *Castilio*, a verie wittie
man, a musicien, a daunser and the best Courtier in all *Spaine*, they
longed verie much to speake with him, and sent incontinentlye for him,
and after they had receyued him honorablye, they caused him to sitt
downe, and beegan to entertein him with a verie greate respect in the
presence of all menne, and fewe there were present that knew him not
to be a *Bergamask* Cowherd. Therefore seeinge those Ladies enterteine
him with such respect, and honour him so muche, they fell all in a
laughyng, the more bicause the seelie felowe spake still his natyue language the meere *Bergamaske* tunge. But the Gentilmen that diuised The woorst
this *Prancke*, had first toulde those Ladyes that emonge other thinges speach in all
he was a great dissembler and spake all tunges excellentlye well, and Italy
especiallye the Countrie speache of *Lumbardye*, so that they thought he
feigned, and manie tymes they beehelde the one the other with certein
marueilinges, and saide: What a wonderfull matter is this, howe he
counterfeyteth this tunge? In conclusion thys communication lasted
so longe that euerye mans sydes aked for laughinge, and he could not
chouse himselfe but vttre so manye tokens of hys noblenesse of birth,
that at length those Ladies (but with muche ado) beleaued he was the
man that he was in deede.'

22. *iustice Silence*. The Second Part of *King Henry IV* was a new
play at this date: cf. *E.M.I.* prol. 11 n. Nicholson suggested that 'a
kinsman to iustice *Silence*' may mean 'a Shallow'.

38. *Briskes feature*. Cf. II. i. 99.

86–7. Cf. IV. viii. 52–3.

124. *strooke* ('struck' F2). See *E.M.I.* IV. vii. 141.

v. iii. 4. *insult vpon* retains the original notion of the Latin *insulto*,
'I leap upon', or 'attack'.

12. *taints*. Cf. II. i. 131.

37. *beare no coales*. See v. i. 17, and note. Cf. Shelton, *Why come ye
nat to Courte*, l. 240, ed. Dyce, 'Will ye bere no coles?'; H. Buttes, *Dyets
drie Dinner*, 1599, E1 (of the palm), 'This tree is of a most aspiring
nature: it will beare no coales. It resisteth all burden, bearing it vpward
with his armes & boughs: Therefore it is an Hieroglyphick or Embleme
of victory and conquest'; and *Rom. and Jul.* I. i. 1.

57. *the wood-yard*, 'an outlying part of Whitehall, just as well known
as the Tilt-yard, or Scotland Yard, between which and the Thames it
was situated' (Cunningham). It is mentioned again in *Love Restored*, 73–4,
'. . . climbe ouer the wall, and in by the wood-yard, so to the tarras'.

68. *viliaco*. Florio, 1598, has '*Vigliacco*, a raskal, a villain, a base,
vile, abiect skuruie fellow, a scoundrell'. Cf. Dekker, *Satiromastix*,
1602, B2, 'before they came near the great hall, the faint-hearted
villiacoes sounded at least thrice'.

74. *camouccio*. Cf. Middleton, *Blurt Master-Constable*, I. ii (1602, B2), '*Laz*. Who so euer Saies you haue a black eye, is a *camooche*'; Dekker and Webster, *The Famous History of Sir Thomas Wyat*, 1607, E2, '*Bret*. . . . what is a Spaniard ? . . . a Spaniard is a Camocho, a Callimanco, nay which is worse a Dondego'. . . .

The *O.E.D.*, in view of the collocation with 'Callimanco' in Dekker, derives 'Camocho' from the Italian *camoscio*, 'a kinde of stuffe worne in Italie' (Florio). *Camouccio* looks like a back-formation from 'camooch' —an unhappy attempt to quote what Jonson conjectured to be the native Italian form. It seems here a pointless term of abuse.

v. iv. 1. *shot-sharkes*. The misprint 'Shotmarkes' in Q1 was perhaps due to mistaking a ligatured 'ſh' for 'M'. Q2's attempt to correct the word by transposing the *r*—'Shot-makers'—shows how the emendator makes recovery of the original word impossible.

4. *George*. Probably a real name: see Dekker and Webster, *Westward Hoe*, iv. i (1607, E4ᵛ), where Luce, blindfold, guesses who is holding her: 'O you are *George* the drawer at the Miter, pray you vnblinde me.'

8. *Neophite*. 'Not in general use till the 19th century' (*O.E.D.*). Cf. *C.R.* III. i. 3, 'Your *neophyte*-player'; iv. 55, 'There stands a *Neophyte* glazing of his face'; *Poet.* I. ii. 123, 'my noble *Neophyte*; my little *Grammaticaster*'.

16. *take mee with you*, go no faster than I can follow, let me understand you. Cf. *Love Freed*, 172, 'Say 't againe, and take me'along'; *Rom. and Jul.* III. v. 141; Swift, *A Tale of a Tub*, 1704, p. 105, 'Pray, said Peter, take me along with you, either you are both Mad, or disposed to be merrier than I approve.'

20. *shaft . . . out of the butt*. A quibble: the 'butt-shaft' or 'butt-bolt' was an unbarbed arrow which could stick in the butts but be extracted.

24. *successe*, achievement, result, whether good or bad.

28. *Kecks* (Q), dry stem of a plant. Cf. Wilkins, *The Miseries of Inforst Mariage*, 1607, F4ᵛ, '*Ilf.* Dost not know me Butler ? *But.* For Kex, dryde Kex'. The dry-nurse in Jonson's *Entertainment at the Blackfriars* is called 'Mistress Kecks'.

37. *gymblet*. Cf. *D. is A.* I. i. 71, where the term is applied to the drawers at 'the Cranes i'the *Vintry*'. 'Faucet' is similarly used in *B.F.* II. ii. 48. Lydgate in his *Assembly of the Gods*, stanza 51, describes Bacchus:

> On hys hede he had a thredebare kendall hood;
> A gymlot and a fauset thereapon stood.

in the false scabberd should refer to some peculiarity in the dress of the boy-drawer, but the context gives no clue to it. Perhaps Carlo objects to a boy serving him—a *neophite*, as he calls him in line 8—and regards him as an intruder.

38. *sir Burgomaster*, the big-bellied jug with a bearded figure in front. Cf. the 'Bellarmines' of a later date.

43. *bite off his nose.* For this animal form of endearment cf. IV. iv. 98, *Alch.* II. iii. 326, 'Slaue, I could bite thine eare.'

50 foll. Whalley noted Dryden's imitation of this episode in Act I of *The Wild Gallant* where 'Trice is discovered playing at Tables by himself'. As C. R. Baskerville remarks (*English Elements*, p. 177), 'Carlo's manipulation of his cups is in the manner of a puppet-show.' Fynes Moryson in his *Itinerary*, 1617, Part III, ii, ch. 4, p. 99, notes that in the Netherlands, 'Some wanting companions to drinke, lay down their hat or cloke for a companion, so playing themselues both parts, of drinking to, & pledging, till they haue no more sence or vse of reason, then the cloke or hat hath.'

69. *If it were the basest filth* . . . Cf. J. Cooke, *Greenes Tu quoque*, 1624, C, 'here master *Pursnet* you shall pledge him. *Purs.* Ile not refuse it were it puddle.'

70. *respectiuely.* Cf. *C.R.* v. iv. 219, *B.F.* I. iii. 57.

75. *on my knee.* Gallants often knelt to pledge a health, especially the health of their mistress. Anaides in *Cynthia's Revels*, II. ii. 93, 'neuer kneeles but to pledge healths'. Cf. *A Yorkshire Tragedy*, 1608, A3, 'Sam. Why then follow me, Ile teach you the finest humour to be drunk in, I learnd it at London last week. . . . The brauest humor, 'twold do a man good to be drunck in't, they call it Knighting in London, when they drink vpon their knees.'

79. *doe me right*, drink a bumper. Cf. *S.W.* IV. ii. 102, and Massinger, *The Bond-Man*, II. iii (1624), E3ᵛ:

> These Glasses containe nothing; doe me right
> As e're you hope for liberty.

v. v. 16. *chang'd his copie*, of a change of style or behaviour. Cf. R. Edwards, *Damon and Pythias*, 1571, B4ᵛ:

> *Aristippus.* Byr lady Wyll, this is good counsell, playnely to iest
> Of women, proofe hath taught mee it is not best,
> I will change my coppy.

20. *Banke-side*, Thames side in Southwark; the Globe, the Rose, and the Hope theatres were situated in it. So named because it was originally a row of houses on a bank or dike made over a swamp.

30. *minion, saker, culverine.* In 'A Table of proportion for the weight and shooting of great Ordnance' given in Captain John Smith's *A Sea Grammar*, 1627, p. 70, the 'Minion' discharges a shot of four pounds, the 'Sacre' a shot of five and a third pounds, and the 'demy Culuering' a shot of nine and one-third pounds. In the enlarged edition of 1692 a fuller table, given on p. 96, shows the advance made in the interval.

32. *case of petrionels*, pair of carbines. See *E.M.I.* III. i. 145 n.

34. *German tapster.* Cf. 'skinker', derived from the Middle Low German 'schencker'.

40. *enough*, done enough. Cf. *The Pleasaunt Historie of Lazarillo de Tormes*, 1586, Bvij: 'hee gaue mee a piece of a sausedge to rost, the

which being almost inough, and the fat dropped and pressed out vpon
thin slices of bread, as the fashion is, and those being eaten. . . .'

46. *farce*, stuff. Cf. *The Two Noble Kinsmen*, IV. iii. (1634, K2), 'what
Broken peece of matter so'ere she's about, the name *Palamon* lardes
it, that she farces ev'ry busines Withall'.

49–53, 60–4. Edmund Gayton in *The Art of Longevity*, 1659, p. 31,
ch. xv, 'Of the Flesh of Swine, Deer, Hares and Bears', thus reproduces
this passage:

First, *of Swine*.

> My Father *Ben*, discoursing of this Grunter,
> In that so famous Play, where old Sir *Punter*
> Being turn'd *Orlando* for the losse of 's dog,
> Did lug the jeering buffon like a hog:
> There in that celebrated *Comedy*,
> (Whether my Father *Ben*, as well as I,
> Met with *Arabian Comments*) the smart Play
> Doth patly what my *ancient Authors* say:
> There's wit to th'height, read it, and try our *Dogma*,
> Whether from both the places we a Hog may
> Not all alike commend; first *Avicen*
> Sayes, Pork's most naturall to men, so *Ben*;
> Hogs flesh is likest mans, saith *Isaak*;
> The same again saith *Ben*, but adds, that Sack,
> A Hogshead full, for a *vehiculum*,
> Will spoile its grumbling in our *medium*,
> (Or middle Region of our Trunk) for Swine,
> Alive or dead, will be still laid with Wine.
> Indeed my Father *Ben* doth there produce
> A reason why they were denied the Jews;
> Because that Nutrimentall Animall
> Of a provoking sap, and *Hogon* all,
> Would have disorder'd and o're-pamper'd those
> Who newly come from Egypts hard dispose:
> Rebels in rough *Mosaick* Discipline,
> How much more Rebels, had they eaten Swine?

53. *strummel-patcht*. See critical note. The epithets are very ambiguous: *strummel* = 'straw', and we adopt Gifford's 'strummel-patcht'
in the sense of 'patched with straw' or 'patched up of straw'.

54. *goggle-ey'd*. Cf. Burton, *The Anatomy of Melancholy*, 1621, Pt. I,
Sec. 2, Memb. 1, Sub. 6, p. 80: 'That famous family of *Ænobarbi*, were
knowne of old, and so surnamed from their red beardes, as the *Austrian*
lippe at this day, and those *Indians* flat noses are propagated, the
Bavarian chinne, and goggle eyes amongst the *Iewes*, as *Buxendorfius*
obserues.' He refers to Buxtorfius, *Synagogo Iudaica*, Hanoviæ, 1604.

Grumbledories. Coined by Jonson on the analogy of 'drumbledory',
a dor-beetle or bumble-bee: cf. *The Triall of Treasure*, 1567, A3ᵛ, 'Thou
goest like a Dromeldory, dreaming & drousy.'

Gigantomachiz'd. Another coinage of Jonson's: the Jews would have fought like the Giants against the Gods; passed from murmuring to open rebellion.

57. *seruetur* . . . Horace, *A.P.* 126–7.

71. *abhorres from*: the Latin *abhorrere ab.*

73. *Long-lane Cannibals* (Qq). See Stow, *Survay*, 1603, p. 382, 'the lane truly called Long, which reacheth from Smithfield to Aldersgate street. This lane is now lately builded on both sides with tenements for brokers, tiplers, and such like'; Dekker and Webster, *North-Ward Hoe*, II. i (1607, B4ᵛ), 'If the Diuel and all the Brokers in long lane had rifled their wardrob they wud ha beene dambd before they had fitted thee thus'.

77. *to been incorporated.* Cf. *S.W.* IV. vii. 2, 'TRV. O, sir! here hath like to been murder since you went.' But it is an unexpected archaism at this date. Spenser has it, e.g. *Faerie Queene*, 1590, II. i. 1, 'To beene departed', iii. 11, 'To beene with Guyon knitt'.

78. *messe.* Cf. *E.M.I.* I. iii. 71.

82. *vnicornes horne* . . . *bezoars stone*, in high repute as antidotes against poison, and often mentioned as fraudulent. Wither, *Britain's Remembrancer*, 1628, f. 58, mentions as preservatives against plague:

> Our *Boezar-stone*; our med'cines Chymicall;
> Or, that high-prized Iewell wherewithall,
> For horne of *Vnicorne* men cheated are.

Cf. Massinger, *The Roman Actor*, ii. i (1629, D1ᵛ):

> His sirrups, Iulips, Bezerstone nor his
> Imagin'd Vnicornes horne comes in my bellie,
> My mouth shall be a draught first.

Guillim argued in *A Display of Heraldrie*, 1610, III. xiv, p. 134, 'Some haue made doubt whether there bee any such *Beast*, as this, or no. But the great esteeme of his *Horne* (in many places to be seene) may take away that needlesse scruple.' Sir T. Browne in the *Pseudodoxia Epidemica*, III. xxiii, analyses the various substitutes on sale in England: 'Nor is it to be omitted, what hath been formerly suspected, but now confirmed by *Olaus Wormius*, and *Thomas Bartholinus* and others, that those long Horns preserved as pretious rarities in many places, are but the teeth of Narhwales, to be found about Island, Greenland and other Northern regions; of many feet long, commonly wreathed, very deeply fastned in the upper jaw, and standing directly forward'; he instances 'the Horn at *Windsor* . . . in his second voyage brought by *Frobisher*'.

The 'bezoar stone' was a calculus or concretion found in certain animals, notably the wild goat of Persia, the lamas of Peru, and the chamois: see Caspar Bauhinus, *De Lapidis Bezaar, Orientalis et Occidentalis Cervini item et Germanici Ortu Natura Differentiis, veroque vsu, ex veterum & recentiorum placitis*, Basle, 1613. Robert Pitt, *The Craft and Frauds of Physick Expos'd*, 1702, pp. 35–6, states: '*Bezoar* has held its name and Reputation almost Sacred with us, tho' exploded long since in almost all the Parts of *Europe*. Dr. *Guybert* in a Discourse, entituled, *Decou Les Tromperies* (sic) *du* Bezoar *de couvertes*, convinc'd the *French*, that they had been impos'd on, by the Trading Physitians returning from the *Indies*, to take off the pretty Trifle at a very great Price. . . . Two *Criminals*, by the King's Command, had Poyson given them, with promise of Life, if *Bezoar* could procure their Pardon. They lost their Lives, and the Stone, and the Physitians their Reputation.'

v. vi. 11. *muske-cod*, literally a small bag or purse used for perfumes, sometimes called simply 'a cod'. Cf. *Ep.* xix 'On Sir Cod the perfumed'; and *Disc.*, 584–5, 'preposterous as our Gallants cloathes, sweet bags and night-dressings'. Hence, 'fop', as in Dekker, *Satiromastix*, 1602, E3, 'It's a sweete Muske-cod, a pure spic'd-gull.'

34. *a dutch purse.* The contemporary purse was usually an embroidered pouch drawn at the top by strings, which ended in tassels. *Dutch*: query, a cheap purse made of coarse holland instead of the usual leather or silk.

36. *the Masters side in the Counter.* For the 'Counters' see *E.M.I.* II. i. 78 note. The four wards of the prison were—in descending order—the Master's side, the Knight's side, the Twopenny ward, and the Hole. Cf. W. Fennor, *The Compters Common-wealth*, 1617, pp. 4, 11; Dekker and Webster, *West-ward Hoe*, III. ii (1607, E): '*Mono*. I will patiently incounter the Counter. Which is the dearest warde in Prison Serjeant! the knights ward? *Amb.* No sir, the Maisters side. *Mono.* Well the knight is aboue the maister though his Table be worse furnisht: Ile goe thither'; and J. Cooke, *Greenes Tu quoque*, 1614, I1v:

> *Hold.* If you haue no monie,
> You're best remoue into some cheaper Ward.
> *Spend.* What Ward shall I remoue in?
> *Hold.* Why to the Two-pennie Ward, is likeliest to hold out with your meanes: or if you will you may go into the Holl, and there you may feed for nothing.
> *Spend.* I, out of the Almes-basket, where Charitie appeares
> In likenesse of a peece of stinking Fish:
> Such as they beat Bawdes with when they are Carted.
> *Hold.* Why sir, doe not scorne it, as good men as your selfe,
> Haue been glad to eate Scraps out of the Almsbasket.

And Wilkins, *The Miseries of Inforst Mariage*, 1607, E1v, 'From the featherbed in the Maisters side, or the Flock bed in the Knights warde, to the straw-bed in the hole'. See the amusing passage in *E.H.* v. ii. 42–51.

42. *Flea.* The usual form in Jonson, but 'flay' is found in *Volp.* I. iv. 27, II. vi. 30, III. vii. 252.

48. *Yohan.* Cf. 'Yaughan' in *Hamlet*, v. i. 60. Cardozo in *The Contemporary Jew in Elizabethan Drama*, p. 130, notes that 'Yohan' is a

name avoided by Jews, but that 'Jew' often means Dutchman or Fleming, and that the name Yaughan was specially affected by the Low Germans.

54–5. For the *familiar* or attendant demon to be got in Germany see IV. iii. 35–6 and note.

75. *Adalantado*, or more correctly 'Adelantado', a grandee or a governor of a province. Cf. *Alch.* III. iii. 50, and *Love's Cure*, II. i (Beaumont and Fletcher Folio, 1647, p. 129), 'Nay, we are all *Signiors* here in Spaine, from the Jakes-farmer to the Grandee, or *Adelantado*'.

79. *Et tu Brute!* Gifford suggests that Macilente holds the light. The words are first found in *The True Tragedie of Richard Duke of Yorke*, 1595, v. i. 53, 'Et tu Brute, wilt thou stab *Cæsar* too?' Shakespeare copied the expression in *Julius Caesar*, III. i. 77, acted in 1599. There can be little doubt that Jonson is burlesquing it. He would know the account in Suetonius, that Caesar died without speaking, though Suetonius also quotes a tradition that Caesar, when Brutus rushed upon him, exclaimed καὶ σὺ εἶ ἐκείνων, καὶ σύ, τέκνον;

v. vii. 8. *paramptorie*, the reading of F1, may be justified by 'parantory' on the lips of Constable Haggise in *B.F.* IV. i. 70, as a vulgarism— the constable's 'mistaking words, as the fashion is, in the *Stage*-practice' (ibid., Ind. 44–5). But, as there is no attempt to develop this form of humour, and the constable is a very practical person, perhaps the correction 'peremptorie' in F2 was authoritative. 'Peramptorie' and 'parramtorie' occur in W. Warner's *Pan his Syrinx*, 1584, N3ᵛ and S3ᵛ.

60. *crosse*. Cf. *E.M.I.* IV. ix. 43.

65. *friday night*, a fast night: see note to *E.M.I.* III. iv.

v. viii. 36. *wilde quick-set beard*. Whalley quotes from the *locus classicus* on beards in Taylor's *Superbiæ Flagellum*, 1621, C7ᵛ:

> And some (to set their loues desire on edge)
> Are cut and prun'de like to a quickset hedge.

63. *forslow*, delay. Cf. Marlowe, *Edward II*, II. iv, 'War. Forslowe no time sweet Lancaster, lets march.'

v. ix. 47. *shot-clog*, 'One who was tolerated because he paid the shot, or reckoning, for the rest; otherwise a mere clog upon the company.'— *Nares.* Cf. *Poet.* I. ii. 15–17, 'What? shall I haue my sonne a stager now? an enghle for players? a gull? a rooke? a shot-clogge? to make suppers, and bee laught at?'; and *E.H.* I. i. 136, 'thou common shot-clog, gull of all companies'.

v. x. 8. *visitation* (corrected to *visit* in F2). Similarly used in *S.W.* III. v. 40, but the word strictly connotes an official or formal visit, e.g. of a client, *Cat.* III. 670, or a visit to the sick, *Volp.* I. ii. 88, III. ix. 45; *S.W.* v. ii. 63. Cf. E. Sharpham, *Cupids Whirligig*, 1607, B2, '*Young*

Lord. Or else I were vnworthie of your loue if I neglect the visitation of so kinde friends as your selfe and my deare mistris. ⟨*Kni.*⟩ Visitation! my wife's not sicke, what visitation?'

20. *Ludgate.* Cf. I. ii. 122.

24. *passion*, emotion.

34. *as 'tis in Euphues.* Quoted from a letter of Philautus in the second part of Lyly's *Euphues and his England* (1580, ed. Bond, ii, p. 123), where the original has 'writing' instead of 'speaking'. Greene had used it twice in 1584, in *Gwidonius, The Carde of Fancie* (*Works*, ed. Grosart, iv. 176) and in Arbasto, *The Anatomy of Fortune* (ib. iii. 216). Burton in the second edition of the *Anatomy*, 1624, p. 451, quotes it, apparently from Jonson, as he gives the same variant. See also *E.M.I.* II. iv. 54.

v. xi. 2. *has the wolfe seene you?* Alluding to the superstition recorded in Pliny, *Naturall Historie* (Holland's translation, 1601), VIII. xxii, 'It is commonly thought likewise in Italie, that the eye-sight of wolves is hurtfull; in so much, as if they see a man before hee espie him, they cause him to loose his voice for the time.' Gifford quotes Vergil, *Ecl.* ix. 53, 54:

vox quoque Moerim
iam fugit ipsa; lupi Moerim videre priores.

5. *Planet strike me dead.* Cf. *E.M.I.* IV. vii. 141.

11. *deceptio visus.* Cf. *G.M.* 970.

24. *Enfans-perdus.* Cf. Raleigh, *The History of the World*, 1614, v, p. 451, 'His Darters and Slingers of the *Baleares*, he sent off before him, to encounter with the *Roman Velites*. These were loose troupes, answerable in a manner to those, which we call now by a *French* name *Enfans perdues*; but when we vsed our owne termes, *the forlorn hope.*' '*Perdu's*' in *M.L.* III. vi. 122.

26. *Pulpamenta.* Cooper in his *Thesaurus Linguæ Romanæ & Britannicæ*, 1578, defines the word as 'A delicate dishe of meate finely seasoned'. Cf. Terence, *Eunuchus*, 426, 'Lepus tute es, pulpamentum quaeris'.

32. *spinster.* Originally, one who spins; then a common law term for an unmarried woman. This use dates from the seventeenth century, but had not yet established itself. With the text cf. the tract of Henry Goodcole, *The Wonderfull Discouerie of Elizabeth Sawyer*, 1621, which supplied material for *The Witch of Edmonton*. In the headline before the text she is spoken of as 'Elizabeth Sawyer, late of Edmonton, Spinster', but in the tract her husband is spoken of.

51. *two-penny ward.* See note on v. vi. 36.

52. *set vp your rest.* Cf. *C. is A.* I. iii. 11.

53. *pomander*, scent-box. Cf. II. i. 98.

54 foll. Baskerville (*English Elements*, pp. 168–9) notes a parallel speech forming the Epilogue to the old play of *Timon* quoted on page 483.

61. *malicing.* Cf. *Poet.* prol. 10, 'within his malic't sides'.

82–4. Imitated by Dekker in *The Wonderfull yeare*, 1603, A3ᵛ (the address to the reader), 'Besides, if that which he presents vpon the Stage of the world be *Good*, why should he basely cry out (with that old poeticall mad-cap in his *Amphitruo*) *Iouis summi causa clarè plaudite*, beg a *Plaudite* for God-sake.'

87. *Fal-Staffe*. Another Shakespearian allusion: cf. v. ii. 22. The final quotation of the Quartos is from Horace, *Epistles*, 1. xix. 37.

Epilogue before the Queen

In the defiant apology which Jonson prefixed to this speech in the Quarto (reprinted in Appendix X, 1), he makes it clear that Elizabeth was impersonated on the public stage. He refers to the precedents 'in diuers Playes' and the practice of the city pageants. Such a play was Peele's pastoral, *The Araygnement of Paris*, printed in 1584. In the Folio version Jonson refers only to a court performance, which doubtless took place as well; and in line 18 he altered the original expression that Elizabeth's 'Figure' had effected the change in Macilente to 'presence'.

Elizabeth was unpopular at the end of her reign, and Nicholson suggests that the Londoners especially resented her treatment of the Earl of Essex. Compare the guarded defence of the Queen in *Cynthia's Revels*, v. xi. 9–27.

W. J. Lawrence (*Shakespeare's Workshop*, p. 101) has suggested that Hamlet's comment on hearing that players are coming to Elsinore (II. ii), 'The humorous man shall end his part in peace', refers to this Epilogue. Sir E. K. Chambers is inclined to agree (*Shakespeare*, i, p. 423). But, if so, it is the only pointed and personal reference in a context of generalities: 'He that plays the king shall be welcome; . . . the adventurous knight shall use his foil and target; the lover shall not sigh gratis; . . . the clown shall make those laugh whose lungs are tickle o' the sere, and the lady shall say her mind freely, or the blank verse shall halt for't.' Professor Dover Wilson's interpretation is simpler, that the words refer to interruptions by victims or their partisans of topical or personal allusions.

8. *our cities torrent*. Cf. *U.V.* xxxv. 16, 'Dowgate Torrent falling into Thames', and Stow, *Survay*, 1598, p. 34, '*Downe* gate, so called (as may be supposed) of the sodaine descending, or downe going of that way from *S. Iohn's* Church vpon Walbrooke into the Riuer of Thames, whereby the water in the channell there hath such a swift course, that in the year 1574. on the fourth of September after a strong shower of rayne, a lad (of the age of 18. yeares) minding to haue leapt ouer the channell, was taken by the feete and borne downe with the violence of that narrow streame, and caryed towarde the Thames with such a violent swiftnesse, as no man could rescue or stay him, till he came against a cart wheele, that stood in the water gate, before which time he was drowned, and starke dead.'

17. *He kneeles*. (Q). From the time of the moral interludes to the beginning of the seventeenth century it was a usual practice for the

actors at the end of the piece to pray for their patrons—for the nobleman in a private performance, or for the King or Queen in the public theatre. Sometimes this prayer formed a part of the epilogue. Thus at the end of Ulpian Fulwell's *Like wil to like*, 1568, the epilogue contains a prayer for the Queen, the Council, the Lords and Commons. Cf. Middleton, *A Mad World, My Masters*, v. ii (1608, H4ᵛ), '*Follywit*. Pray Grandsire, giue me your blessing, [He kneels.] *Sir Bounteous*. Who? Sonne Folliwit? *Follywit [aside]*. This showes like kneeling after the play, I praying for my Lord Owemuch, and his good Countesse, our honourable Lady and mistresse.'

21. *fortunate*. Cf. Ind. 273.
28. *turtle-footed*, slowfooted. Imitated by Ford and Dekker in *The Sun's Darling*, v. i (1656, p. 37):

and Turtle-footed Peace
Dance like a Fairie through his realms, while all
That envie him, shall like swift Comets fall.

31. Revived for Queen Anne in the last lines of *The Entertainment at Althorp*:

Peace vsher now your steps, and where you come,
Be *Enuie* still strooke blind, and *Flatterie* dumb.

33–4. Copied by Massinger and Dekker in *The Virgin Martir*, iv. iii (1622, K1):

Vnmou'd, by *Mars*, as if she were assur'd
Death looking on her constancy would forget
The vse of his ineuitable hand.

Appendix X, 1.
5. *part of the Heauen awry*. Cf. *C.R.* iv. i. 38 n.
8. *President*, precedent: a common spelling.
16. *discours't ouer*, ranged over. A rare use: the *O.E.D.* cites Surrey, *Æneid*, iv. 475, 'With silence [silent] looke discoursing ouer al'.

APPENDIX XX
THE ANONYMOUS PLAY OF 'TIMON'

THE play of *Timon* survives in Dyce MS. 52 and was first printed by Dyce for the Shakespeare Society in 1842. It was obviously written for an academic audience: G. C. Moore Smith, who noted parallels with Wingfield's academic play of *Pedantius*,[1] suggested that it was acted at Cambridge at some date between 1581 and 1600. Dyce suggested 1600 for the date. The scene is laid at Athens: characters in the play are 'Gelasimus, a cittie heyre', 'Pseudocheus, a lying trauailor', 'Philar-

[1] *Modern Language Review*, iii, p. 143.

gurus, a couetous churlish old man', and his son 'Lollio, a cuntrey clowne'. The play is taken from Lucian's *Misanthropos*, and there are verbal borrowings also from Plautus, Juvenal, and Horace: it misquotes the opening line of the *Iliad* (III. i), and makes Timon conclude his curse (v. ii) with Εμεῖο ζώντος γαῖα μικθήτω πυρὶ, a blundering adaptation of Nero's quotation ἐμοῦ θανόντος γαῖα μιχθήτω πυρί. In II. v we have

> I drinke this to thee super naculum.
> *Dem.* This wee doe call at *Athenes* κ'αθ ὅλον

There are epithets like 'macilente Grunnio' (III. iv), 'a wife morigerous' (III. v), and there is a tinge of Plautus' phraseology: 'O foolisher than foolishnes itselfe', Plautus' 'stultior stultissimo';

> My ffreind, a word or two.
> *Pseud.* Yes, if thou wilt, three hundred. (I. iv)—

Plautus' 'Pax te tribus verbis volo. *Suc.* Vel trecentis' (*Trinummus*, 963–4). The style of writing is quite unfitted for the London stage, and there is no record of the play being acted there.

As H. C. Hart noted (*The Works of Ben Jonson*, i, pp. xliii–xlv)— though he exaggerated their number and significance—*Timon* has points of contact with Jonson's work.

Timon, in the epilogue, shakes off his misanthropy as Macilente abandons his envy.

> I now am left alone, this rascall route
> Hath left my side, what's this? I feele throughout
> A sodeine change: my fury doth abate,
> My hearte growes milde & laies aside its hate.
> Ile not affecte newe titles in my minde
> Or yet bee call'd the hater of Mankinde:
> Timon doffs Timon, & with bended knee
> Thus craues a fauour: If our Comedie
> And merry Scene deserue a Plaudite
> Let louing hands loude sounding in the Ayre
> Cause Timon to the Citty to repaire.

This should be compared with Macilente's closing speech in *Every Man out of his Humour*, v. xi. 54–65.

Another passage (I. iv) recalls the first meeting of Amorphus and Asotus in *Cynthia's Revels*. Gelasimus, a rich citizen's heir, son of a miser Philargurus, is attracted by a lying traveller Pseudocheus, who boasts of his exploits in foreign lands:

> at Gades I washt away
> *Non vltra* writt with Hercules owne hand.

Gelasimus says to his page:

> Shall I speake to him, Pædio? he seemes
> A man of greate accompt, that hath orevieu'd

> Soe many countreyes: what shall I saye first?
> Shall I salute him after our manner?
> > *Pseud.* A spruce, neate youth: what, yf I affront him?
> > *Gelas.* Good gods, how earnestlie doe I desire
> His ffellowshipp! was I e're soe shamefac't?
> What yf I send and gyue to him my cloake?
> > *Pseud.* What shall I saye? I saw his face at Thebes
> Or Sicelie?
> > *Gelas.* Ile send it. Pædio,
> Gyue him this cloake; salute him in my name;
> H'st, thou may'st tell him, yf thou wilt, how rich
> My ffather was.

The King of the Antipodes gave Pseudocheus a ring.

> > *Gelas.* Prythee, lett me se it.
> Wilt thou that wee exchainge my Pylades?
> > *Pseud.* I am a man, Ile not denye my ffreind.
> By Joue, my ringe is made of brasse, not gould. [*Aside.*

Compare *Cynthia's Revels*, I. iv. 28 foll.

Gelasimus, when Callimela has rejected him (III. iii), expresses his stupefaction somewhat like Amorphus when Echo flies from him in *Cynthia's Revels*, I. iii. 24–45, but it is a natural prompting, not a stimulus from the fountain of self-love.

> Soe the gods loue mee, I doe nothing see
> That this fonde foolishe girle can blame in mee:
> I am not redde hair'd, and I am noe dwarfe;
> What, then, can shee dislike? are my palmes dry?
> Am I not a gentleman by descent?
> Am I not riche enough? what man is there
> Liues in all Athenes richer than myselfe?
> Am I a foole? my braines howere they are,
> I knowe them well; I am noe foole or asse.

There are minor parallels: Gelasimus has a grotesque coat of arms (I. iii) like Sordido's; Pseudocheus gives him absurd instructions how to woo (I. iv)—a superficial likeness to Amorphus instructing Asotus; in IV. ii Timon lying on the ground comments on the dialogue, like Macilente in *Every Man out of his Humour*, I. ii.

Parallels have also been traced between *Timon* and *Poetaster*: a feeble drinking song to Bacchus has been compared with 'Swell me a bowle with lustie wine' in *Poetaster*, III. i. 8–12; and a cap with ass's ears sent to Timon as a present has been compared with the ass's ears fixed on Asinius Lupus the tribune in the same play (V. iii. 130). Neither parallel has much point; but there does appear to be a connexion between *Timon* and the two earlier plays of Jonson.

Who was the borrower? *Timon* was unprinted; it is definitely the work of an amateur; *Pedantius*, with which the play has some points of contact, was produced at Trinity College, Cambridge, in 1581, so that, as far as this play is concerned, *Timon* was the borrower. Its attempt to revive the classical manner is crude and unscholarly; it is closer to Lucian than to Plutarch; indeed the rhetorician Demeas is borrowed from Lucian. Assuming that Jonson got hold of the manuscript—and it is a large assumption—what use would such childish writing be to him? The idea of his using it as dramatic quarry is grotesque—only less grotesque than the suggestion that Shakespeare used it. Unless we had evidence to the contrary, what reason is there to suppose that the manuscript circulated in London?

Professor Tucker Brooke tries to meet the difficulty by suggesting that Jonson's plays and *Timon* drew on a common source,[1] and Mr. Baskerville has found it in Greene's sharper in *The Defence of Conny catching* (1592), who 'openly shadoweth his disguise with the name of a Traveller' and spins wonderful yarns of his adventures abroad.[2] A common source can be postulated when there is a marked correspondence of plot, as in *The London Prodigal* and Jonson's *Staple of News*, but hardly for mere episodic touches and a few snatches of conversation, and the reasonable inference here is that the amateur copied the practised playwright, and not vice versa. If this is so, the proposed date of 1600 for *Timon* would have to be carried forward to the following year, 1601. But everything about the play is hazy—author, date, place of production. In fact we have no evidence that *Timon* was ever acted at all.

CYNTHIA'S REVELS

PLACE AND TIME IN THE PLAY

THE scene is Gargaphie (Ind. 42), where Cynthia holds her court (ib. 44). The first act takes place in a valley close by, with the fountain in which Narcissus lost himself (I. ii) and the stone into which Niobe was petrified (ib. 85). The rest of the play is acted in various parts of the Court, a private apartment in Act III, the Nymphs' Chamber in Act IV, a gallery or hall in Act V, with Amorphus and Morphides keeping the door (iii. 4). The humorists, as we may call the group of affected courtiers, are finally sent on penance to their several homes 'by Niobe's stone' (xi. 144), whence they return to Court in pairs, singing a palinode. The play is thus confined to a narrow area.

The time occupied by it is one day. Various indications are given of its passing. In II. iv. 5 it is 'a quarter past eleuen'. In III. i it

---

[1] *Tudor Drama*, p. 411 n.
[2] *Early Elements in Jonson's Comedy*, pp. 268–72. But the lying traveller was proverbial, and could be met in any London ordinary; it was unnecessary to search literature in order to find a portrait of him.

484486 *Plays*

is still morning: Amorphus and Asotus go off to dinner (l. 20);
Asotus is to have a lesson 'against after-noone' (17). The lesson is
given in III. v. At IV. iii. 41 it is 'past fiue'. There are references
to 'this' coming 'night' in IV. v. 5, 133. The sports conclude 'with
declining night' in v. xi. 3.

The mottoes on the Quarto title-page 'Quod non dant Proceres.' . . .
'Haud tamen inuideas', are from Juvenal's seventh *Satire*. ll. 90, 93;
the motto on the Folio title-page is from Martial, *Epigrams*, XII. xxxvii.
'Nasutum', is a quibble; literally 'large-nosed', and secondarily 'shrewd'
or 'witty'. The line before is 'Nasutus nimium cupis videri', 'I like a
fine nose, not a polypus.—form, not deformity'. Nasutus and Polyposus
are two of the speakers in the 'Apologetical Dialogue' appended to
Poetaster.

Dedication

11, 12. *For to grace* . . . From Seneca, *Ep*. cxv. 3, 'Quanta esset cum
gratia auctoritas! nemo illam amabilem qui non simul venerabilem
diceret.'

13, 14. *It is not pould'ring*. . . . Cf. *Disc*. 1415–17, 'There is nothing
valiant, or solid to bee hop'd for from such, as are alwayes kemp't, and
perfum'd; and euery day smell of the Taylor.'

24. *Thy seruant, but not slaue*. Lurking beneath the stately compli-
ments of the dedication is a touch of resentment that the satire on bad
courtiers had been unacceptable at court: see too the passages quoted in
vol. iv, pp. 21–2.

The Persons of the Play

Jonson interprets the Greek-derived names in the Induction, 55–74,
for the benefit of the audience. Note that in Jonson's day the Greek
names were pronounced by accent, not by quantity. Sir T. Smith in his
De recta & emendata Linguæ Græcæ Pronuntiatione, 1578, p. 31, argued
against distinguishing the quantity of vowels: 'Itaque in quo nobis cum
inveterato vsu controuersia est? Primum illud est, quod inter longas
vocales et breues differentias obseruamus: aliterque sonamus a & i cum
longæ sunt, quam quando correptæ.' Thus in III. iv. 93, 'Your honour'd
friends, TIMÈ, and PHRONESIS,' and v. xi. 60, 'Who would haue thought
that PHILAVTIA durst', we scan Phronēsis, and Philautīa, because of
φρόνησις, φιλαυτία. Cf. *Time Vindicated*, 199, 'I envie not the Ἀποθέωσις,'
where Jonson writes the long vowel ω but shortens it in scansion.
In v. xi. 80. 'Anaïdes' (Greek ἀναίδης) is mispronounced as four
syllables. Jonson should have known its derivation from αἰδώς.

3. *Crites*. In the Quarto 'Criticus', which survives in F1 in the scene-
heading of I. v. Dekker was the first to suggest that Criticus is a self-
portrait, a Jonson *in excelsis*: 'You must haue three or foure suites of
names, when like a lowsie Pediculous vermin th'ast but one suite to thy
backe: you must be call'd Asper, and Criticus, and Horace, thy tytle's

longer a reading then the stile a the big Turkes: Asper, Criticus, Quintus, Horatius, Flaccus' (*Satiro-mastix*, 1602, D1). And Gifford was of opinion that in these three characters 'Jonson undoubtedly meant to shadow forth himself'. The name 'Criticus' or 'Crites', and the account of him as a retired scholar utterly despised at Court (Ind. 86–8), lend some colour to the attribution, but, as Sir E. K. Chambers says, 'the description of the "creature of a most perfect and diuine temper" in II. iii. surely goes beyond even Jonson's capacity of self-praise' (*Elizabethan Stage*, iii, p. 364). He is inclined to suggest Donne, the 'Criticus of Jonson's lost commentary on the *Ars Poetica*' (*Conv. Dr.* xvi. 416–17). But is it necessary in this play to find personal portraits for the chief characters? Who, in that case, is Arete? As Dekker found Marston and himself in Hedon and Anaides (see note on III. iii. 25–6), Jonson was easy to identify. We have discussed the whole question in the introductory Essay, vol. i, pages 406–12.

The latest critic of these early plays, Professor Oscar J. Campbell, aptly says that Crites is 'attached to the court of the divine Cynthia as a kind of moral laureate'. 'In brief, he is Jonson's notion of an ideal critic of manners and morals' (*Comicall Satyre*, pp. 84–6).

6. *Asotus*. A character in Massinger's *Bondman* is 'Asotus, a foolish Lover, and the sonne of Cleon' (who is rich).

17. *Philautia*, or 'self-love', used by Bacon together with 'wisdom for a man's self' to express the idea of 'selfishness', a word first found in the works of Puritan divines about 1650 (Trench, *Past and Present*, p. 154). Cf. Heywood, *A Challenge for Beautie*, I. ii (1636, B3ᵛ), 'I am not so much infected with that same Court-sicknesse *Philautia*, or selfe-love, to scorne the service of any generous Spirit.' See Professor Campbell's illustrations of self-love as a vice (*Comicall Satyre*, p. 90).

23. *Time*, or 'Honour' (Greek τιμή). In the Quarto Jonson marks the disyllabic character of the word by printing 'TimE'.

The Scene

Gargaphie, a valley and spring of Boeotia sacred to Diana, where Acteon was torn in pieces by his hounds (Ovid, *Met.* iii. 155–6). This does not prevent Amorphus from travelling to the Alps, Venice, and Padua (I. iv. 79, 86).

Induction

9. *the cloake*. Cf. T. Heywood, *The Four Prentises of London*, 1615: '*The Prologue*. Enter three in blacke clokes, at three dores. 1. *What meane you, my maisters, to appeare thus before your times? Doe you not know that I am the Prologue? Do you not see this long blacke veluet cloke vpon my backe? Haue you not sounded thrice? Do I not looke pale, as fearing to bee out in my speech? Nay, haue I not all the signes of a Prologue about me?*'

22. *the cuts*. Straws unequally cut—in this case three straws—were held out with one end evenly placed: he who drew the shortest (or some-

times he who drew the longest) was the one on whom the lot fell. Cf.
Marston, *The Malcontent*, ed. 2; Induction (1604, A3ᵛ),'After supper we
drew cuttes for a score of Apricoks, the longest cut stil to draw an
Apricoke.'
39 margin. *breaches*, breaks, pauses. Cf. 121 below.
41. *saued by his booke*, can read the 'neck-verse' and so escape hanging,
as Jonson himself did after killing Gabriel Spencer (*B.F.* I. iv. 7, 8, III.
v. 262); with a further reference to the Elizabethan custom of posting
up the title of the play and the scene. The title and scene of *Poetaster*
(Induction, 3, 28) and the title of *The Magnetic Lady* (Induction, 74–5)
are marked in this way.
47. *anie of our play-bookes*. 'A thrust chiefly aimed at Lyly', says
Dr. Judson, who instances Cupid in *Sapho and Phao*, 1591, *Galathea*,
1592, *Love's Metamorphosis*, 1601, and Cupid and Mercury in *The Woman
in the Moon*, 1597. Cf. Shirley, *The Coronation*, IV. iii (1640, G4), where
Cupid appears in a masque,

> There's *Cupid* now that little Gentleman,
> Has troubled every masque at Court this seven yeare.

69. *the whetstone*, i.e. Cos (Latin *cos*, 'a whetstone'): cf. II. iii. 99–102,
v. xi. 112. The lying of travellers was proverbial, and an old punishment
of liars was to hang a whetstone round their neck. Cunningham on
I. v. 8, 9 quotes Riley, *Memorials of London*, p. 316, describing the
punishment of John de Hackford in 1364 for preferring a false charge of
conspiracy: 'The said John shall come out of Newgate without hood or
girdle, barefooted and unshod, with a whetstone hung by a chain from
his neck, and lying on his breast, it being marked with the words *a false
liar*.' Cf. John Heywood, *The fifth hundred of Epigrammes*, 'Of a lyar,
98' (*Works*, 1562, Bbij):

> Where doth Francis fabler now lie, Jane?
> At signe of the whetstone in double tunge lane.

Later the whetstone was a reward in lying competitions: cf. *An Admonition to the Parliament, 1570–2*, 1617, p. 14 'Hee'—the minister—'againe
posteth it'—the service—'ouer as fast as he can gallop: for either he
hath two places to serve, or else there are some games to be plaid in the
afternoone as lying for the whetstone . . .' S. Nicholson, *Acolastus his
after-wit*, 1600, G3ᵛ:

> Shepheard, I glory in the happie chance,
> That made me Mistris of so kinde a man,
> And one so well my praises can aduance;
> Good Lord, how long since you the whetstone wan?

70. *entertaines*, engages as a servant.
78. *ingeniously*, ingenuously.
departs withall, parts with.
116. *gentile*, an older spelling—Chaucer has it—matching the Latin

gentilis. Jonson frequently has it, but in *The Forest*, xi. 45, 'That is an essence farre more gentle, fine' corrects an earlier reading, 'That is an essence most gentile, and fine'.

118. *three sorts of tabacco.* Dekker in *The Guls Horne-booke*, 1609, p. 5, appeals to Tobacco to 'make the phantastick *Englishmen* (aboue the rest) more cunning in the distinction of thy *Rowle Trinidado, Leafe* and *Pudding*, then the whitest-toothd Blackamoore in all *Asia*'.

121. *breaches.* Cf. Lewis Sharpe, *The Noble Stranger*, 1640, E3:

> *Pupillus.* But I will speak to her, and because she shall
> Not say I speak without book, this learned
> *Littleton* shall be my prompter—
> *Takes out a booke and holds it in his hand, and looks on it at the breaches.*
> Bright, bright Moon-shine of beauty.

And Macilente's comment in *E.M.O.* III. ix. 69, 70, 'I ne're knew tobacco taken as a *parenthesis*, before.'

135. *better-gather'd*, more composed.

140. *a stoole*; 142. *sixpence.* Cf. *B.F.* v. iii. 63–4, *Ep.* xii. 18; H. Fitz-geffrey, *Certain Elegies*, 1618, in 'The Third Booke, of Humours: Intituled Notes from Black-Fryers', F2ᵛ:

> A Stoole and Cushion! Enter *Tissue slop!*
> Vengeance! I know him well, did he not drop
> Out of the *Tyring-house*?

Dekker, *The Guls Horne-booke*, 1609, p. 29: 'By sitting on the stage, you may (with small cost) purchase the deere acquaintance of the boyes: haue a good stoole for six-pence: at any time know what particular part any of the infants present: get your match lighted, examine the play-suits lace, and perhaps win wagers upon laying tis copper, &c.'

148. *a piece of perspectiue* in this context can only be a reference to a painted cloth used for scenery, like 'the sittie of Rome' in Henslowe's inventory of properties of the Admiral's men in 1598, which was used in Marlowe's *Doctor Faustus.* It cannot be here the peep-show of *Alch.* III. iv. 87, or the optical toy of *U.V.* ii. 9–11.

150. *cracke*, pert boy. Cf. 167 below, II. i. 5, *D. is A.* II. viii. 58, and *Coriolanus*, I. iii. 67–8, '*Val.* 'Tis a noble childe. *Virg.* A Cracke Madam.'

153. *good clothes.* Cf. *E.M.O.* II. vi. 52 (Rich apparell) 'takes possession of your stage at your new play'.

161. *his presence in the tiring-house.* Contrast *B.F.* Ind. 28–30.

162. *booke-holder*, prompter. He is a character in the induction to *Bartholomew Fair* (ll. 45 foll.); cf. *Every Woman in her Humour*, 1609. B3: 'He would sweare like an Elephant, and stampe and stare (God blesse vs) like a play-house book-keeper, when the actors misse their entrance.'

Dekker in *Satiro-mastix*, 1602, M1, makes Horace-Jonson promise not to 'sit in a Gallery, when your Comedies and Enterludes haue entred their Actions, and there make vile and bad faces at euerie lyne, to make Gentlemen haue an eye to you, and to make Players afraide to take your part⟨s⟩.'

166. *enghles.* Cf. *C. is A.* I. iv. 3, 'Ingle'.

175. *immodest and obscene writing.* Cf. *Volp.* ded. 46 'such foule, and vn-wash'd baud'ry, as is now made the foode of the *scene*'.

178. *stale apothegmes.* *Volp.* prol. 23, of his own practice: 'Nor hales he in a gull, old ends reciting.'

179. *farce*, stuff.

181. *laundresse, or hackney-man*, types of lower-class ignorance

182. *common stages.* 'The eyrie of children, little eyases,' in *Hamlet* (II. ii. 335 foll.) 'are now the fashion, and so berattle the common stages —so they call them—that many wearing rapiers are afraid of goose-quills, and dare scarce come thither.' This may be a direct reference to the present passage. The phrase is used also in Nashe's *Summer's Last Will and Testament* (prol. 65 foll.), 'Moralizers, you that wrest a neuer meant meaning out of euery thing, applying all things to the present time, keepe your attention for the common Stage: for here are no quips in Characters for you to reade.' Here, however, the words point to the private performance before Archbishop Whitgift at Croydon, and 'common Stage' means 'public theatre'.

184. *liued . . . vpon another mans trencher.* Juvenal, of parasites, 'aliena vivere quadra' (*Sat.* v. 2).

187. *how soone they had drest it.* Private comments made when criticizing Jonson's slowness in composition: 'you Nastie Tortois, you and your Itchy Poetry brake out like Christmas, but once a-yeare, and then you keepe a Reuelling, & Arraigning.'—Dekker, who said this in *Satiro-mastix* L3ᵛ, put on the title-page of his *Seuen deadly Sinnes of London*, 1606, '*Opus septem dierum*.' So Jasper Mayne's lines in *Jonsonus Virbius*

> Scorne then their censures, who gave out, *thy Witt*
> As long upon a *Comœdie* did sit
> As *Elephants* bring forth.

189. *foot-cloth nags.* *C. is A.* IV. ix. 37.

195. *some three or foure playes.* Gifford quoted *Iack Drums Entertainment*, played by the Children of Pauls in 1600 (1601, H3ᵛ):

> *Sir Ed. Fortune.* I sawe the children of *Powles* last night,
> And troth they pleasde me prettie, prettie well,
> The Apes in time will do it hansomely.
> *Planet.* Ifaith I like the Audience that frequenteth there
> With much applause: A man shall not be choakte
> With the stench of Garlicke, nor be pasted
> To the barmy Iacket of a Beer-brewer.
> *Brabant Iu.* 'Tis a good gentle Audience, & I hope the Boyes
> Will come one day into the Court of requests.

Bra. Sig. I and they had good Playes, but they produce
Such mustie fopperies of antiquitie,
And do not sute the humorous ages backs
With cloathes in fashion.

Other plays are probably Lyly's *Love's Metamorphosis*, 1601, 'First playd by the Children of Paules, and now by the Children of the Chapell'; *The Wisdom of Doctor Dodipoll*, 1600, 'As it hath bene sundrie times Acted by the Children of Powles'; and *Histriomastix*, originally perhaps a play of 1589, and probably revived by the Paul's boys in 1599 (E. K. Chambers, *Elizabethan Stage*, iv, p. 18).

201. *ciuet-wit*, perfumed dandy, Pope's 'courtly Civet-cats' (*Epilogue to the Satires*, ii. 183).

203. *vellets*, 'Veluets' in Q. Jonson has both forms, and also 'vellute' (*M.L.* v. iii. 27), which is closer to the medieval Latin *vellutum*.

207. *prunes his mustaccio*. A metaphor from falconry. When a hawk prunes, or picks her feathers, 'she is lyking and lusty', says the *Boke of St. Albans*, 'and whanne she hathe doone she will rowse hire myghtyly' (Harting, *Ornithology of Shakespeare*). Cf. III. iv. 56, and *Und.* ii. (5) 35 ('proyne').

mustaccio, 'adopted in the sixteenth century, partly from Spanish *mostacho*, and partly from its source, the Italian *mostaccio* (*O.E.D.*).

209–10. *the Old Hieronimo (as it was first acted)*. Cf. *B.F.*, Induction 106–10: 'He that will sweare, *Ieronimo*, or *Andronicus* are the best plays, yet, shall pass vnexcepted at, heere, as a man whose Iudgement shewes it is constant, and hath stood still, these fiue and twentie, or thirtie yeares. Though it be an *Ignorance*, it is a vertuous and stay'd ignorance.' The production was therefore between 1584 and 1589. In January 1597 the play was revived by the Admiral's men, and Henslowe entering it in his *Diary* marks it as new. 'As it was first acted' would therefore refer to the earlier version. In *Satiro-mastix*, 1602, G3ᵛ, Dekker says that Jonson 'took mad Ieronimoes part, to get seruice among the Mimickes'; this would refer to the revival. The King's men had taken the play from the Chapel children in 1602, according to the induction in Marston's *Malcontent*, 1604, A4.

211. *great-bellied*. Cf. *Disc.* 196.

212. *when Monsieur was here*. Francis, Duke d'Alençon and afterwards d'Anjou, a suitor for Elizabeth's hand; he sent her a love-letter in June 1572, and paid three visits to England, the last in November 1579. As Gifford remarked, this visit is spoken of as if it marked an epoch. Jonson has it in *Mercury Vindicated*, 100: cf. Dekker, *The Seuen deadly Sinnes of London*, 1606, v, 'the yeare when *Monsieur* came in'; Middleton, *A Mad World*, IV. ii (1608, F3), 'in *Mounsieurs* dayes'.

216. *shakes his bottle-head*. So *E.M.I.* IV. ii. 51–2, 'shakes his head like a bottle, to feele and there be any braine in it!'

222. *Sall*: (Quarto text) the abbreviation of 'Salomon', i.e. Solomon. So Jonson spells the name *Alch.* II. i. 4, *B.F.* I. iv. 13, 27, 29. Gifford

492 *Plays*

rechristened him 'Salathiel', through not understanding this. See on *Epigram*, cxx.

Prologue

7, 8. Inaccurately quoted in Dekker's *Satiro-mastix*, 1602, E3ᵛ, in a soliloquy of Horace-Jonson:

> The Muses birdes the Bees were hiu'd and fed
> Vs in our cradle, thereby prophecying;
> *That we to learned eares should sweetly sing,*
> *But to the vulgar and adulterate braine,*
> *Should loath to prostitue our Virgin straine.*
> No, our sharpe pen shall keep the world in awe,
> Horace thy Poesie, wormwood wreathes shall weare,
> We hunt not for mens loues but for their feare.

20. *matter aboue words.* In *Poetaster*, v. iii. 551, Marston is advised, 'But let your *matter* runne before your words'. Bacon notes that 'the first distemper of learning' is 'when men study words and not matter' (*Advancement of Learning*, I. iv. 3).

I. i. 1, 2. Gifford inferred from this that the pair entered 'on different sides'. So in Marston's *Malcontent*, v. i (1604, H), '*Enter Maleuole and Maquerelle, at seuerall doores opposite, singing.*'

9. *rouer*. Dyce interpreted 'archer', i.e. one who 'shoots at rovers', but there is no authority for this use of the word.

14–17. From Lucian, *Dialogues of the Gods*, which has suggested part of the dialogue here. *You did neuer steale.* Dial. vii, *ΑΠ*. Ἐρώτα τὸν Ποσειδῶνα, οὗ τὴν τρίαιναν ἔκλεψεν, ἢ τὸν Ἄρη· καὶ τούτου γὰρ ἐξείλκυσε λαθὸν ἐκ τοῦ κολεοῦ τὸ ξίφος, ἵνα μὴ ἐμαυτὸν λέγω, ὃν ἀφώπλισε τοῦ τόξου καὶ τῶν βελῶν.

22. *fether-heel'd couss'.* Cf. ὁ πτερόπους Ἑρμῆς, Philodemus in *Anth. P.* xvi. 234. 4. *Poet.* IV. v. 211, 'feather-footed MERCVRY.'

22–34. From the *Dialogues of the Gods*, xxiv (Hermes complains to Maia), τοσαῦτα πράγματα ἔχω μόνος κάμνων καὶ πρὸς τοσαύτας ὑπηρεσίας διασπώμενος. ἕωθεν μὲν γὰρ ἐξαναστάντα σαίρειν τὸ συμπόσιον δεῖ καὶ διαστρώσαντα τὴν κλισίαν εὐθετίσαντά τε ἕκαστα παρεστάναι τῷ Διὶ καὶ διαφέρειν τὰς ἀγγελίας τὰς παρ' αὐτοῦ ἄνω καὶ κάτω ἡμεροδρομοῦντα, καὶ ἐπανελθόντα ἔτι κεκονιμένον παρατιθέναι τὴν ἀμβροσίαν· πρὶν δὲ τὸν νεωνήτου τοῦτον οἰνοχόον ἥκειν καὶ τὸ νέκταρ ἐγὼ ἐνέχεον. τὸ δὲ πάντων δεινότατον ὅτι μηδὲ νυκτὸς καθεύδω μόνος τῶν ἄλλων, ἀλλὰ δεῖ με καὶ τότε τῷ Πλούτωνι ψυχαγωγεῖν καὶ νεκροπομπὸν εἶναι καὶ παρεστάναι τῷ δικαστηρίῳ· οὐ γὰρ ἱκανά μοι τὰ τῆς ἡμέρας ἔργα, ἐν παλαίστραις εἶναι κἂν ταῖς ἐκκλησίαις κηρύττειν καὶ ῥήτορας ἐκδιδάσκειν, ἀλλ' ἔτι καὶ νεκρικὰ συνδιαπράττειν μεμερισμένον.

26. *a crowde*, 'an ancient Celtic musical instrument of the viol class, now obsolete, having in early times three strings, but in its later form six, four of which were played with a bow and two by twitching with the fingers; an early form of the fiddle' (*O.E.D.*). Cf. *S.S.* I. iv. 45, *H.W.* 275, *Warble vpon a crowde*: cf. the Latin use of *cano*, as in *canere tibia*.

46. *made the whole bodie of diuinitie tremble.* Cf. *Dialogues*, vi. 3,

Zeus admits ὁ δ' ἔρως βίαιόν τί ἐστι καὶ οὐκ ἀνθρώπων μόνον ἄρχει, ἀλλὰ καὶ ἡμῶν αὐτῶν ἐνίοτε.

47. *Saturnius*, Jupiter, son of Saturn.

51. *in decimo-sexto*. A metaphor from the book in which the size of a page is a sixteenth of a sheet. Cf. Brathwaite, *Whimzies*, 1631, p. 196, of the Puritan, 'Hee sets forth in an *Amsterdam* print his *faith* and *workes* in two severall *tomes*, and in two different *volumes*; the first in *folio*, the latter in *Decimo Sexto*.' Hence = diminutive: Lyly, *Mother Bombie*, II. i. 44–6, ed. Bond, 'Looke where *Halfepenie*, *Sperantus* boy, commeth; though bound vp in *decimo sexto* for carriage, yet a wit in *folio* for coosnage'; T.M., *The Ant, and the Nightingale*, 1604, C, the ant is called 'this small Actor in lesse then *Decimo Sexto*'.

52. *charme your . . . tongue*, silence, as if by magic. Cf. *The Taming of the Shrew*, IV. ii. 58, 'To tame a shrew and charm her chattering tongue'.

53. *your snakie tipstaffe*, the caduceus or wand of Mercury with two snakes intertwined at the top of it: he had found the snakes fighting, had divided them with his wand, and then used them as an emblem. Cf. v. iv. 612–15.

56 foll. *Dialogues of the Gods*, vii. 3, of the infant Hermes, χθὲς δὲ προκαλεσάμενος τὸν Ἔρωτα κατεπάλαισεν εὐθὺς οὐκ οἶδ' ὅπως ὑφελὼν τὼ πόδε· εἶτα μεταξὺ ἐπαινούμενος τῆς Ἀφροδίτης μὲν τὸν κεστὸν ἔκλεψε προσπτυξαμένης αὐτὸν ἐπὶ τῇ νίκῃ, τοῦ Διὸς δὲ γελῶντος ἔτι τὸ σκῆπτρον· εἰ δὲ μὴ βαρύτερος ὁ κεραυνὸς ἦν καὶ πολὺ τὸ πῦρ εἶχε, κἀκεῖνον ἂν ὑφείλετο.

63. *girdle*. *Volp.* v. ii. 102.

67. *at Vulcans forge*. *Dialogues of the Gods*, vii. 2 (Hermes has just visited Hephaestus) ΑΠ. τί οὖν; πάντα ἔχεις τὰ ἐργαλεῖα καὶ οὐδὲν ἀπόλωλεν αὐτῶν; ΗΦ. πάντα, ὦ Ἄπολλον. ΑΠ. ὅμως ἐπίσκεψαι ἀκριβῶς. ΗΦ. μὰ Δία, τὴν πυράγραν οὐχ ὁρῶ.

69. *'tis ioy on you*. Cf. 'Shame on you!'

73. *casting-bottles*. *E.M.O.* IV. iv. 75.

pick-toothes. Ib. IV. i. 40.

74. *shittle-cocks*. For shuttle-cock as a Court amusement see II. iv. 39, IV. i. 44.

75. *iealous*, suspicious.

87. *come within me* (Quarto) continues the fencing metaphor of l. 86. Cf. *The Comedy of Errors*, v. i. 34 'Some get within him, take his sword away.'

110. *really*, royally.

122. *repercussive*, reverberating. *C. is A*. i. ix. 57.

I. ii. Echo, according to the old myths, was a mountain-nymph who incurred the anger of Juno by helping to hide Jupiter's unfaithfulness and was changed into an echo as a punishment. She pined away with unrequited love for Narcissus till only voice was left her. Nemesis punished Narcissus for his indifference by letting him see the reflection of his own face in water and making him fall in love with it. Ovid, in telling the story (*Metamorphoses*, iii. 339 foll.), weaves into his verse some mocking answers of the echo (ll. 379–92); the trick was a favourite one with Elizabethan writers. A full list of echo-scenes 'from Euripides to Thomas Hardy' is given by F. L. Lucas, in his edition of Webster, vol. ii, p. 195. The Elizabethan dramatists who used it were Wilson, *The Cobler's Prophesie*, 1594, C2; Peele, *The Old Wife's Tale*, 1595, C3ᵛ; Lodge, *The Wounds of Ciuil War*, 1594, E3ᵛ; Dekker, *Old Fortunatus*, 1600, I. i; Heywood, *Loves Maistress*, 1636, I. i; Webster, *The Duchess of Malfi*, 1623, v. iii; Mason, *The Turk*, 1610, v. i; Shirley, *The School of Compliment*, 1631, IV. v; Randolph, *Amyntas*, 1638, v. viii.

14. *Arise.* Dekker in *Satiro-mastix*, G4, baits Horace-Jonson, 'So, now arise sprite ath Buttry; no Herring-bone Ile not pull thee out, but arise dear Eccho rise, rise deuill, or Ile coniure thee vp.'

17. *conuert*, turn (Lat. *converto*).

25. *trophæe*, Jonson's favourite spelling. Cf. l. 87 below, and the verb 'trophæed' in v. xi. 17.

49–51. The thought is developed in Shakespeare's *Sonnets* i–xxix; in i. 5–8, there is the metaphor from the taper.

54. *Saturnia*, Juno, daughter of Saturn. See Ovid, *Met.* iii. 365.

59. *hearse*, tomb. Gifford compares Lycidas:

> He must not float upon his watery bier
> Unwept, and welter to the parching wind
> Without the meed of some melodious tear.

62. *The humorous aire.* Cf. II. iii. 165, 'humorous as the aire'; *Vision of Delight*, 28, 'Our sports are of the humorous night.'

65–75. Set to music by Henry Youll in *Canzonets to Three Voyces*, 1608, no. viii.

68. *diuision.* See *E.M.O.* III. ix. 135 n.

78–9. *Suffer my . . . eye . . . to taste. E.M.I.* IV. vii. 1.

86. *From Phrygian mountains.* A rock on Mount Sipylus near Magnesia in Asia Minor, presenting at a certain distance the semblance of a weeping woman, was anciently identified with Niobe.

90. *Latona.* Jonson may have confused Diana with her mother Latona, but in view of Catullus' ode to Diana, 'O Latonia, maximi | magna progenies Iovis' (xxxiv. 5, 6) and Virgil's 'nemorum Latonia custos' (*Æneid*, ix. 405), it is reasonable to conjecture 'Latonia', i.e. daughter of Latona, here: cf. 'Saturnius' I. i. 47, 'Saturnia', l. 54 above.

I. iii. 5. *Hyæna. C. is A.* v. v. 19.
Babion, from the French *babion*, a parallel form to 'baboon'.

8. *trauailing motion*, marionette. So of Tucca in *Poet.* v. iii. 195, 'I only know him for a motion.'

17. *I am a Rhinoceros*, I am monstrous and ungainly—the antithesis to 'an essence so sublimated, and refin'd by trauell' (l. 30). Cf. *Poet.* v. iii. 195.

19. *digression*, departure (Lat. *digressio*)—an affected use.

22. *By thy favour, sweet fount.* Like Malvolio's 'By your leave, wax' as he opens Olivia's supposed letter (*Tw. Night*, II. v. 85).

25. *garbe*, fashion. *E.M.O.* II. i. 85 n.

26. *trite*, frayed (Lat. *tritus*).

28. *peece*, individual. Common in Jonson: cf. *Alch.* II. iii. 225.

32. *tender*, exhibit, show forth, as in Polonius's 'you'll tender me a fool', i.e. 'you'll show yourself a fool in my eyes' (C. T. Onions). The 1640 Folio reads 'render', possibly a compositor's attempt to correct the text.

33. *mere extraction*, pure essence.

34. *returne vpon venter*. The form of speculation which Sir Puntarvolo tried in *Every Man out of his Humour* (II. iii. 243–51).

35. *the true lawes of the duello.* Three technical works on duelling had appeared before 1600: *Giacomo di Grassi his true Arte of Defence, plainlie teaching by infallable Demonstrations, and Figures and perfect Rules the manner and forme how a man without other Teacher or Master may safelie handle all sortes of Weapons aswell offensiue as defensiue: With a Treatise of Disceit or Falsinge: And with a waie or meane by priuate Industrie to obtaine Strength, Iudgement and Actiuitie*, 1594, translated by I. G., gentleman, and prefaced by T. Churchyard; *Vincentio Saviolo his Practice. In two Bookes. The first intreating of the vse of the Rapier and Dagger. The second, of Honor and Honorable Quarrels*, 1595; George Silver's *Paradoxes of Defence. Wherein is proued the true grounds of Fight to be in the short auncient weapons, and that the short Sword hath aduantage of the long Sword or long Rapier*, 1599.

It is not necessary to take literally Amorphus's boast that he is the first Englishman to 'enrich his country' with the laws of duelling. Stimulated by two draughts of the fountain, he is posing not only as superior but as anterior to the experts. It is he who arranges the mock-duel of courtship later, and this is a faint first hint.

36. *optiques*. 'Formerly the learned and elegant term' (*O.E.D.*): this would commend it to Amorphus.

46. *My thoughts and I am* . . . For the grammatical attraction of 'am' to the second subject cf. *Volp.* II. ii. 177; *As You Like it*, I. iii. 92–3, 'The love Which teacheth thee that thou and I am one'; *Welth, and Helth*, 1575? Bi, l. 206, 'Seyng that helth and I am met.'

I. iv. 4, 5. *Nec placere* . . . Horace, *Epistles*, I. xix. 2, 3, 'nulla placere diu . . .'

9. *nepenthe*, opiate.

10. *metheglin*, Welsh *meddyglyn*. First described by Sir T. Elyot in *The Castle of Helthe*, 1541, f. 36, 'Metheglyn, whiche is moste used in wales, by reason of hotte herbes boyled with hony, is hotter then meade.' Waspe says to the 'welsh Cuckold' Bristle in *B.F.* IV. vi. 51 rather inconsequently, 'You stinke of leeks, *Metheglyn*, and cheese.'

17. *argued*, proved (Lat. *arguo*).

18. *Lucian. Demosthenis Encomium*, § 15, οὐ γὰρ ὡς τὸν Αἰσχύλον ὁ

496   *Plays*

Καλλισθένης ἔφη που λέγων τὰς τραγῳδίας ἐν οἴνῳ γράφειν ἐξορμῶντα καὶ ἀναθερμαίνοντα τὴν ψυχήν, οὐχ οὕτως ὁ Δημοσθένης συνετίθει πρὸς μέθην τοὺς λόγους, ἀλλ᾽ ὕδωρ πίνων· ᾗ καὶ τὸν Δημάδην παῖξαί φασιν εἰς ταύτην τὴν ὑδροποσίαν ὡς οἱ ἄλλοι πρὸς ὕδωρ λέγοιεν, τὸν Δημοσθένην δὲ πρὸς ὕδωρ γράφειν.

22. *fittons*, fittens, lies. *Promptorium Parvulorum, c.* 1440, 163/1, 'Fyton, or lesynge, *mendacium*'. Emissary Fitton is a newsmonger in *The Staple of News*.

figments. Another courtier Puntarvolo uses the word in *E.M.O.* IV. iv. 5.

leasings. Ent. Alth. 41.

30. *Philargyrus.* Greek φιλάργυρος: he doted on Argurion (IV. i. 209).

42. *some catalogue.* Cf. *Cymbeline*, I. iv. 3–6, 'I could then have looked on him without the help of admiration, though the catalogue of his endowments had been tabled by his side and I to peruse it by items.'

50. *make this gentleman and I friends.* Cf. *E.M.I.* v. iii. 62.

55. *without me*, beyond me. *Sej.* II. 93.

84. *ragioni del stato*, 'discourse of *State*' (Quarto), political considerations, *Volp.* IV. i. 141, *Nept. Tr.* 245. Cf. Bacon, *The Advancement of Learning*, I. ii. 3, 'men bred in learning are perhaps to seek in points of convenience and accommodating for the present, which the Italians call *ragioni di stato.*'

85. *out of his element.* One of Amorphus's affectations: cf. *Twelfth Night*, III. i. 54–6, 'Who you are and what you would are out of my welkin, I might say "element", but the word is over-worn.'

93. *burning of cannes.* The wooden measures then in use had their quantity legally attested by a brand. In *The Taming of the Shrew*, Induction, sc. ii. 86, Sly is indignant that the hostess 'brought stone jugs and no seal'd quarts'.

94. *pulling doune a superstitious crosse.* Stow in his *Survay of London*, 1603, p. 268 records of the Cross in West Cheap that in 1581 the images 'of Christ his resurrection, of the virgin *Mary*, king *Ed.* the confessor' were broken and defaced; in 1595 the image of the Virgin was repaired, but in 1596 'on the east side of yᵉ same crosse, . . . vnder the image of Christs resurrection defaced, was then set vp a curious wrought tabernacle of gray Marble, and in the same an Alabaster Image of *Diana*, and water conuayd from the Thames, prilling from her naked breast for a time, but now decaied' (*W*). Jonson's Catholicism peeps out here, but he need not have substituted the obscene figure of Priapus for Diana.

97–8. *buckets . . . parish church.* Fire buckets were hung up in the choir of the parish church. 'They were originally carried up ladders on men's shoulders, but so early as 1686 Gemelli says, "They have now invented a portable engine which throws the water so high as to quench fires on the tops of the houses." But the water had still to be brought in these buckets' (Cunningham). Cleueland in *The Rebel Scot*, ll. 5–7,

> I am all on fire,
> Not all the buckets in a Countrey Quire
> Shall quench my rage.

And Dryden, of the Fire of London, *Annus Mirabilis*, stanza 229, has 'Some ran for Buckets to the hallow'd Quire.' Jasper Mayne notices the inscriptions in *The Citie Match*, ii. iii (1639, E2):

> *Tim.* What am I sweet Lady?
> My Father is an Aldermans fellow, and I
> Hope to be one in time. *Aur.* Then, Sir, in time
> You may be remembred at the quenching of
> Fired houses, when the bells ring backward, by
> Your name upon the Buckets.

101. *painting of his posts.* Cf. *E.M.O.* iii. ix. 23 n.

108–9. *a most curious . . . as.* A frequent construction: so *Alch.* v. v. 133.

123. *(being altogether vn-trauel'd)*, a good example of Jonson's terseness: 'you being' is clearly suggested by the context.

133. *motley.* Cf. Fletcher, *The Maid in the Mill*, iv. ii, 'What motley stuff is this? Sirrha, speak truth' (Gifford).

149. *a beauer.* P. Stubbes, *The Anatomy of Abuses in England*, 2nd ed. 1583 (ed. Furnivall, p. 50), on 'the diuersity of hattes' mentions 'some of a certaine kind of fine haire. These thei call, Beuer hattes of .xx, xxx, or xl shillinges price fetched from beyond the seas.' Cooke, *Greenes Tu quoque*, 1614, K1ᵛ: '*Scat.* Felts? By this, light, mine is a good Beauer: | It cost me three pound this morning vpon trust.' So W. Fennor, *The Compters Common-wealth*, 1617, p. 33, 'come our Taylor shall furnish you . . . your four shillings dutch felt shall be conuerted to a three pound Beuer.' A four-pound bever is promised in *M.L.* v. ii. 18, but that was 'Set with enamell'd studs'. See M. C. Linthicum, *Costume in the Drama*, p. 229.

152, 154. *French account . . . so neere his head.* The same quibble as in *E.M.O.* ii. i. 113–18.

156. *band*, hatband.

conceited recalls Osric's 'liberal-conceited carriages' (*Hamlet*, v. ii. 159).

162. *after the Italian manner*, i.e. in order to be refused. Cf. Campion's epigram 'ad Calvum' in the *Poemata* of 1595, E4ᵛ:

> Italico vultu donas mihi Calue machæram,
> More Britannorum protinus accipio,
> Id mihi succenses; nunc ergo remittere conor,
> Quo more id faciam non tamen inuenio.

A marginal note adds: 'Italorum comitas est laudanti quiduis amico obtrudere, si autem acceperit tanquam sordidissimum respuere.'

172. *What make you . . . here?* Common in the sixteenth and seventeenth centuries for 'what are you doing' (*O.E.D.*, s.v. 'make', 58).

182. *be not so sad.* 'Probably the burden of some forgotten song' (Dyce, *Remarks*, p. 280). Cf. Randolph, *The Jealous Lovers*, 1632, i. ii:

> *Asotus.* Well, pockets, well,
> Be not so sad; though you are heavy now,
> You shall be lighter.

185. *block*, the wooden shape on which the hat was moulded, and hence the fashion of the hat. *Histrio-mastix*, 1610, D3, '*Mavortius.* Your hat is of a better block then mine. *Philarchus.* Is on a better block, your Lordship means.'

187. *and not so few. E.M.O.* III. ix. 105.

192. *proofe against thunder.* Brathwaite, *Whimzies*, 1631, p. 174, '*Lawrell, hawthorne,* and *Seale-skinne* are held preservatives against *thunder.*'

I. v. 5, 6. *casheere . . . in priuate.* So *E.M.O.* I. ii. 140–2.

9. *a whetstone.* See Induction, 69.

31–2. Repeated in a different context in *Love Restored*, 35–6. From Seneca, *Ep.* 59, 15: 'Omnes istos' (i.e. pleasure-seekers) 'oblectamenta fallacia et brevia decipiunt, sicut ebrietas, quae unius horae hilarem insaniam longi temporis taedio pensat.'

33–5. From Seneca, *Naturales Quaestiones*, praef. 5, 'O quam res est contempta homo nisi supra humana surrexerit!' Quoted also by Daniel in his address to the Countess of Cumberland, ll. 98–9 (*Certaine Epistles* in the Folio of 1601):

> . . . vnlesse aboue himselfe he can
> Erect himselfe, how poore a thing is man!

a man. The article individualizes the description as in the Folio text of *Julius Caesar*, II. i. 67–9:

> the state of a man,
> Like to a little kingdom, suffers then
> The nature of an insurrection.

42. *intention* should mean 'looking intently', like the 'serious and intentiue eyes' of *E.M.O.* Ind. 138, but qualified here by 'mere' seems no more than 'observation'.

64. *motion*, puppets. Cf. *Disc.* 240.

II. i. 5. *cracks.* Ind. 167.

22. *page, boy, and sirha.* Cf. II. iii. 72–4, IV. v. 138–40.

42. *monkie.* Cf. the Palinode, 16.

45. *not suspected*, i.e. used as a bath and not for the cure of disease. A sign of the gallant in *E.H.* IV. ii. 233.

46. *pedant*, a teacher of the language: cf. III. v. 91–3.

48–9. *a rimer, . . . better then a poet.* For this distinction see *Disc.* 2445–9: 'The common Rymers poure forth Verses, such as they are, (*ex tempore*) but there never comes from them one Sense, worth the life of a Day. A Rymer, and a *Poet*, are two things.' Similarly in *The Forest*, xii. 68–9, 'a better verser . . . (Or *Poet*, in the court account)', and *The Fortunate Isles*, 291–9. The distinction goes back to the early days of criticism: Quintilian describes Cornelius Severus as 'versificator quam poëta melior' (x. i. 89). So in the days of the Pleiade, Ronsard writes: 'Il y a autant de difference entre vn Poëte & vn versificateur, qu'entre vn

bidet & vn genereux coursier de Naples, & pour mieux les accomparer,
entre vn venerable Prophete et vn Charlatan vendeur de triacles'
(*Preface de la Franciade, Œuvres*, 1609, p. 583), and Du Bellay, 'Et vous
autres si mal equippez, dont l'ignorance a donné le ridicule nom de
rymeurs à nostre langue (comme les Latins appellent leurs mauvais
poëtes versificateurs)' (*La Deffense et Illustration de la Langue Francoyse*,
1549, ch. xi).

51. *beates a tailour.* Cf. Middleton, *Women beware Women*, I. ii (1657,
H): 'Sord. What, my Ladies Tailor? *Ward.* I, and beat him too. *Sord.*
Nay that's no wonder, He's us'd to beating.'

56. *the lanching of some three ships.* Cf. *E.H.* III. ii. 15–18.

58–60. *he do's hire a stocke.* Cf. Nashe, *Lenten Stuffe*, 1599 (*Works*, ed.
McKerrow, iii, pp. 148–9), on the 'primerose knight of Primero', who is
reduced to forty shillings 'to trie his fortune with at the cardes in the
presence; which if it prosper, the court cannot containe him, but to
London againe he will, to reuell it, and haue two playes in one night,
inuite all the Poets and Musitions to his chamber the next morning;
where, against theyr comming, a whole heape of money shall bee be-
spread vppon the boord, and all his trunkes opened to shewe his rich
sutes' (quoted in Baskerville's *English Elements in Jonson's Early
Comedy*, pp. 273–4).

60. *a verie necessarie perfume for the presence.* Cf. *E.M.O.* Characters,
41. Dr. Judson compares Shirley, *The Lady of Pleasure*, II. ii (*Works*, ed.
Gifford, iv, p. 33), Celestina on Master Haircut:

> He is the sweetest of all men that visit me.
> *Isab.* How mean you, madam?
> *Cel.* He is full of powder;
> He will save much in perfume for my chamber,
> Were he but constant here.

63. *how many great horse.* Cf. *E.M.O.* III. ix. 49–51.

64–5. *the whole, or the halfe pommado.* The *pomado* was vaulting on a
horse, the *pomado reversa* vaulting off again. Henry V, wooing Katharine,
says, 'If I could win a lady . . . by vaulting into my saddle with my
armour on my back, . . . I should quickly leap into a wife.' For the 'whole
pomado' there is a plate and description in W. Stokes's *The Vaultinge
Master*, 1641, plate 11.

67. *how many shirts . . . tennis.* Cf. Dekker, *The Guls Horne-booke*,
1609, p. 24, 'discourse . . . how often you haue sweat in the Tennis-court
with that great Lord.'

II. ii. 24. *Alpine hills.* Chapman has the conceit in *Ouids Banquet of
Sence*, 1595, E3, when Ovid, about to touch Corinna's breast, exclaims:

> See *Cupids* Alps which now thou must goe ouer,
> Where snowe that thawes the Sunne doth euer lye.

28. *nicke all*, hit the mark.

47. *alwayes weares a muffe.* The earliest quotation for 'muff' in the

O.E.D. They were worn by men as well as women in the seventeenth and eighteenth centuries. Pepys in his *Diary* for 30 November 1662 writes: 'This day I first did wear a muffe, being my wife's last year's muffe, and now I have bought her a new one, this serves me very well' (*Diary*, ed. Wheatley, ii, p. 405).

49. *wit enough . . . warme.* Proverbial: see *B.F.* v. iv. 362–3, and *Iohn Heywoodes woorkes*, 1562, 'Epigrammes vpon Prouerbes', *Wit kept by warmth*, 131:

> Thou art wyse inough, if thou keepe thee warme:
> But the least colde that cumth, kilth thy wit by harme.

55. *potato's.* *E.M.O.* ii. iii. 83, 'potato-pies, and such good vnctuous meats', contrasted, as here, with porridge. *Oyster-pyes*, another succulent dish. There is no suggestion of aphrodisiacs, as Cunnngham and Judson think.

57. *prophecie.* The Court-game suggested in iv. iii. 83–6.

59. *cioppini*, high raised shoes with cork soles, apparently Spanish in origin: Minsheu has *chapin*, 'a woman's . . . high cork shoes'. 'The English writers *c.* 1600 persistently treated the word as Italian, even spelling it *cioppino*, pl. *cioppini*, and expressly associated it with Venice, so that, although not recorded in Italian Dictionaries, it was apparently temporarily fashionable there'—*O.E.D.*, which adds that there is little or no evidence of its use in England, except on the stage, but Sir Walter Scott, 'and others after him', have treated it as an English article of dress in the seventeenth century. See Coryat's *Crudities*, 1611, pp. 261–2, quoted in *D. is A.* iv. iv. 68–90, where Jonson has borrowed from it. In the Tradescant collection at the Ashmolean, Oxford, there are two pairs of these chopines and an odd one, the last about 3 in. high, covered with satin and embroidered with silver.

For the lover's wish to be one of the shoes cf. *E.M.O.* iii. ix. 104–6.

77. *two essentiall parts.* Discussed in our introduction, vol. iv, pages 21, 22. The taunt was repeated in *The Forest*, iv. 45–8.

80. *all that comes in his cheeks.* Cf. *Disc.*, 783. Borrowed from the Latin: 'Tu, quaeso, crebro ad me scribe, vel quod in buccam venerit'— Cicero, *ad Atticum*, vii. x., and Martial, xii. xxiv. 415, 'Hic mecum licet, hic, Iuvate, quidquid | in buccam tibi venerit loquaris.'

will blush no more then a sackbut. Not the musical instrument but a butt of sack. Cf. J. Trapp's *Commentary upon Ezra*, ix. 6, 'But he is past grace that is past shame, and can blush no more then a sackbut.'

88. *below the salt.* A large salt-cellar placed in the middle of a long table and serving as a social boundary mark; important guests were distinguished by being placed above it. Massinger, *The City Madam*, i. i (1658, B1ᵛ), describing Lady Frugal's treatment of her ruined brother-in-law,

> My proud Ladie
> Admits him to her Table, marry euen
> Beneath the Salt, and there he sits the subiect
> Of her contempt and scorn.

90. *tissue*, 'a rich kind of cloth, often interwoven with gold or silver'—
O.E.D., comparing *The Romaunt of the Rose*, 1104:

> The barres were of gold ful fyne
> Upon a tyssu of satyne.

92. *illiberall sciences*. Cf. *N.I.* 1. iii. 81–2, 'The arts | Or seuen liberall
deadly sciences | Of Pagery, or rather Paganisme'.

93. *neuer kneeles but to pledge healths*. Cf. *E.M.O.* v. iv. 73 n.

94. *pudding tobacco*. Cf. Ind. 119 n.

98. *to a friend in want* . . . Juvenal, *Sat.* vii. 74–5, 'Non habet infelix
Numitor quod mittat amico, | Quintiliae quod donet habet.'

99. *soldred groat*. In Lodge's *Wits Miserie*, 1596, p. 28, the demon of
Usury buys up cracked angels and makes bargains with them, while the
borrower 'ventures on the crackt angels, some of which cannot fly for
soldering'.

101. *punquetto*, young punk. 'Punquettees' in *Alch.* 11. i. 23. 'One
of the forms may be a misprint'—O.E.D., which apparently inclines to
'punquette' in both passages.

11. iii. With this scene cf. J. Cooke, *Greenes Tu quoque*, 1614, 14ᵛ,
where a neophyte is practising faces: '*Bub.* See, yonder's the companie
that I looke for; therefore if you will set my face of any fashion, pray
doe it quickly. *Sta.* You carry your face as well as eare an *Italian* in the
world, only inrich it with a Smyle, and tis incomparable: and thus much
more, at your first apparance, you shall perhaps strike your acquaintance into an extasie, or perhaps a laughter: but tis ignorance in them,
which will soone be ouercome, if you perseuer.'

1. *You are now within*, i.e. the audience are supposed to imagine a
change to an inner room with Cupid and Mercury invisible in the background. *In regard of the presence*—so the First and Second Folios;
'within reguarde' in the Quarto—'in view of', a rare use of 'regard'.

6. *when the wolfe enters*. An allusion to the Latin proverb, 'lupus in
fabula' (cf. l. 75), our 'talk of the devil'. Cicero, *ad Atticum*, XIII. xxxiii.
4, 'De Varrone loquebamur: lupus in fabula; venit enim ad me'; and
Chapman, *An Humorous Day's Mirth*, I. ii (1599, A3), 'See where he
comes, now must I say, *Lupus est in fabula*, for these latine ends are
part of a gentleman and a good scholler.'

13. *refell*, refute (Lat. *refello*).
pseudodox, a coinage of Jonson's suggested here by the antithesis to
'paradox'.

14. *the index of the mind*. Cicero, *In Pisonem*, i. 1, 'Oculi supercilia
frons voltus denique totus, qui sermo quidam tacitus mentis est'; Quintus
Cicero, *De petit. consul.* 44, 'Voltu ac fronte quae est animi ianua.'

29. *a beard*. The soldier 'bearded like the pard' in *As You Like It*,
11. vii. 150.

30. *intricate face*. Dr. Judson cites Earle, *Microcosmographie*, 1626,
of an attorney, no. 47, 'His skin becomes at last as dry as his parchment,
and his face as intricate as the most winding cause.'

32. *statists face*, statesman's face. Compare the justice in *As You Like It*, 'with eyes severe and beard of formal cut.'
42. *went with a vice.* So *C. is A.* II. vii. 80–1.
44. *puntilio. E.M.O.* II. ii. 22.
47. *northerly*, bleak, as Dr. Judson says, does not fit the context; we should expect 'southerly'.
66. *casting-bottle. E.M.O.* IV. iv. 75 n.
67. *mirrour*, a small glass worn by men in their hats and by women at their girdles. Cf. *Und.* ii (5), 40–1.
81. *smelt*, simpleton. Fletcher, *Loue's Pilgrimage*, v. ii, Incubo of Philippo, who has given him money without waiting to see if he had earned it:

> These direct men, they are no men of fashion,
> Talk what you will, this is a very smelt.

83. *the begger to follow him.* S. *of N.* II. iv. 210–11.
88. *with a cloue.* Cf. *M. Christmas*, 158–60.
pick-tooth. Cf. *E.M.O.* IV. i. 39; *King John*, I. i. 189–90, 'Now your traveller, He and his toothpick at my worship's mess.'; and the Affected Traveller in the Overburian *Characters* (ed. Paylor, p. 11), 'his pick-tooth is a maine part of his behaviour'.
90. *face . . . essayes.* Copied by R. Heath in the *Satyrs* appended to his *Epigrams*, 1650, p. 11:

> his speech is cream,
> Starcht as his beard, takes his hat off by th' brim
> Methodically 'twixt two fingers, while
> His face of Essayes seldom deigns to smile.

his beard an Aristarchus, stiff and formal, like the justice in *As You Like It*, II. vii. 155. There is a quibble on 'starch'd beard' (*Volp.* II. v. 15).
96. *ten constables. E.M.O.* I. ii. 17.
102. *Zani. E.M.O.* IV. ii. 44–5.
106. *bouoli*. . . . Florio, 1598: 'Bouolo, *a snayle, a cockle, a Periwincle*'; 'Fagioli, Fagiuoli, *a kind of pease like vnto a beane, called faseoles, welch beans, or kidney beanes*'; 'Caviare, *a kinde of salt meate used in Italie like black sope, it is made of the roes of fishes.*'
112. *galliard*, a quick dance in triple time, III. i. 9; *Beauty*, 364. Elyot, *The Castle of Helthe*, 1539, f. 50b, 'Vehement exercise is compounde of violent exercise and swift whan they are ioyned together at one tyme, as dansyng of galyardes.'
123. *humours and elements.* See the discussion in Appendix xix, pages 391–5. There are two well-known parallels to Jonson's description: the character of Brutus in *Julius Caesar*, v. v. 73–5—

> His life was gentle, and the Elements
> So mixt in him, that Nature might stand vp,
> And say to all the World, This was a man.—

and the revised character of Mortimer of Drayton's *The Barons Warres*, 1619, canto iii, stanza 40:

> He was a Man (then boldly dare to say)
> In whose rich Soule the Vertues well did sute,
> In whom, so mix'd, the Elements all lay,
> That none to one could Sov'raigntie impute,
> As all did governe, yet all did obay;
> He of a temper was so absolute,
> As that it seem'd, when Nature him began,
> She meant to shew all, that might be in Man.

Julius Caesar was acted in 1599, *Cynthia's Revels* in 1600: so Jonson was the borrower. Drayton borrowed from both.

137. *dares as little to offer an iniurie*. Worked out in *The New Inn*, IV. iv. 54 foll. Cf. *Und*. lix. 14–16.

143–5. From Seneca, *De Vita Beata*, v. 1, 'Potest beatus dici qui nec cupit nec timet beneficio rationis'; vi. 2, 'Beatus est is cui omnem habitum rerum suarum ratio commendat.'

162. *Argurion*. Some hints for the conception of Argurion are to be found in Aristophanes' *Plutus*, and the Lady Pecunia in *The Staple of News* is an expansion (Gifford).

166. *primero*. See *Ep*. cxii n.

II. iv. 6. *reform'd discipline*. The Quarto italicizes discipline with reference to the Puritan ring of the phrase.

7. *lady-bird*, a term of endearment from an older woman to a younger, as Mistress Touchstone to Gertrude, *E.H.* v. i. 158, or the Nurse to Juliet, *Romeo and Juliet*, I. iii. 3.

8. *intricately*. Cf. the Wright quotation in the next note, and *D. is A.* v. iv. 37–8, 'not Intricate, as one would say'.

16. *a strange word*. Cf. Lucian, *Lexiphanes*, 24, ἤν που ῥῆμα ἔκφυλον εὕρῃς ἢ αὐτὸς πλασάμενος οἰηθῇς εἶναι καλόν, τούτῳ ζητεῖς διάνοιαν ἐφαρμόσαι. This is the point which Jonson makes against Marston in *Poetaster*, using Lucian's satire for this purpose: see especially v. iii. 549–58. T. Wright, in *The Passions of the Mind*, 1604, pp. 111–12, criticizes '*Affectation in speech*': 'Some haue a peculiar manner of parley, they speake in print, hunt after metaphors, coyne phrases, and labour extreamely that their wordes may smell of subtilitie, elegancie, and neat deliuerie. . . . If they pen any thing to bee presented vnto the view of the world, you shal euer haue one new coined word or other which neuer saw light before it issued out of the mint of their imagination, and it will beseeme them as well as a peacocks fether a fooles cap. I heard once one of these worthy parolists who had got by the end the word *intricat*; he comming among as wise men as him selfe, tould them, that such a gentleman and he did beare most *intricat* loue one to another: he would haue said intier. Another had got the word *expostulat*, and he imagined it was to require, and so he requested a friend of his, to *expostulat* a

certaine fauour at his lords hands in his behalfe.' Davies of Hereford in
A Scourge for Paper-Persecutors, 1625 (p. 233 in the edition printed with
The Scourge of Folly, 1620), makes Paper personified say,

> And though I grieue, yet cannot choose but smile
> To see some moderne Poets feed my Soile
> With mighty Words that yeeld a monstrous Crop,
> *Embellish,** Blandishment* and *Equipage*
> Such Furies flie from their Muse holy rage.
> And if (perchance) one hit on *Surquedry,*
> Oh he writes rarely in sweet Poesie!
> But he that (*point-blank*) hits *Enueloped,*
> He (Lord receiue his Soule) strikes *Poetry dead.*

* These words are good: but ill vsed: in ouermuch vse sauouring of wittlesse affectation.

27. *had whelpt it her selfe.* Cf. Shadwell, *The Humorists*, ii (1671, p. 15):
'*Drybob.* Besides this Dog I stole from my Mother, who lov'd him as
well as if she had whelp'd him her self.'

39. *shittle-cock.* A fashionable game: in Marston's *What You Will*,
IV. i, Celia sends for her shuttle-cock and plays with it.

45–6. *in painting; and . . . poetry.* It is a sign of early work that Jonson
did not elaborate this with critical specimens, like Lady Politic Would-
be's display in *Volpone*, III. iv. 79–96. Philautia has one reference to a
painting (or a tapestry) in IV. i. 48–9; her only connexion with poetry
is to inspire Hedon's lyric of the Kiss (IV. iii. 242–53).

50. *integrate.* Moria's affectation for 'perfect'.

51. *aggrauate.* *C. is A.* v. vi. 16 '*Iuniper* . . . do not aggrauate my ioy.'

54. *out of measure.* The same quibble as in *E.M.I.* III. i. 95–6.

55. *the swim i' the turne.* At the dancing lesson in Chapman and
Shirley's *The Ball*, II. iii (1639, C2) the master says 'Carry your body in
the swimming fashion'; Massinger, *The Bondman*, III. iii (1624, F1ᵛ), to a
dancer, 'Carry your body swimming.'

57. *from*, differently from. Cf. *Julius Caesar*, II. i. 195–6:

> For he is superstitious grown of late,
> Quite from the main opinion he held once;

Twelfth Night, v. i. 319, 'Write from it, if you can, in hand or phrase.'

70. *the italian print.* For instance, Bartolomeo Grassi, *Dei Veri
Ritratti degl' Habiti di tutte le Parti del Mondo*, Rome, 1585, or, as
Gifford suggests, *Habiti Antichi e Moderni di Cesare Vicellio*, Venice,
1589.

75. *burne juniper.* A common practice at the time to purify the air
(see *E.M.O.* Characters, 53–4) and so Phantaste despises it.

78. *Suburbe-sunday-waiters.* Like the crowd at the Court christening
in *Henry VIII*, v. iv. 68–9, about whom the lord chamberlain rebukes the
porters:

> There's a trim rabble let in: are all these
> Your faithful friends o' the suburbs?

Similarly in *E.M.I.* I. iii. 134 'a suburbe-humor' means a lower type than that in the city.

85. *skin'd a new.* The *O.E.D.* explaining 'clothed', queries 'skin'd anew' and compares Beaumont and Fletcher, *The Scornful Lady*, II. ii, 'Off with your husks; I'le skin you all in Sattin.'

90. *that's counsell,* a secret. Cf. T. Heywood, *King Edward the Fourth*, part i (1600, F1r): '*King.* Faith, whether louest thou better *Harry* or *Edward*? *Hobs.* Nay, thats counsel, and two may keepe it, if one be away.' We still say, 'to keep one's own counsel'.

100. *vbiquitarie.* *E.M.O.* II. iii. 187.

102. *let her passe.* Phantaste analyses herself fully in IV. i. 171–214: she designs a Book of Humours (l. 213) which is to treat of the effects of love 'inwardly' in all temperaments and types of character, and also outwardly by just such foppery and folly as Jonson decided in his own analysis—for instance 'colour'd ribbands and good clothes'.

II. v. The Beggar's Rhyme is much fuller in the Quarto.

Blackingmen, sellers of blacking (and blacking-brushes?).

Corne-cutters. One appears in *B.F.* II. iv. crying 'Ha' you any cornes i' your feete, and toes?'

Sellers of marking stones. 'Buy a very fine marking stone' is one of the cries of Rome (i.e. London) in T. Heywood's *The Rape of Lucrece*, 1608, K2. The marking-stone was 'an earthy stone used for marking cattle, &c.' (*O.E.D.*).

Sow-gelders. Fletcher and Massinger, *The Beggers' Bush*, III. i (Folio, 1647, p. 82): '*Enter* Higgen *like a Sow-gelder, singing. Have ye any worke for the Sow-gelder, hoa?*'

Raylers, makers or fitters of rails. But the *O.E.D.* gives this sense of 'railer' as occurring first in Ogilvie 1882.

Fadingers, those who dance the 'fading' (*Irish M.* 82).

Thomalins, beggarly itinerants. Cf. *The Pinder of Wakefield*, 1632, H1.

Skinkers, tapsters.

Cuttlebungs, cut-purses. Cf. *2 Henry IV*, II. iv. 121, 'Away you cut-purse rascal! you filthy bung, away.'

Hookers, thieves who stole by hooking things: 'hokers, or Angglers' (Harman).

Horne-thums. *B.F.* II. iii. 30 n.

Post-knights, men who gained a living by giving false evidence in law courts. Cf. Nashe, *Pierce Pennilesse*, 1592 (*Works*, ed. McKerrow, i, p. 164), 'A knight of the Post, . . . a fellowe that will sweare you any thing for twelue pence.'

Iags, tatters: 'jag' literally a scrap, a shred of cloth. Cf. *Rustick Rampant* in Cleveland's *Works*, 1667, p. 415, 'To preserve a Shred, or jagg of an incertain ragged Estate.'

muscle-bags, thighs. Modelled on 'honey-bags', which are on the legs of the bees.

14, 15. *discouer . . . a little more too.* *E.M.I.* IV. vi. 75–6.

19. *languishing vpon the rushes.* Compare the picture of Elizabeth Woodville in the Sanctuary at Westminster in Sir T. More's *Workes*, 1557, p. 45 ('The Pittiful Life of King Edward V')—'The Queene her selfe satte alone alowe on the rishes all desolate and dismayde.' Bulleyn, *The Boke of Simples*, ed. 1579, p. 21, 'Rushes that growe vpon dry groundes, be good to strewe in Halle, Chambers, and Galleries, to walke vpon, defending apparell, as traynes of Gownes and Kertles, from dust. Rushes be olde Courtiers, and when they be nothing worth, then they be cast out of the doores, so be many that do tread vpon theim' (Gifford).

24. *a dish of eeles in a sand-bag.* Cf. Middleton and Dekker, *The Roaring Girl*, IV. i (1611, H3ᵛ), 'wriggle in and out, like an eele in a sandbag'.

III. i. 3. *grammaticall courtier*, like the 'courtier elementarie' of II. iii. 48, 'but newly enter'd, or as it were in the *alphabet* . . . of courtship'.

neophyte-player. See *E.M.O.* v. iv. 8 n.

9. *to vndertake the bastinado.* Like Bessus in *A King and no King* and Graccho in *The Duke of Milan*.

11. *beaten to the world.* Plutarch's *Morals*, Philemon Holland's translation, 1603, p. 390, 'one, who hath beene trained and employed all the daies of his life in politike affaires and throughly beaten to the world, and the administration of the common-weale' (τὸν ἐμβεβιωκότα πολιτικαῖς πράξεσι καὶ διηγνωνισομένον).

23. *as to haue taken vp a rush.* Cf. *E.M.O.* I. ii. 56, 'picke your teeth when you cannot speake'; R. Brathwaite, *A Strappado for the Diuell*, 1615, p. 125 ('The Courtier'):

> hauing forgotten
> What he should speake, hee's fingering his button,
> Or some such trifling action, till he store
> Himselfe with wit, which he had lost before.

31. *forespoke*, bewitched.

33. *you must frequent ordinaries.* Cf. *E.M.O.* III. vi. 172–86, *Alch.* III. iv. 47–53; T. Heywood, *The Fair Maid of the Exchange*, 1607, F3ᵛ:

> *Crip.* I could doe more, for I could make enquirie
> Where the best witted Gallants vse to dine,
> Follow them to the tauerne, and there sit
> In the next rowme with a calues head and brimstone,
> And ouer heare their talke, obserue their humours,
> Collect their jeasts, put them into a play,
> And tire them too with payment to behold
> What I haue filcht from them. This I could doe:
> But O for shame that men should so arraigne
> Their owne feesimple wits, for verball theft!
> Yet men there be that haue done this and that,
> And more by much more than the most of them.

48. *light crownes at primero.* Cf. *E.H.* I. i. 37–40 n.

54. *Put case*, originally in a legal sense. Browning uses the phrase.

63. *harken out*, find out by inquiry. *S.W.* I. ii. 24, *Alch.* v. v. 85. Cf. 'to hearken after'.

64. *pay for the silence.* Martial, *Ep.* I. lxvi. 13–14, 'Aliena quisquis recitat et petit famam, | non emere librum, sed silentium debet.'

78. *frame*, an affected substitute for 'form'.

III. ii. 3. *candle-waster*, one who uses up candles by studying late at night. *Much Ado*, v. i. 18.

6. *grogran-rascall.* For grogran or grogram see *E.M.I.* II. i. 9.

11. *smels all lamp-oyle.* Plutarch records of Demosthenes' careful preparation, Πυθέας ἐπισκώπτων ἐλλυχνίων ἔφησεν ὄζειν αὐτοῦ τὰ ἐνθυμήματα (*Demosthenes*, viii).

8. *blanketted.* Dekker inflicts this punishment on Horace-Jonson in *Satiro-mastix*, IV. iii (1602, I3).

30. *perpetuana*, 'a durable fabric of wool manufactured in England from the sixteenth century' (*O.E.D.*). Dekker sneers at Jonson's suit of it in *Satiro-mastix*, I4. It was evidently a very plain cloth: Dekker in *The Seven Deadly Sins of London*, ed. Brett-Smith, p. 32, speaks of 'the sober *Perpetuana* suited Puritane'.

32. *silken disposition.* Cf. 'silken thoughts', III. v. 61, and Chapman, *Hero and Leander*, 3rd sestiad, 45, 'Whose disposition silken is and kinde'.

38. *outsides.* *B.F.* II. v. 115.

60. *all he does, is dictated from other men.* So Demetrius (i.e. Dekker) of Jonson in *Poetaster*, v. iii. 312–13:

I know the authors from whence he ha's stole,
And could trace him too, but that I vnderstand 'hem not full and
whole.

Jonson is putting on Anaides' lips some of the criticisms levelled against himself. Anaides is not a portrait of Dekker, though Dekker probably made this particular charge and so interpreted the whole character to refer to him. See the next note.

III. iii. 8–10, 24–6. Quoted in *Satiro-mastix*, I. ii (1602, C2):

Hor. That same Crispinus is the silliest Dor, and Fannius [misprinted Faninus] the slightest cob-web-lawne peece of a Poet, oh God!
Why should I care what euery Dor doth buz
In credulous eares, it is a crowne to me
That the best iudgements can report me wrong'd.
   Asi. I am one of them that can report it.
   Hor. I thinke but what they are, and am not moou'd.
The one a light voluptuous Reueler,
The other, a strange arrogating puffe,
Both impudent, and arrogant enough.
   Asin. S'lid do⟨st⟩ not Criticus Reuel in these lynes, ha Ningle ha?
   Hor. Yes, they're mine owne.

Professor Campbell well comments that ' Dekker, in order to justify his
attack on Jonson, accumulates unjustified *ex post facto* insults, for himself
and Marston, where clearly none were intended ' (*Comicall Satyre*, p. 85 n.).

8. *dor*, buffoon. So v. i. 19.

13–31. From Seneca, *De Remediis Fortuitorum*, vii. 1. '*Male de te
opinantur homines*. Sed mali: moverer si de me Marcus Cato, si Laelius
sapiens, si alter Cato, si Scipiones duo ista loquerentur: nunc malis
displicere laudari est. Non potest ullam auctoritatem habere sententia
ubi qui damnandus est damnat. 2. *Male de te loquuntur*. Moverer si
hoc iudicio facerent: nunc morbo faciunt. . . . *Male de te loquuntur*.
Bene enim nesciunt loqui. Faciunt non quod mereor, sed quod solent.
Quibusdam enim canibus sic innatum est ut non pro feritate sed pro
consuetudine latrent.'

Jonson in his turn was imitated by Marston in *What You Will*, ii. i
(1607, C2):

> Lam⟨patho⟩. O Sir you are so square you skorne reproofe.
> Qua⟨dratus⟩. No sir should discreete *Mastigophoros*
>   Or the deere spirit acute *Canaidus*
>   (That *Aretine*, that most of me belou'd
>   Who in the rich esteeme I prize his soule,
>   I term my selfe) should these once menace me
>   Or curbe my humors with well gouern'd check,
>   I should with most industrious regard
>   Obserue, abstaine, and curbe my skipping lightnesse.
>   But when an arrogant od impudent,
>   A blushles fore-head, only out of sence
>   Of his owne wants, bauls in malignant questing
>   At others meanes of wauing gallantry
>   *Pight foutra.*
> Lam. I raile at none you well squar'd *Syneor*.
> Qua. I can not tell, tis now grown fashion,
>   Whats out of railyng's out of fashion.

14–16. Cf. *Disc.* 173–4.

17–18. *Chrestus*, the Honest (Greek χρηστός) ; *Euthus*, the Straight-
forward (εὐθύς) ; *Phronimus*, the Sensible (φρόνιμος).

26. *puffe*. *E.M.O.* ii. i. 101.

33–6. From Seneca, *De Constantia*, xiii. 1, 2, 'Quis enim phrenetico
medicus irascitur ? . . . Hunc adfectum adversus omnes habet sapiens
quem adversus aegros suos medicus.'

34. *affects*, feelings.

40. *inginous*, crafty. *N.I.* ii. vi. 66 'inginous'.

iii. iv. With this picture of the Presence Chamber and its frequenters
compare (or contrast) Donne's in his fourth *Satire*, ll. 175 following.

5. *diffus'd*, disordered.

6. *straines*, streaks.

13. *hand-fuls*, hand-breadths, four inches.
fore-top. See *E.M.O.* III. iii. 8 n.
14–19. Imitated by R. Heath in his picture of a 'young proud *Statist*', *Satyrs*, 1650, p. 11:

> Whose face is all Mosaick, intricate,
> And ful of artificial gravitie,
> Talks to himself where e'er he goes, with eie
> By speculation downward fixt, though he
> Looks higher than his foretop, hopes to be
> O'th' Privie Councel: and wil whispring tel
> News known as doubtful as an Oracle.

29. *make legs*. *T. of T.* IV. i. 59.
the cringe Of seuerall courts. Barnaby Rich, *Faultes Faults, And nothing else but Faultes*, 1606, p. 8 (of a traveller), 'if at his returne he hath but some few foolish Phrases in the *French, Spanish,* or *Italian* language, with the *Baselos manos,* the *Ducke,* the *Mump,* and the *Shrugge*, it is enough'; R. Brome, *The Antipodes*, I. vi. (1640, C3ᵛ), 'Who's not familiar with the Spanish garbe, | Th'Italian shrug, French cringe, and German hugge'. The '*venetian Dop*' of v. iv. 249, and the '*Spanish* Stoupe' of *Alch.* IV. iv. 9 may be added.
32. *court-common-places*. In *Disc.* 2281–2, Jonson recommends to a young writer 'some knowne History, or other common-place, such as are in the *Courtier*' of Castigliano, 'and the second booke of *Cicero de Oratore*'. Here the allusion is to more trivial collections, phrase-books such as Amorphus studied for the lesson he gives Asotus in Act III, scene v.
39. *itchie palmes*. Brutus told Cassius he was 'much condemn'd to have an itching palm' (*Julius Caesar*, IV. iii. 10).
42. *Proteus*, the sea-god of the shifting shapes. 'In varying figures, I would haue contended | With the blue PROTEVS'—*Volp.* III. vii. 152–3. In a note on *The Masque of Beauty*, 73, Jonson refers to Virgil's picture of him in *Georgic*, iv. 387–414, where his transformations are described.
48–52. From Juvenal, *Sat.* i. 73–5:

> Aude aliquid brevibus Gyaris et carcere dignum,
> si vis esse aliquid. Probitas laudatur et alget.
> Criminibus debent hortos praetoria mensas.

Cf. *Sej.* I. 13–14.
55. *glazing*, making the face shine like glass. Cf. the palinode (below), 22.
56. *pruning*. Ind. 207.
58. *vnperfect prologue at third musike*. *E.M.O.* Ind. 297–9.
63. *kisse away his hand in kindnesse*. Cf. *Love's Labour's Lost*, v. ii. 323–5:

> Why this is he,
> That kist away his hand in courtesie.
> This is the Ape of Forme, Monsieur the nice.

64. *wreath'd*, with folded arms. *E.M.O.* Ind. 161, 'Sits with his armes thus wreath'd'.

67. *Playes with his mistresse pappes. C. is A.* II. ii. 37–8 n.
salutes her pumps. E.M.O. IV. ii. 34.
69. *for a garter,* to hang a dagger in. *E.M.O.* II. vi. 24–5.
70. *feather in her . . . fanne. E.M.O.* II. iii. 201.
86. *the Arachnean workers,* i.e. the cobweb-spinners. Arachne, a Lydian girl skilled in weaving, challenged Minerva to a trial of skill and was changed into a spider.
96. *illustrous.* A common form of the word in Jonson.

III. v. Compare for an earlier and cruder rehearsal *The Case is Altered,* Act IV, scene iii.
6. *palace of your pleasure.* A reference to the title of William Painter's *The Palace of Pleasure,* vol. i, 1566, vol. ii, 1567.
8. *two turnes.* So Puntarvolo 'steps forward three pases' and 'barely retires one' when he accosts his lady (*E.M.O.* II. ii. 10, 11).
11. *trembling boldnesse.* So in Briske's courtship, *E.M.O.* III. ix. 44–8.
28. *Lindabrides,* the love of the Donzel del Febo or Knight of the Sun. See *The First Part of the Mirrour of Princely deedes and Knighthood,* 1578, translated by Margaret Tiler from the Spanish of Diego Ortunez. The second and third parts of the first book were translated by R. P. in 1585 and (?) 1586. Lindabrides thus became a name for a mistress, and in Marston's *The Dutch Courtezan,* III. i, one man even addresses another as 'My dear Lindabrides'. Scott in *Kenilworth,* ch. xxviii, as Cunningham notes, makes Michael Lambourne say of Amy Robsart, 'I will try to get a sight of this Lindabrides of his'. For other allusions to the romance see *Poet.* I. ii. 157, *E.H.* v. i. 29, *Alch.* I. i. 175, *N.I.* I. vi. 124–5.
36. *humanitian,* humanist.
51. *More then most faire. E.M.O.* Ind. 114 n.
51–2. *let not the rigour of your iust disdaine.* A part-echo of Kyd's *Spanish Tragedy,* I. iv. 71–2, ed. Boas, where Belimperia says of Don Balthazar:

> He shall in rigour of my iust disdaine,
> Reape long repentance for his murderous deed.

53–6. Cf. Marston, *The Insatiate Countesse,* II. ii, 1613, C4ᵛ: Abigail, who has intercepted a love-letter of her husband to another, 'What? and *dedicate to thee*: I marry, heere's a stile so high, as a man cannot helpe a Dog o'er it. He was wont to write to me in the Citie phrase, My good *Abigall*: here's *Astonishment of nature, vnparalleld excelency, and most vnequal raritie of creation.*'
73. *passant,* facing to the right, the heraldic term for walking or facing towards the dexter side of the shield.
76. *guardant,* as above, but with head turned to the spectator.
80. *reguardant,* as above, but with head turned back, looking over her shoulder to the left.
80. *irpe.* Found only here and (as a noun) in the Palinode at the end of the play, l. 1. The origin is unknown; it is most likely some

Court affectation. Professor Skeat (in *N. & Q.*, 8 August 1896) mis-
trusted the text at both points: here he conjectured *yepe*, i.e. active
(*yēap* in Stratmann) written *iepe*, for *i* before a vowel with the variable
value of *y* and *j* comparing 'yerk' and 'jerk'; in the Palinode he conjectured *iapes*, i.e. 'japes' for 'irpes'. But if there had been misprints
in the Quarto, the Folio should have corrected them, as it corrected
'manfrede' to 'vndertake' in *E.M.O.* iv. viii. 110. The *O.E.D.* defines
the noun as 'Some kind of gesture: ? a toss or jerk of the head, the
act of perking', and the adjective as '? perk, smart'. The context of
the present passage, 'shew the supple motion of your pliant bodie',
suggests some kind of movement.

82. *arride*. *E.M.O.* ii. i. 82–7, where the word is criticized.

92–3. *french*, or . . . *italian*. Cf. Chapman, *Monsieur d'Olive*, ii. ii.
(1606, E), a new-made lord invited to enter the presence says 'Faith
I do not care, if I go and make a face or two there, or a few gracefull
legges; speake a little Italian, and away; there's all a Presence doth
require'; Dekker, *The Guls Horne-booke*, v (1609, p. 23), for the young
gallant at an ordinary 'that will be an excellent occasion to publish
your languages, if you haue them: if not, get some fragments of French,
or smal parcels of Italian to fling about the table: but beware how you
speake any Latine there'.

100. *adiection*. *E.M.I.* iv. viii. 5.

104. *ambiguous*. Asotus has picked up 'a new *phrase*' (iii. i. 43) and does
not understand it. 'Sufficient' (able or competent) is another absurd use.

110. *feature*, primarily of the 'make' of the entire body, not of the
face only. In iv. iii. 287 the Folio reads 'feature' for the 'Creature' of
the Quarto. *Alch.* iv. i. 75, *M.V.* 195.

116–17. *And will* . . . Adapted from *The Spanish Tragedy*, ii. i. 7,8,
ed. Boas:

> And she in time will fall from her disdaine,
> And rue the sufferance of your freendly paine.

The Quarto reading, '*If euer you haue seene great* TAMBERLAINE', has
little bearing on the courtship.

119. *more of these play-particles*. Dekker, *The Guls Horne-booke*, 1609,
ch. vii, p. 32: 'To conclude, hoord vp the finest play-scraps you can
get, vppon which your leane wit may most sauourly feede for want of
other stuffe, when the *Arcadian* and *Euphuizd* gentlewomen haue their
tongues sharpened to set vpon you: that qualitie (next to your shittle-
cocke) is the onely furniture to a Courtier thats but a new beginner,
and is but in his A B C of complement.' So the swaggering lover in
Wither's *Abuses Stript and Whipt*, 1613, D3ᵛ:

> His Poetry is such as he can cull
> From plaies he heard at *Curtaine* or at *Bull*,
> And yet is fine coy Mistres-*Marry*-Muffe,
> The soonest taken with such broken stuffe.

Cf. iv. i. 207 below, and *Volp.* v. iv. 41–2.

124. *ruffle it*, 'swagger it' (Quarto). Cf. Camden, *Remaines of a greater worke concerning Britaine*, 1605, p. 221: 'There was a Nobleman merry conceited, and riotously given, that having lately sold a Mannor of an hundred tenements, came ruffling into the Court, in a new sute.'

in red and yellow, substituted for the '*Black* and *Yellow*' of the Quarto, to suggest the fool's motley. '*In white*' (125): cf. the 'cloth of siluer sute' of *Poet.* III. i. 175.

130. *measure*. 'Measures (when spoken of technically) were dances of a grave and dignified kind, performed at Court and at public entertainments at the Temple, Inns of Court, &c. They were not to the taste of Sir Toby, if we may trust Shakespeare; and that the knight was not singular in his dislike appears from Shirley's *Bird in a Cage*: "No, none of your dull *measures*! There's no sport but in your country figaries"' (Gifford).

139. *courting-stock*. In v. iv. 608 and *N.I.* I. vi. 154 'courting-stock' means the lady who is the object of courtship; here it means the properties such as finery and ribbons with which the tailor had provided Asotus at the beginning of the scene, and possibly a chair.

IV. i. 18. *far-fet*. *S.W.* prol. 21; Puttenham, *The Arte of English Poesie*, p. 193, ed. Arber, 'we vse to say by manner of Prouerbe: things farrefet and deare bought are good for Ladies'. The proverb is in *Iohn Heywoodes woorkes*, part i, ch. xi (1562, D4), 'dere bought and far fet | Are deinties for Ladies'.

22. *rebatu*, or rebato, a linen-covered wire frame to which the ruff was pinned, worn by both sexes from about 1590 to 1630.

27. *garbe*. *E.M.O.* II. i. 85.

33. *some Laura, or some Delia*. A gird at Daniel, who was popular in Court circles: in his *Sonnets to Delia*, 1592, xliii, he called his love 'a *Laura*'. Delia is again alluded to in *B.F.* v. iv. 69.

38. *the whole heauen awry*. So in the Quarto ending of *E.M.O.*, appendix X, 5.

39. *coach-horse*. Cf. Chapman, *Monsieur d'Olive*, IV. i (1606, F3), '*Enter D'oliue, Pacque, Dique. Dol.* Welcome little Witts, are you hee Page *Pacque* here Makes choice of to be his fellow Coch-horse?' In the Quarto 'tilt-horse', which suits 'swaggering' better.

49. *the battaile of Lepanto*, Don John of Austria's naval victory over the Turks in 1571. For '*venetian* trumpetter' the Quarto has 'a Dutch Trumpetter'. Shadwell in *The Humorists*, iii (1671, p. 29), has 'Look you Sir, I am no man to be frighted, though you look as big as a Dutch Trumpeter', but there, in a Restoration play, the image has more point.

50–1. *comes euer i' the rereward ... of a fashion*. Like Justice Shallow: 'a' came ever in the rereward of the fashion', says Falstaff (*2 Henry IV*, III. ii. 307.

61. *post-boies horn*. See Truewit's use of it in *S.W.* II. i. 38 fol.

90. *perswade Argurion affect* (Quarto: 'to affect' Folio). Cf. *N.I.* II. v. 137, 'perswade him die for fame'.

107. *short haire*, the city cut as contrasted with the fashion at Court.

116. *sayed on*, tried on. For an example we have Nick Stuffe in *The New Inn* and his wife Pinnacia (IV. iii. 51).

121. *shame-fac'd*. So spelt here and *S.W.* III. vii. 26, and 'shame-fac'tnesse' *N.I.* III. ii. 183. But the correct 'shamefastness' *Und.* xv. 40, *Disc.* 684.

124. *place, and occasion*. Contrast v. vi. 63–5.

127. *relinquish*. *Poet.* II. ii. 221.

132. *march-pane. C. is A.* IV. vii. 40, 'a march paine wench'.

145 fol. *which ladie* . . . From Martial, *Epigr.* IX. xxxvii. 1–6:

> Cum sis ipsa domi mediaque ornere Subura,
> fiant absentes et tibi, Galla, comae,
> nec dentes aliter quam Serica nocte reponas,
> et iaceas centum condita pyxidibus,
> nec tecum facies tua dormiat, innuis illo
> quod tibi prolatum est mane supercilio—

a passage further imitated in *S.W.* IV. ii. 92–101.

149 fol. *There should not a Nymph* . . . From Juvenal, *Sat.* vi. 402–6:

> Haec eadem novit quid toto fiat in orbe,
> quid Seres, quid Thraces agant, secreta novercae
> et pueri, quis amet, quis diripiatur adulter;
> dicet quis viduam praegnantem fecerit et quo
> mense, quibus verbis concumbat quaeque, modis quot.

150. *the verge. E.M.O.* IV. iv. 18 n.

157. *jigg'd the cocke*, kept turning the spigot, and so, always drinking.

167. *done with him*. A coarse equivoque: see *T. of T.* II. iii. 11.

174. *miscelany madams*, traders in miscellaneous articles, such as trinkets and ornaments of various kinds; they had shops in the New Exchange (Nares).

182–3. *come vp to terme, to see motions*. Like Sogliardo in *E.M.O.*, Characters 81.

197. *the very center . . . wherein all lines of loue should meet*. Cf. *L.T.* 130–6.

199. *complexions*, the combination of two elements in one body (as hot and dry, hot and moist)—'the four complexions' of *Love's Labour's Lost*, I. ii. 81.

207. *play-ends*. See above, III. v. 119.

208–9. *stabbing himself* . . . Cf. Dekker, *The Honest Whore*, part i (1604, E1ᵛ), 'How many Gallants have drank healthes to me | Out of their daggerd armes'; W. M., *The Man in the Moone*, 1609, F4 ('A Lover'), 'hee hath let his owne arme blood himselfe, in stead of a Barber-Surgeon, and quaffed an health thereof in praise of his Mistresse, when he hath done'; Cooke, *Greene's Tu quoque*, 1614, H3, 'By the fayth of a Souldier (Lady) I doe reuerence the ground that you walke vpon: I will fight with him that dares say you are not faire: Stabbe him that will not pledge your health, and with a Dagger pierce a Vaine, to drinke a full health to you.'

iv. ii. 4. *deiected*. The sequel to iv. i. 25–32.

32. *the brazen head*. Similarly applied in Chapman's *Monsieur d'Olive*, iii (1606, E3): 'Dol. But *Monsieur Mustapha* there kept state, when I accosted him; slight the Brasen head lookt to be Worshipt I thinke.' For the allusion see *E.M.I.* i. iv. 63.

34. *interpret*. The man who did the talking in the puppet-show was the interpreter, like Squire Tub in *A Tale of a Tub* and Lantern Leatherhead in *Bartholomew Fair*.

39. *carroches*, carriages of a stately and luxurious kind. *D. is A.* i. vi. 214, 'a guilt caroch'; ib. iv. ii. 11, 'the great *Carroch*, sixe horses'.

42. *conniue*. Madam Moria is too unmistakably the ancestress of Mrs. Malaprop to be an authority for Jonson's normal use of words, but Dekker attributes to him a forced use of the word in *Satiro-mastix*, 1602, E3, 'I was but at Barbers last day, and when he was rencing my face, did but crie out, fellow thou makst me *Conniue* too long, & sayes he, Master *Asinius Bubo*, you haue eene Horaces wordes as right as if he had spit them into your mouth.'

44. *close, and open*. *Close* secret, with a suggestion of 'lewd', found also in *E.M.I.* iv. x. 43 and *For*. xiii. 74, 'the close groome and page'. The quibble of 'close and open' shows Moria's muddleheadedness.

45. *happily*. For the spelling cf. *E.M.O.* ii. iii. 307.

iv. iii. 5. *fauoursome*. The only example in the *O.E.D*.

16. *all to bee qualifie*. The obsolete prefix 'to' = asunder, as in Chaucer's 'to-breke', break in pieces. In early English the prefix 'all' is found with verbs preceded by 'to' in the sense of entirely: Judges ix. 53, 'And a certaine woman cast a piece of a milstone vpon Abimelechs head, and all to brake his scull', i.e. completely broke in pieces. 'As these derivative verbs were at length rarely used without *all*, the fact that the *to-* belonged to the verb was lost sight of, and it was written separate, or even joined to *all*, as *al to-torn, al to torn, alto torn*' (*O.E.D.*). Cf. *B.F.* v. iv. 41; *N.I.* v. ii. 70; *M.L.* 1 Chorus, 24, v. ii. 2, 13.

20. *a dictionarie method*. In Sidney, *An Apology for Poetry*, p. 202, ed. Gregory Smith, 'with coursing of a Letter, as if they were bound to followe the method of a Dictionary', and *Astrophel and Stella*, Sonnet xv, 'You that doe dictionary method bring Into your rymes, running in rattling rowes'—the reference is to alliteration. E. Guilpin in *Skialetheia*, 1598, Satire v, describes a courtier, 'Thys is the Dictionary of complements'.

39. *by this watch*. Pocket-watches were introduced into England in 1577.

74. *Fungoso*, i.e. mushroom, upstart: compare the character in the preceding play.

got aboue the cup-board. Cf. Donne, *Sat*. vii. 103–5 (quoted on *E.M.O.* ii. iii. 192), and Harington, *A Treatise on Playe* (*Nugæ Antiquæ*, ed. Park, i, p. 200), 'I have been ever against the opinion of some elder sarvitors, . . . who will mayntayn that till ii of the clocke no gentleman should stand above the cubbard'.

81. *purposes*, or, as Pepys calls it, cross-purposes. Cf. *L.R.* 159, '*Draw-gloues, Riddles, Dreames*, and other prettie *Purposes*'; Burton, *The Anatomy of Melancholy*, 1621, p. 346, speaks of 'vlegames, catches, purposes' as winter games.

83. *prophecies.* We have had a specimen in II. ii. 57–63.

88. *Substantiues and Adiectiues.* E. Phillips, *Mysteries of Love and Eloquence*, 1658 (1685, Gen. Ind. 4), 'A Description of the witty sport of Substantives and Adjectives'.

90. *sirs*, addressed to both sexes. For the use in addressing women see *Antony and Cleopatra*, IV. xv. 85, and *O.E.D.* s.v. 'sir', 9.

125. *has worne the breeches.* Alluding to the proverbial description of a masterful wife, 'The woman wears the breeches'.

146. *Breeches Pythagoricall.* Cf. the quarto version of *E.M.I.* III. iv. 174, 'signior *Pithagoras*, he thats al manner of shapes'; Middleton, *A Trick to Catch the Old One*, IV. v. 76–9, '*Dam.* Pythagorical rascal! *Lam.* Pythagorical? *Dam.* Ay, he changes his cloak when he meets a sargeant.'

152. *whatsoeuer is well taken* . . . H. Porter, *The two angrie women of Abington*, 1599, BI^v, 'She speakes it scornfully, I faith I care not, | Things are well spoken, if they be well taken.'

188. *pain'd slops*, 'a sort of breeches (generally full and bombasted) made of stripes (*panes*) of variously-coloured cloth stitched together, having slips of silk or velvet occasionally intermixed'. Dyce, *Beaumont and Fletcher*, i, p. 15.

212. *wish*, recommend. *Alch.* I. iii. 14.

231. *lyra.* Sidney and Pope use this form.

246. *so melting*, . . . *so delicious.* Ford and Dekker, *The Sun's Darling*, II. i (1656, p. 11):

> 'tis not the *Spring* . . . can heat thy blood
> As't can with one kiss. *Ray.* The rose-lipp'd dawning
> Is not so melting, so delicious.

283–8. Cf. *Merchant of Venice*, III. iv. 69–73.

297. *this gloue.* Cf. the original version of Sidney's *Arcadia*, iii, pp. 159–60, ed. Feuillerat: 'And therewith hee drewe oute a glove of *Pamelas*, done with Murrey silk and golde Lace, and not withoute tender teares kissing yt hee putt yt againe in his bosome, & sange these twoo staves.

> *O sweete glove the witness of my secret Blisse,*
> (Whiche hyding did preserve that beutyes lighte)
> That (opened forthe) my sealle of Comfort ys,
> Bee thow my Starr in this my Darckest nighte . . .'.

golden legacie, a reference to the title of Lodge's *Rosalynde. Euphues Golden Legacie*, 1590.

320. *I care not*, I have no objection.

326. *mammothrept*, a nursling. It is interesting to find that Richard Brathwait misunderstood the passage in the text and interpreted

'mammothrept' to mean 'a severe critic': in *The Smoaking Age*, 1617, O2ᵛ he writes:

> Or what strict Mamothrept that man should bee,
> Who has done Chaucer such an injurie.

350. *muske-cat.* E.M.O. II. i. 97.

352. *frapler*, blusterer.

355. *tuff-taffata*, a kind of taffeta with a nap woven in tufts. With the contemptuous reference cf. *N.I.* II. ii. 42, III. i. 191.

358. *the pencill on your chinne*, tuft, which used to be called an 'imperial' because the Emperor Napoleon III wore one.

359. *garter my hose with your guts.* For this refined threat cf. T. Heywood, *The Four Prentises of London*, 1615, D2: '*Irish.* And by S. Patrick, I'le make him Garter his hose with his guts, that strikes any stroke here'; S. Rowlands, *The Knave of Clubs*, 1611, D:

> I would be-stab his skin like double cuts,
> And garter vp his stockins with his guts.

403. *gloue*; 404. *garter.* Dr. Judson compares S. Rowlands, *Doctor Merrie-man*, 1609, C3ᵛ:

> To giue my Gloue vnto a Gull,
> Is mighty fauour found:
> When for the wearing of the same,
> It costs him twentie pound.
> My Garter as a gracious thing,
> Another takes away:
> And for the same a silken Gowne,
> The Prodigall doth pay.

419. *gold-finch.* Tucca in *Satiro-mastix*, F1ᵛ, calls Sir Quintilian Shorthose 'my noble Gold-finch' after receiving a gold chain from him.

447. *giue her aire.* A contrast to *E.M.I.* II. iii. 53: see note there.

IV. iv. 11. *intergatories.* The form used by Jonson, *Sej.* I. 314, *S.W.* IV. vii. 17, *S. of N.* V. iv. 37.

16. *epitaphs*, 'epithites' in Quarto. So *C. is A.* II. vii. 8.

31. *misprision*, misunderstanding. The verb 'misprize' in the sense of 'mistake' is found *C. is A.* IV. i. 38, *Poet.* I. ii. 112.

53. CVP. 'Cos' in F2: he is Philautia's page and he would fetch the glasses in line 1. But the change is unnecessary.

IV. v. 1. *beuer*, refreshment between meals.

24. *I cannot away with*, I cannot get on with. *Poet.* III. iv. 279; *B.F.* I. vi. 99.

39. *infanted.* The *O.E.D.* quotes as an example Soothern's line censured in Puttenham's *Arte of English Poesie*, 1589, III. xxii, 'And of an ingenious inuention, infanted with pleasant trauaille'. It is unnecessary

to suppose with Dr. Judson that Jonson is poking fun at Soothern here: 'infanted' is merely a courtier's affectation for 'produced'.

45. *I could not construe an author.* An allusive trait which fits Dekker: cf. *Poet.* v. iii. 312–13. Before *Poetaster* both Jonson and Marston resorted to this oblique way of attack—minor touches in a character on the whole irrelevant.

69. *Philautia.* For her dancing see II. iv. 52–61.

71. *the ladie kist mee.* Argurion, we have been told, loves 'your foole aboue all' (II. iii. 179).

74. *my most esteemed page.* Italicized in the Quarto; another affectation; pronounce 'esteeméd'.

78. *And Cynthia had but seene me.* Sir Christopher Hatton first attracted the notice of Queen Elizabeth by his graceful dancing at Court; see the *Entertainment at Althorp,* 261–8.

101. *take our time by the fore-head.* Dionysius Cato, *de Moribus,* II. D. xxvi, 'Rem tibi quam nosces aptam, dimittere noli: | Fronte capillata, post est occasio calua'.

136. *pantofles,* slippers, especially the high-heeled chopins. 'To be up in pantofles' means to be in state: 'to stand upon one's pantofles' is the Elizabethan phrase for 'to stand on one's dignity'.

138. *Sirrah.* Asotus does not repeat the mistake he made in II. iii. 72.

148. *prizers,* competitors in a public contest, especially at fencing, the form of which is minutely copied in this challenge of courtship.

v. i. 12. *No man* . . . From Juvenal, *Sat.* ii. 83, 'Nemo repente fuit turpissimus'. 'Presently', of course, means 'at once'.

19. *court-Dors.* See III. iii. 83.

31. *the true nobilitie* . . . Juvenal, *Sat.* viii. 20, 'Nobilitas sola est atque unica virtus'. So *Und.* lxxxiv (8), 21.

38–9. From Virgil, *Aen.* vi. 129–30, 'Pauci, quos aequus amavit Iuppiter', and Juvenal, *Sat.* xiv. 34–5, 'Quibus arte benigna et meliore luto finxit praecordia Titan'. Here and in v. viii. 23 Jonson interprets 'Titan' as the Sungod, but in *Catiline,* III. 542, he correctly understands the reference to Prometheus.

v. ii. 3. *intend me,* listen to me carefully. Cf. Lat. *intendere animum.*

11. *trussing all the points,* a metaphor from tying the tagged laces which supported the hose.

13. *aped,* an affected spelling of 'apt'.

15. *intrinsecate,* an odd blending of 'intricate' and 'intrinsic'. Shakespeare uses it, *Ant. and Cleop.* v. ii. 302. 'Apparently from Italian *intrinsecato, -sicato,* familiar, confused in sense with *intricato,* intricate' (*O.E.D.*).

17. *colours.* Amorphus's dissertation is a *locus classicus* on the subject. Sidney notes a lover's wearing of 'set colours' in *Astrophel and Stella,* sonnet liv, and the Earl of Newcastle in *The Country Captain,* II. ii, gives an elaborate list: 'Shall I decipher my colours to you now? Here

is Azure and Peach: Azure is constant and Peach is love; which signifies my constant Affection. *Sister.* This is very pretty. *Device.* Oh it saves the trouble of writing, where the Mistress and Servant are learned in this amorous blazon' (Bullen's *Old Plays*, ii, p. 345).

24. *Antagonist.* This is the earliest example of the word in the *O.E.D.*; Amorphus has to explain it to Asotus.

26. *giue him the dor*, make a fool of him. The *O.E.D.* doubtfully suggests a connexion with the Old Norse *dár*, scoff, in the phrase *draga dár at*, to make game of.

43. *pœne*, Lat. *pœna*. This affected spelling is in *S.S.* II. vi. 66, where it has even less justification.

46. *remonstrate*, demonstrate. A common usage.

58. *outrecuidance*, overweening self-conceit. *E.H.* IV. ii. 277–8, 'God doth often punish such pride, and *outrecuidance*, with scorne and infamy.'

61. *a cooke may as soone*, . . . Petronius, *Satirae*, 2, 'Qui inter haec nutriuntur non magis sapere possunt quam bene olere qui in culina habitant.'

64. *passages, and imbroccata's. E.M.I.* IV. vii. 78. *Passages* here of amorous fence: cf. *Sir Gyles Goosecappe*, I. iii (1606, B2ᵛ), 'I am sure I past one *Passado* of Courtship vppon her.'

75. *Sanna.* See Persius, *Satires*, i. 58, 62, where the *ciconia* = stork's bill. Jonson has followed Jerome's interpretation (which differs from the scholiast's) in this passage. Jerome, *Ep.* cxxv (vol. i, § 945, Migne), 'Ne credas laudatoribus tuis, imo irrisoribus aurem ne libenter accomodes; qui cum te adulationibus foverint et quodam modo impotem mentis effecerint, si subito respexeris, aut *ciconiarum deprendes post te colla curvari*, aut manu auriculas agitari asini, aut aestuantem canis protendi linguam.' The Latin *Sanna* = a minicking grimace: Persius, v. 91, 'rugosa sanna', a snarl that wrinkles the face.

79. *pricke out. M.L.* II. ii. 10. A metaphor from putting a tick against an ame in a list of people to be chosen.

v. iii. 16. *tumult* . . . 41. *Knocke that . . . fellow.* There are a number of references to the disorder at Court when people crowded in to see masques or ceremonies. Order was kept—or an attempt was made to keep it—by knocking people on the head. The 'white staff' of the Lord Chamberlain and his officers came into play: see Jonson's *Irish Masque*, 10, 66, and at the performance of his *Masque of Blackness* (*q.v.*) there was a complaint that some ladies were badly hurt by the white staves. So in the Palace Yard, at the christening of Elizabeth, the Porter says (*Henry VIII*, v. iv. 6–8), 'Fetch me a dozen crab-tree staves, and strong ones: these are but switches to 'em. I'll scratch your heads', and his Man denies that he 'spared any That had a head to hit' (21–2). In *The Stratford Letters* (1739, p. 207) Garrard writes on 27 February 1634, 'On Shrove-Tuesday at Night the King and the Lords performed their Masque', i.e. Shirley's *The Triumph of Peace*. 'The Templars were all invited, and well placed, they have found a new way of letting them in by a turning Chair, besides they let in none but such as have tickets sent them beforehand, so that now the keeping of the Door is no trouble.'

20. *Shadowes. S.W.* II. iii. 7, where it almost means 'parasites'.

39. *intrude her* should mean 'thrust her in'. The misuse is another Court affectation.

46. *Husbands are not allow'd here.* So Chloe, who does not want her husband with her at Court, is told 'your husband will be left without in the lobby, or the great chamber, when you shall be put in, i' the closet, by this lord, and by that lady' (*Poet.* IV. ii 59–61). Cf. Chapman, *Byron's Conspiracy*, II. i (1608, D1ᵛ, D2):

> *Henry.* Was he so courted. *Rois.* As a Cittie Dame,
> Brought by her iealous husband, to the Court,
> Some elder Courtiers entertaining him,
> While others snatch a fauour from his wife:
> One starts from this doore; from that nooke another,
> With gifts, and iunkets, and with printed phrase,
> Steale her employment, shifting place by place
> Still as her husband comes.

Everie Woman in her Humor, 1609, F3ᵛ, referring to Court revels, '*Hostis.* Might not a company of Wiues be beholding to thee for places that would be there without their husbands knowledge if neede were?' Sir Edward Peyton, *The Divine Catastrophe of the Stuarts*, 1652, p. 47: 'The Masks and Playes at Whitehal were used onely for Incentives to lust: therefore the Courtiers invited the Citizens wives to these shews, on purpose to defile them in such sort. There is not a Lobby nor Chamber (if it could speak) but would verify this.'

59. *accommodate to the nuptials.* Gloves were presented to the company at a wedding. See *S.W.* III. vi. 88, *B.F.* III. iv. 160–3; in Dekker's *Satiro-mastix*, I. i (1602, B3ᵛ), the host says, 'More Rose-mary and gloues, gloues, gloues: choose Gentlemen; Ladyes put on soft skins vpon the skin of softer hands; so, so'. At Somerset's wedding to Lady Frances Howard in 1613 Sir Ralph Winwood 'had a very fair pair of gloves of three pounds apiece', which he earned by a suit costing about £80; 'the Lord Mayor and Sheriffs had rich gloves sent in requital' for their presents of plate; 'the Lord Burghley, his Lady, and both his daughters, had very fair gloves', though (apparently) they gave nothing. (John Chamberlain, letter of 30 December 1613.)

60. *scholler* . . . 65. *prouost* . . . 66. *masters*—the degrees of the fencing-school, from which Amorphus borrows all his terms for the 'science' of courtship. He had posed as an authority on fencing, I. iii. 35–6.

76. *forsooth.* The city madam's oath, *E.M.O.* II. ii. 14.

91. *white satin reueller.* Cf. III. v. 125.

cloth of tissue, and bodkin, varieties of cloth of gold and silver. For bodkin, or baudkin, see Linthicum, *Costume in the Drama of Shakespeare*, p. 115.

92. *Vlysses-Polytropus*. Ulysses as the type of a traveller: Jonson interpreted the Homeric epithet πολύτροπος as 'man of many wanderings'.

94. *Acolastus-Polypragmon*: ἀκόλαστος 'unbridled', 'lacking in self-control', and πολυπράγμων, 'a busybody'.

98–9. *bare Accost . . . Close*. Baskerville (*Early Elements*, p. 231) points to some analogies with the ritual and terminology of the medieval Courts of Love.

102. *Millaner*, a man, as in *E.M.I.* i. iii. 118.

106. *Wall-eyes*. Cotgrave, 'Oeil de chevre. *A whall, or ouer-white eye*; *an eye full of white spots, or whose apple seemes diuided by a streake of white*.'

108. *a Fanne wauing*. Dr. Judson compares Marmion, *The Antiquary*, ii. 1 (1641, D1ᵛ):

> And then, because I am familiar,
> And daign out of my noblenesse and bounty,
> To grace your weak endeavours with the title
> Of courtesie, to wave my Fan at you,
> Or let you kiss my hand; must we strait marry?

118. *Let's bee retrograde*, as in scene iv, line 10, let's go back.

120. *dispunct*, un-punctilious, impolite. An affected and blundering Latinism: *dispunctus* in classical Latin would mean 'balanced', the credit and the debit sides checked off; and 'dispunct' in sixteenth-century English would mean 'erased'.

121. *state*, canopy. The original meaning; then the chair with the canopy over it. Bacon, *New Atlantis* (*Works*, ed. Spedding, iii, p. 148), 'Over the chair is a state, made round or oval, and it is of ivy.' See v. vi. 3, 4:

> Seated, in thy siluer chaire,
> State in wonted manner keepe.

131. *well-spoken*. It is a dumb show: compare in scene iv. 215–18, where they speak at the 'Better Reguard'.

135. *dutch*. One of the many contemporary references to the drinking habits of this nation. *D. is A.* i. i. 62.

v. iv. 11. *Truchman*, interpreter. *K. Ent.* 261, *A.P.* 157.

13. *chartells*, challenges.

15. *stickler*, a second, to see fair play.

18. *complementaries*, masters of fencing, such as Caranza, who wrote on the 'complements' of duelling.

32. *carries meat in the mouth*, affords entertainment. The ordinary sense is rather, 'brings in money': the *O.E.D.* thinks it may have been used originally of a hawk.

34. *hauings*. *E.M.I.* i. iv. 61.

37. *citticisme*, city manners. A nonce word, apparently found only here. *this elixi'r*, namely, the Court, which transmutes citizens.

40. *prouides coaches.* IV. ii. 38–9.

41. *holds vp the arras.* E.M.O. IV. ii. 35.

49. *reciprock*, Lat. *reciprocus*.

55. *him*, i.e. Crites.

68. *scholaris.* This Latin form is used by Lyly, *Sapho and Phao*, I. iii, and Chapman, *Monsieur d'Olive*, III. ii (misprinted 'Scholares').

96. *the carpe ha's no tongue.* Izaak Walton, *The Compleat Angler*, 1653, pp. 165–6: '*Gesner* sayes, *Carps* have no tongues like other fish, but a piece of flesh-like-fish in their mouth like to a tongue, and may be so called, but it is certain it is choicely good.' Cf. *Alch.* II. ii. 75.

112. *I haue seene the lyons* in the Tower. *M. Aug.* 2, 3, and Dekker, *The Guls Horne-booke*, vii (1609, p. 32), 'a country gentleman that brings his wife vp to learne the fashion, see the Tombs at Westminster, the Lyons in the Tower, or to take physicke'.

122. *prest*, ready for action.

125–6. *meddle with me . . . doe not meddle with my Master.* Asotus is half-quibbling on the phrase 'Meddle with your match' (*E.M.I.* III. v. 121, *B.F.* I. iv. 102).

141. *the tenure of this ensign.* A banner held by the lady to be courted ?

148. *his legge was too much produc'd.* Cf. *Sir Gyles Goosecappe*, IV. ii (1606, G1ᵛ):

> I . . . held my talke,
> With that Italionate Frenchman, and tooke time
> (Still as our conference seru'd) to show my Courtship
> In the three quarter legge, and setled looke,
> The quick kisse of the toppe of the forefinger
> And other such exploytes of good Accost.

152. *french curteau*, the modern French *courtaud*, of which the earlier form was *courtalt*, a small horse with its tail, and sometimes its ears, docked. The process would be completed, says Anaides, by slitting the nose too. Bulwer, *Anthropometamorphosis*, 1650, p. 80, 'The *Indians* Divers have their Noses slit like broken-winded Horses.'

158. *band-string* tied the ruff in front. Some play was made with it at this point: in *The Duchess of Malfy*, II. i. 5, ed. Lucas, Bosola advises Castruchio to 'learne to twirle the strings of your band with a good grace'.

160. *like a stab'd Lucrece.* Even though, as Dr. Judson says, the Lucrece story would be familiar from Shakespeare's poem, the reference here seems to be to some sign. Two printers, Thomas Purfoot and Thomas Berthelet (who printed from 1528 to 1554), had the sign of Lucrece; the device of the latter depicted 'Lucrecia Romana', wild-eyed, open-mouthed, and with dishevelled hair, thrusting a sword into her bosom. Cf. Shadwell, *The Humorists*, iii (1671, p. 30), '*Dryb*. Why look already as sowrely as the Picture of a Stabb'd *Lucrece*'. 'A face . . . worse then GAMALIEL RATSAY's' in *Alch.* I. i. 98–9 similarly suggests a picture in a chapbook.

167. *broun studie. C. is A.* IV. ii. 45.

168. *bird-ey'd.* Cf. W. Bullein's *A Dialogue . . . wherein is a godlie regiment against the Feuer Pestilence*, 1573, p. 85: '*Vxor.* Oh helpe me; my horse starteth, and I had like to haue been vnsadled, let me sit faster for falling. *Civis.* He is a birde eyed iade, I warraunt you, and you are no good horsewoman'; and *Pasquil's Apology*, 1590, Ciij, 'The fellow is bird eyed, he startles and snuffes at euery shadow.' Cf. *Volp.* III. iv. 20. The epithet expresses the startled look of a disturbed bird or a shying horse.

171. *Besso'gno,* besogne, beggarly fellow. Florio has '*Bisogni,* new levied souldiers, such as come needy to the wars'—the original meaning, Shakespeare's 'Bezonian'.

179. *must be partiall,* i.e. etiquette requires us to favour the stranger.

188. *Mungrill,* upstart. Cf. *Ep.* xlviii, 'On Mungril Esquire'.

198. *I lay a discretion.* In *Ent. Blackfriars*, 125–6, Mistress Holdback, the nurse, says: 'I offerd to hold Mr Doctor a discretion, it was a boye', so that this form of wager was not confined to court-circles.

205. *doibt,* a Dutch coin, eighth part of a stiver, half an English farthing.

233. *oblique leere, or the Ianus* must have been something like the '*Sanna,* or Storkes-bill' of v. ii. 75.

235. *Rodomantada,* the form in Florio. Rodomante in the fourteenth book of the *Orlando Furioso* became proverbial as a braggart. Cf. *M. Owls,* 154, 'In his *Rodomant* fashion'.

246–7. Dr. Judson notes that twice in this speech—*sicuratevi* and *vo'*—the second person is used for the courteous third person elsewhere.

249. *Dop,* dip, a very low curtsy, derived from the Middle English *doppen.*

252–3. *As buckets . . .* From Sir John Davies, *Epigrammes,* no. 29, '*In Haywodum*':

> *Haywood,* that did in Epigrams excell,
> Is now put downe since my light Muse arose;
> As buckets are put downe into a well,
> Or as a schoole-boy putteth downe his hose.

Sir John Harington in *The Metamorphosis of Ajax,* 1596, p. 26, writes, 'This Haywood for his Prouerbs & Epigrams, is not yet put downe by any of our country, though one'—a marginal note is 'M. Davies'— 'doth indeed come near him, that graces him the more, in saying he puts him downe'.

260–3. That Amorphus should mangle his Italian was to be expected, but Mercury should have spoken more correct French; one cannot suppose that the printer substituted *mal heureuse* for *malheureux.*

264. *a right Iouialist,* thoroughly cheerful, lit. born under the influence of the planet Jupiter.

297. *mullets,* curling-tongs. Florio, 1598, 'Tanagliette, *little tongs,*

pincers, tanakles mullets'. Dyce (MS.) quotes B. Barnes, *The Divils Charter*, 1607, H1ᵛ:

> I will correct these arches with this mullet,
> Plucke not to hard, beleeue me *Motticilla*
> You plucke to hard.

298. *pinke*, eyelet-hole.

309. *beniamin*, gum benzoin. A corruption of the old form 'benjoin'.

311. *all nose*. Catullus, xiii. 13–14, of a choice unguent:

> Quod tu cum olfacies deos rogabis
> totum ut te faciant, Fabulle, nasum.

312. *I frotted a jerkin.* Middleton notices this extravagance in *A Trick to Catch the Old one*, IV. iii (1608, F3): '*First Creditor.* Come, come sir, what say you extempore now to your bill of a hundred pound: a sweet debt for froating your doublets.' Stow (*Annales*, ed. Howes, 1615, p. 868) says that when Edward de Vere, Earl of Oxford, returned home from Italy in 1576, he brought with him among other luxuries 'a perfumed leather Ierkin'.

313. *titillation*, a means of stimulating or tingling. The *O.E.D.* quotes *Sir Gyles Goosecappe*, II. i (1606, O3): '*Tales.* Nay Ladie hee will perfume you gloues him selfe; most delicately, and giue them the right Spanish Titillation. ⟨*Penelope.*⟩ Titillation what's that my Lord? *Tal.* Why Ladie tis a pretty kinde of terme newe come vp in perfuming, which they call a Titillation.' So *Alch.* IV. iv. 13, 'Your *Spanish* titillation in a gloue'.

314. *Sampsuchine*, oil of marjoram.

315. *nulli-fidian*, lit. a sceptic. W. Bullein, *A Dialogue both pleasaunt and pietifull*, 1579, p. 19: '*Medicus.* Herke in your eare, I am neither Catholike, Papist nor Protestant, I assure you. . . . To be plain, I am a *Nulla fidian*, and there are many of our secte; marke our doynges. *Antonius.* Oh, *Qui dixi⟨t⟩ in corde suo non est deus.*' Here punningly applied to a person of no credit rather than of no faith.

320–3. This list of Eastern perfumes was extracted from Pliny's *Natural History. Phoenicobalanus* is the Egyptian date; *turmerick*, an East Indian plant used as a yellow dye and in curry powder; *sesama*, an oily Eastern plant; *calamus odoratus*, the scented reed of Syria and Arabia; *stacte*, myrrh-oil; *opobalsamum*, balm; *amomum*, an Assyrian perfume; *storax*, a fragrant gum-resin used in medicine; *ladanum*, resin of the lada, a shrub in Cyprus, the *Cistus Creticus*; *aspalathus* (incorrectly given as *aspalathum*), a white thorny shrub, also of Cyprus; *opoponax* (misprinted *opponax* in F1), a gum-resin of South Europe; *oenanthe*, variously explained as the grape of the wild vine, and waterdropwort.

325. *searcing*, finely sifting.

331. *voluptarie*. So Jonson keeps to the correct form of the Latin *voluptarius*; *voluptuarius* is a post-classical form. Cf. *M.L.* I. ii. 41.

340. *smell far worse*. Cf. Martial, II. xii. 4, of a perfumed fopling, 'Postume, non bene olet qui bene semper olet'.

376. *moscardini*, sweetmeats flavoured with musk.

382. *deuant*, front (of his jerkin).

395. *true spanish*. *Alch.* IV. iv. 13–14, 'Your *Spanish* titillation in a glove | The best perfume.'

ambre in the vmbre, ambergris in the dark-brown dye.

400. *diapasme*, 'a scented powder for sprinkling over the person' (*O.E.D.*). The *chaine* is the 'pomander chaine' of l. 407: see *E.M.O.* II. i. 98 n.

404. *the jaw-bones of a sow*. Sir Hugh Platt, *Delightes for Ladies*, 1602, section iv, no. 7, '*A white fucus or beauty for the face*. The iawe bones of a Hogge or Sow well burnt, beaten, and searced through a fine searce, and after grounde vpon a porphire or serpentine stone is an excellent fucus, being laid on with the oyle of white poppey.'

416. *Harlot*, rascal. Used of a man; so *Volp.* v. iii. 65, vi. 14.

433. *a breath like a panther*. *Volp.* III. vii. 215, and Holland's translation of Pliny's *Natural History*, 1601, VIII. xvii: 'It is said, that all four-footed beasts are wonderfully delighted and enticed by the smell of Panthers; but their hideous looke and crabbed countenance which they bewray so soone as they shew their heads, skareth them as much againe: and therefore their maner is, to hide their heads, and when they have trained other beasts within their reach by their sweet savour, they flie upon them and worrie them.'

437. *like a Frenchman*. Cf. Glapthorne, *The Ladies Privilege*, II. i (1640, C3), where Adorni acts a French lover to Corimba: the stage-direction is 'Ador. Acts furiously', and Corimba says:

> Excellently ravishing: this is of force
> To make the hardest hearted Lady love him:
> Can I intreat him but to teach my Cosen
> Some of his French, he will for ever be engallanted.

Livy says of the Gauls, 'Prima eorum proelia plus quam virorum, postrema minus quam femininarum esse' (x. xxviii), and Rabelais copies this tribute to his countrymen, *Gargantua*, I. xlviii.

439–40. *Cupids baths . . . nectar*. From Anacreon, xxvii, γράφε ῥῖνα καὶ παρειάς, | ῥόδα τῷ γάλακτι μίξας. Jonson is very fond of this conceit and elsewhere substitutes 'roses' for 'nectar': *D. is A.* II. vi. 82–3, *G.M.* 536–7, *Und.* ii (5), 21–2, xix. 7, 8. So Propertius, II. iii. 12, 'Utque rosae puro lacte natant folia'.

441. *light all his torches at your eyes*. From the pseudo-Tibullus, III. viii. 5, 6:

> Illius ex oculis, cum vult exurere divos,
> accendit geminas lampadas acer Amor.

This also is a favourite: *Hym.* 737–8; *L.R.* 216–17; *Challenge*, 44–5;

G.M. 534–5; *Und.* vii. 22–4, xix. 1, 2. So Herrick in the *Hesperides*, 1648, p. 131, 'A Nuptiall Song . . . on Sir Clipseby Crew':

> See, a thousand *Cupids* fly
> To light their Tapers at the Brides bright eye.

464. *Buzze*, nonsense! Cf. *S.W.* iv. ii. 49, 50, 'your she-OTTER is comming, your wife. OTT. Wife! Buz. *Titiuilitium*. There's no such thing in nature.' In *N.I.* ii. vi. 70, with a quibble on 'Fly'. In *Hamlet*, ii. ii. 388–9, '*Pol.* The actors are come hither, my lord. *Ham.* Buz, buz!' Various authorities (Aldis Wright, Dover Wilson, C. T. Onions) quote Blackstone's interpretation, 'an exclamation used at Oxford when any one began a story that was generally known before'. This suits the *Hamlet* passage where Hamlet knows of the actors already, but it does not explain the Jonson passages.

467–9. *bitter bob . . . Reuerse.* See v. ii. 64–76. Dr. Judson suggests that at the remark 'Your *frenchified* fool is your onely foole, lady' (l. 461), he leans over Mercury's shoulder in the manner there indicated.

485. *So are most of them.* Another reference to the *morbus Gallicus*.

529. *a wench of the first year.* *Volp.* i. v. 108–9.

534. *Kisses as close as a cockle.* From the Emperor Gallienus' 'Adlocutio ad Sponsos' (Lemaire's *Bibliotheca Classica Latina*, Poet. Lat. Min., vol. iii):

> Ite agite, o iuvenes: et desudate medullis
> omnibus inter vos: non murmura vestra columbae,
> bracchia non hederae, non vincant oscula conchae.

Jonson was fond of the phrase: *Alch.* iii. iii. 69, *Cat.* ii. 344–5, *Hym.* 526. Jonson was imitated by Fletcher, *The Captain*, v. iv (Folio, 1647, p. 71), 'I saw their lips as close upon the bargaine | As Cockles', and Randolph, *The Jealous Lovers*, 1632, ii. xii, 'These eyes are witnesse that descried 'um kissing | Closer then cockles.'

535. *till our very soules mixe.* *Hym.* 512.

542. *seuen, or nine.* Cf. Selden, *Table Talk*, 1689, H4, s.v. '*War*': '*Boccaline* has this passage of Souldiers. They came to *Apollo* to have their profession made the Eighth Liberal Science, which he granted. As soon as it was nois'd up and down, it came to the Butchers, and they desir'd their Profession might be made the Ninth: For say they, the Souldiers have this Honour for the killing of Men, and why should not we have Honour likewise done to us? *Apollo* could not Answer their Reasons, so he revers'd his Sentence, and made the Souldiers Trade a Mystery, as the Butchers is.' Actually in Boccalini's *I Ragguagli di Parnaso*, 1615, i, it is a dispute between Literati and Military men in Parnassus for precedency. Selden has confused two accounts, and his may be the one Jonson had in mind in his two extra sciences.

549. *sir Dagonet.* *E.M.O.* iv. iv. 118–19.

595–6. Judson compares Claudian, *De Raptu Proserpinae*, iii. 197, 'Levius communia tangunt'.

598 foll. Petrarchan conventions, which begin, in a modified form, in John Heywood's 'Praise of his Ladye' in *Tottel's Miscellany*, p. 163, ed. Arber. Shakespeare puts them in perspective in *Sonnet* cxxx. F. G. Fleay compared Daniel's 18th Sonnet to *Delia* (1598), which is adapted from Du Bellay:

> Restore thy tresses to the golden Ore,
>   Yeelde *Cithereas* sonne those Arkes of loue;
>   Bequeath the heauens the starres that I adore,
>   And to th'Orient do thy Pearles remoue.
> Yeeld thy hands pride vnto th'yuory whight,
>   T'*Arabian* odours giue thy breathing sweete:
>   Restore thy blush vnto *Aurora* bright,
>   To *Thetis* giue the honour of thy feete.
> Let *Venus* haue thy graces, her resign'd,
>   And thy sweete voyce giue back vnto the Spheares:
> But yet restore thy fearce and cruell minde,
>   To *Hyrcan* Tygers, and to ruthles Beares.
> Yeeld to the Marble thy hard hart againe;
> So shalt thou cease to plague, and I to paine.

B. Griffin similarly in *Fidessa, more chaste then kinde*, 1596, Sonnet xxxix:

> My Ladies haire is threeds of beaten gold,
>   Her front the purest Christall eye hath seene:
> Her eyes the brightest starres the heauens hold.
>   Her cheekes red Roses, such as seld haue been:
> Her pretie lips of red vermilion dye,
>   Her hand of yuorie the purest white:
> Her blush *Aurora*, or the morning skye,
>   Her breast displaies two siluer fountaines bright,
> The Spheares her voyce, her grace the Graces three,
>   Her bodie is the Saint that I adore,
> Her smiles and fauours sweet as honey bee,
>   Her feete faire *Thetis* praiseth euermore.
> But ah the worst and last is yet behind,
> For of a Gryphon she doth beare the mind.

601–2. *Her nose . . . diall.* R. W. Beninger (*P.Q.* xxii, p. 17) aptly compares Davies of Hereford's grotesque 'Picture of Formosity' appended to the sonnets in *Wittes Pilgrimage*, 1605? where details are similarly elaborated:

>   her eyes are suns, and
> Her Nose, the Gnomon of Loues Diall bright,
> Doth, by those Sunnes, still shadow out that light
> That makes Times longest howres, but Moments seeme:
> For Months, but Minutes, Senses ioy'd, esteem.

Mr. Beninger therefore queries if we are right in thinking that the Folio additions were earlier than the Quarto text (vol. iv, pp. 17–21), but this might be a touch added in revision, like others which we have pointed out.

602. *gnomon*. Puntarvolo postulates a '*gnomon*' for 'the perfection of complement' in *E.M.O.* II. ii. 21.

605. *Yours, if his owne*. Satirized in *E.M.O.* III. vii. 46–7.

608–11, 614–15, 623–4 are in rhyme: only in Jonson's early work is this irregular distribution found. It should mark an emotional moment, and with this excuse lines 608–11 might pass.

610. *guiltie . . . guilt*. The quibble is not uncommon: the great example of it is Lady Macbeth's 'I'll gild the faces of the grooms withal, For it must seem their guilt'.

614. *like the fighting snakes*. Cf. I. i. 53 n.

634. *Ætna*. Cf. Seneca, *Hercules Furens*, 105–6, 'Concutite pectus, acrior mentem excoquat | quam qui caminis ignis Aetnaeis furit.'

650. *exempt*, picked out, choice. Chapman's *Iliad*, ix. 604:

> One girl,
> Of whose faire sex we come to offer seaven,
> The most exempt for excellence.

v. v. 9. *concord's borne of contraries*. Quintilian, I. x. 12, 'Illa dissimilium concordia quam vocant ἁρμονίαν.'

15. *Hermes wand*. Mercury conducted the souls of the dead to the underworld; for the wand see Virgil, *Aen*. iv. 242–4.

17. *the strife of Chaos*. Ovid, *Metamorphoses*, i. 18–21:

> Obstabatque aliis aliud, quia corpore in uno
> frigida pugnabant calidis, umentia siccis,
> mollia cum duris, sine pondere habentia pondus.
> Hanc deus et melior litem natura diremit.

69. *discolour'd*, many-coloured (Lat. *discolor*). *V.D.* 158, *Chl.* 257.

v. vi. 1. *Queene, and Huntress*. This lyric in its stately beauty anticipates the manner of Milton.

4. *State . . . keep*. Cf. *Macbeth*, III. iv. 5, 'Our hostess keeps her state', and the note on v. iv. 62 above. So of the royal seat at the masques, *M. Blackness*, 84; *M. Beauty*, 378.

23. *shine*. So 61 below, scene vii. 41; *Panegyre*, 130; *Und*. xxv. 58; *Poet*. Ind. 11.

74. *broad-seales*. A good example of the freedom of Elizabethan usage. 'Any noun, adjective, or neuter verb can be used as an active verb' (Abbott, *Shakespearian Grammar*, 3rd ed., Introduction, p. 5).

79, 80. *Nothing which dutie . . .* Whalley compares *Mids. N.D.* v. i. 82–3.

93. *conuinceth*, proves.

v. vii. *Cupid, like Anteros*, i.e. the enemy of Love. In *A Challenge at Tilt* and in *Love's Welcome at Bolsover* Jonson interprets 'Anteros' as love requited.

6. *to visit thy . . . court.* The convention of a travelling foreigner visiting a prince or a nobleman is a feature of the primitive masque; an historic instance is dramatized in *King Henry VIII*, I. iv, where 'a noble troop of strangers' land at Hampton Court as if they were 'great ambassadors From foreign princes' (ll. 53–6).

16. *mound*, orb, globe, such as a king carries at his coronation.

28. *neerest to himselfe.* Terence, *Andria*, IV. i. 12, 'Proxumus sum egomet mihi'. Cf. *Sej.* IV. 85–6.

32. *word*, motto. *E.M.O.* III. iv. 86.

Se Suo Modulo. Horace, *Ep.* I. vii. 98, 'Metiri se quemque suo modulo ac pede verum est.'

41. *Curarum Nubila Pello.* Adapted from Ovid, *Epist. ex Ponto*, II. i. 5, 'pulsa curarum nube'.

47. *Petasus*, low-crowned, broad-brimmed, with a wing on either side.

48. *Sic Laus Ingenii.* Untraced: supply 'crescit' or 'pollet'.

52. *an abrase table*, free from markings; the late Latin *tabula rasa* or *abrasa* = virgin paper. Cf. *G.M.* 441–2.

53. *pleights*, plaits.

55. *no deuice.* She bears a white shield.

56. *Omnis Abest Fucus.* Untraced.

60. *Cytheree.* The form 'Cythērē' for 'Cythereia' (Venus) is found in Ausonius; the spelling *-ee* marks the quantity of the last syllable.

v. viii. 3. *This Worke of wit.* The crystal into which she looks: cf. l. 30.

11. *plenilune*, full moon (Lat. *plenilunium*). Swinburne revived the word.

18. *Delia.* She was born on the island of Delos.

21–3. Cf. v. i. 38–9.

v. ix. 3. *Eutaxia*, order (Greek εὐταξία).

6. *officiously*, dutifully (Lat. *officiose*).

7. *cardinall* with a glance at its derivation from the Lat. *cardo*, 'a hinge', as 'frame' and 'moue' show.

11. *state of the presence*, the royal canopy.

17. *Impreses*, a device, especially on a shield at a tilt: cf. *Pericles*, II. ii. 19–44, and in Jonson, *U.V.* xvi. For Jonson's own impresa see *Conv. Dram.* xvii. 578–9.

18. *Symboles.* So in *The Masque of Blackness*, 266–86, Jonson substitutes symbols for impresas 'as well for strangenesse, as relishing of antiquitie'.

40. *good audacitie. Love's Labour's Lost*, v. i. 3, 4, 'pleasant without scurrility, witty without affection, audacious without impudency'.

42. *Divæ Viragini.* In Seneca's *Phaedra*, 51, Hippolytus, praying to Diana as the goddess of the chace, addresses her as 'diva virago'.

45. *watchet*, light blue.

46. *benefique*, 'of good or favourable influence' (*O.E.D.*).

imparteth, gives a share.

48. *seeme double.* Publilius Syrus, 'Inopi beneficium bis dat qui dat celeriter.'

52. *in heaven* as Luna, in *earth* as Diana, in *hell* as Hecate.

v. x. 3. *in a measure.* Amorphus's ambition has been realized (IV. v. 78): Cynthia has seen him 'dance a straine'.

5. *nomenclator.* S.W. III. vi. 13.

9. *in good time.* E.M.I. I. ii. 9, 10.

16. *flights*, long and light-feathered arrows for long-distance shooting. *rovers*, arrows used in 'roving', i.e. at 'a mark selected at will or at random, and not of any fixed distance from the archer'—*O.E.D.*, quoting Markham, *Country Contentments*, 1615, p. 108, 'The Roauer is a marke incertaine, . . . and . . . must haue arrowes lighter or heauier, according to the distance.'

butt-shafts, 'the strong unbarbed arrows used in field exercises' (Gifford). Drayton sings of Robin Hood and his men (*Polyolbion*, song xxvi. 329–32):

> Of Archery they had the very perfect craft,
> With Broad-arrow, or But, or Prick, or Roving Shaft,
> At Markes full fortie score, they us'd to Prick, and Rove,
> Yet higher then the breast, for Compasse never strove.

33. *antiperistasis*, the force of contrast. Silvester's *Du Bartas*, 'The Second Day of the first Week' (Folio, 1641, p. 13):

* Contrary Circumstance

> 'Tis (doubt-less) this *Antiperistasis
> (Bear with the word, I hold it not amiss
> T'adopt sometimes such strangers for our use,
> When Reason and Necessity induce;
> As namely, where our natiue Phrase doth want
> A Word so force-full and significant)

43. *splendidious.* E.M.O. II. ii. 79.

57. *Ignis fatue.* Note that Jonson, taking the phrase over from the Latin, uses the vocative case in *fatue.*

60. *iealous*, suspicious.

72. *resty*, sluggish. S.W. I. i. 172. Cotgrave, 1611, 'Restif . . . Restie, stubborne, drawing backward, that will not goe forward'.

73. *Ex ungue*, sc. leonem. Lucian, *Hermotimus*, 54, says Pheidias conjectured the size of a lion from seeing its claw: φασί γέ τοι τῶν πλαστῶν τινα, Φειδίαν οἶμαι, ὄνυχα μόνον λέοντος ἰδόντα ἀπ' ἐκείνου ἀναλελογίσθαι ἡλίκος ἄν ὁ πᾶς λέων γένοιτο κατ' ἀξίαν τοῦ ὄνυχος ἀναπλασθείς. John Clarke, *Paroemiologia Anglo-Latina*, 1639, p. 64, gives as an equivalent, 'A man may know by your nose what porridge you love'.

112. *Adonis garden.* E.M.O. IV. viii. 29 n.

v. xi. The scene changes without the entrance of a new character, but it sums up the two preceding scenes.

9–22. For the reference to Essex see the introductory essay, vol. i, pp. 394–6. The mention of Niobe in line 16 may be a faint allusion to Mary Queen of Scots, but it is not pressed home like the reference to Actaeon.

23. *make religion*, have conscientious scruples, a latinism (*religionem facere*). Spenser, *Colin Clout's Come home again*, 797–800 (1595, D), 'But we poore shepheards . . . Do make religion how we rashly go, To serue that God', i.e. Love, 'that is so greatly dred'.

36. *tyre of shine*, crown of rays. Cf. v. x. 48.

54. *forehead. Volp.* Ded. 13, IV. ii. 53. Cf. Persius, *Sat.* v. 103–4, 'Exclamet . . . perisse | frontem de rebus.'

58. *neighbour-virtues.* This masquerade in which evils play the part of their contrary virtues recalls the old interludes, e.g. Skelton's *Magnificence*.

95 foll. For the dishumouring caused by imposing a penance or a penalty, and for the choice of Crites to impose it, compare the denouement in *Poetaster*.

112. *the trauellers euill.* See the Induction, 69.

123. *vindicatiue*, from the medieval Latin *vindicativus*.

134. *design*, appoint, assign (Lat. *designo*).

147. *weeping Crosse.* The phrase was 'to come home by Weeping Cross'. Three places in England are still so called, one at Bodicote near Banbury, one near Stafford where the road turns off to Walsall, and a third near Shrewsbury. There were several such crosses at Banbury, and they were so named because the bodies of the dead were set down there on their way to burial. W. Bullein in *A Dialogue both pleasant and pietifull*, 1593, p. 115, says of people fleeced by lawyers, 'in the ende thei go home many miles, by foolam crosse, by weepyng crosse, by beggers Barne, and by knaues Acre, &c.'.

The procession of the penitents would move round the stage for the palinode, and a wayside cross be set up from the trapdoor in the centre (Chambers, *Elizabethan Stage*, iii, p. 107, where for *E.M.O.* read *C.R.*).

149. *Trivia*, an epithet of Diana invoked at the crossways.

152. Midas got rid of the fatal gift of turning everything he touched into gold by bathing in the source of the Pactolus near Mount Tmolus; the river from that time brought down gold dust in its waters (Ovid, *Met.* xi. 136–45). For the *Tagus* cf. *K. Ent.* 312, 'With sands more rich than TAGVS wealthy ore', where Jonson annotates 'A riuer diuiding *Spaine* & *Portugal* and by the consent of Poets stil'd *aurifer*'. 'Aurifer Tagus', Catullus, xxix. 19; Ovid, *Amores*, I. xv. 34. Midas, an Eastern king, of course had nothing to do with the Tagus; Jonson has confused the two gold-bearing rivers.

173. Compare Claudian, *De quarto Consulatu Honorii*, 299, 300, 'Componitur orbis | regis ad exemplum'.

Palinode

This portion of the play is alluded to by Dekker in *Satiro-mastix*, I. ii (1602, C1ᵛ), '*Hor.* Nay sirra the Palinode, which I meane to stitck to my Reuels, shall be the best and ⟨most⟩ ingenious peece that euer I swet for'; and H2^v, when Horace meekly says to Tucca, 'I could be pleas'd (to please you) to quaffe downe, | The poyson'd Inke, in which I dipt your name', Tucca answers, 'Saist thou so, my *Palinodicall* rimester?'

Middleton has used the Palinode in the conclusion of *A Trick to Catch the Old one*, v. ii (1608, H3^v, H4): the Courtesan renounces

> The Glances of a sinnefull eye,
> Wauing of Fans, which some suppose
> Tricks of Fancy, Treading of Toes,
> Wringing of Fingers, byting the Lip,
> The wanton gate, th'alluring Trip;
> All secret friends and priuate meetings—

and Witgood renounces

> Stabbing of armes for a common Mistress,
> Riband fauours, Ribauld Speeches;
> Deere perfumde Iacketts, pennylesse breeches;
> Dutch Flapdragons.

1. *irps*. See note on III. v. 80.

7. *stabbing of arms*. IV. i. 208–9.

flap-dragons. 'A play in which they catch raisins out of burning brandy and, extinguishing them by closing the mouth, eat them' (Dr. Johnson). Marston, *The Dutch Curtezan*, IV. i (1605, F2), '*Tyss.* Nay looke you, for my owne part, if I haue not as religiously vowd my hart to you, been drunke to your health, swalowd flap-dragons, eate glasses, drunke vrine, stabd armes, and don all the offices of protested gallantrie for your sake.' Candle-ends are substituted for the raisins in *New World*, 220. Gifford notes the alleged fondness of the Dutch for them: Barry, *Ram Alley*, II. i (1611, C3^v), 'My brother Swallowes it with more ease, then a Dutchman Does flap-Dragons'; and Daborne, *A Christian turn'd Turk*, I. iv (1612, C4), 'They will devoure one-another as familiarly as Pikes doe Gudgeons, and with as much facility as Dutchmen do Flap-dragons.'

8. *whiffes* expounded in *E.M.O.* III. vi. 136–49.

10. *wauing of fannes*. v. iii. 108.

glickes, gleeks, coquettish glances.

16. *perfum'd dogs*. Dr. Judson quotes Tomkis, *Lingua*, IV. iii (1607, H4), where a recipe is given for a pomander which 'will make you smell as sweete as my Ladies dogge'.

dildo's. *Alch.* v. v. 42, 'MADAME, with a *Dildo*, writ o' the walls', where the reference is indecent. Here it is to such things as 'love-songs for maids; so without bawdry, . . . such delicate burthens of dildos and fadings, jump her and thump her' in *The Winter's Tale*, IV. iv. 192–4.

19. *bracelets of haire*. *E.M.O.* IV. vi. 10.

shooe-ties, gloues, garters. See IV. iii. 403, 404, 412.

20. *rings with poesies*. IV. v. 114–15.

22. *pargetting*, plastering the face with paint. *S.W.* v. ii. 36, 'she's aboue fiftie too, and pargets!'

slicking, making the skin glossy. *Cat.* II. 64–5, 'shee do's sleeke With crums of bread and milke'.

glazing. III. iv. 55.

31. *belying ladies fauours, noble-mens countenance.* *E.M.O.* Characters, 39, 40.

Epilogue

Spoken by Crites? 'Turn'd rimer' would then have point from what he says in II. i. 48–9.

20. *By* (—) *'tis good, and if you lik't, you may.* The point of the joke is that it is the final word on a play which satirizes self-love, and to quote it as from a private conversation not only makes it possible but even makes it more humorous. Naturally it was remembered against Jonson. He refers to it in his next play, *Poetaster*, prologue 15–20:

> Here now, put case our Authour should, once more
> Sweare that his play were good; he doth implore,
> You would not argue him of arrogance:
> How ere that common spawne of ignorance,
> Our frie of writers, may beslime his fame,
> And giue his action that adulterate name.

There are many allusions to the line. J. H., *The House of Correction: or Certayne Satyricall Epigrams*, 1619, A3ᵛ:

> *Tis for a better pen then mine to say*
> *'By God 'tis good, and if you lik't you may.'*

Shirley, *The Wittie Faire one*, III. ii (1633, E3), after Treedle has read a poem of outrageous conceits, 'Now if you like't, you may'. Lewis Sharpe in *The Noble Stranger*, 1640, G3ᵛ, quotes the couplet as 'the inspiration of a confident Poeticall wit'. Jonson's old servant Richard Brome wrote to the Earl of Newcastle on his 'Play called the Variety' (*The weeding of the Covent Garden*, 1658, A4):

> *I would depone each Scene appear'd to me*
> *The Act of wit, each Act a Comedy,*
> *And all was such, to all that understood,*
> *As knowing* Johnson *swore By God 'twas good.*

R. Whitlock, Ζωοτόμια; *or Observations on the Present Manners of the English*, 1654, p. 24, 'Let thy Actions be justified by the Square of Religion and Justice; then say (as a Poet as justly confident) *'Tis good, and if youle lik't you may*: it not being *Arrogance*, but well becoming *Confidence* to scorne the injurious World, when it denyeth merit its due.' Aphra Behn's Epilogue to her play, *Like Father, like Son, or the Mistaken Brothers*, 1682 (in *Rare Prologues & Epilogues, 1642–1700*, ed. A. N. Wiley):

> Impudence assist thee, and boldly try
> To speak for us, and for the Comedy.

Mr. Richards *Speaks.*
I'le do't Gallants, I'le Justify this Play;
'Od Zouns, 'tis good, and if you lik'd you may.

W. Mountfort, *The Injur'd Lovers,* 1688, prologue:

like Brother *Ben* declare,
By God 'tis good, deny't the Slave that dare.

'An Epilogue spoken to the University of Oxford. By Mrs. Cook' in
Poems on Affairs of State, 1698, iii, p. 175:

Twas good old venerable *Johnson's* way,
To force us to th'approving of his Play,
By G—d! 'tis good, & if you lik't, you may.

Originally there was a final couplet preserved in the Edinburgh University MS. (see critical apparatus):

lik't or not lik't, for liking comes by chance
Art hath noe enemy but ignorance.
Ile onely speake.

The aphorism on art is quoted in a similar context in the induction to
E.M.O. 219.

For the punctuation '*By* (—)', cf. *Poet.* III. i. 216 in the Quarto, 'In
their (   ) Courts'; *Und.* xv. 113, 'O   for these'; ib. lviii. 12,
'for a [   ]'.

Ecce rubet . . . Martial, VI. lx (lxi), 3, 4.

POETASTER

Poetaster, or His Arraignment: the title concentrates the play on
Marston (Crispinus) and the cure administered to him in the fifth
act; Dekker (Demetrius) is subordinate. Ovid is depicted as a shallow libertine, powerless to vindicate poetry against such a pretender
to it as Crispinus. In the dedication to *Volpone* (20–30) Jonson put
forth as his ideal of poetry 'the impossibility of any mans being the
good Poet, without first being a good man' and had summarized
his task as being 'able to informe yong-men to all good disciplines,
inflame growne-men to all great vertues, keepe old-men in their best
and supreme state, or as they decline to child-hood, recouer them
to their first strength; . . . the interpreter, and arbiter of nature,
a teacher of things diuine, no lesse then humane, a master in manners, and can alone (or with a few) effect the businesse of mankind.'
Accordingly in this play Horace and Virgil embody the higher type.
Horace, 'the best master, both of vertue and wisdom' (*Disc.* 2592),
is the dramatic counterpart of Crispinus, and the poetic achievement

of Virgil is expressed in the sustained eulogy of Act v, scene i, lines 100–38.

The motto on the title-page is from Martial, VII. xii. 4. The last four lines of this epigram were also printed in the Quarto after the list of the 'Persons' (A1ᵛ), but with a modification: Jonson's 'Ludimus innocuis verbis, hoc iuro . . .' is in the original 'Ludimus innocui: Scis hoc bene: iuro . . .'. Dekker retorted in *Satiro-mastix* (A2ᵛ) by appending to his list of characters an extract from Martial, XIII. ii. 4–8:

Ad Detractorem.

Non potes in Nugas dicere plura meas,
Jpse ego quam dixi. — Qui se mirantur, in illos
Virus habe: Nos hæc nouimus esse nihil.

Dedication

5. *Richard Martin* (1570–1618) of the Middle Temple, called to the Bar in 1602; recorder of London in 1618 just before his death.

6, 7. *A thankefull man . . . needes it.* From Seneca, *De Beneficiis*, III. xvii. 3, 'Gratum hominem semper beneficium delectat, ingratum semel.'

10. *innocence.* He was accused of attacking the law, the army, and the stage (*Apol. Dial.* 82).

11. *vndertaker*, surety. *S.W.* Ded. 10.

12. *the greatest Iustice*, Sir John Popham, lord chief justice from 1592 to his death in 1607. His severity on the bench is noted in the poem to Jonson, 'The State and mens affaires are the best playes', probably by Sir John Roe:

And when I true friendship end,
With guilty conscience let me be worse stonge,
Than with *Pophams* sentence theeves, or *Cookes* tongue
Traitors are.

The Persons

The grouping of the poets is unhistorical: Ovid in *Tristia*, IV. x. 41–54, gives the facts. He was intimate with Propertius and Gallus, and a keen admirer of Horace whom he had heard reading his lyrics, 'Vergilium vidi tantum'; and Tibullus died before Ovid had a chance of meeting him. Ovid never mentions Maecenas.

Pub. Ovid. Virgil. To the view expressed in our introductory essay (vol. i, pp. 432–7), which is also the view of Sir E. K. Chambers (*William Shakespeare*, ii, p. 203), Professor O. J. Campbell (*Comicall Satyre*, p. 130 n.), R. A. Small (*The Stage-Quarrel*, pp. 56–7), Dr. J. H. Penniman (edition of *Poetaster*), and H. S. Mallory in the Yale edition, that these two characters are the historic Ovid and Virgil, and have no Elizabethan counterpart such as Donne for the one or Shakespeare or Chapman for the other, we add some corroboration from internal evidence. In the play there are four passages of poetry definitely assigned to individual authors—the translation of elegy xv in Ovid's first book of *Amores*, in Act I, scene i; the translation of Virgil's picture of Fame from *Aeneid*, IV. 160–88, in Act V, scene ii; and the parodies of Marston and Dekker, which both of them acknowledge, in the same scene, lines 275–92, 302–19. The two translations are authenticated by their authors; Ovid composes his elegy, Virgil reads an extract from his epic. What particle of resemblance is there in either of these pieces to the manner of Donne or of Shakespeare? How could the translations give the audience at the Blackfriars the slightest clue to that effect—such a clue, for instance, as that of Marston's uncouth vocabulary in the effort of Crispinus?

12. *Lupus.* 'Asinius Lupus' in I. ii. 148. Was this personal satire on a magistrate named 'Wolf'? Dekker retorts by calling an intimate of Horace 'Asinius Bubo'.

13. *Tucca.* 'Pantilius Tucca': 'cimex Pantilius', the back-biter, in Horace, *Sat.* I. x. 78, where 'Pantilius' is evidently παν-τίλλειν, the 'all-scratching bug'. Dekker comments on his re-use of this character in *Satiro-mastix*, A3: 'A second Cat-a-mountaine mewes, and calles me Barren, because my braines could bring foorth no other *Stigmaticke* than *Tucca*, whome *Horace*'—i.e. Jonson—'had put to making, and begot to my hand: but I wonder what language *Tucca* would haue spoke, if honest Capten *Hannam* had bin borne without a tongue? Ist not as lawfull then for mee to imitate *Horace*, as *Horace Hannam*? Besides, If I had made an opposition of any other new-minted fellow, (of what Test so euer) hee had bin out-fac'd, and out-weyd by a settled former approbation: neyther was it much improper to set the same dog vpon *Horace*, whom *Horace* had set to worrie others.' Jack Hannam was a captain in Drake's company when they sailed in September 1585 for an expedition against Spain (F. P. Wilson in *M.L.R.* xv, pp. 80–1).

The name 'Tucca' is in E. Guilpin's *Skialetheia*, 1598 ('Satyre Preludium', B8ᵛ), in a satirical description of poetasters courting a mistress:

> A third that falls more roundly to his worke,
> Meaning to moue her were she Iew or Turke:
> Writes perfect *Cat and fidle*, wantonly,
> Tickling her thoughts with masking bawdry:
> Which read to Captaine *Tucca*, he doth sweare,
> And scratch, and sweare, and scratch to heare
> His owne discourse discours'd: and *by the Lord
> It's passing good: oh good!* at euery word.
> When his Cock-sparrow thoughts to itch begin,
> He with a shrug sweares 't a *most sweet sinne*.

15. *Rufus Laberius Crispinus*, i.e. Marston. 'Rufus' because of his red hair: cf. II. ii. 80. Laberius a Roman writer of mimes (Horace, *Sat.* I. x. 6); Aulus Gellius censures his 'verba ignobilia nimis et sordentia' (*N.A.* XIX. xiii), which is Jonson's reason for choosing the name. *Crispinus*, a bad and voluminous poet, challenged Horace to see which of them could write faster (*Sat.* I. iv. 14–16).

16. *Hermogenes.* Horace mentions two musicians of this name, one a Sardinian and hostile critic of Horace (*Sat.* I. ii. 3 foll.), the other surnamed Tigellius.

17. *Demetrius Fannius*, i.e. Dekker. Horace has contemptuous references to a musician Demetrius, whom he calls a monkey (*Sat.* I. x. 18 with the Scholiast's note, and 90) and a backbiter (ib. 78–9), and to a feeble poet named Fannius (ib. iv. 21; 'ineptus', x. 79, 80).

19. *Minos*, an apothecary. Called 'little Minos', III. iv. 178, 360: cf. *Ep.* cxxxiii. 189, where it is used of a fletcher in Holborn. So Gayton in *Pleasant Notes upon Don Quixot*, 1654, p. 39, calls an apothecary '*Pigmy Minos*' and 'little *Minos*'. Is it an allusion to some tradesman who had Marston arrested for debt?

20. *Histrio*, 'a player' (Latin).

21. *Æsop.* A famous tragedian of ancient Rome was so named: see Jonson's epigram to Edward Alleyn (lxxxix. 3).

22. *Pyrgus.* Tucca's page: as there were two of them, Gifford corrected to 'Pyrgi'. 'Pyrgus' in Latin (from the Greek πύργος, a tower) was a tower-shaped dice-box with holes at the bottom: the dice were thrown into the top of it. The word is a variant reading for 'phimus' (Greek φιμός), a kind of cup also used as a dice-box in Horace, *Satires*, II. vii. 17. In Jonson's copy of Scriverius's *Martial*, 1619, p. 273, in the first of the 'Xenia', l. 7, he glossed 'haec est mihi charta fritillus' 'pyrgus' in the margin. The gamester Tucca nicknames his pages 'pyrgi' because he uses them to find out a likely lender; he throws a cast with them for this purpose.

Iulia, 'the Princesse Iulia' (I. iii. 25), daughter of the Emperor Augustus. The authority for identifying Ovid's love with this lady is Sidonius Apollinaris (*Carm.* xxiii. 158–61):

> Et te carmina per libidinosa
> notum, Naso tener, Tomosque missum,
> quondam Caesareae nimis puellae
> ficto nomine subditum Corinnae.

So Jonson in *Und.* xxvii. 17–20. But dates refute this identification: the elder Julia was banished in 2 B.C., Ovid in A.D. 8. His own hints make it clear that his disaster was connected with the detection of her daughter the younger Julia banished in A.D. 9: Ovid's own explanation, as far as he gives one, is that he had seen too much (*Tristia*, II. 102–6).

Cytheris, the mistress of the poet Cornelius Gallus, who celebrated her under the name of Lycoris (I. iii. 30, 31).

Plautia, the mistress of Tibullus, whom he celebrated as Delia (ib. 32–3). In Apuleius' *Apologia*, 406, the name is found in some manuscripts, but the right reading is 'Plania'.

Induction

1 (margin). *Arising in the midst of the stage* by the trap-door through which ghosts appeared and vanished, e.g. in Marston's *Sophonisba*, also

acted at the Blackfriars Theatre, v. i. 40, 'Out of the altar the ghost of Asdrubal ariseth'.

3. *Th' Arraignment.* Envy reads the title which is posted up, as she later reads the scene 'Rome' (l. 28). Cf. *Wily Beguilde*, Ind. (1606, A2), '*Prologue.* How now my honest Rogue; what play shall wee haue here to-night? *Play.* Sir you may looke vpon the Title.'

9. *forc't stings.* Cf. N. Lichefield, *Lopez de Castanheada's First booke of the historie of the discouerie and conquest of the East Indies*, 1582, iii. 8 b, 'Their skinnes be so hard that no speare can pearce the same, albeit it be forced upon it with great strength.'

10. *malic't.* *E.M.O.* v. xi. 61.

14. *these fifteene weekes.* In *Satiro-mastix*, I. ii (D1^v), of an epithalamium which Horace has promised, 'Ile end within this houre. *Tuc.* What wut end? wut hang thy selfe now? has he not writ Finis yet Iacke? what will he bee fifteene weekes about this Cockatrices egge too? has hee not cackeld yet? not laide yet?'

21. *bulke*, breast. Cf. *Hamlet*, II. i. 94–5:

> He raised a sigh so piteous and profound
> As it did seem to shatter all his bulk.

22. *risse.* Cf. *Gram.* I. xix. 30.

26. *promooting.* Cf. 'promoter' in the sense of 'informer'.

28. *ey-strings*, the nerves of the eye, which were 'formerly supposed to crack or break at death or loss of sight' (*O.E.D.*).

30. *preuented*, anticipated.

35. *poet-apes.* *Ep.* lvi, 'On Poet-ape'. Cf. Sidney, *An Apology for Poetry* (ed. Gregory Smith, p. 205), 'the cause why it'—i.e. poetry—'is not esteemed in Englande is the fault of Poet-apes, not Poets.' Dekker in *Satiro-mastix*, E3^r, made Horace describe Crispinus and Fannius as 'these *Poet-apes*'; and Crispinus, crowning him with nettles, says (M1^v), '*All Poets shall be Poet-Apes but you.*'

36. *basiliskes eyes.* Cf. 'Cockatrice', *E.M.O.* I. ii. 220 n.

44. *take my snakes . . . and eate.* Allegorical pictures of Envy (e.g. in the emblem books) depicted her with snakes issuing from her mouth. So Ovid, *Metamorphoses*, ii. 768–70, 'Videt intus edentem | vipereas carnes, vitiorum alimenta suorum, | Invidiam.'

47. *rustie teeth.* Cf. Martial, v. xxviii. 7, of an envious man, 'cui placet nemo': 'robiginosis cuncta dentibus rodit'.

54–5. The rhyming couplet suggests a rounding off of the speech. Envy pauses for her spell to take effect. This failing, she resumes.

Prologue

1. With the gradual sinking of Envy W. J. Lawrence (*Pre-Restoration Stage Studies*, p. 111) compares Harpax in the last act of *The Virgin Martyr*, 'first sinking a little and then disappearing'.

6. *An armed Prologue.* Marston ends *Antonio and Mellida*, acted in 1599 and printed in 1601 (I5^r) with an epilogue which glances at Jon-

son's self-praise in the epilogue to *Cynthia's Revels*: 'Gentlemen, though I remain an armed Epilogue'—evidently spoken by Andrugio who in the final scene 'entered in armour'—'I stand not as a peremptory chalenger of desert, either for him that composed the Comedy, or for vs that acted it: but a most submissive supplyant for both.' Hence Jonson arms his prologue in 'a well erected confidence'. The prologue to Shakespeare's *Troilus and Cressida* (entered on the Stationers' Register 7 February 1603, and probably acted in 1602[1]) clearly replies to this:

> And hither am I come,
> A prologue arm'd, but not in confidence
> Of author's pen or actor's voice.

There is the imitation of Jonson's disciple Randolph in the prologue of his *Aristippus*, 1630:

> Be not deceiu'd, I haue no bended knees,
> No supple tongue, nor speeches steep'd in oyle,
> No candid flattery, nor honied words.
> I come an armed Prologue; arm'd with Arts. . . .

H. Burnell in *Landgartha*, 1641, has a 'Prologue delivered by an *Amazon* with a Battle-Axe in her hand'.

15. *once more*, as in the last line of *Cynthia's Revels*.
22. *base deiection*. Cf. v. iii. 347–9.

I. i. There is some dramatic clumsiness in Jonson's introduction of Ovid in this first scene and his father's trouncing him for poetry in a play entitled *Poetaster*. The father is perhaps a personal reminiscence: the elder Knowell in *Every Man in his Humour* and Marcus Ovid here may be echoes of the bricklayer stepfather. To Jonson, of course, Ovid was a true poet, but this may not have been clear to the audience till later in the play.

5. *gods a mee*, or 'gods me', a colloquial clipping of 'God save me'. Cf. 'God's my life!' *E.M.I.* iv. i. 18.
songs and sonnets. *E.M.I.* iv. iii. 17 n.
9. *cast*, vomit.
17. *by the welkin*. Nym's oath in *The Merry Wives*, i. iii. 88, 'By welkin and her star!'
24. *skeldring captain*, as he professes to be in iii. iv. 155. Cf. *E.M.O.*, Characters, 85.
25. *veluet armes*. *E.M.I.* ii. iv. 76.
35. *castalian mad*, mad on poetry. From the spring of the Muses, Castalia, by Mount Parnassus.
43–84. Based on Marlowe's translation of Ovid's *Amores*, i. xv. Jonson retouched the version in the direction of literalism. With the heading, '*The same by* B. I.', this was appended to Marlowe's original text

---

[1] E. K. Chambers, *William Shakespeare*, i, p. 443.

in the second edition. The only variant in the reprint is 'The frostdrad myrtle' (the Quarto reading) for 'Frost-fearing myrtle' in line 79.

Jonson's changes in Marlowe's text are:

43. *twitst . . . ill*] carpest thou my time is spent so ill,

44. *call'st my verse*] termst my workes

45. *sprung*] come   (Here the rhyme justifies Jonson.)

46. *I pursue not young?*] are refus'd being yong ?

47. *Or*] Nor   *tedious*] brawling

48. *And prostitute my voice*] Nor set my voyce to sale

50. *Which through the world shall*] That all the world may

51. *will*] shall

52. *to the sea*] into sea   *fleet*] swift

53. *And . . . beare*] Ascræus liues, while grapes with new wine swell

54. *Or . . . eare*] Or men with crooked Sickles corne downe fell

55–6. CALLIMACHVS *. . . flowe*]

> The world shall of *Callimachus* euer speake,
> His Arte excelld, although his witte was weake.

57. *No . . . vaine*] For euer lasts high *Sophocles* proud vaine

59. *Whil'st . . . whorish*] While bond-men cheate, fathers hard, bawds whorish

60. *harlots*] strumpets

61. ENNIVS *. . . straine*] Rude *Ennius*, and *Plautus* full of witt

62. *A fresh . . . gaine*] Are both in fames eternall legend writt

63. *Of . . . eare*] What age of *Varroes* name

64. *Of*] And

65–6. *Then . . . frie*]

> Loftie *Lucretius* shall liue that howre
> That nature shall dissolue this earthy bower

67. TYTIRVS *. . . ÆNEE*] *Æneas* warre, and *Tityrus*

69. *fires . . . bowe*] Bowe and fiery Shafts

70. *neate*] sweet

71. *Our*] And

72. *now loues*] loued

73–4. *The suffering . . . feare*]

> Therefore when Flint and Iron weare away
> Verse is immortall, and shall nere decay.

75. *Kings . . . it*] To verse let Kings give place

76. *The*] And

77–8. *Kneele . . . well*]

> Let base conceipted witts admire vilde things,
> Faire *Phœbus* lead me to the Muses springs.

79–80. *Frost-fearing . . . read*]

> About my head be quiuering mirtle wound,
> And in sad louers heads[1] let me be found.

[1] Query, hands.

81. *"Enuie . . . bite*] The liuing, not the dead can enuie bite
83–4. *Then . . . aspire*]

> Then though death rakes my bones in funerall fire,
> Ile liue, and as he puls me downe mount higher.

61. *Accius.* Lucius Accius, an early tragic poet. Marlowe renders by 'Plautus': till Ritschl discovered the real name of Plautus to be Titus Maccius Plautus from the palimpsest in the Ambrosian library at Milan, the name was misread Marcus Accius from the corrupt reading of two prologues.

64. A reference to the lost *Argonautica* of Varro.

67. *Tityrus, Tillage, Ænee*: in the original 'Tityrus et segetes (v.l. fruges) Aeneiaque arma', i.e. the *Eclogues, Georgics,* and *Aeneid.*

70. *neate,* 'culte Tibulle' in Ovid. Cf. *U.V.* xxvi. 52, 'Neat *Terence,* witty *Plautus'.*

76. *gold-bearing Tagus. C.R.* v. xi. 152.

79. *frost-drad* (Quarto) is an incorrect form for 'frost-dreading'. 'Drad' = dread in *Sej.* IV. 265.

81–2. Quoted from Jonson's rendering by Lovelace 'On Sannazaro being Honoured', *Lucasta,* 1659 (ed. Wilkinson, p. 179).

I. ii. Ovid's father is historical: the Apologetical Dialogue (l. 120) quotes *Tristia,* IV. x. 21, 'Saepe pater dixit "studium quid inutile temptas"' of the son's early poetry. An early life of Ovid records that when his father caught him writing poetry and applied the rod, the boy cried out 'Parce mihi: nunquam versificabo, pater'. We may compare lines 103–11 below.

12. *Medea.* A lost work on which Quintilian bestowed qualified praise.

16. *enghle,* minion. *C. is A.* I. ii. 3.
shot-clog. E.M.O. v. ix. 47.

22. *poring into an oxes panch.* A reference to divination from the entrails of victims offered in a Roman sacrifice.

24. *rowle powle, all riualls.* Cf. *T. of T.* II. ii. 15, 'What? Rowle-powle? Maple-face? All fellowes?' and note.

25. *master of worship.* 'Knight of worshippe' in the Quarto. Ovid was descended from an old equestrian family (*Ex Ponto,* IV. viii. 17–18). Tucca harps on this in the Quarto: 'knight Errant' (150), '*Mirror of Knighthood*' (157), 'Knight' (163, 188, 214, 215), but these and all later references to knights and knighthood are altered in the Folio. Dr. Penniman suggests that Jonson may have been rebuked for satirizing knights; at any rate he may have thought it judicious to make no additional enemies after his troubles with the law, the army, and the players.

45. *cropshin.* 'A form of "copshen" or "corpion", meaning an inferior quality of herring' (*O.E.D.*). Nashe, *Lenten Stuffe,* 1599 (*Works,*

ed. McKerrow, iii, p. 216), 'There was a Herring, or there was not, for it was but a cropshin, one of the refuse sort of herrings.'

46. *twang'd.* Cf. *cano* in Latin of the chanted answer of an oracle.

47–52. Compare H. Fitz-Geoffrey's mock depreciation of satire in *Certain Elegies*, Satyre ii (1620, B3ʳ):

> Beshrow me, sirs, if I dare strout in street.
> Wink at a *Window*: a *God-dam-me* greet:
> Vsher a *Lady*: but salute her *Glove*:
> Or *kisse* a Maid for manners more then *Love*:
> Cringe to a *Scriuener*: be conversing seen
> In *Ludgate*, with a broken *Citizen*:
> Turn oft in *Pauls*: call for a stoole o'the *Stage*:
> Or walk attended with my *Hackney* Page:
> Pace *Turnball, Shoreditch, Long-lane*: or *Pickt-hatch*,
> Least I be taken by this heedfull watch.
> These *pickthank* Peasants: that with *Lynceus* eye,
> Inspect mens Actions too Injuriously.

47. *kisse his mistris slippers.* *E.M.O.* iv. ii. 34, 'kissing ladies pumps'.

52. *i'the statute*, the thirty-ninth of Elizabeth (1597–8), ch. 4, by which players were made vagabonds in the eyes of the law unless authorized to act under the hand and seal of some nobleman. In *Histriomastix* (1610, D4ᵛ) Steward takes leave of the players, 'Farewell yee proud (I hope they heare me not) Proud Statute Rogues.'

54. *trickt.* *E.M.O.* iii. iv. 69.

62. *blow your eares.* *E.M.I.* ii. i. 104.

63–4. Ovid in the *Tristia* (v. vii. 27) hearing that his poems were being recited in the theatre to the accompaniment of dancing, says 'Nil equidem feci (tu scis hoc ipse) theatris'.

75. *a younger brother.* Ovid's elder brother practised at the law and died in his twentieth year (*Tristia*, iv. x. 17–18, 31–2).

76. *exhibition.* *E.M.O.* ii. v. 27.

81. *Homer.* 'Maeonides nullas ipse reliquit opes', said Ovid's father: see the Apologetical Dialogue, 121.

82. *must not be spew'd against, but with hallowed lips.* A violent ellipse for a writer who objected to Shakespeare's 'Caesar did never wrong, but with just cause' (*Disc.* 664–5).

86. *boothes*, ale-booths.

87. *in his sleepe.* Varied in *S. of N.* ii. i. 15–16, 'A sordid Rascall, one that neuer made | Good meale in his sleep.'

94. *a Senators reuenue.* Dr. Mallory quotes the money-qualification for a senator—an estate of 800,000 sesterces, which Augustus raised to 1,200,000, i.e. about £8,860 (Suetonius, *Augustus*, 41).

96. *in his litter.* A privilege originally confined to the wives of senators, but men of rank soon indulged in it.

97. *Bias*, one of the seven sages of Greece, who lived about 600 B.C. His *sentences*, or maxims, are mostly to be found in Diogenes Laertius.

101. *apt. T. of T.* IV. i. 126.

102. *disclaime in him. C. is A.* v. xii. 68.

113. *Mis-prize*, misunderstand. *C.R.* IV. iv. 31. Marcus Ovid glances at the legal use of 'misprision', a misdemeanour or failure of duty on the part of a public official. The historical Ovid had a marked fondness for legal metaphor in his poetry: Professor Arthur Palmer noted it in the *Heroides*, viii. 7, ix. 109–10, x. 52.

120. *angels*, the usual quibble on the coin so called. Cf. *Witt's Recreations*, 1641, M7ᵛ, no. 544, ' *Vpon Annas marriage with a Lawyer* ':

> *Anne* is an angell, what if so she be ?
> What is an angell ? but a Lawyers fee.

happy, 'rich', like the Latin *beatus*: cf. *Alch.* I. ii. 119.

124. *little Grammaticaster* is as pointless as 'pretty Alcibiades' (132). When Drayton complained in the preface to *The Barons Wars*, 1603, that 'Grammaticasters *have quarreld at the title of* Mortimeriados, *as if it had been a sin against* Syntaxis *to have inscribed it in the second case* ', there was equal point in his calling them 'inferior grammarians', and in their objecting to a genitive case in the title instead of a nominative, 'Mortimerias'.

129. *Three bookes.* Four authorities are quoted in *E.M.O.* II. iii. 166–7, Plowden, Dyer, Brooke, and Fitzherbert.

130. *Besides, when.* A compressed way of saying 'over and above the time when'; almost equal to 'not to mention the time when'. Shakespeare's 'Moreover that we much did long to see you' (= besides that) in *Hamlet*, II. ii. 2, and 'Seldom when The steeled gaoler is the friend of man' (*Measure for Measure*, IV. ii. 82–3) show the same free use of the conjunction, but one much clearer.

131. *cheu'rill*, of kid's leather, and so yielding, stretching. *Epigrams* xxxvii and liv satirize a pliant lawyer named 'Chev'ril'. A 'cheverel conscience' was a common phrase. Cf. Stubbes, *The Anatomy of Abuses in England*, Book II, i (ed. Furnivall, p. 12), 'the lawiers haue such chauerell consciences, that they can serue the deuill better in no kind of calling than in that'.

136. *haue the law on his side for't.* *B.F.* IV. i. 80, and the opening scene of *Romeo and Juliet*.

139. *traduce* (Quarto), seduce, pervert. A rare use.

140. *Janus. E.M.O.* I. ii. 203.

141. *Intend*, direct your mind to it (Lat. *intendo*).

150. *Cothurnus*, i.e. Lupus, called 'buskin', which was worn in ancient Rome by men of rank. Cf. IV. iv. 15 (Lupus), 'on with my buskins'; v. iii. 87, Tucca to Lupus, 'Touch him. old *Buskins*'.

153. *drachme.* The drachma, a Greek coin, was worth about 9¾*d.*, nearly the same value as the Roman denarius.

156–7. *my flowre o'the order.* The Quarto has 'my most *Magnanimous Mirror of Knighthood*'; cf. *C.R.* III. v. 28 n.; *B.F.* Ind. 143; Dekker, *Satiro-mastix*, 1602, F1ᵛ, '*Tac.* Dost loue her, my finest and first part of the Mirrour of Knighthood?'; *The Honest Whore*, 1630, pt. 2: '*Mut.* Signior *Lodovico*? how does my little Mirrour of Knighthood?'; Butler, *Hudibras*, part I, canto i, 15–16:

> A Wight he was whose very sight wou'd
> Entitle him *Mirror of Knighthood*.

160. *Lucullus*, the conqueror of Mithridates, celebrated for his wealth and magnificence.

161. *stumpe*, strictly of a short man; like 'stub' and 'stock' it could mean 'blockhead'. But Tucca, whose language is perfectly reckless, as in his use of 'cropshin' (l. 45), probably means the former.

162. *a good broach . . . in a mans hat.* Brooches were worn by men, both as an ornament and also to clasp the feather. Cf. *Christmas*, 3; *S. of N.* III. ii. 265; *M.L.* I. vii. 33.

163. *old boy.* Cf. III. iv. 112; *Alch.* v. v. 137; *For.* x. 19.

172. *Agrippa.* M. Vipsanius Agrippa commanded the Roman fleet at Actium; Horace addressed an ode to him (I. vi).

173. *moyles*, mules.

179. *your tongue.* Tucca stammers: see IV. v. 77. Horace in *Satiromastix*, I. ii (1602, C2r), calls him 'lymping tongu'd captaine'.

181. *a talent.* A Greek coin, not a Roman; Jonson may have used it because of its mention in Plautus and the Roman poets.

183. *nut-cracker.* 'Boy, lacquay, or sirrah' at the Court (*C.R.* II. iii. 73), but Tucca would be incapable of calling a boy a 'boy'.

185. *clem*, starve.

187–8. *setter . . . tumbler* refer to obsolete hunting tactics. The setter, approaching a bird, 'layes him downe, and with a marcke of his pawes, betrayed the place of the byrdes last abode, whereby it is supposed that this kynde of dogge is called *Index*, Setter' (Caius, *Of Englishe Dogges*, 1576, Fleming's translation, p. 16). The tumblers, used for rabbits, were so called 'because in hunting they turne and tumble, winding their bodyes about in circle wise' and so keep 'the selly simple Coney away from his hole' (ibid., p. 11). Cunningham compares Davenant, *The Fair Favourite*, II. i (*Works*, 1673, p. 95), 'Cavaliers | That start upon us in the dark, like Tumblers in | A Warren at their Game.' Tucca's pages help him to track out dupes: cf. 'ferret', III. iv. 118. They are rewarded with 'halfe a share' (*infra*, 222).

192. *sixe and fiftie*, i.e. experienced, but not yet an old man.

194. *bald.* *C.R.* IV. v. 101 note.

this chaine. Elizabethan rather than Roman. 'Chains were worn by most citizens, and were provided by the wealthy for their retainers; every well-dressed Gentleman wore a gold chain' (*Shakespeare's England*, ii, p. 115). Cf. v. iii. 41–2.

198. *Better cheape*, cheaper: 'cheape' = market. Cf. *H.W.* 109.

200. *sixe, sixe, drachmes.* Bare numbers were used in this way to express value, but were liable to equivocal interpretations. See *D. is A.* III. iii. 183–4, 'No, Sir, he cost me forty, ere he was set. MER. Turnings,

you meane? I know your *Equiuocks*.' For further examples see III. iv. 165, 'thou hast fortie, fortie, shillings, I meane', and *Alch.* III. iii. 31.

Callimachus, the Alexandrian poet who flourished *c.* 250 B.C. For Ovid's qualified praise of him see I. i. 55–6.

209. *seame-rent suite*. So in *E.M.O.* II. vi. 66 scholars are 'poore seame-rent fellowes'.

210. *emblemes*. *E.M.I.* v. v. 35.

213. *tell*, count.

215. *beuer*. To Asinius Lupus, the tribune, regarded as a sleek, comfortable city-magistrate. The beaver's coat of soft fur gives the suggestion.

229. *stomacke to digest*. A quibble on the Roman 'Digest'.

233. *próphane*. *Alch.* IV. v. 26, v. v. 98.

235. *pouertie*. Cf. the personal passage, *Disc.* 1358.

243. *Muse*: 'soule' in the Quarto. The change takes away the slight tinge of scriptural suggestion and substitutes Pegasus.

248. *desp'rate censures*: 'dudgeon censures' in the Quarto. Horace says of Tucca in *Satiro-mastix*, I. ii (1602, C2ʳ), 'I am too well ranckt *Asinius* to bee stab'd with his dudgion wit.' 'Dudgeon' was the wood used by turners to make handles for daggers.

253–4. From Ovid, *Amores*, III. viii. 3, 4:

> Ingenium quondam fuerat pretiosius auro;
> at nunc barbaries grandis habere nihil.

256. Quoted by T. May, *The Old Couple*, II. i (1658, B2ᵛ):

> 'Tis matterless in goodness who excels:
> He that hath coyn, hath all perfections else.

I. iii. The looser rhythm of lines 1–4, 7–9, 17, 24–8, keeping up a conversational tone, is a sign of early work.

3. *What's here?* The Quarto adds '*Numa in Decimo nono?*' which Jonson probably omitted later because it latinized the English method of dating laws. Further, tradition ascribed to Numa sacred books only on questions of ceremonial law: his reign was peaceful, and he did not legislate on war.

8. *they runne from my pen*. So Ovid of his attempts to write in prose after his father's rebukes:

> Sponte sua carmen numeros veniebat ad aptos,
> et quod temptabam scribere versus erat.

12–14. *in case . . . in too much case*. Cf. Hoby, *The Courtier*, 1561, Aiiiᵛ, 'he was not in case with hys personne to practise the feates of Chiualary.' As in *S. of N.* v. i. 61–2 there is a quibble on Ovid's being cased in a lawyer's gown and studying legal cases.

15. *sprightlie poesies habiliments*. Marston, *The Scourge of Villanie*, Satire vi (1597, E6ᵛ):

> . . . the odious spot
> And blemish that deformes the lineaments
> Of moderne Poesies habiliments.

19. *a supersedeas*, literally an injunction to stay proceedings. A common metaphor: cf. Cooke, *Greene's Tu quoque*, 1614, C2^r, 'Rash. I would my lamentable Louer had beene heere, heere had beene a Supersedeas for his melancholy.'

34. *Corinna*. The name under which Ovid veiled his love:

> Ad leve rursus opus, iuvenalia carmina veni,
>   et falso ('imaginary') movi pectus amore meum.
>
> (Tristia, II. 339–40.)

> Moverat ingenium totam cantata per urbem
>   nomine non vero dicta Corinna mihi.
>
> (Ibid. IV. x. 59, 60.)

58. *obiects . . . abiects*. Cf. F. P., *The Case is Altered. How? Aske Dalio and Millo*, 1604, C3^r, 'this ougly obiect, or rather abiect of nature'; and *Histrio-mastix*, v. i (1610, G2^r), where Sickness says to Poverty,

> O end thy Age! that we may end our dayes,
> Once Obiects, now all Abiects to the world.

61. *Cynthia*, the poetic alias of Hostia, according to Apuleius (*Apol.*, p. 406). In the seventh elegy of the fourth book of Propertius her ghost appears to him with words of reproach for his forgetfulness of her. Jonson's picture of Ovid's sympathy with the poet was suggested by the statement in the *Tristia* (IV. x. 45–6):

> Saepe suos solitus recitare Propertius ignes,
>   iure sodalicii quo mihi iunctus erat.

70. *strooke with the like planet*. *E.M.I.* IV. vii. 141.

II. i. Albius and Chloe reproduce the doting Deliro and tyrannical Fallace of *Every Man out of his Humour*. In the Crispinus of this scene Jonson works off the first strokes of his satire on Marston.

12. *back-side*. *C. is A.* IV. viii. 1.

13. *most strenuously well*. Marston disgorges 'strenuous' in v. iii. 501. We may compare Plautus' 'pancratice atque athletice valere' (*Bacchides*, 248) and 'pugilice atque athletice' (*Epidicus*, 20).

15, 16. For the perfumes and flowers compare *E.M.O.* II. iv. 89–94.

17. *felt*, in reference to a smell, survives in dialect.

19. *well said*, well done. *C. is A.* II. vii. 83.

21, 24. *obsequiously . . . predominant*. The pair affect court jargon: compare Mistress Otter in *S.W.* III. ii. 3, 'It shall not be obnoxious, or difficill, sir', with Dauphine's tribute (26), 'What an excellent choice phrase, this lady expresses in!'

26. *In sincereitie*. One of Chloe's phrases, a mild substitute for an oath: cf. line 46 and IV. ii. 14, 52.

36. *make bumpes*. Compare the lumbering joke on Captain Otter's 'bull-head' in *S.W.* IV. ii. 138–41 when his wife has hit him on the head. Chloe apparently strikes her husband here ('mooues mightily').

41. *poking*, irritating, provoking.

48. *your spoke in my cart*. For this proverbial obstruction cf. Samuel Hieron, *Works*, 1607, i, p. 411, 'Shee should not put in her spoke to withstand the motion, but should rather further her husband in such an honest business.'

50. *pack-needles* . . . A separate branch of the business from the jewellery; it moves Chloe's contempt because it is uncourtly.

hobby-horse, the child's toy, as in *B.F.* I. v. 10.

55-7. "*Gaine . . . frankincense*. From Juvenal, *Sat.* xiv. 203-5:

> Neu credas ponendum aliquid discriminis inter
> unguenta et corium. Lucri bonus est odor ex re
> qualibet.

55. *respects*, gives heed to (Lat. *respicere*).

57. *oade*, woad, as Jonson spells it, *Alch.* III. iv. 97. It supplied the old English blue dye till it was superseded by indigo.

61. *take it . . . in snuffe*. *E.M.I.* IV. ii. 99 n.

66. *disbast*, debased.

67. *hood and . . . fartingall*. Cf. *E.H.* I. ii, where the tailor enters 'with a faire gowne, Scotch Varthingall, and French fall in his armes' for Gertrude, who is on the point of becoming a lady. *Fartingall*: the spelling is suited to the context.

bumrowles, bustles. In Dekker's *The Shoemaker's Holiday*, 1610, C3ᵛ, the sheriff's wife asks, 'Art thou acquainted with neuer a fardingale-maker, nor a French-hood maker, I must enlarge my bumme, ha, ha.'

68. *whale-bone bodies*, the 'straight-bodied city attire' of IV. i. 4. In *Two most vnnaturall and bloodie Murthers*, 1605, B4ᵛ, Calverly, trying to snatch his child from its mother, 'most remorcelesse stabbed at it some three or foure times, all which shee saued the childe from, by taking it on her selfe; and hauing a paire of Whale-bone boddies on, it pleased God his dagger so glanced on them, that she had yet but one wound in the shoulder'.

70. *mummia*. *Volp.* IV. iv. 14 n. Albius's amorous pharmacopoeia tails off into a senseless pun on 'spermacete' and 'citie'.

71. *most best*. *Gram.* II. iv. 25-36.

fæminine. Read 'foeminine', which is a seventeenth-century spelling. So the 1640 Folio.

74. *participate the knowledge*, like *vouchsafe the sight* (deign to look on, 94), is an attempt to speak courtly.

79 (and following). *forsooth*. *E.M.O.* II. ii. 14: it is amusing to find Crispinus using this tame substitute for an oath, 'like a forsooth of the citie' (*Ent. Highgate*, 246). He also misapplies the polite formula 'for fault of a better' (85).

80. *Who* for 'whom'. 'Common in colloquial use as object . . . of a preposition at the end of a clause' (*O.E.D.*).

88. *a gentleman*. This point, which distinguishes Crispinus from Demetrius, is harped on in the play: by Crispinus himself, III. i. 27,

iv. 62, and by Tucca, III. iv. 160, v. iii. 120. When he entered at Brase-
nose College, Oxford, he was described in the University records as
a gentleman's son.

92. For *little legges* as the sign of a gentleman see *E.M.O.* III. iii. 37 n.
Dekker glances at this and other passages of the play in *The Guls Horne-
booke*, 1609, p. 31: 'Now sir, if the writer be a fellow that hath either
epigramd you, or hath had a flirt at your mistris, or hath brought
either your feather'—the 'ash-colour'd feather' of Crispinus's embroidered hat, III. iii. 1—'or your red beard'—his red hair, II. ii. 80—
'or your little legs &c. on the stage, you shall disgrace him worse then
by tossing him in a blancket, or giuing him the bastinado in a Tauerne,
if in the middle of his play, (bee it Pastorall or Comedy, Morall or
Tragedie) you rise with a skrewd and discontented face from your stoole
to be gone. . . .'

97. *my armes*. Marston's arms were *sable*, a fesse dancettée *ermine*
between three fleurs-de-lis *argent*, differenced by a crescent of the last
(*Archaeological Society's Transactions*, vi, p. 499, Visitations of Shrop-
shire). The crescent for an open mouth, the indented fesse for the toes,
and the thorns for the fleur-de-lis are Jonson's attempt at a parody.

108. *God's my passion*. Cf. *E.M.I.* IV. i. 18, 'God's my life!'; *All's
Well that Ends Well*, v. ii. 39, 'Cox my passion!'

110. *cushions in the parlor windowes*. Cf. Middleton, *A Chast Maid in
Cheape-side*, v. i (1630, I3ᵛ):

> *Mis. All.* Let's . . . take a House in the Strand.
> *Allwit.* In troth a match Wench;
> We're simply stock't, with Cloath of Tissue Cussions
> To furnish out bay-windows.

And *How a man may chuse a good Wife from a bad*, III. iii (1602, F3ᵛ):

> *Mis. Ar.* Come spread the Table: Is the hall well rubd,
> The cushions in the windowes neatly laid?

122. *Citi-sin*. Dr. Penniman quotes Dekker, *Lanthorne and Candle
Light*, ii (1608, C2), in the court of Hell, 'The Cittizen is sued here and
condemned for the Citty-sinnes'.

130. *Wife*.—She strikes him; see the next speech.

135. *andirons*. Iron bars, with an upright ornamental pillar to support them in front and a short foot at the other end; the burning wood
was placed on them.

II. ii. 46–8. Condensed from Cicero, *In Cat.* i, § 31, 'Ut saepe homines
aegri morbo gravi, cum aestu febrique iactantur, si aquam gelidam
biberunt, primo relevari videntur, deinde multo gravius vehementiusque
adflictantur, . . .'.

52. Plutarch, *De Exilio*, 1, quotes οὐδὲν πέπονθας δεινὸν ἄν μὴ προσποιῇ.

75. *loue and beautie*. Plato, *Symposium*, 196 e, πᾶς γοῦν ποιητὴς γίγνεται. . .
οὗ δ' ἄν Ἔρως ἐφάψηται.

80. *your hair*. It was red.

86. *a slight banquet*, a light refection, dessert. Albius has picked up some scraps of etiquette: *Timon of Athens*, I. ii. 149, 150:

> *Tim.* Ladies, there is an idle banquet attends you:
> Please you to dispose yourselves.

87. *accost*, draw near.

89. *commended to haue*, praised for having. An affectation.

95. *Hermogenes*. This character is developed from the brief sketch in Horace's *Satires*, I. iii. 1–8:

> Omnibus hoc vitium est cantoribus, inter amicos
> ut nunquam inducant animum cantare rogati,
> iniussi nunquam desistant. Sardus habebat
> ille Tigellius hoc. Caesar, qui cogere posset,
> si peteret per amicitiam patris atque suam non
> quidquam proficeret; si collibuisset, ab ovo
> usque ad mala citaret 'io Bacche!' modo summa
> voce, modo hac resonat quae chordis quattuor ima.

110. *humanitie*, courtesy (Lat. *humanitas*).

160. *staffe*, stave, stanza.

163 foll. The song is filled in from the outline in Martial, I. lvii:

> Qualem, Flacce, velim quaeris nolimve puellam?
> nolo nimis facilem difficilemque nimis.
> illud quod medium est atque inter utrumque probamus:
> nec volo quod cruciat nec volo quod satiat.

187. *delicates*, charms.

203. *Please . . . way*. Mayne, *The City Match*, 1639, IV. iii: '*Plotw.* Nay will you enter? *Tim.* Ladie, Pray will you show the way? *Plotw.* Most Citie like, 'Slid take her by the arme, and lead her in. *Tim.* Your arme sweet Lady.'

208. *I had rather want meate*. Sir H. Cock, writing to Lord Burleigh on 29 April 1602 about entertaining King James at Broxbourn on his way to London, promises to do the best 'as for the shortnes of yᵉ tyme I shal be able, which I hope your honor will take in good parte, remembring, under your good favor, yᵉ olde sayinge, Better to lacke meate than good companie' (*Cecil Papers*).

210. *good legges*. *C.R.* III. iv. 29.

221. *relinquish*. *C.R.* IV. i. 127.

expiate, terminate. An absurd misuse of the word: it should mean to end suffering or life by death, as in *Richard III*, III. iii. 23, where Ratcliff on his way to execution says, 'Make haste; the hour of death is expiate'. So the First Folio reads; later Folios 'now expir'd'.

224. *enghle*, cajole.

III. i. The first three scenes of this act are a dramatizing of Horace's famous Satire I. ix:

> Ibam forte via sacra, sicut meus est mos,
> nescio quid meditans nugarum, totus in illis.
> accurrit quidam notus mihi nomine tantum,
> arreptaque manu, 'Quid agis, dulcissime rerum?'

All the details of the poem are utilized and supplemented.

8. *Swell me a bowle with lustie wine* . . . Cf. I. i. 77–8, *Cat.* I. 499.

9. *Lyæus*, Bacchus, the 'loosener' of care: *Oberon*, 78, with Jonson's note. *Plump*: *Faerie Queene*, III. i. 51, '*Lyæus* fat'; *Antony and Cleopatra*, II. vii. 111–12, 'Come, thou monarch of the vine | Plumpy Bacchus with pink eyne!'

12. *In flowing measure* . . . In *Satiro-mastix*, I. ii (1602, B4), Dekker satirizes Jonson's laboured method of composing a lyric, making him hunt after rhymes and end by quoting this line as 'good'. Jonson quoted the poem to Drummond (*Conv.* v. 96).

15. *frolicke*, sportive.

17. *you'ld naught else, sir, would you?* 'Numquid vis?' (Horace)—the polite formula of Roman leave-taking, 'I suppose I can do nothing further for you'.

19–21. 'Noris nos', inquit, 'docti sumus'. Hic ego 'Pluris | hoc', inquam, 'mihi eris' (Horace).

23. *new turn'd Poet*. His *Pygmalion's Image and certain Satires*, and his *Scourge of Villany, three books of Satires* had been printed in 1598, and the latter reprinted in 1599. But the reference is to II. ii. 76 and the poem on Chloe's cap (85–8 below).

26. *sermons*. The traditional title of Horace's satires was *Sermones*.

29. *To the proportion of your beard*. Cf. Horace, *Sat.* II. iii. 35, 'Sapientem pascere barbam' and the Greek proverb ἐκ πώγωνος σοφός.

31. *enamour'd of this street*. 'Cum quidlibet ille | garriret, vicos, urbem laudaret' (Horace).

32. *againe*. *E.M.I.* I. v. 55.

33. *polite, and terse*, polished and smooth (Lat. *politus, tersus*).

36–7. Repeated from *C. is A.* I. viii. 25–6.

40. *castalian dews*. *E.M.O.* Ind. 335.

46. *a dressing*, more definitely in the Quarto a velvet cap. So in IV. iii. 30 the cap becomes 'the little fine dressing'. Cf. *E.M.I.* III. iii. 36, *Und.* xlii. 28.

49. *siluer bodkin*. Sneered at by Gertrude in *Eastward Ho*, I. ii. 23 as a common ornament of a city dame. Cf. *The Honest Man's Fortune*, IV. i (Beaumont and Fletcher folio, 1679, p. 525):

> They come to steal ⟨your⟩ Napkins, and your Spoons;
> Look to your Silver-Bodkin, (Gentlewoman).

52–3. *gable-ends* . . . *tuscane-tops* . . . *pyramid's*, angular, flat, and pointed dressings. For Tuscan tops cf. James Howell, *Epistolae Hoelianae*, ed. Jacobs, p. 329, '*Fair* Eromena *in her* Toscan tyre'.

67. *your sattin sleeue begns to fret*. This and the reference to Demetrius' decayed doublet (III. iv. 320) provoked a retort in *Satiro-mastix*

(D1): '*Tuc.* Thou wrongst heere a good honest rascall Crispinus, and a poore varlet Demetrius Fanni[n]us (bretheren in thine owne trade of Poetry) thou sayst Crispinus Sattin dublet is Reauel'd out heere, and that this penurious sneaker is out at elboes, . . . Crispinus shall giue thee on olde cast Sattin suite, and Demetrius shall write thee a Scene or two, in one of the strong garlicke Comedies.' Ibid. 14ʳ: 'They haue sowed vp that broken seame-rent lye of thine, that Demetrius is out at Elbowes, and Crispinus is falne out with Sattin heere, they haue.'

69. *bases*. 'A plaited skirt, of cloth, velvet, or rich brocade, appended to the doublet, and reaching from the waist to the knee' (*O.E.D.*).

76. *crost, and so's not that*; i.e. the debt is not crossed off. Cf. the quibble in *Timon of Athens*, I. ii. 154–7:

> More jewels yet!
> There is no crossing him in's humour; . . .
> When all's spent, he'ld be cross'd then, an he could.

91. *Paranomasie, or Agnomination*. Greek παρονομασία, Latin *agnominatio*, an assonance or word-play noted by grammarians as a figure in rhetoric. A good example is Jonson's *Epigram* lxi. He utters a warning against the excessive use of it in *Discoveries*, 1954. *Paranomasie* was a common misspelling in the seventeenth century.

96. *how I sweat*. 'Cum sudor ad imos | manaret talos' (Horace).

102. *with halfe my teeth*. In Juvenal, *Sat.* iii. 301, the victim of a Mohock club asks 'ut liceat paucis cum dentibus inde reverti'.

104. *take mine eares vp by commission*, seizure by legal warrant, as in purveyance or the press-gang.

106. *solœcismes*. Cf. *Satiro-mastix*, H2ᵛ, a neat stroke in Horace's apology to Tucca:

> Hence forth Ile rather breath out *Solœcismes*
> (To doe which Ide as soone speake blasphemie)
> Than with my tongue or pen to wound your worth.

107. *Bolanus*, a hot-tempered man, a friend of Cicero's (*Ep. Fam.* XIII. lxxvii. 2). 'O te, Bolane, cerebri | felicem!' (Horace). Jonson's description of him in the Quarto, '*Romes* Common Buffon', suggests the Carlo Buffone of *Every Man out of his Humour*.

115–29.

> Ut illi
> nil respondebam, 'misere cupis', inquit, 'abire;
> iamdudum video; sed nil agis; usque tenebo;
> prosequar hinc quo nunc iter est tibi'. 'Nil opus est te
> circumagi: quendam volo visere non tibi notum.
> Trans Tiberim longe cubat is, prope Caesaris hortos.'
> 'Nil habeo quod agam et non sum piger; usque sequar te.'
> Demitto auriculas ut iniquae mentis asellus,
> cum gravius dorso subiit onus.—Horace (*Sat.* ix. 13–21).

116. *proue*, make trial, put to proof.

128. *Cæsars gardens* on the Ianiculum across the Tiber, Julius Caesar's legacy to Rome. Shakespeare, misled by North's *Plutarch*, wrongly placed them 'on this side Tiber'.

131. *the plague*. Jonson's addition; in Horace the friend is merely 'ill in bed' (*cubat*).

134. *Phœbus*, the inflicter of pestilence, as in the opening book of the *Iliad*.

150. *the Three Furies*. Some contemporary allusion is veiled under this name and the references to Rhadamanthus and Minos: see *Epigram* cxxxiii. 176–90, describing a voyage up the Fleet ditch:

> Behold where CERBERVS, rear'd on the wall
> Of *Hol'bourne* (three sergeants heads) lookes ore, . . . ⟨They past⟩
> The tripple head without a sop. At last,
> Calling for RHADAMANTVS, that dwelt by,
> A sope-boyler; and ÆACVS him nigh,
> Who kept an ale-house; with my little MINOS,
> An ancient pur-blinde fletcher, with a high nose, . . .

Ianus Temple would be the Inns of Court.

153. *laid*, plotted.

161–206. Adapted from Horace (*Sat.* ix. 22–34):

> 'Si bene me novi, non Viscum pluris amicum,
> non Varium facies; nam quis me scribere plures
> aut citius possit versus? quis membra movere
> mollius? Invideat quod et Hermogenes ego canto.'
> Interpellandi locus hic erat: 'Est tibi mater,
> cognati, quis te salvost opus?' 'Haud mihi quisquam.
> Omnes composui.' 'Felices! nunc ego resto.
> Confice; namque instat fatum mihi triste, Sabella
> quod puero cecinit divina mota anus urna:
> "Hunc neque dira venena nec hosticus auferet ensis
> nec laterum dolor aut tussis nec tarda podagra;
> garrulus hunc quando consumet cumque; loquaces,
> si sapiat, vitet simul atque adoleverit aetas."'

161. *taste*. *E.M.I.* IV. vii. 1.

163. *Varius*, man of letters and friend of Virgil, joint-editor of the *Aeneid* after Virgil's death.

168. *sport with her fanne*. H. Hutton, *Follies Anatomie*, 1619, A8ᵛ:

> And there reposing on his Mistrisse lap,
> Beg some fond fauour, be 't a golden cap:
> Plaies with her plume of Feathers or her Fan,
> Wishing he were accepted for her man.

176. *my long stocking*. *E.M.O.* III. ix. 53.

182. *Is your mother liuing?* In Horace the question is 'Have you any

near relatives who are interested in your safety?' either (1) because
a youth of so many accomplishments could not live long because 'whom
the gods love die young' (Gow), or (2) because Horace is just going to
say that his friend across the Tiber had an infectious disease (Palmer).
Jonson, like Horace, is not clear about the answer, but he seems to
mean, as Nicholson suggests, 'Have you not a mother to praise you
since you praise yourself?'

185. *of the mother*, a quibble on 'mother' in the sense of 'hysteria'.
Cf. *B.F.* I. v. 168.

188. *compos'd in their vrnes.* Horace's 'Omnes composui'. *Compono*
was technically used of placing the bones of the dead together in the
urn after they had been gathered from the pyre.

193. *Sabella*. In Horace 'a Sabine woman', not a personal name.

209–78. From Horace, *Sat.* ix. 35–60:

> Ventum erat ad Vestae, quarta iam parte diei
> praeterita; et casu tunc respondere vadato
> debebat, quod ni fecisset, perdere litem.
> 'Si me amas' inquit 'paulum hic ades'. 'Inteream si
> aut valeo stare aut novi civilia iura;
> et propero quo scis.' 'Dubius sum quid faciam' inquit,
> 'tene relinquam an rem.' 'Me sodes.' 'Non faciam' ille,
> et praecedere coepit. Ego, ut contendere durum est
> cum victore sequor. 'Maecenas quomodo tecum?'
> hinc repetit. 'Paucorum hominum et mentis bene sanae.'
> 'Nemo dexterius fortuna est usus: haberes
> magnum adiutorem, posset qui ferre secundas,
> hunc hominem velles si tradere; dispeream ni
> submosses omnes.' 'Non isto vivimus illic
> quo tu rere modo; domus hac nec purior ulla est
> nec magis his aliena malis; nil mi officit' inquam,
> 'ditior hic aut est quia doctior; est locus uni
> cuique suus.' 'Magnum narras, vix credibile!' 'Atqui
> sic habet.' 'Accendis quare cupiam magis illi
> proximus esse.' 'Velis tantummodo; quae tua virtus,
> expugnabis; et est qui vinci possit eoque
> difficiles aditus primos habet.' 'Haud mihi deero:
> muneribus servos corrumpam; non hodie si
> exclusus fuero desistam; tempora quaeram,
> occurram in triviis, deducam. Nil sine magno
> vita labore dedit mortalibus.'

248. *brize*, gadfly. *E.M.I.* Quarto, v. v. 309, 'Hath the brize prickt
you?' Gifford quotes Dryden's version of *Georgic* iii. 237–40:

> This flying Plague (to mark its quality;)
> *Oestros* the *Grecians* call: *Asylus*, we:
> A fierce loud buzzing Breez; their stings draw blood;
> And drive the Cattle gadding through the Wood.

silkenesse. 'Apparently a mock title, but the text may be corrupt' (*O.E.D.*). It is a satire on the affected usage of Court circles: thus, in *C.R.* iii. ii. 32, 'the silken disposition of courtiers' is contrasted with the description of Crites as 'a piece of serge, or *perpetuana*', and Amorphus prays (ibid. iii. v. 47) for 'silken thoughts' to 'attend this deare beautie'. In *Poet.* iv. ix. 104–5 Ovid worships 'the louing aire, | That clos'd her body in his silken armes'.

273. *extrude.* The opposite of 'intrude', *C.R.* v. iii. 39.

iii. ii. This scene is from Horace's satire ix. 60–74:

> Haec dum agit, ecce
> Fuscus Aristius occurrit mihi carus et illum
> qui pulchre nosset. Consistimus. 'Unde venis?' et
> 'quo tendis?' rogat et respondet. Vellere coepi
> et prensare manu lentissima brachia, nutans,
> distorquens oculos ut me eriperet. Male salsus
> ridens dissimulare: meum iecur urere bilis.
> 'Certe nescio quid secreto velle loqui te
> aiebas mecum.' 'Memini bene, sed meliore
> tempore dicam; hodie tricesima sabbata: vin tu
> curtis Iudaeis oppedere?' 'Nulla mihi' inquam
> 'religio est.' 'At mi; sum paulo infirmior, unus
> multorum. Ignosces; alias loquar.' Huncine solem
> tam nigrum surrexe mihi! Fugit improbus ac me
> sub cultro linquit.

Fuscus Aristius was a literary friend of Horace who addressed *Ode* i. xxii and *Epistle* i. x to him. His amusing reason for leaving Horace, that he could not transact private business on a Jewish sabbath, might have been dangerous to reproduce: Jonson told Drummond that Savile in his *Ende of Nero and the Beginning of Galba*, a translation of Tacitus, durst not translate the last book 'for ye evill it containes of ye Iewes' (*Conv.* xiv. 369–70).

4. *Land-Remora.* The remora was a sucking-fish supposed to hold a ship fast if it clung to it. *E.H.* iv. ii. 14, *M.L.* ii. ii. 25–30; Holland's Pliny's *Natural History*, ix. xxv (1602, i, p. 148), '*Of Echeneis* [i. the stay-ship]. There is a very little fish keeping ordinarily about rockes, named Echeneis. It is thought that if it settle and stick to the Keele of a ship under water, it goeth the slower by that meanes'; Florio's *Montaigne*, ii. xii (ed. Stewart, i, p. 533), 'his Admiral-gally was in her course staied by that little fish, the Latines call *Remora*, and the English a Suck-stone, whose property is, to stay any ship he can fasten himselfe vnto'.

6. *Alcides shirt*, the envenomed robe, steeped in the blood of the Centaur Nessus, which Deianeira, the wife of Hercules, unwittingly sent to him as a death-gift.

III. iii. The arrest is from the closing lines of Horace, *Sat.* ix. 74–8:

> Casu venit obvius illi
> adversarius, et 'quo tu turpissime?' magna
> inclamat voce; et 'licet antestari?' Ego vero
> oppono auriculam. Rapit in ius; clamor utrinque,
> undique concursus. Sic me servauit Apollo.

1. *ash-colour'd feather*. See II. i. 92 n.

19. *By Ianus, and Iupiter*. A classical oath: these two divinities were invoked first in every undertaking; Jupiter sanctioned it by augury, but its successful beginning depended on the blessing of Janus.

25. *exhale*, drag away. I. H., *The Divell of the Vault. Or, The vnmasking of Murther*, 1606, D2, God 'who hath preseru'd our liues . . . Exhal'd vs from the chaps of hell. | And death's deuouring iawes'.

27. *Sweet meat* . . . quoted as an Italian proverb in Florio's *Second Frutes*, 1591, p. 169. *Iohn Heywoodes woorkes*, part i, ch. viii (1562, B4ᵛ), 'Sweete meate will haue sowre sawce, I see now playne.'

III. iv. 2. *gent'man*. Tucca affects this form: it occurs as dialectic in *T. of T.* II. ii. 79, and in verse *Ep.* xc. 12. Udall, *Royster Doyster*, III. iii. 21, 'Beware what ye say (ko I) of such a ientman'.

4. *pilchers*. So v. iii. 409. 'A term of abuse, frequent at the beginning of the seventeenth century. It has been conjecturally explained as meaning "One who wears a pilch or leathern jerkin or doublet", or "One who pilches, a thief"' (*O.E.D.*). Cf. Fletcher, *Love's Cure*, II. ii (1647, p. 131), 'You Dog-skin-fac'd rogue, pilcher, you poore *Iohn*'.

11. *lotium*. 'Stale urine used by barbers as a "lye" for the hair' (*O.E.D.*). *S.W.* III. v. 90.

15. *good-man slaue*. With this ironical prefix cf. *B.F.* III. iv. 113, 'good-man angry-man'; *King Lear*, II. ii. 41, 'goodman boy'.

hooke. Usually in the form 'unhappy hook': *Iohn Heywoodes woorkes*, 1562, Eijᵛ, 'Sens thou art crosse saylde, auale vnhappie hooke.' There is also a suggestion of catching with a hook: compare Mistress Quickly's 'Nut-hook' to the constable in *2 Henry IV*, v. iv. 8.

16. *ramme*, because he butts or batters.

23. *Some wiser then some*. Field, *A Woman is a Weather-cocke*, IV. ii (1612, G4): '*Stan.* Giue me thy sword, or I will kill thee. *Capt.* Some wiser than some, I loue my reputation wel, yet I am not so valiant an asse, but I loue my life better, thers my sword.'

26. *halfe his lendings*, half the six drachmas he borrowed from Ovid senior, I. ii. 200.

50. *centum-viri*, a standing court whose jurisdiction was concerned with suits affecting ownership or transfer of rateable property. Ovid held this office (*Tristia*, ii. 93–6).

57. *Fourescore sesterties*. 'A sesterce was worth about two-pence of our money; so that the whole of Crispinus' debt did not much exceed twelve shillings' (Gifford).

68. *eringo's*, the candied root of the sea-holly used as an aphrodisiac.

84. *hangers*. *E.M.I.* I. v. 81.

87. *acceptiue*, ready to accept. *C. is A.* II. vii. 62.

103. *barbers*. *E.M.O.* IV. iii. 100–1.

106. *errant*, a variant of 'arrant'. Frequent in Jonson in this form.

107. *Poetaster*. Here and in line 293, v. iii. 182 Tucca speaks of Crispinus thus.

115. *Comus*, the god of revelry, who is a character in *Pleasure Reconciled to Virtue*.

Priapus, the god of procreation.

121. *vaile*. As a merchant vessel lowered its topsails or its colours to a king's ship.

126. *two-penny teare-mouth*. So 'two-penny rascall' (204). A reference to the two-penny gallery in the theatre, *E.M.O.* Ind. 312.

fortune, a punning reference to the Fortune Theatre opened in 1600 by Edward Alleyn, situated on the east side of Golding Lane in the parish of St. Giles, Cripplegate. The Admiral's men were acting there. It was burned down in 1621.

the good yeare. Putting together the expletive 'what the good-year?' and the evil influence suggested in 'The good-yeares shall devour them' (*King Lear*, v. iii. 24), the word possibly means 'the devil': see *The Times Literary Supplement*, 17 June 1939, where this suggestion is worked out by W. Alan Rock.

130. *Oedipus*, self-blinded in the plays of Sophocles and Seneca.

131. *hares eies*. *C. is A.* v. xi. 15.

134. *in a tawnie coate*. Gifford quotes T. Deloney, *The Pleasant History of John Winchcomb*, 1630, B4, a widow, and two of her gallants, being at the fair, enter a tavern, where 'They had not sitten long, but in comes a noyse of Musitians in tawny coats, who (putting off their caps) asked if they would haue any musicke'.

135. *Goose-faire*, or Green-goose fair, held on Whitmonday at Bow, near Stratford in Essex: young (or green) geese were the staple food. John Taylor in his *Goose* (1630, p. 110) gives a description of it, but he says 'the Thursday after whitsontide'.

136. *gulch*, glutton. Gifford quotes Brewer, *Lingua*, 1607, v. xvi, 'You muddy gulche, darst looke me in the face?' An actor in the company satirized in *Histrio-mastix* is named Gulch.

139. *Owleglas*, buffoon. An anglicizing of Tyll Eulenspiegel or Ulenspiegel, the hero of a medieval German tale, a version of which was printed in England by W. Copland about 1528. The name is spelt 'Howle-glasse' in *F.I.* 232, 349, 350; '*Vlen-spiegle*' in *F.I.* 237, *Alch.* II. iii. 32; and 'Owle-spiegle' in *S.S.* II. iii. 9.

140. *perstemptuous* probably mimics a mispronunciation of the original of Tucca.

141. *a hundred and fiftie*, the number of a company.

143. *leaders of a legion* of lice, like Falstaff's joke in *2 Henry IV*, III. ii. 162–4: 'I cannot put him to a private soldier, that is the leader

of so many thousands'; S. Rowlands, *Diogenes Lanthorne*, 1607, B4, 'his frieze gowne sconce, wherein he intrenches himselfe, is at least thirtie thousand strong'.

155. *skelder*. *E.M.O*. Characters, 85.

157. *Pantolabus*, 'grab-all', is the nickname for a buffoon in Horace, *Sat*. I. viii. 11. J. Palsgrave, *Ecphrasis Anglica in Comœdiam Acolasti*, 1540, b4, 'And Pantolabus signifieth *omnia capiens* one that is a sweep-stake and all is fysshe that commeth to nette with hym'. Cf. v. 39 below. The Quarto has *Caprichio*, 'freak'.

160. *parcell-poet*, part poet. So Crispinus describes himself, IV. vi. 29: cf. *B.F*. II. ii. 16; *S. of N*., the Persons, 20. In *D. is A*. II. iii. 15 Pug is 'parcel-*Diuell*', and in *Alch*. IV. vi. 33 Face is 'That parcell-broker, and whole-baud, all raskall'.

163. *Minotaurus*, Tucca's way of saying 'bellower'.

164. *rand*, rant.

165–6. *fortie, shillings . . . in earnest*. There are occasional entries in Henslowe's *Diary* of £2 as the first instalment paid for a play; for Henry Porter's *The Two Merry Women of Abington* on 28 February 1599, for a pastoral tragedy of Chapman's on 17 July, for Dekker's *Whore of Babylon* on 18 and 30 January 1600.

168. *to trauell . . . grauell*. A quotation from *Histrio-mastix*, 1600, C3ᵛ, where a company of actors sing,

> Besides we that trauell, with pumps full of grauell,
>> Made all of such running leather:
> That once in a weeke, new maisters wee seeke,
>> And neuer can hold together.

The reference here is probably to Pembroke's men, who in 1593, the second year of their existence, travelled, but had to come back to London and sold their apparel. Tucca is applying the lines, rather pointlessly, to the Chamberlain's men, who were well equipped. The company 'may have been told to leave London for a few weeks' after the Essex rising in which they were implicated (Chambers, *Elizabethan Stage*, ii, p. 206; see IV. iv below). And they may have been forced to travel by the competition of the 'little eyases', e.g. at the Chapel Royal in 1600. This is the reason given in the 1603 Quarto of *Hamlet*, sc. vii. 71–7 (ed. Aldis Wright).

173. *Stiffe toe*, here and in line 304, a slang-term for an actor. *Paunch* in the Quarto.

175. *shifter*, dealer. The Quarto *Twentie i'the hundred* doubled the legal rate of interest: see *E.M.O*. IV. iv. 9. Morecraft, the usurer, is greeted in Beaumont and Fletcher's *The Scornful Lady*, III. ii. 176 (ed. Bond), as 'Good twelve i' the hundred'.

176. *the statute*. I. ii. 53.

184. *be Minos*, act up to your name, be just.

190. *humours, reuells, and satyres*, Jonson's own 'comical satires' of *Every Man out of his Humour* and *Cynthia's Revels*, acted at the Black-friars.

194. *on the other side of Tyber*, the theatres on the Bankside, the Globe, the Hope, the Rose, and the Swan.

199. *copper-lac't.* Copper lace was used for the actors' dresses: see Henslowe's *Diary*, ed. Greg, p. 133, 'Sowld vnto Richard Bradshawe player the 15 of desember 1600 j pownd & ij owences of coope⟨r⟩ lace' for 14s.

201. *your Globes, and your Triumphs.* Cf. *D. is A.* III. iii. 26, 'The *Globes*, and *Mermaides*'. *Triumphs* = pageants.

205. *neufe*, fist. An erroneous form of 'neaf', 'nieve' (*O.E.D.*). 'Giue me your neafe, Mounsieur Mustardseed' (*Mids. Night's Dream*, IV. i. 18).

giue mee a weeke. Cf. the reference to Burbadge and Heming in *M. Christmas*, 133–7, and Chapman, *May-day*, III. iv (1611, G2ᵛ), 'Afore heauen 'tis a sweete fac't child, me thinks he should show well in womans attire: . . . Ile helpe thee to three crownes a weeke for him, and [s]he can act well.'

206. *point-trussers. E.M.I.* I iii. 34.

208. *in King Darius dolefull straine.* Compare Falstaff's 'speaking in passion', in King Cambyses 'vein' (*I Henry IV*, II. iv. 375–6). The quotation cannot be traced.

215–22. Laxly quoted from Kyd's *The Spanish Tragedy*, II. i. 9, 10, 21–2, 25–8. Field, who acted in *Poetaster*, afterwards parodied these lines in *A Woman is a Weathercock*, I. ii.

223. *orrible* (Quarto). A late survival of an older spelling.

224–6. Untraced.

225. *beare a braine*, a quibble on the sense 'be cautious'. Skelton, *Magnyficence*, 1526, l. 1422, 'I counsel you, bere a brayne.'

227. *Demet. Hist.* So 243. Demetrius probably entered with Histrio as a sort of hang-by. Tucca asks Histrio about him in line 318.

230–5. Untraced, but evidently from a ghost scene. '*Vindicta*' was common form. In Peele's *The battell of Alcazar*, 1594, the presenter's opening speech in Act II is interrupted by '*Three ghosts crying* Vindicta'; the Ghost which opens *The True Tragedie of Richard the Third*, 1594, says '*O sitio, sitio, vindicta*'; in *Locrine*, 1595, III. vi, when '*Albanacts* bloodie ghost' enters, '*Alba-ghost. Vindicta, vindicta*'. The expression is satirized in *A Warning for Faire Women*, 1599, A2ᵛ:

> . . . a filthie whining ghost
> Lapt in some fowle sheete, or a leather pelch,
> Comes skreaming like a piggie halfe stickt,
> And cries *Vindicta*, reuenge, reuenge.

Timoria in the Jonson quotation is Greek (τιμωρία) and is not found in any extant play.

242. *Who calls out murder?* From Chapman's *The blinde begger of Alexandria*, 1598, E4:

> Whose there, Come forth for here is murder done,
> Murder, Murder of good prince *Doricles*.
> *Enter* Euribates.
> Who cals out murther Lady was it you.

The drunken Quicksilver in *E.H.* II. i. 110 quotes this among other play-scraps. Perhaps something in the acting of these words had made them notorious; it is odd to find a line of Chapman's ridiculed in a play of which he was part-author.

245. *what sha' call him. E.M.I.* I. iii. 15.

246. *and yet, stay, too.* Nicholson prints 'and "yet, stay" too', commenting 'This "yet stay" appears to me to be his attempt to remember the passage. We have in it "O *stay*", and close to it "*Yet speak*".'

247-54. A second extract from *The Spanish Tragedy*, II. i. 67-75, spoken by Lorenzo, 'the t'other fellow' of line 245.

256-8. Cf. Pistol in *2 Henry IV*, v. iii. 107, 'Why then, lament therefore', and in *The Merry Wives*, I. iii. 33, 'Young ravens must have food.' The source is untraced.

264-5. Unknown.

266. *the Moore*, Muly Mahamet in Peele's *The Battle of Alcazar*.

275. *mangonizing*, trafficking in slaves. Cunningham quotes Cooper's *Thesaurus*, 1565, '*Mango*. A baude that paynteth and pampereth vp boyes, women, or seruauntes to make them seeme the trimmer, thereby to sell them the dearer.' Cf. *Mango*, l. 300.

276-306. The personal satire of these lines is obvious, and in the Apologetical Dialogue appended to the play Jonson admitted it (141-2):

> Now, for the Players, it is true, I tax'd 'hem,
> And yet, but some;

and those 'sparingly'—which would suit the present passage. Thomas Davies in his *Dramatic Miscellanies*, 1783, ii, pp. 81-2, conjectured that these players were members of the Chamberlain's company, a probable view, as Jonson knew Dekker was going to attack him, and the Chamberlain's men acted *Satiro-mastix* as a reply to *Poetaster*. In III. iv. 322 Histrio expressly says of Demetrius 'we haue hir'd him' to produce a play on Horace. T. W. Baldwin in *The Organization and Personnel of the Shakespearean Company*, 1927, pp. 232-4, has offered identifications of the seven actors glanced at in Jonson's text. Histrio is Augustine Phillips, the manager of the company; 'seuen-shares and a halfe' is Richard Burbage, the largest shareholder, though he actually had two shares and a half. Poluphagus (281) is Armin; Aesop (295) is the aged and decaying Heminges; Frisker (299) is William Sly; the 'fat foole' (300) is Pope, who played Falstaff and Belch; the fiddler Aenobarbus (283) is Cowley, who was a musician in *The Seven Deadly Sins*. 'There seems to be no trace in these descriptions of the other two members of the period, Shakespeare and Condell.'

A second attempt at identification was made by Mr. H. D. Gray, 'The Chamberlain's Men and the "Poetaster"', in *M.L.R.* xlii (1947), pp. 173-9. It agrees with Mr. Baldwin for Phillips, Burbage, Pope, and Cowley, but suggests Armin for 'Frisker', Sincklo for 'Poluphagus', and Shakespeare for 'Aesop'. The suggestion is made that Shakespeare by a dirty backstairs intrigue stopped *Cynthia's Revels* from being acted at Court; hence the vindictive satire on the character here and in v. iii. 107–28. This attack on Shakespeare was answered by P. Simpson, 'A Modern Fable of Aesop', in *M.L.R.*, July 1948.

The other company which may be glanced at satirically in this scene is the Admiral's. They were acting near the date of *Poetaster* the three plays which can be identified, from which the Pyrgi recite extracts: *The Spanish Tragedy* (215–22, 247–54) in 1597 and in 1601 and 1602; Henslowe, on behalf of the Admiral's men, paid Jonson for additions; *The Blind Beggar of Alexandria*, published as an Admiral's play in 1598, for a revival of which properties were bought in May and June 1601; and *The Battle of Alcazar*, printed as an Admiral's play in 1594, and revived in December 1597 or at some date between 1600 and 1602.

280. *He will eate a leg of mutton.* Chapman, *May-day*, i. ii (1611, p. 15), 'as neere as you can, when they are in their Mutton, be thou in thy Wood-cocke, it showes resolution'.

281. *Poluphagos*, Greek πολυφάγος, eating to excess.

282. *Barathrum*, abyss, devouring gulf. Suggested by Horace's 'Pernicies et tempestas barathrumque macelli | quidquid quaesierat ventri donabat avaro' (*Ep.* i. xv. 31–2).

283. *Ænobarbus*, 'red-beard'.

287. *accommodate.* For this cant use see *E.M.I.* i. v. 126.

296. *your politician.* So v. iii. 109. Middleton, *A Mad World*, v. i. 59–63 (1608, H), a description of 'my Lords Players': '*Sir Boun.* Good, good, and which is your Polititian amongst you? now yfaith he that workes out Restraints, makes best legs at Court, and has a suit made of purpose, for the companies busines, which is he, come, be not afraid of him.' This suggests a factotum, who represented the company and managed their outside business. Thus we find Heminges was payee for the Chamberlain's men for Court plays from 1599 to 1616 (Chambers, *Elizabethan Stage*, ii, p. 204).

ram vp his mouth with cloues. Cf. v. iii. 121–2.

299. *my zany. E.M.O.* iv. ii. 44–5:

> Hee's like the *Zani*, to a tumbler,
> That tries tricks after him, to make men laugh.

For Tucca to claim 'Frisker', a regular actor of the company, as a copyist was pure folly, and this may be the point of Tucca's outburst in *Satiro-mastix*, 1602, D, 'ile teach thee to turne me into Bankes his horse, and to tell gentlemen I am a Iugler, and can shew trickes'.

305. *glauering*, fawning: 'to glaver' is to talk plausibly. Foxe, *Acts and Monuments*, 1596, f. 1423, 'The Chaunceller with a glauering and smiling countenance, called to the Bishop.' Marston is fond of the word: *The Scourge of Villanie*, 1598, E6, 'Ha, now he glauers with his fawning snowte'; *What You Will*, ii. ii (1607, D3), 'O glauering flatterie'.

308. *pu'ness*, puisnes, novices. So spelt in *Ep.* xcvi. 10; 'pui'nee', *D. is A.* i. i. 5.

315. *confine*, secure.
moderne, ordinary.

318. *halfe-armes*, a dagger only, not a sword and dagger.

319. *motion*, puppet-show. *Ep.* xcvii, 'On the New Motion'.

320. *his dubblet's a little decaied.* See III. i. 67 n.

321-2. *Demetrius, a dresser of plaies*, the 'iourney-man' of IV. vii. 27. The half-pun on 'decker' in the word *dresser* is emphasized by italics in the Quarto. Dekker's collaborations while he worked for the Admiral's and for Worcester's men have been catalogued by Dr. Greg in *Henslowe's Diary*, ii, pp. 258-60. In addition he adapted and altered plays; thus, on 3 November 1602 Henslowe paid him £2 'for mendinge of the play of tasso'.

322. *we*, the Chamberlain's men: see above, 276-306 n. The statement is interesting as showing that Jonson's fifteen-weeks' piece was intended to anticipate the coming attack. In IV. vii. 26-7 Tucca and Crispinus go to see how far Demetrius has got with the play.

328. *this winter.* The closing words of the epilogue to *Satiro-mastix* speak of 'this colde weather'.

329. *No bodie comes.* So in *Hamlet*, II. ii. 334-40, acted by the Admiral's or the Chamberlain's men, there is the famous complaint that the 'eyrie of children', the 'little eyases', are the fashion about 1602, and have seriously damaged the popularity of the older players.

331. *by*, of. *E.M.I.* IV. x. 50 marginal note, '*By Thomas*'.

335. *my Parnassus . . . shall helpe him. Satiro-mastix* was published in 1602 as by Dekker only, but it is highly probable that Marston had a hand in it. The Epistle speaks of '*that terrible* Poetomachia . . . *between* Horace the second, *and a band of leane-witted* Poetasters', and Jonson in the Apologetical Dialogue, 154, speaks of 'the vntrussers'.

343. *gathering*, collection, subscription. So 'gather', *G.M.* 774-5.

345. *well said*, well done.

346-52. From the second act of Peele's *The Battle of Alcazar*, 1594, (Malone reprint, ll. 512, 516-21), with one variant *fore-runners* for 'foretellers' in 352.

353. *penny-biter*, one who bites a (silver) penny to test if it is genuine.

354. *seuen-shares and a halfe*, the manager. Cf. Crashaw, *Steps to the Temple*, 1646, the preface contributed by a friend, 'It were prophane but to mention here in the Preface those under-headed Poets, Retainers to seven shares and a halfe; Madrigall fellowes, whose onely businesse in verse, is to rime a poore six-penny soule, a Subburb sinner into hell'.

355. *play in my name.* There is a good parallel in *Ratseis Ghost. Or The second Part of his madde Prankes and Robberies*, 1605, which records 'A pretty prancke passed by *Ratsey* vpon certaine Players that he met by chance in an Inne; who denied their owne Lord and Maister, and vsed another Noblemans name', B1ᵛ. Ratsey the highwayman gives them leave to play in his name for a week and advises the chief player to try London: 'And in this presage and propheticall humor of mine,

(sayes *Ratsey*) kneele downe, Rise vp, Sir *Simon two shares and a halfe*; Thou art now one of my Knights, and the first Knight that euer was player in England. The next time I meete thee, I must share with thee againe for playing under my warrant, and so for this time adiew.'

368. *ram, vnder his arme-holes*. Cf. Catullus, lxix. 5, 6, 'Fertur | valle sub alarum trux habitare caper'.

370. *twentie drachmes*. Inconsistent with the twenty sesterces of line 182, where the Quarto had 'drachmes'. Jonson forgot to revise the present passage.

375. *Genius*, the classical equivalent of the guardian angel, the rational guiding soul or spirit. Cf. Horace, *Ep.* ii. ii. 187–8, 'Genius, natale comes qui temperat astrum, | naturae deus humanae'.

III. v. This scene is an addition of the Folio, for which we believe it to have been specially written; we have discussed it in the introductory essay (vol. iv, pp. 194–5). It is a free rendering of the first *Satire* of Horace's second book. Like the translations from Ovid and Virgil it is in couplets.

C. Trebatius Testa, a famous jurist, the friend of Cicero who recommended him to Julius Caesar, 'Probiorem hominem, meliorem virum, pudentiorem amicum esse neminem; accedit etiam quod familiam ducit in iure civili singulari memoria, summa scientia' (*Ep. ad Fam.* vii. v. 3). Seventeen of Cicero's letters to him are extant (ibid. vi–xxii). He sided with Caesar in the Civil War, and he had a high reputation as a legal expert in the reign of Augustus.

4. *wants pith*, 'sine nervis' (Hor.).

6. *A thousand verses*. Cf. *Disc.* 2454–64, where Euripides, writing three lines in three days, is told by Alcestis that *he* could have written a hundred in the time, and Euripides' retort that the hundred would not last those three days: 'I have met many of these Rattles, that made a noyse, and buz'de.'

7. *Surcease*, 'quiescas' (Hor.).

13–14. *golden sleep . . . siluer Tyber*. Neither epithet is in the original, and their juxtaposition here is not very happy; but it was an Elizabethan mannerism: cf. *E.M.I.* iii. iii. 19, 20, 'beauties golden tree' of the Hesperides, and 'leaden sleep' of the Dragon; *Macbeth*, ii. iii. 110–11, 'Here lay Duncan, | His silver skin laced with his golden blood.'

14. *thrice*. A. Palmer comments on the Horace, 'The objection that if a man swam thrice across a river he would find himself on the far side from his clothes did not occur to Trebatius'; but it might have occurred to Jonson and been corrected.

23. *burst*, broken. Sly would not pay for the glasses he had 'burst' (*Taming of the Shrew*, Ind. 6), and John of Gaunt 'burst' Shallow's head at the tilt-yard (*2 Henry IV*, iii. ii. 314).

28. *Lucilius, honor'd*. The comma gives a slight emphasis to 'Lucilius'. The first great Roman satirist (148–103 B.C.), who determined the form which satire was to take.

30. *aspire*, attain.

39. *Pantolabus*. III. iv. 157. *Nomentanus* is known only through Horace's mention of him.

50. *both our better*. Cf. *All's Well*, I. iii. 154, 'or were you both our mothers'.

52–3. *in things vniust, Or actions lawfull*. Jonson followed the reading of nearly all the manuscripts of Horace, 'neque si male gesserat . . . neque si bene', where 'gesserat' is an early uncial corruption of 'cesserat', C being mistaken for G (Palmer). The true reading 'Si male cesserat' means 'if matters had gone ill with him'. With 'gesserat' we should require 'rem', 'if he had managed affairs ill'.

55. *votive table*, a reference to the pictures of shipwreck hung by rescued sailors in a Roman temple as a votive offering.

57. *not* = 'ne-wot', 'know not'. See *T. of T.* IV. i. 82 n.

58. *Venusian colonie*. Venusia, the modern Venosa, the birthplace of Horace.

61. *rode*, inroad, foray. *Henry V*, I. ii. 138, 'the Scot, who will make road upon us'.

65. *stile* keeps up the double meaning of the Latin *stilus*, (1) a dagger, (2) a pen. Cf. the Apologetical Dialogue, 97, 'They did prouoke me with their petulant stiles.'

68. *contend*, strain (Lat. *contendo*).

69, 70. *when no malicious thiefe* . . . Horace says simply 'tutus ab infestis latronibus': Jonson's version anticipates the famous lines of *Othello*, III. iii. 159–65.

73. *disease*, discomfort.

79. *Pola Servius*, 'homo taeter et ferus', according to Cicero (*ad. Q. Fr.* II. xiii. 2).

vrne, the judge's urn in which the voting tables were put, as in v. iii. 405.

81. *Canidia*, attacked in Horace's *Satires*, I. viii, and *Epodes* v and xvii: said to have been Gratidia, an old love of Horace.

Albucius. Horace's line 'Canidia Albuci quibus est inimica venenum ⟨minitatur⟩' probably means 'Canidia threatens her enemies with Albucius' poison', but the scholiast Acron interprets 'Canidia filia Albuci'.

83. *Thurius* found only in this passage; so *Scaeva* (89).

104. *Pull the skin ouer the eares of vice*. In the original 'detrahere et pellem, nitidus qua quisque per ora | cederet, introrsum turpis', a reference to the fable of the ass in the lion's skin. But to a seventeenth-century ear the phrase would rather suggest 'Send packing'; a dismissed servant had his coat pulled over his ears (*C. is A.* I. vii. 48).

107. *Laelius*, consul 140 B.C., intimate friend of the younger Scipio, a patron of Terence, and the chief speaker in Cicero's dialogue *De Amicitia*.

108. *from sackt Carthage*. Scipio Africanus the younger.

109. *pierce*, pronounced 'perse'.

111. *Lupus*, L. Cornelius Lentulus, consul 156 B.C. In the present play apt to be confused with Asinius Lupus the tribune.

quick, alive. *famous*, infamous, defaming ('famosis versibus', Hor.).

113. *from sight, and from the iudgement seat*, 'a volgo et scaena' (Hor.), 'from the throng and stage of public life'. Jonson seems to have misinterpreted 'scaena' as 'tribunal'.

115. *Vnbrac't.* 'Discincti' (Hor.), literally 'ungirt', means simply 'without restraint'. The commentator Cruquianus has a story of Lucilius chasing Laelius round the dining-room with a twisted napkin; Jonson glosses 'light sports'.

116. Horace more graphically, 'till the cabbage was boiled'. If Jonson had been literal here, he would probably have been suspected of a personal reference.

133–4. Jonson has worked in here a favourite passage of Martial, *Ep.* x. xxxiii. 9, 10:

> Hunc servare modum nostri novere libelli,
> parcere personis, dicere de vitiis.

He quotes it again in the Apologetical Dialogue, 85, and in the second prologue of *Epicoene*, 4. Cartwright echoed it in his tribute in *Jonsonus Virbius*, 72.

IV. i. 2. *sadnesse*, seriousness.

4. *straight-bodied city attire.* II. i. 68.

5. *loose sacks.* Cf. *Everie Woman in her Humor*, I. i (1609, A3):

> A body prisoned vp with walles of wyer,
> With bones of whales, somewhat allyed to fish,
> But from the wast declining;

and the bill for Katharina's gown in *The Taming of the Shrew*, IV. iii. 131–40, 'a loose-bodied gown, with a small compassed cape, with a trunk sleeve, the sleeves curiously cut'.

13. *my muffe, and my dogge* . . . 20. *my fanne, and my masque.* S. Rowlands, *The Letting of Humours Blood in the Head-Vaine*, 1600, epigram 33, describes a husband who 'makes himselfe a pack-horse to his wife':

> carrying Pearle, so prettie vnder's arme.
> Pearle his wiues Dog, a prettie sweete-fac'd curre, . . .
> Is now not well, his cold is scarcely brooke,
> Therfore good husband wrap him in thy cloake:
> And sweete hart, preethee helpe me to my Maske, . . .
> Heere, take my Muffe: and do you heare good man?
> Now giue me Pearle, and carrie you my Fanne. . . .
> Com to me Pearle, my Scarfe good hisband keepe:
> To be with me I know my Puppie loues.
> Why Pearle I saie: hisband take vp my Gloues.

For the mask cf. *B.F.* v. iv. 44, *S. of N.* 1st Intermean, 56, and Dekker, *The Shomakers Holiday*, 1600, E3ᵛ, Eyre's wife, expecting her husband to be sheriff, says 'It is verie hot, I must get me a fan or else a maske. *Rog.* So you had need, to hide your wicked face.'

15. *Iuno: Hercules* in the Quarto. A wrong oath for a woman: see *Sej.* IV. 438 n.

16. *puffe wings. E.M.O.* III. v. 5 n.

18. *pure laundresses.* The pure linen of the city wives was famous: even Gertrude in *Eastward Ho* (I. ii. 20) approved of it. Cf. Dekker and Webster, *West-ward Hoe*, I. i (1607, A2ᵛ), '*Bir.* I tel thee ther is equality inough betweene a Lady and a Citty dame, . . . name you any one thing that your citizens wife coms short of to your Lady. They haue as pure Linnen, as choyce painting . . .'.

24. *as thick as stones.* A classical simile: cf. Ovid, *Tristia*, I. ii. 47–8 (of sea waves):

> Nec levius tabulae laterum feriuntur ab undis
> quam graue ballistae moenia pulsat onus.

33. *citie mannerly word (forsooth). E.M.O.* II. ii. 14.

37. *minsitiue*, mincing, affected, as the *O.E.D.* queries. The noun is found in *Sir Gyles Goosecappe*, II. ii (1606, B2), ''tis the mind of man, and woman to affect new fashions; but to our Mynsatiues for sooth, if he come like to your *Besognio*, or your bore, so he bee rich, or emphaticall, they care not'.

41. *lyen.* Jonson uses this form in *S.W.* v. ii. 76, *Alch.* IV. i. 46, and 'lien' in *Volp.* IV. v. 81, *B.F.* v. iv. 239–40.

IV. ii. 17. *I do long to ride in a coach*, like Gertrude in *Eastward Ho*, III. ii. Stow says the first English coach was made in 1555. The use of them spread rapidly by 1580 and was a common source of satire against city wives. In 1601 a bill was brought into Parliament to restrain the excessive use of coaches within this realm, but was rejected at the second reading. John Taylor in *The World runnes on Wheeles* (a tract against coaches as injuring the watermen) says a Dutchman, William Boonen, first brought the use of coaches into England in 1564; he was Queen Elizabeth's coachman, 'for indeede a *Coach* was a strange monster in those dayes, and the sight of them put both horse and man into amazement: some said it was a great Crab-shell brought out of *China*, and some imagin'd it to be one of the Pagan Temples, in which the Cannibals adored the diuell: but at last those doubts were cleared, and Coach-making became a substantiall Trade: So that now all the world may see, they are as common as whores, & may be hired as easie as Knights of the post' (*Works*, 1630, p. 240).

26. *fit of a poet*, strain.

33. *habilities. S. of N.* I. v. 119.

57. *clog to your marmaset.* Selden, *Table Talk*, ed. Reynolds, p. 194: 'You shall see a monkey sometime that has been playing up and down

the garden, at length leap up to the top of the wall, but his clog hangs a great way below on this side: the bishop's wife is like that monkey's clog, himself is got up very high, takes place of temporal barons, but his wife comes a great way behind.'

59. *your husband will be left without*. *C.R.* v. iii. 45 n.

iv. iii. 4. *Propertius*. Several touches in this play indicate that Jonson did not know this poet. No friendship existed between Horace and Propertius (see vol. i, p. 419 and note). In i. ii. 107 the 'smoothness' of Propertius' elegies is not only unsound criticism, but a tribute impossible for Horace.

14. *tir'd on*. Used of a hawk tearing flesh with its beak: Gifford compares the legend of Prometheus or Tityus. *Cat.* iii. 200, of Prometheus.

16. *holy-street*. The 'Via Sacra', the principal street of ancient Rome, running through the Forum to the Capitol.

19. *neat*, trim, spruce. So Kent to Oswald in *King Lear*, ii. ii. 37, 'you neat slave'.

28. *thy wedlocke*, like 'coniugium' in Latin, 'thy wife'. So *E.H.* iii. i. 19, *D. is A.* i. vi. 10.

30. *little fine dressing*: 'veluet Cap' (Quarto). The same change as in iii. i. 46.

33. *scroile*, scoundrell (as in l. 19). *E.M.I.* i. i. 46.

50. *In good time*. *E.M.I.* i. ii. 9.

53. *violl*. *E.M.O.* iii. ix. 30.

63–4. *cockatrice . . . punke*. In *Satiro-mastix*, iv. iii, Horace is rated for calling 'modest and vertuous wiues punckes & cockatrices', and for calling citizens bankrupts (as in this scene, ll. 87, 158).

64. *set thee up*, make you elated.

65. *puet*, a sixteenth- and seventeenth-century form of 'pewit', the lapwing: here a quibble.

68–9. *scant-* | *one*. The defective rhyme and metre are difficult to understand in view of Tibullus' statement (l. 95) that the ditty is 'all borrowed' from Horace. We are inclined to suggest 'scant-one, | One such another'. The poem has nothing in it that recalls the work either of Horace or of Jonson.

89. *Canidia*. iii. v. 81.

101. *colledge of criticks*. Cf. Dekker, *The Guls Horne-booke*, 1609, p. 25, the gull at an ordinary may acquire 'the terrible name of a seuere *Criticke*: nay and be one of the Colledge, if youle be liberall inough: and (when your turne comes) pay for their suppers'; and Webster's Induction to *The Malcontent*, 1604, A4ᵛ, 'Nay truly, I am no great censurer, and yet I might have beene one of the Colledge of Critickes once' (Penniman).

103. *Phaeton*. Dekker wrote a play *Phaethon* for the Admiral's men in January 1598 and altered it for a Court performance at Christmas 1600.

110–15. From a similar context in Horace, *Satires*, I. iv. 34–8:

> Faenum habet in cornu; longe fuge: dummodo risum
> excutiat sibi, non hic cuiquam parcet amico;
> et quodcumque semel chartis illeverit omnis
> gestiet a furno redeuntis scire lacuque
> et pueros et anus.

110. *hey in his horne.* The scholiast on Horace explains that a wisp of hay was tied on the horns of a dangerous ox. So Herrick of Oberon, *Hesperides*, 1648, p. 191:

> He's sharp as thorn;
> And fretfully carries Hay in 's horne,
> And lightning in his eye.

lose his best friend. *E.M.O.* Ind. 359–60 n.

113. *tankard-bearer,* water-carrier, like Cob in *E.M.I.*

114. *from the bake-house.* *S.W.* III. v. 26, *S. of N.* 3rd Intermean, 19. Cf. Dekker, *The Belman of London,* 1608, C2, 'But such a noise made they . . . that yᵉ scolding at ten conduits, & the gossiping of fifteene bake-houses was delicate musicke to it'; Massinger, *The Parliament of Love,* IV. v (Malone reprint, 1834–5), 'liue to bee the talke | of the Conduit & the bake howse'.

120–3. This is the line of attack in *C.R.* III. ii. 60–4, and in the present play, v. iii. 310–13.

125. *neufts,* newts. *B.F.* II. ii. 20, vi. 13. The form is intermediate between 'newt' and 'eft': 'an ewt' was corrupted 'a newt'.

132. *Pythagoreans.* Cf. *S.W.* II. ii. 3, *New World,* 199. The Pythagoreans were said to pass through a noviciate of five years' silence.

134. *as fishes.* *New World,* 199, '*Pythagorians,* all dumbe as fishes'.

151. *with her face,* i.e. the mercury used in cosmetics.

159. *look here,* i.e. finger on lip. So v. 57 below.

IV. iv. This scene and its sequel in v. iii. 1–134, where the informer and the magistrate get access to Caesar, are a puzzling episode. Did any contemporary actor play the part of an informer? In the 'Apologetical Dialogue' Jonson, while denying that he had attacked the law and the army, admitted that he had taxed 'some' of the players (ll. 141–2). The actors would be fully justified in resenting such an imputation if there was no foundation for it.

On 7 February 1601, the day before Essex launched his fiasco of a rising and just before *Poetaster* was put on the stage, the Chamberlain's company, at the request of some leading followers of Essex, played *King Richard II.* This we know from the deposition of one of the performers, Augustine Phillips, before Chief Justice Popham on 18 February. The conspirators, he said, specially asked 'to have the play of the deposing and killing of King Richard the Second'. The facts are fully stated by Sir E. K. Chambers in *The Elizabethan Stage* (ii, p. 205). Sir

Poetaster 567

Edmund cautiously asks, 'Can the Aesop episode be a reminiscence of the part played by Augustine Phillips in the Essex innovation?' (ibid. i. 385). Phillips, of course, is not to be identified with Aesop, but there is just a vague hint that players might betray a confidence.

9. *my sword, knaue.* So Justice Clement in *E.M.I.* v. i. 49.

12, 13. *a caduceus*, the snake-tipped staff of Mercury; *petasus*, his winged cap.

15. *coniuration*, conspiracy (Lat. *coniuratio*).

16. *buskins.* Tucca calls him '*Cothurnus*', i. ii. 150.   *act a tragedie*: tragic actors on the classical stage wore the buskin.

38-9. *fasces* combines the Roman practice with the Elizabethan *half-pikes and halberds*. *From the lares*: every Roman house had a *lararium* or shrine of the household gods, containing their images. This is made here to contain the weapons hanging in the hall of a justice of the peace.

iv. v. This fancy-dress performance is recorded by Suetonius, but as a freak of the Emperor Augustus, who is said to have played Apollo in it (*Augustus*, 70). It was known as the 'Caena δωδεκάθεος'. Suetonius also quotes the satire on it. The tone and treatment of the scene are Lucianic, though there is little or no direct debt to Lucian.

Jonson apparently took it more seriously than a modern reader would. In iv. vii. 41-2 he describes it as 'innocent mirth, | and harmlesse pleasures, bred, of noble wit'.

5. *clarified.* Cf. Maplet, *A Greene Forest*, 1567, p. 12, 'To clarifie yᵉ voice, and to helpe them that be hoarse'.

7. *God of reprehension.* Momus takes a leading part in Lucian's *Deorum Concilium*, proposing to clear bastards and barbaric gods out of heaven.

37. *matterie.* Cf. v. i. 128, 'materiall HORACE'.

46. *read in a booke.* 'Stultitiam simulare loco sapientia summa est' was an aphorism of Dionysius Cato, quoted with approval by Erasmus in *The Praise of Folly*, ch. lxii. Editors compare *Twelfth Night*, iii. i. 57-65.

49. *wizard*, wise man.

68. *our sooty brother*, Albius, who plays Vulcan with a blackened face.

horn-booke. A primitive spelling-book, consisting of the alphabet, the Lord's Prayer, the ten digits, set in a wooden frame and covered over with transparent horn to prevent the letters from being worn away.

77. *stut*, stutter. Cf. i. ii. 179-80.

93. *cot-queane.* Originally 'housewife of a labourer's cot'; hence 'rude, ill-mannered woman', and as here 'scold'.

101. *bind thee hand and foot.* So in the *Iliad*, i. 399, 400, Hera (i.e. Juno), Poseidon, and Athena are described as wishing to bind Zeus (Jupiter).

106. *iealous . . . for Thetis.* See the *Iliad*, i. 518-59.

109. *Phrygian frie.* Ganymede was the son of Tros, king of Phrygia, and Jupiter snatched him from Mount Ida.

116. *knocke our chinne against our brest.* A burlesque of κυανέῃσιν ἐπ' ὀφρύσι νεῦσε Κρονίων . . . μέγαν δ' ἐλέλιξεν Ὄλυμπον (*Iliad*, i. 528, 530).

119. *Your nose*, an allusion to the name Ovidius Naso, the 'well-nos'd *poet*' of line 215.

125. The inane passage found at this point in the Quarto is perhaps a reference to a puppet-play. There is a faint suggestion of scriptural phraseology; is it the 'motion of Niniveh'? The omission alters the point of 'Another good iest' (126), referring it to 'thunder thee in peeces.'

129. *collied*, blackened.

133. *skinker*, drawer. In the *Iliad*, i. 571–600, Hephaestus (i.e. Vulcan) mediates between Zeus and Hera and acts as cupbearer to the gods, who laugh at him.

134. *liuers*. The Romans regarded the liver as the seat of love: compare Jonson's terrible translation of 'si torrere iecur quaeris idoneum' (Horace, *Odes*, IV. i. 12) by 'If a fit livor thou dost seeke to toast' (*Und.* lxxxvi. 12).

143. *tongue . . . gent'man vsher to his wit.* Iohn Heywoodes woorkes, 1562, Gij^v, 'Proverbs', II. iv:

> Ye harpe on the stryng, that geueth no melody.
> Your tongues run before your witz, by seint Antonie.

Ray, *Proverbs*, 1678, p. 273, 'Your *tongue* runs before your wit. This is an ancient form of speech; I find it in *Isocrates* his oration to Demonicus'—πολλοῖς ἡ γλῶττα προτρέχει τῆς διανοίας (Isocr. 11A).

151. *blocke of wit.* Cunningham compares *Satiro-mastix*, I. ii (1602, C2), 'but sirra Ningle, of what fashion is this knights wit, of what blocke?'

191. *Running diuision.* E.M.O. III. ix. 135 n.

192. *feast of sense*: *Ent. Bols.* 8, 32. The phrase recalls Chapman's poem, *Ovids Banquet of Sence*, 1595.

210. *Altitonans*, 'thundering from on high', Homer's Ζεὺς ὑψιβρεμέτης.

211. *feather-footed.* *C.R.* I. i. 22.

214. *had better to do.* Cf. *The Golden Book of Marcus Aurelius*, ed. 1546, I. vij, 'I had rather to bee Cato.' For the origin of the idiom see *O.E.D.* s.v. 'Better' *a.* 4b.

217. *soothing*, flattering.

IV. vi. Caesar's sudden intervention in this scene with Lupus and Histrio in his train is the outcome of their intelligence in IV. iv that the gathering was treasonable. It is reserved for Horace to comment on this in scene vii. 37–50; Caesar ignores it, but his description of the 'turbulent informer' in V. iii. 17 shows that he had taken Lupus's measure. Caesar's wrath about impiety (l. 8) hardly tallies with Horace's description of the banquet as 'innocent mirth' and 'harmless pleasures, bred of noble wit' (vii. 41–2). What rouses Caesar is the degradation of his daughter in a company so far beneath her, but there is some inconsistency in the management of the scene.

10. *Euerts*, overtures (Lat. *everto*).

man. For this self-apostrophe see *E.M.I.* III. vi. 22.

11. *panther.* *C.R.* v. iv. 433 n.

29. *parcell-poet.* III. iv. 160.

41. *centaures.* An allusion to the myth of Ixion.

62-3. *Bountie . . . virtue.* The thought is Senecan: cf. *De Beneficiis*, I. xv. 3, 'Cum sit nulla honesta vis animi, etiamsi a recta voluntate incepit, nisi quam virtutem modus fecit, veto liberalitatem nepotari'.

IV. vii. 2. *poultfoot*, club-footed. Applied to Vulcan in *Merc. Vind.* 37.

9. *fawne*, sycophant. Cf. the title of Marston's play, *Parasitaster, or The Fawn*: the prologue flattering the audience, ends

> Now if that any wonder why he's drawn
> To such base soothings, know his play's; *The Fawne.*

Faunus in the later Roman mythology was identified with Pan, and so depicted as 'goat-footed'.

15. *tam Marti, quam Mercurio*, i.e. both with the cudgel and with a libel. The origin of the phrase is unknown.

17-18. Ridiculed in *Satiro-mastix*, IV. ii (H2ʳ). Horace tells Tucca, 'Holde Capten, tis knowne that Horace is valliant, & a man of the sword.'

21. *puck-fist.* *E.M.O.* I. ii. 159 n.

24. *prophet.* Cf. the Latin *vates*, prophet and poet.

little fat Horace. Horace, says Suetonius in his *Life*, 'habitu corporis fuit brevis atque obesus'.

29. *innocence . . . innocent* veil a lost allusion to Marston: in the Quarto text of v. iii. 293 the parody of his verse is subscribed 'Cris: alias Innocence'.

31. Contrary to his usual custom, Jonson does not mark a new scene here with the entrance of new characters.

44. *moths . . . of a state.* B. Rich, *The Honestie of this Age*, 1614, pp. 12-13, 'It hath beene holden for a Maxime . . . that there is not so hatefull a vermine to the common wealth, as those that are Surnamed *The Moathes of the Court*'.

49, 50. *vomit forth Their owne . . . malice.* So Virgil in v. iii. 140-4, and the attack in *Volpone*, Ded. 68-70, on 'inuading interpreters, . . . who cunningly, and often, vtter their owne virulent malice, vnder other mens simplest meanings'.

53. *lapwing-cries.* This bird was supposed to cry at a distance from its nest, in order to lure away the searchers. *Sej.* v. 564, *Und.* xl. 37-8. Chapman, *The Reuenge of Bussy d'Ambois*, v. i (1613, K2):

> Trust not his oathe.
> He will lie like a Lapwing when shee flyes
> Farre from her sought nest, still Here 'tis she cryes.

and Tennyson, *Queen Mary*, III. v:

> The lion needs but roar to guard its young;
> The lapwing lies, says 'here' when they are there.

IV. viii. Charles Lamb included this and the following scene in his *Specimens of English Dramatic Poets*. It is the only passage in Jonson in which his conception of a love-scene is elaborately worked out. Usually he disposes of such episodes and characters rather summarily, avoiding love-making; for instance with Bridget Kiteley in *Every Man in his Humour*, Dame Pliant in *The Alchemist*, and Grace Wellborn in *Bartholomew Fair*.

2. *concluded*, included (Lat. *concludo*).

11. *excites*, summons up (Lat. *excito*).

IV. ix. 6. *lets*, hindrances.

19. *affects*, affections.

28. *quicke* plays on the twofold sense of 'living' and 'swift'.

36–41. Note the gnomic pointing of this passage. It expresses the typical conception of the Renaissance Platonist who worshipped his 'fair' or 'divine Idea', but took care to embody her in an individual. She did not remain a shadowy abstraction. Compare Donne's poem of *The Ecstasy*, which closes on this note after dwelling on spiritual rapture. Lovell in *The New Inn*, III. ii, emphasizes the latter aspect, but his case is exceptional.

40. *plausible*, pleasing.

50. *preying towards stormes*. Cf. *The Faithful Friends*, III. iii (Dyce, *Beaumont and Fletcher*, iv, p. 264):

> My father was a soldier, and that blood
> I took from him which flows within this breast,
> Not, swallow-like, foreseeing of a storm,
> Flags to the ground, but soars up higher still.

91. *retire*. *E.M.I.* (Quarto), I. i. 9.

v. i. This scene and scene ii up to line 56 were excerpted by Charles Lamb for his *Specimens of English Dramatic Poets*. Jonson, he says, 'has here revived the whole court of Augustus, by a learned spell'. He makes the wild comment that 'Virgil, Horace, Ovid, Tibullus, converse in our own tongue more finely and poetically than they expressed themselves in their native Latin', but there is point in his final criticism of 'the scenes between this Louis the Fourteenth of antiquity and his literati. The whole essence and secret of that kind of intercourse is contained therein. The economical liberality by which greatness, seeming to waive some part of its prerogative, takes care to lose none of the materials; the prudential liberties of an inferior which flatter by commanded boldness and soothe with complimental sincerity.'

6. *Cornelius Gallus.* When Octavian was compelled to return to Italy after the battle of Actium in 31 B.C., he sent Gallus to Egypt, where he defeated Antony; after Cleopatra's death, when the country was formed into a province, Gallus was appointed its first prefect (or 'provost', as Jonson calls him). He lost the Emperor's favour, forfeited his office, and committed suicide, 26 B.C.

10. *quarried,* preyed on, as if by a hawk.

11. *out-termes,* mere exteriors. Cf. 'out-formes', *Ep.* cxiv. 4.

19, 20. *if shee bee . . . sciences.* The qualification is important: cf. *Disc.* 1873–6, discussing why a poet should 'have all knowledges'.

32. *Pierian,* of the Muses. Pieria near Mount Olympus was their original home before they migrated, so to speak, to Boeotia.

37. *Contain,* hold ('in contempt'). A very rare use.

39. *president,* precedent. This spelling, due to confusion caused by pronunciation, is found from the fifteenth to the eighteenth centuries.

47. *Where,* whereas.

52. *tempest.* For the use as a verb Gifford quotes *Paradise Lost,* vii. 412.

57. *see not who.* *T. of T.* IV. ii. 34, 'But who haue we here?'

63. *miserie,* miserliness.

72. *out of Campania.* Virgil's favourite residence in later life was at Naples, from which he emerged occasionally to visit Rome, where he had a house on the Esquiline. The story of his reciting to the Emperor parts of his epic is well known: he read three books to Augustus and the other members of his family after the death of Marcellus in 23 B.C.

84. *path-lesse.* Chapman, *Cæsar and Pompey,* 1631, iv, 'striving to entangle men in pathless error'.

moorish, moorlike, barren.

101. *discourse,* thought.

103. *tartarous,* 'having elements of acerbity, unrefined, rough' (*O.E.D.*), which suggests a quibble on 'tartar' in the cant sense of a strolling vagabond.

105–6. *most seuere In fashion, and collection of himselfe.* Quite inappropriate to the never-blotting Shakespeare, but exactly what we should expect of Virgil. 'Vergilium quoque paucissimos die composuisse versus auctor est Varius' (Quintilian, x. iii. 8).

118–23. Cf. Bacon, *The Advancement of Learning,* I. vii. 21, 'As certain critics are used to say hyperbolically, *That if all sciences were lost they might be found in Virgil'. . . .*

128. *material,* full of matter, of sound sense.

v. ii. 9. *with their wants.* In his last hours Virgil asked that the *Aeneid* should be burnt because he had been unable to revise it.

20. *sensuall complement.* With *complement* compare *E.M.O.* I. ii. 22–3, 'all the rare qualities, humours, and complements of a gentleman'.

Sensuall complement is that which completes the character in the eyes of the world.

24. *of purpose.* M.L. II. i. 8.

25. *refuse it not.* Virgil makes a gesture to decline it (Nicholson).

39. *strictly*, concisely: cf. *strictus* in Latin rhetoric.

45. *rapteth.* The verb is formed from the past participle, like 'hoist' and 'graft'.

56–97. From Virgil, *Aeneid*, iv. 160–88.

56–7. *in taile Of that* roused Swinburne to fury. 'This is what Virgil is represented as reading to Augustus—and Augustus as hearing without a shriek of agony and horror' (*Study*, p. 114). But cf. Captain John Smith, *Works*, i, p. 235, 'In the tayle of the Hericano wee were separated from the Admirall'; Drayton, *The Moone-Calfe*, 1627, p. 168:

> When the winde came about with all his power,
> Into the tayle of this approching shower . . .
> And downe the shower impetuously doth fall,
> Like that which men the Hurricano call.—

and Black, *The Adventures of a Phaethon*, 1872, xx. 278, 'The tail of a shower sometimes overtaking us'.

59. *nephew*, grandson, like the Latin *nepos*.

60. *seuerall shelter.* *Alch.* IV. ii. 67, 'That hath the seuerall scale vpon't'.

v. iii. 1–25. The speeches of Lupus are spoken 'within', as Gifford noted. Lines 9–11 have a loose, jerky rhythm, expressive of Lupus's excitement.

20. *auoid him*, turn him out.

31. *perruke* Folio: *Periwig* Quarto. 'Perruck' in the sixteenth century was altered to 'perwyke'; then corrupted to 'perewyke', 'perewig' (*O.E.D.*). Tucca, as he thrusts in, deranges the usher's wig.

37. *puckfist.* IV. vii. 21.

38. There is a Puritan ring about Lupus's phraseology here.

41. *flaggon chaine.* The *O.E.D.* queries, 'a chain bracelet to which a smelling-bottle (F. *flacon*) could be attached'. It was massive, judging from a Lancashire will of 1598, which the *O.E.D.* quotes, 'One flagon cheane viij^{li}'.

43. *party-colour'd.* More suited to the Yeomen of the Guard than to the lictors of ancient Rome.

52. *to begge their land* as a reward for informing. Gifford quotes *Iacke Drums Entertainment*, 1601, C1, 'I haue followed Ordinaries this twelue-month, onely to find a Foole that had landes, or a fellow that would talke treason, that I might beg him.'

56. *then 'tis no libell.* In *Satiro-mastix*, III. i (1602, E4^v), Sir Vaughan offers Mistress Miniver a sealed paper of love-verses: '*Mini.* Ile receiue no Loue libels perdy, but by word a mouth. *Sir Vaughan.* By Sesu tis

no libell, for here is my hand to it.' *Nobody and Somebody*, 1606, I3,
a quibbling speech by Nobody:

> Are libels cast, if *nobody* did make them,
> And *no-bodies* name to them, they are no libels,
> For he that sets his name to any libel,
> Makes it by that no libell.

57. *embleme*. *E.M.I.* v. v. 35.

61–6. A faint echo of Horace's 'Iustum et tenacem propositi virum'
(*Odes*, III. iii. 1–8).

63. *eare*. Cf. IV. vii. 59. Gifford finds in the image of this line a
reference to the cave of 'Dionysius' ear' at Syracuse.

70. *giue*, in the heraldic sense 'display as an armorial bearing'. A. H.
Nason (*Heraldry in Jonson's Plays*, p. 31) notes that the Roman eagles
were in the nature of heraldic bearings and quotes Legh, *The Accedens
of Armory*, f. 38*b*, for Julius Caesar's coat, 'Or, an Eagle displayed with
ii. heddes Sable'.

75. *Giue me my long-sword*. Lupus calls for this property also in
IV. iv. 9.

101–3. From Claude Mignault's commentary on Alciati's *Emblems*,
1600, p. 50, 'Non erit a re alienum, si adiecero, asinum a veteribus
Aegyptiis sapientiae, fortitudinis, laboris indefessi & frugalitatis esse
symbolum.'

109. *politician*. III. iv. 296.

118. *this gent'man*, Crispinus.   *his Achates*, Demetrius: Virgil's
'fidus Achates' (*Aen.* i. 188) is a sort of aide-de-camp to Aeneas.

122. *a bay-leafe*, to sweeten his breath: cf. Martial, v. iv. 1, 2:

> Fetere multo Myrtale solet vino:
> sed, fallat ut nos, folia devorat lauri.

129. *fierce*, rash. *Sej.* v. 542, *Alch.* IV. i. 39.

130. *larger ears*. So in the play of *Timon* a cap with asses' ears is
sent to him. See p. 484.

147. *too wittie in anothers worke*. Martial, preface to his *Epigrams*,
'Absit a iocorum nostrorum simplicitate malignus interpres nec epi-
grammata mea scribat: inprobe facit qui in alieno libro ingeniosus est.'
So in *M.L.*, chorus 2, 46–7.

155. *my three soules*. Cf. Trevisa, *Bartholomaeus de Proprietatibus
Rerum*, 1498, III. vii, p. 53: 'In dyuers bodyes ben thre manere soules:
vegetabilis that yeuyth lyfe and noo felinge, as in plantes and rootes;
Sensibilis, that yeuyth lyfe and felynge and no reason in vnskylfull
beastes; Racionalis, that yeuyth lyf, felyng, and reeson in men.' And
Donne, *LXXX Sermons*, 1640, sermon lxxiv, p. 755, 'First, in a naturall
man wee conceive there is a soule of vegetation and of growth; and
secondly, a soule of motion and of sense; and then thirdly, a soule of
reason and understanding, an immortall soule'. How far Tucca grasped
this evolutionary idea is not obvious; it started with Aristotle whom
Tucca certainly had not read.

158. *rhinoceros*. *C.R.* I. iii. 17.

159. *Hippocrene*, the spring of the Muses near Mount Helicon. The reference is to Maecenas.

160. *be whipt*, the punishment of vagrants, as players were held to be unless they were specially licensed (I. ii. 53).

166. *distastes*, annoyances.

178. *I take no knowledge*. Horace's attitude throughout the 'Apologetical Dialogue'.

186. *deft*, dexterous. *S.S.* II. ii. 2.

187–8. *Make 'hem hold vp their spread golls*, i.e. arraign them, as in 213. Cf. Dekker's retort in *Satiro-mastix*, I. ii (1602, D2), 'Holde, holde vp thy hand, I ha seene the day thou didst not scorne to holde vp thy golles: ther's a Souldiers spur-royall, twelue pence'. *Golls*, hands.

190. *band*, neck-band, collar.

195. *motion*, puppet.

217. *Lex Remmia*, a Roman law dealing with the question of calumny, mentioned by Marcian, *Digest*, 48, tit. 16, s. 1.

251. *Iwusse*. *E.M.I.* I. i. 36.

275–92. Jonson had already satirized Marston's vocabulary in *E.M.O.* III. iv. 21–30.

275. *Ramp vp*, climb up. The image is that of an animal on its hind legs: cf. 'rampant' in heraldry. There is no example of this use in Marston.

my genius. *The Scourge of Villanie*, 1598, opening lines to Detraction:

> Know that the *Genius*, which attendeth on,
> And guides my powers intellectuall,
> Holds in all vile repute *Detraction*.

Ibid. *Sat.* vi. 12–15:

> Think'st thou that *Genius* that attends my soule,
> And guides my fist to scourge *Magnifico's*,
> Will daigne my mind be ranck'd in *Paphian* showes?

Ibid. 107–9:

> What though I bare to lewd Opinion,
> Lay ope to vulgar prophanation
> My very *Genius*?

retrograde. In *C.R.* v. iii. 118 Asotus says 'Let's bee retrograde'. Not in Marston.

276. *nominate a spade, a spade*. Gifford quotes the criticism in *The Returne from Pernassus*, ed. Macray, I. i. 279–82:

> Tut, what cares he for modest close coucht termes,
> Cleanly to gird our looser libertines.
> Giue him plaine naked words stript from their shirts
> That might beseeme plaine dealing *Aretine*.

Our own criticism to the same effect is given in the introduction to *Eastward Ho* (vol. ii, pp. 39, 40).

277. *lubricall*, slippery. Not in Marston.

glibberie also means 'slippery'. Marston, *Antonio and Mellida*, I. i (1602, B4), 'His loue is glibbery; there's no hold ont, wench'; ibid. II. i (C3), 'milke, milke, yee glibbery vrchin, is foode for infants'; ibid. IV. i (G), 'O, you that made open' [*read* wade vpon] 'the glibbery Ice | Of vulgar fauour'. In *Iacke Drums Entertainment*, 1601, B—a play in which Marston's hand can be clearly traced—'Let who will climbe ambitions glibbery rounds, | And leane vpon the vulgars rotten loue.'

278. *defunct*. This use had not established itself by 1601. Not in Marston.

280. *moderne*, slight, trivial. *The Scourge of Villanie*, Sat. ix (1598, G8):

> O what a tricksie lerned nicking straine
> Is this applauded, sencles, modern vain.

But Jonson uses the epithet himself, *Alch.* IV. i. 23, *B.F.* v. iii. 121.

281. *cothurnall buskins*. *Antonios Reuenge*, II. iv (1602, E2ᵛ), 'O now *Tragœdia Cothurnata* mounts', seemingly borrowed from *The Spanish Tragedy*, IV. i. 159, '*Tragœdia cothurnata*, fitting Kings'.

282. *incubus*. The point of the sneer is Marston's metaphorical use in *Antonios Reuenge*, I. i (A4):

> I would haue told you, if the *incubus*
> That rides your bosome, would haue patience

ibid. IV. iv (H4):

> Then death, like to a stifling *Incubus*,
> Lie on my bosome.

283. *spurious snotteries*. *The Scourge of Villanie*, Sat. ii (C2ᵛ):

> O what dry braine melts not sharp mustard rime
> To purge the snottery of our slimie time?

284. *puft-vp lumpe of barmy froth*. *The Scourge of Villanie*, 'In Lectores', B, 'each odd puisne of the Lawyers Inne, | Each barmy froth'; ibid., B4, 'iudiciall *Torquatus*, (that like some rotten stick in a troubled water, hath gotte a great deale of barmy froth to stick to his sides)'; ibid., *Sat.* vi (E6), 'Curio, know'st me? why thou bottle-ale, | Thou barmy froth'; *Iacke Drums Entertainment*, A3, 'You shall haue me an emptie caske that's fur'd | With nought but barmie froth'.

286. *clumsie chil-blain'd iudgement*. *Clumsie* in the sense of 'benumbed with cold'. *Iacke Drum*, C4ᵛ:

> Let clumsie iudgments, chilblain'd gowtie wits
> Bung vp their chiefe content within the hoopes
> Of a stuft drie-fatt.

287. *Magnificates*. *Certayne Satyres* (appended to *Pigmalions Image*), 1598, *Sat*. ii, p. 42, 'The which the female tongues magnificate'; *The Scourge of Villanie*, *Sat*. iii (D2), 'Nay, shall a trencher slaue extenuate, | Some *Lucrece* rape? and straight magnificate | lewd *Iouian* lust'; ibid. 'Proemium' (D8), 'I cannot with swolne lines magnificate, | Mine owne poore worth'. *Magnificates*, magnifies.

bespawles, bespatters with saliva. *Iacke Drum*, i, ii (1601, B3ᵛ):

> Why should your stomacke be so queasie now,
> As to bespawle the pleasures of the world?

288. *conscious*, 'attributed to inanimate things as privy to . . . human activities or secrets' (*O.E.D.*). Cf. 504, 'the often *conscious dampe*'. Neither this nor 'conscious time' can be traced in Marston. Nashe similarly took exception to 'conscious mind' in Gabriel Harvey (*Foure Letters Confuted*, ed. McKerrow, *Works*, i, p. 316).

289–90. *As if his organons of sense would crack The sinewes of my patience*. *Iacke Drum*, iii (E4ᵛ):

> Oh thou omnipotent, infinitie,
> Crack not the sinewes of my patience
> With racking torment.

The Scourge of Villanie, *Sat*. viii (G6ᵛ), 'Abusing all his organons of sence'.

292. *Of strenuous venge-ance to clutch the fist*. *Antonios Reuenge*, v. i (I2):

> The fist of strenuous vengeance is clutcht,
> And sterne *Vindicta* towreth vp aloft.

Also ridiculed in *The Honest Mans Fortune*, ii. iv (Dyce MS. 9, f. 15), after an arrest:

> the strenuous fist of vengance now is clutcht,
> therefore feare nothing.

Marston always made the word three syllables: e.g. in *Antonios Reuenge*, Malone Society's reprint, 1069, 'If my heart beat on ought but vengeance'; ibid. 1071–2, 'if my braine | Digest a thought, but of dire vengeance'; ibid. 1074, 'If blood, heart, braine, plot ought saue vengeance'.

294. *like a Hercules*. Cf. *E.M.O.* Ind. 39 n.

302. *th'vntrussing a* poet. '*The vntrussing of the* Humorous Poet' was the second title of *Satiro-mastix*, and the running title of the play.

304. *bescumbers*, befouls. *The Scourge of Villanie*, *Sat*. ix (G7ᵛ), 'With muck-pit esculine filth bescumbers'. Literally in *S. of N.* v. iv. 62.

312–13. Cf. *C.R.* iii. ii. 60–2.

319. *buy repentance too dear*. Proverbial: cf. Udall's *Apophthegmes* of Erasmus, 1542, ff. 341–2: '*Demosthenes* is reported to haue sailed on a tyme to yᵉ citee of *Corinthe*, enticed & allured wᵗ the fame of *Lais* a

Courtesan there of greate name, to thentente yᵗ he also emong the mo might haue his pleasure of the paramour which all yᵉ worlde spake of. But when she by couenaunte required for one night tenne thousande drachmes, *Demosthenes* feared wᵗ the greatnesse of yᵉ price chaunged his mynde, saying, οὐκ ἀγοράζω τοσούτου μετανοῆσαι. that is: I will not bye repentaunce so dere.' The story is in Aulus Gellius, *Noctes Atticae*, I. viii. 4.

321. *carries palme with it*. A latinism: cf. Varro, *De Re Rustica*, III. xvi. 14, 'Siculum mel fert palmam'. *E.M.O.* III. ix. 9, *U.V.* iii. 6.

322. *motly gull*. Cf. 'motley fool', of the jester in his parti-coloured dress.

327. *viper*. Vipers were anciently believed to eat their way through their parent's body at birth. *Sej.* III. 385, *M.L.* IV. iv. 7.

329–39. Adapted from Horace, *Satires*, I. iv. 81–5:

> Absentem qui rodit amicum,
> qui non defendit alio culpante, solutos
> qui captat risus hominum famamque dicacis,
> fingere qui non visa potest, commissa tacere
> qui nequit; hic niger est, hunc tu, Romane, caveto.

340. *twang'st*. Cf. I. ii. 46.

342. *rise to the vrne*. In a Roman lawsuit, after the speeches and the evidence, the judge called upon the jury to give their verdict: they were said *ire*, or *consurgere, in consilium*, a phrase perhaps implying that they retired to consider their verdict.

355. *Here-hence*. *T. of T.* III. i. 61.

364. *erection*, 'lifting himself up to his true height of place' (Nicholson).

371. *ierking pedants*, schoolmasters plying the birch, a type of narrow-minded severity. Note the company in which Jonson puts the players.

381. *quit*, acquit. *S.W.* I. i. 159, *Alch.* v. v. 164.

383. *generous*, gentle-born (Lat. *generosus*).

385. *case*, pair.

389. *bastinado a mans eares*. Cf. *King John*, II. i. 463–4:

> He gives the bastinado with his tongue:
> Our ears are cudgelled.

391. *pills*. The idea of the vomit is taken from the *Lexiphanes* of Lucian, where a rhetorician with a passion for outlandish words is similarly cured. This was first pointed out by James Upton, who has not had the credit for it, in his pamphlet *Remarks on Three Plays of Benjamin Jonson*, 1749, p. 3.

392. *whitest kind of ellebore*, used by the ancients in treating mental disease. Jonson had in mind the following passage of Pliny, *Natural History*, xxv. v (in Holland's translation, 1601, p. 217): 'The white ⟨ellebore purgeth⟩ by vomit upward, and doth evacuat the offensive humours which cause diseases. In times past it was thought to be a

daungerous purgative, and men were afraid to use it: but afterwards it became familiar and common, insomuch as many students tooke it ordinarily for to cleanse the eyes of those fumes which troubled their sight, to the end that whiles they read or wrote, they might see the better and more clearely.'

394. *tumorous*, *Disc.* 2053.

408. *a beggar vpon pattins*. Cotgrave, 1611, s.v. 'Galoche': 'A wooden Shooe, or Patten, made all of a peece, without any latchet, or ty of leather, and worne by the poore clowne in Winter.'

409. *pilchers*. III. iv. 4.

419. *Parcell-guiltie*, i.e. *Non liquet*, not proven. The expression plays on 'parcel-gilt'. Tucca had voted 'not guilty'; then, hearing the other votes, he tried to 'hedge'.

422. *cantharides*. From Greek κανθαρίς, the blister-fly. Actually the dried beetle or Spanish fly. Pliny discusses them (*N.H.* XXIX. iv, transl. Holland, p. 362): 'Of a causticke and burning nature they are, in so much as they will raise blisters, yea and leaue an escharne vpon the exulcerat place.'

440. *Harpies*. *Gorboduckes* in the Quarto, the title of Norton and Sackvile's play, *The Tragedie of Gorboduc*, 1561, the first English tragedy.

443. *Cargo's*. A term of contempt, apparently derived from the Spanish *cargo*, *carga*, 'burden'. It is also used as an exclamation or imprecation: G. Wilkins, *Miseries of Enforced Marriage*, 1607, IV, 'But cargo! my fiddlestick cannot play without rosin' (*O.E.D.*).

456–62. Horace writes in a similar spirit, *Satires*, I. x. 78–88.

457. *best-best*. *Und.* XXV. 63; Markham and Machin, *The dumbe Knight*, 1608, I2ᵛ, 'My dearest dreade, my best best soueraigne'.

463–529. In Lucian's *Lexiphanes*, Lucian and a doctor named Sopolis administer a draught to Lexiphanes to cure his vocabulary of out-of-the-way words and phrases, archaisms, and Homeric tags, and word-coinages (such as ἐχεγλωττία, 'linguistice', modelled on ἐχεχειρία, 'armistice'). Jonson adapts this passage. ΛΕΞ. Οὐκ οἶδ' ὃ καὶ δράσετέ με, ὦ Σώπολι, σύ τε καὶ Λυκῖνος, πιπίσκοντες τουτουὶ τοῦ φαρμάκου. δέδοικα γοῦν μὴ πτῶμα γένοιτό μοι τοῦτο τῶν λόγων τὸ πῶμα. ΛΥΚ. Πίθι καὶ μὴ μέλλε ὡς ἀνθρώπινα ἤδη φρονοίης καὶ λέγοις. ΛΕΞ.'Ιδοὺ πείθομαι καὶ πίομαι. φεῦ τί τοῦτο; πολὺς ὁ βορβορυγμός. ἐγγαστριμυθόν τινα ἔοικα πεπωκέναι. ΣΩΠ. Ἄρξαι δὴ ἐμεῖν. βαβαῖ· πρῶτον τουτὶ τὸ μῶν, εἶτα μετ' αὐτὸ ἐξελήλυθε τὸ κᾆτα, εἶτα ἐπ' αὐτοῖς τὸ ἦ δ' ὅς καὶ ἀμηγέπη καὶ λῷστε καὶ δήπουθεν καὶ συνεχὲς τὸ ἄττα. βίασαι δ' ὅμως, κάθες εἰς τὴν φάρυγγα τοὺς δακτύλους. οὐδέπω τὸ ἴκταρ ἐμήμεκας οὐδὲ τὸ σκορδινᾶσθαι οὐδὲ τὸ τευτάζεσθαι, οὐδὲ τὸ σκύλεσθαι. πολλὰ ἔτι ὑποδέδυκε καὶ μεστή σοι αὐτῶν ἡ γαστήρ. ἄμεινον δέ, εἰ καὶ κάτω διαχωρήσειεν ἂν ἔνια· ἡ γοῦν σιληπορδία μέγαν τὸν ψόφον ἐργάσεται συνεκπεσοῦσα μετὰ τοῦ πνεύματος. ἀλλ' ἤδη μὲν καθαρὸς οὑτοσὶ πλὴν εἴ τι μεμένηκεν ὑπόλοιπον ἐν τοῖς ἐντέροις. σὺ δὲ τὸ μετὰ τοῦτο παραλαβὼν αὐτόν, ὦ Λυκῖνε, μεταπαίδευε καὶ δίδασκε ἃ χρὴ λέγειν.

The emetic had a chastening effect on Marston's later style; no outlandish phrases are to be found in any of his works printed after *Poetaster*. And this is specially noteworthy in *What You Will*, written and acted before *Poetaster*. Dr. Small notes in *The Stage-Quarrel* (pp. 107–8) that only fifteen of the words or phrases which Jonson ridiculed can be found in Marston's extant works; there are nineteen others unaccounted for, viz. 'retrograde', 'reciprocal', 'lubricall', 'defunct', 'conscious' (applied to inanimate objects), 'inflate', 'turgidous', 'ventosity' or 'ventositous', 'oblatrant', 'furibund', 'fatuate', 'prorumped' in Quarto and Folio; 'obcæcate', 'tropological', 'anagogical', 'loquacity', 'pinnosity' in the Quarto only; 'snarling gusts' and 'quaking custard' in the Folio only. Of these 'turgidous', 'oblatrant', and 'prorumped' furnish the only examples quoted in the *Oxford Dictionary*, which does not recognize 'pinnosity'.

Now granting that Jonson could not resist the temptation to put in a few additional absurdities, would he have exaggerated to this extent? For this reason Dr. Small conjectured that the missing words were in the text of *What You Will* as it was originally acted, but that Marston purged the vocabulary before he printed the play in 1601. Two slight points support this conjecture: 'ventosity' in the Quarto text of line 494 had already been indicated as a Marstonian word in *E.M.O.* iii. iv. 27, and 'the often *conscious*' of line 504 ('*conscious dampe*' in the Folio) implies that it was used in three or four passages at least.

Jonson's satire made a hit; Kempe alludes to it in *The Returne from Pernassus* (part ii, iv. iii): 'O that *Ben Ionson* is a pestilent fellow, he brought vp *Horace* giuing the Poets a pill.' The satire, as Small argues, loses much of its point if Marston had just produced a play free from this barbarous diction, and *What You Will* shows clear traces of revision in the confusion of the character-names before the speeches, Celia with Lucea and Adrian with Andrea (Small, op. cit., pp. 99, 100).

In Lewis Sharpe's *The Noble Stranger*, 1640, G3, there is a kind of inverted parody of Crispinus' emetic. Pupillus is made by Mercutio to swallow 'little pieces of paper rold vp', which are 'certaine Collections out of learned and witty Authors, for all humours in an accomplished wit, namely "Scholastique Inspiration", "the inspiration of a confident Poeticall wit", "the expiring breath of a great warrior", "a wanton lovers rapture"'. Pupillus then delivers speeches on these lines.

468. *reciprocall*. Jonson himself has the word, *C.R.* i. iv. 77, *Ch. Tilt*, 207. As Jonson uses the word in a normal way, the point of the satire here may be in the corrected Folio reading '*reciprocall Incubus*'.

494. *Puffy*. Marston, *Pigmalions Image*, 1598, p. 24, 'puffie as Dutch hose'; ibid. *Sat.* ii, p. 48, 'O worthless puffie slaue'; *The Scourge of Villanie*, *Sat.* iv (D4), 'striuing to get repute | Mong puffie Sponges'.

525. *snarling gusts*. *Antonios Reuenge*, 1602, prol. (A2), 'Whilst snarling gusts nibble the iuyceles leaues, | From the nak't shuddering branch.'

quaking custard. *The Scourge of Villanie*, *Sat.* ii (B8ᵛ), 'Let Custards quake, my rage must freely runne.'

Anagogicall (Quarto), mystical.

Pinnosity (Quarto) (or 'pennosity'?), the capacity for being fitted with wings, wingfulness—to coin a monstrosity which matches the original.

535–58. Modelled on the suggestions to Lexiphanes (op. cit., 347–8). He is advised to study the best poets, Thucydides and Plato, 'fine comedy' and 'stately tragedy'. With lines 549–58 cf. καὶ μήν κἀκεῖνο οὐ μικρόν, μᾶλλον δὲ τὸ μέγιστον ἁμαρτάνεις ὅτι οὐ πρότερον τὰς διανοίας τῶν λέξεων προπαρεσκευασμένος ἔπειτα κατακοσμεῖς τοῖς ῥήμασι καὶ τοῖς ὀνόμασιν, ἀλλὰ ἤν που ῥῆμα ἔκφυλον εὕρης ἢ αὐτός πλασάμενος οἰηθῇς εἶναι καλόν, τούτῳ ζητεῖς διάνοιαν ἐφαρμόσαι καὶ ζημίαν ἡγῇ ἂν μὴ παραβύσης αὐτό που, κἂν τῷ λεγομένῳ μηδ' ἀναγκαῖον ᾖ. Cf. *C.R.* ii. iv. 15–18.

537. *Catoes principles. Dionysii Catonis Disticha de Moribus*, a work of the silver age of Latin literature, popular in the Middle Ages; it is often quoted by Chaucer. Erasmus edited it, and it was a text-book in Elizabethan schools. Drayton in the *Epistle to Henry Reynolds*, describing his early education, says he read the *Sententiae Pueriles* and construed *Cato*.

538. *next your heart*, on an empty stomach. Cf. Greene, *The Second Part of Conny-catching*, 1591, C4ᵛ, 'which stroke such a cold quandary to his stomacke, as if in a frostie morning hee had drooncke a draught of small beere next his heart'.

542. *Shun Plautus, and old Ennius*. So Jonson advises for English youth the 'openest and clearest' authors; 'beware of letting them taste *Gower*, or *Chaucer* at first' (*Disc.* 1799).

544. *But not without a tutor*. So *Lexiphanes*, 347, ἀρξάμενος δὲ ἀπὸ τῶν ἀρίστων ποιητῶν καὶ ὑπὸ διδασκάλοις αὐτοὺς ἀναγνούς.

545–6. *Pindarus*: cf. *Conv. Drum.* ix. 141. Note the scanning 'Orphëus'. The choice of *Musaeus* must be determined by Marlowe's *Hero and Leander*.

547–8. *Lycophron . . . too darke*. The Alexandrian grammarian and poet. Lexiphanes was warned against his *Alexandra* (op. cit., 350), which was a byword for obscurity. Suidas calls it σκοτεινὸν ποίημα, and the poet was known as ὁ σκοτεινός.

551. *matter . . . before words. C.R.* prol. 20, and Tucca's joke, iv. v. 143–4.

553. *Gallo-belgick phrase*. A reference to the latinity of the famous register of news *Mercurii Gallo Belgici: sive, rerum in Gallia, et Belgio potissimum: Hispania quoque, Italia, Anglia, Germania, Polonia, Vicinisque locis ab anno 1588, ad Martium anni 1594, gestarum, Nuncii*. Published at Cologne in 1598, and fifteen volumes appeared up to 1630. It was ornamented with a woodcut of Mercury on a globe. The original compiler was Michael von Isselt. An English translation by R. Bothe appeared in 1614. Cf. *Ep.* xcii. 16.

562. *in that robe*. Perhaps the same as Demetrius' fool's coat and cap in line 577. Cf. *Satiro-mastix*, iv. iii (I4), 'tis not your fooles Cap Master Horace, which you couer'd your Poetasters in'.

568. *in some dark place*. As if Crispinus were a lunatic.

571. *branded*. Roman law prescribed that a false accuser might be

branded on the forehead with the letter K (= Kalumnia). This punishment is conjecturally assigned to the *Lex Remmia*. To the audience branding would suggest the Elizabethan practice: cf. Porter, *The two angry women of Abington*, 1599, M, 'Nor that same hisse that by a fier doth stand, | And hisseth T. or F.'—i.e. traitor or felon—'vpon the hand.'

587–610. Dekker administers a comic parody of this oath to Horace in *Satiro-mastix*, v. ii (M).

590. *Booke-sellers stalls*, where gallants used to meet and read new books. *E.M.O.* III. i. 29–31.

tauernes. Ibid. I. ii. 192.

591. *two-penny roomes*. Ibid., Ind. 312.

'tyring-houses, the dressing-rooms at the theatres.

noble-mens buttries. So in the induction to *The Taming of the Shrew*, 100, the lord orders the players to be taken to the buttery.

592. *puisne's chambers*, at the Inns of Court. Cf. III. iv. 308.

601. *bastoun*. 'Replaced in the seventeenth century by Batoon, and now by Baton' (*O.E.D.*).

605. *vntrussers*. So Dekker's reply is *Satiro-mastix. Or The vntrussing of the Humorous Poet*, with running-title *The vntrussing of the Humorous Poet*.

whippers. An allusion to *The Whipping of the Satyre* by W. I., 1601, an attack on Jonson, Marston, and Breton for their criticism of the follies of the time: see vol. i, pp. 29, 357. So 'these whippers' in the Apologetical Dialogue, 55; cf. *Satiro-mastix*, v. ii (L4), '*Tuc.* Sirra stincker, thou'rt but vntruss'd now, I owe thee a whipping still, and Ile pay it: I haue layde roddes in Pisse and Vineger for thee: It shall not bee the *Whipping a'th Satyre*, nor the Whipping of the blinde-Beare, but of a counterfeit Iugler, that steales the name of Horace.' 'Poet-whyppers' is a phrase of Sidney's in the *Apology for Poetry* (ed. Gregory Smith, p. 180).

609. *hospitall of Fooles*. Cf. the title of Tommaso Garzoni's *The Hospitall of Incurable Fooles, erected in English*, 1600.

630. *apes are apes* . . . Lucian, *Adversus Indoctum*, 4: πίθηκος γὰρ ὁ πίθηκος, ἡ παροιμία φησί, κἂν χρύσεα ἔχῃ σύμβαλα.

632. *Rumpatur* . . . Martial, IX. xcvii. 12.

Apologetical Dialogue

A. W. Ward, *English Dramatic Literature*, ii, p. 360, compares the Aristophanic parabasis and suggests that Jonson appeared *in propria persona* to speak the author's part.

11. *Non annorum* . . . St. Ambrose, *Epistles*, I. xviii, ed. Migne.

13. *Nasutus, Polyposus*. From Martial, XII. xxxvii, quoted on the title-page of the Folio text of *Cynthia's Revels*: see p. 486.

23. *Fates haue not spun* . . . *the coursest thread*. Cf. *Hadd.* 224–5 (and n.), 'the *Parce* spunne | Their whitest wooll'.

38–9. *shot-free* . . . *vn-hit*. From Seneca, *De Constantia Sapientis*,

iii. 3, 'Involnerabile est non quod non feritur, sed quod non laeditur'. Repeated *N.I.* IV. iv. 204–5; *Und.* xxv. 48–50.

45. *barking students of Beares-Colledge*, the dogs of the Bear Garden in Southwark. *G.M.* 1358, *Ep.* cxxxiii. 117. Cunningham refers to Radulph Agas's plan of Elizabethan London, where they are pictured in the foreground. The Butchers' Company sent all their offal from Eastcheap and Newgate Markets to provide food for the King's bears (Ordish, *Early London Theatres*, p. 237).

53. *Teucers hand. Iliad*, xiii. 313–14, Τεῦκρός θ', ὃς ἄριστος Ἀχαιῶν | τοξοσύνῃ.

55. *whippers.* v. iii. 605 n.

62. *high-way stands.* Cf. *Bid-stand*, *E.M.O.* IV. v. 36.

67. Juvenal, *Satire*, iv. 106.

82. *The Law, and Lawyers. Satiro-mastix*, IV. iii (I3), 'th'ast entred Actions of assault and battery, against a companie of honourable and worshipfull Fathers of the law: you wrangling rascall, law is one of the pillars ath land, and if thou beest bound too't (as I hope thou shalt bee) thou't prooue a skip-Jacke, thou't be whipt'.

85. Martial, also quoted III. v. 133–4.

96, 98. *three yeeres, . . . On euery stage.* We can now trace the portraits in only three plays, which were acted by the Paul's boys—Chrisoganus in *Histrio-mastix*, 1599, a clumsy attempt at a complimentary portrait which Jonson interpreted as a caricature, Brabant Senior in *Jack Drum's Entertainment* (1600), and Lampatho in *What You Will* (1601). See vol. i, pp. 25–7.

97. *petulant styles.* Repeated *Volp.* Ded. 74: see III. v. 65.

111. *next*, i.e. to wasps.

113. *grasshoppers.* A Greek proverb: Lucian, *Pseudologistes*, 1, τὸ δὲ τοῦ Ἀρχιλόχου ἐκεῖνο ἤδη σοι λέγω ὅτι τέττιγα τοῦ πτεροῦ συνείληφας, . . . εἰκάζων ἑαυτὸν τῷ τέττιγι ὁ Ἀρχίλοχος φύσει μὲν λάλῳ ὄντι καὶ ἄνευ τινὸς ἀνάγκης, ὁπόταν δὲ καὶ τῷ πτεροῦ ληφθῇ, γεγωνότερον βοῶντι. Also in *Volp.* III. iv. 55, *M.L.* II. v. 45–6.

120–1, 123–4. Translated by Gifford:

> Renounce this thriftless trade, my father cried:
> Maeonides himself—a beggar died.
> To learn the wrangling law was ne'er my choice,
> Nor, at the hateful bar, to sell my voice.

129. *an Epigramme.* Reprinted in the book of *Epigrams*, no. cviii.

130. *lemma*, the argument, heading (Greek λῆμμα).

140. *is such* as the Captain they complain of—in this context Tucca.

143–5. From Martial's preface to his *Epigrams*, 'Spero me secutum in libellis meis tale temperamentum ut de illis queri non possit quisquis de se bene senserit, cum salva jnfimarum quoque personarum reverentia ludant.' Jonson quoted this in his letter to Lord Salisbury (1605) on the subject of *Eastward Ho* (vol. i, pp. 195), and in the Induction to *Bartholomew Fair*, 83–4.

148. *gaue 'hem meat.* Cf. Histrio's statement in III. iv. 327–30, and Tucca's offer to provide 'fresh rags' for Demetrius (ibid. 344).

151. *some better natures.* This includes Shakespeare who 'was (indeed) honest, and of an open, and free nature' (*Disc.* 655–6), and who had administered to Jonson the 'purge' mentioned in *The Return from Parnassus* (ed. Macray, ll. 1809–13).

159. *baffull.* Cf. *D. is A.* IV. vii. 73 (margin), 'Wittipol *baffles him*', and note.

161. *Archilochus fury.* Archilochus of Paros, cheated by Lycambes of his marriage with Lycambes' daughter, lampooned him so bitterly that he hanged himself: Archilochus used the iambic metre. Horace, *Ars Poetica*, 79, 'Archilochum proprio rabies armavit iambo.'

163. *Irish rats.* A common comparison: cf. *S. of N.* 4th Intermean, 54–5; *As You Like It*, III. ii. 164–5, where Rosalind says of Orlando's rhymes to her, 'I was never so be-rhymed since Pythagoras' time, that I was an Irish rat'; and Randolph, *The Jealous Lovers*, 1630, V. ii:

> my Poets
> Shall with a satyre steep'd in vinegar,
> Rime 'um to death, as they do rats in Ireland.

165. *deepe, and publike brands.* From Martial, VI. lxiv. 24–6:

> At si quid nostrae tibi bilis inusserit ardor,
> vivet et haerebit totoque legetur in orbe
> stigmata nec vafra delebit Cinnamus arte.

So *Volp.*, Ded. 140–2.

166. *Barber-Surgeons.* 'The Company of Barber-surgeons was incorporated by Edward IV in 1461; under Henry VIII the title was altered to "Company of Barbers and Surgeons", and barbers were restricted to the practice of dentistry; in 1745 they were divided into two distinct corporations' (*O.E.D.*).

172. *to clothe tabacco* . . . Cf. Martial to his book, III. ii. 3–5, 'Ne nigram cito raptus in culinam | cordylas madida tegas papyro | vel turis piperisve sis cucullus'. So *Ep.* iii. 12, *Und.* xliii. 52, *Disc.* 589–92.

175–9. From Juvenal, *Sat.* xiii. 189–95:

> Quippe minuti
> semper et infirmi est animi exiguique voluptas
> ultio: continuo sic collige quod vindicta
> nemo magis gaudet quam femina. Cur tamen hos tu
> evasisse putes quos diri conscia facti
> mens habet attonitos et surdo verbere caedit
> occultum quatiente animo tortore flagellum?

180–1. Cf. Seneca, *De Ira*, III. v. 7, 8, 'At ille ingens animus et verus aestimator sui non vindicat iniuriam quia non sentit. . . . Ultio doloris confessio est.'

182. *the treasure of the foole, their tongues.* From Plautus: cf. *Disc.* 392–3 n.

194. *scarce . . . a play a yeere.* Cf. *Satiro-mastix*, v. ii (L3ᵛ), Tucca to Horace, 'you Nastie Tortois, you and your Itchy Poetry breake out like Christmas, but once a yeare'; and Jasper Mayne's lines in *Jonsonus Virbius*, 1638, p. 30:

> Scorne then their censures, who gav't out, *thy Witt*
> As long upon a *Comœdie* did sit
> As *Elephants* bring forth.

Contrast the reference in the Induction, 14, to the fifteen weeks in which *Poetaster* was written.

201. *master of art . . .* Persius, *Sat.* prol. 10, 11, 'Magister artis ingenique largitor | venter.' So *P.R.* 15.

208. *stuff'd nostrills.* The opposite of Horace's *emunctae naris* (*Sat.* I. iv. 8). So 'nostrill' = perception in *Sej.* III. 248. Cf. Marston, *Parasitaster*, III. i (1606, F1ᵛ):

> Else your youth shall finde,
> Our nose not stuft, but we can take the winde,
> And smell you out.

210, 211. Juvenal, *Sat.* vii. 27, 'Frange miser calamos vigilataque proelia dele.'

213. *his dumbe candle.* Cf. the satire on 'a candle-waster', *C.R.* III. ii. 3, and 11, 12, and the amusing picture in *Satiro-mastix*, I. ii, of Jonson pumping up a lyric, '*Horace sitting in a study behinde a Curtaine, a candle by him burning, bookes lying confusedly*'.

214. *a more crowne.* *S.W.* I. ii. 20, 'a more portent'; *Cat.* IV. 688, 'for the more authoritie'.

219. *Ibides.* Holland's Pliny, *Natural History*, 1601, VIII. xxvii: 'The . . . device . . . of clystres, we learned first of a foule in . . . Ægypt, called Ibis (or the blacke Storke.) This bird having a crooked and hooked bill, vseth it in steed of a syringe or pipe, to squirt water into that part, whereby it is most kind and holsome to void the doung and excrements of meat, and so purgeth and cleanseth her bodie.'

225. *my next*, i.e. *Sejanus*.

228. *a theatre.* Seneca, *Epist.* I. vii. 11: 'Egregie . . . Epicurus cum uni ex consortibus studiorum suorum scriberet, "Haec", inquit, "ego non multis, sed tibi: satis enim magnum alter alteri theatrum sumus".' In Hamlet's advice to the actor (III. ii), the fool overdoing his part or acting inertly, 'cannot but make the judicious grieve; the censure of the which one must in your allowance overweigh a whole theatre of others'. Jonson may be echoing this.

'say, essay.

232, 239. Jonson's occasional alexandrine: *E.M.I.* II. i. 87 n.

234–5. From Juvenal's picture of a poet, *Sat.* vii. 28–9:

> Qui facis in parva sublimia carmina cella
> ut dignus venias hederis et imagine macra.

The ivy was sacred to Bacchus, god of inspiration: Horace, *Od.* I. i. 29, 'doctarum hederae praemia frontium'; Virgil, *Ecl.* vii. 25, 'Pastores, hedera crescentem ornate poetam'. *S. of N.* IV. ii. 176, *For.* x. 12.

238–9. Repeated in the 'Ode to Himself', *Und.* xxiii. 35–6.

SEJANUS

TIME INDICATIONS IN THE PLAY

IN his prefatory address 'To the Readers' (ll. 6, 7) Jonson admits that he has not observed 'the strict Lawes of *Time*'. The play covers several years of history. The death of Drusus (II. 479) took place in A.D. 23; the trial of Silius (III. 155–369) in A.D. 24; the trial of Cordus, which follows immediately in the play (III. 374–470), in A.D. 25. Titius Sabinus (IV. 115–232) was entrapped in A.D. 28, and Sejanus himself was overthrown in A.D. 31.

The first two acts are connected. In I. 352–4 Eudemus promises Sejanus a private meeting with Livia; the meeting opens Act II. In II. 9 the poisoning of Drusus is planned; in line 479 he is dying. In II. 285, 300, 303 Tiberius and Sejanus decide on the murder of Silius, Sosia, and Cordus. In 494 'They say, the *Senate* sit'.

The meeting of the Senate opens Act III. Silius is cited (155) and kills himself (339); Sosia is proscribed (356); Cordus is accused (373); the case is postponed till the next sitting (464). Sabinus is the 'next' to be destroyed (497). Tiberius is advised to leave Rome (582) and goes to Campania (630, 670).

At this point there is an interval. In IV. 43 Sejanus, who had accompanied his master to Campania, returns to Rome. Sabinus is trapped by informers (115–232). In line 244 Macro advises Caligula to go to Tiberius at Capreae; he goes with Macro (501–2). The younger Nero is arrested, as Caligula would have been, Drusus is confined to the Palace, and Agrippina banished (323–35). 'The night grows fast vpon vs' as the act closes (523).

There is another interval before Act V. In 53 'this morning' with the early calls of clients; so 'to-day' in line 58. Macro has returned (96); he had arrived about midnight (325). Another day passes; for the meeting of the Senate, at which Sejanus is to be overthrown, the watch is to be kept in arms 'when morning comes', and the Senate are to meet 'early' (149–51): 'Night hath many eyes' (169). These orders are carried out (288–90).

The day approaches of Sejanus' fall (368), and the Senate meets 'with the first light' (515). Sejanus is executed (805–6).

CHARACTER-TOUCHES

Jonson has taken scrupulous care in points of detail to knit the plot together and to keep the consistency of character. He strongly believed in the Horatian maxim,

> Servetur ad imum
> qualis ab incepto processerit,

and applied it with special force to the comedy of humours, in which the characters were stationary.

'Good cousin LATIARIS' (I. 21) is employed to entrap his kinsman Sabinus, who trusts him (IV. 110).

Sejanus tells his informer Posthumus, 'Giue ARRVNTIVS words Of malice against CAESAR' (II. 354–5); Tiberius, knowing what Arruntius thinks, marks him out for slaughter (III. 497), but Sejanus preserves him as a stalking-horse under cover of which they can attack others:

> His franke tongue
> Being lent the reines, will take away all thought
> Of malice, in your course against the rest.   (498–500.)

'AFER the oratour' (II. 418) plays a consistent part. His attack on Silius is 'Well worded, and most like an Orator' (III. 283), and Silius talks of his 'bloudying tongue' (328). Afer's 'eloquence' has secured other convictions (IV. 20–4).

Lepidus is 'graue and honest' (III. 367) and obtains a larger portion of Silius' forfeited estate for his children. Compare IV. 273–82.

Gallus, a friend of Agrippina, trims his sails, as he advises her to do (IV. 15). He joins in the attack on Silius (III. 294) and echoes the proposal to burn Cordus' books (469). But he does not deceive Tiberius:

> And GALLVS too (how ere he flatter vs,)
> His heart we know.   (III. 493–4.)

His fate is recorded, 'Feasted to day by CAESAR, since committed!' (IV. 236).

Tiberius mentions the odium he has incurred in promoting Sejanus; he tells Sejanus of it (III. 561–4), and in the famous letter to the Senate even more pointedly, that 'by his particular loue to one' he dared 'aduenture the hatred of all his other subiects' (V. 572–3). Of Sejanus' greatness we are told that his 'fortune is sworne by', and 'More altars smoke to him, then all the gods' (IV. 431–3); so his parasite Natta addresses him as 'the most diuine SEIANVS' and swears 'by his sacred fortune' (V. 42–3).

Swinburne's qualified praise of the 'laboured delineation' of Tiberius—his recorded words 'are wrought into the text, his traditional characteristics are welded into the action, with a patient and earnest fidelity which demands applause no less than recognition'—applies to the poet's careful study of the minor characters.[1]

THE SUMMONS BEFORE THE PRIVY COUNCIL

Drummond, in a confused note, reports Jonson as saying, 'Northampton was his mortall enimie for brauling on a St Georges day one of his attenders, he was called befor ye Councell for his Sejanus & accused both of popperie and treason by him' (*Conv. Dr.* 325–7). References to this accusation are found in the commendatory verses prefixed to the play in the Quarto. Hugh Holland appeals to 'great-Ones':

> Nor make your selues lesse honest then you are,
> To make our Author wiser then he is:
> Ne of such Crimes accuse him, which I dare
> By all his *Muses* sweare, be none of his.

And the anonymous *ΦΙΛΟΣ*, after praising the vividness of the action, says

> Yet some there be, that are not moou'd hereby,
> And others are so quick, that they will spy
> Where later Times are in some speech enweau'd—

men 'so vniust, they will deceaue themselues'.

'Popery' could not be detected in the play; this was no doubt a separate charge. So possibly was the charge of treason. But Chapman's commendatory poem evidently refers to the play being examined by the Privy Council, the members of which—Baron Ellesmere, Lord Chancellor, a patron of artists or, as Chapman puts it, 'fautor of all humane *skils*'; the Earl of Dorset, Lord High Treasurer; the Earls of Northumberland, Worcester, and Devonshire; 'Oraculous Salisburie', and 'Most Noble *Suffolke*'—he eulogizes; Suffolk in particular, who helped the authors when

> our Hearde, came not to drinke, but trouble
> The *Muses* waters.

We have quoted in our introductory essay (vol. ii, pp. 4, 5) one passage which Jonson himself found it expedient to tone down in the Folio—Silius' accusation that

> all best Turnes,
> With *Princes*, do conuert to iniuries—

[1] *A Study of Ben Jonson*, p. 27.

when they are too great to be requited (III. 302–10). The Folio
modified this to 'With doubtfull Princes'.

Speaking of his experience in cases of this kind, Jonson said in
the *Discoveries*, 1334–58, 'I have beene accus'd to the Lords, to the
King; and by great ones', and he tells one form which the accusations took: 'Nay, they would offer to urge mine owne Writings
against me; but by pieces, (which was an excellent way of malice)
as if any mans Context, might not seeme dangerous, and offensive,
if that which was knit, to what went before, were defrauded of his
beginning; or that things, by themselves utter'd, might not seeme
subject to Calumnie, which read entire, would appeare most free'
(ibid., 1351–8).

Here are some isolated extracts of this kind from *Sejanus*, extracts
on which an informer could fasten.

(1)   When men grow fast,
    Honor'd, and lou'd, there is a tricke in state
    (Which iealous princes neuer faile to vse)
    How to decline that growth, with faire pretext,
    And honourable colours of employment,
    Either by embassie, the war, or such,
    To shift them forth into another aire,
    Where they may purge, and lessen.   (I. 159–66.)

(2)   COR. Rarely dissembled. ARR. Prince-like, to the life.
                                                (Ibid. 395.)

(3) The prince, who shames a tyrannes name to beare,
    Shall neuer dare doe any thing, but feare;
    All the command of scepters quite doth perish
    If it beginne religious thoughts to cherish: . . .
    It is the licence of darke deeds protects
    Eu'n states most hated.   (II. 178–84.)

(4)   The way, to put
    A prince in bloud, is to present the shapes
    Of dangers, greater then they are (like late,
    Or early shadowes) and, sometimes, to faine
    Where there are none, onely, to make him feare;
    His feare will make him cruel.   (Ibid. 383–8.)

(5)   Excus'd
    Are wiser sou'raignes then, that raise one ill
    Against another, and both safely kill.   (III. 656–8.)

(6) The whole speech of Macro in III. 714–49 is a cynical profession of his readiness to commit any crime that Caesar suggests
to him.

(7)   The cause, sir? LAC. Treason. ARR. O?
The complement of all accusings? that
Will hit, when all else failes. (IV. 342–4.)

Historical writing came specially under the ban of the authorities.
To criticize the past was to reflect upon the present. A notable
victim was Sir John Hayward, who published in 1599 *The First
Part of the Life and Raigne of Henry IIII*. He was imprisoned for
it, and a second edition, which was called for within a year, was
burnt by order of the Bishop of London. The notes of Sir Edward
Coke, one of his judges, are among the State Papers, and here are
two of them:

'1 he selecteth a storie 200 yere olde, and publisheth it this last yere;
intendinge the application of it to this tyme
2 maketh choice of that story only, a king is taxed for misgovernm^t,
his councell for corrupt and covetous for their priuate, the king censured
for conferring benefits of hatefull parasites and fauorites, the nobles
discontented, the commons groning vnder continuall taxation. here-
vppon the king is deposed.'[1]

A deposition was a highly dangerous subject to discuss. When
Shakespeare's *King Richard II* was first published in quarto in 1597,
the deposition scene was omitted. And under Charles I taxation
could also be dangerous. In Massinger's lost play *The King and the
Subject*, 1638, Pedro, King of Spayne, was made to address his
subjects:

Monys? Wee'le rayse supplies what ways we please,
And force you to subscribe to blanks, in which
We'le mulct you as wee shall thinke fitt. The Caesars
In Rome were wise, acknowledginge no lawes
But what their swords did ratifye, . . .

King Charles read the manuscript at Newmarket, marked this passage, and said 'This is too insolent, and to bee changed'.[2]
Raleigh summed up the attitude of the authorities in the preface
to *The History of the World*, 1614, E4: 'I know that it will bee said
by many, That I might haue beene more pleasing to the Reader, if
I had written the Story of mine owne times; hauing beene permitted
to draw water as neare the Well-head as another. To this I answere,
that who-so-euer in writing a moderne Historie, shall follow truth
too neare the heeles, it may happily strike out his teeth. There is
no Mistresse or Guide, that hath led her followers and seruants into

---

[1] Quoted in Miss M. Dowling's article, 'Sir John Hayward's Troubles over
his Life of Henry IV', in *The Library*, Second Series, xi, pp. 212–24.
[2] Malone, *Variorum Shakespeare*, iii, p. 240.

greater miseries.' Even this history of a far past nearly suffered shipwreck. James the First ordered it to be suppressed. Raleigh had said of Henry the Eighth that 'if all the pictures and Patternes of a mercilesse Prince were lost in the World, they might all againe be painted to the life, out of the story of this King'. 'Too saucy in censuring princes' was James's verdict on this and other comments in Raleigh's survey of English history.

Now one of Tiberius' and Sejanus' victims is the historian Cremutius Cordus,

> A gentleman of *Rome*: one, that hath writ
> Annal's of late, they say, and very well.

So one informer Latiaris tells another, Pinnarius Natta:

> NAT. Annal's? of what times? LAT. I thinke of POMPEI's,
> And CAIVS CAESARS; and so downe to these.

'Those times', Natta comments, 'are somewhat queasie to be toucht'—and he notes down Cordus (I. 75–82). Sejanus, duly informed, reports to Tiberius:

> Then, there is one CREMVTIVS
> CORDVS, a writing fellow, they haue got
> To gather notes of the precedent times,
> And make them into Annal's; a most tart
> And bitter spirit (I heare) who, vnder colour
> Of praysing those, doth taxe the present state,
> Censures the men, the actions, leaues no tricke,
> No practice vn-examin'd, paralels
> The times, the gouernments, a profest champion
> For the old libertie— (II. 303–12.)

So, when he is accused by Satrius:

> I doe accuse thee here, CREMVTIVS CORDVS,
> To be a man factious, and dangerous,
> A sower of sedition in the state,
> A turbulent, and discontented spirit,
> Which I will proue from thine owne writings, here,
> The Annal's thou hast publish'd; where thou bit'st
> The present age, and with a viper's tooth,
> Being a member of it, dar'st that ill
> Which neuer yet degenerous bastard did
> Vpon his parent. (III. 379–88.)

Cordus defends himself in a speech borrowed from Tacitus, which Jonson would have pleaded if he had been attacked for writing it. As in Tacitus, Cordus' books are burnt:

It fits not such licentious things should liue
T' vpbraid the age.   (Ibid. 467–8.)

The only comment is that of Arruntius, 'If th'age were good, they might'. Jonson has been cautious at this point, but the way he has set forth the story of Cordus shows his standpoint unmistakably. In the Quarto, however, he added a sentence to the 'Argument', that the fate of Sejanus was 'a marke of Terror to all *Traytors*, & *Treasons*', and that God and the angels watched to guard the 'Piety and Vertue' of good princes, such as James the First.

Title-page

The motto is from Martial, x. iv. 9, 10.

Dedication

Esme L. Aubigny. Esmé Stuart, Seigneur d'Aubigné (1574–1624), the younger brother of the second Duke of Lennox, whom he succeeded in 1583, gave Jonson hospitality for five years (*Conv. Drum.* 254–5). *Epigram* cxxvii is a warm tribute to him, recording

How full of want, how swallow'd vp, how dead
I, and this *Muse* had beene, if thou hadst not
Lent timely succours, and new life begot.

A tribute to his wife is in *The Forest*, xiii, and an epithalamium on his sister's marriage to Hierome Weston is in *The Underwood*, lxxv.

To the Readers

6–15. Copied by Webster in the preface to *The White Divel*, 1612: 'If it be obiected this is no true Drammaticke Poem, I shall easily confesse it, *non potes in nugas dicere plura meos: Ipse ego quam dixi,* willingly, and not ignorantly, in this kind haue I faulted: for should a man present to such an Auditory, the most sententious Tragedy that euer was written, obseruing all the critticall lawes, as height of stile; and grauety of person; inrich it with the sententious *Chorus*, and as it were life'n Death, in the passionate and waighty *Nuntius*: yet after all this divine rapture, *O dura messorum ilia*, the breath that comes from the vncapable multitude, is able to poison it, and ere it be acted, let the Author resolue to fix to euery scene, this of *Horace*,

—Haec hodie Porcis comedenda relinques.'

8. *a proper Chorus . . . not any . . . since the Auntients.* Jonson had a craving to revive this feature of the Senecan drama: see the argument prefixed to *Mortimer*, and the actual attempt in *Catiline*. A classical chorus is found in Norton and Sackville's *Ferrex and Porrex*, 1562, Kyd's *Cornelia*, 1593, Daniel's *Cleopatra*, 1593, his *Philotas*, 1604, and the Earl of Sterling's *Darius*, 1603, and *Croesus*, 1604. Choruses which did not

conform to the classical type are in Peele's *David and Bethsabe*, 1594, Marlowe's *Faustus*, 1604, and Shakespeare's *King Henry V*, 1599.

16. *Obseruations upon Horace.* Written in Lord D'Aubigné's house (*Conv. Drum.* 85–8), and lost in Jonson's fire (*Und.* xliii. 89–91). In the dedication of *Volpone*, 123–4, Jonson hinted at its publication.

18. *truth of Argument.* Contrast Chapman's attitude in the dedication of *The Revenge of Bussy d'Ambois*, 1613, A3ᵛ, 'And for the autenticall truth of eyther person or action, who (worth the respecting) will expect it in a Poeme, whose subiect is not truth, but things like truth? Poore enuious soules they are that cauill at truths want in these naturall fictions: materiall instruction, elegant and sententious excitation to Vertue, and deflection from her contrary; being the soule, lims, and limits of an autenticall Tragedie.'

20. *Sentence*, the *sententia* of Roman rhetoricians, who applied the word to such general utterances as have a bearing on human life and action. These *sententiae* are frequent in Seneca; Jonson's use of them is discussed in our textual introduction, vol. iv, pp. 335–6. Jonson criticizes the improper use of them in *Disc.* 764, 1819.

26. *in some nice nostrill.* Marston's, for instance, who wrote in the preface to *The Tragedie of Sophonisba*, 1606, A, 'Know, that I haue not labored in this poeme, to tie my selfe to relate any thing as an historian, but to inlarge euery thing as a Poet. To transcribe Authors, quote authorities, & translate Latine prose orations into English blank[1]-verse, hath in this subiect beene the least aime of my studies.'

37. *English.* Richard Greneway's translation of *The Annales of Corn. Tacitus*, 1598 and four later editions. Jonson referred to this when he told Drummond 'The first four bookes of Tacitus ignorantly done jn Englishe' (*Conv. Dr.* 603).

39. *Tacit. Lips. C. Cornelii Taciti Opera quæ exstant. Iustus Lipsius postremùm recensuit. Additi Commentarii meliores pleniorésque, cum Curis secundis. Accessit seorsim C. Velleius Paterculus cum eiusdem Lipsi auctioribus notis. Antuerpiæ, Ex officina Plantiniana, Apud Ioannem Moretum.* cɪɔ ɪɔɔ. *Cum Priuilegijs Cæsareo & Regio.*

40. *Dio. Folio. ΤΩΝ ΔΙΩΝΟΣ ΤΟΥ ΚΑΣΣΙΟΥ ΡΩΜΑΙΚΩΝ ΙΣΤΟΡΙΩΝ βιβλία πέντε καὶ εἴκοσι. Dionis Cassii Romanorum Historiarum libri* xxv. *Ex Gulielmi Xylandri interpretatione.* [Latin couplets by Henri Estienne.] *Excudebat Henricus Stephanus anno M.D.XCII.*

600 . . . 92, i.e. 1600, 1592. For this clipped form of the date cf. *Alch.* IV. iv. 29, '*eighty-eight*' (the Armada year); *M. Augurs*, 123–4, 'that famous matter of *Englands joy* in sixe hundred and three'.

45. *a second Pen.* Chapman's: see vol. ii, pp. 3–5. In the commendatory poem which he contributed to the Quarto Chapman (ll. 220–3) praises the Earl of Suffolk:

> *Who when our Hearde, came not to drinke, but trouble*
> *The* Muses *waters, did a Wall importune,*
> (*Midst of assaults*) *about their sacred Riuer.*

[1] Misprinted 'blak-verse'.

In plain prose, there was trouble over the play, and Suffolk rescued the writers. In this passage of obscure allegory Chapman is evidently associating himself with Jonson.[1] It is plausible to conjecture, as Chapman's contribution to the play was omitted, that he wrote the passages which brought Jonson before the Privy Council. It is difficult to point to any other playwright whom Jonson would have complimented by saying that he had been forced to substitute 'weaker (and no doubt lesse pleasing)' work 'of mine own'. One absurd suggestion about the collaborator may be disposed of. In the *Athenaeum* of 1 May 1875 Dr. Brinsley Nicholson proposed the poetaster Samuel Sheppard, who in *The Times Displayed*, 1646, 6th Sestyard, p. 22, after praising Daniel, Shakespeare, and Drayton, continued:

Ben. Iohnson. So *His that Divine PLAUTUS equalled
Whose Commick vain MENANDER nere could hit,
Whose tragick sceans shal be with wonder Read
By after ages for unto his wit
My selfe gave personal ayd ⟨and⟩ *I* dictated
To him when as *Sejanus* fall he writ,
And yet on earth some foolish sots there bee
That dare make Randolf his Rival in degree.

But this is a speech put in the mouth of Apollo, and means, 'I, the god of song, verbally inspired him'.[2] In the same way in his *Epigrams*, 1651, G6, Sheppard makes Clio say of Spenser, 'I help'd the last to frame his Faerie Queen'.

51. Persius, *Satire* 1. 47–8, the context of which suggested Jonson's next words—

Sed recti finemque extremumque esse recuso
euge tuum et belle.

57. *Quem Palma . . .* Horace, *Epistles*, 11. i. 181. Marston in *Parasitaster*, v. i (1606, H3), has an echo of this passage:

So wee may . . . in the end close all the various errors
Of passages, most truly comicall,
In morall learning, with like confidence
Of him that vowde, good fortune of the sceane
Shall neither make him fat, or bad make leane.

The Argument

9. *before corrupted.* Historically true, but Jonson forgot that he had altered this: see vol. ii, p. 12.

16. *lets*, hindrances.

---

[1] F. G. Fleay first called attention to this passage: when the poem was prefixed to the 1616 Folio all the personal passage with the praise of the Privy Councillors was omitted.

[2] Pointed out by H. E. Rollins in *Studies in Philology*, xxiv, 1927, pp. 511–12, 'Samuel Sheppard and his Prais of Poets'.

24. *ingine. E.M.I.* v. iii. 115.

36. *a long doubtfull letter.* Juvenal's 'verbosa et grandis epistola'.

After 38 the Quarto has a sentence obviously added as a disclaimer of any treason that might be suspected in the subject of the play or Jonson's handling of it. The Quarto was entered on the Stationers' Register on 2 November 1604, before Gunpowder Plot. The two plots which Jonson may have had in mind would be 'that monstrous conspiracy' in 1600 of the Earl of Gowry in Scotland, as he called it in *The Haddington Masque*, 226, and the rising of the Earl of Essex in London in 1601. But, when the Quarto appeared, readers would naturally interpret the passage as a reference to Gunpowder Plot.

The Persons of the Play

1. *Tiberius* (I. 375, 395, 410).

2. *Drusus senior* (I. 105, 106, 112, 113), the son of Tiberius by his first wife Vipsania. The intrigue of Sejanus with his wife Livia is an important episode in the play; they poison him.

3. *Nero*, the eldest son of Germanicus and Agrippina, became heir to the throne when Drusus was poisoned. Sejanus plotted his ruin, and he was banished to the isle of Pontia (IV. 330), where he was starved to death.

4. *Drusus junior*, the second son of Germanicus and Agrippina. He was condemned along with his brother, but Tiberius kept him for some years in a small chamber in a lower part of the palace, intending to put him forward as a leader if Sejanus made any attempt to seize power (V. 153–60). Like his brother, he was starved to death.

5. *Caligula*, Caius Caesar (I. 114, 213), the youngest son of Germanicus, kept the favour of Tiberius by his abject submission, helped to murder him, and succeeded him as emperor.

6. *Lucius Arruntius* (I. 86), a man of high character, suspected by Tiberius of being 'rich and daring, brilliantly accomplished, and with a corresponding public reputation'; Augustus characterized him as 'well worthy' of the highest place, and 'likely to venture on it if the chance were offered him' (*Ann.* I. xiii). Tacitus talks of his 'stainless accomplishments' (ibid. VI. vii). He killed himself in A.D. 37, when he was the victim of an accusation of Macro.

Such was the man whom Jonson selected to comment on the action; he was honest and fearless. He plays somewhat the same part as Asper in *Every Man out of his Humour*.

7. *Gaius Silius* (I. 1, V. 245) served under Germanicus in Germany, and defeated Sacrovir in A.D. 21. Accused of extortion (for which there was justification) and treason in A.D. 24, he killed himself, but not in the Senate house, as Jonson dramatically rounds off his trial in III. 339.

8. *Titius Sabinus* (I. 1, 121; IV. 93; V. 245), a friend of Germanicus, entrapped by Latiaris, who posed as his friend. Jonson makes them cousins, in order to heighten the treachery.

9. *Manius Lepidus*, not Marcus, as Jonson, following Lipsius' text in

IV. 289, calls him. The abbreviated form of the praenomen is M', not M, which stands for Marcus. He was a man of high character, but did not forfeit the favour of Tiberius. Tacitus' eulogy of him is worked into the text at III. 366–8.

10. *Cremutius Cordus* (I. 73, II. 303–4, III. 371, V. 247), writer of a history of his own generation of which only a few fragments remain. His trial is given fully from Tacitus in III. 374–470. When he died Seneca wrote a treatise, *De Consolatione*, to his daughter Marcia. It gives details of his life which Jonson has worked into the play: he had given offence to Sejanus by his sharp sayings, one of which is quoted in I. 542–4.

11. *Gaius Asinius Gallus* (III. 493, IV. 235, V. 248) married Vipsania, the divorced wife of Tiberius. He showed some freedom in his speeches in the Senate; hence the comment in III. 295. In A.D. 30 Tiberius invited him to dinner and had him sentenced to death the same day; he lingered in prison for three years and then died of starvation.

12. *Publius Memmius Regulus* (IV. 439), so called by Jonson in V. 514, was consul in A.D. 31. He is described as an opponent of Sejanus in IV. 439–40. He may therefore be the Regulus casually mentioned as a member of Agrippina's circle (II. 220), though there is no evidence that he belonged to it. In this passage Professor Briggs has suggested Livineus Regulus mentioned in Tacitus' *Annals*, III. xi, as counsel for Piso who was charged with poisoning Germanicus; he also is not known to have been connected with Agrippina.

13. *Marcus Terentius* was a friend of Sejanus and accused on that account in A.D. 32. His spirited defence against the charge is given in Tacitus, *Annals*, VI. viii; it gained him an acquittal.

14. *Graecinus Laco* (IV. 323) was commander of the night-watch (*praefectus vigilum*) in A.D. 31. It was he who executed the dangerous task of taking Sejanus into custody.

15. *Eudemus* (I. 180), the paramour of Livia, with whom he plotted the poisoning of Drusus. When the crime was divulged, he was tortured to get evidence (*Ann.* IV. xi. 4) and killed.

16. *Petilius Rufus*, the betrayer of Sabinus in IV. 93–232.

17. *Lucius Aelius Seianus* (I. 202, 214), son of an *eques* of Volsinii in Etruria—'Borne but a priuate gentleman', III. 554; 'raysed from obscure . . . gentrie', V. 568—rose to the highest offices of state under Tiberius. Jonson follows his career closely. He was murdered on 18 October, A.D. 31.

18. *Latinius Latiaris* (I. 21) the betrayer of Sabinus, whom he entrapped under a mask of friendship. Jonson, to make the betrayal more repellent, calls him a cousin of Sabinus (I. 21, IV. 110).

19. *Lucius Visellius Varro*, consul in A.D. 24, attacked Gaius Silius.

20. *Naevius Sertorius Macro* (III. 647, 714), praetorian praefect, was the main agent in the overthrow of Sejanus. The part he plays in V. 657–89 is not historical. Actually he presented Tiberius' letter to the consul in the Senate and then withdrew to quell a mutiny of the prae-

torian guards who were jealous at the preference shown to the *vigiles*. But the prophecy of v. 750–3 was fulfilled. Arruntius, speaking before his death, described Macro as a worse Sejanus (*Ann.* VI. xlviii. 5). He secured the succession of Caligula, who had him killed with his wife and children.

21. *Cotta Messalinus*, a senator, joined in the attacks on Silius and on Cordus in Act III. He has a bad name in Tacitus, but Ovid, who writes to him from his exile at Tomi, praises him warmly.

22. *Domitius Afer* (II. 418) won the favour of Tiberius by prosecuting Claudia Pulchra, Agrippina's cousin, in A.D. 26 (IV. 21–4). But he did not, as Jonson represents him, take part in the prosecution of Silius (III. 156–317). His oratory is described satirically in II. 418–25, but it is noteworthy that Quintilian thought him the best orator he had ever heard (X. i. 118).

23. *Quintus Haterius*, a minor character in the play in which he is a commonplace satellite of Sejanus. In real life he was famous as an orator: the dictum of Augustus, which Jonson later applied to Shakespeare (*Disc.* 659), was 'Haterius noster sufflaminandus erat'—his oratory needed the drag-chain.

24. *Sanquinius* (V. 454), another minor character, of whom little is known owing to the gap in the text of Tacitus, but later he accused Arruntius (*Ann.* VI. vii. 1).

25. *Pomponius* (V. 400) is noticed with contempt along with Satrius by Tacitus (*Ann.* VI. viii. 10); he too must have been in the lost part of the *Annals*.

26. *Julius Posthumus* (II. 331), more correctly 'Postumus', as the Quarto spells the name—the paramour of Mutilia Prisca, and through her having access to Augusta, the Emperor's mother (II. 331–80).

27. *Lucius Fulcinius Trio*, a notorious informer. Tacitus writes his epitaph: 'celebre inter accusatores Trionis ingenium erat avidumque famae malae' (*Ann.* II. xxviii. 4). He was consul at the fall of Sejanus, whom he supported. He escaped by pretending great anxiety to bring Sejanus' accomplices to justice, but in A.D. 35 he was forced to suicide.

28. *Minutius* (IV. 410, V. 211), or Minucius Thermus, a friend of Sejanus, after whose fall he was denounced by Tiberius and condemned (Tacitus, *Ann.* VI. vii).

29, 30. *Satrius Secundus* and *Pinnarius Natta* (I. 22), two clients of Sejanus, who accused Cremutius Cordus (III. 374–5).

31. *Marcus Opsius* joined with Petilius Rufus in betraying Sabinus (IV. 93–232).

32. *Agrippina* (II. 190, 211; V. 250), granddaughter of Augustus and wife of Germanicus, a woman of high and fearless character; she had distinguished herself in Germany and in Asia. The accusations and intrigues to which she was exposed under Tiberius are fully set forth in the play. Her banishment to Pandataria is noted in IV. 335; she lived there three years and starved herself to death in A.D. 33.

33. *Livia*, or Livilla (I. 279, 340), sister of Germanicus and wife of

the elder Drusus, Tiberius' son, a leading figure in the earlier part of the play which treats of her seduction by Sejanus and her poisoning of her husband in A.D. 23. When this murder was revealed after Sejanus' death she was already dead (Tacitus, *Annals*, VI. ii. 1), but Jonson (in Act V. 875) evidently accepted the account of Dion Cassius that she was still alive and that her mother Antonia caused her to be starved to death when Tiberius spared her (LVIII. xi).

34. *Sosia Galla* (II. 300), the wife of Gaius Silius, involved in his fall in A.D. 24. Her friendship with Agrippina was the real motive for attacking her.

35 foll. *Praecones*, heralds; *Flamen*, priest; *Tubicines*, trumpeters; *Tibicines*, flute-players. *Nuntius*, messenger: see note before v. 833.

Jonson's historical notes printed in the margin of the Quarto were reprinted as an appendix to the text of the play in volume IV on pages 472–85. The Tacitus and Dion references are useless to a modern reader, as they follow the pagination of Lipsius' and Stephanus' editions. Professor Briggs incorporated the Quarto notes in his commentary, amplifying them and, where necessary, correcting them. Our own plan has been to write a brief note on all the characters in commenting on 'The Persons of the Play' and to add in brackets after each character's name line references to Jonson's historical or biographical notes. Where Jonson is indebted to the early texts, we have quoted the passages in full, prefixing an asterisk to the note. Two books which we have found helpful are Professor W. D. Briggs's edition of the play in Heath's Belles-Lettres series and Mr. H. Furneaux's edition of the *Annals* of Tacitus published by the Clarendon Press. In particular Professor Briggs has taken great pains to track out the classical borrowings in the play; we have used his record of some of these which we had overlooked.

I. 7. *shift of faces. Volp.* III. i. 21, of parasites: 'Make their reuennue out of legs, and faces.'

cleft tongues. Cf. v. 38–9, 'A tongue Forked as flatterie'.

11. *by slauerie, not by seruice.* *Tacitus, *Annals*, I. ii, 'Cum . . . ceteri nobilium, quanto quis servitio promptior, opibus et honoribus extollerentur'.

14. *owe vnto our crimes.* Jonson marks his indebtedness to Juvenal, *Sat.* i. 75; he had used it in *C.R.* III. iv. 52, quoting the Latin in the Quarto.

15. *We burne with no black secrets.* *Juvenal, iii. 49–57:

> Quis nunc diligitur nisi conscius et cui fervens
> aestuat occultis animus semperque tacendis?
> Nil tibi se debere putat, nil conferet unquam,
> participem qui te secreti fecit honesti;
> carus erit Verri qui Verrem tempore quo vult
> accusare potest. Tanti tibi non sit opaci
> omnis harena Tagi quodque in mare volvitur aurum,
> ut somno careas ponendaque praemia sumas
> tristis et a magno semper timearis amico.

20. *leane,* have a tendency. Unusual in this intransitive use without a preposition.

30–1. *cut Mens throates.* Juvenal, iv. 109–10:

> Saevior illo
> Pompeius tenui iugulos aperire susurro.

31–2. *sell . . . The emptie smoake.* Martial, iv. v. 7 (addressed to Fabianus, 'vir bonus et pauper linguaque et pectore verus'):

> vendere nec vanos circa Palatia fumos.

Cf. G. Whetstone, *A Mirour For Magestrates of Cyties,* 1584, f. 18*b,* Severus' punishment of Vetronius Turinus for bribery: 'That in the Market place, he should be bounde vnto a Stake, and with a Smoake of greene Stickes and wette Stubble, should be smoothred to death: And duryng the time of his execution, he commaunded a Bedell to crye:

> *With Fume let him die, that Fumes hath sold.'*

33–40. *From Juvenal, iii. 100–8:

> Rides, maiore cachinno
> Concutitur; flet si lacrimas conspexit amici,
> nec dolet; igniculum brumae si tempore poscas,
> accipit endromidem; si dixeris 'aestuo', sudat.
> Nocte dieque potest aliena sumere vultum
> a facie, iactare manus, laudare paratus
> si bene ructavit, si rectum minxit amicus,
> si trulla inverso crepitum dedit aurea fundo.

36. *his watch.* Gifford explained the cumbrous and not too accurate pocket-watch of Jonson's day, which had to be regulated by a public clock: cf. Dekker, *The Guls Horne-booke,* ch. iv (1609, D3ᵛ), 'Besides, you may heere haue fit occasion to discouer your watch by taking it forth, and setting the wheeles to the time of *Powles.*' But W. B. Mc-Daniel (*M.L.N.* xxviii. 5) rejects the anachronism and points out that the Romans had sundials and waterclocks, and signalled the hour, (1) either by a trumpet: Petronius, *Satyricon,* 26, 'Trimalchio lautissimus homo horologium in triclinio et bucinatorem habet subornatum ut subinde sciat quantum de vita perdiderit'; or (2) by a slave announcing the time: Martial, viii. lxvii. 1, 'Horas quinque puer nondum tibi nuntiat et tu | iam conviva mihi, Caeciliane, venis'.

37. *turkise.* Cf. John Swan, *Speculum Mundi,* 1635, p. 296: '*Turcois* is dark, of a skie colour, and greenish. It helpeth weak eyes and spirits, refresheth the heart; and, if the wearer of it be not well, it changeth colour and looketh pale and dim, but increaseth to his perfectnesse as the wearer recovereth to his health.

> *The sympathizing Turcois true doth tell,*
> *By looking pale, the wearer is not well.'*

(This is a misquotation of Donne's *An Anatomy of the World,* 343–4.)

41–55.* Literally from Tacitus, *Annals*, III. lxv. 2–4 (which Jonson cites): 'Ceterum tempora illa adeo infecta et adulatione sordida fuere, ut non modo primores civitatis, quibus claritudo sua obsequiis protegenda erat, sed omnes consularès, magna pars eorum qui praetura functi multique etiam pedarii senatores certatim exsurgerent foedaque et nimia censerent. Memoriae proditur Tiberium, quotiens curia egrederetur, Graecis verbis in hunc modum eloqui solitum "o homines ad servitutem paratos!" Scilicet etiam illum, qui libertatem publicam nollet, tam proiectae servientium patientiae taedebat.'

48. *Pedarij*. Usually explained of the section of the Senate which had not held a curule office and which gave a silent vote (as Jonson understands it): the evidence of Tacitus elsewhere goes to show that they were not precluded from speaking, but they would not be called on by the presiding magistrate so frequently as those who had held the higher offices.

60. *triumphed world*. *Cat.* III. 280, 'The farre-triumphed world'; Ovid, *Amores*, I. xv. 26, 'Roma triumphati caput orbis'.

67. *Our lookes . . . our wordes*. *Tacitus, I. vii. 11, of Tiberius: 'Verba vultus in crimen detorquens recondebat.' Briggs compares Massinger, *The Roman Actor*, I. i:

> So dangerous the age is, and such bad acts
> Are practis'd euery where, we hardly sleepe,
> Nay cannot dreame with safetie. All our actions
> Are cal'd in question, to be nobly born
> Is now a crime; and to deserve too well,
> Held Capital treason.

70–2. *Tyrannes artes . . .* Cf. *Disc.* 1158–60, 'A *Prince* should exercise his cruelty, not by himselfe, but by his Ministers: so hee may save himselfe, and his dignity with his people, by sacrificing those, when he list, saith the great *Doctor* of *State, Macchiavell*'.

77. The line could be made strictly metrical by writing 'I, I think of POMPEI'S', but there is a break and possibly a pause as in line 106, 'I like the prince well. ARR. A riotous youth', and II. 49, 'Ile tell his lordship. SEI. Who is't, EVDEMVS?'

80. *Drusian? or Germanican?* *Tacitus notes (II. xliii. 5) 'Divisa namque et discors aula erat tacitis in Drusum aut Germanicum studiis'. Germanicus died in A.D. 19, but the parties are represented as continuing.

90. *god-like Cato*. 'An attribute giuen to great persons, fitly aboue other humanity, and in frequent vse with all the greeke Poets, especially Homer', whose δῖος Ἀχιλλεύς is cited.—Jonson's note on *K. Ent.* 341.

96. *vnkindly*, unnaturally.

captiue. In very common use in 16th–18th centuries as a verb. Originally pronounced *captive*, as still in Milton (*O.E.D.*).

104. *the last of all that race*. Words used by Brutus himself at the death of Cassius (Plutarch, *Brutus*, xliv), and familiar to English readers from Shakespeare's *Julius Caesar*, V. iii. 99.

106. *A riotous youth.* *Suetonius, *Tiberius*, lii, 'Filiorum neque naturalem Drusum neque adoptivum Germanicum patria caritate dilexit ⟨Tiberius⟩, alterius vitiis infensus. Nam Drusus fluxioris remissiorisque vitae erat.'

109. *nobly*, the syllabic *l* makes the word a trisyllable.

112. *opposing to.* Bacon, *The Advancement of Learning*, II. xi. 3, 'If it be admitted that imagination hath power, and that Ceremonies fortify imagination, . . . yet I should hold them unlawful, as opposing to that first edict which God gave unto man'. 'Resist to', 'obey to' are also found. They copy the usage of the Latin dative.

121. *Sabinus, and my selfe.* *Tacitus (IV. 18) says of this pair 'Amicitia Germanici perniciosa utrique'.

124. *a man most like to vertue.* Jonson has transferred to Drusus Velleius Paterculus' character of Cato (II. 35), 'Homo virtuti simillimus et per omnia ingenio dis quam hominibus propior'.

128–54. *Worked up from Tacitus, II. 72–3, which Jonson cites: 'Induluere exterae nationes regesque: tanta illi comitas in socios, mansuetudo in hostes; visuque et auditu iuxta venerabilis, cum magnitudinem et gravitatem summae fortunae retineret, invidiam et adrogantiam effugerat. Funus sine imaginibus et pompa per laudes ac memoriam virtutum eius celebre fuit. Et erant qui formam aetatem genus mortis, ob propinquitatem etiam locorum in quibus interiit, magni Alexandri fatis adaequarent. Nam utrumque corpore decoro, genere insigni, haud multum triginta annos egressum suorum insidiis externas inter gentes occidisse: sed hunc mitem erga amicos modicum voluptatum uno matrimonio certis liberis egisse, neque minus proeliatorem, etiam si temeritas afuerit praepeditusque sit perculsas tot victoriis Germanias servitio premere. Quod si solus arbiter rerum, si iure et nomine regio fuisset, tanto promptius adsecuturum gloriam militiae quantum clementia temperantia ceteris bonis artibus praestitisset.'

132. *In images, and pompe.* At a Roman funeral the images of the deceased and his ancestors, painted masks usually kept in the lararium, were carried before the corpse; they were worn by relatives. As Drusus died at Antioch, these family emblems could not be sent there from Rome.

141. *Year'd . . . to thirty.* The *O.E.D.* quotes 'twice yeared' (two years old) from a letter of Lord Burleigh.

142. *alike made away.* There is no clear proof that Drusus was poisoned. An absurd version of Alexander's death is that he fell a victim to poison administered by his son and concocted by Aristotle and Antipater.

153–4. *Which, parted . . . Flow'd mixt in him.* Briggs quotes Claudian, *De Consulatu Stilichonis*, i. 33–5:

> sparguntur in omnes,
> In te mixta fluunt, et quae diversa beatos
> efficiunt collecta tenes.

158. *and that they knew.* *Tacitus, II. v: 'Ceterum Tiberio haud ingratum accidit turbari res orientis ut ea specie Germanicum suetis

legionibus abstraheret novisque provinciis impositum dolo simul ac casibus obiectaret.'

167. *second's,* seconders. The chief agent was Gnaeus Calpurnius Piso, consul with Tiberius in 7 B.C., who conferred upon him the command in Syria when Germanicus went to the East in A.D. 18.

168. *damme.* Livia, who married Augustus as her second husband.

175. *Sejanus.* Tacitus sketches his character in the passage cited, *Annals,* IV. i, ii.

183. *Fiftie sestertia,* 50,000 sesterces. Jonson notes, '£375 of our money'.

187. *well like off.* Greene, *Orlando Furioso,* I. i (1599, A4ᵛ), 'Daughter like of whome thou please'.

195. *griefe,* ailment. Cf. lines 276, 294, 338.

199–201. *when men . . . liuing.* Juvenal, *Sat.* viii. 83–4:

> Summum crede nefas animam praeferre pudori
> et propter vitam vivendi perdere causas.

208. *Rhadamanth. Poet.* III. i. 146–9.

212–37. *From the notice of Sejanus in Tacitus, *Ann.* IV. i, ii: 'Genitus Vulsiniis patre Seio Strabone equite Romano et prima iuventa Gaium Caesarem divi Augusti nepotem sectatus, non sine rumore Apicio diviti et prodigo stuprum veno dedisse, mox Tiberium variis artibus devinxit, adeo ut obscurum adversum alios sibi uni incautum intectumque efficeret, non tam sollertia (quippe isdem artibus victus est) quam deum ira in rem Romanam, cuius pari exitio viguit ceciditque. Corpus illi laborum tolerans, animus audax; sui obtegens, in alios criminator; iuxta adulatio et superbia; palam compositus pudor, intus summa apiscendi libido, eiusque causa modo largitio et luxus, saepius industria ac vigilantia, haud minus noxiae quotiens parando regno finguntur.

'Vim praefecturae modicam antea intendit, dispersas per urbem cohortes una in castra conducendo, ut simul imperia acciperent, numeroque et robore et visu inter se fiducia ipsis, in ceteros metus oreretur. Praetendebat lascivire militem diductum; si quid subitum ingruat, maiore auxilio pariter subveniri; et severius acturos si vallum statuatur procul urbis illecebris. Ut perfecta sunt castra, irrepere paulatim militares animos adeundo, appellando; simul centuriones ac tribunos ipse deligere.'

215. *Apicius.* M. Gabius Apicius, the supreme epicure of his age; after squandering eight hundred thousand pounds on good living, he balanced his books, and finding only eighty thousand left, killed himself.

216. *pathick,* catamite. Drayton, *The Moone-Calfe,* 306–8 (*Works,* ed. Hebel, iii, p. 174):

> He lookes like one for the preposterous sin,
> Put by the wicked and rebellious Jewes,
> To be a Pathique in their Malekind Stewes.

217. *the second face.* *Juvenal, x. 63, 'ex facie toto orbe secunda'.

225. *One, and his house.* Briggs compares Claudius, *In Rufinum*, i. 193–4:

> Congestae cumulantur opes orbisque ruinas
> accipit una domus.

249. *they are three.* Sejanus, says Tacitus, plotted after the death of Drusus how to overthrow the sons of Germanicus: 'neque spargi venenum in tres poterat' (*Ann.* iv. xii. 4).

257. *atomi, to' vndoe.* The Latin form, *atomus* (sing.), *atomi* (plur.), was the one chiefly in use in the sixteenth century. Cf. Marston, *The Scourge of Villanie*, Sat. vii (1598, F2ᵛ), 'His very soule . . . Is not so big as in an *Atomus*'. Jonson has it in *Ep.* cxxxiii. 127, but '*Atomes*' in *F.I.* 190. F2, which modernized, dropped the metrical apostrophe: '*atomes*, to undoe'.

285. *feare no colours.* A quibble on the military sense 'fear no foe'. Cotgrave, 1611, '*Aduentureur*. Hazardous, aduenturous; that feares no colours.'

286. *conceited*, witty. *E.M.I.* iii. ii. 29.

300. *the only cabinets.* *Tac., *Ann.* iv. iii. 5, 'Eudemus, amicus ac medicus Liviae, specie artis frequens secretis'.

305. *violet.* The mock-refinement of the epithet deepens its irony.
siege, evacuation.

307. *sleepes with her owne face.* *C.R.* iv. i. 146.

314. *intergatories.* *C.R.* iv. iv. 11.
but, only, merely.

343. *iealous*, suspicious.
Happily, haply. Eudemus is mentioned as a go-between in this intrigue by Pliny, *Nat. Hist.* xxix. 20.

359. *apozems*, decoctions or infusions.

363–5. *Fortune . . . wishes.* From Lucan, *Pharsalia*, v. 581–3, Caesar of himself:

> quem numina nunquam
> destituunt, de quo male tum fortuna meretur
> cum post vota venit.

375 (margin). *One kneeles to him.* Gifford identified as Haterius because of the story in Tacitus, i. xiii, that Haterius entered the palace and flung himself at Tiberius' feet; he was almost killed by the guard because Tiberius tripped over him. Cf. line 388.

*Tiberius' rejection of flattery is vividly recorded by Suetonius, *Life*, xxvii: 'Adulationes adeo aversatus est ut neminem senatorum aut officii aut negotii causa ad lecticam suam admiserit, consularem vero satisfacientem sibi ac per genus orare conantem ita suffugerit ut caderet supinus; atque etiam si quid in sermone vel in continua oratione blandius de se diceretur non dubitaret interpellare et reprehendere et commutare continuo.'

376. *axes, rods*, the *fasces*, bundles of rods with axes tied up in the middle of them, carried before the chief magistrates.

381–3. From Juvenal, *Sat.* iv. 70–1:

> Nihil est quod credere de se
> non possit cum laudatur dis aequa potestas.

383. COR. Briggs notes the inconsistency of this speech of Cordus with his next comment 'Rarely dissembled' (l. 395) and suggests that Cotta was the speaker here, prefixing 'COT.' for 'COR.'.

389–94. *Tacitus, 11. lxxxvii, 'Acerbeque increpuit eos qui divinas occupationes ipsumque dominum dixerant', and *Suetonius, *Tiberius*, xxvii, 'Dominus appellatus a quodam, denuntiavit ne se amplius contumeliae causa nominaret'.

396–7. Briggs compares *Disc.* 1110–15, '*Mores Aulici*'.—'I have discovered, that a fain'd familiarity in great ones, is a note of certaine usurpation on the lesse. For great and popular men, faine themselves to bee servants to others, to make those slaves to them. So the Fisher provides baits for the Trowte, Roch, Dace, &c. that they may be food to him.'

407–9. From Claudian, *De Consulatu Stilichonis*, III. 113–15:

> Fallitur egregio quisquis sub principe credit
> servitium. Nunquam libertas gratior exstat
> quam sub rege pio.

413. *strokes, and stripes. Ep.* lxi.

417. *like a pitcher.* Cf. Plutarch, *De Vitioso Pudore*, xviii, of people easily led by flatterers: διὸ καὶ Βίων ἀπείκαζε τοὺς τοιούτους ἀμφορεῦσιν ἀπὸ τῶν ὤτων ῥᾳδίως μεταφερομένοις. So Chapman, *May-Day*, III. ii (1611, pp. 42–3): 'An arrant Rooke by this light; a capable cheating stocke; a man may carry him vp and downe by the eares like a pipkin.'

427. *Palace-rattes.* Jonson's vague reference to Sextus Aurelius Victor cannot be traced. But the Emperor Constantine 'spadonum & aulicorum omnium vehemens domitor fuit, quos tineas & sorices Palatii appellare solitus erat' (Langius' translation of Nicephorus Callistus, *Historia Ecclesiastica*, 1588), note p. 451. Cf. *S. of N.* IV. iv. 142, in contrast with a worthy courtier 'This is a moth, a rascall, a Court-rat'.

bane, ratsbane, arsenic.

437–8. *Of all wilde beastes . . .* Plutarch, *De Adulatore et Amico*, xix, attributes this saying to Bias, ὅθεν οὐδὲ ὁ Βίας ἀπεκρίνατο καλῶς τῷ πυθομένῳ τί τῶν ζῴων χαλεπώτατόν ἐστιν, ἀποκρινάμενος ὅτι τῶν μὲν ἀγρίων ὁ τύραννος, τῶν δὲ ἡμέρων ὁ κόλαξ. In the *Septem Sapientum Convivium*, ii, it is attributed to Thales, who denies it and ascribes it to Pittacus.

440–6. *From Suetonius, *Tiberius*, xxix (as Jonson notes): 'Dixi et nunc et saepe alias, patres conscripti, bonum et salutarem principem, quem vos tanta et tam libera potestate instruxistis, senatui servire debere et universis civibus saepe et plerumque etiam singulis; neque id dixisse me paenitet, et bonos et aequos et faventes vos habui dominos et adhuc habeo.'

441. *instructed,* provided, equipped ('instruxistis' in Tacitus). *S.W.* IV. iv. I.

442. *dilate*, extended (Lat. *dilatus*).

451. *preuent*, anticipate.

454–502. Closely translated from *Tacitus, IV. xxxvii, xxxviii: 'Per idem tempus Hispania ulterior missis ad senatum legatis oravit ut exemplo Asiae delubrum Tiberio matrique eius exstrueret. Qua occasione Caesar, validus alioqui spernendis honoribus et respondendum ratus iis quorum rumore arguebatur in ambitionem flexisse, huiusce modi orationem coepit: "Scio, patres conscripti, constantiam meam a plerisque desideratam quod Asiae civitatibus nuper idem istud petentibus non sim adversatus. Ergo et prioris silentii defensionem et quid in futurum statuerim simul aperiam. Cum divus Augustus sibi atque urbi Romae templum apud Pergamum sisti non prohibuisset, qui omnia facta dictaque eius vice legis observem, placitum iam exemplum promptius secutus sum quia cultui meo veneratio senatus adiungebatur. Ceterum ut semel recepisse veniam habuerit, ita omnes per provincias effigie numinum sacrari ambitiosum, superbum; et vanescet Augusti honor si promiscuis adulationibus vulgatur. Ego me, patres conscripti, mortalem esse et hominum officia fungi satisque habere, si locum principem impleam, et vos testor et meminisse posteros volo; qui satis superque memoriae meae tribuent ut maioribus meis dignum, rerum vestrarum providum, constantem in periculis, offensionum pro utilitate publica non pavidum credant. Haec mihi in animis vestris templa, hae pulcherrimae effigies et mansurae. Nam quae saxo struuntur, si iudicium posterorum in odium vertit, pro sepulchris spernuntur. Proinde socios cives et deos ipsos precor, hos ut mihi ad finem usque vitae quietam et intellegentem humani divinique iuris mentem duint, illos ut quandoque concessero cum laude et bonis recordationibus facta atque famam nominis mei prosequantur."' The final words are later in the speech: 'Cetera principibus statim adesse: unum insatiabiliter parandum, prosperam sui memoriam; nam contemptu famae contemni virtutes.'

502. For this aphorism of Tacitus Jonson showed a marked preference: he repeats it, *M. Queens*, 730, *G.M.* 1432–3, *Chl.* 292–5.

508. *Antium*, Porto d'Anzio. The statue of *Fortuna equestris* was given by the Equites Romani; there was at Rome no temple of Fortune under this aspect, and Antium was specially associated with the worship of this goddess: 'O diva, gratum quae regis Antium', Horace, *Odes*, I. xxxv. 1.

512. *the Æmilian place.* Tacitus, III. lxxii, 'Isdem diebus Lepidus ab senatu petivit ut basilicam Pauli, Aemilia monumenta, propria pecunia firmaret ornaretque'. 'Basilica' suggests that Jonson may have written 'palace' as a literal equivalent, though the basilica was a court of justice.

515. *th'other Is'le Cithera.* Jonson follows an old correction of the MS. reading 'Cythenum' in Tacitus, *Ann.* III. lxix. 8. The true correction, however, is 'Cythnum', i.e. Thermia in the Cyclades, near the 'other isle' of Gyaros, a well-known place of exile under the early empire. Tiberius sanctioned the change, according to Tacitus, on the ground that Gyaros 'immitem et sine cultu hominum esse'.

516. *religious sister*, Torquata, a vestal virgin.

520. *Pompei's theatre*, the greatest and the first permanent building of this kind in Rome, built by Pompeius after his second consulship in 55 B.C. For Sejanus' statue there see v. 28–30.

537–40. Echoed by Fuller, *The Holy State*, IV. i, maxim vi: 'But princes have their grounds reared above the flats of common men; and who will search the reasons of their actions must stand on an equal basis with them.'

542. *was never ruin'd.* *From Seneca, *Ad Marciam de Consolatione*, xxii. 4, 5: 'Decernebatur illi statua in Pompeii theatro ponenda, quod exustum Caesar reficiebat. Exclamavit Cordus tunc vere theatrum perire. Quid ergo? Non rumperetur supra cineres Cn. Pompeii constitui Seianum et in monumentis maximi imperatoris consecrari perfidum militem?'

551. *riuall*, partner. Cf. *Hamlet*, I. i. 13, 'The rivals of my watch', where the Quarto of 1605 has in the corresponding line 'The partners'.

551–9. *From comments of Drusus quoted in Tacitus, *Annales*, IV. vii, 2: 'crebro querens incolumi filio adiutorem imperii alium vocari. Et quantum superesse ut collega dicatur? Primas dominandi spes in arduo: ubi sis ingressus, adesse studia et ministros. . . . Precandam post haec modestiam ut contentus esset.'

564. *lift.* Used of a ship riding the waves or of a horse rearing: see *O.E.D.* s.v. 3 and 3*e*.

565. *Take that.* *Tacitus, *Ann.* IV. iii: 'Drusus impatiens aemuli et animo commotior orto forte iurgio intenderat Seiano manus et contra tendentis os verberaverat.' Dion, on the other hand, represents Sejanus as having struck Drusus out of sheer insolence.

568. *dull camell.* *E.M.I.* III. i. 38.

575. *A Castor.* Whalley quotes Xiphilinus, ed. Stephanus, 1551, p. 104, of Drusus, τῇ μέντοι ὀργῇ οὕτω χαλέπῃ ἐχρῆτο ὥστε καὶ πληγὰς ἱππεῖ ἐπιφανεῖ δοῦναι, καὶ διὰ τοῦτο καὶ Κάστωρ παρωνύμιον ἔλαβε.

576–9. From Seneca, *Medea*, 150–4:

> Sile, obsecro, questusque secreto abditos
> manda dolori. Gravia quisquis vulnera
> patiente et aequo mutus animo pertulit,
> referre potuit: ira quae tegitur nocet;
> professa perdunt odia vindictae locum.

580. *practice*, treachery.

582. *Chorus—Of Musicians.* For music between the acts see Marston, *The Wonder of Women*, 1606: at the end of Act I, 'the *Cornets* and *Organs* playing loud full Musicke for the Act'; after Act II, '*Organ* mixt with Recorders for this Act'; after Act III, 'Organs, Violls and Voices *play for this Act*'; after Act IV, 'A Base Lute and a Treble Violl *play for the Act*'; after Act V, '*Cornets a short florish*'. In Middleton's *The Phœnix*, 1607, acted by the children of Paul's, at the end of Act II, sig. F3, '*Towards the close of the Musick, the Iustices three men prepare for the robberie*'.

11. 5. *like*, equal, adequate.

11. *abled*. Cf. 'vn-abled', *S.W.* v. iv. 46.

13. *an Eunuch Drusus loues*. *Tacitus, Ann.* iv. x, 'is aetate atque forma carus domino interque primores ministros erat'. As the cup-bearer of a prince, he would taste the wine before his master.

17. *free accesse, and trust*. Briggs compares Seneca, *Oedipus*, 686: 'Aditum nocendi perfido praestat fides.'

36. *among the lesser lights*. Horace, *Odes*, I. xii. 46–8:

> Micat inter omnes
> Iulium sidus velut inter ignes
> luna minores.

48. *Illustrous*. *C.R.* III. iv. 96.

63. *ceruse*, a cosmetic of white lead. *E.M.I.* IV. viii. 113.

74. *addition*, title. *King Lear*, I. i. 138–9, 'Only we shall retain the name, and all th'addition to a king'.

79. *dentifrice*. *Cat.* II. 146 n.

89, 90. *discouerie Of all his counsells*. *Tacitus, Ann.* IV. vii. 4, 'Secreta quoque eius corrupta uxore prodebantur'.

93. *without your sexe*. *C.R.* I. iv. 55.

98. *strike the stars*. So 'hit the starres', Ode on *The New Inn*, 58. A classical hyperbole: cf. Horace, *Odes*, I. i. 36, 'Sublimi feriam sidera vertice'.

108. *so prepare the poyson*. *Tacitus, IV. viii: 'Igitur Seianus maturandum ratus deligit venenum quo paulatim irrepente fortuitus morbus assimularetur.'

123. *made*, prepared, primed. *E.M.I.* IV. xi. 46.

127. *cutis*. The earliest example in the *O.E.D.*, which quotes Massinger, *The Bondman*, IV. iv, 'Your ten-crown amber possets good to smooth the cutis, as you call it'. Jonson generally says 'skin', but this deviation is to suit his Roman play.

137. *vse my fortune . . . with reuerence*. Ausonius, *Ep.* viii. 7, 8:

> Fortunam reverenter habe quicumque repente
> dives ab exili progrediere loco.

Jonson affected the phrase: *Volp.* III. vii. 88–9, *N.I.* v. ii. 58, *Pr. Henry's Barriers*, 405–6, *Und.* xxvi. 23.

140–1. *Ægyptian . . . Parthians*, in reference to the abject homage of orientals. Virgil, *Georgic*, IV. 210–12, of the queen-bee:

> Praeterea regem non sic Aegyptos et ingens
> Lydia, nec populi Parthorum . . . Observant.

For the fame of the Egyptians as bearers of burdens see Aristophanes, *Frogs*, 1406; they built the Pyramids.

141. *bare-foot Hebrewes*. Juvenal, *Sat.* vi. 159, 'Observant ubi festa mero pede sabbata reges.'

150–6. Pieced together from Seneca, *Thyestes*, 25–7, 44–7, 192–5:

Certetur omni scelere et alterna vice
stringatur ensis; ne sit irarum modus
pudorve. . . .
Effusus omnes irriget terras cruor,
supraque magnos gentium exultet duces
Libido victrix: impia stuprum in domo
levissimum sit facinus.
Age, anime, fac quod nulla posteritas probet,
sed nulla taceat. Aliquod audendum est nefas
atrox, cruentum, tale quod frater meus
suum esse mallet.

162. *'Primus in orbe deos fecit timor', Petronius fragm. 27, Statius, *Thebais*, iii. 661.

165. *When the master-prince* . . . Jonson refers to Suetonius, *Tiberius*, 55, probably, as W. D. Briggs suggests, to the concluding comment about Sejanus, 'quem ad summam potentiam non tam benevolentia provexerat quam ut esset cuius ministerio ac fraudibus liberos Germanici circumveniret'.

The dialogue in this interview closely follows the tyrants' maxims of Seneca's *Thyestes* and *Phoenissae*.

170–2. *That nature* . . . Seneca, *Thyestes*, 214–18:

Atr. Ubicumque tantum honesta dominanti licent,
precario regnatur. *Sat.* Ubi non est pudor
nec cura iuris sanctitas pietas fides,
instabile regnum est. *Atr.* Sanctitas pietas fides
privata bona sunt, qua iuvat reges eant.

174. Seneca, *Oedipus*, 703–4:

Cr. Sic odia fiunt. *Oed.* Odia qui nimium timet
regnare nescit: regna custodit metus.

and *Phoenissae*, 654:

Regnare non vult esse qui invisus timet.

178–85. Lucan, *Pharsalia*, viii. 489–95:

Sceptrorum vis tota perit si pendere iusta
incipit, evertitque arces respectus honesti.
Libertas scelerum est quae regna invisa tuetur,
sublatusque modus gladiis. Facere omnia saeve
non impune licet, nisi cum facis. Exeat aula
qui vult esse pius. Virtus et summa potestas
non coeunt; semper metuet quem saeva pudebunt.

W. D. Briggs has pointed out in *Anglia*, xxxix, pp. 247–8, that a first draft of these lines, headed 'A Speech out of Lucan', translating also lines 484–8, is in Harley MS. 4064 on f. 243. A slightly better copy is in Rawlinson Poetry MS. 31 on f. 18. Printed in *U.V.* l.

Note the rhyme here and lines 190–209, 239–77; so III. 625–60, 714–49, v. 1–24: it is expressive of strong emotion.

186–7. Cf. *Mortimer*, I. i. 24–8.

196. *iealous*, suspicious.

197. 'I.e., who rather than fail of proof, would believe the mere evidence of their own thoughts' (Whalley).

198–9. Cf. the proverb νήπιος ὃς πατέρα κτείνας υἱοὺς καταλείπει, quoted in Aristotle, *Rhetoric*, i. 15.

206. *secure*, careless (Lat. *securus*).

None swiftlier . . . Velleius Paterculus, II. cxviii. 2, of Arminius: 'Segnitia ducis in occasionem sceleris usus est, haud imprudenter speculatus neminem celerius opprimi quam qui nihil timeret et frequentissimum initium esse calamitatis securitatem.'

209. *All power's to be feared* . . . From Tacitus, *Histories*, II. xcii, 'Nec unquam satis fida potentia ubi nimia est'.

211. *male-spirited dame*. *Tacitus, *Ann*. I. xxxiii. 6, speaks of her 'indomitus animus' and her courage in saving the bridge over the Rhine in A.D. 15 which secured the retreat of the Roman army ('femina ingens animi', ibid. lxix). In describing her death (VI. xxv. 3) he notes her 'masculine aspirations' ('viriles curae').

220. *Furnius* put to death in A.D. 26 on a charge of adultery with Claudia Pulchra, Agrippina's cousin (IV. lii. 2).

Regulus. See the notes on 'The Persons of the Play' (p. 594).

223. *niece*, granddaughter, like the Latin *neptis*.

235–6. *with hope Of future freedome*. Briggs compares the section 'Vulgi expectatio' in *Disc*. 405–12: '*Expectation* of the *Vulgar* is more drawne, and held with newnesse, then goodnesse; we see it in *Fencers*, in *Players*, in *Poets*, in *Preachers*, in all, where *Fame* promiseth any thing; so it be new, though never so naught, and depraved, they run to it, and are taken. Which shewes, that the only decay, or hurt of the best mens *reputation* with the people, is, their wits have out-liv'd the peoples palats. They have beene too much, or too long a feast.'

252. *detect*, reveal, uncover (Lat. *detego*).

257–9. *Nought is more high* . . . From Juvenal, *Sat*. vi. 284–5:

Nihil est audacius illis
deprensis; iram atque animos a crimine sumunt.

265. *Fautors*, supporters (Lat. *fautores*).

273. *wolues doe change their haire*. A Greek proverb: ὁ λύκος τὴν τρίχα, οὐ τὴν γνώμην ἀλλάττει (Erasmus, *Adagia*, ed. Stephanus, 1558, col. 801).

274–5. *While thus your thought* . . . Tacitus, *Histories*, III. xl. 4, 'Mox utrumque consilium aspernatus, quod inter ancipitia deterrimum est, dum media sequitur, nec ausus est satis nec providit'.

277. *The subiect* . . . Seneca, *Thyestes*, 205–7:

Maximum hoc regni bonum est,
quod facta domini cogitur populus sui
tam ferre quam laudare.

284. *clickt all his marble thumb's.* Jonson's quotations in his Latin note explain his curious metaphor. A gesture of the spectators in the amphitheatre decided the fate of a conquered gladiator; the upturned thumb meant death, the thumb turned down meant mercy. See A. S. Wilkins on Horace, *Ep.* i. xviii. 66, the passage quoted by Jonson.

286–95. *Tacitus, *Ann.* iv. xviii. 1: 'Qua causa ⟨Seianus⟩ C. Silium et Titium Sabinum adgreditur. Amicitia Germanici perniciosa utrique. Silio et quod ingentis exercitus septem per annos moderator partisque apud Germaniam triumphalibus Sacroviriani belli victor, quanto maiore mole procideret, plus formidinis in alios dispergebatur.'

289. *Sacrovir* headed a rebellion in north-eastern Gaul in A.D. 21.

296–300. Tacitus, *Ann.* iv. xix. 1, 'Erat uxor Silio Sosia Galla, caritate Agrippinae invisa principi. Hos corripi dilato ad tempus Sabino placitum'.

313–16. *As if there were that chaos* . . . Cf. *Cat.* iv. 480–8. Adapted from the words of Julius Caesar to Metellus in Lucan, iii. 137–40:

> Te vindice tuta relicta est
> libertas? Non usque adeo permiscuit imis
> longus summa dies ut non, si voce Metelli
> serventur leges, malint a Caesare tolli.

322–4. *Counsels are vnfit* . . . Cf. Tacitus, *Histories*, i. xxi. 5, 'Opportunos magnis conatibus transitus rerum, nec cunctatione opus ubi perniciosior sit quies quam temeritas'. A similar thought in *Cat.* iii. 492–4.

330. 'Εμοῦ θανόντος . . . Milton translated the line in *The Reason of Church Government*, i, ch. v, 'When I dye, let the Earth be roul'd in Flames'. Cunningham aptly compared Louis XIV's 'Après moi le déluge'.

331. *Iulius Posthumus.* *Tacitus, *Ann.* iv. xii. 6: '(Seianus) delegerat Iulium Postumum, per adulterium Mutiliae Priscae inter intimos aviae' (i.e. Augustae) 'et consiliis suis peridoneum, quia Prisca in animo Augustae valida anum suapte natura potentiae anxiam insociabilem nurui efficiebat.'

342–3. *t'extoll The hospitable ladie.* *Ibid. 7, 'Agrippinae quoque proximi illiciebantur pravis sermonibus tumidos spiritus perstimulare'.

349. Jonson's Latin note: '*in animum Augustae valida*' should be '*in animo*'.

350–1. *the words* . . . *of Silius.* Utilized in iii. 272–82.

357. *infinite pride.* *Tacitus, ibid. 5: 'Igitur contumaciam eius insectari . . . ut superbam facundiatte, subnixam popularibus studiis inhiare dominatione apud Caesarem arguerent.'

359. *popular studies*, the devotion of the people.

361–2. *pub- | lique.* So *Oberon*, 202, 'ridge- | Bones'; *G.M.* 1255, 'vnder- | stand'; *M. Owls*, 168, 'whis- | per'; *A.P.* 20, 'bor- | dring'; *Und.* lxx. 92, 'twi- | lights'. This ugly enjambment was a fashion of the time: cf. Donne, *Satire* iii. 68, 'and this blind- | nesse too much light breeds', iv. 13, 'of good as forget- | full'; Herrick, *The Lily in a Christal*

(*Works*, ed. Moorman, p. 75), 'Put Purple Grapes, or Cherries in- | To Glasse'; *Nuptiall Song on Sir Clipseby Crew* (ibid., p. 112), 'And Amber; *Spice-* | ing the Chaste Aire with fumes of Paradise'; ibid (p. 113), 'On then, and though you slow- | ly go'; *A Panegyrick to Sir Lewis Pemberton* (ibid., p. 148), 'But temperate mirth dealt forth, and so discreet- | ly that it makes the meate more sweet'.

369–73. *Our citi's now Deuided* . . . *Tacitus, Ann. iv. xvii. 4: 'Insta-bat quippe Seianus incusabatque diductam civitatem ut civili bello; esse qui se partium Agrippinae vocent, ac ni resistatur, fore plures.'

377. *businesse.* A trisyllable: so iii. 604, *Julius Caesar,* iv. i. 22, 'to groan and sweat under the business'.

381. *second,* support, seconding. Cf. i. 167.

388–90. *And once entred* . . . Cf. *Disc.* 1182–9, 'But *Princes* by harkning to cruell counsels, become in time obnoxious to the Authors, their Flatterers, and Ministers; and are brought to that, that when they would, they dare not change them: they must goe on, and defend cruelty with cruelty: they cannot alter the Habit. It is then growne necessary, they must be as ill, as those have made them.'

395. *whose guardes.* Tacitus, *Ann.* iv. xii. 4, 'Neque spargi venenum in tres poterat, egregia custodum fide et pudicitia Agrippinae impene-trabili'.

397. *too-too.* 'Very common c. 1540–1660' (*O.E.D.*). *D. is A.* iii. iii. 231, *N.I.* ii. vi. 203.

406. *in the wind.* *E.M.I.* ii. iii. 54 n.

416. *the publique hooke.* The body of an executed criminal was dragged from prison to the Gemonian steps by the *uncus* of the execu-tioner, and thence three days later to the Tiber (iv. 283). 'Seianus ducitur unco spectandus', Juvenal, *Sat.* x. 66.

420. *rethorique.* An accepted spelling: cf. the Old French *rethorique* and the Medieval Latin *rethoricus.* But Jonson would probably spell 'rhetorique'.

443. *enuies . . . eyes.* Cf. *Pan.* 83–4, all that kings do,

> discouer'd lies
> Vnto as many enuies, there, as eyes.

Envy in *The Faerie Queene,* i. iv. 31:

> All in a Kirtle of discolourd say
> He clothed was, ypainted full of eyes.

450. *stuck with eyes.* Cf. *I Henry IV,* v. ii. 8, 'Suspicion all our lives shall be stuck full of eyes'.

453. *eares as long.* Imitated in Webster, *The White Divel,* iii. ii. 237–9:

> Were your intelligencing eares as loving
> As to my thoughts, had you an honest tongue
> I would not care though you proclaim'd them all.—

where F. L. Lucas from the text of *Sejanus* emends 'loving' to 'long'.

473. *examp'lesse (examplêss,* Q). Florio has the full and correct form
'exampleless'.

476. "*He threatens many* . . . From Publilius Syrus, 'Multis minatur
qui uni facit iniuriam'.

484. *This's.* A constant abbreviation in Jonson: *T. of T.* II. ii. 52.

should be, 'is said to be'—a form of reported speech. Cf. *Volp.* II.
i. 22.

500. *No tree* . . . Cf. *Mortimer,* I. i. 3, 4.

III. 5. *your father, and his.* 'His' should be 'him': Tacitus records
(*Ann.* III. xliii. 4) that Silius superseded C. Visellius Varro, the father
of the prosecutor, in the command against Sacrovir.

In ancient Rome, where there was no class of professional advocates
taking fees, and where any citizen might come forward as prosecutor
or defender, cases of collusion were not infrequent. Hence Roman
writers often lay stress on the personal hostility of the prosecutor as
a proof of his sincerity.

21. *whips, and furies.* Briggs compares *The Spanish Tragedy,* III. xi.
42–3 (ed. Boas), one of the additional scenes:

> And there is *Nemesis,* and Furies,
> And things called whippes.

23. *shittles,* shuttles.

28. *Fathers Conscript,* strictly *patres et conscripti,* 300 in number, the
conscripti or 'enrolled' members being originally those who were added
at the establishment of the republic to fill the vacancies caused by the
expulsion of the Tarquins and by the gaps made when a number of
senators accompanied them into exile. *Cat.* IV. 65.

35–81. *From Tacitus, *Ann.* IV. 8: 'Ceterum Tiberius per omnes
valetudinis eius' (i.e. Drusi) 'dies, nullo metu an ut firmitudinem animi
ostentaret, etiam defuncto necdum sepulto, curiam ingressus est. Con-
sulesque sede vulgari per speciem maestitiae sedentes honoris locique
admonuit et effusum in lacrimas senatum victo gemitu simul oratione
continua erexit: non quidem sibi ignarum posse argui quod tam recenti
dolore subierit oculos senatus: vix propinquorum adloquia tolerari, vix
diem aspici a plerisque lugentium. Neque illos imbecillitatis damnandos:
se tamen fortiora solacia e complexu rei publicae petivisse. Miseratusque
Augustae extremam senectam, rudem adhuc nepotum et vergentem
aetatem suam, ut Germanici liberi, unica praesentium malorum leva-
menta, inducerentur petivit (55–61). Egressi consules firmatos adloquio
adulescentulos deductosque ante Caesarem statuunt. Quibus adprensis
"patres conscripti, hos" inquit "orbatos parente tradidi patruo ipsorum
(66–8), precatusque sum, quamquam esset illi propria soboles, ne secus
quam suum sanguinem foveret, attolleret, sibique et posteris conformaret.
Erepto Druso preces ad vos converto disque et patria coram obtestor:
Augusti pronepotes clarissimis maioribus genitos suscipite, regite,
vestram meamque vicem explete. Hi vobis, Nero et Druse, parentum

loco. Ita nati estis ut bona malaque vestra ad rem publicam per-
tineant".'

37. *dissolv'd* survives in the phrase 'dissolved in tears'.

47. *communicate*, share (Lat. *communico*).

52. *strooke with time*. An incorrect variant of 'stricken in years',
where the participle simply means 'advanced' for the Middle English
striken, to advance or flow, used of swift motion. Augusta was eighty
years old; Tiberius sixty-five.

84–5. *Let their great titles.* Cf. Claudian, *De Consulatu Stilichonis*, ii.
317–18, 'Titulo tunc crescere posses, Nunc per te titulus'. Quoted in
Hadd. M. 229, Jonson's note.

87. *no riuals, but themselues* . . . A favourite conceit of the time:
cf. Massinger, *The Duke of Millaine*, IV. iii (1623, I3ᵛ):

> Her goodnesse does disdaine comparison,
> And but her selfe admits no parallel.

It goes back to Seneca, *Hercules Furens*, 84–5:

> Quaeris Alcidae parem?
> Nemo est nisi ipse: bella iam secum gerat.

113–27. From Tacitus, *Ann.* IV. ix. The Senate listened with tears
and good wishes, 'ac si modum orationi posuisset, misericordia sui
gloriaque animos audientium impleverat: ad vana et totiens inrisa revo-
lutus, de reddenda re publica utque consules seu quis alius regimen
susciperent, vero quoque et honesto fidem dempsit'.

123. *that charme.* An old superstition: see Jonson's quotation from
Suetonius, and cf. Greene, *Penelopes Web*, 1601, E4, 'He which weareth
the Bay-leafe is priviledged from the preiudice of Thunder'; Webster,
The White Divel, V. iv. 62–4 (ed. Lucas):

> Reach the bayes,
> Ile tye a garland heere about his head:
> 'Twill keepe my boy from lightning.

136. *Vertumnus*, an old Italian god of fruits, who presided over the
changing year. *S. of N.* III. i. 33–8.

154. *Afer* took no part in the prosecution of Silius: he prosecuted
Furnius and Claudia Pulchra. The trial of Silius is based on *Ann.* IV.
xviii, xx, which Jonson has followed closely.

167. *moile*, mule.

174. *impotence*, lack of self-restraint (Lat. *impotentia*).

186. *entertainment*, employment. *C.R.* IV. iii. 372.

188. *sordid-base*. *E.M.I.* II. v. 96.

192. *If I not proue it.* Jonson refers to the formula in Brisson, v,
p. 469, used under Theodosius, Constantine, and later, 'Si te iniuste
interpellavero, et victus exinde apparuero, eadem poena quam in te
vindicare pulsavi, me constringo, atque conscribo partibus tuis esse

damnandum atque subiturum. Et pro rei totius firmitate manu propria firmo, et bonorum morum iudicio roborandum trado.' Cf. v. 603–4.

197–208. Tacitus, *Ann.* IV. xix. 2, 'Precante reo brevem moram dum accusator consulatu abiret, adversatus est Caesar: solitum quippe magistratibus diem privatis dicere; nec infringendum consulis ius, cuius vigiliis niteretur ne quod res publica detrimentum caperet.'

204. *appoint their day*, a literal rendering of 'diem dicere', to name a day for trial, to prosecute.

219. *interess'd*. Florio, '*Interessare*, to interesse, to touch or concerne a mans maine state or fee-simple, to concerne a mans reputation'.

231–2. *I can see*. Tacitus says that Silius 'either said nothing or, if he attempted a defence, made no secret of the person whose resentment was crushing him' (ibid. 4). He probably said nothing to meet the charge of extortion (l. 187), which Tacitus evidently thought true.

243. *Sejanus hates me.* 'Odia Seiani', ibid. 1.

245. *A net of Vulcan's filing.* Vulcan entrapped Venus and Mars in a mesh of finely woven wires and exposed their adultery (*Odyssey*, viii. 266–366). Massinger in *The Roman Actor*, IV. ii (1629, H3), copies the phrase—'taken in a net of *Vulcans* filing'—of the empress detected in adultery.

248. *nostrill*, perception. Martial, I. xli. 18, 'Non cuicumque datum est habere nasum'.

252. *prouoke*. Read *prouokd*, a correction which should have been made in the text. The printer confused the round looped form of the final *d* with the looped form of final *e*.

256–7. Cf. Juvenal, *Sat.* xiii. 164–5:

> Caerula quis stupuit Germani lumina, flavam
> caesariem et madido torquentem cornua cirro?

261. *curl'd Sicambrians*. Jonson's reference is to the collection on the amphitheatre prefixed to Martial's *Epigrams*.

272–8, 288–91, 305–8. *From Tacitus, *Ann.* IV. xviii. 2, 3: 'Credebant plerique auctam offensionem ipsius intemperantia immodice iactantis suum militem in obsequio duravisse cum alii ad seditiones prolaberentur, neque mansurum Tiberio imperium si iis quoque legionibus cupido novandi fuisset. Destrui per haec fortunam suam Caesar imparemque tanto merito rebatur. Nam beneficia eo usque laeta sunt dum videntur exsolvi posse: ubi multum antevenere pro gratia odium redditur.'

275–6. *yours . . . You.* The change from 'thine' and 'thou' of the Quarto in the rest of this speech is noticeable. But 'thou' and 'you' are often interchangeable in contemporary verse. Other examples in Jonson are *E.M.O.* v. vi. 11–13; *Volp.* II. iv. 12, v. 26–7; *S.W.* IV. iv. 174–5; *Alch.* I. i. 63–4, IV. iii. 7–10, v. iv. 142–3; *D. is A.* IV. ii. 7.

285. *famous*, infamous (Lat. *famosus*).

288. *crime*, accusation (Lat. *crimen*).

303. *With doubtfull Princes.* Discussed in vol. ii, pp. 4–5, and on p. 58 above. Briggs aptly quotes Bacon's *History of King Henry VII*,

ed. Lumby, p. 122, of the king's feeling against Sir William Stanley: 'First, an over-merit; for convenient merit, unto which reward may easily reach, doth best with Kings.'

324. *hands of fortune.* Seneca, *De Constantia Sapientis*, viii. 3, 'Et si fortunae iniurias moderate fert, quanto magis hominum potentium, quos scit fortunae manus esse'.

324–5. *Shee her selfe* . . . From Cato's speech in Lucan, ix. 569–70:

> An noceat vis ulla bono, fortunaque perdat
> opposita virtute minas?

Repeated in *N.I.* iv. iv. 154–6. In the summing up of the same speech 'pavido fortique cadendum' (l. 583) is echoed in line 334.

326–31. From Cicero, *Tusc. Disp.* v. i, 'Virtus . . . omnia quae cadere in hominem possunt subter se habet, eaque despiciens casus contemnit humanos' (W. D. Briggs).

335. *the cause, and manner how.* Cf. *Ep.* xxxiii. 3–4.

338. *mock Tiberius tyrannie.* Briggs compares Petronius' suicide in the play of *Nero* iv. vii (1633, H1ᵛ), '*Nero*, my end shall mock thy turanny'.

339. *learne to die.* Tacitus says (*Ann.* iv. xix. 5) 'Silius imminentem damnationem voluntario fine praevertit', but this was not in the Senate.

345. *stalled*, brought to a standstill, stopped from proceeding. The thought is from Manius Lepidus' speech in Tacitus, *Ann.* iii. l. 3, 'Saepe audivi principem nostrum conquerentem si quis sumpta morte misericordiam eius praevenisset'.

356–69. *Let her be proscrib'd* . . . *Tacitus, *Ann.* iv. xx. 2–4: 'Sosia in exilium pellitur Asinii Galli sententia, qui partem bonorum publicandam, pars ut liberis relinqueretur censuerat. Contra M' Lepidus quartam accusatoribus secundum necessitatem legis, cetera liberis concessit. Hunc ego Lepidum temporibus illis gravem et sapientem virum fuisse comperior: nam pleraque ab saevis adulationibus aliorum in melius flexit.'

374. CORVˢ. Here and in v. 421 this contraction for 'us' is used owing to the length of the line. See McKerrow, *Introduction to Bibliography*, p. 323.

376. *Seianus blood-hounds.* Briggs quotes Seneca, *Ad Marciam de Consolatione*, xxii. 5, of Sejanus: 'Et acerrimi canes, quos ille ut sibi uni mansuetos, omnibus feros haberet, sanguine humano pascebat, circumlatrare hominem et iam illum impetratum incipiunt.'

385. *a viper's tooth.* *Poet.* v. iii. 327 n.

387. *degenerous*, Lat. *degener*. *N.I.* iii. ii. 168.

389. *forth a world.* *Ant. and Cleop.* iv. x. 7, 'They have put forth the haven'.

392. *Cassius was the last.* Cf. i. 104 n.

394. *priuate.* *Cat.* iii. 481, 'Nor must I be vnmindfull of my priuate'.

397. *parricide*, traitor (Lat. *parricida*).

407–60. 'In his Sejanus', Jonson told Drummond, 'he hath translated a whole oration of Tacitus' (*Conv.* xviii. 602). This is the speech from the *Annals*, IV. xxxiv–xxxv: 'Verba mea, patres conscripti, arguuntur: adeo factorum innocens sum. Sed neque haec in principem aut principis parentem, quos lex maiestatis amplectitur: Brutum et Cassium laudavisse dicor, quorum res gestas cum plurimi composuerint, nemo sine honore memoravit. Titus Livius, eloquentiae ac fidei praelarus in primis, Cn. Pompeium tantis laudibus tulit ut Pompeianum eum Augustus appellaret; neque id amicitiae eorum offecit. Scipionem, Afranium, hunc ipsum Cassium, hunc Brutum nusquam latrones et parricidas, quae nunc vocabula imponuntur, saepe ut insignes viros nominat. Asinii Pollionis scripta egregiam eorundem memoriam tradunt; Messalla Corvinus imperatorem suum Cassium praedicabat: et uterque opibus atque honoribus perviguere. Marci Ciceronis libro, quo Catonem caelo aequavit, quid aliud dictator Caesar quam rescripta oratione velut apud iudices respondit? Antonii epistulae, Bruti contiones falsa quidem in Augustum probra, sed multa cum acerbitate habent; carmina Bibaculi et Catulli referta contumeliis Caesarum leguntur: sed ipse divus Iulius, ipse divus Augustus et tulere ista et reliquere, haud facile dixerim, moderatione magis an sapientia. Namque spreta exolescunt: si irascare, agnita videntur. Non attingo Graecos, quorum non modo libertas, etiam libido impunita; aut si quis advertit, dictis dicta ultus est. Sed maxime solutum et sine obtrectatore fuit prodere de iis quos mors odio aut gratiae exemisset. Num enim armatis Cassio et Bruto ac Philippenses campos obtinentibus belli civilis causa populum per contiones incendo? An illi quidem septuagensimum ante annum peremti, quo modo imaginibus suis noscuntur, quas ne victor quidem abolevit, sic partem memoriae apud scriptores retinent? Suum cuique decus posteritas rependit; nec deerunt, si damnatio ingruit, qui non modo Cassii et Bruti sed etiam mei meminerint.'

419. *Scipio.* Metellus Scipio, Pompey's father-in-law and colleague in the consulship in 52 B.C.

Afranius, consul in 60 B.C., Pompey's legatus in Spain.

422. *notes*, brands (Lat. *nota*).

423. *Asinius Pollio's writings.* Poet and statesman of the Augustan period (76 B.C.–A.D. 5); he wrote a history of the civil war.

424. *Messalla Corvinus* was next in command after Brutus and Cassius at Philippi: he wrote a history of the war after Caesar's death.

427. Cicero's treatise of *Cato*, answered by Caesar's *Anticato*; both are lost.

431. *Antonius letters* quoted by Suetonius (*Augustus*, xvi, lxix).

Brutus pleadings. Even the subject of them is unknown.

434. The *Epigram's* of Marcus Furius *Bibaculus* are lost: he wrote a poem on Caesar's Gallic wars, and was a master of the turgid style: see *Disc.* 1917 n.

Catullus' attacks on Julius Caesar survive in *Carmina* 29, 54, 57, 93.

441. *confest.* Seneca, *De Ira*, III. v. 8, 'Ultio doloris confessio est' (W. D. Briggs).

453. *their images*. Plutarch in his comparison of Dion with Brutus, ch. v, records that a bronze statue of Brutus was preserved at Mediolanum by Augustus' orders.

457–60. Imitated in the play of *Nero*, iv. v (1633, G2ᵛ), quoted by Briggs:

> This benefit at lest
> Sad death shall give, to free me from the power
> Of such a government; and if I die
> For pittying human chance and *Pisoes* end,
> There will be some too, that will pitie mine.

463. *He puts 'hem to their whisper*. Imitated by Massinger in the trial of Paris, *The Roman Actor*, i. iii (1629, C2), 'He ha's put The Consuls to their whisper'.

466. *Ædiles* probably a trisyllable (see vol. iv, p. 341). North, quoted by the *O.E.D.*, has 'an Ædilis' for the singular number.

471–80. From Tacitus, *Ann.* iv. xxxv. 5, 6: 'Libros per aediles cremandos censuere patres: sed manserunt, occultati et editi. Quo magis socordiam eorum irridere libet qui praesenti potentia credunt extingui posse etiam sequentis aevi memoriam. Nam contra punitis ingeniis gliscit auctoritas, neque aliud externi reges aut qui eadem saevitia usi sunt nisi dedecus sibi atque illis gloriam peperere.' Bacon commented on this passage that 'a wise writer' had 'set it downe, that *punitis ingeniis gliscit authoritas*; and indeed we euer see it falleth out, that the forbidden writing is thought to be a certaine sparke of truth that flieth up in the faces of them that seeke to choke and tread it out' (*A Wise and Moderate Discourse Concerning Church Affaires*, 1641, p. 11).

486–7. *From Suetonius, *Tiberius*, xxi: 'Scio vulgo persuasum quasi, egresso post secretum sermonem Tiberio, vox Augusti per cubicularios excepta sit: "Miserum populum Romanum qui sub tam lentis maxillis erit!"'

489. *iealousie of practice*, suspicion of plotting.

496. *with so good vultures*. The *O.E.D.* explains vultures here as 'persons of a vile and rapacious disposition'—a cynical description of the legal birds of prey, Afer and Varro. Cf. iv. 139–40, 'made The prey to greedy vultures, and vile spies'. But the main reference is to augury: the phrase is a variant of 'bonis' or 'secundis avibus'; it might be suggested by the twelve vultures which appeared to Romulus at the foundation of Rome. In the *Masque of Augurs* the test of the vulture is how high it flies (ll. 352–3). Cf. for this sense v. 597, 'I shall anon beleeue your vultures, Marcvs'.

501. *Dearest head*. So the Greek address φίλτατον κάρα. Cf. 'impudent head' in *Cat.* iv. 488, v. 212; 'Camden, most reuerent head', *Ep.* xiv. 1.

503–29. *From Tacitus, *Ann.* iv. xxxix: 'At Seianus nimia fortuna socors et muliebri insuper cupidine incensus, promissum matrimonium flagitante Livia, componit ad Caesarem codicillos: moris quippe tum erat quamquam praesentem scripto adire. Eius talis forma erat: benevolentia patris Augusti et mox plurimis Tiberii iudiciis ita insuevisse ut spes votaque sua non prius ad deos quam ad principum aures conferret. Neque fulgorem honorum unquam precatum: excubias ac labores ut unum e militibus pro incolumitate imperatoris malle. Ac tamen quod pulcherrimum adeptum, ut coniunctione Caesaris dignus crederetur: hinc initium spei. Et quoniam audiverit Augustum in collocanda filia non nihil etiam de equitibus Romanis consultavisse, ita, si maritus Liviae quaereretur, haberet in animo amicum sola necessitudinis gloria usurum. Non enim exuere imposita munia: satis aestimare firmari domum adversum iniquas Agrippinae offensiones, idque liberorum causa; nam sibi multum superque vitae fore, quod tali cum principe explevisset.'

516. *his daughter*, Julia. The Latin note is quoted from Lipsius.

530–76. *From Tacitus, *Ann.* iv. xl: 'Ad ea Tiberius laudata pietate Seiani suisque in eum beneficiis modice percursis, cum tempus tanquam ad integram consultationem petivisset, adiunxit: ceteris mortalibus in eo stare consilia quid sibi conducere putent; principum diversam esse sortem, quibus praecipua rerum ad famam derigenda. Ideo se non illuc decurrere quod promptum rescriptu, posse ipsam Liviam statuere, nubendum post Drusum an in penatibus isdem tolerandum haberet; esse illi matrem et aviam, propiora consilia. Simplicius acturum, de inimicitiis primum Agrippinae, quas longe acrius arsuras si matrimonium Liviae velut in partes domum Caesarum distraxisset. Sic quoque erumpere aemulationem feminarum, eaque discordia nepotes suos convelli: quid si intendatur certamen tali coniugio? "Falleris enim, Seiane, si te mansurum in eodem ordine putas, et Liviam, quae Gaio Caesari, mox Druso nupta fuerit, ea mente acturam ut cum equite Romano senescat. Ego ut sinam, credisne passuros qui fratrem eius, qui patrem maioresque nostros in summis imperiis videre? Vis tu quidem istum intra locum sistere: sed illi magistratus et primores, qui te invitum perrumpunt omnibusque de rebus consulunt, excessisse iam pridem equestre fastigium longeque antisse patris mei amicitias non occulti ferunt perque invidiam tui me quoque incusant. . . . Atque ego haec pro amicitia non occultavi: ceterum neque tuis neque Liviae destinatis adversabor. Ipse quid intra animum volutaverim, quibus adhuc necessitudinibus immiscere te mihi parem, omittam ad praesens referre: id tantum aperiam, nihil esse tam excelsum quod non virtutes istae tuusque in me animus mereantur, datoque tempore vel in senatu vel in contione non reticebo."'

530. *pietie*, dutiful affection (Lat. *pietas*).

532. *Those, bounties* (Quarto punctuation). Tiberius hesitates as if trying to find a simpler word. Cf. *E.M.I.* iv. ii. 99, 'You, lampe of virginitie'.

541. *a mother, and a grandame*, Antonia and Livia.

574. *aspire*, mount up to, attain. *Ep.* xxviii. 1.

575. *on all watch'd occasion*. Massinger, *The Bond-man*, iv. i (1624, G4^v):

> waite carefully,
> And vpon all watch'd occasions, continue
> Speech, and discourse of me.

597. *hemlocke.* Cf. Greene's *Neuer too late*, 1590, part ii, H2: 'In that sir, your eye dazled and mistooke me, for *Venus*. You gazde against the sunne, and so blemisht your sight, or els you haue eaten of the roots of Hemlocke, that makes mens eyes conceipt vnseene obiects.'

598. *poppie, and . . . mandrakes.* Cf. *Othello*, III. iii. 334–7:

> Not poppy, nor mandragora,
> Nor all the drowsy syrups of the world,
> Shall euer medecine thee to that sweet sleep
> Which thou owedst yesterday.

604–12. *From Tacitus, *Ann.* IV. xli. 4: 'Igitur paulatim negotia urbis, populi adcursus, multitudinem adfluentium increpat, extollens laudibus quietem et solitudinem, quis abesse taedia et offensiones ac praecipua rerum maxime agitari.'

610. *Larded,* garnished, dressed with. *E.M.I.* III. v. 170.

617–20. From Tacitus, *Ann.* IV. xli. 3: 'Et minui sibi invidiam adempta salutantum turba sublatisque inanibus veram potentiam augeri.' *Wanting accesse to him* is not what Tacitus here says: the 'salutantum turba' was Sejanus' own crowded receptions; when these stopped, the envy they excited would cease or at any rate be less.

617. *mine owne strengths.* 'In 15–18th centuries the plural was often used after a plural possessive' (*O.E.D.* s.v. 'strength'). It is frequent in Jonson: see below, v. 310, 590.

637–42. Cf. *Disc.* 1224–9: 'But *Princes* that neglect their proper office thus, their fortune is often times to draw a *Seianus*, to be neere about 'hem; who will at last affect to get above 'hem, and put them in a worthy feare, of rooting both them out, and their family. For no men hate an evill *Prince* more, then they, that help'd to make him such.'

651. *aconite.* From Pliny, *Nat. Hist.* XXVII. ii: 'Hoc quoque tamen in usus humanae salutis vertere scorpionum ictibus adversari experiendo datum in vino calido . . . mirumque exitialia per se ambo cum sint, duo venena in homine commoriuntur, ut homo supersit.' So Webster, *Appius and Virginia*, III. iii:

> APP. O my *Clodius*,
> Observe this rule—one ill must cure another;
> As *Aconitum*, a strong poison, brings
> A present cure against all Serpents stings.

654. *wrastle.* The old form, usual in Jonson.

660. The saying attributed to Aeschylus in Aristophanes' *Frogs*, 1431, 1433:

> οὐ χρὴ λέοντος σκύμνον ἐν πόλει τρέφειν,
> ἢν δ' ἐκτραφῇ τις, τοῖς τρόποις ὑπηρετεῖν.

668. *our courtings.* The 'your courtings' of the 1640 Folio shows ignorance of Elizabethan usage: 'our' = of us, the objective genitive. Cf. *Henry V*, I. ii. 224–5:

France being ours, we 'll bend it to our awe,
Or break it all to pieces.

Jonson examples are *Volp.* v. xii. 145, 'your iudgements' (judgements
of, or upon, you); *M.L.* 2nd Chorus 44, 'his calumnie' (of him); *For.*
ii. 62, 'his feare' (fear for himself).

675. *produc't*, prolonged (Lat. *produco*).

692. *int' themselues*. For the elision before a consonant cf. 'this's':
int' is found before a vowel or *h*, e.g. 'int'a closet' (Chaucer, *Troilus*,
ii. 1215); 'But by the varying soyle, int'one againe are cast' (Drayton,
Polyolbion, iv. 420). And also before *h*: 'And blow her int'his nosthrils'
(Webster, *The White Divel*, iv. ii. 45).

707. *Sauer*. Cf. *Hadd. M.* 228–9:

to his name did bring
The honor, to be *Sauer of his King.*

714–43. Chapman, Jonson's collaborator in the original draft of this
play, puts similar language into the mouth of Baligny in *The Revenge
of Bussy d'Ambois*, II. i (1613, D):

Your Highnesse knowes
I will be honest; and betray for you
Brother and Father: for I know (my Lord)
Treacherie for Kings is truest Loyaltie;
Nor is to beare the name of Treacherie,
But grave, deep Policie. All acts that seem
Ill in particular respects, are good
As they respect your vniversal Rule.

727. *twin'd. Othello*, II. iii. 203–5:

And he that is approved in this offence,
Though he had twinn'd with me, both at a birth,
Shall lose me.

729–30. *draw . . . In compasse*, involve in a trap, overreach.

736–7. Cf. *E.M.O.* I. iii. 145, '"He that will thriue, must thinke no
courses vile'.

748. *vncouth*, strange, unknown. The thought may be illustrated from
the ruined abbeys of Henry VIII's reign and the grants of them to
his nobles.

IV. I, 2. *You must haue patience. . . . I must haue vengeance first.* So
in *The White Divel*, III. ii. 280–1, of Vittoria after her condemnation:
'FRAN. You must have patience. VIT. I must first have vengeance.'

4, 5. *Let it be sodaine . . .* Adapted from Lucan, *Pharsalia*, ii. 14–15:

Sit subitum quodcumque paras; sit caeca futuri
mens hominum fati; liceat sperare timenti.

14. *Choose once to fall* ... Seneca, *De Beneficiis*, II. v. I: 'Nihil aeque amarum quam diu pendere. Aequiore quidam animo ferunt praecidi spem suam quam trahi.'

28. *cause of raging* ... Seneca, *De Clementia*, I. viii. 7, 'Voluntas oportet ante saeviendi quam causa deficiat'.

47. *Tiberius sitting* ... *From Tacitus, *Ann.* IV. lix. 1–4: 'Ac forte illis diebus oblatum Caesari anceps periculum auxit vana rumoris praebuitque ipsi materiem cur amicitiae constantiaeque Seiani magis fideret. Vescebantur in villa cui vocabulum Speluncae, mare Amunclanum inter et Fundanos montes, nativo in specu. Eius os lapsis repente saxis obruit quosdam ministros: hinc metus in omnes et fuga eorum qui convivium celebrabant. Seianus genu vultuque et manibus super Caesarem suspensus opposuit sese incidentibus, atque habitu tali repertus est a militibus qui subsidio venerant. Maior ex eo, et quamquam exitiosa suaderet, ut non sui anxius, cum fide audiebatur.'

48. *Spelunca*. 'The name is still preserved in the modern village Sperlonga, half-way between Terracina and Gaeta, where a cave showing traces of adaptation and decoration can still be seen.'—H. Furneaux on the passage quoted.

68–70. From Seneca, *De Providentia*, I. iv. 15–16: 'Quid miraris bonos viros ut confirmentur concuti? Non est arbor solida nec fortis nisi in quam frequens ventus incursat. Ipsa enim vexatione constringitur et radices certius figit.' Cf. Herrick, *A Panegyrick to Sir Lewis Pemberton*, 108–13 (*Works*, ed. Moorman, p. 148)—of his house:

> But fixt it stands, by her own power,
> And well-laid bottome, on the iron and rock,
>   Which tryes, and counter-stands the shock,
> And *Ramme* of time and by vexation growes
>   The stronger: *Vertue dies when foes*
> *Are wanting to her exercise....*

80. *remoue*, stage of his journey.

93–232. The source is Tacitus' *Annals*, IV. lxviii–lxx, which Jonson has adapted. 'Iunio Silano et Silio Nerva consulibus foedum anni principium incessit tracto in carcerem illustri equite Romano Tito Sabino ob amicitiam Germanici: neque enim omiserat coniugem liberosque eius percolere, sector domi, comes in publico, post tot clientes unus eoque apud bonos laudatus et gravis iniquis. Hunc Latinius Latiaris, Porcius Cato, Petilius Rufus, M. Opsius praetura functi aggrediuntur cupidine consulatus, ad quem non nisi per Seianum aditus; neque Seiani voluntas nisi scelere quaerebatur. Compositum inter ipsos ut Latiaris, qui modico usu Sabinum contingebat,'—Jonson makes them cousins in I. 21—'strueret dolum, ceteri testes adessent, deinde accusationem inciperent. Igitur Latiaris iacere fortuitos primum sermones, mox laudare constantiam, quod non, ut ceteri, florentis domus amicus afflictam deseruisset; simul honora de Germanico, Agrippinam miserans, disserebat.' Sabinus wept and complained, then Latiaris 'audentius iam

onerat Seianum, saevitiam, superbiam, spes eius. Ne in Tiberium quidem convicio abstinet.' So a close friendship to all appearance began
as of men who 'had exchanged confidences on forbidden subjects'. Then
the trap was laid at Latiaris' house: 'tectum inter et laquearia tres
senatores, haud minus turpi latebra quam detestanda fraude, sese
abstrudunt, foraminibus et rimis aurem admovent.' Latiaris takes
Sabinus to a bedroom: 'praeteritaque et instantia, quorum affatim copia,
ac novos terrores cumulat. Eadem ille et diutius, quanto maesta, ubi
semel prorupere, difficilius reticentur.' An attested report of the conversation was then sent to Tiberius. He was condemned: 'et trahebatur
damnatus, quantum obducta veste et astrictis faucibus niti poterat,
clamitans sic incohari annum, has Seiano victimas cadere.'

How was this scene staged? Probably the whole was played on the
upper stage. The 'holes' of line 114—Sir E. K. Chambers queries if this
was a misprint for 'hole'—must be 'betweene the roofe, and seeling'
(95). At line 114 the spies mount a rope ladder into the 'hut' above
and draw it up after them; they drop it again at line 217 and descend.

170 *purchas'd*, won.

175. *at Rhodes.* *Tacitus (*Ann.* IV. lvii. 3) after describing Tiberius'
face full of eruptions and covered with patches of plaster continues:
'et Rhodi secreto vitare coetus, recondere voluptates insuerat', i.e. 'even
in his retirement at Rhodes he had habituated himself to shun society
and to hide his voluptuous life'. Jonson, as Professor Briggs points out,
overlooked 'insuerat'. The exile at Rhodes had taken place in the reign
of Augustus; Jonson speaks of it as if it were taking place at the moment.

176. *upon the heads of Romanes.* Seneca, *Ad Marciam de Consolatione*,
xxii. 4, says of Marcia's father, 'tacitus ferre non potuerat Seianum in
cervices nostras ne imponi quidem, sed escendere'.

217. *bogg'd in . . . lusts.* *Und.* xv. 30, 'bogg'd in vices'.

220. *catch'd.* See *Grammar*, I. xx. 38.

222. *reuerend*, awe-inspiring, formidable (Lat. *reverendus*).

228. *The yeere is well begun.* The day was sacred, and Sabinus is
a sacrifice, as it were, to Sejanus as a god. Cf. Suetonius, *Tiberius*, lxi,
'Nullus a poena hominum cessavit dies, ne religiosus quidem ac sacer;
animadversum in quosdam ineunte anno novo'.

230. *Couer him with his garments.* 'Alluding to the form by which
a criminal was condemned to death: "I, lictor, colliga manus, caput
obnubito, &c."' (Gifford).

247. *to Augustus statue.* Suetonius, ibid. liii, 'Novissime calumniatus
modo ad statuam Augusti modo ad exercitus confugere velle . . .'.

256. *vpon the second*, while supporting. For 'second' cf. II. 381.

259. *Still, do'st thou suffer heau'n?* Cf. *Cat.* III. 235–6.

267. *pull thee by the beard.* Cf. Persius, *Sat.* II. 28–9, 'Idcirco stolidam
praebet tibi vellere barbam | Iuppiter?'

268. *black-lidded eye.* A phrase of Spenser's about Jupiter in *Mother
Hubberds Tale*, 1228; it was suggested by the black brows of the
Thunderer, Homer's κυανέῃσιν ἐπ' ὀφρύσι νεῦσε Κρονίων.

270. *Giant-race.* The Sons of Earth who tried to scale heaven by piling Ossa on Olympus and Pelion on Ossa, and were destroyed by Jupiter.

274. *equall with a prodigie.* Juvenal, *Sat.* iv. 96–7, 'Sed olim | prodigio par est in nobilitate senectus'.

278. *a'most.* This form is found in *Volp.* v. xii. 52, *S.W.* v. iv. 248, *D. is A.* II. vii. 38.

283. *Gemonies.* See Jonson's note on line 309.

284. *fact,* crime.

285. *His faithfull dogge.* *Dion, Rom. Hist.* LVIII. i. 3: τὸ δὲ σῶμα αὐτοῦ κατὰ τῶν ἀναβασμῶν ἐρρίφη καὶ ἐς τὸν ποταμὸν ἐνεβλήθη. καὶ δεινὸν μὲν τοῦτο τὸ πάθος καὶ καθ' ἑαυτὸ ἅπασιν ἦν, ἐδείνωσε δ' αὐτὸ ἐπὶ πλέον τὸ πάθος αὐτοῦ κύων τις τοῦ Σαβίνου, συνεσελθών τε αὐτῷ ἐς τὸ οἴκημα καὶ ἀποθανόντι παραμείνας, καὶ τέλος καὶ ἐς τὸν ποταμὸν ῥιφέντι συνεσπεσών. Tacitus does not mention the dog.

290. *patriot.* Found in Jonson in the modern sense at a time when it commonly meant 'fellow-countryman': thus *Volp.* IV. i. 95–6, 'knowne patriots, Sound louers of their country'; *S. of N.* 1st Intermean 63–4, '*and lou'd the common wealth, as well as e're a* Patriot *of 'hem all*'; *Und.* lxx. 46, 'A perfect Patriot, and a noble friend'; *Disc.* 532–4, 'No good *Christian,* or *Ethnick,* if he be honest, can misse it' (i.e. truth): 'no *States-man,* or *Patriot* should'.

295–311. These lines echo Juvenal's sketch of Vibius Crispus, *Sat.* iv. 86–93:

> Sed quid violentius aure tyranni,
> cum quo de pluviis aut aestibus aut nimboso
> vere locuturi fatum pendebat amici?
> Ille igitur numquam direxit brachia contra
> torrentem, nec civis erat qui libera posset
> verba animi proferre et vitam impendere vero.
> Sic multas hiemes et octogensima vidit
> solstitia, his armis illa quoque tutus in aula.

300–1. *May I pray . . .* Persius, *Sat.* I. 119, 'Men muttire nefas? nec clam, nec cum scrobe.'

302. *With open wishes.* Persius, *Sat.* II. 7, 'Aperto vivere voto'.

313. *religious . . . times.* Cf. 228 above.

315. *all occasion pleaseth.* Seneca, *De Beneficiis,* III. xxvi. 1: 'Sub Tiberio Caesare fuit accusandi frequens et paene publica rabies, quae omni civili bello gravius togatam civitatem confecit: excipiebatur ebriorum sermo, simplicitas iocantium. Nihil erat tutum. Omnis saeviendi placebat occasio. Nec iam reorum exspectabatur eventus cum esset unus.'

330, 335. *Pontia . . . Pandataria,* now Ponza and Vandotena in the Tyrrhenian sea not far from Naples.

336–9. Suggested by Juvenal, *Sat.* xiii. 78–83:

> Per Solis radios Tarpeiaque fulmina iurat
> et Martis frameam et Cirrhaei spicula vatis,

per calamos venatricis pharetramque puellae
perque tuum, pater Aegaei Neptune, tridentem,
addit et Herculeos arcus hastamque Minervae,
quidquid habent telorum armamentaria caeli.

337. *blue-ey'd Maid*, Pallas, Homer's γλαυκῶπις Ἀθήνη.

343. *The complement of all accusings.* Tacitus, *Ann.* III. xxxviii. 1, 'addito maiestatis crimine, quod tum omnium accusationum complementum erat'.

346–9. *Caesars letters . . .* *Ibid. v. iv. 3, 'Simul populus effigies Agrippinae ac Neronis gerens circumsistit curiam faustisque in Caesarem omnibus falsas literas et principe invito exitium domui eius intendi clamitat'.

360. *Greeke-Sinon*, who duped the Trojans into receiving the wooden horse by means of which Troy was captured. 'Greeke' is no doubt suggested by the 'Graeculus esuriens' and 'Graecia mendax' of Juvenal.

363. *night-ey'd.* *Dion, LVII. ii. 4, πλεῖστον γὰρ τοῦ σκότους βλέπων ἐλάχιστα τῆς ἡμέρας ἑώρα: *Pliny, *N.H.* xi. 143, 'Ferunt Tiberio Caesari . . . fuisse naturam ut expergefactus noctu paulisper haud alio modo quam luce clara contueretur omnia, paulatim tenebris sese obducentibus'.

373. *our monster . . .* Juvenal, *Sat.* iv. 2–4:

> Monstrum nulla virtute redemptum
> a vitiis, aegrae solaque libidine fortes
> deliciae.

375. *His lothed person.* Ibid. 14–15:

> Quid agas cum dira et foedior omni
> crimine persona est?

379. *comick face.* Allusing to the masks worn on the ancient stage.

380. *Amid'st his rout of Chaldees.* *Juvenal, *Sat.* x. 94, 'cum grege Chaldaeo'; the astrologers, who professed to predict a person's destiny from the position of the heavens at his birth. *Tacitus, *Ann.* VI. xxi. 1, 2: 'Quotiens super tali negotio consultaret, edita domus parte ac liberti unius conscientia utebatur. Is litterarum ignarus, corpore valido, per avia ac derepta (nam saxis domus imminet) praeibat eum cuius artem experiri Tiberius statuisset, et regredientem, si vanitatis aut fraudum suspicio incesserat, in subiectum mare praecipitabat ne index arcani exsisteret.'

381. *vnkind*, unnatural.

399. *spintries, sellaries*, male prostitutes who practised unnatural lust. *Tacitus, *Ann.* VI. i. 4: 'Tuncque primum ignota antea vocabula reperta sunt sellariorum et spintriarum ex foeditate loci ac multiplici patientia: praepositique servi qui conquirerent pertraherent, dona in promptos, minas adversum abnuentes, et si retinerent propinquus aut parens, vim raptus suaque ipsi libita velut in captos exercebant.' The words

spintry' and 'sellary' are found in Greeneway's translation (1598) of this passage.

400. *new-commented*, newly invented (Lat. *commentus*).

401. Juvenal, *Sat.* xiii. 28–30, speaks of his own age as

> peioraque saecula ferri
> temporibus, quorum sceleri non invenit ipsa
> nomen et a nullo posuit natura metallo.

403. *the ward.* Juvenal, *Sat.* x. 92, calls Sejanus 'tutor principis'.

406. *side. M. Aug.* 408.

408–9. From Persius, *Sat.* ii. 24–5:

> Ignovisse putas quia, cum tonat, ocius ilex
> sulpure discutitur sacro quam tuque domusque?

410. These letters ... *Dion Cassius, LVIII. vi. 3: περί τε γὰρ ἑαυτοῦ πολλὰ καὶ ποικίλα καὶ τῷ Σηϊανῷ καὶ τῇ βουλῇ συνεχῶς ἐπέστελλε, νῦν μὲν λέγων φλαύρως ἔχειν καὶ ὅσον οὐκ ἤδη τελευτήσειν, νῦν δὲ καὶ σφόδρα ὑγιαίνειν καὶ αὐτίκα δὴ μάλα ἐς τὴν Ῥώμην ἀφίξεσθαι· καὶ τὸν Σηϊανὸν τότε μὲν πάνυ ἐπῄνει τότε δὲ πάνυ καθῄρει, τῶν τε ἑταίρων αὐτοῦ τοὺς μὲν ἐτίμα δι' ἐκεῖνον τοὺς δ' ἠτίμαζεν. ὥστε ὁ Σηϊανὸς ἐν τῷ μέρει καὶ τοῦ ὑπερόγκου καὶ τοῦ ὑπερφόβου πληρούμενος ἀεὶ μετέωρος ἦν. ... καὶ μέντοι καὶ οἱ λοιποὶ πάντες ἐναλλὰξ καὶ δι' ὀλίγου τὰ ἐναντιώτατα ἀκούοντες καὶ μήτε τὸν Σηϊανὸν θαυμάζειν ἔτι ἢ καὶ καταφρονεῖν ἔχοντες ἔς τε τὸν Τιβέριον ὡς καὶ τεθνήξοντα ἢ καὶ ἥξοντα ὑποπτεύοντες ἐν ἀμφιβόλῳ ἐγίγνοντο.

414. 'MIN', a correction in F1 of an original 'MAR' found also in Q. 'MAR' survives at line 498. Marcus Terentius does not enter till line 445. Either we have here a cancelled character or a rearrangement.

426. *Heliotrope.* Pliny, *N.H.* XXII. xxi (Holland's translation): 'Concerning Turnsol ... it turneth about with the sun, although it be a close and cloudy day (so great is the loue of this herb to that planet) and in the night season for want of the Suns presence, as if it had a great misse thereof, it draweth in and shutteth the blew floure which it beareth.'

428. *I cannot tell. E.M.I.* iv. vii. 139.

438. POLLVX ... HERCVLES replace an original '*Castor*' and '*Pollux*' found in the Quarto and the first state of the 1616 Folio; the corrections were made in the proof by Jonson. Professor Briggs first explained the changes of reading, and we discussed them in the textual introduction to the play, vol. iv, pp. 336–7. Jonson did not know at first that '*Castor*' was a woman's oath, and '*Hercules*' a man's. He had made the same mistake in *Poetaster*, iv. i. 15, where he made Cytheris say at first 'O *Hercules!*' and corrected this to Juno in the Folio.

466. *feare*, frighten.

473. *Linceus*, one of the Argonauts whose lynx eyes were proverbial. *E.M.O.* iv. iii. 110, where the name is correctly spelt 'Lynceus'.

484. *The Partner* ... Dion Cassius, LVIII. iv. 3. Tiberius κοινωνὸν τῶν φροντίδων ὠνόμαζε, 'Σηϊανός τε ὁ ἐμός' πολλάκις ἐπαναλαμβάνων ἔλεγε.

485–6. Ibid. viii. 4. Tiberius ἀπεῖπε μήτ' ἀνθρώπων τινι θύεσθαι, διότι καὶ ἐκείνῳ (i.e. Sejanus) τοῦτ' ἐγίγνετο.

492. *beleeue, what they would haue.* Seneca, *Hercules Furens*, 313–14:

> Quod nimis miseri volunt
> hoc facile credunt.

494. *without his titles.* *Dion, LVIII. viii. 4, τῇ δὲ γερουσίᾳ περὶ τοῦ Νέρωνος ἀποθανόντος γράφων Σηϊανὸν ἁπλῶς αὐτὸν ὠνόμασε, μηδὲν ὧνπερ εἴθιστο προσθείς.

503. *mated* (Quarto reading), daunted.

507. *against him.* *Dion, LVIII. viii. 3, καὶ ὁ μὲν μετεγίγνωσκεν ὅτι μηδὲν ἐν τῇ ὑπατείᾳ ἐνεόχμωσεν.

516. *he ha's a wife.* The intrigue of Caius with Ennia Thrasylla took place later in A.D. 37.

517–18. *he can looke vp . . .* Juvenal, *Sat.* i. 56–7, of a pandar husband:

> doctus spectare lacunar,
> doctus et ad calicem vigilanti stertere naso.

520. *the rising sunne.* *Dion, LVIII. xxviii. 4, Tiberius to Macro later, εὖ γε τὸν δυόμενον ἐγκαταλιπὼν πρὸς τὸν ἀνατέλλοντα ἐπείγῃ.

v. 3. *I did not liue . . .* Statius, *Silvae*, IV. ii. 12–13:

> Steriles transmisimus annos:
> haec aevi mihi prima dies, hic limina vitae.

Briggs quotes in this act the various imitations of the dramatist John Wilson in his *Andronicus Comnenus*, published in 1664. In IV. iii he has:

> Now I can say I live, and not till now.
> I've elbow-room enough, and space to breathe.
> I can look round me, too. There's not a tree
> That stops my prospect, but I've levelled it.

7. *My roofe . . .* Seneca, *Thyestes*, 885–8:

> Aequalis astris gradior et cunctos super
> altum superbo vertice attingens polum. . . .
> Dimitto superos: summa votorum attigi.

Compare Horace, *Odes*, I. i. 36.

10, 11. *All my desires . . .* Seneca, *De Beneficiis*, II. xxvii. 4, 'Aeque ambitio non patitur quemquam in ea mensura honorum conquiescere quae quondam fuit eius impudens votum' (W. D. Briggs).

17–21. Lucan, *Pharsalia*, iii. 362–6:

> Ventus ut amittit vires nisi robore densae
> occurrunt silvae, spatio diffusus inani,
> utque perit magnus nullis obstantibus ignis,
> sic hostes mihi deesse nocet, damnumque putamus
> armorum nisi qui vinci potuere rebellant.

29. *your statue* . . . *Dion, LVIII. vii: Σηϊανὸν μὲν οὖν ταῦτά τε ἐτάραττε, καὶ πολλῷ μᾶλλον ὅτι ἐξ ἀνδριάντος τινὸς αὐτοῦ τὰ μὲν πρῶτα καπνὸς πολὺς ἀνέθορεν, ἔπειτα δὲ ἀφαιρεθείσης τῆς κεφαλῆς ὅπως τὸ γιγνόμενον ἴδωσιν, ὄφις μέγας ἀνεπήδησεν, ἑτέρας τε εὐθὺς ἀντεπιτεθείσης αὐτῷ, καὶ διὰ τοῦτ᾽ ἐκείνου θύσειν ἑαυτῷ μέλλοντος . . . σχοίνιον περὶ τὸν αὐχένα αὐτοῦ περικειμένον εὑρέθη.*

43. *by his sacred fortune.* Cf. IV. 431.

52–7. *Dion, LVIII. v. 5, ἐν δέ τινι νουμηνίᾳ πάντων συνιόντων ἐς τὴν οἰκίαν τοῦ Σηϊανοῦ ἥ τε κλίνη ἡ ἐν τῷ δωματίῳ ἐν ᾧ ἠσπάζετο κειμένη πᾶσα ὑπὸ τοῦ ὄχλου τῶν ἱζησάντων συνετρίβη, καὶ προϊόντος αὐτοῦ ἐκ τῆς οἰκίας γαλῆ διὰ μέσων σφῶν διῇξεν.*

59–61. *The fate* . . . *Ibid. 6, ἐπειδή τε καὶ ἐν τῷ Καπιτωλίῳ θύσας ἐς τὴν ἀγορὰν κατῄει, οἱ οἰκέται αὐτοῦ οἱ δορυφόροι διά τε τῆς ὁδοῦ τῆς ἐς τὸ δεσμωτήριον ἀγούσης ἐξετράποντο, μὴ δυνηθέντες αὐτῷ ὑπὸ τοῦ ὄχλου ἐπακολουθῆσαι, καὶ κατὰ τῶν ἀναβασμῶν καθ᾽ ὧν οἱ δικαιούμενοι ἐρριπτοῦντο κατιόντες ὤλισθον καὶ κατέπεσον.* Dion says nothing about the servants breaking their necks, which certainly would be a portent.

⁀*declining*, turning aside from, or, as the Quarto puts it, diverging. Cf. *For.* xiii. 59, 60, 'wisely you decline your life, Farre from the maze of custome, error, strife'.

62–6. *Dion, LVIII. v. 7, οἰωνιζομένου τε μετὰ τοῦτο αὐτοῦ τῶν μὲν αἰσίων ὀρνίθων ἐπεφάνη οὐδείς, κόρακες δὲ δὴ πολλοὶ περιπτάμενοι καὶ περικρώξαντες αὐτὸν ἀπέπταντο ἀθρόοι πρὸς τὸ οἴκημα καὶ ὑπὲρ αὐτοῦ ἐκαθέζοντο.*

64. *Flag'd*, flew unsteadily. *O.E.D.* quotes Spenser, *The Faerie Queene*, dedicatory sonnet to the Earl of Essex:

> . . . my Muse, whose fethers nothing flitt
> Doe yet but flag, and lowly learne to fly.

85. *her gratefull image.* Dion, LVIII. vii. 2, *Τύχης τέ τι ἄγαλμα, ὃ ἐγεγόνει μὲν, ὥς φασι, Τουλλίου τοῦ βασιλεύσαντός ποτε ἐν τῇ Ῥώμῃ, τότε δὲ ὁ Σηϊανὸς οἴκοι τε εἶχε καὶ μεγάλως ἤγαλλεν, αὐτός τε θύων εἶδεν ἀποστρεφόμενον.*

86. *Roman king*, Servius Tullius. For a similar relic we may compare Catiline's silver eagle, originally belonging to Marius (*Cat.* III. 563–5).

91. *masculine odours*, a 'strange Epithite', elaborately explained by Jonson in his note on the Coronation Entertainment, 616. He quotes Virgil's 'mascula tura' (*Ecl.* viii. 66); the name was given to the best kind of frankincense. Cf. Herrick, *The Dirge of Jephthah's Daughter* (*Works*, ed. Moorman, p. 361):

> May Virgins, when they come to mourn,
> Male-Incense burn
> Upon thine Altar!

97. *The house of Regulus.* *Dion, LVIII. ix, of Macro, καὶ ὃς νύκτωρ ἐς τὴν Ῥώμην ὡς καὶ κατ᾽ ἄλλο τι ἐλθὼν τά τε ἐπεσταλμένα οἱ Μεμμίῳ τε Ῥηγούλῳ τότε ὑπατεύοντι (ὁ γὰρ συνάρχων αὐτοῦ τὰ τοῦ Σηϊανοῦ ἐφρόνει) καὶ Γραικινίῳ Λάκωνι, τῷ τῶν νυκτοφυλάκων ἄρχοντι ἐπεκοίνωσε.*

100. *a frequent Senate*, a full muster of the Senate (Lat. *senatus frequens*). *Cat.* IV. 63.

103. *adscribe*, subscribe (Lat. *adscribo*)—a rare use.

105. *the place*. *Dion, LVIII. ix. 4, τῆς γὰρ βουλῆς ἕδρα ἐν τῷ ᾿Απολλωνίῳ γενήσεσθαι ἔμελλε.

167–8. *I, With ... Luco, ... are*. For the plural idea cf. *M.A.* 429–30, ' *Jove*, with the Senate ... were'; *Ep.* cxxxiii, 160–1, 'A face ... With great gray eyes, are lifted vp'; *3 Henry VI*, I. ii. 49, 50:

> The queen with all the northern earls and lords
> Intend here to besiege you in your castle.

171. Coleridge criticized this scene as 'unspeakably irrational. To believe, and yet to scoff at, a present miracle is little less than impossible. Sejanus should have been made to suspect priestcraft and a secret conspiracy against him' (*Lectures on Shakespeare*, ed. Bohn, p. 414). Swinburne replies, 'Coleridge, whose judgement on a question of ethics will scarcely be allowed to carry as much weight as his authority on matters of imagination, objects with some vehemence to the incredible inconsistency of Sejanus in appealing for a sign to the divinity whose altar he proceeds to overthrow, whose power he proceeds to defy, on the appearance of an unfavourable presage. This doubtless is not the conduct of a strong man or a rational thinker: but the great minister of Tiberius is never for an instant throughout the whole course of the action represented as a man of any genuine strength or any solid intelligence. He is shown to us as merely a cunning, daring, unscrupulous and imperious upstart, whose greed and craft, impudence and audacity, intoxicate while they incite and undermine while they uplift him' (*A Study of Ben Jonson*, p. 32).

Jonson in the Quarto carefully annotates the ritual of the scene.

177. *vervin*, Lat. *verbena*, but in the plural *verbenae* applied to the boughs and leafage (e.g. laurel, olive, or myrtle) used in sacrifices.

177. *Fauour your tongues*, and 181, *Fauour it with your tongues*. The sacrificial formula '*Favete linguis*', a summons to use words of good omen only, and so a command to be silent. Jonson seems to have hesitated whether to take 'linguis' as dative or ablative case: the latter is correct—'Be favourable with your tongues'.

It is amusing that Herrick in *The Faerie Temple*: or, *Oberons Chappell* (*Works*, ed. Moorman, p. 91) borrows this ritual:

> First, at the entrance of the gate,
> A little Puppet Priest doth wait,
> Who squeaks to all the commers there,
> *Favour your tongues who enter here*.
> *Pure hands bring hither, without staine*
> A second pules, *Hence, hence, profane*.

186. *auerts her face*. *Dion, quoted on line 85.

202. *spiced conscience*, dainty, over-particular. *B.F.* I. iii. 122, *D. is A*. II. ii. 81, *N.I.* II. v. 36. Chaucer's poor Parson 'ne maked him a spiced conscience' (*Prologue*, 526).

204. *sacrific'd vnto.* Dion, LVIII. iv. 4, καὶ τέλος καὶ ταῖς εἰκόσιν αὐτοῦ ὥσπερ καὶ ταῖς τοῦ Τιβερίου ἔθυον.

206. *gigglot*, originally a lewd woman, then a romping girl. *Cymbeline*, III. i. 31, 'O giglet fortune!' N. Udall, *Apophthegmes . . . Floures for Latine spekynge selected . . . oute of Terence*, 1533, f. 104, '*Quid est, inepta?* . . . What is the matter folyshe gyglotte?'

211. *His fortune suffers.* Note the delicate irony after the last scene.

217. *a rope.* *Dion, quoted on line 29.

235. *worthy my fates.* Lucan, *Pharsalia*, v. 653–4:

> Credit iam digna pericula Caesar
> fatis esse suis.

236–8. *Let doubtfull states . . .* Ibid. ix. 581–3:

> Sortilegis egeant dubii semperque futuris
> casibus ancipites; me non oracula certum,
> sed mors certa facit.

242. *Cedar.* Imitated by Fletcher in *The False One*, IV. iii:

> I cut the Cedar *Pompey*, and I'le fell
> This huge Oake *Cæsar* too.

244. *vine*, his wife Livia. Vines were trained upon elms, and Roman literature often expresses this by a marriage metaphor: cf. Catullus, lxii. 54 (Vitis), 'ulmo coniuncta marito'; Columella, XI. ii. 79, 'ulmi vitibus maritantur'.

256. *Things great enough.* Lucan, v. 659, 660:

> Licet ingentes abruperit actus
> festinata dies fatis, sat magna peregi.

257–62. Ibid. iii. 108–12:

> Omnia Caesar erat: privatae curia vocis
> testis adest. Sedere patres censere parati
> si regnum, si templa sibi iugulumque senatus
> exiliumque petat. Melius, quod plura iubere
> erubuit quam Roma pati.

264. *my second.* Ibid. v. 662, 'Vidit Magnum mihi Roma secundum'.

267. *give*, tell. So 297. So in Latin 'dare' for 'dicere': 'iste deus qui sit da, Tityre, nobis' (Virgil, *Ecl.* i. 18).

286. *Vnquit*, not dismissed.

298. *engin*, trickery.

299. *Macro is without.* Dion, LVIII. ix. 4, Μάκρο ἀναβὰς ἅμα τῇ ἕῳ ἐς τὸ παλάτιον . . . τῷ τε Σηϊανῷ μηδέπω ἐς αὐτό ἐσεληλυθότι περιέπεσε, καὶ ἰδὼν αὐτὸν ταραττόμενον ὅτι μηδέν οἱ ὁ Τιβέριος ἐπεστάλκει παρεμυθήσατο εἰπὼν ἰδίᾳ καὶ ἐν ἀπορρήτῳ ὅτι τὴν ἐξουσίαν αὐτῷ τὴν δημαρχικὴν φέροι.

307. *to some roome*, the upper stage where the interview (323–99) takes place.

325. *the noone of night.* G.M. 265. 'Speedily adopted', as Gifford says, by other poets: R. Armin, *The two Maids of More-clacke*, 1609, G3:

> . . . shine glo-worme,
> In the noone of night;

Drayton, *The Man in the Moone*, 37–8:

> Now the goodly Moone
> Was in the Full, and at her Nighted Noone;

Herrick, *Farewell vnto Poetrie*, 17, 18:

> Nay tell the Bell-man of the Night had tould
> Past Noone of night;

Milton, *Il Penseroso*, 67, 68:

> To behold the wandring Moon,
> Riding near her highest noon.

337. *amused*, puzzled. *Alch.* I. iii. 43; Chapman, *Monsieur d'Olive*, II. ii (1606, D3^v), 'I am amused, or I am in a quandarie gentlemen [for in good faith I remember not well whether of them was my words]'.

341. *by night.* Dion, LVIII. ix. 3.

354. *no iealous scruple.* Dion. ibid. 4.

363. *The tribuniciall dignitie*, a title devised by Augustus to avoid the obloquy attending the name of king or dictator. It carried with it the right of veto (*intercessio*), so that the holder could intervene in state business.

389. *a quarter-looke*, a face almost averted. *The Forest*, xii. 29, 'Turne, vpon scorned verse, their quarter-face'. So Shakespeare's 'half-faced fellowship' (*1 Henry IV*, I. iii. 208).

392–4. Senecan in tone: cf. *Thyestes*, 855–9:

> Leo flammiferis aestibus ardens
> iterum e caelo cadet Herculeus, . . .
> iustaeque cadent pondera Librae
> secumque trahent Scorpion acrem.

So for the 'henge', or axis of the earth:

> Nos e tanto visi populo
> digni premeret quos everso
> cardine mundus? (Ibid. 875–7.)

Before 400 (margin). *To the rest*, who have been keeping guard below.

414. *Harpocrates*, the god of silence and secrecy. *S.W.* II. ii. 4, *B.F.* v. vi. 48. The Greek form of the Egyptian Harpechruti, 'Har the child', figured as one by the sign of the finger on the lip; the Greeks misread this as a sign of secrecy.

431–74. The descriptions here and the characterization of upstart greatness (464 foll.) are from Dion, LVIII. v. 2–3: σπουδαί τε καὶ ὠθισμοὶ περὶ τὰς θύρας αὐτοῦ ἐγίγνοντο ἐκ τοῦ δεδιέναι μὴ μόνον μὴ οὐκ ὀφθῇ τις αὐτῷ, ἀλλὰ μὴ καὶ ἐν τοῖς ὑστάτοις φανῇ· πάντα γὰρ ἀκριβῶς καὶ μάλιστα τὰ τῶν πρώτων ἐτηρεῖτο καὶ τὰ ῥήματα καὶ τὰ νεύματα. οἱ μὲν γὰρ οἰκείᾳ ἀξιώσει προύχοντες οὔτε τὰ δεξιώματα παρά τινων πάνυ ἀπαιτοῦσι, κἂν ἄρα καὶ ἐκλειφθῇ τι αὐτῶν οὐκ ἐγκαλοῦσι σφίσιν, ἅτε καὶ ἑαυτοῖς συνειδότες ὅτι μὴ καταφρονοῦνται· οἱ δ' ἐπακτῷ καλλωπίσματι χρώμενοι πάντα ἰσχυρῶς τὰ τοιαῦτα ὡς καὶ ἐς τὴν τοῦ ἀξιώματός σφων πλήρωσιν ἀναγκαῖα ἐπιζήτουσι, κἂν μὴ τύχωσιν αὐτῶν ἄχθονταί τε ὡς διαβαλλόμενοι καὶ ὀργίζονται ὡς ὑβριζόμενοι.

432. *All haile.* See Jonson's note: so *Cat.* III. 670.

435–6. *pale troubled ensigns.* From Juvenal, *Sat.* iv. 72–5, of Domitian:

> Vocantur
> ergo in consilium proceres quos oderat ille,
> in quorum facie miserae magnaeque sedebat
> pallor amicitiae.

442. *his fall more steepe.* Briggs compares Claudian, *In Rufinum*, i. 21–3:

> Iam non ad culmina rerum
> iniustos crevisse queror: tolluntur in altum
> ut lapsu graviore ruant.

450. *huishers.* Cf. Old French *huisier.* Jonson has this form in *Alch.* IV. iv. 45, *D. is A.* II. vii. 33, III. iv. 43, *Ent. Alth.* 250, *For.* xii. 9.

452. *noise,* band of musicians.

454. *Sanquinius* is known in history only as the accuser of Arruntius (*Ann.* VI. vii). The *slow belly* is from Juvenal's sketch of Montanus hurrying to the council-chamber of Domitian: 'Montani quoque venter adest abdomine tardus.'

456. *another.* Haterius: cf. line 622.

458. *liburnian,* Illyrian slaves who acted as court-messengers. A particular kind of sedan-chair, the *liburna,* was named after them.

464–7. *It is a note* . . . A characteristic comment: it is based on Dion but sharpened by personal observation.

489–90. *Rector of an Isle.* *Dion, LVIII. v. 1: ὁ δὲ Σηϊανὸς τοσοῦτος ἦν τῇ τε ὑπεροχῇ τοῦ φρονήματος καὶ τῷ μεγέθει τῆς ἐξουσίας ὥστε συνελόντι εἰπεῖν αὐτὸν μὲν αὐτοκράτορα τὸν δὲ Τιβέριον νησίαρχόν τινα εἶναι δοκεῖν διὰ τὸ ἐν τῇ νήσῳ τῇ λεγομένῃ Καπρίᾳ τὰς διατριβὰς ποιεῖσθαι.

516. *in the temple of Apollo.* For this meeting-place compare the temple of Concord, 777, and the temple of Jupiter Stator in *Cat.* IV. 61.

517. *registered,* Lat. *conscripti.* III. 28 n.

539–40. *the vertue That could giue enuie bounds.* Claudian, *De Consulatu Stilichonis*, iii. 39, 40:

> Solus hic invidiae fines virtute reliquit
> humanumque modum.

542. *fierce,* rash, with a quibble on the word 'tame'. *Poet.* v. iii. 129.

543–649. Jonson has filled in the outline from Dion Cassius, LVIII. ix, x, adding touches from Tacitus and Suetonius. Juvenal describes the letter as 'verbosa et grandis' (x. 71) and Suetonius as 'pudenda miserandaque oratio' (*Tib*. lxv). *Dion says (LVIII. x): κἂν τούτῳ ἡ ἐπιστολὴ ἀνεγνώσθη. ἦν δὲ μακρά, καὶ οὐδὲν ἀθρόον κατὰ τοῦ Σηϊανοῦ εἶχεν, ἀλλὰ τὰ μὲν πρῶτα ἄλλο τι, εἶτα μέμψιν κατ' αὐτοῦ βραχεῖαν, καὶ μετ' αὐτὴν ἕτερόν τι, καὶ κατ' ἐκείνου ἄλλο· καὶ ἐπὶ τελευτῆς δύο τε βουλευτὰς τῶν ᾠκειωμένων οἱ κολασθῆναι καὶ αὐτὸν ἐν φρουρᾷ γενέσθαι δεῖν ἔλεγεν. ἄντικρυς γὰρ ἀποθανεῖν αὐτὸν ὁ Τιβέριος οὐ προσέταξεν, οὐχ ὅτι οὐκ ἐβούλετο, ἀλλ' ὅτι ἐφοβήθη μὴ ταραχή τις ἐκ τούτου γένηται· ὡς γοῦν οὐδὲ τὴν ὁδὸν ἀσφαλῶς ποιήσασθαι δυνάμενος τὸν ἕτερον τῶν ὑπάτων μετεπέμψατο. The reception of Sejanus before, during, and after the reading of the letter is recorded in the same chapter. *τοσαῦτα μὲν ἡ γραφὴ ἐδήλου, παρῆν δὲ καὶ ἀκοῦσαι ἐπ' αὐτῇ καὶ ἰδεῖν πολλὰ καὶ ποικίλα. πρότερον μὲν γὰρ, πρὶν ἀναγιγνώσκεσθαι αὐτήν, ἐπαίνους τε αὐτοῦ ὡς καὶ τὴν δημαρχικὴν ἐξουσίαν ληψομένου ἐποιοῦντο καὶ ἐπιβοήμασιν ἐχρῶντο προλαμβάνοντες ὅσα ἤλπιζον, καὶ προσενδεικνύμενοί οἱ ὡς καὶ αὐτοὶ αὐτὰ δώσοντες. ἐπεὶ δ' οὐδὲν τούτων εὑρίσκετο ἀλλὰ καὶ πᾶν τοὐναντίον ἢ προσεδόκων ἤκουον, ἔν τε ἀπορίᾳ καὶ μετὰ τοῦτο καὶ ἐν κατηφείᾳ πολλῇ ἐγένοντο, καί τινες καὶ ἐξανέστησαν τῶν συγκαθημένων αὐτῷ· οὐ γὰρ πρόσθεν περὶ πολλοῦ φίλον ἔχειν ἐποιοῦντο, τούτῳ τότε οὐδὲ τῆς αὐτῆς συνεδρείας κοινωνεῖν ἤθελον. κἀκ τούτου καὶ στρατηγοὶ καὶ δήμαρχοι περιέσχον αὐτὸν ὅπως μὴ συνταράξῃ τι ἐκπηδήσας· ὅπερ πάντως ἂν ἐπεποιήκει εἰ κατ' ἀρχὰς ἀθρόῳ τινὶ ἀκούσματι ἐπέπληκτο. νῦν δὲ τό τε ἀεὶ ἀναγιγνωσκόμενον ὡς καὶ κοῦφον καὶ μόνον ὂν παρορῶν καὶ μάλιστα μὲν μηδὲν ἄλλο, εἰ δὲ μή, μήτι γε καὶ ἀνήκεστόν τι ἐπεστάλθαι περὶ αὐτοῦ ἐλπίζων διετρίβη καὶ κατὰ χώραν ἔμεινε. κἂν τούτῳ προσκαλεσαμένου αὐτὸν τοῦ Ῥηγούλου οὐχ ὑπήκουσεν, οὐχ ὅτι ὑπερεφρόνησεν (ἤδη γὰρ ἐτεταπείνωτο), ἀλλ' ὅτι ἀήθης τοῦ προστάττεσθαί τι ἦν. ὡς δὲ καὶ δεύτερον καὶ τρίτον γε ἐκεῖνος ἐμβοήσας οἱ καὶ τὴν χεῖρα ἅμα ἐκτείνας εἶπε "Σηϊανέ, δεῦρο ἐλθέ", ἐπηρώτησεν αὐτὸν αὐτὸ τοῦτο "ἐμὲ καλεῖς;" ὀψὲ δ' οὖν ποτε ἀναστάντι αὐτῷ καὶ ὁ Λάκων ἐπεσελθὼν προσέστη. καὶ τέλος διαναγνωσθείσης τῆς ἐπιστολῆς πάντες ἀπὸ μιᾶς γλώσσης καὶ κατεβόων αὐτοῦ καὶ δεινὰ ἐπέλεγον, οἱ μὲν ἠδικημένοι οἱ δὲ πεφοβημένοι, ἄλλοι τὴν φιλίαν τὴν πρὸς αὐτὸν ἐπηλυγαζόμενοι, ἄλλοι δὲ τῇ μεταβολῇ αὐτοῦ ἐπιχαίροντες.

562. *in a free state*. *Suetonius, *Tib*. xxviii: 'Sed et adversus convicia malosque rumores et famosa de se ac suis carmina firmus et patiens, subinde iactabat in civitate libera linguam mentemque liberas esse debere.'

564. *The lapwing*. *Poet*. IV. vii. 53 n.

575. *affie in*, trust in.

582. *no innocence* ... From Seneca, *De Clementia*, I. i. 9, addressed to Nero: 'Ex clementia omnes idem sperant, nec est quisquam cui tam valde innocentia sua placeat ut non stare in conspectu clementiam paratam humanis erroribus gaudeat.'

585. *wearied crueltie*. Ibid. I. xi. 2, 'Ego vero clementiam non voco lassam crudelitatem.'

604–6. *What we should say* ... Quoted with comments by Tacitus (*Ann*. VI. vi. 1) in reference to a trial of Cotta Messalinus, one of the emperor's most cruel agents: 'Insigne visum est earum Caesaris litterarum initium, nam his verbis exorsus est: "Quid scribam vobis, patres conscripti, aut quo modo scribam aut quid omnino non scribam hoc tempore, di me deaeque peius perdant quam perire me cotidie sentio si scio." Adeo facinora atque flagitia sua ipsi quoque in supplicium verterant. . . . Quippe Tiberium non fortuna, non solitudines protegebant quin tormenta pectoris suasque ipse poenas fateretur.' With the slight modification 'quam cotidie perire sentio' the words are quoted vaguely by Suetonius (*Tib.* lxvii) as the beginning of a letter. Suetonius explains them, not as Tacitus, of the torment of conscience, but by Tiberius' sensitiveness to libels cited as evidence in the law courts. See our discussion in the general introduction to the play in vol. ii, page 25.

613. *prouide their safetie.* Like the Latin *prouidere*: so *Volp.* dedication, 78.

622. *porcpisce.* *E.M.O.* IV. iii. 82, 'porpuse'. For the *dancing* of this fish as a sign of storm see *E.M.I.* Quarto, v. iii. 240–1.

648. *apprênded.* The spelling copies the Latin *apprendo*, a syncopated form of *apprehendo*: so *Volp.* v. i. 6, the Quarto text. Gayton in *Pleasant Notes upon Don Quixot*, 1654, p. 214, has

> Conceal'd and smother'd sinns have never end,
> Shame and deprênsion is a better friend.

651. *reuerend.* IV. 222.

670. *betweene you, and I.* *E.M.I.* v. iii. 62.

673. *Typhœus,* one of the Giants who did battle with the Gods. Hesiod describes him as aspiring to the sovereignty of earth and heaven and finally quelled by the thunderbolts of Zeus (*Theog.* 821 foll.).

685. *Phlegra,* or Pallene, a peninsula of Macedonia, where Zeus struck down the Giants.

690–701. *From Juvenal, *Sat.* x. 58–66:

> Descendunt statuae restemque sequuntur,
> ipsas deinde rotas bigarum impacta securis
> caedit et immeritis franguntur crura caballis. . . .
> Pone domi laurus, duc in Capitolia magnum
> cretatumque bovem.

705. *popular ayre.* Horace's 'aura popularis'.

708–9. Dion, LVIII. vi. 1, πρὸς γὰρ τὴν τῶν παρόντων ὄψιν οὐδ' ἂν εἰ σαφῶς θεός τις προέλεγεν ὅτι τοσαύτη δι' ὀλίγου μεταβολὴ γενήσοιτο ἐπίστευσεν ἄν τις.

712. *Moores.* Briggs quotes Herodotus IV. clxxxviii of the sun-worship in Libya.

718–29. Dion Cassius, LVIII. xi: ἔνθα δὴ καὶ μάλιστα ἄν τις τὴν ἀνθρωπίνην ἀσθένειαν κατεῖδεν ὥστε μηδαμῇ μηδαμῶς φυσᾶσθαι. ὃν γὰρ τῇ ἕῳ πάντες ὡς καὶ κρείττω σφῶν ὄντα ἐς τὸ βουλευτήριον παρέπεμψαν, τοῦτον τότε ἐς τὸ οἴκημα ὡς μηδένος βελτίω κατέσυρον, καὶ ὃν στεφάνων πρότερον πολλῶν ἠξίουν, τούτῳ τότε δεσμὰ περιέθεσαν· ὃν δὲ ἐδορυφόρουν ὡς δεσπότην, τοῦτον ἐφρούρουν ὡς δραπέτην καὶ ἀπεκάλυπτόν ἐπικαλυπτόμενον, καὶ ὃν τῷ περιπορφύρῳ ἱματίῳ ἐκεκοσμήκεσαν ἐπὶ κόρρης ἔπαιον, ὅν τε προσεκύνουν ᾧ τε ὡς θεῷ ἔθυον, τοῦτον θανατώσοντες ἦγον. καὶ αὐτῷ καὶ ὁ δῆμος προσπίπτων πολλὰ μὲν ἐπὶ τοῖς ἀπολωλόσιν ὑπ' αὐτοῦ ἐπεβόα, πολλὰ δὲ καὶ ἐπὶ τοῖς ἐλπισθεῖσιν ἐπέσκωπτε. τάς τε εἰκόνας αὐτοῦ πάσας κατέβαλλον καὶ κατέκοπτον καὶ κατέσυρον ὡς καὶ αὐτὸν ἐκεῖνον αἰκιζόμενοι· καὶ οὕτω θεατὴς ὢν πείσεσθαι ἔμελλεν ἐγίγνετο.

727. *fugitive*, a runaway slave (Lat. *fugitivus*).

733–5. From Juvenal, *Sat.* x. 365–6:

> Nullum numen habes si sit prudentia; nos te
> nos facimus, Fortuna, deam caeloque locamus.

739. *Caesars tutor*. Cf. iv. 403.

743. *twelue score off*, i.e. yards, a common length for a shot in archery.

750. *I prophesie*. So in Tacitus, *Ann.* vi. xlviii. 5, Arruntius, after speaking of life under Macro, who had attacked him—'haec vatis in modum dictitans venas resolvit'.

754. *mankind*, human feeling.

764. *deuoure the way*. So Latin 'viam vorare', French 'dévorer l'espace': 2 *Henry IV*, i. i. 47, 'He seem'd in running to devour the way'.

765. *To . . . a new theatre*. Seneca, *Hercules Furens*, 838–9:

> Quantus incedit populus per urbes
> ad novi ludos avidus theatri. . . .

768. *sensiue*. *E.M.I.* ii. iii. 67.

768–76. Juvenal, *Sat.* x. 62–3: 'Ardet adoratum populo caput et crepat ingens Seianus.'

777. *temple of Concord*. Dion, LVIII. xi. 4: ὕστερον δ' οὐ πολλῷ ἀλλ' αὐθημερὸν ἡ γερουσία πλησίον τοῦ οἰκήματος ἐν τῷ Ὁμονοείῳ . . . ἀθροισθεῖσα θάνατον αὐτοῦ κατεψηφίσατο.

779–85. *tread him downe* . . . Juvenal, *Sat.* x. 85–8:

> Curramus praecipites, et
> dum iacet in ripa calcemus Caesaris hostem.
> Sed videant servi, ne quis neget et pavidum in ius
> cervice obstricta dominum trahat.

786–804. Ibid. 67–77:

> Gaudent omnes. 'Quae labra, quis illi
> vultus erat! Nunquam, si quid mihi credis, amavi
> hunc hominem.' 'Sed quo cecidit sub crimine? quisnam
> delator? quibus indicibus, quo teste probavit.'
> 'Nil horum, verbosa et grandis epistola venit
> a Capreis.' 'Bene habet; nil plus interrogo.' Sed quid
> turba Remi? Sequitur fortunam ut semper, et odit
> damnatos; idem populus, si Nortia Tusco
> favisset, si oppressa foret secura senectus
> principis, hac ipsa Seianum diceret hora
> Augustum.

Jonson's translation of 'Quae labra, quis illi vultus erat!' misses the point: as Gifford says, the original is 'the language of contempt, not

of curiosity'. Translate 'What lips he had, what a haughty face!'—
a reference to the scorn habitual to him in his greatness.

814–32. Excerpted from Claudian's picture of the fate of Rufinus in
A.D. 393: as Gibbon remarks, Claudian 'performs the dissection' 'with
the savage coolness of an anatomist'. The criticism applies to Jonson's
copy.

> Vacuo plebs undique muro
> iam secura fluit; senibus non obstitit aetas
> virginibusque pudor; viduae quibus ille maritos
> abstulit orbataeque ruunt ad gaudia matres
> insultantque alacres. Laceros iuvat ire per artus
> pressaque calcato vestigia sanguine tingi.
>
> (_In Rufinum_, ii. 427–32.)

> Hi vultus avidos et adhuc spirantia vellunt
> lumina, truncatos alii rapuere lacertos.
> Amputat ille pedes, umerum quatit ille solutis
> nexibus; hic fracti reserat curvamina dorsi;
> hic iecur, hic cordis fibras, hic pandit anhelas
> pulmonis latebras. Spatium non invenit ira,
> nec locus est odiis. Consumpto funere vixdum
> deseritur sparsumque perit per tela cadaver.
>
> (Ibid. 410–17.)

> Iacet en qui possidet orbem
> exiguae telluris inops et pulvere raro
> per partes tegitur nusquam totiensque sepultus.
>
> (Ibid. 451–3.)

818. _mounting._ An impossible word: Sejanus' head has been struck
off, and the sense is further confused by the account of two sets of
assailants, one mounting at his head, another at his face. Even if the
head was fixed on a stake or a spear, people eager to reach it would
not 'mount' at it. Whalley quoted a note by Sympson, conjecturing
'minting', i.e. aiming. But this word, since the Middle English period,
has been restricted to the north of England. The text appears to be
corrupt.

Before 833. The appearance of a _Nuntius_ is a noteworthy revival:
usually Jonson contented himself with putting a narrative in the mouth
of a character; for instance, Terentius in the preceding scene, or Petreius
in _Catiline_, v. 629–88.

840–1. *From Seneca, _De Tranquillitate Animi_, xi, of Sejanus: 'Quo
die illum senatus deduxerat, populus in frusta divisit. In quem, quicquid congeri poterat, di hominesque contulerant, ex eo nihil superfuit
quod carnifex traheret.'

846. _The girl so simple_ . . . *Tacitus, _Ann._ v. ix (vi. iv): 'Placitum
posthac ut in reliquos Seiani liberos adverteretur, vanescente quamquam
plebis ira ac plerisque per priora supplicia lenitis. Igitur portantur in
carcerem, filius imminentium intellegens, puella adeo nescia ut crebro

interrogaret quod ob delictum et quo traheretur; neque facturum ultra
et posse se puerili verbere moneri. Tradunt temporis eius auctores, quia
triumvirali supplicio affici virginem inauditum habebatur, a carnifice
laqueum iuxta compressam; exim oblisis faucibus id aetatis corpora in
Gemonias abiecta.' *So Dion, LVIII. xi. 5, stating ὡς οὐχ ὅσιον ὂν παρθενευο-
μένην τινὰ ἐν τῷ δεσμωτηρίῳ διολέσθαι.

851. *wittily*, inventively.

855–6. *O act* . . . Seneca, *Thyestes*, 1094–5:

> Aeterna nox permaneat et tenebris tegat
> immensa longis scelera.

859. *Apicata*. *Dion, LVIII. xi. 6: καὶ ἡ γυνὴ 'Απικᾶτα οὐ κατεψηφίσθη
μὲν, μαθοῦσα δὲ ὅτι τὰ τέκνα αὐτῆς τέθνηκε καί σφων τὰ σώματα ἐν τοῖς ἀναβασμοῖς
ἰδοῦσα, ἀνεχώρησε καὶ ἐς βιβλίον γράψασα περὶ τοῦ θανάτου τοῦ Δρούσου κατά τε τῆς
Λιουίλλης τῆς γυναικὸς αὐτοῦ δι' ἥνπερ που καὶ αὐτὴ τῷ ἀνδρὶ προσεκεκρούκει ὥστε
μηκέτι συνοικεῖν, τὸ μὲν τῷ Τιβερίῳ ἔπεμψεν, αὐτὴ δὲ ἑαυτὴν διεχρήσατο.

860. *degrees*, steps. *New World*, 28, *Chl.* 230, 321. Cunningham compares Massinger, *The Roman Actor*, III. ii (1629, F1ᵛ):

> 'Twould rellish more of pollicie to haue them
> Made away in priuate . . . then to haue them drawne
> To the degrees in publike; for 'tis doubted
> That the sad obiect may beget compassion
> In the giddie rout, and cause some sudaine vprore
> That may disturbe you.

867–8. *the sunne Runne backward*, as at Thyestes' banquet.

868–9. *the old Deformed Chaos*. Seneca, *Thyestes*, 831–2:

> . . . iterumque deos
> hominesque premat deforme chaos.

893. *Forbeare*. . . . Claudian, *In Rufinum*, 440–1:

> Desinat elatis quisquam confidere rebus
> instabilesque deos et lubrica numina dicat.

And Juvenal, *Sat.* x. 103–7, of Sejanus:

> Nam qui nimios optabat honores
> et nimias poscebat opes, numerosa parabat
> excelsae turris tabulata, unde altior esset
> casus et impulsae praeceps immane ruinae.

896. *pash*, break violently. Cf. *Iack Drums Entertainment*, 1616, A4:

> I care not to be like the *Horeb* Calfe
> One day ador'd, the next pash't all in peeces.

902–3. From Seneca, *Thyestes*, 613–14:

> Quem dies vidit veniens superbum,
> hunc dies vidit fugiens iacentem.

EASTWARD HO

The Problem of the Authorship

VARIOUS attempts have been made to disentangle the shares of the three authors to whom the *Eastward Ho* is assigned on the title-page —Chapman, Ben Jonson, and Marston. 'J. C.' in a notice of *Eastward Ho* contributed to *Blackwood's Edinburgh Magazine* (September 1821) made a few vague suggestions.[1] Jonson had not the chief part in the writing; it has no bold delineation of character, no highly wrought finish of dialogue, and none of his peculiar richness of humour. 'Neither, on the other hand, is it distinguished by his hardness', such as over-elaboration of character. 'The style bears more resemblance to that of Chapman', but Jonson probably first sketched the plan and revised the whole; he can be traced in the character of Touchstone and in the concluding scenes.

Attempts at a complete analysis have been made by F. G. Fleay, who revelled in this kind of detective work, in his *Biographical Chronicle of the English Drama* (1891), ii. 81; by Professor W. J. Cunliffe in his edition of the play in Gayley's *Representative English Comedies* (1913), iii. 395–501; by Professor T. M. Parrott in his edition of Chapman's comedies (1913); by Dr. Julia H. Harris in the Yale edition of the play (1926); and by Dr. Morse D. Allen in his monograph on *The Satire of John Marston*. W. J. Lawrence touched on the question in the chapter on 'Early Dramatic Collaboration' in his *Pre-Restoration Stage Studies* (1927), pp. 240–72. Two editors, A. H. Bullen in 1887 and Professor F. E. Schelling in 1904, held that the problem of the divided authorship was insoluble. They accepted only the few suggestions that the poet Swinburne made in his study of *George Chapman* (1875).

The introductory essay of our colleague C. H. Herford to the edition[2] was confined to the broad critical aspect of the question; it produced sufficient evidence to show that each of the three dramatists could be traced in the play and reserved fuller treatment for the commentary. Now that we are called upon to face the question we have departed in one respect from the practice of some of our predecessors. We have relied far less on the illusory test of parallel passages and vocabulary, using only the most remarkable as corroborative evidence. Thus 'dilling' (I. i. 79) is not 'a Marston word' because it occurs once in the text of Marston (*What You Will*, II. i. 25, ed. Bullen), and 'well-parted' (I. ii. 163) is not exclusively a Jon-

[1] x. 127–36.   [2] See vol. ii, pp. 27–46.

son phrase when it is found in Shakespeare,[1] Webster and Rowley, and Field. The use of 'Why!' as an interjection has even been quoted as a minor test of Marston's authorship. The desire to press home verbal parallels often carries critics much too far when a text is put under the microscope. And the value of these parallels is diminished by a fact not usually recognized when they are discussed. From the beginning of the seventeenth century there was a tendency for individual dramatic styles in prose dialogue to converge on one more or less established type; somewhat as a modern journal acquires a distinctive style to which all who write for it tend to conform. Resemblances which are purely superficial may be taken too seriously.

We believe the idea of the play to have originated with Marston. Touchstone, the model of *bourgeois* morality, and Sindefy the courtesan, reflect two contrasted types which strongly appealed to him. It is, therefore, natural to find Marston's hand in the opening scenes of the play. He set the characters going. On these points we find ourselves in agreement with Professor Parrott, who further sees in Marston's work a reaction against the sentimental treatment of city life in Middleton and Dekker: *The Dutch Courtesan*, for example, was Marston's counterblast to *The Honest Whore*.

On the other hand, Professor Cunliffe, backed by Mr. Lawrence,[2] thinks that Jonson plotted and organized the execution of the play but contributed nothing to it except perhaps the prologue. Chapman in 1598-9 had written for the Admiral's men a tragedy on a plot drawn up by Jonson (*Henslowe's Diary*, ff. 51ᵛ, 52ᵛ, ed. Greg), but this is an exceptional instance, and Marston is less likely to have worked in this way under Jonson. Personally we find clear traces of Jonson's handiwork, especially in the concluding scenes. This is what we should expect: of the three men he was the best qualified to gather up and round off the final stages of the work.

The middle-class tone of the comedy was carefully observed in one important particular: the writers kept off the classics. Two references to Greek mythology in the play are carefully manipulated. Mildred alludes to the fable that Ulysses, to escape going to Troy,

[1] In the analogous 'dearly parted', *Troilus and Cressida*, III. iii. 96.

[2] Mr. Lawrence further suggested that the Quarto was revised before publication and 'the gaps neatly closed' in order to get rid of offending passages; he explains the abrupt change in Act III, scene ii, as an example, apparently, of this 'neat' closing. He evidently did not know the text of the First Quarto; we have shown in the textual introduction of the Oxford *Jonson* (vol. iv, pp. 495-8) how cuts were made, evidently by the publisher, for the gaps were not closed. See the facsimiles given of A4ᵛ, C1ᵛ, and C2ʳ. A gap was closed only in the famous reference to the Scots on E3ᵛ, E4ʳ: here revision was a necessity, and one of the authors was called in to supply it.

feigned madness, yoking an ass and an ox to the plough and sowing salt (I. ii. 35–8); but her version is that he yoked cats, dogs, and foxes, and she prefaces it with the statement 'I heard a Scholler once say'. The other passage is a Homeric reference to Ulysses sailing past the island of the Sirens, stuffing the ears of his crew with wax and getting himself tied to the mast until he was out of hearing. Touchstone replies to the appeal of his family (v. iv. 1, 2), 'I will sayle by you, and not heare you, like the wise *Vlisses*': 'not heare you' is, again, an inaccurate version, and Touchstone follows it up with, 'I have stopt mine eares, with *Shoomakers waxe*', which effectively gets away from the Greek. The song of 'The Golden Shower' (v. i. 101–9), with its reference to the Danae story, is the only undiluted classical reference in the play, and it may pass muster as a song.

We now take the play scene by scene, beginning with the Prologue:

> Not out of Enuy, for ther's no effect
> Where there's no cause; nor out of Imitation,
> For we haue euermore bin Imitated;
> Nor out of our contention to doe better
> Then that which is opposde to ours in Title—

a reference to the play of *Westward Ho*, which had been acted in the previous year.

The prologue has been assigned to Chapman by Mr. H. Dugdale Sykes because of a verbal resemblance in the opening lines to the prologue of *Bussy d'Ambois* published in 1641; this play had been revived by the King's men on 7 April 1634, and the prologue refers to an authorized performance by another company:

> Not out of confidence that none but wee
> Are able to present this Tragedie,
> Nor out of envie at the grace of late
> It did receive, nor yet to derogate
> From their deserts, who give out boldly that
> They move with equall feet on the same flat;
> Neither for all, nor any of such ends,
> We offer it, gracious and noble friends,
> To your review, wee farre from emulation,
> And (charitably judge)[1] from imitation,
> With this worke entertaine you, a peece knowne,
> And still beleev'd, in Court to be our owne.

As Chapman died a month after the performance on 7 May 1634, this prologue cannot with certainty be attributed to him, and it may

---

[1] Dr. F. S. Boas's punctuation.

be a half-conscious recollection of the prologue of *Eastward Ho*. The tone of this earlier prologue as a whole better suits Jonson, to whom it is usually attributed. 'We haue euermore bin Imitated' fits in with the prologue to *Cynthia's Revels*:

> In this alone, his MVSE her sweetnesse hath,
> Shee shunnes the print of any beaten path;
> And proues new wayes to come to learned eares.

And in his verses upon Brome's *Northern Lass* in 1632 Jonson speaks of

> observation of those Comick Lawes
> Which I, your *Master*, first did teach the Age.

ACT I

This is given by common consent to Marston, the most suitable person to begin the play if, as we believe, he originated the idea of it. Bullen noted a parallel to I. i. 27–9—'I am intertaind among gallants, true: They call me coozen *Franke*, right; I lend them monies, good; they spend it, well'—in *Parasitaster*, IV. i, 'No prejudice dear Garbetza: his brother your husband, right; he cuckold his eldest brother, true; he got her with child, just.' Parrott adds *The Dutch Courtesan*, II. ii. 1–3, 'Nay, good sweet daughter, do not swagger so; you hear your love is to be married, true; he does cast you off, right; he will leave you to the world—what then?'

Nine lines have been excised in the First Quarto from the text of the second scene:[1] the context, with the remark about a 'right Scot' farthingale 'clipping close', suggests that further reflections on the Scotch have been deleted. This is ground for supposing it was a Marston passage.[2]

The rhyming tag at the end with its high moral tone (I. ii. 171–6) is Marston all over. The announcement

> *I intend to prooue*
> *Which thriues the best, the meane or loftie loue—*

recalls the argument of *The Dutch Courtesan*, 'The difference between the love of a courtesan and a wife'. Parrott gives a list of these verse tags at the end of scenes in *The Dutch Courtesan*; for instance, I. i. 169–70, ed. Bullen:

> Well, I'll go to make her loath the shame she's in;
> The sight of vice augments the hate of sin.[3]

---

[1] See vol. iv, pp. 495–6. [2] Vol. ii, p. 38.
[3] Compare in the same play I. ii. 271–2, III. i. 283–4, IV. ii. 47–8, V. i. 113–14.

Act II

Scene i. From this point onward the work is more divided. The Goulding and Mildred passages (53–86, 143–74) we assign to Marston; they complete the portraiture of the first act. The Quicksilver and Touchstone dialogue (1–52, 87–142) has the mark of Jonson's style. The quotation from *The Blind Beggar of Alexandria* (110), '*Who cries on murther? lady was it you?*' he had already used in *Poetaster* (III. iv. 242).

The Marston tag at the close is introduced with '*I haue often read*': so in I. ii. 126, 'I haue read, that olde wit sings'. We know of no Martin Tupper of the period who could have supplied Touchstone with these platitudes; but a tradesman of his conventional stamp could hardly have posed as an original poet.

Scene ii. Here again there has been a deletion after line 10; Security, who is on the stage already, enters at line 11. Most of the scene (1–319) we assign to Chapman; it has touches of his heightened, quasi-epic style such as 'My house is as 'twere the Caue, where the young Out-lawe hoords the stolne vayles of his occupation' (4–6) and the verse-ring of

> *Via*, the curtaine that shaddowed *Borgia*;
> There lie thou huske of my enuassail'd State,
> I *Sampson* now, have burst the *Philistins* bands (34–6).

The vague allusiveness of the Borgia reference is characteristic of Chapman's style. So is the tennis metaphor describing storms at sea:

'What are these Shippes, but Tennis Balles for the windes to play withall? Tost from one waue to another; Nowe vnder-line; Nowe ouer the house; Sometimes Brickewal'd against a Rocke, so that the guttes flye out againe; Sometimes strooke vnder the wide Hazzard, and farewell Master Marchant' (63–8).

It is instructive to contrast Quicksilver's cynicism about marriage (281–306) with Jonson's elaborate treatment of the same theme, based on Ovid and Juvenal, in *Epicoene* (II. ii). The difference of tone is as marked as the difference of treatment. In lines 307–8 Professor Parrott points to a Chapman touch: 'Out of my fortune, what a death is my life bound face to face too.' He compares *Bussy D'Ambois*, V. i. 115–17, where the image is worked out more closely:

> binde me face to face
> To some dead woman, taken from the cart
> Of Execution.[1]–

---

[1] Parrott explains the phrase as a reference to the brutality of Mezentius in Virgil, *Aeneid*, viii. 485–6:

> Mortua quin etiam iungebat corpora vivis,
> componens manibusque manus atque oribus ora.

and *Byron's Tragedy*, v. iv. 38:

> A slave bound face to face to Death till death—

a line repeated in *Euthymiæ Raptus; or the Teares of Peace* (1609).

At or just before the entrance of Gertrude (313 foll.) we seem to return to Marston. There is an allusion to *Hamlet*, phrases of which he was fond of echoing, in lines 316–17, 'he (with a purpose to feede on you) inuites you to supper',[1] which is in Marston's manner, and so is Gertrude's shamelessness in the concluding passage (371–91).

ACT III

Scene i. The style is Jonson's in the first half of the scene (1–39); the Virginia scheme in the second half seems to have been entrusted to Chapman.

Scene ii. Marston's hand is easy to trace up to the entrance of Touchstone, Goulding, and Mildred (1–82): the quick movement of the action; the reference to *Hamlet* ('Sfoote *Hamlet;* are you madde?' in line 6), and naming the footman Hamlet; the song in lines 77–81; and the vulgar indecency of Gertrude's reference to her old relations with Quicksilver, which even Quicksilver finds embarrassing (71–6). This portion of the scene was discussed in our introduction.[2]

The style is firmer, and the action steadier, in what follows (83–200); this is in Jonson's manner, and it is instructive to see him trying to make Goulding talk in character (100–9). Contrast also the terse aphorism, 'Ambition consumes it selfe, with the very show' (138–9) with Mildred's diffuse platitudes, 'Where Titles presume to thrust before fit meanes to second them, Wealth and Respect often growe sullen and will not follow. For sure in this, I would for your sake I spake not truth. *Where ambition of place goes before fitnesse of birth, contempt and disgrace follow*' (I. ii. 31–5). Here again is a sentence with the Jonsonian ring, 'hee that wayes mens thoughts, has his handes full of nothing' (III. ii. 193).

Lines 201–332. This is the only continuous verse passage in the play, which so confused the printer that he set up bits of it in prose (201–8, 280–7, 292–4, 311–21). This abrupt change may be credited to Chapman. Swinburne long ago commented, 'Two allusions, in the mouth of the usurer, one to "the ship of famous Draco" (251), and one to the camel's horns (266), of which we hear something too often from this poet, are in the unmistakable manner of Chapman'.[3] The

---

[1] Cf. *Hamlet*, IV. iii. 17–20: '*King.* Now, Hamlet, where's Polonius? *Ham.* At supper. *King.* At supper! where? *Ham.* Not where he eats, but where he is eaten.'

[2] Vol. ii, p. 44.

[3] *George Chapman*, 1875, p. 59.

latinized form of Drake's name is paralleled by Chapman's tribute to Sir Horace Vere, 'besieged and distrest in Mannheim', *Pro Vere, Autumni Lachrymæ* (1635). The story of the camel's horns is in Erasmus's *Adagia*:[1] 'Camelus desyderans cornua, etiam aures perdidit', with the explanation that the camels, petitioning Jupiter for horns, got them, but he was annoyed and took away their ears. Chapman writes in *Ouids Banquet of Sence* (1598), A2, Dedication: 'But that Poesie should be as peruiall as Oratorie, and plainnes her speciall ornament, were the plaine way to barbarisme: and to make the Asse proude of his eares; to take away strength from Lyons, and give Cammels hornes.' And in *Byrons Conspiracie*, IV. i (1608, G2ᵛ):

> But for a subiect to affect a kingdome,
> Is like the Cammell, that of *Ioue* begd hornes.

And finally in *The Revenge of Bussy D'Ambois* (1613), II. i (D3), the allusion becomes 'pervial':

> A man may well
> Compare them to those foolish great-spleen'd Cammels,
> That to their high heads, beg'd of Ioue hornes higher;
> Whose most vncomely, and ridiculous pride
> When hee had satisfied, they could not vse,
> But where they went vpright before, they stoop't
> And bore their heads much lower for their hornes:
> As these high men doe, low in all true grace,
> Their height being priviledge to all things base.

Further, the abrupt introduction of the camel is a trick of Chapman's style:

> 't wilbe rare,
> Two fine horn'd Beastes, a Cammell and a Lawyer! (265–6.)

Chapman prefers to append an irrelevant suggestion where other writers would use a simile or a comparison. Compare *Monsieur D'Oliue*, V. i (1606, G3): Vandome, begged by Vaumont not to disturb two sleeping ladies, says:

> My Lord, your onely way to deale with women
> And Parrets, is to keepe them waking still.

And *May Day*, II. iv (1611, p. 29):

> *Ang.* Women and fethers? now fie on that affinity.

The parrots and the feathers are dragged in exactly like the camel in *Eastward Ho*.

The situation of Security helping to abduct his own wife, thinking

---

[1] Ed. Stephanus (1558), col. 842.

she is Mistress Bramble, and then proposing to deceive Bramble by disguising her in his own wife's dress is, we have pointed out,[1] in the same vein of humour as the central device of Chapman's *All Fools*, where Gostanzo, the real victim of the deceit, assists, with huge gusto, in making game, as he thinks, of Mark Antonio. There is a slight verbal parallel in the two plays: 'A toye, a toy runns in my head yfaith', says Security (317); 'Troth,-sir, I'll tell you what a sudden toy Comes in my head', says Rinaldo when he is duping Gostanzo (*All Fools*, III. i. 78–9). But the intrigue in *Eastward Ho* is borrowed from the *Novellino* of Masuccio published at Naples in 1476.[2] Pietro Genefra, a Catalan living in Salerno, in love with Adriana, the wife of an Amalfian silversmith Cosmo, inveigles her jealous and witless husband to bring her on board ship when he goes away, making him believe she is the wife of a boatman known to Cosmo, who enters heartily into the fun of the intrigue. Points of detailed resemblance are the promise of Cosmo to make Genefra godfather if he has a child (III. i. 7–13), Cosmo making Adriana kiss Genefra at their sham farewell (ibid. 19–22), and even more suggestively, the tears of the disguised wife when her husband tries to comfort her and she cannot keep a steady face (III. iii. 123–36).

Scene iii. Chapman continues the Virginia episode; the adaptation from the *Utopia* of Sir Thomas More, describing gold as the only metal used by the Virginians for the commonest purposes, and rubies and diamonds picked up on the beach (25–35), is especially in his manner. There is the question of the cancelled lines 41–8: did Chapman write them, or Marston? Drummond's statement about the play is ambiguous,[3] but both this and the other passage[4] which got the authors into trouble occur in what we believe to be a Chapman scene.

A minor indication of Chapman's manner is the Latin stage-direction '*Surgit*' (120): compare in *Bussy D'Ambois* '*Procumbit*' (I. i. 33, ed. Boas). '*Exiturus*' (III. ii. 338) '*Surgit Spiritus cum suis*' (v. iii. 53), '*Moritur*' (v. iv. 146).

Scene iv is by Marston. The parody of *King Richard III*, 'A boate, a boate, a boate, a full hundred Markes for a boate', proves it. Marston had used it in *The Scourge of Villany* (1598), and was to re-use it in *Parasitaster* and *What You Will*.

---

[1] Vol. ii, p. 41.
[2] First pointed out by H. D. Curtis in *Modern Philosophy*, v. 105–8. Professor Parrott gave a full account of the fortieth *novella* from which the episode is chiefly taken, and Dr. Harris in the Yale edition reprinted the Italian text of this and the thirty-fourth *novella* on pages 174–9.
[3] *Conversations*, 273–6, in vol. i, p. 140.
[4] Act IV. i. 178–81.

ACT IV

Scene i. In no other scene of the play is the division of the shares of the three authors so easy to trace. Lines 1–119 are by Marston; in lines 62–4 is an allusion to the drowning Ophelia which is given a characteristically indecent turn.

The brief passage of verse (120–39) is clearly Chapman's, as R. H. Shepherd, Swinburne, and Bullen long ago noted. The repentance here expressed in a philosophic, almost a tragic, vein clashes with Quicksilver's jaunty reappearance later in the scene (199–243) and with the grovelling piety of the concluding scenes. In fact the tone of

> the drift of all vnlawfull courses, . . .
> In the firme order of iust *Destinie*,
> They are the ready high wayes to our Ruines.—

hardly suits a climax in comedy.

Chapman's portion continues to the re-entrance of Quicksilver (185). What follows up to line 283 is Jonson's, not merely because of the alchemist's jargon, but more for such a trait as the comment upon it in lines 219, 220. 'Tush Knight, the tearmes of this Arte, every ignorant Quack-saluer is perfect in.' With Jonson the literary critic is always coming to the surface. The Quicksilver of this part of the scene (with due allowance for his mercurial temperament) relapses very quickly from the repentance he has just expressed. Chapman no doubt meant to give a hint of the final scene: this is a good example of what the authors could agree upon informally at the outset, but in the hurry of composition they overlooked the discrepancy.

Lines 284–98, misplaced in the text, where, as Sir E. K. Chambers has pointed out,[1] they should have followed line 243, are Marston's; they round off the opening of the scene.

Scene ii. Alone of previous authorities F. G. Fleay attributed this scene to Jonson: we agree with him. The style is simpler and clearer than Chapman's or Marston's, and, if it lacks something of Jonson's virility, that is because he is coming down to the level of the city tradesman in order to give a sympathetic picture of Touchstone and Goulding. A further point is that this scene really opens the dénouement, in which Jonson took a leading part.

ACT V

Scene i. Here again we follow F. G. Fleay in ascribing this scene to Jonson. It has his clearness and directness of style; Gertrude

[1] *Elizabethan Stage*, iii, p. 150 n.

in her persistent folly is a species of Jonsonian gull; and the kind-hearted mother, with her attempts at practical proposals, brings in the element of dramatic contrast. Gertrude's childish insistence on Sindefy's name in lines 15–23—

'Nay weepe not good *Sinne* . . . Thy miseries, are nothing to mine, *Sinne*: I was more then promised marriage, *Sinne*, I had it *Sinne*: and was made a Lady; and by a Knight, *Sin*: which is now as good as no Knight, *Sin*: And I was borne in *London*, which is more then brought vp, *Sin*: and already forsaken, which is past likelihood, *Sin*: and in stead of Land i'the Countrey, all my Knights Liuing lies i' the *Counter*, *Syn*, there's his Castle now'—

has a quaint parallel in *Bartholomew Fair*. Another empty babbler, John Littlewit, greets his wife Winifrid in Act III, scene vi, lines 1–10:

'Do you heare, *Win*, *Win*? . . . While they are paying the reckoning, *Win*, I'll tell you a thing, *Win*, wee shall neuer see any sights i'the *Fayre*, *Win*, except you long still, *Win*, good *Win*, sweet *Win*, long to see some Hobby-horses, and some Drummes, and Rattles, and Dogs, and fine deuices, *Win*. The Bull with the fiue legs, *Win*; and the great Hog; now you ha' begun with Pigge, you may long for any thing, *Win*, and so for my motion, *Win*.'

Scene ii. By Jonson, continuing the characters of Act IV, scene ii.
Scene iii. By Jonson. There is a striking parallel to Security's description of prison, 'this *Purgatorie*, to which Hell is a kinde of coole Bathe in respect' (27–8). In *Bartholomew Fair*, II. ii. 42–5, Ursula, the pig-woman, complains, 'who would weare out their youth, and prime thus, in roasting of pigges, that had any cooler vocation? Hell's a kind of cold celler to't, a very fine vault, o' my conscience!'
Scene iv. The references to Ulysses (2), the Sirens (15–16, 32–3), and 'waxe' (16) are details which suggest Chapman. Dr. Harris notes that the unHomeric version of Ulysses stopping his ears with wax that he might not hear the Sirens is also used by Chapman in *The Widdowes Teares*, I. ii (1612, B4): 'But by your leaue *Lycus*, *Penelope* is not so wise as her husband *Vlysses*, for he fearing the iawes of the *Syrens*, stopt his eares with waxe against her voice.' We should have expected Chapman to follow Homer, but Jonson has the same version in *Bartholomew Fair*, III. ii. 46–7.
Scene v. By Jonson. The similarity to the close of *Every Man in his Humour* in the Quarto version of 1601 is strongly marked.[1]

[1] See vol. i, pp. 41–3.

Security here and Thorello in the earlier play illustrate a favourite device of Jonson's stage-craft; he liked to put a check upon the action, to give the suspense of a counter-movement at the climax of a play.[1] Both these characters hark back to their old suspicions of their wives' unfaithfulness after they have acknowledged that there is no ground for it. Security in Act IV, scene i, lines 276–83, is convinced of his wife's innocence. 'Villaine, and Monster that I was, howe haue I abus'd thee.' But in this final scene (183–4) he exclaims, 'Would I were no Cuckold'. 'Cuckold, husband? why, I thinke this wearing of Yellow'—the prison dress—'has infected you.' So Thorello, when his brother-in-law Prospero chaffs him: 'But brother *Thorello*, and sister, you have a spice of the yealous[2] yet both of you' and advises them to be 'smooth-foreheaded'. Thorello at once feels his brow to see if there are horns there, and asks Bianca if she does not play the woman with him. Finally both husbands come round. There is also a close affinity between the characters of Clement and Touchstone in these plays. In this portion of *Eastward Ho* Jonson is to some extent re-using old material.

But the last lines of the scene (205–10) are evidently by another hand. 'The Vsurer punisht' is not true; he is let off lightly: Goulding decrees that the dower he is to give Sindefy is to be 'all the restitution he shall make of that huge masse, he hath so vnlawfully gotten' (178–80). This has some resemblance to the close of *The Alchemist*, where Face escapes scot-free after cheating his partners in villany, and to the close of *Bartholomew Fair*, where Mistress Overdo and Mistress Littlewit, who have been 'green women' in the fair, go quietly to supper—'and no enormities'—at Overdo's house. Touchstone fully approves of Goulding's decision about the usurer, whom he proceeds to banter on his cuckoldom: this again is hardly consistent with the tone of the last lines of the scene which, together with the epilogue, may be assigned to Marston.

The qualities which make the play such a puzzle, considering its parentage—rapidity of movement, ease, and vitality—become intelligible on one hypothesis. Whatever the reason, the authors hurried over their work. A commission given to three authors suggests that a manager wanted the play quickly. So the stream flowed freely, and the writers had no time to check and make it turbid.

[1] He prided himself upon it. See *The Magnetic Lady*, Chorus 4, where Damplay says a fifth act is unnecessary because everybody in the theatre can foresee it. 'Stay, and see his last *Act*, his *Catastrophe*, how he will perplexe that, or spring some fresh cheat' and please the audience with 'some unexpected, and new encounter'.
[2] 'Yellows' and 'jealous', a quibble.

Title

The title was, like 'Westward Ho', a cry of the Thames watermen. Cf. Peele, *Edward the First*, 1593, Malone Society reprint, sc. xxii. 2551-6:

> '*Make a noise, Westward how.*
> *Queene.* . . . woman what noise is this I hear?
> *Potters wife.* And like your Grace it is the Watermen that cals for passengers to goe Westward now.'

The Persons of the Play

8. *Poldauy*, so named from the coarse canvas used for sails.

9. *Sir Petronel Flash.* 'Petronel' = carbine. The name suggests a huffing gallant: cf. *Histrio-mastix*, ii (1610, C4ᵛ), *The Song extempore*:

> Giue your Scholler degrees, and your Lawyer his fees,
> And some dice for Sir Petronell flash.

Middleton, *The Family of Love*, III. ii (1608, D4), 'shall I neuer be rid of these Petronell Flashes?'

16. *Scapethrift.* A character in *Gammer Gurtons Nedle*, 1575, is 'Scapethryft Mayst. Beylies seruante'.

17. *Spendall.* The name appears in an abbreviated form as '*Spoyl.*' in III. i. 54, 64. Virginian adventures were not looked upon as a very reputable class (*S.W.* II. v. 128), and there may have been some personal satire at this point of the play, causing an alteration of the name.

The Prologue

5. *opposde to ours in Title.* Dekker and Webster's *Westward Ho*, acted by the Children of Paul's late in 1604. 'Was good' (l. 6) shows that it was no longer on the stage.

9, 10. *East-ward; west-wards* . . . Cf. I. i. 108-11. There is a hint of the westward journey to Tiburn.

11. *vtterly enforste.* There are the boating scenes on the Thames east of London and Gertrude's journey eastward to find Petronell's castle.

I. i. Stage-direction. *At the middle dore*, at the back of the curtained rear-stage. The three doors are alluded to in *S.W.* v. iii. 5, 6, also played at the Blackfriars. Cf. Heywood, *The Four Prentices of London*, 1615, prologue, 'Enter three in blacke clokes, at three doores'; and Day's *The Travailes of the three English Brothers*, 1607, H4ᵛ, 'Enter three seuerall waies the three Brothers'.

discouering a Gold-smiths shoppe by drawing the curtain. *C. is A.* I. i, the opening stage-direction, 'Iuniper *a Cobler is discouered, sitting at worke in his shoppe* . . .'.

4. *Indeed, and in very good sober truth.* Quicksilver mimics the mild expressions which the citizens used as a substitute for oaths.

6. *a french footboy. C. is A.* v. vi. 31; for his swearing see *E.M.I.* III. v. 170.

18. *tho you be no Alderman.* 'Among the ancient city regulations concerning apparel is the following: "The lord mayor and those knights that have borne the office of mayoralty ought to have their *cloaks* furred with grey amis; and those aldermen that have not been mayors are to have their *cloaks* furred with calabre. And likewise such as have been mayors are to have their *cloaks* lined with changeable taffaty; and the rest are to have them lined with green taffaty."'—Reed's note in Dodsley, 1780.

Ruffins hall. '*West-Smith-field* (now the *Horse-Market*) was formerly called *Ruffians-Hall*, where such met casually and otherwise, to try Masteries with Sword and Buckler. Moe were frighted then hurt.'—Fuller, *The Worthies of England*, 1602, ii, p. 199.

19. *Racket.* Cf. Massinger, *The City-Madam*, v. ii. (1658, L):

> The masters never prosper'd
> Since gentlemens sons grew prentices. When we look
> To have our business done at home, they are
> Abroad in the Tenis-court, . . .

24. *of Quorum,* eminent justices of peace whose presence was necessary to constitute a bench, the commission reading '*quorum unum A B. esse volumus*'.

36. *whit-meate,* with which Fallace entertained Briske, *E.M.O.* iv. i. 39.

38. *light golde.* *C.R.* iii. i. 48; Dekker and Webster, *West-ward Hoe*, i. ii (1607, B1ᵛ), 'there's a great deale of light gold. *Tent.* O sir, twill away in play.'

47. *fought low* implies modest pretensions on the part of a tradesman.

50. *Light gaines* . . . *Iohn Heywoodes woorkes*, 1562, pt. i, ch. xi (Diijᵛ):

> For come lyght winnynges with blessings or curses,
> Euermore light gaynes make heauy purses.

51. *Tis good to be merry and wise.* Ibid. ch. ii (Aiij):

> And whan hasty wittlesse mirth is mated weele,
> Good to be mery and wise, they thinke and feele.

54. *deuise of the Horne.* Elucidated by the picture on a sixteenth-century panel described by J. E. Hodgkin in *N. & Q.* vii. iv. 323: 'It measures 18 in. by 22 in. long. . . . Upon a tree, whose branches extend to each side of the picture, hangs by a red belt with gold tassel an enormous curved horn, the ends upwards. At the extreme left stands a man with black velvet flat-cap and surcoat trimmed with fur, ruff, and gold chains on his breast. He is superintending the action of a man dressed in a purple doublet, profusely slashed, who weares a large felt hat and a cloak, with a dagger in his girdle, and is engaged in thrusting into the large end of the horn an unfortunate wretch, whose trunk and legs (the latter loosely bound together with a rope, the end of which

is held by the gold-chained gentleman) are inverted, and are the only portions of the body visible at that part of the picture. But at the little end of the horn, about 6 feet away as the crow flies, . . . but 9 feet along the curved surface, appears the unhappy head and one arm of the victim. At the right stands a man clad only in a shirt and ragged coat, with . . . a woe-begone expression. . . . On a black ground at the bottom of the picture is the inscription, "This horn embleme here doth showe of suertishipp what harme doth growe". On either side of the tree are the words, in semi-Gothic character, "The Sea of | Trubble". Above the head of the personage in the veluet cap is the citation, "Psalme 37, 26, but he is ever merciful and lendeth and his sede enjoyeth the blessing".' H. C. Hart (ibid. vii. 376) quotes Fletcher, *A Wife for a Month*, iii. iii:

> Thou wilt look to-morrow else
> Worse then the prodigal fool the ballad speaks of,
> That was squeezed through a horn.

61. *of good phrase.* So Bobadill says of Downright in *E.M.I.* i. v. 95–6, 'He ha's not so much as a good phrase in his belly.'

66. *What doe yee lacke Sir?* The city tradesman's regular greeting to a customer: cf. *B.F.* ii. iv. 3. Bacon, *Promus of Formularies*, ed. Durning-Lawrence, p. 5, 'How doe you? They haue a better question in Cheap side w^t lak ye'.

72. *crackling Bauins.* Cf. *1 Henry IV*, iii. ii. 61–2, 'rash bavin wits, Soon kindled and soon burnt'. A 'bavin' was a bundle of brushwood used for lighting fires.

79. *Dilling*, darling.

86. *Court-cut, and long tayle.* The 'old Quipper', as Quicksilver calls him, combines two phrases—on the one hand, 'court-cut' in its simple sense of fashion and 'tayle' of a lady's train; on the other, the popular phrase 'come cut and long-tail' (*Ent. Welb.* 167), originally of horses and dogs of every kind, and then extended to mean 'one and all'.

101. *Marry faugh.* *C.R.* iii. ii. 11, 'Fough, he smels all lamp-oyle.' *flat-cap.* A mark of the tradesman: see *E.M.I.* ii. i. 110.

102. *giue armes*, show armorial bearings.

107–8. *let the Welkin roar, and Erebus also.* So Pistol of Doll Tear-sheet, 'I'll see her damned first: to Pluto's damned lake . . . with Erebus and tortures vile also . . . and let the welkin roar' (*2 Henry IV*, ii. iv. 147–9, 159).

111. *Eous*, the morning-star. The quotation is untraced.

114. *Sattin-belly, & Canuas-backt.* A tradesmen's dress, the front satin with a cheap back: cf. *The London Prodigall*, iii. i (1605, C4^v), where Civet scorns his old-fashioned father's dress, 'a mocado coat, a paire of red satten sleeues, and a canuis backe'; Middleton, *The Mayor of Quinborough*, v. i (1661, I2), 'He (i.e. the mayor) throws off his Gown, discovering his doublet with a satten forepart and a Canvas back.'

116. *sould Ginger-bread in Christ-church.* *B.F.* i. iv. 37. 'The parishes

of St. Ewin, St. Nicholas, and part of St. Sepulchre's were amalgamated into one large parish and called Christ Church' (Bullen). Gingerbread was sold at Bartholomew Fair.

119. *testones*, sixpences.

122. *pent-house*, the projecting roof over the counter of the shop. Cf. *West-ward Hoe*, I. i (1607, A4), 'like pollitick penthouses, which commonly make the shop of a Mercer, or a Linnen Draper, as dark as a roome in Bedlam'.

123. *beare Tankards*. Apprentices had to carry water from the conduits for the use of their masters' household. In Heywood's *The Foure Prentises of London*, I. i (1615, B2), one of the noble apprentices says, 'I left my Tankard to guard the Conduit; and away came I.'

125. *Who calls Ieronimo?* . . . A quotation from *The Spanish Tragedy*, II. v. 4.

136. *shot-clog*. *E.M.O.* v. ix. 47.

138. *Moore fields*. *E.M.I.* II. iv. 9; the 'cudgell vnder thine arme' may be illustrated from the same scene, line 88.

147. *thus I haue read*. With these lines of commonplace morality cf. I. ii. 171–6, II. i. 171–4.

I. ii. Stage-direction. *Bettrice* makes one brief speech, line 65. Her sole function is to lead Gertrude's pet monkey in and out in this scene. Probably a small part was assigned to her before the cancel was made in A4ᵛ of the First Quarto: see the textual introduction, vol. iv, pp. 495–6.

Scotch Varthingall. Noticed in lines 49, 50, where some further comment—query, anti-Scottish suggesting Scotch miserliness—has been cut out of the text. Cf. Dekker and Webster's *West-ward Hoe*, I. i (1607, A2ᵛ), 'I wist this'—i.e. ladies learning from city wives to get what they can from their husbands—'is better wit then to learne how to weare a Scotch Farthingale.'

French fall, or 'falling band', a collar falling flat round the neck.

1. *For the passion of patience*. Cf. Chapman, *The Widdowes Teares*, II. i (1612, D2ᵛ), 'Passion of Virginitie, *Ianthe*, how shall we quit our selues of this Pandresse?'

5. *Medam*. An affected pronunciation: Dr. Harris compares Marston's *The Malcontent*, IV. iv. 1 (1604, F3), '*Maq.* Medam, Medam, are you stirring Medame? if you bee stirring Medam, if I thought I should disturbe yee.'

7. *in any hand*, in any case. Schelling quotes *All's Well*, III. vi. 36–7, 'let him fetch off his drum in any hand'.

8. *pax*, pox. A euphemistic form: Gertrude, forgetting herself, swears unlike 'a forsooth of the city'. *North-ward Hoe*, III. i (1607, D4ᵛ), 'The puncks in her humer—pax.'

Thus whilst she sleepes . . . From the song 'Sleep wayward thoughts, and rest you with my love' in John Dowland's *First Book of Songs or Airs*, 1597.

15. *lichet*, latchet, lace. Coifs were usually tied with strings under the

chin, but sometimes they were pinned to the hair. Gertrude felt that the string was not desirable (Linthicum, *Costume in the Drama*, p. 224).

Stammell petticoate, red linsey-wolsey, and spoken of as inferior. See Beaumont, *The Woman Hater*, IV. ii (1607, G2ᵛ), 'Ist not a miserie, . . . to see a handsome, young, faire enough, and well mounted wench, humble her self in an old stammel petticoate?' So too *Ent. Welb.* 176, 'In Stamel. . . . Scarlet is too deare', which shows what Gertrude's preference would have been.

16. *with two guardes*, ornamental bands or borders, here of plain cloth, and so not lavish enough.

Buffin, 'a narrow grograin or single chamlet . . . made in both wool and silk. Since it cost from one to one and a half shillings a yard, it could not be classed with the *very* cheap materials' (Linthicum, op. cit., p. 71). Mildred would have the woollen, not the silk, variety. Massinger in *The City Madam*, IV. iv, Anne and Mary, after Luke has ruined them, appear 'In buffin gowns, and green aprons'.

Tuf-taffitie cape. Taffeta was 'a thin, fine silk fabric of even texture. . . . But plain taffeta was not rich enough for Elizabethan taste. It must be "tufted", i.e. woven with raised stripes or spots' (Linthicum, op. cit., pp. 123–4).

19. *Cherries*. Richard Harris, fruiterer to Henry VIII, imported the cherry from the Low Countries and made the first orchard at Teynham in Kent (N. F., *The Fruiterers Secrets*, 1604). The high price this fruit fetched is frequently alluded to: Nashe, *Pierce Pennilesse*, 1592 (*Works*, ed. McKerrow, i, p. 173), 'In an other corner, Mistris Minx, a Marchants wife, that wil eate no Cheries, forsooth, but when they are at twenty shillings a pound'; Robert Tofte's translation of Varchi's *The Blazon of Iealousie*, 1615, p. 73:

> When Cherries could not gotten be
> With us, for money, Love, nor Fee:
> I forescore miles, did send in haste,
> Lest that thy longing should be past,
> And for one pound five Pounds I paid,
> Before my man could have them weigh'd.

20. *Grogoram*, or grograin. *E.M.I.* II. i. 9 n. Here the silk variety of grograin is referred to.

21. *pure linnen*, for which the City wives were famous. *Poet.* IV. i. 16–19.

22. *smocks of 3. li. a smock*. 'I haue heard that you haue three score Smocks that cost three poundes a Smocke', says Birdlime in *Westward Hoe*, I. i (1607, A3).

23. *taffata pipkins*, 'small French hats with a large crown pleated into a narrow brim. After 1600 ladies such as Gertrude expected to be, wore large-brimmed, high-crowned felts' (Linthicum, *Costume in the Drama*, p. 231). Cf. Field, *Amends for Ladies*, II. i (1618, C3), 'a finicall taffatae pipkin'.

durance, 'a closely woven, worsted fabric of lasting quality' (Linthicum, op. cit., p. 74).

siluer bodkins. Poet. III. i. 49.

25. *And euer she cried shoute home.* Not identified: Bullen refers to a similar song in *The Roxburghe Ballads,* ii, p. 207, 'Have at a venture', but the resemblance is slight.

30. *Boe-bell.* Cf. line 124; v. v. 168–9. Fynes Moryson, *Itinerary,* 1617, pt. iii, p. 53, 'Londiners, and all within the sound of Bow-Bell, are in reproch called Cocknies.'

34–5. *Where ambition of place* ... Mildred quotes a saying of Louis XI of France, 'à ceux qui lui reprochaient de ne pas garder assez sa dignité: *Quand orgueil chemine devant, honte & dommage suivent de bien près*' (M. Duclos, *Histoire de Louis XI,* 1745, iii, p. 439).

37. *cattes, and foxes, and dogges:* Mildred misreports the scholar. See page 638.

45. *a creature of Gods making.* So Portia of the French lord, 'God made him, and therefore let him pass for a man' (*Merch. of Venice,* I. ii. 50).

46–7. *And euer and anon* ... 64. *And if she will not* ... Untraced.

49. *Does it clip close?* See the opening stage-direction.

58. *beare my hands? light?* Middleton, *A Chast Mayd in Cheape-side,* I. i (1630, B1ᵛ), where a mother complains of her daughter: 'I cannot get her for my life to instruct her Hand thus, before and after, which a Knight will looke for, before and after. I have told her still, 'tis the wauing of a Woman dose often moue a Man, and preuailes strongly.'

80. *Baloone,* a game in which a large inflated ball of leather was driven to and fro by a 'bracer' or flat piece of wood attached to the arm. *Volp.* II. ii. 168.

88. *ye are come.* Touchstone deliberately avoids 'welcome': cf. *C. is A.* IV. i. 1–4.

89. *A 100. li. Land.* This was the yearly rent: cf. II. ii. 249. Touchstone's valuation—'two thousand poundes worth of good land' (IV. ii. 240)—gives the market value of the estate: it included 'Two hundred pounds woorth of wood readye to fell' and 'a fine sweete house' (II. ii. 146–7).

103. *dub'd.* The same equivoke as in *North-ward Hoe,* III. ii (1607, E), 'Sfoot hee may well dreame hees made a Knight: for Ile be hangd if she do not dub him.'

121. *Chittizens* ... 123. *Chittie.* An affected pronunciation: Bullen compares Middleton, *Blurt, Master-Constable,* I. ii. 24, 'this chitty of Venice', but Lazarillo in that passage may be copying the Italian *cittá.*

144–5. *his Castle on his back.* Cf. *Irish M.* 76, and T. Freeman, *Rubbe, And a great Cast,* 1614, B2, epigram 6:

> *Superbus* sold a gallant Mannor place,
> Himselfe with a new-fashion'd sute to grace.
> Meant he himself an Elephant to make,
> In carrying such a Castle on his backe.

The elephant with a castle on his back sometimes appeared in London pageants. The Elephant and Castle was a London inn-sign; 'the elephant, in the Middle Ages, was nearly always represented with a castle on his back. . . . It was, at one time, the form of the "castle" in chess.'— R. Withington in *M.L.N.* xliii, pp. 28–9. Cf. Ovid's 'census corpore ferre suos' (*Ars Am.* iii. 172).

163. *wel parted. E.M.O.*, Characters, 8.

175–6. *tis honest Times expense* . . . i.e. Time is honestly spent on such an apparent trifle as matchmaking when a deeper purpose underlies it.

II. i. 4. *Maister Quicksiluer*. Like the Gobbos in *Merch. of Venice*, II. ii. 40–55, and contrast the insolent 'now I tell thee, *Touchstone*' in line 128.

5. *addition*, title.

6. *trusse my points*, tie the tagged laces which fastened the hose to the doublet.

25. *the Scripture*. Isaiah v. 11, 'Woe unto them that rise up early in the morning, that they may follow strong drink; that continue until night, till wine inflame them.'

27. *a their knees. E.M.O.* v. iv. 73–4 n.

43. *Noahs Arke*. Cf. the 'Overbury' *Characters*, ed. Paylor, p. 78, 'A Franklin': 'he is pleased with any nourishment God sends, whilest curious gluttony ransackes, as it were, *Noahs Arke* for food, onely to feed the riot of one meale.'

45. *at a Conduict. S.W.* III. v. 25.

87. *Holla ye pampered Iades* . . . From the second part of *Tamburlaine*, IV. iii. 1, and constantly parodied. M. R., *Micrologia*, 1629, D6ᵛ, records that to add to the terrors of Bridewell prisoners were yoked to the dung and dust carts of the City:

> Whilst as they passe the people scoffing say,
> Holla, ye pampered Iades of Asia.

88. *a' my fidelitie*. A mincing City oath.

89. *Pulldo, pulldo*. Is Quicksilver thinking of a boat-race? This would suit *showse quoth the Caliuer*, 'bang went the gun'. For this phrase cf. Beaumont, *The Knight of the Burning Pestle*, v (1613, I4), 'sa, sa, sa, bounce quoth the guns'. The *caliuer* was the lightest portable fire-arm except the pistol.

92. *wa ha ho*. The falconer's cry to recall the hawk. Cf. Marston, *The Dutch Courtezan*, I. ii. 238, '*Frec*. Wha, ha, ho! come bird, come'.

93. *counterbuff*. Cf. *Ent. Welbeck*, 198–201.

96. *Ioulthead*, blockhead. *Volp.* v. viii. 17.

107. *hast thou not Hyren here?* Supposed to come from Peele's lost play *The Turkish Mahomet and Hiren the Fair Greek*. The quotation is also found in *2 Henry IV*, II. iv. 150, 165 (on the lips of Pistol); Dekker, *Satiro-mastix*, IV. iii (1602, I4); Middleton, *The Old Law*, IV. i (1656, G4), 'we have *Siren* heere. *Cook. Siren*, twas *Hiren* the faire Greek man.'

110. *Who cries on murther?* . . . *Poet.* III. iv. 242 n.

120. *Westward ho*, to Tyburn in the hangman's cart. Reed quotes Greene, *The Second Part of the Art of Conny Catching*, 1591, Z, 'And yet at last so long the pitcher goeth to the brooke that it cometh broken home: and so long the foists put their villanie in practice that Westward they goe, and there solemnly make a rehearsal sermon at *tiborne*'; and in the *Third Part*, 1592, C, 'the end of such (though they scape a while) will be sailing Westward in a carte to Tiborn'.

121. *dishonest.* So the verb 'honest', *S.W.* I. iv. 3.

127. *Rente*, wages. *Flye with a Duck in thy mouth.* Richard Capel (1586–1656), quoted by Spurgeon, *Treasury of David*, on Psalm ix. 18, has, 'It is (saith Chrysostom) like money, which lying long in the bank, comes home at last with a duck in its mouth, with use upon use' (i.e. compound interest); 'when money is out a great time, it makes a great return: we can stay thus upon men, and cannot we, shall not we, stay upon the Lord, for a large return?' The sense is clearly 'returns with a good profit'. Compare the phrase 'carries meat in the mouth' (*C.R.* v. iv. 32), meaning 'brings in money, is a source of profit', perhaps originally said of a hawk (*O.E.D.*). But Quicksilver's use of the opposite phrase 'fly with a duck in thy mouth' is less clear: apparently he expected, when released from his apprenticeship, to make more money (II. i. 13, 57–8), so that he means 'A good riddance, with profit to myself'.

130–6. Slightly adapted from the opening lines of *The Spanish Tragedy*. Note the punctuation of '*soule*,' (130) and '*flesh*.' (133). Touchstone at first interrupts the quotation; after the second line Quicksilver stops short in drunken stupidity, as Touchstone's question, 'What then, sir', shows. Heywood similarly in *The Fair Maid of the West*, v (1631, p. 57) has

> *Clem.* It is not now as when *Andrea* liv'd,
>   Or rather *Andrew* our elder Iourneyman:

what, Drawers become Courtiers? Now may I speake with the old ghost in *Ieronimo*;

> When this æternall substance of my soule
> Did live imprisoned in this wanton flesh,
> I was a Courtier in the Court of Fesse.

131. *Well said*, well done.

gould ends. II. ii. 44, *Alch.* II. iv. 21 n.

157. *colde meate left.* So III. ii. 60–1; compare *Hamlet*, I. ii. 180–1.

160. *reuerent*, reverend. Cf. Shelley, *The Cenci*, IV. iii, 'His thin grey hair, his stern and reverent brow'.

163. *Lady sir-reuerence.* *T. of T.* I. vi. 25 n. On Touchstone's lips the phrase is a mock apology for using an improper word.

II. ii. The scene is Security's house, with a window 'above'—i.e. on the upper stage—at which Winifred appears, line 203.

1–10. With this description of the character about to enter Dr. Harris compares Chapman's *All Fools*, I. ii. 20–42, Gazetta's description of her husband, and Roderique's description of D'Olive just after he has left the stage in *Monsieur D'Olive*, I. i. 407–20.

2. *Bride-boule*. N.I. Argument, 114.

5. *vayles*, gains over and above his wages.

16. *K. me, K. thee.* Cf. *Iohn Heywoodes woorkes*, 1562, E1ᵛ, 'Ka me, Ka the, one good tourne asketh an other.'

18. *K's.* 'Key' was pronounced 'kay'. In *Hymen.* 896–7 'kayes' rhymes with 'rayes'.

26. *as a scrappe to the nette of villanie*, as a bait to lead the victim into the net. Cf. the *East Anglian Glossary*, 1895, '*Shrap* or *Scrap*, a bait of chaff laid in the winter season to attract sparrows, &c., which are then netted with a contrivance called a "shrap net"'. See vol. iv, pp. 504–5.

31. *Truncks shoote forth.* A quibble on the sense of 'pea-shooter'.

34. *Via.* A joke on 'a way' and 'away!' Florio calls it 'an adverbe of encouragement much used by commanders, as also by riders to their horses'. *D. is A.* II. i. 2, 3, 'Let her goe. | *Via pecunia.*

the curtaine that shaddowed Borgia. Most editors since Reed have illustrated from John Mason's tragedy, *The Turke*, v. iii (1610, K3), where Borgias appears as a ghost and the Turk Mulleasses addresses him,

> Illusiue ayre, false shape of *Borgias*,
> Could thy vaine shaddow worke a feare in him
> That like an *Atlas* vnderwent the earth
> When with a firme and constant eye he sawe
> Hells fifty headed Porter: thus I'de proue
> Thy apparition idle: *runnes at Borgias.*
>   *Borg.* Treason. I liue: Deuils and Furies I am slaine.

But *The Turke* was not acted before 1607–8; the parallel from the curtain is not clear; and the source of the allusion has not been traced.

37. *Dalida*, the Septuagint form Δαλιδά, used by Chaucer, Lydgate, Skelton, and Browne of Tavistock.

39–46. A parody of the ballad preserved in *The Roxburghe Ballads*, ed. Chappell, ii, pp. 495–64:

> When Sampson was a tall young man,
> His power and strength increased than,
> And in the host and tribe of Dan,
>   The Lord did blesse him still.
>
> It chanced upon a day,
> As he was walking on his way,
> He saw a maiden fresh and gay
>   In Timnah.

The tune is in Chappell's *Popular Music of the Olden Time*, i, p. 241. The ballad was entered at Stationers' Hall in 1564; the extant version cannot be older than 1620, the year in which it was assigned to Thomas Symcock.

40. *than*. Cf. Milton, *Nativity Ode*,

> Full little thought they than,
> That the mighty *Pan*
> Was kindly com to live with them below.

63–8. Compare Chapman's rendering of Homer, *Odyssey*, v. 331–2:

> ἄλλοτε μέν τε Νότος Βορέῃ προβάλεσκε φέρεσθαι,
> ἄλλοτε δ' αὖτ' Εὖρος Ζεφύρῳ εἴξασκε διώκειν.—

> So Ulysses fleet
> The winds hurled up and down; now Boreas
> Tossed it to Notus; Notus gave it pass
> To Eurus, Eurus Zephyr made pursue
> The horrid tennis.

65. *vnder-line*. *Iohn Heywoodes woorkes*, 1562, Eij, 'Thou hast striken the ball, vnder the lyne', i.e. too low for correct play.

the house. The sloping roof or 'pent-house' on one side of the court and at the two ends. Cf. *Florios Second Frutes*, 1591, p. 25: '*T*. Whose lot is it to plaie? *H*. Mine, for you are at the house (*alla casa* in the Italian). *I*. Plaie then, and giue me a faire balle.'

Bricke-wal'd. Corrupted from *bricole*, 'a side-stroake at Tennis where-in the ball goes not right forward, but hits one of the walls of the court, and thence bounds towards the aduerse partie' (Cotgrave, 1611).

67. *vnder the wide Hazzard*. The hazards were openings in the inner wall of the court which supported the penthouse; to strike the ball into a hazard was to win a stroke. John Taylor in *A Discouery by Sea, from London to Salisbury* (*Workes*, 1630, p. 24) has the same metaphor for a storm:

> Whilst we, like various Fortunes Tennis ball
> At euery stroake, were in the Hazard all.

'Wide Hazard' means the sea; it was not a technical term of the tennis court.

80–7. So Guilthead of his experience with courtiers, *D. is A*. III. iii. 6–10:

> If I haue a *Businesse* there, with any of them,
> Why, I must wait, I'am sure on't, Son: and though
> My *Lord* dispatch me, yet his worshipful man—
> Will keepe me for his sport, a moneth, or two,
> To shew mee with my fellow Cittizens.

93. *long of*, on account of. *O.E.D.* quotes Swinburne, *Mary Stuart*, III. i. 113, 'That all these Have fallen out profitless, 'tis long of you'.

104. *Thirtie, or Fortie i'th' hundred*. In 1571 Parliament had legalized the rate of interest up to 10 per cent.: cf. *E.M.O*. IV. iv. 9, of a city merchant, 'his wit's after tenne i' the hundred'.

122. *out of ioynt*. *Hamlet*, I. v. 189, 'The time is out of joint'.

134. For a form of one of the *skurvie phrases* cf. *Iohn Heywoodes woorkes*, 1562, Diij, 'He would fayne flee, but he wanteth fethers, some'.

147. *an't*. This variant of 'on't' recurs in III. iii. 44.

173–4. *certainties . . . vncertainties*. Cf. Plautus, *Pseudolus*, 685, 'Certa mittimus dum incerta petimus'.

178. *my sweete Sinne*. A phrase applied to lechery: cf. Guilpin, *Skialetheia*, 1598, B8ᵛ:

> When his Cock-sparrow thoughts to itch begin,
> He with a shrug sweares 't *a most sweet sinne*.

211. *Iewes trumpe*, usurer. Cf. *E.M.O.* III. vi. 74–5, 'I thought he had been playing o' the Iewes trump, I'.

212. *Dice of his bones*. 'I will make dice of his bones' is given as a usurer's threat by Philip Stubbes in *The Anatomie of Abuses*, 1583, p. 127, where Furnivall quotes the same phrase in Thomas Lupton's *Siuquila*, 1580, p. 35, and Samuel Rowlands's *Looke to it: for, Ile Stabbe ye*, 1604, B3. So Nashe of usurers, *Christs Teares ouer Ierusalem* (*Works*, ed. McKerrow, ii, p. 93), 'Huge numbers in theyr stincking Prysons they haue starued, & made Dice of their bones for the deuill to throw at dice for theyr owne soules'. Compare the nine-pins made of usurers' bones with which the Furies play in hell in *Chloridia* 145. Indentures made of usurers' skins are a further development of the idea.

215. *Peeter man*, fisherman, like St. Peter. So the Thames fishing-boats were called 'Peter boats'.

216. *Puritanes skinne*. Quoted in John Spicer's *The Sale of Salt*, 1611, pp. 250–1, in the description of Cathara, a Puritan, with a marginal reference 'Eastward hoe': '*Mad*. Though she be precise in some points, yet she prayeth for the King, Queene, and Prince, she giueth good eare to the Teacher, she commeth to the communion, and I am perswaded there is not any one in the land of those whom you call Puritanes, which wish so many of you, as will not conuert, gon with bagge and baggage, which in defence of the Ghospell, and his Maiestie would not loose each drop of his bloud, though some on the Stage haue deryded them, saying their smooth skins will make the best Vellam. *Rom*. Did you see that Play plaide ? *Mad*. No, but I haue heard of it.'

Before 218. *a riding wan*. 'Houssine, A Switch, or Whisker; (most properly) a riding rod of Hollie ; a Hollie wand' (Cotgrave, 1611). There is no change of scene here: Quicksilver is still on the stage. Elizabethan practice would require an empty stage for this. To mark an exit for Quicksilver, and then imagine a change of scene to Petronel's lodgings and Petronel entering 'followed by Quicksilver' is a purely modern method of stage-location.

220. *blowne vp*. A violent expression for 'closed down'.

222. *Spurre gingling*. *E.M.O.* II. i. 37–9.

244. *Essex Calues*. Fuller, *The Worthies of England*, 1672, s.v. 'Essex', quotes there as proverbial: 'A *learned Authour* telleth us that *Italy* was

so called, *quasi vitalæ*, because the best *Calves* were bred therein. . . . *Essex* may better pretend to the *Name* of *Italy*, producing *Calves* of the *fattest*, *fairest* and *finest flesh* in *England*, (and consequently in all *Europe*,) and let the *Butchers* in *Eastcheap* be appealed unto as the most competent Judges therein. Sure it is a *Cumberland-cow* may be bought for the *Price* of an *Essex-calfe*, in the beginning of the year.'

246. *habilitie*. *L.R.* 268.

249. *commoditie*. Spendthrifts were compelled by usurers to borrow part of the sum in inferior or damaged articles, so as to give the loan the air of a business transaction; this they resold at a lower price, generally to the usurer. Cf. *S.W.* ii. v. 119, *Alch.* iii. iv. 90–9. For the forty pounds of roast beef suggested by Quicksilver (l. 255) cf. Dekker, *Lanthorne and Candlelight*, 1608, D4ᵛ, E: 'Of Ferreting: or the Manner of vndooing Gentlemen by taking vp of commodities': 'vpon a hundred poundes worth of Roasted beefe they could finde in their hearts to venture, for that would away in turning of a hand': they lose 30 per cent., besides fees.

253. *fraile*. A quibble on 'frail', a basket.

260. *laide*, set a watch.

265. *the two Counters*. *E.M.I.* ii. i. 77–8.

274. *There spake an Angell*. Proverbial, as if the suggestion was inspired: cf. *The Faire Maide of Bristow*, 1605, A4ᵛ, 'Why that is well said my wench, ther spak an angel.' There is the usual quibble on the coin of that name: Petronel catches at the words 'ready money'. So Porter, *The Two Angry Women of Abingdon*, sc. vi (Malone reprint, 1359).

277. *foysting*, or fisting, *hound*, evil-smelling. Rudesby in *Sir Gyles Goosecappe*, iv. ii (1606, G3), calls the pages 'my Ladies foysting hounds'.

278. *the Sowe by the right eare*. *E.M.I.* ii. i. 78, 'he has the wrong sow by the eare'.

280. *her new Coache*. Like Chloe in *Poet.* iv. ii. 17–18.

281–306. Contrast *S.W.* ii. ii.

286. *Turne-spit Dog*. Bullen quotes Topsell, *A History of Four-footed Beasts*, 1607, p. 177: 'There is comprehended, vnder the Curres of the coursest kinde, a certaine dog in kitchen-seruice excellent. For when any meat is to be roasted, they go into a wheel, which they turning round about with the waight of their bodies, so diligently looke to their businesse, that no drudge nor scullion can do the feate more cunningly. Whom the popular sort hereupon call Turnspets.'

287. *seruily*. A sixteenth- and seventeenth-century form: see *Venus and Adonis*, 392, 'Seruilly maistred with a leathern raine'.

302. *made a Lady . . .*, married him. Collier quotes Sir George Mackenzie, *Principles of the Laws of Scotland*, 1764, p. 6: 'It is not necessary, that marriage should be celebrated by a clergyman. The consent of parties may be declared before any magistrate, or simply before witnesses: and though no formal consent should appear, marriage is pre-

sumed from the cohabitation, or living together, at bed and board, of a man and woman who are generally reputed husband and wife.'

303. *poynados*. Apparently a wrong form: 'panada' , 'panado', and (in Dekker and Ford, *The Sun's Darling*, II, p. 13) 'ponado', which Bullen prints. A panada was 'a dish made by boiling bread in water to a pulp, and flavouring it according to taste with sugar, currants, nutmegs, or other ingredients' (*O.E.D.*).

307–8. *what a death*. . . . Cf. the essay on the authorship, p. 640.

313. *Thereby lyes a tale*. *The Merry Wives*, I. iv. 134, 'Well, thereby hangs a tale'; *N.I.* I. vi. 118, 'O thereon hangs a history'.

316. (*with a purpose to feede on you*). An echo of *Hamlet*, IV. iii. 17–20:

> *King.* Now, Hamlet, where's Polonius?
> *Ham.* At supper.
> *King.* At supper! where?
> *Ham.* Not where he eats, but where he is eaten.

319. *Iealousie*. The first hint of Security's anxiety about his young wife.

332. *not put on your Hat yet*. The opposite to the usual answer: see *E.M.O.* II. iii. 21.

342. *Nun*. Gertrude's mincing pronunciation, with a quibble on the euphemistic use of 'nun' as in *Und.* xliii. 148, 'the Nun, *Kate Arden*'.

358. *draw all my seruants in my Bowe*, bend to my will, bring under my control. Cf. Dekker and Webster, *North-ward Hoe*, I. iii (B3ᵛ):

> *Bel.* Guiltlesse vpon my soule. *May.* Troth so thinke I.
> I now draw in your bow, as I before
> Suppos'd they drew in mine: my streame of ielozy
> Ebs back againe.

The *O.E.D.* quotes Foxe, 'bend him vnto their bowe', and Bunyan, 'brought wholly to his bow'.

360. *reade on a booke*. *Hamlet*, III. i. 44, Polonius to Ophelia, 'Read on this book'.

III. i. 3. *Virginia*. *S.W.* II. v. 128; S. S., *The Honest Lawyer*, 1606, H4ᵛ, 'Ile to *Virginia*, like some cheating Bankrout, and leaue my Creditour ith' suddes'. *The New Life of Virginea*, 1612, by R. I., Ded. A3 (the attempt) 'accompanied with manifold difficulties, crosses, and disasters', . . . (A3ᵛ) 'by which occasion not only the ignorant and simple minded are much discouraged, but the malitious and looser sort (being accompanied with the licentious vaine of stage Poets) haue whet their tongues with scornfull taunts against the action it selfe, in so much as there is no common speech nor publike name of any thing this day (except it be the name of God) which is more vildly depraued, traduced and derided by such vnhallowed lips, then the name of *Virginea*'.

7–13. Compare Masuccio, *Il Novellino*, xl, '& in tanto se cominciò à stringere la cosa, che Cosmo ò per amore, ò pur per dubio ancora che la moglie non fosse grauida à diuenirli compare il richiefe doue Genefra letissimo gli disse contentarse'. (See page 643.)

19–22. Cf. ibid.: 'la venente sera la naue leuate l'anchore, Genefra hauendo de tutto Andriana pienamente informata, quando hora gli parue chiamò il compare & disse, andiamo in casa che io vò togliere dalla commare licenza, & dopò attenderemo a dare recapito al fatto nostro, il che egli con gran piacer pigliatolo per mano, & ifine à casa dopò vna leggiera collatione, & altri piaceuoli ragionamenti & vinti cinque ducati per la promessa fatta alla commare donati, & da lei tolto l'vltimo finto commiato Cosmo alla moglie riuolto disse abbrazza & bascia teneramente il nostro compare.'

19. wedlocke. Poet. iv. iii. 28.

make you strange. Parrott compares Chapman's *The Gentleman Vsher*, i. ii (1606, B3ᵛ), 'Thanks gracious loue; why made you strange of this?'

38. foreright. iii. ii. 59. Chapman, *Homer's Odyssey,* iii. 244–5 (1614, p. 36):

> Nor euer left the wind his foreright force,
> Since God fore-sent it first.

51. Blew Anchor Tauerne by Billingsgate. Rowlands, *Diogines Lanthorne,* 1607, A4, 'So, take him there at the red Lattice, he has cast Ancker at the blew Ancker for this day'.

iii. ii. 4. *Hamlet.* The Shakespearian allusion in line 6, 'are you madde?', is clear, and Marston was familiar with this play: he has a number of references to it, here and elsewhere. See *E.H.* ii. i. 157; iii. ii. 60–1, 77–82; iv. i. 62.

9. blew coate. E.M.I. ii. iv. 12.

17–18. Cf. *C.R.* ii. i. 55–6.

27. Thanke you good people. Like the Proud One in R. Flecknoe's *Enigmaticall Characters,* 1658, p. 121, 'She looks high and speakes in a majestique tone, like one playing the *Queens* part at the *Bull,* and is ready to say, *Blesse ye my good people all,* as often as she passes by any company'.

35. Ancome, or uncome, an ulcerous swelling.

38. well said, well done.

40–1. But a little higher . . . From Rosseter and Campion's *A Booke of Ayres,* 1601, xvi, which reads 'There, there, O there lies Cupids fire'. Professor Parrott points out that a later version in *The Fourth Booke of Ayres,* 1617, xxii, has the indecent innuendo which is missing in the earlier version.

43. run by your coach. So Stuffe in *The New Inn,* iv. iii. 57, 70.

44. giues no other milke, serves no other purpose. Cf. Middleton, *The Family of Love,* iii. iii (1608, D4): '*Club.* If you be vncleane mistris, you may pure your self . . . but what am I then, that does all the drudgerye in your House? *Mi. Pur.* Thart born to't, why boy, I can show thy Indentures, thou giu'st no other milke: wee know how to vse all i' theyr kinde.'

52. *Honey suckle*. So Ford, *The Fancies Chaste and Noble*, II. ii (ed. Gifford and Dyce, ii, p. 257).

60–1. Cf. II. i. 157.

63–5. Like the ladified Elimine to her sisters Martia and Samathis in Chapman's *The Blinde begger of Alexandria* (1598, D1ᵛ):

> . . . I do not meane,
> To lose my Ladies titles at your handes;
> I may for courtesie and to be term'd
> A gentle Ladie, call you sisters still,
> But you must say, 'And please your ladishippe,
> 'Tis thus and so', and 'As your honor please'.

77–81. Varied from Ophelia's song in *Hamlet*, IV. v. 186–95:

> And will a' not come again?
> And will a' not come again?
> No, no, he is dead,
> Go to thy death-bed,
> He never will come again.
>
> His beard was as white as snow,
> All flaxen was his poll:
> He is gone, he is gone,
> And we cast away moan:
> God ha' mercy on his soul!

83. *with Rosemary*. Cf. the opening stage-direction of Fletcher's *The Woman's Prize*, 'Enter Moroso, Sophocles, and Tranio, with Rosemary, as from a wedding'; Middleton and Rowley, *A Faire Quarrell*, v. i (1617, H4ᵛ): 'It is the Bridegroomes man; harke sir, a word. *Enter Trimtram with Rosemarie. Phy.* Pray you a word sir, your Maister is to bee married to-day. *Trim.* Else all this Rosemaries lost.'

85. *God give you ioy*. A wedding greeting: *E.M.I.* v. iv. 12. *Mistrisse What lacke you*, Goody Tradeswoman: see I. i. 66.

87. *Taffeta hat*, the 'pipkin' of I. ii. 23.

wanion, an altered form of 'waniand', at the time of the waning moon, an unlucky hour. Hence 'with a wanion' as an imprecation, with a vengeance. *D. is A.* v. viii. 33, *S. of N.* 3rd Intermean, 56.

98. *misproude*, wickedly proud, arrogant. *Ent. Blackfriars*, 181.

110. *Sonne* . . . 112. *Sunne. T. of T.* III. v. 53–6, a quibble of the clown Puppy. Donne uses it seriously in the *Divine Poems* on Christ's ascension, 'Joy at the uprising of this Sunne, and Sonne' (*Poems*, ed. Grierson, i, p. 321).

116. *legges* . . . *Armes*. Another quibble, used also in *E.M.O.* III. ii. 31–2; Chapman, *Al Fooles*, III. i (1605, G1), '*Poc.* And if I stood on my armes as others doe. *Dar.* No doe not *Pock*, let other stand a their armes, and thou a thy legs as long as thou canst.'

122. *fourth with* . . . 129. *forth*. In *Al Fooles*, III. i (F2ᵛ) a bashful page is encouraged with 'Forth, boy, I warrant thee!'

127. *Naturall.* A quibble on 'natural' in the sense of 'idiot'.

135. *gallantry indeed*, fine language seriously—not, as now, mere mockery.

136. *saue my breath for my broth.* Cf. Porter, *The Two Angry Women of Abington*, 1594, ed. Gayley, sc. iii. 417–18, 'You may speake when ye are spoken to, and keepe your winde to coole your pottage'.

147–8. *Now, O now* . . . Misquoted from John Dowland's *The First Booke of Songes or Ayres*, 1597, vi:

> Now, O now, I needs must part,
> Parting though I absent mourn.

149. *in Capitall Letters*, with emphasis. In a different context—cuckoldry—Chapman has in *Al Fooles*, IV. i (1605, H1ᵛ), after a quibble about sheets, 'you may set capitall letters on their foreheads'.

150. *What a griefe* . . . Untraced.

156. *girdlestead*, waist.

186. *vagarie*, excursion.

191. *I hope.* Field, *A Woman is a Weather-cocke*, II. iv (1612, D3ᵛ): 'Why I hope she is not the first Ladie that has run away with other womens husbands.'

193. *he that wayes mens thoughts* . . . See page 641.

201. *Compere*, gossip. In *Alch.* III. iii. 11 = comrade.

230. *To my best Nerue*, to the utmost of my strength. 'Nerve' = sinew.

250. *a point de-vice.* A quibble on 'device' and *à point devis*, with great nicety or exactitude, literally 'according to a point'—of exactitude—'that is devised or imagined, i.e. in the best way imaginable' (Skeat). The punctuation *de-vice* suggests a further quibble on 'vice'.

250–1. *the shippe Of famous Draco*, the *Golden Hind*: see *E.M.I.* I. iii. 121 n. 'Draco' for Drake is a Chapman touch, as Swinburne pointed out, contemporary Spaniards used it to suggest 'monster'.

265. *Two fine horn'd Beastes, a Cammell and a Lawyer!* Another Chapman touch, noted by Swinburne. Chapman's three references to the camel's horns are quoted in the discussion of the authorship on page 642.

272. *Quiblyn*, trick. *T. of T.* IV. i. 131.

287. *figent*, fidgety, volatile. E. Guilpin, *Skialetheia*, Sat. iv (1598, Sat. iv), 'an odd figgent iack called *Ielousie*'. Middleton, *A Chaste Maid in Cheapside*, III. iii (1620, G2):

> I neuer could stand long in one place yet,
> I learnt it of my Father, euer figient.

292. *sawce for such sweete mutton.* A glance at the proverb 'Sweet meat must have sour sauce' (*Poet.* III. iii. 27). 'Mutton' could also mean 'prostitute'.

308. *quirck*, a sudden turn. Metaphorically in *Volp.* III. vii. 61.

fyrke, stir up, drive. *Alch.* II. i. 28.

314. *the Deuill to fetch the Lawyer.* A reference to the tale *De Aduocato*

et Diabolo, in the fifteenth-century *Promptuarium Exemplorum* (Percy Society, viii, p. 70). It is on the same theme as Chaucer's *Friars Tale*, and Dr. Furnivall's abstract of it in *Chaucer Analogues* is: 'A grasping lawyer, out to gather prey, met the Devil in the form of a man and could not get quit of him. A poor man, angry with his perverse pig, said: "Devil take you!" But as he did not say it from his heart, the Devil could not take the pig; nor could he a child, to which its mother said: "Devil take you!" When however some townsmen saw the lawyer coming, they all cried out: "May the Devil take you!" And, as they did it from the bottom of their hearts, the Devil carried the lawyer off; as his man bore witness.' The allusive reference in the text is thoroughly characteristic of Chapman.

317. *a toy runns in my head*. Cf. *Al Fooles*, III. i (1606, E4ᵛ):

> *Rin.* Troth, sir, ile tell you what a sudden toy
> Comes in my head—

of a similar trick of planting a disguised wife on a simple knight.

328. *fetch you ouer*, gull you.

III. iii. 10. *Pewter coats*, a humorous phrase for armour: Lyly, *Campaspe*, 1584, v. iii, 'There pewter coates canne neuer sitte so well as satten dublets'.

18. *left there in 79*. An impossible date. The earliest colony was Sir Richard Grenville's expedition sent in 1585 (Hakluyt, *Voyages*, 1600, iii, p. 254). There was a second expedition in 1587 'known as "the lost colony", by some still believed to have found refuge with the Indians of the southern end of Pamlico Sound'—Schelling, quoting Professor Edward Channing's suggestion that the text refers to this.

26. *redde Copper*. Hakluyt, *Principal Navigations*, Hakluyt Soc. reprint, iii. pp. 255, 258, says of trading with the natives of Virginia, 'Copper caryeth the price of all, so it be made red', and 'Our copper is better then theirs: and the reason is for that it is redder'. (Quoted by A. H. Gilbert, *M.L.N.* xxxiii, p. 183.)

27–35. *Why man . . .* Imitated, as Schelling noted, from the *Utopia* of Sir Thomas More, who describes the contempt of the Utopians for gold: 'Of gold and siluer they make commonlye chamber pottes, and other like vesselles that serue for moste vile vses, not only in their common halles, but in euery mans priuate house. Furthermore of the same mettalles they make greate cheynes with fetters and giues, wherin they tye their bondmen. Finally, who so euer for any offence be infamed, by their eares hange ringes of golde; vpon their fingers they were ringes of golde, and about their neckes cheynes of gold; and in conclusion their heades be tiede about with golde. . . . They gather also peerles by the sea side, and Diamondes and Carbuncles vpon certein rockes; and yet they seke not for them; but by chaunce finding them they cutt and polish them. And therwith they decke their yonge infannttes' (Ralph Robyson's translation, ed. Lupton, pp. 175–7).

41–8. The famous passage on the Scots which got the authors into trouble when the Quarto was first published; it was promptly cancelled.

51. *neuer be Scauinger.* 'A petty magistrate, whose province is to keep the streets clean' (Dr. Johnson). Their functions are defined in the Oath of the Scavengers, printed by F. P. Wilson, *The Plague in Shakespeare's London*, pp. 26–7. This was a first step in municipal office, and unpaid.

68. *Cap, and Knee.* For the former *E.M.O.* v. iv. 59; for the latter, *ibid.* 74.

123–36. From Masuccio, *Il Novellino*, xl: 'Andriana che lieuemente si era, mossa, vedendo il marito che egli medesimo con tanta innocentia l'accompagnaua come à femina & giouane li venne certa debole compassione, & cominciò pianamente à plangere & rammaricarse de la fortuna, che a cosi aduerso hauea condotte il suo marito, delche Cosmo che più presso gli staua disse, deh catinella, che piangi forse te duole vedendo qui tuo marito, de certo tu me fai merauigliare, non dubitare doue pouera & mal seruita eri hora signora da tanti beni deuenerai, io so l'amore ch'el mio compare te porta, & renditi secura che ei tenera sempre per donna della persona, & de le facultà sue, che non sono huomini al mondo che sappiano amare, & bene trattare le donne se non Catalani.'

129. *earnes*, feels keen grief.

140. *Porcpisce . . . at London bridge.* *Volp.* ii. i. 40. For the spelling cf. *Sej.* v. 602 n.

150. *supper brought abord . . . Drakes Ship.* For the use made of this pious custom see John Taylor, *Iacke a Lent* (*Workes*, 1630, p. 116), where among the 'secret and vnsuspected places' searched for meat-eaters in Lent are '*Sir Francis Drakes* Ship at Detford, my Lord Mayors Barge', &c.

176. *Cucullus non facit Monachum.* A medieval proverb, the original of which is not definitely traced.

189. *proper taking.* Cf. Lyly, *Midas*, ed. Bond, i. ii. 95, 'These boys be droonk! I would not be in your takings'.

191. *drunken men never take harme.* R. Harris, *Drunkards Cup*, 1619, p. 13, 'A drunken man neuer takes harme'.

iii. iv. 5. *A boate . . . Rich. III*, v. iv. 7, 13, 'A horse, a horse, my kingdom for a horse!' which Marston parodied in *The Scourge of Villanie*, Satire vii. 1, 'A man, a man, a kingdom for a man!'; *Parasitaster*, v. i (1606), 'A fool, a fool, a fool, my coxcomb for a fool'; and literally quoted in *What You Will*, ii. i (1607).

iv. i. The scene changes to Cuckold's Haven on the Surrey side of the Thames about a mile below Rotherhithe Church. Slitgut 'discovers' it 'above', i.e. on the upper stage, by drawing a curtain. A prominent feature was the 'Tree', a tall pole with a pair of horns at the top—'this famous Tree, that is all fruite and no leaues', as Slitgut describes it (ll. 7, 8): 'witherd and pale like the tree in Cuckolds Hauen in a great snow' (*North-ward Hoe*, II. ii, 1607, D4ᵛ):

> the forked Piller, stout and tall,
> Whose leauelesse boughes are neuer seene to bud,
> Though much stone-fruit do from the branches fall.
> *(Pasquils Night-cap*, 1612, p. 51.)

From this eminence Slitgut sees the wreck of Security's boat just below him, Winifred rescued at St. Katherine's, Quicksilver at Wapping, Petronel and Seagull at the Isle of Dogs. No wonder the Tree is described as 'the farthest seeing Sea marke of the World' (l. 285).

In an important note,[1] which we regret to have overlooked, Sir E. K. Chambers has pointed out that the final speech of Slitgut (284–98 in our text) has been misplaced. It should have followed line 243 and closed the first scene of Act IV at that point. There follows a scene outside the Blue Anchor tavern at Billingsgate, to which the Drawer brings Winifred 'new attire'; Security comes there, too, almost immediately, and this should have been the second scene of the act.

There is a parallel to the use made of the upper stage here in the play of Wentworth Smith, *The Hector of Germany* (1615, F4), acted by amateurs at the Red Bull and the Curtain. A shipwrecked character has escaped drowning by climbing a rock.

Enter young Fitzwaters aloft.

Y. *Fytz.* Since I was cast vpon this fatall Rocke, . . .
Here I haue liu'd, fed onely with raw Fish,
Such as the Sea yeelds: and each Shippe I see,
(As dayly there are some furrow this way)
I call vnto for ayde, but nere the neere.

He has hailed three ships, which have refused to take him:

but in happy time,
From this high Rocke, I see a tall Shippe come
Furnisht with all his Sayles: and as it ploughes
The Ocean vp, it rayses hills of snow,
That fly on both sides as they did giue way,
To make a valley for the Shippe to passe:
Their Captaine as I thinke lookes vpon me,
And has took notice of my wauing hand.
Now the Ship turnes and this way ploughes amaine,
As if it meant to runne it selfe aground:
In happy time, now I shall be relieu'd.

Enter[2] *Saxon, Artoise, Mentz, Vandome, and Mendoza.*
Saxon. Twas heere abouts the Gallant beckned me. . . .
Cast Anker here, and let vs question him.

---

[1] *Elizabethan Stage*, iii, p. 150 n.   [2] i.e. on the lower stage.

> *Men.* Yonder he stands, mounted vpon the rocke.
> *Sax.* The very same. What art thou, whats thy name?

Saxon is at first disinclined to rescue an Englishman, but he is over-ruled and says:

> Come downe, and be receiued into our Boate.
> *Art.* That shall be my charge.   *Exit Artoise.*

Nine lines later Vandome says:

> Here comes *Fitzwaters.*   *Enter young Fytzwaters and Artoise.*

And the scene closes with Saxon giving the order 'Launch foorth into the deepe'.

3. *Butcher of East-cheape.* E.M.O. II. ii. 94. For the connexion of butchers with the tree at Cuckolds Haven see *Pasquils Night-cap*, 1612, p. 53: 'some wild Colts' of citizens

> Pull'd down the Post, & threw the horns i'the flood:
> The *Kentish-men* at their next Congregation . . .
> T'erect another made a consultation,
> As like vnto the former as they may:
>   Which was no sooner up: but some againe
>   Which had smal cause for want of horns to plain,
>   Stole them away: . . .
> Which thing when that these curtail'd men espide:
> With certaine *London* Butchers they agreed,
> That they sufficient hornes should still provide,
> For to repaire the Post when it should need:
>   And for reward the neighbouring fields should be
>   Theirs and their heires to hold eternally:
>   Prouided still, that hornes did neuer want,
>   For then they made a forfeit of their grant.
> Thus is the Post repair'd and Fortunes Port,
> Since Citizens first tooke their Hornes away, . . .
> Is nicke-nam'd Cuckolds-Hauen to this day.

4, 5. *in honour of Saint Luke.* Horn Fair at Charlton near Woolwich on Saint Luke's day, 18 October, commemorated a local tradition that King John cuckolded a miller who lived at Cuckolds' Haven, and gave him all the land he could see from his house looking down the river: the miller saw as far as Charlton. But the gift was conditional: he had to walk on Saint Luke's day to the farthest point of the estate, wearing a pair of buck's horns on his head. The fact that the ox was Saint Luke's emblem perhaps determined the choice of saint.

13. *coyle*, noisy disturbance. *Alch.* v. iv. 14, *B.F.* I. iv. 36, 'he keepes such a coyle'. 'Probably a word of colloquial or even slang character, which rose into literary use' (*O.E.D.*).

42. *how weake he is! the weake water* . . . K. Deighton (*The Old*

Dramatists: Conjectural Readings, i, p. 20) proposes to omit the second *weake* as a compositor's repetition of the first.

60. *S. Kath'rins. Alch.* v. iii. 55–6, 'where they use to keepe the better sort of mad-folkes'. Founded by Queen Matilda in 1148 on the north bank of the Thames near the Tower; its site is marked by St. Katharine's docks.

61–2. *her clothes . . . brauely . . .* A glance at *Hamlet*, IV. vii. 176–7, of Ophelia:

> Her clothes spread wide,
> And mermaid-like a while they bore her up.

69. *where the Priest fell in.* Cf. *M. Aug.* 201.

113–14. *Wapping . . . the Gallows.* 'Wapping in the Woze, the vsuall place of execution for hanging of Pirats & sea Rouers, at the low water marke there to remaine, till three tides had ouerflowed them.'—Stow, *A Survay of London*, ed. Kingsford, ii, pp. 70–1. ('Woze' = ooze.) Kingsford quotes Samuel Rowlands, *The Knaue of Hearts*, 1612, Epilogue, F4v:

> For though Pyrates exempted be
> From fatall Tyburnes wither'd Tree,
> They haue an Harbour to arriue
> Call'd Wapping, where as ill they thriue
> As those that ride vp Holbourne-hill,
> And at the Gallows make their Will.

151. *th' eleuation of the Pole*, the latitude. Dragged in for the sake of the quibble.

155. *Frenchyfied. E.M.O.* I. iii. 195, 'FASTIDIVS BRISKE, otherwise cal'd the fresh Frenchefied courtier'.

168–9. *a poore Knight of Windsor.* At this date synonymous with pauper: originally one of the Military Knights of Windsor supported by a benefaction for retired soldiers which was founded in 1349. Cf. B. Rich, *The Fruites of long Experience*, 1604, p. 53, 'after the warres ended, when they returne into their Countrey, it is in their owne choyce, whether they will begge or steale: if he cannot procure to be one of the *Knights of Winsor*, he may easily compasse to be whipt about the streetes at *Westminster*'.

178. *I ken the man weel . . .* 'As he spoke the words the actor', says Bullen, 'mimicked James' Scotch accent.' Most unlikely; this was a sure way of inviting trouble. It need not be more than a sneer at Scottish knights. Or was it this passage with the personal reference in lines 179–81 that made Sir James Murray bring the play to the notice of King James? (*Conv. Drum.* 273–4). 'Thy true friend *Ia.* Moraye' prefixed a tribute 'To the superlatiue Water-Poet *Iohn Taylor*' in *The Nipping or Snipping of Abuses*, 1614:

> For vnto mee, plainely thou doest appeare
> The lofty Plannet of the watry Spheare.

184. *ouershot*, wide of the mark, with a quibble on 'drunk'.

214. *blanche Copper*, whiten it to look like silver.

215. *malleation*, beating with a hammer, 'the proper passion of mettalls' (*Alch.* II. v. 29).

216. *Luna*, silver.

223. *Sublime*, sublimate, convert by heat to vapour and let it cool into a solid form.

224. *Chymia*, chemical analysis. *Alch.* II. iii. 99, *S. of N.* 3rd Intermean 8.

228. *Magisterium*, transmuting the elements. Literally, a master principle of nature. *Alch.* I. iv. 14, II. v. 36.

234. *Achyme*, without chyme: Greek ἄχυμος, without juice.

290. The construction is 'dishonest *Satyre* to honest married Men'.

291. *horne of hunger*, the dinner horn.

293. *horne of aboundance*, a quibble on 'cornu-copiæ' (*E.M.I.* III. vi. 25) and the cuckold's horn. Cf. *2 Henry IV*, I. ii. 42, 'Well, he may sleep in security; for he hath the horn of abundance'.

adornest. Cf. Chapman's pun quoted by Parrott, *Al Fooles*, II. i (1605, D4ᵛ), 'Oh yes, hee adores you, and adhornes mee'; *The Widows Tears*, I. i (1612, B2ᵛ), 'How they adore you for Saints, . . . while you adhorne their temples'. Chapman may have written 'adhornest' here.

headsmen, another quibble (1) chief citizens, (2) cuckolds.

294. *horne of Direction*, the lanterns hung out in the City when the bellman went round calling 'Lantern and candle-light'.

IV. ii. 2. *can*, know.

5. *Cauallaria*, the tenure of land held on condition of knightly service. 'Caballaria, praedium servitio militari obnoxium' (Ducange).

Colonoria, the 'Coloni conditio' (Ducange).

7. *drinke dronke*. Caxton, *The Game and Playe of the Chesse*, ed. 1883, p. 130, 'And not lyue to ete glotonsly & for to drynke dronke'.

8. *a browne dozen*. Cf. 'a round dozen', and Skelton, *Bouge of Courte*, c. 1529, ed. Dyce, l. 393, 'Have at the hasarde; or at the dosen browne'.

Monmouth Capps, flat caps worn by soldiers and sailors. *H. Wales*, 238.

9. *in sea ceremonie*. In the attack on Cadiz in 1596, when Lord Howard of Effingham, who was in command, hesitated to attack by sea till the Earl of Essex had taken the town by land, Raleigh induced Lord Howard to attack: 'When I brought news of this agreement to the Earl, calling out of my boat upon him, *Entramos*; he cast his hat into the sea for joy' (letter of Raleigh in Hadow's *Selections*, p. 168).

11. *a Gravesend Tost*. Cf. John Taylor, *A very Merrie Wherrie-Ferry-Voyage from London to York* (*Works*, 1630, p. 7):

> Twixt *Kent*, and *Essex*, we to *Grauesend* fell.
> There I had welcome of my friendly Host,
> (A *Grauesend* Trencher, and a *Grauesend* Tost)
> Good meat and lodging at an easie rate.

Cornu-copiæ, Pasquils Night cap, 1612, ll. 609–10, suggests that it was a phrase for something worthless:

> There is a Towne, I list not tell the name
> (Nor is the naming worth a Grauesend Tost).

12. *Admiral*, the chief ship of a fleet.

14. *Remora. Poet.* III. ii. 4.

15. *Sconce.* A quibble: (1) fort, (2) the head.

16. *trickes . . . vie. E.M.I.* IV. ii. 95.

23. *by Weeping Crosse. C.R.* v. xi. 147 n.

24. *Malkin*, country wench: so Sindefy was described to Gertrude, II. ii. 336–7.

25. *bite o' the bridle.* Ray, *A Collection of English Proverbs*, 1678, p. 229: 'That is, to fare hardly, to be cut short or suffer want, for a horse can eat but slowly when the bridle is in his mouth. Or else it may signifie to fret, swell and disquiet himself with anger.' T. Twyne, *The Schoolemaster*, 1576, Piiᵛ, 'But after three dayes, when he had sufficiently bit on the bridle, and vexed him selfe . . .'. The second is the usual meaning, but Touchstone here lays more stress on the first.

39. *presentation of the inquest*, report of the committee of inquiry.

68. *weare Scarlet*, the robe of an alderman. *Alch.* I. iii. 37.

72. *Lady Ramsey.* Mary Lady Ramsey, second wife of Sir Thomas Ramsey, who was lord mayor in 1577. She was a benefactress of Christ's Hospital, to which she gave land of the yearly value of £243, and of other institutions. She died in 1596.

graue Gresham. Sir Thomas Gresham, mercer and government financier (1519?–1579) in 1566–7 founded the Royal Exchange, as it was named after Elizabeth's visit to it. Gresham and Lady Ramsey appear in the second part of Thomas Heywood's *If you know not me, you know nobody*, published in 1606, in which the building of the Exchange is a prominent theme.

73. *Whittington, and his Pusse.* Richard Whittington, mercer, thrice lord mayor of London, 'the last of the great medieval mayors' (*D.N.B.*). He died in 1423. The legend of the cat, which has analogues in Indian, Scandinavian, and Russian folk-lore, is first noticed in 1605. In that year a lost play *The history of Richard Whittington, of his lowe byrthe, his great fortune*, played by the Prince's servants, was entered on the Stationers' Register on 8 February.

76. *plaid i' thy life time.* This happened to Gresham in the play *Byrsa Basilica, seu Regale Excambium a Sereniss. Regina Elisabetha in Persona sua sic Insignitum*, by I. Rickets in 1570; it is preserved in Bodleian Tanner MS. 207.

77. *Get-penny. B.F.* v. i. 12.

92. *lay for them*, place officers in ambush to arrest them.

103. *vnreflected*, not turned aside, not diverted. Cf. 'reflect' in the sense to turn aside (Latin *reflecto*). Or possibly, 'without reflexion' in the sense of not having regard for individuals, treating all alike.

115, *fish'd faire, and caught a Frog.* Specially used of unfortunate marriages: see *M.L.* v. ii. 4, and Warner, *Albions England*, xi, ch. 68 (1597, p. 288):

> The Flattries, and the Fooleries, whereby are women wonne,
> With fishing long to catch, perhaps, a Frog, when all is done,
> And all that Sexs Infirmities, his Thoughts did ouer-runne.

So J. Heywood, *Woorkes*, I. xi (1562. D1ᵛ).

124. *Cullion.* E.M.I. III. v. 118.

130. *how euer . . . eyes.* An untraced quotation.

138. *in equipage*, i.e. quick march! The *O.E.D.* interprets the original sense of 'to go in equipage' as probably 'to walk in military array with', referring to Shakespeare's 'To march in rancks of better equipage' (*Sonnet* xxxii).

141. *fyste*, fart.

142. *from a dead man.* From Rabelais, *Pantagruel*, III. xxxvi, 'J'ayme-roys . . . autant entreprendre tirer vn pet d'un Asne mort, que de vous vne resolution'. Cf. *Iohn Heywoodes woorkes*, 1562, D4:

> I shall get a fart of a dead man as soone
> As a farthyng of him, his dole is soone doone.

145. *sir reuerence.* Used as in II. i. 163.

Hunger. . . . Heywood, op. cit., Divᵛ, 'Hunger droppeth euen out of bothe their noses'.

147. *Faire words. . . .* Heywood, op. cit., C1ᵛ, 'It hurteth not the tounge to geue fayre wurds'.

149. *golde ends.* In II. i. 131 used strictly in a trade sense; here of moral tags spoken, as it were, over the counter. Cf. *Volp.* Prol. 23, 'a gull, old ends reciting'.

151–2. *his fetters . . . of gold.* Heywood, op. cit., Biv, 'No man loueth his fetters be they made of gold'. Seneca, *De Remediis Fortuitorum*, xvi. 2, 'Stulti est compedes suas quamvis aureas amare'—an answer to a man complaining that he has lost a good and beautiful wife.

152. *head . . . vnder my childs girdle.* Heywood, op. cit., H1ᵛ:

> And if ye chaunce in aduoutrie to catche him,
> Then haue ye him on the hyp, or on the hyrdell,
> Then haue ye his head fast vnder your gyrdell.

Reginald Scot, *The discouerie of witchcraft*, 1597, VII. ii, p. 130, 'The pope . . . hath placed himselfe in the most loftie and delicate seate, putting almost all christian princes heads, not onelie vnder his girdle, but vnder his foote, &c.'.

153. *as she has brew'd. . . .* E.M.I. II. ii. 34 n.

154. *witlesse to wedding.* Heywood, op. cit., Dijᵛ:

> They went (witlesse) to wedding. Wherby at last
> They both went a begging.

163. *let Pride goe afore.* Ibid., Ciij^v:

> Well well (quoth mine aunte) pryde will haue a fall.
> For pryde goeth before, and shame cometh after.

165. *the first good Cow.* Ibid., Civ^v: 'But many a good cowe hath an euill caulfe.'

171. *melancholy.* The root idea of 'black bile' shades off here to irascibility.

182. *Wapping.* IV. i. 113–16.

185. *carry an M. vnder your girdle,* have the civility to say 'Master Goulding'. Usually in the negative form 'Neare an M by your girdle' (Udall, *Roister Doister,* 1553? III. iii); Chettle and Day, *The Blind-Beggar of Bednall-Green,* ed. Bang, ll. 404–5 (1659, C2): '*Had.* What sayest thou *Franck. Can.* How you base Rogue, nere an (*M.*) under your Girdle, . . . am I no better than your homesome *Franck.*'

190. *Bridewell,* originally a palace of Henry VIII, became a house of correction in 1553.

217. *be couer'd.* The point of this sarcasm is that they had lost their hats.

230. *Gresco.* A card game, only incidentally mentioned by Florio, *Queen Anna's New World of Words,* 1611, '*Massare,* to play or cast at the by, at hazard or gresco'. It was probably identical with the old French dice-game 'A la griesche', for which see Godefroy. 'Gresco' is archaic Spanish for 'griego' (Greek), and the forms with -*s*- in Spanish are imported from Catalan or from French or Provençal through Catalan. The Game may be *Le jeu de grecque* described in the 'Dictionnaire des Jeux' appended to tome iii, *Des Mathématiques. An V de la République,* 1719, p. 19: 'C'est une espèce de tonneau qui a plusieurs fonds à divers étages, tous percés dans le milieu d'un trou rond. On jette dessus des palets ou des écus de six francs. Quand ils passent dans le premier plancher, on compte un certain nombre de points; dans le second, dans le troisième & par terre de même.'

Primero. E.M.O. I. ii. 46.

233. *Bathing Tubbs.* For a similar extravagance see *C.R.* II. i. 44.

252. *encountred.* V. v. 154.

265–6. *God hath done his part in thee.* Proverbial: cf. *The life and pranks of long Meg of Westminster,* 1582, ch. v, where Meg tells a poor maimed soldier, 'Thou art big enough, God hath done his part on thee, A proper man and liue in distresse'.

278. *outrecuidance.* C.R. v. ii. 58.

290. *choppe Logick.* As if Quicksilver had attempted sophistry.

314. *take security.* Petronel means simply: Touchstone quibbles.

v. i. 1. *the Chronicle.* E.M.O. III. viii. 62 (Quarto text).

7. *O hone, hone, o no nera. B.F.* v. iv. 276. 'The Irish Honero' is a tune in the Fitzwilliam *Virginal Book* (given in Chappell, i, p. 85). It is spoken of as a ballad refrain in *North-ward Hoe,* v. i (1607, G1^v), 'O hone, hone, hone, ononero'.

25–6. *Hunger . . . breakes stone walls. Iohn Heywoodes woorkes,* I. xii. 1562, Eiv, 'Some saie, and I feele hunger perseth stone wall'.

28. *And,* if. In modern punctuation 'his Punke—God bless us!' The 'if' clause is an aposiopesis: Gertrude stops short of the implication, 'I could understand his deserting me', and gives a dramatic turn to the sentence by a cry of appeal.

29. *the Knight o' the Sunne. C.R.* III. v. 31 n.

30. *Palmerin of England.* Spoken of with contempt in *Und.* xliii. 30. *Palmerin de Inglaterra* by the Portuguese Francisco de Moraes, 1544, had been translated by Anthony Munday in 1602.

31. *Sir Lancelot? or sir Tristram.* Cf. *Und.* xliii. 69.

39. *still prest,* always ready.

44. *at Winchester.* Painted with the figure of Arthur, and still preserved in the County Hall at Winchester.

46. *Hazard,* the name of a game of dice described in Cotton's *Complete Gamester,* 1674, pp. 168–73.

50. *by bread & salt.* Cf. W. Stevenson, *Gammer Gurtons Nedle,* 1575, ed. Bradley, II. ii. 42–3:

Diccon. But Tib hath tykled in Gammers eare, that you should steale
the cocke.
Chat. Have I, stronge hoore? by bread and salte!—

Nashes Lenten Stuffe, 1599 (*Works,* ed. McKerrow, iii, p. 199): '*Venus,* for *Hero* was her priest, and *Iuno . . .* tooke bread and salt and eate it, that they would be smartlie reuenged. . . .

57. *lay my Ladiship in lauender,* pawn it. *E.M.O.* III. iii. 40. The joke, not a common one, recurs in Chapman's *Monsieur D'Oliue:* D'Olive thinks that he has been appointed ambassador (1606, D4ᵛ):

D'OL. To make the world take notice I am noble
The first thing I will doe ile sweare to pay
No debts vpon my honor.
MVG. A good cheape proofe of your Nobilitie.
D'OL. But if I knew where I might pawne mine honor,
For some odd thousand Crownes, it shal be layd:
Ile pay 't againe when I haue done withal.

60. *waistcoate.* To wear the waistcoat only with no upper garment over it was disreputable: 'waistcoateer' = prostitute.

Peate, a spoilt, self-willed girl. *E.M.O.* Characters, 58.

80–3. Cf. Browne, *Britannia's Pastorals,* I, song ii (1613, p. 31):

A Hillocke . . . where oft the *Fairy-Queene*
At twy-light sate, and did command her Elues,
To pinch those Maids that had not swept their shelues:
And further if by Maidens ouer-sight,
Within doors water were not brought at night:

Or if they spread no Table, set no Bread,
They should haue nips from toe vnto the head:
And for the Maid that had perform'd each thing,
She in the Water-paile bad leaue a Ring.

85. *backe-side.* C. *is* A. IV. viii. 1.

91. *waking dreames.* So Plautus, *Captivi*, 848, in a similar context, 'Hic vigilans somniat'.

120–1. *Thou should'st haue look'd. . . . Iohn Heywoodes woorkes*, 1562, Aiijᵛ:

> Thus by these lessons ye may learne good cheape,
> In weddyng and al thing to looke or ye leape.

122. *blowe at the Cole.* Ibid., Civᵛ, 'Aunt, leat them that be a colde blowe at the cole'.

123. *Selfe doe, selfe haue.* Ibid., Bivᵛ, 'For I did it my selfe: and selfe do, selfe haue'.
The hastie person. . . . Ibid., Aiij:

> In less things then weddyng, hast showth hastie mans fo,
> So that the hasty man neuer wanteth wo.

127–8. *lacke of liking.* Ibid., Aivᵛ:

> And then of olde prouerbes in opening the packe,
> One shewth me openly in loue is no lacke.
> No lacke of liking, but lacke of liuyng,
> May lacke in loue (quoth I) and breede ill cheeuyng.

129. *Cittiner.* A colloquialism: *North-ward hoe*, v. i (1607, G2), 'maister cittiner'.

130. *Iwys.* E.M.I. I. i. 36, 'wusse'.

141. *French-wires.* Cf. *S.W.* Prol. 23, 'citie-wires' n.
Cheat-bread, 'wheaten bread of the second quality, made of flour more coarsely sifted than that used for Manchet, the finest quality'. *O.E.D.* quoting T. Wilson's translation of *Demosthenes' Olynthiacs*, 1570, Ep. Ded., 'Lyke to them that eating fine Manchet, are angry with others that feede on Cheate breade'. One would have expected Gertrude to have eaten manchet.

142. *little Dog.* Poet. IV. i. 13.

150. *intoxicate.* Gertrude means 'excited'.

151. *The legge of a Lark. . . . Iohn Heywoodes woorkes*, 1562, B1:

> For the leg of a larke
> Is better than is the body of a kyght.

155–6. *It's but ill food. . . .* A shrewd retort to line 151.

158. *Lady-bird.* C.R. II. iv. 7.

273. *Chucke.* D. *is* A. II. iv. 2; *Macbeth*, III. ii. 45.

v. ii. 23. *Kindely*, natural.

29. *mortified*, depressed, overcome: but the use is irregular.

33. *Brownist*, a follower of Robert Brown (1550–1633). The sect merged in the Independents.

Anabaptist. This sect arose in Germany in 1521, and began to appear in England about 1534. It advocated adult baptism and community of goods and tried to set up a theocracy. *S.W.* III. ii. 15, 'No Anabaptist euer rail'd with the like licence'.

Millenary, a believer in the Second Advent and the Millennium.

Famely o' Loue. A sect founded by David George or Joriszoon, an Anabaptist of Delft, who claimed to be restorer of the kingdom of Israel. He died in 1556, and was succeeded by 'Harry Nicholas' (*Alch.* v. v. 117). The sect was attacked in John Rogers's *The Displaying of an horrible Secte of Heretiques, naming themselues the Familie of Loue*, 1578, and in Middleton's play, *The Famelie of Loue*, 1607. In 1580 Elizabeth issued a proclamation to suppress it.

34. *Good Fellow*, thief—a humorous ending to the list of sectaries. Cf. Warner, *Albions England*, IX. liii (1597, p. 241):

> If Hypocrites why Puritanes we terme, be ask't, in breefe,
> T'is but an *Ironized* Terme, good-Fellow so spells Theefe.

43. *Knights-Ward*. Explained in *West-ward Hoe*, III. ii (1607, E): '*Mono.* I will patiently incounter the Counter. Which is the dearest warde in Prison Sergeant! the knights ward? *Amb.* No sir, the Maisters side. *Mono.* Well the knight is aboue the maister though his Table be worse furnisht: Ile goe thither.' See *E.M.O.* v. vi. 36 n.

44. *the Hole.* . . . 48. *the Two-penny Ward*, the two lowest wards in the prison. Cf. John Cooke, *Greenes Tu Quoque* (1614, I1v): '*Holdfast.* If you haue no monie, you'r best remoue into some cheaper Ward. *Spendall.* What Ward should I remoue in? *Hold.* Why to the Two-pennie Ward, is likeliest to hold out with your meanes: or if you will, you may go into the Holl, and there you may feed for nothing.' *E.M.O.* v. xi. 51.

55. *cut his hayre*, as Zeal-of-the-Land Busy advised Knock-hum to do (*B.F.* III. vi. 24).

57. *Booke of Martyrs*. *E.M.O.* III. viii. 62.

Sicke-Mans Salue. Thomas Becon's work, *The Sycke Mans Salue. Wherein al faithful christians may learne both how to behaue themselues patiently and thankfully in the time of sicknesse, and also vertuouslie to dispose their temporall goods, and finally to prepare themselues gladly and godly to die*. Written in 1561; seventeen editions appeared up to 1632. See *S.W.* IV. iv. 108.

65. *Intelligencer*, informer. For the promotion cf. Chapman, *Caesar and Pompey*, II. i (1633, C4):

> . . . has *Fronto* liu'd thus long
> In *Rome*? . . . spent all? run thorow worse
> Offices since? beene a Promoter? a Purueyor? a Pander?
> A Sumner? a Sergeant? an Intelligencer?

66. *comming.* *Volp.* II. vi. 74.

69. *Rheume.* *E.M.I.* III. iv. 13–19.

70. *Fish is cast away.* . . . *Iohn Heywoodes woorkes,* I. xi (1562, Dij^v), 'Fishe is caste awaie that is cast in drie pooles'.

75–6. *lay mine eare to the ground.* The vulgar belief that the adder, if the charmer played to it, put one ear to the ground and stopped the other with its tail.

v. iii. 6 (stage-direction). *at the grate.* In Marston's *Antonio's Revenge,* III. ii (Malone Soc. reprint, 844–5), is a stage-direction '*Antonio kisseth Mellida's hand: then Mellida goes from the grate*'. Mellida is imprisoned, and she has heard Antonio lamenting outside her cell: at line 790 she comes to the grate, saying 'O here, here is a vent to passe my sighes'; at line 830 Antonio says to her 'Reach me thy hand'. W. J. Lawrence in *The Physical Conditions of the Elizabethan Playhouse,* p. 67, infers from this passage that there was a grated opening on the ground floor of the tiring-house at a height of about five feet between the rear-stage curtains and one of the entering doors. He cites Security's reference, line 20, to 'yron grates' as a confirmation of the theory.

19. *Case.* A quibble on the architectural sense, the outside face of a building. Compare Marvell's reference to Charles I's imprisonment in '*Caresbrooks* narrow case' (*Poems,* ed. Margoliouth, i, p. 88).

27. *to which Hell is a kinde of coole Bathe.* So Ursula roasting her pigs in *Bartholomew Fair,* II. ii. 44, says of her occupation, 'Hell's a kind of cold cellar to't'.

29, 30. *her New-Moone,* in reference to the horns of the crescent.

54. *eate o' the Basket.* The poor prisoners in the Hole were fed from the scraps and broken meat sent from the sheriff's table or collected in the City. Massinger, *The City Madam,* I. i (1658, p. 5):

> Did not our charitee redeem thee out of prison, . . .
> When the Sheriffs basket and his broken meat
> Were your Festivall exceedings?

The song at the end of Heywood's *The Rape of Lucrece* (1608, K2) entitled 'The Cries of Rome' has for its second cry,

> Bread and—meat—bread—and meat
> For the—ten—der—mercy of God to the
> poore pris—ners of *Morgate,* foure
> score and ten—poore—prisners.

John Cooke's *Greenes Tu Quoque,* 1614, I2^v, has a realistic scene of the basket arriving at the prison. The prisoners used to ask alms of the passers-by in the street: T. Heywood, *A Woman Kilde with Kindnesse,* III. i (1617, D3):

> Agen to prison? *Malby* hast thou seene
> A poore slaue better tortur'd? shall we heare
> The Musicke of his voice cry from the grate,
> *Meate for the Lords sake.*

63. *Rugge gown.* E.M.O. III. vii. 21. The nearest equivalent to sack-cloth which the penitent could secure off-hand.

66. *lay an Execution on him.* Cf. Webster, *The White Divel*, II. i. 291–3 (ed. Lucas): 'A poore quackesalving knave, my Lord, one that should have bene lasht for's lechery, but that he confest a judgement, had an execution laid upon him, and so put the whip to a *non-plus*.'

75. *feeling*, the sense of touch where money is concerned: *D. is A.* III. iii. 78, *S. of N.* II. iv. 158.

87. *winding deuices.* So of Justice 'Bramble' in *T. of T.* v. x. 56: in Chapman's *May-Day*, II. ii (1611, p. 19), Aurelia says of her dotard lover Gasparo, 'The wurse my fortune to be entangled with such a winding bramble'.

v. iv. 2. *Vlisses.* See p. 638.

17. *Mandragora. Sej.* III. 598.

33. *The voyce of the Hyena.* Edward Topsell, *The Historie of foure footed beastes*, 1607, p. 437: 'They are great enemies to men, and for this cause *Solinus* reporteth of them, that by secret accustoming them-selues to houses or yardes, where Carpenters or such mechanicks worke, they learne to call their names, and so will come being an hungred and call one of them with a distinct and articulate voice, whereby he causeth the man many times to forsake his worke and goe to see the person calling him; but the subtill Hyæna goeth farther off, and so by calling allureth him from helpe of company, and afterward when she seeth time deuoureth him, and for this cause hir proper epithite is *Aemula vocis*, Voyce counter-faytor.'

57. *inmure.* Perhaps a printer's misspelling of 'immure'.

v. v. 11. *curious*, particular. Cf. *The Taming of the Shrew*, IV. iv. 36, 'For curious I cannot be with you'.

24. *White-Friers*, 'situated to the south of Fleet-street and east of the Temple, . . . nearly where Salisbury-court and Dorset-street now are. Having been formerly a sanctuary, it long retained the privilege of protecting persons liable to arrest, and thus became the resort of debtors, bankrupts, and profligates of all descriptions' (Nares). The privilege was abolished in Queen Anne's reign. It is noted as a dis-reputable quarter in *Volp.* IV. ii. 35, *Ep.* xii. 2.

44. *in imitation of Maningtons.* Entered on the Stationers' Register on 7 November 1576 as *A woeful Ballad made by Mr. George Mannynton, an houre before he suffered at Cambridge castell*, and printed in Clement Robinson's *A Handefull of Pleasant Delights*, 1584 (ed. Arber, pp. 57–9):

> I waile in wo, I plunge in pain,
> With sorrowing sobs, I do complain.
> With wallowing waues I wish to die,
> I languish sore whereas I lie.

A different version appeared in Ritson's *Ancient Songs and Ballads*, 1877, pp. 188–91.

The reference to Manington and the existence of the ballad dispose of Charles Edmonds's suggestion (*Athenaeum*, 13 October 1883) that Quicksilver is sketched from Luke Hutton, author of *The Blacke Dogge of Newgate*, 1596, who was executed for highway robbery in 1598. He wrote a *Repentance*, entered on the Stationers' Register on 3 November 1595, on which Mr. Edmonds lays stress, but the title (and subject) must have been common for the doggerel of condemned criminals. There was a black-letter ballad (folio broadsheet 1598) which serves to illustrate the text of *Eastward Hoe*, but does not prove the identification: it was entitled *Luke Huttons Lamentation, which he wrote the day before his Death, being condemned to be hang'd at York this last assise for his robberies and trespasses committed*.

48. *An excellent Ditty*. Printed in *Wit and Drollery*, first edition 1606, p. 100, headed 'To the Tune of *I waile in woe, I plunge in paine*: *Or, Labandola shot*': there are variant readings, mostly trivial, but one has some significance; in line 117, '*Shun Vsurers, Bauds*' is changed to 'Shun Usurers bonds', an attractive reading, but Security's song 148-9 confirms the text.

73. *The Ragged Colt. Iohn Heywoodes woorkes*, I. xi (1562, Dij):

> Colts (quoth his man) may proue wel with tatches yll.
> For of a ragged colte there comth a good horse.

77. *Westward*. II. i. 120.

79. *Daughter* rhyming with *after*: *Volp*. I. ii. 74 n. There was a by-form 'dafter' in the sixteenth and seventeenth centuries.

80. *the black Oxe trod o' my foote. T. of T.* IV. vi. 16 n.

90. *Stanze*. A sixteenth- and seventeenth-century form: *Love's Labour's Lost*, IV. ii. 99.

120. *cut your Thongs* . . . Compare *Iohn Heywoodes woorkes*, I. viii (1562, Biv^v), 'I shall Cut my cote after my cloth', and contrast *The Paston Letters*, ii, p. 226, 'Men cut large thongs here of other mens lether'.

138-9. *A shoute in the Prison* 'of joy at the release of the penitent adventurers'—Cunliffe. No: Security has rushed to the grate.

170. *Twier-pipe*. Commemorated in the anonymous tract *Old Meg of Herefordshire*, 1609, Dedication: 'Tweire-pipe that famous Southren Taberer with the Cowleyan windpipe, who for whuling hath beene famous through the Globe of the world.'

185. *Wearing of Yellow*, (1) the prison dress, (2) the colour of jealousy: cf. Herrick, 'How Marigolds came yellow' in *Hesperides*, ed. Moorman, p. 187:

> *Jealous Girles* these sometimes were,
> While they liv'd, or lasted here:
> Turn'd to *Flowers*, still they be
> Yellow, markt for Jealousie.

Compare for the turn of thought here *Every Man in his Humour*, Quarto version, v. v. 388-90.

188. *corasiue*, corrosive.

195. *Innocent*, simpleton. Cf. *Florios Second Frutes*, 1591, p. 143, 'whosoeuer is made a cuckold by his wife, either he knowes it, or knowes it not. . . . If he knowe it, hee must needs be a patient, and therefore a martyr, if he knowe it not, hee is an innocent.'

203. *Children of Cheapside. M. Christmas*, 286.

209. *The Vsurer punisht*. Inconsistent with lines 178–80.

Epilogue

3. *stucke with people. Sej.* II. 450, 'Were all TIBERIVS body stuck with eyes'.

5. *Pageant*, the Lord Mayor's Show. *Und.* xlii. 77–80.

9. *once a weeke*, viz. on Saturday. The Diary of the Duke of Stettin-Pomerania's visit to England in 1602 (printed in *The Royal Historical Society's Transactions*, 1892, new series, p. 26), describing the Children of the Chapel, says: 'Damit sie höfliche Sitten anwenden, ist ihnen aufgelegt, wöchentlich eine comœdia zu agiren, wozu ihnen denn die Königin ein sonderlich theatrum erbauet und mit köstlichen Kleidern zum Ueberfluss versorget hat.' For the Saturday performance see Wallace, *Children of the Chapel at Blackfriars*, p. 125.

VOLPONE

IN our general introduction to the play we touched on the brilliant satire of the legacy-hunter in ancient literature, the records of it in Lucian, Petronius, Horace, Juvenal, and Pliny, all of which would be familiar to Jonson.[1] A later source of satire bearing on the play has been pointed out by Dr. J. D. Rea in the Yale edition—*The Praise of Folly* by Erasmus. The parallels cited in our notes were first pointed out in this edition. Dr. Rea also shows the use Jonson made in the dedicatory epistle to the two Universities of Erasmus's *Epistola Apologetica ad Martinum Dorpium*, a defence of *The Praise of Folly*. Erasmus's great satire takes the form of a sustained harangue and exposition by Folly herself to an imaginary audience who applaud occasionally. She pleads that folly influences and colours every aspect of human life and that, by keeping people cheerful, she is a universal benefactress. The lyric in the second scene of the play,

> Fooles, they are the onely nation
> Worth mens enuy, or admiration

sums up the main idea of much of the work. The great scholar and thinker is 'astride a hobby-horse', to quote one of his own images. Jonson borrows some trappings of the hobby-horse and freely uses

[1] Vol. ii, pp. 50–3.

hints and phrases.[1] But, according to Dr. Rea, Jonson worked up the entire play from Erasmus, so that *Volpone* 'is a product, not so much of genius and originality, as of industry and patience'.[2] To bring the play better into line with Erasmus, we are told that the satire is aimed, not at avarice and greed pursued so far that they pass into open crime, but merely against folly, and 'the keynote of the whole drama' is to be found in Mosca's 'invention', the performance of Nano and his fellows in the second scene.[3] 'Jonson has merely substituted'—merely!—'the group of professional fools as a dramatic equivalent for Folly herself.'

Dr. Rea further illustrates Jonson's lack of original power in drama by stating that Erasmus's colloquy *Alcumista* 'is the source of *The Alchemist*, generally said to have no real source'.[4] In our introduction to that play[5] we gave a full summary of the details taken from Erasmus, and we may refer to this as a terse illustration of the point at issue. For Dr. Rea the finished product is simply the raw material.[6] The artist sinks to the amanuensis.

And Jonson was not even widely read; 'Many, if not most, of the frequent classical quotations in *Volpone* were taken at second hand' from writers of the Renaissance. Dr. Rea instances the Pindar passage in the opening lines of the play, found in Seneca and Erasmus, and the quotation from Sophocles in III. iv. 78 quoted by Libanius. Jonson never read, it appears, his marked copy of the *Greek Dramatists and Lyrists* now in the University Library at Cambridge.[7]

Worse than this, he was capable of atrocious blunders in his Latin. The most extraordinary statement in Dr. Rea's edition is that on pages xxi, xxii:

'I am inclined to think that the suggestion for . . . the pretended death of Volpone, is also to be found in the Latin version of the *Dream* of Lucian—or rather in an easy mistranslation of a passage in it:

'Et consobrinus erat vir supra modum dives, nomine Drimylus: is quoad vivebat, ne obolum quidem donaverat Simari: nam qui daret, quum ne ipse quidem pecunias attingeret? At simulatque mortuus est nuper: universis illis opibus iuxta leges Simon ille, qui coria putria, qui patellam circumlingebat, gaudens potitur: purpura ostroque circumtectus, famulosque et currus, et aurea pocula, et mensas eburnas innexas pedibus possidet, ab omnibus adoratur.

'Jonson's Latin scholarship was not unimpeachable, and a hasty reading of these lines might easily make *simulatque* (which would have

---

[1] See the notes to I. ii. 60–2, 66–81, 112, and Epilogue 6.   [2] p. xxiv.
[3] pp. xxvi–xxvii.   [4] p. xxv.   [5] Vol. ii, p. 99 n.
[6] Libanius is similarly treated. Because Jonson used him for some suggestive details in the fourth scene of Act III, Libanius is the creator of Lady Would-be, and furnishes 'every feature' of her, 'as well as most of the speeches made by and about her'.   [7] Vol. i, p. 265.

been printed *simulatq;*) seem to be a verb, instead of a compound of *simul* and *atque*. The resulting mistranslation, even though instantly corrected, would have been enough to suggest the whole incident.'

For 'an easy mistranslation' read 'an imbecile blunder': how does Dr. Rea suppose Jonson would have translated '*At simulat-que*'? 'But and he pretends'? And does he suppose that Jonson would not have known that with *simulat* the construction would have to be 'At simulat se mortuum esse nuper'? Dr. Rea is driven to this wild theory because no fool pretends to die in *The Praise of Folly*; it is foisted in because Jonson must not be guilty of a scrap of originality. The Latin notes on *Hymenaei*, *The Masque of Queens*, and *The Masque of Augurs* should prove, even to the ill-informed, Jonson's command of Latin.

Dr. Rea's next point is Jonson's imperfect knowledge of Greek: he read his Greek authors in Latin translations rather than in the original Greek. The notes on the Masques will show whether Jonson could quote Greek at first hand, and his copy of Aelian's *Tactica*, 1613, now in the University Library at Cambridge, is carefully annotated, with corrections of the Latin translation which is printed in parallel columns to the Greek text. He probably began Greek at Westminster; Camden's *Greek Grammar* for use in that school was first printed in 1595.

Lastly, it is impossible to pass by Dr. Rea's outrageous suggestion that Sir Politic Would-be is a satire, 'very easy for the audience to distinguish',[1] on Sir Henry Wotton. Twelve pages are devoted to proving it. Every fatuity of which Sir Politic is capable is twisted into a caricature of something Wotton said or did. It is an instructive example of the way in which, when once an identification of this kind is made, evidence can be procured with very little effort. We confine ourselves to one example—Sir Politic's notes; he had valuable information for travellers (IV. i. 5–7); he noted down each day every trivial action in his diary (ibid. 133–44); otherwise the notes are all drawn out of play-books (V. iv. 41–2), a point which Dr. Rea has failed to illustrate. But he does quote as bearing on the question the tribute of Wotton's intimate friend Donne. Writing when Wotton was going to Venice as ambassador, Donne said:

> After those learned papers which your hand
> Hath stor'd with notes of use and pleasure too,
> From which rich treasury you may command
> Fit matter whether you will write or do.[2]

---

[1] The name, apparently, was a clue. 'As Wotton was pronounced Wooton, Sir Pol. Would-be is not a bad parody of Sir Hen. Wotton'. Note the joke on 'poll' and 'hen'; how many of the audience saw it?

[2] *Poems of Donne*, ed. Grierson, i, p. 215.

'Learned papers', 'rich treasury'—how does such a tribute square with Sir Politic's drivel? Jonson respected Wotton as a poet. He knew by heart Wotton's poem 'How happy is he borne, or taught'; he quoted it to Drummond at Hawthornden, and his autograph copy of it is preserved at Dulwich College.[1]

An element of conjecture necessarily enters into attempts to identify stage-characters, but, after this folly about Wotton, it is pleasant to turn to Dr. Samuel C. Chew's suggestion (in *The Crescent and the Cross*, 1937, p. 269) that Jonson had the erratic Sir Anthony Shirley in mind in depicting Sir Politic. It need not be taken as an attempt at a complete picture, but the two had certainly some traits in common. And there is a clue at the close—the proposal to ship Sir Politic away to Zante or Aleppo and put his adventures in 'The Book of Voyages'. In October 1600 there had appeared *A True Report of Sir Antonie Shirlies Journey overland to Venice, from thence to Seaton, Antioch, Aleppo, and Babilon, and so to Casbine in Persia*. The book was suppressed on 21 October as unlicensed, and the printers, R. Blore and J. Jaggard, were fined. An authorized version by William Parry, Shirley's fellow-traveller, appeared in 1601, *A new and large Discourse of the Travels of Sir Anthony Shirley*.

There is an earlier identification, quite untrue, recorded by John Aubrey on the authority of 'old Thomas Tyndale Esq.' that Volpone was drawn from Captain Thomas Sutton (1532–1611), the founder of the Charterhouse. Aubrey says he 'fed severall with hopes of being his Heire. 'Twas from him, that B. Jonson tooke his hint of the Fox; and by Seigneor Volpone is meant Sutton. The later end of his dayes he lived in Fleetstreet at a Wollen drapers shop, opposite to Fetter-lane; where he had so many great chests full of money, that his chamber was ready to grone under it, and Mr. Tyndall, (who knew him, and I thinke had money of him on mortgage during his lawe suite. V. ye Lord Staffords case in Cokes Reports) was afrayd the roome would fall. . . . The Earle of Dorset [I thinke Rich] mightily courted him, & p^rsented him, hopeing to have been his Heire: and so did severall other great persons.' 'An attempt had even been made to induce him to name Prince Charles as his heir, whilst the Prince was still a younger son, to whom an estate worth at least 6000*l*. a year would be no unwelcome gift. To this proposal Sutton steadily refused to listen' (S. R. Gardiner).[2] Sutton was a soldier and financier: an excellent account of him is in the eighteenth chapter of Gerald S. Davies's *Charterhouse in London*, 1921. Sutton was Captain of Berwick in 1558, Master General and Surveyor of

[1] Vol. i, pp. 135, 157.
[2] *History of England 1603–1612*, ed. 1883, ii, p. 213.

Ordnance in the north of England from 1570 to 1594. He is said to have made £50,000 by 1580; he leased the manors of Gateshead and Wickham, which was a coal area. In later life he lived at Hackney and then at Stoke Newington. It is easy to see from Aubrey's gossip how the legend of his sitting for the portrait of Volpone arose, but a knowledge of the true facts of his life completely refutes the imputation. Gifford disposed of it in the Memoir of Jonson which he prefixed to his edition.

PLACE AND TIME IN THE PLAY

Jonson claimed in the prologue to have observed the laws of the drama as laid down by the best critics:

> The lawes of time, place, persons he obserueth,
> From no needfull rule he swerueth.

The scene is Venice, in the houses of Volpone, Corvino, and Sir Politic Would-be, in the streets and in the Scrutineo, where the trial is held. The unity of place is maintained while the actors are allowed freedom of movement.

The time of the action is one day. The play opens after sunrise: 'Good morning to the day' (I. i. 1). Voltore makes 'early visitation' (I. iii. 4). Lady Politic Would-be calls but is put off till 'Some three houres, hence' (I. v. 98): she keeps the appointment in the afternoon (III. iv). Celia is brought to Volpone, who tells her that 'but this morning' he had been the mountebank outside her window (III. vii. 149). The 'sundry times' when he had appeared 'in seuerall shapes' (ibid. 148) are by a dramatic economy rare in Jonson not included in the play. Jonson perhaps forgot that Mosca had discovered Celia 'but yesterday' (I. v. 116). The judgement of the Court of Venice is to be given 'ere night' (IV. vi. 61); it is given in the concluding scene.

Dedication

1. *most equall Sisters*. Gayton, *Pleasant Notes upon Don Quixote*, 1654, pp. 20, 21: 'We will therefore end this perplexed piece of controversy (as our father *Ben* hath given example,) who dedicating his *Fox* to the two Universities of this Iland, Fox-like (knowing they alwaies quarrelled for Antiquity) in a most handsome and unenviable compellation, stil'd them *most equall Sisters*.'

2. *presently*, instantly.

11. *heare so ill*, a latinism, *tam male audiunt*, have such an evil reputation. *Alch.* I. i. 24, *Cat.* IV. 823, *B.F.* IV. i. 73, *L.R.* 163; Spenser, *The Faerie Queene*, I. v. 23, 'If old *Aveugles* sonnes so euill heare'.

13. *fore-head*, shame. *C.R.* v. xi. 54.

Volpone

683

23. *a good man.* From Strabo, *Geographica*, I. ii. 5: ἡ δὲ ποιήτου ⟨ἀρετὴ⟩ συνέζευκται τῇ τοῦ ἀνθρώπου, καὶ οὐχ οἷόν τε ἀγαθὸν γενέσθαι ποιήτην μὴ πρότερον γενηθέντα ἄνδρα ἀγαθόν. Coleridge commented: 'I quite agree with Strabo, as translated by Ben Jonson in his splendid dedication of the Fox—that there can be no great poet who is not a good man, though not, perhaps, a *goody* man. His heart must be pure; he must have learned to look into his own heart, and sometimes to look *at* it; for how can he who is ignorant of his own heart know anything of, or be able to move, the heart of any one else?' (*Table Talk*, ed. H. N. Coleridge, 1865, p. 281).

23–30. *He that is said . . .* The germ of the idea is in Horace, *Ep.* II. i. 126–31:

> Os tenerum pueri balbumque poeta figurat,
> torquet ab obscaenis iam nunc sermonibus aurem,
> mox etiam pectus praeceptis format amicis,
> asperitatis et invidiae corrector et irae,
> recte facta refert, orientia tempora notis
> instruit exemplis, inopem solatur et aegrum.

But, as Castelain has shown, Jonson is drawing directly on Minturno, *De Poeta*, 1559, p. 8: 'Hoc deplorandum quòd in ea tempora incidissent, isq; rerum esset status, cum nulla dicendi ratio uigeret, ipsaq; uis Poetarum penitus cecidisset, quæ quondam pacatis, tranquillisq; in ciuitatibus floruisset, conandum uerò, ut quam publicè colere non possent, eam priuatim tota mente amplecterentur. Quidnam . . . potest, aut debet praeclarius uideri, quam id meditari, quo pueros ad omnem disciplinam possis informare; uiros ad uirtutes omnes hortari, Seniores in optimo statu retinere, aut si repuerascere incœperint, ad pristinam firmitatem reuocare, populum mira cum uoluptate erudire, ac rapere quô uelis, unde libeat abducere. Nec uerò quicquàm puto tam mirabile, quàm ex ita frequenti hominum multitudine unum eminere, qui tanquàm Deus, aut certè Deorum interpres, & arbiter naturæ, doctorq; rerum et divinarum et humanarum, ac morum magister id uel solus, uel cum paucis efficiat, quod natura omnes facere posse uideantur, illudq̄; tum maximè, cùm omnis oratio ex carminibus constabat.'

24. *informe*, shape, mould (Lat. *informo*).

24–5. *yong-men . . . growne-men . . . old-men.* So *Ep.* lxxxv. 3, 'Where I both learn'd, why wise-men hawking follow'. The accent falls on the first syllable in the contrasted words: cf. Herrick, *Hesperides*, 1648, p. 190:

> Have ye beheld (with much delight)
> A red-Rose peeping through a white?

29. *a master in manners. Disc.* 2394–5, 'the wisest and best learned have thought her' (i.e. poetry) 'the absolute Mistresse of manners'.

35. *abused name.* Cf. 'that prophaned name!' (*Poet.* IV. vi. 30).

43–52. Rea compares Erasmus, *Epistola Apologetica ad Martinum Dorpium* (ed. 1703), 2 DE, 'Huiusmodi rationibus ipse mihi persuasi, ut semper innoxias & incruentas haberem literas, nec eas ullius mali nomine contaminarem.' Ibid. 8 E, 'Atque eandem cautionem in omnibus seruare curaui, ne quid obscœne scriberem, ne quid pestiferum moribus, ne quid seditiosum, aut quod cum ullius ordinis iniuria coniunctum uideri posset. . . . At ego in tot iam editis voluminibus, cum tam multos candidissime laudarim, quæso, cuius unquam denigraui famam ? cui uel leuissimam adspersi labem ? Quam gentem, quem ordinem, quem hominem nominatim taxaui ?'

46. *foule, and vn-wash'd baudry.* Cf. *Ep.* ii. 11, a disclaimer of 'lewd, prophane, and beastly phrase'.

49. *my youngest infant.* A glance at the attack on *Sejanus*, which brought Jonson before the Privy Council.

51. *what nation, Societie, or generall order, or state.* So in the appeal to Lord Salisbury on *Eastward Ho* (vol. i, p. 195), 1605, 'let Mee be examind, both by all my workes past, and this present, and not trust to *Rumor*, but my Bookes . . . whether, I haue euer (in any thing I haue written priuate, or publique) giuen offence to a Nation, to any publique order or state, or any person of honor, or Authority . . .'. Jonson had been credited with attacking the Court in *Cynthia's Revels*, the army, the law, and the stage in *Poetaster*, and the Scots in *Eastward Ho*.

55. *that are intirely mine.* A reference to collaboration in *Sejanus* and *Eastward Ho*, both of which had got him into trouble.

57. *mimick*, actor, as in *Poet.* iii. iv. 278–306.

buffon. For instance, Carlo Buffone in *Every Man out of his Humour*.

59, 60. *ingenuously . . . disease. Disc.* 2329–31, 'A man, that is on the mending hand, will either ingeniously confesse, or wisely dissemble his disease'. From Erasmus, *Epistola Apologetica*, I2, 'Et tamen quia nemo nominatim incessitur, arrident omnes, et suum quisque morbum aut fatetur ingenue, aut dissimulat prudenter'.

62. *I know . . . Epist. Apol.* 11 c, 'In quosdam adeo sunt iniqui, ut nihil tam circumspecte dici possit, quod non aliqua ratione calumnietur'.

63. *obnoxious to*, liable to (Lat. *obnoxius*).

65–70. *Application . . .* Discussed in *E.M.O.* ii. vi. 147–79. Cf. Chapman, *Al Fooles*, 1605, prologus:

> Who can shew cause, why th'ancient Comick vaine
> Of *Eupolis* and *Cratinus* (now reuiu'd,
> Subiect to personall application)
> Should be exploded by some bitter splenes ?
> Yet merely Comicall, and harmlesse iestes
> (Though nere so witty) be esteem'd but toyes,
> If voide of th'other satyrismes sauce ?

Marston in *Parasitaster*, 1606, A2, tells the 'equall Reader', 'As for the factious malice, and studied detractions of some few that tread in the same path with me' (i.e. writers of comedy), 'let all know, I most easily neglect them'; and similarly in the prologue:

> Spectators know, you may with freest faces
> Behold this Scene, for here no rude disgraces

Shall taint a publique, or a priuat name,
This pen at valer rate doth value fame,
Then at the price of others infamy
To purchase it.

69, 70. *vtter . . . meanings. Epist. Apol.* 11 B: 'Quid autem mirum, si tales, quales modo diximus, propositiones aliquot eligant, ex magno decerptas opere, quarum alias faciunt scandalosas, alias irreuerentiales, alias male sonantes, alias impias hæresim sapientes? non quod hæc mala reperiant illic, sed quod ipsi secum adferant.'

71. *rak'd vp*, covered, like glead with embers raked over it.

74. *whose faces they intrench.* Milton, *Par. Lost*, i. 600–1, 'his face Deep scars of Thunder had intrencht'.

petulant stiles. Poet. Apol. Dial. 97.

76. *grau'd.* Chapman, *Hero and Leander*, iii. 35, 'Joy grauen in sense, like snow in water, wasts'.

78. *patriots*, fellow-countrymen.

prouiding, foreseeing. *Sej.* v. 613.

84. Horace, *Sat.* II. i. 23, translated in *Poet.* III. v. 41–2.

87. *misc'line interludes*, Lat. *ludi miscelli* (Suetonius, *Caligula*, 20), a variety entertainment, with the suggestion of a medley, a hotchpotch.

89. *filth of the time*: 'garbage' in the Quarto; cf. *Poet.* Apol. Dial. 46, 'To swallow vp the garbadge of the time'.

91. *prolepse's*, anachronisms.

92–3. *brothelry . . . pagan. Epist. Apol.* 10 F, 'Quod si placet, cur non eadem opera quicquid à poetis hodie scribitur aut luditur, ad hanc excutiant legem? quot illic reperient obscœna, quot ueterem paganismum olentia?'

93. *I cannot but be serious.* Ibid. 8 B: 'Quid enim eo sanctius, quid augustius, quid æque resipiens ac referens illa cœlestia Christi dogmata? at hoc, ut omittam barbari factitijque sermonis sordes & portenta, ut omittam omnium bonarum litterarum inscitiam, ut imperitiam linguarum, sic Aristotele, sic humanis inuentiunculis, sic prophanis etiam legibus est contaminatum, ut haud sciam an purum illum ac sincerum Christum sapiat.'

105. *reduce*, bring back (Lat. *reduco*).

108. *in the best reason of living.* Cf. Aristophanes, *Frogs*, 1008–10:

> AI. τίνος οὔνεκα χρὴ θαυμάζειν ἄνδρα ποιητήν;
> ΕΥΡ. δεξιότητος καὶ νουθεσίας, ὅτι βελτίους τε ποιοῦμεν
> τοὺς ἀνθρώπους ἐν ταῖς πόλεσιν.

112. *off industrie*, intentionally (Lat. *de industria*).

113. *with what ease.* Similarly in *S.W.* prologue 1, 14, 15.

119. *not alwaies ioyfull.* As when a knave is exposed or trounced, e.g. Pyrgopolinices in the *Miles Gloriosus*.

124. *elsewhere.* In his commentary on the *Art of Poetry* announced in the address to the readers in *Sejanus* as ready for publication.

141. *Cinnamus the barber.* From Martial, VI. lxiv. 24–6:

> At si quid nostrae tibi bilis inusserit ardor,
> vivet et haerebit totoque legetur in orbe
> stigmata nec vafra delebit Cinnamus arte.

Cf. *Poet.* Apol. Dial. 164–9.

After 146. *my house in the Black-Friars* (Quarto). Coryat, *Traveller for the English Wits*, 1616, wishes to be remembered to 'Maister Beniamin Iohnson the Poet, at his chamber at the Blacke Friers'.

The Argument

An acrostic argument is also prefixed to *The Alchemist*, copying those found before all the plays of Plautus except the *Bacchides*.

Prologue

8. *profit . . . pleasure.* From Horace, *Ars Poetica*, 343–4:

> Omne tulit punctum qui miscuit utile dulci,
> lectorem delectando pariterque monendo.

A favourite quotation: *E.M.O.* Induction, 202; *S.W.* 2nd prologue, 1, 2; *S. of N.* epilogue, 1, 2.

9. *as some.* A reply to Marston, who had written in the prologue to *The Dutch Curtezan* (1605, A2):

> Yet thinke not, but like others raile we could,
> (Best art Presents, not what it can, but should)
> And if our pen in this seeme ouer slight
> We striue not to instruct, but to delight. . . .
> Sit then, with faire Expectance, and suruay
> Nothing but passionate man in his slight play,
> Who hath this onely ill: to some deem'd worst,
> A modest diffidence, and selfe mistrust.

The charges of railing and slowness in production are discussed in the Apologetical Dialogue to *Poetaster*, 185 foll.

23. *a gull, old ends reciting.* So poets are advised, *C.R.* ind. 178–9, not to 'way-lay all the stale *apothegmes*, or olde bookes, they can heare of'.

The Persons of the Play

Volpone, 'an old fox, an old reinard, an old craftie, slie, subtle companion, sneaking lurking wily deceiver' (Florio, *A Worlde of Wordes*, 1598). Later it was bandied about as a political nickname, e.g. of 'this old dissembler', James Ley, Earl of Marlborough, Lord Treasurer 1624–8, who did not pay the judges and tricked them when they asked for their pay: 'He was wont to be called "Vulpone", and I thinke he well deserved it now as ever' (Whitelocke, *Liber Famelicus*, Camden Society, p. 108). Sacheverell in the famous sermon 'On the Perils from False

Brethren', preached in St. Paul's on 5 November 1709, described the Whig ministers as 'wily Volpones' (p. 22) in reference to the nickname of Sidney, Earl Goldolphin, also Lord Treasurer. He had been referred to under this name in 1695 in a private letter of Francis Gwyn of Ford Abbey to Harley (Historical MSS. Commission, *MSS. of the Duke of Portland*, vol. iii, 1894, pp. x and 567). Thomas Burnet wrote to George Duckett (*Letters 1712–1722*, ed. Nichol Smith, p. 10) on 6 October 1712: 'I must tell you, I disapprove of the name *Harlequin*' (for Harley) 'because it has been used before, and likewise of the word *Volpone* for the very same reason. . . . call him *Mosca*, who out-tricked *Volpone* himself, and got all his wealth into his hands, vid. Ben Johnson's Fox.'

Mosca, 'any kinde of flye' (Florio). Erasmus, *Adagia*, 1558, iv. vii. 43: '*Μυῖαι* olim dicebantur qui delectabantur aliena mensa. . . . Apud Athenaeum libro sexto parasitus quispiam se muscæ confert, Δειπνέω ἄκλητος μυῖα. id est, Quod inuocatus cœnitare amo, musca sum.'

Voltore, 'a rauenous bird called a vultur, a geyre or grap. Also a greedie cormorant' (Florio): *Und.* xxxiii. 9 (of lawyers), 'gowned Vultures'. Erasmus, *Adagia*, i. vii. 14, 'Captatores testamentorum & haeredipetae, vulgata metaphora uultures appellantur, quòd senibus orbis ceu cadaueribus inhient'. He illustrates from Seneca, *Ep.* xcv. 43, 'Amico aliquis aegro adsidet: probamus. At hoc hereditatis causa facit: vultur est, cadaver expectat', and Martial, vi. lxii, in reference to a father who has lost his only son: 'Cuius vulturis hoc erit cadaver?'

Corbaccio, 'a filthie great rauen' (Florio).

Corvino, 'of a rauens nature or colour' (Florio, 1611).

Avocatori in Jonson a judicial body. Contareni, *The Commonwealth and Government of Venice*, 1599, L. Lewkenor's translation, p. 85, describes them rather as prosecutors who 'pleaded and made report vnto the . . . xl. men for small causes, for greater to the Senate, for greatest of all to the greater Councell, if so they shall think good'. They punished 'lewd & wicked men, that trespasse . . . wickedly against any citizen, or member thereof in particular' (p. 84).

Politique Would-bee. The preface to Wither's *Faire-Virtue*, 1622, A4, nominally by the publisher, says: 'I entreated him to explaine his meaning, in certaine obscure passages. But, he told me, how that were to take away the employment of his *Interpreters*. Whereas, he would purposely, leaue somewhat remaining doubtfull, to see, what Sir POLITICKE WOVLD-BEE, and his Companions, could picke out of it.' Jasper Mayne, *A Sermon against False Prophets Vindicated*, 1647, p. 21, to Francis Cheynell: 'Here, Sir, methinks, being a *Poet*, I see a piece of *Ben Johnson's* best *Comedy*, the *Fox*, presented to me; that, *you*, a *Politique Would-be* the *second*, sheltring your self under a *capacious Tortoise-shell*.' Saint-Evremond wrote a comedy *Sir Politick Would-be*, 'a la manière des Anglois' (*Œuvres Meslees*, 1709, i, pp. 251–348), with the scene at Venice: for a speech borrowed from *Volpone* see on iv. i.

Prologue, 17, 18. Interesting as showing how joint plays were written.

Coadjutor, as Beaumont and Fletcher, each author writing a definite portion of the play: *Sejanus* had been originally written in this way. *Novice*, a second hand who was learning his business. *Journeyman*, 'where a part of the play was put out to an underwriter, as one act of *The Arraignment of London* was to Cyril Tourneur' (Fleay, *Biographical Chronicle*, i, p. 373). In Randolph's *The Jealous Lovers*, 1632, III. v, Asotus assures two poets,

> nor ⟨shall you⟩ work iourney-work
> Under some play-house poet, that deals in
> Wit by retail.

Cf. 'a Cobler of Poetrie called a play-patcher'—Dekker, *News from Hell*, 1606, Hᵛ.

Tutor, one who superintended and corrected: Jonson, says Falkland in *Jonsonus Virbius*, 1638, p. 5,

> Vs'd not a tutoring hand his to direct,
> But was sole *Workman* and sole *Architect*.

21. *quaking custards*. An allusion to the huge custard set on the Lord Mayor's table at the city feasts for the fool to jump into (*D. is A.* I. i. 97). It appears from Jonson's reference to have been burlesqued on the stage. The epithet 'quaking' is from Marston (*Poet.* v. iii. 525).

23. *a gull, old ends reciting*. Whalley suggested a reference to Marston's *Malcontent* where there are some fifty couplets, proverbial especially. But his *Parasitaster*, acted in 1604, would suit better: the gull would be Gonzago, who has been dubbed 'an over-coloured Polonius'. For the phrase cf. *Rich. III*, I. iii. 336–7:

> And thus I clothe my naked villany
> With old odd ends stolen out of holy writ.

26. *make Bet'lem a faction*, make the inmates of Bedlam a set of your supporters: the reference is to the 'monstrous, and forc'd action', which Shakespeare had criticized in *Hamlet*, III. i, players who had neither the accent 'nor the gait of Christian, pagan, nor man', imitating humanity abominably and seeming as if 'some of nature's journeymen' had made them.

28. *iests, to fit his fable*. In *Disc.* 1819, Jonson noted as a blot on contemporary comedy 'the forcing in of jests'.

33–4. Samuel Butler, *Characters and Passages from Note-Books*, ed. Waller, p. 407: 'Ben: Johnson in saying (in one of his Prologues) All Gall and Coprace from his Inke he drayneth, only a little Salt remaineth &c., would in these more Censorious times be chargd with a kinde of Nonsense, for though Gall and Coprace be used in Inke *Salt never was*.'

35. *he'll rub your cheeks*. Horace, *Sat.* I. x. 3, of Lucilius, 'sale multo urbem defricuit'.

36. *a weeke after*. Cf. *Hon. Wales*, 291–2:

> As in your eares s'all leave a laughter,
> to last upon yow six dayes after.

i. i. 2. *Open the shrine.* The curtain of the inner stage would be drawn.
8. *shew'st like a flame.* From Pindar, *Olympian Ode*, i. 1, 2:

> Ἄριστον μὲν ὕδωρ, ὁ δὲ χρυσὸς αἰθόμενον πῦρ
> ἅτε διαπρέπει νυκτὶ μεγάνορος ἔ ἔξοχα πλούτου.

Quoted in Lucian's dialogue, *Somnium seu Gallus*, § 713, whence Jonson may have borrowed it: he advised Drummond to read Pindar 'for delight' (*Conv.* ix. 141), but he himself shows little knowledge of him.

14–16. Seneca, *Epist.* cxv. 12, 13: 'Accedunt deinde carmina poetarum quae affectibus nostris facem subdant, quibus divitiae velut unicum vitae decus ornamentumque laudantur. . . . Denique quod optimum videri volunt seculum aureum appellant.'

16–20. From a fragment of the Danae of Euripides, preserved by Athenaeus, *Deipnos.* iv. 159:

> ὦ χρυσέ, δεξίωμα κάλλιστον βροτοῖς,
> ὡς οὔτε μήτηρ ἡδονὰς τοιάσδ' ἔχει,
> οὐ παῖδες ἐν δόμοισιν, οὐ φίλος πατήρ
> οἷας σὺ χοὶ σὲ δώμασιν κεκτημένοι.
> εἰ δ' ἡ Κύπρις τοιοῦτον ὀφθαλμοῖς ὁρᾷ,
> οὐ θαῦμ' ἔρωτας μυρίους αὐτὴν ἔχειν.

Seneca translates the passages in *Epistle* cxv. 14, and tells the story that when the play was acted the audience rose in anger at this passage and clamoured for the play to be suppressed, but Euripides came forward and begged them to wait till they saw the fate in store for the character to whom these views were attributed. Jonson's rendering in line 17 gains in dramatic point from the childlessness of Volpone.

19. *Venus*, Homer's χρυσέη Ἀφροδίτη, Virgil and Ovid's 'aurea Venus'.
25–8. *Thou art vertue* . . . From Horace, *Sat.* ii. iii. 94–8:

> Omnis enim res,
> virtus, fama, decus, divina humanaque pulchris
> divitiis parent; quas qui construxerit, ille
> clarus erit, fortis, iustus. sapiensne? etiam, et rex
> et quicquid volet.

31. *purchase*, winning, acquisition. Cf. 'purchast', *E.M.I.* ii. v. 119.
35. *no mills for yron.* N.I. iv. iv. 268, 'His mils, to grind his seruants into powder'. The point of the allusion is the waste of timber: see *The Commons Complaint* by Arthur Standish, 1611, and his *New Directions of Experience . . . for the Planting of Timber And Firewood*, 1613, p. 4, 'the making of Iron and Glasse, hath beene, & is the greatest decay of Woods'.
37. *glasse.* 'Venice, where the scene is laid, and the neighbouring island of Murano, being famous for their manufacture of glass' (Whalley). In *The Costlie Whore*, i. ii (1633, B4), Alfrid says:

> I have a commission drawne for making glasse.
> Now if the Duke come, as I thinke he will,

Twill be an excellent meanes to lavish wood.
And then the cold will kill them (i.e. the poor), had they bread.
   Hat. The yron Mills are excellent for that.
I have a pattent drawne to that effect;
If they goe up, downe goes the goodly trees.
Ile make them search the earth to find new fire.

Massinger, in *The Guardian*, II. iv (1655, I6ᵛ), enumerating financial knaves such as engrossers of corn, inclosers of commons, usurers, includes

> Builders of Iron Mills, that grub up Forests,
> With Timber Trees for shipping.

38. *furrow-faced sea.* Cf. R. Carew, *A Herrings Tayle*, 1598, A2, of the Sun:

> To climbe the Easterne hils, and with light skips to play
> Betweene the wrinckles of the furrow faced sea.

40. *vsure*, a by-form of 'usury'.
42. *Dutch.* E.M.I. III. iv. 42–4 n.
46–7. A fine irony in view of Volpone's fate later (v. xii. 121–4).
53. *the thresher.* From Horace, *Sat.* II. iii. 111–21:

> Si quis ad ingentem frumenti semper acervum
> porrectus vigilet cum longo fuste, neque illinc
> audeat esuriens dominus contingere granum,
> ac potius foliis parcus vescatur amaris;
> si positis intus Chii veterisque Falerni
> mille cadis, nihil est, tercentum milibus, acre
> potet acetum; age si et stramentis incubet unde-
> octoginta annos natus, cui stragula vestis,
> blattarum ac tinearum epulae, putrescat in arca:
> nimirum insanus paucis videatur, eo quod
> maxima pars hominum morbo iactatur eodem.

58. *Romagnia*, or Rumney wine, a sweet wine of Greek origin, very popular in England. Coryat notes it at Venice: 'Some of these wines are singular good, as their Liatico; which is a very cordiall and generose liquor: their Romania, their Muscadine, and their Lagryme di Christo' (*Crudities*, 1611, p. 288).
  Candian wines. Malmsey wine came from Greece and Crete (Candy). Cf. *Newes from Bartholomew Fayre*, A2ᵛ, 'He sent to *Turkie* and *Candie* | For Muscadell and good malmesey'; ibid. B2, 'But chiefly those that came from Candy | And bring vs in true harted malmesey'.
66. *Hold thee*, hold for yourself: *Cat.* v. 578 n.
71. *cocker vp my genius*, the Latin 'genio indulgere'.
88. *bearing them in hand*, deluding with false hopes. Gifford quotes Barry, *Ram-Alley*, II. (1611, D1):

> Yet will I beare some dozen more in hand,
> And make them all my gulls.

89. *the cherry.* An allusion to the game of chop-cherry or bob-cherry, in which one tries to catch with the teeth a suspended cherry. Cf. Herrick's poem 'Chop-Cherry' in *Hesperides* (*Works*, ed. Moorman, p. 142).

I. ii. The cynicism of this interlude in the choice of performers would not appear repulsive in Jonson's day. Compare the Masque of Melancholy in Ford's *Lover's Melancholy* (III. iii) and the fashion of visiting Bedlam as one of the sights of London (*S.W.* IV. iii. 24). The antique flavouring from Lucian and Diogenes Laertius gives the show a distinctive touch. For the allusions see W. Bang's discussion in *Mélanges Godefroid Kurth*, 1908, pp. 351–5.

4. *the false pase of the verse*, loose four-stressed verse such as had been used in the moralities; Jonson uses it again for Iniquity the Vice in *D. is A.* I. i. 44 foll.

6. *here.* Pointing to Androgyno.

7, 8. *That iuggler . . . first from Apollo.* From Lucian, *Gallus*, 708, of Pythagoras, τὸν σοφιστὴν λέγεις, τὸν ἀλάζονα . . . 726 ὡς μὲν ἐξ Ἀπόλλωνος τὸ πρῶτον ἡ ψυχή μου καταπταμένη ἐς τὴν γῆν ἐνέδυ εἰς ἀνθρώπου σῶμα . . . μακρὸν ἂν εἴη λέγειν.

8. *fast and loose.* Nares quotes Sir John Hawkins on the nature of this game which seems to have been a precursor of the three-card trick. 'A leathern belt is made up into a number of intricate folds, and placed edgewise upon a table. One of the folds is made to resemble the middle of the girdle, so that whoever should thrust a skewer into it would think he held it fast to the table; whereas, when he has so done, the person with whom he plays may take hold of both ends and draw it away.' Bets were made whether the fold was fast or loose. It was a favourite trick with gipsies: see *G.M.* 178, 1250.

9–17. From Diogenes Laertius, *De Philosophorum Vitis*, VIII. i. 4, 5, of Pythagoras: τοῦτόν φησιν Ἡρακλείδης ὁ Ποντικὸς περὶ αὑτοῦ τάδε λέγειν ὡς εἴη ποτὲ γεγονὼς Αἰθαλίδης καὶ Ἑρμοῦ υἱὸς νομισθείη· τὸν δ' Ἑρμῆν εἰπεῖν αὐτῷ ἑλέσθαι ὅτι ἂν βούλοιτο πλὴν ἀθανασίας. αἰτήσασθαι οὖν ζῶντα καὶ τελευτήσαντα μνήμην ἔχειν τῶν συμβαινόντων. . . χρόνῳ δ' ὕστερον εἰς Εὔφορβον ἐλθεῖν καὶ ὑπὸ Μενελέω τρωθῆναι. ὁ δ' Εὔφορβος ἔλεγεν ὡς Αἰθαλίδης ποτὲ γεγόνοι καὶ ὅτι παρ' Ἑρμοῦ τὸ δῶρον λάβοι καὶ τὴν τῆς ψυχῆς περιπόλησιν. . . . ἐπειδὴ δ' Εὔφορβος ἀποθάνοι μεταβῆναι τὴν ψυχὴν αὐτοῦ εἰς Ἑρμότιμον, ὃς καὶ αὐτὸς πίστιν δοῦναι θέλων ἐπανῆλθεν εἰς Βραγχίδας καὶ εἰσελθὼν εἰς τὸ τοῦ Ἀπόλλωνος ἱερὸν ἐπέδειξεν ἣν Μενέλαος ἀνέθηκεν ἀσπίδα, . . . ἐπειδὴ δ' Ἑρμότιμος ἀπέθανε, γενέσθαι Πύρρον τὸν Δήλιον ἁλιέα· καὶ πάντα πάλιν μνημονεύειν πῶς πρόσθεν Αἰθαλίδης, εἶτ' Εὔφορβος, εἶθ' Ἑρμότιμος, εἶτα Πύρρος γένοιτο. ἐπειδὴ δὲ Πύρρος ἀπέθανε, γενέσθαι Πυθαγόραν καὶ πάντων τῶν εἰρημένων μεμνῆσθαι. These transmigrations are also in Lucian's *Gallus*.

9. *Æthalides*, the herald of the Argonauts, who had from his father Mercury the gift of remembering everything: so Apollonius Rhodius, *Argonautica*, i. 640:

> τείως δ' αὖτ' ἐκ νηὸς ἀριστῆες προέηκαν
> Αἰθαλίδην κήρυκα θόον, τῷπέρ τε μέλεσθαι
> ἀγγελίας καὶ σκῆπτρον ἐπέτραπον Ἑρμείαο

σφωιτέροιο τοκῆος, ὃς οἱ μνῆστιν πόρε πάντων
ἄφθιτον· οὐδ' ἔτι νῦν περ ἐποιχομένου Ἀχέροντος
δίνας ἀποφάτους ψυχὴν ἐπιδέδρομε λήθη.

12. *Euphorbus.* Lucian, *Gallus,* 727, ἐπείπερ Εὔφορβος ἐγενόμην . . . ἐμαχόμην ἐπ' Ἰλίῳ καὶ ἀποθανὼν ὑπὸ Μενέλεω χρόνῳ ὕστερον ἐς Πυθαγόραν ἦκον.

goldy-lockt. From Lucian, op. cit. 721: ὁπότε Εὔφορβος ἦσθα, χρυσὸν καὶ ἄργυρον τῶν βοστρύχων ἐξημμένος ἦεις πολεμήσων τοῖς Ἀχαιοῖς . . . σὺ δὲ καὶ τότε ἠξίους χρυσῷ ἀναδεδεμένος τοὺς πλοκάμους διαγωνίζεσθαι.

13. *the Cuckold of Sparta,* Menelaus.

17. *the Sophist of Greece,* Pythagoras. Lucian, op. cit. 729, τὰ Πυθαγόρου δὲ ἤδη λέγε. ΑΛΕΚ. τὸ μὲν ὅλον, ὦ Μίκυλλε, σοφιστὴς ἄνθρωπος ἦν.

18–23. Lucian, op. cit. 730–3, ἀποδυσάμενος δὲ τὸν Πυθαγόραν τίνας μετημφιέσω μετ' αὐτόν; ΑΛΕΚ. Ἀσπασίαν τὴν ἐκ Μιλήτου ἑταίραν. . . . ΜΙΚ. τίς δὲ δὴ μετὰ τὴν Ἀσπασίαν ἀνὴρ ἢ γυνὴ αὖθις ἀνεφάνης; ΑΛΕΚ. ὁ κυνίσκος Κράτης. ΜΙΚ. ὦ Διοσκόρω τῆς ἀνομοιότητος, ἐξ ἑταίρας φιλόσοφος. ΑΛΕΚ. εἶτα βασιλεύς, εἶτα πένης καὶ μετ' ὀλίγον σατράπης, εἶτα ἵππος καὶ κολοιὸς καὶ βάτραχος καὶ ἄλλα μυρία· μακρὸν δ' ἂν γένοιτο καταριθμήσασθαι ἕκαστα· τὰ τελευταῖα δὲ ἀλεκτρύων πολλάκις, ἤσθην γὰρ τῷ τοιούτῳ βίῳ.

19. *Aspasia,* famous as the mistress of Pericles.

meretrix. John Martiall in *A Treatyse of the Crosse,* 1564, p. 139, had used this Latin word before, but it was not acclimatized, in spite of quibbles on 'merry tricks' (see *E.M.I.* IV. ii. 88–97 n.).

21. *as it selfe doth relate it* . . . 24. *as in the Coblers cock.* Lucian's *Gallus* is a dialogue between a cobbler Micyllus and the cock who relates the transformations.

23. *brock.* badger.

26. *his great oath, by quater.* As Bang points out, from Plutarch, *De Placitis Philosophorum,* i. 877, εἴ τις θείη ἓν καὶ δύο προσθείη καὶ τρία καὶ τούτοις τέσσαρα, τὸν τῶν δέκα πληρώσει ἀριθμόν . . . διὸ καὶ ἐφθέγγοντο οἱ Πυθαγόρειοι ὡς μεγίστου ὅρκου ὄντος τῆς τετράδος,

οὐ μὰ τὸν ἁμετέρᾳ ψυχᾷ παράδοντα τετρακτὺν
παγὰν ἀενάου φύσιος ῥίζωμά τ' ἔχουσαν.

And Lucian, *Vitarum Auctio,* § 543, in the dialogue between Pythagoras and a purchaser: ΠΥΘ. Εἶτ' ἐπὶ τουτέοισιν (διδάξω) ἀριθμέειν. ΑΓΟ. Οἶδα καὶ νῦν ἀριθμεῖν. ΠΥΘ. Πῶς ἀριθμέεις; ΑΓΟ. Ἕν, δύο, τρία, τέτταρα. ΠΥΘ. Ὁρᾷς; ἃ σὺ δοκέεις τέτταρα, ταῦτα δέκα ἐστὶ καὶ τρίγωνον ἐντελὲς καὶ ἡμέτερον ὅρκιον. ΑΓΟ. Οὐ μὰ τὸν μέγιστον τοίνυν ὅρκον τὰ τέτταρα, οὔποτε θειοτέρους λόγους ἤκουσα οὐδὲ μᾶλλον ἱερούς. In the Pythagorean system number was regarded as the principle of harmony of the universe and of moral life. The τετρακτύς was a *trigon* (τρίγωνον, triangle) which represented the number ten as a triangle of four, viz. ∴ .

golden thigh. Diogenes Laertius, VIII. i. 11, λόγος δέ ποτ' αὐτοῦ παραγυμνωθέντος τὸν μηρὸν ὀφθῆναι χρυσοῦν. So Lucian, *Gallus,* 729. Explained as alchemic in *Alch.* II. i. 92.

28. *how elements shift.* Explained in Diogenes Laertius, VIII. i. 25.

32. *old doctrine*, pre-Reformation teaching as distinct from the 'new learning'. This was written in Jonson's Catholic days.

34. *On fish . . . a carthusian.* Cf. Massinger's joke on the severity of Carthusian rule in *The Guardian*, III. i (1655, K), 'Live like a Carthusian on Poor-John', i.e. dried hake. The Pythagoreans did not eat fish.

35. *dogmaticall silence.* There is a serious reference to the five years' silence enjoined on the Pythagoreans in *Disc.* 384–5. Micyllus in Lucian objects to the Cock, who claims to be the transmigrated philosopher, λάλος εἶ καὶ κρακτικός, ὁ δὲ σιωπᾶν ἐς πέντε ὅλα ἔτη οἶμαι παρήνει (*Gallus*, 709).

42–6. Dr. Rea finds an interesting source for this satire on the Puritans in the *Annotationes* of Gilbert Cousin (Cognatus) to his edition of Lucian (Basel, 1602). In the 'Argumentum' prefixed to the *Gallus* Cousin refers to the other accounts of Pythagoras' transformations, and adds: 'Stoicorum etiam fastum ridet, qui alioqui mollissimi vultus, vestiumque severitate, vitæ continentiam præ se ferebant. Peculiariter tamen eos notat, qui obtentu sanctimoniæ fœdam cauponam exercent, speciosisque titulis severo vultu, sapientiæ opinione cultu externo simplicioribus imponunt.' Jonson had already in the induction to *Every Man out of his Humour* (38–43) applied to the Puritans some traits of Juvenal's picture of the Stoics.

46. *natiuitie-pie.* The Puritans to avoid the popish syllable *-mas* in 'Christmas' called it the Nativity: so 'Christ-tide' in *Alch.* III. ii. 43.

51–3. Adapted from Lucian, *Gallus*, 734, Οὔκουν, ὦ ἀλεκτρυών, ἐπειδὴ πάντων σχεδὸν τῶν βίων ἐπειράθης καὶ πάντα ἦσθα, λέγοις ἂν ἤδη σαφῶς ἰδίᾳ μὲν τὰ τῶν πλουσίων ὅπως βιοῦσιν, ἰδίᾳ δὲ τὰ πτωχικά, . . .

60–2. Suggested by Erasmus, *Mor. Enc.* 406 C, D: 'Horum studium erat, Deorum ac fortium virorum laudes encomiis celebrare. Encomium igitur audietis, non Herculis, neque Solonis, sed meum ipsius, hoc est, Stultitiæ.'

66–81. 'The whole song follows Erasmus closely.'—Rea. *Mor. Enc.* 436 C: 'Ac per Deos immortales, estne quidquam felicius isto hominum genere, quos vulgo moriones, stultos, fatuos, ac bliteos appellant, pulcerrimis, ut equidem opinor, cognominibus? . . . 437 A, B. In summa, non dilacerantur millibus curarum, quibus hæc vita obnoxia est. . . . Adde huc, quod non solum ipsi perpetuo gaudent, ludunt, cantillant, rident, verum etiam cæteris omnibus quocumque sese verterint, voluptatem, iocum, lusum, risumque adferunt. . . . Unde fit, ut . . . omnes . . . impune permittant, quidquid vel dixerint, vel fecerint. . . . 437 D. Quid quod summis etiam Regibus adeo sunt in delitiis, ut nonnulli sine his prandere, nec ingredi, nec omnino vel horam durare possint. . . . 438 B. Iisdem ferme de causis hoc hominum genere mulieres gaudere solent impensius, utpote ad voluptatem et nugas natura impensiores. . . . Sed tamen hoc ipsum mire in fatuis meis usu venit, ut non vera modo, verum etiam aperta convitia cum voluptate audiantur, adeo ut idem dictum, quod si a sapientis ore proficiscatur, capitale fuerat futurum: a morione profectum, incredibilem voluptatem pariat.'

73. *Tongue . . . treasure. Poet.* Apol. Dial. 182.

75. *free from slaughter*, a lax way of saying 'with impunity'.

For the rhyme *laughter* and *slaughter* see Marston's comment on the pedant who 'has vowde to get the consumption of the lungues, or to leue to posteritie the true orthography and pronunciation of laughing' (*Parasitaster*, IV, 1606, G1). It was an unsettled point. Jonson in *Ent. Althorp*, 72–3, and *Merc. Vind.* 229–30, rhymes 'daughters' with 'laughters'; but the rhyme of 'laughter' and 'after' (in various forms) is found in *Volp.* prol. 35–6, *Ent. Althorp*, 242–3, *Ent. Highgate*, 259–60, *Hon. Wales*, 291–2, *Ep.* lxxiii, 7, 8. In *A Mids. Night's Dream*, II. i. 54–5, both Quartos and Folios print 'coffe' and 'loffe' for cough and laugh; and Chapman in *Enthymiæ Raptus*, 1609, B4, rhymes 'aloft' with 'nought', and with 'thought' in *The Georgicks of Hesiod*, 1618, p. 2. Burton in *The Anatomy of Melancholy*, 1621, p. 545, has 'Sanguine are soon cofte', i.e. caught. It is a pity Jonson did not discuss the point in his *English Grammar*.

88. *kite*, Lady Would-be. She is rechristened 'shee-wolfe' in v. ii. 66.

89. *gor-crow*, carrion crow. *gor-* connected with 'gore', is 'mud, filth'. Compare Florio's definition of *corbaccio* as 'a filthie great rauen'.

93–6. *a fox . . . gaping crow*. Horace, *Sat.* II. v. 55–7:

> Plerumque recoctus
> scriba ex quinqueviro corvum deludet hiantem,
> captatorque dabit risus Nasica Corano.

Dr. Rea quotes Porphyrio's note on this passage: 'Hoc allegoricè posuit ex fabula Æsopi, in qua scriptum est, ut vulpis corvum illuserit, cum eum vidisset caseum ferentem, dicens se esse illo meliore voce, et provocans ut clamaret. Quod cum facere voluisset, caseum demisit ac perdidit.' So v. viii. 11–14.

98–109. Suggested, as Dr. Rea points out, by Lucian, *Gallus*, 719:

Ἄκουε δὲ ἤδη καὶ τὸ ἐνύπνιον· ᾤμην γὰρ τὸν Εὐκράτην αὐτὸν ἄπαιδα ὄντα οὐκ οἶδ' ὅπως ἀποθνήσκειν, εἶτα προσκαλέσαντά με, καὶ διαθήκας θέμενον, ἐν αἷς ὁ κληρόνομος ἦν ἁπάντων ἐγώ, μικρὸν ἐπισχόντα ἀποθανεῖν· ἐμαυτὸν δὲ παρελθόντα ἐς τὴν οὐσίαν τὸ μὲν χρυσίον καὶ τὸ ἀργύριον ἐξαντλεῖν, σκάφαις τισὶ μεγάλαις ἀέναόν τε καὶ πολὺ ἐπιρρέον, τὰ δ' ἄλλα, τὴν ἐσθῆτα καὶ τραπέζας καὶ ἐκπώματα καὶ διακόνους, πάντα ἐμὰ ὡς τὸ εἰκὸς εἶναι. εἶτα ἐξήλαυνον ἐπὶ λευκοῦ ζεύγους, ἐξυπτιάζων, περίβλεπτος ἅπασι τοῖς ὁρῶσι καὶ ἐπιφθόνοις.

105. *foot-clothes*. C. is A. IV. ix. 37 n.

107. *moyle*. For a lawyer's mule see *E.M.O.* II. iii. 17.

112. *ambitious*, towering. So 'ambitious fire' II. iv. 6. Erasmus, *Mor. Enc.* 408 B, D, of pretenders to philosophy, 'Quamvis autem sedulo fingant, tamen alicunde prominentes auriculæ Midam prodeunt. . . . Quod si qui paulo sunt ambitiosiores, arrideant tamen et applaudant, atque asini exemplo τὰ ὦτα κινῶσι.'

120. *And hundred, such as I am*. A subtle touch of insincerity inserted thus early to give a first hint of the dénouement.

I. iii. Dr. Rea happily remarks, 'This and the following scenes are really a Roman *salutatio*, i.e. the morning visit of clients to their patron so often referred to and described by the satirists.' He compares Lucian's ninth *Dialogue of the Dead*, 'Simylus and Polystratus': Polystratus, very old and childless, explains how he was courted: ἕωθεν μὲν εὐθὺς ἐπὶ θύρας ἐφοίτων μάλα πολλοί, μετὰ δὲ παντοῖά μοι δῶρα προσήγετο ἀπανταχόθεν τῆς γῆς τὰ κάλλιστα. . . . ἐραστὰς εἶχον μυρίους. ΣΙΜ. 'Εγέλασα· ἐραστὰς σὺ τηλικοῦτος ὢν ὀδόντας τέτταρας ἔχων. ΠΟΛ. Νὴ Δία τοὺς ἀρίστους γε τῶν ἐν τῇ πόλει· καὶ γέροντά με καὶ φαλακρόν, ὡς ὁρᾷς, ὄντα καὶ λημῶντα καὶ κορυζῶντα ὑπερήδοντο θεραπεύοντες, καὶ μακάριος ἦν αὐτῶν ὄντινα ἂν καὶ μόνον προσέβλεψα.

10. *of S. Marke*, i.e. at a goldsmith's shop in the market-place.

26. *know your own good*. Jonson is fond of ringing the changes on Virgil's 'O fortunatos nimium, sua si bona norint'. Cf. 1. v. 2, *G.M.* 1457–8, *Und.* lxiv. 1, 2.

35. *write me, i' your family*, a reference to the 'Houshold Book', in which the names of servants and retainers were entered. Cf. *Disc.* 621–3, 'Poetry in this latter Age, hath prov'd but a meane *Mistresse*, to such as have . . . given their names up to her family.' *Family*, household (Lat. *familia*).

52–66. The satire on lawyers here and on doctors in scene iv, as Dr. Rea has pointed out, borrows from Cornelius Agrippa's *De incertitudine et uanitate scientiarum* (revised edition, 1540?), cap. xciii, 'De arte Aduocatoria': Law is 'ars uetustissima & fraudulentissima suasorio cooperimento subdole adornata. Quæ non est alia, quam scire iudicem persuasione demulcere, & ad omne arbitrium uti, scire iuribus vel inuentis glossis ac commentis leges quascunque pro libidine fingere & refingere, uel iniquis quibusque diuerticulis illas subterfugere, aut fraudulentam litem prorogare.'

57. *And re-turne; make knots, and vndoe them*. Rhythmically a good line with the pause after 're-turne' and with a slight emphasis on 'make' in contrast to 'vndoe'. Gifford's 're-return; could make knots' is intolerable.

58. *faked counsell*. Cf. Herrick's lines to 'M. John Weare, Councellour' (*Works*, ed. Moorman, p. 202):

> Sooner the inside of thy hand shall grow
> Hisped, and hairie, ere thy Palm shall know
> A *Postern-bribe* tooke, or a *Forked-Fee*
> To fetter Justice, when She might be free.

63. *perplexed*, involved in doubt.

64–5. *that would not wag*, . . . From Cornelius Agrippa, cap. xciii, 'De arte Aduocatoria': 'nam ut nullus eorum loquitur, nisi ad mercedem, ita nec tacet nisi ad praemium.'

66. *cecchine*, sequin. '*Zecchino*, a coyne of gold currant in Venice' (Florio, 1598). It was worth about nine shillings.

70. *swim, in golden lard, vp to the armes, in honey*. Perhaps this overwrought image is meant to emphasize Mosca's insincerity. Lard, liquid gold, and honey are clotted fluids for a swimmer. Simpler forms of the expression are in Dekker's *Old Fortunatus*, 1600, G2ᵛ:

> Vnlesse he melt himselfe to liquid gold, . . .
> He cannot raine such shewers: . . .
> His soule (by infernall couenants) has he sold,
> Alwaies to swimme vp to the chin in gold.

And Sir T. Chaloner's translation of *The Praises of Folie*, 1549, ed. Ashbee, p. 25, 'takyng it for a singuler and onely delight, as if they swamme vp to the chinnes in a sea of honey'—a loose rendering of Erasmus' original, *totasque sese melle perungunt*, 'they anoint themselves all over with honey'.

76 (anon.). Addressed to the caller (in this case Corbaccio) who has knocked within.

78. *Put businesse i' your face. Ep.* xxviii. 7, 'H'has tympanies of businesse, in his face'.

I. iv. 11. *slumbers*, dozes.

20–1. *Most of your Doctors* . . . Agrippa, *De Vanitate*, cap. lxxxiii, 'De Medecina operatrice': 'Tota præterea medendi operatrix ars nullo alio fundamento quam fallacibus experimentis superexstructa est, . . . non minus uenefica quam benefica, ut sæpissime & fere semper plus periculi sita medico ac medicina, quam ab ipso morbo.' Cf. *Ep.* xiii, 'To Doctor Empirick'.

27–35. From Cornelius Agrippa, ibid.: 'Qui certe unus ille atque communis cum carnifice honos est, homines scilicet accepta mercede occidere: atque ex homicido, unde supplicium cunctis lex statuit, nullique concessa impunitas, ij soli capiunt præmia. Hoc tamen interest, quod carnifex non nisi ex iudicum sententia necat noxios, medicus autem præter omne iudicium perimit etiam insontes. . . . Experimenta per mortes agunt, & artem suam nostris periculis discunt.'

23–4. *your physitian* . . . Publilius Syrus, 'Male secum agit aeger medicum qui heredem facit.'

36. *apoplex*. 'Apoplexie', I. ii. 125.

52. *scotomy*, dizziness. Middleton and Rowley, *The Old Law*, III. ii (1656, G1ᵛ), a drunken scene: 'I have got the Scotomy in my head already.'

68. *preuent*, anticipate.

73. *palpabile. Merc. Vind.* 82, 167.

potabile, 'a preparation of nitro-muriate of gold deoxydized by some volatile oil, formerly esteemed as a cordial medicine' (*O.E.D.* s.v, 'potable'). Cf. George Baker's translation of Gesner, *The Newe Iewell of Health, wherein is contayned . . . the vse and preparation of Antimonie, and potable Gold*, 1576.

124. *Rooke goe with you*. Be 'rook'd', or fooled. For 'rook' = simpleton see *E.M.I.* I. v. 88.

140. *giue 'hem words*, deceive them, like the Latin *dare verba*. Cf. Guilpin, *Skialetheia*, 1598, epig. 5, 'Of Matho':

> Matho in credite bound to pay a debt,
> His word engagde him for, doth still replie,

That he will aunswere it with sophistrie,
And so deferres daily to aunswer it:
Experience now hath taught me Sophistrie,
He gaue me his word; that is, he coussend me.

141. *Poure oyle into their eares*, of fulsome compliment, cheat in a plausible manner.

142-3. *What a rare punishment* . . . Seneca, *Epist.* cxv. 16, 'Nulla enim avaritia sine poena est, quamvis satis sit ipsa poenarum.'

144-50. From Pliny, *Nat. Hist.* vii. 167-8, '. . . tot morbi, tot metus, tot curae, totiens invocata morte ut nullum frequentius sit votum. . . . Hebescunt sensus, membra torpent, praemoritur visus auditus incessus, dentes etiam ac ciborum instrumenta.'

156. *Æson*, Jason's father, who had his youth renewed by Medea's magic.

158. *cheated on*, cheated. *D. is A.* v. vi. 54, *Merc. Vind.* 70.

I. v. 9. *orient*, of pure lustre. *Cat.* II. 105.

14. *doubles the twelfe caract.* Cf. Cartwright, *The Lady Errant*, IV. i:

> Diamonds, two whereof
> Do double the twelfth Caract.

For 'caract' see *E.M.I.* III. iii. 22. The forms 'twelfe', 'twelf', were in use from the fourteenth century to the seventeenth.

17. *diamant*, the middle English form of 'diamond': Jonson constantly uses it.

22. *The weeping of an heire* . . . Publilius Syrus, 'Heredis fletus sub persona risus est'.

37. *Nothing bequeath'd them* . . . Horace, *Sat.* II. v. 68-9:

> Invenietque
> nil sibi legatum praeter plorare suisque.

So Polystratus in Lucian's *Dialogues of the Dead*, ix. 3, 'Ἐς τὸ φανερὸν μὲν ἕκαστον αὐτῶν κληρονόμον ἀπολιπεῖν ἔφασκον, . . . ἄλλας δὲ τὰς ἀληθεῖς διαθήκας ἔχων ἐκείνας κατέλιπον οἰμώζειν ἅπασι φράσας.

39. *a blind harper.* Proverbial, especially in the phrase 'Have at you, blind harpers', of random shots among a crowd. Cf. *Iohn Heywoodes woorkes*, Proverbs II. vii (1562, I):

Proface. Have among you blynd harpers (sayde I) The mo the merrier.

Ballads with this title were entered on the Stationers' Register on 22 July 1564 and 22 July 1565 (Arber, i. 260, 294).

39-43. *He knowes no man* . . . From Juvenal, *Sat.* x. 232-6:

> Sed omni
> membrorum damno maior dementia, quae nec
> nomina servorum nec vultum agnoscit amici
> cum quo praeterita cenavit nocte, nec illos
> quos genuit, quos eduxit.

46–8. Adapted from Martial, *Ep.* 1. lxxxiv:

> Uxorem habendam non putat Quirinalis
> cum velit habere filios, et invenit
> quo possit istud more: futuit ancillas
> domumque et agros implet equitibus vernis.
> Pater familiae verus est Quirinalis.

57–9. Adapted from Juvenal, *Sat.* x. 191–4:

> Deformem ac taetrum ante omnia vultum
> dissimilemque sui, deformem pro cute pellem
> pendentesque genas et tales aspice rugas
> quales, umbriferos ubi pandit Thabraca saltus,
> in vetula scalpit iam mater simia bucca.

59. *helpe* to abuse him. *S.W.* III. v. 92.
63–4. Juvenal, x. 214–15:

> . . . qui vix cornicines exaudiet atque tubarum
> concentus. Clamore opus est ut sentiat auris
> quem dicat venisse puer.

Culverin, a hand-gun.
75. *to take my pearle*, which is tight in Volpone's clutch.
96. *to night. E.M.I.* II. ii. 9.
101–2. *let loose their wiues.* Coryat in his *Crudities*, 1611, p. 265, notes that Venetian gentlemen 'do euen coope vp their wiues alwaies within the walles of their houses' for fear of infidelity. 'So that you shall very seldome see a Venetian Gentlemans wife but either at the solemnization of a great marriage, or at the Christning of a Iew, or late in the euening rowing in a Gondola.'
105. *the face, to be dishonest. E.M.O.*, Characters, 60–1, Fallace 'only wants the face to be dishonest'.
108. *The blazing starre of Italie.* In Markham's *The Dumb Knight*, I. ii (1608, B1ᵛ), Prate, echoing this passage and III. vii. 195–6, says to his wife Lollia,

> . . . for thy selfe my *Lollia*,
> Not *Lollia Paulina*, nor those blasing starres,
> Which makes the world the Apes of Italy,
> Shall match thy selfe in sun-bright splendency.

a wench O' the first yeere. C.R. v. iv. 529–30.
110–11. *whiter then a swan . . . lillies.* Martial, *Ep.* 1. cxv. 2, 3:

> Loto candidior puella cycno,
> argento, nive, lilio, ligustro.

The correct reading here is 'loto cycno', but Jonson's 'all ouer' shows that he accepted the reading 'toto'.
120. *windore.* From an imagined etymology 'wind-door'; Jonson frequently uses it.

121–2. *the first grapes* . . . Catullus, xvii. 15–16:

> Et puella tenellulo delicatior haedo,
> asseruanda nigerrimis diligentius uvis.

II. i. 1. *to a wise man.* S[t]. Ambrose, *De Officiis*, III. xiv, 'Sapienti patria mundus est'; cf. *Rich. II*, I. iii. 275–6:

> All places that the eye of heaven visits
> Are to a wise man ports and happy havens.

4. *salt*, wanton.

10. *mens minds, and manners.* A reference to the *Odyssey*, i. 3, πολλῶν δ' ἀνθρώπων ἴδεν ἄστεα καὶ νόον ἔγνω: 'qui mores hominum multorum vidit et urbes', as Horace translates it, *A.P.* 142.

12. *height*, latitude. Tomkis, *Albumazar*, I. v (1615):

> My Almanack, made for th' Meridian
> And height of Iapan, giu't th' East India company.

13. *quote*, take mental note of.

14. *with licence.* Cf. Howell, *Epistolae Ho-elianae*, i, § 1, 3, 'I have got a warrant from the Lords of the Council to travel for three years anywhere, *Rome* and *St. Omers* excepted' (1615). As late as 1765 Blackstone noted that the King might prohibit any of his subjects from going into foreign parts without a licence.

17. *my lord Ambassador.* Sir Henry Wotton, who was at Venice from 1604 to 1612 and for two later periods.

18. *vents*, publishes. *Disc.* 58, 'venting newes'. Very common from about 1600 to about 1750 (*O.E.D.*).

22. *a rauen.* 'About the year 1477 a raven bred on Charing Cross, the harbinger of a mighty plague that lasted three years'—F. P. Wilson *The Plague in Shakespeare's London*, p. 3. On 29 September 1860 a cormorant lodged in the steeple of Boston church; this was ominous because the *Lady Elgin*, with the member for Boston and his son on board, were lost at sea that morning (*Fenland Notes and Queries*, i, p. 206). The swallows on Cleopatra's ship before Actium are recorded as ominous by Plutarch and by Shakespeare (*Ant. and Cleop.* IV. xii. 3).

that should build. The 'should' marks reported speech. Cf. Holinshed's account of King Alfred's burial at Winchester: 'The bodie of King Alured was first buried in the bishops church: but afterwards, because the Canons raised a fond tale that the same should walke a nights, his sonne king Edward remoued it into the new monasterie which he in his life time had founded' (*Chronicles*, 1586, i, ch. xvi, p. 149).

29. *curtizans. E.M.I.* II. v. 46.

30. *the spider, and the bee* . . . Proverbial: cf. Beaumont, *The Triumph of Honour*, sc. iv:

> Sweet poetry's
> A flower, where men, like bees and spiders, may
> Bear poison, or else sweets and wax away:
> Be venom-drawing spiders they that will;
> I'll be the bee, and suck the honey still.

35. *Another whelpe.* Stow, *Annales* (1615, ed. Howes, p. 844), under the year 1604: 'Sunday the 5. of August, a Lionesse named *Elizabeth,* in the Tower of London, brought forth a Lions whelpe, which Lions whelpe liued not longer then till the next day'; ibid., p. 857, 1604–5, 'The 26. of February was an other Lion whelped in the Tower of London by the foresaid Lionesse, which was taken from the Dam assoone as the same was whelped, and brought vp by hand according as the king commanded: but this Lions whelpe also dyed about some xvi. dayes after in the moneth of March. Thus much of these whelpes haue I obserued, and put in memory, for that I haue not read of any the like in this land, before this present yeere. . . .'

36. *The fires at Berwike.* Carleton writes to Chamberlain on 15 January 1605 (*Domestic State Papers, James I,* I. xii. 9), 'We heare of a strange apparition on holydowne hilles' (Halidon Hill) 'neere Barwick of armies and fighting men, and such volies of shott were thought to be heard, that it gaue the alarum to both ye borders.'

37. *the new starre.* 'On October 17, 1604, Kepler had discovered the new star which had burst out in the constellation *Serpentarius,* and which surpassed Jupiter in brightness' (E. B. Knobel in *Shakespeare's England,* i, p. 455).

40. *three porcpisces* . . . 46. *a whale.* Stow, op. cit., p. 880, under 1606: 'The 19 of Jan. a great Porpus was taken aliue at Westham, in a smalle creeke a mile, & a halfe within the land, and presented to *Franc*^ses^ *Gofton* Esquire, cheefe auditor of ye Imprests, and within few dayes after, a very great Whale came vp within 8. mile of London whose bought was seene diuers times aboue water, and Judged to exceede the length of the longest ship in the riuer, and when she tasted the fresh water and sented the land she returned into the Sea.' For the portent Sir Politic finds in the whale cf. Chamberlain's letter to Carleton on 19 November 1602 (*S.P.D., Elizabeth,* cclxxxv. 59): 'Our Commissioners and the Danes are met at Breme; the Queenes ship that carried them, comming backe with other in her companie, met with a huge number of whales on the coast of Holland, that indured many shot and plaide many gambols. The like number hath not been seene together, specially in these parts, for they say above two hundreth ⟨years⟩. Here is much descanting what they should portend more then the tempest that followed.' For the form 'porcpisce' cf. *Sej.* v. 622.

49. *Stode-Fleet.* Stode, now Stade, at the mouth of the Elbe, 22 miles north-west of Hamburg.

50. *Arch-dukes* (so Folio for *Arch-duke* of Quarto), the title given to the Infanta Isabella and her husband Albert when the Spanish Netherlands were ceded to them before the death of Philip II of Spain.

51. *Spinola's whale.* Ambrosio Spinola (1569–1630), general in chief of the Spanish army in the Netherlands from 1604. With Sir Politic's suggestion compare *S. of N.* III. ii. 87–94, and in Charles Herle, *Worldly*

Policy and Moral Prudence, 1654, p. 27, the cock-and-bull story of 'Spinola's Whale that should have been hir'd to have drown'd London, by snuffing up the Thames and spouting it upon the City'.

53. *Stone, the foole.* Two anecdotes of him survive. (1) Carleton writes from Greenwich to Winwood, 10 March 1605, on the Earl of Nottingham's voyage to Spain as ambassador (*Memorials*, ii, p. 52): 'There was great execution done lately upon *Stone the Fool*, who was well whipt in *Bridewell* for a blasphemous speech, *That there went sixty Fools into* Spaine, *besides my Lord Admiral and his two Sons.* But he is now at Liberty again, and for that unexpected Release, *gives his Lordship the Praise of a very pittifull Lord.* His Comfort is, that the news of *El Señor Piedra* will be in *Spaine before our Ambassador.*' (2) Selden, *Table-Talk*, ed. Reynolds, pp. 62–3: 'A gallant is above ill words. An example we have in the old lord of Salisbury, who was a great wise man. Stone had called some lord about court, fool, the lord complained, and has Stone whipped: Stone cries, I might have called my lord of Salisbury fool often enough, before he would have had me whipped.'

55. *Mass'.* 'A vulgar or jocular shortening of Master, usually followed by a proper name or an official title' (*O.E.D.*). So Jonson often uses it.

58. *To fit our English stage.* Cf. *Tw. Night*, III. iv. 121–2, Fabian of Malvolio: 'If this were played upon a stage now, I could condemn it as an improbable fiction.'

70. *in cabages.* An importation from Holland, as Whalley notes. Gifford quotes Evelyn, *Acetaria. A Discourse of Sallets*, 1699, p. 17: ''Tis scarce an hundred Years since we first had *Cabbages* out of *Holland*. Sir *Anth. Ashley*, of *Wiburg St. Giles* in *Dorsetshire*, being (as I am told) the first who planted them in *England*.'

73. *Limons.* D. *is* A. IV. iv. 25; in use from the sixteenth to the eighteenth centuries.

74. *Colchester-oysters*, famous from Roman times. Howell, *Epistolae Ho-elianae*, I, § 2. xi, 'I have sent for your welcome home (in part) two Barrels of *Colchester* Oysters, which were provided for my Lord *Colchester* himself; therefore I presume they are good, and all greenfinn'd.'

Selsey-cockles. In the list of presents to Lord Ellesmere to enable him to entertain Queen Elizabeth at Harefield in 1602 Mr. Robert Sackvil sends 'Cellsie Cockelles, xij^c' (*The Egerton Papers*, Camden Society, p. 352).

76. An Alexandrine: *E.M.I.* II. i. 87. So III. vii. 15.

81–2. *meat was cut So like his character. Character* = cipher. Serving up meat cut in fantastic shapes was a fashion of the time: *Cymbeline*, IV. ii. 49, 50: 'But his neat cookery! he cut our roots In characters'; Fletcher and Massinger, *The Elder Brother*, IV. i. 15, 'And how to cut his meat in characters'.

88. *Bab'ouns. Sir Gyles Goosecappe*, I. i (1606, A2), 'A my worde

(*Will*) tis the great Baboone, that was to be seene in Southwarke.'
Alch. v. i. 14 'Babiouns'.

90. *Mamaluchi.* This plural of Mameluk follows the Italian form.
According to Sir Politic, these Egyptians live 'neere to *China*'.

94. *aduises*, dispatches: the word has a diplomatic ring. 'Avises',
M.L. i. vii. 41.

113. *grammar.* The first Italian grammar in English was William
Thomas's *Principal Rules of Italian Grammer, with a Dictionarie*,
1550: it was followed by Henry Grantham's translation of Scipio
Lentulo's *An Italian Grammar*, 1575; Desainlieu's (Claude Holyband),
*The Italian schoolemaister: Contayning Rules for the perfect pronouncinge
of the Italian tonge*, 1597; John Sandford, *A Grammer to the Italian
Tongue*, 1605.

114. *cry'd Italian.* Sir Politic's affectation for 'taught', suggested by
the variations of pitch in pronouncing Italian.

117. *out-side, and mere barke.* Daniel, *Hymen's Triumph*, ii. iv (1623,
p. 291):

> And neuer let her thinke on mee, who am
> But euen the barke, and outside of a man.

ii. ii. Coryat in his *Crudities*, 1611, pp. 272–5, gives a full description
of the Venetian mountebanks: 'although there are Mountebanks also
in other Cities of Italy, yet . . . there is a greater concourse of them in
Venice then else where, and that of the better sort and the most eloquent
fellowes.' The name is derived from *montare* and *banco*, 'because these
fellowes doe act their part vpon a stage, which is compacted of benches
or fourmes, though I haue seene some fewe of them also stand vpon the
ground when they tell their tales, which are such as are commonly called
Ciar⟨l⟩atanoe's or *Ciarlatans*. . . . The principall place where they act,
is the first part of Saint *Marks* street that reacheth betwixt the West
front of S. *Marks* Church, and the opposite front of Saint *Geminians*
Church. In which, twice a day, that is, in the morning and in the afternoon, you may see fiue or sixe seuerall stages erected for them: those
that act vpon the ground, euen the fore said Ciarlatans being of the
poorer sorte of them, stand most commonly in the second part of S.
Marks, not far from the gate of the Duk⟨e⟩s Palace. These Mountebankes
at one end of their stage place their trunke, which is replenished with
a world of new-fangled trumperies. After the whole rabble of them is
gotten vp to the stage, whereof some weare visards being disguised like
fooles in a play, some that are women (for there are diuers women also
amongst them) are attyred with habits according to that person that
they sustaine; after (I say) they are all vpon the stage, the musicke
begins. Sometimes vocall, sometimes instrumentall, and sometimes both
together. This musicke is a preamble and introduction to the ensuing
matter: in the meane time while the musicke playes, the principall
Mountebanke which is the Captaine and ring-leader of all the rest, opens
his truncke, and sets abroach his wares; after the musicke hath ceased,

he maketh an oration to the audience of halfe an houre long, or almost an houre. Wherein he doth most hyperbolically extoll the vertue of his drugs and confections:

> *Laudat venales qui vult extrudere merces.*

Though many of them are very counterfeit and naught. Truely I often wondred at many of these naturall Orators. For they would tell their tales with such admirable volubility and plausible grace, euen *extempore*, and seasoned with that singular variety of elegant jests and witty conceits, that they did often strike great admiration into strangers that neuer heard them before: and by how much the more eloquent these Naturalists are, by so much the greater audience they draw vnto them, and the more ware they sell. After the chiefest Mountebankes first speech is ended, he deliuereth out his commodities by little and little, the iester still playing his part, and the musitians singing and playing upon their instruments. The principall things that they sell are oyles, soueraigne waters, amorous songs printed, Apothecary drugs, and a Commonweale of other trifles. The head Mountebanke at euery time that he deliuereth out any thing, maketh an extemporall speech, which he doth eftsoones intermingle with such sauorie iests (but spiced now and then with singular scurrility) that they minister passing mirth and laughter to the whole company. . . . I haue obserued maruelous strange matters done by some of these Mountebankes. For I saw one of them holde a viper in his hand, and play with his sting a quarter of an houre together, and yet receiue no hurt; though another man should haue beene presently stung to death with it. He made vs all beleeue that the same viper was linealy descended from the generation of that viper that lept out of the fire upon S. *Pauls* hand, in the Island of Melita now called Malta, and did him no hurt. . . . Also I haue obserued this in them, that after they haue extolled their wares to the skies, hauing set the price of tenne crownes vpon some one of their commodities, they haue at last descended so low, that they haue taken for it foure gazets, which is something lesse then a groat.' It will be seen how closely this later account of an eyewitness tallies with Jonson's scene; Jonson probably got all his facts from Florio. A passing reference to the *circulatores* (or chiarlatani) in Erasmus' *Moriae Encomium*, 478 C–479 A, would not take him very far.

P. L. Duchartre's *The Italian Comedy*, tr. Weaver, 1929, on page 63 reproduces an engraving by Giacomo Franco 1610 of Comedians and Charlatans in the Piazza of St. Mark. There are three platforms with performers, and one ground ciarlatano. In the foreground, watching the nearest comedians, is a cosmopolitan crowd, including one 'Inglese'.

Killigrew in *Thomaso*, part i, IV. ii (*Comedies and Tragedies*, 1664, pp. 360–1), has quoted freely from Volpone's speech to the crowd in his Lopus the Mountebank. He borrows with only slight alteration lines 75–86, 151–70, 173–85, 228–98; these are put on the lips of a mountebank at Madrid.

5. *quacksaluers.* Cotgrave, 1611, s.v. 'Charlatan': 'A Mountebancke,

a cousening drug-seller, or pratling quack-saluer, a tatler, babler, foolish prater, or commender of trifles.'

14. *lewd*, ignorant.

22. *Scoto of Mantua*, a professional actor and the leader of an Italian company licensed by the Duke of Mantua; his real name was Dionisio (K. M. Lea, *Italian Popular Comedy*, ii, pp. 360–1). In England he was known as a juggler: in the Foreign State Papers of Elizabeth's reign, cxxxvii. 596, Valentyne Dale writes to Lord Burghley from Paris on 25 March 1576, 'There is one Scotto an Italian that playeth such knocks as ffeates doth vppon the Cardes who commeth to shewe the Quenes Matie. sum of his toyes, he hath ben made ⟨much⟩ of in this Court, and hath ben in the Emperores court, and maketh him self a ioyle fellow.' In Nashe's *Unfortunate Traveller*, 1594, F3 (*Works*, ed. McKerrow, ii. 252), '*Scoto*, that dyd the iugling tricks before the Queene, neuer came neere him' (i.e. Cornelius Agrippa) 'one quarter in magicke reputation'; McKerrow (ibid. v, p. 378) quotes the *Defensative against Supposed Prophecies* of Henry Howard, Earl of Northampton, 1583, Y3^v–4, 'I was present my selfe when diuers Gentlemen & noble men, which vndertooke to descry the finest sleights, that Scotto the Italian was able to play by Leiger du main before the Queene: were notwithstanding no less beguiled then the rest'; and John Harvey, *A Discoursive Probleme concerning Prophesies*, 1588, p. 50, 'If there be any wonders . . . wrought now adaies are they not performed either by incantations, such as the sorcerers of *Pharao* vsed . . . or else contriued by the deceitfull leigerdemaine, and Craftie conueiance of shifting iuglers, and cogging impostors, such as amongst infinite other of the same foisting crue, namely *Scoto* and *Feates* vsed, seeming likewise in apparance to have done, and vndone that, which in very truth they coulde neuer doo, or vndoo, but made semblance thereof by the diuels sophistry, and their owne counterfet sleights.' King James, in his *Dæmonologie*, Book I (*Workes*, 1616, p. 105), says of the things Satan will do for magicians, 'As in like maner he will learne them many Iuglarie trickes at Cardes, dice, and such-like, to deceiue mens senses thereby, and such innumerable false practiques, which are proued by ouer-many in this aage; as they who are acquainted with that Italian called Scoto yet liuing can report.'

28. *Zany*. *E.M.O.* iv. ii. 44.

36. *the portico, to the procuratia*, the Procuratie Vecchie with an arcade of fifty arches running along the north side of the Piazza di San Marco. It was built in 1517 as a residence for the Procurators of St. Mark, important state officials from whose ranks the Doge was usually chosen.

41. *cold on my feet*, *U.V.* xxxiv. 68, of Inigo Jones. G. Torriano, *Piazza Universale di Proverbi Italiani*, 1666, p. 147: 'Haver freddo a'piedi . . . *to have cold at ones feet, viz. through poverty and want, to be fain to sell ones wares and commodities at a low rate, nay to lose.*'

44. *Buttone*. Described as a brother-mountebank, and otherwise unknown.

45. *a'Sforzato*. '*Sforzati*, gallie-slaues, prisoners perforce' (Florio, 1598).

46. *Cardinall Bembo's—Cooke.* Pietro Bembo (1470–1547), the great humanist. The dash before 'Cooke' marks a pause for the actor, suggesting a more scandalous dependant than a cook.

47. *attach'd,* suggested by the legal sense 'arrested' or 'accused'.

49. *these ground Ciarlitani.* See Coryat's description quoted at the head of this scene.

52. *Tabarine,* a zany in a troop of Italian comedians, headed by Zan Ganassa, who visited France in 1572. M. Jal, in the *Dictionnaire critique d'histoire et de biographie,* notices him as 'Italien de Venise', who lived at Paris in the sixteenth century, King Charles IX standing godfather to his son according to the lost records of the parish of St. Germain l'Auxerrois. The name means 'short cloak'; cf. English 'tabard'.

59. *turdy-facy-nasty-paty-lousy-farticall.* Modelled, as Upton notes, on similar compounds in Aristophanes, e.g. the songs of Philocleon μέλη ἀρχαιομελισιδωνοφρυνιχήρατα (*Wasps,* 220).

61. *'scartoccios.* 'Scartóccio, a coffin of paper for spice, as Apothecaries vse. Also a charge made readie for any musket or ordinance' (Florio, 1598).

64. *oppilations,* obstructions (Lat. *oppilatio*).

65. *salad-eating.* Compare the taunt in *Hymenaei,* 25–8.

71. *canaglia.* 'Canaglia, Canagliaccia, raskalitie, base people, the skum of the earth, raskallie people onelie fit for dogs companie' (Florio, 1598). French, 'canaille'.

77. *terra-ferma,* the continental possessions of the old Venetian State.

80. *splendidous.* 'Splendidious', *E.M.O.* II. ii. 79.

83. *cocted,* boiled (Lat. *coctus*).

104. *mal caduco,* the falling sickness.

105. *tremor-cordia,* palpitation of the heart.

retyred-nerues, shrunken sinews.

107. *iliaca passio.* Trevisa, *Bartholomaeus,* 1495, VII. xlix, 'This passyon callyd Colica hath a cosyn that hyghte *Iliaca passio,* and hath that name of a gutte that hyghte Ilion.' Holland, *Pliny,* 1601, ii. 39, defines it as 'the paine and ringing of the small guts'.

108. *torsion of the small guts,* gripes.

114. *Zan Fritada,* or Fritata (Ital. *fritata,* 'pancake'). The name is taken from a zany commemorated by Thomaso Garzoni, *La Piazza Vniuersale di tutte le Professioni del Mondo,* ed. 1605, p. 749, in a chapter on the crowd at Venice: 'Basta (per toccarne qualcuna) che da vn canto della piazza tu vedi il nostro galante Fortunato insieme con Fritata cacciar carotte, et trattener la brigata ogni sera dalle vintidue fino alle vintiquattro hore di giorno, finger nouelle, trouare historie, formar dialoghi, far calesselle, cantare all' improuiso, corucciarsi insieme, far la pace, morir della risa, alterarsi di nuouo, vrtarsi in sul banco, far questione insiemi, e finalmente buttar fuora i bussoli, & venire al quamquam delle gazette, che vogliano capire con queste loro gentilissime, & garbatissime chiacchiere.'

119. *Broughtons bookes.* Hugh Broughton (1549–1612), a divine and

rabbinical scholar, and a strong Puritan: he wrote a number of learned monographs and controversial pamphlets. His collected works were published by John Lightfoot in 1662. Jonson satirized him in *The Alchemist*, II. iii. 237–8, 'a most rare scholler; And is gone mad, with studying BRAVGHTONS workes'.

121. *Hippocrates* (460– after 350 B.C.) as the originator, and *Galen* (*c.* A.D. 130–? 200) as the systematic exponent of the theory of humours, would appeal to Jonson: for the former cf. *Conv. Drum.* 141.

130. *Raymund Lullies great elixir.* Raymond Lull or Lully (1235–1315), a native of Majorca. See on *Alch.* II. v. 8. Bacon, *Of the Advancement of Learning*, II, ch. xvii. 14, criticized him as one of those who 'deliver knowledges in such manner, as men may speedily come to make a show of learning who have it not'.

131. *Danish Gonswart.* Not satisfactorily identified. Two names have been suggested. (1) By L. H. Holt—the Dutch theologian, a precursor of Luther, Johan Wessel (*c.* 1420–89), whose full name was Wessel Harmeus Gansfort (or Ganzevort); the surname is from Gansfort or Gösewort, the Westphalian village from which his family came. But he was a theologian, not a chemist. (2) By Mr. B. H. Newdigate, Berthold Schwarz, a monk of Fribourg, who invented guns; his real name was Konstantin Anklitzen. The English translation of *Pancirolli Rerum Mirabilium Libri Duo* (1785, p. 384) says: ''Tis said he was a Chymist, who sometimes for Medecines kept Powder of Sulphur in a Mortar, which he covered with a Stone. But it happened one Day as he was striking Fire, that a Spark accidentally falling into it, brake out into a Flame, and heav'd up the Stone. The Man being instructed by this Contingency, and having made an Iron Pipe or Tube together with Powder, is said to have invented this Engine.' Sebastian Munster calls Schwarz a Dane.

132. *Paracelsus.* See *Alch.* II. iii. 230 n.

with his long-sword. Famous both in fact and legend. Melchior Adam, *Vitae Germanorum Medicorum*, 1620, p. 35: 'Domi, quod Oporinus amanuensis ejus sæpè narravit, nunquam nisi potus ad explicanda sua accessit: atq; in medio conclavi ad columnam τετυφωμένος adsistens, apprehenso manib. capulo ensis, cujus κοίλωμα hospitium præbuit, ut aiunt, spiritui familiari, imaginationes aut concepta sua protulit. Alii illud, quod in capulo habuit, ab ipso *Azoth* appellatum, medicinam fuisse præstantissimam, aut lapidem philosophicum putant.' So Butler in *Hudibras*, Part II, canto 3:

> Bumbastes kept a devil's bird
> Shut in the pommel of his sword,
> That taught him all the cunning pranks
> Of past and future mountebanks.

And H. Peacham, *The Truth of our Times*, 1638, p. 43: 'Wherefore Paracelsus (that glory of Germany, for his depth of knowledge in the nature of Minerals) to shew his true happinesse therein, when he travelled by the way, and came to his Inne at night, the first thing hee did, he would lay his sword upon the Table, professing hee would not give the same to the Emperour of Germany: it was a long broad sword, and had engraven upon the blade this:

Alterius non fit qui suus esse potest.

As being the Embleme of his Liberty: In the pommell (which was hollow, and to be opened with a skrew) were all his chiefe Quintessences, and spirits of Metalls and Hearbs, wherewith hee cured the most desperate Diseases, gaining hereby infinite treasure and summes of money.' Browning, who quotes the first two of these passages in a note on his poem of *Paracelsus*, says the 'Azoth' was simply laudanum.

140. *the signiory of the Sanitâ*, organized in 1485, the 'health-masters', as Lewkenor calls them in his additions to Contareni's *The Common-wealth and Government of Venice*, 1599, p. 183: 'They haue authority to giue licence to phisicians to practise, and to Mountebankes, & Chiarlatanes to go vp and downe the countrey, & to preach in the markets.'

156. *in fumo. Alch*. IV. v. 58.

159. *to bee a foole borne*. Dr. Rea quotes the preface to Paracelsus' *De Generatione Stultorum*, prologus (*Opera*, 1659, ii, p. 382), 'Eò difficilius sanantur, qui stulti nati sunt. Is enim affectus nec morbus est, & est insuper incurabilis.' He has other parallels, most of them rather vague, to support his view that the mountebank's speech as a whole is based on the writings of Paracelsus.

168. *balloo*, more correctly 'balloon' (*E.H.I.* ii. 80). Coryat, describing St. Stephen's Piazza at Venice, says: 'Here euery Sunday and Holy-day in the euening the young men of the citie doe exercise them-selues at a certaine play that they call Baloone, which is thus: Sixe or seuen yong men or thereabout weare certaine round things vpon their armes, made of timber, which are full of sharp pointed knobs cut out of the same matter. In these exercises they put off their dublets, and hauing put this round instrument vpon one of their armes, they tosse vp and downe a great ball, as great as our football in England: sometimes they will tosse the ball with this instrument, as high as a common Church, and about one hundred paces at the least from them.'

180. *Montalto*, Felice Peretti, Cardinal di Montalto in 1570, Pope as Sixtus V in 1585. His grand-nephew Alessandro was nominated Cardinal di Montalto at Sixtus' first consistory.

Ferneze. Alessandro Ferneze, Pope Paul III in 1534; there was a later Cardinal Ferneze.

the great duke of Tuscany. The office was created by Pius V in 1569, who conferred it on Cosimo de' Medici.

181. *gossip*, godsib or godfather.

189. *gazets*. The gazet was coined at Venice for circulation in the Levant; Jonson here gives its value at about three farthings, and Coryat agrees with him: to go to the top of St. Mark's tower, he says, 'will

cost thee but a gazet, which is not fully an English penny' (*Crudities*, p. 185).

202. *aches.* A disyllable, as in *The Tempest*, i. ii. 370.

203. *for the nones*, for the nonce, for the occasion. So *G.M.* 2 prologue, 31, *Ent. Welb.* 100; and 'at ones' (= at once) *Ep.* lxviii. 3. ME 'for þe nanes,' literally with a view to the one (thing or occasion).

210. *muccinigo*, moccenigo, worth about ninepence.

212. *the banner of my front. The Widow*, iv. i (1652, F4ᵛ):

> Where did I hear late of a skilfull fellow,
> Good for all kind of Malladies? true, true sir,
> His flag hangs out in town here, i' th' Cross Inn,
> With admirable cures of all conditions,
> It shews him a great travelling, and learnd Emperick.

Ibid. G1ᵛ: '*Scæna 2. Enter* Latrocinio *and* Occulto, (*a Banner of Cures and Diseases hung out.*)'

bagatine, worth about the third part of a farthing. '*Bagatino, Baggatino*, a little coyne vsed in Italie, a nickname for a kitlin or whelp as we say, a pug, a puffe, a puppie' (Florio, 1598).

215. *tosse your handkerchiefes.* Daniel Martin, *Parlement nouveau*, 1637, describing the sensation made at Paris by the later famous Tabarin of 1623 and his associate Montdor, says when they had advertised their drugs, 'il y avoit presse à qui jetteroit le plus tost son argent noué dans le coin d'un mouchoir ou dans un gant, sur l'echaffaut, pour avoir une petite bouette d'onguent, enveloppée dans un billet imprimé, contenant l'usage d'ycelui et la façon de s'en servir' (quoted by M. Sand, *Masques et Bouffons*, ii, p. 299).

219. *double pistolet.* Middleton and Rowley, *The Spanish Gipsy*, i. v (1653, C1ᵛ), 'I'd not be so lind For my Cap full of double Pistolets'; Fletcher and Massinger, *The Spanish Curate*, i. i (Folio 1647, p. 27):

> And perhaps give a double Pistolet
> To some poor needy Frier, to say a Masse
> To keep your Ghost from walking.

The pistolet was a Spanish gold coin worth from 16*s.* 8*d.* to 18*s.* at the date of the play.

246. *virginall iacks.* The jack was 'an upright piece of wood fixed to the back of the key-lever, and fitted with a quill which plucked the string as the jack rose on the key's being pressed down'—*O.E.D.*, which notes that Shakespeare (as Jonson does here) erroneously applied the term to the key: so in the following: Dekker, *The Gull's Hornbook*, ch. iii (1609, C3ʳ), of a cold morning—'so that thy teeth (as if thou wert singing prick-song) stand coldly quauering in thy head, and leap vp and downe like the nimble Iackes of a paire of Virginals'; Taylor, *The Penniless Pilgrimage*, 1618, E4, 'The next day I trauelled ouer an exceeding high mountaine, called mount *Skene*, where I found the valley very warme before I went vp it; but when I came to the top of it, my

teeth beganne to daunce in my head with colde, like Virginall iackes.'
The idea came from Rabelais, *Pantagruel*, ii (1505, p. 215), 'les dents
leur tressailloyent comme font les marchettes d'vn clauier d'orgues, ou
d'espinette, quand on iouë dessus'.

II. iii. 3. *Flaminio*. Flaminio Scala, professionally known as Flavio,
published at Venice in 1611 a collection of scenari, *Il Teatro delle Favole*.
He was a noted actor in the Comedy of Arts.

4. *Franciscina*, the servant-maid of the Comedy of Arts. In Jacomo
Callot's *Balli di Sfessania* (Florence? 1630?) she is dressed as a dancing-
girl with a tambourine.

8. *Pantalone di besogniosi*, a stock Venetian character in the Comedy
of Arts; 'de' Bisogniosi' is a jocular quasi-family name—of the pedigree
of Paupers. He was a lean old man, wore loose slippers, a black cap
and gown, and a red dress. He was commonly depicted as a jealous
dotard or as a cuckold, and this is the point of Corvino's allusion. Compare Day, Rowley, and Wilkins, *The Travels of Three English Brothers*,
1607, E4ᵛ, where Will Kemp arranges to play with an Italian Harlaken:
'*Harl*. Marry, sir, first we will haue an old Pantaloune. *Kemp*. Some
jealous Coxcombe. *Harl*. Right, and that part will I play.' He goes on
to say, 'And wee must haue an *Amorado* that must make me a Cornuto.'

13. *This three weekes*. Sir Politic has forgotten the 'aduises' he had
'on wensday last' in II. i. 94.

II. iv. 3. *bolting*, springing.
from her eyes. Cf. the *Anacreontea*, xxvi. 4–8:

> οὐχ ἵππος ὤλεσέν με,
> οὐ πεζός, οὐχὶ νῆες·
> στρατὸς δὲ καινὸς ἄλλος
> ἀπ' ὀμμάτων με βάλλων.

4–7. *Hath shot himself* . . . Ibid. xiii. 13–20, of Eros:

> ὡς δ' οὐκέτ' εἶχ' ὀιστούς,
> ἤσχαλλεν, εἶτ' ἑαυτὸν
> ἀφῆκεν εἰς βέλεμνον·
> μέσος δὲ καρδίας μὲν
> ἔδυνε καί μ' ἔλυσεν·
> μάτην δ' ἔχω βοείην.
> τί γὰρ βάλωμεν ἔξω,
> μάχης ἔσω μ' ἐχούσης;

9. *liuer*. In classical poetry spoken of as the seat of the violent passions, such as jealousy or love. Cf. *Und*. lxxxvi. 12, where Jonson
translates Horace's address to Venus, 'si torrere iecur quaeris idoneum'
by 'Iff a fit livor thou dost seeke to toast'.

33. *your epilogue*, the beating.

II. v. 4. *dole of faces. Sej.* I. 7, 'We haue no shift of faces.'

11. *copper rings. The Wandering-Jew, Telling Fortunes to Englishmen*, 1640, F2, 'Gloves under his Girdle like an Usurer, and Rings on his fingers like a Juggler.'

12. *toade-stone*, really a petrified sea-urchin, something after the nature of an agate, but supposed in medieval times to be taken from the head of a toad. It was worn in rings as an amulet and believed to be an antidote against poison.

13. *cope-stitch.* As Rea suggests, a stitch like that used in embroidering the straight edge of a cope. Cf. Gobelin stitch, 'a short upright stitch, also called Tapistry' (*O.E.D.*), and blanket stitch, a long stitch used to oversew the edge of blankets.

15. *starch'd beard.* Cf. *Disc.* 1417–20, *De mollibus et effœminatis*, 'The exceedingly curious . . . gumming, and bridling their beards.'

17. *moother*, hysteria: of course with an equivoque. *fricace*, massage.

21. *lady vanitie.* Jonson has left the Comedy of Arts and turned to the old morality plays. Lady Vanity is a character in R. Wever's *Lusty Juventus* (1549–69), in *The Contention between Liberality and Prodigality*, 1602, and in the interlude acted in the play of *Sir Thomas More*, IV. i. Cf. 'Vanity the puppet' in *King Lear*, II. ii. 33, and Jonson's later reference in *D. is A.* I. i. 41–3, where a Vice is called for.

22. *a dealer.* S. Rowlands, *The Letting of Humour's Blood*, 1600, Ep. 29, 'A gentlewoman of the dealing trade'; *Pericles*, IV. vi. 23–4, Lysimachus asks at the brothel, 'How now, wholesome iniquity, have you that a man may deal withal?'

57. *a locke*, a girdle of chastity.

70–1. *make thee an anatomie . . . read a lecture. E.M.I.* IV. vi. 36–7, 'they must ha' dissected, and made an *Anatomie* o' me, first'; *Und.* xxv. 37–9:

> When her dead essence (like the Anatomie
> In Surgeons hall)
> Is but a Statists theame, to read Phlebotomie.

II. vi. 14. *osteria*, inn.

25. *officious*, dutiful. *C.R.* v. ix. 6.

29. *cataplasme*, poultice.

34. *some young woman*, such as Abishag the Shunammite in David's last years.

42. *delate*, inform against (Lat. *delator*, an informer). *Disc.* 1596.

53. *flexible*, easy to manipulate.

64. *a fever.* Juvenal, *Sat.* x. 217–18:

> Praeterea minimus gelido iam in corpore sanguis
> febre calet sola.

74. *comming*, yielding. *Cat.* III. 372, *S.W.* v. i. 77, *D. is A.* IV. iv.180.

88. *thratled.* A sixteenth- and seventeenth-century form of 'throttle'.

92–5. Horace, *Sat.* II. v. 75–6:

Scortator erit: cave te roget; ultro
Penelopam facilis potiori trade.

II. vii. K. Brunner pointed out an analogy to the Celia story in
Gower's *Confessio Amantis*, v. 2643–825, which Gower took from the
Roman des Sept Sages—the story of a steward who betrayed his wife
to a king.

2, 3. L. H. Holt, quoted by Rea, compares the situation in Plautus'
Amphitruo, 912–16, where Jupiter has to explain away the reproaches
of the husband whose disguise he has assumed:

> Ego expediam tibi.
> Non edepol quo te esse impudicam crederem;
> verum periclitatus sum animum tuom
> quid faceres et quo pacto id ferre induceres.
> Equidem ioco illa dixeram dudum tibi,
> ridiculi causa.

8, 9. For the thought cf. Juvenal, *Sat.* vi. 347–8:

> 'Pone seram, cohibe.' Sed quis custodiet ipsos
> custodes? Cauta est, et ab illis incipit uxor.

III. i. Jonson's own views on parasites whom he had observed in
noblemen's houses are set forth in the *Discoveries*, 1586–1635, but the
consummate type is sketched here and fitted into the framework of
the play as the arch-contriver of the intrigue. Slight hints from Athenaeus, pointed out by Dr. Rea, colour this soliloquy, but they are only
hints. Athenaeus gives a number of extracts from Greek comedy describing the parasite. With line 8 compare Diodorus of Sinope in *The
Heiress* (vi. 239 b):

> βούλομαι δεῖξαι σαφῶς
> ὡς σεμνόν ἐστι τοῦτο καὶ νενομισμένον
> καὶ τῶν θεῶν εὕρημα.

The banquets of Zeus, he says, originated parasites. With lines 12–15
compare Alexis in *The Pilot* (237 b):

> δύ' ἐστι, Ναυσίνικε, παρασίτων γένη,
> ἐν μὲν τὸ κοινὸν καὶ κεκωμῳδημένον,
> οἱ μέλανες ἡμεῖς. θάτερον ζητῶ γένος,
> σεμνοπαράσιτον ἐκ μέσου καλούμενον,
> σατράπας παρασίτους καὶ στρατηγοὺς ἐμφανεῖς.

With lines 23–5 compare Aristophon in *The Doctor* (238 b):

> βούλομαι δ' αὐτῷ προειπεῖν οἷός εἰμι τοὺς τρόπους·
> ἄν τις ἑστιᾷ, πάρειμι πρῶτος ὥστ' ἤδη πάλαι
> ‹τοῖς νέοις› ζωμὸς καλοῦμαι. δεῖ τιν' ἄρασθαι μέσον
> τῶν παροινούντων, παλαιστὴν νόμισον αὐτάργειόν μ' ὁρᾶν.
> προσβαλεῖν πρὸς οἰκίαν δεῖ, κρίος· ἀναβῆναί τε πρὸς
> κλιμάκιον . . . Καπανεύς· ὑπομένειν πληγὰς ἄκμων.

And Antiphanes in *The Ancestors* (238e):

> τὸν τρόπον μὲν οἶσθά μου
> ὅτι τῦφος οὐκ ἔνεστιν, ἀλλὰ τοῖς φίλοις
> τοιοῦτός εἰμι δή τις τύπτεσθαι μύδρος,
> τύπτειν κεραυνός, ἐκτυφλοῦν τιν' ἀστραπή,
> φέρειν τιν' ἄρας ἄνεμος, ἀποπνῖξαι βρόχος,
> θύρας μοχλεύειν σεισμός, εἰσπηδᾶν ἀκρίς,
> δειπνεῖν ἄκλητος μυῖα, μὴ 'ξελθεῖν φρέαρ,
> ἄγχειν φονεύειν μαρτυρεῖν ὅσ' ἂν μόνον
> τύχῃ τις εἰπών, ταῦτ' ἀπροσκέπτως ποιεῖν
> ἅπαντα.

To these commonplace notices of the diner-out Jonson added the intellectual refinement of Mosca; he is the consummation of the type which began with Brainworm.

4. *whimsey*, whim. *S. of N.* IV. iv. 80–1: in *F.I.* 69 it means 'dizziness'.

9. *clot-poules*. The form 'clot' survives in dialect: 'clots' = clownes, *M.L.* I. vi. 26.

17. *bait*. So the parasite in *Disc.* 1588, 'makes baites for his Lordships eares': cf. Persius, *Sat.* i. 22, 'Tun, vetule, auriculis alienis colligis escas?'

19. *the belly, and the groine*. *E.M.O.* v. iv. 31.

21. *revénnue*. The usual stressing of the word during the seventeenth and eighteenth centuries.

22. *lick away a moath*. A trick of the parasite in all ages. Cf. Theophrastus, *Characters*, ii, The Flatterer: καὶ ἄλλα τοιαῦτα λέγων ἀπὸ τοῦ ἱματίου ἀφελεῖν κροκύδα, καὶ ἐάν τι πρὸς τὸ τρίχωμα τῆς κεφαλῆς ὑπὸ πνεύματος προσενεχθῇ ἄχυρον καρφολογῆσαι. Valeria, Sulla's last wife, first attracted his notice at the theatre by picking a thread from his cloak (Plutarch, *Sulla*, 35).

III. ii. 6. *mate*. For the contemptuous use cf. *The Taming of the Shrew*, I. i. 58, 'To make a stale of me amongst these mates'.

13–16. From Seneca, *Medea*, 199, 200:

> Qui statuit aliquid parte inaudita altera,
> aequum licet statuerit, haud aequus fuit.

vnequall, unjust (Lat. *iniquus*).

22. *obsequy*, obsequiousness (Lat. *obsequium*).

56. *pietie*, filial affection (Lat. *pietas*).

65. *issue of the earth*, obscure, of unknown parentage (Lat. *terrae filius*).

III. iii. 5. *Being, all*, the Quarto punctuation: cf. *M. of Q.* 71 (autograph MS.), 'For we, all, stay'.

delicates, favourites (Lat. *deliciae*).

10. *as it is little, is prittie.* Cf. *Love's Labour's Lost*, I. ii. 21, 'pretty, because little'; J. Taylor, *Epigram* 17 (*Works*, 1630, p. 264):

> *Euery thing is prettie when it is little*
>
> There is a saying old, (but not so wittie)
> That when a thing is little, it is prettie:
> This doating age of ours it finely fits;
> Where many men thought wise, haue pretty wits.

III. iv. Lady Politic Would-be's patter in this scene is borrowed from the treatise of the fourth-century rhetorician Libanius of Antioch called *De Muliere Loquaci*, of which Jonson made ample use in *Epicoene* later. He used the edition of the French scholar Morellus published at Paris in 1597. A husband, driven mad by his wife's loquacity, appeals to a court to give him hemlock in order that he may escape her. ἔστι δ' οὐκ ἀσφαλές, οὔτε τὸ χεῖρον, οὔτε τὸ βέλτιον ἀγγεῖλαι· φύεται γὰρ ἐξ ἑκατέρων λόγων σωρός· ἐντεῦθεν γὰρ ἐπ' ἄλλο μεταπηδᾷ (p. 9). For the 'storme' (39) and 'torrent' (64) cf. φεῦ τῆς ἐπομβρίας τῶν ῥημάτων (p. 9); εἶθ' ὥσπερ ἐκλαθομένη τῶν μεγίστων, ἑαυτὴν εἰς ἀνάμνησιν κονδυλίζει· ἐγὼ δὲ φρίττω, ῥεῦμα ἕτερον ἐπερχόμενον ὁρῶν (p. 10); καθάπερ πλοῖον θάλασσα, ὑπεράνεσχέ με τῆς γυναικὸς ὁ κλύδων (p. 13). For the dream (44–8) cf. ἐπειδὰν δὲ πάντα ἀναλώσῃ . . . τὰ ἡμέτερα, πάλιν τὰ τῶν γειτόνων, κἂν μηδὲν ἔτι φαίνηται, ὀνείρατα διηγεῖται, πλάττουσα κἀκεῖνα μὰ τοὺς θεοὺς ὡς ἔμοιγε δοκεῖ (p. 11). The literary criticism of lines 78–97 is elementary in Libanius: ἡ δὲ μνήμη τῶν χορηγιῶν, ἐπὶ τοὺς τραγῳδοὺς αὐτὴν παρέπεμψεν· κἀνταῦθα ὑεῖ ῥαγδαίως τοὺς πρώτους εὑρόντας τραγῳδίαν λέγουσα, καὶ τοὺς ἐνδειξαμένους καὶ ὅτῳ τρόπῳ τὸ σχῆμα ηὐξήθη, καὶ τί συνεισήνεγκεν ἕκαστος· ἐγὼ δὲ δεινότερα πάσχω τῶν ἐν ταῖς τραγῳδίαις κολαζομένων. μὴ γὰρ οἶδεν ἡ γυνὴ στῆναί ποι τοῦ λαλεῖν· οἱ ποταμοὶ πρότερον ἂν σταῖεν ἢ τὸ ταύτης στόμα. πᾶσα γὰρ πρόφασις λόγων ἀφορμή (pp. 10, 11). Lines 84–5 reproduce the thought of the last words, and lines 76–8 are from a later passage: σὺ δέ, εἶπον, εἰ μὴ ἐμέ, ἀλλὰ καὶ τὸν σοφώτατον ποιητὴν αἰσχύνθητι λέγοντα, Γύναι, γυναιξὶ κόσμον ἡ σιγὴ φέρει. ἡ δ' εὐθύς, καὶ τίς οὗτος ὁ ποιητής, καὶ τίνος πατρός, καὶ ποίου δήμου· καὶ πότε ποιεῖν ἤρξατο, καὶ πῶς ἐτελεύτησε· καὶ τὴν ἡμέραν ἐνταῦθα κατέτριψεν ἡ γυνή (p. 18).

10. *Is this curle . . .* 16. *is red.* Juvenal, *Sat.* vi. 492:

> 'Altior his quare cincinnus?' Taurea punit
> continuo flexi crimen facinusque capilli.
> Quid Psecas admisit? quaenam est hic culpa puellae,
> si tibi displicuit nasus tuus?

Similarly Massinger, *The Bondman*, II. i (1624, E), Corsica to her maid Zanthia:

> Carelesse Harlotrie,
> Looke too't, if a Curle full, a winde, or Sunne,
> Take my complexion off, I will not leaue
> One haire vpon thine head.

12. *wash'd your eies.* *T. of T.* II. ii. 136, 'where were your eyes then? out at washing?'

18. *One haire* . . . Martial, II. lxvi. 1–4:

> Unus de toto peccaverat orbe comarum
> anulus, incerta non bene fixus acu.
> Hoc facinus Lalage speculo, quo viderat, ulta est,
> et cecidit saevis icta Plecusa comis.

20. *bird-ey'd. C.R.* v. iv. 168. At the word 'forsooth' Lady Would-be turns upon her woman with a threatening gesture, and the latter starts back as if to avoid a blow.

27. *More carefully* . . . Seneca, *De Brevitate Vitae*, xii. 3, of dandies consulting with their barber, 'dum de singulis capillis in consilium itur' —'Qui non comptior esse malit quam honestior?'

38. *entertaynément.* So 'commandément' in *The Faerie Queene*, III. iii. 11, and *The Merchant of Venice*, IV. i. 446. Jonson spells the word 'command'ments' in *D. is A.* II. ii. 44.

39. *my Volp.* So 'Bob' for Bobadill, *E.M.I.* IV. iii. 16, 'Sir Puntar' for Puntarvolo, *E.M.O.* v. i. 66, and in this play 'Sir Pol' for Sir Politic Would-be (e.g. IV. i. 131).

47. *the golden mediocritie.* Lady Would-be, forced to make up a dream on the spur of the moment, takes refuge in high-sounding nonsense.

51. *the passion of the heart,* heartburn (Lat. *cardiaca passio*).

52. *Seed-pearle.* Burton, *The Anatomy of Melancholy*, ed. 1632, p. 376, discussing the cure of melancholy, says '*those smaller vnions which are found in shells amongst the Persians and Indians,* by the consent of all writers, *are very cordiall,* and most part availe to the exhilaretion of the heart'.

53. *Tincture of gold,* the *aurum potabile* again. 'For gold in phisik is a cordial', Chaucer, *Canterbury Tales*, Prologue A, 443.

corrall. Burton, op. cit., p. 376, quotes Levinus Lemnius as saying that carbuncle and coral '*drive away childish feares, Diuels, ouercome sorrow, and hung about the necke represse troublesome dreames*'.

54. *mirobalanes.* An Eastern plant formerly used in medicine. Burton, op. cit., p. 383, '*Mirabolones,* all fiue kindes, are happily prescribed against melancholy and quartan agues. *Brassivola* speakes out *of a thousand* experiences, hee gaue them in pills, decoction, &c.'

55. *a grasse-hopper. Poet.* Apol. Dial. 113–14.

56. *Burnt silke.* Gilbert the Englishman (fl. 1250) in his *Compendium Medicinae*, printed in 1510, f. cccxlviij *b*, mentions a popular remedy for the small-pox: 'Vetulae provinciales dant purpuram combustam in potu. habet enim occultam naturam curandi variolas. Similiter pannus tinctus de grano' (Freind, *History of Physic*, ii, p. 283).

59. *english saffron.* Formerly much used both in confectionery and medicine. The county of Essex was noted for it; hence the name of Saffron Walden. Harrison in his *Description of England* has a chapter on the industry (iii, ch. viii), which died out in the eighteenth century.

61. *Buglosse.* Burton, op. cit., p. 373: 'Buglosse is hot and moist, and therefore worthily reckoned vp amongst those hearbs, which expell

melancholy, and exhilerate the heart. . . . It is an excellent cordial, and against this malady most frequently prescribed.'

63. *scarlet-cloth.* Used, like the burnt silk of line 56, for the treatment of small-pox. John of Gaddesden, court doctor under Edward II, cured a son of Edward I by wrapping him in scarlet cloth. In his *Rosa Anglica*, 1492, f. 51, he says: 'Dein capiatur scarletum rubeum & involvatur variolosus totaliter vel in panno alio ru⟨beo⟩. Sic ego feci de filio nobilissimi regis angliae qui patiebatur istos morbos & feci omnia circa lectum esse rubea. Est bona cura. & curavi eum in sequenti sine vestigiis variolarum' (Freind, as in line 56). Jonson appears to have believed in the use of scarlet cloth: see *D. is A.* iv. iv. 38, *Ent. Blackfriars*, 160.

74. *concent*, harmony (Lat. *concentus*).

76. *the Poet.* Sophocles, *Ajax*, 293.

79. *Which o' your Poets?* The literary lady in Juvenal, *Sat.* vi. 434–6:

> Illa tamen gravior quae cum discumbere coepit
> laudat Vergilium, periturae ignoscit Elissae,
> committit vates et comparat.

80. *Guerrini.* Giovanni Battista Guarini (1537–1612), the author of the *Pastor Fido*; see 86 below.

Aretine. Pietro Aretino (1492–1556), comedian and satirist; see 96–7 below.

81. *Cieco di Hadria*, 'the blind man of Adria', Luigi Groto (1541–85). He translated the first book of the *Iliad* (1570), and celebrated the battle of Lepanto (1572); he also wrote tragedies, comedies, and pastorals. He made a sensation as a blind actor in O. Giustiniani's version of the *Oedipus* of Sophocles at Vicenza in 1585, and he annotated an edition of the *Decameron*, which was published at Venice in 1588.

86. *Pastor Fido*, Guarini's pastoral (1590), a masterpiece of diction, had a great influence on style. An English version appeared in 1602. Jonson's own verdict on the poem is quoted by Drummond, *Conv.* iv. 64–5. The reference to plagiarism from him points, as F. G. Fleay first suggested, to Daniel, whose masque, *The Vision of the Twelve Goddesses*, had been performed at Court on 8 January 1604 and his pastoral, *The Queen's Arcadia*, at Oxford before the Queen on 30 August 1605. Compare the criticism in *The Return from Parnassus*, Part II, i. ii. 241–6:

> Sweete hony dropping *Daniell* doth wage
> Warre with the proudest big Italian,
> That melts his heart in Sugred sonneting.
> Onely let him more sparingly make vse
> Of others wit, and vse his owne the more:
> That well may scorne base imitation.

'Fitting the time, and catching the court-eare' points to Daniel; see the note on *The Forest*, xii. 68–9.

90. *Montagnie.* The Quarto spelling shows the pronunciation: cf. Bacon's 'Montaigny saith prettily' (*Essay* xli). For Jonson's opinion

of essayists and their plagiarisms see *Disc.* 719–29. Marston and Webster borrowed freely ideas and aphorisms from Montaigne, sometimes quoting verbatim: see C. Crawford's *Collectanea*, ii, pp. 1–63.

93. *Petrarch.* English borrowings from Petrarch's love poems begin with Wyatt, who translated thirteen sonnets. Comment on the practice is frequent. It begins with Sidney, *Astrophel and Stella*, 1591, sonnet xv:

> You that old *Petrarchs* long deceased woes
> With new borne sighes, and wit disguised sing;
> You take wrong wayes, those far-fet helps be such,
> As doe bewray a want of inward tutch,
> And sure at length stolne goods doe come to light.

Drayton in the lines to Antony Cooke prefixed to *Ideas Mirrour*, 1594, says of his sonnets in that collection:

> Yet these mine owne, I wrong not other men, . . .
> Nor filch from *Portes* nor from *Petrarchs* pen,
> A fault too common in thys latter tyme.

Hall in the *Virgidemiarum*, 1597, Book IV, ii, p. 17, speaks of

> an, *Hos ego*, from old *Petrarchs* spright
> Vnto a Plagiarie sonnet-wright.

And Book VI, i, p. 93:

> Or filch whole Pages at a clap for need
> From honest *Petrarch*, clad in English weed.

95. *Dante is hard.* Cf. Florio, *A Worlde of Wordes*, 1598, Epistle Dedicatorie, a4: '*Boccace* is prettie hard, yet vnderstood: *Petrarche* harder, but explaned: *Dante* hardest, but commented. Some doubt if all aright.' Breton, *The Court and Country*, 1618, B4ᵛ, makes a countryman say, 'I will say as one *Dante*, an Italian Poet, once said in an obscure Booke of his, *Vnderstand me that can, I vnderstand my selfe.*'

96–7. *Aretine.* The reference is to sixteen obscene designs by Giulio Romano engraved by Marc Antonio Raimondi, for which Aretino wrote sixteen *Sonnetti lussuriosi*, 1523. Cf. iii. vii. 60 below, *Alch.* ii. ii. 44.

100. *O'y me.* Cf. the Italian *ohimè, oimè* in Torriano.

110. *Plato.* As accurate as Sempronia's quotation from Thucydides, *Cat.* iv. 718.

112. *Assassinates.* Cf. Martial, viii. l. 26, 'ut iugulem curas'. The earliest example of the verb in the *O.E.D.* is dated 1618.

125. *coœtanei.* Cf. the use of '*soloecisme*', iv. ii. 43. Usually Lady Would-be's verbal extravagances are English.

iii. v. 3, 4. The husband in Libanius (op. cit., p. 12) appeals to the Court, ῥύσασθέ με φωνῆς ἀπαύστου.

5. *The bells, in time of pestilence.* Cf. *S.W.* I. i. 183–4; *Ep.* cxxxiii. 173–4:

> Cannot the *Plague*-bill keepe you backe? nor bells
> Of loud SEPVLCHRES with their hourely knells?

See F. P. Wilson, *The Plague in Shakespeare's London*, pp. 177–8.

7. *The cock-pit.* *S.W.* IV. iv. 14 n. There were cockpits in St. Giles-in-the-Fields (afterwards the Phoenix theatre), St. James's Park, and at Whitehall.

9–11. From Juvenal, *Sat.* vi. 438–42, in a similar context:

> Vincuntur rhetores; omnis
> turba tacet, nec causidicus nec praeco loquetur,
> altera nec mulier: verborum tanta cadit vis,
> tot pariter pelves, tot tintinnabula dicas
> pulsari.

19. *gondole.* A form in use from the seventeenth to the nineteenth century. 'Gondola' in IV. v. 149.

23. *lightly*, commonly.

36. *primero.* Jonson plays on the technical terms of the game—'goe lesse', 'draw', 'encounter'. With the first cf. *S.W.* III. v. 105, *P.R.* 310. For *draw* (= pluck a card from the pack) and *encounter* cf. *Ep.* cxii. 18, 19:

> That both for wit, and sense, so oft doth plucke,
> And neuer art encounter'd.

Encounter quibbles on the senses of love-meeting.

III. vi. 1. *here conceald.* Mosca takes him to one of the side-doors of the stage. In sc. vii. 13 he sends him off-stage into the 'gallery' of this opening.

III. vii. 39. *There's no such thing in nature.* *S.W.* IV. ii. 50.

43–5. *takes his meate.* From Juvenal, *Sat.* x. 228–31:

> Huius
> pallida labra cibum accipiunt digitis alienis,
> ipse ad conspectum cenae diducere rictum
> suetus hiat . . .

48. *Iigge*, farce.

51. *Whose lippes are i' my pocket.* Cf. John Heywood, *Witty and Witless*, MS. facsimile, f. 4*a*:

> So much the bettyr, and yow so muche the wurs.
> That ye may now put yowr toong in yowr purs.

60. *Aretine.* III. iv. 96–7.

61. *quirke*, sudden twist.

84. *Applying fire to a stone*. Cf. *Iohn Heywoodes workes*, Pt. II, ch. ii (1562, Fiijᵛ):

> Her carrain carkas (saide he) is so colde,
> Because she is aged, and somewhat to olde,
> That she kylth me, I doo but roste a stone.

88–9. *t'vse his fortune, With reuerence*. *Sej*. II. 137 n.

95. *Eate burning coales*, like Portia.

99. *rotchet*, the red gurnet.

100. *some slaue*. As Tarquin threatened Lucrece.

118. *locust*, a consuming plague. More appropriate on the lips of Deacon Ananias denouncing the swindlers in *The Alchemist*, v. v. 13–14, 'Locusts Of the foule pit'.

119–20. *Crocodile* . . . From Juvenal, *Sat*. vi. 273–5:

> Uberibus semper lacrimis semperque paratis
> in statione sua atque expectantibus illam
> quo iubeat manare modo.

For the proverbial tears see *Batman vppon Bartholome*, XVIII. xxxiii (1582, p. 359): '*Phisiologus* saith, that if the Crocodile findeth a man by the brim of the water or by the cliffe, he slayeth him, if he may, and then he weepeth vpon him, and swalloweth him at the last.'

127. *more comming*, ready to meet advances. So II. vi. 74, *S.W.* v. i. 77.

133. *whether*. The old form of 'whither', which Jonson frequently uses.

144. *cope-man*, dealer.

152–3. *contended With blue Proteus*, e.g. before Menelaus captured him (*Odyssey*, iv. 456–8). *Blue*, sea-colour, the *caeruleus Proteus* of Virgil, *Georgic*, iv. 388: see *M. Beauty*, 73, with Jonson's note.

the horned Floud. The Achelous who fought with Hercules for the hand of Deianeira; he assumed three shapes, those of a bull, a serpent, and the trunk of a man with the front of an ox (Sophocles, *Trachiniae*, 9–14). This embodiment of a river-god symbolized both the roar of the torrent and the branchings of the stream. See Jonson's note on *M. Blackness*, 46.

161. *the great Valois*. In 1574 the Doge and senators of Venice entertained Henry of Valois, Duke of Anjou, King of Poland, on his way back to France when the death of his brother Charles IX made him king as Henry III. For an account of the entertainment see J. A. Symonds's *Shakspere's Predecessors in the English Drama*, 1884, pp. 331–6.

162. *Antinous*, the favourite of the Emperor Hadrian, famous for his youthful beauty.

166–73. The opening lines of this song are from the beautiful fifth poem of Catullus:

> Vivamus, mea Lesbia, atque amemus,
> rumoresque senum severiorum
> omnes unius aestimemus assis.

Soles occidere et redire possunt:
nobis cum semel occidit brevis lux,
nox est perpetua una dormienda.

Jonson reprinted this poem and the snatch of song which follows Volpone's speech at lines 236–9 in *The Forest*, v and vi. 'Come, my Celia' is in Cotgrave's *Wits Interpreter*, 1655, p. 141.

Lines 171–3 are quoted in Burton, *The Anatomy of Melancholy*, ed. 1624 (part i, sect. 2, number 5, sub. 5).

180–3. These lines, as Gifford noted, have reference to the well-known Spartan attitude towards theft. Dryden, *Limberham*, v. i: '*Wood*. I have been taken upon suspicion here with Mrs. *Tricksy*. *Aldo*. To be taken, to be seen! Before *George*, that's a point next the worst, Son *Woodall*.' Fletcher and Massinger in *The Lover's Progress*, iv. i (Folio, 1647, p. 86):

> *Clar*. But I have sworn unto my Lady never
> To sinne again.
>   *Leon*. To be surpriz'd—the sinne
> Is in it self excusable; to be taken
> Is a crime, as the Poet writes.

184. *serene*. 'A light fall of moisture or fine rain after sunset in hot countries, formerly regarded as a noxious dew or mist' (*O.E.D.*): from the French *serein*. *Ep*. xxxii. 10.

192. *the braue Ægyptian queene*, Cleopatra. She challenged Antony to spend one hundred million sesterces on one meal; this is how she won the wager: 'Ex præcepto ministri unum tantum vas ante eam posuere aceti cuius asperitas visque in tabem margaritas resolvit. Gerebat auribus cum maxime singulare illud et vere unicum naturae opus. Itaque expectante Antonio quidnam esset actura detractum alterum mersit et liquefactum obsorbuit' (Pliny, *N.H*. ix. 120–1).

193. *Dissolue*. *Alch*. ii. ii. 76 n.

194. *both the eyes of our St. Marke*. No image of St. Mark adorned in this way is recorded at Venice, but there were two famous carbuncles. One in the Treasury of St. Mark, 'an exceeding great Carbuncle which was bestowed on the Senate by Cardinal Grimannus' (Coryat, *Crudities*, 1611, p. 216). Edmund Warcupp, *Italy*, 1660, p. 11, also mentions this, but calls it a ruby, and further says that the *corno* or coronation cap of the Doge, 'the Mitre or Bonnet (as we call it) with which every new Duke is Crowned', had 'at the very Top, a Carbuncle of inestimable value'. *L'occhio di San Marco* might have been a popular name for one of these jewels. Evidently Jonson is using in this passage some information which he had obtained from Florio.

195. *Lollia Paulina*. Pliny, *N.H*. ix. 117: 'Lolliam Paulinam, quae fuit Gaii principis matrona, ne serio quidem aut solemni caerimoniarum aliquo apparatu, sed mediocrium etiam sponsalium cena, vidi smaragdis margaritisque opertam, alterno textu fulgentibus toto capite crinibus spira auribus collo monilibus digitisque. Nec dona prodigi principis fuerant sed avitae opes, provinciarum scilicet spoliis partae.'

200–1. *but worth a private patrimony* . . . Juvenal, *Sat.* i. 138, 'una comedunt patrimonia mensa'.

201–4. 'This is a strain of luxury taken from the Emperor Heliogabalus' (Whalley). Cf. Lampridius, *Heliogabalus*, 20: 'Comedit . . . linguas pavonum et lusciniarum. . . . Exhibuit et Palatinis ingentes dapes extis mullorum refertas, et cerebellis phoenicopterum et perdicum ovis et cerebellis turdorum et capitibus psittacorum et fasianorum et pavonum. 23 Fertur et promisisse phoenicem conviviis . . . 30 Sexcentorum struthionum capita una cena multis mensis exhibuit ad edenda cerebella.'

213. *thy bathes.* Lampridius, op. cit. 19, 'Non nisi unguento nobili aut croco piscinis infectis natavit.'

iuly-flowers. This is a perverted form of 'gillyflower'.

215. *milke of vnicornes.* Imaginary, even in an age which believed in the unicorn and used its powdered horn as medicine.

panthers breath. *C.R.* v. iv. 433–4.

216. *cretan wines*: 1. i. 58. The Earl of Shrewsbury, when keeper of Mary Queen of Scots, petitioned for a larger allowance on account of her habit of bathing in wine (Lodge, *Illustrations of British History*, i, p. 490).

217. *prepared gold, and amber.* *E.M.O.* ii. vi. 107–8; *Alch.* ii. ii. 76, iv. i. 137.

218. *vntill my roofe whirle round.* Juvenal, *Sat.* vi. 304–5, 'cum bibitur concha, cum iam vertigine tectum ambulat'.

221–4. Cf. Massinger, *The City Madam*, iii. ii (1658, p. 43):

> And when you appear
> Like *Juno* in full majesty, and my Neeces
> Like Iris, Hebe, or what deities else
> Old Poets fancie; your examin'd wardrobes richer
> Then various natures, and draw down the envy
> Of our western world upon you.

223. *Erycine*, Venus, the Lady of Eryx in Sicily.

225. *weary'd all the fables of the gods.* Martial, x. v. 17, 'delasset omnes fabulas poetarum', and Herrick's imitation, *Hesperides*, 'To Electra' (*Poems*, ed. Moorman, p. 58):

> Ile come to thee in all those shapes
> As *Jove* did, when he made his rapes: . . .
> And kissing, so as none may heare,
> We'll weary all the Fables there.

234. *trans-fuse our wandring soules.* From the fragmentary lyric in Petronius' *Satyricon*, 79:

> Et transfudimus hinc et hinc labellis
> errantes animas.

236–9. From Catullus, vii. 9–12:

> Tam te basia multa basiare
> vesano satis et super Catullo est,
> quae nec pernumerare curiosi
> possint nec mala fascinare lingua.

263. *Nestor's hernia*, a quotation from Juvenal, *Sat.* vi. 326.

III. viii. 4. *so courteous.* Randolph, *The Jealous Lovers*, 1632, I. vii:

> I would your just sword would so courteous be
> As to unrip my heart.

14. *like Romanes*, kill ourselves fearlessly, like Cato or Brutus.

15. *like Grecians*, dissolutely. Upton cites the verb *pergraecari* in Plautus, to revel or carouse.

16. *Saffi.* '*Saffo*, a catchpole, or sergeant' (Florio, 1598).

20–1. *Guilty men* . . . Dyce quotes Petronius, *Satyricon*, 125, 'Dii deaeque, quam male est extra legem viventibus: quicquid meruerunt, semper expectant.' In his MS. notes he adds that the thought is found in Cicero and Seneca.

III. ix. 22. *foist's* . . . *I shall sent 'hem*. Voltore quibbles on two distinct words, (1) foist, a rogue, and so a piece of roguery (cf. *E.M.I.* IV. iv. 17), (2) foist, a stench.

32. *disclaiming in him*. *C. is A.* v. xii. 68.

36. *stated*, settled, safely placed.

38–9. A reference to treasure found in old monuments. From Plautus, *Pseudolus*, 410–13:

> Erum eccum video huc Simonem una simul
> cum suo vicino Calliphone incedere.
> Ex hoc sepulcro vetere viginti minas
> ecfodiam ego hodie quas dem erili filio.

42. *successe*, result.

43. *old rauen*, Corbaccio.

55. *Scrutineo*, senate-house.

IV. i. With this scene compare Saint-Évremond's imitation in his comedy of *Sir Politick Would-be* with the scene at Venice, I. iii, Sir Politick to Mr. de Riche-Source, a great projector: 'Chaque Païs a ses Usages; c'est pourquoi je vous recommande ces choses: Premierement le Pas grave, & la Contenance composée; cela sent son Personnage. Pour vos Discours, ne dites jamais rien que vous croyiez; comme aussi ne croyez rien de ce qu'on vous dira: que toutes vos Actions soient réglées par les Loïx, dont je porte un *Compendium* sur moi. De Religion, vous vous accommoderez à celle du Païs en apparence; & pourrez en effet en avoir une autre, si vous n'aimez mieux n'en avoir point du tout, ce que je laisse purement à votre choix.' A marginal note says '*Cela est imité de la COMÉDIE de* Ben.Johnson *intitulée VOLPONE* or *The FOX*, Act. iv. Sc. i'. This second Sir Politick plans a pigeon-post with the Levant to secure information, and is overheard by a spy.

9. *I haue better.* 'This captious kind of wit (such as it is) occurs in Donne:

> "Your *only* wearing is your grogaram."
> "Not so, sir, I have more."—Sat. iv.' (Gifford.)

12. *garbe*, outward bearing. '*Il pensieri stretti, ed il viso sciolto* was the advice of Sir Henry Wotton to Milton, when he was going on the tour of Italy' (Whalley).

24–5. Sir Politic, like most shallow persons, is pattering a catchword of the time—the formula 'Cuius regio eius religio' of the Religious Peace of Augsburg, 1555.

26. *Machiavel* of course said nothing of the kind.

Bodine, Jean Bodin (1530–96), from whom Hobbes borrowed his theory of sovereignty. His *Six Livres de la Republique*, 1576, was the starting-point of modern political science. He advocated toleration solely on opportunist grounds: complete religious unity was impossible; why wreck the State in a vain effort to obtain it? For Sir Politic's idea cf. Day, *The Isle of Gulls*, iii. i (1606, F1ᵛ): '*Lis.* Thou speak'st like a Christian; prethee, what Religion art of? *Man.* How manie soeuer I make use of, Ile answere with *Piauano Orlotto*, the Italian: I professe the Dukes onely.'

28. *your . . . forke, at meales.* Knives for eating purposes began commonly to take the place of fingers in 1563, and forks were not in much use before 1611. Thus in 1616 Jonson makes a projector plan

> The laudable vse of forkes,
> Brought into custome here, as they are in *Italy*,
> To the sparing o' *Napkins.* (*D. is A.* v. iv. 18, 19.)

Breton, in *The Court and Country*, 1618, D2ᵛ, makes a countryman tell a courtier, 'But for vs in the Country, when we haue washed our hands after no foule worke, nor handling any vnwholesome thing, wee neede no little Forks to make hay with our mouths, to throw our meat into them'. Coryat noticed the general use of forks in Italy, and Italy only, in his travels, and gives an elaborate account of it (*Crudities*, 1611, pp. 90–1), adding that, on using a fork in England afterwards, he was quipped on the subject by being called 'furcifer'.

34. *Preposterous*, inverting the natural (or in this case the conventional) order (Lat. *praeposterus*).

40. *Contarene.* The reference is to the *De Magistratibus et Republica Venetorum*, 1589, of Cardinal Gasparo Contarini, an English translation of which by Lewis Lewkenor appeared in 1599.

41. *my Iewes.* The 'my' is unusual: it is modelled on the indefinite use of 'your', as in 'Your *Spanish* iennet is the best horse' (*Alch.* iv. iv. 9).

46. *proiects.* Sir Politic is a mild example of the projector; the type was fully developed in Meercraft in *The Devil is an Ass.*

54. *States,* a member of the States-General of Holland.

64. *defalk,* reduce the amount. Cf. Daniel, *Philotas,* i (*Poems,* 1605, B3ᵛ):

> See how these vaine discoursiue Booke-men talke, . . .
> And doe not see how much they must defalke
> Of their accompts, to make them gree with ours.

72. *cautions,* precautions.

91. *arsenale.* Fully described in William Thomas's *The historie of Italie,* 1561, ff. 74ᵇ–75ᵇ.

102. *Soria,* Syria. P. Ferrarius, *Lexicon Geographicum . . . cum indice copiosissimo Latino-Italico,* Milan, 1627, p. 735, had 'Syria *Soria* Italis . . . Prou. maxima Asiæ'. Sir Politic out of affectation uses the Italian form.

104. *where,* whereas.

106. *Lazaretto.* The first lazaretto or pest-house was established on the island of Santa Maria di Nazaret after the plague of 1423; a second during the plague of 1576 on the island of Sant' Erasmo.

110. *onions.* Regarded as 'the best fortification against the plague. . . . Three or four peeled onions left on the ground for ten days would gather all the infection in the neighbourhood.'—F. P. Wilson, *The Plague in Shakespeare's London,* p. 9: his authority is *Present Remedies against the Plague,* 1594, B3ᵛ. Cf. Fletcher, *The Mad Lover,* II. i. 124–5, 'The plague . . . I'll cure it with an onion.'

136–46. Cf. Theophrastus, Character xvi, The Superstitious Man: καὶ τὴν ὁδὸν ἐὰν ὑπερδρομῇ γαλῆ, μὴ πρότερον πορευθῆναι ἕως διεξέλθῃ τις, ἢ λίθους τρεῖς ὑπὲρ τῆς ὁδοῦ διαβάλῃ, . . . καὶ ἐὰν μῦς θύλακον ἀλφίτων διαφαγῇ πρὸς τὸν ἐξηγητὴν ἐλθὼν ἐρωτᾶν τί χρὴ ποιεῖν.

140. *burst,* broke. *Poet.* III. v. 23.

141. *ragion del stato. C.R.* I. iv. 84.

142. *moccinigo.* II. ii. 210.

144. *I cheapen'd sprats.* Coryat, *Crudities,* p. 258, notes with surprise that the Venetian 'Gentlemen and greatest Senators, a man worth perhaps two millions of duckats, will come into the market, and buy their flesh, fish, fruites, and such other things as are necessary for the maintenance of the family'. He commends the English gentleman who 'employeth his Cooke or Cator about these inferior and sordid affaires'. W. Thomas, *The historie of Italie,* 1549, f. 83ᵇ, also notes this habit of the Venetian gentleman.

IV. ii. 2. *plaies both,* i.e. plays fast and loose. See I. ii. 8.

25. *massácre.* 'Spenser stresses *massa·cre,* Shakespeare and Marlowe *ma·ssacre*', *O.E.D.,* comparing Spenser's *Amoretti,* x:

> See how the Tyrannesse doth ioy to see
> The huge massacres which her eyes do make.

29, 30. A sneer at the indiscriminate creation of knights by King James I: cf. *Alch.* II. ii. 86–7.

35. *the courtier*. Castiglione's great manual, *Il Cortegiano*, 1528. Hoby's translation first appeared in 1561. The third book discusses the behaviour of women in the spirit indicated by Lady Would-be.

41. *perséuer*. The usual pronunciation down to the middle of the seventeenth century; Shakespeare always uses it (*O.E.D.*).

48. *Sporus*, a favourite of Nero who made him a eunuch, dressed him as a woman, and publicly went through the form of marriage with him in A.D. 67.

51. *white-Friers nation*. *E.H.* v. v. 24 n.

53. *fore-head*. *C.R.* v. xi. 54.

55. *fricatrice*, prostitute. The earliest example in the *O.E.D.*

59. *state-face*. *Revenge for Honour*, I. ii (1659, p. 9):

> Your sage and serious Courtier, who does walk
> With a State face, as he had drest himself
> Ith' Emperors glasse, and had his beard turn'd up
> By the'irons Roial.

60. *carniuale*. Cotgrave, 1611, 'Carnavalée: f. A wench thats growne as licentious, or is vsed as licentiously, as the Carnaval: (ou qui est chevauchée tout le long du Carnaval).'

62. *Marshall*. An officer of a court of law who had the charge and custody of prisoners, and who kept order; he was frequently entrusted with the keeping of a prison. Dol in *The Alchemist*, I. i. 120–1, tells Subtle and Face,

> I'll not be made a prey vnto the *marshal*,
> For ne're a snarling dog-bolt o' you both.

63. *disc'ple*, discipline, i.e. whip. Cf. *The Faerie Queene*, I. x. 27:

> And bitter *Penance* with an iron whip,
> Was wont him once to disple euery day.

72. *your nose*. It was red (III. iv. 16). The simile, as Gifford notes, is prettily turned in Suckling's *Ballad of a Wedding* (*Fragmenta Aurea*, 1646, p. 38):

> Her Cheeks so rare a white was on,
> No Dazy makes comparison,
> (Who sees them is undone).
> For streaks of red were mingled there
> Such as are on a Katherne Pear,
> (The side that's next the Sun.)

But it occurs earlier in Sidney's *Arcadia*, 1590, ed. Feuillerat, p. 219: her cheeks

> *like the fresh Queene-apples side*
> *Blushing at sight of* Phœbus *pride*.

IV. iii. 4. *callet*. Bullokar, 1616, '*Callette*, a Lewd Woman.' Harington, in *Orlando Furioso*, 1591, xx, st. 97, 'this old ilfauord spitefull callet', comments in the margin, 'Callet is a nickname that they vse to a woman, it signifies in Irish a witch'. Cf. '*Kitt-Callot*', *G.M.* 252.

18. *see* in Folio: altered from the 'vse' of the Quarto because of the equivoque with 'conceiue'. Peregrine takes it for an overture.

23. *salt-head*: a quibble as in *E.M.O.* IV. iii. 80, (1) 'salt' as opposed to 'fresh'; (2) 'salacious': cf. 'Sir POLITIQVE bawd', line 20.

IV. iv. 12. *croakers*, Corbaccio's.

14. *mummia*. Egyptian mummy was formerly a recognized article of medicine. Sir T. Browne, *Urn Burial*, ed. Evans, p. 80: 'The Ægyptian Mummies, which Cambyses or time hath spared, avarice now consumeth. Mummie is become Merchandise, *Mizraim* cures wounds, and *Pharaoh* is sold for balsams.' Counterfeit mummy, procured by drying dead bodies in ovens, was once an extensively practised fraud. Shirley, *The Bird in a Cage*, I. i (1633, C), 'make Mummy of my flesh, and sell me to the Apothecaries'.

20. *Much!* The ironic use as in *E.M.I.* IV. vi. 53.

21. *Mercury*, as the god of eloquence.

22. *the French Hercules*. 'The *Gallic* or *Celtic* HERCULES was the symbol of eloquence. LVCIAN has a treatise on this *French Hercules*, surnamed OGMIUS: he was pictured old and wrinkled, and drest in his lion's skin; in his right hand he held his club, in his left his bow: several very small chains were figured reaching from his tongue to the ears of crowds of men at some distance.'—Upton. The link between the Greek hero and the Celts was supplied by the quest of Geryon's cattle in the West: Hercules, returning homeward through Gaul, founded there Alesia and Nemausus, and became the father of the Celts.

IV. v. 7. *monstrous*, the syllabic *r* makes the word a trisyllable; 'monsterous' is a seventeenth-century spelling.

45–7. *being plac'd . . . benefit.* From Tacitus, *Annals*, IV. xviii. 3, quoted on *Sej.* III. 305–7.

48. *extirpe*, root out (Lat. *exstirpare*).

50–2. From Juvenal, *Sat.* vi. 284–5, quoted on *Sej.* II. 257–9.

54. *fact*, crime.

61–2. *vice . . . vertue.* Juvenal, *Sat.* xiv. 109, 'Fallit enim vitium specie virtutis et umbra'.

79. *Mischiefe doth euer end*, i.e. goes on consistently. Whalley's plausible conjecture 'Mischief doth never end' is supported by the passage of Valerius Maximus (IX. i. 2), 'Neque enim ullum finitur vitium ibi ubi oritur.' 'Euer', which Jonson twice passed in the proofs of the Quarto and the Folio, cannot be regarded as a misprint.

81. *lien. Engl. Gram.* I. xix. 37 gives the past participle '*lyne* or *layne*'. *bed-red.* In use from the fourteenth to the eighteenth century (OE. *bedreda*).

85. *stale*, decoy.

97. *sols.* Coryat, *Crudities*, p. 250, values the sol at a halfpenny.

110. *made you*, wrought you. *E.M.I.* IV. xi. 46.

118. *partrich*, partridge: a common form in Jonson. Pliny, *N.H.* x. 102, 'Neque in alio animali par opus libidini.'

124. *well-timber'd gallant*. *E.M.O.* Ind. 327.

here. Corvino touches his forehead, making with his fingers the letter V, the sign of the cuckold. There is a reference to the horn-book (*Poet.* IV. v. 68).

130. *catholique*, the Folio reading, is better suited to Venice than the 'Christian' of the Quarto.

138. *cue*. 'Qu:' in the Quarto: cf. *Disc.* 2188-90, 'For the consequence of Sentences, you must bee sure, that every clause doe give the Q. one to the other, and be bespoken ere it come.' The etymology of the word, with this abbreviation, has not been satisfactorily explained.

139. *lay'd*, plotted, designed. *Poet.* III. i. 153.

155. *turn'd a stone*. Fletcher and Massinger, *The Spanish Curate*, IV. iv. 40 (Folio, 1647, p. 41):

> *Iamy*. I am turn'd a stone with wonder,
> And know not what to thinke.

IV. vi. 3. *hyæna*. A type of treachery: cf. Milton, *Samson Agonistes*, 748-9, Samson to Delilah:

> Out, out *Hyæna*; these are thy wonted arts,
> And arts of every woman false like thee.

But, as Dr. Rea notes, it was the voice of the hyena (*E.H.* v. iv. 33), not its tears, that duped its victims.

21. *conuince*, overpower, convict (Lat. *convinco*). *B.F.* I. i. 20, *S. of N.* v. iv. 69, *Ep.* cxxxiii. 152.

32. *strappado*. Coryat saw this torture in Venice: 'On the fourth day of August being Thursday, I saw a very Tragicall and dolefull spectacle in Saint *Markes* place. Two men tormented with the strapado, which is done in this manner. The offender hauing his hands bound behind him, is conueighed into a rope that hangeth in a pully, and after hoysed vp in the rope to a great heigth with two seuerall swinges, where he sustaineth so great torments that his ioynts are for the time loosed and pulled asunder; besides such abundance of bloud is gathered into his hands and face, that for the time he is in the torture, his face and hands doe looke as red as fire' (*Crudities*, p. 254).

33. *the racke hath cured the gout*. Webster, *The Devil's Law-Case*, III. ii. 174:

> . . . in England
> Cured a' th' Gowt, by being rackt i' th' Tower.

Marston, *The Malcontent*, III. i (2nd ed. 1604, E2ᵛ): '*Bianca*. Why the racke: al your Empericks could neuer do the like cure vpon the gout the racke did in *England*: or your Scotch boote.'

52. *their constancy abounds*. From Juvenal, *Sat.* xiii. 237, 'Cum scelus admittunt' (sc. *mali*), 'superest constantia'.

58. *I haue an earthquake in me*. Massinger, *The Emperor of the East*, IV. iv (1632, I4), 'what an earth-quake I feele in mee'.

82. *cortines*, curtains (low Latin, *cortina*). Jonson affects this form: v. ii. 84 below, *Alch.* IV. ii. 7, *Nept. Tr.* 248.

89–91. From Juvenal, *Sat.* x. 254–5:

> Cur haec in tempora duret,
> quod facinus dignum tam longo admiserit aevo?

93. *the deuill, and all*, 'the whole confounded lot; all or everything bad' (*O.E.D.*). The phrase, here addressed to Voltore, is used with reference to lawyers in Nashe, *Pierce Pennilesse*, 1592 (*Works*, ed. McKerrow, i, p. 162), 'they say the Lawyers haue the Deuill and all', and Dekker, *Iests to make you Merie*, 1607, B1ᵛ, 'And what newes (quoth he) at Westminster; Mary sayes the other Lawyers get the Diuell and all: What an Asse replied the Citizen is the diuell: if I were as he I would get some of them.'

v. i. 6. *apprehended*: 'apprênded' in the Quarto, copying the Latin 'prendo', the syncopated form of 'prehendo'. So it would scan here and in III. viii. 17, IV. iii. 7, but the word has three syllables in IV. ii. 21, v. iv. 40.

v. ii. 7, 8. *It were a folly* . . . From Plautus, *Pseudolus*, 576, 'Nam ea stultitiast, facinus magnum timido cordi credere.'

15. *playd thy prise*. *C.R.* v. iii. 9.

23. *Too much light*. *T. of T.* I. i. 56–7:

> Hilts, can you see to rise? *Hil.* Cham not blind Sir
> With too much light.

30–2. *but if Italy* . . . From Plautus, *Epidicus*, 306–7:

> Nullum esse opinor ego agrum in agro Attico
> aeque feracem quam hic noster Periphanes.

52. *shift a shirt*, i.e. through his violent gestures. Whalley instances the Italian preachers of his day.

62. *sadly*, seriously.

90. *Clarissimo*, a grandee of Venice.

91. *crumpe*, curl up. *you* is ethic dative. For the image of the *hog-louse* cf. *S.W.* II. iv. 141–2, where Daw is advised to be as melancholy as a hog-louse: 'I would roule my selfe vp for this day, introth, they should not vnwinde me.'

98–105. From Lucian, *Gallus*, 722, describing Zeus: ὁπότε ἠράσθη τῆς Ἀργολικῆς ἐκείνης μείρακος, οὐκ ἔχων ἐς ὅτι ἐρασμιώτερον αὐτὸν μεταβάλοι οὐδὲ ὅπως ἂν διαφθείρειε τοῦ Ἀκρισίου τὴν φρουράν—ἀκούεις δήπου ὡς χρυσίον ἐγένετο. . . . οἷς ἂν παρῇ ⟨χρυσὸς⟩, καλούς τε αὐτοὺς καὶ σοφοὺς καὶ ἰσχυροὺς ἀπεργάζεται τιμὴν καὶ δόξαν προσάπτων καὶ ἐξ ἀφανῶν καὶ ἀδόξων ἐνίοτε περιβλέπτους καὶ ἀοιδίμους ἐν βραχεῖ τίθησι. 724 ὁρᾷς ὅσων ἀγαθῶν ὁ χρυσὸς αἴτιος, εἴ γε καὶ μεταποιεῖ τοὺς ἀμόρφους καὶ ἐρασμίους ἀπεργάζεται ὥσπερ ὁ ποιητικὸς ἐκείνος κεστός. Cf. Horace, *Odes*, III. xvi. 1–8.

103 (margin) *Cestus*. See Jonson's note on *Hymenaei*, 407–8, 'that beauteous CESTON' 'Of *louers* many-colour'd blisse': in which he

translates Homer's description in *Iliad* xiv. 214–16. See also *Challenge at Tilt*, 50–1.

104. *Acrisius*, the father of Danae, who locked her up in the tower.

v. iii. 7. *vellets*. A sixteenth-century form of 'velvet': *C.R.* Ind. 203.

9 (margin). *trauerse* 'appears to indicate a low, movable screen, probably of a non-structural kind' (E. K. Chambers, *Elizabethan Stage*, iii, p. 26).

21. *in their garters*. Suicide, as in Harington's *Orlando Furioso*, 1591, x, stanza 37:

> Nor maist thou die in quiet and tranquillitie:
> But burned might'st thou be, or cut in quarters,
> Or driuen to hang thy selfe in thine owne garters.

Cf. *Mids. N. D.* v. i. 348, 'if he . . . had . . . hanged himself in Thisbe's garter'.

32. *salt*, salt-cellar.

51. *beene a wittoll*, connived at your wife's dishonour.

63. *foure eyes*. Corbaccio wears spectacles.

65. *Harlot*. Applied to a man: see *C.R.* v. iv. 416.

68. *the three legges*. An allusion to the riddle of the Sphinx.

97. *law . . . conscience*. *D. is A.* iii. ii. 42–3.

102. *eat lettuce*. Rea quotes Martial, *Ep.* iii. lxxxix:

> Utere lactucis et mollibus utere malvis:
> nam faciem durum, Phoebe, cacantis habes.

Cf. 'costiue' in line 101.

105. *my habit of Clarissimo*. 'Most of their gownes are made of blacke cloth, and ouer their left shoulder they haue a flappe made of the same cloth, and edged with blacke Taffeta. Also most of their gownes are faced before with blacke Taffeta' (Coryat, *Crudities*, p. 259).

119. *The Fox . . . curst*. Cursed, that is, for escaping. Cf. Harington's *Orlando Furioso*, 1591, xxiii, st. 27:

> Winners may bost, when leesers speake their fill,
> Best pleasd was he, when as she wisht him worst,
> As still the foxe fares best when he is curst.

And Greene, *Friar Bacon*, iv. i (1594, G3ᵛ), '*Miles*. Tis no matter, I am against you with the old prouerb, The more the fox is curst, the better he fares.'

v. iv. In a letter of Diderot to Sophie Volland, 5 September 1762 (*Lettres*, ed. Babelon, ii, pp. 152–5), there is a story of a trick played by Lord Chesterfield on Montesquieu at Venice which might have been suggested by this scene, especially if Chesterfield had seen *Volpone* acted. Discussing with Montesquieu the characteristics of Englishmen and Frenchmen, Chesterfield agreed that the French were superior in wit, 'mais en revanche ils n'avoient pas le sens commun'. Montesquieu agreed, but said the two qualities could not be compared. The dispute lasted several days. Montesquieu went about Venice, sightseeing, inquiring, talking freely, and every evening making notes of his observations. A stranger called on him, a badly dressed Frenchman, who said he had lived in Venice twenty years and made a point of helping his countrymen there. 'On peut tout faire dans ce pays, excepté se mêler des affaires d'État. Un mot inconsidéré sur le gouvernement coûte la tête, et vous en avez déjà tenu plus de mille. Les Inquisiteurs d'État ont les yeux ouverts sur votre conduite, on vous épie, on suit tous vos pas, on tient note de tous vos projets, on ne doute point que vous n'écriviez. Je scais de science certaine qu'on doit, peut-être aujourd'huy, peut-être demain, faire chez vous une visite. Voyez, monsieur, si en effet vous avez écrit, et songez, qu'une ligne innocente, mais mal interprétée, vous coûteroit la vie.' Montesquieu in consternation collected all his papers and burnt them. When Chesterfield returned to the house, Montesquieu told him of the visit, and that he had burnt his papers and ordered a carriage for 3 a.m. Chesterfield carefully discussed the situation: it was unnatural; who was the man? how did he know his facts? The authorities would be secret enough, and this beggar, if he learnt from them, would not betray his masters. Finally, Chesterfield in a tentative and hesitating way suggested that he might have been sent 'par un certain milord Chesterfield qui auroit voulu vous prouver par expérience qu'une once de sens commun vaut mieux que cent livres d'esprit, car avec du sens commun . . . — Ah scélérat, s'écria le président, quel tour vous m'avez joué! Et mon manuscrit! mon manuscrit que j'ai brûlé!'

5. *booke of voyages*. One of the numerous collections of travels, such as Hakluyt's, which were then in vogue.

6. *guld story*, virtually 'the story of his gulling'. For this use of a past participle cf. *Merch. of Venice*, III. ii. 97–8:

> Thus ornament is but the guiled shore
> To a most dangerous sea,

where 'guiled' means 'treacherous'.

21. *Bolognian sausages*. The *mortadella* of Bologna is still famous. Sir Thomas Gresham imported it to England from Rotterdam.

23. *tidings*. The state-word was 'intelligence' (II. i. 68).

42. *out of play-bookes*. See *C.R.* III. v. 118–22.

43. *essayes*, on which Jonson looked with contempt (*Disc.* 719-29).

45. *fraile*, a rush basket used for packing figs and raisins. *The Times* of 19 September 1933 had an account of a frail-maker.

49. *curren-but*, a cask for holding currants or currant-wine. 'Currans', *B.F.* I. iii. 141.

54. *tortoyse-shell*. Coryat, *Crudities*, p. 258, 'Amongst many other strange fishes that I haue obserued in their market places' (i.e. at Venice) 'I haue seene many Torteises, whereof I neuer saw but one in all England.'

55. *Fitted*. 'Apted' (Q): cf. *Poet.* I. ii. 101.

67. *a cart*. Cf. R. W., *The Three Lords and Three Ladies of London*, 1590, B2ᵛ: '*Wil*. What is it' (viz. the impresa of a shield) 'in sadnesse?

Wit. A Tortoys my boy, whose shell is so hard, that a loaden cart may goe ouer and not breake it.'

77. *motion . . . in Fleet-street. E.M.O.* ii. iii. 147.

78. *the faire,* Bartholomew Fair, so vividly depicted in Jonson's later play.

83. *The freight of the gazetti,* the theme of the news-sheets. 'Gazetta' so called from the coin gazet (ii. ii. 189); or possibly from *gazzetta,* the diminutive of *gazza,* 'magpie', with the idea of 'chatter', 'tittle-tattle'. *S. of N.* i. v. 11, *Ep.* xcii. 16.

v. v. 6, 7. *My Foxe Is out on his hole.* An allusion to the children's game of Fox-in-the-Hole. The players 'hopped on one leg, and beat one another with gloves or pieces of leather tied at the end of strings'— Halliwell. Chapman, *The Gentleman Usher,* v. iv (1606, K2): '*Pog.* Come on my Lord *Stinckerd,* Ile play Fox, Fox, come out of thy hole with you ifaith. *Med.* Ile runne and hide me from the sight of heauen. *Pog.* Fox, Fox, goe out of thy hole; a two leg'd Foxe, A two leg'd Fox. *Exit with Pages beating Medice.*'

out on his hole. For this use of 'on' cf. 'on's' = of his in *Coriolanus,* ii. i. 176, 'at very root on's heart'; *K. Lear,* iii. iv. 111, 'all the rest on's body cold'.

v. vi. 17. *ouer-leauen'd,* transformed, not merely modified. *Ep.* xcvii. 20, 'Onely his clothes haue ouer-leauen'd him.'

18. *wine-fat,* vat.

25. *a'knowne,* acknown, acknowledged. Chaucer, *Boethius,* 17, 'Þat I confesse and am a-knowe'.

v. vii. 10. *piscaria,* fish-market, on the Grand Canal.

candle-rents, rents from property which is continually deteriorating. Chapman, *The Georgics of Hesiod,* 1618, pp. 17–18:

> Let neuer neate-girt Dame . . . be heard to faine
> With her forkt tongue; so far forth as to gaine
> Thy candle rent (she calls it).

20. *no end of your wealth. Iohn Heywoodes woorkes,* 1562, Divᵛ, of a miserly man and wife:

> They know no ende of their good: nor beginnyng
> Of any goodnesse. suche is wretched winnyng.

v. viii. 2. *gun-stones,* stone balls for cannon. F. Cunningham, writing in 1875, said, 'They are still to be seen in India, piled in heaps by the side of the huge native guns in the old fortresses.' For the idea cf. *E.M.O.* i. i. 26–7.

13. *dropt your cheese.* See on i. ii. 94–6.

16. *cap.* 'The dress of a commandadore (officer of justice), in which Volpone was now disguised, consisted of a black stuff gown and a red cap with two *gilt buttons* in front' (Gifford).

17. *iolt-head. E.H.* ii. i. 96.

20. *valure*, 'apparently an alteration of OF. *valur* or *valeur*, "valour", after forms in *-ure*' (*O.E.D.*).

27. *Basiliske*. *E.M.O.* i. ii. 220, 'Cockatrice' n.

v. ix. 4. *solœcisme*. iv. ii. 43.

5. *biggen*, a skull-cap of lawn or silk worn by lawyers, called a 'night-cap' in *S. of N.* v. i. 104, *M.L.* i. vi. 21. Cf. Mayne, *The City Match*, 1639, iv. vii:

> One whom the good
> Old man his Uncle kept to th' Inns of Court,
> And would in time, ha made him *Barrester*;
> And raisd him to the sattin *Cap*, and *Biggin*.

The idea is from Erasmus' satire on theologians, *Mor. Enc.* 470 A, 'Quare nolite mirari, si videtis caput illorum tot fasciis tam diligenter obvinctum in publicis disputationibus, alioquin enim plane dissilirent': a note of Lijster adds, 'Id potissimum videmus in Doctoribus apud Parisios, quorum capita tot fasciis obvoluta, ut vix possint evolvere sese.'

14. *This's*. *Sej.* ii. 484.

v. xii. 9, 10. *Possession*, the entrance of the evil spirit into the body, *obsession* the attack from without.

25. *vomits crooked pinnes*. In *A Tryal of Witches at the Assizes Held at Bury St. Edmonds . . . on the Tenth day of March, 1664. Before Sir Matthew Hale K^t, 1682*, p. 21, Samuel Pacy, a merchant of Lowestoft, deposed about his two children, supposed to be bewitched: 'At other times They would fall into Swounings, & upon the recovery to their speech they would Cough extreamly, & bring up much Flegme, and with the same crooked Pins, and one time a Two-penny Nail with a very broad head, which Pins (amounting to Forty or more) together with the Two-penny Nail were produced in Court, with the affirmation of the said Deponent, that he was present when the Said Nail was Vomited up, and also most of the Pins.'

27. *His mouth's running away*. Cf. Darrell, *A true Narration of the strange and grevous Vexation by the Devil, of . . . William Somers of Nottingham*, 1600, p. 19: 'He was also continually torne in very fearful manner and disfigured in his face: wherein somtimes his lips were drawne awry, now to the one syde now to the other: somtimes his face and neck distorted, to the right and to the left hand, yea somtimes writhen to his back.'

28, 29. *in his belly . . . in his throate*. Samuel Harsnet, *A Discouery of the fraudulent practises of Iohn Darrel*, 1599, p. 213, quotes Somers's confession of his imposture: 'I did moue first the calfe of my legge, then my knee-bone, which motion of the knee will likewise make a motion or rising of the thigh. Also by drawing and stopping of my wind, my bellie would stirre and shewe a kind of swelling. The bunch (as p. 214 they tearmed it) about my chest, was by the thrusting out of my breast. Likewise my secret swallowing did make the ende of my windepipe to moue, and to shew greater then vsually it is: Againe, by mouing of my iawes, one bunch was easily made in the side, my cheeke neere mine eare: and about the middle of my cheeke with the ende of my tongue thrust against it. These motions by practise I woulde make very fast, one after another: so that there might easily seeme to bee running in my bodie of some thing, from place to place.'

31. *blew toad.* Ibid., p. 53, 'The booke of the boye of Burton' (Thomas Darling, another of Darrell's tools) 'sayeth, that towards the end of the fast for his pretended dispossession, *he began to heaue & lift vehementlie at his stomacke, and getting vp some fleagme and choler said (pointing with his finger, and following with his eyes) looke, looke, see you not the mouse that is gone out of my mouth? and so pointed after it, vnto the farthest part of the parlor.*'

50. *proper,* handsome.

64. *Your voice . . .* Plautus, *Mostellaria,* 576, 'Scio te bona esse voce, ne clama nimis.'

73–4. *I was borne . . .* Plautus, *Mostellaria,* 562–3, 'Ne ego sum miser, | scelestus, natus dis inimicis omnibus.'

85. *uncase,* strip off his disguise.

99, 100. Cf. (in a different context) Horace, *Sat.* i. i. 78–9, 'Horum | semper ego optarim pauperrimus esse bonorum.'

101–2. Seneca, *Ep.* cxix. 12, 'Sic divitias habent quomodo habere dicimur febrem, cum illa nos habeat.'

116. *Saffi.* III. viii. 16.

120. *hospitall, of the Incurabili.* Depicted in Graevius's *Thesaurus Antiquitatum Italiae,* v, pt. i, p. 200.

125. *mortifying of a Foxe.* A quibble on the cookery term. Cotgrave, 1611, '*Faisander.* To mortifie fowle, &c.; to make it tender, by hanging it vp, or (otherwise) keeping it some while after it is killed.'

131. *monasterie of San' Spirito,* on the Giudecca Canal, opposite the island.

136. *grand canale,* nearly two miles long, the 'main street' of Venice. Coryat describes it in his *Crudities,* p. 163.

139. *berlino,* pillory.

146–8. *Now, you begin . . .* Juvenal, *Sat.* xiii. 237–9:

> Quod fas
> atque nefas, tandem incipiunt sentire peractis
> criminibus.

Epilogue

1. The seasoning of a play. Plautus, *Poenulus,* 1370–1:
> Nunc, quod postremum est condimentum fabulae,
> si placuit, plausum postulat comoedia.

6. *fare iouially . . .* 'Valete et plaudite' was an ending to a Latin comedy, but Dr. Rea points here to the ending of the *Moriae Encomium,* 'Quare valete, plaudite, vivite, bibite, MORIÆ celeberrimi Mystæ', with Gerard Lijster's note, 'His verbis utebatur recitator fabulæ discessurus e proscænio. De suo addidit, Vivite, bibite. Et vivere proprie est genialiter vivere.'

'70

HOUSTON PUBLIC LIBRARY
CENTRAL LIBRARY

This book may be kept for FOURTEEN DAYS.
With due notice, it may be renewed once
for the same period. A charge is made for
overdue books.

S-1-69-20M-1